BEHAVIOR THERAPY

TECHNIQUES AND EMPIRICAL FINDINGS · THIRD EDITION

John C. Masters
Vanderbilt University

Thomas G. Burish
Vanderbilt University

Steven D. Hollon
Vanderbilt University

David C. Rimm

Harcourt Brace Jovanovich College Publishers
Fort Worth   Philadelphia   San Diego
New York   Orlando   Austin   San Antonio
Toronto   Montreal   London   Sydney   Tokyo

Preface

Behavior therapy clearly has matured since the 1950s, when it emerged from the experimental laboratory as a system of psychotherapy. Even though some of the early and sweeping claims about the efficacy of behavior therapy clearly have not been supported by empirical research, over the intervening years both practice and research have revealed a breadth, richness, and effectiveness that confirm the central importance of behavior therapy techniques among clinical procedures. For example, behavior therapy alone cannot fully eradicate the aberrant thought processes and behavior patterns associated with the schizophrenias, but decades of careful, innovative empirical work show that behavior therapy techniques are valuable to the larger clinical picture. Similarly, behavior therapy procedures are an integral part of intervention programs, targeting such varied issues or conditions as infantile autism, mental retardation, parent effectiveness training, the various nonpsychotic emotional disorders and behavior problems, substance abuse, and personality disorders.

Perhaps the single greatest virtue of the behavior therapy tradition has been a steadfast commitment to a rationally guided empiricism. Such a commitment provides for the continual development of new techniques and the refinement and validation of current ones, and it serves as a check against the unrestrained enthusiasm of adherents and the unfounded negative allegations of detractors. We also believe that behavior therapy's historical commitment to empirical verification of its claims has strengthened other domains of applied psychology.

Some areas have developed significantly in the field of behavior therapy, while the field has changed surprisingly little in other ways since the initial edition of this text in 1974. Important trends continue, such as the extension of behavioral principles to the understanding and treatment of physical (medical) disorders and the investigation of the role of cognitive processes in the evolution and treatment of disordered thought, emotion, and behavior. Indeed, this Third Edition includes two new areas of specialization: behavioral medicine and cognitive-behavioral intervention. For most other topics we cover, the bulk of research since the late 1970s has extended and refined work that began in that decade or before. In a maturing field, one that has already proved its worth and is beginning to realize its limitations, this is to be expected.

Our efforts in the Third Edition represent an attempt to capture the growth and refinement of behavior therapy in a similarly mature fashion. We have tried to provide a fair, reasoned, and balanced treatment of the field—one that is neither unduly critical nor unabashedly enthusiastic. We believe that the behavior therapy perspective has added a great deal to the science and the discipline, but we also realize that much of value can be derived from other domains as well. And always, above all else, we clearly recognize and constantly attempt to note how much remains to be done.

We would like to express our appreciation

for the significant contributions of Donna Free-
dle, Deborah Keim, and Regina Perry, whose
diligent word processing, proofreading, and
permission garnering were a cornerstone to the
preparation of this edition. We thank Jennifer
Vasterling for her skilled assistance in the
preparation of the new chapter on behavioral
medicine. And finally, recognition is extended
to Denise Matt for her many contributions to
this volume, including the preparation of the
various indices.

John C. Masters
Thomas G. Burish
Steven D. Hollon
David C. Rimm

Acknowledgments

We wish to acknowledge the following reviewers, whose recommendations greatly improved the quality of this Third Edition:

Laurence A. Bradley, Wake Forest University
Nancy L. Eldred, San Jose State University
Louis R. Franzini, San Diego State University
David S. Holmes, University of Kansas
Paul M. Lehrer, University of Medicine and
    Dentistry, New Jersey
Richard M. McFall, Indiana University, Bloom-
    ington
Martin K. Moss, Wright State University
Ronald J. Prinz, University of South Carolina
David G. Schlundt, Vanderbilt University
David G. Weight, Brigham Young University

Contents

1

The Nature of Behavior Therapy

Before we present specific types of behavior therapy techniques or the problems and contexts for which they are appropriate, we must first define behavior therapy. In Chapter 1, we will discuss behavior therapy's origins, its basic assumptions, and its relationship to empirical and theoretical aspects of the scientific method and behavioral assessment. Behavioral assessment and interviewing are then presented, and the chapter concludes with ethical considerations, which are of particular importance.

What Is Behavior Therapy?

We include under the label *behavior therapy* any of a large number of specific techniques that employ psychological (especially learning) principles to change human behavior constructively. Often behavior therapists deal with behaviors that are maladaptive, that are obviously self-defeating and interfere in some way with the welfare of others. Perhaps just as often, the behavior therapist is called upon to assist a client with a specific aspect of personal growth or improvement, in the absence of what others would describe as "psychological problems." Thus, for example, individuals not notably lacking in assertiveness might, nevertheless, seek assertion training. Those who have poor social skills might profit immensely from social skills training through contingency management or cognitive procedures.

The term *behavior* is interpreted broadly to encompass covert responses (e.g., emotions and implicit verbalizations), when such can be clearly specified, as well as overt responding. The techniques used in behavior therapy are relaxation, systematic desensitization, assertion training, modeling, operant conditioning, self-control procedures (including biofeedback), extinction, and aversive conditioning, as well as certain techniques aimed at modifying cognitions.

Since the term *behavior therapy* was introduced in the late 1950s,[1] the field has undergone many significant developments—some of them quite recent. Not surprisingly, all behavior therapists are not in perfect agreement with respect to certain issues. One issue of contention is the fundamental question of which techniques or approaches belong to behavior therapy and which do not. This is well illustrated by the conflicting points of view of Arnold Lazarus (1976, 1977), who espouses a kind of eclecticism in his multimodal approach, and Joseph Wolpe (1976a, 1976b), who favors behavior therapy techniques that are, in his view, directly tied to established learning principles. Much of the controversy focuses on the role of cognitions in mediating maladaptive behavior and the use of cognitive techniques in changing behavior (Beck, 1984; Coyne & Gotlib, 1983; Ellis, 1977). This important issue will be discussed in Chapter 9.

The term *behavior modification* has sometimes been used in relation to behavior therapy. As

[1]According to Lazarus (1971, 1977), the term *behavior therapy* was first used by Skinner, Solomon, Lindsley, and Richards in 1953, but apparently these authors did not use it again. Eysenck independently used the term in 1959. It is now in common usage.

has been frequently noted (Franzini & Tilker, 1972; Wilson, 1978), the two terms have not been applied consistently. Some writers (e.g., Kanfer & Phillips, 1969) equate the two terms. Others (e.g., Lazarus, 1971) note that *behavior therapy* usually refers to counterconditioning methods (for instance, systematic desensitization and assertion training), whereas *behavior modification* stresses operant procedures. Still others (Wilson, 1978; Wolpe, 1973) subsume all such procedures under behavior therapy. The authors of this text also prefer to use the all-encompassing label of "behavior therapy." Although this may seem somewhat arbitrary, the important issue is not the differentiation of general terms to lump groups of behavioral techniques together, but rather, to identify more focused classes or categories of related techniques. The individual chapters in this book represent such categorizations.

The Origins of Behavior Therapy

Were it possible to review everything that has been written concerning the improvement of psychological condition, we could find approximations to every technique practiced by modern behavior therapists. Franks (1969b) has described a variety of early applications, including Pliny the Elder's use of aversive conditioning in the treatment of alcoholism. Other examples include the use of operant conditioning on the royal cavalry by the son of a Chinese emperor to effect the assassination of his father (Kreuger, 1961), as well as the application of procedures similar to reciprocal inhibition (see Chapter 2) that were reported in Paris in 1845 (case described in Stewart, 1961). Wolpe (1969) recounts an interesting case reported by Leuret of a patient suffering from debilitating obsessions. Treatment involved having the patient engage in competing responses (reciting songs), with food contingent on such behavior. In the

1800s, Alexander Maconochie, a captain in the British Royal Navy, successfully used what today might be called a token economy to control the behavior of prisoners in a British penal colony on Norfolk Island in the South Pacific (see Pitts, 1976).[2]

As Franks (1969b) intimated, although these examples are of some historical interest, they should not be viewed as the major antecedents of modern behavior therapy. Vastly more influential were 1) the writings of Pavlov (1927, 1928), whose experiments on what is now called classical, or respondent, conditioning are well known to students of introductory psychology; 2) the work of Thorndike on reward learning (1898, 1911, 1913), a major precursor of what is now called instrumental, or operant, conditioning; and 3) the writings and experiments of Watson and his associates (Jones, 1924; Watson, 1916; Watson & Rayner, 1920), which pointed to the application of Pavlovian principles to psychological disorders in human beings—which was an interest that Pavlov himself later developed (see Franks, 1969b).

Within the confines of academic psychology in the United States, a strong interest in the theoretical and empirical aspects of behaviorism has persisted from the early writings of Thorndike and Pavlov to the present day. Behaviorism defined in various ways, therefore, has been an important part of experimental psychology for most of the twentieth century. With respect to the systematic *application* of behaviorism to human problems, only since the 1950s has an interest developed that in any way approximates the early academic interest in its theoretical or empirical aspects. Sporadic reports of attempts to apply behavior therapy to problems of a clinical nature can be found in the earlier literature. Yates (1970), for example, listed 28 such appli-

[2]Pitts notes, "Maconochie's superiors were disturbed with his lack of orthodoxy and openly repudiated his successes. Maconochie was soon recalled to England" (1976, p. 146). When psychologists began to set up token economies in the 1960s, similar objections were widespread.

cations appearing from 1920 to 1939, and Gesell (1938) cited 57 early references to learning procedures for dealing with children's problems (see Lazarus, 1977). However, the long-term impact of these early reports does not appear to have been great. Developments in applied science tend to lag behind developments in pure science, but a delay of some 40 years requires explanation (Franks, 1969b).

One factor in the lack of interest in behaviorism's applications may have been the overbearing and dogmatic manner in which early behaviorists such as Watson presented their case to the public. Willis and Giles (1978) note that such religious zeal may have had the effect of alienating, or even frightening, practitioners who might otherwise have been friendly to the behavioristic view. Another factor contributing to the failure of mental health practitioners to incorporate principles of scientific behaviorism is that throughout the first part of the century therapy was generally restricted to psychiatrists. Psychiatrists' training generally was psychoanalytic in nature and so did not include the principles of an experimentally based psychology. The logical professional person to stress such principles in his practice would, of course, have been the clinical psychologist. However, clinical psychology as a recognized profession only came into its own after World War II.

It is interesting that early theoretical efforts (i.e., post–World War II) aimed at integrating clinical psychology and behaviorism often involved nothing more than translating Freudian concepts into behavioristic language (e.g., Dollard & Miller, 1950). The usefulness of such translations is largely predicated on the assumption that psychoanalysis is an effective means of treatment. In general, however, therapists using procedures from psychoanalysis and related dynamic schools of therapy have failed to provide hard data to support this crucial assumption. In an early but very influential paper, Eysenck (1952) presented data suggesting that neurotic individuals receiving psychotherapy might not fare any better than those who did

not receive such treatment, with approximately two-thirds of each group showing improvement. We should point out that Eysenck's data did not come from a controlled experiment but, instead, were derived from a survey of psychiatric outcome studies and from insurance company and hospital records.

While some other investigations have tended toward similar conclusions (e.g., Appel, Amper, & Schefler, 1961; Levitt, 1963, dealing with a population of children), the many problems associated with such investigations have led certain writers (for instance, Kiesler, 1966; Paul, 1967; Smith & Glass, 1977) to question seriously the validity of the "two-thirds improvement rate" dictum. For one thing, an obvious danger exists in lumping together all psychotherapists and patients in an attempt to come up with an overall improvement rate. Bergin (1966), for example, in reviewing psychotherapy outcome studies (involving several forms of therapy), found that while average improvement for non-treated patients approximated that for patients receiving therapy, the treated patients showed more variability. In other words, treated individuals tended to show greater change, though it was as likely to be in the undesirable as in the desirable direction.[3] Because psychotherapy showed inconsistent and inconclusive results, the above findings have motivated many individuals to question seriously the overall value of the psychotherapeutic enterprise and to seek out alternatives.

One such alternative was behavior therapy. Two books that were of paramount importance in establishing the foundations of this new discipline were Skinner's *Science and Human Behavior* (1953) and Wolpe's *Psychotherapy by Reciprocal Inhibition* (1958). Skinner provided a basis for the belief that much of human behavior can be understood in terms of the principles of operant

---

[3]With respect to the studies reviewed by Bergin, Bandura (1969, p. 55) has made the observation that when more "stringent and socially meaningful" improvement measures were employed, the effects of treatment were relatively less positive.

conditioning. Wolpe went further and offered a conceptualization of human neurosis in terms of Pavlovian and Hullian learning principles (with a sizable dose of neurophysiology). Far more important, he outlined specific therapy techniques (for instance, systematic desensitization and assertion training) aimed at dealing with neurotic behavior. Wolpe also provided impressive case history outcome data to support the value of his reciprocal-inhibition techniques. Another significant early contribution was Eysenck's *Behavior Therapy and the Neuroses* (1960).

The first behavior therapy journal was established by Eysenck in 1963, entitled *Behavior Research and Therapy*. Many such journals have followed, covering applied behavior analysis, behavior therapy, experimental psychiatry, cognitive therapy, and research. Behavior therapy texts also began to appear in the late 1960s, which were followed by specialized therapy textbooks. Topics have included self-control, cognitive approaches, behavioral approaches to children and families, treatment of alcoholism, and assertion training. Needless to say, the literature on behavior therapy has become extremely broad since the field's rebirth in the post–World War II period.

Numerous behavior therapy conferences, and professional organizations such as the Association for the Advancement of Behavior Therapy and the Behavior Research and Therapy Society, have become well established. Considering that before midcentury the term *behavior therapy* was not even part of the psychological vocabulary, the growth of the field has been a little short of phenomenal.

Some Major Postulates of Behavior Therapy

1. *Relative to psychotherapy, behavior therapy concentrates more on behavior itself and less on a presumed underlying cause.* Behavior therapy approaches differ considerably in the emphasis they place on underlying processes in maladaptive behavior. Therapists interested in operant conditioners have the strongest philosophical commitment to remaining at a purely behavioral level. Some are even unfriendly to methods such as systematic desensitization that, theoretically at least, are dependent on the existence and manipulation of events below the level of overt behavior (such as visual imagery and anxiety).

For example, some methods (e.g., systematic desensitization) emphasize alleviating maladaptive anxiety, whereas others focus primarily on the overt maladaptive behavior. A therapist interested in contingency management might deal with the snake phobic simply by providing reinforcement for successively greater approach behaviors to a snake (since the problem is construed to be a snake avoidance behavior), whereas a therapist devoted to systematic desensitization would conceptualize the problem in terms of an underlying cause—anxiety—and attempt to alleviate this internal state. While anxiety is by no means as "public" as overt avoidance behavior, it is a state of arousal that has definite, detectable physiological characteristics (for instance, the galvanic skin response). In other words, although anxiety is an internal mediating response, it is a good deal less obscure than underlying entities typically postulated by schools of dynamic psychology (e.g., Oedipal conflict and organ inferiority).

Those interested in behavior therapy have always been cautious about dealing with cognition, although a blanket rejection of concepts that refer to covert events or processes is now relatively rare. This is reflected most clearly in the recent upsurge of interest in cognitive methods, which are treated in detail in Chapter 9. Thus, certain cognitive approaches, such as Ellis's rational emotive therapy, are included in this text because they share many of the assumptions common to the more traditional behavior therapies. Rational emotive therapy, however, may also be correctly described as a depth approach. According to this perspective, our snake phobic avoids snakes because he or she is anxious, but the anxiety is generated by irrational thoughts (self-verbalizations) that follow from a faulty system of beliefs. In sharp contrast to the traditional depth approaches, the kinds of cognitive activity so essential to Ellis's theoretical position can be specified in a relatively concrete and unambiguous manner.

For purposes of comparison, consider how a psychoanalyst might conceptualize a snake phobia. He or she would agree that the snake phobic does experience anxiety when confronted with a snake, but below this anxiety might be the unconscious perception of phallic-like properties of the snake. At a more basic level, there might be repressed thoughts of castration, and at an even more fundamental level, a sexual love of the mother, also repressed. For some behavior therapists such as Wolpe, the underlying anxiety can be detected by independent means, and for Ellis, cognitions conceived of as self-verbalization can readily become overt verbalizations subject to public scrutiny, but many of the underlying events postulated by psychoanalysis are, according to its own theory, quite inaccessible.

Psychoanalytic and related dynamic approaches were created and have been perpetuated largely by individuals trained in the field of medicine (psychiatrists). It is not surprising, then, that "models" of human maladaptive behavior associated with such approaches have tended to borrow rather heavily from concepts associated with physical illness. Hence, these dynamic conceptualizations have come to be identified with such labels as the "medical model" or the "disease model." In the medical model of psychological disorder, maladaptive behavior is *symptomatic* of an underlying pathological state, or state of disease. To cure the patient suffering from "mental illness," this model also assumes that it is necessary to eliminate the inner state of pathology. That is, treating symptoms alone would be of no benefit and in the long run might be harmful, since the inner disease could be expected to intensify.[4] It is interesting that the psychodynamic adaptation of this model of illness is considerably more stringent on the matter of symptomatic treatment than is the parent physical medicine model (witness the symptomatic treatment of cystic fibrosis, or the widespread, symptomatic treatment of the common cold).

A corollary of postulate 1 is that behavior therapy tends *not* to follow the medical model. Again, this is a matter of degree. Were behavior therapy limited to operant conditioning, we could say that it rejects the medical model, and in particular, the concept of the symptom. However, when we speak of anxiety-mediated avoidance or self-verbalizations that give rise to maladaptive behavior, in a sense we are treating overt behavior as symptomatic of something else. This "something else," however, is not thought of as a disease state, related to overt behavior in a mysterious or poorly specified fashion. Instead, it refers to internal events *triggered by external stimuli* that serve to mediate observable response. Another important difference is that in behavior therapy, "internal" events are a good deal more accessible to the client, as well as to the therapist, than are those of psychodynamic theory. Learning (hence behavior therapy techniques) can affect basic physiological processes, such as the functioning of the immune system—which are clearly internal. This domain will be discussed in detail in Chapter 11.

The accessibility of the cause of the patient's suffering is critical to his welfare. To illustrate, one of the authors served as therapist for a patient who had been hospitalized for most of his adult life. The patient, a 40-year-old male who

---

[4]Emphasis on underlying causes of mental illness did not originate with Freud. As Ullmann and Krasner (1969) have noted, the so-called moral treatment of the eighteenth and nineteenth centuries, which in certain respects was similar to behavior therapy, was criticized because it did not remove the underlying cause of the illness.

was diagnosed as having anxiety neurosis, was well above average in intelligence and had attended college briefly. During the course of his lengthy hospitalization, he had been repeatedly exposed to therapists who expounded the traditional medical model. He firmly believed that his problems emanated from his "mental sickness" and could not be convinced that the behavior of others, how tense he felt in certain situations, or what he said to himself in certain situations was especially relevant to his discomfort. That is, he believed that until "the doctors" cured him of his "disease," there was nothing he could do. To all who knew him well, the man appeared to be in genuine misery much of the time. In other words, whatever gains he accrued from failing to work actively on his problems were far exceeded by his evident distress.

The attitudes of individuals who are assigned to help patients obviously are equally critical in treatment. A psychiatrist, or psychiatric nurse, whose training has provided no alternatives to the disease model will not be inclined to view self-defeating behavior on the part of the patient as a consequence of stimulus events (especially contingencies of reinforcement). Consider a hospitalized patient who one day put his hand up the dress of an attractive ward nurse who happened to get in range. At a subsequent staff meeting, the decision was made to make no efforts to communicate to the patient the inappropriateness of such behavior, or to arrange contingencies so that future behaviors of this sort would be less likely to occur. After all, since the patient was mentally ill, what could one expect? From the patient's point of view, he had engaged in a behavior that (taken by itself) most males would find reinforcing, and presumably it was reinforced. Unfortunately for the patient, our culture tends to deal harshly with males who publicly fondle unwilling females, so this episode was put to no therapeutic use and might even have increased the likelihood of such maladaptive behavior by this patient in the future.

The examples just presented will be all too familiar to anyone who has spent any time on a traditional psychiatric ward. Adherence to the disease model has diverted attention from the events that account for maladaptive behavior and, indeed, has encouraged such behavior. Behavior therapy does not reject every aspect of the medical model, but it does categorically reject the premise that maladaptive behavior is primarily a function of a relatively autonomous, highly inaccessible mental disease.

Symptom Substitution Psychodynamic approaches (especially psychoanalytic theory) predict that removing a symptom while ignoring the underlying cause will result in either the recurrence of that symptom or the appearance of a substitute symptom. At one time it was strongly suggested that the hypothesis of symptom substitution follows the medical model, but this requires qualification. If by symptom substitution we mean the appearance of new symptoms as a result of the removal of old ones, this doctrine is *not* consistent with the medical model of physical illness, which *does* allow for symptomatic treatment and does not ordinarily anticipate untoward consequences. Thus, the physician in viewing fever as a symptom of an invasion of bacteria does not expect aspirin therapy or alcohol rubs to cause the appearance of a new ailment. Even certain psychiatric adaptations of the medical model allow for treatment that can best be described as symptomatic. Most psychiatrists who prescribe tranquilizers or electroshock therapy would not argue that they are attempting to alleviate psychopathology at its most basic level, nor would they expect new and terrible symptoms to appear after prescribing such treatment.

In others words, the hypothesis of symptom substitution (one could use the term *doctrine,* because this is what it has become) does not follow from the medical model per se, but primarily from one specific psychiatric derivative of the medical model—namely, psychoanalytic theory.

With respect to the psychoanalytic view of maladaptive behavior, the analogy is often made to a closed hydraulic system. If something within the system gives rise to a buildup of pressure, this may cause a surface to rupture and fluid to rush out. However, merely sealing the rupture (analogous to treating symptoms) only increases the likelihood that a rupture will occur elsewhere. Were this analogy truly appropriate to human psychological functioning, symptom substitution would be a very plausible notion.

Naturally, the critical question from our point of view is whether symptom substitution is likely to occur. As Bandura (1969) cogently points out, it is not possible to disprove this doctrine once and for all, because therapists who apparently believe in symptom substitution have specified neither the nature of the substitute symptom nor the circumstances under which it should occur. On the other hand, it is possible for the behavior therapist to state *his or her own* version of the hypothesis (Cahoon, 1968) and to test it to see if symptomatic treatment may indeed prove harmful. Generally, efforts in this direction (and there have been many) have involved employing behavior therapy to eliminate or to weaken an undesirable behavior, waiting a reasonable period of time, and then querying the individual as to whether or not he has experienced a new symptom. Reviews of empirical findings (including case histories and controlled experiments) indicated that the evidence is overwhelmingly against symptom substitution (see Bandura, 1969; Lazarus, 1971; Wolpe, 1969), and this issue is seldom debated today.

As other writers (e.g., Bandura, 1969) have noted, there are circumstances in which one maladaptive response may substitute for another. He cites the example of antisocial behavior that has been suppressed by punishment. If the individual lacks a socially acceptable response that could serve the same end, he or she is likely to engage in another antisocial response. Wolpe (1969) notes that symptom substitution may occur when a particular overt act is eliminated, but the underlying autonomic (emotional) response remains. For example, if compulsive hand washing is suppressed, the individual might conceivably learn another maladaptive anxiety-reducing response. Thus, there is no axiom of behaviorism that precludes the substitution of one maladaptive behavior for another. But from a practical point of view, it is a phenomenon only rarely observed.

2. *Maladaptive behaviors are, to a considerable degree, acquired through learning, in the same ways that any behavior may be learned.* No currently popular theory of human behavior or personality would take issue with the view that human beings, to a large extent, are products of their environment. However, behavior therapy specifies rather precisely *how* the environment may influence people, in terms of established learning principles (e.g., classical and operant conditioning, modeling).

While maladaptive behavior differs from adaptive behavior in terms of its impact on the individual and those around him or her, healthy and unhealthy ways of responding are generally viewed as fundamentally alike in other respects. Both ways of responding directly reflect the individual's learning history and follow from the same general principles of learning.

Clearly, no modern behaviorist would take the position that *all* maladaptive behavior is merely a consequence of an unfortunate learning history. We would be hard pressed to argue that the immediate behavioral deterioration following a traumatic central nervous system accident arises from the sudden acquisition of a large number of new habits (i.e., learned responses). There are also behavioral characteristics clearly associated with inheritable genetic anomalies, and few therapists would maintain that mental retardation arises exclusively, or even primarily, from unusual learning experiences.

Many American behaviorists stress the importance of certain biological predispositioning factors in accounting for maladaptive behavior (see Herrnstein, 1977). Seligman's "preparedness" is one such factor, discussed in Chapter 2 (de Silva, Rachman, & Seligman, 1977; Seligman, 1971). British behaviorists (most notably Eysenck & Eysenck, 1968) have long emphasized constitutional or biological factors of this general nature.

3. *Psychological principles, especially learning principles, can be extremely effective in modifying maladaptive behavior.* It seems reasonable to assume that a correspondence exists between the degree to which a particular response was learned (as opposed to having been genetically determined) and the ease with which it can be modified. Current conceptualizations of behavior therapy see environmental and biological factors as interactive. This interaction is of more direct concern in some instances (e.g., the context of behavioral medicine) than in others (any of the range of behavioral or cognitive techniques directly addressing overt, generally social, behavior problems). The point is that biological factors are indeed important within the field of behavior therapy, and there is a clear recognition of significant ways experience as well as biological factors, learning, and physiology—in short, nature as well as nurturance—must be considered in conceptualizing clinical problems and in developing effective behavioral treatments. Of course, the fact that a response can be modified through learning does not *prove* it was acquired through learning. For example, it is likely that certain components of human sexual arousal are innate. Yet everyday experience suggests that we can learn to be aroused (and later inhibit such arousal—see Chapter 8) in the presence of stimuli that initially were "neutral" (such as articles of clothing or pornographic literature).

The degree to which people in a position of social control are aware of the importance of relatively straightforward learning principles can have a major bearing on the welfare of their charges. Consider the case of a child who very early in life is diagnosed as severely mentally deficient (say the child has Down's syndrome).

This child has two serious strikes against him. First, assuming the diagnosis is correct, there is something wrong with the way his brain functions, and it is unlikely that he will ever behave in a totally normal manner, no matter what kind of treatment he receives. Second, once he has been labeled severely mentally deficient, a great many people (including some professionals) may automatically assume that he is totally incapable of learning. As a result, instead of receiving the extra attention necessary to learn such functions as elementary speech, the child is treated in a custodial manner and fails to acquire many basic skills that he may be quite capable of learning.

Perhaps to a lesser extent, persons labeled as autistic, schizophrenic, or even epileptic are frequently victimized by others who severely underestimate their ability to learn. In such instances, the unfortunate individuals are likely to develop a major learning deficit, thereby fulfilling the misguided prophecy.

4. *Behavior therapy sets specific, clearly defined treatment goals.* Behavior therapy does not hold that maladaptive responses emanate from a "disturbed personality." The goal of the therapist and client is to help alleviate the specific problems that are interfering with the client's functioning, often by treating these problems in a relatively discreet manner. For this reason, early critics (see Breger & McGaugh, 1965) complained that behavior therapy ignored states such as general unhappiness. The behavior therapist prefers to determine the specific events that lead to broad statements such as "I'm unhappy all the time" and "Life isn't worth living." The analogy may be made to physical medicine, wherein the patient who feels "generally poor" is asked to indicate specific ailments that are often treated separately. The criticism that the physician is thereby ignoring his patient's "general health" would not seem to be justified.

The Importance of Stimulus Control The term *stimulus-response* (S-R) is often associated with behavioristic psychology.[5] We prefer to avoid its usage, because for many it has a highly simplistic connotation that does not do modern behavior theory justice. Yet a fundamental precept is that behavior is largely under stimulus control, and when the behavior therapist establishes his or her objectives, they are conceived of in terms of specific responses occurring lawfully in the presence of specific stimuli. Thus, the therapist using systematic desensitization is not usually trying to free his client of "fearfulness," but rather of specific fears (e.g., of high places or certain animals). And the operant conditioner would not attempt to increase the likelihood of all types of behavior in all circumstances, but rather of specific responses to specific stimuli. Even cognitive methods, which are not usually thought of as exemplifying S-R psychology, postulate lawful stimulus-response relationships, with S and R bridged by the client's thoughts and emotions.

5. *Behavior therapy rejects classical trait theory*. The concept of psychological traits has been a subject of controversy and debate for three-quarters of a century (see Bem & Allen, 1974; Mischel, 1968, 1973). A *trait* is a predisposition to behave similarly in a wide variety of situations. To illustrate, suppose that in a given situation person A is rated more aggressive than person B, who, in turn, is judged more aggressive than person C. A strong trait conception of aggression would hold that the same rank order would occur in a *different* situation. While most lay people, and many psychologists, find the no-

tion of psychological traits intuitively appealing, research findings suggest that behavioral consistency (i.e., across situations) is the exception, not the rule.[6] Not surprisingly then, alternatives to trait "psychologizing" have been put forth in order to deal with the problem of how best to conceptualize and to predict human behavior.

As Endler and Magnusson (1976) note, two alternatives to trait psychology are situationalism and interactionism. *Situationalism,* which is diametrically opposed to trait psychology, maintains that behavior is under direct stimulus control and, therefore, is highly situation-specific. Consistency of response, then, is more or less a direct function of stimulus or environmental consistency. Thus, person A behaves aggressively in a given stimulus situation because he or she has been conditioned to act that way in the presence of such stimuli. Advocates of situationalism would have no reason to expect person A to behave aggressively in a discriminably different external environment unless there were a common learning history.

Interactionism is a midway position. Advocates maintain that behavior is best accounted for as an interactive function of external stimuli *and* person variables (e.g., cognitions, traits, physiological states). Actually, there are several versions of the interactional view. Some are essentially statistical. For those familiar with analysis of variance, in a Situation X Trait factorial design, one looks at the magnitude of each of the main effects in comparison to the Situation X Trait interaction. If the latter is markedly greater, this is taken as support for the interactional position. Other versions of the interactional perspective are more theoretical in nature, including formulations by Mischel (1973) and Bandura (1978), wherein the person variables are mainly cognitive. Eysenck's position (e.g., Eysenck & Eysenck, 1968) may also be described as interactional, with person variables

---

[5]Certain writers (Lazarus, 1977; Locke, 1971) have suggested that we should not equate behavior therapy with behavioristic psychology (or behaviorism). It is true that contemporary behavior therapy, with its increasing emphasis on cognitive processes and procedures, such as self-management, has gone well beyond the "pure" behaviorism of John B. Watson or B. F. Skinner. It should be noted, however, that much of the philosophical underpinning provided by classical behaviorism is still manifest in the theory, practice, and general perspective on maladaptive behavior that characterizes approaches to modern behavior therapy.

[6]As Mischel (1968) notes, consistency of traits associated with intellectual ability has somewhat more empirical support.

having a psychophysiological flavor (for instance, conditionability).

An interactionist, such as Bandura or Mischel, might account for person A's aggressive behavior in a given situation as having been cued by external stimuli, but only after the person has processed, or "cognitively transformed"—to use Mischel's term (1973)—the stimuli. Further, interactionists note that individuals, in part, *determine* their stimulus environment by selecting certain situations and avoiding others. Additionally, they may modify those external environments by their actions. Bandura (1978) uses the term *reciprocal determinism* to characterize this complex ongoing process. To illustrate, person A may seek a stimulus environment where inducement to aggression is likely (a seedy waterfront bar), may process stimuli in a way that further increases the likelihood of aggression (view the behavior of another patron as bellicose), and may, by his own actions, change the environment (assault that patron).

Thus far we have mentioned three general approaches to conceptualizing the causes of human behavior: trait psychology, situationalism, and interactionism. What position do behavior therapists take? We noted previously that behavior therapists stress the importance of stimulus control and stimulus specificity. This is most clearly the case among radical behaviorists, who would strongly favor the situationalism perspective. Not surprisingly, behavior therapists whose social learning orientation stresses the role of constructs, such as cognitions, are partial to an interactive view (Bandura, 1977a; Mischel, 1973). What behavior therapists *share* is a disenchantment of classical trait psychology. That is, behavior therapists hold that, in the absence of additional information, a person's behavior in one set of circumstances is generally a rather poor indicator of how the person will respond in a situation that is markedly different. Stated positively, in the absence of additional information, the best predictor of how a person will act in the present situation is how

that person behaved in the same or similar situations in the past. The "additional information" might involve assessment of the individual's cognitions or physiological state. For example, if a person views two very different situations as similar on one important dimension ("people reject me wherever I go"), his or her behavior or emotional responsiveness may nevertheless be similar (withdrawal, depression). On the other hand, if the person sees two quite similar situations as different because of very subtle changes, his or her behavior may also be different in each. We will deal with this and other issues related to behavioral assessment later in this chapter.

6. *The behavior therapist adapts the method of treatment to the client's problem.* Many forms of traditional psychotherapy provide essentially one method of treatment, regardless of the specific nature of the client's presenting complaint. While it is true that the psychodynamic therapist may occasionally opt to provide "support" rather than to attempt to get at the root of the problem, this is usually a stopgap procedure. If we assume, as in the case of psychoanalytic and related approaches, that present difficulties usually stem from a lack of insight into critical childhood experiences, a single approach aimed at achieving such insight is plausible. Similarly, if an individual's present problems are usually symptomatic of a need for unconditional positive regard, client-centered therapists are quite justified in providing this as the principal mode of treatment.

In terms of the problems with which they are confronted, behavior therapists are willing to assume a more varied etiology, although, obviously, learning is stressed. However, there is nothing in present learning formulations that suggests that maladaptive responses are acquired very early in life, or that they necessarily are mediated by the same pervasive mental state (e.g., a low self-concept). As we shall see later in the chapter, behavior therapy does not require that the precise learning conditions that give rise to present difficulties be known. The point is that the behavior therapy conceptualization of how psychological disorders develop does not justify the use of what Bandura has called an "all-purpose, single method" therapy. Instead, the therapist will employ different procedures, depending on the nature of the problem: A person fearful of flying may be desensitized; a man who is timorous in the presence of attractive women may receive assertion training; the alcoholic may be offered aversive conditioning; the parent whose child frequently throws tantrums may be instructed in operant principles; the obese person may be taught principles of self-control; and so on.

If practitioners tend to view all psychological disorders as emanating from a common internal state or process, and especially if they believe that state to be "unconscious," it is unlikely that they will interpret the client's "presenting" complaint as the client's *real* problem. The client, who is ruled by powerful but unconscious thoughts and impulses, is considered not competent to portray what is troubling him or her in anything but a superficial and distorted manner. In fact, the present authors have known psychodynamically oriented therapists who universally assume that the client's true thoughts and feelings are, in fact, diametrically opposed to those he or she expresses during initial therapy sessions.

Behavior therapists, on the other hand, are considerably more likely to accept the client's presenting complaints as valid (if she did not suffer from these complaints, she would not have sought professional help). Naturally, one need not be an experienced professional practitioner to know that, in any initial encounter, people are not always candid. The therapist, after all, is a stranger and, regardless of his or her formal credentials, time is required to establish an atmosphere of trust and confidence. Any experienced clinician will recall many cases involving clients who, after a few sessions, readily admitted to problems that were of far greater concern to them than the problems they initially had presented. It is also very common for

clients during the course of therapy to report problems unrelated to their initial complaints. Thus, experienced behavior therapists do not assume that they have "a complete picture" of their clients after spending a single hour with them. At the same time, the client is generally viewed as an essentially competent source of pertinent information whose basic problems may be specified without spending hundreds of hours on "uncovering" therapy.

7. *Behavior therapy concentrates on the present.* Individuals beginning therapy often expect that they will be asked to delve into their early childhood experiences in minute detail. In fact, psychoanalytic and related approaches, which have predominated in the United States throughout most of this century, do strongly emphasize the importance of uncovering (i.e., "working through") early events assumed to be critical.[7] Psychoanalytic theory holds that a client's insight into these experiences is of curative value. Behavior therapists, however, ask two critical questions of this postulate. First, how can we be sure that the content of such insights adequately describes actual childhood events? From a behavioral perspective, insights presented to the therapist represent a particular class of verbal behaviors, subject to the same principles of learning that influence other behaviors. Verbal conditioning wherein an experimenter is able to increase certain types of classes of verbal response by selective reinforcement, has been repeatedly demonstrated in the laboratory. Given the presumably higher levels of motivation of most clients, we might expect influences of this nature to be even more potent in the therapeutic situation. A combination of selective

---

[7]Actually, among psychodynamic schools, thinking has tended to evolve in the direction of greater emphasis on dealing more directly with present difficulties. This can be seen when one compares orthodox psychoanalysis (Freud, 1922–1923) with the modified analytic approach of Alexander (Alexander & French, 1946) or the psychoanalytic ego psychology of Rappaport (Gill, 1967).

reinforcement and verbal modeling could easily account for findings wherein clients tend to characterize their own behavior in terms of the orientation of their particular therapist. The situation is analogous to that of a student adopting the idiosyncratic language of a favorite professor or an admired friend. Considerations of this nature have led Bandura to suggest that what has been labeled "insight" in the therapeutic interview might better be characterized as "social conversion."

Second, assuming the validity of insights obtained in psychotherapy, does it follow that they will necessarily lead to reduction in maladaptive responding? Consider the clients who are known as war neurotics (Grinker & Spiegel, 1945). They are quite able to describe traumatic combat experiences that relate to their presenting complaints in a manner far too plausible to discount. Yet despite their apparent insights, their problems seem to remain. For example, one of the present authors treated a veteran who had served as bombardier through 50 combat missions and who, 20 years later, was still fearful of high places and of loud noises resembling the sounds of exploding flak or machine-gun fire (before the war he had experienced neither fear). Whereas such insight appeared to be of little value, both fears were alleviated through systematic desensitization. We are not suggesting that every phobic person is able to recall precipitating traumatic events; Lazarus (1971) has presented data to the contrary.[8] But persons who can, nevertheless, would seem to remain phobic.

[8] Lazarus reported on 100 patients whose presenting complaints included phobic reactions, only 2 of whom could recall traumatic experiences that were clearly relevant. On the other hand, approximately 35 percent of a sample of students who reported having irrational fears were able to recall some traumatic experience that could account for their fear (Rimm, Janda, Lancaster, Nahl, & Dittmar, 1977). Also, in the Lazarus report, it is not clear whether vicarious traumatic experiences were taken into account. The typical snake phobic has never experienced pain or injury

To be fair, we should note that recent innovations in psychoanalytic therapy have included brief, time-limited models for short-term psychotherapy, and these frequently include a focus on the present rather than on lengthy probing into historical insights (e.g., Davanloo, 1980; Malan, 1976; Sifneos, 1979; Strupp & Binder, 1984). There is still a major difference, however, between psychodynamic therapies in general and behavior therapy regarding whether or not historical insight is curative. The necessity for detailed explorations of the client's childhood is generally rejected in behavior therapy, although a certain amount of biographical information is usually considered helpful. (See the discussion of intake interviews later in this chapter.)

8. *Behavior therapists place great value on obtaining empirical support for their various techniques.* As we have suggested, behavior therapy has undergone many changes, but one critical aspect has remained more or less invariant: Behavior therapy is very self-conscious when it comes to scientific validation of its technique (Kanfer & Phillips, 1970). This self-critical attitude is, in truth, an important *defining* characteristic of behavior therapy. As we will see in the section that follows, empirical evidence can be in more than one form, with greater degrees of scientific control providing greater degrees of certainty. The behavior therapist does *not* assume that a technique is effective because it derives from a widely held theory, or because an authority has labeled it effective in the absence of supporting evidence, or because common sense suggests it is effective. Naturally, our thinking is affected

in the presence of a snake but has probably witnessed negative emotional responses on the part of others (especially in the movies or on television, where snakes are almost always depicted as deadly). Similarly, the reader may know persons who, after seeing the movie *Jaws*, were fearful of swimming in the ocean. Most contemporary behaviorists would take the position that fears are acquired in a variety of ways, including direct conditioning, vicarious conditioning, and via the transmission of information (Rachman, 1977).

by factors of this nature that may serve as the source for hypotheses about human behavior. The essential point, however, is that these hypotheses must be put to the test.

Behavior Therapy and the Scientific Method

The essence of science is understanding, typically confirmed through prediction. Any scientific endeavor aims at establishing lawful relationships among observables, so that given one set of events, one can anticipate the occurrence of another set of events. In psychology, one such set of events might be the behavior leading to a high score on an IQ test. The second set might be behaviors leading to a high grade point average at college. If a relationship does exist between these two measures (and a positive relationship does exist), we are then able to predict IQ from grade point average, or vice versa, with some degree of accuracy. Naturally, the degree of predictability will be directly related to the strength of the relationship between the two measures. In this example, no effort is made to manipulate IQ or grade point average. It is possible to determine the degree of relationship between them because they vary naturally. An investigation of this nature is empirical because it is based upon systematic observation, and such investigations are often referred to as *correlational studies*.

This is not an experiment, however. In an experiment, one set of events involves actual manipulations of some sort, with the effect of these manipulations constituting the second set of events. That is, the experimenter performs a specific activity and observes its measurable effects. If we were to provide subjects with a drug presumed to alter the level of intellectual functioning and then measure its effect on IQ (or grade point average), we would be engaging in an experiment.

With respect to any mode of psychological therapy, the most fundamental question to be answered is, Does the treatment work (i.e., is it beneficial, does it do what it is hypothesized to do)? To find this out, we must present the treatment and observe the consequences—in other words, conduct experiments. Therefore, throughout the remainder of this text, when we use the term *empirical findings*, we are normally referring to experiments, whether they are at the primitive case history level or are well-controlled investigations.

Levels of Experimentation and Believability

Assuming that we have adopted a scientific approach, what sort of evidence do we need to be convinced that treatment X is an effective means for dealing with problem Y? To simplify the discussion, assume that alternative treatments are lacking in scientific support. The question is, then, Does treatment X work? Since no one would anticipate that any single approach to human maladaptive behavior will always be maximally effective, the question is best stated in a probabilistic manner: Given the nature of problem Y, what is the probability that treatment X will result in an appreciable improvement? Let us consider sources of empirical information that should help answer this question.

Case Histories Usually initial support for new treatment methods can be found in published case histories. The client—viewed as patient rather than as experimental subject—is treated by the practitioner, whose principal goal is to alleviate suffering. Following treatment, the degree of improvement is assessed (perhaps by comparing the client's pretreatment verbal report with that obtained following treatment). Sometimes follow-ups are performed, perhaps after one month or one year, to determine if the client has maintained the reported improvement.

The case history method may be viewed as a crude experimental technique. While it is true that the therapist is actively *doing* something with his or her client and observing the results, controls are obviously lacking. First, assuming that objective evidence is provided that the client did indeed show improvement (which was maintained at some reasonable follow-up), we cannot specify with certainty the factors that led to the improvement. While it might have been specific aspects of the technique (in other words, any therapist using the same technique would have obtained improvement with any such client), the therapist in a clinical setting is doing a great deal more than merely mechanically applying a technique. In some measure, she is probably providing her client with the expectation that he will get better, in which case improvement could be considered as a placebo effect. She is probably also providing reassurance and support, which by themselves might be helpful to a given client. Even if the therapist were interacting with her client in what might be considered a mechanical manner, her personal characteristics (demeanor, manner of dress) might be expected to have some bearing on the outcome. Such factors can influence the credibility of the therapist, and credibility may have considerable bearing on how persons react to communications of a clinical nature (see Kazdin & Wilcoxon, 1976).

Again, assuming that the client's improvement was real, the improvement might have been quite unrelated to therapy—witness the high rate of spontaneous remission reported initially by Eysenck (1952). When we consider that the client typically spends 1 hour per week in therapy and 167 hours engaged in other activities, it can come as no surprise that the other activities may have a far greater impact than formal treatment.

Finally, truly objective assessments of improvement are not usually reported in the case history literature. Typically, the reader must rely on the therapist's impression of the client's self-report. Thus, we have two possible sources of bias, and either can have a compromising effect on objectivity.

Getting back to hypothetical problem Y, suppose the only information the therapist has is that treatment X was reportedly used successfully in a solitary case involving this problem. What, then, is the likelihood that it will work in a present case? Obviously, there is no way to provide a reasonable answer. If there seemed to be no danger in employing the treatment, and especially if problem Y were of a particularly serious nature, results of the single case would probably be sufficient to motivate most therapists to carry out the treatment, taking care to monitor its effects along the way.

Instead of just a single case history, suppose that there are, say, 20 such case histories, all treated by the same clinician, and that 19 patients reportedly showed marked improvement. Naively, we might therefore conclude that the probability of success in the present case would be 19/20, or .95. Considering the aforementioned difficulties inherent in the case history method, though, we could not fairly make such a statement. On the other hand, assuming that people who publish case histories have standards of objectivity and honesty, the finding may be taken as rather suggestive.

Now, suppose that five therapists, each at a different clinic or hospital, provided separate reports. Each report described roughly 20 clients who suffered from problem Y and received treatment X. Suppose the improvement rate was approximately 95 percent for each of the five therapists. While one therapist might be hopelessly prejudiced, or even fraudulent—or have certain unique personal characteristics that actually account for the improvement—the likelihood that all five reports would be so "contaminated" seems rather remote (Paul, 1969a). Thus, these findings would strongly suggest that when a therapist applies treatment X to problem Y, it is very likely that the client will improve.

Given this kind of information, any therapist would be far more comfortable employing the treatment than he or she would be given the solitary case history. It is still possible that treatment X, taken by itself, is totally worthless, with improvement resulting entirely from non-specific factors, or because the patients would have shown the same rate of improvement without treatment. If nonspecific factors were crucial, we could argue that the treatment as a whole was still effective and should not be abandoned, although a more economical alternative would be to administer only the nonspecifics. If almost every client could be expected to improve spontaneously, this fact would be well known. Let us take a medical example. If problem Y happened to be a severe wrist fracture, and if treatment X resulted in complete healing in three days 95 percent of the time, few would argue that such results would have been obtained without treatment, because the typically long healing time for a fracture is well known. Moreover, few would be convinced of the curative powers of mustard packs on the basis of reliable findings that individuals who used them almost always recovered from colds within three weeks, because it is also well known that colds seldom last that long even without any sort of treatment.

As noted, the medical examples rest on the assumption that people are reasonably familiar with the natural course of the problems in question. However, in the case of psychological disorders, this is often not true. First, people seem a good deal more reticent to discuss their psychological problems than they do their broken bones, bouts with the flu, and the like. (Considering societal attitudes toward individuals who have a history of "mental illness," this is not surprising [see Farina, Gliha, Boudreau, Allen, & Sherman, 1971; Farina & Ring, 1965].) In the main, the sharing of experiences is what leads one to expect that relief from a cold should come within a week or two. If people generally do not share knowledge of their psychological difficulties, how is the lay person to have any knowledge of the rates of spontaneous remission for such disorders? Further, even if people *always* discussed such matters openly, the pejorative language the lay person some-

times uses to characterize such disorders ("psycho," "mental breakdown") is vague, and it is therefore unlikely that agreement could be reached as to rates of recovery. This same argument applies to many professionals.

Let us return to our original question. To what extent can we believe in the efficacy of a treatment, given only case history data? From the above, it would seem that the more positive outcomes we have (especially when reported by practitioners working independently from one another), the more reason we have to believe that the treatment is indeed effective; case histories *can* provide legitimate evidence. However, because of the aforementioned limitations inherent in this approach, such evidence can never be taken as absolutely conclusive that the specifics of a particular treatment are beneficial.

Controlled Experiments *Controls* in an experiment refer to any of a sizable number of procedures employed to ensure that the results can be interpreted in a relatively unambiguous, straightforward manner. Experimental control is not an either-or matter; rather it exists in degrees, depending on the rigor programmed into a particular investigation. The greater the number of carefully instituted control procedures, the more conclusive the results.

Psychological researchers typically employ one of two general strategies of control. The group strategy, the more common of the two, is illustrated in its simplest form in the following experiment. We begin with a sizable number of individuals (subjects), let us say 30. On a random basis, 15 are assigned to one group and 15 to the other. The first group receives a particular treatment, and this group is designated the *experimental, or treatment, group.* The second group does not receive the treatment, and so is designated the *control group.* Usually, response measures are taken at the start and at the conclusion of the experiment, and the two groups are compared with respect to the average, or mean, degree of change. If the average degree of change does not differ at all between the two groups, the obvious conclusion is that the treatment had no effect. This is rare, however, since *chance factors* (events over which the experimenter has no control) would probably account for some difference between the groups. *Inferential statistics* are used to help the experimenter decide whether the obtained group differences are large enough to be considered "real" (i.e., very probably did not occur by chance and *are*, therefore, generalizable). When such is the case, the result is usually stated as follows: "Treatment X was found to have a significant effect on behavior Y." Throughout this text, whenever the term *significant* is used within the context of an experimental finding, it means that the findings may be viewed as trustworthy and would replicate if the study were repeated.

A second general strategy for controlled experiments involves having each subject serve as his or her own control. To illustrate, a particular behavior (e.g., nail biting) is selected for investigation. For each subject, the frequency of occurrence of nail biting is established during a baseline (pretreatment) period. Then a treatment is instituted—perhaps the subject is instructed to punish himself for nail biting by snapping a rubber band around his wrist. By the end of this period a record of nail biting frequency will probably show a great decrease. Up to this point, the experimental design might be termed an AB design. A and B refer to two segments: A, the baseline during which the frequency of a presenting complaint is established; and B, the treatment phase, following which the frequency is again assessed to determine if the treatment was effective. Often this sort of design is expanded into an ABA or ABAB form. In laboratory experiments, where permanent changes are typically not sought, the ABA design ends with a return to baseline (i.e., the treatment is terminated). If the frequency of the behavior returns to baseline levels, this suggests that the treatment was indeed effective. For true problem behaviors where one would not want to leave the individual unchanged, an

ABAB design might be employed where the treatment is instituted a second time. If the frequency of the target behavior once again declines, then treatment is reinstituted. This strengthens the argument that the treatment was indeed effective. However, the astute reader will have noticed that inherent in the ABA or ABAB designs is the assumption that the treatment is not effective once withdrawn—and certainly the hope of any therapeutic intervention would be to achieve generalized and lasting changes in behavior that extend beyond the period of treatment. Thus, these designs would not be particularly appropriate for testing treatments that are expected to make lasting changes in a target behavior.

In this last instance, an AB–Follow-up design would be most appropriate, with a separate untreated control group. In this case, both the experimental and control groups would receive a baseline assessment (A), with a second assessment after treatment for the treatment group and after an equivalent period of time for the control group (B). At this point, we would expect differences in the frequency of the problem behavior if the treatment is effective. Some time later, a third assessment of the frequency of the problem behavior would demonstrate whether treatment gains have been maintained during a period after the treatment itself was discontinued (Follow-up).

There are many controlled experimental designs that may be used to test the effectiveness of treatment, and we need not review all of them here. The experimental design an investigator chooses necessarily depends, in part, on the nature of the problem being investigated. For example, if we were interested in determining the effects of systematic desensitization on an airplane phobia, the simple subject-as-his-own-control strategy might be rejected, since the subject would not be expected to revert to his pretreatment avoidance of flying following the administration of the treatment. Working within an operant framework, however, when reinforcing events control behavior in a simple, straightforward fashion, we could expect a presentation and then a withdrawal of reinforcers to result in an increase in the reinforced response followed by a return to baseline—and this might be demonstrated in a single individual. When appropriate, this strategy has the advantage of being economical (few subjects are required), and as Sidman (1960)—one of the most vigorous opponents of the large-group statistical approach—has pointed out, it allows for examination of unusual individual patterns of response that are lost when the focus is on group averages. For the study of therapeutic outcomes in individual clients, the experimental analysis of single cases has distinct advantages, and researchers have given attention to ways the single-subject methodology can be effectively employed to assess behavior change (Barlow & Hersen, 1984).

On the other hand, Paul (1969a) has argued that in terms of establishing cause-and-effect relationships, the large-group strategy (in particular, the factorial approach, which simultaneously examines the effects of many relevant factors) is the more powerful of the two. Paul would not maintain, however, that the subject-as-his-own-control strategy does not contribute to establishing the validity of a particular technique (especially if different experimenters working in diverse settings report similar results). Both strategies can be considered useful in supporting the efficacy of therapy techniques, though generally the large-group statistical methodology is the more popular of the two (most of the research reported in this text employs this approach).

One more factor needs to be controlled in research on the effectiveness of therapeutic interventions. This is the degree to which the treatment procedure as understood by the client is believable or credible, since more credible treatments will achieve greater effectiveness. A client, for example, is likely to work harder to follow a therapist's instructions when the treatment procedure "makes sense" to him or her than when it does not. It is particularly impor-

tant to control for this (i.e., to keep believability equal) when two forms of treatment are being experimentally compared. In short, the therapeutic rationale, regardless of the theory from which it is drawn, may have a powerful effect on the subjects. Thus, a truly valid comparison between any two treatments necessitates that they be similar with respect to credibility or believability; this determination can only be made empirically. A common approach is to question the subjects regarding credibility after the rationale has been presented: for example, "How logical is the treatment?" "How effective do you think it will be?" (Borkovec, Kaloupek, & Slama, 1975). The important point is that experimenters must not *assume* the two treatments are equally credible, because frequently they are not (Borkovec & Nau, 1972).

Needless to say, these general comments are not intended to provide you with the skills necessary for carrying out therapy research. In specifying such an adequate control treatment, many factors specific to the particular investigation must be taken into account, and an appreciation of such factors probably requires extensive training and experience. On the other hand, we hope that you have been alerted to the crucial role of control groups of this nature (so often missing in research) and will be somewhat better able to evaluate the degree of experimental control when reading the psychological literature.

Finally, we must give some consideration to *ethics*. In therapy research involving untreated controls, placing subjects in control conditions raises an obvious ethical issue of potentially denying needed treatment. After all, is not the experimenter denying therapy to individuals in need? Actually, most subjects in such experiments are not individuals who deliberately seek out treatment in a clinic. Instead, they are generally persons who are functioning relatively well but who have a specific difficulty and who volunteer for what they are told is an "experiment" that is to focus on that difficulty. Perhaps the most important point to be made is that the experimenter is not withholding a treatment that is *known* to be effective. Indeed, this is the whole point of the investigation. If it turns out that therapy subjects fare no better than controls, this is evidence the control subjects were not denied effective treatment. If therapy subjects do fare better, the experimenter is now in the excellent position of being able to offer the control subjects a treatment that now has scientific support. In fact, this is often done, with control subjects receiving the (effective) experimental treatment after the major part of the experiment is concluded. If there is a legitimate ethical issue, it is related to the fact that experimenters often do not provide control subjects with this option.

Outcome Measures Throughout this section we have been referring to possible *improvement* occurring as a result of the application of therapy, but how is such improvement determined? We will return to the very important topic of *behavioral assessment* later in the chapter, but for the present we will examine three general types of measures that may be employed to assess treatment effectiveness: behavioral, subjective or self-report, and physiological (see Table 1–1).

Often, *behavioral measures* directly sample the target behavior under investigation. Selected examples of problem areas frequently treated by behavior therapists are listed in the left-hand column. In the next column are behavioral response measures frequently used in investigations of these problems.

Self-report (*subjective*) measures may be derived from an interview or from a paper-and-pencil test (Meyer, Liddell, & Lyons, 1977; Tasto, 1977). Usually in research, response measures are related to the target problem in a relatively straightforward way.

In therapy outcome research, *physiological* measures such as heart rate, blood pressure, and skin resistance are often used to confirm findings obtained by behavioral or self-report measures, although in some cases they may themselves constitute the most basic outcome measures (e.g., if the target problem is reduction of blood pressure or modification of penile tumescence). Complicated and expensive hardware is usually involved, and reasonable expertise is required in its use.

A fourth class of response measures, used less frequently, includes *reports of significant others* regarding the behavior of the subject. Researchers in the area of alcoholism frequently rely on such reports, but care must be taken to obtain the subject's prior informed consent.

Since the intercorrelations among the various classes of measures are often low (Cohen, 1977), most experimenters opt to include a minimum of two such classes. For instance, in research with agoraphobics, Krawitz, Rimm, and Zimmerman (1978) employed as their behavioral measure the number of levels the subject was able to climb on a fire department training tower (much like a fire escape), as well as the individual's subjective report of fear at each level. For logistical reasons, physiological measures were not employed by Krawitz and associates, but when feasible, at least one such measure is recommended.

Follow-up Outcome Assessment If the treatment is to have any practical value, its positive effects must have a degree of durability. For this reason, it is important that therapy research include follow-up measures. Frequently, such measures are the same as those employed in the experiment proper, although sometimes novel *in vivo* measures are added (see Hersen & Bellack, 1977). A major issue is the amount of time that the experimenter should allow to elapse before taking follow-up measures. Certainly, a period of only two or three days could not possibly allow for a convincing demonstration of the stability of treatment effects. On the other hand, certain writers (see Paul, 1969a) have pointed to problems inherent in attempting follow-ups on a truly long-term basis. For example, two years after treatment, a sizable number of subjects may not be available, and among those who are, some may be

Table 1–1 **Common Target Problems and Typical Response Measures**

Target Problem	*Behavioral Measure*	*Self-report Measure*	*Physiological Measure*[a]
Fear of heights	Number of stories climbed on fire escape; how close subject will go to edge of a rooftop; how long subject will remain on top of a building	Self-report of anxiety (say, on a 10-pt. scale) while on a fire escape, etc., or while *imagining* engaging in such an activity	(For any phobic response) Skin resistance, heart rate, skin temperature, respiration rate
Fear of small animals	How close subject will get to a caged animal; how long subject will remain seated next to the cage	—	—
Overweight	—	Self-report of type and amount of food consumed during the day	—
Lack of assertion	Objective ratings of subject's assertiveness in role-played situation, including loudness of voice, latency, fluency, assertiveness of content of speech, eye contact	Self-report of anxiety (or perhaps anger) while in role-play situation or imagining it	Skin resistance, heart rate, blood pressure
Orgasmic disorder	—	Self-report of anxiety while engaging in sex-related activity (or imagining such activity); self-report of pleasure while engaging in real or imagined situation; self-report of frequency of sexual intercourse and frequency of orgasm	—
Sexual impotence	—	—	Skin resistance, heart rate, penile circumference or volume
Tension headaches	—	—	Muscle action potentials (EMG)

[a]In some cases, the specific choice of a measure is obvious (e.g., penile volume in the case of impotence), but frequently the choice is less clear (e.g., researchers differ on what is the best physiological measure of anxiety).

unwilling to participate. Also, successful treatment would not ordinarily protect the subject from adverse learning experiences during a long follow-up period that might cause the reappearance of the same maladaptive behavior. The longer the follow-up period, the more likely regression is to occur; and if it does occur, it is not reasonable to conclude that the treatment was ineffective.[9]

One factor we should take into account is the frequency with which the subject is likely to be exposed to stimuli that, prior to treatment, typically gave rise to maladaptive behavior. For instance, a dog phobic individual, following systematic desensitization, might be expected to have frequent *in vivo* encounters with dogs. If the improvement associated with treatment was of a transient nature (e.g., if the therapist induced a temporary sense of confidence in the subject, but the subject's *in vivo* emotional or cognitive responses to real dogs had not changed), the subject would quickly learn that he or she was not "cured" after all. Here it is likely that a follow-up of, for instance, two months would reveal the lack of durability of the treatment. Individuals treated for, say, fear of flying might be expected to engage in relevant experiences no more than once or twice a year. In such cases, a much longer follow-up would be highly desirable.

---

[9]There are also some interesting paradoxes worth thinking about. Consider an investigation where treatment consists of removing the individual from an environment that regularly reinforces what society considers to be inappropriate behaviors and placing him or her in an environment that reinforces appropriate behaviors (e.g., a hospital or a token economy). If, after successful treatment, the client is returned to the original environment, the individual's *failure* to "relapse" could be taken as evidence that the assumptions of treatment were not valid (i.e., if the maladaptive behavior really were under the control of these contingencies, it should return).

From the perspective of potential consumers—that is, therapy clients—cost-versus-gain (i.e., cost effectiveness) considerations are paramount in determining the duration of a follow-up. How many months (or years) of relative psychological well-being justify X therapy sessions at Y dollars per session? Clearly, no single answer can be provided because many subject-related variables are involved. Given a *specific* subject (or client) population, an experimenter could make an empirical determination, for instance, by asking the subjects. These data could then be used as a partial basis for deciding on a reasonable follow-up duration.

Analogue Experiments Controlled behavior therapy experiments are usually of the analogue variety. The experimenter's treatment of his subject is a somewhat simplified analogue for the practitioner's treatment of his patient in the clinical setting. The subjects are volunteers taken from a nonclinical population (i.e., they would be classified as "normal"). Ordinarily, in a given experiment, each subject suffers from the same problem. Treatment, which is administered in a stereotypical fashion, deals only with the specified problem. As early researchers have noted (see Kanfer & Phillips, 1970; Paul, 1969a), for reasons of ethics and experimental control, the analogue approach is a desirable way of investigating the efficacy of treatment. However, the real purpose of carrying out analogue research is to provide practitioners with better methods for dealing with clinical problems (for instance, problems of hospitalized patients or of clients who seek out patient therapy).

The critical question is, then, To what extent can we expect analogue results to generalize to clinical populations? Paul (1969a) has concluded that generalizability depends upon the degree to which the variables studied in the laboratory share the essential characteristics of the variables in the clinical context. Some of these characteristics would include severity and duration of the target problem, the existence of other problems possibly correlated with the target problem, and levels of motivation.[10]

Critics of analogue research have noted that in many studies target problems have not been especially relevant to the subject's everyday functioning, either because subjects showed the problem only to a mild degree or because subjects were not required to confront the problem stimuli or situations very often (for instance, fear of snakes in people who live in a large city). Subjects for analogue studies are very often recruited from introductory psychology courses. And there is reason to believe that subjects so chosen may not see their problems as interfering with their lives very much. The difficulty in obtaining subjects who regard their problems as relevant seems to be more related to the *method of subject selection* than to the population from which the subjects come. For instance, Little, Curran, and Gilbert (1977) found that introductory psychology students volunteering for a study on social anxiety (supposedly because they

---

[10]Motivation is so frequently invoked as an explanation (often *post hoc*) for therapeutic success or failure that it has virtually become a cliché. This is unfortunate, because if by *motivation* we mean a set of external reasons (contingencies) for behavior change, then motivation is of paramount importance (witness the striking changes in ward behavior when token economy approaches are instituted). It is likely that anyone who has ever worked with patients hospitalized in a Veterans Administration hospital will testify to the frustration encountered in attempting to motivate patients to improve and thereby to leave the hospital, when leaving the hospital often leads to a substantial loss of veterans' benefits. An honest dialogue between therapist and patient might be as follows:

Therapist: Let me help you behave in a normal manner and then you can be discharged.
Patient: What! Do you think I'm crazy?

This is in no sense a criticism of the hospital per se, but rather of a system that inadvertently rewards maladaptive, dependent behavior.

had problems in heterosexual interaction) showed relatively little social anxiety in the laboratory test. In contrast, Royce and Arkowitz (1977) recruited socially anxious subjects from a similar population but screened out subjects whose responses on a questionnaire suggested that their problem was not very debilitating. Subjects who were unwilling to deposit $10 (refundable at the end of the experiment) were also screened out. The final sample of subjects was a fraction of the number originally contacted by the experimenters. In terms of a variety of behavioral and self-report measures, subjects selected in this manner did show relatively high levels of social anxiety.

However, given even the most stringent subject selection procedures, it seems fairly clear that generalization of results to clinical settings can be expected to be a good deal less than perfect. The final test of whether a treatment method works in a clinical setting must be conducted in a clinical setting. Herein lies an important function of case history data. If we can conclude from analogue research (and certainly our conclusion should be based on more than one experiment) that the specifics of treatment X are effective in dealing with a class of problems Y, and if a sizable number of different therapists in different clinical settings report a high success rate (based on a large number of patients or clients) in dealing with a similar class of problems, this argues very strongly for the clinical or practical value of the treatment. Naturally, positive findings from controlled research conducted in a clinical setting will add to the strength of such a conclusion.

In summary, whether a particular technique X is of practical value in dealing with a given class of maladaptive behaviors, Y, is a matter of empirical findings. Controlled analogue experiments can provide convincing evidence that the technique is effective for certain populations. Nonspecific control groups, the use of different experimenters, the inclusion of several relevant response measures, and a reasonable follow-up all contribute to the believability of such findings. The degree to which analogue findings can be generalized to clinical settings is a function of commonality of essential factors. Extensive case history findings and, when feasible, controlled research in the clinical setting, coupled with analogue findings, may provide conclusive evidence that the specific technique is of practical value.

Behavior Therapy and the Accumulation of Empirical Findings

In 1965, one of the authors attended a seminar conducted by a prominent behavior therapist who expressed the view that since the principles for modifying human behavior were already well established, psychologists should concentrate their efforts on dealing with matters of ethics. In other words, the "data were in," and the question was how to use the data in an ethical and a socially constructive fashion. When one reviews the vast accumulation of empirical knowledge since then (much of which has appreciably altered the "behavior" of the practicing behavior therapist), it is clear that such a statement was quite premature. At that time, the empirical support for the effectiveness of systematic desensitization and assertive training was relatively weak, the "extinction" methods (e.g., implosive therapy) were virtually unresearched, the important work of Bandura and his associates on modeling procedures and fear reduction had not yet appeared, behavioral approaches to self-control were largely in the conjectural stage, and the important role of cognitive factors in influencing behavior was neither widely appreciated nor empirically supported. Indeed, behavioral medicine and health psychology are not yet recognizable fields. Clearly, a wealth of clinically and theoretically relevant information has accumulated since 1965. If, indeed, the data were by no means entirely collected then, would such a statement be correct

today? Given existing trends, the answer is firmly in the negative.

For scientific purposes, in this case understanding effective principles of behavior change, this answer is welcome—as it should be in science. And from the point of view of the dedicated practitioner, this is crucial. If practitioners incorporate some of these procedures in their practice, they must not be oblivious to subsequent findings that indicate that the procedures, as described here, are in need of modification. To ignore such findings is to perform a disservice to their clients. A fundamental defining characteristic of behavior therapy is its insistence that clinical practice be subject to continual modification as new factual data appear. To ignore these data is, in considerable measure, to fail to appreciate what behavior therapy is all about.

Behavior Therapy and Theory

A reader unfamiliar with developments in academic psychology may be surprised to learn that the role of theorizing has been, for some time, a subject of considerable controversy. While the majority of psychologists are quite comfortable dealing with issues on a theoretical level, others decidedly are not. The most vigorous, and certainly the most publicized, criticisms of psychological theorizing came from Skinner and his followers (Rachlin, 1977a, 1977b; Skinner, 1950, 1953, 1971, 1974). Over the years they have held that psychological theories have not contributed a great deal to the establishment of functional relationships—that is, lawful relationships between variables. They have been especially uncomfortable with the practice of postulating hypothetical inner causes, sometimes referred to as "hypothetical constructs" or "intervening variables," to account for observable behavior. Examples of such constructs are the id, ego, and superego of Freudian psychology; the habit strength (S^hR) of Hullian learning theory; the expectancies of

Tolmanian learning theory; and the thoughts and images that cognitive behavior therapists believe are important determinants of human behavior (Beck, 1984; Coyne & Gotlib, 1983; Ellis, 1977; Meichenbaum, 1977). This controversy has cooled in recent years, even though some psychologists (generally those embracing an operant framework) continue to eschew the use of theory or theory building.

Constructs of this nature, as they are employed so often, provide what appears to be an explanation of behavior. But sometimes they really are circular pseudoexplanations that provide nothing more than a label for the behaviors they are postulated to explain. Consider the person who cries a great deal. An observer might say, "That's because he is an emotional person." But how does the observer know that the subject is emotional? Usually because he infers it from the crying behavior. What the observer is really saying is, "That person cries because he is emotional, which I infer from his crying." The circularity is obvious, and it is equally obvious that nothing *has* been explained. Unfortunately many people (including many psychologists) seem to believe that something has been explained, and as Skinner notes, the effect is to "allay curiosity and bring inquiry to a stop" (1974, p. 14). Psychological theories, especially theories of personality, have not infrequently postulated constructs of the above nature, and the criticisms of the Skinnerians have considerable foundation. However, many psychologists, including the present authors, take exception to what they view as a *blanket* rejection of the scientific value of postulating constructs. Let us examine this issue further.

The nature of hypothetical constructs is that they have "surplus meaning" (Bower & Hilgard, 1981)—that is, having been postulated, they assume a status not entirely dependent on a specific instance of observable behavior. For example, a person whose crying is attributed to "emotionality" will be assumed to be emotional, even when he is not observed to be crying.

While it is true that in the above example accounting for crying in terms of emotionality was circular, it is still possible that the construct "emotionality" has scientific value. This will be the case if we can conceptualize emotionality in terms of certain specific properties that give rise to predictions about behaviors other than crying.

The major problem with hypothetical constructs, as they have so often been used in psychology, is that their defining characteristics have not been specified to the degree of precision necessary to allow for clear-cut predictions. Given a broad theory with a large number of such vaguely defined constructs, it is possible to "explain" virtually any observable behavior *after* it has been observed. A theory that by nature of its ambiguity has numerous built-in loopholes and escape clauses is almost impossible to disprove, and both its scientific value and clinical ability are severely limited.

The essential problem with so many psychological constructs is not that the label *mentalistic* can be attached to them, but rather that they do not have clear-cut procedures to implement them or do not lead to clear-cut predictions. Many notable advances in the study of human learning and memory have come about in considerable measure because theorists have been careful to describe hypothesized underlying processes in relatively clear and concrete terms. Excellent examples of this include work on conceptual organization involving mnemonics, clustering, and visual images that have been shown to have a profound effect in enhancing learning and recall (e.g., Bower, 1972b; Houston, 1976; Paivio, 1971). These experimenters were willing to postulate mental events, but they did it in a way that allowed for unambiguous hypotheses. Some of these cognitive hypotheses have met with dramatic experimental support, while others have not. The important point is that careful theorizing of this nature, whether called "mentalistic" or not, has contributed appreciably to our knowledge of learning and memory.

Some psychologists argue that theoretically based hypotheses of this nature are still irrelevant, inasmuch as the functional relationships with which they are associated would have been found even in the absence of any theorizing. Technically, this argument is impossible to refute, but at best it suggests a grossly inefficient approach to research. Consider how unlikely it would be that a researcher who resolutely disregarded the construct "visual imagery" would just happen to instruct his subjects to memorize pairs of nouns by visualizing the objects which they represent interacting in a scene (Bower, 1967; Paivio & Yuille, 1967). Similar statements can be made regarding the likelihood of developing behavior therapy procedures such as systematic desensitization, covert modeling, implosive therapy, or cognitive methods, while denying the importance of mediational processes such as visual imagery, self-verbalization, and anxiety.

The argument that theory is irrelevant is somewhat more cogent when the theory in question makes predictions that everyday experiences render obvious. For example, a "theory" of gravitation that merely makes the qualitative prediction that objects tend to fall to the ground is hardly in need of a test, nor would there be any need for empirical verification of a theoretically derived assertion that males generally tend to be sexually attracted to females. If theorizing were limited to predictions of such an obvious nature, it would clearly be a waste of time.

The important point is that modern science is replete with examples of theorizing that have given rise to predictions not at all obvious or trivial. This is perhaps best seen in atomic physics, where it has been necessary to postulate the existence of new, subatomic particles having very peculiar properties, with subsequent experimentation validating their existence. For example, the *neutrino*, assumed to have a negligible rest mass (but detectable energy and momentum), was postulated, in part, to satisfy the law of conservation of momentum. The neutrino

hypothesis gave rise to experiments that indeed supported the existence of this very strange particle. Einstein's special theory of relativity gave rise to even more dramatic and unusual predictions (e.g., that the mass of a body should vary with its velocity).[11] We can readily point to similar, although usually less dramatic, examples in psychology, including theoretical hypotheses leading to the aforementioned human learning experiments, to numerous short-term memory studies, to a large number of empirical investigations found in the mathematical psychology literature, as well as the theoretical considerations leading to the development of the cognitive therapy methods discussed in detail later in this text. Thus, it would seem clear that theory (in particular, the postulating of hypothetical constructs) does have an important role to play in science, including psychology, provided that such theory leads to testable predictions of a nontrivial nature.

The Importance of Simplifying Assumptions

It is a truism to say that human behavior is profoundly complex. We can postulate an almost endless number of plausible factors, both internal and external, to account for virtually any observable response made by an adult human being. Given this state of affairs, how is it possible to study or observe behavior in a manner that will allow for meaningful prediction? (In this regard, we should point out that the practitioner is every bit as concerned with prediction as the scientist. His focus is simply upon individual clients rather than on subjects

[11]It is interesting that Skinner (1971), the arch foe of psychological theorizing, advocates that psychology adopt the strategy of physics, with its emphasis on environmental causation. In fact, much of the progress of modern physics can be attributed to the physicists' willingness to deal with states or processes that initially could not be observed directly. Obviously, modern physics is not antienvironmental, but it is by no stretch of the imagination antitheoretical.

in an investigation.) An important part of the answer to this very fundamental question is that the observer *must be willing to make certain simplifying assumptions.* To illustrate what is meant by a simplifying assumption, any student of high school physics will be familiar with the formula for the distance traveled by free-falling bodies, $S = 16t^2$, where S is the distance fallen, and t is the elapsed time. This formula is only an approximation, however, for it ignores air resistance—which itself is a complex function of atmospheric conditions—and the shape, texture, and velocity of the object. It also ignores the fact that the "constant" number (16) is not really constant, but varies with the distance from the object to the earth's center. Whenever such factors are deliberately ignored, we say a simplifying assumption is being made.

It is essential to realize that, even with the several simplifying assumptions, it is possible to use the formula $S = 16t^2$ to make remarkably accurate predictions. However, if Isaac Newton had insisted on taking into account every conceivable factor in theorizing about free-falling bodies, it is quite likely that he would have given up in sheer frustration, thus depriving the world of an important formulation. A similar point is made by Skinner: "If Gilbert or Faraday or Maxwell had had even a quick glimpse of what is now known about electricity, they would have had much more trouble in finding starting points and in formulating principles which did not seem 'oversimplified' " (1971, p. 159).

Few would argue that the complexity of a falling rock in any way approximates the complexity of the human behaving organism. Imagine, then, the task of the scientist or practitioner who attempts to take into account every conceivable causal factor in predicting what a person is going to do in any given situation. It would be impossible. As with the physicist, the student of human behavior has no choice but to make simplifying assumptions. This is exactly what the behavior therapist does. Suppose he is presented with a child who shows a high frequency of tantrum behavior. He will probably assume that such behavior is reinforced, perhaps by parental attention. This particular conception, or "model," of what is going on will enable him to gain whatever information is necessary to support or to reject the assumptions on which it is based. If support is found, the therapist will be in a position to make concrete suggestions to the parents. If it is not, he will be forced to find an alternative approach. The point is that by making simplifying assumptions, the therapist (and theoretician, as well) will not be so overwhelmed by possibilities that he will be thrown into a virtual state of paralysis.

The behavior therapist is well aware he is making such simplifying assumptions. He would not take the position, for example, that parental attention is the sole factor maintaining tantrum behavior, or, on a more general level, that one can explain all of human behavior in terms of the principles underlying behavior therapy. Instead, he would argue that the behavioral "model," based upon such principles, is very *useful* in the prediction and modification of the way people behave. He does not claim to have a total understanding of human behavior which, as Kanfer and Phillips (1970) have noted, is probably not even *necessary* for effective treatment.

Behavioral Assessment

Recent years have witnessed a sharp increase in the number of experimental and theoretical publications dealing with the area of behavioral assessment. Throughout much of its early development, behavior therapy concentrated its efforts on evolving conceptually rigorous, empirically based *treatment* techniques. As we noted earlier, testing such techniques necessitated the development of assessment procedures, but such procedures, in general, were unstandardized and lacking in conceptual sophistication. More recently, publications dealing with various aspects of behavioral assessment have come to provide a good level of scientific rigor not apparent even 5 years ago, and there is now a journal devoted solely to research on behavioral assessment.

Traditional Assessment Versus Behavioral Assessment

A traditional psychological assessment battery might include a Rorschach (projective test), a Bender-Gestalt (test of organic brain damage), and a paper-and-pencil personality inventory, such as the popular Minnesota Multiphasic Personality Inventory (MMPI). For purposes of comparison, let us consider the MMPI. It consists of 550 items—for example, "My father was a good man," "Everything tastes the same," "I sometimes have the urge to hurt people with sharp objects." The subjects respond by indicating that a given item is or is not applicable to them. On the basis of their responses, subjects are assigned a score on each of several traditional dimensions or traits of psychopathology (e.g., schizophrenia, hysteria, depression).

Another paper-and-pencil questionnaire, which is more appropriate for the behavior therapist, is the Fear Survey Schedule (FSS). The Geer FSS (Geer, 1965)—the most prominent of several versions—consists of 51 items, each representing a common fear, for example, sharp objects, criticism, auto accidents. The items are rated on a seven-point scale, indicating the degree to which the subject experiences a given fear. The FSS is used as a screening device to determine what specific fears or phobias the subject reports. In comparing the MMPI and the FSS, several general points can be made. The interested reader should also refer to the Conflict Resolution Inventory presented and discussed in Chapter 3. This inventory illustrates how interpersonal conflicts can be presented behaviorally in an assessment instrument.

1. *Conceptually,* behavioral assessment is more *direct* than traditional assessment. *Intuitively* (or in terms of face validity), self-report that one is terrified of high places is more directly related to acrophobia than, let us say, to endorsement

of the statement "Everything tastes the same" would be to schizophrenia. The point regarding conceptual directness is even more obvious in comparing, for example, a measure of ego strength derived from the Rorschach with a behavioral measure of acrophobia that involves how close an individual will go to the edge of a high building. The latter comparison, however, might tend to obscure the following point.

2. *Methodologically,* traditional and behavioral assessment do not necessarily differ in any systematic way. Note that both the MMPI and the FSS are paper-and-pencil tests that involve endorsements of specific items. These are self-report measures, but the same point can be made for behavioral and physiological measures. Thus, observing motor activity as a reflection of catatonic schizophrenia illustrates the use of a gross behavioral measure in a traditional way. Observing how close an individual will go to the edge of the roof illustrates the use of a gross behavioral measure within the context of behavioral assessment. Similarly, skin conductance as a measure of the use of schizophrenia illustrates the use of a physiological measure in traditional assessment, whereas skin conductance specifically in the presense of a phobic scene (or penile erection given erotic stimuli) exemplifies the behavioral use of physiological measurements.

3. Relative to traditional assessment, behavioral assessment tends to *focus on specific rather than on global entities.* Typically, traditional assessment attempts to tap into pervasive, global traits (e.g., schizophrenia, ego strength). In contrast, and this relates to its emphasis on directness, behavioral assessment deals with modes of response that are of a more situationally specific nature. The degree to which this is the case will depend on the individual orientation of the behavior therapist—that is, on whether he or she is partial to situationalism or interactionism (see p. 9). The notion of relative specificity is clear when we consider how the FSS is used: The practitioner, in general, is not interested in a global measure of a trait called "fearfulness,"

but rather in specific fears of specific stimuli or situations.

4. Relative to traditional assessment, behavioral assessment is much more *oriented toward treatment*. While traditional assessment devices such as the MMPI may have some utility in terms of treatment decisions (e.g., an elevated score on the schizophrenia scale of the MMPI might increase the probability that antipsychotic medication will be prescribed), they were not designed for this purpose. Behavioral assessment devices, on the other hand, are a particularly integral part of any behaviorally oriented treatment program. An indication on the FSS that the client is terrified of high places, when corroborated by other behavioral assessment data, may be used to establish that acrophobia constitutes a problem for the client and may point to a specific technique as the "treatment of choice" (e.g., systematic desensitization instead of a cognitive behavior therapy technique). Similarly, a low baseline for cooperative social behavior in a child may be indicative of a problem in this area and may suggest the use of operant procedures in enhancing this behavior.

Identifying a problem in need of treatment and identifying the appropriate treatment are sometimes separate tasks. This is the case when more than one treatment is available for the same problem. This is well illustrated in examining the behavior therapy literature on the treatment of phobias. Among the techniques that have been successfully employed are systematic desensitization, assertion training, modeling, extinction procedures, and cognitive behavior therapy.

While the specifics of a particular case may indicate that one of the above techniques is more appropriate than the others, often this is not so, and the therapist must make an essentially arbitrary decision. In practice, therapeutic decisions are sometimes made on the basis of habit, which is not particularly comforting and has motivated thoughtful writers such as Wolpe (1977) to argue for the assessment of individual differences in response to the various treat-

ments available. Traditionally, behavior therapy has been preoccupied with whether a given treatment helps the *average* person. Clearly, we must also be concerned with what works best for whom. Throughout this text, we shall attempt to address both of these crucial questions.

Approaches to Behavioral Assessment

As we intimated earlier, there is at present no widely accepted, standardized behavioral assessment *battery*. There are, however, comprehensive, systematic approaches to, or models for, behavioral assessment (see, for instance, Adams, Doster, & Calhoun, 1977; Ciminero, Calhoun, & Adams, 1986; Kanfer & Saslow, 1969; Lazarus, 1976). Adams and associates provide what they call the Psychological Response Classification System (PRCS). The PRCS is seen as an alternative to traditional disease-model conceptualizations (most notably, those found in the Disease and Statistical Manuals of the American Psychiatric Association: DSM-I, 1958; DSM-II, 1967; DSM-III, 1979). In contrast to the DSMs (but characteristic of behavioral assessment schema), the PRCS is designed to classify responses rather than people. Response systems are divided into six broad categories: motor, perceptual, biological, cognitive, emotional, and social (see Adams, Doster, & Calhoun [1977] for the specifics). Lazarus (1976) regularly employs what he calls the BASIC ID as a conceptual guideline in his approach to behavioral assessment (Lazarus would probably prefer the term *multimodal assessment*). The anacronym BASIC ID, chosen in part with tongue in cheek, reflects the author's desire to provide the broadest possible basis for assessment. Thus, it is important that the therapist explore with the client (and with significant others, when appropriate) each of the elements listed below. Like the PRCS, which in many respects is very similar, the BASIC ID is essentially a response classification scheme. Naturally, the therapist will wish to specify the contextual or environmental stimuli associated with each response system. The categories of the BASIC ID include the following:

Behavior. Simple and complex motor and verbal behavior

Affect. Anger, anxiety, joy, depression, love, sexual arousal

Sensation. Visual, auditory, olfactory, gustatory, tactile, erotic sensations

Imagery. Visual images

Cognition. Beliefs, thoughts, self-verbalizations, *self-efficacy*

Interpersonal Relationships. Responses vis-à-vis others, including the therapist

Drugs. Drug and state history, but also refers to other aspects of client's physical being, including physical appearance and dress; patterns of exercise and diet

Note that in the Cognition category we italicized "self-efficacy." We did this to bring this construct to your attention because we believe it has far-reaching potential in relation to assessment and, even more generally, in relation to the fundamental processes involved in behavioral change. Research by Bandura (1977b; Bandura, 1978) and others suggests that individuals may be excellent predictors of how well they will be able to master potentially aversive situations. According to Bandura, prior learning experiences provide individuals with a sense of ability to cope, of confidence, or of *self-efficacy* vis-à-vis problem situations. Self-efficacy is easy to assess and correlates very highly with behavior in the target situation. To illustrate, in a recent preliminary investigation with agoraphobics, subjects were asked whether they could perform 15 separate tasks that subjects in such a population have difficulty confronting—for example, being a certain distance from home, being in crowds, riding in elevators. The subjects differed considerably in relation to the specific tasks, but far more interestingly, their own predictions were accurate 81 percent of the time

(and the figure would have been higher had their ratings not been merely dichotomous). Bandura (1977a) also presents convincing data for the predictive power of self-efficacy ratings following behavior therapy involving systematic desensitization and participant modeling. A beginning procedure for assessing self-efficacy might involve little more than asking clients the following questions (Bandura, 1977a):

1. Do you think you are able to . . . (carry out the target behavior)?

   Yes   No

2. How confident are you about what you just said?

   0%————————————100%

   Not confident at all   Completely confident

General guidelines such as those provided by Adams and his associates and by Lazarus are very useful in cuing therapists to aspects of the client's behavior (broadly defined) that might otherwise go unobserved. Shortly, we will present a portion of a sample *initial* interview incorporating many elements of these systems. The primary purpose of the initial interview is to begin to define the client's major problem areas (and strengths). Once a client and therapist decide to work on a specific problem area, the focus of assessment shifts, temporarily at least, to a determination of the treatment most appropriate for the client's problem. Behavioral assessment at this level is discussed in relation to each of the behavior therapy techniques as they are presented throughout the remainder of the text.

Another obvious goal of the initial interview is to establish rapport. In certain respects, the behaviorally oriented initial interview is similar to the interview that therapists of other orientations conduct. The therapist's way of relating to his client, while not necessarily communicating "unconditional positive regard," nevertheless should be marked by warmth and a concern for the client's welfare. Throughout this text, we present evidence for the efficacy of behavior therapy procedures when efforts have been made to minimize such nonspecific factors, and you may wonder why they are emphasized. First, no therapy can succeed if the client perceives his therapist as cold and indifferent; the client will drop out of treatment as a result. Second, a major task for the therapist is to obtain a good deal of information from his client (some of which will be potentially embarrassing), and an atmosphere of warmth and acceptance will facilitate this goal. Third, it is reasonable to suppose that a therapist who is seen as understanding and caring will be a more potent source of social reinforcement for progress in treatment than would one who is perceived as cold and uninterested.

For anyone who had observed the consulting-room manner of a behavior therapist, the above points may seem too obvious to mention. Unfortunately, those who have not very often assume that the behaviorist interacts with his client in a cold, "objective" fashion, as Pavlov might have interacted with his dogs. Not so.

The Initial Interview

While most therapists are not comfortable with a rigid interview format, some degree of structure is desirable. For initial interviews, the following order of events is illustrative:

1. Delineation and elaboration of the presenting problem, setting of initial goals (e.g., to begin treatment)
2. Delineation of other current problem areas
    3. Delineation of strengths
    4. Gathering of background information

For some clients, one session may be adequate to accomplish the above, but frequently two or three sessions are required. Needless to say, the therapist does not cease the process of assessment after a few hours. As we noted earlier, ongoing assessment is very much a part of any behavior therapy treatment regimen and, in fact, is highly desirable *after* the termination of treatment (i.e., during the follow-up).

As Lazarus (1971) has noted, one focus should be the delineation of the problem behavior with respect to when it occurs and what factors maintain it, rather than focusing on why the individual is behaving in such a maladaptive fashion. Novice therapists have an unfortunate tendency to begin with "why" questions, which has the effect of putting clients off (it makes them feel as if they are on the witness stand). For the learning therapist, the first few moments of an initial interview may be very awkward indeed.[12] Not infrequently, the client says nothing, waiting for the therapist to make the first move. At such times, the therapist might ask the client, "What's happening?" or simply smile and shrug his shoulders (communicating the same thing). Frequently, this will be followed by the client verbalizing his "presenting complaint." The degree to which problems are clearly specified will vary considerably from client to client, but usually a considerable amount of questioning will be in order. Consider the following example:

> The client is a male, 31 years old. He is married and works as a shipping clerk.

Therapist: How can I help you?

Client: I wanted to talk to someone. I have this problem. (Pause) Maybe I'm really a sicky . . . . I don't know. (Client takes a deep breath and clears his throat. Therapist observes that the client is neatly dressed and well groomed, but gives the appearance of a person who wishes not to be noticed. He is 5-feet-8 or -9 and of slight build. His posture is

---

[12]While we disagree with Roger's contention that positive regard, empathy, and genuineness are sufficient conditions for the client's improvement (Rogers, 1961), we have found that the interviewing skills of students are vastly enhanced as a consequence of some training in the use of nondirective techniques. In our experience, four to six hours of such training is sufficient.

slightly stooped. He speaks in a low, somewhat monotonous tone.)

Therapist: Okay . . . let's talk about your problem.

Client: Let me start at the beginning. About 6 months ago I was in a Safeway supermarket. For no reason, I got, like, really nervous and panicky. I just got out of there, really fast. I even left a whole shopping cart piled with groceries.

Therapist: Can you recall how you felt at the time?

Client: Just really nervous . . . shaky. I remember it was hard to breathe.

Therapist: Can you recall anything that happened, right before you got nervous . . . say, in the supermarket, or before you went shopping?

Client: (Pause) No. Like I say, it was out of the blue. Since then, it has been happening a lot. And it's getting worse.

Therapist: When you say "getting worse," do you mean that the nervousness is happening more often lately?

Client: Yeah, that's what I mean. Now it is like almost every day.

Therapist: Let's see if we can pinpoint things a little. What sorts of situations seem to make you the most nervous. When are you the most uptight?

Client: Well . . . supermarkets. My wife has to do all the shopping now. And movie theaters . . . . I sometimes make myself go, but I don't enjoy myself. I feel so uptight . . . especially before they, you know, dim the lights. And, oh yeah, shopping centers are really bad. Two weeks ago we drove up to visit my mother-in-law in Arlington. We were in that great big shopping center at Tyson's Corners, and I had to get out of there. It made my wife mad because she's really looking forward to shopping at that new store . . . Bloomingdale's.

Therapist: I'm wondering whether the experience at Tyson's Corners has anything to do with your making an appointment here?

Client: Yeah, that pretty much was it.

Therapist: Let's try something. Close your eyes and pretend, or imagine, you're back at the shopping center. Right before you felt nervous. Describe the scene like you are there right now.

Client: The thing is, anymore, I get nervous just thinking about it. But when did I start to panic . . . we'd just walked into a department store, not Bloomingdale's . . . can't remember the name.

Therapist: That isn't important. Go ahead and describe the scene.

Client: Okay . . . . (Pause) There are lots of people all around. Seems like thousands, strangers. The lights are bright . . . . (Client momentarily catches his breath and taps his fingers nervously on the arm of the chair.)

Therapist: Anything else?

Client: That's all I can remember.

Therapist: How did you feel when you imagined the scene?

Client: Pretty nervous. You could probably tell.

Therapist: Can you recall the events that happened before you felt panicky? What led up to feeling this way?

Client: That day we slept late, and had lunch at a deli, and then went to the shopping center. Nothing really happened.

Therapist: Do you happen to recall what you were thinking before you felt panicky?

Client: I don't know . . . maybe that I might panic.

Therapist: What happened after you felt panicky?

Client: I told my wife I had to get out of there . . . and we left.

Therapist: How did you feel when you got out of there?

Client: Relieved. Like I could breathe again.

Therapist: Do you usually leave the situation when you feel panicky?

Client: Yeah, if it's possible.

Therapist: Okay, now try and tell me when you are least likely to feel uptight. In other words, when do you feel, well, safe?

Client: Safe . . . that's a good way to put it. When I'm by myself . . . or just with my wife, or a few friends.

Therapist: What about at work? Let's see, you're a shipping clerk, right?

Client: Work is fine . . . . I can handle that.

Therapist: What about just being outside?

Client: It depends . . . like, I don't know, it's really crazy. I can walk my dog at 6 a.m., or late at night, and I'm okay.

Therapist: Do you think that is because at 6 a.m. or late at night you aren't likely to come across a lot of people?

Client: You know, that's really what it is. Crowds . . . strangers.

Therapist: What is a crowd like . . . I mean, how many people before you feel really nervous?

Client: (Long pause) You know, I can't really say, because it depends. Like, if I'm in a room with a whole bunch of people, if I'm standing near the door, it doesn't bother me very much. The worst thing is to be jammed smack in the middle. (Voice trembles, client takes a deep breath.)

Therapist: I can see that just thinking about this bothers you, but look, I think we're getting somewhere. The crowd isn't so bad, if you have a kind of escape route?

Client: That's it. Exactly it. That's crazy, isn't it. I mean, am I crazy?

Therapist: No, and as a matter of fact your problem is probably a lot more common than you realize.

Client: It is hard to believe other people are so . . . screwed up . . . their wives have to do the shopping. (Said with disgust)

Therapist: How many people know about this problem you have about being uptight in crowds?

Client: I haven't told anyone, except Fran, my wife, and she doesn't know how bad it is.

Therapist: Usually people with your sort of problem don't tell other people about it, which is why everybody thinks it's so rare. But really, like I said, it's fairly common.

Client: That does surprise me. Maybe I'm not such a freak after all. But I'm afraid things are gonna really get out of hand. Can . . . this sort of problem be overcome? (Client leans lightly in the direction of the therapist, eyes wide, mouth drawn.)

Therapist: Well, the track record with your kind of problem is actually pretty good. Of course, I'm going to need some more information, but right now, I bet you're pretty tense talking about all this. Am I right?

Client: Yes. (Sighs)

Therapist: Okay, then let's spend a few minutes doing some exercises to help you relax. (Therapist talks client through a few of the basic relaxation exercises described in Chapter 2. The concentration is on breathing.)

Note: Thus far, the therapist has delineated and partially elaborated the problem. In listening to what the client has said, he has not observed any indication of psychotic thinking and he notes the client's affect is appropriate to the content of his speech. He provides the client with assurance that he is not "crazy," that his problem is not uncommon, and that the prognosis is favorable. The relaxation exercises will increase the client's comfort level, and facilitate communication. The exercises should also enhance the therapist's credibility as a helping person.

The therapist further elaborates the problem and sets an initial goal:

Therapist: Let's talk more about how these bouts of anxiety affect your life. What aspect of your life is most disrupted?

Client: Well, it is taking the pleasure out of life. I used to love to go to the movies . . . hell, I even enjoyed shopping. (Laughs)

Therapist: You mentioned there was no problem at work.

Client: Right. No problem there. I do my job well, but then, it isn't very challenging. (Sighs, then gazes out the window)

Therapist: Sounds like you might have some mixed feelings about your job, which I'd like to explore. But right now, how would you say your problem affects your marriage? By the way, how long have you and Fran been married?

Client: A year. My first, her second. Well, the main thing is, we aren't doing things together, like going places where there are a lot of people. I'm causing her to miss out on some things, and I really feel bad about it. I love her, and try to treat her well. We don't fight, at least not very much.

Therapist: Do you think your problem has had any effect on your sex life?

Client: (Pause) I'll say this, when we first got married, sex was great. We'd, well, go to it just about every night. Now, maybe once a week . . . I'm just not in the mood anymore. I don't know whether that ties in with my problem or not.

Therapist: Well, I think that is something we are going to want to explore. Can you think of other areas of your life affected by your getting nervous in crowds?

Client: Not too much left. (Laughs, sarcastically)

Therapist: Okay, let me, right now, give you a homework assignment, and then I want to get some more information. I'd like you to make some notes on these 3-by-5 cards. Would you fill one of these out every time you have one of those bouts of nervousness? Let's fill one out together so you'll know what to do. Take you being nervous at Tyson's Corners. (Therapist and client complete the accompanying card. [See Figure 1–1.])

Therapist: I think we can start a treatment program for your nervousness soon, and this information will really help.

Note: While the client's job is not (apparently) affected by the anxiety bouts, it is a source of conflict. The therapist notes that the presenting complaints began 6 months after the client was married. The client seems to believe his problem is detracting from his competency as a husband. The therapist notes that treating a wife well includes not fighting. He wonders how assertive the client is with his wife, and whether his diminished interest in sex reflects unexpressed anger.

The therapist now attempts to delineate other important problem areas:

Therapist: I'm looking at one of the forms you filled out in the waiting room (Fear Survey Schedule). According to this, you are afraid of high places. Is that a serious problem?

Client: Not really. Maybe if I get over my problem with crowds, we could work on it.

Therapist: Okay. Can you think of some other things that bother you or that you might get uptight about?

Client: Not right now . . . . (Laughs) But give me time.

Note: Most clients report at least some depression. We strongly recommend that the client's affective state be dealt with early on.

Therapist: Do you ever get depressed?

Client: Well, my problem has been getting to me, lately especially.

Therapist: Tell me how depressed you get.

Client: It isn't that bad really. I've never thought

Date and time: April 24   3:00 p.m.

Difficulty: Very nervous, trouble breathing.

Situation::   Tyson's Corners, department store very crowded, can't see exit.

Prior events: Had lunch in deli with wife. Worrying I might panic in shopping center.

What you did: Left shopping center.

Consequences: Felt relieved; wife said she was disappointed.

Figure 1–1 *A "homework assignment" card to help a client identify the whats, wheres, and whens for a problem behavior or reaction.*

about, you know, doing myself in or anything like that. I just want to get over my problem.

Therapist: Fair enough. After all, that's why you're here. So far we've been talking about negative things . . . you know, what's wrong with your life. Now, let's talk about some positive things . . . like the sorts of things you feel good about in relation to your present life. Including the kinds of things you like about yourself.

Note: Following this the therapist begins to gather background information. Topics usually covered include relationships with parents and siblings, religious background, schooling, dating, marital and sexual history, experiences with drugs and alcohol, the client's physical health, and current interpersonal relationships not previously dealt with.

Clients, especially those who have been exposed to more traditional forms of psycho-therapy, frequently engage in seemingly endless discussion of their past life (traditional approaches may even reinforce such behavior). From the point of view of the behavior therapist, this can be very counterproductive since it is antithetical to the "here-and-now" orientation, which stresses problem solving rather than passive reflection. Clients should be gently dissuaded from undue dwelling on such past experiences. At the same time, however, care should be taken not to communicate to the client that he is forbidden to bring up relevant background material that, perhaps through embarrassment, he avoided during the initial interview.

Behavior Therapy and Ethical Considerations

In 1975, the board of directors of the Association for the Advancement of Behavior Therapy appointed a committee to develop a statement of ethics that would apply to all types of human intervention (including, of course, behavior therapy).[13] The statement is presented at the end of this section.

Ethical considerations have always been a concern of professional psychologists. Among behavior therapists, this concern about ethical issues intensified during the 1970s for a variety of reasons.

Thousands of research and clinical reports have indicated that behavior therapy interventions can change the way people behave *and probably* the way they think and feel. This is not to suggest that traditional psychotherapy is ineffectual, but behavior therapy, with its immense data base, now projects a relatively more powerful image in the eyes of behavior therapists and the lay public alike. Increments in power necessitate increments in choice and responsibility, *ergo,* a greater preoccupation with ethical issues.

A basic reason for concern about professional conduct by behavior therapists stems from the very nature of behavior therapy. To the extent that behavior therapy eschews the traditional disease model, behavior therapists cannot use "curing the sick" or "eliminating illness" as ethical referents (see Krasner, 1976a). What, then, is the basis for deciding which among out client's behaviors are "good" and which are "bad"? Obviously, no simple answer is forthcoming, although Krasner makes the following observation:

> A major point that derives from the social learning model is that the goal of helping individuals is to enable them to learn how to control, influence, or design their own environment. Implicit in this is a value judgment that individual freedom is a desirable goal and that the more an individual is able to affect his environment, the greater is his freedom. (1976a, p. 646)

We think that behavior therapists in general share Krasner's observation.

[13]The committee members were Drs. Nathan H. Azrin, Richard B. Stuart, Todd R. Risley, and Stephanie B. Stolz.

The Association for the Advancement of Behavior Therapy statement on ethical issues for human services appeared in the November 1977 issue of *Behavior Therapy* (8, v–vi) and reads as follows:

A. *Have the goals of treatment been adequately considered?*
   1. To insure that the goals are explicit, are they written?
   2. Has the client's understanding of the goals been assured by having the client restate them orally or in writing?
   3. Have the therapist and client agreed on the goals of therapy?
   4. Will serving the client's interests be contrary to the interest of other persons?
   5. Will serving the client's immediate interests be contrary to the client's long-term interest?
B. *Has the choice of treatment methods been adequately considered?*
   1. Does the published literature show the procedure to be the best one available for that problem?
   2. If no literature exists regarding the treatment method, is the method consistent with generally accepted practice?
   3. Has the client been told of alternative procedures that might be preferred by the client on the basis of significant differences in discomfort, treatment time, cost, or degree of demonstrated effectiveness?
   4. If a treatment procedure is publicly, legally, or professionally controversial, has formal professional consultation been obtained, has the reaction of the affected segment of the public been adequately considered, and have the alternative treatment methods been more closely reexamined and reconsidered?
C. *Is the client's participation voluntary?*
   1. Have possible sources of coercion on the client's participation been considered?
   2. If treatment is legally mandated, has the available range of treatments and therapists been offered?
   3. Can the client withdraw from treatment without a penalty of financial loss that exceeds actual clinical costs?
D. *When another person or an agency is empowered to arrange for therapy, have the interests of the subordinated client been sufficiently considered?*

1. Has the subordinated client been informed of the treatment objectives and participated in the choice of treatment procedures?
2. Where the subordinated client's competence to decide is limited, has the client as well as the guardian participated in the treatment discussions to the extent that the client's abilities permit?
3. If the interests of the subordinated person and the superordinate persons or agency conflict, have attempts been made to reduce the conflict by dealing with both interest?

E. *Has the adequacy of treatment been evaluated?*
1. Have quantitative measures of the problem and its progress been obtained?
2. Have the measures of the problem and its progress been made available to the client during treatment?

F. *Has the confidentiality of the treatment relationship been protected?*
1. Has the client been told who has access to the records?
2. Are records available only to authorized persons?

G. *Does the therapist refer the clients to other therapists when necessary?*
1. If treatment is unsuccessful, is the client referred to other therapists?
2. Has the client been told that if dissatisfied with the treatment, referral will be made?

H. *Is the therapist qualified to provide treatment?*
1. Has the therapist had training or experience in treating problems like the client's?
2. If deficits exist in the therapist's qualifications, has the client been informed?
3. If the therapist is not adequately qualified, is the client referred to other therapists, or has supervision by a qualified therapist been provided? Is the client informed of the supervisory relation?
4. If the treatment is administered by mediators, have the mediators been adequately supervised by a qualified therapist?

2
Relaxation and Systematic Desensitization

Relaxation training and systematic desensitization are, in many ways, the backbone of behavior therapy. In traditional or modified form, they have been the focus of more clinical and research attention, for a longer period of time, than any other behavioral techniques. For both historical and contextual reasons, therefore, we start our review of behavior therapies with a focus on these two techniques.

Relaxation Procedures

Relaxation training is such a ubiquitous component of behavior therapy that it has been referred to as "behavioral aspirin" (Russo, Bird, & Masek, 1980). In general, relaxation techniques refer to any strategies aimed at reducing arousal. Some procedures involve active components, in which an activity (e.g., muscle tensing) is used to aid in the eventual reduction of arousal, whereas others are passive in nature and involve components that focus solely on relaxation and tranquillity. Relaxation procedures can be used either as a component of a more elaborate behavioral intervention, such as systematic desensitization, or as major therapeutic tools in their own right.

Background

Relaxation strategies have been used for centuries as integral components of major philo-

sophical, theological, and therapeutic traditions. Their current use in behavior therapy, however, stems primarily from the work of Edmund Jacobson. In the early 1930s, as part of his PhD thesis in psychology, Jacobson conducted the first psychophysiological study of relaxation (McGuigan, 1984). He found that when subjects deeply relaxed their skeletal muscles, they would not show a normal startle response to a loud noise. Later, after he had earned his MD and was working with patients, including some who were highly anxious individuals, Jacobson (1938) developed a technique he called "progressive relaxation," which was designed to bring about a deep state of muscle relaxation. Jacobson believed that such a state could reduce arousal in both the central nervous system and the autonomic nervous system and as a result could restore or promote psychological and physical well being. This view was consonant with the then-popular James-Lange theory of emotion, which held that there was a close and interactive relationship between bodily states (e.g., muscle tension) and emotional states (e.g., feelings of anxiety). Thus, it followed that by reducing skeletal muscle tension, a person could reduce anxiety and its negative consequences. As we will describe in more detail in the next section, Jacobson's progressive relaxation procedure was time consuming, often requiring the client to attend 50 or more training sessions. It also was characterized by an active approach to relaxation in which subjects were first instructed to contract their muscles and produce feelings of tension and then to let go of the tension and focus on feelings of relaxation.

At about the same time that Jacobson was developing his active form of relaxation training, Johannes Schultz (1932), a German physician, introduced a passive form of controlling arousal. Schultz was interested in producing an optimal homeostatic level of arousal, which may involve an increase or a decrease in one's current level of physiological arousal depending upon the circumstances. He did not believe that a deep state of relaxation was necessarily an optimal physiological state, arguing instead that the optimal level of arousal depended on the task or the circumstances at hand. In practice, however, most behavior therapists use autogenic training to produce a state of relaxation and consider the procedure—albeit incorrectly—as simply a relaxation technique.

Schultz had studied hypnosis and was impressed with its effects on both physical and emotional symptoms. However, he viewed the considerable dependence on a therapist to produce the hypnotic state, and the often short-term nature of posthypnotic effects, as drawbacks to the procedure (Pikoff, 1984). Therefore he sought to develop an autosuggestion technique whereby a person could self-produce, after a minimal amount of training, physiological changes that would result in an optimal level of arousal. He called this technique *autogenic training* (or self– ["auto"] initiated ["genic"] training). As we will discuss later, this procedure focuses a person's attention on internal sensations such as warmth and heaviness (sensations often associated with hypnosis). Schultz and his subsequent collaborator, Luthe (Schultz & Luthe, 1959), believed that the mental and physical tranquillity brought about by focusing on these sensations could eventually lead to permanent relief from physiological and emotional problems (Pikoff, 1984).

In the 1950s, a major development led to the emergence of progressive relaxation and its progeny as the technique of choice over autogenic training and other passive forms of relaxation. That development was Joseph Wolpe's (1958) adoption of progressive relaxation as an essential component of systematic desensitization. Wolpe, like Jacobson, believed that muscle relaxation was a physiological state that was incompatible with anxiety. Since Wolpe's procedure (described in detail later) required a relatively anxiety-free state in order to decondition formerly anxiety-provoking stimuli, progressive relaxation became a key component of his intervention technique. However, since Jacobson's procedure was much too long for the behavioral technique that Wolpe had in mind, Wolpe modified it so that muscle relaxation could be taught within approximately 6 to 10 sessions.

In the late 1960s and the 1970s, amid the rise of biofeedback and cognitively based therapies and the increasing acceptance of Eastern philosophical and medical practices into Western culture, passive relaxation procedures such as autogenic training, meditation, and guided imagery began to become more widely incorporated into behavioral therapies and research. Moreover, relaxation procedures were increasingly used as isolated techniques, not only as part of a more comprehensive procedure such as systematic desensitization. Early applications of relaxation as an independent treatment were generally with clients who had chronic, generalized anxiety problems, although in recent years the scope of application has increased dramatically. Another major influence on the development of relaxation techniques was the demand for quicker and more cost-effective methods of teaching relaxation. Therapists did not want to devote 50 sessions to teaching relaxation, and clients wanted to learn "self-help" approaches to relaxation. As a result, an astonishing array of relaxation procedures emerged, including a large number of self-help manuals and audio cassette programs.

Do all of these different relaxation procedures produce similar effects, or are some superior to others? Looking only at therapist provided techniques, the research literature suggests in general that there are more similarities than differences among the effects produced by various forms of relaxation. However, many clinicians believe that the differences that do exist (e.g., passive or active approach, few or many training sessions) are important, at least with some kinds of people or dysfunctions (Borkovec & Bernstein, 1985). As a result, most behavior therapists seem to prefer to use one or two kinds of relaxation procedures. Progressive relaxation is the most popular relaxation procedure used, perhaps in large part due to the historical developments noted above, and it is the one to which we will devote most of our attention in this chapter. Following our presentation of progressive relaxation, we will briefly describe other forms of relaxation training.

Assessment

Perhaps because behavior therapists use relaxation training so often, many apply it almost indiscriminately whenever anxiety seems to be a major problem. Fortunately, because relaxation training usually is of some help, and rarely does any harm, there is little risk in using it. On the other hand, good clinical technique dictates against the indiscriminate use of any procedure, because even if a procedure does no harm, it may delay the use of a more effective approach. Therefore, the therapist should consider several assessment issues before he or she begins relaxation training (Bernstein & Given, 1984).

First, the therapist should determine whether maladaptive anxiety, tension, or related emotions are part of the client's problem. Often this can be determined during an initial interview with the client. Self-reports of anxiety or behavioral indications of tension often emerge in this situation. In other cases, psychological tests or rating scales will suggest that the client suffers from maladaptive anxiety. Sometimes anxiety is more indirectly implicated. For example, in some cases the behavior therapist might suspect anxiety because the client may have exhibited potential escape-avoidance behaviors,

such as drug abuse, aggression, truancy, and so on. In other cases, symptoms such as insomnia, unusual weight loss or gain, sexual dysfunctions, increased irritability, hypertension, muscle contraction headaches, and concentration problems may be signs of maladaptive anxiety.

Second, assuming that anxiety is part of the client's problem, the therapist should determine whether anxiety reduction should be the primary or immediate focus of treatment. Take the case of a freshman referred to a therapist by his adviser for "test anxiety." The student is highly anxious about tests—so much so that he claims he cannot concentrate enough to study, and that when the examination is handed out he becomes so distressed that his mind goes blank, losing whatever knowledge he did have. Clearly, anxiety is part of this student's problem. Does this mean the therapist should immediately administer relaxation training? Not necessarily. First the therapist should determine why the student is anxious about tests. If the primary reason he does poorly on tests is that he does not know how to study and therefore is likely to fail most tests, then his anxiety is most understandable! In this case, study skills training might be the first order of business, with relaxation training becoming a secondary focus. If the student is anxious primarily because of unrealistic fears or maladaptive self-statements, then systematic desensitization or a cognitive behavioral approach (see Chapter 9) might be the optimal therapeutic strategy. In this case, relaxation training is likely to be a component of therapy, but not necessarily the primary focus.

In our experience, relaxation training by itself is rarely an adequate intervention for any problem. Rather, it is usually an *adjunctive intervention*—that is, an intervention that forms an important component of a more comprehensive treatment program. The second goal of assessment, therefore, is to determine whether or how relaxation skills fit into the overall approach to the anxiety-related problem.

Finally, the therapist should rule out any organic or physical causes for the client's anxiety or anxiety-related symptoms. This caveat is especially important when relaxation training is being used for stress-related somatic symptoms such as headaches, hypertension, tinnitus, pain, and so forth. In these cases, the therapist should ensure that the client has been seen by a physician and is complying with any prescribed medical interventions. In such situations, it is best for the therapist to inform the client's physician, with the client's consent, that he or she is seeing the patient for relaxation training. Regardless of how successful relaxation training is in reducing anxiety and distress, clients should not be encouraged to alter any medical regimen (e.g., decrease their medication dosage) without their physicians' approval.

Procedure

After the behavior therapist has determined that relaxation techniques are appropriate, he or she should explain the nature of and rationale for the procedures in sufficient detail that the client understands what is about to occur and is motivated to cooperate. The presentation should include an explanation (a) of the nature of and the role that anxiety is playing in the client's problem, and (b) of how relaxation training would be expected to help (Bernstein & Given, 1984). Clients are much more likely to practice relaxation training and to cooperate with the therapist if they understand why they are learning the technique and what benefits they are likely to experience from its regular use. In some cases, the therapist may feel it important to assure clients that they will not become hypnotized or in anyway lose control by being relaxed. Rather, they will be fully conscious and aware, but very relaxed and calm. The therapist should emphasize that relaxation is a skill that the client develops him- or herself—and one that the client can use in a variety of situations.

Once the client accepts the rationale of relaxation and is motivated or at least willing to begin training, the therapist should present in some detail the specific procedure that will be used. An example follows, taken from Bernstein and Borkovec (1973), of an introduction to relaxation training. It is intended as a general guide, illustrating one way of presenting the technique, not as a script to be memorized. In actual clinical situations, the presentation should be made at a level and a pace that matches the client's ability to understand and to absorb the material, and in a style that is natural to the therapist.

The procedures I have been discussing are called progressive relaxation training. They were first developed in the 1930s by a physician named Edmond Jacobson and in recent years have been modified to make them simpler and easier to teach. Basically, relaxation training consists of learning to tense and then relax various muscle groups throughout the body, while at the same time paying very close attention to the feelings associated with both tension and relaxation. In addition to focusing on tension and relaxation in your muscle groups, I will help you to learn to recognize tension as it occurs in everyday situations. The procedure has two basic objectives: First, to help you become aware of tension levels before they are so high that they cause problems or discomfort; and second, to be able to reduce tension completely and on your own.

Learning to relax is very much like learning any other kind of skill such as riding a bike or typing—the only way to get good at it is to practice. I cannot make you good at relaxation—you are responsible for doing that. And the way to do it is simply to practice everyday. Without practice the technique will not do you much good.

Now, I mentioned earlier that I will be asking you to tense and relax various groups of muscles in your body. You may be wondering why, if we want to produce relaxation, we start off by producing tension. The reason is that, first of all, everyone is always at some level of tension during waking hours; if a person were not tense to some extent, he or she would simply fall down. The amount of tension actually present in everyday life differs, of course, from individual to individual, and we say that each person has reached some adaptation level—the amount of tension under which she or he operates day to day.

The goal of progressive relaxation training is to help you learn to reduce muscle tension in your body far below your adaptation level at any time you wish to do so. In order to accomplish this, I could ask you to focus your attention, for example, on the muscles in your right hand and lower arm and then just let them relax. Now you might think you can let these muscles drop down below their adaptation level just by "letting them go" or whatever, and to a certain extent you probably can. However, in progressive relaxation, we want you to learn to produce larger and very much more noticeable reductions in tension, and the best way to do this is first to produce a good deal of tension in that muscle group (i.e., raise the tension well above adaptation level) and then all at once release that tension. The release creates a "momentum" which allows the muscles to drop well below adaptation level. The effect is like that which we could produce with a pendulum which is hanging motionless in a vertical position. If we want to swing far to the right, we could push it quite hard in that direction. It would be much easier, however, to start by pulling the pendulum in the opposite direction and then letting it go. It will swing well past the vertical point and continue in the direction we want it to go. Another important advantage to creating and releasing tension is that it will give you a good chance to focus your attention upon and become clearly aware of what tension really feels like in each of the various groups of muscles we will be dealing with today. In addition, the tensing procedure will make a vivid contrast between tension and relaxation and will give you an excellent opportunity to compare the two and appreciate the difference in feelings associated with each of these states.

Do you have any questions about what I've said thus far? (1973, pp. 19–20)

After any questions are answered, the therapist should carefully identify for the client each of the muscle groups that will be included in the tension-relaxation exercises and should demonstrate how to tense the muscles. The therapist should inquire as to any injuries or disabilities that might cause pain or discomfort if certain groups of muscles are tense, or might in any other way interfere with muscle tensing. If such restrictions do arise, the therapist should not ignore these muscle groups but rather take special care in dealing with them, either by limiting the amount or the suddenness of the tensing or by passively focusing on relaxation without prior tensing.

The client should next get into a comfortable position. The use of a recliner chair aids this process greatly and is recommended. Tight clothing (especially neckties) should be loosened, the client's legs should not be crossed, and all parts of the body should be supported by the chair. If the client wears contact lenses, he or she might wish to remove them.

So far, the instructions could apply to most types of progressive relaxation. What happens now, however, depends largely on the specific method of progressive relaxation training the therapist intends to employ. If the traditional Jacobsonian procedure is followed, for example, the therapist would spend the rest of the session focusing on one muscle group. We will present here a modified version of Jacobsonian relaxation that involves the tensing and relaxing of 14 muscle groups followed by several minutes of guided relaxation imagery. The whole procedure takes about 35–40 minutes. In many ways, this procedure follows the general methods recommended by Bernstein and Borkovec (1973).[1]

[1]Because of space limitations and because abbreviated forms of relaxation are the most popular today—both when relaxation is used as a component of a multifactorial treatment, such as systematic desensitization, and when it is used as an independent treatment technique—we have elected to focus on this approach. However, it should be noted that a growing number of behavior therapists are returning to a more Jacobsonian approach to relaxation. As suggested earlier, Jacobson's approach differs from its later modifications in being more time consuming. However, it also differs in some aspects of its underlying theory and in its training methods. For example, in Jacobson's view, tensing muscles can produce neuromuscular changes that do not facilitate immediate relaxation, and therefore a quick tension-relaxation sequence is not the best way to teach muscle relaxation. Also, more than most modified versions of relaxation, the Jacobsonian approach emphasizes differen-

At this point, we would briefly interview the patient to determine what imagery will be used following muscle tensing and relaxing. Although sometimes "canned" imagery can be used (e.g., lying on a raft on a glorious day with a warm breeze blowing), such imagery is not always effective (some people have a great fear of being on a raft or by water). Hence, it is best to ask clients about a place in their experience that they find very comfortable and peaceful. The therapist should help the client to describe the setting in sufficient detail that the therapist can guide him or her through the image after the muscle tensing and relaxing has been completed. However, it is also important not to become overly detailed in describing the scene—it is best to let the client embellish the description in his or her mind. The goal is to provide enough detail to direct and to stimulate the client's imaginative process.

The client is now ready for the muscle tension and relaxation instructions. Table 2-1 lists the 14 muscle groups and the methods of tensing that we recommend. The introduction to

tial relaxation—that is, teaching clients to tense only the muscles that are necessary to perform this or that activity, while specifically keeping other muscles relaxed. In this way, the focus is on teaching an individual to perceive levels of muscle tension in each major muscle group, and on controlling the tension levels so that tension is produced only when necessary and only in those muscles in which it is necessary. Detailed descriptions of the Jacobsonian approach can be found in Jacobson (1938, 1970, 1977) and in McGuigan (1984). In our view, Jacobsonian relaxation probably produces deeper levels of relaxation and teaches clients more control over their muscle tension levels than do abbreviated forms of relaxation. However, as we will discuss later, research suggests that in the majority of clinical cases (see Lehrer, 1982, for possible exceptions) abbreviated forms of relaxation can produce highly acceptable therapeutic effects, and presumably can do so much more efficiently than Jacobsonian procedures. It is for these reasons that abbreviated forms of relaxation are so widely employed among behavior therapists.

the first muscle group, the dominant arm, might go something like the following:

> I want you to start the relaxation procedure by taking a deep breath and holding it . . . and letting it out. This will help you to relax. And another . . . and hold it . . . and let it out. Good. Imagine that with each breath you inhale not only air but also relaxation, and that this relaxation spreads from your lungs throughout your body, and that as you exhale you push out any tension in your body. Take another deep breath and hold it . . . and let it out. Good. . . .
>
> Let's begin by tensing the muscles of the right hand and arm by clenching your fist and bending your arm at the elbow, as if to show off your biceps. Tense these muscles *now*. Good. Hold it. . . . Feel the tension. . . . Feel the tightness. . . . *Relax*. Let go of all the tension. Let your hand and arm fall down to a comfortable position. Feel the relaxation as it spreads through your fingers . . . hand . . . lower arm . . . and through your upper arm to your shoulder. Notice the difference between the feelings in your right hand and arm and your left hand and arm. These are the pleasant feelings of relaxation. . . .
>
> Okay, let's again tense the muscles of the right hand and arm by making a fist. . . .

This same general pattern should be followed for each of the muscle groups listed in Table 2-1. The therapist should keep in mind the following general principles, as outlined by Bernstein and Given (1984).

1. Instruct the client how to tense the muscles.

2. The client is to start tensing when the therapist says "now." Maintain tension for 5–7 seconds, focusing the client's attention on the feelings of tension with appropriate phrases.

3. The client should release the tension and initiate relaxation upon the cue word "relax." Instruct the client to focus on the feelings of relaxation as they replace the feelings of tension. Use appropriate phrases to help direct the client's attention to the relaxation for about 30–40 seconds.

Table 2–1 **Instructions for Tensing Muscle Groups**

Muscle Group	Method of Tensing
1. Dominant hand and arm	Make a tight fist, curl toward shoulder, bend arm to elbow
2. Nondominant hand and arm	Same as dominant
3. Forehead and eyes	Open eyes wide and raise eyebrows. Make as many wrinkles as possible on your forehead
4. Upper cheeks and nose	Frown, squint eyes, wrinkle nose
5. Jaw, lower face, neck	Clench teeth, protrude chin. Corners of mouth should be pulled down
6. Shoulders, upper back, chest	Shrug shoulders and pull shoulder blades back as far as possible as though trying to have them touch one another
7. Abdomen	Bend forward slightly at waist, protrude stomach, tighten muscles as much as possible, making them very hard
8. Buttocks	Squeeze buttocks together, push down into chair at same time
9. Dominant upper leg	Push large muscle on top of thigh against smaller areas on bottom of thigh. Make muscles hard, press them against each other
10. Dominant lower leg	Pull toes up till they point toward head. Stretch and harden muscles in calf
11. Dominant foot	Point toes outward and downward, stretching foot
12. Nondominant upper leg	Same as dominant
13. Nondominant lower leg	Same as dominant
14. Nondominant foot	Same as dominant

4. Repeat the tension-relaxation cycle for the same muscle group (Steps 1–3). This time allow the client a bit longer (40–50 seconds) to enjoy the relaxation.

5. Ask the client to signal (e.g., by raising a finger) if the muscle is not completely relaxed. If the client signals, repeat the tension-relaxation cycle, using slightly different descriptions to highlight the sensations. Again, ask the client to signal if the muscles are not completely relaxed. If they are not, repeat the tension-relaxation cycle once more. Then move to the other muscle groups, making a mental note to interview the client about the problem after the procedure is over. During this interview, try to determine an alternate approach to relaxing the muscles (different method of tensing, use of imagery, etc.) that might be more useful.

6. Very often, when asked to tense one set of muscles, a client will proceed to tense other groups automatically. For example, while making a fist, clients might be observed to catch their breath, grit their teeth, or squint. Obviously, this interferes with relaxation induction. Therefore, after the first exercise, it is good to suggest to the client that he or she tense *only* the muscle group under consideration, making a conscious effort *not* to tense other muscles. This is especially crucial after several groups of muscles have been relaxed since the client may inadvertently tense muscles that have already undergone the tension-relaxation cycle. All of this

should be pointed out, with an indication that while the habit of tensing muscles other than the target group is quite common, it is important that it be unlearned.

7. Repeat Steps 1–5 with the next muscle group.

After all 14 muscle groups are relaxed, the therapist should focus attention on feelings of relaxation throughout the entire body, again using breathing as a focus. For example, the therapist might say something like the following:

> Your whole body should now feel very comfortable and relaxed. I want you to let the relaxation go deeper and deeper, in your right hand and arm . . . left hand and arm . . . [name all muscle groups]. If you notice any tension remaining, let relaxation from another part of your body flow in to replace the tension. Take a deep breath, . . . hold it, . . . and breath out any tension. Let your entire body now feel comfortable, relaxed, very pleasant, very peaceful. . . .

After the client has had about 30 seconds to focus on total body relaxation, the therapist should begin the guided imagery. The therapist should initially guide the client into the scene that previously had been agreed upon, using a relaxed, peaceful cadence and voice. Encourage the client to embellish the images. If individualized imagery is impractical or impossible for some reason—for example, if the relaxation induction is in a group setting—the therapist has at least three options. One is not to use imagery at all. A second option is to use some universal relaxing images, such as lying on a beach or in a field. A final option is to use neutral imagery. For instance, the client could be asked to imagine a blue ball, to watch the ball grow slowly until it becomes a curtain of blue, and then to see a small yellow triangle up in the right-hand corner, and so on. Such imagery sometimes helps to prolong the sensations of relaxation by keeping clients' attention focused on relaxing,

or at least on nonarousing images, rather than on the concerns that brought them to therapy in the first place.

To terminate the relaxation procedure, the therapist can count backward from 5 to 1, telling the client that he or she will become more and more alert with each number, although continuing to feel very comfortable and relaxed. On 3, the therapist might instruct the client to move his or her hands and legs a bit; on 2, open the eyes, on 1, feel alert and awake, but still very relaxed. The therapist should then interview the client about the induction. The therapist might ask the client to indicate on a 10-point scale how he or she feels, with 10 being as anxious as the client has ever felt, and 1 indicating a feeling of complete relaxation. Most individuals receiving relaxation induction for the first time report relatively low levels of tension, usually 3 or lower on the 10-point scale. With increasing practice, the anxiety rating falls further, and after a few additional sessions it is not uncommon for the client to report a rating of 1. The therapist might also ask questions such as, Were there any muscle groups that did not become fully relaxed? (If so, a new approach to those muscles should be discussed.) Was the imagery successful? Does the client have any questions?

The therapist should then instruct the client to practice the relaxation skills once, or preferably twice, a day. It is usually helpful for the therapist to arrange with the client a specific schedule for doing so the first week—when and where the practice will occur. The client can be given a reminder sheet that lists the muscle groups and how to tense them and the proper sequence he or she should follow (similar to Table 2-1). Some therapists give the clients an audiotape of the session to aid in home practice. We endorse this procedure as long as it is time limited. The goal of relaxation training is eventually to have the client self-relax, not to become dependent on a tape. Thus, over time the client should become increasingly less dependent on outside help to produce the relaxation.

If, after approximately three sessions of directed relaxation, the client appears to be successful at becoming deeply relaxed both during the session and at home, as determined by client report, the therapist can begin to combine the 14 muscle groups into 5 or more groupings as follows:

1. Both hands and arms
2. All facial muscles
3. Chest, shoulders, upper back, stomach
4. Buttocks in both upper legs
5. Both lower legs and feet

Following the fifth muscle group, the client should again be instructed to use the relaxation imagery. However, the therapist should give the client more responsibility for directing the imagery.

After the client has successfully learned this modification and is able to relax deeply, he or she can be instructed to relax the five muscle groups without tensing first by focusing on the natural tension in each muscle group and then, by using the cue word "relax," to release the tension and let the muscles become deeply relaxed. After the final muscle group is relaxed, the client should be encouraged to self-direct him- or herself in 45 to 60 seconds of relaxation imagery.

As a final step, most therapists teach the client *cue-controlled relaxation.* This step involves instructing the client to relax by simply saying "relax" to himself or herself, focusing briefly on sensations of relaxation in each of the five major muscle groupings and concentrating briefly on the relaxation imagery. The intention of teaching cue-controlled relaxation is to allow the client to relax quickly and unnoticeably in almost any setting, from waiting in the car at a stop light to sitting in a meeting. However, reviews of the literature have raised some questions about the effectiveness of this procedure (e.g., Grimm, 1980), and in our experience few

individuals ever master it. Therefore, we generally do not lead clients to expect that they will be able to achieve adequate relaxation by using a cue-controlled procedure. However, we do advocate instructing clients who have learned to relax in ideal settings to begin practicing in less than ideal settings, beginning first with fairly comfortable situations (e.g., sitting at one's desk at work or relaxing at home with the television on) and then gradually moving on to more demanding circumstances.

Additional Comments It is inevitable that some relaxation sessions, either in the therapist's office or at home, will be momentarily interrupted by loud noises or a knock at the door (despite a "Do Not Disturb" sign!). It is often best to handle these interruptions by telling the client to expect them occasionally and to use them as part of the learning experience. That is, the client should regard these interruptions as opportunities to apply the relaxation skill under challenging circumstances and should try to relax through the interruptions rather than become angered or disrupted by them. The client can use a specific image or relaxation sensation as a focal point during these times. After the client appears able to relax under ideal conditions, the therapist might in fact wish to program in a few such distractions during training.

Probably the most common error beginning therapists make is to rush the relaxation exercises. And even if the therapist proceeds at an appropriate speed, the client is likely to proceed too rapidly, especially if the base level of tension is high. The client will gain little relaxation from going through the exercises rapidly in a calisthenic fashion. Practitioners differ somewhat with respect to the duration of the tension and relaxation phases, but most agree that the tension phase should be at least 5 seconds, with a minimum of 10 seconds for relaxation. Most recommend somewhat longer periods for the relaxation.

Finally, we cannot stress enough that the procedures outlined above are *guidelines,* not rules.

Clients differ tremendously, and these differences must be considered in the relaxation training. Some clients may do best if the progression from 14 muscle groups to the passive relaxation of 5 muscle groups proceeds with more intervening steps. Some clients have a hard time imaging. A few will find that muscle tensing makes it harder, not easier, to relax, preferring instead to relax each muscle group without the tensing stage first. As we stress throughout this text, individual differences must be recognized and flexibly handled in any therapeutic interaction, including the administration of relaxation procedures.

Negative Effects While the majority of individuals undergoing relaxation procedures will experience a considerable increase in feelings of relaxation and a decrease in subjective distress and physiological arousal, there have been some reports of negative effects occurring in a small percentage of individuals. For the most part, these negative effects can be subsumed under the heading "relaxation-induced anxiety" (Heide & Borkovec, 1983). For example, there are reports of individuals being afraid to relax (see Lehrer, 1982) and of others showing increased anxiety (e.g., Heide & Borkovec, 1983) or physiological arousal (e.g., Norton, Rhodes, Hauch, & Caprowy, 1985) during relaxation. Some clients even experience panic attacks (Cohen, Barlow, & Blanchard, 1985). These negative effects do not appear to be limited to any single type of relaxation; they have been reported with an array of procedures including progressive relaxation training (e.g., Borkovec & Grayson, 1980), meditation (Heide & Borkovec, 1983), and EMG biofeedback (Budzynski, Stoyva, & Peffer, 1980).

How common is relaxation-induced anxiety? In part, the answer depends on one's definition of the phenomenon and on the type of subject being relaxed. In one of the most sophisticated empirical investigations in the area, Heide &

Borkovec (1983) administered one session of progressive relaxation and one session of meditation (similar to transcendental meditation) to each of 14 highly anxious subjects (i.e., subjects who reported experiencing moderate or severe anxiety 40 percent or more of each day). The researchers found that 31 percent of the subjects reported increased levels of anxiety during progressive relaxation and 54 percent during meditation. In contrast, Jacobsen and Edinger (1982) reported that approximately 5 percent of the patients seen in their clinical experience developed side effects to relaxation. Edinger (1982) surveyed 116 behavior therapists who had employed some form of relaxation training with a total of more than 17,500 patients. Other than intrusive thoughts, the percentage of patients experiencing any type of side effect ranged from 0.38 percent (psychotic symptoms) to 9.28 percent (fear of losing control). Overall, the data suggest that relaxation-induced side effects are relatively uncommon, except perhaps in a subgroup of individuals who are highly anxious. However, although uncommon, these side effects do occur with sufficient frequency that most behavior therapists who routinely employ relaxation procedures will observe them in their practice.

At present, we can only speculate on why some individuals show paradoxical increases in anxiety during relaxation training. Lehrer (1982) has suggested that some of the cases may be due simply to poor technique on the part of the therapist. According to Heide and Borkovec (1984), other explanations have generally focused on one of five theories:

1. Relaxation may be associated with the release of cognitive, physiological, or sensory side effects that some, especially chronically tense individuals, find unpleasant.

2. Some individuals may fear losing control during relaxation.

3. Some individuals, especially those with high levels of anxiety, may fear that by focusing

on themselves and their feelings, they will experience their own anxiety, and that this experience might extenuate the feelings further.

4. Some individuals may find it aversive to engage in any sort of self-focused attention, of being alone with themselves.

5. Some individuals may engage in worrisome cognitive activity about miscellaneous matters (e.g., financial problems) unrelated to relaxation.

Fortunately, if people do show side effects to relaxation, they tend to be mild (Edinger, 1982), to appear during the initial sessions (Cohen et al., 1985), and to remit if the therapist switches to another type of relaxation procedure (Heide & Borkovec, 1983) or continues to expose the client to additional relaxation sessions with the same procedure (Cohen et al., 1985). The general conclusion, therefore, appears to be that negative effects to relaxation training are relatively uncommon and that when they do occur they usually can be successfully handled. As in all therapeutic interventions, however, the therapist must be continually alert to the possibility that side effects can develop, even with procedures as apparently innocuous as relaxation training.

Other Major Relaxation Techniques

Although progressive relaxation training is probably the most widely used relaxation technique among behavior therapists, an astounding array of other relaxation procedures are available. These other techniques vary from carefully developed procedures on which a fair amount of research has been conducted (e.g., autogenic training), to age-old procedures that are associated more with religion and philosophy than with behavior therapy (e.g., forms of meditation such as Maulavi), to popular self-help techniques on which there is little if any controlled research. Probably the two procedures other than progressive relaxation training that are most commonly used by behavior therapists are autogenic training and EMG biofeedback.

Autogenic Training As we noted earlier, autogenic training is a passive form of controlling arousal that was developed by Johannes Schultz (1932) about the same time that Jacobsen introduced progressive relaxation training. Autogenic training has enjoyed widespread popularity in Europe, where it was originally introduced, for a number of years, but has become widely known in this country only recently. Pikoff (1984) has reported that although there are thousands of foreign-language references on autogenic training, as of the early 1980s there were only approximately 30 references in English, although the number has been growing in more recent years.

At the core of autogenic training is a set of six psychophysiological exercises that involve the use of short "formulas," or autosuggestions, that the client focuses on. According to the authors of the technique, the formulas emphasize feelings of "heaviness and warmth in the extremities, regulation of cardiac activity and respiration, abdominal warmth and cooling of the forehead" (Schultz & Luthe, 1969, p. 6). The six exercises are prescribed in a specific sequence, and the client must master one before the next is introduced. The first exercise involves formulas that focus on feelings of heaviness. The training procedure proceeds as follows:

As soon as the patient is settled into a relaxed position with eyes closed, the first formula (for heaviness in the limbs) is introduced. The therapist begins in a calm voice, "I am at peace . . . my right arm is heavy . . . my right arm is heavy . . . my right arm is heavy . . . I am at peace . . . my right arm is heavy . . . my right arm is heavy . . . my right arm is heavy." The trainee then continues this monologue silently for about 20 seconds and concludes this first cycle by vigorously flexing the arms, taking a deep breath, and opening the eyes. While repeating the phrase the patient is encouraged to visualize the words, perhaps in the form of a film or neon sign and to establish mental contact with the relevant organ. At the same time the trainee is reminded to maintain a casual attitude toward his or her performance. This basic attitude, variously described as "attentive passivity," "relaxed watchfulness," or "passive concentration," is, in fact, considered the bedrock of autogenic training. It is an orientation toward watching and waiting rather than striving, of "allowing" rather than "forcing." In practice it means the trainee will simply repeat the formula and pay attention to the part of the body involved. If he or she experiences the desired sensation, fine. If not, it will come eventually. . . . Following a 1-minute rest interval the cycle of monologue-recovery-rest-interval is repeated 2 more times with each rest time devoted to a discussion of the patient's precise sensations during the preceding monologue. The three repetitions take about 5 minutes and constitute the standard set for a given formula. Patients are expected to practice three such sets per day at home, recording reactions in a diary that is discussed with a therapist at weekly meetings. At approximately 1-week intervals, the heaviness formula is successively modified to include additional parts of the body in cumulative fashion: "My right and left arm are heavy" (Week No. 2); "My right, left arm, and right leg are heavy" (Week No. 3); etc. After 4–6 weeks of practice the heaviness formula has typically been condensed to, "I am at peace . . . my arms and legs are heavy . . . my arms and legs are heavy . . . my arms and legs are heavy."

At this time the second formula, "warmth" in the limbs is usually introduced. . . . (Pikoff, 1984, pp. 620–621)

After the client has mastered the six exercises, the therapist can introduce two types of supplementary exercises. The first involves concentration exercises, which enhance the client's ability to generate vivid mental images. The second involves specialized exercises that have been developed to produce specific psychophysiological effects. The therapist selects the exercises most appropriate for the client's particular problem.

The English-language research literature on autogenic training is relatively sparse and contains many studies that are either poorly controlled or do not adhere closely to the description of autogenic training provided by Schultz and his followers. Among the better controlled studies, there are data to suggest that autogenic training can be effective in treating a variety of problems, including insomnia (e.g., Nicassio & Bootzin, 1974), Raynaud's Disease (e.g., Surwit, Pilon, & Fenton, 1978), and migraine headaches (e.g., Blanchard, Theobald, Williamson, Silver, & Brown, 1978). Overall, autogenic training shows considerable promise as a therapeutic technique, but additional research is clearly warranted.

EMG Biofeedback   *Biofeedback* refers to a number of procedures that provide information (feedback) to a subject about one or more biological responses. For example, a subject might receive feedback from a meter that indicates what his or her skin temperature is—as determined by sensors attached to the subject's fingers. The general purpose of biofeedback is to teach a person to use the feedback to gain conscious control of a biological response over which the subject previously had little or no control.

Since biofeedback is basically a self-control procedure that is used for a variety of problems, it is discussed at length in Chapter 10. But the topic is equally pertinent here, because biofeedback, especially electromyographic (EMG) biofeedback, is often used as a general relaxation technique. In fact, next to progressive relaxation training, there is probably more controlled research on the stress-reducing effectiveness of EMG biofeedback than there is of any other single relaxation procedure.

Most applications of EMG biofeedback involve attaching three small electrodes to the forehead to measure tension levels primarily from the muscles in the upper facial area. This type of biofeedback is usually referred to as frontalis EMG biofeedback, since the electrodes rest most proximally above the frontalis muscles. Early researchers believed that the tension levels of these muscles were a good index of the general tension levels of other muscles in the body and, therefore, assumed that if one could learn to relax these muscles, relaxation of other muscles would follow. Since Jacobson and others have shown that general decreases in muscle tension are associated with general reductions in anxiety in other physiological indices (e.g., heart rate), they assumed that frontalis EMG biofeedback would be a useful way to produce deep relaxation.

Unfortunately, research on the relaxation effects of frontalis EMG biofeedback does not support some of its early claims about its effectiveness. In fact, the majority of controlled research indicates that although frontalis EMG biofeedback does produce a significant decrease in the EMG levels of the frontales muscles, the decrease is usually not accompanied by significant decreases in the EMG levels of other muscles, in self-reports of anxiety and other negative affects, and in indices of autonomic arousal (see Burish, 1981). Moreover, controlled research on clinical populations generally suggest that when EMG biofeedback is effective, it is generally no more so than less expensive relaxation procedures, such as progressive relaxation training (Burish, 1981; Lehrer, 1982). However, EMG and other types of biofeedback have generated more positive results in other areas (see Chapters 10 and 11).

Theory of Relaxation Techniques

Given that relaxation techniques of one type or another have been used for thousands of years, that they have received considerable research attention in recent years, and that large amounts of money are spent for self-help books on relaxation and on professional training in relaxation skills, one would assume that there is a solid theoretical basis for the use of relaxation techniques. Surprisingly, this is not the case. Most writers do not discuss the theoretical basis for relaxation training, and many who do make rather obvious statements to the effect

that muscular tension underlies the development and maintenance of many problems that clients bring to treatment, and therefore the removal of muscular tension will help to resolve the problems and prevent their recurrence.

Among the theoretical explanations that have been provided, perhaps the most thorough is that of McGuigan (1984). McGuigan's theory revolves specifically around Jacobsonian progressive relaxation training, but it has implications for other kinds of relaxation techniques as well. He begins by asserting that the mind and body are complex interacting systems, with each directly affecting the activity of the other. Most mental processes, he suggests, begin when muscles of the eyes and speech regions tense, and there is a direct correspondence between the activation of these muscles and subsequent mental activity. A similar process occurs with emotions. A direct correspondence exists between the generation and intensity of emotions, and the generation and intensity of muscle tension in select parts of the body. It follows, therefore, that by learning to control muscle tension, we can directly control—through changes in the activation of neuromuscular circuits—mental activity and emotion. McGuigan puts it as follows:

> In regard to the clinical application of progressive relaxation for psychiatric difficulties, it has been noted that any interruption of neuromuscular circuits will eliminate thoughts, preventing them from occurring. . . . Undesired thoughts, such as those of phobias and worries, can be eliminated by relaxing the speech muscles (tongue, lips, jaws, throat, and cheeks, for verbal mental activity) and the eye muscles (for eliminating the visual components of thought). . . . By consistently relaxing those covert skeletal muscle components, the tranquility of the neuromuscular circuits can relax away worry, phobia, or depression. (1984, pp. 20–21)

Although few other theorists go as far as McGuigan in equating muscle tension with emotion and mental activity, most have at least suggested that there is a close connection. For example, Jacobson held that when people are relaxed, they think more clearly and are better able to solve their own problems (Lehrer, 1982). Wolpe (1982) has suggested that the effects of deep muscle relaxation on the autonomic nervous system produce a state that is physiologically incompatible with anxiety. Therefore, to the extent that a person's problems are due to anxiety—to its consequences on behavior, on problem-solving ability, on healthy physiological response, or on maintaining a positive affect—he or she can ameliorate the problems by relaxing.

The following points summarize the mechanisms that have been suggested as mediating the effects of relaxation techniques:

1. Increased awareness of muscle tension
2. Increased ability to control muscle tension
3. Increased ability to control autonomic activity
4. Increased ability to control cognitive activity, including concentration

The sequence of Nos. 1–4 generates the following responses:

5. Decreased muscle tension
6. Decreased physiological arousal
7. Decreased feelings of anxiety and other negative emotions
8. Decreased worry

Finally, although we have implied that all relaxation techniques may exert their effects for similar reasons, we should note that this is a point of some controversy. Some, such as Benson (1975), do indeed espouse a unitary theory of relaxation which holds that all relaxation techniques produce a similar integrated state. Benson suggests that the hypometabolic state we call relaxation is generated by the provision of four elements, each of which is common to most relaxation methods: (a) a quiet environment, (b) a constant stimulus to dwell upon, (c) a passive attitude, and (d) a comfort-able position permitting a minimum of muscle tension.

In contrast to this view, Davidson and Schwartz (1976; Davidson, 1978) have argued that different types of relaxation techniques lead to different patterns of psychological and physiological changes. For example, somatically focused techniques, such as progressive relaxation training, are most likely to produce somatic changes, whereas cognitively oriented techniques, such as some forms of meditation, are most likely to produce cognitive changes. Techniques such as progressive relaxation with imagery and autogenic training, which contain both somatic foci (muscle tensing and relaxing, attending to feelings of warmth and heaviness in specific body parts) and cognitive foci (imagery), would be expected to affect both types of outcome measures. While relatively little research has been directed toward the specific effects hypothesis as applied to various relaxation techniques, the hypothesis has focused more attention on procedural differences between relaxation strategies and on different patterns of response to relaxation techniques both between and within individuals. These are areas of considerable importance in our theoretical understanding of how relaxation may exert its effects.

Empirical Findings

In the paragraphs that follow, we focus on representative research that has been conducted on relaxation training that was considered as the only form of intervention rather than as a component of a multifaceted treatment approach (such as systematic desensitization or anxiety management training). We seldom advocate the use of relaxation training as a sole intervention technique, preferring instead to incorporate it into a more comprehensive treatment program. Nonetheless, an understanding of the specific effects of relaxation training is of obvious importance regardless of whether relaxation is being used as a sole intervention or as an adjunctive component of a broader treatment package.

As you might expect, the major use of relaxation training has been for anxiety or stress-related problems. For example, Borkovec, Grayson, and Cooper (1978, Experiment 2) randomly assigned 36 highly anxious college students to one of three groups: (a) progressive relaxation training, (b) relaxation without the muscle tensing component, or (c) no-treatment control. Both relaxation groups received nine sessions of individual training as follows: Sessions 1–3 involved 14 muscle groups; Sessions 4–5, 7 muscle groups; Sessions 6–7, 4 muscle groups; and Sessions 8–9, a four-group recall procedure. Dependent measures included daily ratings of percent of each day that subjects felt tense, the average severity of the tension, and self-measured pulse rate. The results indicated in general that, compared to the control group, progressive relaxation training significantly reduced reported daily tension levels throughout treatment and at the five-month follow-up. The relaxation without tensing group fell somewhere between the other two groups and was not significantly different from either. An important methodological feature of this study was an attempt to control for any demand characteristics that might, by themselves, account for the treatment outcome. To reduce the likelihood of such effects, the authors used a "counterdemand" procedure in which they specifically suggested that subjects *not* expect any treatment effects until after the seventh treatment. The fact that the treatment effects occurred even during these counterdemand sessions suggests that the treatment itself, not the subjects' expectations, accounted for the results.

A later study by Borgeat and his colleagues (1983) also indicated that therapists' suggestions do not play a major role in the outcome of relaxation procedures. Over an eight-week period, the researchers taught both progressive relaxation training and autogenic training to two groups of college students. One group was told that progressive relaxation was likely to in-

duce more sleepiness and mental images than was autogenic training, while the other group was given the reverse expectations. The results showed that these differential suggestions had no effect on outcome.

In a study of the effects of relaxation training on anxious versus nonanxious individuals, Lehrer (1978) used a "2 × 2" design. The first 2 refers to the subjects—individuals diagnosed as having anxiety neuroses versus individuals with no apparent anxiety problems—and the second 2 indicates the form of treatment—progressive relaxation training versus no treatment.[2] Relaxation subjects received four sessions of an abbreviated form of Jacobsonian relaxation that involved tensing and relaxing 35 muscle groups. Similar to some of Jacobson's early work, treatment outcome was assessed by measuring subjects' physiological responses to aversive tones. Subjects' physiological reactions to a series of milder tones and self-reports of anxiety were also collected. Results generally indicated that relaxation training decreased physiological reactivity—both defensive reactivity to aversive tones and natural orienting responses to nonaversive tones—in both the anxious and the nonanxious groups, with the decrease being greater for patients in the anxious group. By the end of training, the autonomic responses of the anxious subjects decreased to a level similar to that of the nonanxious subjects. Interestingly, self-reported anxiety decreased more in the nonanxious than in the anxious group.

Miller, Murphy, and Miller (1978) studied the effects of two relaxation procedures in reducing anxiety reactions to a commonly stressful situation: dental treatment. Patients identified by a dentist as being highly anxious during treatment were randomly assigned to one of three groups: (a) progressive relaxation training, (b) frontalis EMG biofeedback, or (c) no-treatment control. Following the initial den-

---

[2]The study also included a fifth group that received alpha biofeedback, but unfortunately only nonanxious subjects were included in this condition.

tal appointment, during which actual dental work occurred, treatment subjects received 10 sessions of individual relaxation training or biofeedback in a room adjacent to the dentist's office. Two weeks after relaxation treatment ended, a second dental appointment was scheduled. The data indicated that the two treatment groups achieved significant and comparable reductions in frontalis EMG, as compared to the no-treatment control group. In addition, while the state anxiety and the dental anxiety self-reports of subjects in all groups decreased from their first to their second appointment, those of the subjects in the two relaxation groups decreased significantly more than did those of the control subjects.

A major stress-related problem that frequently is treated with relaxation techniques is hypertension. Brauer and his colleagues (1979) randomly assigned 29 patients who had elevated blood pressures to one of three groups: (a) therapist-directed progressive muscle relaxation training, (b) audiotaped progressive muscle relaxation training, and (c) nonspecific psychotherapy. All patients were treated for 10 weeks, with blood pressures being taken at the baseline and posttreatment times and six months following the termination of treatment. The results indicated that all three groups showed comparable declines in blood pressure following treatment (*M* decrease of 8.4/3.9mm Hg). However, the therapist-directed relaxation training group continued to improve following treatment, and by the six-month follow-up, patients in this condition had significantly lower blood pressures (*M* decrease of 17.8/9.7mm Hg) than did the patients in either of the other two conditions.

Agras and his colleagues (1980) were interested in determining whether the blood pressure reductions produced by relaxation procedures persisted after the therapist concluded the relaxation induction. Obviously, if the effects of relaxation procedures occur only during relaxation practice, then fewer major health consequences would be expected (unless, of course, a person could practice relaxation all

day long!). The investigators addressed this question by hospitalizing five hypertensive patients and monitoring their blood pressure continuously for six days. During each of Days 3 to 5, the patients were given three sessions of progressive relaxation training followed by relaxation imagery. The results indicated that relaxation training was effective in producing immediate reductions in both systolic and diastolic blood pressures. More importantly, the data also showed that the effects persisted well beyond the practice sessions, and for some patients were especially evident during the night while they were sleeping. These results suggest that the effects of relaxation can last well beyond the actual relaxation induction.

In later studies, Agras and his colleagues (1983; Southam, Agras, Taylor, & Cramer, 1982) approached in another way the question of the long-term effects of relaxation on the lowering of blood pressure. Hypertensive patients were assigned either to a progressive relaxation training group or to a no-treatment control group. Some of the patients were followed up to 15 months after their treatment had ended. By fitting the patients with ambulatory blood pressure monitors, the investigators were able to collect blood pressures several times throughout the day, including while patients were at work. The results indicated that patients who received relaxation training showed significantly greater reductions in diastolic blood pressure than did the control patients, both immediately after treatment and at the 15-month follow-up, and both in the clinic and the workplace.

Interestingly, another study by Agras and his colleagues (1982) suggests that, contrary to the studies described previously, client expectations can have a considerable effect on the use of relaxation procedures, at least with regard to blood pressure levels. Thirty subjects under medical supervision for hypertension received relaxation training and were told either that the training would cause immediate reductions in blood pressure or that it would cause no reductions, and perhaps even slight increases in blood pressure, until after the third session. Graphs of expected results were shown to the patients to bolster the expectancy effects. The results showed a mixed pattern: there were no effects for expectancy on diastolic blood pressure, but effects did appear for systolic blood pressure. Subjects who were told to expect immediate improvement produced significantly greater reductions than did clients who were told to expect delayed improvement. Apparently, for some types of individuals, the effects of relaxation procedures on blood pressure levels can be modified by well-orchestrated expectancy manipulations.

As will be noted in more detail in Chapter 11, relaxation procedures can be effective on their own or as an adjunctive treatment for a large number of health or medically related problems besides hypertension, including acute (e.g., Kaplan, Metzger, & Jablecki, 1983) and chronic pain (e.g., Turner, 1982), asthma (Creer, 1982), the side effects of cancer chemotherapy (e.g., Burish & Carey, 1984), postpartum distress (e.g., Halonen & Passman, 1985), headaches (e.g., Blanchard et al., 1982), Raynaud's disease (e.g., Surwit, Allen, Gilgor, & Duvic, 1982), and postsurgical distress (e.g., Wilson, 1981). Relaxation procedures have also been used for a vast array of other problems, including insomnia (see Borkovec, 1982), temper outbursts (e.g., Harvey, Karan, Bhargava, & Morehouse, 1978), nightmares (e.g., Miller & DiPilato, 1983), agoraphobia (e.g., Michelson, Mavissakalian, & Marchione, 1985), and speech anxiety (e.g., Gatchel, Hatch, Watson, Smith, & Gaas, 1977).

While the great majority of evidence suggests that relaxation can be highly effective for a broad array of problems, there are some problems for which relaxation procedures may be of relatively little assistance. For example, Kirkland and Hollandsworth (1980) randomly assigned highly test-anxious undergraduates to groups that received (a) meditation, (b) cue-controlled relaxation training, (c) instruction and test-taking skills, or (d) no treatment. The treatment groups each received five 90-minute training sessions. Results indicated that following training, the skills acquisition group reported significantly higher grade point averages, more effective test-taking skills, and less attentional interference during tests than did the other three groups, which did not significantly differ from each other. It is likely that the students were anxious for good reason—they lacked adequate skills—and that the inculcation of such skills was essential to the improvement of their GPA and, consequently, to meaningful reductions in anxiety. As we will see many times in this book, relaxation or fear-reduction procedures alone are usually inadequate when skill deficiencies are the root of a problem.

Automated Relaxation In 1969, Lang recommended that investigators might use tape-recorded relaxation training instructions to insure comparability of training from subject to subject and from study to study. Tape-recorded relaxation procedures also have the clinical advantage of being more efficient than traditional methods of training since they do not require the presence of a "live" therapist. Paul and Trimble (1970) conducted the first study directly comparing live versus taped relaxation. They concluded that live relaxation was more effective, especially in reducing physiological indices of arousal. Since that time, numerous other studies have compared the two procedures (e.g., Beiman, Israel, & Johnson, 1978; Carey & Burish, 1986; Israel & Beiman, 1977; Russell, Sipich, & Knipe, 1976). The findings have been consistent: live relaxation is usually more effective than, and at least equal to, taped relaxation, especially with regard to physiological measures. In some studies, taped relaxation is more effective than no treatment; in others it is not (see reviews by Borkovec & Sides, 1979; Hillenberg & Collins, 1982; Lehrer & Woolfolk, 1984).

Why is live training better? There are several potential reasons, although none has been adequately subjected to empirical tests. First, in live training the instructions are paced according to the individual client's needs and responses. The training, therefore, is maximally sensitive to individual differences. In contrast, taped training provides standardized instructions designed for the average person and is relatively insensitive to any unusual client needs. Second, in live training the therapist can use visual cues and patient comments to help recognize, diagnose, and correct any problems the patient may be having with the relaxation procedure, whether or not the client is actually aware of such problems. As in other therapeutic interactions, such observations can be of critical importance in designing or modifying intervention strategies. Finally, factors such as personal attention, a warm interpersonal relationship, and therapist support and suggestion are each likely to be stronger in live versus taped training. These factors may also help to bolster the treatment effect for some clients. Overall, we highly recommend that, whenever possible, live relaxation be provided rather than taped relaxation. However, taped procedures may produce some therapeutic changes and thus can be preferable to no treatment. They also can be used for adjuncts (e.g., for home practice) to live instructions.

Home Practice Since relaxation training is a learned skill, most therapists believe that a person must practice them regularly if he or she is to become efficient at the procedure. Relaxing once or twice a week in the therapist's office is not thought to be adequate to instill self-relaxation skills. Research exploring the value of home practice has been mixed. For example, Blanchard et al. (1983) taught progressive relaxation to over 100 patients who had chronic headaches. Patients were given 10 individually administered sessions and were told to practice them at home for about 20 minutes daily. The patients were also asked to record in a daily diary how often they practiced and the frequency and severity of their headaches. Results indi-

cated a small but significant ($r = 0.19$) correlation between frequency of practice and improvement in headache symptoms. Another interesting finding was that patients whose headaches decreased became more faithful in practicing the skills as treatment progressed, whereas patients whose headaches did not improve showed no such increase in home practice. Home practice has also been associated with treatment gains in several other studies (e.g., Hillenberg & Collins, 1983; Hoelscher, Lichstein, & Rosenthal, 1986; Wadden, 1983).

In contrast, some research has not supported the value of home practice. For instance, Taylor and his colleagues (1983) used a hidden electronic device embedded within a special tape recorder to determine whether their hypertensive patients were practicing at home. For comparison purposes, patients were also asked to report how often they practiced. The investigators found two interesting results. First, the patient-reported and electronically monitored records of home practice correlated highly ($r = 0.88$), with only a small amount of overreporting of practice on the part of patients. Second, there was not a significant relationship between home practice and treatment outcome (i.e., changes in blood pressure). Other studies have reported similar results (see Hillenberg & Collins, 1982).

Overall, the research literature on the value of home practice is relatively meager, and the results of the studies that have been conducted are inconsistent. Because we do not know of any data indicating that home practice does harm, and a lot of theory indicating that it is essential, we continue to strongly advocate its use. Obviously, however, additional research is warranted.

Additional Issues As with other behavioral interventions, there is considerable intersubject variability in response to relaxation training. Surprisingly, relatively few studies have been conducted to determine what individual difference factors might be associated with treatment outcomes. However, among those that have been reported, one factor has repeatedly emerged: pretreatment anxiety level. As we discussed previously, Heide and Borkovec (1983) suggested that paradoxical increases in anxiety following relaxation were most likely to occur in highly tensed clients. Carey and Burish (1985) found that cancer patients who had high pretreatment anxiety showed fewer reductions in negative effect and physiological arousal after relaxation training than did patients who had comparatively moderate or low anxiety at the base level time. This finding agrees with results in other areas and suggests that, with some types of problems, the more severe the symptom is to begin with, the more difficult it is to treat.

Another factor that affects outcome is the length of training. A full course of training in Jacobsonian relaxation procedures requires 50 or more sessions, and a full course of autogenic training can require a similar amount of time. Abbreviated forms of both procedures usually require at least 8 to 10 sessions. Unfortunately, some investigators provide considerably less training, and not surprisingly they report limited therapeutic success. For example, after an extensive review of the literature, Hillenberg and Collins (1982) found that the studies that did not show a significant difference between the relaxation procedure and the no-treatment control group used an average of only 2.3 training sessions. The studies that showed significant treatment effects averaged twice that many training sessions. Regrettably, Hillenberg and Collins noted that only 5.6 percent of all studies used at least 10 sessions.

Systematic Desensitization

Systematic desensitization, developed by Joseph Wolpe (1958, 1969, 1973, 1982), is aimed specifically at the alleviation of maladaptive anxiety. The technique involves pairing relaxation with imagined scenes depicting situations that the client has indicated cause him or her to feel anxious. The therapist usually operates on the assumption that if the client is taught to experience relaxation rather than anxiety while imagining such scenes, the real-life situations will cause the client much less discomfort. Some of the considerable clinical research literature supporting the efficacy of desensitization is reviewed in a later section of this chapter.

Background

Systematic desensitization was formally introduced by Wolpe in 1958. However, its clinical roots go back to at least 1924 when Mary Cover Jones published a report on the elimination of a fear of rabbits in a small boy. Jones's therapy included, among other things, the pairing of eating a desirable food (which presumably produced positive feelings) with a gradual introduction of the rabbit. In Wolpean terms, eventually the pairing of the rabbit with the pleasurable feelings associated with eating replaced the previously learned association of the rabbit with a fear response. This process, however, was not articulated until Wolpe refined it in his book *Psychotherapy by Reciprocal Inhibition,* in 1958.

In the 1950s, Wolpe was producing fears or phobias in cats. He would place the cat in a cage, sound a buzzer, and then electrically shock the cat. Not surprisingly, the cat developed a conditioned fear response to the sound of the buzzer and to the cage itself. In other cats, Wolpe first paired the buzzer with food so that initially the animal showed positive or appetitive responses to the sound of the buzzer. After such appetitive conditioning occurred, Wolpe changed the contingencies so that the buzzer now signaled shock. This sequence of conditioning produced a conflict situation for the cat, in which a stimulus presumably had both positive and negative consequences associated with it. Wolpe called the result an "experimental neurosis." In both types of conditioning, the result was that the animals began to show anxietylike responses to the sound of the buzzer. Wolpe noticed that these conditioned fear responses also had another effect: they inhibited eating. Wolpe reasoned, as apparently did Mary Cover Jones, that if anxiety was able to inhibit eating, perhaps eating could inhibit anxiety. To test the notion, Wolpe conducted the following experiment. Because the animals showed the greatest anxiety in their home cages, and relatively less anxiety in cages physically different from their home cages, he began by presenting food pellets in these different cages. After he observed them eating in those cages, he transferred them to cages more like their home cages and fed them again. This process of gradually reintroducing the home-cage stimuli was continued until the animal showed no signs of anxiety in the home cage. By an analogous procedure, the buzzer was paired with food until it, too, elicited no apparent anxiety.

Wolpe described his procedure as a *counterconditioning* process, whereby old and unadaptive associations (e.g., between a buzzer and fear responses) were replaced by new associations (e.g., between a buzzer and approach responses), which were produced by pairing the stimulus (buzzer) with something positive in nature (eating) until this new association was strong enough to replace the old one. Wolpe assumed that if this procedure could work with animals who had "experimental" neuroses, perhaps it could also work with human fears.

Following his research with cats, Wolpe (1958) began to search for responses in humans that would inhibit anxiety and that could be used therapeutically. Apparently, in spite of Mary Cover Jones's work, he believed that eating was not an effective way to countercondition fear responses in humans (Wolpe, 1958). Based on Salter's conditioned reflex therapy (1949), Wolpe decided to try assertion training to produce responses antithetical to anxiety. For many individuals, this did not work out satisfactorily, and so Wolpe searched further. Wolpe described what happened next:

> Soon afterwards I had the good luck to come across Edmond Jacobson's *Progressive Relaxation*

(1938). Here was a description of an anxiety-inhibiting response that [did what I was looking for]. . . . I began to give relaxation training to patients for whose neuroses assertion was not applicable. (1982, p. 135)

Because Jacobson's relaxation procedure was very time consuming, as we have already seen, Wolpe modified it so that more modest relaxation skills could be taught in 6 to 10 sessions. Finally, Wolpe dealt with the practical difficulty of gradually introducing actual feared objects into the therapeutic setting:

> I therefore began to explore the possibility of making use of imaginary situations in place of real ones, being encouraged in this by the writings of practioneers of hypnosis. I was delighted to find that magnitudes of experienced anxiety diminished progressively when I repeatedly presented imaginary situations that were weakly anxiety arousing. (1982, p. 136)

These ingredients—a counterconditioning paradigm, the use of relaxation as a response antagnostic to anxiety, and the use of imagined situations rather than *in vivo* exposure to feared objects and situations—are the basic concepts of Wolpean systematic desensitization as we practice it today.

Wolpe's description of systematic desensitization in his *Psychotherapy by Reciprocal Inhibition* stimulated a tremendous amount of research. Many of the early studies conducted in the 1960s (e.g., Davison, 1968; Lang & Lazovik, 1963; Lang, Lazovik, & Reynolds, 1965; Paul, 1966; Rachman, 1965) were well controlled and already are regarded as classics. By 1970, most researchers accepted the conclusion that systematic desensitization could be effective in reducing conditioned anxiety, and their research began to focus not as much on treatment outcome per se as on the mechanisms responsible for its effectiveness, and on whether there were ways of improving its effectiveness. As we will see in later sections of this chapter, this research led to developments in two major areas. First, the basic counterconditioning theory of desensitization proffered by Wolpe was challenged, and several other theories were offered to explain the effects of desensitization. Second, several investigators recommended modified forms of systematic desensitization that differed in one or more notable ways from Wolpe's procedure. For example, Goldfried and Goldfried (1977) recommended a self-controlled desensitization, in which a client first imagined an anxiety-provoking scene and then imagined himself or herself appropriately handling the situation until the scene caused no anxiety.

Today, the term "systematic desensitization" is usually restricted to procedures that closely follow Wolpe's recommended technique. Therapists almost always use relaxation training to induce a response antagonistic to anxiety, and the anxiety-provoking stimuli are usually presented in imagination rather than *in vivo*. Assertion training, which has become a technique in its own right, is now infrequently used as a component of systematic desensitization. Assertion procedures are discussed in detail in Chapter 3.

The Theory of Desensitization

Although systematic desensitization is regarded as an effective strategy for reducing conditioned fears, behaviorists do not universally agree on the mechanisms responsible for this effect. Several of the theories that have been proffered in this regard follow.

According to the Wolpean view, desensitization reflects the process of *counterconditioning* (Wolpe, 1958, 1969, 1982). Counterconditioning in this context means the substitution of an emotional response that is appropriate or adaptive to a given situation for one that is maladaptive. For Wolpe, in most instances the maladaptive emotion is anxiety, a state he associates with the activity of the sympathetic nervous system. People learn through classical conditioning to experience excessive levels of sympathetic ex-

citation in the presence of certain stimuli. The task of the therapist is to teach the client a response that competes with and effectively inhibits sympathetic activity. Wolpe called this process *reciprocal inhibition*—a term borrowed from the physiologist Sherrington (1906)—because anxiety (or sympathetic activity) was *inhibited* by a response that was incompatible with, or the *reciprocal* of, anxiety.[3] As we suggested, there are several responses Wolpe assumed that are capable of inhibiting sympathetic activity, including relaxation, assertion, and sexual behavior. Physiologically, these classes of behaviors are assumed to have in common a predominance of parasympathetic nervous activity, which according to Wolpe inhibits sympathetic activity. Concretely, then, the Wolpean interpretation of desensitization is as follows:

A phobic client is taught relaxation. If the client can maintain this state of relaxation while imagining phobic scenes, relaxation rather than anxiety will become conditioned to the phobic cues. That is, parasympathetic activity will have replaced sympathetic activity as the predominant response to the phobic situation. It is assumed that anxiety reduction will generalize from imaginal to actual phobic stimuli.

A major alternative interpretation for desensitization is *extinction*. This view holds that anxiety reduction results from the fact that, in

---

[3]Although we are using the terms "reciprocal inhibition" and "counterconditioning" rather interchangeably in this chapter, technically they refer to somewhat different processes. Specifically, in the desensitization context, counterconditioning and reciprocal inhibition both require that the anxiety-evoking stimulus be paired with the response that inhibits anxiety (e.g., relaxation) if the stimulus is to lose its anxiety-evoking qualities. However, unlike reciprocal inhibition, the counterconditioning hypothesis does not posit underlying neurophysiological mechanisms (such as parasympathetic versus sympathetic dominance).

desensitization, the fear-evoking conditioned stimulus is presented repeatedly without any adversive consequences, which results in an eventual decay of the conditioned response. Ample data exist to suggest that repeated exposure to fear-evoking objects can indeed lead to reductions in anxiety (see Kazdin & Wilcoxon, 1976). Interestingly, Wolpe himself (1976c) viewed desensitization as an extinction procedure, although the inclusion of a competing response such as relaxation is a marked departure from extinction as it is usually conducted. Whether or not we wish to view desensitization as an instance of the general extinction *procedure* is really semantic. The more germane question is, Do desensitization and extinction reflect the same underlying *process* or mechanism? Theorists have attempted to deal with this question by comparing desensitization with extinction; the results have been mixed. However, even if desensitization were always found to be superior to extinction, we could still argue that the relaxation component somehow facilitates a more basic extinction process. At present, our knowledge of the neurophysiology of learning simply does not permit a definitive answer to this question.

Habituation provides an explanation that is similar to extinction. Habituation refers to the decrement of a person's response to a stimulus when the stimulus is repeatedly presented. A person is most likely to become habituated to a stimulus that is repeated under conditions of low arousal. Since systematic desensitization presumably produces, via relaxation training, low levels of arousal during the stimulus presentation, it provides an optimal setting for habituation to occur. This explanation, therefore, holds that the conditioned stimulus does not become "reconditioned" to elicit relaxation instead of anxiety, but rather that the person simply becomes habituated to it and therefore no longer shows an emotional response when it is introduced. Obviously, there are considerable similarities between extinction and habituation hy-

potheses. Levin and Gross note that the major difference is a technical one:

> It has been suggested that habituation and extinction may have the same underlying mechanisms. Typically, however, habituation has been used in reference to the decrement of unconditioned responses, whereas extinction has been applied to conditioned responses. (1985, p. 188)

Some researchers have indicated that the effects of systematic desensitization may be due largely to *nonspecific factors,* such as positive expectancy or demand characteristics. This view stems in part from two observations. First, most researchers and clinicians try to induce a positive expectancy toward treatment outcome when using systematic desensitization (or almost any other technique), and we know from other research that such expectancies can effect behavior. Second, some research has suggested that the effects of desensitization can be achieved if a therapist omits the relaxation training, the hierarchical arrangement of the anxiety-provoking stimuli, or the pairing of relaxation with the hierarchy items (see Kazdin & Wilcoxon, 1976). This observation has indicated to some (e.g., Wilkins, 1971) that explanations that include factors such as positive expectancy make more sense than do reciprocal inhibition or extinction. To test this hypothesis, several researchers have included in their studies credible placebo groups, which presumably controlled for nonspecific factors such as positive expectancy. In a review of over 100 controlled investigations of desensitization, including those with placebo comparison groups, Kazdin and Wilcoxon (1976) concluded that nonspecific treatment effects such as expectancy may play a role in the desensitization outcome.

Theorists have offered additional explanations for the effectiveness of systematic desensitization, including operant shaping, modeling, attention control, and self-instruction training (see Kazdin & Wilcoxon, 1976). Some have even suggested that the effectiveness of desensitization is partially the result of the client's "unconscious fantasy of merging with the therapist as a mother substitute" (Silverman, Frank, & Dachinger, 1974), although this hypothesis has been challenged roundly (Condon & Allen, 1980). No single explanation of desensitization has been endorsed by the majority of researchers who have investigated the problem. It is likely that no single explanation is always correct; rather, different explanations may account for the effectiveness of desensitization with different subjects who have different problems treated by different therapists.

Desensitization as Coping Whether we think of desensitization as reflecting counterconditioning, extinction, or habituation, the traditional view is that the client is in some sense "deconditioned" to the feared stimulus. That is, the client is not required to *do* anything (engage in any deliberate activity) in the phobic situation in order to realize the benefits of therapy. Some researchers, on the other hand, believe that desensitization is better conceived as a coping or self-control technique wherein the client is taught *how* to relax in the phobic situation. For example, Goldfried suggested that systematic desensitization should be construed

> as more of an active process, directed toward the learning of a general anxiety-reducing skill, rather than [as] the passive desensitization of specific adversive stimuli. . . . During the process of systematic desensitization, the client is taught to become sensitive to his proprioceptive cues for attention and to react to these cues with his newly acquired skill and muscular relaxation. . . . According to this view, then, what the client learns is a means of actively coping with anxiety, rather than an immediate replacement of it. (1971, pp. 228–229)

Goldfried, like others who take an active coping view of desensitization, has suggested a number of modifications in the desensitization procedure to promote self-control training. For

instance, clients were not to terminate a scene whenever it caused them anxiety; rather they were to continue imagining the scene while attempting to relax away the anxiety. Hierarchies also need not be constructed around a single theme but, instead, could include scenes from a diversity of anxiety-eliciting situations (Denney, 1982). These and other changes are akin to those used in anxiety management training, which we will discuss in more depth in Chapter 10. The goal here is to point out that the process of desensitization has been modified over the years in a number of ways by different groups of investigators, with a large number of them suggesting that it should be viewed as a method of teaching active coping skills to emotionally distraught individuals.

Desensitization and Cognitions Cognitive interpretations of desensitization fall into two broad categories. The first emphasizes that the phobic object is really not dangerous after all. Desensitization helps the client to realize this and to *deal with his thoughts vis-à-vis the phobic object more rationally* (or less irrationally). In one early formulation, London (1964) argued that in desensitization the client learns to discriminate between the actual feared stimulus and the imagined stimulus. He or she also learns that experiencing images of frightening events does not lead to dire consequences. Both elements contribute to therapeutic success. Beck (1976) has suggested a somewhat related interpretation: because a client is relaxed when presented with the phobic image, he or she is better able to think about it objectively. The client may then come to the conclusion that the fear really is irrational. Ellis's (1962, 1971b) conceptualization of phobic behavior points to a similar interpretation of desensitization. He assumes that anxiety and avoidance behavior result primarily from self-verbalizations of an irrational nature. Such self-verbalizations are discouraged in desensitization, which could readily account for the techniques' effectiveness.

The second category of cognitive formulations instills in clients the belief that *they are less fearful, or will be, as a result of treatment.* There have been several experimental variations on this general theme. In one, the phobic subject is given false physiological feedback (e.g., heart rate reduction, Valins & Ray, 1967; increasing skin resistance, Lick, 1975) indicating that the person really was not that afraid of the formally feared stimulus, possibly paralleling the client's subjective experience in actual desensitization. False feedback research is discussed and evaluated in Chapter 10. For our present purpose, it suffices to say that results of the efficacy of such techniques tend to be conflicting. When positive results are reported, they typically tend to be weak.

The Method of Systematic Desensitization

Systematic desensitization is a valuable tool in assisting clients to overcome anxiety reactions that are conditioned responses to specific situations or events. Specific anxiety reactions fall into two categories.

Problems in the first category are the reactions resulting from irrational anxiety; for clients who experience such anxiety, desensitization may be very helpful. An anxiety reaction is considered irrational if the client has sufficient *skills* for coping with whatever it is he or she fears, but habitually avoids the target situation, or if that is impossible, performs below his or her actual level of skill. For example, a skillful and experienced driver, following involvement in an accident, may avoid driving altogether or may drive with less apparent skill because his or her attention is impaired by a high level of anxiety.

Problems in the second category are those in which the fear is rational, either because the individual is lacking in pertinent skills, or because the target situation is inherently dangerous, or both. For clients who have such problems, desensitization alone probably will not be adequate and, in fact, may be inappropriate. For instance, we could expect a novice driver to avoid attempting to negotiate a treacherous ice-covered mountain road. Successful desensitization might have fatal consequences, and most therapists would opt instead to help the client to increase his or her driving skill.

The therapist must decide which of the client's anxieties are irrational and which arise from rational considerations. If the particular problem is primarily one of irrational anxiety, desensitization may well be an appropriate treatment, depending on other factors to be discussed shortly. It is essential that the therapist consider very carefully whether the anxiety is irrational, even when the client is convinced that desensitization is needed.

Consider a client who spent the greater part of his leisure hours in seedy bars. One of his stated therapeutic goals was to lose his fear of getting involved in barroom brawls so that he would be in a position to "beat the shit out of everybody in the place." He was not physically large and possessed no particular combative skills. The therapist pointed this out, with the suggestion that were the client to be desensitized to this fear, and were he then to engage in such behavior, he would not remain desensitized very long.

Clinicians frequently encounter individuals who desire heterosexual interactions but report intense anxiety when such interactions arise. The beginning therapist may be tempted to employ desensitization immediately, on the assumption that the client has all the appropriate skills necessary to sustain such an interaction but is inhibited by anxiety. Quite often, however, such is not the case with the client. The individual may be anxious because he knows he is lacking in necessary social skills (asking for a date, giving compliments, small talk, dancing, etc.), and instruction in these areas (perhaps including assertive training—see Chapter 3) might be more appropriate than desensitization. Therapists can determine whether their clients' problems result from a lack of skill by questioning them—or if their replies are vague, by asking them to role-play how they would handle certain situations. If it appears that the client's anxiety does not result from an objective lack of skills (or from an objectively dangerous situation), systematic desensitization may be an appropriate treatment.

Determining the Feasibility of Desensitization for a Given Client

As we saw in our discussion of relaxation procedures, there is evidence that with certain problems, the more serious the symptoms are, the less likely that some interventions will be effective. Clinical experience along with some research (Lang & Lasovik, 1963) suggest that this principle applies to systematic desensitization in at least one regard: there is a negative correlation between success in desensitization and the number of phobias the client reports. We cited the Fear Survey Schedule (Wolpe & Lang, 1964) in Chapter 1 as a useful instrument for assessing the nature and intensity of a client's fears. If we assume that a "much" or "very much" afraid response for an FSS item defines a phobic reaction, an individual with, say, 1 to 3 such responses would probably be amenable to desensitization. The client with 8 to 10 such responses probably would be a poor candidate for desensitization, at least as it is traditionally employed. For instance, for a male client who seemed fearful of virtually everything—meeting his brother-in-law, driving on the freeway, flushing the toilet, men riding motorcycles, crawling under a house, and so forth—the attempted desensitization was to no avail.

What about the intensity of the fear, or its duration, or whether the client acquired the fear suddenly or in a gradual fashion? None of these factors appear to have much bearing on whether desensitization will or will not be effective (de Silva, Rachman, & Seligman, 1977).

What about the type of fear? As we suggested earlier, desensitization may be very helpful to the client, provided the fear does not stem from an actual deficiency in certain skills. This is

well illustrated in the area of test anxiety. Numerous studies have shown that test anxiety can indeed be reduced as a result of desensitization; however, in most instances, a commensurate increase in grade point average is *not* reported (Anton, 1976). This is understandable when we realize that desensitization does nothing to enhance the client's study or exam-taking skills, or his or her attitudes toward studying. For essentially the same reason, we saw earlier that relaxation procedures alone are often not effective in altering grade point averages. In a similar vein, assertive training usually is more effective than desensitization in enhancing dating *behavior* in shy individuals (Curran & Gilbert, 1975; Marzillier, Lambert, & Kellett, 1976), although desensitization may be effective (at least temporarily) in reducing dating *anxiety*. Evidence (Evans & Kellam, 1973) shows that desensitization is more effective with so-called simple phobias (e.g., fear of heights, dogs, loud noises) than with social phobias, including agoraphobia, perhaps in part because social fears may reflect deficiencies in social skills.

One potentially important predictor of the degree of success in desensitization is the client's *arousability,* as measured by spontaneous fluctuations in the electrical conductance of the skin, or the *galvanic skin response* (GSR). Lader, Gelder, and Marks (1967) found that clients high in arousability did not respond as well to desensitization as did clients showing low arousal. Lader (1967) reported that social phobics and agoraphobics, who are generally somewhat less responsive to desensitization than simple phobics, were higher in arousability than simple phobics (the simple phobics did not differ from normal individuals). High-arousal individuals also acquire laboratory fears more readily, and their fears are more difficult to extinguish (Hugdahl, Fredrickson, & Ohman, 1977).

Measuring arousability may present a problem because many practitioners do not have the necessary recording equipment (or the skills to use such equipment). Further, normative data on arousability are not readily available. We can only recommend that clinicians who frequently employ systematic desensitization gain access to the appropriate equipment (a polygraph, or a less expensive GSR recording device) and learn how to use it. Clinicians, of course, may generate their own informal normative data in relatively short order.

Based on the foregoing discussion, let us assume that a client appears to be an appropriate candidate for desensitization—that is, he or she suffers from only a small number of phobias, the phobias do not reflect a major skill deficiency, and the level of arousability is not high. The therapist should now determine the degree to which the client is able to imagine scenes by having him or her imagine an emotionally neutral, but familiar, scene (e.g., the neighborhood post office) and indicate afterward the extent to which the image was clear or real. If the client reports being unable to create a reasonably clear image, which is somewhat unusual, the therapist may present a different scene, or several scenes if necessary, to see if practice facilitates imagining. If the client still reports being unable to experience a reasonably clear image, this probably should be taken as a counterindication for systematic desensitization, and the therapist should choose an alternative strategy such as *in vivo* desensitization, modeling, or perhaps a cognitive approach.

When the client reports that he or she is imagining a clear image, the therapist should then present a scene that the client considers frightening. Again, the image needs to be clear. Sometimes individuals can imagine neutral or pleasant scenes, but will block on unpleasant scenes, and so will need additional practice to imagine unpleasant scenes. If the client reports a clear image, the therapist needs to determine if this causes anxiety.

Research (Grossberg & Wilson, 1968; Rimm & Bottrell, 1969) suggests a positive relationship between related clarity of a frightening image and level of arousal as indicated by physiological measures. However, the correlation is by no means perfect. Some individuals can imagine quite clearly scenes that ought to be frightening to them without experiencing the expected emotional response. This is rare, occurring in only 1 out of 10 individuals according to Wolpe (1969). With such individuals, desensitization may not be very effective. On the other hand, for some phobics, the anxiety may be attached to cues that are nonvisual. Consider a person who develops an earthquake phobia as a consequence of having experienced an actual earthquake. It is likely that intense anxiety would be triggered by sensations of even a very slight tremor, associated, for instance, with the passage of a large truck or a train. The therapist might ask the client to attempt to imagine these sensations. If this is successful in eliciting anxiety, the therapist and client can then create a hierarchy having as its core the imagining (i.e., feeling) of slight tremors.

To illustrate, consider the case in which a woman's fear of flying was seriously interfering with her life (see Rimm & Somervill, 1977, p. 91). Her husband was working halfway around the world and the only feasible way to join him was to fly. She developed the phobia after a turbulent flight about a year before treatment. When asked to imagine herself flying in a plane, she reported having difficulty experiencing anxiety because it just did not seem real. The therapist then introduced several nonvisual external cues or prompts, related to the experience of flying:

1. The therapist emits a loud hum, simulating the engines.

2. The therapist says, "This is Captain Roberts. I hope you are enjoying the flight tonight. Folks, we are going to be running into a little turbulence in a few minutes, so we are asking you to remain in your seats. Thank you."

3. The therapist resumes the steady hum, then places his hand on the client's chair, shaking it so as to simulate turbulence.

This procedure was very effective in generating anxiety. The cues or prompts, of course, were incorporated into the treatment proper.

Certain researchers (e.g., Brady, 1967; Munjack, 1975; Munjack & Ranzani, 1974) have reported good results (but sometimes side effects) using quick-acting barbiturates to facilitate relaxation, while others (Ley & Walker, 1973; Slater & Leavy, 1966; Wolpe, 1982) have reported inducing relaxation by having the individual inhale a mixture of carbon dioxide and oxygen. However, these practices are not widespread, and most practitioners do not have the facilities or the license to use them. A somewhat more feasible strategy is to find a response other than relaxation that successfully combats anxiety. Thoughts of sexual activity or of eating, or of any kind of pleasurable activity, are appropriate. Assertive responses are also likely candidates. Laughter is also an effective anxiety inhibitor, and case history data support its use in desensitization (Smith, 1973; Ventis, 1973).

Finally, desensitization (or some other intervention) will not be effective because the client feels conflict about letting go of the fear. For instance, one client with a phobia of driving a car was making little progress in desensitization. Treatment of this phobia was temporarily discontinued when it became apparent that the client was fearful of looking for a job; being unwilling to drive effectively precluded job seeking, since public transportation in the area was virtually nonexistent. Another example is an agoraphobic who is unhappy about her inability to leave the house, but at the same time is concerned about losing disability payments if she were to overcome her fears. These examples highlight the importance of identifying possible motives for maintaining a phobia and determining—and sometimes facilitating—a client's resolve to deal with them.

In summary, then, before embarking upon desensitization, the therapist should

1. Determine that the client suffers from relatively few phobias.
2. Determine that the client's fears do not reflect a major skill deficit.
3. Determine that the client's arousability is not unusually high.
4. Determine that the client can imagine negative scenes with appropriate emotion, using external prompts if necessary.
5. Determine that deep muscle relaxation (or a practical alternative) can induce relaxation.
6. Determine the client's motivation to overcome the phobia and his or her willingness to resolve any conflicting motives that might maintain the phobia.

Given all of these elements to review, a novice to systematic desensitization is likely to question whether anybody would be a good candidate for treatment. However, the many positive laboratory and clinical findings (some of which are reviewed later in the chapter) suggest that most individuals qualify.

The Desensitization Procedure

After the therapist has determined that a client is a good candidate for desensitization, he or she can initiate the treatment. Three basic steps are involved in traditional desensitization: (a) training the client in progressive muscle relaxation (or some other relaxation procedure); (b) constructing a hierarchy of anxiety-eliciting items, ranging from the least anxiety evoking to the most anxiety evoking; and (c) pairing relaxation with exposure to the anxiety-evoking stimuli composing the hierarchy.

Even before the therapist begins to progress through each of the three basic stages, he or she should introduce the basic concept of desensitization to the client in terms that are understandable and that instill maximum confidence in the therapist and the technique. It is helpful to indicate to clients not only that systematic desensitization can be effective, but also to tell them *why* it is effective. This presents something of a problem since, as we noted, authorities do not agree on why desensitization is effective. We can only suggest that the therapist select the interpretation he or she thinks is best substantiated, and base the rationale on this. When using, for instance, the counterconditioning explanation, the therapist might say:

At the beginning of treatment, we are going to teach you how to become really relaxed. Then you are going to imagine scenes related to your fear, starting with ones that are only a little frightening and working your way up. Because I will be introducing the scenes in a *graduated way,* and because you will be relaxed when you imagine them, before long you are going to be able to imagine situations related to [phobic object] and actually feel comfortable at the same time. And if you can *imagine* [phobic object] and still feel calm, then when you come across an actual [phobic object] out there in the real world, you will find you are not afraid anymore.

This is just a brief and sketchy example of the type of rationale that should be provided; the actual introduction to the technique should be guided by the nature of the problem, the characteristics of the client, and the specific procedures used by the therapist. Much of the rationale presented earlier for relaxation training can be incorporated into the initial presentation for desensitization.

Training in Relaxation The first step in desensitization is to teach the client to relax. As we saw earlier, although Wolpe believed that a state of relaxation (or another reciprocally inhibiting state) is essential to desensitization, he viewed the extended procedure advocated by Jacobson as overkill: a more moderate state of relaxation, produced in 8 to 10 sessions, is adequate for the purposes of desensitization. The progressive relaxation procedures we detailed earlier in the chapter are the ones most commonly used, and the therapist can introduce them to the client in much the same way as we described. After the client shows an ability to relax in the office or clinic setting, he or she should be instructed to practice relaxation in progressively less ideal circumstances, such as in distracting or stressful environments. But the therapist should be careful not to push a client too quickly in this regard. A client's failure to relax could provide a setback in therapy by reducing his or her self-confidence and feelings

of mastery regarding relaxation. At any rate, the therapist should not attempt to pair relaxation with the hierarchy items (Step 3, p. 67) until he or she is satisfied that the client is sufficiently skilled to produce and maintain a moderately deep state of relaxation.

Constructing the Hierarchy The construction of the hierarchy usually begins early in the course of desensitization, when the client is also learning relaxation skills. The hierarchy is a list of anxiety-evoking scenes or stimuli, usually thematically related, that are arranged according to the degree of anxiety they bring about. The scenes depict realistic, concrete situations relevant to the client's problem. They may involve situations that the client has experienced or anticipates experiencing. It is important to point out that primary responsibility for generating the items to be included in the hierarchy belongs to the client, who has first-hand knowledge of what sorts of situations cause him or her anxiety. While some research has suggested that progress may be achieved using a hierarchy that is not specifically tailored to a given client, individuals who have the same phobia have had different learning histories and cannot be expected to respond in precisely the same manner to a particular scene. Therefore, we recommend that whenever possible, the therapist should construct and use individualized hierarchies rather than "canned" hierarchies that may be available for common problems such as airplane phobia, test anxiety, and so forth.

Although it is the client's responsibility to identify hierarchy items, the therapist should provide as much structure and aid as necessary. He or she might begin by suggesting a homework assignment in which the client writes down on index cards details describing a variety of scenes or situations pertinent to the phobia. Since the completed hierarchy will be graduated with respect to the degree of anxiety elicited by the different scenes, the client should select scenes that create intense anxiety (9 and 10 on the anxiety scale), moderately strong anxiety (7 and 8), moderate anxiety (5 and 6), mild anxiety (2, 3, and 4), and little or no anxiety (1 and 2). The therapist might specifically assist the client in identifying anchor points for the hierarchy, such as an item that would be a 1 or a 2 on the anxiety scale. If the client were dog phobic, perhaps seeing a chained white toy poodle 100 yards away might qualify. The therapist should point out to the client that he or she must describe the scene in enough detail so that when the therapist presents the scene during desensitization, the client will indeed be imagining the correct scene. If the client presented the poodle scene, the therapist might ask where the dog is located, what it is doing, what it is chained to, something about the neighborhood, and perhaps the time of day. Having provided an anchor for the low end of the hierarchy, the therapist then can establish the high anchor by requesting the client to list an item that would evoke a 9 or a 10 on the anxiety scale. The client might suggest having an unchained German shepherd approach him or her. As before, the therapist must gather additional, detailed information. It should be pointed out to the client that the anchor points are not to be viewed as absolute. If the client thinks of new items that might be higher or lower than the anchors, he or she should simply adjust the ratings of the old anchors accordingly.

Clients should be instructed that, when doing their homework, they should try to come up with scenes or situations that represent all 10 levels of anxiety, so that the hierarchy is uniformly graduated. The total number of hierarchy items, of course, will depend on the severity and the breadth of the phobia, as Marquis and Morgan (1969) have pointed out. These authors suggest that in most cases 10 items are sufficient, although for very severe anxiety reactions, the gaps in the 10-item hierarchy may be too large to bridge. Also, for phobic reactions that have generalized to a variety of situations, 10 items may not be sufficient to cover all relevant situations. As a rule of thumb, the client might be instructed to develop a 10- to

15-item hierarchy, and if the severity or breadth of the phobia reveals this to be inadequate, additional items can be introduced during the course of desensitization.

When the client returns with the completed hierarchy, the therapist should examine the scene descriptions with the client to ensure that they are sufficiently detailed. Since the client has rated each item on the 10-point anxiety scale, it is now possible to present the hierarchy in graduated fashion. However, the client may have made scaling errors in setting up the hierarchy (e.g., an item rated as a 4 elicits more anxiety than another item rated as a 6). While the consequences of such an error are not disastrous, errors of this nature will probably slow up therapy. As a safeguard against such errors, the therapist might ask the client to order the items in terms of the amount of anxiety elicited, independent of the previous anxiety ratings. If no inconsistencies appear between the prior ratings and the rankings, the hierarchy may be considered complete enough to begin therapy. If inconsistencies do appear, the therapist should point this out and should ask the client to rerate the discrepant items.

Following are four sample hierarchies. So that you can gain a better sense of how a therapist presents desensitization hierarchies, we have listed the initial items in the first two hierarchies here in the same manner that therapists relate them to clients. The remainder of the items are given in abbreviated form. The other two hierarchies are presented entirely in abbreviated form. Note that these scenes are greatly simplified; our intention is only to provide you with a general feel for hierarchy construction.

The first hierarchy was used by an author of this text with a 40-year-old male who had developed a fear of heights shortly after his discharge from the army air corps during World War II. He was a navigator and had flown many combat missions; he attributed his phobia to his wartime experiences. The items are in order of increasing anxiety.

1. You are beginning to climb the ladder leaning against the side of your house. You plan to work on the roof. Your hands are on the ladder, and your foot is on the first rung.

2. You are halfway up the ladder, and you happen to look down. You see the lawn below you and a walkway.

3. Driving with the family, road begins to climb.

4. Driving with family on California coastal highway, with dropoff to the right.

5. Standing on California seashore cliff, approximately 30 feet from edge.

6. Standing on California seashore cliff, approximately 6 feet from edge.

7. Driving with family, approaching mountain summit.

8. In commercial airliner, at the time of takeoff.

9. In commercial airliner, at an altitude of 30,000 feet.

10. In airliner, at an altitude of 30,000 feet with considerable turbulence.

11. Standing on a California seaside cliff, approximately 2 feet (judged to be a safe distance) from the edge and looking down.

12. Climbing the town water tower to assist in painting, about 10 feet from ground.

13. Climbing the town water tower, but about 20 feet from ground.

14. On the catwalk around the water tank, painting the tank.

Paul (1969b) has distinguished between *thematic* hierarchies, referring to hierarchies in which items are related to the same basic theme or label (for instance, height in the above example), and *spatial-temporal* hierarchies, in which the individual fears a specific situation or event and where the items are graded according to how close they are in space (e.g., distance from seaside cliff and height on water tower, in the above hierarchy) or in time to the target situation. Paul would refer to the first hierarchy as a *combined* hierarchy, since it is both thematic and spatial.

The second hierarchy, also constructed by an author of this text, was used for an insurance salesman in his early forties. The man experienced anxiety primarily when anticipating professional contacts with coworkers or clients, especially when he felt that there was a possibility of failure. It is a thematic hierarchy.

1. You are in your office with an agent, R.C., discussing a prospective interview. The client in question is stalling on his payments, and you must tell R.C. what to do.

2. It is Monday morning and you are at your office. In a few minutes you will attend the regularly scheduled sales meeting. You are prepared for the meeting.

3. Conducting an exploratory interview with a prospective client.

4. Sitting at home. The telephone rings.

5. Anticipating returning a call from the district director.

6. Anticipating returning a call from a stranger.

7. Entering the Monday sales meeting, unprepared.

8. Anticipating a visit from the regional director.

9. A fellow agent requests a joint visit with a client.

10. On a joint visit with a fellow agent.

11. Attempting to close a sale.

12. Thinking about attending an agents and managers' meeting.

13. Thinking of contacting a client who should have been contacted earlier.

14. Thinking about calling a prospective client.

15. Thinking about the regional director's request for names of prospective agents.

16. Alone, driving to prospective client's home.

17. Calling a prospective client.

The next hierarchy, reported by Wolpe (1982, p. 152), was successfully employed with a 24-year-old female student. One of her problems was debilitating examination anxiety. Since the target situation seems rather specific, the hierarchy that follows is best described as spatial-temporal.

1. Four days before an examination.
2. Three days before an examination.
3. Two days before an examination.
4. One day before an examination.
5. The night before an examination.
6. The examination paper lies face down before her.
7. Awaiting the distribution of examination papers.
8. Before the unopened doors of the examination room.
9. In the process of answering an examination paper.
10. On the way to the university on the day of an examination.

Note that the first five items lie along a very natural temporal continuum. One might have expected "On the way to the university . . ." to be the next item, but instead this item is at the very top of the hierarchy. Similarly, "The examination paper . . ." item, contrary to what might have been expected, is not especially near the top of the hierarchy. This particular example illustrates how idiosyncratic hierarchies are and how important it is for the therapist to ensure that the order of items is imposed by the client, rather than by the therapist on "logical" or "intuitive" grounds.

The last hierarchy is reported in Marquis and Morgan (1969, p. 28). It was used with an individual who was extremely sensitive to criticism, especially in relation to the general subject of mental health. It is a good example of a thematic hierarchy.

1. Friend on the street: "Hi, how are you?"
2. Friend on the street: "How are you feeling these days?"
3. Sister: "You've got to be careful so they don't put you in the hospital."

4. Wife: "You shouldn't drink beer while you are taking medicine."
5. Mother: "What's the matter, don't you feel well?"
6. Wife: "It's just you yourself, it's all in your head."
7. Service station attendant: "What are you shaking for?"
8. Neighbor borrows rake: "Is there something wrong with your leg? Your knees are shaking."
9. Friend on the job: "Is your blood pressure okay?"
10. Service station attendant: "You are pretty shaky, are you crazy or something?"

Before starting desensitization, the client should be asked to think of a scene that he or she is able to imagine clearly and that gives rise to pleasant, relaxing sensations. During desensitization, the client may be asked to imagine these scenes in order to facilitate relaxation between the presentation of hierarchy items. Scenes used by our clients have included the following: sitting on the front step of a mountain cabin drinking beer. It is a warm, clear day and it is late in the afternoon; on a massage table being massaged after a vigorous workout; lying on a beach, all alone, on a glorious day, feeling the warm sun on your back and hearing the waves rhythmically lap up on the shore. It is probably a good idea to encourage the client to practice imagining the scenes at home until he or she becomes adept at immediately bringing the appropriate images to mind when requested to do so.

Sometimes, even though the hierarchies were carefully constructed and the client reports being able to imagine them vividly, the therapist may make little progress in desensitizing the client. One possibility is that the content of the hierarchy is inappropriate. For example, Goldenberg (1983) described a medical student who received only modest relief after being desensitized for test anxiety. Upon further discussions with the student, it was discovered that his underlying fear was actually disappointing his parents, and that doing poorly on examinations was only one example of the many potential failure situations that he dreaded. This is another illustration of how the therapist must be careful to explore in some depth the nature of the client's fears before constructing the hierarchy, and not to conclude hastily that the anxiety situations first reported by the client adequately describe the basic problem. However, even the most experienced therapists sometimes do not discover until they are well into the desensitization procedure that the hierarchy content is incorrect. When that occurs, the therapist needs to reassess not only whether a different hierarchy would be more effective, but also whether the problem as reanalyzed is still treated best by desensitization.

Pairing Relaxation and the Hierarchy Scenes The client and the therapist are now ready to begin the actual desensitization procedure. Clients, by now, have had several occasions to practice relaxation on their own. Usually they experience little difficulty in inducing self-relaxation in a matter of several minutes, perhaps by using the cue-controlled procedure we discussed earlier in this chapter. If for some reason clients cannot induce a state of relaxation approximating 1 on the anxiety scale (certainly no higher than 2), additional guided instruction is in order. However, clients should be encouraged to practice relaxation on their own until they can induce the desired state of relaxation quickly. When clients do indicate they are at or near 1, and there are no visible signs of anxiety—such as irregular breathing or movement in the extremities or around the mouth—they may be prepared for the first hierarchy scene.

The clients are told they are going to be asked to imagine a scene and that they are to imagine it as clearly as possible. They are told to imagine only the scene presented. They should imagine the scene as they would actually perceive it, in contrast to imagining an observer viewing them in the situation. (Imagining seeing themselves in the phobic situation is another

method of fear reduction, which will be discussed in Chapter 4.) Clients are advised that if the scene begins to change, they should make it revert to its original form. They are then instructed to signal by raising a finger when they have gained a clear image of the scene and are told to signal again if they experience any anxiety while imagining the scene. If the clients do not signal anxiety, how long should they continue to imagine scenes? At one time, it was common practice to employ brief durations, on the order of 5 to 10 seconds (Paul, 1969a; Wolpe, 1969). However, research findings point to the value of longer exposure durations, possibly as long as 30 seconds (Ross & Proctor, 1973; Sue, 1975; Watts, 1973). Longer exposures appear to favor greater and more permanent fear reduction. On the other hand, some clients report difficulty holding scenes for this length of time, and long intervals make it more likely that they will change the scene in a way that will interfere with progress up the hierarchy. We have found the following procedure to be a useful compromise. The first time the scene is presented, if no anxiety is signaled, the client continues to imagine it for about 10 seconds. When the scene is presented for the second time, the interval is increased to 25 to 30 seconds.[4] The initial brief presentation has the effect of allowing the client to practice for the second, longer interval.

The therapist now presents the first hierarchy scene to the client in a detailed fashion. If no anxiety is signaled when 10 seconds have elapsed, the client is instructed to stop imagining the scene. The client's level of anxiety should be assessed, even in the absence of a

---

[4]Keep in mind that these intervals begin *after* clients have signaled a clear image. The time necessary to generate such an image will vary as a function of the complexity of the scene (Wolpe, 1982). These time intervals, as well as other parameters associated with desensitization, are not etched in stone. As new laboratory findings appear, old treatment procedures require modification, which is what an empirically based behavior therapy is all about.

signal. Some clients habitually fail to report small amounts of anxiety, and over several hierarchy scenes these increments could swell to levels that would interfere with treatment. This assessment can be accomplished easily by quietly asking the client where he or she is on the 10-point anxiety scale. If no anxiety is signaled and no increase in rated anxiety is reported (which usually means the client is still at 1), and no signs of anxiety are apparent after an interval of 15 to 30 seconds, the client should be ready for the second presentation of the same scene.

The procedure is precisely the same for the second presentation, except that the interval is increased to 25 to 30 seconds. In particular, the second presentation should include about as much detail as the first. Merely saying "Imagine the scene again" does not provide the client with sufficient structure (Watts, 1974). If the client does not signal anxiety during the second presentation, and if there is no increase in rated or visible anxiety, the therapist should verify that the image was indeed clear before introducing the next hierarchy item. The therapist should make similar inquiries from time to time throughout the treatment procedure. Sometimes clients are able to avoid anxiety by suppressing or otherwise modifying the scenes so as to eliminate noxious elements. As an illustration, one of the authors of this text treated a client who was able to imagine without anxiety interpersonal scenes, which in real life elicited considerable anxiety, simply by blotting out the faces of the people involved. The therapist pointed out that this was self-defeating, and with a little additional practice the client was able to include the missing faces.

Especially with beginning therapists, there is a strong tendency to reinforce the subject for not signaling anxiety. This may manifest itself in the therapist's saying (sometimes with a note of relief in his or her voice), "Good." While we could argue that such a practice is therapeutic because it rewards and thereby strengthens the tendency to relax while imagining, there is the very real danger that what is being strength-ened is the tendency *not to report anxiety.* This is especially likely to be the case if, in addition to praising the client for not signaling anxiety, the therapist remains silent (or subtly conveys discomfort or displeasure) following the client's anxiety signals. To guard against this effect, we recommend that the therapist have some standard instruction whenever he or she wishes the client to cease imagining a scene, independent of whether anxiety was signaled: "Now I want you to stop imagining the scene" will probably suffice.

If the client signals anxiety while imagining any hierarchy scene, the therapist should immediately request that he or she stop imagining the scene, and should take steps to return the client to his or her former state of relaxation. For many clients, simply suggesting that they relax once again will result in deep relaxation in very short order. For others, several minutes may be required before they indicate they are at or near 1 on the anxiety scale. In such cases, a more efficient procedure would be to have the client imagine the previously described pleasant scene. The positive feelings arising from imagining the pleasant scene are usually sufficient to overcome the remaining anxiety. If after about 1 minute of imagining the pleasant scene (with the client indicating a clear image) anxiety is *still* reported, the therapist might inquire which muscles still feel tense and then have the client perform the tension-relaxation exercises on those muscle groups. Regardless of the procedure used to induce relaxation following an anxiety signal, it is important for the therapist to ensure that the client has attained a state of deep relaxation before desensitization is resumed. If there are no physical signs of anxiety, and if the client rates him- or herself at or near 1, the therapist can assume that the client has reached such a state.

The time elapsing between the anxiety signal and the resumption of desensitization is simply the period of time required to reinstate relaxation. If the anxiety signal occurred during the first presentation of a particular hierarchy scene, following relaxation induction, the same scene is presented again.

If during the second presentation anxiety is still signaled, this may indicate that the client is not yet ready for the second scene. If the scene in question is the first (lowest) in the hierarchy, the client and therapist must think of a new scene even less anxiety provoking than the present one. If the scene is not the first in the hierarchy, then the client may still be feeling some anxiety attached to the preceding scene. Therefore, following relaxation induction, the preceding scene is again presented. One or two presentations are usually enough to remove any residual anxiety associated with this scene, although the therapist must corroborate this by the absence of an anxiety signal from the client. After this step, the scene in question should be presented again.

A repeated signaling of anxiety at this point may indicate that the client is not sticking to the scene presented. Instead, he or she may be making modifications or additions so that the scene actually corresponds to a scene higher on the hierarchy. Such activity can be determined by asking the client to describe in detail what it was that he or she experienced. This inquiry should deal not only with what the client visualized, but also with what ruminative self-verbalizations he or she engaged in. Indeed, the client might visualize the scene as it was presented, but might verbalize to him- or herself a catastrophic circumstance not directly associated with the scene. For instance, we observed an individual being desensitized for a fear of flying. He was especially fearful when flying over open water. An inquiry revealed that when imagining such a scene, he would ruminate on the possibility of being eaten by sharks were the plane to crash into the sea. If the client has been changing the scene, or ruminating, in this manner, the therapist should remind him or her that it is essential to stay with the scene as presented. This is usually sufficient to enable the client to imagine the scene without an increase in anxiety. If, in fact, the client indicates that he or she *has* been imag-

ining the scene as it was presented, and the hypothesis that the previous item was not completely desensitized has been ruled out, the therapist must now assume that the gap between the present and the prior item is too great, and an additional hierarchy item must be constructed. Therapists should not hesitate to modify hierarchies during the course of the desensitization process, if necessary. As with all hierarchy items, the primary source must be the client, although the therapist might suggest that it be somewhat similar in content to the two adjacent hierarchy items and that it give rise to a degree of anxiety about midway between the degree of anxiety elicited by the two adjacent items.

If the client does not signal anxiety during the first presentation of a given scene but does during the second presentation, following relaxation induction, the therapist should present the same scene again. If anxiety is not signaled, the item may be considered completed (although a cautious therapist may wish to present it an additional time). If the client *does* signal anxiety, the therapist should revert to the strategies just described.

This completes our discussion of the basic desensitization procedure, which is normally followed until the hierarchy has been successfully completed. However, before leaving the procedure section of this chapter, we must consider several additional important points relating to the mechanics of desensitization.

Transition From One Session to the Next

Therapists commonly begin a desensitization session with the last item that was successfully completed during the previous session. This provides continuity between sessions and also serves as a check on whether any relapse has occurred.

Therapists also commonly avoid ending a given session with an anxiety signal, because the client is likely to recall the events associated with the conclusion of the last session. To ensure that the session does end on a pleasant note, care should be taken *not* to present new hierarchy items during the last few minutes of the therapy hour. Instead, the time may be spent on other activities—for instance, discussing the progress of therapy.

Length of the Desensitization Session

Wolpe (1982) reported that a typical desensitization session lasts 15 to 30 minutes. And Marquis and Morgan (1969) suggested that few individuals can tolerate much more than 20 minutes of continuous desensitization. While desensitization cannot be described as painful, it does require considerable effort and concentration on the part of the client; in most instances, 20 or 30 minutes is a reasonable upper limit. In fact, practical considerations often limit the time that can be devoted to desensitization. Assuming the standard 50-minute therapeutic "hour," at least a portion of the time will be spent discussing the course of therapy and relevant life experiences. If the additional time required for the initial relaxation induction is added to this, it is unlikely that the remaining time will be more than 20 or 30 minutes.

On the other hand, if time is available, and if the client is able to maintain an adequate level of concentration and motivation, there is no theoretical reason for limiting the duration of the session. In fact, Wolpin and Pearsall (1965) reported successfully eliminating a phobic reaction in a single, continuous 90-minute session.

Desensitization for Multiple Phobias

Another question pertains to what strategy a therapist should employ when the client wishes to work on more than one phobia, which is often the case (although Wolpe, 1969, reported that few clients evidence more than four phobias). Both Lazarus (1964) and Wolpe (1969) treated two or more phobias simultaneously, setting up separate hierarchies for each, and often drawing from each hierarchy during any given session. We consider this strategy more efficient than treating the separate hierarchies sequentially.

Real-life Contacts with the Phobic Stimuli

Frequently the therapist must make a decision regarding whether or not clients should be encouraged to place themselves in situations depicted in the hierarchy *prior to* the completion of therapy. Both Bandura (1969) and Wolpe (1969) believed that such *in vivo* contacts may be beneficial, and Garfield, Darwin, Singer, and McBreaty (1967) reported that such a procedure facilitated desensitization. However, a word of caution is in order. It would probably be most unwise to encourage clients to place themselves in situations corresponding to hierarchy items to which they are not yet desensitized. While they might have some generalization of improvement from already completed hierarchy items to such situations, the reverse could very easily be the case. That is, clients might experience intense anxiety in such situations, which by the process of generalization might then cause previously desensitized scenes to give rise to anxiety. If this were to occur, it would retard therapy, especially in clients who viewed the experience as a failure, indicating that the therapy was not really "working."

Even if clients' attempts to test themselves are in keeping with the progress already made in desensitization, they may inadvertently find themselves suddenly confronted with a situation much higher on the hierarchy. For instance, a man being treated for sexual impotency arising from anxiety may have reached the stage where he can fondle his partner while maintaining an erection. If, however, his partner were to demand suddenly that they engage in coitus, the ensuing anxiety might result in loss of erection and feelings of failure combining to effect a serious setback to therapy. Unless the therapist can ensure that situations corresponding to a given hierarchy level are not likely to be transformed into more anxiety-provoking situations, it would probably be best to discourage such *in vivo* activity until the hierarchy is complete.

The Importance of Relaxation

Is a structured relaxation procedure a necessary ingredient in desensitization? Some studies suggest that it is, while other findings seem to indicate the opposite (see Kazdin & Wilcoxon, 1976). Schubot (1966) found that a structured relaxation procedure was necessary only for subjects who were initially *extremely* phobic. Moderately fearful subjects attained the same degree of improvement whether or not relaxation was paired with anxiety. It seems likely, however, that individuals seeking therapy for their phobias would be more like the extreme phobics than the moderate phobics in the Schubot study, which suggests the importance of relaxation in a clinical setting.

In Chapter 7, we present several techniques (flooding, implosive therapy, graduated extinction) that are at least somewhat helpful in alleviating phobias. These extinction techniques do not incorporate any form of structured relaxation, indicating that procedures akin to deep muscle relaxation are not always necessary for fear reduction. However, considering the evidence supporting the value of relaxation in systematic desensitization, and since its inclusion is unlikely to do harm, we recommend its use.

The Importance of the Ascending Hierarchy

As we have indicated, the standard desensitization format requires that scenes be presented in graduated fashion. Items are ranked according to the amount of fear each elicits, and the least fear-arousing ones are presented first. While this procedure is clearly effective, Krapfl (1967) found that presenting the hierarchy in *descending* order was about as effective in reducing snake-phobic behavior as the standard ascending-order procedure, and Richardson and Suinn (1973) reported improvement in test anxiety when their subjects were exposed to only the three *highest* hierarchy scenes. By a process of generalization, we would expect that eliminating anxiety from the highest items of the hierarchy would result in an automatic reduction of anxiety associated with the lower items. Thus, the procedure of presenting items in the descending order might seem to be more efficient. However, it should be pointed out that when items high on the hierarchy are presented first, the intense anxiety associated with them will probably necessitate many presentations before clients are successfully desensitized. This is in contrast to the relatively few presentations required when the usual ascending order is employed. In other words, the descending order procedure may not necessarily be more efficient. More important, as Bandura (1969) has pointed out, the descending order procedure may cause the client considerable momentary distress (rarely encountered when the standard method is used), which may cause him or her to terminate the therapy prematurely.

Empirical Findings: Case Histories

As is often the case, many therapists adopted and employed systematic desensitization long before the publication of the first reasonably well controlled experiment supporting its efficacy (see Lang & Lazovik, 1963). Probably the primary reason for this was the high success rate reported in the literature by practitioners, most especially Wolpe (1952, 1954, 1958, 1961). In Wolpe's most definitive work, *Psychotherapy by Reciprocal Inhibition* (1958), he reported that of 210 clients treated, nearly 90 percent were either cured or much improved with a mean of only 31 sessions. Many of these 210 individuals, however, were treated with procedures other than systematic desensitization (for instance, assertion training), although Paul (1969b) concluded after reviewing all of Wolpe's published data that Wolpe's success for desensitization alone was 92 percent. A "success" for Wolpe (1961) meant that the intensity of the original problem (e.g., snake phobia) was reduced by at least 80 percent, as measured by the clients' ratings.

Wolpe (1958) provided data indicating that for other forms of therapy, primarily psychosomatic, the success rate did not exceed 60 percent. Comparisons of this nature are fraught with difficulty, since the groups (those treated by Wolpian methods versus those treated by traditional methods) may not be comparable with respect to the intensity or nature of the presenting complaints, the duration of therapy, the criteria for assessing improvement, or the number of dropouts. Also, success in the clinic, even with such a large number of individuals, does not prove that a particular method really works (see Chapter 1).

Hain, Butcher, and Stevenson (1966), using systematic desensitization augmented by other procedures, reported improvement in 78 percent of the 27 patients they treated. Lazarus (Paul, 1969b) treated 220 individuals using systematic desensitization. Using improvement criteria similar to Wolpe's, Lazarus obtained a success rate of 85 percent, although many of the individuals in the sample received other forms of behavior therapy. Later Lazarus did report higher relapse rates (as high as 40 percent) one to three years after treatment, and this was an important consideration in developing his multimodal approach to behavior therapy (Lazarus, 1971, 1976). These findings notwithstanding, the early positive reports, along with the many hundreds of case histories in the literature, clearly suggest that desensitization is effective with a wide range of anxiety-related disorders, and the improvement does tend to endure.

Perhaps because the number of case histories reporting the successful use of systematic desensitization with some of the more common anxiety-related disorders is so great, researchers turned to using the case study approach to test the efficacy of desensitization with several not as common anxiety-related disorders. For example, Brown (1978) reported the case of Mr. M., a 22-year-old male who complained of experiencing extreme anxiety whenever he had to drive past a cemetery after dark. To avoid passing a cemetery, Mr. M. usually would not drive at night under any circumstances. However, if he was forced to go past one after dark, he would have an "overwhelming compulsion" to stop the car and look at the back seat. Mr. M.'s treatment consisted of self-administered, *in vivo* desensitization with sexual arousal serving as an anxiety inhibitor. Specifically, Mr. M. would imagine scenes of sexual activity with his wife until he became extremely aroused, at which point he would drive past a cemetery. He spent approximately 30 minutes each day doing this. After several weeks, Mr. M. reported that his fear of driving past cemeteries had completely disappeared. Moreover, treatment effects were maintained at a one-year follow-up. Other unusual case histories appearing in the literature include reports of desensitization used in the treatment of blood phobia (Elmore, Wildman, & Westefeld, 1980), handwriting anxiety (Cornelio, Levine, & Wolpe, 1980), and even mannequin phobia (Waranch, Iwata, & Wohl, 1981).

In addition to reporting the use of systematic desensitization with unusual target problems, recent case histories have focused on novel technological variations of desensitization procedures. Schneider (1982), for instance, used optical lenses to alter depth perception in the *in vivo* desensitization treatment of acrophobia (the fear of heights). The *in vivo* hierarchy of fear-arousing situations consisted of different levels of the stairwell of an eight-story building. At each level, the subject was instructed to relax as much as possible and then to look out the window to the ground below through binoculars held backwards. Because the binoculars were held in such a manner, the apparent distance to the ground was magnified by seven. Thus, the subject had the visual effect of ascending a building that was 56 stories high! When the subject removed the binoculars at the end of the desensitization procedure, the actual eight-story height was nonthreatening. These procedures were repeated, with the subject ascending increasingly taller buildings until he could keep his level of anxiety low at virtually any "apparent" height.

Another interesting use of technology with desensitization procedures has been the use of radio transmitter contact to guide people who have driving phobias through *in vivo* desensitization. In one case report, Levine and Wolpe (1980) began the treatment of a 55-year-old male driving phobic by having him drive behind a therapist who was in another car. The subject and the therapist maintained contact through the use of a radio transmitter. By continuing voice communication with the therapist, the subject was able to increase the actual distance between himself and the therapist, eventually becoming able to drive with little anxiety even when the therapist was completely out of sight and the range of the radio transmitter. In another case report, Rovetto (1983) used a similar desensitization procedure with a 34-year-old driving phobic. But in addition to maintaining subject-therapist communication via radio contact, the therapist monitored the subject's physiological arousal with a telemetric transceiver. By monitoring the subject's physiological arousal, the therapist was able to determine objectively whether or not the subject was ready to progress to the next level of the hierarchy. After 12 sessions, the subject was able to drive alone without exhibiting any physiological or subjective indices of anxiety. Treatment effects were maintained at a nine-month follow-up.

Thus, the findings provided by the many published case reports indicate that systematic desensitization is not only effective with a variety of common anxiety-related disorders, but is also quite effective with some rather unusual disorders. Case histories have also provided several innovative technological advances in the implementation of systematic desensitiza-

tion. On the other hand, as we noted in Chapter 1, the case history method cannot establish the final validity of technique. Therefore, let us examine some of the experimental evidence pertinent to systematic desensitization.

Empirical Findings: Experimental Evidence

Systematic desensitization has been one of the most widely researched of all behavior therapies. Early research focused on treatment outcome, comparing traditional desensitization procedures to placebo or no treatment control conditions. In contrast, much of the recent research has focused on the treatment outcome of modified desensitization procedures, comparing them to traditional desensitization and to alternate treatment procedures. Many of the structural modifications of desensitization involve cognitive techniques (e.g., rational restructuring, self-instructional training), which are discussed in detail in Chapter 9. The present chapter will provide an overview of those studies which have assessed traditional desensitization procedures and several of the major non-cognitively oriented modifications.

Individual Treatment Lang and Lazovik (1963) published the first controlled experiment testing systematic desensitization. The experiment, and a considerable amount of the research that followed, employed snake-phobic individuals as subjects. The decision to use this phobia as the target behavior in this and in many other research projects was partly from the fact that fear of harmless snakes is relatively common in our culture. Additionally, the symbolic sexual significance of the snake in psychoanalytic writings (Fenichel, 1945) is well known, and researchers felt that if any maladaptive behavior could be considered symptomatic of an underlying psychosexual conflict, it should have been fear of harmless snakes. If the psychoanalytic point of view is generally correct, we would predict that snake avoidance is very difficult to dislodge—and that alleviation of this fear, when it did occur, would almost certainly be followed by symptom substitution.

Lang and Lazovik (1963) found appreciably greater reduction in the behavioral measure of snake avoidance for subjects who had undergone desensitization than for nontreated control subjects, who showed almost no change. Similar, though somewhat weaker, results were obtained when the measure of change was the subjects' ratings of how they felt in the presence of the test snake. Interestingly, in a follow-up six months later, the difference between the desensitization group and the controls on both measures was somewhat greater than it had been immediately following treatment. Care was taken to determine whether new symptoms (phobias) appeared, and the evidence for symptom substitution was negative.

By adhering to the rules of sound experimental logic, Lang and Lazovik were able to provide convincing evidence that the set of procedures labeled *systematic desensitization* does result in behavior change. It is quite possible, however, that such a behavior change has little to do with the specifics of desensitization, but results instead from the fact that the subjects *perceived* the procedure as therapeutic and expected it to work.

To check on the possibility of placebo effects, Lang, Lazovik, and Reynolds (1965) presented desensitization to one group of snake phobics and what they called pseudotherapy to a second group. The pseudotherapy, or placebo procedure, included some of the elements of the desensitization procedure, but excluded crucial elements that, according to Wolpe (1958, 1969), were necessary for improvement. This procedure included, as well, a general discussion of different aspects of the subject's life. These experimenters found greater improvement in the desensitization subjects than in the pseudotherapy subjects, who behaved very similarly to subjects who had received no treatment of any kind in the previous study (Lang & Lazovik, 1963). Thus, it seemed reasonable that the suc-

cess obtained by Lang and Lazovik in their original study could not have been the result of a simple placebo effect.

Since the original studies of Lang and his associates, a multitude of studies examining the efficacy of systematic desensitization procedures has been conducted (see Hatzenbeuhler & Schroeder, 1978, for a review of desensitization used with childhood disorders; Kazdin & Wilcoxon, 1976, for a review through 1974; and Levin & Gross, 1985, for a review of the role of relaxation in desensitization procedures). An examination of the experimental literature reveals that, in most of these reports, desensitization was found to be superior to placebo or to treatment component controls (i.e., comparison groups that received one or more, but not all, of the major components of desensitization, such as relaxation). Furthermore, desensitization appears to be of value for a variety of problems.

The following are some areas that the experimental literature has covered. Clearly, the list is not exhaustive. We are not presenting desensitization as the treatment of choice in each of these areas. The point is simply that desensitization is of potential value for a broad range of problems.

Acrophobia (Pendleton & Higgins, 1983)

Agoraphobia (James, Hampton, & Larsen, 1983)

Alcoholism (Hedberg & Campbell, 1974; Lanyon, Primo, Terrell, & Weiner, 1972)

Anticipatory nausea and vomiting associated with cancer chemotherapy (Morrow & Morrell, 1982)

Asthma (Moore, 1965)

Dating anxiety (Curran, 1975)

Dental fear (Bernstein & Kleinknecht, 1982; Harrison, Carlsson, & Berggren, 1985)

Fear of flying (Howard, Murphy, & Clarke, 1983)

Fear of insects (Emmelkamp & Straatman, 1976)

Fear of water (Ultee, Griffioen, & Schellekens, 1982)

Nightmares (Miller & DiPilato, 1983)

Racial anger (O'Donnell & Worell, 1973)

Sexual disorders (Andresen, 1981; Evaraed & Dekker, 1982)

Speech anxiety (Lent, Russell, & Zamostry, 1981)

Stuttering (Moleski & Tosi, 1976)

Test anxiety (Leal, Baxter, Martin, & Marx, 1981; Romano & Cabianca, 1978)

In summary, the experimental literature supporting the efficacy of traditional systematic desensitization is considerable. There can be little doubt that the technique is useful, not only with problems of a clearly phobic nature but also with many anxiety-related disorders. Moreover, systematic desensitization may even be effective when the maladaptive behavior is not related to anxiety in an obvious way (e.g., aggression emanating from anger).

In the next three sections, we will look at variations of traditional desensitization procedures.

***In Vivo* Desensitization**   Rather than have the client imagine a hierarchy of anxiety-provoking stimuli, many therapists prefer to use *in vivo* desensitization procedures in which the client is asked actually to confront a hierarchy of real-life fear-related situations. Empirical support of *in vivo* desensitization procedures is largely positive, indicating that these procedures are at least equivalent in their effect (e.g., James, Hampton, & Larsen, 1983) if not superior (e.g., Ultee, Griffioen, & Schellekens, 1982) to imaginal desensitization procedures for some disorders.

In vivo procedures may be particularly useful with clients that have trouble vividly imagining anxiety-provoking situations. To test this hypothesis, Dyckman and Cowan (1978) divided snake phobics into three groups based on their ability to imagine scenes vividly. Subjects in these high, medium, and low vivid groups were assigned to imagined scenes or *in vivo* desensitization treatment conditions. In general, subjects in the *in vivo* condition improved more in reduction of avoidance behavior than did subjects in the imagined scene condition. In addition, the data revealed that in the condition that used an imaginal hierarchy, subjects who were good imaginers improved more than subjects who were poor imaginers. *In vivo* desensitization was especially helpful for this latter group.

Automated Desensitization   Automated desensitization refers to the presentation of the desensitization instructions to the subject through mechanical means (most commonly a tape recorder), with a resultant reduction in contact with a live therapist. There are three primary reasons for using automated desensitization. First, because the procedure involves less therapist time, it is usually less expensive than therapist-directed desensitization. If automated desensitization produces the same outcome as therapist-directed desensitization, it can be a more cost-effective procedure. Second, automated desensitization has several other practical benefits. For example, it allows clients to receive treatment at their own convenience, and the number of clients receiving simultaneous desensitization is limited only by the number of automated devices available. Finally, the use of automated desensitization assures consistency in the desensitization procedure from subject to subject and from study to study. This consistency can be attractive to researchers who strive to generate highly reliable intervention packages.

The technique presented by Cotler (1970) illustrates the mechanics of automated desensitization. Subjects were snake phobics who were selected on the basis of a questionnaire and a behavioral avoidance test. During a second session, each subject was presented with an explanation of desensitization and a statement of the purpose of the study, all on tape. An experimenter then answered any questions concerning the tape, and if the subject desired to participate, a future appointment was arranged. For the remainder of the treatment, the subject had no contact whatsoever with a live experimenter or therapist.

Over the next several sessions, the subject was given relaxation and visualization instructions, as well as instructions on how to use the automated apparatus, all on tape. In subsequent sessions, a standard 16-item hierarchy was presented. The subject controlled the progress of the tape with five buttons located near his hand. He was to use the first button whenever he wanted to visualize a hierarchy scene or to concentrate on relaxation. The second and third buttons were to be pressed when the subject could imagine the hierarchy scene with little or no anxiety; depressing the buttons advanced the tape to a higher item in the hierarchy. The fourth and fifth buttons were to be pressed when the subject experienced higher levels of anxiety while imagining the hierarchy scene, and this recycled the tape to a previously presented set of relaxation instructions. The subject followed this procedure until he or she was able to imagine all hierarchy scenes with minimal anxiety.

Using this highly mechanical procedure, Cotler found that subjects experienced a marked reduction in self-rating of anxiety in the presence of a harmless snake and an appreciable increase in the tendency to approach the snake, with the improvement lasting through the one-month follow-up. Control subjects showed little or no improvement.

The success of automated desensitization does not imply that the role of the therapist in these procedures is not important. In the studies on automated desensitization, the therapist is always at least implicitly available (e.g., he or she is in the next room or can be reached by phone). *Some* clinical interaction is almost always required for comprehensive behavioral assessment, and perhaps for hierarchy construction and for follow-up. Furthermore, the relative

success of automated tapes may be dependent on the quality of the therapist's voice in the tape. For example, Morris and Suckerman (1974) found that snake phobics who listened to a taped therapist speaking in a "soft, melodic, and pleasant voice" improved significantly more in reduction of avoidance behaviors than did snake phobics who listened to a taped therapist speaking in a "harsh, impersonal, and business-like" voice. In fact, subjects in the "cold" therapist condition fared no better than those in a no-treatment control group.

In general, the literature suggests that automated desensitization can be a highly effective therapeutic procedure (e.g., Donner & Guerney, 1969; Harrison, Carlsson, & Berggren, 1985; Lang, Melamed, & Hart, 1970). A study by Evans and Kellam (1973) suggests that, at least in some situations, automated desensitization can compare favorably to live desensitization. In this study, 24 patients diagnosed as having phobic anxiety were randomly assigned either to a live treatment group, in which desensitization was administered by a therapist according to standard procedures, or to an automated treatment group, in which desensitization instructions were delivered during therapy by prerecorded tapes. The actual structure of the procedure (i.e., progression through the hierarchies and representation of the items) was the same for both groups. As indicated by patient ratings of anxiety and psychiatrist ratings of fear, both treatments produced beneficial results with no significant differences in improvement between groups.

Desensitization in Groups As with automated procedures, group desensitization has the obvious advantage of allowing more individuals who are in need of help to receive treatment. Although few recent studies have assessed group desensitization procedures, early experimental evidence supporting the effectiveness of these procedures is impressive. The first such report came from Lazarus (1961), who worked with patients who were mainly either height phobic, claustrophobic, or sexually impotent males. Subjects received group desensitization, traditional interpretation, or traditional interpretation plus relaxation. Based on self-report, a much larger number of individuals receiving group desensitization showed improvement than did individuals in either of the other two conditions. One of the more remarkable aspects of this study was the administering of stringent behavioral tests to participants who indicated they had improved. One month after the completion of therapy, the height phobics were required to stand on the roof of an eight-story building and to count cars passing in the street below for two minutes; and claustrophobics had to remain in a small cubicle for five minutes without distress. Lazarus reported that all but two participants among the height phobics were able to complete their task.

In the 15 years after the publication of the Lazarus study, a sizable number of additional studies supported group desensitization. Representative of these are Rachman's (1966a, 1966b) study with spider phobics, Paul and Shannon's (1966) study with college students suffering from interpersonal anxiety, Wright's (1976) experiment with students fearful of speaking up in class, and an investigation by Sue (1975) using snake phobics. Several studies have shown that desensitization can be effective in dealing with test anxiety (Anton, 1976; Taylor, 1971; Zemore, 1975).

Procedures vary somewhat from study to study. More often than not, a common hierarchy is used (e.g., Wright, 1976; Zemore, 1975). The hierarchy may be developed by the group, or it may come from another source, with the group collectively ranking the scenes (Zemore, 1975). Subjects may generate their own hierarchies, writing the items on cards. Group desensitization proceeds with the experimenter merely instructing the members to imagine the scene described on Card No. 1, and so on. In certain studies (e.g., Anton, 1976), the subjects' anxiety level is not assessed by the experimenter; that is, no procedure for signaling anxiety is provided. Others do provide for anxiety signals, with the group staying with a given scene until it can be comfortably imagined by each member (Zemore, 1975). If treatment involves individualized hierarchies, a good procedure is to instruct subjects, in advance, to return to the previous hierarchy card if after two or three visualizations of a given scene anxiety still persists (Sue, 1975).

Conclusion Systematic desensitization is in its third decade of rigorous empirical examination—longer than almost any other behavioral technique. The weight of the evidence is clear and is widely recognized, even among many non–behaviorally oriented therapists: desensitization is highly effective in treating a variety of phobic and anxiety-related disorders. This conclusion is based primarily on research that examined traditional desensitization procedures, but automated, *in vivo*, and group desensitization can also be highly effective.

Although there is little debate about whether or not systematic desensitization works, there is not agreement on why it works. Perhaps a variety of different, potentially therapeutic components are combined in desensitization. Some individuals and some types of problems may need only one component to demonstrate treatment gains, while others may require the composite therapeutic package. Indeed, most of the current developments in the desensitization area involve either basic research into its conceptual underpinnings or conceptually based refinements and innovations in the procedure itself. This research is likely to generate a greater understanding about the nature of systematic desensitization and a more potent array of desensitization-based clinical interventions.

3
Assertion Training

Assertion training is one of the most popular clinical techniques and research topics among behavioral psychologists. It is almost impossible to pick up a major behavioral journal and not find an article on assertion training or, more broadly, social skills training. What Bellack wrote several years ago is equally true today: "If someone were to read uncritically, he or she would get the impression that social skills deficits are at the core of a vast majority of behavioral dysfunctions" (1979, p. 158).

There have been many definitions of the term "assertiveness." These definitions usually take one of three approaches: defining what assertive behavior is in absolute terms; defining what assertive behavior is *not* by differentiating it from related concepts, such as aggression; and defining assertive behavior in relative terms by focusing on the relationship between assertive behaviors and their interpersonal consequences. In absolute terms, most writers would probably agree that assertive behavior has the following three characteristics:

1. Assertive behavior is interpersonal behavior involving the honest and relatively straightforward expression of thoughts and feelings.
2. Assertive behavior is socially appropriate.
3. A person behaving assertively is taking others' feelings and welfare into account.

Taking an absolute approach, Christoff and Kelly (1985) have suggested that there are three general categories of assertive behavior. The first is *refusal assertiveness*. This type of assertiveness refers to a socially appropriate and skillful blocking of, or at least refusal to acquiesce to, the attempts of others either to impose their goal-directed behaviors on you or to interfere with your ongoing, goal-directed behavior. Take the case of a freshman who is waiting in line at a checkout counter when two other students—say upperclassmen—step in front of him. Refusal assertion in this situation would refer to socially appropriate behavior that attempts to stop the others from cutting in line. For example, the freshman could say, "I am sorry, but I was here first." Another example of refusal assertion involves the situation where a student asks her roommate to do a favor, such as returning a book to the library, that imposes on the roommate's planned behavior. In this instance a refusal assertion response could be, "I'm sorry, I really don't have time to return your book right now. If you can't do it yourself, perhaps you can find someone else who has the time."

Refusal assertiveness has received the most research attention and represents the popular lay conception of what "assertive behavior" means (i.e., standing up for your rights and not letting other people take advantage of you [Christoff & Kelly, 1985]). One of the reasons that refusal assertion has received so much attention and research is that in most cases people tend to agree on what constitutes an unreasonable request and what constitutes appropriate refusal behavior. As a result, clinicians and researchers are often able to study and treat refusal assertion problems in a fairly rigorous, replicable, straightforward fashion. We will devote a considerable portion of this chapter to describing techniques aimed at increasing refusal assertion.

The second type of assertiveness is *commendatory assertiveness*. This refers to the ability to express positive feelings, such as appreciation, liking, love, admiration, praise, and gratitude. Wolpe (1982, pp. 127–128) offers the following examples of commendatory assertions:

1. "That's a beautiful dress."
2. "That was a clever remark."
3. "I love you."
4. "That was right on target."
5. "You handled him very skillfully."

The ability to express positive emotions in a sincere, warm, socially appropriate manner is an important interpersonal skill, and it can be successfully taught by using many of the same techniques that are used to instill refusal assertiveness. However, the kinds of situations that require commendatory assertions, and the actual commendatory behaviors appropriate to these situations, tend to be more diverse and complex than those associated with refusal assertions. For example, the appropriate ways to express positive feelings toward your coworkers are often quite different from those appropriate to expressing these feelings to your mother or to your spouse. Of course, it is always important to consider the nature of a given situation in choosing an appropriate response, assertive or otherwise. Our point here is that this type of consideration tends to be especially important with commendatory assertions.

Finally, there is *request assertiveness*. According to Christoff and Kelly, this form of assertiveness occurs "when one makes requests of others in order to facilitate meeting one's needs or attaining one's goals" (1985, p. 375). Most writers include the qualification that to be considered assertive, the request should not violate the rights of others. Request assertions can be made by themselves (e.g., "I believe my test was scored incorrectly. Could I make an appointment to go over it with you?") or in conjunction with either refusal assertions (e.g., "I am sorry, I was here first. *I suggest you go to the back of the line.*") or commendatory assertions (e.g., "I really like you. *Would you go out to dinner with me on Friday night?*"). As with other types of assertion, being able to make request assertions in appropriate situations is an important interpersonal skill that frequently can help an individual attain desired goals.

In summary, defining assertiveness in absolute terms involves the identification of certain behaviors that, by definition, are assertive. These behaviors include refusing to be taken advantage of, expressing both positive and negative feelings, and making requests of others. While from the absolute perspective these behaviors may always be assertive, it is important to emphasize that they may not always be socially appropriate or produce an optimal social or interpersonal effect. For example, "No, I'm afraid I cannot do that right now" might be an appropriate response to the question "Would you mind driving me to the store right now?" but would not be an appropriate response to a grimacing neighbor who is pleading "Help me, I think I'm having a heart attack." It is one thing to learn *how to behave assertively*; it is another to learn *when* to behave assertively.

A second approach to defining, or at least clarifying, what assertion means is to identify what it is not. The primary differentiation made by behavior therapists is between assertion and *aggression* (e.g., Gambrill, 1985; Goldenberg, 1983; Hollandsworth, 1977). Aggressive behavior can be characterized in a variety of ways. However, a common definitional thread suggested by most writers is that aggression involves a hostile or coercive expression of one's own desires without adequate concern for the rights of others. Some (e.g., Alberti, 1977) have argued that for behavior to be labeled aggressive, an *intent* to aggress must be present.

However, intentions are often difficult to ascertain. For our purposes, aggressive behavior is behavior that would be expected to have an *unnecessarily* negative impact on the welfare of others. What we mean by "unnecessarily negative" will become clear later in the chapter.

The third approach to defining assertion focuses on the relationship between behaviors and their consequences. According to this approach, assertive behavior enables a person to accomplish his or her objectives without creating adverse consequences for others. Schlundt and McFall (1985) have discussed definitions of this sort under the topic of social competence. "Social competence" refers to any behavior that enables an individual to achieve valued interpersonal outcomes; whereas "assertion" refers more particularly to behaviors that accomplish the objectives of refusing to be taken advantage of, expressing positive and negative feelings, and getting others to do what you want in a way that does not impose upon their rights.

Defining assertion according to this relativistic framework has the advantage that only behaviors that are socially appropriate in a given situation are considered to meet the definitional criteria. However, defining assertive behavior in terms of outcomes can pose considerable challenges for behavior therapists. How do therapists decide what behaviors to teach in assertion training, since any given assertive behavior can be as inappropriate as it can be appropriate, depending on the situation? Some authors (e.g., McFall, 1981) have argued that empirical research is needed to determine what behaviors should be taught in assertion training. This kind of research involves investigations referred to as "social validation studies," so named because they are designed to determine whether a given behavior is socially appropriate or valid. For example, Mullinix and Galassi (1981) broke assertive behaviors into four different components and assessed whether each component was socially valid—that is, whether its addition to an assertive response was judged to improve the social appropriateness or sensitivity of the response. The four components

were (1) describing the problem (e.g., why one was returning the shirt to the store), (2) requesting a behavior change (e.g., "I want you to quit calling me"), (3) making an empathic statement, and (4) making a threat. Eighty-eight men and 88 women were presented with examples of assertive behaviors that involved one or more of the above components and were asked to rate their appropriateness and how they would respond to them. The results indicated that requesting a behavior change or making an empathic statement did not add to the rated appropriateness of the response over simply describing the problem, and that making a threat actually detracted from the perceived effectiveness and appropriateness of the response. These findings suggest that although certain behaviors may be considered assertive (e.g., asking someone to change a behavior or threatening them if they continue to act in a certain way), they are unnecessary or may even be counterproductive.

Finally, assertion training refers to any therapeutic procedure designed to teach clients to behave more assertively. Assertion training essentially takes a response acquisition approach to behavior therapy—that is, it usually focuses on learning a new repertoire of responses. However, it is important to keep in mind that knowing what responses to teach clients is not always as clear and straightforward as implied by many of the more popular books on assertion training. Being an effective behavior therapist requires an in-depth knowledge of effective ways to handle the multitude of situations that clients will identify as problems. Knowledge of the empirical research on assertion training, especially on social validation of assertive behaviors, will help considerably in this regard. However, therapists often have to rely on their own social and clinical experience. The danger is that *the uncritical teaching of assertive behaviors can cause harm to clients if the behaviors are inappropriate or are used inappropriately.* The best safeguard against this danger is to assess each situation on its own merits and to attempt to identify the behaviors that will help a given client obtain the desired consequences with a minimum of negative effects.

Background

Present-day assertion training techniques are based to a large degree on the writings of Andrew Salter (1949, 1964) and Joseph Wolpe (1958, 1969; Wolpe & Lazarus, 1966). Although Salter's *Conditioned Reflex Therapy*, published in 1949, was the first major work extolling the virtues of assertive-type behavior, the writings of Wolpe and his followers have had considerably greater impact than those of Salter. There are several likely reasons for this. First, the psychiatric and psychological establishments were probably more amenable to considering a learning-based or behavioral approach in 1958 (when Wolpe's *Psychotherapy by Reciprocal Inhibition* was published) than they were in 1949. During the intervening decade, influential books on the behavioral approach were widely read (e.g., Dollard & Miller's [1950] *Personality and Psychotherapy* and Skinner's [1953] *Science and Human Behavior*), which created a more accepting attitude for behaviorally based interventions. Second, for Wolpe, systematic desensitization and assertion training were closely tied theoretically, and the relatively early acceptance (in some quarters, at least) of desensitization certainly facilitated the acceptance of his assertion training. Third, the manner in which Salter presented his views had the effect of antagonizing a good number of clinicians who otherwise might have made very effective use of his techniques. He attacked psychoanalysis with unmitigated vengeance, and since most clinicians of the day had at least some investment in psychoanalytic thinking, this could hardly endear him to them. He advocated assertion (his term was *excitatory*) procedures for virtually every conceivable psychological disorder and for every client who was seen as suffering from inhibition. In sharp contrast to Wolpe, Salter appeared to pay little heed to the consequences of spontaneous, impulsive behavior—a fact that

could do little to enhance his credibility in the eyes of conservative clinicians. Thus, it was not difficult for many to dismiss Salter and his excitatory therapy and thereby fail to appreciate the considerable merit in his approach.

Salter presented his techniques somewhat tersely in *Conditioned Reflex Therapy*, along with a large number of illustrative case histories. His six excitatory exercises (Salter, 1949, pp. 97–100) are summarized below:

1. The use of *feeling talk*, which involves practice in expressing literally any feeling. Some of Salter's examples include "I detest the man and everything he stands for"; "I like soup"; "Darling, I love you with all my heart"; "Now, that was stupid of me!"

2. The use of *facial talk*, which involves practicing facial expressions that normally go with different emotions.

3. Practice in expressing a contradictory opinion when one disagrees.

4. Practice in the use of *I* (e.g., "I found the New England fall breathtaking," rather than, "One finds the New England fall breathtaking.")

5. Practice in agreeing when complimented (e.g., "Yes, I like this tie, too," rather than, "What, this old thing!")

6. Practice in improvising and acting spontaneously.

Salter's approach mainly includes applying these exercises in conjunction with a great amount of exhortation to the client to behave more assertively. As we will see shortly, current approaches to assertion training rely heavily on the type of practice or rehearsal characteristic of Salter's excitatory exercises.

Wolpe, who was using assertion training when Salter's book appeared, was further encouraged by Salter's writings (Wolpe, 1969). Although both Wolpe and Salter have stressed the importance of behaving in an assertive manner, notable differences exist between their approaches. First, Wolpe did not assume that every client is primarily in need of assertion training, although he employed it frequently, often with relaxation or desensitization. Second, whereas Salter viewed assertiveness (excitation) as a generalized trait, Wolpe did not. Thus, for Wolpe, the mere fact that a client may have no difficulty expressing resentment or hurt to a fellow employee in no way ensures that he can behave similarly with his wife. As we shall learn in a later section, the research literature supports Wolpe on this point. Third, Wolpe was considerably more concerned with the interpersonal consequences (especially negative) of assertive acts. Some of the particulars of the Wolpian approach (and that of Lazarus [1971], which is similar) are incorporated into the "Methods" section of this chapter.

There are considerable similarities between the writings of three additional individuals or groups of individuals and present-day assertion training techniques. One is J. L. Moreno (1946, 1955), who founded *psychodrama*. Psychodrama is a staged dramatization of the real-life attitudes and conflicts of the participating clients. It strongly emphasizes spontaneity and improvisation, which are elements that Salter stressed. As a role-playing strategy, psychodrama is similar to behavior rehearsal (described in the methods section), one of Wolpe's principal assertion techniques. In fact, behavior rehearsal was originally referred to as "behavioristic psychodrama" (Wolpe, 1982). However, the goals of psychodrama, including catharsis and insight, are not usually thought of as consistent with a behavioral approach.[1]

A second writer whose contributions bear similarities to current assertion training practices is Kelly (1955). His *fixed-role therapy*, described in detail in Chapter 4, is an interesting mixture of cognitive and behavioristic psychology. It involves developing a personality

[1]Both Strum (1965) and J. L. Moreno (1963) have suggested a possible *rapprochement* between a behavioral and a psychodramatic point of view. To learn more about psychodrama, see J. L. Moreno (1946, 1955), Lippitt and Hubbell (1956), or Z. T. Moreno (1965).

sketch of a fictitious individual who is free of the anxieties and behavioral inadequacies troubling the client and then instructing the client to assume this role. By behaving in a manner consistent with the role and by adopting the fictitious person's way of perceiving the world, the client eventually should no longer feel that he or she is assuming a role. The role-playing features of fixed-role therapy are similar to the behavior rehearsal techniques used in assertion training.

More recently, several cognitively oriented writers have furthered our understanding of unassertiveness and have contributed procedures that are often incorporated into the current practice of assertion training. Perhaps the first major influence was Albert Ellis (1962, 1971b, 1973), who is primarily associated with rational emotive therapy, a vastly influential cognitive approach discussed in detail in Chapter 9. Ellis frequently advocated practices and procedures that bear a notable resemblance to present-day assertion training (e.g., stressing the self-defeating nature of nonassertive behavior and providing homework assignments involving assertive behavior). Ellis's contribution to assertion training is apparent in more recent writings by others in the field, such as Schwartz and Gottman (1976), who suggested that unassertive individuals often suffer from an inner "dialogue of conflicts" which might best be approached with more cognitively oriented treatment techniques. As we will describe later in the chapter, the addition of cognitively oriented procedures to the assertion training package has been perhaps the most noticeable change in assertion training procedures since the mid-1970s.

The Theory of Nonassertiveness

Consistent with most other behavioral theorizing, assertive behavior generally is thought to be more reinforcing than nonassertive behavior, so that most people will come naturally to make assertive responses. Appropriately expressing positive feelings toward loved ones, asking for desired objects, and standing up for your rights are all behaviors that usually lead to desired outcomes. Why, then, are some people not willing or able to act assertively? One of the first and most comprehensive theories of nonassertiveness was put forth by Wolpe (1958, 1969, 1973, 1983; Wolpe & Lazarus, 1966), who suggested that many behavior problems, including nonassertion, were due simply to maladaptive conditioning. Specifically, he suggested that in nonassertive individuals, cues that usually lead people to exhibit assertive behavior (e.g., a person cutting in front of you in line) instead elicit *anxiety.* Wolpe assumed that, to a considerable degree, assertion and anxiety are incompatible. Thus, if a person is anxious in the presence of these cues, it is unlikely that he or she will be assertive. The task of the therapist is to countercondition these cues so that they elicit assertive behavior, not anxiety. As Wolpe put it, "Assertiveness training is mainly used to decondition unadaptive habits of anxiety response to other people's behavior" (1983, p. 118). Wolpe suggested that unassertive individuals often develop these "unadaptive habits of anxiety response" because in their early life they were taught to believe that the rights of others are more important than their own, and that people should never impose their own views or needs on other people.

Cognitive theorists have offered views that are compatible with Wolpe's notion, but they emphasize the cognitive rather than the emotional aspects of assertion problems. In general, they suggest that unassertive individuals often suffer from negative expectations and self-statements that block the initiation or execution of assertive behaviors (Hollon & Beck, 1986). Alden (1984) has suggested that the cognitive style of nonassertive individuals is in some way similar to that of depressed individuals. Specifically, she found that nonassertive subjects, like depressed individuals, were generally unwilling to attribute positive outcomes to themselves, i. e., to their own ability or effort. Rather, they attributed them to external factors, such as luck. Assertive (like nondepressed) individuals, in contrast, were more likely to attribute positive outcomes to their own good qualities. Similarly, work by Bandura (1977) on self-efficacy expectations suggests that individuals who choose nonassertive responses do so because they do not expect that assertive behaviors will result in desired outcomes.

A physiologically based study by Dayton and Mikulas (1981) is consonant with both the Wolpe and cognitive theories. These investigators asked both assertive and nonassertive college students to imagine responding nonassertively, assertively, or aggressively to a variety of hypothetical conflict situations. While the students were imagining the situations and their responses, blood volume changes were recorded from photoplethysmographs attached to the subjects' fingers. The results suggested that, in general, imagining the conflict situations increased arousal in all subjects. For assertive subjects, imagining an assertive or aggressive response reduced their arousal significantly more than imagining a nonassertive response, whereas the opposite response pattern was true for nonassertive subjects. Assuming that arousal reduction was a desired or reinforcing state, these data suggest that nonassertive subjects find nonassertive behavior reinforcing, and assertive subjects find assertive behavior reinforcing.

McFall (1976) has suggested that skill deficits often underlie nonassertive behavior. That is, some individuals have never had experiences that enable them to acquire the ability to emit assertive behaviors. The person who does not know how to behave assertively would be expected to be anxious in conflict situations and to have negative expectations regarding his or her ability to effect appropriate outcomes. McFall's work (e.g., McFall & Lillesand, 1971; McFall & Marstern, 1970) has shown that direct training of assertive behaviors using modeling, coaching, rehearsal, and feedback (all of which are discussed later in the chapter) can lead to effective therapeutic results without having to address anxiety or cognitive expectations directly.

From a behavioral point of view, the data on anxiety (emotion), cognition, physiology, and skill all seem to fit together nicely. They generate a picture of nonassertive individuals as having little self-confidence in their own skills and efforts and feeling considerable subservience to the rights and desires of others. Such individuals probably regard their own desires and goals as being of secondary importance and become anxious and aroused when contemplating the assertion of those desires or goals in the presence of others. To reduce this anxiety, these individuals do not exhibit or even think about exhibiting assertive behavior, and instead act unassertively, even though such behavior may result in a failure to attain desired goals. Presumably in some individuals, such a state of affairs may have resulted in their never learning how to execute assertive behaviors skillfully, while in others these skills may be present but inhibited due to anxiety or negative expectations. As we will discuss in more detail later, usually this state of affairs is situation-specific— that is, it pertains to some situations but not necessarily to others (e.g., a person may have no trouble being assertive at work but cannot do so at home). Thus, even though we may refer to "assertive individuals" or "nonassertive individuals" in this chapter, we are doing so only as a semantic convenience. It is our strong view that problems related to assertiveness are and must be treated as being situation specific.

Methods of Assertion Training

Determining the Need for Assertion Training

Given the plethora of articles and books on the topic, it is somewhat surprising that clients rarely ask for assertion training. Usually the therapist must inform the client of its availability and potential value. This is normally done after the therapist has decided, tentatively perhaps, that assertion training might be beneficial. This decision may be based solely on a relatively routine behavior therapy interview. However, many behavior therapists are relying increasingly on the use of assertion inventories to help them determine whether unassertiveness is a problem and, if so, in what specific situations this problem occurs. Some of the most widely used assertion scales are described in Table 3–1. Perhaps the most carefully constructed of all assertion scales (see Beck & Heimberg, 1983) is the Conflict Resolution Inventory (McFall & Lillesand, 1971).

The Conflict Resolution Inventory (CRI), which is reprinted in Table 3-2, was designed as a research instrument for measuring how college students typically respond to unreasonable requests. It is divided into two sections. The first includes 8 questions designed to assess how important being assertive is to the client (as determined primarily by being able to say no to a variety of demands). The second section includes descriptions of 35 hypothetical situations in which a request is made of the client. The client is to indicate how he or she would respond, and would feel about that response, on a 1-to-5 scale ranging from "I would *refuse* and would not feel uncomfortable about doing so" to "I would *not refuse* because it seems to be a reasonable request." The reliability data on the CRI are generally acceptable, with test-retest coefficients ranging from .86 (1 week) to .85 (4 weeks) to .56 (10 weeks) (e.g., Galassi et al., 1978; Kern & McDonald, 1980). The CRI also appears to be a sensitive measure of treatment-induced changes and, in general, to have good validity (see review by Beck & Heimberg, 1983).

The CRI is designed to measure a specific subclass of assertive behaviors, namely refusal assertions. Thus, the therapist using this scale should be aware that high scores reflect a problem with behaving assertively in only one type

Table 3-1 Descriptive Information on Common Assertiveness Scales

Scale	Type of Assertive Behavior Addressed	Target Population	No. of Items	Response Format	Source of Items	Reading[a] Grade Level	Comments
Wolpe–Lazarus Assertiveness Schedule (Wolpe & Lazarus, 1966)	hostile and commendatory assertion	clients	30	none	clinical experience	I: 8–9 D: 8–9	Not intended as research scale; yes–no scoring format sometimes adopted
Wolpe–Lazarus Schedule (revised) (Hersen, Bellack, Turner, Williams, Harper, & Watts, 1979)	hostile and commendatory assertion	clients	30	yes–no	original scale	I: 7 D: 10–12	Formalized version of original scale
Assertion Inventory (Gambrill & Richey, 1975)	positive and negative assertion	students, clients	40	5-point scale	literature review; reports of students and clients	I: 10–12 D: college grad.	Assesses both discomfort and probability of responding
College Self-Expression Scale (Galassi, Delo, Galassi, & Bastien, 1974)	positive and negative assertion, self-denial	students	50	5-point scale	literature review	I: 8–9 D: 10–12	Assesses range of situations and target persons
Adult Self-Expression Scale (Gay, Hollandsworth, & Galassi, 1975)	same	adult	48	same	CSES and original items	I: 8–9 D: 8–9	Adults drawn from community college sample
Rathus Assertiveness Schedule (Rathus, 1973a)	positive and negative assertion	general	30	6-point scale; no midpoint	literature review; student diaries	I: 8–9 D: 10–12	May confuse assertion and aggression
Assertion Questionnaire (Collner & Ross, 1976)	same	male drug addicts	40	4-point scale; no midpoint	literature review; original items	I: 7 D: 8–9	May be scored for overall assertion or by individual content area
Conflict Resolution Inventory (Part II) (McFall & Lillesand, 1971)	refusal of unreasonable requests	students	35	5-point categorical scale	empirically generated from student report	I: 8–9 D: 10–12	Only specifically focused assertion scale

Adapted from Beck & Heimberg (1983).
[a]I = items, D = directions.

Table 3–2 **Conflict Resolution Inventory (CRI)**

1. How assertive do you think you usually are compared to other people your age in this culture? To indicate how you would honestly rate yourself, place a check mark on the following scale.

1%	more assertive than 25%	more assertive than 50%	more assertive than 75%	99%

2. Compared to other people your age in this culture, how assertive would you like to be in order to feel satisfied with yourself?

1%	more assertive than 25%	more assertive than 50%	more assertive than 75%	99%

3. In a few sentences, could you please describe what you mean by "assertiveness."

4. Do you feel that the ability to say "no" is an important part of being assertive?

Yes _____   No _____   Maybe _____

If yes or maybe, how important a part is it?

1	2	3	4	5
slightly important		moderately important		very important

5. Compared to other people your age in this culture, where do you think you stand in saying no to something you don't want to do?

| 1% | say no more readily than 25% | say no more readily than 50% | say no more readily than 75% | 99% |

6. Compared to other people your age in this culture, where would you LIKE to stand in saying no to something you don't want to do?

| 1% | say no more readily than 25% | say no more readily than 50% | say no more readily than 75% | 99% |

7. How much of a problem do you feel you have when it comes to saying no to people regarding things you don't want to do?

| Not much of a problem | A mild problem | A moderate problem | A significant problem | A very significant problem |

8. Would you volunteer to participate in a clinic in which people were taught how to refuse requests with which they didn't wish to comply?

Yes _____   No _____   Maybe _____

Table 3–2 *(continued)*
_____

Directions

Read each situation carefully. Decide which of the five responses (A–E) below you would be most likely to make if the situation *actually* happened to you. Mark the response you select in the appropriate box on the answer blank supplied. Try to consider each situation separately, not letting your reaction to one situation influence your reaction to other ones.

Alternatives

A I would *refuse* and would not feel uncomfortable about doing so.

B I would *refuse* but would feel uncomfortable doing so.

C I would *not refuse* but would feel uncomfortable because I didn't.

D I would *not refuse* even though I might prefer to, but would not feel particularly uncomfortable because I didn't.

E I would *not refuse* because it seems to be a reasonable request.

CRI Situations
_____

1. Suppose you want to sell a book for $5. A mere acquaintance of yours says that he/she really needs the book, can't find it anywhere, and can only pay $3 for it. You are sure that you can easily get $5 for it.
2. Suppose it were a friend who needed the book, but you were broke and needed $5 to pay off a debt.
3. Suppose it were a mere acquaintance who needed the book, but you were broke and needed the $5 to pay off a debt.

_____

4. An acquaintance of yours asks you to go with him/her to get something to eat and you know that he/she will not go if you refuse to accompany him/her.
5. Suppose a mere acquaintance asks you to go with him/her to get something to eat; you know that he/she will not go if you refuse to accompany him/her, but you have just finished eating.

_____

6. Your roommate is constantly borrowing dimes from you in order to buy Cokes, but he/she never pays you back. You are getting rather annoyed at this and have decided to stop lending them out to him/her. Now he/she asks to borrow a dime.
7. Suppose this person were merely an acquaintance from down the hall who kept borrowing dimes and not repaying them.
8. Suppose your roommate is constantly borrowing dimes from you in order to buy Cokes, but he/she never pays you back. You are getting rather annoyed at this and have decided to stop handing them out to him/her, and besides you're really low on money and have put yourself on a tight budget.

_____

9. An acquaintance of yours is going to fly home over the weekend and will have to miss a class on Friday. Even though you are not enrolled in that class, he/she asks as a favor that you go to the class and take notes on Friday. (You are free at that hour.)

10. Suppose it were a close friend who asks for this favor, but you are somewhat pressed for study time since you have an exam on Friday.

11. Suppose a mere acquaintance asks the favor, but you have an exam Friday afternoon.

12. A slight acquaintance of yours asks to borrow $5 until next week. You have the money, but you would have to postpone buying something you wanted until the loan was repaid.

13. A student you do not know well is chairman of the dorm's fund-raising campaign. He/she catches you when you don't have anything special to do and asks you to help out by soliciting room-to-room for about 3 hours.

14. Suppose that your roommate is the fund-raising chairman, but that he/she needs your help right when you should be studying for an exam.

15. Suppose the chairman, who is someone you don't know too well, needs your help right when you should be studying for an exam.

16. A friend in one of your classes borrowed your class notes several weeks ago, then failed to return them at the next class, thus forcing you to take notes on scrap paper. Now he/she is asking to borrow your notes again.

17. Suppose that the person who borrowed your notes were someone you had only met in class and did not know too well.

18. Suppose that it is your friend who is asking to borrow your notes again, but that there is going to be an exam on the next day of class.

19. Suppose that your classroom acquaintance is now asking you to borrow your notes again, but the exam is scheduled for the next day of class.

20. You live in a dorm. Suppose someone, whom you don't know, calls on your phone one night. He/she says that the phone of the person he/she is trying to reach seems to be out of order. He/she asks if you would go get this person. You don't even know the person the caller is trying to reach, and you are expecting an important phone call yourself.

21. A class project has been planned. There are several things left to do before the project is finished, but instead of asking the other members to do the work, the chairman, whom you hardly know, asks if you would help him/her do it. You have already done your share of the work.

22. Suppose the chairman, who asks you to finish the project, were your best friend, but that you have already done your share of the work and had made plans to do something else.

23. Suppose the chairman, who asks you to help finish the project, was someone you hardly knew, and that you had already done your share of the work and had made plans to do something else.

24. A person you do not know very well is going home for the weekend. He/she has some books which are due at the library and he/she asks if you would take them back for him/her, so they won't be overdue. From where you live it is a 25 minute walk to the library. The books are heavy, and you hadn't planned on going near the library that weekend.

Table 3–2 (continued)

25. You have volunteered to help someone, whom you hardly know, to do some charity work. He/she really needs your help but when he/she calls to arrange a time, it turns out that you are in the middle of exams.

26. You know you have a lot of schoolwork to do, but an acquaintance of yours, whom you do not know very well, asks you to go to a concert with him/her.

27. You are studying for an exam but your best friend asks you to go to a concert with him/her. He/she makes you feel that if you were a true friend you would go.

28. What if you are studying for an exam and it was someone whom you hardly knew who asked you to go with him/her to the concert.

29. You have been standing in the ticket line at the movie theater for about 20 minutes. Just as you are getting close to the box office, three people, who you know only slightly from your dorm, come up to you and ask if you would let them "cut" in front of you.

30. You are in the thick of studying for exams when a person whom you knew only slightly comes into your room and says "I'm tired of studying. Mind if I come in and take a break for a while?"

31. You and two close friends are looking for a 4th person with whom to share an apartment. Now your two roommates come to you and say that they have found someone they would like to ask. However, you know this person and secretly dislike him/her.

32. On your way back to the dorm, you meet a slight acquaintance who asks you to carry a heavy package home for him/her since he/she is not going home for a while, but it would be quite cumbersome since you are carrying packages of your own.

33. A friend of yours comes to your door selling magazine subscriptions. He/she says it would be a personal favor if you bought one since he/she is trying to win a scholarship in a sales contest. He/she is offering a good price, but you are only mildly interested in the magazines being sold.

34. In the above situation, suppose that you not only couldn't find any especially interesting magazines on your friend's list, but that you also felt that they were slightly overpriced.

35. A young high school boy comes to your door selling magazine subscriptions. He says it would really help him if you would buy one since he is competing for a college scholarship. You can't find any especially interesting magazines on his list, and in any case, you feel they are slightly overpriced.

	Scoring Key	
ITEM	ASSERTIVE	NONASSERTIVE
1.	1,2	3,4
2.	1	2,3,4
3.	1	2,3
4.	1	3,4
5.	1	2,3,4
6.	1	3,4
7.	1	2,3,4
8.	1	2,3,4
9.	1	—
10.	1	2,3,4
11.	1	2,3,4
12.	1	2,3,4
13.	1	2,3,4
14.	1,2	3,4
15.	1	2,4
16.	1	2,3
17.	1	2,3
18.	1	2,3
19.	1	2,3
20.	1	3,4
21.	1,4,5	2,3
22.	1	2,3
23.	1	3,4
24.	1	2,3
25.	1	2,3,4
26.	1	2,3
27.	1	2,3,4
28.	1	2,3,4
29.	1,2,5	3
30.	1	2,3,4
31.	1,2	3,4
32.	1	3,4
33.	1,2	3,4
34.	1	3,4
35.	1	2,3

From McFall & Lillesand (1971).

Note: 1 = A, 2 = B, 3 = C, 4 = D, and 5 = E for the response alternatives provided to subjects for the "Alternatives" section of the inventory.

of situation—namely, refusing unreasonable requests. Other scales have been developed to assess assertive behaviors in other types of situations. For example, the Assertion Inventory (Gambrill & Richey, 1975) assesses a variety of assertive behaviors, including refusal assertions, commendatory assertions, and request assertions. The Interpersonal Situation Inventory (Goldsmith & McFall, 1975), which was designed for middle-aged men, collects information on a wide range of social skills, including assertiveness, interview behaviors, and dating behaviors. The Assertion Self-Statement Test (Schwartz & Gottman, 1976), which is based on a cognitive-behavioral model of assertiveness, measures the frequency of positive and negative self-statements associated with a variety of situations rather than assertive behavior per se. To date, no direct comparison studies of the relative validity of the various assertion scales have been published. Most therapists choose a scale based on the characteristics and problems of the client being assessed (e.g., whether the cause is seen as due to maladaptive cognitive expectations, anxiety, or behavioral skill deficits).

Evaluation of Assertiveness Inventories

The CRI and other assertiveness inventories clearly provide a wealth of potentially useful information. In general, we highly recommend their use as an aid in assessing the existence and nature of assertion problems. However, some words of caution are in order.

First, in general there are few *normative data* on the various assertion scales. That is, we do not have a reliable psychometric basis for determining what a "normal" or "appropriate" score is for adults, students, children, and other populations. This issue is often addressed in research settings by having a control or comparison group of apparently normally functioning subjects, or by ignoring the issue of "normal" assertiveness and simply being concerned with pre- and postchanges as a result of inter-

vention. But in a clinical context, such approaches are usually not satisfactory. Thus, we must be careful when interpreting what a given assertion inventory score means in relation to what is normal or appropriate assertiveness. It is important to keep in mind that what is appropriate behavior may vary as a function of age, sex, socioeconomic status, and other client characteristics, as well as being due to situational variables.

Second, a scale may indicate that a person is not unassertive, but this does not necessarily mean that the person is *appropriately* assertive. For example, suppose a client indicates that he or she would certainly turn down a request to borrow a car, and would do so comfortably. In actual situations, the client's model behavior might well be aggressive rather than assertive: for example, "Hell, no. . . . It happens to be my damn car!" Clearly, most assertiveness inventories would not pick this up. Third, the results of using a particular inventory are limited to the domain of situations from which that inventory samples. For example, scores on the CRI reflect problems in refusing unreasonable requests but do not reflect behavior relevant to commendatory or request assertions. Overall, questionnaires such as the CRI are potentially valuable, and we encourage their use, but mainly as *initial* screening devices.

Finally, although assertion inventories can provide information about whether an assertion problem exists, most scales provide little information about *why* the person has the problem. As we will discuss shortly, in some cases, the person may not know how to be assertive; in other cases, he or she may know how to handle unassertive requests but may be too anxious or afraid to do so; and in still other cases, the person simply may not be able to appraise the situation as demanding an assertive response.

Elements from the CRI, or any of the other assertion inventories, can be readily incorporated into a clinical interview with whatever degree of structure the therapist deems appropriate. Whether or not the therapist employs a structured assessment device, he or she should search for indications of interpersonal difficulty in the client's interview behavior. Finally, information gained from questionnaires and interviews should be supplemented by direct observation of the client's actual performance, either in the natural environment or through role-playing.

Assessing the Nature of an Assertion Problem

After a therapist determines, or strongly suspects, that the client has an assertion problem, the next step is to determine more explicitly the nature of the problem. Such a determination is important because the specific treatment used may to some extent depend on the specific nature of the problem behavior.

The first step in assessing the nature of an assertion problem is to identify the types of situations the client finds difficult to handle. Although information from the various assertion inventories may prove useful, an in-depth behavioral interview is often the most useful tool in developing a list of the client's problem situations. Some therapists also find it quite useful to have clients keep a behavioral diary in which they record day-to-day situations that are perceived as difficult or problematic. Having the client record information about the nature of the situation, the thoughts and emotions experienced, and the behaviors used to handle the situation can provide a wealth of useful diagnostic information.

Once the presence and nature of the assertion problems are identified, the next step is to analyze why the client is unable to behave assertively. Often, anxiety is a prominent feature of assertion problems. Sometimes this anxiety is directly manifest when the client attempts to engage in an important interchange, as in the case of the student who becomes hopelessly flustered whenever he asks an attractive girl for a date, or the loyal employee who becomes tongue-tied when asking his boss for a much deserved raise.

Sometimes the anticipatory anxiety is so intense that the individual avoids the situation, which leads to immediate frustration and sometimes long-term negative consequences, such as depression. As we noted previously, Wolpe (1982) has suggested that much, if not most, nonassertive behavior is associated with high levels of anxiety, and therefore that anxiety-reduction (e.g., through systematic desensitization or guided exposure) is an important component of assertion training.

Although anxiety about being assertive is common clinically, it must be kept in mind that this anxiety can be due to several different factors. In some situations, it can stem from negative self-statements made by the person. For instance, an individual may say to herself, "I know that if I say no to him, he'll never ask me out again. And no one else will ask me out either. I'm not very attractive or much fun. I'd better not lose what I've got. I can't afford to say no!"

In other cases, the anxiety may be more realistically based. That is, certain persons may feel anxious about being assertive because they are not skilled in how to express assertive intentions. As a result, they may feel that they probably will mess up any attempt to be assertive. For example, one of us observed an interview with a male college student who was despondent over his inability to establish satisfying relationships with women. He did not appear to believe that he was lacking in requisite skills, but it was obvious to us that he was. When asked to role-play a particular incident involving an initial overture to an attractive female in the college student union, his verbalizations were insensitive and clumsy. No wonder women usually refused to go out with him! Understandably, he began feeling anxious whenever he was in mixed company and thought about assertively asking out a woman.

In the above example, the client's verbal description of his own behavior when attempting romantic overtures was clearly at odds with his manner of responding when he role-played a sample situation.

Contradictions of this nature are not at all uncommon, and when they occur it is likely that the role-played behavior is far more accurate than the client's verbal characterization of how he typically handles such a situation. While behavior rehearsal is an important component of assertive therapy, it is also an invaluable diagnostic technique, and we recommend its use. In fact, a number of researchers have developed structured role-playing assessment devices for identifying assertion and other social skills problems (see Fisher-Beckfied & McFall, 1982; Herson, Bellack, & Turner, 1978; Arkowitz, Lichenstein, McGoven, & Thies, 1975).

Several patterns of behavior can be identified as maladaptive and might be appropriately replaced by assertive behaviors. These maladaptive behaviors can include anger, passive-aggressive behavior, jealously, and shyness. In assessing a client's problem, the therapist needs to be sensitive to these types of behaviors as cues that assertion training may be appropriate. In the paragraphs that follow, we discuss each of these maladaptive behaviors.

Sometimes a client will have difficulties expressing anger directly and as a result may express it in an ambivalent or apologetic fashion, producing an unsatisfying and ineffective performance. Inability to express anger sometimes directly leads to a passive-aggressive mode of dealing with hostility. _Passive aggression_ is the label clinicians give to behaviors designed to punish another in an indirect fashion (often by inducing guilt). If the individual is skilled at this, he will be spared immediate retaliation on the part of his victim, who will usually fail to label his assailant's behavior as aggressive or punitive. Unfortunately for the individual who regularly exhibits passive aggression, sooner or later his victim will begin to feel resentment and will avoid the assailant. Individuals exhibiting consistent patterns of passive-aggressive behavior would not be expected to have many lasting, satisfying relationships; this situation often drives them to seek therapeutic help.

Of the various types of interpersonal problems amenable to assertion training, those associated with unexpressed (or indirectly expressed) anger are among the most difficult to deal with. Persons who have considerable difficulty expressing anger often believe not only that it is wrong to express anger overtly, but that it is equally wrong to "think angry thoughts." In fact, this belief is an explicit ethic of certain organized religions. Unfortunately, individuals who have such indoctrinated beliefs are not immune to the hurtful behavior of others. This means that they are as susceptible to anger as any of us, even though they are forbidden to admit this to themselves, let alone to a therapist. Thus, the therapist has a multifold task. First, he or she must correctly identify the degree to which the client experiences hostility in daily interpersonal interactions. In this regard, it is helpful for therapists to reflect on whether they themselves (or the "average" person) would experience anger in the situations in question, and whether or not the client's facial expression and tone of voice reflect anger. Some clients, when faced with the possibility that certain situations may be annoying or anger inducing, respond with "It wasn't that important," or "It isn't worth getting angry over." A high frequency of responses of this nature may well reflect a good deal of unexpressed anger. Nor should the therapist be misled by the statement, "When I get mad, I really blow my top," which can usually be translated as, "Although I'm rarely justified in showing or even feeling anger, some situations clearly are so wrong and unfair that I must react."

Once the therapist has gathered sufficient evidence that unexpressed hostility is a problem, the next task is to convince the client of this, which is no minor undertaking. Telling a client—who believes that feeling anger is immoral—that he is angry may be likened to confronting a Victorian spinster with the observation that she is oversexed. A premature confrontation would likely alienate the client, who might smile and nod his head in agreement, but inwardly experience a swell of resentment toward the therapist. This reaction could result in the client's terminating therapy. We recommend that the therapist first establish feelings of trust and confidence and that the subject of the client's hostile feelings be dealt with in a graduated fashion. For some clients, this might mean dealing with mildly angry feelings occurring in relatively insignificant situations. For others, the general area might be approached by using synonyms (admittedly of a euphemistic nature) for "angry" or "hostile": for example, "I get the feeling you are a bit irritated at your wife," or "Do you find that it is somewhat annoying when your father interrupts you like that?" Once the client is persuaded that he or she has angry feelings, assertion training can commence.

Jealousy is another emotion that may signal problems with assertiveness. Jealousy has a variety of meanings in our culture, but we are specifically referring to feelings of anxiety and resentment when threatened with losing one we love to a competitor. Extreme jealousy, especially when unfounded, has destroyed many relationships, and therapeutic strategies for dealing with this problem might well include a combination of systematic desensitization (Chapter 2), assertion training, and some of the cognitive techniques to be presented in Chapter 9.

Whereas occasional feelings of mild jealousy are inevitable and normal, many individuals refuse to admit to such feelings, perhaps because they place them in the same category as pure anger or selfishness. Certain persons are imbued with an ethic of totally unselfish love that realistically cannot exist between a man and a woman engaged in a love relationship. Given normal expectations and a normal degree of possessiveness, individuals will sometimes experience jealousy. Often one partner will deliberately try to induce such a feeling in the other, to test that person's love or to manipulate the person's behavior. If the partner regularly fails to respond, this may drive the other to more

drastic action (e.g., consummated sexual encounters rather than casual flirting at a cocktail party). As an illustration, Wolpe (1958) described the case of a man whose wife was engaged in an extramarital affair that he condoned, but also resented. Only when he forcefully made his feelings known did his wife terminate the affair, and most willingly at that.

As in the case of hostility, the therapist must decide whether the client is experiencing jealousy. Again, asking the question, "Would the average person feel some jealously in such a situation?" will probably prove to be of diagnostic value. Problems involved in persuading the client to acknowledge these feelings (and to see the therapeutic benefit of expressing them in a reasonable way) are similar to those raised in connection with unexpressed anger. Here, too, we recommend the gentle approach.

Finally, in addition to emotions such as anxiety, anger, and jealousy, assertion problems can be associated with other factors. For example, some clients do not know how to communicate positive comments, to give compliments or show affection—even though they may in fact feel affection or love for another. These clients will often identify themselves as shy persons. Thus, a client might tell his therapist that he loves his wife, but that he "doesn't have to tell her" because she "knows"—that is, she can "read between the lines." Not infrequently, the client implies that it is the other party's *responsibility* somehow to know that she is loved or appreciated. It is well to point out that in any relationship involving intense feelings, subtle cues are often missed, and feelings of affection, warmth, and love must be made very explicit, at least occasionally. Generally, clients seem more willing to own up to honest, but inadequately communicated, positive feelings than to resentment or anger, probably because our culture is far more permissive about the expression of positive feelings. On the other hand, many persons (men, especially) believe that expressing love and affection is indicative of weakness. Here the therapist's task may be to turn this attitude around on the client by indicating how straightforward expressions of positive feeling are interpreted by most people as a sign of strength and confidence. In addition, there are others who feel unsure of themselves and inadequate in expressing positive feelings. Assertion training may help these individuals develop greater self-confidence in expressing their positive feelings.

As we emphasized previously, when assessing whether assertiveness is or is not a problem for a client, you must keep in mind that assertiveness (or the lack of it) is not a pervasive trait. That is, a person may be quite assertive in one situation, yet tremulous and ineffective in another seemingly related set of circumstances. It is absolutely essential that the therapist be aware of this, lest he or she come to premature and fallacious conclusions that will impede the course of treatment. This theme also underlies our emphasis on identifying problem situations as the first step in approaching assertion training. On numerous occasions, the clinician is confronted with a smiling, verbally facile client who presents the superficial picture of an individual supremely confident and competent in virtually any social interchange. The therapist might easily conclude that assertion training is the last thing such an individual requires. Yet careful interviewing (including role playing) will often reveal significant situations in which the client shows a lack of assertiveness. This is well illustrated by the confident, boisterous businessman who is regularly intimidated by his wife when he attempts to make certain kinds of decisions, or by his children when he attempts to apply verbal discipline. Another example is the cool and highly articulate professional woman who, while espousing feminism, will, upon careful questioning, admit that she is frequently the victim of unscrupulous and unsatisfying sexual conquests because she is unable to say no. On the other side of the coin, clients may evidence extreme anxiety and apparent lack of self-confidence or social skills during an initial interview, not be-

cause this is their habitual manner of social interaction, but because they are unaccustomed to situations wherein they are expected to reveal to a virtual stranger highly troublesome and embarrassing facets of their personal lives.

In summary, diagnosing problems pertaining to a lack of assertiveness may be facilitated by the use of structured self-report and role-playing assessment devices, although a precise pinpointing of areas of difficulty normally requires careful behavioral interviewing. Assertion training is usually in order when the client is unable to express feelings in a manner that is both personally satisfying and socially effective. Indications for assertion training include obvious signs of interpersonal anxiety or habitual avoidance of important interpersonal interactions, as well as obvious or subtle signs that the client is experiencing intense, but unexpressed emotions, especially anger, resentment, and jealousy. Lack of assertiveness should be seen as a behavioral deficit related to specific situations rather than as a general personality trait. Before beginning assertion training, the specific situations that are troublesome for a client should be identified.

Presenting the Concept of Assertion Training to the Client

We will assume that the therapist is now convinced that some of the client's problems are due to a lack of assertion. The next task is to inform the client about assertion training and to enlist his or her cooperation. Although this has not been subject to controlled research, most behaviorists place considerable emphasis on inducing a positive, enthusiastic attitude toward assertion training before attempting the actual procedures. In part, this is because assertion training, like most other behavior therapy techniques, requires a good deal of active participation on the part of the client, necessitating reasonable motivation. As we pointed out in the prior section, the initial prospect of behaving assertively in certain situations may be anxiety provoking or even frightening to the client. It is likely that for many clients in need of assertion training, significant prior attempts (perhaps in childhood) at assertion were met with highly unpleasant consequences. While appropriate assertion is usually met with positive consequences, the client may not be convinced of this. As we noted earlier, it is also possible that the client lacks appropriate assertion skills and that producing these skills—or the confidence that they can be learned—is the first step toward motivating a client to want to act assertively.

The therapist might stress the negative effects of nonassertion (frustration, resentment, lack of satisfaction) the client is currently experiencing and the feelings of personal well-being and relief, as well as increased interpersonal satisfaction, that will very likely follow from increased assertiveness. The therapist might find it useful to identify individuals whom the client admires as models of appropriate assertive behavior.

Some writers (Alberti & Emmons, 1978; Lange & Jacubowski, 1976) suggest that individuals have an unalienable "right" to be assertive, and there can be little doubt that imbuing the client with this belief sometimes has a powerful motivating effect. However, it is our judgment that the risks associated with presenting assertiveness as a *right* far outweigh the therapeutic or motivational value. First, while we would anticipate that most of the client's assertive behaviors will be met with positive consequences, sometimes the consequences will be negative, and negative consequences are more frustrating when behaviors are motivated by a sense of righteousness. A righteous attitude may encourage the client to persist in a particular behavior in the face of negative feedback; such an experience is likely to be disheartening as well as self-defeating. Second, we agree with Ellis (1962, 1971b) and other cognitive therapists that certain value-laden beliefs contribute heavily to human suffering (see Chapter 9 for a discussion of Ellis). Cognitive therapists take great pains to point out to their clients that such

beliefs are often of an arbitrary nature. Within such a therapeutic context, it would be logically inconsistent to present assertiveness as an absolute right.[2] Third—and this, too, relates to the views of Ellis and other cognitive therapists—to the extent that assertion is presented as a right, clients are likely to assume that they *should* be assertive. This almost invariably leads to what we call "assertion neurosis": clients observe that they are not assertive in every conceivable situation. They then repeatedly castigate themselves for this seeming imperfection, generating a good deal of unnecessary distress in the process.

In our experience, a constructive alternative to presenting assertion as a right is to emphasize that behaving assertively is *self-enhancing*, whereas lack of assertiveness is frequently *self-defeating*. In particular, we have found that characterizing a client's behavior as "self-defeating" (and, naturally, giving reasons *why* it is self-defeating) almost always produces the needed motivation to change.

The following dialogue between a therapist and an adult male client who has admitted that he is bullied by and greatly resents his brother-in-law illustrates this point.

Therapist: From what you've been saying, it seems clear that you feel a lot of resentment and anger toward your brother-in-law. What do you think about feeling like that? I mean, is it a good, or pleasant, way to feel?

Client: Well, no. Sometimes I feel I'm going to lose control and hit him. That would be terrible.

Therapist: What else do you feel around him?

[2]Readers bothered by our eschewal of assertion as an absolute right should note that we do not therefore view assertion as a *wrong*. Instead, we would agree with Heimberg and associates (1977) that it is of little avail to think of assertiveness in terms of absolute values. To be sure, we do sometimes speak to clients about rights, but within a legal context, which is quite a different matter.

Client: Like I said, I'm pretty upset and nervous, and when I'm over at his house for dinner I don't feel like eating. I don't want to offend my sister, so I eat, but afterward I feel like throwing up.

Therapist: So, in other words, your brother-in-law's way of acting makes you angry and anxious and downright sick to your stomach? Sounds like you are pretty miserable around him.

Client: Yes, pretty miserable. Like I was saying, he's not the only one, but it's worse around him.

Therapist: Just pretend for a minute that you were the sort of person who could tell him off whenever he was bothering you. Whenever he was on your back, bullying you the way he does. How would you feel then?

Client: Well, if I did tell him off, he'd say something to hurt my feelings. It wouldn't be worth it.

Therapist: But suppose you were so effective at telling him how you felt that he really got the message and left you alone, and even treated you with admiration and respect. How do you suppose you would feel then?

Client: That's hard to imagine. If I could do it—I mean beat him at his own game—I'd feel a lot better. I just want him to leave me alone, and I would enjoy visiting my sister a lot more. But I don't think I could ever do it. . . . I'm just not that way.

Note: As is so often the case early in assertion training, the client fails to make a distinction between assertion and aggression. Unless the client is assisted in making this important distinction, it is unlikely the client *will give himself permission to behave more assertively.*

Therapist: When you say you're "not that way," do you mean you just aren't comfortable being aggressive, and maybe hurting other people's feelings?

Client: Yeah. I mean I don't like it when other people treat *me* that way. Do you understand?

Therapist: I think I do and I really see your point. You don't like it when your brother-in-law bullies you and you don't want to be a bully. Fair enough. But, you know, being *assertive* isn't the same thing as being *aggressive.* Aggression is like you don't give a damn about how other people feel. When you're being assertive, you *do* care about how the other person feels, but you also care about how you yourself feel.

Client: I guess I can kind of see the difference. Being assertive isn't like putting people down. Hmmm . . . I don't know . . . maybe telling him how I feel *would* be the right thing to do.

Therapist: Look, I don't want to play God and tell you what is right and wrong. But I'll say this: You'll be a lot more honest if you tell him how you really feel. And if you're like most other people, you'll feel better afterward. Especially if you say it in a way that doesn't make him feel like some kind of monster. And you know something else? There is a pretty good possibility that your brother-in-law doesn't even *realize* how he's been getting to you. If you make him aware of it, then he has a choice.

Client: You almost make it sound like I'd be doing him a favor.

Therapist: I wasn't thinking along those lines, but that is a darn good point. He may be bullying a lot of other people . . . you know, turning them off, and not even knowing it.

Client: (Long pause) I think he does. I really think he does. Maybe I could help him. (Laughs)

Therapist: That is quite possible! But don't lose track of yourself in the process. The main thing about being more assertive is that *you'll* feel better, and probably like yourself more. And your brother-in-law will take you more seriously. Being nonassertive can sometimes be *very* self-defeating.

Client: Self-defeating. Yeah . . . that's a good way to put it. But the thing is, I always get tense and, you know, clam up when anyone criticizes me, and especially when they make fun of me. You mean I'd be better off if I just made up my mind to . . . speak up?

Therapist: Yes. There are some things we can do to help you express your feelings.

At this point the therapist would briefly describe the method and rationale of assertion training. He might point out that role-playing responses within the "safe" confines of the consulting office can result only in increased effectiveness in interpersonal situations, and that when a person is behaving assertively, it is very difficult for him to experience anxiety. Certain writers (Wolpe & Lazarus, 1966) have recommended presenting the client a sample case history to provide him with a more concrete notion of what is in store.

In introducing the subject of assertion training, the therapist should take care not to suggest that these procedures are designed only to help people to express negative feelings. The early clinical and research literature stressed this aspect of assertion, but the fact is that a very broad spectrum of interpersonal behavior can be enhanced by assertion training.

Implementing Assertion Procedures

As Wolpe has pointed out, "The quintessence of assertive behavior is to do toward others what is reasonable and right" (1983, p. 120). How do you teach individuals to do what is reasonable and right, to do it skillfully, and to do it without feelings of fear or anxiety? There are many ways, all of which qualify as assertion training.

That is, assertion training per se does not refer to a specific set of procedures, but rather to the use of any of a large number of procedures to increase assertive behavior. In fact, McFall (1976) has argued that any educational procedure designed to increase the frequency of appropriate assertion (or other) behaviors is a valid technique in clinical behavior therapy. In the following pages we present several of the more common techniques used to increase assertive behaviors. Our descriptions of these techniques are based on our own clinical experience and writing (e.g., Hollon & Beck, 1986; Rimm, 1977a, 1977b), the clinical experiences and writings of others (e.g., Gambrill, 1985; Lazarus, 1971, 1976; Wolpe, 1958, 1969, 1973, 1983), and a large number of experimental investigations.

Behavioral Rehearsal

By far the most commonly used assertion training technique is *behavioral rehearsal,* which is the acting out ("rehearsing of behaviors") of appropriate and effective ways to handle real-life situations that are troublesome for the client. For example, the therapist and client may role-play how to respond to a domineering and demanding boyfriend. The goals of behavioral rehearsal are to learn how to modify currently maladaptive (e.g., unassertive) ways of responding by replacing them with new responses. Behavioral rehearsal accomplishes this without undue anxiety by repeatedly role-playing them until they are part of one's repertoire. Behavioral rehearsal differs from other forms of role playing, such as psychodrama, by focusing on behavior change as an end in itself, not as a technique for identifying or working through presumed conflicts.

When used to promote assertive behavior, behavioral rehearsal is usually done first in the therapist's office. The client normally identifies (sometimes with the therapist's help) a situation in which he or she does not act assertively. The client then plays himself or herself, while the therapist assumes the role of the significant "other" person with whom the client has trouble interacting. In carrying out this role, the therapist must portray the other person with some degree of realism. Since the client is normally the only source of information about the other person, he must tell the therapist how to behave. The client might model the behavior outright, or if this is too anxiety provoking or awkward, he might simply describe the behavior to be modeled, with the therapist filling in the details.

Having set the stage, the client usually initiates the vignette with behavior that is *typical* for him or her in such a situation. The therapist responds according to his or her role, and this, in turn, is met by the client's response, and so on. Normally, exchanges of this nature are quite brief, and sometimes the nature of the target task is such that only the client need make a response. For example, a client may wish to learn how to deal with a salesclerk that persists in ignoring him. Here the therapist might say, "Pretend I'm that clerk. Role-play what you would say [did say] to me." The client would then terminate the exchange with a single statement such as, "Excuse me, I'm sorry but when you are through, would you wait on me?"

On the basis of such initial role-played behaviors, the therapist is in an excellent position to assess whether assertion training is required for the situation just acted out, and if so, to pinpoint the exact behaviors of the client in need of changing. If deficiencies are apparent, the therapist may opt to provide corrective *feedback*. This feedback should be immediate, specific, and presented in as positive a fashion as possible. Following the feedback, the role-played scene should be repeated. This procedure might be continued until both client and therapist agree that the response is appropriately assertive and is accompanied by minimal anxiety. Alternatively, following the client's initial response, the therapist might immediately *model* a more adequate response that the client

would then have an opportunity to imitate. The therapist can also use coaching, in which the principles and strategies underlying assertive behavior are described. However, the most desirable strategy probably should incorporate immediate feedback, modeling, and coaching (Edelstein & Eisler, 1976; Hersen, Eisler, & Miller, 1974; Hersen, Eisler, Miller, Johnson & Pinkston, 1973; Kazdin, 1976b). Consider the following example.

A male college student has difficulty making dates with women. In the present situation, he is attempting to ask for a date over the telephone. He has introduced himself and has engaged the woman in the appropriate amount of small talk. Both client and therapist agree that it is now time to ask for the date.

Client: By the way (pause) I don't suppose you want to go out Saturday night?

Therapist: Up to actually asking for the date you were very good. However, if I were the woman, I think I might have been a bit offended when you said, "By the way." It's like your asking her out is pretty casual. Also, the way you phrased the question, you were kind of suggesting to her that she doesn't want to go out with you. Pretend for the moment I'm you. Now, how does this sound: "There is a movie at the Varsity Theater this Saturday that I want to see. If you don't have other plans, I'd very much like to take you."

Client: That sounded good. Like you were sure of yourself and liked the woman, too.

Therapist: Why don't you try it.

Client: You know that movie at the Varsity? Well, I'd like to go, and I'd like to take you Saturday, if you don't have anything better to do.

Therapist: Well, that certainly was better. Your tone of voice was especially good. But the last line, "if you don't have anything better to do," sounds like you don't think you have too much to offer. Why not run through it one more time.

Client: I'd like to see the show at the Varsity, Saturday, and, if you haven't made other plans, I'd like to take you.

Therapist: Much better. Excellent, in fact. You were confident, forceful and sincere.

Some of the principles discussed in Chapter 5, "Contingency Management I," are incorporated in the above dialogue. One was the use of plentiful *reinforcement* in the form of praise from the therapist. The second was the use of the *principle of successive approximations.* After the client's first attempt at imitating the therapist, the therapist praised those components of the client's response that reflected improvement. Had the therapist insisted on a perfect performance, almost anything the client said would have missed the mark. However, when the therapist attends to *any* improvement discernible in the client's behavior, such improvement, instead of being lost, persists through the next response. Rewarding *improvement, rather than absolute levels of performance,* is labeled *shaping,* which, as we consider in Chapters 5 and 6, is an essential ingredient of behavior modification. Also stressed in these same chapters is the importance of dealing with relatively small segments of behavior at a time. In assertion training this means that initially, at least, protracted monologues are not modeled by the therapist, who opts, instead, to *work on effecting improvement in small portions of the client's behavior.* Ordinarily, the therapist deals sequentially with segments of an interaction, until the interaction is complete. Then he or she might have the client "put together" (i.e., rehearse) the entire sequence, thus simulating the interaction as it would actually occur.

Note that in the above dialogue, the therapist attended not only to the content of the client's verbalization, but to *voice tone* as well. Most

would agree that assertive behavior consists of a good deal more than responses with assertive content. Assertion trainers pay considerable attention to a variety of paralinguistic and nonverbal components of the client's behavior, including the following:

Paralinguistic *Components*	Nonverbal *Components*
Response latency	Eye contact
Amplitude of response	Facial expression
Duration of response	General posture
Tone of voice	Lean of body (toward or away from other person)
Speech dysfluencies	

The use of video tapes can be an especially helpful technique for monitoring and then showing clients their nonverbal characteristics and for recording progress in the alteration of habitual behaviors. They can also be used to demonstrate progress for clients—something that can be especially important for nonassertive subjects who are uncertain of how convincing they appear when they are trying to act assertively, or who are convinced that they are not getting any better.

Frequently, it is helpful if *role reversal* is used in enacting a difficult situation. In role reversal, the therapist assumes the client's role while the client plays the role of the other person in the interaction. For example, the client may play a domineering, arrogant roommate while the therapist pretends that he or she is the client and role plays how the client might repond to the roommate. Role reversal can be helpful in providing a more realistic context in which the therapist may model appropriate behavior for the client. Additionally, assuming the role of the other person encourages the client to experience the sorts of feelings that the other person (any person) would plausibly experience in a given situation. This is especially valuable if the client has unrealistically negative expectations of how other people will respond to more assertive overtures. For instance, consider the client who is reluctant to express disagreement with his employer lest it offend the boss. By engaging in role reversal, the client has the opportunity to observe the therapist modeling disagreement in a tactful and well-reasoned fashion and to observe his own emotional reaction to this. He may be surprised to realize that the modeled response did not elicit especially negative feelings after all, and this would provide added impetus for trying out the new behavior *in vivo*.

The following illustrates the technique of role reversal, as well as the procedures and principles described in the preceding discussion. The client is a teenage girl, about to graduate from high school. She is not an especially good student and has no desire to attend college, but her mother, who dominates her, is insisting that the girl do so.

Therapist: Well, it is apparent to me that you really don't want to go to college. It is also clear that you've given it a great deal of thought. Now what happens when you discuss this with your mother?

Client: We don't exactly *discuss* it. She tells me what is best for me, and that I am immature and don't know my own mind, and that I'll regret not going to college for the rest of my life.

Therapist: And how does that make you feel?

Client: Angry inside and pretty frustrated. I can't seem to get a word in edgewise, but if I did say what I really felt, it would hurt her, so I don't. I just go to my room and cry for a while.

Therapist: Just to see how you do come across in this situation, let me play your mother and you be yourself. You direct the play and

make sure I act like your mother. Ready? Here goes. (As mother) When are you going to apply to State? You haven't done it yet, have you?

Client: No. You know, I don't really want to go.

Therapist: I know you're not old enough to know your own mind! You are very immature and you'll regret not going to college the rest of your life. If I didn't love you I wouldn't say these things. Now, I insist that you apply!

Client: (Long sigh) Oh, all right. (Role play ended) That's actually what I'd say. To get her off my back.

Therapist: Well, you begin by telling your mother how you really felt, and that sounded good. But then, after she said her piece, you backed down, angry and frustrated. Let's try reversing roles for a minute. You be your mother and I'll be you. You start.

Client: Okay. (As mother) Why haven't you applied to State College yet?

Therapist: (As client) To tell you the truth, Mom, I've thought about it a great deal, and I don't want to go to college.

Client: (As mother) I absolutely insist that you apply. You aren't really very grown up and you don't know your own mind. Do as I say. I love you and it's for your own good.

Therapist: (As client) Mom, I know you care a great deal about me and that is important. But, like I said, I thought it over very carefully. I wouldn't enjoy college and I know I wouldn't do well. (Role play ended) Now, why don't you try something like that? You be yourself and I'll be your mother. (As mother) I insist you apply to State. I love you and it's for your own good.

Client: (As client) I know you love me, and I appreciate it. But I've thought about it a lot and know I won't do well. I really don't think it would be a good idea. I'm sure it wouldn't be.

It takes two to lie. One to lie & one to listen

Therapist: That was certainly much better! How did you feel?

Client: A little anxious.

Therapist: Let's try it again.

Note: Certain writers in the area (e.g., Lange & Jakubowski, 1976; Lazarus, 1973) stress the importance of empathy in assertive behavior and we wholeheartedly concur. In the above, the therapist modeled an empathic response vis-à-vis the mother, and the client readily incorporated it. Empathic responses are not likely to be seen as aggressive, ergo they probably will not threaten the client or the people with whom the client is to interact.

The interaction continues until the client reports little or no anxiety while engaging in the interchange.

Therapist: Would the conversation end with that?

Client: No, I don't think so. She'd probably say I was a disappointment to her. That really gets to me, and she knows it, and I wouldn't know what to say.

Therapist: Let's try to reverse roles again. You begin with the statement about disappointment.

Client: (As mother) Why do you insist on disappointing me?

Therapist: (As client) Well, I don't want to disappoint you, and if I am, that makes me feel bad. But this is an important decision that I have to make for myself. You know I value your opinion and I don't want to seem disrespectful, but I've looked at this from all angles, and I know it would be best if I take that job instead of going to college. (Role play ended) How did that sound?

Client: Really good. It was like you were disarming her. Putting it that way would have made her less angry.

Therapist: Now, you try it. Just the last part. (As mother) Why must you disappoint me?

Client: Well, that isn't what I want to do and I'm really sorry if I am. You know I respect your opinion very much, but this is an important decision and it has to be made by me. I've really thought it over and over and know it would be best if I took the job and didn't go to college.

Therapist: Very good. You came across forcefully, but you didn't sound harsh or unkind. Also, your eye contact is getting much better, and that is important. Did you feel anxious at all?

Client: No, as a matter of fact, I felt pretty good while I was talking.

Therapist: How would your mother respond to what you just said?

Client: I really don't know. I've never asserted myself that much before.

Therapist: Do you think you feel comfortable enough to try that sort of thing out?

Client: Yes, but with a little more practice.

Therapist: Okay, let's go through the whole thing now. (As mother) Why haven't you applied to State yet?

Behavioral rehearsal is sometimes divided into two subcategories, overt and covert. *Overt* refers to rehearsal in which the client and therapist actually act out a given situation. *Covert* rehearsal is the practicing of new behaviors in one's imagination. For example, the client may be asked to imagine how he would respond to a domineering father who insists, contrary to the client's wishes, that he attend medical school. The therapist might assist the client in crafting a script for the covert scene, including how the client would approach the father one evening while the father was working in his study, would walk to the front of the father's desk, would initiate the topic and make his thoughts known, and would respond to protests or orders from the father. Covert rehearsal can be used in place of or to supplement overt rehearsal. However, we generally recommend that it be used as a supplement, since in most cases—especially if there is any suspicion that the client does not have the requisite skills to display effective assertive behavior—overt rehearsal allows more opportunities for the therapist to "observe" the maladaptive behavior and to teach the client appropriate modifications, usually in successive approximations.

As a supplement, covert rehearsal has several advantages. For example, it can be used as an intermediary step between overt in-session rehearsal and the actual display of assertive behavior in the real-life situation (Bellack, 1985). It also lends itself to being used as a homework assignment between therapy sessions. A client might be asked to imagine, at least three times a day, behaving assertively in two different situations similar to real-life encounters, such as giving a compliment to a friend or asking a girl out for a date. Homework assignments should be as specific as possible and should always be within the range of behaviors that the therapist believes the client can handle successfully, so that they generate success experiences (Christoff & Kelly, 1985). Difficult situations should only be assigned for overt rehearsal after the client is appropriately assertive in comparatively less challenging situations and has shown all the requisite skills to handle more difficult interactions.

In addition to helping a client practice assertive behavior between sessions in a safe and non-demanding manner, covert rehearsal may also aid in the generalization of assertive skills. By continually rehearsing assertive behaviors covertly in a variety of new situations not specifically rehearsed during therapy sessions, the client learns to apply the general principles of assertiveness to a broad spectrum of situations. The client can gain confidence in this manner and can always check back with the therapist during the next session to go over any problems that emerge during the covert practice. Assertion training generally is not terminated until the therapist is confident that the client will, on his or her own, display appropriate assertive behavior in new situations that were not specifically dealt with in therapy.

The Use of a Hierarchy

The situations that are role-played in behavioral rehearsal, be they overt or covert, are sometimes presented in a hierarchical order. This is so for two reasons. First, many clinicians believe that a gradual increase in the difficulty of the rehearsed interactions increases the likelihood that the client will be able to complete them successfully and will not become discouraged. Second, a good deal of deconditioning may occur during behavioral rehearsal and, as with systematic desensitization, this deconditioning might be enhanced if the interactions are presented in a graduated hierarchy. However, unlike systematic desensitization, in which the hierarchies are carefully structured and thoroughly detailed, in assertion training hierarchies are usually less formal or rigid, although they should follow the same general principles (see Chapter 2). Ordinarily, scenes in the hierarchy are ranked from the least to the most anxiety provoking, although in assertion training it may also be useful to have clients consider the degree to which scenes make them frustrated, jealous, irritated, or helpless, especially with clients who do not deem it appropriate to admit when they are anxious.

Constructing a detailed hierarchy and methodically going through it is a time-consuming undertaking, and some therapists may feel it is not necessary or expedient to demand such precision when dealing with assertiveness problems. In fact, some therapists begin behavioral rehearsal with situations that are creating the most distress in the client's life, dispensing with a hierarchy altogether. With the proper social support for working on difficult situations, many clients can be taught to behave assertively through repeated application of the modeling, coaching, rehearsal, and feedback methodology, without a need for a hierarchy.

However, it is our view that the novice to assertion training may find a fairly detailed hierarchy desirable, since it provides structure as well as valuable diagnostic information. We feel that the premature presentation of an item (i.e., interaction) can be more damaging in assertion training than in desensitization. This is especially true if the assertive item has to do with the expression of hostility. Getting a client to "tell off" his father (even in a supposedly "safe" role-playing context) before he is ready for this may threaten him to the point of terminating therapy. If the client's lack of assertiveness encompasses expressing negative feelings toward a therapist, the therapist may be unaware of what is happening, only to discover after several subsequent meetings have been canceled that he or she has "lost" the client who was "doing so well." Therefore, we recommend that the newcomer to assertion training employ a desensitization-type hierarchy until he or she feels that this procedure can be dispensed with.

The following are sample hierarchies. The first two items are presented in detail, and the remainder are given in abbreviated form. The items are in order of increasing difficulty of behaving assertively, as perceived by the client. As in desensitization, situations should be presented in realistic detail.

The first hierarchy is for an accountant who was bullied by his immediate supervisor.

1. Your supervisor is sitting at his desk. For the past three days, you've been working overtime and you'd like to leave the office 20 minutes early to attend to your son's birthday party. You walk up to his desk and begin to make the request.

2. Your supervisor walks by as you are seated at your desk one morning. In spite of the fact that you are always punctual, he says, in a very sarcastic tone, "Were you late today?"

3. Your supervisor observes (inaccurately) that you and the others have been taking excessively long coffee breaks.

4. Your supervisor unjustly accuses a colleague of yours of acts of dishonesty.

5. You approach your supervisor to request that your vacation, scheduled for September, be changed to August.

6. You have been working overtime all week. Your supervisor requests that you do so again. You want to refuse.

7. Your supervisor makes sarcastic comments about your leaving the office early on Wednesday to meet with your psychotherapist.

8. You approach your supervisor to ask for a much-deserved raise.

9. You want to inform your supervisor that if a raise is not granted you will leave the firm.

The second hierarchy is for a 25-year-old woman having an affair with an older married man who appears to be indifferent to her feelings.

1. Late one night, he telephones you from his apartment, insisting that you visit him immediately. He seems not to care whether or not this is inconvenient for you.

2. He was to meet you at 5:00 p.m. at the railroad station. You haven't eaten and it is cold and rainy. He shows up at 7:30, offering no excuse.

3. He phones to tell you he may not be able to see you the following weekend, offering no reason.

4. He refuses to discuss the future of your relationship.

5. You complain about his mistreatment, and he calls you a "bitch" and won't respond further.

6. He says he can't see you because Bonnie (another girlfriend) is in town.

7. You want to tell him off, but you fear losing him as a result.

8. You want to tell him to change or you will end the relationship.

9. You want to tell him you no longer wish to see him.

The Minimal Effective Response

As we have indicated, assertion is the appropriate expression of feelings. Deciding whether a particular act is appropriate is, of course, a matter of social judgment. As we discussed earlier, identifying what behaviors to teach is often the most difficult part of assertion training. Ordinarily, the decision is made jointly by client and therapist. In this process, it is of utmost importance that the therapist be sensitive to the client's values. Assertive behavior can produce both positive and negative outcomes, depending on the client's values. A study by Kelly and associates (1980) nicely illustrates this point. Subjects were shown videotaped examples of assertive and compliant behaviors in situations involving refusal. Each subject rated the actor on the videotape on a skillfulness and an attractiveness dimension. Actors portraying assertive responses were rated as more skillful but less attractive than actors portraying compliant responses. The drop in attractiveness ratings was most pronounced when the actor was a female portraying an assertive response. The therapist, in determining what behaviors to teach, must be sensitive to how much the client values "standing up for one's rights" versus "being liked and well thought of." The therapist should not presume that the same way of responding is appropriate for every person, but instead should approach each client on an individual basis.

Since many of the problems the therapist will deal with involve a failure on the part of the client to stand up for his rights, some general guidelines for determining appropriate behaviors in such situations may be helpful. In expressing feelings such as hurt or anger, a good rule of thumb is to stress implementing the *minimal effective response,* which is behavior that would ordinarily accomplish the client's goal with a minimum of effort and of apparent negative emotion (and a very small likelihood of negative consequences). The person who is concerned about other people's opinions as well as about being appropriately assertive can often obtain the best possible consequence by using the minimal effective response. Consider how a person might deal with a chatty couple interfering with his enjoyment of a movie. Assume the

couple has been engaged in loud whispering for about five minutes, and no one has yet asked them to refrain. A minimal effective response might be, "Gee, I wonder if you'd mind being a little more quiet? I'm having trouble hearing," whispered in a friendly tone of voice. Naturally, one could engage in overkill, with a loud and angry, "If you don't shut the hell up, I'll call the usher and have you kicked out." However, a response of this nature, while it might get the job done, would probably cause the complainant to feel guilty, unnecessarily anger or distress the target couple (who, after all, may have been unaware they were causing a disturbance), and irritate all innocent bystanders within earshot.

The following are frequently occurring annoying situations, with sample minimal effective responses.

A gas station attendant fails to clean your windshield:
I wonder if you'd mind getting the windshield? It's kind of dirty.

A waiter charges you for dessert you didn't have:
I believe you've made an error in the check. Would you mind checking it again?

The night before an important exam a friend drops in to chat; 20 minutes later he is going strong:
Hey, you know, I've got this exam tomorrow, and I've really got to study. How about getting together tomorrow night?

Your date is 30 minutes late. He offers no excuse:
I was getting a little worried (while glancing at your watch).

A friend continually interrupts you:
I'm sure you don't realize this, but sometimes I get kind of flustered when you interrupt (with a friendly smile).

Escalation

Assertive responses of the relatively mild nature illustrated above are quite effective in most cases. *Sometimes, however, they are met with un-*

responsiveness or even belligerence, and steps should be taken to prepare the client for this. In fact, many clients won't even attempt a minimal effective response in the real world unless they feel that they can go beyond this if necessary. Once clients have shown themselves to be adept at the minimal effective response (in the consulting room or in imagination), the therapist can model successively more negative or more threatening counterresponses. Training in *escalation* (a term borrowed from McFall & Marston, 1970) increases the client's confidence, and research findings suggest it may facilitate generalization of assertive behavior (Neitzel, Martorano, & Melnick, 1977). However, the therapist should take special care to keep these escalations within the realm of *plausibility* and to remind the client that such counterresponses, after all, are rather unlikely to occur. This caution is important because individuals who are timorous in such situations have probably done a thorough job of intimidating themselves with anticipated dreadful consequences to any assertive acts on their part. The last thing the therapist wants to do is to reinforce these ruminations. On the other hand, the therapist should also help the client to feel prepared for any event that might occur. The following, in summary form, is an example of an escalation involving the noisy couple in the movie theater. In implementing this, the methods of modeling, coaching, rehearsal, and feedback should be used.

Complainant: I wonder if you would please be a little more quiet. I'm having difficulty hearing. (After five minutes of silence, the chatter resumes)

Complainant: Look, would you please be a bit more quiet? I simply can't hear the movie (First-order escalation)

Spokesman for the culprits: Sorry. (Silence for remainder of movie)

The therapist may wish to extend this into a second-order escalation. The second complaint

is met with "Jeeze, what's that guy so uptight about?"—followed by continued chatter. Now, an appropriate response might be: "Look, if you people don't quiet down, I'm simply going to call the manager," which might be followed by this counterresponse: "(Extended sigh) Okay, buddy, okay," and silence for the remainder of the movie. Or, "This guy gets on my nerves. Let's leave."

Note that at each step the therapist structures things so that the client's assertions are met with ultimate success. While it might be argued that appropriate assertiveness in the real world is not *always* met with success, the fact is that it usually *is* successful, and overly emphasizing negative consequences in therapy will only reinforce already powerful tendencies toward inhibition. Perhaps the best way to prepare a client for a potential failure experience is to emphasize that no matter what happens, the client should feel good about having spoken up and acted assertively. It would be wrong to give someone the impression that assertive strategies always lead to getting what he or she wants. However, clients can be convinced that behaving assertively works better than either passive or aggressive responses, and that they really have no other choice, even if assertion does not work perfectly. The greatest emphasis, however, should be placed on the potential positive consequences of behaving assertively.

The client may raise the possibility that, during the course of an escalated encounter, the other person may resort to physical violence or corresponding threats. The likelihood of this happening is probably much lower than most clients realize. In our experience, people who frequently behave in a bullying manner easily succumb to verbal assertiveness, so the interchange rarely reaches the point of physical threats or violence. This is especially true for the client who is taught to avoid backing an opponent against the wall. This is best accomplished by having the client concentrate on ways to inform the other person that what he or she is doing is a source of personal inconvenience, discomfort, or, when appropriate, hurt, rather than on tactics involving personal attacks or insults.

Consider the following situation. You are in serious need of some cash, but the clerk at the convenience market you frequent refuses to cash your check because he is new and he does not know you. You might say, "To tell you the truth, this makes me feel kind of funny. After all, I've been a good customer here for some time, and I do need the money very badly." From personal experience, this usually works. However, in a far more foolish and impulsive vein, you might back him into a corner with: "Look, you moron, I've been cashing checks in here for more than a year." Most people do not respond with increased friendliness to being called a moron. Additionally, if the clerk is given to violence, calling him a moron will do little to suppress this response. Keep in mind that the source of your distress in this situation has little to do with any enduring "trait" (such as a lack of intelligence) the clerk might possess. It is his present behavior that is annoying, and telling him this in an objective and straightforward manner is a good deal more honest (and usually more effective) than engaging in inflammatory name-calling. Similarly, for the customer who has just been shortchanged, the problem is not that the waiter is "a liar and a cheat" (although indeed he may be). Rather, the event causing distress is this specific instance of change-making behavior on the part of the waiter, and this is what is in need of correction.

Cognitive Techniques

Thus far we have focused primarily on techniques for directly changing overt behaviors. Until about 1976, assertion problems were considered to be due primarily to skill deficits or inhibition caused by anxiety, and therefore, treatments were aimed at teaching—through procedures such as modeling, coaching, rehearsal, and feedback—the client how to fashion appropriately assertive responses. As we saw in the "Background" section, recently it has been hy-

pothesized that dysfunctional cognitions may play an important role in the genesis and maintenance of assertion problems. Specifically, cognitivists have suggested that nonassertive behavior may result from *response inhibition*, which is due to irrational beliefs, maladaptive self-statements, or low self-efficacy expectations, such as "If I assert myself, no one will like me"; "I have no right to make a request or demand of anyone else"; "One should always turn the other cheek, no matter what"; or "I just can't do it, so why try?" As a result of the response-inhibition hypothesis, clinicians have begun to introduce a number of cognitive restructuring techniques into their assertion training programs.

In general, the cognitive techniques used in assertion training are identical to those described in detail in Chapter 9 (e.g., rational emotive therapy, rational restructuring, self-instructional training, etc.). The goal of these techniques is to replace maladaptive cognitions that lead to inhibition or fear with more appropriate thinking that will allow the individual to behave assertively. In some cases, the successful initiation of assertive behaviors itself will help to reduce these inhibitions. This may be due to increases in feelings of self-confidence and mastery that result from repeated success experiences. Likewise, in some cases removing the inhibitions is sufficient to allow the person to behave assertively. Thus, it is not surprising that the literature often suggests that either behavioral techniques, such as behavioral rehearsal, or cognitive techniques, such as rational restructuring, can be equally effective in increasing assertive behavior (e.g., Hammen et al., 1980; Kaplan, 1982; Safran, Alden, & Davidson, 1980; Valerio & Stone, 1982). However, in general, we recommend that *both* behaviorally and cognitively focused techniques be used when working with unassertive clients. This recommendation is based both on our clinical experience, the clinical experience of our colleagues, and on data that suggest a combination of cognitive and behavioral treatments is never less effective than either alone, and in some cases is more effective (e.g., Linehan et al., 1979; Jacobs & Cochran, 1982).

Self-efficacy and Assertion

Bandura (1977a), who originated the concept of self-efficacy, has argued that self-efficacy is a potent predictor of behavior and behavior change (e.g., becoming more assertive). Presumably, anything from therapy that imparts to the client a real sense of being able to cope will increase the likelihood of success *in vivo*. The hypothesis has far reaching implications, is intuitively appealing, and enjoys research support (e.g., Hammen et al., 1980; Kazdin, 1980; Lee, 1984). Therefore, it is worthwhile to explore how we might incorporate the concept of self-efficacy into assertion-training procedures.

First, it is important to understand what self-efficacy refers to. A positive sense of self-efficacy is based on two expectations: (1) that a particular response will be effective in a given situation, and (2) that the client is able to carry out the particular response (Bandura, 1977a). Self-efficacy expectations are thus different from outcome expectations, which refer in a more limited sense to "a person's estimate that a given behavior will lead to certain outcomes" (Bandura, 1977a, p. 193). Some nonassertive individuals believe that assertive behaviors may be effective in a given situation (outcome expectancy), but are not confident that they can produce those behaviors, perhaps because their lack of self-confidence is due to dysfunctional self-statements or due to repeated failure experiences in the past. Other nonassertive individuals may believe neither in their ability to act assertively nor in the instrumental value of assertive behaviors.

In regard to the first expectation associated with positive self-efficacy, it is clear that the client's expectation that a given response will work will be based, in part, on prior life experiences, but things can be done to enhance this belief. Thus, the therapist, using coaching, can give reasons why a particular act ought to be effective in accomplishing the client's goals. Further, Kazdin's work (1974d, 1976b; Pentz & Kazdin, 1982) suggests that *positive consequences* to the model, as well as the use of *several models*, facilitate assertion. We can expect that observing (or imagining, as Kazdin's subjects did) several models experiencing positive consequences will enhance a client's belief that a particular response will, indeed, be effective. When logistically possible, *in vivo* modeling will provide convincing evidence of the efficacy of a response—for example, the therapist models sending an overdone steak back (assuming it really is overdone!) or returning a garment that is the wrong size. In suggesting this, we are assuming positive consequences; needless to say, the therapist should orchestrate such real-life interactions carefully. The therapist can also have the client focus on significant others whom the client knows are capable of behaving assertively. This will help broaden the range of models that the client can look at in modifying behavior outcome expectations. Often it is not necessary to convince a client that a particular act will work. Rather, the client need only be convinced that trying out the behavior is a worthy experiment and that whether or not the strategy works is an empirical question.

Once clients are convinced that a particular behavioral tactic will meet with success or at least that it is worth trying, how can *they* (as opposed to the therapist) perform it effectively? That is, how can we increase in the client the second expectation associated with self-efficacy? Evidence shows that response feedback, in the form of comments from the therapist, or via audio or videotape, facilitates subjects' assertiveness (e.g., Edelstein & Eisler, 1976; Melnick, 1973; Muehlenhard & McFall, 1983). One function of feedback is to provide the client with information that his or her response was indeed effective or appropriate.

As we noted earlier, experimental evidence generally supports the situation-specific view of assertiveness. In the last edition of this text, we noted that efforts to program generalization into assertion training treatment packages (i.e., to ensure that what is learned in therapy is *not* situation-specific) had generally met with little success. Over the past few years, however, this trend has reversed, so that generalization of assertion skills to new situations is now often reported in the literature (e.g., Kazdin, 1982; Kazdin & Mascitelli, 1982; Pentz, 1980; Twentyman, Pharr, & Connor, 1980). Why the change? We might speculate that changes in how assertion training is now provided (e.g., more emphasis on cognitive factors associated with self-confidence and on covert rehearsal in which clients are encouraged to generate their own assertion tactics) have led to an increase in clients' sense of self-efficacy in dealing with situations that are different from those specifically targeted in therapy. A therapeutic strategy to facilitate generalization might involve *considerable structure early on, but with a gradual fading out of modeling.* By the end of treatment, virtually all the client's assertion tactics would be self-generated, which, presumably, would provide the client with a sound reason for believing that he or she can deal effectively with novel situations. *Specific attention to these self-beliefs should also be part of the therapy.*

The strategy we have just suggested is somewhat akin to Bandura's "self-directed mastery" (Bandura, Jeffrey, & Gajdos, 1975—see Chapter 4 of this text), which is used in conjunction with participant modeling. In cases dealing with snake phobics, Bandura and his coworkers reported that self-directed mastery experiences resulted in greater reduction of fear of actual snakes. But perhaps more importantly, the mastery experiences were also associated with higher levels of confidence for effectively dealing with snakes in *novel* situations. Presumably, such strategies would also facilitate a more generalized expectancy of being able to behave assertively and, indeed, of actually behaving assertively in novel situations.

Consistent with the points we have made in this section about self-efficacy and its attainment as a goal of assertion training, some data suggest that changes in self-efficacy following therapy can be used as predictors of future assertive behaviors. For example, Valerio and Stone concluded from their study of the effectiveness of behaviorally and cognitively focused assertion procedures that no matter what procedure they use,

> increased self-efficacy was [positively] associated [at the posttest and three-month follow-up times] with self-report of more assertive behavior, a higher quality of assertive performance on behavioral measures, a higher incidence of self-reported assertive behavior and comfort with that behavior in the natural environment, a greater occurrence of positive self-statements, and a higher reported satisfaction with treatment. (1982, p. 167)

Similar findings have been reported by Kazdin (1979) and Hammen et al. (1980).

The following is a summary of the main points associated with the various assertion training procedures we have advocated.

1. The specific situations that are of concern to the client are identified.

2. What the client typically does and thinks in these situations is assessed.

3. A specific situation is chosen and the client role plays his or her response.

4. The therapist provides specific verbal feedback, stressing positive features and presenting inadequacies in a friendly, nonpunitive fashion.

5. The therapist models more desirable behavior, with the client assuming the other person's role when appropriate (role reversal).

6. The therapist provides coaching, explaining general principles underlying the desired behavior.

7. During modeling, the therapist enuciates positive self-statements that accompany the behavior.

8. The client then attempts the response again.

9. The therapist rewards improvement using a shaping or successive approximations strategy. Steps 5, 6, 7, and 8 are repeated until both therapist and client are satisfied with the response and the client can engage in the response feeling little or no anxiety and making no negative self-statements.

10. Once the client can handle a situation that formerly had evoked mild anxiety, the therapist moves on to a situation higher on a hierarchy of problem situations.

11. The interaction, if it is at all lengthy, should be broken up into small segments and dealt with sequentially. Then the client and therapist may wish to run through the entire interaction for the purpose of consolidating gains.

12. Between sessions, the therapist instructs the client to practice in imagination responding assertively to several specific situations. The client is also told to attend to self-statements made during this covert rehearsal. The results are discussed at the next therapy section.

13. In an interchange involving the assertive expression of negative feelings, the client should be instructed to begin with a relatively mild response (the minimum effective response). However, he or she should also be given stronger responses in case the initial responses are ineffective.

14. In rehearsing the assertive expression of negative feelings, objective statements pertaining to annoying or hurtful behaviors on the part of the other person are far superior to personal attacks, which are often irrelevant and have the effect of backing the other into a corner.

15. The therapist may wish to fade out the modeling of assertive responses and have the client assume more and more of the responsibility for generating assertive tactics, both in covert rehearsal and *in vio*. Homework assignments can be given to facilitate generalization.

16. The therapist should determine whether the client is effective in self-generating assertive responses to novel situations, both from self-reports by the client and from significant others identified by the client.

17. The therapist assesses the client's belief that he or she can act assertively in novel situations. If the client is showing assertive behavior in novel situations and is expressing positive self-efficacy, termination of therapy should be considered.

The Use of a Cotherapist

We have found that assertion training at times may be considerably expedited if two therapists see the client at the same time. While we know of no controlled research investigating this, the rationale behind the use of a cotherapist is highly plausible. First, as we have emphasized earlier, one of the more difficult aspects of assertion training can be deciding what precisely is an appropriately assertive response in a given situation. Certainly, in matters of social judgment, the adage "two heads are better than one" is applicable. Second, and related to this point, the credibility of a novel response presented to the client can only be enhanced by the fact that *two* ("expert") observers agree on its appropriateness. Third, research findings suggest that two persons acting as models facilitate assertive behavior better than a solitary model (Kazdin, 1976b). In behavior rehearsal, the presence of a cotherapist means there are two individuals available to assume the role of the "other person," and it is far more likely that the role will be portrayed in a plausible manner. This is obviously the case when the client has difficulty being assertive with members of both sexes, and one therapist is male and the other female. Cotherapists would have a similar advantage if the client has difficulty with authority figures as well as peers, and the therapists differed markedly in age. Finally, two therapists verbally reinforcing increased assertiveness on the part of the client should have far more impact than a solitary therapist.

Naturally, it is not always feasible to have cotherapists (if fees are an issue, it might be prohibitively expensive), and the standard one-to-one therapy arrangement can be quite effective. Under such circumstances, the therapist may want to enlist the help of another individual occasionally (e.g., the male ward psychologist may ask a nurse to assume the role of the male patient's wife).

Assertion Training in Groups

In Chapter 2, we presented evidence that systematic desensitization can be effectively and economically presented within a group setting. Findings in the laboratory and clinic indicate that the same holds true for assertion training (e.g., Berah, 1981; Christoff et al., 1985; Landau & Paulson, 1977; Lange & Jacubowski, 1976; McIntyre, Jeffrey, & McIntyre, 1984; Rathus, 1972; Rimm, 1977b; Rimm, Hill, Brown, & Stuart, 1974; Stalce & Pearlman, 1980).

Aside from obvious economic considerations, there are several compelling reasons for supposing that group assertion training *ought* to be superior to individual treatment. The arguments in favor of group assertion training are essentially the same as those for the use of cotherapists. The group, consisting (usually) of two therapists and 5 to 10 clients, can provide a ready consensus for what is appropriately assertive in a given situation, multiple models— as well as a varied assortment of "target" persons—for assertion exercises, and massive social reinforcement for individuals' improved performances.

For most groups, training is similar to individual treatment in that it includes modeling, coaching, rehearsal, and feedback with plenty of social reinforcement. After a member presents a particular problem to the group, he or she is asked to role-play his or her typical response, which is then evaluated in a nonjudgmental and friendly manner by other members of the group. Each member of the group is expected to assume some responsibility for training fellow members, although ordinarily the therapists will provide guidance for the others

in the group. After the member's initial response has been evaluated, one of the therapists might say, "Now, let's decide what would be an appropriately assertive response in this situation." In an inexperienced group, this statement will often be met with silence, and one of the therapists may have to provide the necessary response, although care should be taken to wean the members away from such overreliance on the therapists. Once the alternative response has been put forth, it is discussed by the group until agreement is reached that it is indeed appropriate. This response is then modeled by a group member volunteering for the task, or by one of the therapists if no one volunteers. Since modeling the response is a learning experience for the actor as well as for the observer, it is generally more productive if a member rather than a therapist acts as the model.

Initially, a good deal of encouragement by the therapist may be required by modeling. Praising the model's performance will increase the likelihood that group members will volunteer for such tasks in the future. It is rare for a model's performance to be inadequate, partly because the appropriate response has already been agreed upon. But if one of the therapists does consider the performance lacking, he or she might follow it up with "That's certainly in the right ball park. But what about the following?" Whereupon, he or she will model the response. Once an effective response has been modeled, the member originally presenting the problem is asked to rehearse it and is praised by all members of the group for any improvement. As usual, the therapist then inquires as to how the member felt. If the member indicates anxiety, he or she is asked to repeat the response. Normally, the level of anxiety considerably diminishes during the second attempt. Also, what the client was thinking or saying to himself or herself when rehearsing the assertive response should be discussed. What other group members might have been saying to themselves could also be elicited and discussed. Group discussion of negative or dysfunctional self-statements, how they interfere with assertiveness, and how to eliminate them should follow.

There are some groups for which group training as just described may be inappropriate. For example, the authors have found that for groups consisting of extremely withdrawn members (ordinarily chronic inpatients in a mental hospital), behavior rehearsal is difficult or threatening. We recommend that such a group be presented with a graduated series of exercises that normally lead up to behavior rehearsal when the majority of group members are ready. Such exercises usually fall into broader classification of social skills training. *Greetings* and *free association* are nonthreatening warm-up exercises. Greetings simply require that a given member turn to his neighbor and say, "Hello _____, how are you?" The neighbor replies, "Fine, _____, how are you?" The recipient then turns to a third member, and a similar exchange of greetings occurs, with the process continuing until each member has participated. Warmth, good eye contact, and a loud and assertive tone of voice should be reinforced. Free association begins with a member saying a word, to which his or her neighbor responds. The exercise continues until each member has participated. Brief latencies and emphatic voicing should be reinforced. In these and the remaining exercises, the therapists participate as any other group member, although they must make sure to model the style of response they wish their clients to acquire. These exercises serve the function of shaping some of the component verbal and nonverbal behaviors that represent an assertive response.

As we noted earlier, many individuals have trouble with commendatory assertions—that is, with expressing positive feelings. A group exercise called *exchanging compliments* is designed to increase skill (as well as comfort level) in this area. A group member turns to another member and warmly and emphatically provides the other with a compliment. Example: "Gee, _____, I really like the way you are wearing your hair today." The recipient is encouraged to accept the compliment with a positive acknowledgement. Example: "Thank you, that makes me feel good," or "Thanks, I thought I'd try something different." Self-disparaging comments (for instance, "Are you kidding? It's a mess") are gently but firmly discouraged, as are automatic and insincere countercompliments.

Positive self-statements require that each member tell the group something about himself or herself that he particularly likes (Example: "I like my sense of humor," or "I am pleased with my taste in clothes"). *Small talk* is probably the most difficult (albeit beneficial) of the exercises. Here, a member who is "it" designates two other members by name and gives them a topic for "small talk" ("Harry and Louise, discuss the weather"). As usual, good eye contact, spontaneity, and a warm, assertive tone of voice are reinforced. Quite frequently, members are initially reluctant to participate because they feel they have nothing to say. The therapist should stress that it usually does not make a great deal of difference what is said in small talk, and that the participants are by no means on trial. Often an individual who is uneasy in this exercise will assume the role of the "friendly interrogator," bombarding his or her partner with questions, but revealing nothing of himself or herself. In fact, many people consider this to be good conversational style. Within limits, question asking should be encouraged, but the client should be reminded that the ultimate goal is to learn to engage in a mutually satisfying conversation.

Sometimes, individuals find themselves engaged in conversations on subjects about which, *objectively*, they know very little. In these situations, it would be good if the individual could change the subject, and we recommend a variant of small talk requiring practice in doing just this. A smooth transition of the subject (and avoidance of such hackneyed and rather rude ploys such as "Not to change the subject, but . . .") is warmly reinforced. Another potentially useful variation involves having members practice breaking into an ongoing conversation.

These exercises by no means exhaust the possibilities available to an assertion training group. We would encourage therapists to be innovative in their approach. However, a word of caution is in order. It would be unwise to encourage group members who are already deficient in the ability to make judicious social discriminations to participate in behaviors that, outside the group, would be subject to ridicule or censure. Thus, exercises involving intimate physical contact, the venting of rage, self-disclosures of a startling nature, blatant sexual overtures, and language that society would view as shockingly profane are to be discouraged. However, individuals participating in group assertion training are led to believe (often explicitly) that they will be interpersonally more effective if they engage in direct applications of what they have learned. Given this expectation, it would be nothing short of cruel to provide them with responses that would tend to shock or offend people outside the group setting.

Assertion Training in the Treatment of Antisocial Aggression

Thus far, we have concentrated on problems of social inhibition or timidity, whether the repressed feelings were of a negative or a positive nature. A growing body of research and clinical evidence suggests that assertion training may be very useful with clients who show self-defeating and socially disruptive patterns of aggressive behavior (Fehrenbach & Thelen, 1981; Foy, Eisler, & Pinkson, 1975; Huey & Rank, 1984; Pentz, 1980; Rimm, 1977a, 1977b; Thelen, Fry, Dollinger, & Paul, 1976).

We have included some instances of verbal abuse in this chapter. Unfortunately, antisocial aggression is not so limited. Acts of violence, including murder, aggravated assault, and rape, are increasing in frequency in the United States, and in almost all technologically advanced so-

cieties. Often it is possible to conceptualize acts of aggression, including physical violence, in terms of a lack of a repertoire of assertive verbal behaviors, or a reluctance to use such behaviors (Rimm, 1977b; Freedman, Rosenthal, Ranaboe, Schlundt, & McFall, 1978). Take the following case of a former mental patient:

> While on a weekend pass, the patient had sought lodging in a hotel. He was standing in the lobby when another man inadvertently jostled him. The patient might have said, "Hey, please be careful," which could be described as assertive; instead he said nothing and stabbed the man with a knife, receiving a year in prison for this needless act of violence. It is probably more than a coincidence that the words "mute" and "violence" have a common root. (Rimm, 1977b, pp. 101–102)

Feshbach (1970) and others draw a theoretically and clinically useful distinction between *instrumental-mediated* and *drive-* (or anger) mediated aggression. Instrumental aggression is a means to gain tangible reinforcement—for example, boxing for a lot of money. If anger is involved, it is not the principal motivation, and intense anger may be self-defeating; thus, the prizefighter who "blows his cool" will probably not be very effective in the ring (Rimm, 1977b). On the other hand, anger-mediated aggression is marked by intense emotionality (when the onset is gradual, the term *hostility* is often used instead of anger). If physical or psychological injury is a consequence, it is an end in itself rather than a means to an end.

Whereas assertion training may be helpful in cases of anger-mediated aggression, in general it is *not* of much value in dealing with antisocial aggression of a purely instrumental nature. The latter is maintained by potent external reinforcement (e.g., money) that would not accrue were the client to substitute assertion for aggression. However, many people may resort to violent and aggressive behavior because they lack the skills needed to achieve their ends using more peaceful means. For example, Freedman et al. (1978), in a study comparing delinquent and nondelinquent adolescent boys, showed that delinquents lacked the specific skills needed to handle a variety of social situations, whereas the nondelinquents had them. Such data suggest that with proper intervention, some instances in which aggression is used as a means to an end might be replaced by less destructive, more appropriate ways to realize important personal goals.

Another useful distinction bearing on the applicability of assertion training to antisocial aggression has been put forth by Megargee (1966). Megargee observed that some acts of aggression reflect *overcontrol,* whereas others reflect *undercontrol.* Without implying the existence of invarient traits, the individuals who are characteristically overcontrolled have been taught not to express anger. Typically, they keep their anger to themselves until it reaches a level that is virtually uncontrollable, at which point an outburst is likely, perhaps of a violent nature. In contrast, undercontrolled aggression suggests a learning history that favored the expression of anger, given even the slightest instigation. A style of undercontrolled aggression may be inferred from repeated acts of verbal or physical abuse, particularly in the absence of apparent guilt or remorse (Rimm, 1977b).

While this has not been researched, clinical experience and common sense suggest that *overcontrolled aggression is more amenable to assertion training* (or to virtually any other clinical intervention) *than undercontrolled aggression.* Overcontrolled aggressive patterns are associated with intense feelings of guilt and remorse, and clients usually welcome the opportunity to modify their behavior. In contrast, persons showing patterns of undercontrolled aggression typically have a learning history of plentiful reinforcement for such behavior, usually from their peers. Individuals showing such patterns of behavior often come from socioeconomic backgrounds where the subculture is relatively tolerant of aggression. Such individuals usually seek help, if at all, only *after* they have changed their status in some important way (e.g., obtained employment, moved to an environment less permissive to-

ward aggression, become involved in a love relationship that is now in jeopardy because of aggressive behavior). Sometimes they seek help at the request of the court, the alternative being to go to jail. (In our experience, such individuals are the most difficult to work with.) Males showing the pattern of undercontrolled aggression sometimes take great pride in their ability to overpower, frighten, or intimidate others, seeing this as a reflection of masculinity. Persons showing the undercontrolled pattern usually are, at best, ambivalent about changing. Not surprisingly, research suggests that individuals with overcontrolled aggression have more problems with assertion than either individuals with undercontrolled aggression or individuals without aggression-related problems (Quinsey, Maguire, & Varney, 1983).

The following example (adopted from Rimm, 1977a, pp. 87–89) illustrates assertion training with a client showing overcontrolled aggressive behavior. The client, a 22-year-old Caucasion male, had completed six months of a three-year enlistment in the military. On two occasions, he had been involved in fights in the barracks; the second time he cut the arm of another male with a trenching tool. The wound was not serious, and the incident was never repeated. He was very disturbed by his own behavior, but did not seek military psychiatric assistance because he feared, with some justification, that admitting to such an incident might result in a psychiatric or disciplinary discharge. Finally, he sought help from a private practitioner. During the first session, the following information was uncovered.

The client, John, was an only child. His parents had been divorced when he was 7, and he had been reared by his mother. Although he was never physically punished, he recalled numerous instances when he was severely chastised by his mother for virtually any display of anger, which was "un-Christian." He reported that his mother's favorite saying was, "If you can't say anything good about somebody, don't say anything," and he felt guilty if he engaged in the most trivial gossip with peers. He stated that while growing up he never engaged in fighting, in part because no one had ever taught him how.

Therapist: The second time, you know, when you went after the guy with your shovel. Tell me about that.

Client: My God, I think I could have killed him. I really went bananas.

Therapist: What made you so mad?

Client: He asked me whether I stole from his locker. I've never stolen anything in my life, except maybe a piece of fruit from a stand.

Therapist: Well, that *is* a heavy accusation, but there are other ways of handling situations like that. Has he ever bugged you before?

Client: Yeah, he sort of made comments like that before. I just clam up, but I'm really angry inside. Once I went to the latrine and threw up.

Therapist: Sounds like you let your feelings build up until you couldn't control them. Maybe if you would say how you feel in situations like this, your feelings wouldn't build up.

Client: The things I want to say are crazy. Like "you rotten dog." It's wrong to say things like that. Or to cuss. Everybody else does, but I can't.

Therapist: So, in other words, you don't say anything but get sick inside, and finally you take a whack at someone with a shovel.

Client: Well, that was the first time I did that. But what if I do it again? I really feel messed up.

Therapist: Look, I think that a lot of your problem is that you just don't know what to say. Let's do a little play acting. I'll be Dick, the guy you hit, and you be yourself . . . just don't swing at me, that's against the rules. Ready?

Therapist: (As Dick) Man, did you take a shirt from my locker?

Client (Silent, but discernibly upset.)

Therapist: Well, you didn't say anything. How did you feel?

Client: Even though we were play-acting . . . first, I got uptight, and then mad.

Therapist: It's good that you are aware of your feelings, but it would be better if you had said something. Let me play you and show you what I mean. You be Dick. Just say what Dick said.

Client: Okay. . . . (As Dick) Hey, did you take my shirt from my locker? (said somewhat tremulously)

Therapist: (As client) No, I damn sure did not. And it makes me madder than hell when you accuse me.

Client: It makes me uncomfortable to swear.

Therapist: I'm glad you told me, and I guess I can see why. What about this. (As client) I certainly did not. And I resent your saying that.

Client: I guess I could say that.

Therapist: Okay, then I'll be Dick. (As Dick) Hey, did you take my shirt from my locker?

Client: I did not. (Tremor in voice). That makes me angry.

Therapist: How did you feel?

Client: Kind of tense.

Therapist: Well, this is new for you, and I'm not surprised. Let's try it again.

The rehearsal continued until the client reported feeling comfortable.

Client: I see what you're getting at. But the thing is, by the time he accused me of stealing his shirt, I was already so angry at him I'm not sure . . . well, that I could pull it off . . . maybe, but I don't know.

Therapist: Okay, then let's go back to the very first time he made you angry, and let's practice what we just did, so that your feelings don't build up. Let's just work on each incident.

Assertion training with a client showing undercontrolled aggression is seen in the following example (also adopted from Rimm, 1977a, pp. 90–91). The client, a 20-year-old college freshman, had been reared in a southside Chicago ghetto. When in high school, he had been a member of a gang. Rumbles with other gangs were commonplace. He indicated with some pride that his gang was the terror of his high school and was quick to point out that because of his physical strength, and his prowess with his fists, chains, and knives, he was held in high esteem by his comrades. Upon leaving the ghetto and enrolling in an essentially middle-class university, the contingencies of reinforcement changed drastically. Early on he was involved in one or two fistfights, but quickly learned that while he might frighten others with such behavior, he was shunned rather than admitted. His combative behavior vis-à-vis males was extinguished in short order, and he reported having some friends. His present difficulty was with females. More specifically, his girlfriend had broken off with him because he had beaten her up.

Therapist: Well, what exactly happened?

Client: Two weeks ago . . . it was Saturday night . . . we were talking and Loretta told me she had been seeing this other dude. Dumb bitch! I slapped the shit out of her. I'd go after the dude, but that's against the honkey rules. (Said with sarcasm)

Therapist: I'm not sure it's as simple as black and white. But you are right if you mean middle-class rules are different from the rules of your ghetto, which is pretty frustrating for you, I guess. I know that if I had to go and live in your ghetto, I'd be frustrated and scared.

Client: Scared, shit! You'd be *dead*. But I'm not scared. I can take care of myself.

Therapist: Fair enough. But why are you here seeing me?

Client: Okay, man. You got me. I don't *always* do the right thing. I quit frightening dudes . . . but this shit with Loretta has got me down. She had it coming, but now she won't even talk to me.

Therapist: I'm not going to say what you did was right or wrong. But I know one thing, it was self-defeating. Whether she had it coming or not, you ended up hurting yourself.

Client: No argument. But what am I supposed to do when she tells me she's been screwing around with another dude? Kiss her behind?

Therapist: Well, I certainly wouldn't. But tell me something. Did you have an understanding or agreement that she was only going to date you?

Client: The night I beat her up . . . it all started with me telling her I didn't want her seeing anybody else. She told me she didn't like being ordered around, and she *was* seeing this guy. That's when I hit her.

Therapist: Well, you asked me a moment ago what you were supposed to do with Loretta. First, let me find out what you did say. Pretend this is Saturday night and Loretta is sitting next to you. Like you are actually in the situation. Say what you said, the way you said it.

Client: Baby, I don't want you seeing any other guys, you understand?!!

Therapist: Sounds like you really cared about her, and didn't want to risk losing her. I can understand that, but what you said was pretty heavy. Like, if I were Loretta, it would have made me defiant. Let me show you a different way you might have handled it. Pretend I'm you and I'm talking to Loretta.

Therapist: (As client) You know, honey, I really care for you. It's your choice, but I'd feel better if you didn't see anybody else.

Client: That doesn't sound much like me talking. But the bitch would lap it up. (Laughs)

Therapist: Well, put it in your own words. Pretend you are talking to Loretta. Go ahead.

Client: Baby, I really dig you. Don't go messing around with other dudes, okay?

Therapist: How did you feel saying that? Comfortable? Uptight?

Client: Okay, I guess.

Therapist: To me, it sounded a lot better. You told her you cared, and you didn't sound so aggressive. But don't you think you still *told* her not to see other guys instead of asking her? Remember, she really and truly does have a choice, and telling her she doesn't is only going to drive her away.

Client: (With resignation) You're right.

Therapist: Why don't you try it again. Pretend Loretta is really sitting next to you.

Client: Baby, I *really* dig you. I know it's up to you, but I'd prefer that you didn't see other guys.

Therapist: I thought that was really good. Did it feel okay?

Client: Yeah. I guess I feel less mad when I say it like that. But I keep thinking, what if she says, "Screw you, I'll see who I want"?

Therapist: If you said to her what you just said in here, the way you said it, she might go along with you. But if she said no, she wouldn't say it in such a bitchy way, and you wouldn't get so mad.

Client: Maybe not so mad, but I'd still be plenty pissed off. What do I do then?

Therapist: Okay, let's practice what you would do then. Suppose Loretta says, "I dig you too, but to tell you the truth, I don't want to get that tied down right now."

Whether the problem is overcontrolled or undercontrolled aggression, assertion training lends itself well to a group setting. However, a word of caution is in order. In assigning clients to a particular therapy group, special attention should be paid to clients who have a high potential for undercontrolled aggression. They are likely to intimidate other group members, especially if the other members are inclined to be inhibited in the first place. One possibility is to assign such persons to groups set up for the explicit purpose of dealing with problems of undercontrolled aggression, where each member is likely to show this pattern of behavior (for obvious reasons, novice or thin-skinned therapists should not lead such a group).

The following (from Rimm, 1977a, p. 111) illustrates group assertion training for undercontrolled aggressive behavior. Bob, a 23-year-old construction worker, has volunteered to participate in behavior rehearsal. His primary difficulty is with supervisors. His usual pattern is to barrage them with verbal abuse whenever he perceives he is being criticized unjustly, but on one occasion he lost a job because he struck his foreman. With such a group it is important that the therapist or cotherapist take a gentle but firm hand. It is also a good idea to lay down ground rules at the *outset*, such as no physical violence or threats of violence.

Therapist: Okay, Bob, why don't you tell the group what happened.

Bob: I've been on this construction job for 2 months. Okay? And the foreman comes up to me and says, "You better get your ass to work on time!" Well, I don't take any shit, see, and I told him what I thought of that. Hell (laughing) he just walked away with his old tail between his legs!

Therapist: Let's play-act the situation. But remember, no actual fighting or you are out of the group. Bob, pick out somebody to play the foreman.

Bob: Art, old buddy, you look like enough of a turd to be the foreman. (Said playfully)

Art: Well, screw you! But what the hell, okay.

Art: (As foreman) You'd better get your ass to work on time.

Bob: (In a very threatening voice, with clenched fists) *You* get off my back, you dumb bastard, 'fore I bust your ass!

Therapist: How did you feel just after you said that? Angry? Uptight?

Bob: Good. Maybe kind of pissed off.

Cotherapist: Okay, group, what do you think about Bob's response?

Jim: Right on, Bob. You scared the pee out of that uppity mother!

Bob: You're damned right. You know, I was *never* late on that job.

Steve: These foremen think they're God almighty.

Therapist: Well, maybe they do come on that way. But let's face it. Bob has lost six jobs in the last two years. And sooner or later nobody in this town is going to hire him. Doesn't look like the foremen are going to change.

Cotherapist: I think it is kind of up to Bob.

Art: I think Miss Goody-Two-Shoes over there is telling you you gotta learn to be an ass kisser, Bob.

Bob: The *hell* with that noise! Sure, I don't like losing jobs . . . who does? But I'd rather not work than take crap.

Therapist: I don't think you have to. Remember, the main purpose of this group is to teach people how to stand up for themselves, *without* getting into trouble. Like losing your job.

Bob: Well, what *am* I supposed to do when this bastard picks on me?

Therapist: That is a very reasonable question. We will show you.

In the preceding pages, we have gone over various assertion training procedures in some detail. Assertion training is clearly among the most challenging of the treatment packages presented in this text, largely because so much in the way of social judgment is required of the therapist (Galassi, 1978). The reader interested in carrying out assertion training is advised to consider carefully what we have said, and to do additional reading as well. There are, after all, many books devoted exclusively to this topic (e.g., Alberti & Emmons, 1978; Bower & Bower, 1976; Cotler & Guerra, 1976; Dawley & Wenrich, 1976; Galassi & Galassi, 1977; Lange & Jakubowski, 1976; Lazarus & Fay, 1975; Liberman, King, DeRisi, & McCann, 1975; Osborn & Harris, 1974; Phelps & Austin, 1974; this list is not exhaustive!). We also suggest working with an *experienced* assertion trainer before striking out on your own. Be advised that assertion training is probably second only to sex therapy in attracting self-styled experts, who in reality do not have requisite credentials or skills.

Potential Adverse Effects of Assertion Training

While training in assertiveness has many potential benefits, there are also some possible adverse effects. The most frequently documented negative effect is that assertive individuals, while usually rated high on characteristics such as handling social conflict and leadership, occasionally are rated relatively low on scales of likability or desirability (Kean, St. Lawrence, Himada, Graves, & Kelly, 1983; Kean, Wedding, & Kelly, 1983; Kelly, Kern, Kirkley, Patterson, & Kean, 1980; Kelly, St. Lawrence, Bradlyn, Himada, Graves, & Kean, 1982; Kern, 1982). Further research has highlighted some of the factors associated with this general finding. First, potential decreases in likability, when they occur, almost always do so *following refusal assertions.* Commendatory assertions rarely have this effect. Second, the level of assertiveness of the rater may affect how he or she evaluates assertiveness. Not surprisingly, assertive individuals tend to rate assertive behavior more positively than passive individuals (Gormally, 1982). Third, stereotypes or biases can affect the view one takes of assertion behavior. For example, the literature on whether assertiveness in males is rated as more or less attractive than assertiveness in females has produced all possibilities of results, including that assertive males are more likable than (e.g., Kelly et al., 1980), less likable than (e.g., Schroder, Rakos, & Mo, 1983), or as likable as (e.g., Kern, 1982) assertive females. Kern and his colleagues (Kern, Cavell, & Beck, 1985) have suggested that a critical variable in such studies may be the subjects' attitudes toward females' roles in society. Those with more conservative and traditional attitudes toward the roles of females are more likely to devalue assertiveness in them, whereas those with more liberal, egalitarian opinions tend to view it more positively. Finally, Gormally (1982) has suggested that how likable you view assertive individuals may depend on whether they are being assertive with someone else, in which case you may admire their behavior, or with you, in which case you may not be as complimentary.

A second potential negative effect is *escalation*, a topic we have already covered in some detail. The point here is that, in some cases, people will respond to assertive individuals, especially assertive individuals who were previously passive and never stood up for themselves, with increased attempts to control the person's behavior, sometimes through aggression. While this is relatively uncommon, it can happen, and clients should be taught to deal effectively with these situations.

Finally, sometimes assertiveness is ineffective because of *environmental restraints*. Perhaps the most notorious example is military boot camp. A new marine recruit going through boot camp may feel quite correctly that his rights are being trampled upon and that he is being bossed around beyond what any human should have to

endure! However, deciding to be assertive with the drill sergeant is usually not a good idea, not necessarily because of skill deficits or inappropriate response inhibition on the part of the recruit, but because the environment simply does not tolerate such behavior. Obviously, as we have emphasized throughout the chapter, part of any assertion training program is the realistic assessment of when and under what circumstances it is appropriate to be assertive.

In summary, we want to emphasize that assertive behavior has many benefits, and it usually results in increased esteem, liking, and respect from others. But in some instances, with some types of assertiveness, adverse consequences are possible. To the extent feasible, therapists must prepare the client to avoid or to handle such situations should they arise.

Empirical Findings

Assessment

Assertiveness Inventories Research on the reliability and validity of assertiveness scales is limited, but the data that do exist are generally quite favorable. Table 3-3 summarizes many of the reliability data on eight of the more commonly used assertiveness scales. The figures for test–retest reliability are generally good, with the majority of studies reporting reliability coefficients of .70 and higher. Note, however, that the investigations have generally studied short test–retest periods, ranging from 1 to 10 weeks. Data are needed on the reliability of the scales over longer periods of time, for example at 6- and 12-month intervals. As Table 3-3 shows, there are relatively few data on the internal consistency of most assertiveness scales. Again, however, the data that do exist are generally in the acceptable range.

The validity data on assertion inventories can be divided into three areas: (a) sensitivity of the inventories to treatment effects, (b) correlations

Table 3-3 Summary of Reliability Information

Scale	Sample	Test–Retest Reliability	Interval	Internal Consistency	Cited In
Wolpe-Lazarus Assertiveness Schedule	—	none	—	none	Wolpe & Lazarus (1966)
Wolpe-Lazarus Assertiveness Schedule (revised)	male and female psychiatric patients	0.56 males, 0.79 females, 0.65 overall	1 week	0.85 males, 0.63 females, 0.78 overall (split half)	Hersen et al. (1979)
Assertion Inventory	male and female students	0.87 discomfort, 0.81 response probability	3 week	none	Gambrill & Richey (1975)
College Self-Expression Scale	male and female students	0.90	2 week	none	Galassi et al. (1974)
		0.88, 0.88, 0.81	1 week, 4 week, 10 week	none	Kern & McDonald (1980)
Adult Self-Expression Scale	community college students	0.88, 0.91	2 week, 5 week	none	Gay et al. (1975)
Rathus Assertiveness Schedule	college students	0.78	5 week	0.77 (split 1/2), 0.86 (split 1/2), 0.76 (cor. split 1/2), 0.73 (K-R 20)	Rathus (1973), Futch et al. (1982), Quillan et al. (1977)
	college students seeking assertion training			0.59 (students), 0.86 (sig. others)	Mann & Flowers (1978)
	criminal offenders	0.80	11–15 days	0.80 (split)	Heimberg & Harrison (1980)
	junior high school students	0.76, 0.83 (short form)	8 week	0.77 (split 1/2)	Vaal (1975)
Assertion Questionnaire	young male drug addicts	0.86	1 week	none	Callner & Ross (1976)
Conflict Resolution Inventory	college students	0.81, 0.85, 0.54	1 week, 4 week, 10 week	none	McFall & Lillesand, 1971; Kern & McDonald (1980)
	college students	0.83 assertion scale, 0.70 nonassertion scale, 0.56 global scale	3 week	none	Galassi et al. (1978)

Adapted from Beck and Heimberg (1983).

with other assertion scales, and (c) correlation with behavioral indices of assertion (Beck & Heimberg, 1983). Relative to traditional psychology assessment inventories, the validity data for these scales are quite good. For example, the CRI has been found to be sensitive to differences between treated and untreated subjects (e.g. Kazdin, 1982; McFall & Lillesand, 1971; Muehlenhard & McFall, 1983), to correlate significantly with other assertion scales (e.g., correlations in the .50-.90 range [see Frankel, 1977; Galassi et al., 1974; Kern & McDonald, 1980]), and to relate surprisingly well to role-played refusal behavior ($r = .69$ in McFall & Lillesand, 1971). Overall, the CRI seems to fare as well as or better than other assertion inventories across all categories of validity studies. However, several other scales also do quite well, including the College Self-Expression Scale and the Rathus Assertiveness Inventory. The remaining scales have relatively less validity data on which to base a firm conclusion, although according to the data that do exist, there is reason to be optimistic (Beck & Heimberg, 1983).

Behavioral Measures of Assertion   Many research investigations include a behavioral as well as a self-report measure of assertion. The most common approach to behavioral assessment is to put the subject in a role-playing situation and to assess the subject's responses. For example, Kazdin (1980, 1982) and his colleagues (Kazdin & Mascitelli, 1982a, 1982b; Pentz & Kazdin, 1982) usually include in their studies a "behavioral role-playing test," in which the subject is asked to respond to several tape-recorded situations in which an assertive response is appropriate. The situations are usually given both at pretest and posttest times, with several new situations being presented at the posttest to measure generalization. Valerio and Stone (1982) carried the role-playing test one step further. After the subject responded to the tape-recorded antagonist, the tape came back on with an increasingly insistent statement. The persistence continued until the subject

complied or stopped responding, or until a total of five statements were made by the antagonist. In most studies that use behavioral role-playing tests, the subjects' responses are tape-recorded or videotaped and later scored by raters. Early investigations usually provided only a global measure of assertiveness, but more recent research has moved toward the specific delineations of multiple response attributes. For example, Kazdin and his colleagues usually record (a) overall level of assertiveness, (b) latency of response after the signal to respond, and (c) duration of the response. Eisler, Hersen, and Agras (1973b) have proposed the following specific behaviors as pertinent to assertion:

Duration of looking at target person

Frequency of smiles

Duration of reply

Latency of reply

Fluency of speech

Compliance

Request that other person change behavior

Affect

Overall ratings of assertiveness

Factor-analytic studies (Pachman et al., 1978) lend support to a definition of assertion in terms of many of the above components. Specifically, eye contact, response duration, request for change, and compliance correlated with global ratings of assertion (in the case of compliance, the correlation was, of course, negative).

A second behavioral strategy includes measuring assertion in contrived situations within the laboratory context. This approach usually involves having a confederate maneuver the subject into a situation in which an assertive response is appropriate (e.g., Curran & Gilbert, 1975; Goldsmith & McFall, 1975; Hemmen, Jacobs, Mayol, & Cochran, 1980). For example, Kaplan (1982) gave subjects a questionnaire and asked them to go to an adjoining room to complete it. The room had two desks with a chair under each, and a third chair off to the side of the room with 20 journals piled on it. Another student (a confederate) was seated at one desk with his feet propped up on the chair under the other desk. To be scored as assertive, the subject had to ask the other student to remove his feet. Several researchers have raised questions about the extent to which either role-playing tests or contrived laboratory *in vivo* tests of assertion are valid indices of the degree to which a person will be assertive in more naturalistic situations (e.g., Christoff & Kelly, 1985; Jacobs & Cochran, 1982). For example, Bellack, Herson, and Turner (1979) found that in a population of psychiatric patients, behavior in role-playing tests was not highly related to behavior in naturalistic settings, even when the role-playing situation was designed to be highly similar to a naturalistic situation.

As a result of such concern, researchers are increasingly using a third type of behavioral observation: a contrived test in a naturalistic, as opposed to a laboratory, setting. For example, Pentz arranged to have a student released from class to run an errand. Although the teacher allowed the student to leave the classroom he did not give the student a "hall pass" to document this permission. Once in the hallway, a confederate teacher stopped the participant and asked, "Where's your pass? [pause] You know you can't go roaming the halls without one." (1980, p. 78). The student's response was then scored for assertiveness.

Overall, there are few data on the reliability or validity of behavioral measures of assertiveness. As we have noted earlier, sometimes behavioral measures correlate highly with self-report measures, but often they do not (Beck & Heimberg, 1983). Behavioral measures do tend to be sensitive to treatment interventions—that is, they tend to show change (improvement) with subjects who received assertion training but not with those who did not receive training. However, the fact that role-playing tests may not be highly related to more naturalistic

behavioral interactions suggests that sensitivity to treatment effects may in some situations largely reflect an artificial commonality between the therapy that involves role-playing and a dependent variable that involves role playing or at least fairly contrived *in vivo* testing. Regrettably, as in many areas of behavior therapy research, the validation of behavioral measures has not received adequate attention.

Case Histories

Since the inception of assertion training procedures, a sizable number of case histories employing these procedures have been published. In the majority of these reports, assertion training was not the only method used. Frequently, relaxation training and systematic desensitization were also employed, as in the large-scale reports of Wolpe (1958) and Lazarus (1963). Although case histories of assertion training have provided a good deal of suggestive evidence, the recent explosion of studies investigating assertion procedures has led to a predominance of controlled experimentation in the assertion training literature. In fact, many of the implications which originally arose from the findings of case histories have now been supported by well-controlled experiments. A more valid and current assessment of the efficacy of assertion procedures is to be found in the following section, which presents results of controlled experimentation. Nevertheless, a brief sampling of the case histories in which assertion training was used as the primary intervention will help illustrate the broad spectrum of problems for which this method may be useful.

Salter presented 57 case histories in *Conditioned Reflex Therapy* (1949), and apparently the majority were exposed to at least some of his excitatory exercises. Unfortunately, details are lacking. What may be of interest to the reader is the wide variety of problems that have been dealt with using Salter's approach. A partial list includes fear of the dark, blushing, fear of public speaking, suicidal tendencies, homosexuality and alcoholism. As we have suggested earlier, Salter's universal diagnosis is inhibition, and it is not surprising that he used his excitatory procedures for almost any presenting complaint.

More recently, therapists have successfully implemented assertion training as an intervention for a diverse array of behavioral problems ranging from pervasive anxiety (Cautela, 1966a) to sexual deviance (e.g., Stevenson & Wolpe, 1960). Cases successfully treated with assertion training include a battered woman who was able to leave her husband after receiving training (Meyers-Abel & Jansen, 1980), a male stutterer who typically withheld anger until he experienced an emotional outburst (Wolpe, 1958), and a compulsive hand washer who had the urge to inform others of his homosexuality and to harm them with a sharp object (Walton & Mather, 1963a).

A particularly illustrative case history is one in which Lazarus (1971) describes a twenty-eight-year-old lawyer named Sam who came to therapy with complaints of claustrophobia and feelings of being "nervous, confused, and unfulfilled." Although Sam had a very successful career in law, he viewed himself as "a failure and a loser." His inability to share his feelings in a direct fashion without "attacking" affected his capacity to maintain interpersonal relationships. He was divorced, had a tenuous relationship with his parents, had no close friends, and usually felt uncomfortable around other people. A noteworthy feature of the assertion procedure that Lazarus used was his emphasis on training Sam to communicate in a nonaggressive manner that the behavior of another person was hurtful. That is, he taught Sam to respond to others honestly without "attacking" them. After only four sessions, Sam's anxiety and claustrophobia were gone. Lazarus's presentation of this case is especially valuable in that a sizable portion of the patient-therapist dialogue is included.

An analysis of case study reports by Wolpe (1958) suggests that assertion training may be one of the briefer forms of behavior therapy. Wolpe tabulated the results of behavior therapy

for 88 clients, and in 5 cases, assertion training was the primary focus of treatment. The mean number of interviews was approximately 16 for these cases, in contrast to a mean of over 45 interviews for all clients. Naturally, assertion training may require many more sessions, as in the case reported by Wolpe (1954) of a socially inadequate female who required 65 interviews. Occasionally, the therapist encounters an individual so "phobic" about assertion that it is necessary to apply desensitization to this dimension before implementing assertion procedures, as in a case reported by Wolpe and Lazarus (1966).

Experimental Results for Individual Treatment

In the earlier editions of this book, we were able to describe in some detail most of the experimental investigations of assertion training published in the behavior therapy literature. However, as we predicted (Rimm & Masters, 1979), research on assertion training has burgeoned such that well over 100 experimental investigations of assertion procedures have been published within the last several years. These investigations have led to significant advances in the effectiveness of assertion training techniques and in our appreciation of the broad array of dysfunctions that can be ameliorated with assertion interventions.

In the paragraphs that follow we have attempted to be representative and illustrative, rather than exhaustive, in our review of assertion training outcome studies. That is, for the most part the studies chosen are aimed at giving the reader a flavor for the typical (or in some cases the better) research that has been reported on a given topic and are intended to illustrate the nature and variety of approaches that have been taken in this area of inquiry.

Prior to the 1970s, experimental research on assertion training successfully demonstrated that behavioral approaches such as behavioral rehearsal significantly increased assertiveness over no-treatment control procedures and over various comparison interventions, such as advice giving (e.g., Friedman, 1968; Lazarus, 1966; Sanders, 1967). During the 1970s, therapists gave more emphasis to developing new and more powerful techniques for increasing assertive behaviors, including the use of cognitive and cognitive-behavioral procedures. For example, McFall and Lillesand (1971) assigned nonassertive male and female college students to one of three groups: (a) overt rehearsal with modeling and coaching; (b) covert rehearsal with modeling and coaching; or (c) assessment-placebo control. All subjects were seen for two 20-minute sessions. Outcome was assessed with both a self-report index (the CRI) and the behavioral role-playing test. On the average, subjects in the treatment groups showed greater increases in assertiveness than those in the control group; subjects receiving covert rehearsal improved somewhat more than those receiving overt rehearsal. The authors suggested that this latter finding could have resulted from the fact that as part of the overt rehearsal procedure, subjects heard immediate playbacks of their tape-recorded rehearsal responses, whereas covert rehearsal subjects did not receive such feedback. To the extent that their practice responses were inadequate, covert rehearsal subjects were therefore confronted with their ineptitude, and as a result might have responded to the overt rehearsal procedure with avoidance behavior, which in turn may have had a negative effect on their learning.

The separate and combined effects of overt and covert rehearsal have been the focus of several more recent investigations. For example, Kazdin (1980) assigned nonassertive adults to one of five conditions formed by a 2 (covert vs. overt rehearsal) $\times$ 2 (elaboration of training vs. no elaboration of training) + 1 (delayed treatment control) design. By "elaboration of training," Kazdin meant the process by which subjects were instructed to go beyond the specific scenes presented in therapy and to elaborate upon them or to introduce variations into them

as they saw fit. Treatment led to significant increases in assertiveness in all four interventions, as indicated both by self-report and behavioral role-playing indices. Covert and overt rehearsal generally produced equivalent changes. However, subjects who received elaboration of training procedures improved more than subjects who did not receive elaboration.

This study (and others by Kazdin and his colleagues) contained several methodological strengths that are worth highlighting. First, it assessed assertiveness not only at the preintervention (baseline) and immediate postintervention times, but also at six months after treatment. Importantly, treatment effects were maintained at the *follow-up period*. Second, the postintervention testing included novel role-playing situations in order to assess the subjects' ability to generalize any assertion skills they learned to new and presumably unrehearsed situations. Data indicated that significant *generalization* did occur in all four treatment groups. Finally, Kazdin provided an index of the *clinical importance* of subjects' changes by comparing their performance to that of a group of subjects who did not consider themselves to have social skills problems. As a result, the experimental design allowed the investigator not only to determine how much the subjects improved (by looking at pretest vs. posttest differences), but also whether that improvement was substantial enough to make the subject indistinguishable from individuals who did have apparent assertion problems. The data suggested that the assertion training interventions brought subjects' performance to levels not significantly different from those of individuals who had no apparent assertion problems.

A follow-up study by Kazdin (1982) explored whether a condition that combined covert and overt rehearsal was superior to either type of rehearsal alone. A delayed treatment control group was also included. The results suggested that while either overt or covert rehearsal alone is effective, their combination leads to significantly greater improvements, both at the posttest and follow-up (eight months) times. Additional studies in this series (Kazdin & Macitelli, 1982a, 1982b) suggested that the further addition of homework assignments (practicing assertive responses in several real-life situations outside the therapist's office) to behavioral rehearsal procedures increased further the effectiveness of training. Overall, these data suggest that, in general, the more comprehensive the training procedures, the stronger the treatment effect.

Another major line of recent research in the assertion training area has involved comparing behavioral treatment to cognitive and cognitive-behavioral treatments (see Hollon & Beck, 1986, for a review of this area). In one of the first comprehensive and well-controlled studies in this area, Linehan, Goldfried, and Goldfried (1979) randomly assigned adult females to one of five groups: (a) behavioral rehearsal, including modeling, role-playing, and feedback; (b) systematic rational restructuring (see Chapter 9), in which clients were taught to identify, reevaluate, and change negative self-statements made in response to the same situations used for role playing in the behavioral rehearsal conditions; (c) combined behavioral rehearsal–systematic rational restructuring; (d) attention control, in which the therapist simply interacted with clients in an unstructured discussion; and (e) waiting list control. All interventions were administered during eight individual sessions held once weekly. Outcome was assessed on both self-report and behavioral role-playing tests at posttest and eight week follow-up times. The pattern of results was complex, but in general suggested that the behavioral, cognitive, and cognitive-behavioral treatments were each effective in increasing assertion behavior.

There have been many other comparisons of behavioral, cognitive, and combined cognitive-behavioral interventions. Most of these studies have found no differences among the various treatments, but there have been several exceptions. Unfortunately, these exceptions are

not consistent in outcome (see Hollon & Beck, 1986).

In our view, much of this inconsistency is due to at least two factors. The first is illustrated in a study by Valerio and Stone (1982). Nonassertive female college students who expressed an interest in becoming more assertive were randomly assigned to one of four treatment groups: (1) behavioral rehearsal; (2) cognitive self-statement, which emphasized the importance of identifying and eliminating negative self-statements and replacing them with positive self-statements; (3) combined behavioral rehearsal–cognitive self-statements; and (4) waiting list control. Treatments were administered via audio tape during four individual sessions. Treatment outcome was assessed by an unusually broad array of both behavioral and cognitive measures, including (1) a self-report scale (CRI); (2) behavioral record card, on which clients self-recorded performance in assertion-related real-life experiences; (3) behavioral role-playing assessment tests, consisting of role-played responses to 20 taped situations; (4) extended behavioral role-playing assessment, in which after the client responded to a tape stimulus situation, the antagonist on the tape continued to respond with increasingly more insistent statements (up to five such statements); (5) assertiveness self-statement tests, in which clients rated how often 16 positive and 16 negative self-statements characterized their thoughts in the role-playing situations; and (6) an irrational beliefs test, which assessed clients' agreement with 100 irrational statements. Treatment outcome was measured immediately after the interventions were completed and at a three-month follow-up.

The results strongly supported the effectiveness of each treatment over the control group, and in general suggested, as has most research, that there were no significant differences among the behavioral, cognitive, or behavioral-cognitive interventions. However, when differences did occur, they did so *on outcome measures that reflected the emphasis of the treatment.* For example, the behavioral rehearsal groups scored better than the cognitive group on the behavioral role-playing tests, and the cognitive group scored better than the behavioral rehearsal group on the cognitive measures (Assertiveness Self-Statement test and Irrational Belief test), with the combined cognitive-behavioral group doing as well as the better of the behavioral-rehearsal-alone or cognitive self-statement-alone groups. The overall point is that, to some extent, whether or not a behavioral or a cognitive group appears to be superior to the other may depend on the specific dependent variables that are being assessed. Not surprisingly, behavioral outcome variables seem to be more sensitive to behavioral interventions, while cognitive outcome variables may be more sensitive to cognitive interventions.

A second factor that might account for some discrepancy in outcome among studies pitting cognitive against behavioral interventions involves individual differences among clients. As we have suggested several times, assertion problems are neither uniform across individuals nor persistent within individuals; rather they can involve a number of underlying problems (e.g., skill deficit vs. response inhibition) and can be more or less specific to a limited array of situations.

Based on this appreciation of the diverse nature of assertion problems, some investigators have attempted to determine the extent to which individual difference variables affect the outcome of assertion interventions. For example, Pentz (1981) had ninth-grade students who had difficulties either being assertive or aggressive complete a battery of individual difference tests that measured variables such as state anxiety, self-efficacy, and verbal reasoning ability. The students were then assigned to one of six treatment groups formed by a 3 (overt modeling, covert modeling, no modeling) × 2 (type of modeling scenes: all involving teachers vs. teachers, parents, or peers) factorial design. Training consisted of three 55-minute group

sessions in which the modeling scenes were presented via audio tape. Outcome was measured on a behavioral role-playing test. Multiple regression analyses indicated that, although the effectiveness of therapy was related to the specific type of treatment, individual differences among students were even more important determinants of outcome. Specifically, low anxiety and high verbal reasoning were highly related to positive outcome.

Safran, Alden, and Davidson (1980) also underscored the importance of individual difference variables. These investigators randomly assigned female college students who sought assertion training either to a behavioral skills training group that included modeling, feedback, and behavioral rehearsal or to a cognitive restructuring group that included instructions in identifying maladaptive self-statements and the implementation of cognitive coping strategies. Prior to receiving treatment, the students were identified as being either high or low anxious, based on a median split of their scores on the discomfort scale of the Assertion Inventory. After six two-hour sessions, outcome was assessed on a number of behavioral and self-report measures. The results showed that the success of the treatments depended on the students' anxiety levels: high-anxiety students benefited more from behavioral training on behavioral measures and tended to benefit more from cognitive training on cognitive measures, whereas low anxiety students benefited equally well from behavioral or cognitive procedures.

In summary, several studies (e.g., Hammen et al., 1980; Pentz, 1980, 1981; Safrin et al., 1980) suggest that the degree to which a given assertion training intervention is successful may depend as much on the individual characteristics of the client as on the specific nature of the treatment or the problem. To date, only a few investigators have published research in the area, and there are not enough data to reach firm conclusions about which kinds of individual differences interact with which kinds of treatments to produce which kinds of effects. Thus, although we know that individual differences are important, additional work must be done before we will know enough to predict *a priori* which differences will have which effects.

In addition to investigating the relative effectiveness of different types or components of assertion interventions, and to assess the contribution of individual difference variables for treatment outcome, recent research has documented the plethora of problems for which assertion training techniques can be used. For example, several investigations have examined the efficacy of assertion training with individuals who experience difficulty in heterosexual (dating) interactions (see Curran, 1977). In one such investigation, Twentyman and McFall (1975) reported that assertion training was superior to a nontreated control condition in terms of both physiological arousal during a behavioral test and subjective anxiety. Further, treatment subjects were rated by others as having more social skills than control subjects, and they reportedly began to date more often. In a novel approach, Christensen, Arkowitz, and Anderson (1975) had dating-shy males and females interchange written feedback. After each date, subjects filled out forms describing two aspects of their partners' physical appearance and dress, two aspects of their partners' behavior that they liked, and one aspect of their partners' behavior that they wished changed. Contrary to what the experimenters had anticipated, practiced dating *without* such feedback was generally superior to dating with feedback. In spite of efforts to structure the feedback so as to accentuate the positive, some subjects reported that it made them feel nervous.

Curran (1977), in reviewing research on the treatment of dating anxiety, points to three possible deficits in the etiology and maintenance of dating anxiety: conditioned anxiety, skills deficiency, and faulty cognitive appraisal. He recommends a multidimensional approach that takes into account the possible contribution of all three deficiencies.

Assertion training has also been suggested for a variety of other tasks, including modifying Type A behavior (Thurman, 1985), helping the physically disabled to accept their disabilities (Morgan & Leung, 1980), and improving performance by athletic coaches (Miller, 1982). Wolff and Desiderato (1980) have even presented evidence that the effects of assertion training can transfer to people close to the client. These investigators assigned college freshmen to an assertion training group, a discussion-oriented control group, or a no-treatment control group. As expected, assertion training was effective in increasing assertive behavior and reducing social anxiety. More intriguing, however, was the finding that the roommates of students receiving assertion training showed significantly greater increases in assertion than did the roommates of students in the other two groups. Clearly, research on assertion training substantiates the claims of behavior therapists that assertion techniques are valuable not only for helping passive individuals become more assertive but also for dealing with an unusually wide array of other problems in which factors such as poor self-esteem, social anxiety, or social skill deficits may play a role.

Experimental Results for Group Treatment

As mentioned earlier, there are several convincing reasons for suggesting that group procedures are a cost-effective approach to assertion training. Experimental results have provided evidence that this is indeed the case. Group assertion training has been employed successfully with a number of populations, including nonassertive women (Rathus, 1972), alcoholic inpatients (Hirsch, 1975), juvenile delinquents (Sarason, 1968), aggressive adults (Rimm, Hill, Brown, & Stewart, 1974), agoraphobics (Emmelkamp, Haut, & deVries, 1983), anorgasmics (Kukiansky, Sharpe, & O'Connor, 1982), and various professional groups (e.g., nurses; McIntyre, Jeffreys, & McIntyre, 1984). Furthermore, group assertion training procedures have changed behaviors in addition to assertiveness. For example, Stake and Pearlman (1980) measured levels of self-esteem in a group of women who underwent group assertion training. Self-esteem increased significantly in this group from pretesting to follow-up. Data obtained from a no-treatment group, which controlled for nonspecific aspects of the training experience thought to affect self-esteem (i.e., a competent woman teacher–leader model and individualized attention in a supportive atmosphere), indicated no differences from pretesting to follow-up.

Group assertion training has been compared with several other strategies. In one such study, Hedquist and Weingold (1970) compared assertion training with a social learning approach that stressed problem solving. The sole response measure was a subjective report of *in vivo* assertion. After six weeks of treatment, both groups showed greater improvement than a control group, but the treatment groups did not differ from each other. At a six-week follow-up, group differences were no longer significant. In contrast, Percell, Berwick and Biegils (1974) reported that group assertion training was more effective than relationship therapy in increasing self-rated assertion and self-acceptance and in decreasing anxiety. But as Rimm (1976) noted, traditional approaches, including relationship therapy, generally require more time than most behavioral approaches. If the number of treatments is limited, as it was in the study by Percell and his associates, such a study is better viewed as a controlled investigation of group assertion training than as a comparison of two bona fide treatments. Thus, results of studies such as these should be interpreted with caution.

Lazarus (1974) has noted that assertion training may be of value in dealing with depression. Lewinsohn and his coworkers (e.g., Lewinsohn & Shaffer, 1971; Libet & Lewinsohn, 1973) have theorized that depression may be largely due to lack of reinforcement, including social reinforcement. In one study (Libet & Lewinsohn, 1973), depressives in a group situation initiated considerably fewer social interactions and were less likely to respond positively to the behaviors of others. In addition, when another group member reinforced (for instance, praised) a depressive, the recipient tended to wait longer before replying, suggesting that depressed people may inadvertently discourage others from providing praise or other forms of social reinforcement.

Group assertion training, then, would seem to be a logical treatment strategy for depressives, and research findings support this notion. LaPointe and Mimm (1980) compared assertion training with a cognitive training package derived from Beck (1967a). The female subjects, respondents to a newspaper ad, were seen over a six-week period for two hours per week. Following treatment, subjects in both the assertion training and the cognitive treatments obtained significant decreases in self-reported depression. But a third group of subjects, who had undergone an insight (placebo) treatment, reported no such decreases. Further, on subjective mood ratings, 90 percent of the assertion training subjects reported improvement, compared with 83 percent of those receiving cognitive therapy and only 36 percent of the placebo group. The results of the two-month follow-up are difficult to interpret: while improvement on self-reported depression was maintained for both assertion and cognitive groups, the placebo subjects showed comparable low scores. Sanchez, Lewinsohn, and Larson (1980) also assessed the effects of assertion training on depression. The investigators gave depressed outpatients either group assertion training—which included modeling, behavioral rehearsal, feedback, and homework—or "traditional" outpatient group psychotherapy, using an insight orientation. The groups met for 90 minutes twice weekly for five weeks. Attendance at both groups was 70 percent or greater. Results indicated that assertion training, as compared to traditional psychotherapy, produced both significantly greater increases in self-reported assertiveness and significantly greater decreases in depression.

Several efforts investigating the efficacy of group procedures have focused on variations in the training techniques. For instance, Berah (1981) studied the effects of scheduling on group training. Her results indicate that there were no differences in the effectiveness of a massed practice group, which underwent six hours of assertion training on each of two consecutive days; a distributed practice group, which met twice weekly for 90-minute sessions; and a combination group, which underwent an initial six-hour session, followed by four weekly 90-minute sessions, although all assertion groups showed greater increases in assertiveness than a no-treatment group. These data suggest that the scheduling of sessions can be guided by convenience without loss of effectiveness.

In another study, Huey and Rank (1984) compared the effects of counselor-led and peer-led group assertion training on black adolescent males who were selected for their aggressive classroom behavior. The investigators found that although both counselor-led and peer-led assertion groups were more effective than comparison groups in reducing aggressive classroom behavior and increasing assertive behavior, there were no differences between the two assertion training groups.

Finally, Kaplan (1982) compared behavioral, cognitive, and behavioral-cognitive group procedures. As was often the case for individual treatment (e.g., Hammen et al., 1980), there were no differences among the assertion training groups on a variety of self-report and behavioral measures. Moreover, each of the assertion training groups were significantly more effective than a placebo treatment group in increasing assertive behavior. Interestingly, Kaplan found that only participants in the cognitive groups increased their *positive* cognitions about assertion, whereas participants in both the cognitive and behavioral groups decreased their negative cognitions. Overall, however, each of the three groups was equally effective in increasing assertiveness.

In summary, we can draw three general conclusions. First, it is evident that group procedures may be used successfully for a variety of target problems and with different populations. Second, when compared with commonly used therapies, group assertion training appears to be equally effective both in increasing assertiveness and in decreasing depression. Finally, no distinct superiority reliably emerges for any specific type of group assertion training procedure.

4

Modeling and Behavior Rehearsal Procedures

Introduction

The consideration and use of modeling procedures as a formal technique in behavior therapy began in the late 1950s. Although there is a relatively broad range of clinical procedures by which modeling can effectively alter problem behaviors and promote adaptive ones, the basic modeling procedure is quite simple. It involves exposing the client to one or more other individuals—actually present (live), filmed (symbolic), or even imagined—who demonstrate behaviors that the client wishes to adopt. Exposure to models also includes exposure to the cues and situations that surround the model's behavior, so that not only the behavior but also its relationship (appropriateness) to relevant stimuli are demonstrated. The procedure also encourages the client to make changes in his or her affective and attitudinal determinants and correlates of these behaviors (Bandura, 1977b; Bandura, Adams, & Beyer, 1977; Bandura, Jeffery, & Gajdos, 1975). For example, a snake-phobic patient, after observing a model perform approach behaviors toward a snake (picking it up, letting it crawl around in his lap), would be expected to show not only an increase in the approach behaviors he is willing to perform toward the snake, but also an increase in feelings of personal competence regarding potential en-

counters with the reptile and a decrease or total elimination of the fear he previously felt toward snakes. To take another example, a client fearful of social situations and unskilled in self-presentation may easily acquire such skills by observing models, practicing the skills covertly by imagining herself interacting with others, and subsequently participating in social interactions (e.g., job interviews) more effectively *and* with less anxiety.

Clinicians and researchers have published a substantial number of reports regarding the use of modeling procedures in treating a remarkably broad variety of behavior problems. The range of disorders, problem behaviors, or needed skill training that modeling procedures have addressed includes assertion training—see also Chapter 3 (Kazdin, 1982; Pentz & Kazdin, 1982); depression (Frame, Matson, Sonis, Fialkoo, & Kazdin, 1982); medical and dental fears (Bernstein & Kleinknecht, 1982; Roberts, Wartele, Boone, Ginther, & Elkins, 1981); alcoholism (DeRicco & Neimann, 1980; Kendall & Finch, 1980); self-control skills in children—(impulsivity) (Kendall & Braswell, 1982); test anxiety (Harris & Johnson, 1980); effective parenting (Webster-Stratton, 1982); sexual dysfunction (Nemetz, Craig, & Reith, 1978); gender identity confusion in children (Hay, Barlow, & Hay, 1981); social skills training (Matson, 1982); and phobias (Biran & Wilson, 1981).

131

Basic Functions Modeling Procedures May Serve

There are four basic functions that modeling procedures serve. By observing a model, a client can learn new, appropriate behavior patterns; thus, modeling can serve an *acquisition* function. Instances of a client actually acquiring totally new or novel behavior patterns simply by observing a model are quite rare. (The use of modeling to promote the initial acquisition of language in an autistic or psychotic child [Lovaas, Berberich, Kassorla, Klynn, & Meisel, 1966; Risely & Wolf, 1967] is an example of this.) Rather, modeling behavior more commonly provides social *facilitation* of that behavior by inducing the client to perform it at more appropriate times, in more appropriate ways, or toward more appropriate people. Modeling may also lead to the *disinhibition* of behaviors that the client has avoided because of fear or anxiety. And, while disinhibiting behaviors, modeling may promote the *vicarious* and *direct extinction* of the fear or other emotional reactions associated with the person, animal, or object toward which the behavior was directed.

Much of the early work with modeling procedures concentrated on the elimination of phobias or fearful behavior by exposure to models, and hence was involved primarily with the disinhibition of approach behaviors toward the feared stimuli and the vicarious extinction of that fear (e.g., Bandura, Grusec, & Menlove, 1967b, 1968; Ritter, 1968a, 1968b, 1969a, 1969b, 1969c). The most obvious interpretation of modeling would lead one to expect that it is a technique limited to the treatment of behavior deficits; that is, it is for individuals whose repertoire of social behaviors is so deficient that they are unable to, or are inhibited from, behaving appropriately in certain circumstances. However, the range of behavior problems modeling may be used to treat is extremely broad. For example, problem behaviors may be eliminated by instilling alternative behaviors that are incompatible with the problem behaviors (see Chittenden, 1942; O'Connor, 1969, to be discussed later). Modeling is also an effective technique for eliminating the fears and anxieties associated with avoidance behavior. Evidence shows that avoidance behaviors motivated by fears are not eliminated simply by replacing them with alternative, incompatible approach behaviors. Rather, as we discuss later, exposure to fearless models produces vicarious extinction of the fear and anxiety that promote the phobic avoidance behaviors (Bandura, Blanchard, & Ritter, 1969).

Although we will not deal with it in detail here, we should note that therapists have also studied the role of modeling in the etiology of behavior problems. For example, Turkat (1982) has demonstrated that reactions to physical disease, such as the avoidance of work, are influenced by the degree to which the patient's parents were work-avoidant when ill, and such patients also report higher medical utilization rates and a poorer quality of life. Garlington and Derico (1977) have also demonstrated how peer models may influence drinking behavior (both by modeling and social reinforcement) and thus play a potential role in the etiology of drinking-related disorders, such as alcoholism. These investigators found that college student subjects exposed to a peer confederate who varied the rate at which he drank beer closely matched their own drinking rates to the confederate's. This occurred whether the modeled drinking rate was either higher than the subject's—thus potentially leading to excessive consumption—or lower, which suggests the possible therapeutic uses of modeling. A study by Caudill and Lipscomb (1980) provides evidence that this may be the case. These investigators found that alcoholics who observed a confederate drink wine at high and low rates altered their own wine consumption accordingly. There is some indication that alcoholics are not as influenced by low-rate models (Caudill & Lipscomb, 1980; DeRicco & Niemann, 1982), but other findings suggest that the inclusion of

Figure 4–1 *Component processes proposed by Bandura in a social learning analysis of observational learning and imitative performance.*

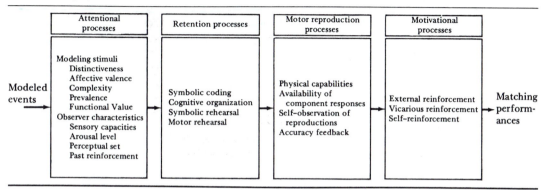

From Bandura (1977b).

Two primary types of characteristics of a modeling setting contribute to its effectiveness for securing and maintaining the attention of an observer: the characteristics and behaviors of the model and the characteristics of the observer. Within the category of modeling stimulus characteristics that should affect attention, the distinctiveness of the model or the behavior needs little discussion: attention-getting models or attention-getting behaviors get attention! There are some trade-offs, however. A model who is *distinctive* by being unusual—a clown for children, professorial-looking gentleman for adults—may promote attention but detract from subsequent imitative responses if he is perceived as too dissimilar from the observer. Note that attention-securing characteristics of a modeling *procedure* that enhance the distinctiveness of the model or of the behaviors in question need not involve the distinctiveness of the model or the behaviors per se if an observer's attention is secured in others ways (viz., when an autistic child is slapped on the thigh during a language learning session in order to orient the child to the model who is providing the words and attempting to instill them in the child's other vocabulary). Other procedural aspects of the modeling situation that may affect attention include

1. The *affective valence* of the behavior being demonstrated. Is it a pleasant behavior to perform, or is it one that has intrinsic or anxiety-provoking aversive properties, such as assertiveness for a mild-mannered client?

2. The *complexity* of the behavior pattern (a complex sequence of behaviors may need to be broken down into shorter, simpler components) and the functional value of the behavior for the observer. Is it a behavior that is needed for success in his job?

3. The *prevalence of models* exhibiting the behavior. If all the nurses on a ward display assertiveness toward one another in securing favors, at the very least inadvertent attention is likely.

The selection of model characteristics that will be particularly salient or effective for a given client is a difficult task and often cannot be made accurately on an a priori basis using clinical judgment. A priori or clinical judgments often reflect the personal theories of the clinician, either those he or she holds about personality factors or more general social theories about the development of behavior patterns and attentional sensitivities, and these personal theories may not be totally valid or accurate. The best criterion for the selection of any aspect of treatments is an empirical testing of the particular client for sensitivities, proclivities, characteristics, and so forth.

A client's attention to modeled events is also affected by characteristics of the observer. Physical characteristics are important: the observer must be able to see and hear the model in order to perceive the modeled stimuli. There is certain to be an optimum level of arousal—hyperanxious individuals may be as inattentive as those who are heavily drugged, catatonic, or nearly asleep. And the observer's focus (knowing what to look for) is also important: an individual who is looking for particular modeled behaviors will be more likely to attend and focus properly upon them—the modeling of asking a woman for a date will be more effective if the client is prepared to observe how nicely the model is dressed as well as how skillfully he puts his verbal request. Finally, attention to models may be considered an appropriate, adaptive behavior whose own contingencies will affect how well it is accomplished. Individuals with behavior problems who are often in contact with others whose behavior is more appropriate can be encouraged to attend to the behavior of those models by providing positive contingent consequences for social attention. This point is not an unimportant one for the utilization of modeling procedures, since many individuals with behavior problems or deficits are surrounded in everyday life by others who are behaving appropriately and thus constitute appropriate models if properly attended to. Effective models can be those on television and in movies as well as the actual individuals with whom a client interacts or whom a client observes.

There are two main classes of processes that enhance an observer's retention of modeled behavior patterns: coding or organization, and rehearsal or practice. An individual's ability to describe behavior in words provides a unique cognitive capability that can enhance learning and retention significantly. *Symbolic coding* describes any sort of procedure that reduces an observed behavior to a form that can be easily retained. For example, describing an action in words constitutes symbolic coding, as when a film narrative follows an actor's behavior (something that a therapist could do during a live modeling session) or when an observer describes (either covertly in thought or overtly to someone else) what he or she is seeing.

Organizational factors can be implicit in any verbal coding and are also likely to affect retention. An observer is most likely to remember and subsequently to execute a behavior pattern that "makes sense" by being relatable to something that is already known. For example, while a client is observing a model display appropriate interaction with a member of the opposite sex, the therapist might comment, "Notice how he leans forward when she is talking, clearly listening with interest, and how he periodically makes direct eye contact with her and smiles, showing an obvious enjoyment in the conversation." The descriptive terms "interest" and "enjoyment" not only provide a symbolic code for the particular behaviors being displayed but also integrate the appropriate behaviors for the specific modeling context into the broad classes of behavior connoting interest and enjoyment. This allows the observer to be somewhat creative in an actual situation, because it draws other behavioral capabilities he or she may have that also connote interest and enjoyment.

Rehearsal or practice is another component of successful modeling that can not only promote retention of a modeled behavior pattern but can also allow for progressively more accurate and more effective delivery in the natural context. As Figure 4-1 indicates, rehearsal may be covert and symbolic or it may be totally overt (motor). Overt behavioral (or "motor") rehearsal is simply practice and can be accomplished through role playing, in which the client draws upon the modeling to create appropriate role behavior and the therapist or another individual—or even several individuals (e.g., in a group therapy context)—adopts complementary roles.

Symbolic rehearsal has not been studied extensively, perhaps because it seems eminently reasonable to expect that thinking back over a modeled behavior sequence would allow additional opportunities to provide a symbolic code for various constituent behaviors and the detection of points at which the behavior of the model was not well grasped. Indeed, in an early study, Kazdin (1978) varied the degree to which clients employed a summary verbal code for modeled assertive behavior. He found that covert modeling (imagining an assertive model) that was combined with a verbal code of the modeled behavior influenced both the acquisition and maintenance of the assertive behavior.

The motor reproduction component of Bandura's modeling analysis also may be conceptualized as having two major subcomponents. One deals with the basic capability of an individual to behave in a certain fashion: the goal behavior that is modeled must be one the observer is physically capable of and has the necessary component responses for. Generally, the problem of physical capability seldom arises in a therapeutic encounter designed to promote changes in social and personal behavior, but making certain that a client has the necessary component behaviors for a complex behavior pattern is quite important. Training an autistic child to speak may have to include training in phoneme production before words can be attempted; only after a lexicon has been established can sentence training begin. Similarly, enhancing a shy client's interpersonal skills may require the separate modeling of purely motor and postural behavior toward others (e.g., the "listening interestedly" posture) and of what one says in a given interpersonal context before these two components can be successfully combined into a smooth interpersonal interaction.

The final component in the modeling analysis is devoted entirely to output and includes the processes that will incline an observer to reproduce behavior patterns acquired by observation. The processes proposed by Bandura are entirely based upon reinforcement. The external reinforcement component is simple and straightforward: it can be praise by the therapist for successful and accurate role playing in the treatment context, or it can be the successful performance of the behavior pattern in the natural context (e.g., competent interpersonal behavior resulting in obtaining a date with an attractive woman or man). Indication of the positive consequences that follow the modeled behavior is an important component of the modeling scenario. This provides vicarious reinforcement for the observer, encouraging the person to expect that his or her own behavior will be successful in producing positive consequences if it accurately matches that of the model. Finally, self-evaluative processes provide additional incentive to adopt previously modeled behavior in a natural context. These are most likely to be covert (pride and satisfaction in the accomplishment of new behavioral skills), and as such, may operate as reinforcers. Self-evaluations also provide important feedback of information related to competent behavior. The strong motivational value of any reinforcement accompanying the actual display of skills acquired by modeling underscores the importance of practicing a new skill within the treatment context and carefully planning the first opportunities to display the newfound behavior pattern in the natural context to maximize the likelihood for successful and positive consequences.

An interesting example of some model characteristics that may promote imitative performance in an everyday context is contained in a study that contrasted the effectiveness of various staff members as models of social skills for hospitalized patients. In a hospital setting, one of the most accessible modeling sources is the staff, who may demonstrate a variety of appropriate behaviors and useful social skills in their interaction with one another and with the patients. One therapeutic program (Wallace, Davis, Liberman, & Baker, 1973) included a "social interaction hour" as part of daily ward routine. During this hour, the professional staff modeled appropriate social behavior by attending and participating in various interpersonal activities. To evaluate the effectiveness of staff models, a number of different procedures were successively employed. In addition to a simple attempt to evaluate the effectiveness of model availability by having models present on some occasions and absent on others, the different members of the treatment staff served as models on various occasions so their differential effectiveness could be assessed. The researchers found that the presence and participation of staff at the social interaction hours greatly increased the proportion of patients who participated, and that the nursing staff appeared to be more potent models, producing more participation, than did the remainder of the professional staff (a clinical psychologist and his assistant). This latter finding may have occurred because the nurses had the most direct contact with—and supervisory control over—the patients; the psychologist and his assistant were primarily consultants. Patients thus appeared to be more responsive to models who possessed more "social power" in terms of direct control over daily events, a fact that was clearly demonstrated in early nonclinical research (Bandura, Ross, & Ross, 1963; Rosekrans & Hartup, 1967).

A particularly important factor that may influence the actual adoption or implementation of modeled behaviors is the self-efficacy belief, held by the model. The concept of belief in self-efficacy has been of particular interest since Bandura proposed it in an attempt to identify a common component of different therapeutic interventions that might account for success in treating similar disorders. Self-efficacy belief, in this analysis of modeling processes, might best be considered to transcend or participate in all of the constituent processes. Thus, for example, strong self-efficacy belief would enhance attention (if it existed prior to an instance of modeling), foster coding and covert practice and other retention processes, promote self-monitoring of motor activity, and motivate actual matching performances. In a later section we will give more detailed consideration to self-efficacy processes in behavior change.

Types of Modeling Procedures

Many applications of modeling involve the participation of the client in the modeled behavior immediately after the demonstration by the model, with the therapist reinforcing the client's successful performance. Procedures involving client participation are referred to by a variety of labels. For example, if the modeling sequences involve the systematic, graduated presentation of increasingly difficult behaviors (as they almost always do), the term *graduated modeling* is often used. The parallel of this presentation procedure to that utilized in systematic desensitization is clear. Generally, the senses of the various terms are self-evident:

1. Graduated modeling
2. Guided modeling (usually gradual)
3. Guided modeling with reinforcement
4. Participant modeling (usually gradual)
5. Modeling with guided performance (usually gradual)
6. Contact desensitization
7. Covert modeling (imaginal)
8. Modeling with response-induction aids and self-directed mastery experiences
9. Coping modeling and mastery modeling

"Graduated modeling," "guided modeling," and "guided modeling with reinforcement" usually describe procedures for the acquisition or facilitation of new patterns of behavior. "Participant modeling" and "contact desensitization" usually describe procedures dealing with fear, anxiety, and avoidance behaviors. Of course, the systematic, gradual manner in which fearless models demonstrate progressively more daring behavior is indeed gradual or graduated, so the term *graduated modeling* is applicable as well, although it is not typically used. Some use the term *participant modeling;* others prefer *contact desensitization.* Procedures termed "contact desensitization" invariably involve body contact with the therapist in the guiding of the client's participation, and thus may also be termed "modeling with guided performance." For example, in climbing a ladder following a model's demonstration, an acrophobic may be assisted by the model, who puts her hand around the client's waist. Or a model, after interacting closely with a snake, may place the client's hand on his, gradually moving it onto the snake. While there may be cogent reasons for separating modeling procedures that involve physical contact with the model from those that involve more distant demonstration and independent participation by the client, the importance of this distinction awaits empirical confirmation.

Covert modeling is a purely imaginal procedure in which a client uses descriptions and instructions about appropriate behavior to construct an image of a model performing the target behaviors. Response induction aids—the inclusion of materials or procedures designed to aid a client in performing a desired response (e.g., allowing a snake-phobic individual to wear heavy gloves when first handling a snake during participant modeling)—have also been used, as have the inclusion of time periods during the course of treatment when a client can practice the target behaviors independently and can direct his own self-mastery over the behavior problem.

Finally, researchers have contrasted the effectiveness of "mastery" models, who demonstrate target behaviors without error or trepidation, with that of "coping" models, who demonstrate initially flawed and hesitant behavior but gradually improve as they cope with new demands (e.g., Roberts, Wurtele, Boone, Ginther, & Elkins, 1982). In this same vein, studies have shown that models who demonstrate the desired behavior only intermittently (e.g., who do not always respond in an assertive fashion) are essentially as effective as models who are totally consistent in their behavior (Brody, Lahey, & Combs, 1978). This finding indicates that

research studies, which tend to employ consistent modeling cues, can be generalized to natural settings, in which modeling stimuli are likely to be irregular or inconsistent.

In general, most procedures can be reduced to a form of simple modeling (observation of a model), participant modeling (with some enacting of target behaviors during a modeling sequence), or covert modeling (purely imaginal), and these are the terms that will be in primary use throughout the chapter. Descriptions of the actual procedures used in a given case study or investigation will make clear the degree to which graduated performance, self-mastery experiences, reinforcement, or other ancillary components are included.

Early Research on Modeling Procedures Although intense and sustained interest in modeling as a behavior change procedure did not begin until the early 1960s, the fact that social learning could readily occur through the observation of others had long been recognized (e.g., Miller & Dollard, 1941). In fact, a most interesting and informative study of the effectiveness of modeling with children occurred as early as a half century ago.

Chittenden (1942) used symbolic models to alter children's hyperaggressive reactions to frustration, replacing them with cooperative, constructive behaviors in the same circumstances. The children selected for treatment were excessively domineering and hyperaggressive. Tests of aggressive tendencies, and for the relative lack of cooperative behaviors, included (a) situations in which two children were placed in a room with only one valued and attractive toy, and (b) behavior observations of the children in a nursery school setting. The treatment for one group of these hyperaggressive children consisted of the observation and discussion of 11 15-minute playlets involving dolls. In each little play, dolls representing preschool children were depicted in interpersonal conflicts common to the children of that age, and the plot of the playlet then demonstrated both an aggressive and a nonaggressive, cooperative solution to the problem. The *consequences* of these two solutions differed radically: aggression was shown to lead to unpleasant consequences, while cooperation was depicted as resulting in rewarding circumstances (cf. Bandura, 1965). For example, in one playlet involving a conflict between two boys over a wagon, the aggressive solution depicted a fight during which the wagon was broken. The cooperative solution involved the two boys' taking turns playing with the wagon, obviously enjoying themselves as they played.

The results, shown in Figure 4–2, are quite clear. Compared with a pretest measure of both cooperativeness and aggressiveness, children were much less domineering and substantially more cooperative after viewing the series of playlets. The investigators made these observations in a situation in which children found themselves in a room with another child, but with only one toy. Other observations also found an increase in cooperativeness and a decrease in aggression, which extended to typical real-life social situations. Another important aspect of this experiment was the inclusion of a follow-up observation conducted 30 days after treatment. Ratings of behavior in the nursery school indicated that the children were maintaining the decreases in aggressiveness and increases in cooperation. Modeling procedures can also be adapted for use in modifying the ag-

Figure 4–2 *Amount of cooperative and dominating behavior displayed by hyperaggressive children in a nursery school before and after exposure to symbolic modeling treatment.*

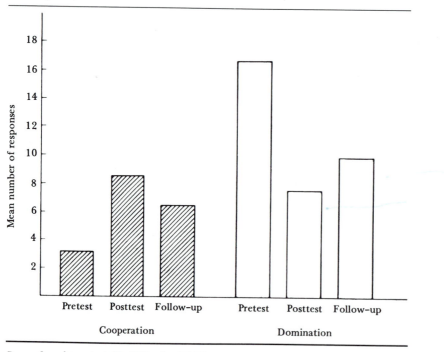

Drawn from data reported by Chittenden (1942).

gressive behavior of older children (see Gittelman, 1965). This procedure frequently includes the enactment of irritating and aggression-provoking situations along with the modeling of nonaggressive ways of coping with them.

Acquisition and Facilitation of New Behavior Patterns by Modeling

Before detailing procedures for the acquisition and facilitation of new behavior patterns, we first should discuss procedures for the training of imitation itself as a generalized response. In the case of severely retarded or psychotic patients, behavior patterns already established may include only repetitive, bizarre, meaningless, or self-stimulatory behavior, accompanied by attention and responsiveness to others that is minimal or totally absent. In other cases, minimal social responsiveness may not include a tendency to imitate or acquire any new behavior patterns by observing others. In these instances, training in imitation itself is a prerequisite to the use of modeling procedures to teach new behavior patterns.

Reinforcement Training of Imitative Responses

Individuals who work with severely disturbed or retarded clients, either adults or children, may encounter the problematic instance of a client who shows no propensity or ability to imitate at all. In such instances, the therapist may find it necessary to teach the client to imitate modeled responses or to use a method to increase imitation. The question, then, is whether or not it is possible to influence the rate of imitation using reinforcement techniques.

Baer, Peterson, and Sherman (1967), for example, worked with three 9- to 12-year-old severely retarded children who evidenced no imitation whatsoever in their daily interactions with others. Furthermore, when an adult engaged the children in extended play, these children steadfastly failed to imitate such simple responses as clapping hands or waving, even though it was obvious that the responses were clearly within their capability.

Training was conducted during mealtime, once or twice a day, three to five times a week. The experimenter would say "Do this" and would model a simple response such as raising his arm. Any response by the child that vaguely resembled arm raising would be rewarded by food, which was delivered a spoonful at a time. The experimenter also said "Good!" just before putting the spoon into the subject's mouth. If the child made no response, the experimenter would gently guide the child's arm through the appropriate motion and then offer the reward. Gradually such assistance was faded out. After each child demonstrated the reliable imitation of one response, he was taught to imitate another one. For one subject, 130 responses were demonstrated.

Out of the lengthy series of different responses demonstrated to each child, most imitation was reinforced. For some imitative responses, however, there was no delivery of food; the experimenter merely said "Good!" and then demonstrated the next response. Only responses that were imitated upon their first demonstration received this treatment.

After a series of responses was demonstrated and their imitation (even if guided) was reinforced, the children tended to imitate new behaviors demonstrated by the experimenter at their first demonstration. Furthermore, as long as *some* of the imitative responses were reinforced, the children continued to imitate essentially *every* new response demonstrated. At a later point in the experiment, when each child was imitating nearly every demonstrated response, the experimenter began reinforcing other responses performed by the child, responses that were *not* imitative. With this change in reinforcing procedure, the children's imitation behavior rapidly decreased, until after a short while they were imitating almost none of the experimenter's demonstrated responses.

Reinstatement of the contingency produced a rapid reacquisition of the tendency to imitate. The reversal and reinstatement periods indicated that reinforcement did indeed control imitative behavior.

Other work has confirmed that seriously debilitated patients, both adults and children, who show a deficit in learning by imitation can be taught via reinforcement procedures to acquire new behavior patterns and skills through modeling (Gresham & Nagle, 1980; Matson, 1982; Sarason & Sarason, 1981). For example, following earlier work by Goldstein and his colleagues (Goldstein et al., 1973; Gutride, Goldstein, & Hunter, 1973), Chartier, Ainley, and Voss (1976) demonstrated the effectiveness of vicarious reinforcement for enhancing the imitative adoption of socially appropriate behaviors in chronic psychotic patients (average hospitalization: 15 years). In this study, patients viewed a seven-minute videotape twice. Then the researchers observed and recorded the frequency of the patients' socially appropriate behaviors: initiating conversations, talking, maintaining eye contact, and maintaining an appropriate interactive posture (leaning forward).

The modeling scenes on the videotape depicted an interaction between a young white female and a young white male, in a patient role, being interviewed. Some modeling episodes depicted appropriate social interaction on the part of the patient: frequent eye contact, initiation of exchanges, nods, smiles, and complete responses to inquiries. Other episodes depicted inappropriate behavior by the model patient: infrequent and brief replies, and no eye contact or smiles. In some episodes, the interviewer rewarded model patient behavior with praise for individual behaviors and a gift of cigarettes and candy at the end of the interview; in others, the interviewer punished the model patient behavior by behaving in a curt and rude fashion and withholding the cigarettes and candy at the end; in still other episodes, the model patient behavior produced no noteworthy reactions from the interviewer.

In general, two of the modeling conditions enhanced socially appropriate behavior in the patients who viewed the videotape: seeing examples of *inappropriate behavior* that elicited *punishing* reactions from the model interviewer. Thus, not only did vicarious consequences enhance generalized imitation, but here was specific evidence that the "negative" modeling effect enhanced proper behavior. Modeling incorrect or undesired behaviors is a precarious procedure because it remains for the observer to conclude what alternative behaviors there are to the ones for which the model is being punished and then to respond accordingly. When there are many alternatives to an inappropriate behavior, not all of which are appropriate responses, negative modeling may not achieve the desired effect of shifting behavior away from the inappropriate and toward the appropriate. On the other hand, when there are few alternatives to an undesired or inappropriate behavior, the likelihood is probably much higher that an observer will indeed respond to the depiction of inappropriate, punished behavior by shifting his own response in the proper direction. Children as young as 3 and 4 years can profit from negative modeling when the number of alternative behaviors is not great (Masters, Gordon, & Clark, 1976). For example, when a model is confronted with two alternative behaviors (such as crossing at the light or in the middle of the block), displaying one and receiving negative consequences (crossing in the middle of the block and nearly being hit by a car) may lead to an observer's adopting the clear alternative behavior.

In a study concerned with the training of institutionalized retarded children to enhance their social imitation, Marburg, Houston, & Holmes (1976) examined the effects of having a model directly reinforce children for imitative responding. In this investigation, children encountered either the same model over three sessions or a different model for each of the three sessions, so that the effects of multiple models could be assessed. The researchers found that over the three sessions the children progressively increased the number of modeled behaviors that they imitated; and thus, exposure to multiple models neither enhanced nor reduced the children's learning to imitate. Within each session, there was a small set of modeled behaviors for which the children were not reinforced if imitation was shown. The children's tendency to imitate such nonreinforced behaviors was taken as evidence of generalization of the imitative tendency. Over the three sessions, the children did indeed increase their imitation of nonreinforced behaviors, and the use of multiple models significantly increased the acquisition of a generalized tendency to imitate. Additionally, when the children's tendencies to imitate a totally new model were assessed in a posttest, the observers found that previous exposure to multiple models inclined the children to be imitatively responsive to new individuals whose behavior they observed. These results, when combined with other findings—such as those from Bandura and Menlove (1968), which shows that multiple models increase the likelihood that phobic children will engage in the most fearless approach behavior—indicate that the use of multiple models is particularly advisable when generalization to new models or behaviors is desired (as in the instance above, where imitation itself was the goal response) or when the most feared behavior within a phobia is one of the outcome goals of treatment.

As mentioned earlier, it is probably only in rare instances that *totally* new behavior patterns are acquired by modeling (or any other procedure, for that matter). Most frequently, patients are capable of performing some elements of desired behavior patterns, but their performance is inhibited by fear or anxiety. Or the behavior patterns are only weakly elicited by appropriate stimuli or so poorly practiced that their infrequent occurrence is ineffective, meets punishing consequences, and has thus led to total nonperformance (extinction or suppression). Nevertheless, the facilitation or organization of adaptive behavior patterns also includes the acquisition of some behavior elements, and to some extent the *patterning* or organization of the elements may be new and therefore "acquired." In the sections that follow, most applications of modeling will be targeted to the development of new patterns of responding that replace maladaptive ones or that fill a major deficiency in behavioral capability. However, we will not dwell upon whether acquisition or facilitation is occurring, since the central issue is the consideration of the effectiveness of various modeling procedures in behavior change.

Modeling With Reinforced Guided Performance

One class of behavior is occasionally totally absent, and any form of modeling treatment for it truly involves acquisition. We are speaking here of the acquisition of language skills by mute psychotic children. The modeling procedure utilized in the treatment of these children has been labeled *modeling with reinforced guided performance* (Bandura, 1971). This procedure is similar to modeling with guided participation, which we discuss later in the chapter. In essence, this technique involves the modeling of a desired behavior (in this case, a sound or word), possibly guiding the patient's performance (e.g., by shaping the mouth into an "O" for production of the "oh" sound—what is termed a "manual prompt"), and reinforcing the behaviors of the patient that re-create or approximate the modeled behavior. When working with patients who have extreme deficiencies in their behavioral repertoires, it may even be necessary to use specific means to gain their attention and to train them to be responsive to modeling cues.

In treating psychotic children (or other patients whose behavioral repertoires are extraordinarily limited or whose contact with the environment is poor), initial treatment usually aims toward increasing the scope of their social and intellectual capabilities—a goal that ultimately involves the development of linguistic skills. Let us consider closely the pioneering procedure utilized by Lovaas and his colleagues for the establishment of linguistic competencies in autistic children (Lovaas, Berberich, Kassorla, Klynn, & Meisel, 1966; Lovaas, Berberich, Perloff, & Schaeffer, 1966; Lovaas, Dumont, Klynn, & Meisel, 1966; Lovaas, Freitag, Nelson, & Whalen, 1967).

In this procedure, the therapist confronts the child, sitting directly in front of him at close quarters. This placement maximizes the likelihood that the child will attend to the responses being modeled by the therapist. Continued attention is maintained by the therapist's physically reorienting the child if he turns away. Episodes of bizarre or self-stimulatory behavior are interrupted and halted by behaviors on the part of the therapist to command the child's attention, such as a sharp word or even a slap on the thigh. A film is available (Lovaas, 1966) that illustrates this procedure effectively. The film also contains striking examples of the effectiveness of these procedures. For example, in one instance, a girl is being asked to name the color of a yellow crayon. As the therapist attempts to elicit this response from the girl, she behaves in an increasingly bizarre fashion, flapping her arms and grimacing. The therapist then slaps her on the thigh and again attempts to elicit the name of the color, and the girl responds, "Yellow," in a calm and straight-forward manner.

Figure 4-3 depicts the course of verbal imitation in a previously mute autistic child. This case is especially illustrative since it demonstrates how, when the acquisition of a totally new and complex behavior pattern is required, treatment must begin with the modeling of simple components of the desired complex response (note the similarity to the successive-approximations procedure discussed in Chapter 5). In this instance, "baby" was modeled for several days; simple sounds such as "e" and "pa" were imitated first. Furthermore, initial imitation may not occur immediately, and in this example even the simplest sounds were not imitated during the first 10 days of treatment. It seems possible that "pa" plus "e" were elements whose similarity to the component sounds of "baby" aided in the capability of imitating that word. Once some word imitation had occurred, the rate of subsequent imitation of new words indicated that mute children may possess greater linguistic competence than is generally thought. Nonetheless, the common element in the acquisition of new linguistic units is the prior modeling of those sounds and words.

Another procedure for initial word learning described by Humphrey (1966) has been reported by Bandura (1969). In this procedure, children sit in a darkened room and view pictures of objects projected on a screen, while hearing the appropriate word through earphones. Learning presumably involves the linkage of the verbally modeled labels to the visually modeled objects. At first the child may not be required to reproduce the words himself. Subsequently, however, the individual may be rewarded for correct productions of the acquired words. The pictures presented may include people, animals, objects, or even activities. Humphrey (1966) presented slides depicting the patients themselves interacting with peers in natural settings.

The procedures discussed thus far are not limited to the treatment of autism in children. Quite similar methods have been used in the treatment of echolalic children (Coleman & Stedman, 1974; Risely & Wolf, 1967) and young children whose speech is deficient or defective (Sloane, Johnston, & Harris, 1968). You may wish to consult these sources for detailed procedural descriptions.)

When simple imitation occurs, and when the child begins to show verbal responsiveness to commands and requests, these behaviors are typically reinforced. For example, in training competence in language skills, the initial task is acquisition of words and sentences and the use of these words and sentences to label appropriate objects and actions. The use of contingent reward increases the likelihood that the child will attend, imitate (accurately), and subsequently use the acquired language skills. Lovaas (1967) has shown clearly how the use of con-

Figure 4–3 *Growth of verbal imitation during the initial 26 days of treatment by an autistic child who was previously mute.*

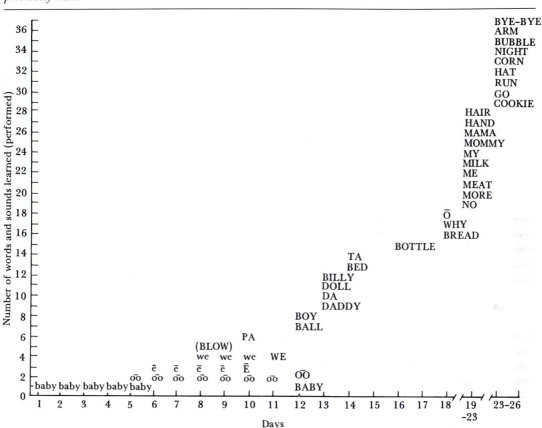

From Lovaas, Berberich, Perloff, and Schaeffer (1966).

tingent reward increases the accuracy of imitative responding. As we can see in Figure 4-4, when an autistic child was rewarded for the accurate imitation of modeled responses, there was increased correct imitation; when reinforcement was *not* contingent on the child's imitative responding, accurate imitation clearly decreased.

The use of reinforcement with modeling procedures is important in the expansion of language abilities into the realm of abstract con-

ceptual function, especially as this is contained in language. For example, consider therapeutic procedures designed to teach a child prepositional constructions and to respond to abstract queries from others. Initially the child might be given an instruction to put a toy "on the table." If he fails to respond appropriately, the therapist may repeat the request while guiding the child's hand, executing the behavior for him and, in the process, illustrating the "meaning" of the preposition. In this instance, we might say

Figure 4–4 *Proportions of modeled responses correctly and incorrectly reproduced by an autistic child as a function of reward contingency: during periods when rewards were contingent on the correct reproduction of the modeled response and when they were contingent on the passage of a certain amount of time (□—□: correct R; △---△: incorrect R).*

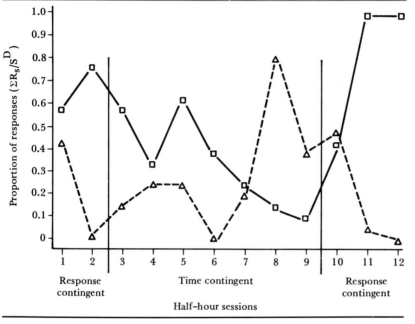

From Lovaas (1967).

that the meaning is modeled by the child's observation of his own guided behavior. Subsequently, the therapist will arrange the objects so that an accurate verbal description of their placement requires use of the preposition. In the process of training, various relationships (on, in, over, on top of, under, beneath, near, away from, etc.) will be modeled, a procedure that encourages the child to generalize his experience and to form a rule for the use of prepositional phrases. These same general procedures may be used to facilitate the child's acquisition of increasingly complex linguistic and conceptual capabilities, including verbal responding to abstract queries, such as "What did you do yesterday?" or "Where are you going to-

morrow?" Careful planning allows the initial teaching of such cognitive skills to involve queries that can be modeled (e.g., "What did you do yesterday?" at first could be responded to by acting out the answer).

Since speech is not only a linguistic-cognitive skill but a social skill as well, language training must involve verbal social interaction and appropriate spontaneous speech. Procedures for training these functions in mute children can also apply to patients who are not mute but whose speech lacks social appropriateness. In this training procedure, the goals include the use of acquired language skills to express feelings and desires, to ask for and communicate information, and in general to use speech to initiate and maintain social interaction. Withholding desired objects from the child or preventing desired activities creates an occasion for the child to verbalize his or her desires. The subsequent granting of these wishes constitutes reinforcement for the elicited verbal behavior. Encouraging patients to tell stories concerning pictures and to venture opinions, predictions, and comments concerning the persons and activities represented develops narrative skills. Again, gradually more complex and novel recountings should be rewarded. After specific training of this sort, the individual may be guided into real social interactions with other individuals whose approval and friendly social responsiveness will continue to reinforce appropriate social verbal behavior.

We have concentrated on the example of linguistic skills for two reasons: such skills are a prerequisite to appropriate social interaction, and the systematic application of both modeling and reinforcement procedures is a good example of how the *combined* or multimodal use of behavior techniques works effectively with behavior problems. The combination of modeling and reinforcement procedures is effective in training appropriate social behaviors other than those intimately linked to language. The general procedures remain the same: obtain the patient's attention, and illustrate the behaviors by modeling. Then, often in steps of increasing difficulty (again, compare graduated modeling, discussed later in the chapter), physically guide behavior that is difficult to match. Next, reinforce behaviors that the individual initiates in the appropriate circumstances.

Guided Behavior Rehearsal

Bandura (1971) proposed that the impact of modeling will be maximized if the client follows it by practice or rehearsal that is guided toward the most accurate or skillful reproduction of modeled acts. This practice is clearly more beneficial when done in a natural context than in the therapist's office. Ascher and Phillips (1975) reported a treatment procedure for individuals lacking in social skills that involves the recruitment of nonprofessional, socially competent individuals to serve as both models and guides. In this program, the therapist recruits a model-guide who is similar to the patient in such characteristics as age, sex, socioeconomic status (SES) level, and occupation. The model-guide is introduced to the patient during regularly scheduled sessions with the primary therapist and then begins the modeling component of treatment. The therapist and guide jointly plan details of modeling and shaping the client's behavior, and the guide may accompany the client into situations that cause him great difficulty, modeling the appropriate behavior and then reinforcing the patient's efforts, attempting to shape improvement. Prior to a modeling interlude, the therapist may also use imaginal desensitization to reduce any anticipatory anxiety that may occur in the actual situation. This treatment program thus provides a good example of the combination of modeling procedures with other behavior therapy techniques. In their proposal of the technique, Ascher and Phillips (1975) provided four case illustrations of the effective treatment of disorders ranging from severe and inappropriate procrastination to the elimination of socially inappropriate self-deprecation and negativism.

Guided behavior rehearsal has been implemented in a number of innovative ways. In one investigation, a procedure termed "rehearsal modeling" was used (McCordick, Kaplan, Finn, & Smith, 1979). In this study, groups of test-anxious students received a core treatment of cognitive behavior modification (Meichenbaum, 1972) plus other study skills training, observation of a videotaped model, or a rehearsal modeling. After observing the videotaped model, each student in turn modeled the coping behavior he or she had just observed for other students in their group. The rehearsal led these students to report significantly less test anxiety than did those in any of the other treatment conditions. In another study, Kendall and Finch (1978) treated disturbed children for behavioral impulsivity. Children who were taught verbal self-instructions via a modeling procedure and then experienced a response-cost for erroneous task performance were found to slow their performance, decrease their errors, and be rated as less impulsive by classroom teachers. This study illustrates how rehearsal can include an ancillary behavioral treatment procedure, in this case involving contingency management.

Modeling is also useful to facilitate patterns of behavior that are seldom performed or that have been replaced by problematic behavior. Thus, less frequent but more appropriate behavior patterns may be strengthened by modeling and utilized as an incompatible response in the elimination of the more common problem behaviors. Withdrawal or isolation behaviors and, at the other extreme, aggressive behaviors are two good examples of behavior patterns in children that have been treated in this manner. As we shall see later in a detailed example, anxiety over self-disclosure has been treated in adults, with particular success (e.g., Bruch, 1975; Scheiderer, 1977).

The combination of modeling and reinforcement procedures has been used to facilitate needed behaviors and competencies in the treatment of delinquents. In one instance involving delinquent boys (Sarason & Ganzer, 1969), methods of coping with common problem situations were demonstrated by models and then rehearsed and perfected. A variety of complex skills was included, such as self-control, coping with job demands, and interacting with authority figures, as well as handling negative influences from peers. Finally, it has also been found that contingency management procedures concentrated on one member of a group produce behavior changes in others who observe that individual.

The Use of Modeling for Skill Facilitation

There is a growing literature illustrating the effectiveness of modeling for the facilitation (and to some extent the acquisition) of many different

types of skills, including social skills, cognitive and problem-solving skills, self-control skills, safety skills, parenting skills, and health behavior or medical self-help skills. In recent years there has been a particular emphasis on behavioral treatment procedures to facilitate social skills. Although contingency management has been a common technique for this purpose, many studies have reported modeling to be effective.

Eisler, Blanchard, Fitts, and Williams (1978) contrasted social skills training with and without a modeling component and found that modeling was essential to teach social skills to psychotic patients, though it appeared unnecessary for nonpsychotics. This probably illustrates more the importance of its acquisition function for this population and less its facilitative use. Matson (1982) found that modeling was effective in training retarded adults in conversation skills only when it was part of an "independence training" package that also included social reinforcement, instruction, performance feedback, shaping by successive approximations, and self-monitoring and evaluation. Similarly, in an intervention program with chronic psychiatric patients Matson and Stephens (1978) found that a training package involving instructions, modeling, role playing, and feedback was effective in reducing aggressive behaviors (arguing and fighting) on the ward, and treatment efforts were still evident in a three-month follow up. Finally, Sarason and Sarason (1981) reported on the effectiveness of a modeling and role-playing procedure to increase the cognitive and social skills of high school students having a high probability of delinquency on dropping out of school.

Within the domain of social skills training, modeling appears to be most effective when it is combined with other treatment procedures. The studies just described illustrate the effectiveness of such "packages." Consistent with this conclusion, Barton (1981) reported that, in training prosocial skills to children, modeling alone was ineffective in increasing their sharing. Another study found that children's sharing was enhanced only when modeling was combined with the treatment at a psychiatric clinic. In this study, the treatment conveyed more accurate expectations about the process and led to fewer canceled appointments and fewer dropouts. Other reports of health-related skills modeling include the use of peer modeling films, for example, to teach diabetic children to self-inject insulin (this film focused both on reducing children's anxiety and on skill acquisition) (Gilbert, Johnson, Spillar, McCallum, Silverstein & Rosenbloom, 1982) and to improve the children's oral hygiene (Murray & Epstein, 1981).

Treatment of Social Isolation by Modeling: An Example   An early study by O'Connor (1969) presents a good example of the use of symbolic modeling procedures to correct severe behavior deficits in young children. Children in this project all showed extreme social withdrawal, tending to isolate themselves from adults and other children. (Such a behavior problem may indicate either lack of requisite social skills *or* fear of the avoided social interaction.) Half of the children observed a sound film that vividly portrayed a variety of social interactions between a child and others. A number of interaction scenes were depicted, each successive one containing increasingly energetic activity (graduated modeling). In each activity sequence, a child model was first shown observing the social activity from a distance, then later joining in and interacting with other children. A second group of socially isolated children observed a control film that did not contain a graded series of social interactions and portrayed no behaviors particularly incompatible with isolate, withdrawn behaviors. O'Connor also observed nonisolated children in the same environment to obtain a measure of "normal" social activity.

Following these treatments, the children were given the opportunity for social interaction, and the extent of their participation was measured (see Figure 4–5). Children who had not observed the film depicting social interac-

Figure 4–5   *Extent of social interaction shown by withdrawn children before and after a treatment session that utilized symbolic modeling (—). The dashed line (- - -) illustrates the behavior of control-group children who saw no filmed models. The dotted line (...) represents the amount of social interaction displayed by nonwithdrawn children who were observed at the time of the pretest.*

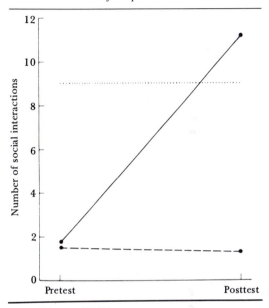

From O'Connor (1969).

tion remained quite withdrawn, showing no improvement in their social skills. Children who had observed the modeling films, however, showed an impressive gain in the number of social behaviors displayed, and the frequency of their social interactions approached (and in some cases, even slightly surpassed) the nonisolate baseline frequency. One criticism of the study is that the measure of behavior change occured *immediately* after the experimental manipulation, and there was no long-term follow-up. However, the reinforcing value of the skills acquired makes it likely that the children would maintain the social interaction behaviors.

More recent work using modeling with guided participation confirmed the effectiveness of modeling procedures in expanding the social repertoires of withdrawn children. Ross, Ross, and Evans (1971) presented a case study in which the extreme social withdrawal of a 6-year-old child was effectively treated with participant modeling procedures. A seven-week treatment program utilized an adult model. Initially, the child was trained in generalized imitation both by reinforcement for imitative acts and by direct exhortation by the primary therapist (not the model) to reproduce the model's behaviors. Seventeen individual 90-minute sessions ensued, containing a variety of modeling stimuli. In a graduated series of social interactions, the model approached and interacted with other children. Symbolic modeling presentations, such as pictures, stories, or movies, were also used. The model provided the child information about interaction—such as the unlikelihood of adverse consequences—and demonstrated, along with the therapist, role-play examples of appropriate social behavior in hypothetical social situations (which were sometimes humorous, to reduce the child's anxiety). In a graduated series of joint participations in social interactions, the model interacted with other children while the child patient accompanied him. Finally, modeling and interactions demonstrated social skills (games, tricks, slang speech) for the child, who was then encouraged to practice them. This case study thus provides a good example of the many ways in which a participant modeling procedure may be elaborated or combined with other techniques (direct instruction, reinforced practice) to treat a given behavior problem. As one might expect, observational measures of the child's actual social interaction before and after therapeutic intervention, plus a comparison of the child's social behavior with that of more socially competent peers, indicated significant improvement as a result of treatment. Initially, the child's social interaction scores were significantly lower than his peers'. But after the seven-week treatment program, and again after a two-month follow-up, his social interaction levels and skills were indistinguishable from his peers'.

Use of Modeling Techniques To Enhance Self-disclosure and To Reduce Interview Anxiety: An Example Therapists have shown serious interest in using modeling procedures to reduce clients' anxiety during therapeutic interviews and to foster the degree of self-disclosure that can provide important diagnostic and background information for the therapist. Bruch (1975) contrasted the effectiveness of coping and mastery models on the interview anxiety of psychiatric inpatients. A videotaped model interview, 36 minutes in length, was shown to patients and multiple assessments of interview anxiety were then taken. Coping models were portrayed as initially hesitant in the taped interview and then gradually becoming more confident in their interaction with the interviewer. Coping models also displayed various coping techniques (taking deep breaths, relaxing themselves) and verbalized self-instructions—that they supposedly covertly administered to themselves during the interview—to relax, to take one question at a time, and to pause for thought before answering a question. Mastery models exuded confidence during the entire interview tape. Bruch found that coping models produced the most consistent improvement in the clients' interview anxiety, especially when the models evidenced positive affect after their improved, more confident behavior.

Other aspects of interview or self-disclosure modeling that are of potential importance are the status of the model (Doster & McAllister, 1973), the type of information revealed (Doster & Brooks, 1974), and the length or detail of behavioral modeling or instructional modeling (McGuire, Thelen, & Amolsch, 1975; Scheiderer, 1977). Although model similarity has been viewed as an important factor in maximizing a client's adoption of social behaviors (Ascher & Phillips, 1975; Rosekrans, 1966), Doster and

McAllister (1973) found that a model with assumed clinical expertise (identified as a clinical intern) was more effective in producing self-disclosure than one introduced as a peer of the client.

Doster and Brooks (1974) utilized the interviewer himself as a model in videotaped sequences that showed self-disclosure of either positive or negative personal information. Although the investigators anticipated that seeing an interviewer disclose unfavorable personal information would reduce clients' tendencies to disclose information about themselves, the unfavorableness of the information provided in the modeling sequence had no significant effect upon client self-disclosure. McGuire and colleagues (1975) varied the length of behavioral or instructional modeling on self-disclosure. For short modeling sequences, 2 minutes in length, instructional modeling enhanced self-disclosure more than behavioral modeling, but neither produced a particularly high level of disclosure. Longer behavioral modeling sequences (25 minutes) significantly increased self-disclosure, while longer instructional modeling was no more effective than short. The implicit recommendation is clear: when the available time for a modeling procedure is severely limited, then precise, explicit instructions are favored over a brief interlude of behavioral modeling. When more time is available, the modeling sequence should be longer, and it should be behavioral in nature, illustrating the self-disclosure (or other) behavior that is desirable.

Facilitative Modeling in Group Contingency Management Procedures

One inadvertent component of a contingency management that focuses on one individual within a group is the fact that it is observed by other group members. This provides the opportunity for observational learning by individuals whose behavior was not necessarily targeted for modification. Periodic reports in the literature

have noted the positive effects of reinforcement procedures on individuals who only observe the reinforcement of another and do not receive any themselves (Christy, 1975; Kazdin, 1973b; Ollendick, Shapiro & Barrett, 1982). Working with moderately mentally retarded children, Kazdin (1973b) used a contingency management procedure designed to improve attentive behavior toward lessons. Verbal social reinforcement was dispensed when a target child was paying attention to his or her lesson, but the reinforcement did not designate the exact behavior upon which it was focused (e.g., "Good, I like what you're doing!"). The target child sat at a table with a second child whose behavior was not reinforced. Over a 38-day period, social reinforcement for attention was periodically applied and then withdrawn to demonstrate its effect. The attending behavior of both the child being reinforced and the other child at the table was recorded. Figure 4–6 presents the results for Jane, one of the target children, and for Laura, a girl who simply observed the contingencies. Not only did the contingency management procedure produce appropriate changes in the behavior of the observing children, but improvements in attending behavior tended to persist in the observing child during any period when the target child was being reinforced—even when the reinforcement was reversed so that nonattending behavior was being reinforced. This latter finding, which was not limited to Laura, indicates that the observing child appears to generalize the first modeled contingency to all subsequent periods of observed reinforcement. If the initial intervention places a contingency on attending behavior, the observing child acts as if subsequent interventions utilize the same contingency, even when the process has actually been reversed. While this tendency toward overgeneralization may characterize only retarded children, it nevertheless suggests a precaution in the use of contingency procedures in group settings: nontarget children who might observe the contingency should be exposed to it initially, when target

Figure 4–6 *Modeling effects of a contingency management program to increase attentive behavior in one child (BASE: no experimental intervention; RFT ATT: reinforcement of attentive behavior for target child (Jane) only; REV: reversal of contingency through a return to base period conditions; RFT INATT: reversal of contingency through a switch to the reinforcement of inattentive behavior; RFT ATT: return to contingency reinforcing target child for attentive behavior). The dotted lines represent the mean amount of attentive behavior for each phase.*

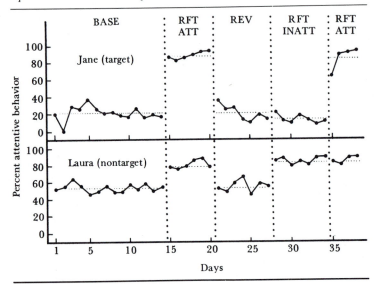

From Kazdin (1973b).

behaviors are being reinforced, and not merely during any subsequent reversal period that might be included to confirm the effectiveness of the contingency procedure.

In a study that involved even younger children, Christy (1975) reported the successful modeling of contingencies within a preschool group setting. In two separate classrooms, three children who seldom remained sitting for any length of time were rewarded with both verbal and food reinforcers for staying in their seats. Not only did this contingency improve the in-seat behavior of target children, but observing peers who were also low in initial in-seat behavior improved as well. By the end of the study, which lasted about two months, all children in the classes showed increases in the amount of

time they remained sitting. Christy also noted that negativistic behavior on the part of the observing peers (being upset over not participating in the reinforcements) appeared only fleetingly (in the form of requests for rewards too) and did not interfere with the success of the management procedure for either the target procedure or the observing peers.

Another modeling function that may be embedded within contingency management procedures relates to the training of contingency managers, such as the counselors, therapists, or ward staff who are charged with implementing the program. Gladstone and Spencer (1977) found that mental retardation counselors who observed a model counselor reinforce severely retarded children for various personal hygiene behaviors subsequently increased their use of contingent praise with the children. Thus, group contingency management programs that also have multiple staff may contain implicit training procedures, through modeling, for the orientation of new staff.

The success of the group application of behavior modification techniques reinforces the possibility of developing treatment centers on the model of "schools." Assistants could be trained to administer all assessment techniques, both behavioral and paper-and-pencil, as well as many modification procedures. Professionally trained individuals then could devote their time to the construction of new therapeutic programs and the evaluation of current therapeutic procedures, tasks to which their training is directly suited. As Ritter (1969b) has suggested, such an institution might include laboratories suited to various live and filmed treatments. Information obtained from the results of live treatment could be used in producing the filmed and taped treatment demonstrations. In addition, a team of technicians could be trained to do guided behavior rehearsal when laboratory treatment would be difficult or less efficient (e.g., with street-crossing phobics or subjects with problems of generalization). Ollendick and associates (1982) reported that observing others be reinforced for performing a behavior may lead the observers initially to increase the desired behavior but subsequently to *decrease* it. Thus, it is probably of particular importance to combine vicarious reinforcement treatment procedures with other behaviors, such as guided behavior rehearsal, to ensure long-lasting effects.

Disinhibition and the Vicarious Extinction of Fear and Anxiety by Modeling

Modeling has proven to be effective in influencing many different types of behavior that are fear or pain related. The predominant focus in this area has been upon the elimination of avoidance behavior that is motivated by fear of a person, object, or situation. In these instances, the treatment has clearly proved effective at encouraging approach (nonavoidant) behaviors and, at the same time, producing vicarious extinction of the fear. Recently, however, some attention has focused on the role of modeling in the tolerance or avoidance of pain, which is another factor that may motivate avoidance behavior. In addition, the fear associated with the anticipation of pain (such as that preceding a visit to the dentist) may evoke disruptive or tantrum behavior, especially when avoidance is not possible.

It seems clear that naturalistic modeling, such as the behavior of parents (Turkat, 1982) or the depiction of scenes on television (often termed symbolic modeling), may lead to the acquisition of fear or avoidant behavior. Yet evidence is accruing that modeling may increase pain tolerance and reduce disruptive behavior associated with pain-related situations. For example, Thelen and Fry (1981) found that adults who were exposed to pain-tolerant models were able to tolerate pain (holding their hand in ice water) for a significantly longer period of time, though they still reported equally high levels of subjective discomfort. Earlier, Craig and Niedemayer (1974) reported that subjects who observed a model tolerating high levels of shock not only were more likely to accept similarly high levels themselves but also showed no increase in autonomic arousal, as did control subjects. Melamed and her colleagues (Melamed et al., 1975(a); Melamed et al., 1975(b); Melamed et al., 1978), as well as others (Stokes & Kennedy, 1980), have repeatedly shown that children who view videotapes of a child model coping well in a dental office will display significantly less disruptive behavior.

In the use of modeling to reduce fears, *sensitization* rather than desensitization may occur. For example, Melamed and colleagues (1978) report that young children with previous treatment experiences benefited most from viewing desensitization modeling, whereas those who had no prior dental experience actually became more fearful. At the present time, little is known regarding the factors that may shift the impact of modeling from vicarious extinction to the intensification of fear. These results suggest that modeling cues contain fear-evoking elements as well as the presentation of fearless responses. And clients whose own fears are not based upon a full comprehension of everything in a given situation that they would find fearful may be more influenced by the new fear-evoking cues in the modeling stimulus than they would by the cues that might lead to vicarious extinction. This interpretation is compatible with the conceptual, desensitization-related theory behind graduated modeling (see below) and suggests (a) that graduated modeling will be particularly appropriate for the treatment of fears based on little knowledge or experience, and (b) that graduated modeling stimuli may best include graduated exposure to the fear-related elements of the context as well as to fearless behaviors.

Several components may enter into an overall modeling procedure designed to eliminate fears and anxieties and to allow free performance of behaviors that had been inhibited. These components are often combined to maximize the effectiveness of treatment, as will be discussed below. Nevertheless, for the sake of clarity, the three primary procedural concerns will be discussed separately. We will then provide two detailed examples of the use of modeling techniques to treat quite divergent behavior problems involving fear and avoidance behaviors.

Graduated Modeling

In a manner similar to the systematic exposure sequencing in desensitization, it is usually best to expose fearful clients to models who perform behaviors that are progressively more and more threatening, as perceived by the client. To expose a snake-phobic individual to a professional snake handler interacting closely with a giant anaconda would do little to lessen the person's fears. The client observing such a scene would be likely to elicit an intense emotional response, which would not dissipate during observation (compare the discussion of implosive therapy or flooding/response prevention in Chapter 30 of Bandura, 1971) and which might promote avoidance behaviors (looking away, shutting eyes, etc.) during the modeling sequence. For these reasons, it is generally best to graduate, or order, the behavior patterns performed by the model so that sequences that are minimally anxiety provoking to the client are performed first. Note, however, that some investigators (e.g., Bandura, 1971) feel that though the graduated modeling procedure is an aid to the effectiveness of modeling, it is not a prerequisite, and repeated exposure to the model's performances of highly anxiety-provoking behavior patterns might also prove effective, though they might require a longer series of treatment sessions.

Bandura and colleagues (1967b) treated children who were extraordinarily fearful of dogs by exposing them to peer models who fearlessly interacted progressively more closely with a dog. Treatment consisted of eight 10-minute sessions held over the brief period of four days. Groups of four children observed the model, whose sequence of behaviors lasted only three minutes during each session. During the first sessions, the model's behaviors included patting the dog (which was confined in a pen) and feeding her. Beginning with the fifth session, the modeled tasks were performed outside the pen, and the model walked the dog around the room. During the last two sessions, the model climbed into the pen with the dog and continued his friendly interactions with her.

Since the purpose of the study was to evaluate the effectiveness of graduated modeling, these investigators used several treatment procedures: two modeling procedures and two control conditions. In one modeling condition, the context of treatment was positive, designed to buoy the children's spirits and to make them happy and relaxed (responses presumably incompatible with fear). Thus, in that modeling condition, the children were introduced to a party atmosphere (hats, prizes, games) before the modeling sequence. In a second condition, no attempt was made to alter the children's general affective state; they simply sat at a table and observed the model. In the two control conditions, the party atmosphere was created, but there was no modeling sequence; the dog was simply present in the room (penned during the first sessions, on a leash afterward) in one control condition and absent in the other.

The children's fear of dogs was assessed by means of an approach test in which they were exposed to a live dog and asked to approach it, feed it, and spend time alone with it in a room. Their behavior was assessed before treatment, immediately after the completion of 10 treatment sessions, and then 30 days later. During the posttest and follow-up test assessments, children were exposed not only to the dog used during treatment, but also to a dog of vastly different appearance. Figure 4–7 illustrates the effectiveness of these various treatment procedures. It is quite clear that the context in which the modeling occurred had little impact on the effectiveness of the modeling procedure, and simple exposure to a dog in the positive atmosphere or to the positive context alone also had little effect on the children's fear. There was clear evidence of the generalized effectiveness of treatment as well. The children in the modeling conditions were more likely to perform extremely threatening behaviors (remaining alone in the room with either dog) than were children in either control condition.

As noted earlier, graduated exposure to fear-evoking behaviors or to elements of a fearful context may be an important part of any modeling treatment designed to reduce fear and enhance fearless behavior. Indeed, desensitization procedures involving imaginal representations of fearless approach behaviors might be viewed as containing elements of symbolic covert modeling that is graduated in nature. Consequently, graduated modeling is seldom reported as a treatment procedure by itself but rather as an aspect of treatment given

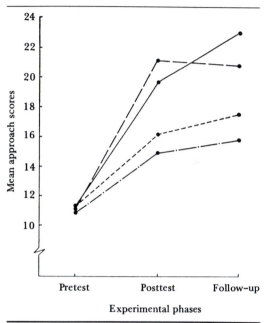

Figure 4–7 *Mean approach scores achieved by children before and after various treatment conditions and after a follow-up period of one month (●—●: model + positive context; ●– – –●: model + neutral context; ●–·–·●: dog + positive context; ●–--●: positive context).*

From Bandura, Grusec, and Menlove (1967b).

another name. Thus, for example, Nemetz, Craig, and Reith (1978) report the effectiveness of a symbolic modeling procedure for the treatment of debilitating sexual anxiety in woman. The modeling treatment involved videotapes that depicted graduated sexual behaviors and was accompanied by relaxation training. This treatment produced decreases in anxiety as well as improvements in both sexual behaviors and attitudes. The point is that graduated modeling is broadly applicable and is likely to be a component of a modeling treatment whose label (participant, covert, symbolic, etc.) does not identify the graduated component explicitly.

Diversified Modeling: The Use of Multiple Models and Contexts

The use of multiple models is one procedure that may promote generalization of treatment effects. While the client might presume single models to have some special talents that allow them to be fearless, this is less likely to be the case among a group of divergent models (Bandura, 1971). Furthermore, multiple models are likely to vary slightly in the ways in which they demonstrate fearless behavior, thus providing greater latitude of behavior possibilities for the client to adopt.

We have already noted that the symbolic presentation of models is generally no less effective than the use of models actually present. An advantage of symbolic presentation is that the same modeling sequences may be presented to a number of clients at different times without requiring the services of the model in each instance. Consequently, more elaborate procedures involving equipment and numerous individuals may be filmed, relieving the client or therapist of the organizational and financial burden of repeatedly assembling them. Symbolic presentation allows the economical utilization of multiple models.

It is not surprising, then, that the effectiveness of multiple models for fear reduction has been tested by exposing individuals to films of various models demonstrating fearless behavior. In a study similar to that described in the preceding section, Bandura and Menlove (1968) exposed dog-phobic children to a series of eight three-minute films that depicted models interacting with a dog in gradually more threatening ways. One group saw films that included models of both sexes and varying ages interacting with a variety of dogs of all sizes and degrees of fearsomeness (these factors increased gradually as treatment proceeded). In a control condition, the children saw films of Disneyland and Marineland.

The children's actual avoidance behaviors were tested before treatment, immediately after treatment, and 30 days later. As Figure 4–8 il-lustrates, the two modeling conditions were more effective than the control in increasing the children's capabilities to interact fearlessly with a dog. The effect of multiple modeling is most apparent when we examine the data on children's capabilities for performing the terminal interaction behavior in the assessment scale: to remain alone in a room confined in the pen with the dog. Figure 4–9 illustrates these data. It is clear the multiple-model procedure was the only one that actually induced such fearless behavior, and its effectiveness was, if anything, improved after the 30-day follow-up.

Participant Modeling and Contact Desensitization

Several terms in the literature are used relatively interchangeably to describe basically the same modeling procedure: participant model-

Figure 4–8 Median approach scores achieved by children in the treatment and control conditions before and after treatment and after the follow-up period (●—●: multiple model; ●---●: single model; ●····●: control group).

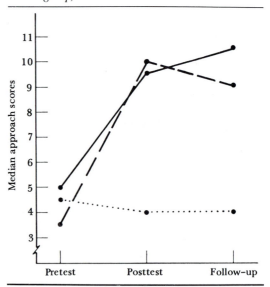

From Bandura and Menlove (1968).

Figure 4–9 *Percentage of children from each treatment condition who performed the terminal approach behavior immediately following treatment and one month later. (The behavior of the treated controls was assessed immediately after their treatment, which occurred during the follow-up period.) (Dotted bars: multiple model; hatched bars: single model; open bars: control.)*

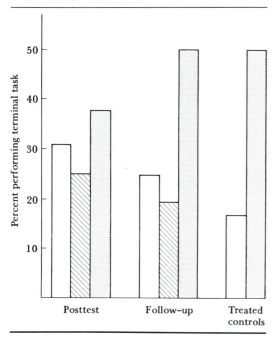

From Bandura and Menlove (1968).

ing, modeling with guided participation, and contact desensitization. Since there is a tendency for one or the other term to be used consistently by a particular author, the divergence may indicate personal preference for a term rather than an actual difference in procedure. As we noted earlier, it would appear that a major factor determining the use of the term *contact desensitization* is the inclusion of actual physical contact between the therapist and client. In general, all terms may be reduced to the general procedure of *demonstration plus participation,* and the participatory portion typically involves guidance by

the therapist, either verbally or by actual physical contact. For the remainder of this chapter, we use the general term *participant modeling* to refer to the general technique of modeled demonstration plus client participation, employing other terms only when describing the work of investigators who prefer those terms.

Before turning to a detailed description of participation modeling procedures, we should first consider the factors that seem responsible for the effectiveness of the technique (studies bearing upon this question are presented in a subsequent section). A primary factor is clearly that of *vicarious extinction.* Observing a model perform a feared behavior in the absence of dire consequences constitutes a learning situation in which the cues that tend to induce avoidance behavior are present, but the avoidance behavior does not occur. Furthermore, if the anxiety generated by the observation of the feared stimulus (e.g., a snake) or behavior (e.g., approaching the snake with a gloved hand) is minimal, it may dissipate during the performance, thus allowing the client to be relatively free of anxiety in the presence of the stimulus, which would reduce the tendency for that stimulus to evoke anxiety.

Another factor that has been inadequately stressed in the literature is the *acquisition of technical knowledge and information* via modeling. In the extinction of a snake phobia, the client learns technical details concerning how to handle a snake gently but effectively so it will not get away. Similarly, in treating a water phobia (described later in the chapter), technical skills of swimming, treading water, floating, and so on are undoubtedly important and fear reducing. Information may also serve an important function in reducing fear or revulsion, as in the case when a client learns, by experience, that a snake is not slimy or deathly cold, does not immediately strike, and so forth. A client can acquire technical skills by observation and polish them during the participation procedure; thus, the person acquires information through observation of the model's behavior and direct experience during participation.

The acquisition of technical knowledge and information is intimately related to the direct acquisition of skills during the demonstration phase. These skills are likely to reduce anxiety due to ignorance of how to behave and to improve the chance that the client will successfully participate in the feared activity, thus gaining needed practice and reinforcement (success) for the newly acquired behaviors. The acquisition of information is related to another factor—namely, the *direct extinction of fear,*—which tends to occur when anticipated dire consequences fail to materialize during the participation phase. The disconfirmation of such expectancies, accompanied by a diminution in level of anxiety, reduces the degree to which the stimulus continues to evoke that anxiety.

Finally, the continued *presence of the therapist* is an important factor for at least three reasons. First, his or her presence provides social (emotional) and physical (contact) support during the participation phase. Second, the continued presence of the therapist is likely to prevent or at least minimize any problems that may develop during the participatory phase (e.g., if a snake starts to escape, or an acrophobic client stumbles while on the steps of a ladder).

The participant modeling technique is applicable to a variety of behavior problems characterized by fear of animals, insects, or people (e.g., Denny, Sullivan & Thiry, 1977) and of rather nonspecific stimuli, including height, water, closed places, or dental treatment (Bernstein & Klein Knecht, 1982; Speltz & Bernstein, 1979). Persons in the individual's typical surroundings can also be employed as therapists. Matson (1981), for example, reported the successful use of mothers in the participant modeling treatment of their children's fear and avoidance of other adults. Throughout the range of problem behaviors to which this technique may be applied, the basic procedures remain the same: graduated demonstration plus graduated participation. In addition, there is at least one early report that a period of self-directed practice following a participant modeling procedure enhances the

generalization of efforts (Smith & Coleman, 1977).

The following sections present detailed examples of participant modeling procedures, one adapted for the treatment of a snake phobia and the other for the fear of water. The basic procedures clearly may be adapted to a wide range of other behavior problems.

Treatment of Fear of Snakes by Participant Modeling: An Example   Often, research on modeling procedures utilizes snake-phobic individuals as subjects. While this type of "analogue" study (snake phobics are analogous to "real" clients with "true" phobias) has been criticized, snake phobias *are* widespread and numerous individuals restrict their vacations in the country, refuse to go barefoot in the grass or attend picnics, have nightmares, and in many other ways limit their behavior (or their job opportunities, such as for those requiring outside work) because of this phobia. Thus, the snake phobic does seem to be particularly representative of clinical phobias.

Initially, a therapist must acquire a snake known to be docile and relatively unmenacing in appearance (e.g., a Florida hognose). Pet store managers or other suppliers of reptiles are knowledgeable in this area. Typically, after an initial session or portion of a session in which the technique is generally outlined, the procedure may commence. First the client will be asked to enter the room containing the snake, which is enclosed in a glass cage on the other side of the room. The client is told that the door will remain open throughout the treatment sessions and that he may leave at any time. Then he will be asked to stand, or sit, at whatever distance from the cage he feels comfortable. (There are some constraints on this: the client should be in the room and able to view the snake and subsequent modeling interaction clearly.) The therapist then slips on a pair of gloves, opens the top of the glass cage, and touches the snake briefly (but not hesitantly). If this interaction causes undue distress to the client, the individual can reposition himself farther away from the cage. In addition, the therapist may verbally reassure the client that the snake cannot escape from the cage. Throughout the entire series of modeling demonstrations, the therapist-model should behave with ease, confidence, and a lack of hesitancy and should show warmth toward the client.

After these introductory interactions, the therapist may proceed to the major sequence of modeled interactions with the snake, which are as follows:

I. Gloved hand procedure
    A. Stroke the snake's midsection, then tail, then top of head.
    B. Raise the snake's midsection, then tail, then head.
    C. Grasp the snake gently but firmly a few inches from the head and about six inches from the tail, remove it from the cage (taking care not to approach the client or swing the snake obviously closer to him).
    D. Comfortably handle the snake, modeling how easy and comfortable the interaction process can be, how the model is in complete control, and so forth. This facet of the procedure should continue for several minutes (it may be wise to time it to ensure adequate length), until external indications show that the client's anxiety level is rather low.

II. Bare hand procedure
    A–D. The above procedure should be repeated by the therapist-model using his or her bare hands.

Throughout the entire procedure, care should be taken not to allow the client to become unduly agitated. If the client reports intense fear, or if the therapist observes such fearfulness, the procedure should stop, the snake should be returned to the cage and the lid replaced, and the therapist should support and reassure the client, perhaps making some relaxation suggestions. If such an interruption is necessary, the procedure should subsequently be restarted at an earlier phase in the graduated sequence than the one that evoked anxiety and then should carefully progress through the various modeled interactions.

When these two modeling sequences have been successfully completed, the client may be asked if he is willing to approach the snake. By this time, most clients will agree; however, if a client is not willing, continued demonstration sequences should be undertaken with lengthy exposure to calm, controlled, pleasant-appearing interactions with the snake. When the client agrees to approach the snake, the therapist should pick the snake up and hold it while he asks the client to don the gloves and briefly touch the snake's midsection. When the client successfully does so, the therapist should give reinforcement and support—for example, "I'll bet that is the first time in your life you ever touched a snake. Good for you!"

The client may then be asked to stroke the midsection, then touch and stroke the tail, and finally touch and stroke the top of the head. Should the snake extend its tongue, the therapist might matter-of-factly note that it is harmless, merely a sensing device for sound.

When the gloved touching and stroking behaviors have been completed, the client should be asked to hold the snake in his gloved hands. He may be instructed to place his hand loosely about the midsection of the snake and hold it there until he feels fairly comfortable (the therapist continues to support the snake). If these actions appear to cause some anxiety (or, perhaps, excitement) in the client, the therapist could suggest that he take a deep breath to induce relaxation. When the client's progress is apparent, praise should be given.

The procedure continues, with the client holding (in gloved hands) the snake's tail, then its head. Finally, he may be asked to support the entire snake. This progression is not rapid, of course. Time is allowed at each step for the client to become comfortable, and praise is given for progress. If at any point the client expresses anxiety, the therapist should immediately take the snake back (calmly) and offer reassurance before returning to the participation process. The availability of the therapist to intervene if any problems develop is an important part of the procedure, and the therapist should make certain that the client realizes this. Some investigators and therapists suggest that it is important, at the beginning of the participation phase, to have contact between the therapist and client (Ritter, 1969b, 1969c). In the present case, this might be accomplished by having the therapist place a bare hand on the snake's midsection, with the client placing his *gloved* hand on the therapist's hand and then sliding it off the therapist's hand and onto the snake (similar procedures should be added to other components of the modeling sequence described above). The choice of including therapist contact procedures such as these appears to depend on the therapist's personal experience and preference.

Treatment of Water Fears by Participant Modeling: An Example It should be clear from the above example that overcoming fears of quite specific objects includes the acquisition of approach skills, as well as the vicarious extinction of fears and anxiety. There are many instances of unreasonable fears that appear to be attached more to the requisite behaviors involved in an activity and their individual consequences than to the particular stimulus object itself. Thus, a fear of water, which prevents the participation in, and enjoyment of, water activities may not be precisely a fear of water (since there may be little fear of showering, bathing, etc.), but of activities such as swimming in deep water, submerging the head, and so on.

Hunziker (1972) developed a procedure designed to reduce fear of water activities and to allow previously fearful individuals to enjoy them. This program included 54 individualized modeled behaviors and was designed for group treatment. When administering such a treatment regime to groups, an attempt is typically made to include a sufficiently lengthy series of graduated stimuli to prevent even the most timid participants from experiencing overwhelming anxiety following transition from one step to the next. Clearly, if such a program is used to treat an individual, it may be shortened (or perhaps lengthened) and tailored to the individual's unique pattern of fearfulness.

At each step, ideally, treatment participants should be asked to rate their level of anxiety in order to ensure that anxiety reduction has accompanied each step. Any modeled sequence might be repeated if some clients indicate that anxiety is still present (at a level of, say, 4 or higher on a 10-point scale). An effective adjunct is to sequester one of the clients as an aide, preferably a client who is likely to do well. His demonstrated successes will provide a second modeling stimulus, creating a situation of multiple models. At the therapist's choice, there may be guided participation, carried out verbally or manually, as well as reinforcement for success. Hunziker's utilization of this procedure eliminated all these factors—the clients simply tried each behavior sequence after it was modeled—yet he found participant modeling to be more effective than modeling without such participation.

Below are listed some of the 54 steps proposed by Hunziker. The treatment regime is primarily designed for use in a swimming pool. Such a setting provides a body of water with an even bottom, with depths specifically marked, and with no currents or dropoffs. Furthermore, safety measures and closer supervision can be maintained in such a setting. Generalization might be assessed at an ocean beach or lakeshore, although the client might require further treatment, since each of these settings includes stimuli that may be fear provoking and that are not handled in the specific treatment program. The 54 steps are as follows:

1. Sit on the edge of the pool.

2. Sit on the edge of the pool with your feet in the water.

4. Stand in the pool and hold onto the side.

7. Not holding the side, splash water in your face.

8. Hold the side and blow bubbles in the water.

13–15. Not holding the side, put your face in the water.

22–24. Hold the side, put your face in the water, and lift one foot off the bottom.

25–27. Hold the side, put your face in the water, and lift both feet off the bottom.

28–30. Hold the kick board and put your face in the water with one foot off the bottom.

37–39. Without any support, put your face in the water and take both feet off the bottom.

Note: Steps 1–39 were performed in approximately 3 ½ feet of water.

40. Where the water is 12 feet deep, sit on the side.

42. Where the water is 12 feet deep, slide into the pool and hold onto the side.

46–48. Where the water is 12 feet deep, hold onto the kick board and submerge completely.

53. Kneel on the side where the water is 12 feet deep and push off the side into the pool.

54. Stand on the side where the water is 12 feet deep and jump into the pool.

Note: Each of the inclusive steps was demonstrated by the therapist for one inch, three inches, and five inches of water.

Additional Modeling Procedures

Coping Models Versus Mastery Models

One distinction that the literature is making is that between coping models and mastery models. *Coping models* initially display flawed or fearful performances, and gradually, as the modeling sequence continues or in subsequent modeling depictions, become increasingly competent in the target behavior pattern. *Mastery models,* on the other hand, show flawless performance from the very beginning, depicting the ideal imitative goal for the observer.

Roberts and his colleagues have reported on the effective use of coping models to reduce children's fears of hospitalization (Roberts, Wurtele, Boone, Ginther & Elkins, 1982). In this study, children viewed a slide show about two children entering a hospital for tonsillectomies. The children also gave a recorded narrative describing what they saw and what happen to them. Both the children's narratives and the depicted behaviors illustrated coping: they acknowledged their anxiety but also showed how they overcame it through such means as talking to themselves, relaxing, or changing the way they thought. This procedure proved effective in reducing children's medical fears relative to those in a control group. In an early investigation contrasting coping and mastery modeling procedures, Meichenbaum (1972b) found that filmed coping models were more effective in reducing anxiety than were filmed mastery models. Subsequently, research on the effectiveness of covert modeling found the same effects when the behavior of models was merely imagined (Kazdin, 1973b).

The mechanisms governing the effectiveness of coping versus mastery models have not yet been clearly investigated, but it seems logical to propose that one possible mediating factor is the implicit graduated nature of the coping model scenario, thus reducing coping modeling to a specialized case, or simply a renaming, of graduated modeling. Coping models have also been interpreted as being more similar to an observer in that they, too, initially possess the same behavioral difficulties or deficits (Kazdin, 1974b). It is probably not fruitful to argue about the relabeling of coping versus mastery modeling, especially since there has been no research focused on this question. Such research might compare graduated modeling—using obviously competent (mastery) models who gradually display more difficult, more complex, or more fear-provoking behavior—with coping modeling, in which the model's initial performance is actually flawed or obviously anxiety laden. Pending such deeper examination of the question, the research on both graduated modeling and coping versus mastery models supports the effectiveness of a graduated, coping sequence of modeled behaviors over the simple illustration of flawless goal behavior.

Covert Modeling

Just as desensitization began as a primarily imaginal technique and was elaborated to include *in vivo* procedures, modeling techniques were initially overt or *in vivo,* and imaginal or covert procedures were introduced sometime later. The concept of covert modeling was proposed initially by Cautela (1971b) and subsequently elaborated by Kazdin (1974a, 1974b, 1974c, 1974d, 1975). The procedure is quite simple: clients imagine a model performing the goal behavior, rather than actually observing a live or filmed model. The effectiveness of covert modeling procedures has been assessed in a number of investigations and case studies, and the types of problems treated range from phobias and lack of assertiveness to alcoholism and obsessive-compulsive behavior.

In standard covert modeling procedures, clients practice visualizing scenes, typically ones that are described by the therapist. During the treatment course, the therapist will describe a scene, including the model, the modeled behaviors, and any ancillary objects or components of the scene's context, and the client will signal by raising a finger (or some other minor act) when he or she has clearly visualized the scene. At this point, the therapist will allow the scene to continue for a period of time, such as 15 seconds, and then terminate the visualization. If the behavior problem is one for which the systematic

graduation of modeled acts would be appropriate—for example, the elimination of a phobia (note how this would resemble desensitization with the addition of an imagined model) or the gradual training of assertiveness—the scenes may be arranged in a preestablished order proceeding from easy to difficult, least fearsome to most, and so on. Scenes typically contain a clear description of the behavior and the consequences to the model of his or her performance: good consequences when appropriate or desired behavior is illustrated, and aversive consequences when the behavior is undesired and changeworthy ("negative" covert modeling).

An interesting example in the literature describes the potential use of covert modeling with children through the utilization of stories or verbally described fantasies. Treating a child who consistently set fires, Stawar (1976) repeatedly told him a story, including visual illustrations with dolls, in which a boy similar to the client found some matches, but instead of striking them and setting fires, gave them to his mother who praised him and gave him candy. The child was involved in the storytelling and was asked to tell it back to the therapist, including descriptions of the consequences for the good behavior of turning in the matches. Simultaneous with treatment, a minimal contingency management program was instituted that matched the story: the mother was instructed to praise and reward the child if he brought any matches to her at home. After only two treatment sessions, several structured trials in which matches were placed in obvious locations in the child's home revealed that in 19 out of 23 instances he returned the matches to his mother, while on the remaining trials he either overlooked the matches or ignored them. While there had been four incidents of fire setting in the three months before therapy, during a seven-month follow-up there were no further instances, and on at least one occasion the child spontaneously brought some matches he found to his mother.

Covert modeling has enjoyed more active research interest in recent years than just about any other category of modeling treatment. This research has not merely focused on the basic effectiveness of covert modeling, it has also contrasted it with other techniques. In addition, several components of the covert modeling procedure have been tested for effectiveness. One unique aspect of the technique is that it allows an individual to visualize *himself* as the model, potentially augmenting his personal involvement in the procedure and the degree to which it will affect his subsequent behavior. An imagined model who is not the client himself may be particularly similar—or dissimilar—to the client. The therapist can manipulate this by the verbal descriptions he or she provides to the client to invoke the covert modeling scene. Dimensions of similarity that have been studied include similarities unrelated to the problem at hand (age, physique, sex) or the degree of coping or mastery displayed by the imagined model early in the series of scenes. While coping and mastery are clearly dimensions describing the competence of a model in displaying goal behavior, coping models have also been interpreted to be similar to a client (since they evidence initial nonmastery of the goal behavior, as does the client) and mastery models dissimilar. Imagined modeling scenes may also vary in terms of the number of models depicting the desired behavior.

Covert modeling is generally most effective when the imagined models are most similar to the client. Kazdin (1974d), for example, examined the effectiveness of imagining oneself as the model, as opposed to imagining someone else in that role. Subjects were individuals with a severe fear of snakes. In this study, the fear-relevant similarity of the model was also varied by having clients imagine scenes in which the model gradually coped with the fear, eventually displaying fearless approach behavior, or scenes in which the model displayed mastery behavior from the very start. There was also a no-model control condition. The results, illustrated in Fig-

ure 4–10, indicated quite clearly that some forms of model similarity are of distinct importance, and others are not. Imagining oneself or someone else as the model proved to have no differential effect (the tendency for self-model conditions to be slightly lower than other-model conditions is not significant). However, the other dimension of similarity—whether the model was a coping or mastery one—proved to be quite significant. Coping models produced much greater behavior change than did mastery models. Interestingly, imagining a mastery model was effective only when the model was someone else, probably because imagining oneself as totally unafraid or courageous under

Figure 4–10 *Effectiveness of covert modeling in promoting approach behaviors toward a phobic object (snake). Depicted are the mean number of approach responses at a premeasurement, a postmeasurement immediately following treatment, and during a follow-up conducted approximately three weeks after treatment was concluded (SC: self-coping model; SM: self-mastery model; OC: other-coping model; OM: other-mastery model; NM: no-model scene control).*

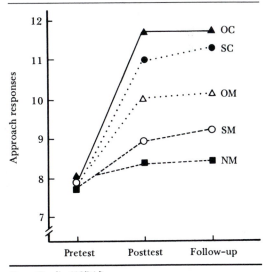

From Kazdin (1974d).

precisely the conditions that are most frightening to one is difficult and generally unbelievable. As Figure 4–10 illustrates, the changes produced by the various modeling conditions proved to be stable during a follow-up period of approximately three weeks.

Another dimension of similarity that has been examined is the relevance of that similarity to the problem. In a study also concerned with fear reduction, Kazdin (1974b) contrasted similarity factors that were irrelevant to the problem behavior, in this case the age and sex of the model. The results of this investigation indicated that problem-irrelevant dimensions of similarity for an imagined model do contribute to the effectiveness of a covert modeling procedure, the greatest change being produced by a coping model who was of the same age and sex as the client. Although Kazdin interpreted age and sex as components of a similarity dimension that is irrelevant to fear, we should note that some might dispute this interpretation, especially given prominent sex-role stereotypes regarding general fearfulness. In this case, dissimilar models were older (not younger) and of the opposite sex, and the safest conclusion may be that Kazdin's study indicates the importance of instructing clients to imagine models who are of the same age and sex as themselves, and perhaps similar in other physical characteristics as well (height, weight, general build, and so forth). Extensive evidence shows that covert modeling procedures can be effectively employed to increase assertive behavior.

In two early investigations, Kazdin (1974c, 1975) demonstrated the particular effectiveness of having clients imagine multiple models and positive consequences for imagined assertive behavior. In his procedure, Kazdin utilized four treatment sessions comprised of 35 individual scenes that clients are to imagine. In one investigation, the scene descriptions were prerecorded and not presented directly by the therapist. The following is an example of a scene that models assertive behavior and produces positive consequences:

1. The person (model) is eating in a restaurant with friends. He (or she) orders a steak and tells the waiter he (or she) would like it rare. When the food arrives, the person begins to eat and apparently finds something wrong with the steak.

2. He (or she) immediately signals the waiter. When the waiter arrives, the person says, "I ordered the steak rare, and this one is medium. Please take it back and bring me one that is rare."

3. In a few minutes, the waiter brings another steak and says he is very sorry this has happened. (Kazdin, 1975, p. 242)

The effectiveness of multiple models and positive consequences may be seen clearly in Figure 4–11 (Kazdin, 1975). On an assessment device (Conflict Resolution Inventory), in which a refusal is an index of assertiveness, imagining multiple models who were successful produced the greatest increase in assertiveness, significantly greater than the other modeling conditions, as well as the no-model control. Note that all of the covert modeling conditions were superior to the no-model control, indicating that imagining multiple and/or positive consequences simply improves upon the already established effectiveness of covert modeling. Interestingly, Kazdin's seminal research also found (1974c) that the use of multiple stimuli (e.g., several waiters in the above example for assertive training, or several snakes or dogs to reduce fear and avoidance behaviors) does not improve upon the effectiveness of covert modeling.

There is growing evidence in the literature on covert modeling that elaborating imagined scenes involving initial failure (e.g., the modeled behavior initially does not result in success and must be repeated or intensified) and subsequent success improves the effectiveness of covert modeling for initiating assertive behavior. Nietzel and associates (1977) contrasted straightforward covert modeling with a procedure that included "reply training": scenes in which assertion initially produces noncompliance, which must be responded to with contin-

Figure 4–11 *Effects of multiple models and positive consequences on assertiveness as indexed by the Conflict Resolution Inventory (SR: single model, positive consequences [reinforcement]; SNR: single model, no positive consequences; MR: multiple model, positive consequences [reinforcement]; MNR: multiple model, no positive consequences; NM: nonassertive model control condition).*

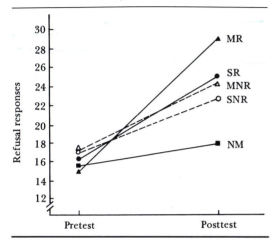

From Kazdin (1975).

ued assertion and finally elicits compliance. An illustrative scene is as follows:

1. The person has just moved into a new apartment with two other friends. They have been looking for a fourth person with whom to share the apartment. The two friends come to the person and inform him (or her) that they have found a fourth person. The proposed roommate happens to be someone that the person secretly dislikes.

2. The person looks directly at the two friends and says, "I wish you had talked to me beforehand. He (or she) is someone I don't particularly want to live with."

3. One of the friends immediately responds, "Well, it's too late now, we've already asked him (or her)."

4. The first person replies, "I don't think it is too late. I want to talk this over with you before we make a final decision. Let's discuss it right away."

5. The other friend then says, "I guess you're right. We should all have a say in this." (Nietzel et al., 1977, p. 185)

On a variety of measures, including the Conflict Resolution Inventory used by Kazdin (1975), adding reply training to a scene that depicted the model coping with initially ineffective assertion produced significantly greater improvement in clients than did covert modeling alone or placebo treatment (imagining scenes that called for assertion but without an assertive model or no-treatment control conditions). However, on a truly behavioral test of assertion conducted four months after treatment—an actual telephone call soliciting volunteer work involving an onerous task (McFall & Twentyman, 1973)—all treatment groups, including the control, did not differ from one another or from a random group of individuals having no assertion problems in terms of their ability to decline a persistent request. This may indicate that covert modeling with reply or coping training may produce rapid changes in assertion, but covert modeling in general, or even the focusing of attention on situations requiring assertion (the placebo manipulation), may produce subsequent behavior change over a period of time. Perhaps the reason is that clients attempt assertive behavior, are forced to cope with initial instances of noncompliance, and essentially learn assertiveness by a process of trial and error, the motivation for which was supplied by the treatment that drew attention to assertive contexts.

Many studies support the importance of elaborating covert modeling treatments by detailing the imagery inherent in the procedure (e.g., Kazdin, 1979; 1980), by developing descriptive verbal or symbolic codes for the covertly modeled behaviors (e.g., Kazdin, 1979), or by augmenting covert modeling with behavioral rehearsal (e.g., Hersen, Kazdin, Bellack, & Turner, 1979; Kazdin, 1982; Kazdin & Mascitelli, 1982). This literature is consistent in demonstrating the increased effectiveness of covert modeling when it is either elaborated covertly or accompanied by overt elaborations, such as rehearsal. In addition, at least one report suggests that overt rehearsal is especially important for children and adolescents. There is some indication that covert procedures are not as effective in adolescents as for adults (Pentz & Kazdin, 1982), although a case report does exist on the successful use of covert modeling to treat cross-gender motor behavior (feminine mannerism) in a preadolescent boy. Thus, the question of age differences in the effective use of covert modeling is still open.

Covert modeling techniques for assertiveness or for simply committing behaviors that are difficult or interfered with by hesitancy have been creatively adapted to other behavior problems. Hay and his colleagues (1977a) provided two case studies for the utilization of covert modeling in the treatment of alcoholism and obsessive-compulsive behavior. In the case of alcoholism, scenes were designed to promote assertive behavior in so-called trigger situations— ones in which the client was most likely to begin drinking. Covert modeling was thus intended to promote generalized self-control, which would increase the client's assertive capability to say no to others when invited to go drinking and to deliberately leave trigger situations. For example, a scene might involve an invitation by some old drinking buddies to join them in a night on the town, followed by an assertive refusal on the part of the client and his resolute departure from the scene. In the case of obsessions or compulsive rituals, covert modeling treatment involved the covert rehearsal of behavior that would ordinarily have been interfered with by the rituals; for example, deliberately walking out of a room while ignoring urges to check that the lights were off or that the door was shut. In this procedure, the covert scenes were really more rehearsal than explicit modeling of new

behavior patterns, and the treatment concentrated upon behaviors relative to only one ritual at a time (e.g., leaving a room without checking the lights, with separate, subsequent concentration on leaving a room without checking the door).

In general, the literature indicates that covert modeling is an effective procedure for treating a variety of behavior problems, though it is especially good for assertive training. As noted earlier, it has the creative advantages of tailoring a modeling procedure to the specific problems of individual clients, while at the same time offering a pragmatic savings by preventing the necessity for preparing form modeling stimuli, such as films or videotapes or the provision of live models. Not much research has been designed to test comparatively the effectiveness of covert and overt modeling, but in at least one investigation involving the treatment of fears (Cautela, et al., 1974), no difference existed between the two procedures on four out of five measures, both subjective and behavioral. Further research seems called for, since null results are potentially untrustworthy because of possible flaws in experimental procedure that might preclude significant results. For example, one can never be certain that the covert, cognitive representations by the client are full or accurate renditions of the desired behavior. However, while we cannot make a firm statement regarding the equivalence of covert and overt modeling techniques, covert modeling clearly seems to be effective as an independent behavior therapy technique.

Self-modeling: The Use of Videotaped Feedback in the Therapeutic Context

One procedure that clearly involves modeling, although it has not always been so labeled, is the use of videotaped feedback to a client as he or she rehearses a new behavior pattern or skill. Actually, this procedure involves more than modeling alone, since a therapist typically will comment during the showing, pointing out examples of particularly adept behavior as well as examples of behaviors that are still ineffective or in need of further modification. "Self-modeling," then, includes the demonstration of behavior (both adept and inept), the information inherent in seeing one's own behavior (about exactly which behaviors were adept and which were not), and the selective reinforcement or denotation by a therapist of the behaviors that have been appropriately modified, plus the denotation of behaviors that are still in need of change.

Videotape feedback has been used in a variety of ways, some of which do not truly constitute modeling, despite their therapeutic relevance. Viewing one's own behavior may have a motivating effect—for example, as it clearly reveals negative components. Such feedback has been used to motivate alcoholics to change their behavior or to overcome "resistance" in therapy by clearly revealing aspects of behavior that are either denied or misconstrued (Griffiths, 1974). Milby, Meredith, and Rice (1981) report the effectiveness of videotapes of a client reciting his obsessive thoughts for the elimination of that obsession. Bandura (1971) has also suggested that the effectiveness of modeling will be enhanced if it is followed by the guided rehearsal of observed behavior patterns and skills. Rehearsal followed by videotaped feedback with the therapist commenting could be interpreted as a form of "vicarious" guided rehearsal in which the client learns how to evaluate his own behavior and subsequently guide it toward competence.

A particularly instructive study is also one of the earliest. Arnkoff and Stewart (1973) contrasted the effects of modeling and of videotape feedback, singly and together, on skills in solving personal problems. In this experiment, young adults were first given some behavioral problems (pretest) involving situations that might easily be encountered by individuals similar to them. For example, one problem involved meeting a deadline for handing in some work.

The night before the task had to be finished, a friend calls to say he has two tickets to an extremely attractive recreational event. First, subjects were given the opportunity to ask whatever questions they might have about missing information. They then proposed several solutions to the problem and noted which one they thought best. Skill at solving personal dilemmas such as those represented in the problem was assessed by determining the number of questions a subject asked, the quality of the questions (good to poor), and the quality of the solution chosen.

There were four different treatment procedures: videotape feedback, modeling, videotape feedback plus modeling, and a control condition. For videotape feedback, the subject's performance was taped as he solved two training problems, and the tape was played back while the experimenter gave commentary feedback on the relevance of the subject's questions and the quality of the final solution chosen. In the modeling condition, the subject was shown videotapes of two different people solving problems similar to those used in the pretest and commenting on their own strategies (question relevance, etc.) as they worked. The models were shown to make occasional mistakes in strategy, which they then corrected and commented upon. In a third condition, both modeling and videotape feedback were utilized in an additive fashion. In the control condition, subjects solved the pretest problems, as well as the two training problems utilized in the videotape procedures, but their behavior was not videotaped or commented on by the experimenter. After all subjects had completed the pretest and treatment phase, they then solved several posttest problems and their performance was compared to the pretest to evaluate any change.

The results indicated that both modeling and videotape feedback are effective in improving aspects of personal problem solving, but neither appeared to be better than the other, nor was improvement greater when both modeling and videotape feedback were utilized. Modeling, videotape feedback, and both together were effective in increasing the number of questions subjects asked to extract additional information about the problem situation, but only the conditions involving modeling differed significantly from the control condition. Ratings of the quality of the questions asked indicated that videotape feedback and modeling were equally effective in enhancing the quality of questions, whereas the combination of both techniques produced no further improvement. There was some indication that videotape feedback was slightly superior to modeling in enhancing subjects' skills at asking particularly essential questions. Ratings of the quality of the various solutions provided by subjects did not reveal any effects due to the treatment procedures, but the quality of the solution rated best tended to be higher in all treatment groups than in the control.

The results of this study indicate that videotape feedback is effective as a modeling procedure, but that it adds little to what can be gleaned from observing models other than oneself. In the present instance, it may be that a procedure in which models demonstrate both trial *and* error—exhibiting skilled behavior plus behavior that is flawed but which is then corrected—includes components of videotape feedback that are particularly effective. While this interpretation requires further validation, it does suggest that modeling sequences should not depict error-free performances, although any depicted inappropriate or flawed behavior should be corrected before the sequence ends. Even if videotaped feedback is no more effective than modeling, it has the advantage of being specifically matched to the problem behaviors of a particular client, since it occurs during the client's own rehearsal. It also allows the therapist to use a modeling procedure without assembling an armamentarium of modeling tapes or films to cover a broad spectrum of behavior problems.

Most recent research has characterized self-modeling primarily as a vehicle for feedback about one's own behavior. It has been used suc-

cessfully to enhance motor skills in handicapped children (Dowrick & Dove, 1980), as a significant adjunct to overt modeling and instructions in the treatment of public speaking problems (Marshall, Parker, & Hayes, 1982), and as a self-confrontation component in a broader treatment program of assertiveness training (Thelen & Lasoski, 1980). Nevertheless, when combined with other intervention procedures, self-modeling feedback does not always augment the other procedures, though ceiling effects may have simply prevented the demonstration of feedback effects when other techniques were particularly potent.

Response Induction Aids and Self-directed Mastery as Augmentations of Participant Modeling Procedures

Experimental work on participant modeling has been directed toward the elaboration of such techniques in ways that enhance effectiveness. One such procedure is the introduction of response induction aids that facilitate the elicitation of participant behavior during the therapeutic interaction. In a study utilizing individuals with crippling snake phobias (e.g., a geologist who was nearly incapable of fieldwork), Bandura and his associates (1974) contrasted the effectiveness of various amounts of induction aids. The aids used within the participant modeling context included having the therapist hold a snake securely by the head and tail (giving complete protection), asking clients to don either lightweight or heavyweight gloves in order to touch the snake, introducing a snake much less fear provoking in nature, and reducing the amount of time a client was asked to participate in contact with the snake. Most response aids could be classed as part of the systematic graduation of participation, either temporal (varying the duration of participant contact) or physical (how securely the snake was restrained, how protected the client's hand was during participation).

The surprising finding of the investigation was that a moderate amount of response aids proved to be the treatment procedure of choice. Both medium and high levels of aid enhanced the ability to approach the snake used in therapy, but when a new snake was introduced to test generalization, a moderate number of response aids produced the best generalization, as indicated by Figure 4–12. The investigators also found that both moderate and high amounts of response aids produced the greatest cognitive changes in clients, in terms of their general loathing of snakes (see Figure 4–13). This latter finding is important, given the role of attitudinal and attributional factors as mediators of behavior change (Bandura et al., 1975, 1977; Davison & Valins, 1969; Valins, 1966; Valins & Ray, 1967).

There seems little reason to argue whether response induction aids are an addition to the technique of participant modeling or simply constitute ways in which the graduation of temporal and physical components of the technique can be varied. Bandura and his associates (1975) conclude that participant modeling should be graduated moderately—that is, the degree of graduation should be tailored to the individual client.

A second augmentation of participant modeling procedures, one that relates to basic conceptualizations of processes mediating modeling-produced behavior change, is an increasing tendency to stress the cognitive and attitudinal components of modeling procedures (Bandura et al., 1975, 1977). Bandura and his colleagues (1975) proposed that participant modeling

Figure 4–12 *Degree to which snake phobics were able to approach snakes after treatment with a low, moderate, or high number of response induction aids. On the left is indicated the degree to which approach responses could be performed toward the snake used in treatment. On the right are the approach scores involving a new, unfamiliar snake (generalization) (●—●: high aids; ●- - -●: moderate aids; ○- - -○: low aids).*

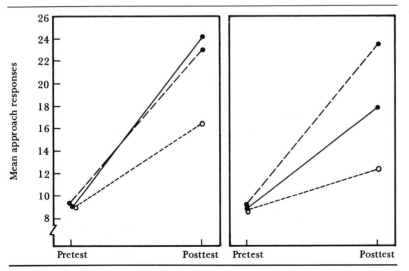

From Bandura, Jeffery, and Wright (1974).

Figure 4–13 *Changes in attitudes (general loathing of snakes) as a function of participant modeling treatment with low, moderate, or high degrees of response induction aids. (●——●: high aids; ●- - -●: moderate aids; ○- - -○: low aids)*

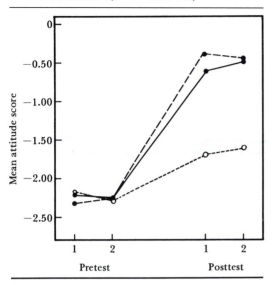

From Bandura, Jeffery, and Wright (1974).

procedures be augmented by including lengthy practice periods during treatment. During these periods, clients approach feared stimuli, practicing and perfecting the approach responses by themselves, with no externally administered response aids or therapist guidance. Bandura has termed these periods experiences *of self-directed mastery.*

In one investigation (Bandura et al., 1975), severe snake phobics were treated with one of several conditions: participant modeling alone, participant modeling in combination with self-direct mastery (toward the snake used in treatment), or participant modeling in combination with varied self-directed mastery (toward the snake used in treatment). During the treatment regimen, participant modeling with response induction aids when necessary was used until

clients were able to perform a number of different behaviors involving an actual snake. The treatment procedure lasted approximately one hour. Following the participant modeling portion of the treatment, some clients were not given any further therapy, some were allowed to interact alone for an hour with the snake used in the participant modeling portion of treatment (self-directed mastery), and some were allowed to interact alone for an hour with both the therapy snake and a distinctively different one (varied self-directed mastery). The researchers gauged the effectiveness of treatment by assessing the degree to which clients would approach the snake used in therapy or a totally new one (different from either of the snakes in the varied self-directed mastery condition).

As may be clearly seen in Figure 4–14, both types of self-directed mastery experiences enhanced clients' abilities to approach both familiar and new snakes to a greater degree than participant modeling alone. In addition, the degree of fear reduction was stable and still present at a one-month follow-up assessment. Attitudinal changes accompanying the behavior change were measured. As indicated in Figure 4–14, clients experiencing participant modeling with self-directed mastery periods showed lesser degrees of fearfulness regarding potential encounters with snakes and enhanced degrees of faith in their ability to handle effectively any actual encounter with a snake in the natural environment. Interestingly, the individuals whose self-directed mastery experiences were *not* varied showed greater changes in both behavior and attitude. A likely explanation is that an early self-directed mastery experience that contains new items of a threatening nature constitutes a premature test of fearlessness that may effectively reduce some of the gains made through the modeling experience. It may thus be advisable to allow varied self-mastery experiences only after nonvaried ones have occurred, although it is not yet clear what the potential gains might be from such a procedure, since the nonvaried self-mastery experiences provided

Figure 4–14 *Attitudinal changes following participant modeling with and without self-directed mastery components. On the left, changes in fears of future encounters with snakes. On the right, changes in the sense of personal potency (perceptions of self-competency). (PRE: before treatment; PM: following participant modeling treatment; SDP: after self-directed performances [for the two conditions that included them]; POST: at the posttreatment assessment; FU: at the follow-up assessment;* ■ · · · ■: *participant modeling;* ○- - -○: *self-directed mastery components;* ●——●: *varied self-directed mastery components.)*

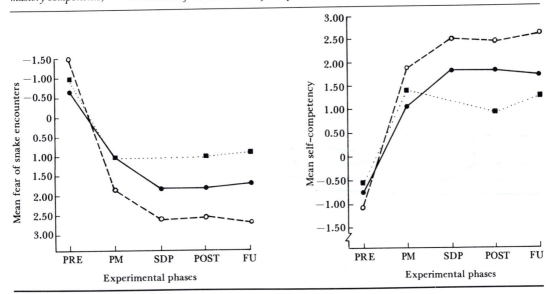

From Bandura, Jeffery, and Gajdos, (1975).

good therapeutic success that was both enduring and highly generalizable.

Vicarious Punishment Procedures

Aversion procedures are discussed at length in Chapter 8, but a related procedure merits brief mention here. Typically, the goal of modeling procedures is to enhance behavioral capabilities or to reduce fear. However, modeling may also be used to associate fear or anxiety with undesired behaviors in order to promote their control or elimination.

There are not many reports of vicarious aversion procedures, despite the fact that they have an implicit ethical advantage as an aversive procedure that does not actually inflict any harm to the client. Rosenthal and his colleagues (Rosenthal, Linehan, Kelley, Rosenthal, Theobald, & Davis, 1978) report the use of vicarious shock in the treatment of nail biting. In this study, clients either imagined themselves receiving shocks contingent on nail biting (covert sensitization) or viewed a trained model receive shocks. The vicarious shock treatment was typically more effective than the imaginal and clearly effective when these clients were compared to controls. The best treatment procedure, however, was one that included both the observation of a punished model and a few trials of shock to the clients themselves. While this procedure did include a direct punishment procedure, it illustrates how such treatments may be combined with modeling in ways that enhance effectiveness and reduce the amount of direct aversive experience by the client.

Role Therapies Related to Modeling Procedures: Fixed-role and Exaggerated-role Therapy

Some techniques of therapy, not generally considered behavior therapies, rely heavily on modeling procedures. Consider, for example, the *fixed-role* and *exaggerated-role* therapies proposed by George Kelly (1955). In fixed-role therapy, the therapist, often with some collaboration by the client, composes a role that includes desired behavior patterns. This sketch, and some role playing by the therapist, constitute a model for the client. In a fixed-role sketch, the role a client is to assume includes overt behaviors as well as behaviors that are less available to observation by others, such as feelings, attitudes, and points of view. If a client cannot change his attitude or point of view upon request, he may still be able to adopt overt behaviors that are in line with the views and feelings he hopes to achieve as a result of therapy. Fortunately, there is a strong tendency for changes in behavior to *evoke* changes in attitudes and other cognitive activities; hence, changes in overt behavior may be the desired therapeutic procedure to gain attitudinal change.

Nonetheless, role sketches generally contain descriptions of both behaviors *and* attitudes whose adoption by the client is the goal of therapy. The client is to adopt the behavior patterns in the sketch over an extended period of time, often several weeks. The behaviors in the sketch are often at great variance with the client's typical behaviors, and some difficulty is usually encountered. The client is instructed to act *like* a person whom the character sketch would fit, not to try to *be* him. There is stress on the experiential, simulatory aspect of the role adoption in order to minimize any threat the client might feel about actualizing broad changes in his life.

The fixed-role sketch presented below was developed for a college-age client who requested therapy for severe self-consciousness. He was extremely ill at ease with others, compulsive in his attempts to be errorless in the completion of every task, and subject to swings of mood, from cool placidity to hyperirritability. In this sketch, since the role is to be considered practically an entire personality, the central character is given a new name: Kenneth Norton. The client, then, is to assume the role of Kenneth Norton; to behave and feel as Kenneth Norton would. Note how the fixed-role sketch describes Kenneth Norton's behavior and feelings in great detail, specifying just exactly how the client is to act when he assumes this role. For example, the client was quite self-concerned and gave many examples of his tendency to examine his every motive. Kelly (1955), in composing the fixed-role sketch, rolled this into a single behavior prescription (and, in this case, *pro*scription): be so concerned with other people that there is not time left to examine yourself; note also how satisfying and enjoyable are certain of their behaviors. Thus, the role even includes what stimuli are to be reinforcing for the person.

Kenneth Norton is the kind of man who, after a few minutes of conversation, somehow makes you feel that he must have known you intimately for a long time. This comes about, not by any particular questions that he asks, but by the understanding way in which he listens. It is as if he had a knack of seeing the world through your eyes. The things which you have come to see as being important, he, too, soon seems to sense as similarly important. Thus he catches not only your words but the punctuations of feeling with which they are formed and the little accents of meaning with which they are chosen.

Kenneth Norton's complete absorption in the thoughts of the people with whom he holds conversations appears to leave no place for any feelings of self-consciousness regarding himself. If indeed he has such feelings at all, they obviously run a poor second to this eagerness to see the world through other people's eyes. Nor does this mean that he is ashamed of himself; rather, it means that he is too much involved with the fascinating worlds of other people with whom he is surrounded to give more than a passing thought to soul-searching criticisms of himself. Some people might, of course, consider this itself to be a kind of fault. Be that as it may, this is the kind of fellow Kenneth Norton is, and this behavior represents the Norton brand of sincerity.

Girls he finds attractive for many reasons, not the least of which is the exciting opportunity they provide for his understanding the feminine point of view. Unlike some men, he does not "throw the ladies a line," but, so skillful a listener is he, soon he has them throwing him one—and he is thoroughly enjoying it.

With his own parents and in his own home he is somewhat more expressive of his own ideas and feelings. Thus his parents are given an opportunity to share and supplement his new enthusiasms and accomplishments. (Kelly, 1955, pp. 374–375)

With practice, clients can adopt prescribed roles such as these. Thus, their behaviors are changed for at least a short period of time. However, one is still faced with the problem of maintaining such changes in behavior. It is seen as important that new behavior patterns be practiced in as many different approximate contexts as possible, and care should be taken to help the client "try them out"—first in situations that will allow the new behaviors to be reinforced. In the case of Kenneth Norton, Kelly reported the following anecdote indicating that the role behaviors of Kenneth Norton met with positive consequences in at least one instance when the client met a girl, a former classmate, after a movie:

> The girl works in the candy counter in the lobby (of the theater) and she and he had a twenty-five- to thirty-five-minute talk. She seemed

quite interested in him and the role worked better with her than with anyone else. In fact, by the time the conversation was finished she was paying him several compliments, saying that he had changed since he had gone away to college, obviously implying a change for the better. The conversation was so rewarding to the client that he did not leave until the manager of the movie came along and implied that he was taking too much of her time. (1955, p. 394)

Kelly's fixed-role therapy is more sweeping than other role-therapy techniques, perhaps because his procedure is embedded within an entire theory of personality. Often therapists with a behavioral bent will make use of what is known as *exaggerated-role training,* a procedure of instructing patients deliberately to adopt prescribed, but limited, roles that are designed to correct highly specific behavioral problems. Wolpe and Lazarus described the case of a college student who complained of severe feelings of uneasiness when dining at his girlfriend's house. The problem became exacerbated when, during dinner, his mouth would become so dry that he could not swallow his food. The following short role was prescribed:

> The next time you dine at her house I want you to act as if you were a wealthy and important businessman . . . not 22-year-old Peter. As you sit at the table, I want you to look at each person and see him as you think he would appear in the eyes of this mature and wealthy businessman. (Wolpe & Lazarus, 1966, p. 134)

In this case, we may surmise that the use of the label "businessman" was sufficient to produce in the client a clear notion of all the attendant social behaviors that would characterize a businessman at the dinner table. More important than the client's success in acting out all the behaviors a businessman would perform, perhaps, is his success in avoiding anxiety, which certainly would *not* have characterized an effective businessman. It seems likely that by behaving like a businessman (including the cognitive aspects that were embodied in that role, such as a feeling of competence or superiority), many internal stimuli eliciting the anxiety were removed. Probably it was not the sight of his girlfriend or her father that produced anxiety, but rather the client's thoughts in that situation: "What can I say to impress them? How do I talk to her father when I don't even know him?" and so on. Thus, it seems reasonable for the therapist to determine the cognitive components of any set of maladaptive behaviors so that he may devise a role that includes cognitive components that supplant those which elicit anxiety or other maladaptive behaviors.

Investigations of the Effectiveness of Modeling Procedures

Various Modeling Procedures Contrasted

Research on modeling as behavior therapy technique often contrasts various types of modeling procedures instead of selecting particular modeling protocols and contrasting them with a nonmodeling technique. Ritter (1969b) drew a distinction between contact desensitization, in which the therapist manually guides or assists the client's participation; demonstration plus participation, in which any guidance is verbal only; and live modeling, with no participation. She then compared these three techniques in terms of their effectiveness for the elimination of acrophobia. Subjects exhibiting a severe degree of fear of heights were given but a single 35-minute treatment session utilizing one of these techniques. Treatment took place on the roof of a seven-story building, a flat roof with a 41-inch-high concrete railing. The pace of treatment was governed by feedback from the subjects concerning how comfortable they were with the various tasks they were asked to perform. As in a desensitization procedure, when-

ever a subject reported feeling some discomfort at the completion of a task, that task was repeated. This procedure differs from the typical desensitization procedure, in that a discomforting task might not be repeated until one of somewhat more difficulty had been completed successfully (Ritter, 1969c).

In all procedures, the therapist first performed the behaviors to be acquired. These consisted of several behaviors. First, the therapist would stand on each of five rungs of a wooden ladder for two 30-second intervals; then for two 30-second intervals, she would stand on an 18-inch-high chair, and on a 29 ½-inch-high stool, all positioned 11 inches from the roof railing. Finally, the model would climb to the eighth rung of an elevator penthouse wall ladder, 8 feet above the roof's surface.

In the *contact desensitization* procedure, the therapist, after demonstrating each behavior, assisted the subject in her performance of modeled response. For example, in working on ladder climbing, the therapist might walk alongside the subject, an arm around her waist, while approaching the ladder. Then, as the subject ascended the ladder, the therapist might follow behind with hands placed on the subject's waist. Finally, when the subject was standing on the upper rungs of the ladder, the therapist might place her hands on the subject's legs. In the *demonstration-plus-participation* procedure, following the therapist's demonstration, the subject would be guided verbally through her replication of the therapist's modeled behaviors. In the *live modeling* procedure, the therapist demonstrated the behavior while the subject sat toward the center of the roof and observed. The therapist also asked occasionally how the subject was feeling and only proceeded to model more difficult behaviors when the subject was able to observe the preceding behaviors with little or no discomfort.

Before treatment, each subject was given a height avoidance test that included the behaviors described above. Points were given for each behavior the subject could already perform, the maximum score being 44, and only those individuals accumulating 18 points or fewer were included as subjects in the experiment. Following the modeling procedures, the subjects were again administered the height avoidance test, with only a 5-minute rest period. Thus, the total time included in treatment amounted to a bare 40 minutes.

The results of this study are shown in Figure 4–15. Treatment by contact desensitization produced a greater increase in the number of fearless behaviors performed than did either of the other two procedures, and the demonstration plus participation produced a greater increase than did live modeling.

It is clear from this study that the greater the interaction between therapist and client in a modeling procedure, the greater the effectiveness of treatment. The question that remains is, Which of the components of this interaction enhance the effectiveness of treatment? Certainly one factor is the provision of social reinforcement by the therapist as the client actually demonstrates mastery of new behaviors. The client's own self-administered reinforcers, such as positive self-comments or feelings of pride, doubtless contribute to the successful acquisition and maintenance of behaviors previously feared.

The presence of the therapist and the encouragement he or she gives, whether verbal or physical, probably has a calming effect—similar to the relaxation portion of a desensitization procedure. An indication that this is the case comes from the results of an experiment by Rimm and Madieros (1970), in which demonstration plus participation was coupled with relaxation training for one group of subjects, while another group received demonstration plus participation or relaxation training alone. The subjects, all severely frightened of snakes, showed an equally striking reduction in their snake phobias when demonstration plus participation was employed, regardless of the inclusion of relaxation training. Subjects who received relaxation training showed no substantial relief from their fears.

Figure 4–15 *Mean number of approach behaviors shown by individuals before and after treatment by live modeling, demonstration plus participation, or contact desensitization procedures (——: contact desensitization; — —: demonstration + participation; . . . : live modeling).*

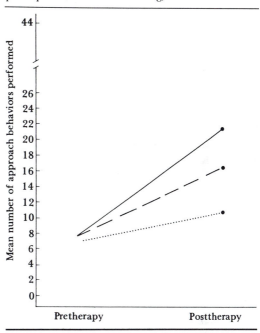

From Ritter (1969c).

The finding that relaxation training, which appears to be important in desensitization procedures, had no observable effect may indicate that subjects receiving demonstration-plus-participation procedures were already sufficiently calm and relaxed to allow the completion of fearful behaviors, such as the actual handling of a snake. It is also possible that the effectiveness of demonstration plus participation, for reasons that remain unclear, is so powerful that the addition of ancillary techniques such as relaxation training cannot offer improvement, since the effectiveness is already so great. Further research should clarify this point.

In an extensive study, Bandura and colleagues (1969) compared the relative effectiveness of *symbolic modeling, live modeling plus participation,* and *desensitization* for the reduction of snake phobias. Symbolic modeling consisted of a 35-minute film depicting young children, adolescents, and adults engaging in progressively more frightening and more intimate interactions with a snake. This procedure also contained elements of a desensitization procedure. Subjects were taught to induce and maintain deep relaxation throughout the period during which they viewed the movie. Further, they were in control of the progression of the film and were instructed to stop the film whenever a particular model performance was anxiety provoking, to reverse the film to the beginning of the aversive sequence, and to reinduce deep relaxation.

Desensitization utilized a 34-item hierarchy containing scenes that the subjects were to imagine while in a deep state of relaxation. These scenes ranged from relatively innocuous activities, such as looking at pictures and toy replicas of snakes, to the imagined handling of live snakes. In the live-modeling-plus-participation condition, subjects repeatedly observed intimate snake interaction behaviors modeled by the experimenter. Then they were aided by joint participation with the experimenter in the performance of progressively more threatening approach responses toward a king snake. The experiment also had a control condition, in which subjects participated in the assessment procedures that were administered before and after the treatments utilized in the other conditions.

It is noteworthy that the various treatments required differing amounts of time to administer. Subjects continued in a treatment procedure until either they achieved the terminal criterion (e.g., observing the model perform the most threatening behavior or imagining the most fearful item on a hierarchy) or the treatment had consumed 5¼ hours, not including time for relaxation training. The modeling treatments both took somewhat more than 2 hours, while systematic desensitization required an average of 4½ hours to achieve the criterion, a significantly longer period of time.

Following treatment, subjects were presented with the opportunity to interact with a snake, either the one included in the treatment and pretest phases or another snake of distinctively different appearance (generalization). One stringent measure of the effectiveness of a treatment is the percentage of subjects who will perform the behavior previously rated *most* threatening. Fully 92 percent of the subjects in the modeling-with-participation treatment condition were able to interact this closely with a snake. On the other hand, only 33 percent of the subjects in the symbolic modeling condition, 25 percent in the systematic desensitization condition, and none in the control condition were willing to interact so intimately with a snake. Subjects from the symbolic modeling, systematic desensitization, and control groups who would not perform the most intensely threatening interaction with a snake were subsequently given the live-modeling-with-guide-participation treatment. The average length of this subsequent treatment was 1 hour and 20 minutes. After this treatment had been administered, 96 percent of all subjects were able to make the most threatening approach response to the snake used during treatment, and 70 percent showed the complete elimination of avoidance behavior toward the generalization snake as well. These results indicate that participant modeling is a powerful and extremely rapid technique for the elimination of fears.

At this point it would be helpful to comment upon the relationship between behavioral and attitudinal changes that presumably result from these therapeutic techniques. In an early study by Bandura and his colleagues (1969), subjects were given an attitude scale testing their attitudes toward snakes. They were also requested to fill out a semantic differential. Changes in approach behavior toward snakes were positively related to attitude change as measured by both the semantic differential ($r = .55$, $p < .01$) and the attitude scales ($r = .58$, $p < .01$). Interestingly, there was no relationship between the degree of initial fearfulness (initial number of intensity of fears) in other areas of functioning and the degree of behavioral change. The subjects' initial attitudes toward snakes also did not affect the extent of improvement in their approach behavior toward snakes effected by the various treatments. Bandura's subsequent work (Bandura et al., 1974, 1975) has highlighted the role cognitive components play in achieving therapeutic effectiveness (see the section on response aids and self-mastery above, as well as the final section of this chapter).

Hersen, Eisler, and Miller (1973) compared demonstrative modeling, symbolic modeling (instructions), and practice in the encouragement of assertive behavior. In this investigation, scenes from the Behavioral Assertiveness Test (Eisler, Miller, & Hersen, 1973) were described to nonassertive psychiatric patients who were then asked to role-play how they would act. In the practice condition, patients were simply encouraged to "do better" after each scene, while in the instruction condition, specific suggestions for behavior change were given (e.g., talk louder, say what you expect others to do, look directly at others during the interaction). There were two modeling conditions, one in which a videotape depicted assertive behavior for each scene, and one in which the videotape was accompanied by the instructions described above. Not surprisingly, practice with no specification of the desired behavior had little effect on assertion, while the combination of demonstrative modeling and instructions specifying desired behavior (symbolic modeling) significantly enhanced a variety of types of assertive behavior (duration of verbal replies, overall assertiveness, requests for new behavior from another person, duration of eye contact with another person). For some individual types of assertive behavior, modeling alone or instruction alone was as effective as modeling plus instructions. Only direct instruction produced changes in voice loudness, and only demonstrative modeling re-

duced bland compliance. Overall, however, these findings indicate that the combination of demonstrative modeling with symbolic components (instructions) that denote specific behaviors for acquisition is probably the most potent form a modeling treatment can take. The effectiveness of modeling alone or instruction alone on different categories of behavior may indicate that some specific types of behavior are particularly responsive to simpler, nonredundant procedures, although at this point it is probably impossible to specify those behavior types in advance.

Jaffe and Carlson (1976) used both demonstrative and instructional modeling as treatment procedures to increase the social behavior of chronic psychiatric patients. These investigators found that either modeling procedure was effective, and it is interesting to note that the patients generalized many treatment effects to a variety of ward situations. Patients who had had either demonstrative modeling (a videotape of appropriate social responding during a ringtoss game) or specific instructions on how to behave appropriately improved in such categories as amount of care needed, seclusiveness, the social behavior scale (see Farina, Arenberg, & Guskin, 1957), and in observations of on-ward other-oriented behavior and reciprocated social behavior.

Modeling Procedures Contrasted With Other Behavior Therapy Techniques

Many investigations have compared the relative effectiveness of behavioral modeling procedures with other treatment procedures. Some have been between variants of a modeling procedure—such as behavioral modeling (demonstration), instructional modeling, or descriptive modeling (role playing, with the role defined by a written or verbal description of a model's behavior)—whereas others have contrasted modeling with techniques such as desensitization or practice. The evidence regarding differential effectiveness is somewhat mixed, perhaps because of the wide variety of problem behaviors that have been utilized, ranging from phobias in adults to the inadequate question-asking behavior of mildly retarded children. Demonstrative and instructional modeling have been found to be effective treatment procedures, often equally so. Modeling and desensitization also seem to be similarly effective in treating fears, even though one procedure concentrates on the acquisition of fearless approach behaviors, while the other concentrates on the elimination of anxiety with no attention to approach behavior.

Ritter (1968b) contrasted contact desensitization and what she termed "vicarious desensitization." Although we have included contact desensitization as a modeling procedure in this chapter, we should note that the actual technique combines the experience of modeling with graduated practice that, in the case of fearful behaviors, constitutes a component of *in vivo* desensitization. For that reason, we are considering it as a variant and to some extent a non-modeling procedure in the present discussion. On the other hand, vicarious desensitization is more directly a modeling procedure in which a model demonstrates gradually more fearless behavior but the observer does not participate. The careful reader will already have noted that contact desensitization resembles the *imitation* paradigm discussed earlier and vicarious desensitization resembles the *observational learning* paradigm.

Ritter (1968b) utilized a group desensitization procedure for the elimination of snake phobias in young children. In her procedure, peer models were employed to demonstrate fearless and bold interactions with snakes. Initially, children were given an avoidance test in which they were required to move from a point 15 feet away from a caged snake to a point 1 foot away. Other tasks involved standing in front of the snake, looking down at the snake, touching the cage with a gloved hand or with a bare hand, or inserting a gloved hand and then

a bare hand into the cage up to the wrist. Further tasks involved the lifting of the snake or taking it out of the cage. Only children who could not hold the snake within the cage with a gloved hand for five seconds were included in the study.

Children were given two treatment sessions that lasted approximately 35 minutes each and that were spaced one week apart. Seven to eight children participated in each treatment group. In one condition, which involved *contact desensitization,* the children observed an adult experimenter taking a snake out of the cage, sitting with the snake, and petting it. This continued until one of the subjects appeared to be willing to participate, at which time the experimenter encouraged the child to put on a glove and to place his hand on her hand while stroking the snake. Gradually then, the child was encouraged to stroke the snake himself, first with a gloved hand, then with his bare hand. When several children had become bold enough to stroke the snake, the children were encouraged to take turns being therapist and client, one stroking the snake and the other beginning with his hand on the first child's and gradually moving it to the body of the snake.

In a *vicarious desensitization condition,* there were five peer models at each session. These were boys and girls who had expressed no fear at all of snakes prior to the experiment. In each session, these models were seated in a corner of the room. After the experimenter had removed the snake from the cage, she encouraged the models to perform tasks that had been included in the avoidance task, such as stroking the snake with a gloved and then a bare hand, lifting the snake with first gloved and then bare hands and so on. The children who were subjects were not encouraged to participate directly with the snake. They did, however, take charge of the demonstrators in a game, during which they sent the demonstrator from the room, called him back in, and instructed him to perform the various fearless interactions with the snake, at which time they could again observe his behavior.

Following the treatment procedures, all children were again administered the snake avoidance test. There was also a control group of children who were administered the avoidance test and then, following a period of time equivalent to that consumed by the treatment for the other two groups, were given the avoidance test again.

The behaviors required in the avoidance test, some of which were described earlier, culminated in a task requiring that the snake be held approximately five inches from the face for 30 seconds, after which the subject was asked to sit in a chair with his arms at his side while the snake was in his lap for 30 seconds. *All* of the items in the avoidance test were performed successfully by fully 80 percent of the children who had received contact desensitization. Significantly fewer children in the vicarious desensitization condition performed all of these items, whereas none of the children in the control condition performed all items. Statistical analyses revealed that children in both treatment groups evidenced highly significant increases in their abilities to interact closely with snakes when compared with children in the control condition. It was also evident that children in the contact desensitization condition improved in their ability to interact intimately with snakes to a significantly greater degree than did children who received vicarious desensitization.

Clearly, group procedures can be highly effective in the administration of observational learning techniques for the elimination of fears. Although little research has been done, it seems quite apparent that these techniques also lend themselves to group application for the treatment of problems in which the goal may be the addition of behaviors to the client's repertoire.

Research on Components of the Participant Modeling Procedure

Blanchard (1969, 1970) isolated several components of the participant modeling procedure and compared the individual contributions to specific and generalized behavior change. Three components were separated from a demonstration-plus-participation procedure: the modeling component, the provision of *verbal information*, and the provision of *direct contact* with the feared object. Four subjects simultaneously participated in a treatment procedure, but each subject was in a different condition. To one subject, the therapist administered a demonstration-plus-participation modeling procedure. Behind a one-way mirror, two other subjects observed. One of these who observed listened via earphones to the verbal interchange between the therapist and the participating subject, whereas the other observer merely watched. Of these three subjects, then, the participating subject received modeling, verbal information, and direct contact with the feared object; the second subject, modeling and verbal information; and the third, only modeling. A fourth subject (the control) received none of these treatment procedures.

Before treatment, each subject was tested to determine how closely he would approach a live snake. Following treatment, the subjects were twice again administered this test, once with the same snake that had been included in the earlier test and in the treatment procedure, and once with a different, unfamiliar snake, in order to assess the generalization of the treatment effectiveness. The terminal behavior in each assessment was the subject's picking up the snake from a glass cage with bare hands, holding it close to his face, and then allowing it to crawl around freely on his lap, with his arms at his side. Blanchard also gathered data concerning the subject's general fear of snakes (*affect*) and their liking (*attitude*) toward snakes.

Figure 4–16 illustrates the changes in behavior, affect, and attitude produced by the various procedures. The modeling component appears to account for 60 percent of the observed change in behavior and 80 percent of the recorded changes in affect and attitude, with the guided participation responsible for the remainder. It is interesting that information

Figure 4–16 *Percentages of change in approach behavior, fearfulness, and attitudes exhibited by individuals who received various components of modeling and guided participation treatment procedures (solid bars: modeling + information + participation; hatched bars: modeling + information; dotted bars: modeling; open bars: control).*

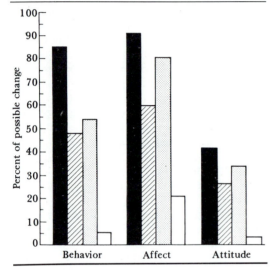

From Blanchard (1969).

indication that the provision of extensive verbal information may prove rousing since the two procedures containing information began at a higher level of arousal. However, in all procedures, there was a dramatic reduction of arousal during observation of, or *participation* with, the live snake.

In testing subsequent improvement, Blanchard measured subjects' abilities to approach

Figure 4–17 *Mean degree of fear arousal elicited by approach to the feared object: level of arousal following the initial approach, and by subsequent repetitions of the approach, shown by individuals who participated in treatment or observed the treatment of others with or without information influences (○——○: modeling + information + participation; ●– – –●: modeling + information; ●- - -●: modeling).*

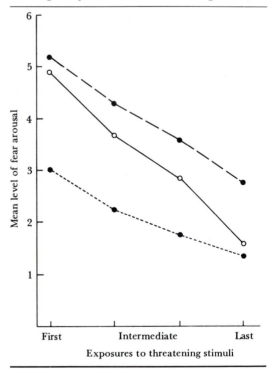

From Blanchard (1969).

appeared to add nothing to the effectiveness of the general technique, but the information was limited to verbal renditions of the nonslimy nature of snakes, the harmlessness of their tongues, their poor vision, and the like—and giving highly phobic people such verbal information may even prove arousing. It is still the case, certainly, that the modeling procedure and the subsequent participation provides both vicarious and first-hand information on how to handle snakes and how they do, indeed, feel and behave.

Blanchard also gathered ratings of fear arousal at several times throughout the three modeling sequences. Figure 4–17 illustrates the effect of these procedures on arousal at the various points during treatment. Again, there is an

the snake used in treatment and a new, generalization snake as well. The entire modeling-plus-information-plus-participation procedure proved to be the most effective in reducing fear toward the snake that was used during treatment. However, subjects who only observed the therapist modeling the desired behavior, without participating or hearing the verbal interchange, proved to be the least fearful of the new, generalization snake. Thus, there is some indication that modeling *without* participation by the client constitutes a procedure that is to be preferred when the behavior to be changed will necessarily occur in many different situations or toward many different objects. If extensive generalization must occur before changes in environmental contingencies, produced by the client's changed behavior, elicit the desired behavior in new situations, the therapist may choose to conduct a rather lengthy simple modeling procedure instead of utilizing a less extensive exposure to a demonstration-plus-participation procedure.

Instructions and Narratives as Augmentations of Modeling Therapy

While Blanchard's research concentrated on modeling and information techniques for fear reduction, several other investigations have been designed to elucidate the role that instructions or narratives accompanying actual modeling may play in achieving or accentuating the effectiveness of modeling procedures for the acquisition of new behavior patterns. Edelstein and Eisler (1976) contrasted modeling and modeling plus instructions and feedback (therapist commentary on the appropriateness of behavior) in the treatment of a schizophrenic hospital inpatient. To improve the social skills of the patient, first a simple modeling procedure was utilized. Then instructions and feedback were added after from 6 to 18 sessions, depending upon the particular social skill being modeled. Modeling alone was found to increase the display of appropriate affect in social en-

counters, but only after the inclusion of instructions and feedback were positive changes in eye contact, use of appropriate head and hand gestures, and assertiveness noted.

Not surprisingly, recent research on a number of different modeling procedures has increasingly included instructions as part of the base "package" of treatment. For example, the work of Kendall and his colleagues on impulse control typically includes self-instructions along with a modeling component (e.g., Kendall & Braswell, 1982; Kendall & Finch, 1978; Kendall & Zupan, 1981). Similarly, Matson included it in his package for independence training (Matson, 1982), and many procedures for reducing fear include an instruction component focused upon the description of what an individual may expect in a fear-evoking context, such as a dental office (Melamed, 1978; Stokes & Kennedy, 1980).

Modeling and Role-playing Techniques Contrasted

Role-playing techniques have not frequently been contrasted with direct modeling, but at least one such comparison was attempted in an early study. Lira, Nay, McCullough, and Etkin (1975) used self-regulated symbolic modeling and self-regulated role playing in the treatment of avoidance behavior (snake phobias). The symbolic modeling procedure consisted of a videotape depicting a competent male model gradually but confidently approaching a snake. The procedure, termed *self-regulated role playing,* was actually a combination of role-playing instructions with verbal descriptions of competent, fearless behavior toward a snake. Subjects were given a one-page description of a John or Jane Harris, a person similar to the subject but who had had extensive experience with snakes. They then heard a 10-minute audiotape that described positive approach behaviors toward a snake (including all the specific behaviors illustrated by the videotape model) and were instructed to put themselves in the role of John or Jane Harris while listening to the description and to imagine themselves approaching a snake. The role-playing procedure thus resembles the covert modeling procedure described by Cautela (1971b) and Kazdin (1974a–1974d) and could be interpreted as an inadvertent comparison of overt and covert modeling procedures. The investigators found that their modeling procedure had no effect on subjects' subsequent fearless behaviors toward a real snake, while the role-playing manipulation increased subjects' fearless approach behaviors and reduced avoidance attitudes toward possible encounters with snakes. These effects were maintained during the two-month follow-up period.

Investigations contrasting the effectiveness of modeling treatments with other forms of behavior therapy have commonly elaborated on the modeling procedure by combining it with components of other techniques. The work of Hersen and colleagues (1973), described above, is one example since they included a treatment that combined demonstrative modeling with specific verbal instructions. Graduated modeling, which depicts fearless approach behaviors toward a phobic object or activity, draws heavily on the procedures basic to systematic desensitization. In a comparison of modeling and desensitization treatments, Denney and Sullivan (1976) elaborated further upon the modeling technique by combining videotaped modeling sequences with both verbal narrative and relaxation instructions. In this investigation, individuals with a serious fear of spiders were treated either by imaginal and videotaped desensitization procedures, videotaped modeling-plus-relaxation instructions, or modeling alone. In the imaginal desensitization procedure, subjects either imagined graduated scenes of spiders or scenes that included an individual interacting with the spider. Similarly, the videotaped scenes, whether combined with relaxation instructions or not, either included scenes of spiders alone (videotaped desensitization) or of individuals interacting with spiders (videotaped modeling).

One rationale for this investigation was to determine whether mere visual exposure to the feared object—an automatic component of any modeling sequence—was primary in determining the effectiveness of the modeling technique, or whether the actual modeling—the depicted behavior of the model—was the primary effective component. These investigators found that desensitization and modeling treatments were equally effective in reducing behavioral avoidance and self-rated anxiety. The desensitization procedure that involved imagining scenes containing individuals interacting with a spider corresponds to covert modeling, whereas the modeling procedure that contained spiders amounts actually to videotaped (rather than imaginal) desensitization. The investigation found that imaginal desensitization, visual desensitization (where the phobic object is viewed), behavioral modeling, and covert modeling all produced equivalent relief from unrealistic anxiety and needless avoidance behavior. The one condition in which individuals were shown scenes of the phobic insect with no relaxation instructions or other desensitization procedures produced no improvements in phobic behavior, indicating that the desensitization and modeling procedures were effective because of components other than simply displaying the feared object—that is, specifically because of the desensitization or modeling components.

In an investigation that demonstrated the effectiveness of modeling techniques for altering cognitive and intellectual coping behavior in retarded individuals, Bondy and Erickson (1976) contrasted modeling and reinforcement procedures for increasing the question-asking behavior of mildly retarded children. This was a unique investigation in that it contrasted modeling and contingency management procedures for effecting behavior change. The researchers found that modeling by itself did not greatly enhance question asking, but modeling combined with a token reinforcement procedure produced significant improvement. Reinforcement alone also produced improvement in question asking, but the combination of modeling and reinforcement allowed a faster rate of improvement immediately after the treatment procedure was instituted. This study provides some evidence for the productive interaction of modeling and contingency management techniques, especially when it is important to produce some initial changes in behavior that can be specifically reinforced.

One final investigation should be discussed. Horne and Matson (1977) contrasted a large number of behavior therapy techniques in their effectiveness for treating test anxiety: modeling, desensitization, flooding, and instruction in study skills. Modeling was accomplished by audiotapes supposedly from a group treatment of test-anxious students who initially expressed a great deal of anxiety, but gradually, over the course of 10 sessions, made fewer and fewer anxious statements as they interacted with one another. Modeling and desensitization consistently produced significant reductions in test anxiety, general anxiety, and pulse rate following an actual midterm or final examination. Flooding was also effective in reducing test anxiety as measured by the Sarason Test Anxiety Scale (Sarason, 1958), but it had no effect on the pulse rate index of anxiety following an actual test situation. In addition, subjects indicated that they did not like the flooding procedure, despite its partial effectiveness, because of the psychological discomfort it produced. Clients greatly preferred the modeling procedure, with desensitization being somewhat less recommended.

A Summary of Comparative Research Results

The comparative investigations of modeling as a behavior therapy technique have indicated that it can be effectively applied to a variety of populations—from the retarded to the psychotic and the institutionalized—and to a variety of behavior disorders—from the primarily cognitive (such as test anxiety or phobic avoidance) to the

social (the insertion of social skills or individually positive patterns into insufficient individual repertoires). The use of instruction or narratives generally enhances the effectiveness of modeling, probably by providing cognitive structure in the denotation of specific behaviors or implicit attitudes (such as appreciation or fearlessness) held by models that can be adopted through role playing. The voluminous research has provided important clarification for the clinical use of modeling procedures and certainly signifies their increased utility.

Efficacy Cognitions and Successful Behavior Change

It has become common to label the participant modeling procedure an *enactive* one in order to distinguish it from simple modeling, which is called *vicarious* because it involves only observation and no behavioral enactment. In theorizing about processes by which behavior change is accomplished, the component differences between these two types of modeling have become especially significant. Bandura (1977b; Bandura, Adams, & Beyer, 1977) has proposed that an important cognitive factor mediating the effectiveness of behavior therapy procedures is the degree to which individuals acquire the expectancy that they will be able to perform the new or goal behaviors toward which the change procedures are oriented. Bandura distinguishes between expectancies of self-efficacy—anticipation of personal mastery of a difficult behavioral problem—and expectancies of response outcome—anticipation that a behavior, if performed, will produce a rewarding outcome or positive consequence. These two expectancies are actually quite different. One can know full well that effectively asking a girl for a date is likely to be successful (positive response outcome) but still have serious or total doubt about one's ability to solicit a date with skill (self-efficacy expectancy).

Bandura has argued that self-efficacy expectancies are crucial to effective behavior change, because they mediate the likelihood that a person will attempt a goal behavior in the natural context—that is, outside the treatment situation. In addition, self-efficacy expectations also influence how strongly a behavior will be persistently maintained in the face of failure. Since efficacy expectations are considered determinants of behavior, they are potentially important factors in behavior change that is accomplished by any therapeutic intervention. However, we could argue that they are especially likely to be influenced by a technique such as participant modeling because it provides the person with experiences of personal mastery during the course of treatment as he or she participates in and actually demonstrates components of the goal behaviors.

In fact, the early research on self-efficacy expectancies was conducted primarily in the context of participant modeling techniques. In an experiment with severely snake-phobic adults, modeling and participant modeling procedures were contrasted, in terms of both the degree to which they changed individuals' self-efficacy expectancies (that they would be able to behave fearlessly with respect to snakes) and the degree to which actual behavior change was accomplished. As Figure 4–18 illustrates, both modeling procedures produced changes in self-efficacy over a control group, but by far the largest changes occurred as a result of participant modeling. Efficacy expectancies about fearlessness in the presence of snakes different from the one used in the treatment procedure were also changed, indicating a good degree of generalization. Although the actual behavior of phobic individuals toward both similar and dissimilar snakes became more bold as a function of modeling treatment, participant modeling was the more potent technique, as indicated in Figure 4–19. Research has suggested additional procedures that can be integrated into the therapy situation and that can enhance the development of efficacy expectation. Bandura and Schunk (1981) found that the setting of proximal, readily attainable subgoals promotes

Figure 4–18 *Effects of participant and nonparticipant modeling treatments on self-efficacy expectancies. The two assessments during the posttest were made before and after behavioral avoidance tests with two snakes (Participant modeling, ●—●: similar threat; ○—○: dissimilar threat. Modeling, ●- - -●: similar threat; ○- - -○: dissimilar threat. Control, ●· · ·●: similar threat; ○· · ·○: dissimilar threat).*

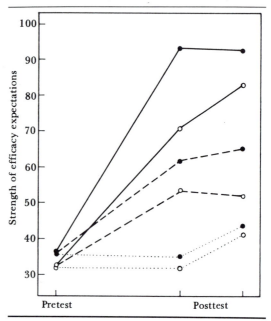

From Bandura, Adams, and Beyer (1977).

motivation, successful attainment, and feelings of competence, whereas distal, more difficult goals do not.

More recent research by Bandura and his colleagues has confirmed that efficacy beliefs influence both psychological variables, such as the level of fear for phobic objects or difficult behaviors, and actual performance as well. Bandura, Reese, and Adams (1982) employed a treatment procedure for spider phobics involving a model who demonstrated fearless behavior toward spiders, along with various coping behaviors (e.g., how to pick it up by putting a plas-

Figure 4–19   *Combined presentation of self-efficacy expectancies for successful fearless performance and actual degree of fearless behavior with respect to similar threat (snake used in treatment) and dissimilar threat (generalization) as a function of participant and nonparticipant modeling treatments. The two assessments during the posttest were made before and after behavioral avoidance tests of self-efficacy expectancies with the two snakes (Participant modeling, ○—○: efficacy expectancy; ●—●: behavior. Modeling, ○– – –○: efficacy expectancy; ●– – –●: behavior. Control, ○- - -○: efficacy expectancy; ●- - -●: behavior).*

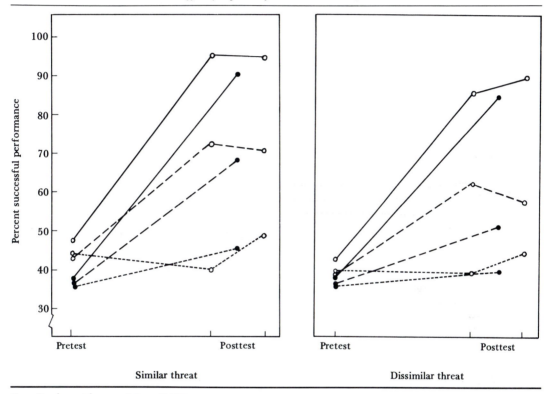

From Bandura, Adams, and Beyer (1977).

tic cup over it and sliding a thin piece of card-board underneath). By varying the length and extent of treatment, it was possible to include different levels of self-efficacy beliefs and then to examine the relation between these beliefs and subjects' actual behavior with spiders. As may be seen in Figure 4–20, subjects' levels of self-efficacy were strongly related to their ability to demonstrate fearless behavior. The case is

made even more strongly by noting that group differences in self-efficacy (on the left in the figure) affected behavior were mirrored in the behavior of individual subjects as they proceeded from low to high levels of self-efficacy (on the right in the figure).

One implication from this research involves the use of efficacy expectancies as a criterion for the assessment of therapeutic effectiveness.

Figure 4–20 *Mean performance attainments as a function of differential levels of perceived self-efficacy. (The left panel shows the performances of subjects whose self-percepts of efficacy were raised to different levels. The right panel shows the performances of the same subjects at different levels of self-efficacy.)*

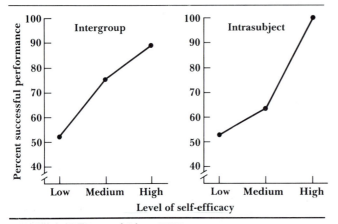

From Bandura, Reese, and Adams (1982).

Bandura et al. (1977) found that there was a close correspondence between individuals' efficacy expectancies and the degree to which they could perform fearlessly, as Figure 4–21 shows. Even when a treatment procedure was reasonably effective in reducing fear for an entire group of clients, some individuals held a reduced expectancy for successful performance, and it was those individuals who did poorly in a real behavioral task that involved confronting the phobic object, a snake. More recently, research has demonstrated that efficacy beliefs can predict which clients will relapse and which will not, how long before a relapse would occur, and even in which situations a relapse was most likely to occur (Condiotte & Lichtenstein, 1981).

There are some caveats, of course. On the one hand, efficacy expectancies should be better predictors of successful behavior change than, say, behavior immediately at the termination of treatment, because those behaviors may be influenced by temporary and nongeneralized factors, such as the presence of an influential other (e.g., the therapist), or specific situational constraints (Bandura, 1982a, 1982b; Lee, 1983). On the other hand, efficacy expectancies themselves may have a weakened relationship to subsequent behavior as a function of factors such as the misjudgment of future situations or task requirements, unanticipated situational constraints, or even inadequate or inaccurate self-knowledge.

Overall, the message is twofold. First, self-efficacy expectancies can be used as an assessment of treatment effectiveness in increasing the competent performance (or elimination) of problem behaviors (and not necessarily just for modeling treatments). Second, some attention should be given in any treatment procedure to altering the individual's self-efficacy expectancies in addition to changing the problem behavior itself, since changes in efficacy beliefs may augment the actual behavior change and promote generalization of changed behavior patterns.

Figure 4–21   *Influence of self-efficacy expectancies on the probability of successful accomplishment of fearless behavior. On the left, the relationship between self-efficacy expectancies and probability of performance for modeling and control conditions (●—●: participant modeling; ●- - -●: modeling; ○- - -○: treated controls). On the right, the relationship between the two variables when fearless behavior was measured toward similar and dissimilar (generalization) threats, with the various treatment condition data combined (●—●: similar threat; ○- - -○: dissimilar threat).*

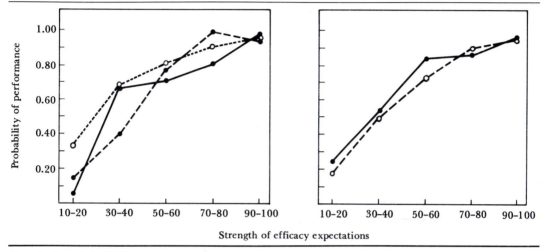

Strength of efficacy expectations

From Bandura et al. (1977).

5
Contingency Management I: Basic Procedures and Techniques

In this chapter, we examine procedures involving the contingent administration of rewarding (reinforcing) consequences or events. Clinicians all too frequently focus on the elimination, or extinction, of maladaptive behaviors and ignore the more positive goal of strengthening adaptive behaviors that are infrequent or of initiating adaptive behaviors that are absent from an individual's repertoire. Where possible, it is surely preferable to eliminate a maladaptive behavior by increasing the frequency of a desirable, competing behavior (which cannot be performed at the same time as the maladaptive behavior). Eliminating a response by punishment may be ineffective if the client has no alternative response. Moreover, the use of extinction procedures for individuals whose lives are replete with punishment or who seldom enjoy reinforcement may alienate or depress them and consequently prove ineffective. Too often, for instance, the therapist encounters children whose parents punish them when they misbehave but do nothing when they behave properly. In such cases, a primary goal may be to teach the parents techniques of contingency management that employ reinforcement rather than punishment. Contingencies of reinforcement are often an alternative to other means that may be effective but less desirable in producing behavior change.

Depending on the nature of the presenting problem, the therapist may need to employ varying combinations of modification techniques. For example, if the problem involves the complete absence of a desirable behavior, and the behavior appears to be one that the client lacks the ability to perform, the therapist may need to shape his performance of this behavior by the procedures of *successive approximation*. In such a case, the therapist could utilize observational learning techniques to instigate some initial performances of the behavior, followed by the judicious use of reward to establish the behavior firmly in the person's repertoire and ensure its performance in appropriate situations (*discrimination training*). To take a second example, one may have to punish a maladaptive behavior of very high frequency in order to clear a "slot of time" into which a new behavior may be inserted. For self-destructive children, punishment is often effective in inhibiting their persistent tendency to injure themselves or to engage in hyperactive behavior so that more human rewards—such as love and affection—can be made contingent upon more acceptable forms of behavior, such as smiling, passive social contact (sitting in an adult's lap), or quiet play. In short, the management of reinforcing contingencies can be an important addition to other treatment procedures as well as a powerful tool for behavior change in its own right.

References in this chapter and the next are to many studies that were completed when contingency management procedures came to be an important technique of behavior therapy, generally the 1970s. During this period, there was a great deal of research on the utilization of such procedures in a variety of settings and for the treatment of a variety of behavior problems. Subsequently, however, many procedures or their applications to particular behavior problems have generated less research attention, primarily because early reports clearly demonstrated their effectiveness, and methods of implementation needed little further refinement. We have continued to describe this early research and, in a number of instances, to quote from them examples of the implementation of various techniques because the treatment effectiveness remains valid and procedures of implementation are still current.

The Role of Reinforcement in the Learning of Social Behaviors

Learning theorists generally agree about the factors responsible for the acquisition and maintenance of human behavior. However, they differ in the emphasis they place on any one factor. Thus, theorists who are primarily concerned with observational learning as a source of human social behavior are likely to argue cogently that the observation of others is a powerful, perhaps even primary, source of behavior acquisition for both child and adult. Theorists with an operant bent are likely to acknowledge the usefulness of observational learning but are quick to point out that even though the observation of another person provided the original learning situation, a person will continue to perform the behavior only if it is rewarded. They will also argue that behaviors that produce contingent aversive consequences (i.e., are punished) may be observed but not adopted into the individual's own behavioral repertoire.

We do not intend to take sides in the value-laden arguments concerning which process of learning is more important for the development of personality behaviors in human beings. Clearly, while an operant philosophy stresses the importance of reward and punishment in the acquisition, maintenance, and extinction of human behavior, it also acknowledges, at least minimally, factors other than reinforcement and punishment (e.g., classical conditioning and observational learning). It is true, however, that major operant theorists, such as Skinner, eschew the use of punishment and sidestep the use of other techniques of behavior change if positive reinforcement procedures are applicable.

Definition of Terms

Reinforcement

The terms *reinforcement* and *reward* are often used synonymously, and to a considerable extent they do overlap in meaning. A *positive* reinforcer is an event, behavior, privilege, or material object that will increase the probability of occurrence of any behavior upon which it is contingent. A smile or a compliment directed toward you from another person is an event that would be likely to act as a reinforcer and will increase the probability that you will behave again, sometime in the future, in the same manner that elicited the event. Note that we say *likely*. Although the therapist often anticipates what will act as a reinforcer, technically he cannot be certain of this until he observes that the contingent presentation of the speculated reinforcer does, indeed, affect the behavior of the person in question (Becker, 1971; Skinner, 1966).

Similarly, the privilege of performing a high-frequency behavior can act as a reinforcer: children's disruptive behavior in the classroom may be eliminated and their quiet, studious behavior strengthened if they are allowed to be rowdy or have a recess only *after* they have been quiet for a set period of time. Related to this, the privilege of performing a behavior may become a reinforcer if a person has been deprived of that behavior for awhile (Konarski, Johnson, Crowell, & Whitman, 1981; Konarski, Johnson, Crowell, & Whitman, 1982). Finally, a reinforcer can be a tangible, material reward. Yet, while material rewards are indeed quite effective in the control of behavior, the social reinforcement value of another person's friendly, loving, approving, or simply attending behavior is also a powerful factor in the control of behavior, and social reinforcement is certainly a more common occurrence across all situations in the natural environment than the dispensation of material rewards.

Contingent reinforcers *increase* the frequency of a behavior. By definition, there are two types of reinforcers, positive and negative. A *positive reinforcer* is any stimulus event whose contingent *presentation* increases the rate of performance of a response. A *negative reinforcer* is any event whose contingent *withdrawal* increases the rate of performance of a response. As Skinner has so aptly put it, "The kinds of consequences which increase the rate (of a response) ('reinforcers') are positive or negative, depending upon whether they reinforce when they appear or disappear" (1969, p. 7). As the reader may already have concluded, a negative reinforcer is usually the termination of a punishment or punishing stimulus. Chapter 8, "Punishment and Aversion Procedures," covers in some detail the use of the contingent termination of punishment as an integral component in avoidance conditioning procedures. Appendix A contains a more complete discussion of the definition of reinforcers and reinforcement and of schedules of reinforcement in general.

Contingency

In its simplest form, to make a reinforcer contingent is to dispense it *following* a desired behavior (one whose frequency is to be increased) and to take care that the reinforcer is dispensed *only* following desired behaviors. Later in the chapter we discuss principles designed to increase the effectiveness of the contingent dispensation of reward.

There is little doubt that the contingent dispensation of reinforcement is an effective method for controlling behavior. It has been clearly demonstrated that noncontingent reinforcement fails to control behavior, whereas the contingent application of the same reinforcer does exert effective control. If an office worker receives a raise every three months, regardless of the quality of his work, his performance is less likely to improve than if he is working under a system employing bonuses and raises based on merit (i.e., contingent on good performance). Similarly, the contingent application of a stimulus or event that has no value to an individual is ineffective in altering the behavior upon which it is contingent. In such cases, the therapist either should employ a stimulus that can be demonstrated to have reinforcing properties or should directly establish a reinforcing value for the neutral stimulus by pairing it with an established reinforcer. Chocolate candy will not be a powerful reinforcer for the child who dislikes, or is allergic to, chocolate, nor will the opportunity to play baseball be an effective reinforcer for the child who dislikes physical activity and prefers to play chess. In a later section, we will discuss procedures for discovering the stimuli and events that are reinforcing for a given person or group.

Contingent Reinforcement and the Undermining of Intrinsic Interest

A topic of great interest in psychology since the early 1970s has been a phenomenon reported by Lepper, Greene, and Nisbet (1973) termed either the "undermining of intrinsic interest" or the "overjustification effect." Briefly, the finding was that if children were reinforced for engaging in an activity that had already been of some interest to them, when the reinforcement contingency was withdrawn they showed less interest in the activity than they had before it was reinforced. Thus, for example, if children spent some time during the day spontaneously engaging in picture drawing, after a period when they were rewarded for drawing they would tend to spend less time drawing than they had before. This effect was interpreted in a cognitive fashion—that is, that the reinforcement overjustified the activity. After a period of being reinforced for an activity, the reinforcement becomes the justification for it (rather than an intrinsic interest in the activity), so when the reinforcement is withdrawn the activity is abandoned because the justification for engaging in it is gone.

At first, this phenomenon suggests that reinforcement contingencies to develop behavior patterns or increase their frequency might "enslave" the individual so that he or she would only perform the desired behaviors when the reinforcement contingency was in effect (see the discussion of intrinsic and extrinsic reinforcement in Appendix A). However, this has rarely proved to be the case in the actual implementation of contingency management programs, including token economies, especially when care is taken to promote generalization and to use procedures such as fading to phase the management program out (Davidson & Bucher, 1978; Fisher, 1979; Marholin & Steinman, 1977; Vasta, 1981). In addition to generalization and fading procedures, whenever possible it also is advisable that reinforcement be made contingent on the product of an activity, especially the quality of that product (e.g., not only increasing social behavior but having that behavior be appropriate). The research literature on the question of undermining intrinsic interest suggests that the effect does not occur when aspects of behavior, such as its quality or excellence (e.g., achievement in school, as in part of the Achievement Place program described later in this chapter) rather than simply its occurrence of frequency, are the target of reinforcement.

What is Contingency Management?

Contingency management involves the *contingent presentation* and *withdrawal* of *rewards* and *punishments*. Although the therapist may use such procedures herself, often it is more feasible and effective that she train others to function as contingency managers—such as parents and teachers, individuals more closely involved in the life of the individual under treatment than the therapist herself. Furthermore, as detailed later, clients can be trained in contingency management so that they may exercise self-control over their own problem behaviors.

Obviously more skills are involved than the mere dispensation of reinforcements. To take just a few examples, the therapist must discover a number of rewards or reinforcers that can be manipulated and are effective for the individual whose behavior is to be altered. Even prior to this step, the therapist must determine the behaviors to be changed, their frequency of occurrence, the situations in which they occur, and the stimuli or reinforcers that appear to be responsible for the maintenance of these maladaptive behaviors in the natural environment. These assessment procedures may reveal that an individual's problematic behavior is due not to the presence of inappropriate behaviors but rather to the absence of appropriate behaviors. In that case, subsequent contingency management procedures must be directed toward the shaping of new behaviors as much as the elimination of problem ones. In a nutshell, assessment and pretreatment procedures include establishing a baseline rate of frequency, instituting procedures for measuring behavioral change, and assessing the behaviors to be treated and the reinforcers to be employed in treatment.

All of these skills are involved in contingency management and make it a complex and sophisticated procedure, even though many accuse a reinforcement analysis of behavior of being rather simplistic. In this chapter, we will focus primarily upon the contingent management of reinforcers, although some attention will be given to mild punishers such as contingent withdrawal of reinforcement (e.g., time-outs or response cost procedures). A direct treatment of contingent punishment will be found in Chapter 8, "Punishment and Aversion Procedures."

There are a number of separate components to the design and implementation of a sound program of contingency management. These components are of particular interest and importance to those planning to establish such a program or who are intent upon learning principles of contingency management in a particularly thorough and detailed fashion. Of all the behavior therapy procedures we discuss, the use of reinforcement, and to some extent punishment, through the management of contingencies has perhaps the longest and richest history. This is because it draws upon the entire field of the experimental analysis of behavior, more commonly known as operant or instrumental conditioning.

Much of the detailed substructure of contingency management procedures will be unnecessary for the person interested simply in gaining a general understanding of reinforcement-based procedures for behavior change, though a good acquaintance with operant psychology is a necessary prerequisite. See Appendix A for a brief introduction to the general principles of reinforcement that form the foundation of all contingency management procedures.

Elements of Contingency Management Programs

Below we discuss a number of the elements that make up a contingency management program, from the characterization of the problem behavior, its frequency, and what seems to con-

trol it to the effective implementation of a contingency-based intervention and the assessment of its outcome. In many ways, this is an ideal set of elements: not all will be included in a given program, but were it not for limitations of time, cost, manpower, and so on, the inclusion of all these elements would constitute an exemplary intervention with every likelihood of success.

Baseline Measurement

In the assessment procedures that should precede any contingency manipulation, the therapist must establish the relative frequency or infrequency of the behavior(s) in question. This procedure is applicable to many behavior therapy techniques, but it is perhaps most important in the application of operant techniques, whether in the office, home, school, or institution. There are several sources of information concerning the frequency of a behavior.

In what might seem to be the most direct assessment, the therapist can ask the client for, or simply listen to, his or her account of the presenting complaint. This source of information has its problems, however, since people are not objective observers of their own behavior or of others'. Experience shows that a behavior to which one objects may seem all too frequent, even though in actuality it occurs quite rarely, and a behavior that one desires may seem never to occur. Depressed individuals may be particularly subject to such distortions (cf. Lewinsohn & Amenson, 1978). Often an individual's concern with the frequency of a behavior makes him a less discriminating observer in that he does not notice, and hence cannot report, the situations in which the behavior does or does not occur. This makes it difficult for the therapist to move from the assessment of frequency to the assessment of when, where, or under what conditions the behavior tends (not) to occur.

In cases when the clients are children, they are often referred by their parents, and the therapist may utilize the parental complaints as assessment information. This source is problematic since parents can speak only for the frequency of behaviors in their presence, and they themselves may be powerful eliciting stimuli for behaviors that occur only rarely otherwise—or that frequently occur in other situations. In fact, one study (Schnelle, 1974) found that parents frequently were inaccurate reporters of such an objective behavior as attendance at school. The therapist cannot tell all from the parents' report alone.

Clients and individuals who refer clients generally do not count behaviors, draw graphs, or in other ways attempt to objectify their impressions of behavior. Thus, it is often up to the therapist to direct them in the techniques of generating good baseline data. For example, they may be instructed in the procedure of time-sharing observations. Once each five minutes, say, a parent will be instructed to note simply whether the child is or is not performing the questionable behavior. Furthermore, the parent should record the observation only in a certain situation—for example, in the house—and not to count those times (or not to record them on the same sheet) when the child performed the behavior in the yard. In the same fashion, clients can be instructed in the observation of their own behavior, although clearly the fact that they are their own observers may affect the behavior in question.

It is also possible to use *direct observational report* or specimen description. In this procedure, the observer, whether she is the client herself or the parent, teacher, friend, or sibling (Doleys, Doster, & Cartelli, 1976; Lavigueur, 1976), or even an observer employed by the therapist (Johnson, Christensen, & Bellamy, 1976; Wahler & Erickson, 1969), simply notes the time and place for each occurrence of the behavior in question. Clearly, this technique is cumbersome, especially for a behavior that occurs with any great frequency; however, it is fairly comprehensive and can be reduced to tabular or graphic

form, thereby allowing a clearer picture of the frequency of the behavior in question. The client can be asked to bring this information to the therapist, who may then plot a graph of the behavior. Furthermore, it may be desirable to have the client, his parents, teachers, or other observers plot the data as they are gathered, or perhaps once a day, to provide a continuing picture of the behavior in question. This procedure is especially useful during the period of behavior *change*, since it may act as a powerful reinforcer for the individuals whose manipulation of contingencies is effecting the change.

Incidentally, the direct observational report is not a bad practice in the utilization of *any* technique of behavior change because it allows the rapid recognition of progress (or the lack thereof). As we discuss later, assessment is not limited to the period before behavior change, but should be an ongoing process that occurs throughout the intervention period and afterward during the follow-up.

Clearly, the most effective technique of behavior measurement, whether for baseline data or for data regarding behavior change during and after therapy, is the utilization of trained observers to observe the client in the situations where the maladaptive behavior tends to occur. Training competent observers is an arduous process, and expensive as well. But it is a worthy endeavor and instruction manuals are available.

Occasionally the therapist himself may act as observer; for instance, when he attends a class in which a child typically exhibits disruptive behavior, or monitors the interaction between mother and child in the waiting room before an appointment. These procedures are clearly the most accurate, and were it not for economic limitations, they would surely be the preferred assessment technique. They are expensive, however, and may not always be possible. Videotaping behavior or firsthand observation by the therapist, even for a limited period of time, will increase the likelihood that he has accurate information concerning the behavior in question.

Recording the Frequency of Behaviors

When working with problem behaviors, the therapist is often concerned less with problems of discriminative performance of behaviors (learning to perform them in the appropriate situations) than with problem behaviors performed in appropriate situations that occur too frequently or too infrequently. For example, the therapist does not record the total frequency of aggressive behavior a child may show throughout the entire day. Rather, the necessary information may include the frequency of aggression *at home, toward parents,* or *toward other children at school* versus *toward other children at home,* and so on. Thus, there are two basic considerations when setting up a program of frequency recording: (1) designating the behaviors to be recorded *and* the situations during which they are to be recorded; and (2) training observers (who may be the client himself, parents, teachers, or—although not very likely—the therapist himself or persons in his employ). The latter procedure should include the provision of tallying materials and instruction in the art of constructing a graph or chart that summarizes the frequency information.

Defining and Designating Behaviors and Situations to Record

Typically, the therapist must sift through the presenting complaints and any observational material she may have concerning the client's behavior in order to arrive at a description of the problem behaviors and the situations in which they seem to occur. If the evidence (information) at this point appears reasonably complete, little may need to be done in the way of further specification of the frequency of the problem behaviors. However, it is always a good idea to gather specific data on behavioral frequencies since these data either will confirm the initial impressions or disconfirm them by demonstrating that the behavioral frequency is not as high or as low as supposed, or that the situations originally designated are not the ones in which the behavior occurs inappropriately or with a maladaptively high or low frequency. Thus, gathering frequency data during the early part of a modification sequence may provide corrective feedback to an inaccurate behavioral diagnosis.

You may have noted that we have discussed only the frequency of behaviors and not their intensity. Often the intensity of an act is an important consideration in identifying changeworthy behaviors. A soft-spoken "Excuse me, but the end of the line is back there" is assertive in content but may be said so softly and mildly that it does not qualify as a truly assertive act. Similarly, the aggressive and hyperactive conduct of the class bully toward his peers may comprise the same behaviors as normal rough-and-tumble play, but be exaggerated in intensity until they render harm. Although frequency within a situation or toward a particular person should indeed be recorded during the assessment phase of contingency management, other aspects of behavior, such as intensity, may be taken into account in the *definition* of the behavior to be given to observers. Thus, if interpersonal aggression constitutes the potential problem behavior, observers who record the behavior must have a clear definition of the aggressive behavior that they are to assess. The therapist can give definitions most clearly through examples, both of behaviors that fit the definition and of those that resemble it but are not of concern at the moment. In the above example of the aggressive child, the observers would be given not only examples of aggressive acts toward peers but also examples of rough-and-tumble play that are *not* to be considered aggressive.

Finally, observers should be sensitive to the events that precede and follow the behaviors under scrutiny. For effective behavior change, a range of important information is generally required. Some of the most important information concerns the events that act as stimuli for a particular behavior pattern and the events that follow it, potentially acting as reinforcers or punishers. Later in this chapter we will discuss the importance of maintaining stimuli in the natural environment. Often a complete behavior change program must consider the potential necessity for altering aspects of the environment, such as the behavior of others with whom the client interacts frequently, if those aspects appear to be maintaining or strengthening the problem behavior. For example, in the hypothetical case of an aggressive child, behavioral assessment might reveal that aggression against siblings is most likely when the child repeatedly asks for something from his busy mother and is consistently ignored by her. The consequent frustration the child feels, plus the fact that an aggressive act *will* elicit the mother's attention, may account for the occurrence of aggression within the family context. The child is more likely to act aggressively when in a state of frustration (stimulus), and that action is effective in eliciting the valued attention from the mother (reinforcer).

Training Observers

Observation of frequency of occurrence should actually involve *behavioral events*—that is, *units* that include the performance of a behavior *and* the consequences that accrue. These can be recorded as separate frequencies. For example, if a child exhibits tantrum behavior at home, the therapist might first attempt to ascertain the response of the parents (the parents can be quite accurate in reporting their own behavior in this case). Let us say that the parents have tried to ignore the tantrums, attempting a simple extinction procedure (Chapter 7, "Response Elimination and Extinction Procedures"). The child reacts, however, by howling longer and longer, louder and louder, until the parents give in to the child's wishes most of the time just to silence him. Undoubtedly the parents' behavior has two effects: (1) it increases the length and loudness of the tantrum, since increasing both of these characteristics has led to attention get-

ting (success) and thus has been reinforced; and (2) it increases, or at least maintains, the frequency of tantrums, since they are usually successful in removing the frustration of desire.

Parents of a child such as this might be asked to fill in a chart, listing the numbers of tantrums per day and noting their response to each tantrum. They should also estimate the amount of time each tantrum endured. Table 5-1 illustrates what such a chart might look like.

Typically, contingency management techniques train *parents, teachers, siblings, peers,* and other individuals in the client's immediate environment to act as therapists. Part of this training must involve teaching them to observe and record behavior. Initially it will often prove wise to have these individuals read materials that explain how to observe the behaviors of individuals, not their personality characteristics, and how to analyze behavior *consequences* in order to understand and change behaviors. Fortunately, there are several good books on the techniques of observation that are written so laypeople can readily understand them (e.g., Becker, 1971; Blechman, 1985; Patterson & Gullion, 1976). The therapist may wish to discuss these books with the paratherapists and instruct them in the techniques she prefers for the gathering of frequency information, the skills involved in making graphs, and so on. She may also provide them with prepared observation charts on which they are to record behavior observations. As new behaviors are to be modified, new charts should be prepared, and the therapist should reinstruct the observers in the observation of these particular behaviors. At some point, however, it may be appropriate to train a naive individual to intervene as a "paratherapist," and this will involve providing training in more than the simple skills of observation and recording.

Training Contingency Managers

In recent years, there has been rising attention to the problem of enlisting individuals in the natural environment as contingency

Table 5-1 **Instances of Tantrum Behavior and Parental Responses to Tantrums Over a Seven-Day Period: Sample Behavior Chart**

Days	Tantrums	Duration (minutes)	Response
1	1	4	Comforted child when he slipped and banged head during crying
2	1	5	Told child to be quiet but finally gave cookie to quiet him down
	1	6	Ignored until couldn't stand it; gave cookie
3	1	5	Ignored
	2	6	Ignored
	3	8	Ignored until child took cookie himself; spanked child
4	1	4	Ignored; child stopped spontaneously
5	1	4	Company present; gave child cookie to quiet him
	2	5	Ignored; finally gave in
6	1	8	Ignored; went into bathroom, had cigarette, read magazine until child quieted himself
	2	4	Ignored; just as I was about to give in, child stopped
7	1	3	Ignored; child stopped, began to play

managers. This makes ample sense since it is, generally, precisely those individuals who provide the eliciting stimuli and maintaining reinforcers that promote problem behaviors. Often the person to be trained as a contingency manager is an individual whose own behavior may be totally or partially responsible for the deviant behavior and who is highly motivated to act in ways that will promote change. Parents, for example, may be extremely concerned about their child's behavior and acknowledge their own inability to cope with it. Ample evidence (Berkowitz & Graziano, 1972) shows that

parents can be trained to be effective behavior therapists in their use of contingency management procedures, and often this training may be minimal. For highly motivated individuals, simply learning about operant principles and the ways that social consequences affect behavior (by reading Patterson & Gullion, 1976; or Becker, 1971) can promote self-initiated changes in the way they interact with the individual displaying the problem behavior. Today there are a number of concise and simply written manuals directed at parents, as well as ones for therapists who undertake the training of parents. There are an increasing number of manuals for behavior change addressed to teachers, as well.[1]

In the treatment of children, parents are almost invariably involved, and their efforts may be used to supplement a more rigorous treatment program in settings such as the school, hospital, or clinic. Early studies reporting various methods of training parents and their almost uniform success have been surveyed by Berkowitz and Graziano (1972).

Other methodological advances, such as the "bug in the ear," have enhanced the effectiveness with which parents (or other individuals) may be trained. The "bug" is a small one-way communication device worn in the ear that receives messages sent by a therapist observing an interaction from an unobtrusive vantage point. In this way, a therapist can objectively survey a child's behavior and cue parents to behave in a rewarding or punishing fashion contingent upon desired or problem behaviors. This technique, which has been successfully used in a number of cases, initiates not only a contingency management program but also helps to train parents or other significant individuals to recognize target behaviors and to produce appropriately reinforcing or punishing consequences.

A similar bugging procedure can be used to track problem behaviors and assess treatment effectiveness. Johnson et al. (1976) reported an investigation in which children with problem behaviors wore a small radio transmitter that was

activated either periodically by a timer or by parents at predetermined times that problem behaviors were likely to occur (e.g., bedtime). These authors found that audio recordings on which problem behaviors could be identified by sound revealed decreases in the behaviors over a period of treatment. In addition, when parents were allowed to designate times when they thought problem behaviors would be most likely, they selected times when indeed the frequency of such behavior was greater. At these times, there was also a greater frequency of ineffective behavior on the part of the parents, such as negative behavior or the use of authoritarian commands. The audio sampling technique was thus an adjunct in the training of parents to substitute contingency management techniques for their ongoing ineffective attempts at controlling their children.

Interest in contingency management was accompanied from the very outset by a recognition of the need to train contingency managers in a systematic fashion. Thus, there was a concerted effort to develop standardized procedures for the training of contingency managers and to assess the success of implemented training programs. Procedural steps identified as components of extensive training programs include the assessment of the organizational environment (family or institutional setting), identification of any concerns expressed by family members or staff, an explicit program of training with a full explication of the terms and goals of the program, and a system of monitoring during the execution of the program. Parents, teachers, or peers are thus occasionally trained as observers, contingency managers, and experimenters (to the extent that data are gathered to demonstrate the effectiveness of the management program) (Hall, Axelrod, Tyler, Grief, Jones, & Robertson, 1972). An important component of training is the provision of feedback about the adequacy of management behavior. When Doleys and colleagues (1976) trained parents in a group using lecture and role-playing procedures accompanied by written

---

[1]For manuals for parents, see Alvord (1973), Becker (1971), Carter (1972), Gnagey (1975), Patterson (1975), Patterson & Gullion (1976), Rettig (1973), Smith & Smith (1976). For therapists to train parents, see DeRisi & Butz (1974); Fleischman, Horne, & Arthur (1983); Kozloff (1973); Miller (1975). For manuals addressed to teachers, see Becker (1971); Blechman (1985); Buckley & Walker (1970); Carter (1972); DeRisi & Butz (1974); Diebert & Harmon (1973); Homme (1971); Martin & Lauridsen (1974); Rettig & Paulson (1975); Shepphard, Shank, & Wilson (1973); Smith & Smith (1976); Sulzer-Azároff & Mayer (1977); Swift & Spivack (1975); and Zifferblatt (1970).

material, they found little change in the ways that the parents interacted with their children. In a second phase of training, the authors gave feedback to parents regarding the adequacy of their management, and parents heard recordings of some of their interactions with their children, as well as recordings of other parent-child interactions. Following this phase, there were significant changes in the parents' behavior and these changes were maintained over a 30-week follow-up. In short, the training of contingency managers is not necessarily simple, but it is likely to be worthwhile, because it provides an extension of contingency management procedures to the natural environment.

Self-monitoring In some contingency management situations, the primary source of information about problem behaviors is the individual himself. Therefore, an important aspect of many contingency management programs is the accuracy with which individuals can monitor their own behavior so that they may accurately report instances of the problem behaviors before, during, and after treatment. This is an activity in which most clients, whether children or adults, of average intelligence or mildly retarded, can be trained. In many instances, self-monitoring in and of itself appears to have beneficial effects. Self-monitoring probably is successful in changing behaviors because increased attention to problem behaviors, the context in which they tend to occur, and the consequences they elicit prepares the individual to inhibit these problem behaviors, to substitute alternative patterns of action, or to avoid contexts in which the problem behaviors are likely to occur. There is more consistent evidence that self-monitoring maintains behavior previously modified by contingency management, especially children's classroom behavior (Bolstad & Johnson, 1972; Drabman, Spitalnik, & O'Leary, 1973; Glynn, Thomas, & Shee, 1973; Kaufman & O'Leary, 1972).

The broadest generalization that can be made about self-monitoring is that accuracy should not be assumed. Clear attentional factors limit how accurate a person will be in self-monitoring. If an individual is in a contingency management program, the monitoring of behavior other than the one that is being reinforced is significantly less accurate than the monitoring of that same behavior when other behaviors are *not* being reinforced as part of a treatment program (Epstein, Miller, & Webster, 1976). In the school situation, Thomas (1976) has reported that self-monitoring of behavior, such as time-in-task, ranges from a relatively inaccurate 56 percent correct to 95 percent correct. When self-monitoring involves recording behavior that is to be reinforced (monitoring desirable rather than problem behaviors), errors tend to be in the direction of allowing more reinforcement than is actually justified. There is also little evidence that practice alone improves the accuracy of self-monitoring. In the Thomas (1976) study, some children appeared to become more accurate over time, whereas others appeared to get worse.

There is one study that reports the use of self-monitoring to implement the effectiveness of a token contingency management program that, by itself, was failing to modify behavior. Seymour and Stokes (1976) trained adolescent girls whose actions were unaffected by a token system to self-monitor those behaviors that were the targets of reinforcement. In their training procedure, a therapist dispensed token rewards for the girls' accurate self-monitoring of target behaviors, as well as verbal behavior that was likely to elicit praise from the staff. This training procedure resulted in an increase in both the target behaviors eliciting token reinforcement and the verbal behavior producing an increased level of social praise. It appears that a number of different types of positive benefits may accrue from accurate self-monitoring, and that training in self-monitoring is easily implemented. In the basic design of a contingency management program, specific attention should be given to the usefulness of the self-report from the individual under treatment, both in terms of accurate assessment of the frequency of problem and target behaviors and in terms of the beneficial effects that may accrue from the self-monitoring itself.

Frequency Recording in Assessment, Treatment, and Follow-up

The sequence of behavior modification contains three periods, each of which involves gathering information on the client's behavior. During *assessment,* the recording of frequency information will confirm the behavioral diagnosis, and observation in general will give information concerning the maintaining stimuli, the discriminative occurrence of the behavior in question, and so on. During *treatment,* continued tallying of behavior frequencies will indicate whether the modification procedures are indeed effective. Finally, the frequency of a problem behavior (or lack thereof) should be recorded as a *follow-up* for some time after the termination of treatment to verify the continuing success of treatment. Careful training in objective procedures in frequency recording for this last phase is essential since evidence shows that uninstructed individuals may be quite inaccurate, particularly in the assessment of posttreatment change (Schnelle, 1974).

Consider Figure 5-1, which presents a record of the frequency of a problem behavior during a seven-day treatment period. This record is not a good one for several reasons. First of all, if Days 1, 2, and 3 are the baseline period, the behavior appears to be increasing in frequency; clearly, it is not being performed at a stable rate. If the therapist intends to determine whether improvement will be due to the treatment procedure he or she subsequently designs or to other factors, treatment should not begin until a stable frequency is observed. Otherwise, any improvement noted during treatment may be due to the inconsistent frequency of this behavior, which seems to be characterized by such fluctuations.[2]

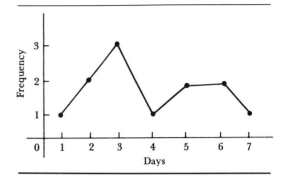

Figure 5-1 *Graph of the frequency of a problem behavior across seven treatment days. The data are presented in Table 5-1.*

During treatment, the therapist must know if the frequency of a behavior is indeed changing so he or she can modify treatment if no frequency changes are being observed (or if it changes in the wrong direction), and so treatment can be terminated when the desired end frequency is reached and is stable. In Figure 5-1, if treatment extended to Day 7, we do not know if it in fact has been effective because the behavior is still as frequent as on the first day. If treatment extended only to Day 4, termination would have been premature, because there was a short recurrence on Day 5 with a subsequent decline on Day 7.

Because the termination of treatment may involve the client's return to his normal environment, the undesirable behaviors may well return: old contingencies that reinforce the maladaptive behaviors are reinstated, and the individual may again be exposed to models who

[2]When the primary goal is simply to lower (as in the present example) or to increase the frequency of a problem behavior as quickly as possible, an extended baseline frequency measure may be deemed unnecessary. It is always best, however, to include baseline measurement even in these cases.

exhibit the maladaptive behavior. Long-term follow-up periods have not been as characteristic of research on operant techniques as they have been for, say, desensitization. Possibly this is because most research studies have concentrated on the effectiveness of certain techniques to produce rapid change and have not considered total treatment programs designed to influence natural contingencies in the environment, or thereby to produce enduring change. Figure 5-1 shows little evidence of a follow-up period, and given the ups and downs of the frequency of tantrum behavior, it would not be surprising if the frequency rose again after Day 7. Without a follow-up, then, there would be no way to tell whether the cessation of treatment on Day 7 was wise or unwise.

Figure 5-2 shows what a total graph might look like. If Days 8–12 (3–7 on Figure 5-1) are the treatment period, it is clear that there is an average level of two tantrums per day from Day 1 to Day 7, then a ragged, but fairly clear, downward trend on Days 8–12, and finally a reasonably good indication that tantrums continued to be absent at the end. Note that this is a hypothetical graph, and a five-day follow-up is *not* a long one. Note also that even if a tantrum occurred occasionally—say, once every four days—during an extended follow-up, the graph would make it clear that the frequency was greatly reduced after treatment. Moreover, a client keeping this graph would not be likely to misinterpret isolated, single occurrences as a full-blown recurrence of the problem, and thus would not likely become disheartened.

Identifying Maintaining Stimuli

Another integral part of problem behavior assessment—and again, an appropriate procedure in the use of nearly all behavior therapy techniques—is the identification of the particular stimuli, situations, or other conditions that consistently precede (elicit) the maladaptive behavior and those that consistently follow maintaining factors, or reinforcers. Determining eliciting stimuli often helps in the subsequent assessment of maintaining reinforcers, in the discovery of exactly which stimuli are effective reinforcers, and in the determination and description of the social and physical environments that elicit the maladaptive behavior and into which more adaptive behaviors must be programmed. Close questioning of the client will provide insight into the determinants of his or her behavior, although direct observation

Figure 5-2 *Frequency of a particular target behavior over a 17-day period. The frequencies for days 6–12 are also presented in Figure 5-1 and in tabular form in Table 5-1.*

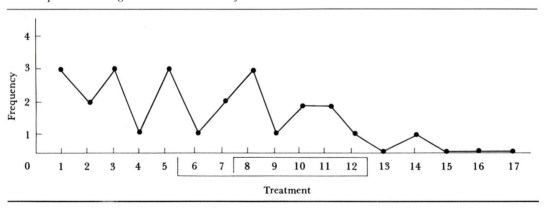

may be necessary and nearly always provides more detailed and more objective information than the client report.

The thrust of any initial questioning should be toward the last several times the behavior occurred. There is little point, at first, in seeking general, characteristic times when the behavior occurs or is absent, because the client is not usually predisposed to observe his or her own behavior in terms of times, situations, events, or people who stimulate it (unless, of course, this is not the first maladaptive behavior the therapist has treated for a particular client). For example, if severe procrastination were the problem, the following dialogue might result:

Therapist: So you say that you continually defeat yourself by putting things off until it is too late?

Client: Yes . . . it really seems to be a terribly self-destructive sort of behavior. . . . I can't understand why I do it.

Therapist: Well, let's think back to the last time you kept putting something off until it was too late. Can you recall when something like this happened recently?

Client: Well, it was just this morning, if you want to know the truth. I was supposed to have taken the storm windows off, now that it's getting hot. I didn't do it last night and then didn't have time to get to it this morning because I had to come here.

Therapist: What did your wife say?

Client: What did she say? She nagged at me a little last night, but not much. There was a good baseball game on that I wanted to see. But this morning she really let me have it. She said that she thought I was doing it just to hurt her, and then she cried. I comforted her and apologized and promised to take them off when I got back from here.

Therapist: Did you go through this last year, too?

Client: No, believe it or not, I took them off just as the weather began to get warm.

Therapist: What did your wife say?

Client: Nothing. Oh, yes, I believe she made a few nasty comments about how it was the first time I had taken them off early and how she hoped I had (sneeringly) "finally gotten rid of your laziness." But that's all.

It is clear from this dialogue that the consequences for the desired behavior were less positive than the ones for procrastinating. Putting off the household chore allowed the client to watch a baseball game. And the next morning, his wife's final pleas led to a highly reinforcing, tender scene between them. Further interviewing would likely uncover additional instances in which procrastination allowed immediate reinforcement that outweighed any eventual punishment for the procrastination itself.

Let us consider another example illustrating the importance of gaining an initial understanding of systematic relations between stimuli, behaviors, and consequences. Problem behaviors, and problem contingencies associated with them, are often imbedded in long sequences. For instance, parents and other adults (teachers, counselors, coaches) may inadvertently deter the performance of desired behaviors, especially when these behaviors are in long sequences. In teaching a child to dress himself for school, a mother may repeatedly enter the child's room while he is dressing and berate him for not being ready yet. Thus, each time the child puts on a few more clothes he is punished by his mother's complaints over his slowness, and even when completely dressed, he may face a minor scolding for having been so slow. Any reward at this time may also be inconsequential, because the behavior was not performed perfectly; the effect of a small reinforcer is likely to be minimal, and indeed, it may be completely without effect since it follows a number of punishments and comes after a long delay.

In each of these examples, it is the therapist's task to determine quite concretely the component behaviors in any general category of behavior or behavior sequence and to gather precise information concerning the antecedent stimuli and the rewards and punishments consequent upon these behaviors. In the second example, the therapist would discern this information from interviewing the mother or observing the mother-child interaction. And treatment, in this case, would clearly involve training the mother in more effective procedures of contingency management than those she already uses.

Assessment of Effective Reinforcers

When the therapist has decided to treat a particular problem behavior by means of contingency management, he or she should clearly specify the reinforcers prior to the actual initiation of treatment. In most instances, at least some of the effective reinforcers will have become clear during the assessment of maintaining stimuli. Often such stimuli are quite general, such as attention by mother or teacher, help given when dependent whining occurs, capitulation to petty or veiled hostile threats, and so on. Clearly some of these reinforcers (e.g., capitulation to threats) are unlikely to be useful during the course of treatment. However, other reinforcers—positive attention, smiles, short play periods, quiet times between parent and child or husband and wife—although rather general, may prove useful when they are applied contingently in a therapeutic regimen. A client's statements concerning his or her desires for attention, recognition, social acceptance, or even small objects will prove informative in a search for effective reinforcers. On the other hand, the therapist should be cautious about speculations concerning items or events that seem likely to serve as reinforcers or punishers for a given person or group. At least one early study (Bassett et al., 1977) found that mental health workers are not particularly accurate in predicting the events that clients themselves nominated as reinforcers.

It is clear from these considerations that the use of material reinforcers is not as common as

the naive picture of a behavior modifier suggests. Therapists do not lurk in dark corners, pockets bulging with candies to be contingently dispensed upon the performance of desired behaviors. For children or hospitalized patients, therapists are likely to employ material or token rewards with greater frequency than for the typical adult patient, whereas contingency management performed in the natural environment by parents, teachers, family members, and so forth will most likely involve social or behavioral reinforcers (smiles, attention, verbal comments), since they are by far the most common reinforcers in such environments.

When it becomes necessary to seek out and identify various reinforcers that are effective for a particular client, empirical methods are clearly preferable, and there are several alternative procedures. One uses the *Mediation-Reinforcer Incomplete Blank* (referred to as MRB) and a *reinforcer-rating scale*. The MRB, created by Tharp and Wetzel (1969), is a modified incomplete-sentences test including 34 sentence stems—such as "The thing I like to do best with my (mother/father) is _____" or "I will do almost anything to get _____"—that represent social and material reinforcers. These examples are intended for children or adolescents, but they can easily be changed to suit clients of various ages and walks of life. It is noteworthy that many material reinforcers, and nearly all social reinforcers, will have *mediators*—persons typically delivering them—who are truly part of the reinforcing system and must be considered when designing a contingency-management program. Actually, the mediators will typically become auxiliary therapists, who carry out the management program in the natural environment.

Because the reinforcers that have been defined as effective for a client may appear to vary in their effectiveness, it is sometimes desirable to employ a reinforcer-rating scale. While this is simply a scaling of reinforcer effectiveness and may be done in a variety of ways, one procedure that has been employed effectively

(Tharp & Wetzel, 1969) involves the use of a nine-point scale ranging from "highly reinforcing; never fails to be effective (9)" through "reinforces fairly well; moderately effective (5)" to "has reinforcing property of a very low or indeterminate power (1)." The interviewer or primary therapist who has had initial contact with the client is the person who rates the client.

Another method of defining reinforcers, and the procedure most applicable to children or adults who have limited capabilities for communication, is the *Reinforcing Event Menu* (REM). This technique, formulated by Homme (1971), is a variant of the MRB. A REM is simply a list, or a collection of pictures, of a variety of material reinforcers with their dispensers (for instance, mother giving a hug is a reinforcing *event*—the hug is a reinforcer that might be *ineffective* if delivered by another mediator), as well as of activity reinforcers. When the client is actually involved in the manipulation of his own

behavior, as discussed in Chapter 6, he may be allowed to select from this menu the reinforcers he wishes to work for.

Closely allied to the REM technique are the *reinforcement survey schedules*. In the reinforcement survey schedule for adults (Cautela & Kastenbaum, 1967), there are four major sections: one refers to reinforcing persons, objects, or easily imaginable activities; the second section, to items or activities that are more difficult to imagine; the third, to situational contexts; and in the final section, the person is asked to list the sorts of activities that are engaged in with low frequency (e.g., 5 times a day) or high frequency (20 times a day). Table 5-2 presents a sample of items from the various classifications. The procedure has obvious application in the contingency management of individuals in private settings or institutions.

There is a children's reinforcement survey schedule that is applicable primarily to children

Table 5-2 **Reinforcement Survey Schedule: Sample Items**

Section I: Objects and Activities

	Not at All	A Little	A Fair Amount	Much	Very Much
Eating					
Ice cream	———	———	———	———	———
Fruit	———	———	———	———	———
Cookies	———	———	———	———	———
Solving Problems					
Crossword puzzles	———	———	———	———	———
Figuring out how something works	———	———	———	———	———
Nude men	———	———	———	———	———
Nude women	———	———	———	———	———
Watching Sports					
Football	———	———	———	———	———
Baseball	———	———	———	———	———
Golf	———	———	———	———	———
Reading					
Adventure	———	———	———	———	———
Mystery	———	———	———	———	———
Sexy	———	———	———	———	———
TV, Movies, or Radio	———	———	———	———	———

Table 5-2 *(Continued)*

Section I: Objects and Activities

	Not at All	A Little	A Fair Amount	Much	Very Much
Shopping					
Clothes	_____	_____	_____	_____	_____
Auto parts & supplies	_____	_____	_____	_____	_____
Sleeping	_____	_____	_____	_____	_____
Being Right					
In an argument	_____	_____	_____	_____	_____
About your work	_____	_____	_____	_____	_____
Being Praised					
About your appearance	_____	_____	_____	_____	_____
About your work	_____	_____	_____	_____	_____

Section II: Situations I Would Like to Be in

How much would you enjoy being in each of the following situations?

1. You have just led your team to victory. An old friend comes over and says, "You played a terrific game. Let me treat you to dinner and drinks."

not at all ( )   a little ( )   a fair amount ( )   much ( )   very much ( )

2. You are sitting by the fireplace with your loved one. Music is playing softly on the phonograph. Your loved one gives you a tender glance and you respond with a kiss. You think to yourself how wonderful it is to care for someone and have someone care for you.

not at all ( )   a little ( )   a fair amount ( )   much ( )   very much ( )

Now, place a check next to the number of the situation that appeals to you most.

Section III: Activity Or Preference Frequencies

List the things you do or think about more than:

5	10	15	20 times a day
_____	_____	_____	_____
_____	_____	_____	_____
_____	_____	_____	_____

from 5 to 13 years of age (Phillips, Fischer, & Singh, 1977). Table 5-3 presents some sample items from this schedule. In an initial evaluation, the scale achieved an overall test-retest reliability of .60, a value that is significant but also indicates that children assign reinforcing value to different items, events, and persons at different times. For the subcategories, the test-retest reliabilities were generally lower except for distinct objects such as toys (reliability: .88). These results indicate that the determination of reinforcer effectiveness is an important component of contingency management and should be repeated if a treatment period is long enough for reinforcement preferences to change.

Clearly these techniques can be used in a variety of contexts, by teachers in the classroom, by parents in the home, or even by therapists on an in-patient ward. Token economies utilize this principle when the therapist makes amply clear the variety of possessions and privileges that tokens can be traded for and insists that patients sample the reinforcers that may be purchased with tokens. Since the types of stimuli a child finds reinforcing may differ for various classes of children, a single reinforcement survey may

not be adequate for all. Recognizing this Dewhurst and Cautela (1980) have proposed a reinforcement survey schedule for special needs children which focuses upon those labeled behaviorally disturbed, learning disabled, autistic, mentally retarded, or developmentally delayed.

The issue of deficiency effective punishers is analogous to that for reinforcers. Although there are no punishment survey schedules, Cautela (1977) does have an aversive events inventory. If punishment is to be part of the management program, the ethical considerations alone obligate the therapist or contingency manager to be certain that aversive events used

---

Table 5-3 **Children's Reinforcement Survey Schedule Excerpts**

Check off valued reinforcers according to child's report:

Food	Visit to the seashore
Candy (What kind?)	A family picnic
Ice Cream (Favorite flavor)	An airplane ride
Potato chips	Visiting a friend
Toys	Social
Racing cars	Playing with friends
Dolls	Being praised (by whom: father, mother, etc.)
Entertainment	Being hugged or kissed
TV (favorite program)	Girl Scouts, Boy Scouts, or other clubs
Movies (what kind: Western, horror, etc.)	Learning
Sports and Games	A new language
Playing football	Piano lessons
with other kids	School work
with your father	Reading
Swimming	Science
Tennis	Gym
Checkers	Helping around the house
Fishing	Setting the table
Music, Arts & Crafts	Making the bed
Playing a musical instrument (what?)	Going on errands
Building models	Personal Appearance
Working with clay	Getting new clothes
Singing	Getting a haircut
Excursions	Dressing up in a costume
Ride in the car	

as punishers actually are punishing in their effects; otherwise the client, a child, is subjected to purposeless discomfort. It is also important to find the least aversive stimuli that are effective. In this vein, there are effective punishers that are actually quite mild, including "icing" (placing an ice cube in a child's mouth for the count of three) (Drabman, Ross, Lynd, & Cordura, 1978), the contingent use of citric acid (lemon juice) (Altman, 1977; Mahew & Harris, 1979) or ammonia (Altman, Haavik, & Cook, 1978), exercise (Luce, Deliquadrix Hall, 1980), immobilization (Bitgood, Crowe, Suarez, & Peters, 1980), or even the performance of a household chore (Fischer & Nehs, 1978).

Effectiveness of Training in Contingency Management

As we have noted, it will often be necessary to train parents, spouses, teachers, nurses, and others in the techniques of reinforcement delivery according to prescribed contingencies. In most instances, this will involve a general introduction to behavior therapy principles—though not necessarily calling them such, since most people do not view social interaction in terms of reinforcers, punishers, and models, nor are they acquainted with the general rules of reinforcer delivery such as immediacy, schedules, and time-outs. There are manuals written expressly for this purpose (e.g., Patterson & Gullion, 1976), and it is common therapeutic practice to insist that individuals who are to be the agents of a contingency management program read such a manual before the therapist schedules further appointments or begins his or her behavioral assessment.

We have noted how the training of these agents may be accomplished effectively via thorough, but brief, training programs. It is now time to give some consideration to evidence that training procedures are indeed effective. Much of this evidence is almost historical by

now. One of the first reports of contingency management using an agent other than the therapist employed the psychiatric nurse as a "behavioral engineer" (Ayllon & Michael, 1959). In their procedure, Ayllon and Michael used psychiatric nurses to carry out contingency management programs of extinction, reinforcement for incompatible behaviors, escape and avoidance training, and satiation. Clear instructions were given, for example:

> Reinforcement is something you do for or with a patient, for example, offering candy or a cigarette. Any way you convey attention to the patient is reinforcing. Patients may be reinforced if you answer their questions, talk to them or let them know by your reaction that you are aware of their presence. The common-sense expression "pay no attention" is perhaps closest to what must be done to discourage the patient's behavior. When we say "do not reinforce a behavior," we are actually saying "ignore the behavior and act deaf and blind whenever it occurs." (1959, p. 325)

Ayllon and Michael reported clear evidence of the effectiveness of their training procedures in changing patient behaviors as accomplished by the behavior engineer nurses. They achieved striking reductions in problem behavior, such as patient intrusions into the nurses' office. Effective contingencies were also put into operation for training self-help skills, such as feeding, so the nurses could direct their efforts away from types of patient care that were necessary only because the patients did not have these self-help skills.

A classic example of the successful employment of contingency management procedures using mothers as agents is that of Wahler, Winkel, Peterson, and Morrison (1965). Employing such procedures occasionally requires a good deal of space and the use of observers whose time and availability may be expensive and difficult to secure. However, in actual clinical practice, observers can be replaced by parental or client report (not a particularly desirable alternative), by closed-circuit television and videotape recording of the client *and* agent's behavior (most preferred), or perhaps by therapist observation of the client's behavior. Wahler's procedure included two sessions devoted to the classification of mother-child interaction, during which the mother was instructed to play with her child in a playroom just as she would at home. Two observers recorded the mother and child's behaviors and these records were analyzed for (1) the child's deviant behavior; (2) the child's behaviors that were incompatible with the problem behavior; and (3) the mother's ways of reacting to the various incompatible behaviors.

Following this step, the therapist instituted training to modify the mother's reaction to the various behaviors. In general, Wahler's procedures always involved the elimination of a problem behavior by strengthening an incompatible one. The mother was shown the baseline data and given an interpretation of them (the problem behaviors, incompatible behaviors, her reactions and their effects, etc.). She was then instructed that in future play sessions she was to ignore completely the problem behavior and respond in any approving way to the incompatible behaviors only. A signal light in the playroom served as an aid to help her respond. She was to keep an eye on the light and respond in an approving way *only* when it was lighted. Thus, the light was a device to aid in teaching the mother procedures of effective contingency management while she was actually interacting with her child. The mother and child were still observed during interaction, and when it became clear she was responding accurately, the use of the signal light was discontinued.

Wahler and colleagues (1965) also reported the successful treatment of several young children with a variety of problems. One child exhibited extreme dependency which, when thwarted, led to aggressive outbreaks of hitting and kicking in nursery school. Another child exhibited extreme "stubbornness," or oppositional behavior, toward her parents, refusing to cooperate or to obey their requests. A third

child was oppositional to the point of commanding his parents, who acquiesced and allowed him to determine his own bedtime and foods, and even when the parents would play with him. In each case, the mother was carefully taught to ignore the problem behavior and to respond with exhilarant approval and acceptance toward incompatible behaviors.

For example, in treating the oppositional child, the mother was instructed to ignore any stubborn behaviors, but to respond warmly whenever he exhibited any sort of cooperation; since a reduction in oppositional behavior was not proceeding rapidly, Wahler and colleagues (1965) also instructed the mother in the use of a time-out procedure: following each stubborn response, the child was to be put in a room adjacent to the playroom and left alone for five minutes. If he exhibited tantrum behavior, he was to be left alone in the room until the tantrum ceased (negative reinforcement contingent upon quieting down).

Figure 5-3 illustrates the cumulative recording of *oppositional* and cooperative responses during periods of treatment and reversal (stubbornness was complied with, as during baselines). A horizontal line of the graph indicates 0 frequency (no new responses), a climbing line indicates repeated instances of response (the sharper the incline of the line, the greater the frequency of responses). Arrows indicate times when the mother used time-outs. Clearly the mother had gained control over oppositional behavior by the judicious use of ignoring and punishing on the one hand (with time-outs); on the other, consistently warm responses to cooperation ensured that the child continued to behave cooperatively.

In a laudatory and successful attempt to provide psychological services to a rural, poverty-ridden area, Wahler and Erickson (1969) established a community program based upon contingency management procedures to handle child behavior problems in a population of 100,000 residents. This program also illustrates the extremely cost-effective application of

Figure 5-3 *Cumulative record of oppositional and cooperative behavior over a baseline period and sessions utilizing various types of contingency management (—: oppositional; ---: cooperative).*

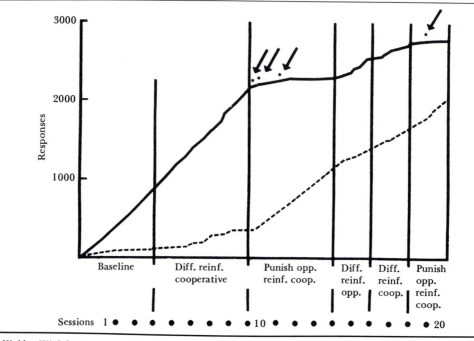

From Wahler, Winkel, Peterson, and Morrison (1965).

behavior therapy techniques given very limited professional resources. A county health clinic with but a single social worker was the source. First of all, Wahler, who was a consulting psychologist to the clinic, spending a maximum of 10 hours a month there, initiated a drive to recruit volunteer workers. In the treatment of an individual case, a child, his or her immediate family, and any other closely involved persons (e.g., teachers) were interviewed by the clinic's professional staff. The intent of the interview was to establish fairly objective descriptions of the problem behaviors and the consequences that typically followed instances of these behaviors. The behavioral diagnosis produced by the interview thus included a list of the problem behaviors, plus a compilation of likely reinforcers.

The volunteer worker was then familiarized with the interview data. He or she was also introduced to the principles of contingency management. Wahler stressed to the volunteer that the deviant behaviors were probably being maintained by social reinforcement from individuals in the child's environment. The person then listened to a brief verbal essay on principles of reinforcement, punishment, and extinction. Finally, Wahler devised a therapeutic regimen by considering which social agents in the child's environment were most likely responsible for the maintenance of the deviant behavior, and how their reinforcing contingencies might be changed in order to modify the child's behavior.

The volunteer worker was first to obtain at least two one-hour observations of the child's behavior to confirm the hypotheses drawn from the interview. The consulting psychologist and the volunteer worker then contacted the social agents whose reinforcing behavior seemed most easily modifiable and who were also likely to produce changes in the child's behaviors. As the volunteer worker became more experienced, he or she met with the social agents alone and then held separate meetings with the consulting psychologist. At first, both the psychologist and the worker met with the social agents at biweekly intervals. Throughout treatment, the volunteer worker made one-hour observations of the child's behavior once each week.

During two years of operation, the clinic treated 66 cases involving one or more problem behaviors. There was a general and significant reduction in the frequencies of various problem behaviors, such as classroom disruptive behavior, school absences, and home disruptive behavior. Simultaneously, study behavior increased both at home and at school. Furthermore, the average length of treatment declined significantly, from an average of 19 weeks per case prior to the initiation of the contingency reward program to an average of only 5 weeks.

Although it is desirable to train contingency managers by observing them in direct contact with the individuals whose behaviors are to be changed, it is not unusual to work with the contingency managers alone. Mothers who themselves have come for treatment may be given instruction in management techniques to improve the behavior of their children and to reduce their own stresses at home. Mira (1970) reported the results of a massive contingency management program that treated 82 cases. In this particular instance, all referrals were children, and in most of the cases, only a parent or teacher was seen (only 11 percent of the cases involved both manager and child attending sessions in which management training was given and practiced).

The managers learned first to delineate the troublesome behavior by receiving instruction in describing behaviors in noninterpretive ways.

Then they learned to record the frequencies of the target behaviors on a standard behavior record form that is commercially available. Finally, they were trained in contingent application of reinforcing consequences that were appropriate to the person involved and the setting in which the problem behavior occurred. The frequency was still recorded in order to assess the effectiveness of the technique.

In this program, the behaviors treated included self-care skills (dressing, feeding, going to the toilet), inappropriate social behavior (lying, screaming, hitting, throwing furniture), educational or rehabilitation behaviors (wearing hearing aids, doing physical therapy exercises, completing academic assignments), and self-mutilation (teeth grinding, skin picking, head banging). As we have noted, managers tended to complain about behaviors they wished the child to stop doing, and therapists were required to turn the therapy program toward problems of acceleration—what the managers wished the child *would* do. Drooling was "eliminated" by teaching a child to swallow, and running off was "eliminated" by teaching a child to walk beside his mother during shopping.

To be classified as successful, a manager had to complete two management goals (behavior changes) successfully. Success was measured by the use of independent observations and recorded changes in the child's behavior, and not solely by the verbal reports of the managers. Fifteen percent of the managers successfully modified the sample presenting troublesome behavior and then dropped out of the program; 46 percent of the managers who met with the therapists at least once did successfully modify at least two problem behaviors. Interestingly, teachers, school social workers, and psychiatrists were no more successful than parents in learning to become effective contingency managers.

When a contingency manager is trained to assume control that has already been established by another person (e.g., a therapist or investigator), a primary training-related problem is the actual transfer of control from the current manager to the new one. This might involve preparing a teacher or parent to assume control, or the client himself as he learns to exert self-control in place of an external management system controlled by someone else. Although there are some examples of the transfer of control from an initial "expert" manager to someone more consistently a part of the setting in which the contingencies are applied, this is not typically the case. More often, contingency managers are trained before intervention and are aided as they bring the contingencies to bear on the target behaviors. When an external manager is utilized, often that person serves as a model for the individual being trained; for instance, a "token helper" may work with a teacher to implement a contingency system and then withdraw from the classroom when training is complete (e.g., Ringer, 1973).

More frequently, an external control system will precede training in self-control, so that as the latter is instilled, the therapeutic contingency system may be withdrawn. Since we consider self-control in greater detail in another chapter, it is unnecessary to devote a great deal of space to it here. One study, though, is worthy of discussion as an example of the effectiveness of training in self-management. Glynn, Thomas, and Shee (1973) contrasted the effectiveness of training in self-control with preceding periods of group contingency management for the maintenance of on-task behavior in second grade children. During initial control phases, an observer determined whether or not children had been concentrating on their work during specified 30-second intervals, and the entire class earned one minute of free time for each interval they had behaved appropriately. Other back-up reinforcers were used in succeeding group contingency periods, such as the availability of toys and puzzles during the earned free time. There was also a period when a single child was in charge of judging whether different reading groups were all on-task at designated times (a group contingency). Finally, children were given training in self-control and

then allowed to determine their own contingent reinforcement.

Training in self-control involved the four basic components initially designated by Bandura and Perloff (1967): (1) *self-assessment* of appropriate behavior, (2) *self-recording* of the instance of appropriate behavior, (3) *self-control* of effective reinforcers, and (4) *self-administration* of the reinforcer. Glynn and colleagues (1973) gave children a card on which they could record, by a checkmark, whether or not their behavior had been appropriately on-task. A beep sounded at random moments and children were to judge their behavior in terms of what they were doing when the beep occurred. Finally, children were allowed to determine how much free time they had earned and then to take advantage of it at the end of the day.

The results are illustrated in Figure 5-4. Children's on-task behavior increased during class or group contingencies, and the contingencies became increasingly effective over time, perhaps because of practice or the addition of new back-up reinforcers. The self-control contingency produced on-task behavior nearly 100 percent of the time during the three periods when it was in effect.

Reducing Problem Behaviors: Contingency Management Procedures for Behavior Elimination

Often the goal of a treatment program is not an increase in the frequency of a desired target behavior but rather the elimination of behavior that is problematic, counterproductive, or of low social value. A number of different procedures for behavioral elimination are available to the behavior therapist, such as punishment or extinction techniques that are discussed elsewhere (Chapter 7, "Response Elimination and Extinction Procedures," and Chapter 8, "Pun-

Figure 5-4 *A comparison of group contingencies with self-control over contingent reinforcement for increasing on-task behavior in the classroom.*

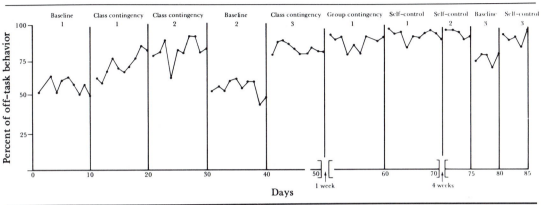

From Glynn, Thomas, and Shee (1973).

ishment and Aversion Procedures"). Contingency management procedures include both punishment and extinction techniques, but since they will be covered more fully in subsequent chapters, we will deal only briefly with them here. There are four procedures worthy of attention: *contingent punishment, time-out, response cost,* and *differential reinforcement.* First, however, let us give some attention to issues of reinforcement *versus* punishment as techniques for changing behavior.

Reinforcement Versus Punishment

It is clear that punishment can be effectively used to modify behavior and that there may be particular behavior problems that respond better, or perhaps exclusively, to aversive procedures. And while there may be a choice between using positive reinforcement and punishment procedures, there are several good reasons for preferring alternative techniques, such as contingency management with positive reinforcers (or observational learning techniques, extinction procedures, assertive training, or cognitive methods). First of all, when effective al-

ternative techniques are available, it is difficult to justify using techniques that cause pain and suffering even if they, too, are effective. Second, punishment often produces a number of side effects that may be quite undesirable. And finally, while punishment may be used cautiously and effectively by the experienced behavior therapist, some spouses and parents use it *ineffectively,* and consequently it becomes ineffective for the individual in question even in the hands of an expert. A more detailed discussion of aversion techniques is found in Chapter 8, "Punishment and Aversion Procedures." For present purposes, let us simply cite some examples of the undesirable side effects and imprudent uses of punishment that may be encountered in contingency management procedures.

A major side effect of punishment is the potential training it provides by reinforcing other behaviors that allow the avoidance or termination (negative reinforcement) of punishment. Ceasing to perform the behavior being punished is but one way to avoid the punishment. Becker (1971) has clearly pointed to some common alternative behaviors individuals turn to when punishment is imminent:

Cheating	Avoiding the punishment that goes with being wrong
Truancy	Avoiding or escaping the many punishments that go with school failure, poor teaching, punitive administration of school
Running away from home	Escaping the many punishments parents can use
Lying	Avoiding the punishment that follows doing something wrong
Sneaking	Avoiding being caught "misbehaving"
Hiding	Avoiding being caught

Often the persons in a client's natural environment who are to become contingency managers must be weaned from a dependence on punishment. The point is made succinctly in the case cited below, reported by Tharp and Wetzel (1969).

> Alan's parents were fundamentalist protestants who imposed strong limitations on their son's freedom for relatively minor offenses. When his school grades began to deteriorate they reacted by almost totally restricting him to his room and depriving him of TV, the use of the phone, etc. The father was a rigid martinet whose job kept him away from home three or four days a week. Both parents felt that anything but total submission to parental authority subverted the rules of man and God.
>
> Alan was a bright, conscientious, and mildly withdrawn 16-year-old, but this crushing limitation drove him to run away from home. He turned himself in to the juvenile probation lockup and announced that he would rather go to the State reform school than go home. When his parents arrived he refused to go home with them

> and said if he were forced he would run away immediately.
>
> Finally the boy agreed to go home after several telephone conversations among probation officers, the father, and our Project, the essence of which was that the restrictions would be lifted and our help would be immediately available.
>
> The parents agreed to an intervention program based on weekly grade notices from Alan's teacher. On the basis of grades, Alan earned points which governed the hours he might spend away from home, watch TV, and use the phone.
>
> The program began effectively, although the boy was suspicious since it appeared to be nonpunitive.
>
> His suspicions soon proved well founded. Although he earned enough points to allow a greater degree of freedom than he had previously been granted, his parents meddled with the plan. Despite repeated discussion and instructions for the BA [Behavior Analyst], they insisted on searching for reasons to punish Alan. One Sunday Alan had enough points to go off with some friends, but as he started for the door his father prohibited him from leaving because he had received a low grade in one subject that week. "You haven't got time to play if you can't keep up your studies," was the way his father justified the action.
>
> The parents were obviously adding punitive features to the program, many of which were not revealed to the BA, and the boy threatened to run away again, protesting that his father and mother were not honoring their promise not to apply restrictions. When the BA deplored these actions the parents explained that they would like an "altered" program which would eliminate the reinforcement features and the point system. "We'd want to use your program as a guideline without being so formal." "We like the weekly grade notes, because we don't have to wait six weeks for Alan's report card." (To this they might have added that such an arrangement made it possible to keep *au courant* with their son's failures for punitive purposes without accepting the responsibility of rewarding his successes.) (Case No. 56., pp. 129–130)

While this example may be an extreme one, it clearly points out the necessity for extensive training, and perhaps modification of contingency managers themselves, in order to secure effective results for the total program.

Contingent Punishment

Punishment involves the dispensation, on a contingent basis, of negative or aversive consequences for a given behavior. In general, most descriptive statements of the factors that influence the effectiveness of reinforcers apply to punishers also. These concerns include scheduling, temporal gradients of delay, and types of punishers (tangible punishers; social punishers, such as disapproval; activity punishers, such as withdrawal of privileges to do certain things; and token punishers, such as demerits). However, a number of ethical concerns relate to the use of punishment and other types of aversive control and must be weighed carefully in any decision to use them as methods for changing behavior. Both the concerns and the techniques for using contingent punishment will be covered in Chapter 8. We have already discussed procedures for the identification of effective punishers and illustrated how mildly aversive stimuli can still serve as effective punishers.

Time-out Procedures

Time-out refers to the contingent isolation (seclusion) or ignoring of an individual following an instance of inappropriate or problem behavior. Somewhat paradoxically, it can be classed as both an extinction and a punishment procedure, because it combines elements of both. To effect a time-out, an individual is isolated for a relatively brief period in a room or other enclosure that contains no positive or potentially reinforcing elements. Time-outs can also be accomplished by withdrawing major rewards, such as social attention (e.g., by ignoring), but as just noted, if alternative sources of reinforcement are available, the time-out is not being effectively implemented. Time-out can be considered an extinction procedure because its contingent implementation prevents reinforcement for the behavior in question. Simultaneously, it can be considered a punishment to the degree that incarceration in the sterile time-out environment constitutes an aversive experience.

Although time-out procedures technically involve a contingent removal of all major reinforcing consequences by withdrawing the individual from them, occasionally a sort of time-out can be instituted by removing the individual from only the primary sources of reinforcement. When a single person is a major source of reinforcement, removing that person can constitute essentially a time-out experience. This procedure is especially helpful when the continued presence of that person makes it difficult to prevent an undesirable behavior from being reinforced. Thus, a mother may be instructed to get a good magazine, go to the bathroom, and lock herself in when her child's temper tantrum erupts, coming out only when all is quiet. This method is also especially helpful when the behavior to be eliminated is an extraordinarily compelling one that *demands* attention (reinforcement) from those present.

In a very early report Wolf and associates (1964) described the elimination of tantrum behavior in a 3½-year-old autistic boy. The child was placed in a room by himself when he had a tantrum and was allowed to come out only when the tantrum ceased. Wahler, Winkel, Peterson, and Morrison (1965) instructed mothers in the use of time-out procedures to eliminate obstructive and tantrum behavior while reinforcing cooperation. Time-outs for tantrum behavior were combined with the ignoring of obstructiveness. Very few time-outs were necessary in order to eliminate the tantrums, and the obstructiveness was eliminated rapidly. More recently, time-out procedures have been used to eliminate aggression in the classroom (Wilson, Robertson, Herlong, & Haynes, 1979), misbehavior in retarded children (Pendergrass, 1972), self-stimulation in autistic children (Koegel, Firestone, Kramme, & Dunlap, 1974), and perseverative speech (Reichle, Brubakken, & Tetreault, 1976). As we stress throughout Chapter 8, punishment techniques should *always* be used in conjunction with the procedures designed to build in desirable alternative behaviors. Punishment is an adjunct to other procedures. The use of time-outs is no exception. Care should also be taken to gauge the length of time-outs carefully. Long ones may be overly punitive, even abusive, and short ones may be ineffective (although not always—the ones used by Solnick, Rincover, & Peterson [1977], whose effects are illustrated in Figure 5-5, were only 10 seconds in length). For seclusion, five minutes is a reasonable rule of thumb for initial implementation.

There are some conditions under which an effective time-out is essentially impossible. A primary example is the case of an individual prone to self-stimulatory activities that are presumably reinforcing. A report by Solnick and associates (1977) is particularly illustrative in this instance. These investigators designed a contingency program including time-outs to reduce the frequency of tantrum behavior in a 6-year-old autistic child. Figure 5-5 illustrates the effectiveness of this program. Much to their surprise, the initial effects of the time-out periods were reinforcing, producing an increase in the frequency of tantrums. When it became apparent that the sterile time-out environment provided almost ideal conditions for self-stimulatory behavior (handflapping, etc.), the possibility that this provided reinforcement was tested by making the opportunity to engage in self-stimulation contingent upon tantrums. This revealed the reinforcing effectiveness of the behavior, and the investigators then instituted physical restraint from self-stimulation as a contingent consequence for tantrums. As Figure 5-5 shows, there was an immediate decline in tantrum frequency to zero. The moral of this story is, of course, that the therapist should never be totally confident that a procedure will be overwhelmingly effective, and when it proves not to be, analysis of the situation to determine why will usually suggest appropriate alternative procedures.

Time-outs are typically most effective when they thoroughly remove reinforcing stimuli. "Punishing" a child by sending him to his room is not likely to be effective when there are reinforcers such as television, books, and perhaps even a saved snack available. Nevertheless, it is still rather harsh to isolate an individual completely, and evidence shows that isolation from certain common reinforcers, such as social contact, proves effective (Foxx, Foxx, Jones, & Kiely, 1980; Foxx & Shapiro, 1978; Griffiths, Bigelow, & Liebson, 1977; Mansdorf, 1978). In these procedures, the time-out involves exclusion from social contact (ignoring) or participation in activities for a period of time. There is some question whether such "time-outs" from specific reinforcers are not better viewed as a sort of response cost procedure instead, as the next section will make clear.

Response Cost

Response cost refers to the contingent *removal* or *withdrawal* of a reinforcer following inappropriate or problem behavior. This particular category of behavior elimination techniques is not totally distinct from others that we have discussed. For example, if the reinforcer that is removed is quite valuable, the implementation of a response cost may be quite aversive and will be, in effect, a contingent punishment. If the response cost involves the withdrawal of the presence of an individual who was a central source of social reinforcement, then it may not only be aversive but constitute a time-out. And, as we will make clear below, if the withdrawal of a particular reinforcer is accompanied by the intentional contingent reinforcement of behavior that is an alternative to the problem one, then response cost may be part of a program of differential reinforcement.

Response cost will be discussed subsequently in this chapter as well as later, along with procedures of aversive control, because it is typically an aversive experience for the individual involved. Note, however, that response cost procedures are often integral components of contingency management programs, such as token economies or contingency contracts, since to-

Figure 5-5 *Effects of time-out on tantrum behavior with and without the opportunity for self-stimulation during the time-out period.*

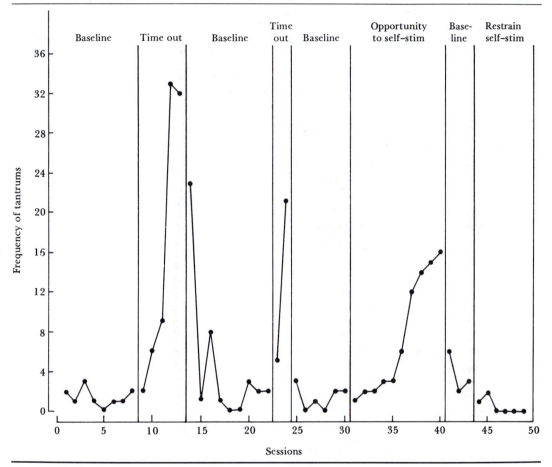

From Solnick, Rincover, and Peterson (1977).

kens or points can easily be both added and subtracted during a period of time before they are totaled and redeemed for back-up reinforcers (e.g., Doty, McInnis, & Paul, 1974). Response cost procedures have been successfully utilized to eliminate a wide variety of behavior problems ranging from cognitive-emotional behavior such as anxiety depression, in which case anxious and depressive behavior (e.g., crying) resulted in a response cost (Reisinger, 1972), to more social, motor behaviors such as perseverative speech (Reichle et al., 1976) and hyperactive behavior (Wolf, Hanley, King, Lachowicz, & Giles, 1970), and even to seeming cognitive capabilities such as the academic performance of mildly retarded individuals (Arnold, Forehand, & Sturgis, 1976).

Differential Reinforcement

Differential reinforcement refers to the implementation of clearly different degrees of positive reinforcement for two behaviors, one of which is to be eliminated and replaced by the other. Generally, it involves the careful *non*reinforcement (e.g., ignoring) of problem behaviors along with careful and clear reinforcement of target behaviors whenever they occur. It is sometimes referred to as a specific schedule of reinforcement, labeled DRO (*differential re*inforcement of *o*ther behavior). In some instances, it is not a specific behavior but a type of behavior that is reinforced. For example, a mother who does not respond to verbal requests by her child even as they grow louder and more petulant, but then finally "gives in" when they reach the level of a loud, rude, insistent demand is inadvertently reinforcing the high frequency of persistent verbal, intrusive behavior. This might be termed a DRH schedule—*differential re*inforcement for *h*igh-frequency responding. The mother who clearly ignores her child when he is too loud or insistent but quickly responds to gentle, polite requests is implementing a DRL schedule—*differential re*inforcement for *l*ow-frequency responding. Most often, however, differential reinforcement is a DRO procedure of extinction whose goal is the elimination of a particular problem behavior and the reinforcement of an alternative, desired behavior. It is as much a technique to maximize the effectiveness of extinction as it is a goal in and of itself. Since it typically involves positive reinforcement, it is also often more acceptable than a punishment-based intervention to eliminate maladaptive responding (Kazdin, 1980).

When extinction procedures are being used, there are cogent reasons for providing reinforcement contingent upon alternative behaviors. If the performance of the behavior being extinguished requires some time for completion, the individual is obviously going to do *something* during the time previously taken up by the performance of the undesirable behavior.

If this behavior is adaptive and desirable, it may be made the object of the reinforcement formerly contingent upon the undesirable behavior. This is also a good time to model, shape, or otherwise train the client in specific alternative behaviors appropriate to the situation at hand. We cannot assume that the client will automatically emit socially desirable and adaptive behaviors once the maladaptive behavior is eliminated.

A second reason for the training of alternative behaviors while target ones are being extinguished is concerned with the individual's responses to decreased reinforcement. The beginning of extinction (immediately following the time when reinforcement is no longer forthcoming) is accompanied by emotional responding and occasionally an *increase* in the frequency of the maladaptive response, often called an "extinction burst" (especially in high-magnitude behaviors, such as tantrums). This may be trying for the agents who must tolerate the behavior without responding in a manner that is reinforcing. Emotional responding, ranging from irritability to temper tantrums and crying, does tend to extinguish relatively rapidly, and one may suspect that the provision of reinforcement, now contingent upon other behavior, is in large part responsible. At any rate, when a high-frequency behavior is being extinguished, it is almost imperative to provide reinforcement contingent upon other behaviors, both to maintain some level of behavior in the extinction settings and to avoid creating a reinforcement vacuum that is an arousing and clearly uncomfortable state of affairs. Such a reinforcement vacuum is an example, perhaps, of the time-out procedures described in the next section.

Designing a program of extinction involves the assessment of the contingencies currently operating and the planned elimination of such contingent reinforcement. Often these contingencies involve social reinforcement, and the reinforcing agents can be retrained to make their attention, responsiveness, smiles, and so on contingent upon behaviors *other* than the undesirable one, and to stand mute, look away, or divert their attention to someone else when the maladaptive behavior occurs.

In a now-classic study, Allen and Harris (1966) treated a girl whose face, neck, and various other body parts were covered with open sores and scabs from nearly a year's worth of scratching herself. Her mother was trained to withhold all reinforcement upon the child's scratching behavior (attention, restraining physical contact, etc.) while simultaneously reinforcing the desirable behaviors. The mother was also given instruction in gradually phasing out the established reinforcement schedule. By the end of six weeks, the child's face and body were clear of all sores and scabs, and a four-month follow-up revealed no reestablishment of the scratching behavior.

As part of a procedure to treat alcoholism, Mertens and Fuller (1964) encouraged the extinction of alcoholic drinking by instructing friends of the client to dispense their usual social behaviors (attention to client, talking, joking, general carousing) as long as he came to the local tavern and drank soft drinks only. As soon as he drank an alcoholic beverage, they were immediately to withdraw all their reinforcement (ignore the client and, if necessary, leave the tavern). Note how discrimination training immediately becomes a part of extinction procedures, since the client is essentially required to discriminate that a new behavior is now instrumental in obtaining reinforcement, while an old one is not.

Differential reinforcement is perhaps most effective when there is a clear and desirable alternative behavior, incompatible with the problem behavior, that can replace or "crowd out" the undesirable one. Sometimes nonbehavior or "doing nothing" is considered to be a behavior, and reinforcement is dispensed when the individual is quiet or clearly trying to suppress the problem behavior. This has been found to be less effective than targeting an alternative, incompatible response for reinforcement (Leitenberg, Burchard, Burchard, Fuller, & Lysaght, 1977).

Differential reinforcement procedures will receive additional treatment in the chapter on extinction procedures. For the moment, we need only note that this technique has been used to treat a wide variety of problem behaviors, including sibling conflict (Leitenberg et al., 1977), compliance in preschool (Goetz, Holmberg, & LeBlanc, 1975), inappropriate classroom behavior (Deitz, Slack, Schwarzmueller, Wilander, Weatherly, & Hilliard, 1978), psychosomatic dermatosis (Dobes, 1977), aggression and self-injurious behaviors (Dougherty & Lane, 1976; Koegel et al., 1974; Luiselli & Greenridge, 1982), food rumination (Conrin, Pennypacker, Johnston, & Rast, 1982), and separation anxiety (Neisworth, Madle, & Goeke, 1975).

Coverant Control: Covert Positive and Negative Reinforcement

The utilization of covert, cognitive, and emotional behavior has been increasingly emphasized in the therapeutic context. While systematic desensitization has always involved a large covert element in terms of the use of imagery to re-create anxiety-producing behaviors and contexts, other behavior therapy techniques and processes have only gradually been seen to have covert components that can be put to effective use. Thus, there is now covert modeling, covert sensitization, covert extinction, and covert reinforcement. Credit for the introduction of reinforcement-related covert processes should probably be given to Homme (1965), who introduced the concept of *coverant control*, "coverant" being a summary term for *covert operant*.

Covert reinforcement refers to the reflection upon positive scenes or recollections (covert positive reinforcement), or upon scenes that involve the termination of an imagined aversive state (covert negative reinforcement), contingent upon or following a target behavior whose frequency is to be increased. The evidence on the effectiveness of covert reinforcement has been mixed, with the negative evidence falling into two classes: studies indicating that some theoretically important aspect of covert reinforcement, such as its contingency upon the target behavior, is actually unimportant for successful treatment (e.g., Bajtelsmit & Gershman, 1976); and studies indicating that the actual employment of a covert reinforcement technique resembles another treatment procedure, such as counterconditioning, and not contingency management, where the reinforcing stimulus just happens to be covert.

To be sure, there are a number of reports in the literature indicating the successful employment of covert reinforcement procedures. Manno and Marston (1972) contrasted covert reinforcement and covert sensitization as procedures for the treatment of obesity. The covert sensitization procedure was a standard one (see Chapter 8) in which clients were to imagine picking up a tasty morsel and, just as they were about to pop it into their mouth, to imagine becoming extremely ill, to vomit, and then to stop vomiting and feel better just at the moment that they imagined putting the piece of food down. The sensitization model is twofold: one part is counterconditioning (the classical conditioning of the aversive properties of imagined discomfort to thoughts of food and eating), and the other part is contingency or instrumental learning (the act of resisting temptation is negatively reinforced by *subsequently* feeling better). In the covert positive reinforcement procedure, clients imagined the same scene at the very beginning, but rather than imagining themselves becoming sick as they were about to eat the food, they were to imagine saying, "I don't want it." Afterward, an imagined friend whom they would like to impress would compliment them on their self-control. In this model, the compliment by the friend is the positive reinforcer that is contingent upon the imagined act of self-control. Manno and Marston (1972)

found that both these treatment procedures produced an equivalent weight loss, one significantly greater than that obtained in a control condition, by the end of a four-week treatment program. There was even further weight loss by the end of a three-month follow-up period.

In a more experimental investigation, Epstein and Peterson (1973) achieved verbal conditioning effects by having subjects imagine positive or aversive scenes after guessing various numbers from 0 to 100. Subjects were told to imagine either a positive or a negative scene whenever the experimenter cued them. They were then unknowingly cued to imagine positive scenes after any number ending in a 1, 2, or 3, and negative scenes after numbers ending in 7, 8, or 9. The results indicated a significant increase in numbers ending in 1 to 3 and a significant decrease in those ending in 7 to 9.

The results of these two studies indicate that contingent covert events can produce behavior change in both the experimental setting and in treating a real behavior problem. Some critical investigations, however, have questioned the importance of contingency in the effective use of covert reinforcement techniques (Hurley, 1976; Ladouceur, 1974; Marshal et al., 1974). Hurley (1976), for example, contrasted covert reinforcement techniques with a covert noncontiguity procedure that took the reinforcing image out of a contingent relationship with the imagined response, and with a covert exposure procedure in which the reinforcing scenes were replaced with presumably neutral scenes. These procedures proved equally effective in the treatment of both fear and avoidance components of snake phobias, a finding that undermines the interpretations of the effectiveness of covert reinforcement techniques.

In an investigation involving the treatment of test anxiety, Bajtelsmit and Gershman (1976) compared covert reinforcement, an attention-focusing control, and two other conditions involving reinforcement: one in which the reinforcement was contingent upon *anxious* test-related behaviors, and one in which the reinforcing scene *preceded* the desired behavior. The results indicated that covert reinforcement treatment was superior to a no-treatment control condition, but not superior to the attention-focusing control condition, indicating that its effectiveness might have been due to attentional components alone. More damaging were the findings that improvement was also found when the reinforcing scene was contingent upon the anxious test-related behaviors rather than upon nonanxious or coping behaviors. There was also improvement in the condition in which the reinforcement preceded the target behavior, which is a total violation of contingency.

In conclusion, covert reinforcement procedures can be utilized effectively in the treatment of various behavior problems that require the establishment of new behaviors. However, current evidence seriously undermines the conceptualization of the technique as one of contingency management in which the reinforcing stimulus simply happens to be covert. Alternative explanations include the possibility that imagined reinforcing scenes have counterconditioning properties that decrease anxiety or other negative associations with the desired behavior patterns supposedly being reinforced that may have been preventing their occurrence. It may also be that the imagining of positive scenes have motivating properties that enhance the likelihood that associated behaviors will be performed when the person next encounters a context in which they would be appropriate. Thus, while there appears to be ample evidence that covert events presumably having a positive valence have an *apparent* reinforcing effect upon behaviors that they follow (e.g., Masters, Furman, & Barden, 1977; Masters & Santrock, 1976), the observed effect may not be due to the contingent reinforcing properties of the covert event but rather to other processes that are at the moment not clearly defined. Note that despite the enthusiasm of some for self-reinforcement procedures (e.g., Thoreson & Mahoney, 1974), others believe it

may be a less potent contingency management technique than externally controlled consequences, especially in the case of a major personal or interpersonal crisis.

Contingency Contracting

A procedure of contingency management in which the contingencies are clearly spelled out in advance and individuals, both those showing the problem behaviors and others acting as contingency managers in the field, make formal agreements about the elements to be in effect is called *contingency contracting.* This particular procedure initially received its clearest statement in work by Homme (1971) and Stuart (1971; Stuart & Lott, 1972). The categories of problem behavior that have most often been addressed by contingency contracting procedures are marital problems, delinquency and adolescent acting out, studying problems and other academic or school-related behaviors, and problems relating to self-control, such as drug abuse, weight control, alcoholism, and the personal scheduling of work and recreation.[3]

[3]See the following references for procedural descriptions. For marital problems (Jacobson, 1978; Stuart, 1969; Weiss, Birchler, & Vincent, 1974; Weiss, Hops, & Patterson, 1972); for delinquency and adolescent acting out (Blechman, Olson, Schornagel, Halsdorf, & Turner, 1976; Kifer, Lewis, Green, & Phillips, 1974; Stuart, 1971; Stuart & Lott, 1972; Switzen, Deal, & Bailey, 1977; Weathers & Liberman, 1975); for studying problems and other academic or school-related behaviors (Blechman, Taylor, & Schrader, 1981; Bristol & Sloane, 1974; Cantrell, Cantrell, Huddleston, & Woolridge, 1969; Homme, 1971; Kelley & Stokes, 1982; Speltz, Shimamura, & McReynolds, 1982; Whitman & Dussault, 1976); and for problems relating to self-control, such as drug abuse (Boudin, 1972; Frederiksen, Jenkins, & Carr, 1976), weight control (Aragona et al., 1975; Mann, 1972), alcoholism (P.M. Miller, 1972), and the personal scheduling of work and recreation (Whitman & Dussault, 1976).

In and of itself, contingency contracting implies little more than a clear specification of target behaviors and the reinforcers that will be made contingent upon them. In practice, however, it is typically adapted to the context for which it is intended, and striking differences may pertain between a self-contract that an individual endorses for promoting personal change (e.g., self control [Whitman & Dussault, 1976]) and the contracts that are prepared for reducing marital conflict or family problems with an adolescent child (Frederiksen et al., 1976; Stuart, 1971). Although the focus of the contract is upon an aspect of behavior intended for change, an important side effect has been noted: Franzini and Grimes (1980) report that the contracts tend to reduce attrition (dropping out) from therapy, at least for treatment dealing with the difficult problem of weight control.

In a personal contingency contract, one intended for self-control and involving few if any other individuals, a system may be established that resembles a private application of "Grandma's Rule"—that is, specific behaviors have to be accomplished (e.g., studying for one hour straight) before others may be engaged in (e.g., calling a girl friend on the phone). Personal contingency contracts are readily established using actual objects or privileges as reinforcers and have been used to address behavior problems as diverse as sleep disorders (Framer & Sanders, 1980), alcohol abuse (Rosenberg, Upper, Connors, & Dicroce, 1982), or dietary compliance in renal patients (Kean, Price, & Collins, 1981).

When circumstances make it difficult to establish one-to-one correspondences between desired behaviors and reinforcers, a personal token system can be worked out (Samson-Fisher, Seymour, Montgomery, & Stokes, 1978; Whitman & Dussault, 1976). In this type of system, points can be assigned to various activities depending upon their degree of unattractiveness or difficulty, and reinforcing events or activities may then be purchased, with more attractive items costing more points. The contract consists largely of defining target or desired behaviors, providing operational definitions, and then assigning their point value. For example, studying behavior may be the target and it could be defined as the actual time spent reading, writing, solving problems, or working from workbooks. For one course, 20 points might be earned by studying 4–6 hours during the week, whereas for another course, 20 points might require only 3–5 hours (presumably the latter course would be less disliked than the first). A date or simply time spent with a friend might "cost" 40 points over a weekend, or perhaps a half hour could be purchased on a weekday using points accrued on that particular day. All the target behaviors as well as the reinforcing items or acts are spelled out clearly in advance, and the point system or set of target behavior–reinforcing event pairs are "contracted for" in terms of the established contingent relationships. Research indicates that the most effective contracts are those that are informative about both treatment strategies and expected outcomes, and effectiveness is further enhanced if the contract elicits statements from the client that he will participate fully in specific aspects of the overall treatment program (Seidner & Kirschenbaum, 1980).

Another common contract is the interpersonal one, in which two or more individuals examine their own behavior, how others would like them to behave, and how they would like others to behave and then establish a contract in which one person delivers a reinforcer or behaves in a way that the other person would prefer in return for the other person's rendering of a reinforcer or behaving in a desired fashion. This sort of contract is guided by the principle of reciprocity ("to get, you must give"), and the assumption that in many or most interpersonal conflict situations, the people involved control one another's reinforcers. For example, in the family with an obstreperous adolescent, keeping his room clean may be a reinforcer for the parents, and allowing some degree of privacy ("Stay off my back") may be a potent reinforcer for the adolescent (Blechman, Olson, Schornagel, Halsdorf, & Turner, 1976).

A contingency contract would arrange a barter system in which each might be made contingent upon the other.

Stuart (1971) early on proposed four major assumptions about interpersonal contingency contracts, and they are worth reviewing here. First, being reinforced by others should be considered a privilege *to be earned* rather than a right. Second, reciprocity should govern the interpersonal exchanges covered by the contract, so that receiving positive reinforcement from others depends upon (is *contingent* upon) providing reinforcements to them. Third, the value or importance of a particular behavioral exchange will depend upon the value and frequency of the positive reinforcements exchanged. (Implicit in the second and third assumptions is a point that should be noted: exchanges should be balanced, containing reinforcers of the same magnitude for each participating individual. If cleaning up a room is a particularly unpleasant risk, but one that is highly reinforcing to parents, a simple "Your room looks nice" or "Humph, I see you didn't leave your room in its usual mess," are not likely to be truly reciprocal reinforcers likely to promote future instances of tidying up). Finally, Stuart proposes the assumption that designating rules for interactions actually increases freedom rather than constrains it. This assumption says simply that knowing the rule governing the exchange of reinforcers—that is, knowing the contingencies—allows one to make informed choices. If the price of generating desired behavior in others is not worth the paying, then one can choose not to pursue that behavior, although in choosing not to "pay" for other people's behavior by behaving in a certain way oneself, one loses the privilege of demanding such behavior from them.

A particularly common type of contingency contract is a *deposit contingency*, in which individuals agree to commit money or valuables (generally in the form of a deposit to the therapist) as a "bet" on successful treatment, and this money is lost when therapeutic gains are not made or if treatment is prematurely terminated. This is essentially a contractual response cost procedure and has been used successfully for many treatment goals, including assertive training (St. Lawrence, 1981), weight loss (Jeffrey, Thompson, & Wing, 1978), and smoking cessation (Paxton, 1980, 1981). This type of contract is more frequently used to promote adherence to the treatment program than for achieving "success."

It should be clear by now that principles of contingency contracting often involve training in interpersonal skills that are applicable to group contexts (families, classrooms, or even the workplace). The establishment of a contract involves the designation of problem behaviors, the identification of effective reinforcers, the establishment of priorities for behavior change both in oneself and in others, and the agreement to a contract that will implement the change. Weathers and Liberman (1975) have outlined a contingency contracting exercise that illustrates some of the considerations in the preparation of a contingency contract between parents and an adolescent. This outline is depicted in Figure 5-6. While all these steps will not necessarily precede the formation of a given contract, the outline illustrates well the way a procedure of contingency management can resemble procedures of conflict resolution and interpersonal negotiation in its implementation.

Token Systems and Token Economies

In this section, we are concerned with systems of contingency management that employ token reinforcers. The distinction between token *systems* and token *economies* is intended to denote the fact that individual programs of contingency management may employ token reinforcers—perhaps along with material, social, and activity reinforcers—without necessarily developing a full-fledged token economy. Gold stars, points marked on a sheet taped to the refrigerator or kept on the teacher's desk, or even

Figure 5-6 *Schema for the Family Contracting Exercise in contingency contracting. The steps outlined with circles are for the parent(s), and the ones outlined with squares are for the adolescent child.*

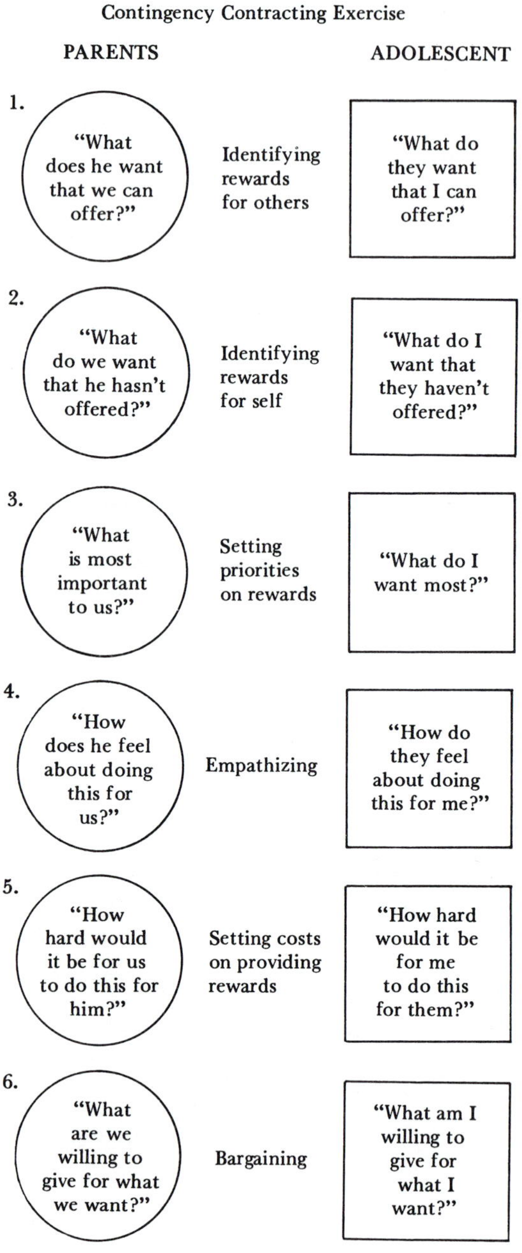

Contingency Contracting Exercise

PARENTS   ADOLESCENT

1.
"What does he want that we can offer?" — Identifying rewards for others — "What do they want that I can offer?"

2.
"What do we want that he hasn't offered?" — Identifying rewards for self — "What do I want that they haven't offered?"

3.
"What is most important to us?" — Setting priorities on rewards — "What do I want most?"

4.
"How does he feel about doing this for us?" — Empathizing — "How do they feel about doing this for me?"

5.
"How hard would it be for us to do this for him?" — Setting costs on providing rewards — "How hard would it be for me to do this for them?"

6.
"What are we willing to give for what we want?" — Bargaining — "What am I willing to give for what I want?"

From Weathers and Liberman (1975).

money are token reinforcers that may be used in either individual or group management. Occasionally, however, particularly in institutional settings such as a hospital ward or school classroom, it is worthwhile to develop an entire economy in which tokens are dispensed contingent upon a wide range of desired or target behaviors. In the latter case, the resultant complex token system is worthy of being termed a token economy. We will be concerned primarily with token economies because of their uniqueness and complexity, but consideration will also be given to the use of token systems in the contingency management of problem behaviors evidenced by an individual.

Token economies are not really unnatural. Indeed, any national economy with a currency system is in every sense a token economy: any currency consists by definition of token or symbolic "reinforcers" that may be exchanged for items that constitute a more direct form of reinforcement. Whereas the individual in society works to earn tokens (money) with which he purchases his dwelling place, food, recreation, and so on, most institutions provide such comforts noncontingently and hence cease to encourage many adaptive behaviors that are appropriate and effective in the natural environment (Gelfand, Gelfand, & Dobson, 1967). Interestingly, there is one report of a token economy in which the back-up reinforcers that could be purchased by tokens were actually items on sale at a local merchandise store (Carpenter & Casto, 1982). This illustrates the clear analogue between token systems and the monetary systems in natural economies.

Advantages and Disadvantages of Token Reinforcement Systems

The establishment of a system of token rewards, even though it is a difficult undertaking, contains a number of inherent advantages. First of all, the individual under treatment may select the specific back-up reinforcer he considers himself to be working for. Essentially, all individuals are continually presented with a "menu" of reinforcing events and can, at any time, work for the reinforcer of their own choice. The use of a menu removes the necessity for determining a single reinforcer that has some value for all individuals under treatment or the tedious process of defining different reinforcers for each person. The use of easily managed tokens also removes the necessity for the contingent dispensation of bulky, messy, or otherwise unmanageable reinforcing events. Perhaps the primary advantage, however, is the ability, by manipulating the rate of exchange, to allow individuals to work over extended periods of time for a single, highly potent reinforcer. At the same time, the staff is able to dispense tangible (if basically symbolic) reinforcement after each response with very short temporal delays. Both of these factors serve to increase the effectiveness of the reinforcer.

Certainly there are disadvantages to token systems, though it is generally conceded that they far outweigh the advantages. Typically (except for permanently institutionalized individuals), any particular token system is not the usual system of reinforcement that prevails outside the institution, or even within an institution outside a specific treatment program (e.g., in schools where a token system may be used to promote studying one subject but not another). Clearly, to increase generalization, an individual's reliance upon a token system should be phased out once the requisite behaviors are established, and the token reinforcers should be replaced by reinforcers more appropriate to the natural environment, such as social reinforcement or money (Fairweather, 1964). Even token systems relying on money must fade out money as reinforcers for activities that are not reinforced by money in the natural environment. Another disadvantage concerns the process of exchange. The institution or staff monitoring the token system must maintain a supply of exchange items—a store, in effect. Again, the use of money as the unit of exchange reduces the problem.

A major difficulty and, as such, a disadvantage concerns the initial establishment of the token system, especially as it applies to each individual in a group. Often severely debilitated individuals must be taught to value the tokens, to discriminate that they have exchange value. Sometimes a verbal explanation will suffice. At other times, as with severely retarded individuals or some psychotics, it is necessary to shape the individual in the use of the token system. Often getting individuals to value the tokens can be accomplished by a sort of free distribution before contingencies requiring the individual to earn his token rewards are put into effect.

One of the initial decisions that must be made concerns the use of groupwide or individualized contingency systems. In a groupwide system, all patients earn tokens at the same rate for any particular behavior and are required to pay the same number of tokens for the same privilege or desired item. In an individualized token economy, the rate of pay and exchange may be different for all patients involved. Patients just beginning the system may be required to pay fewer tokens for a particular privilege, and at the same time may earn more for various behaviors than do more seasoned patients whose rate of performing appropriate behaviors has already improved. Clearly, the group contingency is more easily administered, although its effectiveness for some patients may be reduced since it is not tailored to their individual behavioral capabilities. It seems rigid, however, to assume that a group contingency cannot have individual components injected into it. Liberman (1968) describes an instance of a woman who screamed loudly at a lunch table after being accidentally pushed by a table mate. The decision was made to impose upon her an immediate fine of one token each time this occurred. Individualized components such as these could easily be handled within the context of a group contingency system.

Procedural Details in the Establishment of Token Systems and Economies

Basic Requisites of Token Systems   In setting up a token system, there are three basic considerations. First, as in all contingency management procedures, it is necessary to *identify the target behaviors*. Little further needs to be said concerning this prerequisite, except that such response identification will clearly be necessary in the later determination of reinforcement rate, or magnitude, and whether procedures of response cost will be necessary.[4] Obviously, response cost is applicable only when there are behaviors to be eliminated, or when, as treatment progresses, behaviors learned initially are to be phased out in favor of others that were too difficult, too complex, or undesired at the beginning of treatment. For example, a patient who spends much of his time in bed may be allowed to purchase bedtime by earning tokens in another activity. As treatment progresses and he spends more and more time out of bed earning tokens, the cost of bedtime may also be raised with little or no inflation in the number of tokens earned for the performance of desired behaviors.

Second, the therapist must *define the currency*. This is generally simple and may depend in large part upon the resources of the institution to provide tangible tokens. In the past, items such as poker chips, points on a tally sheet, gold stars, numbers shown on an electric counter, plastic slips resembling credit cards, or holes punched in a ticket have served as tokens.

Finally, the therapist must *devise an exchange system*. This poses a twofold problem. Initially it must be determined exactly what items or privileges tokens may be exchanged for and how often exchanges can take place. If exchange is allowed only once a year, it is unlikely that a token system will succeed, since the value of the token is sure to become obscured in the waiting. As in all instances employing reinforce-

ment techniques, effective reinforcers must be defined, and these may well vary depending on the population being treated. Examples of such reinforcers—termed *back-up reinforcers*—include tangibles, such as money, food, and toys, or intangibles, such as behavior privileges (ward privileges, passes, special trips to movies, shows, pools, etc.). Note how the latter is a direct utilization of the Premack principle concerning the use of preferred activities as reinforcers.

A second important aspect of the exchange system concerns the establishment of *rates* of exchange. We are speaking of two rates of exchange, the number of tokens earned by the performance of a certain activity and the number of tokens required to be surrendered in payment for a desired item or privilege. Each of these may change during the course of a treatment regimen. At first, nonpreferred behaviors should earn large numbers of rewards, enough so that extensive numbers of nonpreferred behaviors are not required to earn minimally valued items or privileges. Cases and research studies cited throughout this chapter and the next contain examples of exchange rates found to be effective.

Considerations in the Establishment of a Token Economy

Token economies for groups are truly complicated social and economic systems whose construction can be summarized, but not fully represented, in a single discussion. Fortunately, there are several excellent and detailed descriptions of token economies that describe in great detail the procedures, rules, and general considerations for such systems and that have been written in a specific, concrete manner that will facilitate the institution of such systems in any institutional ward (see Ayllon & Azrin, 1968b; Schaefer & Martin, 1969; Thompson & Grabowski, 1972, 1977).

In their account, Ayllon and Azrin (1968b) organize much of their presentation around a

---

[4]Response cost procedures involve the *removal* of a reinforcer contingent upon a designated response. Docking pay for late arrival or denying a privilege because of misbehavior are both examples of response cost. See the section in this chapter for an extended discussion.

series of "rules" to be followed in establishing and maintaining an effective token system. Many of these "rules" are those cited earlier for the establishment of any contingency management procedures, with individual clients or groups. Let us briefly consider several of these again as they apply to the token economy.

Control Over the Dispensation of Reinforcement

The typical contingencies that spontaneously exist in an institution are often related to the bizarre or unusual behavior of the patient. Extreme self-mutilating behavior may be reinforced by personal physical restraint given by ward attendants, and a paranoid ideation is likely to get a response from at least somebody on the ward. Furthermore, many powerful reinforcers, such as food or cigarettes, are often dispensed noncontingently, and an attempt to make reinforcers such as these contingent upon appropriate behavior are often resisted by staff and hospital administrators alike under the assumption that patients have a "right" to have these things on a noncontingent basis (Lucero, Vail, & Scherber, 1968). A token economy must be based on control over powerful back-up reinforcers for which tokens are redeemable. The tokens can then be made contingent upon desired behavior patterns. Although there has been little research directly comparing the effectiveness of different types of reinforcers, there seems little doubt that the commodities backing up tokens can be potent reinforcers. In fact, Elliott, Barlow, Hooper, & Kingerlee (1979) contrasted the effectiveness of token reinforcers with the social reinforcement delivered by staff and found the token reinforcers to be significantly more effective.

Staff Coordination

All staff members (the contingency managers) in contact with a patient form opinions regarding the important aspects of the case based on their own observations of the patient. Everyone observes a slightly different aspect of any patient's total behavior system, and thus different staff members may come to strikingly different conclusions concerning the problem and may present these conclusions to the patient, thereby promoting confusion. As Ayllon and Azrin have so succinctly put it:

> One staff member may tell a patient she is not cooperative enough, another that she has not yet learned to live with herself. Other contradictory objectives often given: she must not form too dependent a relationship on others vs. she must learn to be more dependent or to relate more to others; she must not be rigid vs. she must show more perseverance; she must show more diversity of actions vs. she must develop a better concentration on one thing; she must have a better personal appearance vs. she must not be obsessed with personal appearance; she must learn to acquiesce to authority figures vs. she must show more independence of action. (1968a, pp. 196–197).

As the suggestions to follow clearly indicate, the behavior of staff members toward the patient must be coordinated and must follow closely specified procedures for observing, recording, and responding to (reinforcing) target behaviors.

Defining Target Behaviors: Response Specification

Both those to be changed and the eventually desired behaviors must be specified as concretely and elaborately as possible in ways that require a minimum of interpretation by staff or patient. For example, uncooperative behavior can include many things. However, when defined as "ignores requests regarding the taking of medication," a certain behavior is clearly specified and differentiated from all other behaviors that are also uncooperative but are not part of the particular set of problem behaviors characterizing patients on a certain ward. Schaefer and Martin (1969) have noted how the achievement of "good personal hygiene" includes

No dirt on feet	Clean fingernails
No dirt on legs or knees	Nicely combed hair
No dirt on hands or arms	Daily change of underwear
No dirt on neck or face	Clean socks or stockings
No evidence of body odor	Neat and recent shave (men)
No residue in the navel	Suitable cosmetics (women)

This is a long list, and certainly the *total* number of criteria would constitute an extremely long chain of behaviors to require from a patient who performs few of them at first, or at the onset of his experience with a token system. Note, however, the extreme specificity of each item.

Specifications also include defining the "pay rates" (number of tokens earned) for each behavior and establishing rules for how a patient gains access to those tasks that not all patients may do on a particular day. Also to be specified is the amount of time a patient must spend at a task before it is considered completed, plus what constitutes adequate performance. Of course, the desired behaviors selected should be within the eventual competence of the patients participating in the economy. In a management procedure designed to eliminate problem behaviors, there should be clear, positive contingencies for desired behaviors that are currently infrequent (in many instances, they may be opposite to—or mutually exclusive of—the problem behavior). Rather than noting what is *not* to be done, it is better to define positive alternatives to undesired behaviors and to establish contingencies for them. Often, these replacement behaviors and contingencies are not specified. For example, in the rules and contingencies that originally governed a residential treatment program for children and adolescents

(Achievement Place—Bailey, Wolf, & Phillips, 1970), a variety of behaviors received points, but an even more clearly specified set of negative behaviors lost points. In this particular instance, many of the negative behaviors could have been rephrased, resulting in a more positive and less punitive-appearing contingency management program. The list of rules presented to the boys might have been rephrased as follows:

1. Ask permission if you wish to leave your seat.
2. Talk with your classmates before class, and ask permission if you must talk while in class.
3. Focus your attention on the teacher, the board, and the work on your desk in order to avoid daydreaming or gazing out the window.
4. Position your desk properly at the beginning of class and leave it that way.
5. Work quietly.
6. Focus your attention on your own work so as to avoid disturbing others.
7. Work for the whole period.

Although it is a disadvantage that these rephrasings are so long, note that they are all positive in nature, specifying the behavior desired and in many instances the problem behavior to be eliminated. In this way, positive behaviors that are mutually exclusive alternatives to the problem behaviors are clearly spelled out, thus aiding their adoption and the concurrent elimination of the problem behaviors. This is perhaps the most compelling reason to design a contingency management procedure for an individual or in an institution in a positive manner, clearly specifying the desired behaviors as well as the problem ones.

Specifying Reinforcers

Another necessary procedure, similar to the clear identification of desired and changeworthy behaviors, is to specify concretely and elaborately the reinforcer to be administered.

Within a strictly token economy, this is a second-order process, involving the communication to the patient of various "real" reinforcers he can purchase with his earned tokens.

A wide variety of items maximizes the likelihood that tokens will come to have potency as reinforcers for all patients. In many instances, it is wise to vary the forms of a known reinforcer in order to discover slight variants that themselves can act as "new" reinforcers. In their token economy, Ayllon and Azrin (1968b) were able to maximize the continued effectiveness of a variety of reinforcers as a result of this technique. Prior to the installation of the token economy, patients had used bulk tobacco and rolled their own cigarettes. Variation showed that brand, filter versus nonfilter, and even smoking versus chewing tobacco were all reinforcers of varying potency for different patients. Similarly, flavors of soda; colors of bedspreads, floor mats, and throw cushions; and even whether one "purchased" low or high beds were preferences that varied among the patients. The larger the variety of reinforcers for which tokens may be traded, the greater the likelihood that tokens will be of maximal value for each and every participant in the economy.

Observing ward patients can be an important source of information about general behavior patterns that all or most patients frequently display. This information is important in determining activity reinforcers that may be utilized as privileges exchangeable for tokens. Occasionally, the therapist encounters patients whose behavior is so regressed that they appear to value few, if any, items and certainly no activities. Ayllon and Azrin (1968a) have demonstrated that *enforced sampling of activities* is an effective way to increase their reinforcing properties, as seen in the frequency with which patients will exchange hard-earned tokens to purchase the activities.

In three instances, these investigators demonstrated the effectiveness of procedures designed to increase the value of outdoor walks, music, and movies as reinforcers. Each of these behaviors was minimally attractive to the ward patients at first. However, patients were required to sample each activity before deciding whether or not to spend tokens in order to participate more fully. For example, patients were required to assemble outside before deciding whether or not to pay for a walk. Those who decided not to pay then returned indoors. There was a music room in the ward, and in a second experiment, patients were assembled for three minutes just outside the door to this room before deciding whether to pay in order to enter. The door to the room was left slightly ajar so that the music could be heard. In a third study, patients viewed five minutes of a weekly ward movie before being invited to view the remainder for the price of a token. In all studies, patients were given the opportunity to purchase any of the activities for a period of several weeks prior to the sampling procedure. Then, after the sampling had been required for several weeks, it was discontinued and the patients' continued rate of purchasing of the activities was observed. As Figure 5-7 clearly shows, sampling markedly increased the rate of purchasing of the sampled activities, and even after it was discontinued, the activities continued to be purchased at a much higher rate than before the sampling experience. Clearly, such a sampling procedure can prove invaluable when one is dealing with the patients who appear to find few, if any, activities reinforcing.

While reinforcement is clearly the backbone of a token system, it should be noted that tokens can serve other functions as well. Perhaps the most important is that of providing *information* regarding the behavior that effectively earns tokens: it is clearly the behavior targeted for increase, it is judged appropriate by the staff, it is likely to bring reinforcement in the future, and so forth. Patients recognize these factors. In fact, one study reports that patients in a day hospital setting actually saw the tokens (points) they earned as indicators of how well they were doing in the program rather than as avenues to purchasing rewards (Turner & Luber, 1980).

Figure 5-7 *Numbers of patients selecting various activities and numbers of activities selected as a function of reinforcer sampling: outdoor activity (walks), listening to music, and watching movies.*

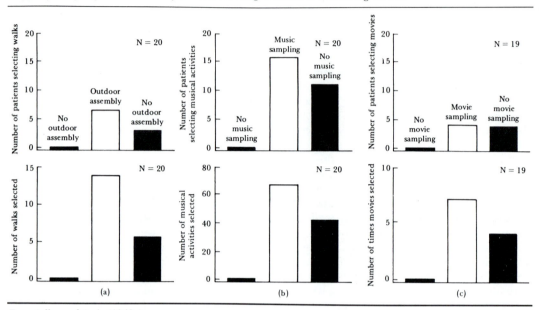

From Ayllon and Azrin (1968a).

Specification of the Contingency and Magnitude of Reinforcement

How many tokens, smiles, ignorings (turning one's back and walking off, or simply changing the subject), *when* to reinforce, *whom* to reinforce with *which* reinforcers—all of these points must be crystal clear to the staff that implements the contingencies of the token economy. Additionally, since reinforcement is the heart of the procedure, it is strongly recommended that systematic, direct observation of the reinforcement procedures be used to coordinate and assure the proper implementation of the contingencies.

Laws of supply and demand are as important in the token economy as they are in the economy of nations. Jobs that are strenuous, tedious,

or that take a long time may be deserving of higher pay. However, if these jobs are attractive for other reasons, so that they are preferred by a majority of patients, they can be devalued—reduced to lower pay—in order to encourage patients to select others jobs (or they may be used as reinforcers). Occasionally, it may be feasible to adjust the number of tokens earned for a specific task for each patient, awarding a higher number of tokens for tasks the patient least prefers or the therapist deems most therapeutic for that particular patient (Ayllon & Azrin, 1968b). Also, sometimes the qualifications for a job will not permit all patients to sign up for it, and this exclusivity may merit greater token reward. Ayllon and Azrin (1968b) have reported that the job of tour guide through the ward required only 10 minutes of a patient's time, but earned 10 tokens; yet a popular job, such as sweeping the floor, although physically demanding and requiring about three hours, earned only 5.

Another contingency decision involves the determination of the number of tokens that must be traded for each back-up reinforcer. This question is clearly correlated to the problem of determining how many tokens a job earns, since both considerations affect a patient's access to the back-up reinforcers. Supply and demand are important here, as well. If the bus to town is of limited capacity, the cost of town passes may be high, whereas if the opportunity to play ping-pong is unlimited, the cost may be low for that activity (Ayllon & Azrin, 1968b). On an individual level, the cost for a particular reinforcer can be reduced to encourage a particular patient to partake of that item or activity. An obvious example would be when visits with the ward psychologist can be purchased with tokens, a high price could prevail for talkative patients whereas the cost would be nil for patients who are relatively uncommunicative (Ayllon & Azrin, 1968b).

Fading Procedures

The goal of most therapy programs is eventually to withdraw the particular, intentional contingencies that constitute the program while the changed behavior patterns continue to persist. Thus, it is wise to select for change—at least at first—behaviors that will continue to be reinforced after training. It is not uncommon for token economies to include progressive liberation from the token system as behavioral improvement is noted. In an example cited later, not all patients on a given ward were included in the token economy, and the contingency managers clearly specified from the start that the goal of that token program was to "promote" individuals to a regular ward routine.

A token program—or an individual's participation in it—should be gradually faded out as appropriate behavior patterns are developed. This can be achieved by increasing the length of time between token administrations or redemptions, by decreasing the number of token rewards earned by target behaviors, by increasing the number of tokens required to earn the back-up reinforcers, or by some combination of these procedures. There has been little research on this point, but when utilizing the procedures of decreasing the number of tokens earned, or when increasing the number of tokens required to purchase a given back-up reinforcer, it seems advisable to begin to make the back-up reinforcers freely available to a limited extent. In this way, fading out the token program would not necessitate the deprivation of back-up reinforcers or the frantic performance of appropriate behavior at an inappropriately high rate so as to guarantee the continued availability of the back-up reinforcers.

As the preceding discussion illustrates, the design and implementation of a token system, especially one that is established as a full economy, is both detailed and complicated. The richness of a well-developed system can only be appreciated by close scrutiny of one that has been designed and put into operation. That level of detail is not necessary for our discussion at this point, but see Appendix B, which contains specific examples of procedures used in token economies that were established in large institutions generally serving psychotic patients.

In this chapter, we have presented most of the basic procedures and techniques of contingency management. Although examples of their implementation to the treatment of a variety of behavior problems were also included, our primary concern has been the description of the foundational contingency management procedures. In the next chapter, we will turn our attention more directly to the application of contingency management procedures, to the treatment of cognitive and behavioral problems, and to the factors that promote effective treatment outcomes.

6

Contingency Management II: Application and Outcome

Contingency Management Research and Case Studies of Reinforcement Procedures

Of all the techniques of behavior therapy, the procedure of manipulating reinforcing events in contingency management is certainly based on the greatest amount of empirical research in laboratory settings. Furthermore, most case studies concerned with contingency manipulations are presented in the form of research studies having only a single subject. This is the direct result of—indeed, constitutes—one of the major research design contributions operant psychology has made to the field in general: the single-subject research design. Let us consider briefly two of the methodological issues that have been of concern in establishing the validity of research on contingency management. These issues also have relevance for designing effective implementations of contingency management programs in individual cases and for assessing their therapeutic success or failure.

Issues of Research Design

The most common research procedure utilizing a single subject is the *reversal design,* in which information is gathered concerning the frequency of a target behavior in a designated sit-

uation (baseline), the contingency is applied (initial intervention) and then removed (reversal—similar to baseline), and finally the contingency manipulation is reinstituted. Frequency is monitored throughout the changes in contingency, and even afterward if the stability of change is under investigation. The data are then examined to see if the frequency of the target behavior was stable during baseline, if it changed markedly during intervention (increasing if it is the recipient of reinforcement, decreasing if an incompatible behavior is the recipient), if it returned to baseline frequency during reversal, and then if it increased or decreased appropriately when the contingency was reestablished. If all these criteria are clearly met, then the researchers can conclude that the power of the contingency manipulations to affect the target behavior has been duly demonstrated.

Another procedure to evaluate the effectiveness of a contingency is the *multiple baseline design.* This is employed in cases involving behaviors that are changeworthy but which one would not want to reverse to their original condition. For example, if a self-mutilating behavior such as head banging is the target, then we might wish to institute a contingency that promotes the frequency of a desirable behavior that is incompatible with head banging and causes a reduction in the frequency of such self-mutilation. However, we would not then want to withdraw this contingency simply to observe whether head banging abruptly resumed. Indeed, it would be unethical to do so. The multiple baseline procedure is based upon the reasoning that one way to evaluate the effectiveness of a particular behavior change technique is to observe its effect on one behavior and then apply it to other behaviors as well. If all the behaviors to which a contingency is applied show similar changes in probability frequency or intensity as the contingency is applied, it is reasonable to conclude that the contingency and constituent reinforcers are responsible for effecting the observed changes in behavior.

These designs are not without their critics, and many of their comments are well taken. One criticism is that the use of only a single subject limits the confidence with which the results may be interpreted as valid for other individuals and thus for general usage. We may never be certain that the individual in question was not atypical in a manner that predisposed him or her to respond to the contingency manipulation differently from the way in which others would respond. Of course, this same criticism can be applied to research involving groups of subjects or clients: a small group can be unrepresentative of the population at large. The clear answer to this criticism is replication, or utilization of the manipulation in a number of individual cases with successful results in each. Fortunately, the operant literature is so extensive that there are few manipulations that have not been replicated a significant number of times, enough to inspire confidence in their effectiveness.

A given investigation or case study can be flawed in many ways. The reversal and multiple baseline designs both rely heavily on baseline data, and some studies omit the baseline period of frequency recording. In some ways, this is understandable and is comparable to the necessary, but often omitted, inclusion of a non-treated control condition in studies of drug or psychotherapy effectiveness. That is, when a potential curative action is available, it is difficult to justify delaying (for baseline) or omitting (in control subjects) its employment, especially when the behavior problem or illness in question is extremely debilitating. Of course, there are times when baseline data are irrelevant, such as when a profoundly retarded individual has never emitted a particular response or when a self-mutilating child engages in head banging instantaneously and continually the moment restraints are removed.

A second potential problem that may apply even when baseline frequency data are gathered is that the data must be stable. Occasionally, data are reported in which the baseline frequency, although quite high, let us say, is clearly declining during the baseline period. Thus, even though a subsequent manipulation appears to produce a further decline, we cannot strongly argue that the decline present during baseline measurement would not have continued and the frequency of the behavior been reduced even if the contingency manipulation had not been instituted. Consequently, it is well to gather baseline data until a fairly stable frequency is obtained, one that appears to be neither increasing nor decreasing.

We should reiterate at this point that the assessment of baseline information is important for the practicing therapist, since it is by comparison with the baseline frequency that he can assess the effectiveness of the contingency management program he has devised for a particular client. Without such information, it is difficult to determine whether parents, teachers, or any other contingency managers are accurately effecting the planned contingencies or, if the planned contingencies are being properly executed, whether they are showing any effective control of overt behavior. The therapist must make such decisions if he or she is to evaluate the effectiveness of current manipulations for future clients with similar behavior problems.

Before continuing, let us present some brief examples of the type of investigations often found in this literature. One of the clearest reported examples of the reversal design in case studies is a classic case reported by Allen, Hart,

Buell, Harris, and Wolf (1964). This is a pleasant example since it illustrates quite clearly the way in which changes in one behavior can be paralleled in an opposite way by changes in a mutually exclusive behavior, thus providing evidence that the frequency of one behavior can be manipulated in order to manipulate (indirectly) a different, but related, behavior. In this particular case, Ann, a nursery school child, was quite isolated from other children in the school she attended, spending 45 percent of her time alone, 35 percent interacting with adults, 10 percent of her time near, but not interacting with, children, and 10 percent in actual interaction with other children. From an initial analysis of the situation, it appeared that Ann possessed several skills that encouraged teachers to interact with her, such as advanced language and conceptual development and a long attention span for teacher-initiated projects. Furthermore, her slow, halting speech appeared to be another factor eliciting teacher attention. Initial observation also indicated that the nursery school teachers granted attention to Ann when she was with them or was playing alone, but rarely when she was with other children, as though for fear of disrupting such activities. Figure 6-1 illustrates the relative frequencies of Ann's interactions with adults and children at the nursery school.

Baseline measurement covered five days of observations and revealed a somewhat stable, high frequency of interaction with adults (although a downward slope is rather noticeable and one or two days more of observations would have been in order to demonstrate stability) and a quite stable, low frequency of interaction with children. Following baseline, the teachers were instructed to pay as little attention as possible to Ann when she was engaged in solitary play or approached one of them, but to grant and actively offer such attention when she was playing with other children. As Figure 6-1 illustrates, the effects were striking and immediate. After five days of this contingency, the teachers were instructed to reverse the con-

tingency and to attend to Ann during solitary play and to respond to her when she was in their presence or made attention bids to them. Clearly, the behaviors of playing with children and interaction with adults were under the control of the nursery school teachers' attention-giving behavior, since the frequencies of these two behaviors reversed again. Finally, the original "therapeutic" contingencies were reinstituted after five days, and the frequencies of these two categories of behavior again changed. Follow-up checks conducted over a period of two weeks indicated that the changes in these two behaviors appeared to be rather enduring.

In general, the reversal design is more common than the multiple baseline procedure, probably because most behaviors that are the object of case studies or small-group experiments involve behaviors for which a reversal to baseline as a part of the procedure would not be unethical or cause irreparable harm. Later we will discuss an example of the use of contingency management procedures in an academic setting to increase accurate performance and on-task behavior (Hay, Hay, & Nelson, 1977b). The results (which are presented in Figure 6-2) revealed that when on-task behavior was contingently reinforced, only on-task behavior improved; later, when accuracy was also contingently reinforced, it, too, became more frequent.

Validity Problems in Recording Behavior

As a processor of information, the human observer is probably incapable of refraining from interpretation when observing and recording behavior. The individual's theoretical bias may not only alert him to the occurrence of phenomena to be recorded, but may also predispose him to misinterpret other, unrelated events as instances of the phenomenon he is to observe and record. Often, in experiments requiring the recording of behavior, more than one observer is employed, and comparison of the reports of several observers constitutes what

Figure 6-1 *Percent of social interactions with adults and with other children shown by an isolated child as a function of reinforcement for peer interaction.*

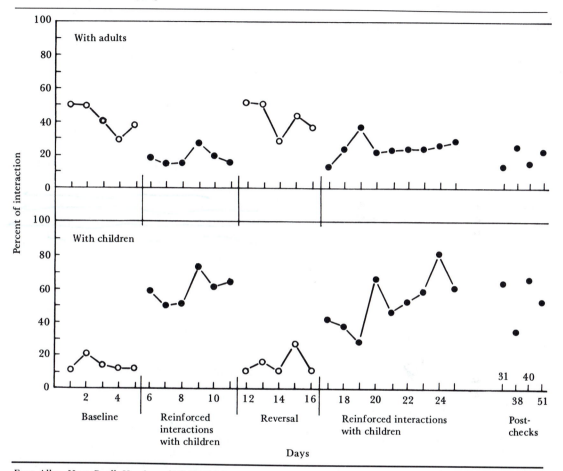

From Allen, Hart, Buell, Harris, and Wolf (1964).

is called *rater reliability*. The assumption is that phenomena—in this case, instances of a behavior—that are consistently reported independently by, say, two separate observers are trustworthy and probably represent observations of events that actually occurred.

Unfortunately, this is an overinterpretation of the power of rater reliability since it implies

that reliable observations (more than one observer recording the same event) are *valid* observations. This does not follow, primarily because it does not rule out the possibility that both observers share many of the same biases and expectancies. That shared biases may influence raters' records and evaluations was shown clearly in seminal research by O'Leary

Figure 6-2 *Relative efficacy of on-task and achievement (academic) contingencies for increasing on-task behavior, rate of work, and accuracy of work (on-task behavior:* ———*; percentage rate: . . .; percentage accuracy: - - -).*

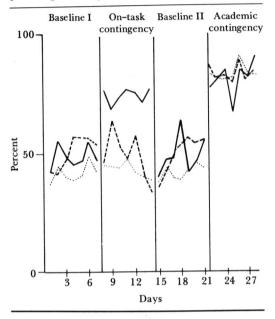

From Hay, Hay, and Nelson (1977b).

tancy tended to be confirmed in observations recorded: individual raters expecting an increase in disruptive behavior recorded such an increase, and individual raters expecting a decrease recorded a decrease.

We must quickly add that further evidence shows that training individuals to record behavior in *clearly and specifically defined categories* can reduce, or even eradicate, this source of error due to shared biases. Kent and colleagues (1973) found that the raters' expectations affected their *global evaluation* of the extent of behavior change they observed, but that the *specific behavioral recordings* produced by the same observer did not show any effect of expectancy. Thus, we emphasize the importance of defining target behaviors *specifically* and *thoroughly* when training individuals to record behavior and of employing rigorous, well-thought-out training procedures in either self-monitoring or the monitoring of others.

Contingency Management of Diverse Behaviors, Competencies, and Behavior Problems

and his colleagues, (Kass & O'Leary, 1970; Kent, O'Leary, Diament, & Dietz, 1973; O'Leary & Kent, 1973; Romanczyk, Kent, Diament, & O'Leary, 1973).

In one study (Kass & O'Leary, 1970), three groups of observers each observed the same videotape of two disruptive children in a simulated classroom. One group was told that soft reprimands were anticipated to be effective in reducing disruptive behavior, while another group was told that such reprimands were expected to increase disruptive behavior. The third group was given no information. It was clearly demonstrated by an analysis of the reports of these raters that each group's expec-

The range of behavior problems to which contingency management techniques have been applied is practically as broad as the imagination. As long as behavior can be defined so that it can be observed, it is possible to attempt to alter it by manipulating contingent consequences. Some behaviors are simple to define. Disruptive behavior in the classroom can be designated as any out-of-seat behavior. Instances of enuresis leave telltale signs and could be quantified by size of wet spot or number of drops, if this were a meaningful thing to do. Other behaviors may have more arbitrary definitions that are limited only by the creativity of the therapist or investigator. Creativity itself has been shaped, as we shall see. If pain is defined as verbal *reports* of pain, it, too, can be made the target of contingency management. This conceptual compromise in definition (*reports* of a problem rather than an actual, objective recording of it) has also been used to apply contingency management procedures in the treatment of depression.

The application of contingency management procedures has largely focused on shaping desired behavior, but specific procedures (e.g., differential reinforcement) have also been used to reduce or eliminate problem behaviors. While we will reserve any intensive concentration on contingency management procedures in the elimination of behaviors until later when we focus on extinction procedures (Chapter 7, "Response Elimination and Extinction Procedures"), clearly there are behavior problems "to be eliminated" that consist of a behavior *deficit,* and we will give some attention to those. In this class of problems are included writer's block, inappropriate gender identity, and even constipation.

To indicate the range of specific behavior problems that contingency management procedures have targeted, Table 6-1 lists a number of examples of different behaviors and competencies that have responded favorably to intervention by the management of contingencies, most of which have been reported in the literature since 1970. Long though it is, this list is not totally exhaustive.

As the years have passed, the diversity of behaviors, competencies, and behavior problems subjected to contingency management procedures has expanded significantly. Behavioral indices of competencies, such as creativity or even IQ, have been sensitive to contingencies, and this will be discussed in greater detail in a subsequent section. Presenting complaints that have been generally categorized as having a physical or physiological base, such as hyperactivity or reports of pain, or as emotional, such as fear or psychosomatic paralysis, have been re-

conceptualized in ways that allow contingency management to be utilized. Thus, for example, pain is construed as *verbal reports* of pain, and those reports are the target of treatment. Similarly, hysterical paralysis can be treated by attempts to increase those behaviors that are prevented or interfered with by the nonphysical paralysis. In another direction, contingency management procedures have been adapted to ecological problems requiring the control of behavior for large populations. In this vein, techniques have been developed to promote large-scale decreases in such things as littering or the consumption of fuel oil and electricity. We will conclude this discussion with some examples of the diversity that characterize the applications of contingency management procedures.

Gender Role Behaviors

One of the most unusual applications of contingency management procedures involved the case of a young child, a boy whose effeminate behavior indicated that he was developing a feminine gender identity (Rekers et al., 1976). By age 5, this child had a long history of cross-dressing and cross-gender play and even made many open statements about his preference to be a girl. When given opportunities, he preferred female role behaviors, female activities, and objects typically associated with females. An independent clinician had judged him to be a high risk for adult transsexualism. The parents decided that they would seek treatment for the boy to alter his feminine mannerisms.

Initially, concentrating a therapeutic procedure on overt behaviors would not have been considered in a case such as this because of the strong assumption that gender identity is a deeply rooted cognitive and emotional phenomenon that determines overt behaviors but is not determined by them. This assumption did not guide the present intervention. The therapists decided to develop a twofold treatment program, one part directed toward training the

Table 6-1 **Behaviors and Competencies Responsive to Contingent Management**

Target	Behavior/Competency	Population	Outcome	Source of Report
Social	Social & emotional behaviors	Handicapped children	Increased	Cooke & Apolloni (1976)
	Prosocial verbal behavior	Delinquent adolescent	Increased	Emshoff, Redd, & Davidson (1976)
	Elective mutism	Normal children	Eliminated	Calhoun & Koenig (1973)
	Mutism	Adults	Improved	Sherman (1965); Straughan (1968)
	Social interaction	Chronic psychotic adults	Increased	Fichter, Wallace, Liberman, & Davis (1976)
	Social interaction	Retarded adolescents	Increased	Williams, Martin, McDonald, Hardy, & Lambert (1975)
	Reluctant speech	Preadolescents	Decreased	Williamson, Sewell, Sanders, Haney, & White (1977)
	Sharing, praising	Children	Increased	Rogers-Warren & Baer (1976)
	Social speech	Retarded children	Increased	Mithaug & Wolfe (1976)
	Social greeting	Retarded children	Increased	Stokes, Baer, & Jackson (1974)
	Positive reinforcement of children	Adult teacher	Increased	Breyer & Allen (1975)
	Social skills	Predelinquent adolescents	Increased	Maloney, Harper, Braukmann, Fixsen, Phillips, & Wolf (1976)
	Peer interaction, obedience	Delinquent adolescents	Increased	Hobbs & Holt (1976)
	Extreme withdrawal or passivity	Children	Improved	Allen, Hart, Buell, Harris, & Wolf (1964); Brawley, Harris, Allen, Fleming, & Peterson (1969); Johnston, Kelley, Buell, Harris, & Wolf (1963); Johnston, Kelley, Harris, & Wolf (1966)
	Sharing	Children	Increased	Warren, Rogers-Warren, & Baer (1976)
	Social disruption	Children	Decreased	MacPherson, Candee, & Hohman (1974); Drabman, Spitalnik, & Spitalnik (1974); Sanders & Glynn (1977)
Self-control	Hyperactivity/ attention span	Retarded children	Decreased/ increased	Alabiso (1975)
	Hyperactivity	Children	Decreased	Wulbert & Dries (1977); Ayllon, Layman, & Kandel (1975)
	Hyperactivity and aggression	Children	Decreased	Allen, Henke, Harris, Baer, & Reynolds (1967); Hall, Lund, & Jackson (1968)
	Obesity	Children	Decreased	Epstein, Parker, McCoy, & McGee (1976)
	Obesity	Adults	Decreased over short term	Hall, Hall, DeBoer, & O'Kulitch (1977)

Table 6-1 **(Continued)**

Target	Behavior/Competency	Population	Outcome	Source of Report
Self-control (continued)	Classroom disruption	Children	Decreased	Todd, Scott, Bostow, & Alexander (1976); Robertson, DeReus, & Drabman (1976); Ayllon, Garber, & Pisor (1975)
	Family interaction	Mother and adolescent	Improved responsibility	Blechman, Olson, Schornagle, Halsdorf, & Turner (1976)
	Constipation	Young child	Eliminated	Wright & Busch (1977)
	Enuresis	Children	Eliminated	Finley, Wansley, & Blenkarn (1977)
	Enuresis	Adolescent	Eliminated	Popler (1976)
	Assignment task completion	Adult prisoners	Increased	Milan & McKee (1976)
	Fire setting	Child	Eliminated	Stawar (1976)
	Pollakuria (frequent urination)	Adult	Decreased	Masur (1976)
	Public masturbation	Adult	Decreased	Mellström & Gelsomino (1976)
	Rumination	Infant	Eliminated	Linscheid & Cunningham (1977)
	Hirschsprung's disease	Child	Controlled	Epstein & McCoy (1977)
	Classroom task attention	Children	Increased	Hay, Hay, & Nelson (1977b); Marholin & Steinman (1977)
	Academic task completion	Children	Increased	Rapport & Bostow (1976)
	Homework	Children	Improved	Harris & Sherman (1974)
	School attendance	Predelinquent	Improved	Alexander, Corbett, & Smigel (1976)
	Curfew obedience	Adolescents	Improved	Alexander, Corbett, & Smigel (1976)
	Self-control	Normal adult	Improved	Whitman & Dussault (1976)
	Writer's block	Adult	Eliminated	Passman (1976)
	Dressing & feeding	Adult psychotic patients	Improved	Ayllon & Michael (1959)
	Personal grooming & responsiveness to verbal directions	Retarded children and adults	Improved	Bensberg, Colwell, & Cassell (1965); Girardeau & Spradlin (1964); Minge & Ball (1967); Roos (1965)
	Toilet training	Retarded children	Improved	Giles & Wolf (1966); Hundziak, Mowrer, & Watson (1965)
	Self-mutilation	Children	Decreased	Allen & Harris (1966)
	Character disorders	Adult	Improved	Jones, Stayer, Wichlacz, Thomes, & Livingston (1977)
	Adherence to a medical regime	Adult	Improved	Hart (1979)
	Adherence to a medical regime	Children	Improved	Margrat & Papadopoulu (1977)

Table 6-1   (Continued)

Target	Behavior/Competency	Population	Outcome	Source of Report
Cognitive-emotional	Complex language	Autistic child	Acquired	Stevens-Long & Rasmussen (1974)
	Creativity	Children	Increased	Henson (1975)
	Intelligence score	Handicapped children	Increased	Smeets & Striefel (1975)
	Intelligence/ vocabulary	Normal children	Increased	Clingman & Fowler (1976)
	Creativity	Normal children	Increased	Glover & Gary (1976)
	School performance	Adolescent	Improved	Schumaker, Hovell, & Sherman (1977)
	Reading/ comprehension	Autistic child	Improved	Rosenbaum & Breiling (1976)
	Preacademic skills	Deviant preschool children	Improved	Rowbury, Baer, & Baer (1976)
	Study rate/test performance	Young adults	Improved in below average	Bristol & Sloane (1974)
	Reading and language	Children	Improved	Van Houten, Hill, & Parsons (1975)
	Arithmetic competence	Children	Improved	Hundert (1976)
	Autisticlike behavior	Child	Eliminated	Moore & Bailey (1973)
	Anxiety and depression	Adult	Eliminated	Vasta (1975); Reisinger (1972)
	Phobia	Adults	Eliminated	Marshall, Boutilier, & Minnes (1974)
	Conversion reaction	Adult	Eliminated	Kallman, Hersen, & O'Toole (1975)
	Anxiety and hyperdependency	Children	Improved	Wahler & Polio (1968)
	Autism	Children	Improved	Lovaas (1968); Wetzel, Baker, Rooney, & Martin (1966)
	School phobia	Children	Eliminated	G. R. Patterson (1965)
	Psychogenic seizures	Adult	Improved	Gardner (1967)
	Psychogenic blindness	Adult	Improved	Brady & Lind (1961)
	Maladaptive or reduced responsiveness of various sorts in schizophrenics	Adult	Improved	Ayllon & Azrin (1968a); King, Armitage, & Tilton (1960); Peters & Jenkins (1954); Schaefer & Martin (1966); Thompson & Grabowski (1972, 1977)
	Inappropriate gender identity	Child	Made appropriate	Rekers, Yates, Willis, Rossen, & Taubman (1976)
	Pain	Adult	Eliminated	Cautela (1971c)
	Stuttering	Adults	Reduced	Ingham & Andrews (1973)

boy's mother in contingency management procedures so that she could reinforce masculine play behaviors and extinguish or punish feminine behaviors, and a second part directed toward the modification of feminine mannerisms, such as a stylistically flexed elbow or a feminine manner of running.

First, the boy's mother was trained to reinforce masculine behaviors by smiles and compliments and to ignore feminine behavior by turning away from the child and withdrawing. Then, after a few sessions with both masculine and feminine toys available so that the mother could act appropriately, the father was introduced into the situation as a contingency manager, and some specific verbal prompts telling the boy not to play with the feminine toys were included. At the beginning of this phase of treatment, the child consistently played with feminine toys, but with the initiation of the contingency, preference for masculine toys began to develop immediately. After approximately 55 10-minute therapy sessions, the therapist tested for generalization by allowing the child to play alone. The boy rapidly reestablished feminine play. This inclined the investigators to include an additional 20 sessions, with sessions specifically designed to promote generalization. The child played alone in the room, and when a hidden observer noted the initiation of feminine play, the mother was instructed to enter the room and prompt the child not to play with those items. By the 75th session, the child showed good generalization, and even when given the opportunity to play with new toys while by himself consistently preferred the masculine toys.

In a second phase of treatment, the targets were some stylistic feminine mannerisms. These were a feminine style of elbow flexing and of running. The investigators developed a game involving throwing and running, and the child was told he could earn tokens by playing. He was given an advance amount, and during the game he lost one token for each instance of a flexed elbow or feminine running, at which point an assistant verbally admonished him and demonstrated the proper way to throw or run. Figure 6-3 illustrates the effects of this treatment phase on these two aspects of feminine behavior. While stylistic behaviors were being treated in formal sessions, the parents were trained, using videotapes of their child's behavior, to recognize inappropriate target behaviors, and they instigated in the home environment contingencies similar to those used in the treatment sessions. The behaviors appeared to decrease in that setting as well and no further treatment was implemented. In a follow-up assessment more than two years later, an independent clinical psychologist noted a clear change in the boy's gender identity. Not only had the particular behaviors under treatment changed, but he also displayed a marked alteration in overall play patterns, interpersonal relationships, and in contact and interaction with his father. Despite the fact that, of necessity, the treatment intervention had been highly focused on a small sample of behaviors, there was clear generalization to multiple aspects of the child's overall patterns of behavior. The formal posttherapy diagnosis was "no cross-gender identification."

There has been discussion in the literature about the ethics of such "sex appropriate" interventions and about the accuracy of identifying future psychological or behavioral problems (i.e., in adulthood) from the behavior of a young child (Nordyke, Baer, Etzel, & LeBlanc, 1977; Rekers, 1977; Winkler, 1977). These concerns are valid and deserve some consideration here. Certainly, intervention into aspects of behavior where there is a range of choice should take into account the preferences and advantages to be gained by the individual being treated. Elsewhere we have noted that aspects of sexual preference have become accepted as just that: preference and not aspects of pathology. Thus, they merit intervention only if they cause problems for the individual or, possibly, for

Figure 6-3 *Changes in two feminine stylistic behaviors in a young boy before and after contingency management intervention to develop a masculine style for the two behaviors (●—●: fixed elbow; ▲—▲: feminine running).*

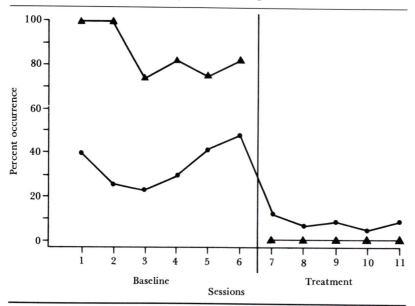

From Rekers, Yates, Willis, Rosen, and Taubman (1976).

society (through misbehavior). The issue becomes particularly thorny when the individual at hand is a child, for whom society limits free choice and assigns it to parents or guardians (or, indirectly, to therapists). It is compounded when one raises the very legitimate question of whether stylistic sex-labeled behaviors in a young child are actually indicative of an eventual gender identity and sexual preference. Even if they are not, does the mere fact that the behaviors have caused concern for the parents make them eligible for change? Perhaps so, if that would improve the quality of life for the child by relieving the parents' concerns. Perhaps not, if it would indeed tamper with an eventual gender identity that would have been more satisfactory. As with every question, there are two sides to this issue, and each case will have different merits. The point, however, is that behavior change interventions into gender-related behaviors, especially with children, must be considered very carefully before being undertaken—from an ethical as well as a scientific perspective (cf. Wolfe, 1979).

Hyperactivity and Hyperkinetic Children

Another behavior problem not typically assumed to be amenable to contingency management, or to any other behavior therapy technique for that matter, is childhood hyperactivity. This disorder is generally diagnosed in young children, primarily boys, and drug treatment utilizing a stimulant (methylphenidate-Ritalin) is commonly prescribed, especially by general care physicians. However, when contingency management procedures are used, they frequently prove comparable in effectiveness to drug treatment of the same disorder. In one of the earliest investigations (Kauffman & Hallahan, 1973), a hyperactive, destructive boy was placed in a teaching program that was highly structured and focused on reinforcement for proper classroom behavior and good academic responsiveness. Within six days of exposure to this classroom regimen, the incidents of rough physical behavior declined from an initial average of 50 per day to fewer than 10.

In another early report (Christensen & Sprague, 1973), two equivalent groups of hyperactive children, one receiving drug treatment and the other not, were given equivalent behavioral treatment involving a monetary reward for sitting quietly. Children not receiving drugs were given a placebo tablet similar in appearance to the medication received by the other group, who actually got a dose of methylphenidate. Figure 6-4 illustrates the results of 13 different sessions. While the drug itself did have an effect, analysis revealed that the contingency system reduced the activity levels of *both* groups of children, so that even those receiving the drug showed still further activity reduction during the conditioning phase. Further, during all of the conditioning sessions but one, the difference in activity between the drug and placebo groups was *not* significant, indicating that on many occasions the behavioral treatment was not significantly less effective than the combined behavioral and drug treatment.

In a subsequent investigation, Ayllon, Layman, and Kandel (1975) contrasted the effectiveness of drug and behavioral treatment of hyperactivity in children's math and reading classes. Their behavioral intervention included token reinforcement, not for reduced activity, but simply for correct academic responses involving either math or reading. This was compatible with results of other investigations indicating that attention, both span and focus, can be manipulated through contingencies, and that

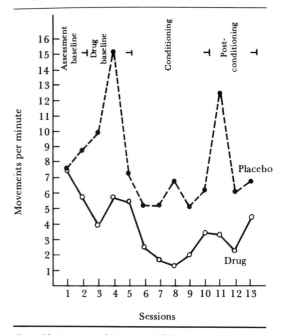

Figure 6-4 *Effects of contingency management on reducing hyperactivity, both alone (with a placebo drug) and in combination with drug treatment.*

From Christensen and Sprague (1973).

increased attention is incompatible with hyperactivity and distractibility (Alabiso, 1975). In the study by Ayllon and his colleagues, following a baseline assessment, the children were first given drug treatment, then the drug was withdrawn and the behavioral treatment instituted. Medication alone reduced hyperactivity from about 80 percent to 20 percent but had little effect on academic competence. When the behavioral treatment was introduced, hyperactivity also fell to 20 percent, but there was a simultaneous increase in academic competence, and accurate performance improved from an initial level of 12 percent to a staggering level of over 85 percent. The results of this study indicate that an effective contingency management procedure for reducing hyperactivity in the classroom context may involve contingencies directed not toward motoric hyperactivity itself but rather toward behavioral competencies requiring nonhyperactive behavior, such as increased attention.

Other investigations have demonstrated the relative advantage of behavioral treatments for hyperactivity (Shafto & Sulzbacher, 1977; Wulbert & Dries, 1977). It still appears that drug treatment does have some effectiveness in reducing aspects of motor hyperactivity (e.g., increases in repetitive hand movements) (Wulbert & Dries, 1977) and slurred speech with higher dosages (Shafto & Sulzbacher, 1977). A formal program of behavioral intervention in the treatment of hyperactivity still does not exist, but the evidence thus far indicates that such treatment has promise, and side effects, if any, are beneficial rather than debilitating. In almost all cases, attentional and cognitive capabilities of children appear to be increased with behavioral treatment, and often these adaptive capabilities may themselves be the target of management.

Psychosomatic Disorders, Anxiety, Depression, and Pain

There is increasing use of behavioral procedures in the treatment of what might be termed emotional or "psychological" disorders, such as anxiety, depression, fears or phobias, and even such venerable diagnostic classifications as a psychosomatic conversion reaction. In each case, the standard procedure is to implement a behavioral diagnosis, focusing upon some specifiable behavior that may be managed in the alleviation of the disorder. In some cases, such as a "conversion reaction," the nonphysiological paralysis or other disability may be used to designate those behaviors that are prevented by the disability, and these become the focus of treatment. Kallman, Hersen, and O'Toole (1975), for example, treated a man who was re-

peatedly afflicted by a "drawing over" reaction to pain in his back that prevented him from straightening up or moving his legs. Repeated hospitalizations and even orthopedic surgery had proved unhelpful. The behavioral treatment consisted of social reinforcement for behaviors gradually approaching walking: first standing, then standing straight, and finally walking. After 18 days of treatment, the distance the man could walk had increased from 0 to more than 100 yards. When he was discharged from the hospital following the initial behavioral treatment, the patterns of social reinforcement in his home environment, which had presumably been maintaining the initial behavior problem, rapidly reestablished the problem and within a month the man was rehospitalized. During the second phase of treatment, a family retraining program was implemented after videotapes of family interactions revealed that family members consistently ignored positive initiatives by the man. After this second intervention, improvement was maintained over a 12-week follow-up.

Another emotional problem that has been treated by contingency management procedures is that of anxiety and accompanying reactive depression. Reisinger (1972), for example, treated a young woman who was rejected and ridiculed by her associates, felt that everyone hated her, and tended to cry often and without provocation. The target behaviors for the behavioral intervention were determined to be crying and a mutually exclusive positive social response, smiling. After gathering baseline information on the frequencies of these two behaviors, a 6-week treatment period levied token reinforcement and response cost procedures against the two target behaviors. The woman was hospitalized and the target behaviors were observed by ward staff, who were instructed to reward instances of smiling and to level fines for instances of crying. The woman showed an immediate and rapid increase in smiling and a decrease in crying. During an extinction period, when neither rewards nor fines were utilized, there was some decline in therapeutic gains, but the behaviors did not revert to baseline. Interestingly, even when a reverse contingency was established for a short period—so that crying was reinforced and smiling fined—baseline frequencies were not reestablished, although the behaviors did respond to the contingencies. When the original contingencies were reestablished, but with social rather than token reinforcement, smiling did again increase in frequency and crying dropped almost to zero frequency. At the end of the 20th week, the patient was discharged.

Pain is another potentially psychological disorder that has been subjected to contingency management. To some extent, the effort described earlier (Kallman, Hersen, & O'Toole, 1975) to increase walking by a client who complained of back pain may be considered an indirect treatment of pain through contingency management procedures to increase those behaviors that supposedly cause pain. Cautela (1977) reported the use of covert positive reinforcement in the direct management of pain, utilizing a procedure that includes having patients visualize a highly reinforcing scene whenever they experience pain. Since Cautela's overall treatment regimen also includes thought stopping (shouting "Stop, relax" at the onset of pain), it seems reasonable to attribute any effectiveness of this procedure to a distracting or even relaxing process rather than to one in which contingency is important. Sand and Biglan (1974) reported another attempt to reduce pain that seems more clearly one of contingency management. They presented a case of a 10-year-old boy suffering recurrent abdominal pain. Treatment consisted of establishing a token system focused on reducing *reports* of pain and increasing behaviors incompatible with having pain (school attendance). The program was successful, and this approach exemplifies the general model of a behavioral attack on seeming psychological problems: define target behaviors that are mutually exclusive of the problem behavior, determine any maintaining factors in the

present environment (e.g., "secondary gain," social reinforcement by others), and eliminate maintaining factors while shaping mutually exclusive alternative behaviors. In the present instance, being absent from school was probably a maintaining factor for reports of pain while school attendance was a mutually exclusive target behavior, so reinforcing school attendance had a doubly beneficial effect.

Population or Ecological Uses of Contingency Management

Contingency management has also been applied to problems related to environmental ecology or social welfare. One issue has been the use of electrical power. The general approach to instilling self-control and restraint in resource consumption has been a combination of information, feedback, and incentives. Consumers are given information about energy, feedback regarding their own personal consumption rates, and then contingent incentives for altering their behavior. Hayes and Cone (1977) achieved significant reductions in electricity use through the utilization of payment for reduced consumption and found that neither information nor feedback enhanced the effectiveness of a basic contingency of reward. Kohlenberg and his colleagues (1976) directed their efforts toward reducing "peaking" in electrical usage— the tendency for consumers to utilize electrical energy at high rates during particular periods of each day. These investigators found that a combination of feedback plus incentives was most effective and produced a 50 percent reduction in peak usage, indicating that the motivational impact of information was not great.

In similar research, Seaver and Patterson (1976) found that both feedback and incentives were required to produce a decrease in fuel-oil consumption for home heating. This investigation utilized mere commendations of praise for the incentives and still achieved a significant reduction in consumption. Gasoline consumption has also been the target of contingency management, but in two diverse fashions. Foxx and Hake (1977) found that offering incentives ranging from money to interesting experiences (touring a mental health facility) contingent on reduced gasoline usage produced a significant 20 percent reduction in the mileage driven by college students. In an alternative approach, Everett, Hayward, and Meyers (1974) utilized contingency management procedures to increase bus ridership. These investigators provided tokens, exchangeable for a variety of backup reinforcers, to all individuals boarding a particular bus, and ridership rose to 150 percent of baseline. This procedure is of note since it demonstrates the extension of token reinforcers into the natural environment from broad applications of contingency management.

The range of applications of contingency management to natural environments and common problems continues to increase. One of the earliest reports dealt with reducing litter in metropolitan areas. As the times changed, so did the ecological problems that were responsive to contingency management intervention. Other problems have included the control of urban disruption and unemployment by judicious use of reinforcers commonly available. Pierce and Risley (1974a, 1974b) reported two interventions that utilized different available reinforcers to promote job training and membership in an urban recreation center. After observing that participation in a federal job training program produced pay that was in no way contingent upon performance, but merely upon physical attendance, the investigators were given the opportunity to redesign the contingency system so that the number of hours of attendance credited to a given individual was proportional to the ratings of the quality of job performance. The result was a striking increase in job performance ratings to near perfect levels. The investigators note that the new contingency required only a change in emphasis:

from *hours* worked as the basis for pay to hours *worked* (low performance ratings indicating that the individual had not been working). In other words, the schedule was altered from an interval one (*hours* worked) to a ratio one focusing on the behavior (hours *worked*). In a second study, these investigators effectively increased attendance at an urban recreation center by manipulating the hours that the center was open. Youths who brought in new members were given extra time in the recreation center, and this produced dramatic increases in membership. In order to control disruptive incidents at the center, the closing time for the entire center was moved forward a few minutes for each disruptive offense, a response cost procedure that produced the almost total elimination of behavioral disruption incidents. This may also have represented a time-out that utilized a group contingency to achieve control over the behavior of a few individuals.

A final focus of ecological contingency management has been to instill appropriate or desired behaviors or preferences, particularly in children. It is common in Southern rural Head Start classes for children from economically impoverished homes, whose home diets differ significantly from those provided by the school system, to refuse to eat the foods at school. In response to this problem, Madsen, Madsen, and Thompson (1974) devised a contingency system in which teachers praised and rewarded (with sugar-coated cereal) each instance of eating the food provided by the school and gave additional rewards and praise to children who finished their entire meal. The resultant increase in meal consumption by initially reluctant children was of major importance since these children came from homes where the diet was not simply different but basically deficient in nutritional requirements. Although the reinforcer itself did not meet standards of good nutrition, it promoted nutrition through the behavior being reinforced.

Another example of contingency management programs designed to increase desired behavioral competencies and preferences is the use of reinforcement techniques to teach children appropriate shopping behavior (Barnard, Christophersen, & Wolf, 1977). As the reader surely recognizes, this is a particularly important skill in a consumer-oriented society such as our own. In this case, parents were trained to respond contingently to the shopping behavior of their own children, focusing upon selections that they considered appropriate. Rapid and significant increases were achieved in appropriate choices by the children involved, and parents independently indicated that they were satified with the improvements in their children's behavior. As increased attention is given to the definition of appropriate and adaptive behaviors within our society, the research literature consistently indicates that contingency management procedures can play an important role in developing those behaviors in individuals who need them most or at times when responsible behavior by members of society becomes most critical.

Educational Applications of Contingency Management

Ever since the introduction of gold stars, and perhaps even earlier, explicit contingency management has played a role in the development of intellectual and academic responding. Early work concentrated largely on procedures remediating defects (e.g., Staats & Butterfield, 1965). As attention has focused on specific programming applications of contingency management, though, a variety of behavioral and competency goals have emerged as targets for management techniques. Thus, not only have contingency management procedures been developed to improve attentional skills, work accuracy, and the reduction of classroom disruption, but there have also been repeated demonstrations that highly generalized competencies,

such as tested intelligence or creativity, are amenable to improvement under appropriate contingency arrangements.

In this section, we will focus on the different techniques and varying foci of contingency management procedures in the educational context. The classroom and other teaching and learning settings have provided an important area of concern for both researchers and practitioners interested in adapting contingency management procedures for educational use. The educational setting has been a laboratory for the development of techniques and research regarding their effectiveness, and ethical issues related to behavior modification research in the social institution of schools are a prime concern. The first group to focus on ethical issues was the National Commission for the Protection of Human Subjects, which raised the following issues: determination of classroom goals, legitimacy of rewards and aversive controls in the classroom, conceptualizations of behavior therapy procedures as manipulative and mechanistic, who can implement the procedures, and accountability. Although the discussion of these issues continues, one conclusion seems clear: the responsibility for preventing any potential misuse of contingency management procedures in the educational setting is best assigned as a shared one among parents, teachers, and behavior therapy practitioners and researchers. As will soon become apparent, the teacher, and often the parent as well, plays an important role in the implementation of contingency management procedures designed to have a beneficial effect on educational performance and competency.

Controlling Disruptive Behavior

Often the control of disruptive behavior in the classroom involves the training of teachers in contingency management procedures to be applied to individual children. In one of the early uses of this procedure, Ward and Baker (1968) trained three elementary school teachers to identify problem behavior instances in four children identified as having disruptive behavior. They learned to cite specific incidents of inappropriate behaviors (and not to say "He's *always* bad") and to identify *when* to reinforce *which* appropriate behavior. Teacher attention for task-relevant behaviors and the ignoring of undesirable behavior were the therapeutic procedures. Overall, the total amount of teacher attention remained the same, but it was redistributed to be applied contingently to task-relevant behavior. The children's deviant, disruptive behavior declined significantly. Moreover, the children no longer differed significantly from controls in terms of the number of incidents of problem behaviors, although they had had a significantly greater rate of such incidents before treatment.

One of the most frequent, and apparently most effective, ways to reduce disruptive behavior in the classroom is through the use of group or interdependent contingencies. In these contingencies, misbehavior by a single child produces consequences for the entire group, such as missing recess, whereas good behavior by all involved may produce a groupwide reinforcing experience, such as additional recess time. The procedure is often one of both contingent reinforcement and response cost. Thus, in the elementary classroom, one form in which token systems may be involved is through what has been termed the "good behavior game." The rules are as follows: first, the teacher lists the rules of the classroom on the board, following which the class is divided into two teams and their names are put on the board. Whenever any *individual* disobeys a rule, his entire team receives a point. At the end of the day, the team with the fewest points receives a special privilege, usually an opportunity for free time or some other valued classroom commodity. The schedule is interdependent since the (mis)behavior of a single child has consequences for his entire team (group). The game itself is largely based on the notion of response cost, although in the final analysis, one team does re-

ceive a reward in return for its good behavior relative to the other team. Figure 6-5 illustrates the striking behavior change that invoking this contingency system can have on the behavior of all the children in a classroom.

Often, a child's own peers are the sources of reinforcement for attention-maintaining disruptive classroom behaviors. Thus, training peer contingency managers has long been recognized

---

Figure 6-5 *Amount of talking and out-of-seat behavior in two classes (math and English) while the "good behavior game" is and is not in effect.*

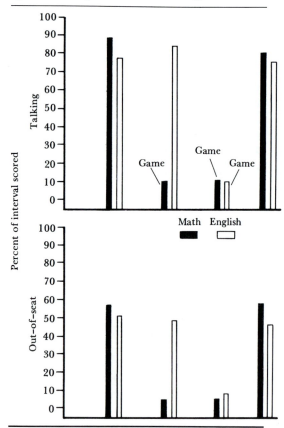
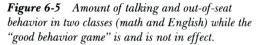

From Harris and Sherman (1973b).

Figure 6-6 *Effectiveness of a peer contingency management system in controlling problem behaviors of disruptive children in a classroom.*

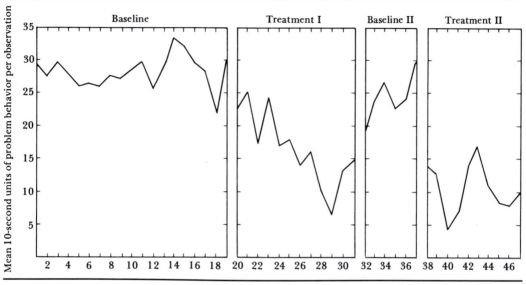

From Solomon and Wahler (1973).

as a successful procedure for reducing classroom disruption (Solomon, 1973; Solomon & Wahler, 1973). Solomon and Wahler (1973), for example, examined an elementary school classroom for teacher and peer determinants of disruptive behavior and found that the problem behaviors of five disruptive children were consistently the target of social attention by all the other children in the room. Five other children were trained in the contingent dispensation of social reinforcement, and they were taught classes of "problem" and "desirable" behaviors. During treatment periods, they were to reinforce "desirable" behaviors and to specifically ignore "problem" behaviors. Figure 6-6 illustrates the results. Even though most of the children in the classroom responded in a reinforcing fashion to the disruptive children's problem behaviors, the introduction of a small group of peers who selectively ignored the problem be-

haviors and shaped more desirable ones had a significant impact on the amount of disruption, reducing it significantly when the appropriate contingencies were in effect.

Maximizing Academic Performance and Teaching Academic Skills

In the classroom setting, contingency management can be applied to studying, attention, and other directly educational behaviors, as well as to the elimination of disruptive behaviors that indirectly affect the educational process. Several studies have indicated the effectiveness of contingency procedures in improving accurate learning directly. Lovitt, Guppy, and Blattner (1969) utilized free time and listening to the radio as reinforcers for spelling accuracy in a fourth grade class. During a baseline period, there was a median of 12 perfect spelling papers per week. Then a free-time contingency system was introduced, in which those pupils receiving perfect scores on one day (there were four tests each week) were relieved from having to take the spelling tests for the remainder of the week. During this period there was a median of 25.5 perfect papers per week, a highly significant increase. In the third phase, the same contingency was in effect, with the additional stipulation that on any day when 100 percent of the students received perfect scores, the entire class could listen to the radio for 15 minutes. For this phase

there was a median of 30 perfect papers per week, a significant increase over Phase II. Figure 6-7 depicts the results of this study.

This is clearly not an isolated result. Evans and Oswalt (1968) found that peer influence may also play a powerful role (it may be inferred from the effectiveness of Phase III in the study by Lovitt et al. [1969] that peers with perfect scores wanted to listen to the radio, so they may have pressured the children who had less than perfect scores).

This report presented four studies in which reinforcing activities for the entire class (early

Figure 6-7 *Number of perfect papers for each week throughout three consecutive experimental phases. I: traditional classroom instruction in spelling. II: perfect papers rewarded by release from any further spelling tests that week. III: same as Phase II with one additional reinforcer—whenever the entire class had perfect papers, all children were allowed to listen to the radio for 15 minutes. The* p *values indicate the significance level for any difference between adjacent phases.*

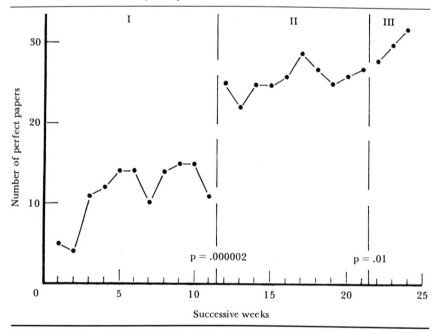

From Lovitt, Guppy, and Blattner (1969).

recess, story reading, early noon dismissal) were contingent upon the improved performance of from one to three individuals whose work was judged by the teacher to be less than their ability would suggest. In all cases but one, the target children showed significant improvement when the contingencies were in effect. The one instance wherein the contingency appeared to be ineffective involved the requirement that a child doing poor work in social science answer a question correctly to gain early class dismissal for afternoon recess. A similar procedure had proved effective when the reward was early dismissal for morning recess. Perhaps afternoon recess, because of the shorter afternoon sessions, is less reinforcing than morning recess. Even more plausibly, it may be that the age of the children was the determining factor. Teachers reported that fourth grade peers made several attempts to influence the target child, while no such attempts were observed among sixth graders. Interestingly, the two studies with the most striking effects involved fourth graders, whereas one of the two involving sixth graders showed only minimal improvement in the target child's performance, and the other showed none at all.

Chadwick and Day (1971) worked with underachieving elementary school students assigned to an experimental classroom. Percentage of time spent at work, work output per minute, and accuracy were measured during three phases: a baseline period, a treatment period involving both token and social reinforcement, and a treatment period involving only the social reinforcement. Students spent time doing workbook assignments and exercises. With the combined token and social reinforcement, the percentage of time at work, rate per hour, and accuracy all substantially increased, as shown in Figure 6-8. In addition, after termination of the token reinforcement, even though the amount of time at work decreased, rate and accuracy of work were maintained.

There are a number of studies indicating that reinforcement procedures can be used effectively to maximize pupil's attending behavior, but must involve the contingency management of individual students (Bushell, Wrobel, & Michaelis, 1968; Walker & Buckley, 1968; Zimmerman, Zimmerman, & Russell, 1969). These procedures are similar to the procedures we discussed previously. Breyer and Allen (1975) reported a successive "last resort" use of a token economy format to induce a teacher's use of positive comments in her first grade classroom. Several other investigators have documented the importance of shifting teachers' personal contingency management styles to include more praise and less punishment (Broden, Hall, Dunlap, & Clark, 1970; McLaughlin & Malaby, 1971).

There is ample evidence now that academic progress can be influenced by contingency management. A variety of procedures has been used to increase children's work output, including making access to recreational activities contingent upon completing a majority of assigned tasks (Rapport & Bostow, 1976; Rowbury, Baer, & Baer, 1976), issuing daily report cards (Schumaker, Hovell, & Sherman, 1977), drawing up contingency contracts with college students (Bristol & Sloane, 1974), and instituting contingencies for the accurate completion of homework assignments (Harris & Sherman, 1974).

Many programs for the use of token reinforcers in the classroom setting are sufficiently complex to justify the term *token economy*. Often the procedure for communicating the rules and regulations of the economy are essentially a contingency contract, so the contingency contracting and token systems often are combined (e.g., McLaughlin & Malaby, 1971; Williams & Anandam, 1973). A good example is the classroom token economy for fifth and sixth grade children described by McLaughlin and Malaby (1972a). During one phase, tokens were awarded for good behavior (completing assignments) and

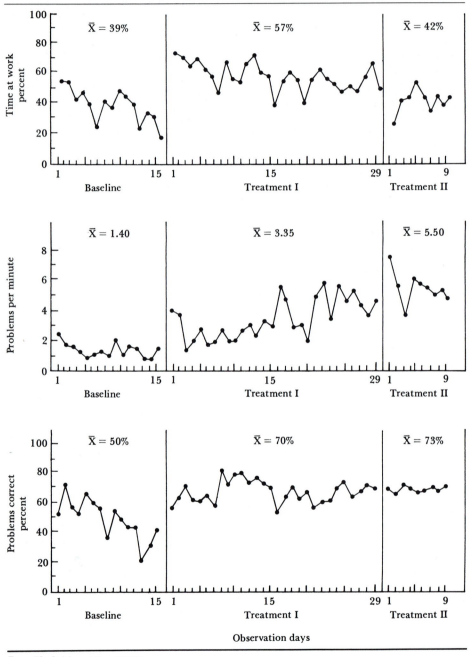

Figure 6-8 *Percent of time spent working, rate of work output, and accuracy of work:* (top) *number of minutes spent working on assignments divided by the total time assigned to the task;* (middle) *the number of exercises and problems completed divided by the total number of minutes spent working;* (bottom) *the number of problems and exercises completed correctly divided by the total attempted (both correct and incorrect).*

From Chadwick and Day (1971).

withdrawn for bad, and these tokens could be traded for the backup reinforcers after five days. As Figure 6-9 reveals, the children showed immediate improvement in the percent of assignments, although their performance was somewhat irregular. When the token system was changed so that tokens would be redeemed sooner—after four days—the irregularities all but disappeared and performance was uniformly high. During the period in which token contingencies were shifted so that quiet behavior, not task completion, was the target, task completion very rapidly approached the base rate. Finally, when the token system was retargeted to task completion, that behavior again improved, though it appeared not to be as regular as before.

These results imply that two considerations should guide the implementation and maintenance of a token economy: (1) the time when tokens can be redeemed for backup reinforcers should not be too far from the time the tokens are earned; and (2) if the same token system is shifted from one target behavior to another and then back (or possibly to a third target behavior), it may lose some of its effectiveness from producing consistent performance of the desired behavior. The latter point is supported by the findings of R. L. Williams and Anandam (1973). These investigators implemented a contingency contract in a high school class utilizing a point system. The points (redeemable for free time) could be earned by appropriate social behavior in class, appropriate academic behavior,

---

Figure 6-9 *Effectiveness of a contingency management program (classroom token economy) to increase task completion in four subject areas. Token 1: period when token reinforcers could be redeemed after 5 days. Token II: period when tokens could be redeemed sooner, after 4 days. Quiet behavior: baseline period for task completion, tokens contingent on quiet behavior.*

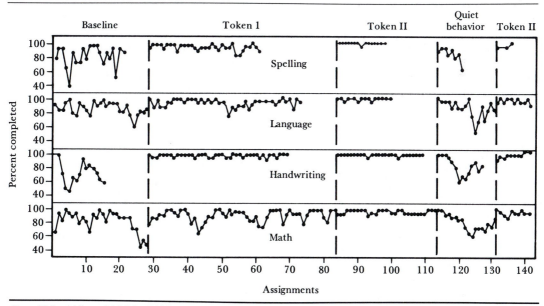

From McLaughlin and Malaby (1972a).

or good academic performance during a given class period. Grades were given *daily* as assessments of academic performance, and these grades could themselves be turned in for points. By the end of the quarter, the overall academic performance of students in the class with the point system was significantly higher than that of the students in a regular class. One possible explanation for this is that students in the experimental class were given reinforcing and evaluative feedback regarding their ongoing academic performance on a daily basis, a procedure that resembles the second token system of McLaughlin and Malaby (1972a) in that the reinforcement rapidly followed the target behavior.

An important distinction has arisen between task-related contingencies and achievement-related or accuracy-related contingencies. Sometimes, the contingent consequences utilized in an educational setting are focused on the completion of tasks or the maintenance of on-task attention, and the accuracy of completed work is not related directly to contingent outcome. There is some evidence that task-oriented contingencies can influence such things as the rate of task completion and the number of tasks completed but have little or no impact on accuracy or level of achievement (Ferritor, Buckholdt, Hamblin, & Smith, 1972; Hay, Hay, & Nelson, 1977b).

On the other hand, there is evidence that reinforcing academic achievement produces concomitant improvements in the attentional behaviors necessary for such achievement. Marholin and Steinman (1977) found that reinforcement based on attentional, on-task behaviors in fifth and sixth grade children increased those behaviors, but only when the teacher was in the room. When reinforcement was made contingent on the rate and accuracy of solving math problems, however, not only did such accuracy improve, but classroom disruption interfering with on-task attention also declined significantly. Hay and colleagues (1977b) contrasted the relative efficacy of on-task and achievement contingencies in an elementary school classroom. The results are illustrated in Figure 6-2, presented earlier in this chapter. When children were praised for attention to their work (on-task behavior), their attending behavior increased, but their work was neither more rapid nor more accurate. When praise was made contingent upon accurate performance and quality of work, not only did accuracy improve but so did the rate of work and the mean amount of time spent on-task, even though neither was the object of reinforcement.

Many reports of academic contingency management outline procedures that focus contingencies on both study behavior and performance quality (Bristol & Sloane, 1974), but the results of Hay and associates (1977b) underscore the importance of the achievement or accuracy contingencies in an academic contingency management program and indicate that when only the end goal (accuracy) of academic competence is the object of reinforcement, even young children are aware of the means (on-task behavior) and respond accordingly. Programs combining achievement and task-related contingencies are certainly advisable, however, for populations in which there is not a common associative knowledge of the instrumental behaviors required to reach an academic goal. Focusing contingencies on accuracy or attainment rather than simply working at a task is also an important mechanism to sustain, or at least avoid diminishing, any intrinsic motivation an individual may have to perform behaviors or work at particular tasks. Research on the "overjustification" hypothesis has shown that reinforcement contingencies for simple task work may, when withdrawn, lead to reduced levels of interest in and work on such tasks (Lepper, Greene, & Nisbett, 1973). However, when the contingency involves reinforcement for the *quality* of performance, interest in a task or the motivation to continue a given behavior is not eroded and the behavior may continue at an increased frequency after the reinforcement contingency is withdrawn. There is also evidence that the persistence of behavior following the termination of a reinforcement contingency is enhanced if individuals are made to *believe* that despite the presence of the contingency they were performing the behavior because they wanted to, or because of other, internal motivation-related reasons, even though it is clear to an objective observer that the contingency was actually responsible for the increased frequency of behavior in question (Grusec, Kuczynski, & Simutus, 1978; Miller, Brickman, & Bolen, 1975).

We should note one limitation of achievement-oriented contingencies. There are at least three reports indicating that the ability level or overall performance level of the student influences the effectiveness of the contingency program (Bristol & Sloane, 1974; Du Nann & Weber, 1976; Rosenfeld, 1972). In examining the effectiveness of contingency management on university courses, the impact of contingencies on studying appears to be broad (Bristol & Sloane, 1974), but only students of below-average ability (Bristol & Sloane, 1974) or with low or medium grade averages (Du Nann & Weber, 1976), showed significant improvements in overall achievement (e.g., performances on tests). On the other hand, Rosenfeld (1972) found that reinforcement for passing tests in arithmetic in a sixth grade classroom increased performance, but only for middle- and high-IQ children. The evidence, then, of the specific effects of ability levels on the success of contingency management interactions is conflicting, but the message is clear. It is advisable to bear in mind the limitations that ability may place on the manageability of some academic behavior classes, such as achievement, as compared with others requiring effort, motivation, or the acquisition of strategies, such as studying, or the focusing on tasks.

Two academic competencies that have often been the target of contingency-based intervention strategies are children's developing verbal and quantitative abilities. The major thrust up to the present has been toward the development and implementation of programs to improve verbal skills, principally reading. While there have been some reports of successful contingency management of verbal production skills, such as composition and writing (e.g., Brigham, Graubard, & Stans, 1972), the focus of attention on reading is not surprising.

Enhancing Verbal and Quantitative Abilities

The role of contingency management procedures in the realm of academic and intellectual functioning originally was one of the controlling disruptive behavior in the learning context, but current efforts also embrace training relating to verbal and, to a lesser extent, quantitative skills. Efforts relating to reading have focused on comprehension of the material being read. Lahey, McNees, and Brown (1973) implemented a program of praise and penny rewards for correct answers about reading content from sixth grade children whose comprehension level was two years below grade level. Not only did the children begin to produce more accurate answers, but their level of comprehension rose to become appropriate for their grade level. Rosenbaum and Breiling (1976) demonstrated the applicability of management procedures to enhance reading comprehension in a severely disturbed (autistic) child. Prompts, modeling, and physical guidance (for motor behaviors such as pointing to correct answers) were used to produce correct responding, which was then reinforced with candy, praise, and attention. After training, the child maintained comprehension at 100 percent as long as the reading occurred in a social setting (e.g., a classroom) and maintained performance even after the contingent enforcers were withdrawn.

Much of the work regarding the development of one verbal skill—speech—involves the use of modeling procedures for the acquisition of speech sounds and basic word capabilities (see Chapter 4, "Modeling and Behavior Rehearsal Procedures"). It is noteworthy, however, that the overall program of acquisition invariably includes contingent reinforcement for the production of accurate speech sounds or communicative content. In this area, attentional behaviors are also important prerequisites for eventual achievement of competence. Often the most difficult problem is the prevention of either the wandering of attention or the occurrence of behavior that interferes with learning. It has been shown, for example, that self-stimulation by autistic children clearly interferes with ongoing learning, and an important component of an overall management program includes the elimination of behaviors that compete with learning as well as the shaping of attentional and other behaviors that promote it (Koegel & Covert, 1972).

One characteristic of verbal skills is that they are likely to be generative. Even though only given examples of content, sentence structure, or writing style are the target of reinforcement, subsequent writing or speech is likely to contain new content and new sentences—in short, new behaviors that are the product of the acquired skill (Brigham et al., 1972; Stevens-Long & Rasmussen, 1974). In one investigation, for example, an autistic child was taught through modeling and contingent reinforcement to use simple and compound sentences to describe pictures (Stevens-Long & Rasmussen, 1974). At the end of training, the child produced not only both types of sentences but also *novel* compound sentences when descriptions were given for a new set of pictures.

Less attention has been paid to the use of contingency management programs for the development of quantitative skills, but the evidence nevertheless indicates that such procedures are effective. Kirby and Shields (1972) used an adjustment fixed-ratio schedule to increase the arithmetic accuracy of a seventh grade student. The adjusting schedule required first 2, then 4, then 6, and finally 16 problems to be solved correctly before praise was dispensed. Figure 6-10 illustrates the effectiveness of the management program during contingency

periods as opposed to baseline (or reversal periods that are a return to baseline). These investigators found (as have others), that the achievement contingency also promoted on-task, attentional behavior, as illustrated in Figure 6-11.

Other work on mathematical skill training has revealed both generality and limits to its effectiveness. Rosenfeld (1972) found that achievement training produced improvements primarily in children in the middle- to high-IQ range, and so a child's intellectual capabilities should be assessed before implementing a contingency management program for mathematical achievement. On the other hand, there seems to be clear evidence that math-related intervention programs are effective for children in schools in low socioeconomic or ghetto areas, where achievement motivation may be a problem. McMillan (1974) found that a monetary contingency program was effective in increasing arithmetic progress and overall accuracy among sixth grade ghetto children. Spiegel (1973) utilized a point-token system, with backup reinforcers ranging from sports items and cosmetics to time at the school's pool table, to promote a variety of academic behaviors and skills including punctuality, arithmetic achievement, and reading achievement among ninth graders from an inner-city school. All the behaviors and competencies under management improved significantly. An important component of these treatment programs that may underlie their applicability to a broad range of individuals, many of whom have no enthusiasm for education, is the flexibility of token or monetary reinforcers. The reinforcers can be used to purchase backup rewards that the individual selects for himself, which maximizes their reinforcing value.

Effects on Basic Competence: Creativity and Intelligence

Creativity is a difficult concept to define, but it generally refers to the production of unusual or diverse content having elements that are not

Figure 6-10 *Effectiveness of a contingency management procedure to develop quantitative skills (arithmetic accuracy) in a seventh-grade student. Treatment 1 and 2: the contingency periods.*

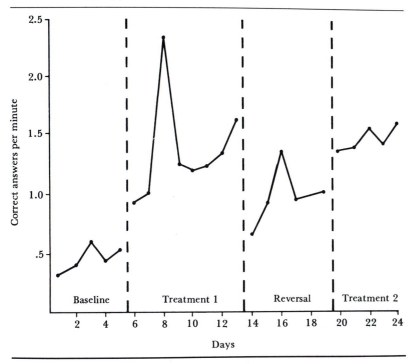

From Kirby and Shields (1972).

commonly produced by others. Diversity of form has been a common operational definition of creativity for purposes of investigation, and thus a variety and diversity of phrasing or sentence construction could constitute one form of verbal creativity, while the creation of new shapes or objects would be judged as an example of creativity resulting from manual or motor behavior (e.g., in artistic or architectural endeavors). Initially, one might think that contingency management procedures would be inappropriate or ineffective in the development of creative behavior, but this is not at all the case (Skinner, 1953). Although contingencies must

be exacted for only those behaviors that actually occur, it is clear that much behavior is governed by production rules (e.g., syntax) that allow new instances of behavior to occur that fit into larger categories. There is clear evidence that children may learn, through contingency management procedures, the rules that produced behaviors that others will call creative.

The principle of "generative" contingency management is simple: the contingency is such that all examples of a particular class of behavior are reinforced and behaviors that do not fit that class are not. When the class is creativity, the typical characteristic of a behavior that will

Figure 6-11 *Effectiveness of a contingency management procedure focused on accuracy in related behaviors: on-task, attentional behavior.*

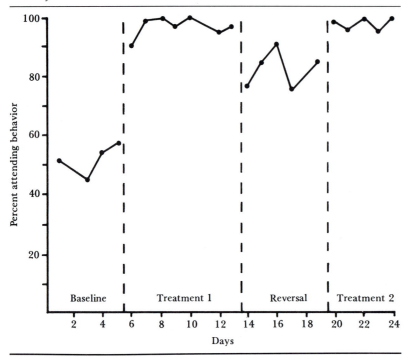

From Kirby and Shields (1972).

allow it to fall into that class is that it is unusual in some specified way. This principle is well demonstrated in a study by Goetz and Baer (1973). These investigators attempted to increase the creativity shown by preschool children in their play with blocks. Creativity was defined in two ways: (1) as a function of the number of different shapes and buildings that a child produced; and (2) in terms of the number of new forms appearing in a given play period that had *not* appeared previously. The contingency management procedure was one in which the nursery school teacher gave social reinforcement (enthusiasm, interest, expressions of delight) whenever the child placed blocks in a

way that created a form that had not previously been created on that particular day. There were 20 different possible forms, ranging from circles, fences, ramps, and arches to balances (a multistory structure for which the upper portion is broader than the base) and subdivisions (two or more enclosures bounded on one side by a common fence). The results of this procedure for three children are presented in Figure 6-12. Children rapidly become very "creative" in their daily block play, eventually producing nearly all the different forms possible during each period of block play.

Other investigations of the impact of contingency management procedures on creativity

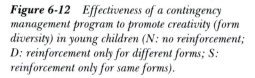

Figure 6-12 *Effectiveness of a contingency management program to promote creativity (form diversity) in young children (N: no reinforcement; D: reinforcement only for different forms; S: reinforcement only for same forms).*

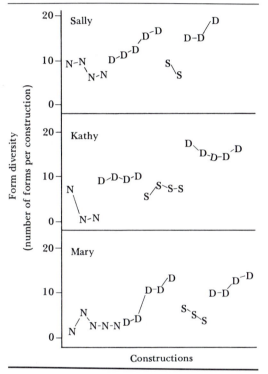

From Goetz and Baer (1973).

have demonstrated its applicability to very different types of creativity. Maloney and Hopkins (1973) defined creativity in written compositions in terms of the number of different adjectives, action verbs, and sentence beginnings contained in a single written piece. When points, exchangeable for extra recess, were made contingent upon the written creativity of fourth, fifth, and sixth grade students, they not only produced compositions containing these selected aspects of creativity, but when their com-

positions were given to independent judges for evaluation, those produced after the creativity training were judged more creative. These findings are confirmed by the work of others using still different assessment indices for creativity. Henson (1975) rewarded children ranging from gifted to learning-disabled for divergent responding on three measures of the Wallach-Kogan Creativity Test and produced improvement. Glover and Gary (1976) used team points as reinforcers for verbal creativity by fourth and fifth grade students and found that their scores on the Torrance tests of creativity improved.

Another competence that is often assumed to be stable, perhaps even hereditary and therefore generally resistant to environmental intervention, is intelligence. Naturally, intelligence is a concept that must be measured using particular measurement instruments, and it is often argued that "intelligence is what intelligence tests measure," and no more. That is in many ways a philosophical argument and need not concern us now. What is important is that scores on intelligence tests are often good predictors of educational performance and, just as importantly, the knowledge that a teacher may have a child's intelligence score may significantly influence the way he or she behaves toward that child.

Evidence shows that reinforcement conditions influence the intelligence scores that an individual obtains on standardized intelligence tests. Edlund (1972), for example, gave children candy contingent upon correct responses to items from the Stanford-Binet intelligence scale. Two groups of children with equivalent scores on Form L of the Stanford-Binet were administered Form M of the same test. In the control group, only standard instructions and procedures were used, but in the experimental group, candy was contingent on correct responding. The experimental children were found to have higher IQ scores on the second test than they had on the first, and their IQ scores for the second test were significantly higher than the scores of children in the control condition. Thus, the contingency program produced generalized effects; and it was not simply the case that children were taught the correct answers by direct reinforcement. Holt and Hobbs (1979) devised a token reinforcement system in which children either earned tokens contingent on correct responses to items in the WISC or lost them for incorrect responses (response cost). Both procedures improved children's subsequent IQ scores.

In another study, Clingman and Fowler (1976) equated three groups of children in terms of their IQ scores on the Peabody Picture Vocabulary Test. They then administered a second form of the test, giving children in one condition contingent candy for correct responses, children in a second condition candy that was not contingent on accurate responding, and children in a control condition no reinforcement at all. Children with initially low IQ scores showed significant improvement when correct answers produced contingent reinforcement, but children with middle- or high-level IQ scores initially showed no improvement. This result is not surprising, since it is likely that improvement with respect to either achievement or ability/competency, such as IQ, will be greatest for those scoring low initially because they have the greatest room for improvement. These results indicated that contingency procedures can provide needed *incentives* that will enhance the accuracy of a test for populations of poorly motivated individuals.

The ability of appropriate contingency conditions to improve intelligence scores extends to atypical populations, such as the handicapped. Smeets and Striefel (1975) introduced a contingency for correct responding on the Raven Progressive Matrices as it was used to test multihandicapped deaf children and adolescents. Reinforcement administered immediately after responding significantly improved the children's scores.

From these results it would appear that the influence of contingent reinforcement on tested intelligence is mediated largely by motivational factors. When producing correct answers results in reinforcement, children who otherwise might have been able to respond correctly, but under other conditions did not do so, are now motivated to produce accurate responses. It is also possible that contingency programs of longer duration that focus on skill dimensions (e.g., verbal ability) may enhance IQ scores through changes in the competence that is the target of the contingency.

Contingency Management With Retarded Individuals

Typically, contingency management of the severely retarded has been applied both to behavior management and to the actual teaching of new skills. Most often, self-help skills are seen as most advantageous to the patients. Thus, there is extensive literature on classroom attentiveness (Kazdin & Allsy, 1980), toilet training (Azrin, Sneed, & Foxx, 1973; Giles & Wolf, 1966; Hundziak, Mauer, & Watson, 1965; Siegel, 1977), personal grooming (Horner & Keilitz, 1975), mealtime behavior (Plummer, Baer, & LeBlanc, 1977), and social skills (Frankosky & Sulzer-Azaroff, 1978; Karen, 1985). Other common behaviors subjected to contingency management procedures are self-injurious behavior (Griffin, Locke, & Landers, 1975; Solnick, Rincover, & Peterson, 1977), aggression and disruptive behavior (Griffin et al., 1975; Plummer et al., 1977), and self-stimulation (Wells, Forehand, Hickey, & Green, 1977).

The skills and habitual behavior patterns that seem simple may actually be rather complex for the retarded individual when they are broken down into their constituent behaviors. The need for a successive approximations approach is often a major consideration. For example, Minge and Ball (1967) used the following succession of responses to teach severely retarded girls to stand up and get undressed, providing food and praise as reinforcers:

I. Standing up
   A. Stands up, with technician providing
      1. Gentle lift under arm or shoulder plus spoken direction
      2. A light touch and gesture plus spoken direction
      3. Upward gesture plus spoken direction
      4. Spoken direction only
   B. Stands up with technician at least five feet away, giving
      1. Upward gesture plus spoken direction
      2. Spoken direction only

II. Undressing: Pants
   A. Use elastic-banded cotton pants. Child should be seated, with pants nearly off; over one foot only. She removes them, with technician
      1. Placing patient's hands on pants and helping pull them off, plus spoken direction
      2. Pointing to pants, plus spoken direction
      3. Giving spoken direction only
   B. Patient is seated with pants at both knees. She removes them with technician
      1. Pointing at pants, plus spoken direction
      2. Giving spoken direction only
   C. Patient either seated or standing, pants all the way up. She takes them off when the technician
      1. Points at the pants, plus spoken direction
      2. Gives spoken direction only

Bensberg, Colwell, and Cassel (1965) worked with severely retarded boys, training one patient at a time during two 15–30-minute sessions daily. Behaviors shaped included dressing and undressing, toileting, washing hands and face (and other personal grooming), and self-feeding. At the beginning of the training, the four patients to be trained had an average score of 27.9 on a test of social maturity; a three-patient control group's average was 28.5. After three months, the trained patients' average score was 59.5 compared to an average of 34.2 for the control group. All trained patients were amenable to simple verbal instruction by the end of eight months of training. It should also be noted that the staff, as well as the patients, benefit from the results of contingency training in self-care. Bensberg and associates found that "those employees who actually had contact with the [patients] . . . were tremendously heartened by the project. Their job changed from drab, custodial care to one of active participation in helping" (1965, p. 678).

One interesting aspect of social behaviors, particularly positive ones, is that they are generally reciprocal. In communicative involvement, for example, eye contact is a mutual social behavior that occurs not when one individual is looking at another but when both are doing so. Other behaviors, such as verbalization or even pointing something out to another person, generally require a form of response on the other person's part. While on one level this is simply an interesting observation about social interaction, it may have important ramifications for severely retarded individuals who may require explicit reinforcement conditions to develop and maintain any sort of rudimentary social interaction.

A particular contingency that has been used to promote social interaction among the retarded is known as a "backscratch" contingency (Powers & Powers, 1971; Williams, Martin, McDonald, Hardy, & Lambert, 1975). This is a contingency in which person B is rewarded contingent upon certain behaviors by person A and, contrariwise, person A is reinforced by behaviors shown by person B. Since social behaviors are mutual, this sort of schedule provides the motivation for person B to *elicit* the behaviors of person A that are being reinforced. Since one part of social interaction is attention to other individuals, a backscratch contingency also makes person A particularly salient for person B and vice versa. Interest of this sort of contingency arose from initial observations that social interaction contingencies involving some individuals in a group also appeared to produce increases in social interaction among group members whose contingencies were not being managed (Buell, Stoddard, Harris, & Baer, 1968; Kirby & Toler, 1970; Zimmerman et al., 1969).

Following an initial observation by Powers and Powers (1971), Williams and his colleagues (1975) instituted backscratch schedules of reinforcement for three social behaviors—eye contact, verbalization, and pointing—in two dyads of severely retarded women. The findings are illustrated in Figure 6-13, which depicts the social interaction rates of one of the women. Not only did the backscratch contingency produce increases in social responding, but these increases generalized toward settings in which the contingency was not applied. Although the generalization produced social responding that was not itself contingently reinforced, it was also the case that social responsiveness increased only during those periods when the contingency was in effect during daily dyadic sessions. In addition, even though responding was higher during the second contingency than during the first, it still fell to zero when the contingency was withdrawn. These results indicate that a backscratch type of contingency is worthy of consideration in any attempt to establish rudimentary social responding, although careful consideration must be given to the maintenance of responding developed by the contingency after it is discontinued. The role that such contingencies may play in the development of social responsiveness and other public behaviors by both those being reinforced and those merely observing seems clearly worthy of additional study.

Although we have concentrated our discussion on the use of contingency management to promote the acquisition of adaptive behaviors in retarded individuals, this is not to say that these techniques cannot be used to control disruptive behavior in retarded individuals. It is clear from the above discussion that positive reinforcement is effective for retarded individuals, and evidence shows that time-out is an effective punishing technique.

Hamilton and associates (1967) effectively controlled the aggressive and destructive behavior of severely retarded patients by contingently confining them to a barren time-out area for periods ranging from 30 minutes to 2 hours. Bostow and Bailey (1969) described the modification of disruptive and aggressive behaviors through the use of positive reinforcement and time-out procedures. In one case, the loud and abusive verbal behavior of a 58-year-old retarded woman was controlled by wheeling her to a corner of the ward and depositing her carefully on the floor after each abusive outburst. She was lifted into the wheelchair only after 2 minutes had passed and there was a 15-second period of silence. Furthermore she was given a treat, a favorite object, or attention when she remained quiet. As a test, the manipulation was omitted for a period (a return to baseline) and then reinstated. As Figure 6-14 illustrates, the time-outs plus positive reinforcement were quite effective in eliminating the abusive verbalization (screaming). It is also noteworthy that the administration of a tranquilizer (Prolixin Enanthate) was ineffective in controlling the patient's vocal outbursts. A comparison of the effectiveness of the tranquilizer and the contingency procedures is obvious from Figure 6-14.

In a second case described by Bostow and Bailey, the aggressive behavior of a 7-year-old retarded boy was effectively controlled by the same procedures. The time-out consisted of being placed in a specially constructed booth (4 feet by 2 feet by 5 feet 5 inches high), which was closed on all sides, but open at the top. Time-out was contingent upon aggression toward other children in the playroom. Whenever two minutes passed without an aggressive response, the boy was given a small amount of milk, a carbonated drink, or a bite of cookie. Not only were these procedures dramatically effective in decreasing aggressive behavior, they also increased positive, acceptable social interactions.

Figure 6-13 *Effectiveness of a "backscratch" contingency to increase three social behaviors, eye contact, verbalization, and pointing, in severely retarded women: in the treatment context (mealtime sessions) and in a generalization context (the ward). Individual = direct reinforcement for target behaviors. Backscratch = reinforcement of one individual when another individual performs the target behaviors (●: eye contact; ×: verbalization; △: pointing; ○: touching). The two subsections with open circles (○——○) chart the percent of touching.*

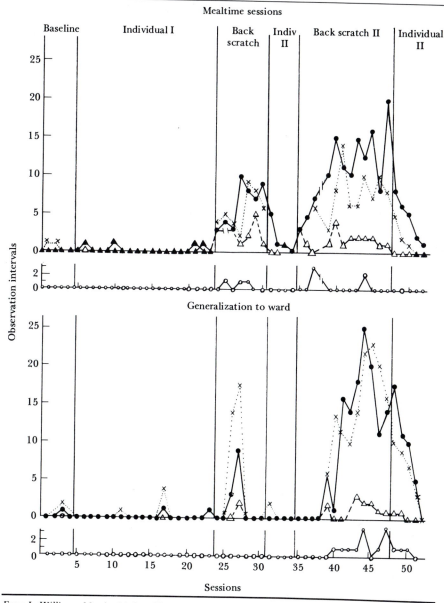

From L. Williams, Martin, McDonald, Hardy, and Lambert (1975).

Figure 6-14 *Elimination of verbal tantrums by contingency management procedures involving time-out from reinforcement and positive reinforcement for quiet behavior.*

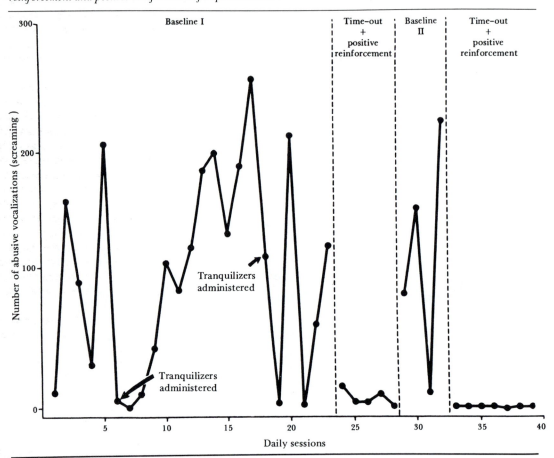

From Bostow and Bailey (1968).

During the treatment phases, the child was observed to approach other children occasionally and to hug and embrace them.

Some research has focused on the advantages of different types of schedules for learning by retarded children and adults. Generally, when contingency procedures are utilized to promote learning, continuous schedules are employed in which physical, social, or token reinforcers follow every correct response. It is not possible to forward any general statement about particular schedules that may be advantageous for learning by the retarded. One study, however, concludes that whereas different schedules may have various effects on the rate of responding, there is no indication that the accuracy of learning is improved by a given schedule (Stephens, Pear, Wray, & Jackson, 1975). In other words, although a certain schedule may increase the number of correct responses in a 10-minute period because answers are being produced more rapidly, the proportion of all answers that are correct appears to remain the same.

Contingency Management Programs for Delinquent or Predelinquent Children and Adolescents

Contingency management programs, particularly those involving token or point systems, are becoming more common in the treatment of delinquency. Often the focus of management programs, particularly for predelinquent youth (individuals for whom the projected likelihood of delinquency is high), is on academic or social skills that will provide behavioral capabilities in social or educational settings that are alternative to delinquent acts (Kazdin & Bootzin, 1972).

Maloney and colleagues (1976), for example, designed a program to teach conversation-related skills to predelinquent girls who resided at Achievement Place for Girls, a cottage-based residential treatment program for predelinquent girls similar to the Achievement Place program that will be described later in this section. The skills that were the subject of training included verbal behavior, such as volunteering information relevant to a conversation before others asked for it, and nonverbal behavior, such as the placement of hands or facial expressions during the conversation. The sessions of training were incorporated into the overall token system that governed behavior in the cottage, so that those engaging in the desired behaviors were awarded tokens. At the end of training, videotapes of conversation behavior were judged by individuals who would be important for the girls' future success in the community, such as probation officers and social workers. Their judgments indicated that the average frequency of appropriate or skilled conversation behavior went from as little as 23

percent before treatment to as high as 100 percent in several instances.

Csapo and Agg (1976) implemented a program for the treatment of school dropouts that involved a year-long school program with points redeemable for cash awarded for approved social and academic behaviors. The youths in this program showed a slow but steady growth in all academic areas, and six months after the termination of the program, there were fewer and less serious offenses recorded for juveniles in the treatment group than for similar youths in a control condition.

Many reports concerning the behavioral treatment of delinquents describe practices appropriate to the classroom or to a cottage system of institutionalization: 5–20 delinquent or predelinquent children housed in a "cottage" with a small resident staff and occasionally a married couple (Hobbs & Holt, 1976). In this section, we concentrate on procedures relevant to these settings. Most procedures discussed, however, are drawn from the token economy, especially the work of Ayllon and Azrin (1968b). Clearly, only a slight adaptation of the token economy for institutionalized psychotics described in the preceding section would be necessary to make it applicable to delinquents in a large institution.

An outstanding example of a cottage-based residential treatment program employing token economy principles with delinquent and predelinquent boys is Achievement Place, a cottage-style rehabilitation unit to which boys are remanded by the court after being judged "predelinquent" (quilty of minor offenses but deemed likely to advance to more serious crimes). The techniques and procedures utilized at Achievement Place have been described several times in the literature (Bailey et al., 1970; Phillips, 1968; Phillips et al., 1971) as they have been applied to various problems and as they have evolved to become more effective.

The tokens used in this system were quite simple: points were earned upon the performance of various target behaviors. Typically the target behaviors selected were social, self-care, and academic behaviors and competencies. At first, the system was on a weekly basis, with tokens being exchanged once a week for desired reinforcers. Later, however, a daily point system was invoked because of irregularities that developed in the boys' behaviors. The two or three days following cashing in of points were characterized by a decrease in target behaviors and consequently fewer points were earned (this is characteristic of an interval schedule, which the weekly cashing in amounted to, superimposed upon the typically continuous schedule of awarding points after cash performance of a target behavior). In the final system, points were cashed in each day, but the privileges (reinforcers) purchased could not be used the next day until a minimum number of points were

earned on that day. Points were tallied on index cards that the boys carried with them. The prices of privileges were typically kept constant, but occasionally they were changed as the value or importance of the privilege seemed to vary (watching TV cost more in winter). Overall, the system was designed so that an individual who performed all the target behaviors expected of him and who lost a minimum number of points in fines could obtain all desired privileges without performing extra tasks.

In the Achievement Place economy, points could be both earned and lost. Table 6-2 presents the various target behaviors that were desirable and undesirable, and the points they earned or lost (this is from a weekly cash-in system requiring approximately 7,000 points to

Table 6-2   **Behaviors and the Number of Points They Earn or Lose**

Behaviors Earning Points	*Points*
1. Watching news on TV or reading the newspaper	300 per day
2. Cleaning and maintaining neatness in one's room	500 per day
3. Keeping one's person neat and clean	500 per day
4. Reading books	5–10 per page
5. Aiding house parents in various household tasks	20–1000 per task
6. Doing dishes	500–1000 per meal
7. Being well dressed for an evening meal	100–500 per meal
8. Performing homework	500 per day
9. Obtaining desirable grades on school report cards	500–1000 per grade
10. Turning out lights when not in use	25 per light
Behaviors Losing Points	
1. Failing grades on the report card	500–1000 per grade
2. Speaking aggressively	20–50 per response
3. Forgetting to wash hands before meals	100–300 per meal
4. Arguing	300 per response
5. Disobeying	100–1000 per response
6. Being late	10 per minute
7. Displaying poor manners	50–100 per response
8. Engaging in poor posture	50–100 per response
9. Using poor grammar	20–50 per response
10. Stealing, lying, or cheating	10,000 per response

From Phillips (1968).

"live well"). Most of the target behaviors, both those earning and those losing points, were formalized and explicit and were listed on the house bulletin board. Few contingencies were not as explicit, although there were some of this sort (e.g., boys might earn or lose points for good or poor manners while guests were in the house). Finally, some privileges had no point price, but were auctioned off once a week. An example of one such privilege, which stressed responsible interpersonal behavior, was the position of "manager" over other boys in the execution of some household task for a week. Such a manager would be personally responsible for the maintenance of bathrooms, the basement, the yard, and had the authority to award or withdraw points from the boys who worked under his direction. The manager himself, however, earned or lost points as a function of the house parents' judgment concerning the quality of the job he directed.

The token system at Achievement Place was designed to influence various target behaviors (and could, of course, be adapted to any number of potential target behaviors if it were desired to incorporate them into the system), and data were gathered to monitor its effectiveness (Phillips, 1968; Phillips et al., 1971). Typically, baseline data were gathered concerning the frequency of the behavior under no constraints; then some constraint, often the use of tokens, was inserted; then perhaps another procedure for comparison was inserted; then back to baseline or the use of threats; and finally a return to the effective procedure.

One target behavior at the outset (Phillips, 1968) was the use of aggressive statements. Often, aggressiveness was noted in court, academic, or psychological reports, but typically there was no real evidence of aggressive *behavior*, but rather of aggressive *statements* ("I'll kill you" or "I'll smash that car if it gets in my way"). Consequently, aggressive statements were monitored for a three-hour period daily. During baseline, no constraints were imposed. Then came a period during which the house parents

"corrected" the boys ("Stop that kind of talk"). Subsequently, fines were levied for a period of time (20 points per statement), which was followed by a period of no fines, but threats ("If you boys continue to use that aggressive talk I will have no other choice but to take away points"). Finally, the fines were reinstated. Figure 6-15 shows the results. Clearly, the use of fines completely controlled the emission of aggressive statements. Other experimental monitoring and manipulations concerned bathroom cleaning, punctuality, completion of homework, bad grammar (Phillips, 1968), promptness, room cleaning, saving money, and keeping up with current events by watching the news (Phillips et al., 1971). In the final instance, "news quizzes" were introduced, which could be answered by watching (and learning from) the evening news. Various manipulations included the possibility of earning the following:

1. 100 points for each question correctly answered

2. 600 points for each correct answer

3. 600 points earned for each correct answer if 40 percent of the quiz were answered correctly; 600 points lost for each incorrect answer

4. 600 points lost for each incorrect answer but no points gained for correct ones

As Figure 6-16 indicates, a combined reward-fine system appeared most effective. When only rewards were used, 600 tokens were not consistently any more effective than 100 tokens, nor was a punitive fine-only system as good as the reward-fine system. It was also clear that the reward-fine procedure was a greater inducement to watch the news, because by the end of that period, 100 percent of the boys watched the news each evening.

In any contingency management system, an important question concerns the selection or designation of the individual enforcing the contingencies. Often the manager is the therapist, investigator, or some other adult, such as a behavioral technician (in a hospital), a parent (in

Figure 6-15 *Number of aggressive statements by each of three youths under various conditions: baseline, correction, 20-point fines, no fines, and 50-point fines. Arrows indicate threats to fine.*

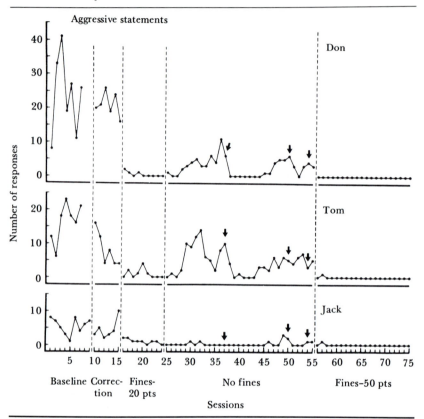

From Phillips (1968).

the home), or perhaps a designated child (e.g., in a classroom). It is possible to ask, then, whether any type of selection system is best. Should the therapist or investigator specify who is to be the contingency manager? Should the individuals participating in the program have some input? The answer is not clear, but some of the experimental work at Achievement Place speaks to this question (Phillips, Phillips, Wolf, & Fixsen, 1973).

Phillips and his colleagues (1973) contrasted the effectiveness of several systems in the context of their Achievement Place cottage system. In one experiment, they contrasted the effectiveness of having the teaching parents for the cottage assign both the tasks each boy was to complete and the points that completion earned (but they could not subtract points for tasks not completed), or the points lost for one completion (±500) with having a peer manager who

Figure 6-16   *Mean percent correct answers on daily news quiz as a function of various contingency management procedures for watching the news program.*

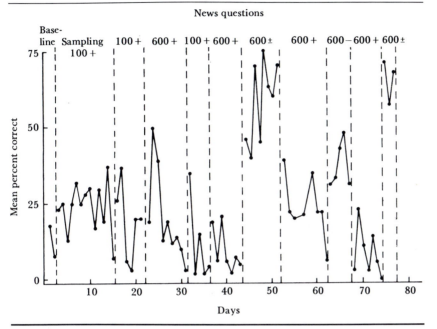

From Phillips, Phillips, Fixsen, and Wolf (1971).

had purchased, with points, the privilege of being manager and who could both award points and levy response costs. As Figure 6-17 illustrates, the purchased management system was more effective, although it is not clear whether this was because it had a peer manager or because it had a manager who could both award and take away points.

In a second experiment, Phillips and colleagues (1973) contrasted two forms of peer management: one in which the peer purchased the privilege of managing, and a second in which the boys elected their peer manager by secret ballot. As Figure 6-18 illustrates, these two systems also were essentially equivalent in effectiveness.

The differences among these diverse systems come when one assesses the degree to which the boys *preferred* one system over another. The boys clearly preferred the elected manager system in which the elected peer controlled both rewards and response costs. The system in which a boy could purchase the managership was by far the least preferred system. These results indicate that there are clearly two separate aspects to a contingency management system: the degree to which it is effective and the degree to which it is preferred by those participating in it. Although effectiveness was not influenced by preference, the possibility that more preferred systems may incline individuals to participate more enthusiastically and not to

Figure 6-17 *A contrast of the effectiveness of a peer manager, who had purchased the management privilege and could both award reinforcement (points) and levy response costs, with the effectiveness of adult managers, who gave individual task assignments and were able to award points only for tasks completed (but could not levy response costs).*

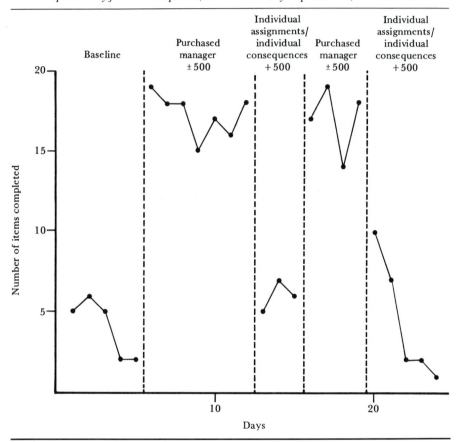

From Phillips, Phillips, Wolf, and Fixsen (1973).

drop out prematurely would suggest that when equally effective programs are available, the one preferred by the participants should be selected.

Achievement Place has become the prototype for what are termed *Teaching-Family* group home treatment programs. In a large evaluation study, Kirigin, Braukmann, Atwater, and Wolf (1982) contrasted the effectiveness of 12 replications of Achievement Place with 9 group homes for juvenile offenders. Children in Achievement Place Teaching-Family programs were found to have significantly fewer alleged criminal offenses. Since truancy and running away from the programs were not different for the two

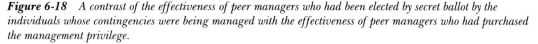

Figure 6-18 *A contrast of the effectiveness of peer managers who had been elected by secret ballot by the individuals whose contingencies were being managed with the effectiveness of peer managers who had purchased the management privilege.*

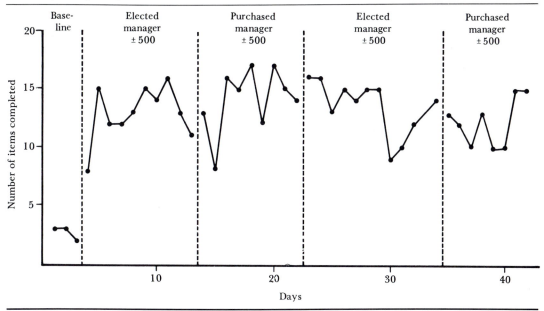

From Phillips, Phillips, Wolf, and Fixsen (1973).

types of programs, this indicates that it is the actual program of a Teaching-Family home that rehabilitates deliquent youth.

Up to now we have been concerned with the operant treatment of less deviant behaviors shown by delinquents or predelinquent children and adolescents in institutional small-group settings. Clearly, the principles of contingency management and the token economy are applicable to the reformatory setting and for the control of more highly deviant behaviors than have yet been discussed in this section. Let us close our discussion of delinquency, then, with a case study illustrating the use of contingency management techniques to treat delinquent behavior in the reformatory setting (Burchard & Tyler, 1965).

This case involved a 13-year-old boy who had been institutionalized since the age of 9 for offenses including stealing, starting fires, bed wetting, and cruelty to animals and small children. Upon various occasions, this child was diagnosed as psychopathic and even schizophrenic. During the year immediately preceding the contingency management intervention, the child had spent 200 days in an isolation room for a variety of offenses, including glue sniffing, attempted escape, breaking and entering, and smearing paint on the walls and curtains of his room. It was most obvious that the use of the isolation room as a punisher by the untrained staff was completely ineffective. Indeed, it was discovered that the staff felt sorry for the isolated child and brought him snacks in the isolation room. The isolation room also allowed the boys in adjacent rooms to communicate with this boy.

The contingency intervention lasted five months, during which time the child was taken off all medication and given no other psychotherapy. Upon displaying any unacceptable behavior, the child was placed in the isolation room. Contingencies were also established to promote acceptable behavior. For each hour during the day that the child was *not* in isolation, he received a token. If he stayed out overnight, he was given three tokens upon waking up. These tokens could be exchanged for cigarettes, soda, trips to town, movies, and the like. The opportunity to exchange tokens was given daily. The system evolved with improving behavior. After a while (two months), the child was required to stay out of isolation for two hours, not just one, in order to gain a token, and there was a *bonus* of seven tokens for each 24-hour period completed without isolation. Finally, the time-out period was shortened from three hours to two hours, thus allowing the child greater time with the staff and other inmates.

Isolation was used relatively rarely—18 times in the first month of treatment and only 12 times in the last. Still, there was a clear effect upon the child's behavior. In addition to the slight (33 percent) decline in the use of isolation, the offenses for which it was invoked became much less serious. During the first month of treatment, these included glue sniffing (twice), stealing while on a field trip, stealing from the staff, fighting, and sniffing from a stolen bottle of bleach. During the fifth month, the offenses included running in the dormitory, disrupting the classroom at school, and insolence to staff.

The token system of Achievement Place, described earlier, was also used to improve the academic behavior of delinquents. Completion of homework, good grammar, and keeping up with current events are examples of academically relevant behaviors that can be manipulated

within the homestyle treatment situation. The reinforcement system can also be expanded to cover the school setting (Bailey et al., 1970; Meichenbaum, Bowers, & Ross, 1968). Bailey and associates (1970) presented two experimental case studies in which the poor academic behavior of delinquent children was improved via reinforcement techniques. In one instance, five boys were placed in a special classroom and worked on mathematics during a summer session. A number of rules governed behavior in this classroom and were communicated to the boys:

1. Do not leave seat without permission.
2. Do not talk without permission.
3. Do not look out the window.
4. Do not tilt the desks.
5. Do not make noise.
6. Do not disturb others.
7. You should work for the whole period.

These "rules" were derived from complaints of the boys' public school teachers. (The reader may wish to refer to the previous section, where the first six rules are given a positive rephrasing that retains their content but makes them more goal-oriented.)

After a period of baseline measurement of rule violation, several manipulations were sequentially applied. The boys were required to carry a daily report card home (to Achievement Place), on which the teacher supposedly checked "yes" or "no" for each of the rules: 1,000 points were to be awarded if all checks were for "yes," the points to be spent for three popular privileges (snacks, television, outdoor privileges); a single "no" lost them these privileges, and 6,000 points were required to earn them back. In fact, the teacher rated *all* boys "yes" for all rules, without regard to their actual rule obedience. Following this procedure, there was a period during which a child could violate a rule 10 percent of the time he was observed and still receive a "yes" (the boys were watched by observers during classtime through a one-way window, and these observers, not the teacher, made the yes and no decisions). Next there was a period when a "yes" was not required to earn the privileges. And finally the procedure with observers (and a "yes" required for privileges) was reinstated. Only during the periods when the boys' rule-obeying behavior was accurately assessed and reinforced did their class performance improve. During the final period, rule violators were essentially absent and studying occurred at all times during the class period.

Phillips and colleagues (1971) reported several other successful applications of a treatment-

or home-based contingency upon academic performance. One case is worth citing, because in it the investigators eventually reduced the number of days per week the student earned privileges from his daily report card. The report card with all yeses could earn the privileges just mentioned. During some periods of the study, the report card was dispensed with entirely, and at the end, instead of five daily report cards per week, the boys brought one to the home on only two of the five days (Tuesdays and Fridays). Figure 6-19 illustrates the results. Clearly, the daily report card and attendant contingent rewards were effective in increasing study behavior, and

Figure 6-19 *Effect of contingent reinforcement based on a daily report card as a determinant of study behavior and rule violations: baseline period, periods of daily report cards and of no report cards, and a period during which report cards were utilized only twice weekly.*

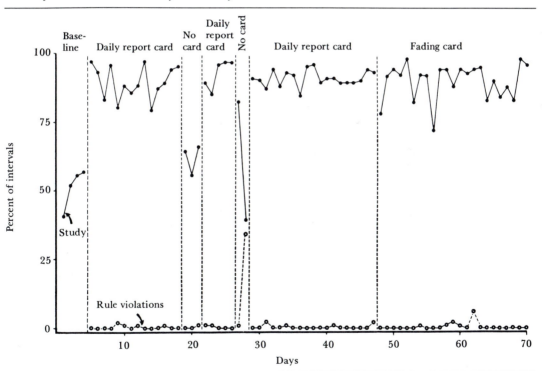

From Bailey, Wolf, and Phillips (1970).

although there was greater variability, this improved studying was maintained when the frequency of the use of the contingency system was reduced.

Contingency Management With Institutionalized Adults: Prisons and Hospitals

Following the initial lengthy reports of token economy systems in hospital settings (e.g., Ayllon & Azrin, 1968b; Schaefer & Martin, 1969), there have been increasing reports regarding the use of contingency management programs within the confines of large institutions, such as prisons or hospitals. In this section, we will describe some of the programs that have been developed for use in institutions of confinement with individuals and groups evidencing severely problematic behavior, such as adjudicated criminals or individuals diagnosed as psychotic.

Prisons

Since the early 1970s, there has been interest in the use of contingency management systems, primarily token economies, in prisons (Bassett, 1974; Bassett & Blanchard, 1977; Bassett, Blanchard, & Koshland, 1977; Geller, 1974; Johnson & Geller, 1974; Kennedy, 1976; Milan & McKee, 1976; Saunders, 1974). Generally, these economies are designed to promote productive behavior within the prison setting. Except for highly focused programs, such as those concentrating on inmate education (e.g., Clements & McKee, 1968), they seem unlikely to have any major rehabilitative effect.

Token economies in penal institutions are more complex than those used elsewhere, largely because inmates are not so behaviorally debilitated as are hospitalized psychotics, and the range of behaviors and reinforcers is larger than may be used in the classroom setting. The complex token system of Achievement Place is probably the closest example that we have already discussed of the sort of economy that can be established inside prison walls.

A good example of a complex token economy that contains analogies to the economic system of society is one reported by Milan and McKee (1976). In this program, inmates earned points for target behaviors and were able to spend them for backup reinforcing activities and objects by writing "checks" against their central account. Token points were awarded on the basis of inspections by the staff, who judged inmates' personal appearance, completion of an assigned maintenance task, and the like. Inmates also received praise by the staff when their performance merited the assigned points.

Point records were kept in two places. There was a master sheet kept by the staff that recorded the number of points that had been assigned to each inmate and noted the behaviors that had merited the reinforcement. At the same time, when an inmate was awarded points, he was instructed to add them to his "checkbook balance" so that he would know how many points he currently had to spend on backup reinforcers. Since a long-term accumulation of points might produce a decline in their reinforcing value (because they had seldom been spent on backup reinforcers), inmates were allowed to carry over only 600 points in their personal accounts from the end of each week to the beginning of the next.

Although the basic economy did not have built-in response costs for inappropriate cellblock behaviors, there were response costs for abuse of the token economy itself. For example, one abuse was writing checks for backup reinforcers when there were inadequate points in the account. Such point overdrafts were charged interest, at the rate of 10 percent per day for each day the account remained overdrawn. Another abuse was failure to pay for a backup reinforcer. This was generally confined to the entering of reinforcing areas (e.g., the television room) without first depositing a check in a deposit box by the door. When this infraction occurred, the inmate was fined the hourly cost of the area and given his choice of leaving or paying, in addition to the already levied fine, the required cost of the area.

One of the most significant requirements with any behavioral management system is that it be conducted in a clear and consistent fashion. A contingency contract, for example, is often an implicit part of a token economy because it constitutes an initial communication to the individuals involved of the target behaviors, the contingent reinforcers that will be awarded, and any response costs that may be levied. While it might be assumed that some minor monitoring would be required during the time that a system is in operation, there is evidence that in complex token economies—perhaps primarily in penal settings—overall monitoring is of immense importance because of the dramatic changes that occur when overall supervision is lacking (Bassett & Blanchard, 1977; Saunders, quoted in Trotter, 1974).

A particularly telling example of how a program can deteriorate in very abusive ways has been provided by Bassett and Blanchard (1977). These investigators describe a prison token economy they established that had both reinforcement and response cost components. After the program had been in operation for approximately 10 months, the program director had to be away for a relatively short time (4½ months). During his absence, the only overall supervision came from a consultant who was able to allot two days per month of consultation time to the program. While the program director was absent, the behavioral technicians involved in managing the program and assigning the token rewards and response costs rapidly altered the system, primarily in terms of the response costs that were assessed. Although the original program had specified the target behaviors for which token reinforcers were to be awarded, it was *not* a component of the system to levy a response cost when the target behaviors were not performed to criterion (if the behaviors were poorly or inadequately performed, reinforcement was simply to be withheld). The technicians, however, rapidly instituted an additional response cost so that failing to perform a target behavior did not simply fail to earn an inmate tokens, it began to cost him some of the tokens he had already accrued. More importantly, the system rapidly became more punitive in other ways. There were basic changes in the system in terms of the number of behaviors for which response costs were levied.

As Figure 6-20 illustrates, upon the departure of the program director, the number of behaviors producing response costs consequences immediately began to rise, as did the actual number of response costs levied by the behavioral technicians. In addition, the magnitude of response costs was escalated for given infractions, and often different technicians would levy different degrees of response cost for the same infraction. For one behavior, there is a recorded instance of a technician levying a fine of 10–25 tokens in one day, and then a fine of from 250–1,000 tokens for the same infraction a day or two later. One of the immediate consequences was a startling increase in the number of inmates dropping out of the program. Whereas fewer than 4 percent of the inmates enrolled opted to quit the program during the 10-month period before the director left, more than 21 percent left the program during the 4½ months that he was absent. Upon his return, the dropout rate was less than 2 percent over nearly a two-year period. It is important to note also that after the director returned, even though there continued to be a larger number of behaviors producing response costs than there had been before his departure, the rate at which response costs were actually dispensed immediately dropped and returned to its initial level. This is clear evidence that one primary factor for the maintenance of low levels of problem behavior in a token economy is not the number of behaviors that produce reponse costs but simply the consistency with which the token system is run.

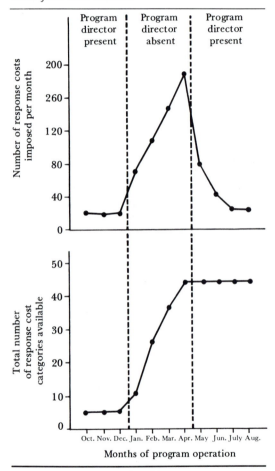

Figure 6-20 *Changes in the use of response cost in a prison setting as a function of whether or not the program director is present: number of fines recorded per month and number of categories of behavior for which fines were recorded.*

From Bassett and Blanchard (1977).

Individual Self-control Management Programs

Individual token economies amount to personal contingency contracts in which the contingent reinforcers are tokens or points redeem-able for other backup reinforcers. The system devised for a male college student by Whitman and Dussault (1976) is a good example of a focused individual economy that was developed for an individual outside an institutional context. In this particular case, four priority groups were established for behaviors whose frequency was to be increased: performance and attendance in classes and a part-time job, personal care and grooming, social contact and daily care of living quarters, and miscellaneous periodic housekeeping chores. Higher priority behaviors received greater numbers of points. A set of priority groups was also established for backup reinforcers, with the more powerful reinforcers costing more points. For example, being with a girlfriend cost 25 points a day, reading other than for class assignments cost 10 points, and walking for exercise or pleasure cost only 5 points. This economy, based on a point system that needed only a record book for recording points earned plus those spent for backup reinforcers, illustrates how individual economies can be established in ways that allow for self-monitoring and thus the self-control of behavior and behavior change after the initial intervention of a therapist-consultant to establish the economy.

Institutionalized Psychotics

In describing the design of token economies, we repeatedly referred to two well-known token economies designed primarily for inpatient psychotic adults: the token system at Anna State Hospital in Illinois (Ayllon & Azrin, 1968b) and the one at Patton State Hospital in California (Schaefer & Martin, 1969). Another program worthy of discussion at this point is the one established by Fairweather and his colleagues at the Palo Alto (California) Veterans Administration Hospital (Fairweather, 1964; Fairweather et al., 1960; Fairweather, Sanders, Maynard, & Cressler, 1969; Fairweather & Simon, 1963).

Fairweather's concern for the effective treatment of institutionalized psychotics appears to have arisen from follow-up studies indicating the general ineffectiveness of all treatment programs. In their earliest work, Fairweather and colleagues found that nearly 70 percent of chronic psychotic patients return to the hospital within 18 months after discharge, regardless of the brand of treatment received while in the hospital (Fairweather & Simon, 1963; Fairweather et al., 1960). He speculated that a primary reason for the ineffectiveness of treatment programs was the general lack of procedures designed to train marketable skills, increase self-direction, and ensure appropriate interpersonal behavior—generally, to establish the competence in social interactions and vocational activity that is necessary for an independent life outside the hospital. Given these considerations, Fairweather (1964) designed a group treatment program intended to establish, within the hospital, behavior competencies in social skills, problem solving, and general self-management.

The patients involved were generally diagnosed as schizophrenic and were matched on the basis of diagnosis, age, and length of hospitalization. One group of patients received the conventional hospital program of treatment, while the remainder participated in a program involving patient-led problem-solving groups. Generally, the treatment programs were quite similar, except for two hours each day, when the one group held group work assignments and decision-making sessions. In addition, an incentive system allowed the patients to receive money and pass privileges as contingent rewards for the development of social and self-directive behavior. The system was divided into four levels, each progressively more complex.

It was left to the groups to evaluate and modify the behavior of a single member. The staff did not interfere in this process, and the group met each day to discuss how individual members were proceeding in the development of competence and to decide ways in which an individual's progress could be fostered. Once each week the group met with the staff and gave their recommendations concerning their evaluation of each member's competence, actions taken over problem behavior, and the suggested passes and monetary rewards for individual patients. The staff then acted upon these recommendations (it could approve or disapprove each one) and, on some occasions, rewarded or penalized the *entire group* as a function of the appropriateness of the group's decision-making behavior. It should be noted that although the monetary and pass privilege rewards were important in the early part of the experimental treatment program, subsequently there was strong evidence that the patients were rewarded by self-reinforcement (pride, perhaps) of their own accomplishments, and there were clear indications of social approval and disapproval for various behaviors.

The experiment lasted for a period of 27 weeks, and behavioral measures were gathered throughout this period and again six months after its termination. Results clearly indicated that the experimental program with its contingent rewards for interpersonal responding improved patient behavior in a variety of areas. By the end of the treatment phase, the patients on the experimental ward showed much less pathological behavior during periods of observation and were much more likely to be observed in interaction with groups of three or more individuals. Patients from the experimental ward were also less likely to be silent, as a group, during the weekly ward meetings and were more likely to participate in these meetings on an individual basis.

But these are behaviors relevant to the hospital setting and the treatment programs itself. What of generalized effects? There were striking ones. Patients on the experimental ward stayed in the hospital for less time, and follow-up reviews found that they more often spent time with their friends and were more likely to be gainfully employed.

Reports of contingency management systems for the treatment of institutionalized psychotics have continued to appear in the literature, but there have been few if any programs of the scope of those proposed by Ayllon and Azrin (1968b), Schaefer and Martin (1969), or Fairweather and his colleagues (Fairweather, 1964;

Fairweather et al., 1960, 1969; Fairweather & Simon, 1963). Generally, reports focus on particular components of treatment programs or propose tests of particular token systems by comparing them with untreated controls (e.g., Claeson & Malm, 1976; Nelson & Cone, 1979). Overall, the most inclusive use of contingency management in the treatment of institutionalized psychotics has been the broad token economy, of which the systems described in this chapter and in Appendix B are representative. These programs have consistently been found to be effective (Kazdin, 1982).

Let us now turn our attention to a particularly imaginative program of group treatment for psychotic patients that specifically targets their deinstitutionalization and reintegration into the community.

Mainstreaming: The Lodge System for Incorporating Patients Into Society

We have expressed concern about the problem of generalizing treatment results from the office or institution to the natural environment. To the extent that token economies re-create the economic and vocational nature of the normal environment, the likelihood that patients will be able to rejoin the community on a permanent basis increases. There are still a number of impediments to perfect generalization. For example, the token economy typically resides within the structure of the institutional setting and the behavioral interactions of patients or inmates are limited to other patients or inmates and staff. Further, the token system mimics, but is not identical to, the reward system in society. Such problems are not insurmountable, and they do not entirely dissipate the potential effectiveness of a token, or other reinforcement-based, system within the institutional setting. Still, the extent to which any treatment regimen can be extended to include behavior in the natural environment seems likely to enhance its effectiveness. In addition, it is important to note

that there has been much contemporary concern with "mainstreaming," the integration of atypical individuals (such as the handicapped child) into natural settings of community and schools rather than sequestering them in special institutions. An important question, then, regards the degree to which contingency management systems can be integrated into natural settings. We have already discussed token economies in the classroom, and the question may now be raised concerning the degree to which contingency management systems for individuals with more serious behavior problems can be made compatible with the normal social and economic environment.

Fortunately, there is a clear example of at least one way a treatment program for institutionalized psychotics can be extended into the natural environment via the establishment of a treatment-related setting within the community. Fairweather and his colleagues (Fairweather et al., 1969) established a lodge (formerly a motel) within the community to which patients were transferred after they had achieved a minimal level of social competence. After patients had developed a variety of vocational, self-care, and social skills, which enhanced group cohesiveness, they were either discharged from the hospital to the community directly or to the lodge. The lodge was not a halfway house and was not staffed by professional personnel. Patients in the lodge were responsible for their own behavior, including financial affairs, the purchasing and cooking of food, and even (with the advice of the local physician) the dispensation of required medications. The patients living at the lodge were also in charge of operating an independent business providing custodial services, painting, hauling, and yard work for commercial and private customers in the community.

Initially, the daily operations at the lodge were supervised by a staff member. But the supervision was rapidly eliminated when the patients proved capable of managing their own affairs; the introduction of many new patients to the lodge setting over a three-year period proved that initial supervision is probably unnecessary except when a lodge is being established. The business operated by lodge members was actually quite profitable, turning a profit of $52,000 in less than three years. One of the responsibilities of lodge members was the dispensation of this income as "wages." There was a weekly allocation of funds to various lodge members, with the amounts dependent upon the extent of personal responsibility a patient had within the group enterprise and the extent of his productivity.

The lodge was established as part of a therapeutic experiment concerned with training patients in community-relevant skills by means of involving them in the natural environment. There was a control group of patients who had received the benefits of hospital training in the skills mentioned above, and who were eligible for outpatient treatment following discharge, but who did not participate in the lodge setting. Measurements were taken to establish patients' capabilities for continued independent existence within the community.

One important criterion for any hospital program is the ability to become and remain gainfully employed. As illustrated in Figure 6-21, when the lodge closed—more than three years

Figure 6-21 *Percentages of time that patients in the lodge and typical hospital programs were employed full time over a 40-month period (the crosshatched bar is the lodge group; the solid bar is the control group).*

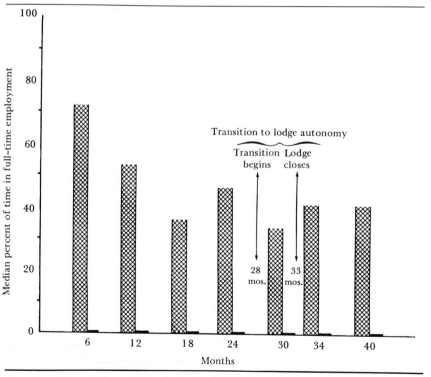

From Fairweather, Sanders, Maynard, and Cressler (1969).

after the initiation of the program—nearly 40 percent of the lodge patients were employed full time, whereas fewer than 3 percent of the control patients were so employed. On all comparisons, the lodge patients were clearly and significantly more integrated into the community. Their continued ability to remain productive members of the community is the definition of a successful outcome for an institutional treatment program.

Achieving Long-term, Generalized Treatment Effects

It is clear that the goals of any contingency management program will include lasting changes in behavior that will generalize to appropriate, new situations and that may eventually include additional desirable behaviors beyond the ones targeted in the program. In this section, we will discuss procedures to enhance generalization, then consider the evidence regarding the stability and generalization of behavior changes achieved through contingency management procedures. At this point, our concern is focused on proposals that have been made for specific procedures that may be integrated into contingency management programs to augment stability and generalization.

At the very outset, any procedure that enhances the self-control of behavior is likely to promote changes that are durable and generalized. Since there is subsequently an entire chapter devoted to self-control techniques, we will not belabor this point here. However, the concerned reader may wish to refer directly to self-control materials (Chapter 10).

Procedures to Enhance Generalization

Multiple Contingency Managers In general, contingency management procedures have focused so narrowly on the initial establishment

of behavior change that concerns about generalization effects have been secondary. One type of generalization training proposed is the inclusion of multiple sources of contingent reinforcement, either multiple therapists or contingency managers in therapeutic settings, or individuals (e.g., parents) outside the specific treatment context who can provide continuity in contingency management across contexts. Stokes, Baer, and Jackson (1974) found that the mere inclusion of a second contingency manager promoted generalization of newly acquired social behaviors in retarded children. Emshoff, Redd, and Davidson (1976) found that the inclusion of a second contingency manager in the treatment context, along with a gradual increase in the range of target behaviors that were reinforced, promoted generalization in the home setting. Ayllon, Garber, and Pisor (1975) utilized parents as auxiliary contingency managers for the control of disruptive classroom behaviors in a particularly ingenious way. On days when individual students displayed a low level of disruption, a "good behavior letter" was sent home to their parents, who, presumably, gave the children additional reinforcement. When letters were sent only after a day of little disruption (i.e., were contingent upon good behavior), the frequency of misbehavior in the classroom declined from 90 percent to a mere 10 percent. On the other hand, during a period when the letters were sent on a random basis and were not contingent upon good behavior, disruption frequency rose to 50 percent. A return to the contingent letter reduced the rate to zero. This research illustrates how individuals outside a treatment or target setting can be enlisted in the management program, in this case without any specific training in management procedures.

Training in Behavioral Management Procedures Another procedure for increasing the generalization of treatment effects is to train the people commonly in the company of the individual in a variety of settings. In at least one study (Glogower & Sloop, 1976), giving parents training in general behavior management principles promoted generalization of treatment effects, presumably because parents could extend contingency management procedures into new contexts as well as to problem behaviors not originally part of the treatment program. Parental "homework assignments" to monitor problem behaviors at home and record their own reactions have also been shown to encourage the generalization of treatment effects for children (Bernal, 1969; Bernal et al., 1968).

Assessment for Inappropriate or Unintended Stimulus Control A relatively unusual procedure to promote context generalization is to assess for inappropriate stimulus control. Occasionally, in the treatment of severely debilitated individuals (e.g., autistic children), inadvertent attention to an irrelevant stimulus in the treatment context produces changed behavior that is only elicited in the presence of that stimulus. Rincover and Koegel (1975) examined the generalization of newly acquired behaviors to additional contexts. While they found that 6 out of the 10 autistic children with whom they were working showed appropriate generalization, 4 did not. Studying these children carefully revealed that they were selectively responding to a stimulus in the original treatment room that was incidental to the behavior being shaped or the contexts in which it would be appropriate. When this stimulus was introduced into the new context, their behavior generalized. The results of this investigation underscore the importance of checking for inadvertent "superstitious" learning during contingency management, although the probability of such learning is likely to be so low that this possibility should be examined ony when generalization fails to occur.

Partial Reinforcement and Fading Procedures Long-lasting behavior change can be attempted through a variety of procedures. The use of partial reinforcement schedules is an obvious one, and evidence shows that this is indeed effective (Atthowe, 1973; Koegel & Rincover, 1977). Perhaps the most common procedural component of contingency management

programs designed to promote the continuation of improvement is the gradual fading out of specific contingent reinforcement systems so that naturally occurring reinforcement and the observation of models can take over the task of maintaining behavior. In one study, for example, a mother was taught to shape her child's appropriate behaviors by attending to them, and her attending was maintained by having her record instances of it on a wrist counter (Herbert & Baer, 1972). Fading consisted of changing from daily recording to an intermittent schedule in which the number of days when no recording was done gradually increased. In another study, Hall and associates (1972) gradually faded out both social (mother's attention) and token (money) reinforcers for wearing an orthodontic device. In both these studies, follow-up checks revealed the maintenance of the desired behaviors. Finally, similar to fading procedures is the inclusion during a follow-up period of "refresher courses" in contingency management (Wahler, 1975) or "booster shots" (Patterson, 1974a, 1974b; Patterson, Cobb, & Ray, 1973). In this procedure, whenever follow-up assessment reveals that behavior problems are returning or that socialization agents are failing to be effective contingency managers, a short period of retraining ensues as a sort of fading of contingency management training.

Evidence for Stability and Generality of Behavior Change

Effecting a behavior change by contingency management or any other procedure is of little import if the change does not endure and the new behavior pattern or competency becomes prevalent in contexts other than the specific one in which treatment occurred. One aspect of the accountability of behavior therapy, or any psychotherapy or behavior-change discipline for that matter, is the degree to which evidence is sought regarding the endurance and generality of behavior change. Unfortunately, the literature has been generally lacking in careful evaluations of how robust changes are that have been achieved through contingency management (Forehand & Atkeson, 1977; Keeley, Shember, & Carbonell, 1976). One review even proposed that many therapists ignore generalization issues and adopt what might be termed a "train and hope" philosophy (Stokes & Baer, 1977). The isolated examples of particularly rigorous evaluation in some areas, such as the use of parents as contingency managers, often indicate that the stability and generality of behavior change is not particularly good (Forehand & Atkeson, 1977). Our concern at this point is not to present a detailed evaluation of the outcome literature but rather to discuss some of the factors influencing the temporal stability, context generality, and behavioral generality (changes in behaviors not directly the target of intervention) of behavior changes produced by contingency management procedures and to provide some examples of procedures designed to enhance these important outcome variables.

Simple Context Generalization There is clear evidence that generalization does tend to occur in settings reasonably similar to those in which contingencies were originally altered during the management program (Bucher & Reaume, 1979). O'Leary, O'Leary, and Becker (1967) treated a 6-year-old child who was diagnosed as an "immature, brain-damaged child with a superimposed neurosis." The child was demanding and aggressive toward a younger brother and tended to fight and cause general destruction of household items. Treatment was diverted toward three classes of behavior: deviant (kicking, hitting, pushing, name calling, and throwing objects); cooperative (asking for a toy, requesting the sibling's help, conversing, and playing within three feet of his sibling); and isolate (playing or simply being alone, with no physical, verbal, or visual contact with the sibling). Cooperative behavior was then reinforced by a therapist who put an M&M into the child's mouth and simultaneously said, "Good." This schedule was then thinned to become in-

termittent; only every fourth response was reinforced. After five days of treatment, token rewards were introduced (checks on a blackboard that were worth reinforcers such as candy, comics, puzzles, and other small toys). The number of checks needed for various prizes was gradually increased. Eventually it took several days to earn enough checks for a reinforcer. A time-out procedure was made contingent upon kicking, hitting, and the like. Any instance of deviant behavior was followed by isolation in the bathroom for at least five minutes, and the child had to be quiet for a period of at least three minutes before he could come out.

The percentage of time spent in cooperative play rose dramatically—essentially doubling—and after 40 days there were no instances of deviant behavior requiring the use of the time-out procedure. Isolate behavior (solitary play) increased in frequency, even though it was not specifically treated. This is an instance of the generalization of treatment effects to behaviors different from those under treatment, but whose frequency of occurrence is unaffected by the occurrence of the maladaptive behaviors. In the present instance, the increase in isolate behavior was considered a desirable outcome since it did not prohibit cooperative behavior at other times and appeared to have taken the place of the deviant aggressive behaviors.

The various changes in this child's behaviors eventually eliminated all deviant behaviors in all settings. Occasionally, aggressive behaviors were reported in the school situation. However, during the year encompassing this treatment, both the parents *and teachers* in contact with this child reported marked progress. Incidents of deviant aggressive behaviors were greatly reduced in both settings, and there was evidence that following treatment there was a stable tendency to play cooperatively with a neighbor's child.

Natural Contingencies and Context Generalization Certainly if a child or adult is returned to an environment where the contingencies are clearly in favor of the originally maladaptive behavior, this behavior is quite likely to increase in frequency. Similarly, if the natural environment of a client is not reinforcing of a newly acquired behavior or is reinforcing of a mutually exclusive alternative behavior, the newly acquired behaviors are likely to decrease in frequency.

Fortunately, a thorough analysis of the home or natural environment will allow the anticipation of such problems, and when parents, spouses, or teachers are involved in a contingency management program, the natural environment is being altered in such a way as to encourage the continued performance of newly acquired behaviors and the continued absence of formerly problematic ones. In the next section, we will discuss how the training of individuals in the natural environment in contingency managment techniques promotes generalization. In this sense, contingency management is a good adjunct to other techniques of behavior therapy to ensure the longevity of a therapeutic change in behavior patterns. But in many instances, such precautions are unnecessary. Many times, contingency management procedures are intended to establish increases in the frequency of prosocial behaviors that naturally tend to evoke reinforcing consequences and generalization outside the treatment context.

A good example of the way some behaviors may influence natural contingencies in ways that will maximize the likelihood of generalization is a study by Cooke and Apolloni (1976). In this investigation, four handicapped children were trained in positive social-emotional behaviors (e.g., smiling, sharing). After training had induced increases, some untrained children were allowed to interact with the subjects in a generalization setting. Not only did training produce increased social-emotional behavior by the subjects, but there were also "spillover" effects in that the *un*trained children also began to display more positive social-emotional behavior. In this case, initial generalization effects may have been enhanced or made more enduring through the induced positive behaviors displayed by the untrained children, although this hypothesis was not directly tested.

Some authors (Baer & Wolf, 1967) have used the term *behavior trap* to refer to the concept that the initial behavior manipulation (by contingency management or other therapy procedures) of a few client behaviors may provide an "entry" to an environment that provides naturalistic reinforcement contingencies that maintain those behaviors and shape new, related ones as well. Although we have not specifically discussed this possibility, it seems clear from evidence and theorizing that analysis of the environments into which the client will move following therapeutic intervention will provide information concerning the behaviors likely to gain reinforcement and thus be maintained. This means also that an attempt should be made to assess or predict how a client's current environment will respond to newly established behaviors, and then, *if necessary,* to work with that environment to encourage the likelihood that therapeutically induced behaviors will be reinforced and maintained.

Other Procedures to Enhance Generalization In the study by O'Leary and colleagues (1967), although there was some generalization from home-based management procedures, the generalization was not perfect. In fact, the child was placed in a classroom that utilized behavior therapy principles to establish total control over his school behaviors. A lack of generality in instances like this is not surprising, since home and school are distinctively different situations with different social agents. Wahler (1969) reported two cases, one involving the contingency management of oppositional behavior in a 5-year-old boy and one involving study behavior in an 8-year-old boy. Figure 6-22 presents the results of a contingency management program for treating the oppositional behavior of the 5-year-old boy. At first, only the parents were trained to give attention to cooperative (nonoppositional) behavior and to utilize time-out procedures contingent upon oppositional, argumentative behavior in the home. By the ninth session, there was a great increase in cooperation at home, but no change at school. When

Figure 6-22 *Cooperative behavior in home and school setting during baseline periods of contingency management in the home alone or in both the home and school (●——●: home behavior; ○----○: school behavior).*

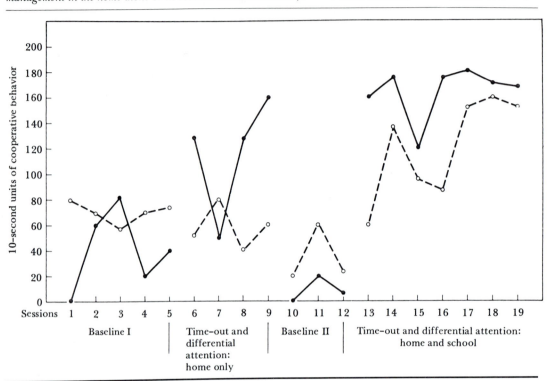

From Wahler (1969).

the changed contingencies and time-out procedures were removed, the behavior reverted to baseline. Finally, however, when contingency management occurred in *both* home and school, cooperative behavior increased in both settings.

Merely because a particular contingency manager is available in different contexts does not mean that there will be generalization across those contexts. Another type of generalization that merits discussion is the degree to which the *contingency manager* exacts the appropriate contingencies in different situations. This is not likely to occur. Miller and Sloane (1976) trained parents of nonverbal children to administer cer-

tain contingencies for their children's vocalizations. The parents were to attend to the child's vocalizations during a snack period, before which there was a short period during which a snack was prepared. After training, parents were significantly more attentive to the child's vocalizations during the snack period, but training had no effect whatsoever on the degree to which they attended to vocalizations during the presnack period. These findings suggest that the clear specification of a setting or time period during which management is to occur may incline an individual contingency manager— parent, teacher, or whomever—to implement the contingencies *only* in that context or during that time period, even though it would seem obvious that there is little reason to make such fine discriminations.

Having more than one individual act as a contingency manager is likely to promote generalization of the target behavior to new contexts. Stokes, Baer, and Jackson (1974) trained four institutionalized retarded individuals in a social greeting response (hand waving). They found that initially this response did not occur toward various staff members who were not involved in the training. When a second individual was involved in the training, the response generalized and was observed to be stable over periods of from one to six months. Emshoff, Redd, and Davidson (1976) trained delinquent adolescents to increase their positive comments about peers. Half the adolescents received training designed to promote generalization in which different contingency managers participated in various sessions and the general context of the session (usually a social game such as Ping-Pong) was varied. The remainder of the adolescents worked with the same set of managers across sessions and the same game was utilized each time. Observations to determine generalization were made in the residential home where the adolescents lived, and these revealed generalization to the home context both during training and afterward.

One rather obvious technique to promote generalization is to adjust the schedule of reinforcement. For example, contingency management that includes a partial rather than a continuous schedule of reinforcement for the target behavior will produce better generalization to extratherapy or extratraining settings (Koegel & Rincover, 1977). The investigators also found that the maintenance of a target behavior pattern in a generalization setting is enhanced by the presence of noncontingent reinforcement. These findings deserve some comment, since neither a partial schedule nor the presence of *noncontingent* reinforcers would necessarily promote generalization into a new and highly divergent context. One of the factors governing generalization is probably the expectancy that the target behavior will be reinforced in that setting. If a generalization environment is highly discrepant from the training environment, even a partial schedule of reinforcement is unlikely to generate an expectancy of reward. However, if the new environment has some similarities to the training environment (e.g., the presence of adults who may reward a child for on-task behavior), a partial schedule in training accustoms the individual to instances of the behavior that are not reinforced. So, initially, exploratory performances of the target behavior in the new context that do not meet with reinforcement are not likely to produce rapid extinction, and repeated performances of the behavior enhance the likelihood that it will, in fact, be reinforced. Similarly, there is no reason to expect that noncontingent reinforcement will promote the maintenance of a target behavior in a new environment unless it somehow increases the expectancies that contingent reinforcement will occur and decreases expectancies that punishments are forthcoming.

One reason that generalization is likely to occur is that the individual fails to discriminate between the generalization setting and the one in which the behavior change was accomplished. Sometimes generalization is less a failure to discriminate than simply the result of an active attempt to determine similarities between the generalization context and the treatment setting. Training a child to be socially responsive to peers may generalize to diverse contexts if the important element is the *presence* of peers and not *where* they happen to be. In this example, we would expect generalization to new contexts where peers are present but not to contexts in which the salient individuals are adults. Even when there is generalization, then, there is also some discrimination.

Generally, then, a contingency management program can be modified to enhance the likelihood of generalization in two ways: by the incorporation of specific training to promote generalization; and by the careful assessment of discriminations, particularly inappropriate ones, that the individuals under treatment may make to reduce the likelihood that target behaviors will generalize into new contexts.) We have already discussed several training procedures that should enhance the likelihood of broad and appropriate generalization of therapeutic results from a contingency management program. We have also given attention to assessment procedures for inappropriate or unintended stimulus control, and the study by Rincover and Koegel (1975) illustrates how the introduction of stimuli associated with desired behaviors into a new situation promotes generalization to that situation. Recall that in the Rincover and Koegel study (p. 279), 6 out of 10 children showed generalization to the new setting and 4 did not. A careful analysis of those 4 children's behavior in the therapy setting revealed that they were responding selectively to a stimulus in the room that should have been irrelevant and incidental to the performance of the target behavior. When that stimulus was introduced into the novel setting, the 4 children then showed the desired generalization.

It is noteworthy that the incidental stimulus was different for each of the 4 children. One, for example, discriminated the presence of a table and chair, and when these were introduced into the novel setting, generalization occurred. Another child required the experimenter to touch his elbow (this touch had been an inadvertent prompt during training). Both social and physical stimuli, then, can play a role in the development of inappropriate discriminations. In addition to speaking to the broad question of generalization, the results of Rincover and Koegel (1975) may also indicate a particular, and selective, sensitivity of autistic children to odd, inappropriate stimuli during the course of learning. More important, these findings suggest that when generalization fails to occur, one remedial procedure is to examine performance in the therapy context to determine whether

inappropriate discrimination is occurring. Although these investigators promoted generalization by adding the inappropriate stimuli to the generalization context, a more likely remedial practice would be to repeat the behavior change program after removing inappropriate stimuli from the setting. More research on this procedure for enhancing therapeutic generalization is clearly warranted.

The use of delayed reinforcement has been proposed as a technique to enhance generalization. In this procedure, reinforcement is delivered after the individual has moved into one or more new contexts following the performance of the desired behavior. Fowler and Baer (1981) evaluated the effectiveness of delayed reinforcement for context generalization and found that late reinforcement, delivered only after children had been in several different settings, promoted generalization. The title of their report—"Do I have to be good all day?"—captures the essence of this procedure from the perspective of the individual being trained.

Spillover Effects to Other Individuals
The beneficial effects of a contingency management program may extend to individuals other than the one whose behavior patterns are the target of treatment, such as those who associate with the individual—e.g., classmates (Strain, Shores, & Kerr, 1976) or siblings (e.g., Arnold, Levine, & Patterson, 1975; Resick, Forehand, & McWhorter, 1976). We have already discussed one example of how a contingency applied to one individual's behavior can affect the behavior of another—the backscratch contingency (Williams, Martin, McDonald, Hardy, & Lambert, 1975)—which was shown to improve mutual social interaction when the behavior of one child produced reinforcers for the other. Most other examples of spillover effects, however, are presumably the consequence of factors other than a backscratch contingency, and a number of different mechanisms have been proposed to account for this sort of generalization.

A primary mechanism for spillover effects is modeling (see Chapter 4, "Modeling and Behavior Rehearsal Procedures") or observational learning by individuals who are not the target of intervention (Christy, 1975; Fantuzzo & Clement, 1981; Kazdin, 1977; Strain, Shores, & Kerr, 1976). Christy (1975), for example, applied contingencies for in-seat behavior to three target children in a class. Peers in the class who also showed low initial levels of in-seat behavior subsequently displayed an abrupt increase in such desired behavior, and by the end of the investigation all the children in the class demonstrated improved sitting.

Another factor may be generalization of treatment techniques by the parent, teacher, or other contingency manager to individuals other than those whose behavior is the focus of treatment. When the behaviors exhibited by different individuals are the same, generalization is more likely to be due to the tendency of the contingency manager to respond in a consistent fashion to the same behavior patterns (Arnold et al., 1975; Resick et al., 1976). In some cases, the magnitude of the spillover effect is remarkable. Arnold and colleagues (1975) contrasted the improvement shown by siblings in families where they as well as the target child were actively involved in the treatment program with that shown by siblings in families where only the target child was the focus of treatment. The investigators found that although the improvement shown by the treated siblings was larger, it was not significantly so.

Although spillover effects seem to occur, perhaps with some regularity, it is certainly not advisable to rely upon them when more than one individual in a family, class, or other group displays problem behavior. Broad training in contingency management procedures, which is often part of parent or teacher preparation for a contingency management intervention (e.g., Patterson & Gullion, 1976), is likely to produce a broad degree of behavioral control by that individual, but this is not an acceptable substitute for the targeting of those individuals who exhibit problem behaviors or behavior deficits for which a contingency management remediation program is being developed.

Outcome Investigations Contrasting Different Procedures

While there is not a wealth of data, there are a number of investigations that have compared different types of contingency management procedures with one another or with other intervention techniques. Often the goal of such research is the design of specific treatment "packages" that either combine different behavior therapy procedures or determine the optimum combination of components within a given behavior therapy procedure. For example, Bondy and Erickson (1976) compared modeling and token reinforcement procedures as effective ways to increase question asking in mildly retarded children. They found that modeling alone was not a particularly effective procedure to induce question asking, but token reinforcement was. However, modeling *plus* token reinforcement produced eventual performance that was equivalent to the token reinforcement procedure alone, and the combined procedure produced changes significantly more rapidly at the onset of treatment.

Van Houten, Hill, and Parsons (1975) in two experiments analyzed the effectiveness of different components in an academic contingency management procedure designed to increase academic performance and peer interaction. The components were (1) establishing time limits for composition completion; (2) self-scoring for early performance feedback; (3) teacher praise; and (4) public posting of highest scores. Introducing the various components increased both academic performance and the extent to which pupils commented on their own and others' work. The researchers concluded that all the components together provided an effective treatment package. Taken together, these two investigations support a growing tendency toward componentized behavior therapy treatment packages, in which several treatment procedures are simultaneously brought to bear on a given problem. Unfortunately, there has not been a broad foundation of combinatorial research to substantiate the generalization that combined treatment or multiple-component methods are to be preferred because of more powerful, more long lasting, or more generalized effectiveness. Nevertheless, that seems to be a reasonable generalization that applies to contingency management procedures and probably to other behavior therapy techniques as well.

The majority of outcome comparative research relating to contingency management techniques has addressed the relative contributions of reinforcement and punishment (response cost) or time-out procedures. Interestingly, of four investigations addressing this question directly, three found that reinforcement and response cost procedures were equally effective (Hundert, 1976; Iwata & Bailey, 1974; Kaufman & O'Leary, 1972), whereas one concluded that reinforcement was to be preferred

over response cost (McLaughlin & Malaby, 1972b). It is difficult to determine any major differences among these investigations that could account for the single discrepancy. Hundert (1976) found the two procedures equally effective for increasing children's attending behavior and improving accuracy on arithmetic problems. Iwata and Bailey (1974) similarly found positive effects on arithmetic performance and reductions in rule violations and off-task behavior. Kaufman and O'Leary (1972) found equivalent effects for the reduction of disruptive behavior and increasing reading skills. The study by McLaughlin and Malaby (1972b) targeted only the reduction in inappropriate verbalization, and found that reinforcing quiet behavior was better than levying a response cost for inappropriate talking. In general, then, it would appear that either procedure is effective and considerations of the moment or the individual context should be used to decide which is preferable. Naturally, if the final decision seems equivocal, ethical considerations regarding the use of punishment procedures when alternatives are available would press for the use of contingent reinforcement rather than response cost.

7

Response Elimination and Extinction Procedures

Problem behaviors can be reduced and eliminated in a number of ways. *Desensitization* (Chapter 2) and *counterconditioning* (Chapter 8) reduce fear-motivated avoidance behaviors. *Graduated extinction* and aspects of *implosive therapy* are similar to these procedures and will be discussed in this chapter. The contingent use of *punishment* (Chapter 8) can be designed to eliminate problem behaviors by suppression. *Negative practice* and *satiation,* to be discussed here, can be interpreted to work in this way also. *Modeling* with guided participation can be used to reduce avoidance behavior, and its procedures are similar to both systematic desensitization and graduated extinction. Finally, *contingency management* procedures (Chapters 5 and 6) involve the withdrawal of contingent reinforcement for problem behaviors and the institution of reinforcement contingent upon alternative behaviors. This chapter, therefore, is not the only one in this text that is concerned with the elimination of problem behavior, even though the title clearly earmarks this focus. The content merely reflects the presentation of procedures other than those more directly related to the focal topics of other chapters, especially procedures that involve the process of extinction.

Extinction typically refers to the unlearning of a behavior. The behavior's frequency either is reduced or the response is eliminated entirely as a function of nonreinforced occurrences. An avoidance behavior, for example, may be consistently reinforced by the termination of fear after the individual successfully avoids the fear-provoking context or stimulus. In this example, avoidance behavior would be consistently negatively reinforced by the termination of the aversive state of fear. In a respondent or classical conditioning model, each pairing of the conditional and unconditional stimulus constitutes a "reinforcement."[1] Consequently, we can accomplish extinction by eliciting the performance of the learned, conditional response through evocation by the learned, conditional stimulus, without the unconditional stimulus simultaneously occurring with the conditional stimulus. Thus, the conditional stimulus should be

---

[1]In this discussion, we use the term *conditional* rather than the more commonly known term *conditioned,* but the two terms are equivalent in meaning. "Conditional" is a more descriptive term, indicating that certain conditions must be satisfied before something is true. For example, a conditional response in the classical conditioning paradigm is elicited by the conditional stimulus only if certain conditions have occurred: repeated pairings of the conditional and unconditional stimuli. The unconditional stimulus elicits the response in question unconditionally—that is, without the need for prior conditions. The term originally used by Pavlov (1927) would have been more correctly translated into English as conditional; it is the term now commonly employed in experimental psychology.

"deconditioned" and lose its power to evoke the conditional response.

An example of this would be the fear that the sight of a dog provokes in a person after he or she has been bitten by one. Running away or carefully avoiding dogs would reduce this fear and would reinforce the avoidance behavior. If the individual is forced to remain near a dog and is not bitten, the fear should be extinguished because the unconditional stimulus (being bitten) does not occur. Desensitization (Chapter 2) contains components of an extinction procedure: fearful stimuli are imagined but the actual source of fear (e.g., falling if acrophobia is being treated; being bitten if a snake phobia is being treated) does not occur. In desensitization, however, only a minimal degree of fear undergoes extinction on each trial, since the stimulus is imagined under conditions of minimal anxiety. In imploding and flooding, or response prevention (discussed in this chapter), a maximal amount of fear is elicited during extinction trials.

Much of the research described for these methods is classic, and both the research studies and the case histories for many extinction procedures are drawn from the early literature. There are several reasons for this. First, some extinction procedures are drawn from pioneering work by individuals such as Pavlov (1927) or Dunlap (1932). Other procedures became a focus of attention during the 1950s and early 1960s, resulting in a relatively extensive amount of definitive research. Finally, for most extinction and response elimination procedures (generally the noncognitive ones), there has been little development in techniques of application or in their application to new behavior disorders, resulting in a general paucity of recent research or case studies. This does not mean that the techniques themselves are invalid or passé—although extinction procedures of the sort grouped in this chapter are employed with less frequency than many others in the behavior therapy armamentarium, and with but a few exceptions they are generating relatively little

current research. Nevertheless, they do constitute an important group of intervention procedures for the elimination of many classes of problem behavior.

We will discuss six basic procedures: extinction by contingency management procedures, graduated extinction, covert extinction, negative practice, stimulus satiation, and anxiety induction procedures including both implosive therapy and flooding (response prevention).

Contingency Management

In many ways, the simplest and most direct procedures for extinguishing problem behaviors involve contingency management. In these procedures, contingent reinforcers that are maintaining the problem behaviors are eliminated, typically by instructing the social agents in the individual's environment to change their patterns of reinforcing behaviors toward the individual. An ancillary procedure that is often employed involves the simultaneous reinforcement of an alternative, more acceptable behavior, perhaps with the same reinforcers as those that previously had maintained the problem behavior. This technique is commonly referred to as *differential reinforcement*. When an alternative, desired behavior is not reinforced, a contingency management extinction procedure may involve simply the withdrawal of contingent reinforcement, not in the manner of response cost—which involves the loss of already acquired reinforcers—but in terms of the absence of any reinforcement occurring contingent upon (immediately after) the problem behavior. We have devoted two chapters to contingency management procedures, and it is appropriate to begin this chapter with a focused discussion of the contingency management techniques that can be used specifically to eliminate undesirable patterns of behavior: the withdrawal of contingent reinforcement either alone or in combination with the reinforcement of alternative behavior.

The Withdrawal or Prevention of Contingent Reinforcement

Generally, this extinction procedure is not employed by itself, since the withdrawal of contingent reinforcement alone involves no specification of alternative behaviors. In some instances, however, it is clear that the person being treated is already capable of performing alternative, more appropriate behaviors, and it is expected that no "behavioral vacuum" will be created by the extinction of the problem behavior. In one of the first reported case studies, extinction procedures were applied to the aggressive, demanding, dependency behaviors exhibited by a young boy (Williams, 1959, n. 25). These behaviors had developed during an extensive illness during which the child required special care and attention. After he recovered from his illness, the parents attempted to extinguish these behaviors by withdrawing some of the attention he had previously enjoyed. The child, however, protested so intensely that the parents were forced to continue the excessive attention and, by yielding to the boy's demands, may have inadvertently reinforced the increased intensity of his protests. In treating the child's bedtime tantrums, the parents were instructed to put the child to bed each night in a calm fashion and, once all bedtime routines were completed and there were obviously no problems, to ignore his subsequent raging protests. As depicted in Figure 7–1, the tantrums disappeared in very short order—a matter of days.

In executing any program of behavior extinction, the procedures must be assiduously and consistently employed if they are to be effective. This is well illustrated by the case just described. Sometime after the bedtime tantrum behaviors were extinguished, the child received some attention from an aunt when he mildly protested being put to bed, and the bedtime raging was soon completely reinstated. A second extinction procedure was conducted, with rapid success, as shown in Figure 7–1. We should be mindful that the permanence of an extinction

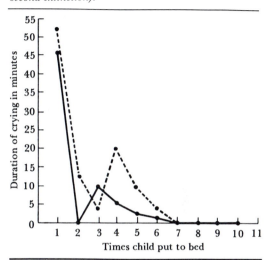

Figure 7–1 *Duration of crying in two successive extinction programs (●—●: first extinction; ● - - - ●: second extinction).*

From Williams (1959).

procedure depends on the *continued nonreinforcement* of random occurrences of the problem behavior. Thus, all persons who come into contact with the individual must be instructed in the management of their own reinforcing behavior, and each person must consistently avoid inadvertent reinforcement of the behavior under treatment.

In an institutional setting, Ayllon and Haughton (1964) treated excessive somatic complaints of two psychotic patients. Figure 7–2 shows the course of extinction for these behaviors in each of the two patients. In order to test the efficacy of the extinction procedures, periods of ignoring the somatic complaints were alternated with periods during which the complaints were reinforced. The effects were striking. In both cases, the complaints declined sharply when they were unreinforced.

We have discussed elsewhere the use of contingent *time-out*—the systematic isolation of an individual from any and all reinforcers—as a

Figure 7–2 *Frequency of somatic complaints during a baseline period and when such complaints were ignored or rewarded with attention.*

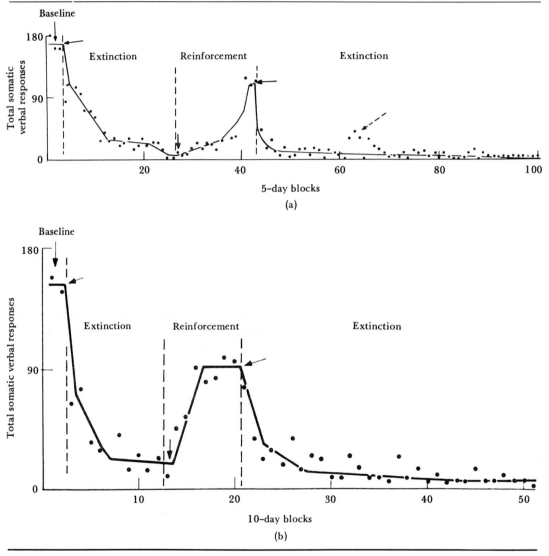

5-day blocks

(a)

10-day blocks

(b)

From Ayllon and Haughton (1964).

method to reduce problem behavior. Often this procedure is considered one of punishment, because isolation is usually an aversive experience. Implicit in the time-out procedure, however, is the prevention of any *contingent* reinforcement for the behavior in question, and the overall reinforcement withdrawal is elaborated through the withdrawal of most incidental or ancillary reinforcers typically available in the environment.

One report in the literature regards a reinforcement withdrawal procedure that is an alternative to the time-out technique (Mansdorf, 1977). In this case, the behavior problem was the refusal by a woman patient to maintain appropriate personal hygiene, specifically to shower on a regular basis. Requests to shower resulted in total noncompliance, either in the form of a tantrum or in the form of total non-responsiveness (remaining mute in bed). An analysis of the behavior indicated that noncompliance, especially in the form of unresponsiveness, was accompanied by social attention from the ward staff, the continued availability of television or music, which could be listened to while lying in bed, and the contingent availability of personal items in a purse. During treatment, noncompliance produced the immediate withdrawal of all the reinforcers that typically were freely available during the noncompliant period (reinforcer isolation). After a five-minute period, if the patient complied, the reinforcers were reinstated. As Figure 7–3 illustrates, the treatment was extremely effective and the patient maintained compliance throughout a six-month follow-up period.

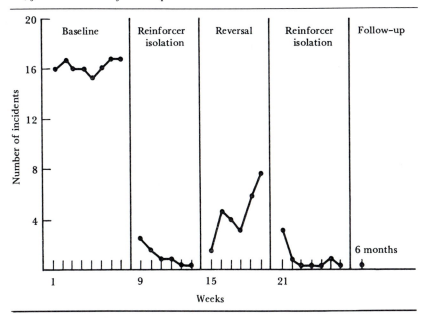

Figure 7–3 *Effectiveness of contingent isolation from reinforcement (modified time-out) for the reduction of noncompliant behavior.*

From Mansdorf (1977).

Any problem behavior that is potentially being maintained by the reinforcers it elicits is a prime candidate for extinction procedures involving the withdrawal of reinforcement. This would certainly be true for psychogenic disabilities that produce positive reinforcement through advantages or sympathy and negative reinforcement through the avoidance of aversive consequences, as well as for other behavior problems that enjoy "secondary gain." A good example is provided by a case of hysterical leg paralysis (Goldblatt & Munitz, 1976). This case involved an Israeli soldier who had developed a leg paralysis so complete that he had neither motor control nor sensation in either of his legs. It was possible, in fact, to insert pins into his legs at any point all the way up to the groin with absolutely no signs of pain. The patient was, however, observed to move his legs in his sleep.

The extinction procedure illustrates a broad-spectrum intervention. First, the patient was told that because there was nothing physically wrong with his legs, he would not be entitled to any pension benefits (which include such things as monetary payments and freedom from taxation on cars, which in Israel amounted to twice the cost of the car itself). To allow any benefits from a placebo effect, a drug was introduced that was said to have proved extremely successful on soldiers serving in Vietnam. The patient was gregarious and enjoyed evenings on the ward, so he was told that one part of the drug treatment involved putting him to bed at eight o'clock each evening. As part of the procedure that inadvertently involved a modicum of punishment, the drug, which was administered by inhaling, turned out to have a particularly aversive aroma.

The drug treatment began two days after the patient was told he would receive no pension, and it occurred twice daily. Only one hour after the initial treatment, the patient demonstrated to a crowd of amazed patients and staff that he could move his toes. By the second day of treatment, toe movement came easily, then leg movement. By the fourth day, he was able to

walk haltingly without crutches. After six days he was able to walk perfectly, kick a soccer ball, and even do cartwheels.

Clearly, there are two primary processes in the establishment of many extinction regimens: (1) determining the effective, maintaining reinforcers; and (2) manipulating the behavior of agents who appear to be delivering the reinforcers that maintain the problem behavior. Although we discussed the training of contingency managers in Chapter 5, it is worth some additional consideration here, because a major component in many training programs involves teaching managers to withhold various forms of reinforcement, often social attention, that are automatically elicited by problem behaviors.

A good example of this was provided by Budd, Green, and Baer (1976). These investigators trained a mother to withhold social attention to undesired behavior by her daughter and to institute a brief time-out procedure for noncompliance. The particular behaviors that the mother was trained in are instructive since the fact that they involve eliminating an inadvertent contingent social reinforcer is not readily apparent. One facet of training focused on eliminating the mother's tendency to repeat instructions when the child did not immediately comply. Another facet involved training the mother not to issue instructions to the child while the child was engaging in inappropriate behavior but rather to wait until five seconds after the inappropriate action had ceased. The mother was also trained to reduce her physical interventions to force or aid her daughter's compliance and to wait at least one minute before intervening to help her daughter comply with an instruction.

All these procedures involve the elimination or slowing of some type of response the mother was making during periods when her daughter was either not complying with an instruction or engaging in inappropriate behavior. Across the term of treatment, the mother gradually learned to control her own responsiveness to her daughter's behavior, and the daughter increased her proportion of compliant behavior to nearly 100 percent, while the proportion of inappropriate responding dropped to near zero. Another point of this example is that many behaviors by social agents are intended to elicit desired, appropriate behavior (e.g., repeating a command to elicit compliance) when in fact they may be maintaining the undesired behavior. Even behaviors that are intended as contingent *punishers* may actually operate as *reinforcers*. In two early cases (Brown & Elliot, 1965; Madsen, Becker, Thomas, Koser, & Plager, 1968), for example, investigators found that the scolding by teachers in an attempt to reduce children's out-of-seat behavior actually was maintaining it. When teachers were instructed to *ignore* the problem behavior (and to reinforce appropriate behavior with positive attention), it rapidly declined in frequency. An extinction procedure, then, is often worthy of consideration when the problem situation appears to contain ineffective punishment or prompting by social agents, since these intended punishments or prompts may in fact be the reinforcers that are maintaining the problem behavior.

One method to reduce the frequency of problem behaviors is to reduce the effectiveness of the reinforcers that appear to be maintaining them. Later we will discuss two procedures that are assumed to work in this fashion. Satiation, for example, through the repeated presentation of a single reinforcing stimulus, is assumed to reduce the reinforcing valence of that stimulus and thus its effectiveness. Another procedure, negative practice, involves the forced repetition of the behavior to be eliminated. Negative practice theoretically works through the buildup of response inhibitions (through fatigue) that mitigate against the performance of the problem behavior, but any intrinsic reinforcing properties of the problem behavior itself, or of its immediate effect upon the environment, may be reduced because of the satiation effects that are the automatic components of repeated performances. These are theoretical questions that we need not attempt to answer here, but it is ap-

propriate at this point to discuss one contingency management procedure in the literature that appears to involve extinction through the *neutralization* of reinforcement.

In an analysis of compulsive checking behavior, Rabavilas, Boulougouris, and Stefanis (1977) adopted the hypothesis put forward initially by Gray (1971) that compulsive behavior produces "safety signals," events that have accompanied successful avoidance behavior in the past and thus have acquired reinforcing value. Checking to see that one has tightly turned off the faucet or switched off the lights may be reinforcing regardless of what the case proves to be: finding the light on makes one glad that a check was made, and eventually checking and finding them off has intrinsic reinforcing properties in addition to the more direct reinforcement from a cessation of worry. If a reinforcement withdrawal model is applied to this behavior, we could propose that enforced checking be required of the individual, including many checks *beyond* the point when the individual would normally have stopped spontaneously (typically a "magic number," which may be different from one client to another). By this procedure, the checks should lose their reinforcing value and thus no longer be able to reinforce the compulsive behavior. Rabavilas and colleagues (1977) applied this "overchecking" treatment to four patients who had been successfully treated for other compulsions but retained the checking one. Although the treatment procedures were not consistently well implemented and the patients did not consistently follow the instructions, remarkable improvements were obtained nevertheless. The extinction model of enforcing the performance of problem behaviors to the point where either external or intrinsic reinforcement fails to occur seems adaptable to cognitively based ritualistic behavior, such as checking.

At times, the predominant problem in designing an extinction procedure is the designation of conditions under which a behavior may be performed while contingent reinforcement is prevented or neutralized. This is often most difficult for behaviors that appear to possess intrinsic reinforcing properties or for which the reinforcement is an almost immutable part of the environment or the person's own response system. A good example of an adept response to this problem is contained in a case study reported by Davis (1976). This case concerned a young married man who, despite his strong heterosexual interests and satisfaction, was bothered by recurring homosexual fantasies. One analysis of the fantasy system is to propose that sexual fantasies (probably of any type) are likely to be maintained by the automatic and reinforcing arousal responses that occur during and following the fantasy period. The extinction procedure proposed for this case relied on the apparently natural sequential components of the human sexual response (Masters & Johnson, 1966) of excitement, plateau, orgasm, and resolution. In the male, a characteristic of the resolution phase is a period of refraction, during which time renewed arousal and erection are difficult or impossible. The extinction procedure utilized with this client involved enforced homosexual fantasies for five minutes immediately following intercourse and during the refractory period when the potentially reinforcing sexual arousal would be eliminated. During a seven-week treatment period, the client was able to engage in the extinction procedure nine times. Despite this seemingly low number of "treatments," the frequency of homosexual fantasies decreased from an average of eight per week to zero by the fifth week, and they remained absent until the end of treatment.

Differential Reinforcement

As we noted earlier, it is unlikely that an extinction program will include only the elimination of reinforcement without the concurrent shaping of alternative behaviors that are appropriate. As with the use of punishment in the

elimination of problem behavior (see Chapter 8), the provision of an alternative response is likely to increase the effectiveness of other procedures for the elimination of problem behaviors. A good example of this is contained in the study by Madsen and colleagues (1968) that was cited earlier. In treating behaviors disruptive of classroom decorum, these authors instructed teachers to ignore children's standing behavior rather than attempt to control it with punitive reprimands and commands ("Sit down!"). As indicated by Figure 7–4, periods when the teachers ignored the problem behaviors were characterized by a lower incidence of such behaviors. However, when teachers were later instructed to praise the alternative, desired behavior of sitting down, the rate of standing was lower yet.

In a classic study, Ayllon and his colleagues reported many examples of the effectiveness of reinforcement withdrawal and the shaping of alternative responses in the control of problem behaviors. In one case (Ayllon & Michael, 1959), a female patient's psychotic verbalizations appeared to be maintained despite verbal and physical punishment (from other patients), simply because the nurses often listened carefully to these strange verbalizations in an attempt to "get at the roots of her problems." When the nurses were instructed not to attend to the psychotic talk and, simultaneously, to reinforce any verbalizations that made sense, the percentage of verbalizations that were clearly psychotic declined from 91 percent to less than 25 percent.

Ayllon and Haughton (1964) treated the psychotic verbalizations exhibited by three female patients by instructing ward staff to withhold social and tangible reinforcement from these patients whenever they were engaging in psychotic talk. Figure 7–5 shows the effectiveness of this extinction regimen for one of these patients. Initially, the staff was instructed to reinforce psychotic verbalizations and to ignore the patient, look bored, and so on whenever she made more normal verbalizations. Then, to

Figure 7–4 *Extinction of positively reinforced behavior. Number of children standing during class time: baseline periods, periods when standing received verbal admonishment, and periods when incompatible behavior was positively reinforced.*

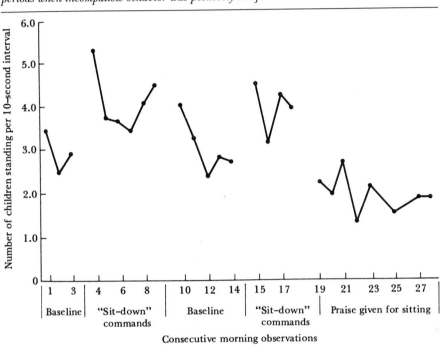

From Madsen, Becker, Thomas, Koser, and Plager (1968).

demonstrate the effectiveness of these contingencies, they were to reverse the procedure, ignoring the problem verbalizations and attending to the normal ones. It is clear from the frequencies shown in Figure 7–5 that these procedures were effective in increasing normal talk and extinguishing psychotic verbalizations.

Differential reinforcement has also been used to treat reasonably complex social and personality problems in both children and adults. In an army psychiatric hospital, for example, a differential reinforcement procedure was used to treat soldiers diagnosed as having character and behavior disorders (Jones, Stayer, Wichlacz, Thomes, & Livingstone, 1977). Target behaviors were derived that constituted positive social stimuli or behaviors, such as proper appearance or completing cooperative work tasks, and were reinforced with token rewards. Inappropriate behaviors, including belligerence, tardiness, or social withdrawal, were treated by being ignored or by a response cost procedure that involved point loss. Following treatment, the soldiers were discharged to duty and their behavior was compared with that of soldiers who had the same initial psychiatric diagnosis but who had not completed the treatment program. Fully 80 percent of the treatment group received a

Figure 7–5 Influence of reinforcement or extinction of psychotic talk upon incidence of neutral speech and the influence of reinforcement or extinction of neutral speech upon the incidence of psychotic talk (●——●: psychotic verbal response; ○- - -○: neutral verbal response).

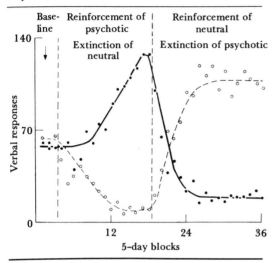

From Ayllon and Haughton (1964).

there a 50 percent reduction in conflict, but there was an accompanying increase in instances of generally appropriate interaction as well. The suppression of conflict behavior was also observed to be rather general and instances of this class of behavior were less frequent even on nights when the parents were not implementing the differential reinforcement contingency.

Thus, one procedure for implementing a differential reinforcement regimen that does not necessarily involve the withdrawal of reinforcement is to increase the degree to which alternative or mutually exclusive behaviors are reinforced relative to the problem behavior. Another interesting example of this, which illustrates how differential reinforcement can be used in a self-control or self-modification fashion, was provided by Dobes (1977). This case involved a woman with a 15-year history of chronic dermatosis on the back of her neck because of nervous scratching, which became even worse in times of stress. The self-modification program that was devised involved having the woman solicit reinforcement from her peers for decreased scratching and consequent reductions in the ugly rash that was produced. Improvement was marked and over a 2-year period the dermatosis continued to be ameliorated.

A common implementation of differential reinforcement procedures involves a combination of reinforcement for alternative behavior with a response cost contingency for the target behavior. Although this is perhaps more particularly an example of providing an alternative behavior while instituting an aversive control procedure, it is appropriate at this point because of its similarity to other differential reinforcement procedures. You may wish to refer to this section when reading Chapter 8 on procedures of aversive control, since the point is made in that chapter regarding the importance of providing alternative, reinforced behaviors to replace the problem behaviors that are to be eliminated.

positive evaluation from their unit 11 months after discharge from the program, while only 52 percent of the control group received such an evaluation.

Another use of differential reinforcement for rather complex social interaction involved instances of sibling conflict (Leitenberg, Burchard, Burchard, Fuller, & Lysaght, 1977). In this investigation, six families were studied, and parents were trained to reinforce behaviors alternative to sibling conflict. When reinforcement was withdrawn from any conflict behavior and applied to other behaviors in general, the frequency of conflict reduced by 50 percent. When the differential reinforcement was applied to a behavior specifically alternative to the conflict interactions, not only was

Combinations of aversive contingencies with the differential reinforcement of desired alternative behaviors have been utilized in the treatment of diverse behavior problems. Reichle, Brubakken, and Tetréault (1976) combined time-out procedures with the reinforcement of incompatible behavior in the elimination of perseverative speech in a psychotic child. In a contingency contract procedure, Aragona, Cassady, and Drabman (1975) contrasted a differential reinforcement procedure, including response cost, with a response-cost-alone treatment of obesity. In this instance, the differential reinforcement was for exercise and weight loss as indicated on graphs kept at home. The response cost component involved a monetary loss for failure to meet a weight-loss goal. Whereas both the differential reinforcement and response cost groups lost an equal amount of weight during the program, after an eight-week follow-up the weight loss was significant only in the group treated with the differential procedure that combined reinforcement with response cost. Differential reinforcement, including response costs or physical restraint, has also been used to reduce aggressive and self-injurious behavior (Repp & Deitz, 1974) and stereotyped body contortions (Barkley & Zupnick, 1976) in retarded children.

Often a program of differential reinforcement to control problem behavior in children can be established using the parents as contingency managers and employing reinforcers that are commonly available in the home and appropriate for the context in which the behavior change is required. Knight and McKenzie (1974), for example, trained parents to eliminate bedtime thumb sucking by regulating the contingency of bedtime reading so that it occurred only when there was no thumb sucking. Dougherty and Lane (1976) treated a case of self-injurious behavior in a 2-year-old girl that occurred at bedtime. In this instance, the parents utilized a pacifier both as an alternative behavior (sucking it) and as a contingent reinforcer, withdrawing it upon the occurrence of head banging and reinstating it contingent upon a full minute of non–self-injurious behavior. Bach and Moylan (1975) treated a 6-year-old boy who was incontinent of both urine and feces by training his parents to use monetary rewards for appropriate toilet behavior and ignoring instances of the problem behavior, such as pant soiling.

An important point to remember about the institution of differential reinforcement contingencies is that they may often involve simply a rearrangement of contingencies already in effect, through a shift in the behaviors upon which common reinforcers are contingent. This is well illustrated in a case presented by Neisworth and Moore (1972). The asthmatic responding of a 7-year-old boy was considered to be maintained by the attention it brought from his mother, who in fact suggested this possibility after several therapeutic interviews. The parents were trained to avoid reinforcing, through either attention or the administration of medication, all instances of bedtime asthmatic attacks: after a fond good night, the child's bedroom door was closed and no further interaction occurred until morning. The child was also told that if he coughed less frequently on a certain night than he had the night before, he would be given lunch money the next day (instead of taking a prepared lunch). As Figure 7–6 illustrates, the effects of this differential reinforcement regimen on bedtime asthmatic attacks were striking, and over a 10-month follow-up, the frequency of attacks remained near zero. Incidentally, the parents also reported that daytime coughing had declined and there were pediatric reports that the child's health was generally improved, indicating the parents' training in differential reinforcement procedures had perhaps generalized to instances of the problem behavior that occurred at times other than those treated.

Another pertinent example of the way natural contingencies may be rearranged to effect

---

Figure 7–6 *Effectiveness of differential reinforcement, including the avoidance of any reinforcement for the problem behavior, on reductions in bedtime asthmatic responding in a young boy.*

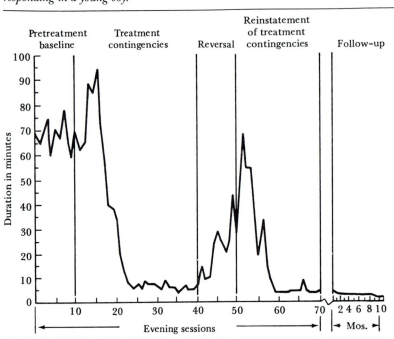

From Neisworth and Moore (1972).

---

appropriate behavior change is contained in the case of a 4-year-old child whose separation anxiety was eliminated through a differential reinforcement procedure (Neisworth, Madle, & Goeke, 1975). In this instance, the reappearance of the mother, which is precisely the goal of anxious separation behavior and a reinforcer that is likely to maintain it over time, was made contingent upon periods of nonanxious behavior, such as social involvement with other children or with the nursery school staff (the mother remained out of sight of the child and was cued to return when nonanxious behavior was exhibited by the child). Figure 7–7 illustrates the success of this treatment. During the

treatment period, a fading procedure was instituted during which the length of time that the child had to display nonanxious behavior before the mother returned was gradually increased. The length of time that the mother remained, upon her return, was simultaneously decreased during the fading aspect of the treatment period. Because of the fading procedure, the child's anxious behavior dropped to zero. The child's anxious behaviors were significantly decreased from the very start of treatment and after only 18 sessions of fading, the child's ability to tolerate separation in a totally nonanxious fashion was maintained consistently throughout a six-month follow-up.

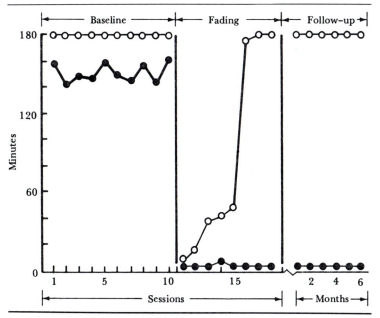

Figure 7–7 *Effectiveness of differential reinforcement in the elimination of separation anxiety in a young child (●—●: duration of anxious behaviors; ○—○: mean length of the delay interval. In the fading period, reappearance of the mother was made contingent upon nonanxious behavior, and the length of nonanxious behavior required for reinforcement was gradually increased.*

From Neisworth, Madle, and Goeke (1975).

Graduated Extinction

Graduated extinction is a technique designed to eliminate avoidance and fearful behaviors by the gradual reexposure of the individual to the fear-evoking stimuli. This procedure is similar in some ways to *in vivo* desensitization and the techniques of implosion and flooding (or response prevention), which are discussed later in this chapter. But graduated extinction also differs from these procedures in several ways. For example, this method provides no competing response (e.g., relaxation) to replace the response of anxiety, whereas desensitization, at least in one interpretation (Wolpe, 1958, 1969), proposes that relaxation provides a competing response to anxiety and arousal. Similarly, graduated extinction assumes no psychodynamic determinants as does the theorizing behind implosive therapy, nor is any specific care taken to prevent avoidance responses or to direct the treatment procedure only to behaviors that are presumed to have been acquired via the process of avoidance conditioning. (See the discussion later in this chapter of implosion and flooding as response prevention therapies.)

Graduated extinction can be seen as a technique of response prevention. It is unlike other response prevention techniques in that fearful, avoidance responses are not prevented by physically restraining the individual or by having him re-create fearful stimuli and situations in his imagination without, at the same time, avoiding or escaping from them. Rather, graduated extinction proceeds by the systematic presentation of aversive stimuli, beginning with extremely weak versions that do not elicit avoidance or defensive behavior and gradually moving on to more aversive scenes. Avoidance behavior can be prevented by always presenting stimuli that are too weak to elicit the avoidance behavior. After minimally aversive stimuli have been presented, slightly more aversive stimuli will no longer elicit the avoidance behaviors, although if they had been presented initially, avoidance would have occurred (Bandura, 1969). An alternative interpretation states that the initial presentations of minimally aversive stimuli allow behaviors to occur that are alternatives to avoidance behaviors, and that these competing responses are likely to generalize to other situations and complex stimuli that are somewhat more aversive (Bandura, 1969).

The use of the graduated extinction technique is not new. Herzberg (1941) treated a patient suffering from agoraphobia of such intensity that she refused to leave the house alone. Treatment initially consisted of having the woman walk by herself in a park, a sort of outing she did not fear greatly. The settings for her walks were gradually expanded to streets, first quiet and then busy ones, until finally she was able to walk almost anywhere she wished without experiencing her previously debilitating anxieties. Several other early reports used this technique successfully with patients suffering from agoraphobia (Jones, 1956; Meyer, 1957; White, 1962).

Grossberg (1965) treated a woman who was unable to complete graduation requirements at her college because she could not complete a required public-speaking course. Before treatment by graduated extinction, she had received tranquilizers, group therapy with other individuals troubled by speech phobias, and 30 hours of individual psychotherapy. Grossberg treated the problem with 17 sessions, during which the woman faced progressively larger audiences and delivered speeches that gradually became longer and longer. Indeed, in the beginning, the patient merely read passages from books to the therapist alone, both in his office and in a small empty classroom. Gradually an audience was introduced, and the classrooms in which the speeches were delivered were varied in different sessions to induce greater generalization (other generalization-encouraging procedures included having the patient imagine she was speaking to her public-speaking class). The patient first sought treatment after she was required to deliver a one-minute speech, but after treatment, she was able to complete six required speeches, and she received a B in the speech class.

Although graduated extinction procedures have almost invariably been applied to problems involving anxiety, they can be extended to other behavior problems where the goal is a behavioral capability that can be gradually approximated by other behaviors. Arora and Murthy (1976), for example, utilized a retraining program in the treatment of writer's cramp that involved behavioral tasks that successively came to resemble writing. The case involved a 19-year-old student who had experienced a gradual onset of difficulty in writing that eventually produced a total inability to write unless he held the pencil in his hand like a knife in stabbing position. Treatment involved having the young man initially hold a paintbrush between his index and middle fingers and draw circles of increasingly smaller diameters. Subsequently other shapes, such as spirals and straight lines, were introduced and finally block letters. After this, the same sequence was used with a soft lead pencil and finally with a pen. At the conclusion of treatment, the client could write comfortably for up to a half hour, and he maintained this improvement throughout a six-month follow-up. An alternative, and perhaps more correct, way to continue this particular use of the procedure would be as a gradual shaping, through successive approximations, of the behavior that was prevented by the cramp.

The details of designing a graduated extinction program do not require lengthy discussion. In essence, this technique requires only that the therapist be adept at devising a series of behavior prescriptions, systematically arranged in a hierarchy that proceeds from behaviors that are so minimally anxiety provoking or inhibiting that they can be performed with reasonable ease to behaviors successively more anxiety provoking.

There has been little research on the use of graduated extinction other than that which can be inferred from the literature on systematic desensitization. Often in studies of component factors within the desensitization procedure, a control condition involves presenting the serialized hierarchy of anxiety-provoking stimuli in the absence of relaxation instructions. The results of such studies, as they reflect on the efficacy of a graduated extinction procedure, are mixed. Studies such as these are generally concerned with the extinction of fear responses to *imagined stimuli* and not with the extinction of fear of the actual performance of *behaviors*. Davison (1968b) found that snake phobics who were administered by the same hierarchy of items as those imagined by desensitization subjects, but without relaxation instructions, showed smaller decrements in fear and would not approach the feared object as closely as would desensitized subjects. Krapfl (1967), also studying snake-phobic subjects, found no difference between a variety of treatment conditions immediately after treatment, but after a six-week follow-up period, desensitization and graduated exposure to stimuli (graduated extinction) produced greater approach responses than did the random presentation of fear-provoking items or two control procedures.

The results of two early studies (Davison, 1968b; Schubot, 1966) indicate that the graduated presentation of stimuli produces greater

levels of anxiety in subjects than does desensitization (graduated presentation of stimuli coupled with relaxation). Recall again that these studies are concerned with stimuli, not with responses. The finding that anxiety levels are greater when relaxation is omitted may imply that treatment via graduated extinction should proceed even more carefully, methodically, and slowly than the presentation of the hierarchy in systematic desensitization. Indeed, this caution may be responsible for the negative findings reported by Davison (1968b). In this study, the speed with which subjects were able to advance through the hierarchy in the desensitization condition determined how rapidly they could advance through the hierarchies in the graduated extinction condition. Thus, the desensitization condition was tailored to the individual subjects, whereas the graduated extinction one was not, and progress in the latter condition may have been too rapid.

There is some evidence that both systematic desensitization and graduated extinction are more effective if the period of exposure to each threatening image or item is long rather than short. No parametric studies have been attempted to determine the exact optimum length; such studies would probably be of little use, since clients will certainly differ in the vividness and effectiveness of their imagery, the rapidity of anxiety decline, and other factors that influence the effectiveness of the procedure. In some early research, Sue (1975) contrasted short exposures of 5 seconds with long exposures of 30 seconds, and the results are illustrated in Figure 7–8. This investigation involved snake-phobic individuals, and on a behavioral avoidance test, as well as on a fear-survey schedule, longer exposures proved to be more effective in eliminating fears.

In some studies of systematic desensitization, the importance of muscular relaxation is tested through the inclusion of a control condition that involves the systematic presentation of fear-provoking stimuli without relaxation. At first, the findings that these procedures produce little

Figure 7–8 *Effects of graduated extinction and desensitization with long or short exposure durations on the reduction of avoidance behavior (□- - -□: no-treatment control; △—△ : short-exposure extinction; □—□ long-exposure extinction; ○- - -○: short-exposure desensitization; ○—○: long-exposure desensitization).*

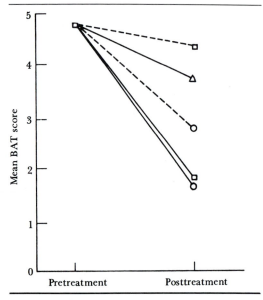

From Sue (1975).

posures to the phobic stimulus become longer as treatment progresses. Other research indicated that graduated extinction incorporating such feedback may be successfully applied to the treatment of phobias (Becker & Costello, 1975; Leitenberg, Agras, Butz, & Wincze, 1971). No specific interpretation of the apparent importance of feedback has been directly tested. An obvious one would be that feedback constitutes reinforcement in the form of externally acknowledged success, which strengthens the courageous behavior of exposing oneself to a fear-provoking stimulus.

One bit of evidence in support of the reinforcement interpretation of feedback comes from an investigation by Becker and Costello (1975). These investigators treated snake phobics with a graduated extinction procedure involving feedback, and included evaluations of fearfulness both before and after treatment and in generalization contexts as well. In this procedure, clients had control over the length of their own graduated exposure to snakes, and the treatment involved increasing lengths of visual exposure only, with no manual or other types of contact. Although clients exposed to a graduated extinction procedure improved in their abilities to confront snakes relative to a control group, their fearfulness immediately after treatment was no less than that of the control group. This finding might be interpreted to imply that feedback about how long the client had been able to remain in visual contact with the snake in each trial provided reinforcement for increasingly long exposures, even though fearfulness declined no more than in the control group. However, in generalization tests that involved snakes at the zoo, slides of snakes, and so on, there was a significant reduction in fear as compared to the control group. Interestingly, upon a follow-up assessment 30 days after the conclusion of treatment, not only were treatment gains maintained in the ability to tolerate exposure to snakes, but at this time a significant improvement in fearfulness was noted. This is in keeping with findings noted in research on

or no therapeutic gain might seem to indicate the ineffectiveness of graduated extinction procedures. It appears, however, that one component of graduated extinction procedures that is absent in these control conditions may play a major role in promoting their effectiveness. This is the typical procedure of providing clients with feedback regarding how long they remained exposed to a fearful stimulus on each trial—feedback that invariably reveals how exposure length increases over successive trials. Leitenberg, Agras, Thompson, and Wright (1968) found that graduated extinction procedures for the elimination of phobias were severely weakened if the patient was not kept informed of the degree to which successive ex-

systematic desensitization (e.g., Lang & Lazovik, 1963) that there may be a lag between changes in self-reported fear and changes in avoidance behavior. In their report, Becker and Costello (1975) compare their results using graduated extinction to those obtained in earlier studies involving the systematic desensitization of similar phobias (Lang & Lazovik, 1963; Lang, Lazovik, & Reynolds, 1965; Lang, Melamed, & Hart, 1970). In all cases, comparison indicated that graduated extinction was equally as effective, if not slightly more so.

A number of studies with animals indicate the potential effectiveness of graduated extinction. It has been clearly shown that graduated introduction to aversive stimuli produces a more rapid elimination of emotional responding than presentation at full intensity (Kimble & Kendall, 1953; Poppen, 1968). A stimulus that elicits one response (e.g., anxiety) can come to evoke an entirely different response if it is initially imbedded in the context of a number of other stimuli that evoke the new response, and then the latter stimuli are gradually removed until only the new stimulus remains (Terrace, 1966).

In an early but quite comprehensive study, Poppen (1970) compared a number of procedures, including graduated counterconditioning (similar to desensitization, but with a competing response other than relaxation), graduated extinction, flooding, nongraduated counterconditioning, and regular extinction, in terms of their efficacy in reducing the inhibition of rats to press a bar after such pressing had been punished by shock. In this experiment, the treatment procedures were carried out as follows: initially, a tone was paired with a shock so that eventually it alone would suppress a bar-pressing response. In the graduated extinction condition, subjects heard the tone initially at a quite low intensity, then the intensity was gradually increased. In the graduated counterconditioning group, the tone was presented at its full intensity (used during training) and was accompanied by food rewards. And in the flooding procedure, the aversive stimulus was presented at its full intensity for durations of 10 minutes at a time. The effects of these various treatments are shown in Figure 7–9.

The regular extinction procedure was least effective in producing rapid recovery of the suppressed response. Graduated extinction and graduated counterconditioning both showed the most rapid alleviation of the response suppression, and each produced the greatest improvement in the very first session. Only after 10 sessions had the other techniques come to produce equivalent amounts of release from the response suppression induced by the prior aversive experience.

Covert Extinction

Covert extinction is one of a family of techniques in which the reinforcing, nonreinforcing, or punitive consequences of a behavior are imagined. Covert sensitization, a technique discussed more fully in Chapter 8, involves the imagining of a problem behavior with a noxious or aversive correlate that persists in imagination as long as the problem behavior is imagined to be occurring. *Covert positive reinforcement* requires that a patient imagine a behavior and then be reinforced for it. *Covert negative reinforcement* requires that a patient imagine himself or herself to be in an anxiety-provoking situation, and then, just as the anxiety peaks, shift to an imagined scene in which he is performing a behavior, the frequency of which is to be increased. For example, a client might imagine he is tied to a chair with a snake about to strike and then, when this image is vivid and truly anxiety provoking, shift to a scene in which he is delivering a public address before a large audience. Clearly, this is a procedure of covert, or imaginal, avoidance conditioning. Both forms of covert reinforcement are discussed in Chapters 5 and 6.

Covert extinction requires the client to imagine herself performing a problem behavior and then to imagine that a common reinforcing

Figure 7–9 *Recovery from response suppression displayed by subjects in each of 5 treatment conditions during 10 extinction sessions. Suppression ratio: a value of 0 indicates complete suppression of the response, and a value of .5 indicates freedom from response inhibition (★- - -★: graduated counterconditioning: ★——★: graduated extinction; ▼- - -▼: flooding; ●- - -●: counterconditioning: ●——●: regular extinction).*

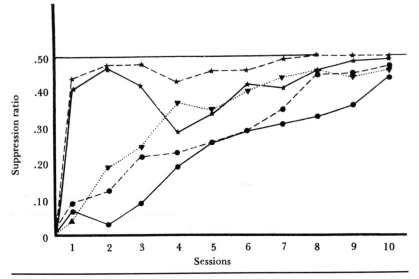

From Poppen (1970).

stimulus does *not* occur. Thus, the client imaginally "performs" behaviors in the absence of contingent reinforcement conditions that are effective in promoting the extinction of overt behaviors. Like systematic desensitization, implosive therapy, and other behavior therapy techniques involving the patient's imagination, covert extinction initially includes the therapist's verbal descriptions of scenes to be imagined. Initially, the client can be told the rationale behind extinction procedures, that her problem behavior is being maintained by reinforcement from the environment, and the treatment will involve the elimination of that reinforcement in the imagination. Then, the client is given several covert extinction trials in the office and homework assignments—that is, trials she is to perform by herself between sessions.

To take an example, a client who complains of stuttering in social situations may be asked first to imagine that he is in a common situation, that he stutters, and that the stuttering evokes no response from others:

> You are sitting in your school cafeteria. Choose a place in which you usually sit. (Pause) You can hear and see students walking around, eating and talking. (Pause) You are eating your favorite lunch. (Pause) There is an empty seat near you. (Pause) A pretty blond girl comes over and asks you if she can sit down. (Pause) You stammer, "Ya . . . ya . . . ya . . . yes." She absolutely reacts in no way to your stuttering. (Cautela, 1971b, pp. 193–194)

After the client has gone through the total scene, he can be quizzed to determine if the scene was vivid and real. Then he can be asked to imagine it on his own, without the therapist's verbal descriptions. He is asked to signal the therapist, for example, by raising the little finger on one hand, when the scene is finished, and the therapist can again ask about its clarity (Cautela, 1971b).

Guided by laboratory evidence that extinction is most rapid when extinction trials are massed (Lawson, 1960; Pavlov, 1927), each therapy session can have as many as 20 imagined scenes, 10 with the therapist verbalizing the scene and 10 with the client on his own. The client should be required to practice the scene 10 times each night at home, to modify the scene on some trials, and to encourage extinction effects in a variety of situations. These procedures are justified by reference to classic laboratory studies of the effects of massed practice, distributed practice (Pavlov, 1927), generalization of extinction (Kimble, 1961), and secondary extinction (Pavlov, 1927). However, these citations appear to be post hoc, and there have been no studies indicating the effectiveness of these various procedures, although they do seem reasonable. Actual clinical sessions usually concentrate on specific important situations involving the problem behavior until all such common situations have been covered. To continue Cautela's example, a stutterer can be given scenes "such as stuttering in response to a professor's question, stuttering whenever the patient is asked directions, and stuttering over the phone (in this case, he is assured that there is absolutely no reaction on the other end)" (Cautela, 1971b, p. 194).

There has been little research on the effectiveness of covert extinction and there are relatively few case studies. Cautela has given the following examples of scenes used in the treatment of a variety of problem behaviors:

1. A hospitalized patient was considered functionally blind, i.e., he claimed he could not see, but observation by a number of individuals indicated that the patient had almost normal vision. . . . Evidently, many situations had become . . . discriminative stimuli for not focusing on a particular object, since not focusing was reinforced by helping behavior. The staff was advised to tell the patient that even though he did not realize it, he was being made helpless by people paying attention to him when he was stumbling around, etc. A staff member presented scenes to the patient in which he was to imagine that he was stumbling over or couldn't find a chair, but that no one helped him or talked to him.

2. In a training school, a boy's disruptive behavior was reinforced by the laughter of his classmates and the attention of his teacher. . . . In the case described here, the teacher and students would not cooperate with the therapist by ignoring the boy's disruptive behavior. Therefore, covert extinction was employed. The boy was asked to imagine performing the disruptive behavior, but no one noticed him. The disruptive behavior was eliminated in three weeks.

3. In many cases of multiple phobias, the husband, wife, or parents of the patient cannot follow the instructions not to reinforce certain behavior because they feel it would be cruel or that the patient would become angry. In these cases, the patients are asked to imagine that they are expressing the phobic behavior, but that no reinforcement is provided by others. The following is a typical example of treatment of fear of being left alone:

You are home with your husband. He says he wants to go bowling. You tell him you don't want him to go because you are afraid of being left alone. But he says, "I'm sorry, I'm going anyway," and he leaves you alone.

4. A homosexual who was reinforced for going into "gay" bars by admiring glances and approaches by other homosexuals was given the following scene:

I want you to imagine you are walking into your favorite bar. You hear the music and the noise of talking and glasses tinkling. You expect to be noticed, but no one notices you. They all act as if you weren't even there. It seems very strange . . . they pay no attention to you at all. This procedure can be combined with covert sensitization toward sexual urges toward males. (1971b, pp. 195–196)

In the available evidence (clinical case studies), there is no indication of any ill effects consequent to the use of covert extinction procedures, although it is conceivable that there might be some. For example, if an individual's stuttering is provoked by the anticipation of other people's response, that portion of the covert extinction scene describing the initial social encounter and consequent stuttering might so sensitize the individual that he would find it difficult to imagine the nonresponse of that other person. Implied here is the possibility of a hierarchical covert extinction procedure, although this possibility has received no attention in the literature as yet. For the time being, covert extinction is probably a technique the behavior therapist should have in his armamentarium, but it remains for future research to clarify the true extent of its effectiveness.

Covert extinction is a technique of relatively recent derivation and merits continued research on factors influencing its effectiveness. It is included in this discussion because of the strong evidence that other techniques involving imagined stimuli (systematic desensitization, implosive therapy, covert sensitization; see especially Chapter 9 on cognitive methods) are effective in the modification of problem behaviors. However, the amount of research on this procedure has not been great, lamentably, and the technique awaits more extensive empirical validation, as do other covert treatment procedures, such as covert positive reinforcement and covert negative reinforcement.

Negative Practice

Theoretically, there could be discussion as to whether *negative practice* constitutes a technique designed to extinguish—as opposed to suppress—behaviors. (Note its resemblance to aversive behavior rehearsal, discussed in Chapter 8). Negative practice has often been employed to eliminate small motor behaviors, usually tics, without the prominent establishment of some observable alternative response. Consequently, we include it in our discussion of extinction procedures.

In 1932, Knight Dunlap published a book entitled *Habits, Their Making and Unmaking*, in which he propounded a treatment procedure for the elimination of small motor habits that had become problematic. The technique ran quite clearly against common sense in that Dunlap proposed practicing the behaviors not to perfect their performance but to eliminate them; hence the term *negative practice*. Actually, in Dunlap's original presentation of the technique and reports of successful application, negative practice was not limited to small motor acts, as it is generally today, but was used in the treatment of enuresis, homosexuality, and masturbation, as well as of tics, typing errors, stuttering, and speech blocking.

Theoretical and empirical support for the procedure of *massing practice* in order to extinguish behaviors came primarily from a different source, experimental psychology (Hull, 1943). Hull proposed that one consequence of the repeated performance of a behavior is the buildup of fatigue, which was aversive to the organism. On the other hand, one consequence of any rest period is the dissipation of this fatigue, which was pleasurable and thus constituted a negative reinforcer (see Chapter 5). The fatigue and other aversive events associated with practice eventually predispose the organism to inhibit further practice (reactive inhibition). Since the aversive effects of fatigue and boredom occur *simultaneously* with the performance of the practiced behavior, they become conditioned to them (classical conditioning), thus attaching aversive properties to the behaviors themselves (conditioned inhibition). Since reactive inhibition (fatigue) dissipates after the practiced behavior ceases, the negative reinforcement of such dissipation is paired with the act of not performing the practiced response. Thus, lengthy practice produces inhibition of the practiced behavior and reinforces the habit of *not* responding. Consequently, extensive practice may eventually eliminate the behavior practiced.

Within his theory of behavior, Hull hypothesized the construct of *reactive inhibition*, symbolized I_r. Since I_r builds up as a function of the repeated performance of an act, Hull proposed that by the process of classical conditioning, the response of inhibition might become conditioned to the performance of an act and the cues that elicited the act, since it was paired with them. He termed such inhibition *conditioned inhibition*, symbolized $_sI_r$. The buildup of conditioned inhibition is maximized when a behavior is performed in such rapid succession that the reactive inhibition from one response has not dissipated when the behavior begins to occur again, thus allowing such inhibition to become conditioned to the beginning of the behavior and to the eliciting cues. Finally, when such conditioned inhibition has become powerful enough to prevent the behavior from occurring at all, it is effectively extinguished (actually, suppressed). Since the repetition of motor acts is more likely to produce fatigue and other aversive consequences than is the repeated performance of less "tangible" behaviors (e.g., thoughts), the concept of negative practice is usually reserved to describe the treatment of problem motor behaviors (e.g., tics) by forced repetition (massed practice). As we shall see later in this chapter, proponents of implosive therapy and flooding (response prevention), which also involve the repetitive presentation of stimuli and the repetitive elicitation of the response of anxiety, account for the proposed effectiveness of these techniques with different theoretical rationales.

In applying the technique of negative practice to the treatment of a problem behavior, the essential procedure is the patient's repeated performance of the act with little rest. Unfortunately, there is no rule of thumb for determining the duration of periods of repeated performance or the duration of rest periods. In one study that varied these two factors, Yates (1958) treated a patient who suffered from four different tics—an eye-blink tic, a throat-clearing tic, a nasal tic (explosive exhalation), and a complex stomach contraction breathing tic. Initially, the patient practiced her tics for 1 minute and then rested for 1 minute. There were two sessions per day (one with the therapist, one at home), with five practice trials in each session. In subsequent experiments with the same patient, the periods of massed practice were extended to 15 minutes and even 1 hour, and the rest periods extended to 15 minutes, 1 hour, several days, and even up to several weeks. Figure 7–10 shows the patient's ability to produce the tics voluntarily over the course of 300 sessions, which included all the different experimental lengths of practice and rests.[2] The decline in the ability to perform the tics is relatively uniform across the sessions, indicating that no procedural variation was more effective than any other. This is, of course, an extensive case study and contains a number of methodological problems, such as the lack of counterbalancing of the order in which the various lengths of practice and rest were enforced. Nevertheless, this provides evidence that the technique can be effective, even though it is not possible to recommend durations of practice and rest periods that maximize success. As may be seen in other case studies, there is little consistency in the durations that have been employed.

Early studies and case histories report the use of negative practice to treat a variety of small motor behaviors, such as errors in piano or organ playing (Wakeham, 1928, 1930), spelling errors in typing (Holsopple & Vanouse, 1929; Poindexter, 1936; Ruhl, 1935), or simple maze learning (Kellogg & White, 1935). These early reports were poorly executed, and the results were thoroughly mixed, some positive and some negative. Nevertheless, these early studies indicated that negative practice does not apply to all behavior problems, especially those involving inhibition. For example, Fishman (1937) treated two cases of speech blocking (inability to speak for a short time after beginning to say

---

[2]Although these data represent the patient's ability to reproduce the tic voluntarily, she also reported a significant decline in the involuntary occurrence of those tics in social situations outside the treatment situation.

Figure 7–10 *Frequency of the voluntary performance of four tics during treatment by massed practice.*

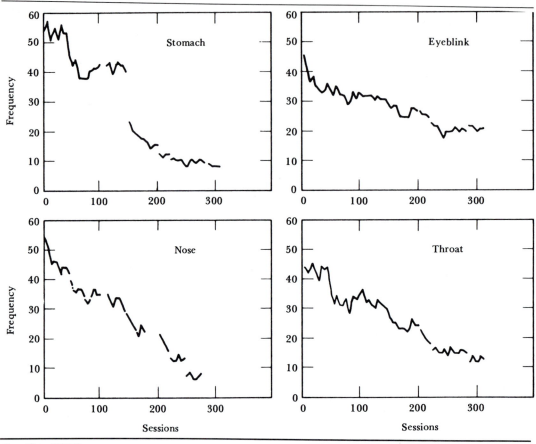

From Yates (1958).

something) and three cases of stammering. After treatment by negative practice, both speech-blocking patients showed *increases* in the frequency of their problem, whereas the stutterers all showed improvement. Case (1940) treated 39 stutterers, achieving total remission of stuttering in common social situations for the 10 individuals who completed the treatment regimen. He also treated three cases of speech blockage, which became worse as a result of treatment (Case, 1940). Rutherford (1940) used negative practice to eliminate grimacing and unusual body movements made by cerebral palsied children when they spoke. Negative practice also improved their speech.

Overall, results have been inconclusive for negative practice. Yates (1958; see the description of this case earlier in the section) achieved what appeared to be positive results in the treatment of tics, but treatment of the same patient by H. G. Jones (1960) revealed no increase in the prevalence of the tic upon transfer to him.

However, Jones noted that there was not a perfect generalization of treatment effects from the voluntary reproduction of a tic in the clinical setting to involuntary occurrences in the natural environment: "Despite the improvement, . . . the patient is still a tiquer. Her tics are far less noticeable, are more easily brought under control and cause far less social embarassment, but can be temporarily exacerbated by illness and by social and vocational frustrations" (Jones, 1960, p. 257).

Walton (1961) treated a young boy who had multiple tics by giving prolonged periods of negative practice on the primary tic and shorter periods on the others. Walton also used a sedative to induce the earlier occurrence of involuntary rest periods (times during the period of practice when the patient can no longer produce the response even though he tries). Treatment produced a significant reduction in the involuntary performance of the tics that was maintained over a one-year follow-up period. Walton (1964) also treated another child with an 11-year history of head shaking plus two other tics (hiccuping and explosive exhaling) with 109 sessions of massed practice, which ranged from ½ to 1½ hours in duration. A sedative drug was also employed in the treatment of this child. Treatment achieved a significant reduction in the frequency of the tics over a five-month follow-up period.

Lazarus (1960) successfully treated a child whose stuttering was also accompanied by unusual head and mouth movements. Clark (1967) applied the technique of massed practice to three patients suffering from the Giles de la Tourette syndrome (involuntary explosions of obscene utterances), two of whom remained free of symptoms over a four-year follow-up period. Mogel and Schiff (1967) described the extinction of a young girl's problematic behavior of "head bumping" after a single treatment session involving two minutes of massed practice. Apparently, the voluntary performance of this behavior in the presence of the therapist proved quite embarrassing, and the success of

this procedure might as easily be understood in terms of punishment. It is noteworthy, of course, that since many clients are embarrassed by their tics, any embarrassment that accompanies the sessions of negative practice may prove to be an additional factor in successful treatment. This hypothesis would predict differential effectiveness for negative practice treatment regimens that involved extensive use of home (solitary) practice sessions in addition to office sessions.

Most applications of negative practice have involved a target behavior that was often involuntary and seldom had intrinsic reinforcing properties that might have been responsible for its maintenance. An exception to this is an investigation reported by Delahunt and Curran (1976), in which a negative practice regimen was applied to help clients stop smoking. The negative practice component of treatment involved having clients increase their rate of smoking to 1½ or 2 times normal for two days and then not smoke for one day. After three initial treatment sessions, containing no negative practice, the two negative practice procedures were to be effected successively, over a six-day period prior to the fourth session.

In this investigation, there was, in addition to a control group that received exhortations to stop smoking, a self-control group in which clients learned self-control strategies, such as self-reinforcement and punishment techniques, the insertion of incompatible behaviors where smoking was once a common response, and strategies for the breaking of behavioral chains. There was also a condition in which negative practice was combined with self-control strategies. After the fourth treatment session, all clients were instructed to stop smoking for as long as possible.

The results are illustrated in Figure 7–11. Both self-control and negative practice were equally effective in producing initial abstinence, but only when self-control skills were combined with negative practice was there any long-term reduction in smoking or continued total

Figure 7–11 *Effectiveness of negative practice and self-control training, both alone and in combination, upon reductions in smoking. (× : control group; ■: group NP; ●: group SC; ○: group SC/NP; ▲: group NS).*

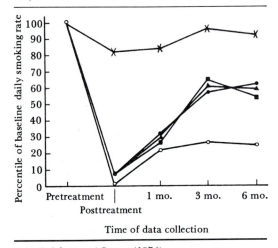

From Delahunt and Curran (1976).

One recent study demonstrates the effectiveness of negative practice in the treatment of fears (Pendleton & Higgins, 1983). The negative practice procedure involves having clients re-create the symptoms of their anxiety, such as trembling, tension, and so on, and to practice them repeatedly without attempts to exercise control over them. In this investigation, acrophobic subjects were treated either by negative practice, by systematic desensitization, or by relaxation alone. Both self-report measures and a behavioral index revealed that negative practice and desensitization were of approximately equal effectiveness. Although the use of negative practice to treat fears is not new and has been proposed as one form of "symptom scheduling" (Newton, 1968), it has received relatively little attention. Thus, it is difficult to draw any firm conclusions about its advantages or disadvantages in the treatment of fears, though the scant evidence that does exist suggests that it is a potentially effective procedure in this regard.

There is one case study in which negative practice failed to be successful, despite the fact that the behaviors treated were similar to those treated successfully by other therapists (Feldman & Werry, 1966). In terms of design and data collection, this is one of the better studies of the effects of negative practice. The patient, an adolescent boy, had two tics, one of which was treated (a head jerk) and one of which was left untreated for control purposes (an eye-blink tic). The data also included the

abstinence (Table 7–1). This result indicates that for behaviors that have an intrinsic attractiveness and reinforcing value for the individual, negative practice must be supplemented with additional behavior control techniques if any long-term behavior change is to be achieved and recidivism avoided.

Table 7–1 **Proportion of Subjects Reporting Total Abstinence at Each Testing Occasion**

| Treatment Group | Posttreatment | Follow-up Occasion | | |
		1 month	*3 months*	*6 months*
Control	2/13	0/13	0/13	0/13
Nonspecific	5/9	4/9	2/9	1/9
Negative practice	4/9	2/9	1/9	2/9
Self-control	7/9	3/9	2/9	2/9
Combined treatment	8/9	4/9	4/9	5/9

number of *involuntary* performances of the tic during the first 15 minutes of each treatment session, which served as a "warm-up period" and during which no negative practice (forced voluntary performance of the tic) occurred. Feldman and Werry found that negative practice produced a significant increase in both the treated and the untreated tics, and an old tic, which had been gone for some time, reappeared. The practice sessions were five minutes in length, and the tic was practiced only once per session. The patient was instructed to practice two other times each day; thus, the three daily practice periods were short and the rest periods quite long and probably variable.

Some authors (Yates, 1970) feel this study casts serious doubt on the effectiveness of negative practice. It is, of course, more a case study than an actual experiment, and the time lengths and frequencies of the practice and rest periods are not particularly similar to those employed in other cases reported in the literature (see cases just described). Furthermore, the head-jerk motion in the treated tic caused dizziness, and this factor limited the length of the massed practice sessions. No rationale is given, however, for the use of only one practice session per treatment session or the decision to have only three sessions per day. Perhaps the dizziness produced by practicing the tic was of long duration.

Like the other techniques discussed in this chapter, the therapeutic use of negative practice has produced mixed results, and there has been very little research concerning the overall effectiveness of the technique or the possibility that it should be applied only to certain classes of disorders—for example, behavioral problems that do not themselves include response inhibition. It seems reasonable to propose that caution be used in the employment of this technique, less because it may prove ineffective than because there are indications that, with some classes of behavior (e.g., speech blocking), negative practice actually exacerbates the problem. Overall, negative practice does appear to have merit, but it is seldom the focus of research to-

day. A renewal of research interest would allow more extensive evaluation of this technique.

Stimulus Satiation

Stimulus satiation is one of the less common techniques of response elimination, but it nonetheless deserves mention. Related to drive theories of behavior (e.g., Hull, 1943), the technique of satiation is designed to reduce the attractiveness of stimuli whose valence is so positive that they motivate behaviors that allow the individual to observe, touch, smell, or possess the stimuli (see Chapter 8 for a more detailed discussion of changing the valence of stimuli). The procedure of satiation involves the repeated presentation of such stimuli to the client until the attractiveness of the stimuli is reduced.

The most famous example of the use of satiation is a case reported by Ayllon (1963) involving a psychotic patient who had hoarded towels throughout her nine-year hospitalization. Although the staff consistently removed hoarded towels from her room, the patient managed to keep 19–29 towels on hand. The program of satiation involved allowing the patient to keep towels in her room and delivering additional towels to her. Towels were handed to the patient in her room, without any comment. Initially she received 7 towels each day, but within three weeks the number was increased to 60 per day. During the first week, whenever a towel was delivered, the patient would say, "Oh, you found it for me, thank you." By the second week, she typically announced that she did not need any more, and by the third week, she was asking that the towels be taken away. Nevertheless, satiation continued, and by the sixth week, the patient was removing the towels from her room herself. Figure 7–12 shows the number of towels in the patient's room at various weeks before, during, and after treatment.

In many instances, stimulus satiation is necessarily confounded with negative practice since a particular behavior on the part of the patient

Figure 7–12 *Number of towels hoarded during a baseline period, a satiation period when towels were given to the patient; and following the satiation period (second baseline).*

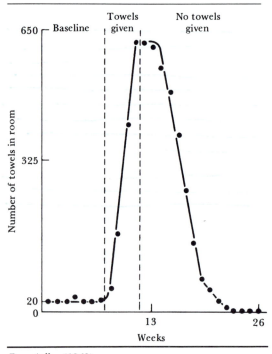

From Ayllon (1963).

shorter treatment; the latter group did not differ from a nontreatment control.

Clearly, there is also the possibility that aversive control is operating in this instance. Other investigators have utilized a satiation procedure in the treatment of smoking, but in the context of aversive control. In these studies, patients are exposed to hot, smoke-filled air, often from an external source, while going through the motor behaviors of smoking (Franks, Fried, & Ashem, 1966; Wilde, 1964). There is clearly a satiation with respect to the stimulus of smoke; however, the aversive nature of the smoke is typically cited for any success achieved by this procedure. Furthermore, data are not typically reported on the extent to which the attractiveness of smoke as a stimulus is altered.

There has been little research on the process of satiation other than that done in the laboratory with children (Gewirtz & Baer, 1958a, 1958b) and animals (Woodworth & Schlosberg, 1954). These studies support the conclusion that satiation experiences weaken the power of reinforcers and reduce the frequency of associated behaviors. Despite the paucity of reports in the literature, satiation appears to be a technique worth considering, especially as an alternative to aversive counterconditioning, when the inappropriately attractive stimulus is one that may be readily dispensed to the point of saturation (e.g., towels may be so dispensed, but there is no evidence that sexual behavior toward inappropriate objects might be eliminated by enforced exposure and interaction with these objects). Certainly, however, research is needed to specify the categories of stimuli and behavior that respond to this technique and the procedural details that determine the effectiveness of the procedure. Caution should be exercised in any decision to employ this technique, although unlike many other extinction techniques described in this chapter, there is no indication in the published literature that satiation may exacerbate the behavior under treatment. The published literature is sparse and dated, however, so this possibility cannot be ruled out. As for negative practice, the technique of

may be necessary to provide the stimulus. For example, in treating problematic smoking behavior, patients may be required to chain smoke for extended periods of time, thus massing the practice of the minor motor behaviors in the overall act of smoking. Marrone, Merksamer, and Salzberg (1970) treated smoking behavior by having patients chain smoke for either 10 or 20 hours straight. They found that either satiation period produced total abstinence from smoking immediately following treatment. However, at the end of a four-month follow-up period, the group that had received the longer satiation (practice) period showed greater abstinence than the group that had received the

satiation could profit from at least a modest renewal of research interest to clarify issues such as these.

Anxiety Induction Therapies

There are two basic categories of anxiety induction therapies that we will discuss in this section, implosive therapy and flooding (or response prevention). Both of these procedures are designed to eliminate avoidance behavior and the anxiety that elicits it through a basic extinction procedure: inducing anxiety but preventing any escape or avoidance behavior so that neither the anxiety nor the avoidance behavior will be reinforced by relief. Another component related to the extinction assumptions is largely informational: the anxiety may be construed as partially an expectancy of terrible and aversive outcomes (whose avoidance produces relief), and the arousal of anxiety without any subsequent avoidance behavior or aversive consequences disconfirms the expectancy for dire outcomes, thus extinguishing it.

Despite some common assumptions or working hypotheses, there are significant differences between implosive therapy and flooding that will become clear in the following discussions of these two techniques. Both techniques are of relatively recent origin and the research literature regarding their effectiveness, the validity of their underlying assumptions, and the relative importance of their various procedural parameters is still growing. The research contains some conflicting results that make overall conclusions rather difficult. Nevertheless, following the discussion of each procedure, we will attempt a tentative evaluation of the anxiety-inducing procedures in general and their promise as behavior therapy techniques.

Implosive Therapy

Implosive therapy is a technique designed to eliminate avoidance behaviors by the process of extinction. The first description of the pro-

cedure and use of the term "implosion" appeared in 1961 in a public presentation by Thomas Stampfl. The first written discussion of the technique appeared a few years later (London, 1964), and numerous theoretical and research papers followed, largely by Stampfl, Levis, Hogan, and Kirchner.[3] We will consider the results of studies testing the effectiveness of implosive therapy later, in a separate section.

In implosive theory, the object of treatment is to avoid anxiety-generating situations and behaviors. A primary assumption for this theory is that such avoidance behaviors are learned because they keep a person from experiencing anxiety (Hogan, 1969; Stampfl & Levis, 1967a). Such defensive avoidance behavior is usually learned in childhood, from situations in which an individual was punished, rejected, or deprived in some manner (e.g., aversive environmental events, such as being cut or burned or falling down; parental punishment, such as slapping, spanking, or deprivation; or peer group experiences, such as being bullied, ostracised, or pummeled). Although these assumptions, as well as others that we discuss later, are reasonably similar to those held by more psychodynamically oriented theorists, learning principles are invoked to account for the initial acquisition of such anxieties and to justify the various procedural details of implosive theory. Following the two-factor theory of learning from aversive consequences (Mowrer, 1960; Solomon, 1964), (1) various behaviors, feared situations, or phobic objects are persistently avoided and that (2) such avoidance behaviors are consistently covertly reinforced by the termination of anxiety each time these behaviors, situations, objects, or people are avoided.

In order for extinction of avoidance responses to occur, the patient must be prevented

---

[3]The classic theoretical and research citations of this technique include Hogan (1963, 1966, 1968, 1969), Hogan and Kirchner (1967), Kirchner and Hogan (1966), Levis (1967), Levis and Carrera (1967), Stampfl (1967), Stampfl and Levis (1967a, 1967b, 1968).

from performing the avoidance behavior, if only in his imagination, and forced to experience the intense anxiety in the absence of any real aversive consequences. When such anxiety is experienced without the occurrence of actual aversive consequences, such consequences will cease to be anticipated and the anxiety will dissipate. The avoided behaviors and stimuli will not be perceived without any attendant anxiety, and the tendency for these behaviors and stimuli to evoke anxiety will undergo extinction. In the words of Stampfl and Levis,

> The fundamental hypothesis is that a sufficient condition for the extinction of anxiety is to re-present, reinstate, or symbolically reproduce the stimuli (cues) to which the anxiety response has been conditioned, in the absence of primary reinforcement (the actual punishment, rejection, or deprivation). (1967a, pp. 498–499)

In theory, and somewhat in actual procedure, implosive therapy is similar to flooding or response-prevention techniques (discussed in a later section). There are several distinct differences, however. Implosive therapy is based upon clearly specified assumptions concerning the psychodynamics of the individual under treatment. Earlier we noted that childhood trauma is proposed to be the source of most avoidance behaviors. The theory of implosive treatment, according to Hogan, specifies that imagery in treatment be generally directed toward the "usual conflict areas that the therapist, from experience, knows concern most individuals." These areas of conflict include "fears, rejections, prior humiliations or deprivations, or conflicts related to expression of fear of aggression, sexual problems of various types, and guilt-related behavior" (1968, p. 423). Stampfl (Stampfl & Levis, 1968) has explicitly stated that the concerns of various psychosexual stages postulated by Freud (toilet training, anal experiences, infantile sexuality, aggression, etc.) are the substance of treatment.

Like several other behavior therapies, implosive therapy uses visual imagery rather than actual performance of avoided behaviors or exposure to feared stimuli. It would appear that this is a necessary procedure of treatment, since the therapist, in his attempts to evoke the maximum amount of anxiety, is likely to describe images that include projected traumata clearly beyond actual experience (see the descriptions presented later in the section). There is some theoretical inconsistency at this point, because the technique is supposed to induce the patient to re-create the original life trauma, while in practice the trauma that the patient is to imagine transcends that of actual human experience. One may speculate that such imagined elaboration is seen as necessary for the induction of a level of anxiety equivalent to that which presumably accompanied the original traumatic experience.

Typically, in implosive therapy scenes of avoided behaviors and stimuli are presented in a hierarchical fashion, beginning with the least anxiety-provoking items. Although this appears to be in the manner of desensitization, it should be clear from the case excerpts that follow that the initial steps in an implosive therapy hierarchy do elicit intense anxiety. Flooding, or response prevention techniques, requires that images related to specific behavioral problems be presented for sufficiently long periods to allow the dissipation of anxiety. Presentations that are too short may produce increased *sensitization* to the feared stimuli and behaviors. The theory of implosive therapy makes no specification regarding the dissipation of anxiety; it only states that anxiety must be experienced without any actual aversive consequences.

In the practice of implosive therapy, it is important to prevent the patient from engaging in any avoidance behavior or otherwise limiting the effectiveness of the reinstitution and magnification of the anxiety associated with the imagined scenes (Hogan, 1969). Psychotics have been observed to interrupt their participation in a therapy session by rolling up their eyes and dissociating. Less disturbed patients may ask questions or in some other verbal way interrupt the provocation of anxiety. In any event, should such dissociation occur, the therapist is obligated to stop the client at this point and begin the presentation again. The therapist must constantly monitor the responses of the patient, interpret those responses, and act accordingly. Any foot wiggling or other body movement that may dilute the experience of anxiety must be stopped. Although crying is often a part of a genuine emotional reaction, if the therapist judges it to be an attempt to elicit sympathy, it should be ignored.

Let us now turn to some examples of implosive procedures. As one researcher (Hogan, 1968) has noted, the patient's involvement is limited only by the creativity of the therapist, who may imitate the growls and roars of animals, touch the patient's arm as an animal is described slithering over his body, or even use electrical devices, such as a fan to simulate a buzz saw mutilating his body.

Stampfl and Levis (1967) have outlined in detail the areas of conflict that generally constitute the domain for implosive treatment. The eight primary areas of concern and the elements of relevant implosive scenes are as follows:

Orality. Many scenes will be destructive (see "Aggression"), involving the eating, biting, spitting, and sucking of various objects, including other human beings (cannibalism).

Anality. General anal scenes involving anal retention and expulsion (cf. Erickson, 1950), often in social situations.

Sexual Concerns. In addition to dynamically oriented Oedipal and primal scene depictions, this area includes scenes of castration, cunnilingus, fellatio, homosexuality, and bestiality.

Aggression. Scenes include interactions with others in which the patient expresses anger, hostility, and aggression. The target is usually a parent, sibling, spouse, or other significant figure. It is usual to include body mutilation, including the death of the patient himself.

Rejection. In this area, scenes depict the patient being deprived, abandoned, rejected, shamed, or left helpless. For example, one scene described by Hogan (1969) depicted the client as a baby whose mother came into the dark, shabby room in which he had been abandoned, squirted milk from her breasts upon the floor rather than feed him, and said how unwanted he was.

Loss of Impulse Control. These scenes are centered about problems of impulse control. Patients are to imagine scenes in which they clearly lose control and act out sexual or aggressive impulses. Incorporated also are scenes of the consequences of such impulsive acting out, such as being relegated to the back ward of a mental hospital for life.

Guilt. These scenes generally depict the patient confessing his responsibilities for a variety of wrongdoings that may have been described in other implosive sessions. He may imagine himself in a courtroom with his parents and loved ones present, or in front of God. God or the court may then condemn him to eternal hell, or sentence him to death, and the sentence is then visualized. Thematically the punishment is generally related to the unpardonable sins confessed by the patient.

Central or Autonomic Nervous System Reactivity. The patient may be required to imagine aspects of his own responsivity that may themselves heighten his anxiety. Thus, scenes may depict his own heart racing, perspiration pouring forth from his body, muscular tension, or involuntary incontinence.

Stampfl and Levis (1967) feel that most of these areas will be touched upon during the treatment of any particular client. Certainly, within any one area the total scene depicted will overlap with other areas: for example, sexual behaviors will certainly elicit moral judgments from others; and the imaginary performance of inhibited sexual, aggressive, oral, anal, or similar behaviors is likely to be equated with a loss of control. Furthermore, single scenes may combine multiple elements.

The following transcription of excerpts from the treatment of a snake-phobic individual (Hogan, 1968; Hogan & Kirchner, 1967) will give the reader some idea of the emotional intensity of the implosive themes. Before the therapeutic interaction, the treatment method had been explained to the client, and in discussions with the patient the therapist had gleaned specific material that he could incorporate into imagery later in the session. Note the intensity of the description and the total involvement that the therapist tries to elicit from the client.

> Close your eyes again. Picture the snake out in front of you, now make yourself pick it up. Reach down, pick it up, put it in your lap, feel it wiggling around in your lap, leave your hand on it, put your hand out and feel it wiggling around. Kind of explore its body with your fingers and hand. You don't like to do it, make yourself do it. Make yourself do it. Really grab onto the snake. Squeeze it a little bit, feel it. Feel it kind of start to wind around your hand. Let it. Leave your hand there, feel it touching your hand and winding around it, curling around your wrist.

In this second excerpt, the level of anxiety is raised and the tempo of the presentation is increased.

> Okay, now put your finger out towards the snake and feel his head coming up. No, it is in your lap, and it is coming up. Its head is towards your finger and it is starting to bite at your finger. Let it, let it bite at your finger. Put your finger out, let it bite, let it bite at your finger, feel its fangs go right down into your finger. Oooh, feel the pain going right up your arm and into your shoulder.

In the third section, the level of anxiety is increased as the animal begins to attack the person's face or vital organs.

> Okay, feel him coiling around your hand again, touching you, slimy, now he is going up on your shoulder and he crawls there and he is sitting on your chest and he is looking you right in the eye. He is big and he is black and he is ugly and he's

coiled up and he is ready to strike and he is looking at you. Picture his face, look at his eyes, look at those long sharp fangs. . . . He strikes out at you. (T slaps hand.) Feel him bite at your face. Feel him bite at your face, let him bite; let him bite; just relax and let him bite; let him bite at your face, let him bite; let him bite at your face; feel his fangs go right into your cheeks; and the blood is coming out on your face now . . . feel it biting your eye and it is going to pull your eye right out and down on your cheek. It is kind of gnawing on it and eating it, eating at your eye. Your little eye is down on your cheek and it is gnawing and biting at your eye. Picture it. Now it is crawling into your eye socket and wiggling around in there, feel it wiggling and wiggling up in your head.

Research on Implosive Therapy Several investigators have focused on the response elimination mechanism hypotheses that are the foundation of the theory of implosive therapy. One question concerns the degree to which phobic or implosive therapy evokes physiological fear responses, which are then dissipated because the fear is disconfirmed. Similarly, any tendency toward avoidance responses would be eliminated because they were previously reinforced by the reduction of fear following escape from the fearful stimulus or situation. Clear and consistent evidence shows that imagined fearful scenes are indeed fear provoking. Edelman (1972), for example, examined the physiological responses of individuals whose responsiveness involved either increases in heart rate or increases in GSR during fear. His findings indicated clearly that fear scenes induce fear-related physiological responding, and the particular type of physiological fear response observed is the one that typically characterizes the individual. May (1977a) confirmed the physiological responsiveness of individuals to fear-related stimuli and found that often internally generated phobic thoughts produced greater fear-related physiological responding than did descriptive statements or pictures presented by someone other than the individual himself (e.g., the therapist).

There appears to be confirming evidence that changes in physiological arousal during a therapy session occur in a pattern consistent with the original interpretation of the extinction mechanisms by which implosive therapy is supposed to work. McCutcheon and Adams (1975) found that a 20-minute period of implosive treatment increased physiological indices of anxiety (GSR) throughout the treatment session, and a behavioral test of fear following a single session did not indicate that the implosive experience had been effective. In a second study, these investigators lengthened the treatment period to 60 minutes and found that treatment period produced first an increase in physiological responding and then a decrease. Following a single treatment of this greater length, a behavioral fear test indicated improvement for individuals experiencing an implosive treatment involving imagery relevant to the fear, as contrasted to a comparison condition that involved implosive imagery unrelated to the individual's particular fear. Similarly, Orenstein and Carr (1975) found that a physiological indicator of fear—heart rate—rose at first during a 40-minute treatment session and subsequently declined. Figure 7–13

illustrates the course of heart rate during a treatment session of implosive therapy as compared to a control condition in which individuals heard extensive information about the lives and habits of the phobic stimulus (a rat).

The most direct evidence in support of the extinction hypothesis underlying implosive therapy comes from another aspect of the Orenstein and Carr (1975) study. After completing the implosive treatment regimen, clients completed a behavioral avoidance test. These investigators found a relatively high correlation (+.52) between the degree to which physiological responses indicative of anxiety were aroused during the treatment session and the decline in self-reported fear during a subsequent behavioral avoidance test. Because of the size of the sample, this correlation is not statistically significant, but it indicates a direction for future research that might reflect directly upon some of the extinction hypotheses underlying implosive and flooding therapies.

Despite the consistency of research findings relating to the presumed factors contributing to the effectiveness of implosive therapy, research on the actual effectiveness of implosive therapy

Figure 7–13 *Course of heart rate during a single treatment session (heart rate averaged over 5-minute blocks of time)(■——■: implosive therapy; ○- - -○: provision of extensive information about the phobic stimulus).*

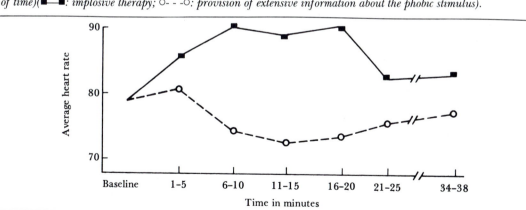

has been quite mixed. Using the MMPI as a criterion for therapy effectiveness, Levis and Carrera (1967) found that out patients treated by eight-hour-long sessions of implosive therapy had a larger number of T scores drop into the normal range than did patients who received conventional treatment or no treatment at all. This study does not indicate the degree to which problem behaviors were modified, nor does it propose any theoretical rationale for the capability of implosive therapy to induce changes in paper-and-pencil measures of mental status, such as the MMPI. The instrument was chosen primarily because it was a common instrument in other studies evaluating psychotherapy effectiveness (e.g., Barron & Learly, 1955; Gallagher, 1953; Kaufmann, 1950; Mogar & Savage, 1964; Schofield, 1950, 1953).

Hogan and Kirchner (1967) treated clients who had an intense fear of rats, utilizing a single implosive therapy session or relaxation training paired with neutral imagery. Clients treated with implosive therapy were to imagine touching a rat, having a rat nibble at their fingers, then bite them on the arm, and eventually sink its fangs into their neck, claw about in their hair, and eventually even devour their eyes. The single treatment session lasted, on the average, only 39 minutes. Following treatment, 20 of 21 subjects treated with implosive therapy opened the cage of a live rat, and 14 of 21 actually picked up the rat. Only 3 of the 22 control group subjects would open the cage, and 7 refused even to enter the room. Physiological monitoring during treatment showed that the pulse rate declined during the session, indicating that anxiety was abating and that extinction might thus be occurring.

Fazio (1970) compared implosive therapy with irrevelant imagery and discussion in the treatment of roach phobias. Subjects treated with irrelevant imagery and discussion were given implosive therapy with respect to irrelevant fears (being attacked by a bear, burned by a forest fire, etc.) and discussions of the feared insect, its living habits, and how harmless

it really was. Fazio found that the irrelevant imagery and discussion were more effective than implosive therapy, or implosive therapy plus discussion, in enabling subjects to touch or hold a live roach. It is noteworthy that these were three treatment sessions of a half hour each, and that all therapy was delivered via a tape recorder. In a second study including groups treated by implosive therapy, irrelevant imagery implosion, or discussion only, Fazio found that discussion-only treatment produced the greatest increase in approach behaviors toward the feared insects. Indeed, of three implosive therapy subjects who were treated, even though they were not judged phobic, two became sensitized to roaches as a result of treatment. As we discuss later, this result may indicate that the implosive therapy sessions were too short, but in any case it poses significant reservations regarding the direct effectiveness and safety of the implosive technique.

Hodgson and Rachman (1970) attempted to reduce anxiety associated with snakes by exposure to anxiety-provoking images that were unrelated to the snake phobia. One group of subjects (adolescent girls) heard a 40-minute tape describing interactions with a snake, similar to the one cited earlier in this chapter. In a second condition, subjects heard descriptions of terrible scenes unrelated to snakes (e.g., automobile crashes) for 30 minutes, and then only the last 10 minutes of the implosion tape. In another condition, this same sequence was given, but the last 10 minutes of the implosion tape were heard 24 hours after the irrelevant implosive imagery session. Finally, there was one condition involving 40 minutes of pleasant, nonanxiety-provoking images. There was no positive effect found for implosive therapy. In fact, on a self-rated fear inventory, implosive therapy subjects subsequently reported an increase in fear of snakes, whereas subjects who heard the 40 minutes of pleasant images reported a decrease. Furthermore, subjects who heard the 10 minutes of implosive therapy immediately following unrelated anxiety-provoking images reported a decrease in fear, whereas those who heard the 10 minutes of implosive therapy after a 24-hour interim reported an increase. In discussing their failure to find the strikingly positive effects of implosive therapy reported by other investigators (e.g., Hogan & Kirchner, 1967), Hodgson and Rachman noted that there appeared to be a greater probability of improvement in subjects who were tested some time after the end of the implosive therapy session, when anxiety generated during the treatment session had dissipated to some degree. It should be further noted that Hogan and Kirchner (1967), who did not use tapes (as did both Fazio [1970] and Hodgson and Rachman [1970]), found that imagery and timing effective with one subject was not necessarily effective with another. This observation would seem to preclude the use of taped implosive descriptions. The findings of McCutcheon and Adams (1975), discussed previously indicate that the length of the implosive therapy session might have been too short to produce therapeutic gains.

There have been a number of studies contrasting the effectiveness of implosive therapy with that of systematic desensitization. These studies also have produced conflicting results and are unanimous only in that none of them showed implosive therapy to be superior to systematic desensitization. Mealiea and Nawas (1971) matched 50 snake-phobic college women on a behavioral avoidance test and fear thermometer scale and then assigned them to treatment by systematic desensitization or by implosive therapy or to one of three control conditions. Subjects received five 30-minute sessions. On a follow-up test one month later, only subjects treated with systematic desensitization showed a significant decrease in phobic behavior. Subjects treated with implosive therapy did not differ from subjects in the control conditions. Hekmat (1973) reports similar results on a study involving women with rat phobias.

In a study of similar design, Willis (1968; Willis & Edwards, 1969) found that systematic

desensitization was significantly more effective than implosive therapy in reducing avoidance behavior in mice-phobic female college students. Subjects treated with implosive therapy showed no less avoidance behavior than did subjects in a control condition.

In the one investigation that comes closest to indicating a superiority of implosive therapy over desensitization, Crowe and associates (1972) contrasted desensitization, implosive therapy, and a contingency management procedure (reinforced practice at contact with the phobic object). The reinforced practice procedure proved to be more effective than desensitization in the treatment of the phobia, and implosive therapy fell in between; not significantly less effective than reinforced practice, but not significantly more effective than desensitization either.

In an early study, Barrett (1967, 1969) found no difference in the effectiveness of systematic desensitization and implosive therapy, but he still concluded that systematic desensitization was a preferable form of treatment for the reduction of fears. In this study, both systematic desensitization and implosive therapy produced significant decrements in avoidance behavior (a noteworthy finding, since this is one of the few comparative studies in which implosive therapy produced results different from those in a control group), but the effect of implosive therapy was found to be more variable. That is, while there was a significant degree of average improvement in the implosive therapy group, some of the subjects improved a great deal, whereas others improved hardly at all. On the other side of the coin, Barrett concluded that implosive therapy was more "efficient" than systematic desensitization, because the same amount of average improvement was accomplished in only 45 percent of the time required by systematic desensitization. Systematic desensitization subjects received 4 training sessions and up to 11 systematic desensitization sessions; implosive therapy subjects received 2 50-minute interviews followed by up to 2 sessions of implosive therapy (of unspecified duration).

A number of studies have reported no differences between systematic desensitization and implosive therapy (Borkovec, 1970; Carek, 1969; Jacobson, 1970; McGlynn, 1968; Mylar & Clement, 1972). Mylar and Clement (1972) contrasted the effectiveness of implosive therapy and desensitization in the treatment of public-speaking anxiety and found them equally effective, even after a one-month follow-up period. In a well-designed study, Borkovec (1970, 1972) contrasted the effectiveness of systematic desensitization and implosive therapy under two conditions of expectancy. Some subjects were led to believe that the therapy they were receiving was effective by being shown false physiological "data" indicating reductions in fear, and some subjects were shown false physiological records but not led to believe these were at all indicative of the progress of therapy. Systematic desensitization and implosive therapy both produced decreases in pulse rate in the presence of the phobic object. However, there was no indication that either type of therapy increased the subjects' actual approach behaviors toward the phobic object, although there was an effect due to expectancy: subjects who thought that the treatment was reducing their fear showed greater increases in approach behavior than subjects having no such expectation, and subjects with a positive expectancy touched the object more rapidly during the post test than did no-expectancy subjects.

Evaluation of Implosive Therapy Although the initial reports of the effectiveness of implosive therapy were quite glowing (Hogan & Kirchner, 1967; Levis & Carrera, 1967; Stampfl, 1967), the total body of research does not support the effectiveness of this technique, and the major research journals have published little research since the mid- to late 1970s. Furthermore, there has been a great deal of criticism concerning not only the effectiveness of implosive therapy, but also the proposed theory (Stampfl & Levis, 1967a) underlying it (Morganstern, 1973). Finally, the methodological sophis-

tication of most research in this area is quite poor, making any conclusions from the research literature exceedingly difficult (Morganstern, 1973).

Theoretically, the incorporation of psychodynamic themes into implosive imagery is an important part of therapeutic procedure: it promotes the description of stimuli that are truly related to the hypothesized original traumatic learning situation. However, Hogan (1968, 1969), one of the most prolific of implosive therapists, uses little if any direct psychodynamic imagery in his treatment procedure (see the extensive example cited earlier). Since Hogan (Hogan & Kirchner, 1967) claims such striking successes, this would seem to indicate that the psychodynamic content of implosive themes may be unnecessary, but this has not been directly tested. Except at the very outset, research concerning the effectiveness of implosive therapy has generally failed to include any psychodynamic considerations, so this issue may be moot.

Both systematic desensitization and implosive therapy propose that patients must be prevented from making avoidance responses and that the low (systematic desensitization) or high (implosive therapy) levels of anxiety must be replaced by nonanxious responses (systematic desensitization) or allowed to extinguish when an expected aversive event fails to occur (implosive therapy). However, Borkovec (1970, 1972) included a control condition in which subjects were instructed to make imaginary avoidance responses when imagining implosive scenes. This group also showed some reduction in arousal to the feared stimulus and did not show the increased arousal that implosive therapy theory would predict.

A number of aspects of the implosive procedure vary from study to study, and their effects have not been investigated systematically. The inclusion of psychodynamic themes is one. Another involves the hierarchical presentation of the implosive scenes (Stampfl & Levis, 1967a). No clear rationale is presented for the hierarchical presentation of scenes other than that scenes higher on the hierarchy are likely to be close to the actual scene of the original trauma and consequently have been repressed. Presumably, it would have been difficult or impossible for the client to imagine them earlier because of such repression, which is eliminated as scenes lower on the hierarchy lose their tendency to provoke anxiety. Some investigators have included the hierarchical presentation of scenes (Barrett, 1967, 1969; Hogan & Kirchner, 1967; Levis & Carrera, 1967), whereas others have omitted this part of the procedure (Mealiea & Nawas, 1971). It is impossible to evaluate the effectiveness of their procedures from the research results, since the projects differed in a number of ways. Studies also vary in the length of the implosive therapy sessions, and recent work (McCutcheon & Adams, 1975) would imply that the use of short sessions should work against any potential effectiveness.

A number of possible alternative explanations for the effectiveness of implosive therapy have also been ignored in the literature. For example, in many presentations of implosive scenes, the subject is asked to imagine various approach behaviors toward the feared object (e.g., Fazio, 1970). This procedure, in effect, includes the covert and symbolic modeling of such approach behaviors. This technique is entirely unrelated to the basic theoretical notions of implosive therapy and more similar to systematic desensitization since it places emphasis on the observation of symbolic stimuli in the absence of anxiety (see Chapter 2).

Another generally uncontrolled factor in studies on implosive therapy (and many other techniques, as well) is the presence of cognitive factors that might affect approach behaviors toward phobic objects and thereby influence the behavior outcome interpreted as due to other aspects of the therapy. The study by Borkovec (1970, 1972), cited earlier, indicates that a client's expectancy of success may be one such important cognitive factor. Further, Borkovec found that expectations that treatment would be

effective were more closely related to overt behavioral measures of fear than to physiological measures of fear, such as pulse rate, which were affected by both implosive therapy and systematic desensitization treatments. This indicates that cognitive components in any treatment regimen may have effects independent of other components of treatment. The evidence here, too, is somewhat mixed. Dee (1970) found that implosive therapy preceded by positive instructions was somewhat more effective than implosive therapy without such instructions. On the other hand, Layne (1970) found no expectancy effect in a study in which implosive therapy itself produced no significant effect.

A particularly important variable that has been little studied within individual experiments is the length of the exposure time to the implosive stimulus. Exposures (session lengths) that are too short are likely to produce sensitization rather than a reduction in anxiety (Eysenck, 1968; Staub, 1968; Wolpe, 1958, 1969) or simply to be ineffective (McCutcheon & Adams, 1975). Although there has been no research on this question with respect to implosive therapy, some investigators have broached the question in studying the effectiveness of flooding, or response prevention, procedures (Rachman, 1969; Siegeltuch & Baum, 1971).

Another untested assumption in implosive therapy concerns the necessity of presenting descriptions of the fear-eliciting stimuli that are dramatic, exaggerated, and clearly unlikely to be (or to have been) encountered in the normal course of events (having snakes gouge your eyes out, swallowing them, finding yourself sexually involved with a parent). In implosive therapy, the necessity for such scenes is usually derived from the emphasis on psychodynamic themes, from the argument that such intense scenes do, somehow, approximate the original traumatic learning situation, or from the assumption that repressed memories and fears can be approximated by such creative descriptions. In practice, the presence of psychodynamic scenes and the creative dramatization of hypothesized repressed material are two ways in which the procedures of implosive therapy differ from those of flooding. Consequently, let us now turn to a discussion of the latter technique before concluding our evaluation of both implosive therapy and flooding procedures.

Flooding (Response Prevention)

Flooding and *response prevention* are two names for the general technique of exposing an individual to anxiety-provoking stimuli while preventing the occurrence of avoidance responses. As we noted earlier, the theoretical rationale for these techniques is generally the same as that for implosive therapy. The techniques differ in that they do not involve the psychodynamic interpretations common to implosive therapy, nor do they include the extensive and theatrical thematic elaborations in the presentation of the phobic stimuli. In some instances, especially in experimental work with animals, exposure may be to the actual feared stimuli rather than to imagined versions. Obviously the extreme situations commonly presented in implosive therapy do not lend themselves to *in vivo* presentations.

The technique of flooding has its roots in experimental work on the establishment and extinction of avoidance responses, work that contributed also to the techniques of aversive control involving avoidance learning (Solomon, 1964; Solomon, Kamin, & Wynn, 1953). Interestingly, this work appeared just prior to the original statements of implosive therapy (Stampfl, 1961), and it is cited in the theoretical statements concerning the mechanisms underlying extinction during implosive therapy (Stampfl & Levis, 1967).

Briefly, in his work on avoidance conditioning, Solomon (1964; Solomon et al., 1953) found that if an unavoidable shock is preceded by a warning signal (for instance, a light), that signal comes to evoke intense emotional responding in the organism being conditioned (presumably because of the anticipation of the aversive stimulus). If that organism is then given the opportunity to escape the shock, say, by jumping out of the the portion of the cage containing the shock conductor, then very quickly it begins to make that escape response as soon as the light comes on. At that time, of course, the escape response has become an avoidance response, since it occurs before the onset of shock and allows the organism to avoid the punishment.

Once such an avoidance response has been established, Solomon found that the animal would continue to avoid the potential shock for hundreds and hundreds of trials, never waiting long enough to ascertain whether the shock would actually occur. This is, of course, one characteristic of avoidance responses: they are quite persistent, and since they do not include "reality testing," they may persist long after the avoided aversive consequences have ceased to exist. In the theoretical model of flooding and implosive therapy, such avoidance responses might have been established long before the individual comes for treatment, perhaps as early as childhood.

Discovering the persistent nature of the avoidance response, Solomon naturally became interested in what procedures, if any, would successfully modify this response. One effective procedure he found (Solomon et al., 1953) was to introduce the animal into the area from which he typically escaped in order to avoid the shock, to actuate the stimulus that supposedly signaled the future onset of shock, and then to prevent the animal from leaving the area and omit the aversive event (shock). Presumably, after a number of trials in which the avoidance response was prevented, the light (the cue that elicited anxiety) would no longer elicit anxiety, and when the animal was not prevented from performing the avoidance response, it in fact would refrain from avoidance behaviors and appear calm and nonanxious. Further research on the effectiveness of this technique has explored various parameters promoting effective extinction of avoidance responding, such as the length of each trial during which the organism is prevented from performing the avoidance response (Baum, 1966, 1968, 1969a, 1970).

Use of the term *flooding* (Polin, 1959) appeared about the time implosive therapy was being developed, and the first use of the technique on human clients was reported by Malleson (1959) that same year. Using a hierarchy similar to that employed in systematic desensitization, Malleson instructed patients to feel more and more frightened as he progressed through the hierarchy. At first, there was an increase in distress, following which Malleson reported that clients showed a recovery of composure and eventually a complete cure. A flooding technique was also reported by Boulougouris and Marks (1969), accompanied by complete recoveries by phobic patients.

In the 1970s, there was an increase in reports of flooding procedures and their effectiveness in treating a variety of disorders, such as phobias (Yule, Sacks, & Hersov, 1974), anxiety neurosis (Girodo, 1974), post traumatic stress disorder (Black & Keane, 1982; Keane & Kalorzek, 1982), obsessive-compulsive behavior (Hackman & McLean, 1975; Levy & Meyer, 1971; Meyer, Robertson, & Tatlow, 1975; Rachman, Marks, & Hodgson, 1973; Rainey, 1972), agitated depression (Hannie & Adams, 1974), psychogenic urinary retention (Glasgow, 1975; Lamontagne & Marks, 1973), somatic complaints (Stambaugh, 1977), and social withdrawal in children (Kandel, Ayllon, & Rosenbaum, 1977). Despite the fact that it is certainly one of the most unpleasant of the behavior therapies (Horne & Matson, 1977), this evidence seems to show that flooding can be used successfully to treat a variety of behavior disorders, that it may be utilized as an adjunct to other behavior therapy procedures such as modeling (Horne & Matson, 1977; Rachman, et al., 1973; Uno, Greer, & Goates, 1973), and that it can occasionally prove superior to other behavior treatments and be successful after another treatment has failed (Kandel et al., 1977; Yule et al., 1974).

One class of behavior disorders, obsessive-compulsive behavior, seems most amenable to treatment by *in vivo* flooding procedures. There are two methods for implementing flooding in such cases: the imposition of a time restriction for any compulsive activity, so that it must be stopped before the anxiety is reduced (e.g., Poole & Bodeker, 1975); and the maximization of all stimuli that appear to set off the anxiety that produces the compulsive behavior (e.g., Meyer et al., 1975). Poole and Bodeker (1975), for example, treated a young women, who compulsively rocked for a period of time before retiring, by simply limiting the amount of time that she was allowed to engage in the rocking behavior. Initially she reported that the premature termination of the compulsive behavior resulted in increased anxiety, but by the end of treatment, she was able to go to bed without rocking and the anxiety was gone. The compulsion was still absent at the end of a six-month follow-up period.

Meyer and colleagues (1975) report a procedure that is perhaps more common for the use of flooding in treatment of compulsions. Their client, a woman, was made extremely anxious by anything associated with death. By the time she sought treatment, her fiancé had become a source of anxiety because before they met, his wife had died and the client associated this death with him. Even newspapers, which might have articles on disasters and deaths, and nearly everything else elicited anxiety, and she would have to wash and change her clothes after even the most distant encounter. Treatment involved "contaminating" both the therapist and herself by the strongest means possible. First a hierarchy of anxiety-provoking stimuli was generated. The top item involved dead bodies, so she and the therapist proceeded to the hospital mortuary where they both handled a dead body thoroughly. Subsequently other sources of anxiety were directly confronted; for example, she handled the picture of a man who had been shot to death in the street. Compulsive rituals were prevented with the help of the therapist on the initial day of treatment (he did not leave until she was preparing to go to bed), and she successfully resisted any tendency to ritualize on the second day. By the 12th day after the initial flooding, ritualization had successfully been avoided, even though problematic stimuli had been encountered (e.g., a suitcase containing her dead father's personal effects). Over an eight-month follow-up period, although some anxiety persisted, the desire to perform cleansing rituals was gone and the client's adjustment was apparently a good one. She had married the "contaminated" fiancé and was successful in her work.

A number of studies have reflected upon various parameters of the flooding technique, many of which utilize animals as subjects. While caution must be used in generalizing such results to human beings, Baum (1966, 1968, 1969a) has found consistently that procedures of response prevention can extinguish experimentally established avoidance responses. In one study, it was apparent that the presence of fearless models can result in social facilitation during the flooding experience and hasten recovery of normal behaviors in fear-producing situations (Baum, 1969b; see Chapter 4 on modeling procedures). Indeed, Baum tends to interpret the effectiveness of models in terms of vicarious response prevention (Baum, 1970; see Chapter 4).

Several investigators have also found that the more non–fear-related behavior the animal engages in during flooding, the more effective the flooding treatment (Baum & Poser, 1971, Spring, Prochaska, & Smith, 1974). Baum has also found that short durations of response prevention (5 minutes) are effective in treating avoidance behaviors established by typical avoidance conditioning (the animal was allowed to escape the shock on initial trials and then learned to avoid the shock by escaping prior to its onset). However, when avoidance learning was preceded by a series of unavoidable shocks, only a response prevention period of long duration (30 minutes) was effective in extinguishing the avoidance response. In an earlier study,

Baum (1969a) showed that 1-minute response prevention periods were ineffective in eliminating avoidance responses, whereas periods of 3 or 5 minutes allowed successful extinction to occur. As for implosive therapy, it appears that sessions that are too short will be ineffective, and the occurrence of adaptive, alternative behaviors in the presence of the feared stimulus may enhance the effectiveness of flooding.

Lederhendler and Baum (1970) have demonstrated not only the increased effectiveness of longer response prevention periods, but also that extinction is facilitated when the animals are forced to move about and explore during the period of response prevention. The authors interpreted these results to indicate that the occurrence of "nonfear" behaviors (approach behaviors or relaxation, for example) may be important factors in the successful employment of flooding procedures. Thus, once again the importance of providing alternative behaviors during treatment designed to eliminate problem behaviors is apparent.

One study examined the effects of the therapist's presence and the use of visual material (slides) to enhance visualization of the flooding material (Sherry & Levine, 1980). In this study, the scenes were also presented either directly by the therapist or by audio tape. The audio tape presentation was as effective as the live, but there was an overall enhancement of effectiveness due to the therapist's presence during a session. Interestingly, the provision of visual material did not increase the effectiveness of treatment.

As with systematic desensitization, flooding may be conducted imaginally, using verbal descriptions of fear-provoking stimuli and their imagination by the client, or *in vivo* with the actual feared objects or contexts re-created in the therapeutic setting or at appropriate locations to which the client is transported. Evidence consistently shows that flooding using imaginal stimuli is effective and may occasionally be preferable when the stimuli in question would be difficult to utilize for actual exposure experiences. Girodo (1974) reported the successful use of flooding in imagination for the treatment of anxiety that had proved intractable in the face of yoga meditation treatment. Wijesinghe (1974) reported the successful use of flooding while the patient was in a hypnotic trance for the treatment of a vomiting phobia. This case provides a good example of some advantages to the imaginal type of treatment since some of the stimuli involved social situations, such as standing in a crowded subway train.

Blanchard (1975) reports an interesting use of imaginal flooding in the treatment of a debilitating revulsion. In this case, a woman came to feel revolt and anger at the sight of infants or pregnant women. It happened that in an earlier pregnancy her own fetus had died in the seventh month and a spontaneous abortion did not occur for two months. She had known that the fetus was dead and her physician advised her to wait for a spontaneous abortion to occur. During that period, she repeatedly visited her obstetrician and, in the waiting room, was consistently engaged in conversation by other expectant mothers about how her pregnancy was going, weren't babies lovely, and so forth. Not surprisingly, through these experiences both anger and revulsion were apparently conditioned to both pregnant women and babies. After only two flooding sessions involving images of interactions with pregnant women and infants, the woman reported that the scenes no longer elicited hostility or anger. As Figure 7–14 illustrates, the flooding produced significant improvements in the woman's ability to approach pregnant women in a behavioral test, as well as in her attitudes toward them. Treatment benefits extended to her interaction with her husband (she had been separated for a time before therapy), as one might expect, but those benefits seem to be nonspecific outcomes of overall therapeutic interactions and not the result of flooding treatment.

There has been some investigation of the differential effects of imaginal and *in vivo* flooding treatment. Boulougouris and Bassiakos (1973)

freely combined imaginal and *in vivo* flooding in the treatment of three clients. Although all three improved, the behavior of two of the clients suggested a possible role that imaginal flooding might play in the extinction of fearfulness that *in vivo* flooding might not. Two of the three clients "abreacted" during the flooding sessions at a point when they were recalling in imagination earlier experiences that seemed likely to have provided the initial maladaptive learning for their obsessions. Improvement seemed to occur rapidly after that point. This suggests that while recollection of the original learning experience is not necessary for a successful treatment, it may provide the substance for imaginal components of flooding that allow an original and major stimulus for anxiety to become neutralized. This suggestion is highly speculative, but it appears to warrant exploration.

There are two investigations in which imaginal and *in vivo* flooding have been contrasted, both involving the treatment of agoraphobia (Emmelkamp & Wessels, 1975; Watson, Mullet, & Pillay, 1973). In both studies, while imaginal flooding proved to have beneficial effects for the extinction of anxiety, therapeutic progress appeared much more striking with *in vivo* flooding or "practice" sessions. As we have noted elsewhere, many fear-eliciting stimuli do not lend themselves to *in vivo* presentation, and with many others it would be particularly difficult to include actual practice sessions as part of the treatment. Nevertheless, it would be important to know if the apparent tendency for *in vivo* flooding to have enhanced effectiveness extends to many different categories of fear-eliciting stimuli, or whether it is limited to the treatment of fears that have highly specifiable and commonly encountered stimuli, such as open places (agoraphobia).

Since one basic hypothesis underlying flooding is that anxiety occurs during the period when an avoidance response is prevented, then patients on anxiety-reducing medication would be poor candidates for this type of treatment.

Figure 7–14 *Effectiveness of imaginal flooding during the psychotherapy of a woman with debilitating revulsions. Effects are illustrated upon approach behavior toward the objects of revulsion, and attitudes toward individuals conceptually related to the object of revulsion. Numbers and arrows on the absissa indicate individual therapy sessions.*

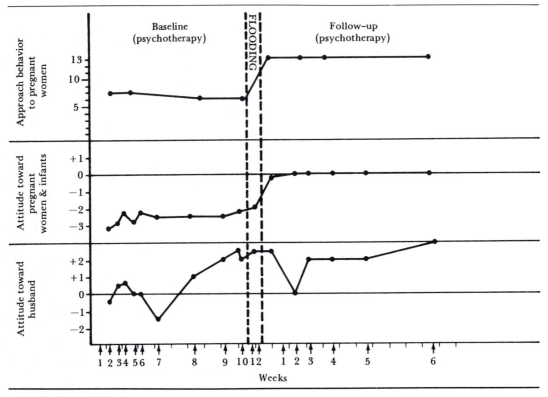

From Blanchard (1975).

Little research has focused on this possibility, and unfortunately the results are mixed. In one study, Kamano (1972) found that individuals who had been given fear-reducing drugs (amobarbital and chlordiazepoxide) actually showed increased avoidance behavior after a flooding treatment. On the other hand, in a study with rats, Baum (1973) found that a fear-reducing drug, chlorpromazine, produced a lower level of avoidance behavior during flooding than did a control manipulator (injecting water) or the injection of a stimulant, methylphenidate. Following treatment, however, there were no differences in the effectiveness of the flooding treatment for the extinction of the avoidance behavior, and Baum suggested that tranquilizing or relaxing drugs might be used to reduce the aversive nature of a flooding treatment regimen.

There are other studies regarding drugs in the use of flooding treatment of phobias in humans to indicate that relaxing drugs such as thiopental (Hussain, 1970, 1971) or tranquilizing/relaxing drugs such as diazepam (Marks, Viswanathan, & Lipsedge, 1972) actually appear to make a flooding treatment more effective. Results of this sort suggest that it is not the amount of fear that occurs during flooding, but rather the prevention of any avoidance behavior in the presence of the fear-provoking stimulus that produces the elimination of both the avoidance behavior and, to some extent, the fear. On the other hand, one study has suggested that at least one drug (bruntal), which reduces anxiety, interferes with the effectiveness of flooding (Chambless, Foa, Groves, & Goldstein, 1979). There are insufficient data to resolve this question, and further research seems clearly warranted, though research interest in this procedure seems to have waned significantly.

Several studies have compared flooding with systematic desensitization in terms of effectiveness and brevity of treatment. Strahley (1965) found flooding more effective than systematic desensitization, although there was no nontreatment control in this study. Yule and associates (1974) found flooding to be effective in eliminating a noise phobia after desensitization had failed, and the resulting improvement was maintained during a 25-month follow-up. Brock (1967), in an experimental analogue study, found no significant differences in effectiveness between flooding and systematic desensitization, but again the no-treatment control was absent. De Moor (1970) found both flooding and systematic desensitization to be effective in reducing fear, with some suggestion that systematic desensitization produced better results at a later, follow-up test. As with other studies, however, there are problems with this experiment because of the use of inappropriately short periods of flooding (though they were four times as long as the periods of relaxation training). Suárez, McCutcheon, and Adams (1976) also found flooding to be effective, but less so than systematic desensitization. In working with speech-anxious college students, Calef and MacLean (1970) found that flooding and systematic desensitization both produced improvements on the Taylor Manifest Anxiety Scale and on a personal-report scale of speaker confidence, but no measure of actual public-speaking behavior was included.

Rachman (1966a) treated three subjects who had spider phobias with flooding and compared them to three subjects treated earlier by systematic desensitization and three subjects in a no-treatment control. In Rachman's flooding procedure, subjects were to imagine fear-provoking scenes for 2 minutes while the therapist "vivified" the experience through verbal elaboration. There were 10 trials per session with 20 minutes of flooding. This study found that flooding produced no improvement on either an actual avoidance test or the fear thermometer, whereas systematic desensitization did result in improvement.

In a well-designed and well-executed study, Boulougouris and associates (1971) gave phobic clients six sessions of flooding, followed by six sessions of systematic desensitization, or six sessions each in the reverse order. After the initial six sessions, they found that flooding produced greater improvement in terms of ratings by therapist and an independent medical assessor on both total phobic behavior and behavior related to the phobia under treatment, and in terms of skin conductance measures of anxiety during a discussion of the phobic object. When the investigators analyzed measures taken after either the flooding or desensitization sessions, regardless of whether they came first or second in the overall treatment, flooding produced greater improvement than systematic desensitization on five out of seven measures of anxiety and phobic behavior. In terms of mean scores, flooding showed greater positive effects than systematic desensitization on all seven.

There have been two types of investigations involving the use of modeling and flooding treatments for the management of anxiety: studies that assess the comparative efficacy of the two procedures, and studies that explore the possible advantages of combining modeling and flooding procedures. The results regarding the relative effectiveness of modeling and flooding treatments are mixed. Rachman and his colleagues (Hodgson, Rachman, & Marks, 1972; Rachman, Hodgson, & Marks, 1971; Rachman et al., 1973) had reported several studies contrasting modeling alone, flooding alone, or a combination of the two in terms of their effectiveness for eliminating obsessive-compulsive behavior problems.

In these investigations, the modeling procedure also included a graduated exposure to eliciting stimuli and thus represents an amalgam of graduated extinction and modeling techniques. In these investigations, both modeling and flooding appeared to have therapeutic effectiveness, but there was little indication that a combined treatment package was any better. As one patient remarked, "I *know* other people don't have trouble with this, therefore watching you doesn't help at all." This may indicate that the modeling procedure utilized was simply weak and effective only for some patients. The investigators did note that modeling appeared to be of particular value to some patients but not to others, although there was no way to determine this in advance. Interestingly, one study, which utilized rats as subjects, produced results indicating that observing another individual in the presence of a fear-provoking stimulus does not make an avoidance response enhance the effectiveness of a flooding procedure for the elimination of similar phobic avoidance behaviors (Uno et al., 1973).

In a study that compared modeling, desensitization, and flooding procedures in the treatment of test anxiety, Horne and Matson (1977) found that modeling was most effective, followed by desensitization and then flooding. Preferences of individuals undergoing treatment also seemed to follow this order. Although nearly all individuals reported satisfaction with modeling and about half did with desensitization, even though flooding had a significant effect in reducing test anxiety, the individuals who

experienced this treatment said that they would not recommend it to others because of the discomfort it produced.

Thus, the evidence appears mixed regarding the relative effectiveness of flooding and modeling procedures. It is difficult to provide any real conclusion, since there are only a few studies in the literature and they have included widely varied types of fearful behavior. It seems appropriate to conclude that flooding was an effective treatment in most cases, even though its effectiveness was occasionally less than that of an alternative treatment procedure. A tentative recommendation with regard to modeling versus flooding procedures is that when there seems to be little reason to select one or the other in terms of likely effectiveness, modeling should be chosen rather than flooding because of the latter's implicit aversive characteristics.

Flooding has also been compared to graduated extinction in its effectiveness in eliminating fearful behavior. Everaerd and colleagues (1973) utilized both imaginal and *in vivo* flooding in the treatment of agoraphobia and contrasted its effectiveness with a successive approximation procedure. The treatments were equally effective in producing an improved ability to tolerate open spaces. But the successive approximation procedure also led to decreased levels of generalized anxiety, whereas flooding produced increased levels of anxiety, as indicated on a phobic anxiety scale. Kandel and associates (1977) treated two young boys who showed extreme social withdrawal by both flooding and systematic exposure to peers. Treatments were implemented through the cooperation of several peers who acted as social stimuli. For one boy, flooding was introduced first and followed by the systematic exposure treatment. The reverse order was used for the other child. When flooding was used first, social interaction immediately rose from 0 to 60 percent, but generalized to a new setting only when flooding was again introduced in that context. The use of systematic exposure produced similar effects. Taken together, these investigations indicate that there is no reason to believe that flooding procedures are either more or less effective than graduated extinction. The selection of one treatment program over the other should depend on other factors, such as ease of implementation and preference of the individual (or parents, in the case of children).

There is one report in the literature contrasting the effectiveness of flooding and thought stopping in the treatment of obsessions (Hackman & McLean, 1975). Although both treatments were effective, flooding tended to produce greater overall improvement and greater reduction in avoidance behavior.

A recurrent theme in much of the recent literature on behavior therapy is the design of treatment regimens that address a client's problems with more than a single therapeutic procedure if there are different goals to be accomplished for an overall effective outcome. This is illustrated in two studies by Marshall, Parker, and Hayes (1982) in which flooding, skills training, and modeling procedures were all applied to the treatment of a public speaking phobia. Although each of the procedures, separately, showed some effectiveness, the combination of all was judged to be most powerful and efficient. The type of overall "package" that emerges is one that includes a focus on new behaviors and competencies to be acquired as well as the elimination of problem behaviors, cognitions, or fears. This broad spectrum approach is reflected also in the concern for providing alternative behaviors when punishment is used (see Chapter 8) and in the upsurge of interest in social skills training (see Chapters 5 and 6).

Evidence for the Effectiveness of Implosive Therapy and Flooding (Response Prevention): An Evaluation

There is no question that the results of studies concerned with the effectiveness of implosive therapy and flooding (or response prevention) are mixed, and many of the early studies tended to be so methodologically poor as to be inconclusive (Morganstern, 1973). In general, however, the studies evaluating the effectiveness of flooding procedures have generally been better designed and executed than those that evaluated implosive therapy. Until the mid-1970s, there were few studies of flooding involving human patients (as opposed to animals), so the effectiveness of flooding had to be interpreted cautiously. Although this period showed an upswing in research on these procedures (e.g., Marshall et al., 1982), there has been little in the way of recent research on issues relevant to these techniques.

In this section, we have discussed implosion and flooding separately because they have diverse origins and, to some extent, theoretical groundings. Since some therapists who employ implosive techniques still develop stimuli for particular patients through the use of psychodynamic rationales, whereas those who employ flooding do not, and since implosion involves the distinct elaboration of anxiety-provoking stimuli but flooding does not, and since because of this elaboration implosion is necessarily an imaginal technique while flooding may be either imaginal or *in vivo*, perhaps there are reasons to maintain this distinction. However, discarding for the moment any consideration of psychodynamic components of anxiety-eliciting stimuli, it is perhaps most straightforward to consider the class of anxiety-inducing therapeutic procedures as a single category and then distinguish subclasses on the basis of procedural differences in implementation. There would be, then, imaginal and *in vivo* procedures. The subclass of imaginal procedures would involve the elaboration of imaginal stimuli beyond the bounds of reality in order to maximize the induced anxiety (implosion) and include only descriptions of events and stimuli that are possible occurrences in the life of the client (flooding). The significance of the latter distinctions has not been established by research, but this seems an important direction for future inquiry.

All the techniques rely upon a basic assumption that the anxiety-eliciting properties of stimuli or events may be extinguished if the anxiety is elicited *and* dreaded outcomes do not occur and avoidance behavior is prevented. Some evidence is accruing that this is indeed the mechanism by which the procedures gain their effectiveness, but much more research is warranted in this regard.

It continues to be difficult to provide an overall evaluation of the effectiveness of implosive or flooding procedures. Although there is a relatively large number of reports in the literature—both case studies and experimental investigations—a proportion of them continue to report either a failure of the basic technique or less therapeutic effectiveness in comparison with another form of behavior therapy. Although there seems to be dwindling interest in anxiety induction procedures, perhaps for humane or ethical reasons, a more conclusive evaluation may be possible in the future as research results accrue. One noteworthy observation from a review of the present literature is the general absence of recent reports on abortive effects, such as sensitization or maladaptive increases in anxious responding, as a negative consequence of treatment. Indeed, Shipley and Bouderwius (1980) specifically surveyed 70 practitioners to determine the frequency of negative side effects. Of nearly 3,500 cases treated, only two clients were reported to have suffered adverse side effects. Thus, it seems reasonable to conclude tentatively that anxiety-inducing techniques are a valid set of procedures for the treatment of anxiety-related behavior disorders. But it may be preferable to use alternative behavior therapy techniques when they can be readily implemented, because there is little evidence that they will be less effective, there is some evidence that they will be more effective, and there is evidence that they will be preferred to anxiety-inducing techniques by the client or patient because of the aversive characteristics of implosive and flooding procedures.

Thus, although the techniques appear to have generated some positive results, more research is clearly necessary before specific statements can be made with regard to their effectiveness. In the absence of such research, the clinician should consider carefully any inclination to employ these techniques. If they are utilized, it seems most prudent that therapeutic procedures be matched carefully—to the point of identity—with those presented in the literature, including even the details of the therapist's monologue in implosive therapy (see the earlier example in this chapter). Tapes exist modeling the styles of presentation. Finally, the possibility of inadvertent sensitization and other potential ill effects demands that the use of implosive therapy and flooding be accompanied by caution at least as great as that employed in the use of techniques of aversive control.

8

Punishment and Aversion Procedures

In many cases, the goal of behavior change is to eliminate a troublesome, inappropriate, dangerous, illegal, or damaging pattern of behavior. A treatment goal for an alcoholic is the elimination, or at least the reduction, of drinking. A person who exhibits deviant sexual behavior, especially if it includes the coercion of others or the involvement of children, should acquire abilities of restraint and should learn to find different sexual activities attractive. The aggressive or intrusive child must learn to inhibit such behavior in contexts where it is unacceptable and must acquire alternative behaviors that are both effective and socially agreeable. In many of these cases, a corollary goal for behavior change is the development of alternative patterns of behavior that are adaptive and appropriate, and that conform to social standards. A reduction in deviant sexual behavior may thus be paired with an increase in skills relating to appropriate sexual interaction and an increase in the frequency of such behavior. The hyperactive, aggressive child will be advantaged if reductions in aggression or intrusive behavior are accompanied by increased cooperative and responsive patterns of social interaction.

Techniques of aversive control, especially punishment, are appropriate for situations that require the elimination of problem behaviors. As we note elsewhere (see Chapters 5 and 6), other techniques may be effective in reducing maladaptive behavior through the strengthen-

ing of alternative, adaptive behavior. When there is a choice, the more positive, nonaversive therapeutic procedures are preferable if only on ethical grounds. Although this chapter concentrates on punishment and aversion techniques, this emphasis does not reflect their frequency of use. In fact, they are *not* used frequently. Because aversion procedures are indeed aversive, they must be employed only when effective alternatives are unavailable and with special attention to issues of ethics and the overall welfare of clients. In addition, they must always be implemented with special care and precision. For these reasons, we treat aversion procedures in some detail, but we again caution against overgeneralizing or exaggerating their role in the broad armamentarium of behavior therapy techniques.

Although it is true that aversive control measures are uniquely qualified to eliminate maladaptive behavior, the range of techniques and processes constituting aversive control is often underestimated. Therapists tend to give too little attention to the ways that such measures can be used to *enhance adaptive behavior*. In this chapter, we will be concerned with the entire range of impact that punishment and aversion procedures can have on behavior. These include (1) punishment to reduce the frequency of maladaptive behavior; (2) sensitization and aversive counterconditioning—the conditioning of aversive characteristics to stimuli and behaviors that replace or counter their positive characteristics; (3) negative reinforcement to increase the frequency of adaptive behaviors that prevent or terminate aversive consequences; and (4) appetitive counterconditioning—the conditioning of positive characteristics to stimuli or behaviors that are currently neutral or aversive but that should be attractive.

Thus, there are two basic dimensions to the techniques of aversive control: (1) the dimension of *contingency,* in which either the onset or the termination of an aversive stimulus is made contingent upon a particular behavior; and (2) the dimension of *counterconditioning,* in a classical conditioning model, in which the *valence* or attractiveness of either a behavior or a stimulus is altered through being paired with the aversive event itself (thereby lowering the attractiveness) or with the termination of the aversive event (thereby increasing the attractiveness because the termination of an aversive event is a positive experience).

Some examples will illustrate procedures that utilize these different influences and their effects upon behavior. Let us take the case of a small child who repeatedly snitches cookies from the cookie jar against his parents' wishes. The child takes cookies because he really likes them, and because they reduce his appetite and let him get away with not eating very much dinner, including the green vegetables and milk he dislikes. The goal of behavior change is to eliminate cookie snitching. One method of aversive control would be contingent punishment: mother could slap the child's hand or sternly lecture him after catching him in the act. Another type of punishment would be *response cost:* mother could tell the child that there will be no television that evening because of his bad behavior. A counterconditioning procedure could also be used: mother could sit the child down and insist that he eat cookies until he is green in the face and feels terrible, an experience likely to reduce the attractiveness of cookies in the future and assist in self-control. Alternatively, if a house rule is that the child may have crackers before dinner, but not cookies, a

positive counterconditioning procedure could enhance the attractiveness of crackers: mother might allow the child to read a new comic book or watch "Sesame Street" while eating a couple of crackers before dinner. Similarly, attempts could be made to enhance the attractiveness of vegetables and milk by allowing the child to watch interesting television shows only as long as the vegetables and milk are being consumed.

Many behavior therapy procedures utilizing aversive control combine contingency and counterconditioning aspects or contain more than one contingency or counterconditioning procedure. A male client who wishes to change a homosexual orientation may be involved in a treatment procedure, such as the following. A slide of a nude male is displayed on a screen. After a few seconds, an unpleasant electric shock is administered to the client's wrist (punishment contingent upon incipient sexual arousal and lingering attention to a homosexual stimulus). The shock continues for a second or two while the nude slide continues to be displayed. This is a counterconditioning procedure in which the pain and anxiety associated with the shock can become attached, through classical conditioning, to the homosexual stimulus, replacing the standard positive valence of the stimulus. The client may also be given the option of pressing a button that terminates the slide of the nude male and replaces it with one of an attractive nude female, at the same time terminating the shock. This involves both contingency and counterconditioning. The positive feeling of relief associated with the termination of the shock reinforces the client's behavior of diverting attention away from a homosexual stimulus and toward a heterosexual one. The positive feeling of relief and anxiety reduction that lingers during the first few seconds of viewing the nude female slide imparts a positive valence to such stimuli and has anxiety-reducing value that is counter to the anxiety-producing quality heterosexual stimuli may have had for the client previously. An extention of this treatment would include enhancing the attractiveness of clothed females and would also be likely to include positive training (through modeling and contingency management) for appropriating social skills with women.

In this chapter, we will be concerned with the effectiveness of procedures that involve aversive stimuli or experiences for changing both overt behavior and cognitive components, such as the attractiveness or preferred status of certain activities or stimuli. Although aversive events are involved in the procedures, we will not always be concerned simply with the elimination of a problem behavior. As the preceding example illustrates, procedures designed to alter a person's sexual orientation may have two separate goals: elimination of the frequency of homosexual behavior and the attractiveness of homosexual stimuli, and the simultaneous enhancement of heterosexual behavior and coordinate increase in the attractiveness of heterosexual stimuli. In that example, the termination of the aversive stimulus (shock) constituted a positive event spelling relief from pain and anxiety, and these attributes of the aversive control procedure were used to augment desired forms of behavior and preferences.

In the process of discussing both the suppressing and augmenting effects of aversive control procedures, we will also repeatedly examine two very basic conditioning processes that are used to interpret the cognitive and behavioral effects: operant and classical conditioning. Contingent aspects of aversive procedures achieve their effects on behavior according to principles of operant or instrumental conditioning: the contingent onset of an aversive stimulus is a punisher and should reduce the frequency of the behavior on which it is contingent; the contingent termination of an aversive stimulus is a positive experience that operates as a reinforcer, increasing the frequency of any behavior on which it is contingent; and the contingent termination or withdrawal of a reinforcer is aversive and will act to decrease the frequency of the behavior on which it is contingent. Counterconditioning procedures concentrate on the opportunities for classical conditioning to occur, in which charac-

teristics of the aversive stimulus or its termination may become associated with stimuli or behaviors that occur at the same time. Behaviors or stimuli that occur during aversive stimulation tend to acquire negative characteristics, such as the tendency to evoke anxiety, whereas those that occur at the termination of aversive stimulation tend to acquire positive characteristics, such as the tendency to reduce anxiety or to promote a feeling of well-being.

Definition of Terms

In this chapter, we will cover two broad classes of aversive control procedures, punishment and counterconditioning. Several different learning processes may be involved in a given procedure of aversive control, but these two basic classifications provide the clearest method of grouping different techniques according to their primary modus operandi.

Recall from the chapters on contingency management procedures that two types of reinforcers exist: positive and negative. The contingent application of a positive reinforcer, or the contingent termination or withdrawal of a negative reinforcer, increases the frequency of a response. In this chapter, we define the opposites of these two procedures as constituting *punishment*. Punishment involves the withdrawal of a positive or rewarding stimulus, or the application of an aversive, unpleasant stimulus. Throughout this chapter, the terms *punisher*, *aversive stimulus*, and *aversive event* are used interchangeably, since even the mere withdrawal of positive reinforcers is generally aversive. In the techniques that we will discuss, those involving the contingent administration of an aversive stimulus, such as shock, are referred to as *contingent punishment* procedures, whereas techniques involving the termination or withdrawal of positive events (reinforcers) have more specific names. *Response cost* is a general term for the contingent withdrawal of reinforcement, and *time-out* refers to a specific procedure in which an individual is isolated from social contact or general access to reinforcing objects or activities for a period of time. Time-out may include withholding a specific reinforcer, but usually the term refers to the general isolation from all reinforcers inherent in the normal social environment.

The other classification of aversive control techniques involving counterconditioning includes two distinct types. The most common procedure involving counterconditioning is *sensitization* or *aversive counterconditioning*. Whereas punishment includes the contingent, *consequent* application of a negative reinforcer, aversive counterconditioning involves the *simultaneous* application of a negative stimulus (aversive event). That is, the negative stimulus is applied *at the same time* the individual is perceiving the stimuli that elicit the problem behaviors or is performing the problem behavior. The goal of this procedure is to eliminate problem behavior, not by suppressing performance, but by altering the effectiveness or the *valence* of the eliciting stimulus rather than by affecting the problem behavior itself. It is termed "aversive counterconditioning" for theoretical rather than descriptive reasons. The effectiveness of this technique is due to the classical conditioning of the internal discomfort produced by the aversive stimulus to the perceptual derivatives (sight, sound, smell, taste) of the stimulus (or response), so that eventually the stimulus (or response) alone is no longer attractive and may now in fact produce feelings of discomfort similar to those produced by the aversive stimulus. (This model is discussed in the section on theoretical concerns.)

"Aversive" refers to the nature of the stimulus typically employed (emetics, electric shock, paralyzing drugs, imagination of noxious scenes). "Counterconditioning" refers to the assumption that the original, positive, appetitive value of the stimulus was learned (conditioned); this procedure replaces or counters that learning by substituting the discomfort and desires for avoidance that accompany the aversive stimulus. Note the similarity between this analysis and Wolpe's theoretical conceptualiza-tion of the effect of desensitization (relaxation responses replace anxiety responses through a process of counterconditioning).

A second type of counterconditioning depends upon the one negative reinforcing component that is inherent in every aversive experience: its *termination*. In this procedure, the termination of an aversive event and the attendant lingering positive experience of relief and anxiety reduction are paired with a stimulus or behavior that currently has low attractiveness or may even be aversive (e.g., a picture of a nude female for a male homosexual). The counterconditioning intended in this procedure is the replacement of a neutral or negative valence with the positive reactions generated by the termination of an aversive stimulus. This procedure may be termed *appetitive counterconditioning*, which describes the goal of increasing the attractiveness of paired stimuli or behaviors. Appetitive counterconditioning is most often, and most naturally, combined with aversive counterconditioning. Maladaptive behavior and preferences are elicited during continuing aversive stimulation (e.g., a male homosexual views slides of nude males while experiencing a prolonged shock), but then the aversive stimulus is terminated when the client performs an appropriate behavior or sees a stimulus whose attractiveness is to be increased (when the client presses a button, the male slide is replaced with one of a nude female and the shock is terminated).

Within the class of counterconditioning procedures that combine both aversive and appetitive counterconditioning, a distinction is sometimes made between aversion-relief and anxiety-relief counterconditioning. In both cases, the "relief" portion of the term refers to the appetitive counterconditioning that occurs during the period of relief that follows the termination of the aversive stimulus. *Aversion-relief* refers to procedures in which an actual aversive stimulus is experienced, such as a shock or nausea. In some procedures, a client may be allowed to *avoid* the aversive stimulus by actively doing something before it occurs, which reduces the anxiety that accompanies anticipation of the aversive stimulus. For example, a male homosexual client may receive a shock while viewing a slide of a nude male, but the shock may occur only after 5 or 10 seconds of viewing, or perhaps after as many as 20 seconds. Once the slide is projected, anxiety presumably arises in the client because of the anticipation of shock. If he presses a button to switch to the slide of a nude female before the shock occurs, some aversive counterconditioning may still have occurred because the anxiety was paired with the viewing of the nude male. Some relief will also occur because the anxiety dissipates as soon as the nude female slide appears. In classical learning theory terms, aversion-relief counterconditioning corresponds closely to escape learning, whereas anxiety-relief counterconditioning corresponds to avoidance learning. We will not consider these two procedures separately, because even though differences have been demonstrated between escape and avoidance learning paradigms, there has been no consistent demonstration of differences in effectiveness between aversion-relief and anxiety-relief counterconditioning.

Ethical and Procedural Concerns in the Use of Aversive Control Techniques

The pros and cons of employing aversive control *must* be considered carefully. There is a deserved general distaste for intentionally caused pain or discomfort, and the potential for harm that accompanies some aversive stimuli cannot be taken lightly. Society has generally frowned upon the intentional infliction of pain except under certain well-specified conditions and at the hands of particular agents. Parents may spank their children with little formal justification, but the schools are generally more cautious about using this technique of punishment. Parents may send their children to bed without supper, but institutions are occasionally

prevented from depriving patients of cigarettes or meals even when the attempt is not to punish, but to create more powerful reinforcers. Legal authorities have been able to order the execution of individuals (military authorities may do so quite summarily during time of war, and the old Blue Laws of Connecticut specified that a father could kill a disobedient son [Blue Laws of Connecticut, 1861, Section 14, p. 69]), but the use of torture has long been prohibited. Certainly there are many inconsistencies between the formal, legal sanctions and the informal, societal sanctions granted certain forms of punishment, and it is quite unfortunate that so many obviously inhumane practices continue to have any sanction at all, especially since they may be ineffective in controlling behavior.

Unfortunately, by definition, aversive control will always involve the infliction of discomfort, physical or mental. The mere approval by a client of the use of aversion techniques does not necessarily justify them. Clearly, however, a client's informed approval is necessary before application of these techniques can be considered. Probably the two most basic justifications for the use of aversion procedures are (1) evidence or professional judgment that they will be effective in changing a person's behavior in the desired direction, leaving no residual ill effects, either physical or mental; and (2) evidence or judgment that no alternative, nonaversive procedures are likely to be effective. Such cautions in the use of aversion techniques point to the negative aspect of aversive control: more than any other type of behavior modification procedure, aversion techniques have an inherent possibility of causing physical or psychological harm to a client if they are used incorrectly.[1] Note, however, that they contain the *possibility*, not the *probability*, of causing harm.

---

[1] This admonition extends to other techniques that are not grouped with procedures of aversive control but which are nevertheless aversive in nature: *viz.*, implosive or flooding (response prevention) techniques for the elimination of fears (Chapter 7).

Aversive control must never employ punishing consequences at an intensity likely to harm an individual. When *misused,* harm is often a possible result.

The point is clear: the use of aversion techniques *must* be carefully considered and monitored to ensure that the client is in no physical danger. In no case should they be employed without the direct supervision of doctorally trained therapists who are experts in the use of such techniques. A great many safeguards are absolutely necessary to preserve the safety and rights of any client undergoing treatment utilizing aversion techniques, including (1) the client's voluntary, informed consent to the use of aversion techniques; (2) his clear understanding of the right to withdraw such consent at any time, even after treatment has begun; (3) clear evidence of due process according to current legal and moral consent; and (4) legal representation for individuals who are not responsible for their own decisions (e.g., children, some handicapped individuals, or psychotic patients). Many treatment decisions are basically the responsibility of the therapist, but in some instances—and particularly in the case of aversion techniques—that decision cannot rest solely in the hands of the therapist. It should involve consultation with others, such as those responsible for the physical care of the client, hospital administrators if the client is institutionalized, family members or guardians, and the client himself.

Considerations Promoting the Selection of Aversive Control Procedures

The types of disorders contained in the case studies and research reports covered later in this chapter provide a range of examples of problems for which aversion procedures are often deemed appropriate. One broad class of problems for which aversive control is almost invariably the treatment of choice includes the behaviors that physically damage a person and are so frequent or poorly controlled that a decisive intervention procedure is imperative. For example, highly disturbed children and adults may occasionally develop patterns of self-destructive behavior that cause extensive physical harm. Paradoxically, it appears that these behaviors are often maintained by the attention of parents or institutional staff who offer interpersonal contact while physically restraining these patients. That the physical contact offered by caretakers is responsible for these behaviors is indicated in studies showing that self-abusing behavior does indeed decrease in frequency when it ceases to elicit attention and care from others. As an interesting ethical perspective, when seriously maladaptive behavior is likely to respond only to aversion procedures, it may be unethical not to employ them, although this would only be the case when there is insurmountable evidence that aversion procedures are effective and alternative ones are not (Turnbull, 1985).

A basic problem with handling self-destructive behaviors by simple nonreinforcement or extinction procedures is the length of time an extinction procedure requires. Often, also, there is an increase in the frequency of the behavior when reinforcement is initially withdrawn. Although these factors may be tolerated when less dangerous responses are under treatment, self-destructive behavior in psychotic patients often reaches such proportions that the patient's life is endangered. For example, it is not uncommon for self-destructive children to break their own noses, keep their eyes constantly blackened, tear out their nails, or even tear large quantities of flesh from their bodies by gnawing, scratching, or gouging with objects. One such boy hit himself 2,750 times in the space of 1½ hours when restraints were removed and an extinction procedure was instituted. Thus, extinction may be unethical to use in place of punishment.

In the treatment of deviant responses requiring rapid inhibition, intense punishment is an extremely effective procedure. More "humane" treatment of self-destructive patients often involves long-term hospitalization (often for life), during which time the patient is almost continuously restrained. Restraint procedures include using "camisoles" (straitjackets) or tying the patient's arms and legs to the head and foot of a bed, thus effectively keeping him from injuring himself. Such restraints have severely debilitating effects, including demineralization of bones, shortening of tendons, and an increasing loss of the ability to move. Clearly, nonpunitive treatment of patients is not always more "humane" than aversion procedures. As we discuss later, a very few intense punishments can effectively eliminate maladaptive behaviors and provide the opportunity for training in alternative behaviors that are adaptive.

Although our society shows great concern over the use of aversive consequences outside the legal or family domain, not all of this concern centers on the possibility of harm to the individual. Some concern centers on the possibility of inadvertent changes in behavior that can happen rapidly and beyond a therapist's control because of the powerful effects of aversion techniques. However, the fact that negative consequences can be a powerful procedure of behavior therapy need not be a liability. Indeed, though it does make necessary the use of extreme care during application, the fact that aversive events may exert rapid and decisive control over behavior is a primary advantage of this technique.

These considerations refer primarily to the use of contingent punishment as an aversive control technique. Another class of behavior disorders has generally been judged appropriate for treatment by aversion techniques, but for different reasons. Often a problem behavior pattern occurs with high frequency or causes distress to a client because it is strongly elicited by inappropriate stimuli or because it is intrinsically highly rewarding. Consider the heterosexual individual who is overly immersed in sexual desire (a newly coined syndrome of "sexual addiction"). Such an individual who wishes to change his habitual sexual behavior may seek assistance because persons of the opposite sex continue to be so attractive that sexual behavior

cannot be controlled, or because even if overt sexual behavior is avoided, continued intense sexual attractions is exceedingly frustrating.

In short, a client with behavior problems in which the valence of a stimulus or of a behavior itself must be altered—either increased or decreased—is a likely candidate for the aversive control procedure of counterconditioning. Experiences resulting from the abuse of powerful drugs are often highly rewarding, and the effects of such immediate rewards often outweigh later negative consequences, thereby resulting in frequent, habitual drug usage. Similarly, sexual deviations immediately provide rewarding consequences of great strength and maintenance. Behaviors that are intimately linked to highly rewarding, maintaining consequences may require the manipulation of extremely aversive consequences, in addition to counterconditioning procedures, if they are to be brought under effective and long-lasting control.

Aversion techniques, then, may be appropriate for gaining control over behaviors that are either highly rewarding or physically damaging, when control is unlikely to be achieved by other means, or when it must be achieved quickly in order to prevent further damaging effects from the client's current behavior. However, even when aversion procedures are appropriately and carefully employed, certain problems may arise following their use. Such problems, of course, can be prevented or minimized with proper precautions.

Potential Side Effects From Aversive Control Procedures

Conditioned Emotional Responses and Inappropriate Avoidance Responses

Intense punishment has the capacity to condition anxiety to all stimuli and behavior at the time of punishment (aversive counterconditioning). Any response that serves to terminate the punishment or to remove the anxiety-evoking stimuli will be reinforced by the termination of that anxiety. Hence, it is possible for avoidance responses, which carry their own reinforcement (the termination of the internal state of anxiety), to develop and become powerful new responses to the stimuli that previously elicited the punished response, as well as to other stimuli that are present during punishment. It is common to feel discomfort when entering a room in which an unfortunate aversive experience has occurred. Another example may be seen in the behavior of a dog who becomes hand-shy after punishment administered by his master's hand rather than by a rolled-up newspaper. This procedure constitutes escape training with some aversive counterconditioning.

Punishment intensity is a factor that may enter into the possible development of a conditioned emotional response. As noted earlier, in aversive counterconditioning, the aversive stimulus is presented during the performance of the undesired response or during the presentation of stimuli that usually evoke the undesired response. The purpose of this procedure is to alter the valence of these stimuli or responses by conditioning the emotional concomitants of punishment directly to them. In this case, obviously, the therapist would want punishment of sufficient intensity to elicit an emotional response, because the emotional response would not be problematic: it is the desired outcome. Even in this case, however, punishment of too great an intensity may drive the client from therapy: the client may have conditioned the emotional response to the entire therapy situation! One may, of course, err in the other direction by administering an aversive stimulus whose intensity is too mild. In such cases, the desired counterconditioning, or inhibition of behavior, will not be accomplished. The stimulus must be truly aversive to accomplish the desired ends. Careful consideration by the therapist is necessary in selecting the proper intensity. Granting the necessity to avoid physical harm, a rule of thumb might be to adjust the intensity (awareness) of the punishment employed to the maximum that will be endured by the client.

In contrasting techniques of positive control (reinforcement) with aversive control, it has also been proposed that punishment is generally inefficient because aversive stimuli of high intensity create a general disruption in behavior and thereby impede learning. Undoubtedly, this is true to some extent, but we should note that the problem is not unique to aversive control. It has long been known that reinforcement of high magnitude disrupts learning, and the retention of acquired behavior patterns and preference for these patterns is also disrupted by the use of high-magnitude rewards.

Behavioral Rigidity

Another potential problem is that changes in behavior accomplished by aversion procedures may be of such strength that they become a rigid part of the person's repertoire and may not be replaced, temporarily or permanently, with different behaviors when they are more appropriate. When working with children, often the problems presented are those of behaviors that are appropriate for adults, but judged inappropriate when displayed by children. For example, sexual curiosity or exploratory sexual behavior by children may be deemed quite undesirable and severely punished. Although such punishment may effectively inhibit the sexual behavior, a child who is severely punished for exploratory sexual behavior may develop anxiety as a generalized response to sexual behavior and stimuli. Later in life, when sexual behavior is deemed appropriate and even desirable, such a person may find himself impotent, inhibited, or simply unmotivated toward appropriate sexual encounters. At this point, the results of prior "successful" behavior therapy may become grist for further modification procedures!

Often the suppression of behavior by punishment is extremely transitory, and the behavior may reappear within a relatively short period of time unless other modification procedures have established behaviors alternative to the punished ones. However, some classes of behavior seem extremely sensitive to punishment. Behaviors related to an organism's survival *(consummatory behaviors)*, such as eating, drinking, and sexual behavior, are extremely sensitive to punishment, and caution should be used when working with such behaviors, especially if some flexibility is desired, not general inhibition.

Generalization of Punishment Effects and the Availability of Alternative Behaviors

When a behavior is punished within a given stimulus context, care should be taken to provide an alternative behavior deemed appropriate and acceptable. Suppression of a behavior by punishment may produce either extensive behavioral inhibition—the individual will do nothing at all in the relevant situation—or, if no specific alternative is provided, the next behavior in the individual's personal hierarchy may appear, and this behavior may not be appropriate either. For example, if a child were punished for physically assaultive behavior toward his parents when he did not get his own way, the assaultive behavior might drop out, but the child might yell, stomp out of the room, or even cry (a response typical of an earlier period in his development). Modeling the appropriate skills of asking with tact and politeness would be good accompaniments to such treatment, since they would probably meet with a modicum of success from appreciative adults and become relatively enduring components of the child's behavioral repertoire.

The therapist can also prevent the uncontrolled generalization of punishment effects by clearly labeling the behaviors being punished and designating the alternative behaviors that are acceptable and that will not elicit negative consequences. Discriminations may also be encouraged by clear labeling that designates not only the appropriate and inappropriate behaviors, but also the times, places, conditions, and people in whose presence the desired behaviors are appropriate and will elicit reinforcement rather than punishment.

Negative Modeling

Another problem that may arise from the use of aversion techniques is the client's acquisition of the skill and predilection for administering similar aversive stimuli to others. Thus, a child who is punished physically by his parents for assaultive behavior in the home may become quite well behaved at home but be physically aggressive toward his peers and adults in other situations. This problem is most likely to arise with children, especially when the modification procedures occur in a naturalistic environment, such as the home (see the chapters on contingency management procedures).

Premature Use of Aversion Techniques

Finally, one of the more hidden negative components of aversion techniques, primarily punishment, is their tendency to be reinforcing to the agents applying them, because they control a behavior in another individual that was bothersome or aversive to them. For example, the use of strong punishment to control the intrusive behavior of a child may, by its effectiveness, incline a parent to use punishment in future instances with increasing frequency. Techniques of aversive behavior control may also provide a reinforcement outlet for anger, one that may be considered legally or even professionally sanctioned. Recall the example cited earlier of the Connecticut law allowing a father to kill a disobedient son, an extreme instance in which legal justification would sanction an incident that may have been solely motivated by the anger of a father. There is always the possibility that an aversion technique, such as punishment, will produce more rapid (often immediate) changes in behavior than will a positive alternative, and this might incline someone to adopt the aversion technique even when more humane alternatives are appropriate and would have as lasting or even more lasting effects.

Summary

In short, we must stress the fact that aversion techniques, especially punishment, are rarely utilized *alone*. Their effectiveness will be maximized and potential problems minimized when they are used in conjunction with other techniques designed to promote more effective behavior patterns. Such combined procedures can hasten the change process. They can also complement improvements in the person's behavior by eliminating undesired behaviors while simultaneously adding desired ones. But, whenever possible, alternative procedures to those of aversive control are surely to be preferred.

During the early 1980s, there appears to have been a reduction in the amount of published research dealing with procedures of aversive control. We have noted elsewhere (see the chapters on contingency management) how other techniques have received increasing attention (e.g., social skills training). One interpretation for these apparent trends is that there is an increasing concern with the ethics of employing aversion procedures when more positive alternatives might be available. Supporting this interpretation is the increase in examples being provided for *mild* aversive stimuli (e.g., water squirts) that may serve as effective punishers, thus supplanting more aversive and potentially less ethical means. Another factor influencing a shift of attention to other techniques may be a sensitivity to the need to provide training in alternative, adaptive behavior while at the same time employing aversion techniques to eliminate maladaptive ones (cf. Josiassen, Fantuzzo, & Rosen, 1980). For example, the aversive deconditioning of inappropriate sexual behavior (e.g., pedophilia) may be paired with social skills training for appropriate social and sexual behavior (Josiassen et al., 1980). This is not to say that there has been a wholesale rejection of

aversion procedures. Rather, it still is recognized that in some instances, such as cases requiring the rapid cessation of harmful behavior or changes in the valence or attractiveness of stimuli, aversion procedures may be the treatment choice—and, as noted earlier, it might even be unethical to employ less effective but nonaversive procedures, because of the harm that would ensue from their ineffectiveness (Turnbull, 1985).

Punishment: Procedures of Contingent Aversive Control

The use of contingent punishment is the most common aversion technique employed in naturalistic socialization and is often incorrectly viewed as the essential, or only, method of aversion control. There are several ways in which punishment can be employed. First of all, punishment can be administered immediately following the occurrence of a problem behavior. This procedure typically produces rapid suppression of the punished behavior, although the behavior may recur if there is no alternative behavior that the individual can perform successfully in situations that usually elicit the problem behavior. It is also important for punishment to occur immediately following the problem behavior, because the longer the lag between the termination of behavior and the occurrence of punishment, the less effective the punishment will be in suppressing the behavior.

If punishment is applied *while* the behavior is actually occurring, it must be terminated as soon as the behavior terminates. This timing is important, because the negative reinforcement inherent in the termination of a punishment will reinforce the act of terminating the problem behavior. It is also likely, in this procedure, that since the aversive event and the problem behavior overlap in time, the problem behavior will acquire an aversive valence by virtue of having been paired with the aversive event—an example of counterconditioning that combines with punishment to foster a change in behavior.

A caution so obvious it hardly bears mentioning is that some problem behaviors may well be exacerbated by the use of punishment. Obviously, in such cases, punishment should not be employed. Examples of such behaviors include certain aggressive responses for which punishment might well be seen as counteraggression and could serve as an inappropriate model, thus increasing subsequent aggression. Tantrum behavior is another class of behaviors generally exacerbated by punishment. Finally, any behavior that is a common response to punishment or anxiety is not likely to be reduced by punishment. Attention seeking, nonassertive dependency, and the attachment or dependent behaviors of young children are common examples of this class of behavior.

The therapist should always take into account several dimensions of punishment procedures, to maximize the likelihood that the punishment procedure will be effective in the suppression of problem behavior. These procedures are noted in Table 8–1. For greatest effectiveness, a contingent aversive stimulus should be of maximal appropriate intensity from the very start, should be of the greatest intensity possible (but not so intense as to inflict physical damage, totally disrupt behavior, or produce a conditioned emotional response), should follow a problem behavior immediately, and should follow every occurrence of a problem behavior. Whenever possible, the therapist should note or suggest an alternative behavior so the individual can use it to "crowd out" the problem behavior, while at the same time providing some satisfying outcomes (reinforcements) in place of those that may have been maintaining the problematic patterns of action.

The judicious use of punishment as a procedure of behavior change is in fact one of contingency management. Punishment is typically dealt with separately, because its major objective is to reduce the frequency of problem behavior rather than to develop adequate, adaptive be-

havior patterns and skills. Punishment also typically employs an aversive stimulus, and thus has potential negative considerations that are common to aversive control procedures but not to the typically positive stimuli used in contingency management. In our consideration of punishment as a relatively broad class of techniques, we will include some procedures whose aversive components are minimal, such as response cost in which reinforcers are explicitly withdrawn following inappropriate or maladaptive behavior. This procedure is quite clearly one of contingency management and involves reinforcers rather than directly punishing or aversive stimuli. Nevertheless, the withdrawal of reinforcement is at the very least a mildly aversive experience, and its effect is to reduce the frequency of behavior patterns on which it is made contingent. For these reasons, we have classed response cost as an aversion procedure rather than one of contingency management. Clearly, though, punishment is most properly considered an aversive control technique using a contingency management technique.

The effectiveness of punishment is strongly influenced by the degree to which the aversive stimulus employed has a clear onset and offset. This is probably because the clear definition of the punishment in terms of the time of its occurrence maximizes the clarity of both the contingency with which it is dispensed and any contingencies that may surround its termination. For example, a punishment may be delivered contingent upon the occurrence of a prohibited or maladaptive behavior, and the punishment may terminate only after the behavior itself has ceased. This set of contingencies includes both punishment for the inappropriate behavior and (negative) reinforcement for ceasing or inhibiting it (the contingent termination of punishment constitutes a negative reinforcer for inhibition). The consequence of such considerations of clarity has been a relatively narrow focus upon a limited number of aversive stimuli that are used in procedures of contingent aversive control. Although extremely intense aversive

Table 8–1 **Variables Related to the Administration and Effectiveness of Contingent Punishment**

Manner of Introduction of Punishment

The introduction of punishment at full intensity is likely to maximize its effectiveness (Azrin, Holz, & Hake, 1963; Brethower & Reynolds, 1962; Masserman, 1943).

An abrupt, substantial increase in the current intensity of an aversive stimulus will increase the degree of behavioral suppression (Azrin, 1959, 1960; Holz & Azrin, 1963).

Intensity of Punishment

The greater the intensity of the aversive stimulus, the greater the suppression of behavior produced (see section on conditioned emotional responses, however) (Azrin, 1958, 1959; Estes, 1944; Holz & Azrin, 1962).

However, punishment whose intensity is gradually increased will have reduced effectiveness. Also, in the naturalistic application of punishment, a clear statement of the contingency and information about behavioral alternatives to the punished behavior may make a low-intensity punisher as effective as a high-intensity one.

Immediacy of Punishment

A contingent aversive stimulus should be applied immediately following a problem behavior (Azrin, 1956; Azrin & Holz, 1966).

In the naturalistic application of punishment, a verbal reinstatement of the contingency may make a delayed punishment as effective as an immediate one (Parke, 1974).

Scheduling of Punishment

A continuous schedule of punishment (aversive stimulation following each instance of the problem behavior) is more effective than intermittent punishment (Azrin, Holz, & Hake, 1963; Estes, 1944; Zimmerman & Ferster, 1963).

Availability of Alternative Behaviors

The effectiveness of any punishment will be maximized if alternative modes of behavior are available that are appropriate for the contexts in which the punished act typically occurs, and that produce the same or similar result as the punished behavior.

Note: The references listed here are the classic studies of the contingent punishments.

states can be effected through the use of drugs (nausea, temporary inability to breathe, and resultant anxiety), these states arise and dissipate rather gradually so their contingency upon specific behaviors is likely to be vague. For severe behavior disorders, electric shock has repeatedly been shown to be an effective stimulus, even though its use calls for the most judicious care and expertise in order not to harm the client. Response cost procedures, such as the contingent withdrawal of specific reinforcers or contingent social isolation (time-out procedures), are also effective punishment techniques, and they are more directly adapted to use with a broad range of clients (children or adults) and can be employed in the natural environment by parents, teachers, or other social agents with whom the person interacts.

Contingent Aversive Control With Mild Aversive Stimuli

Clinical research on punishment procedures has expanded the range of stimuli used far beyond the simple electrical or "faradic" aversion treatments that were initially most common. To call these additional procedures "mild" is perhaps an exaggeration, but in most instances, they are moderately or even minimally aversive. In this section, we will examine a number of procedures that employ the contingent administration of an aversive stimulus, and in the next section, the use of aversion procedures employing electric shock will be considered. Then we will return to another class of mild aversion procedures, those involving the *withdrawal* of positive stimuli (response cost techniques).

The range of stimuli that have aversive characteristics is extremely broad: almost any stimulus can be made to be aversive by greatly increasing its intensity. Even a behavior itself, once positive and attractive, can be made aversive by forced and repeated performances (e.g., negative practice, overcorrection, and aversive behavior rehearsal). Some examples of mild aversion procedures include brief physical restraint, bright light, loud noises, bitter substances or noxious aromas (e.g., lemon juice, ammonia, soap in the mouth, smoke), rubber band snapping, simple scolding or criticism, visual isolation, or forced exercise.

Physical restraint for self-injurious behavior, when it constitutes the most frequent form of social contact, may operate as a reinforcer rather than a punisher (Bucher & Lovaas, 1968). This is especially true when the behavior being restrained is one that precludes other forms of reinforcement. For example, when a self-injurious child frequently self-mutilates, all contact must attempt to control that behavior; even if it did not, the problem behavior—such as head banging—would not allow the child to maintain attention or interaction with others. In some cases, however, when restraint is not needed for immediate control, brief restraint that is immediately contingent upon a problem behavior may act as a punisher. Bucher and associates (1976) applied this technique to the treatment of children who engaged in pica (the ingestion of inappropriate food and small objects). In this procedure, when the child began to touch or grasp the inappropriate object, the therapist shouted "No!" and then held the child's arms behind him or to his side. Struggling was responded to by placing the child on the floor with the therapist's knee pressed gently on his back. A reasonable suppression of the pica was achieved, but there was little generalization to settings outside the treatment room. We should also note that the best suppression was obtained when the restraint was contingent upon the very earliest detectable segment of the pica response. This is a truism for essentially all punishment procedures. Contingent aversive intervention at the earliest point in the deviant response sequence is most effective in producing subsequent inhibitive self-control (see the discussion of Berecz [1976] following).

Many undesirable behaviors occur at times or in settings that are difficult to predict or to have a therapist present and monitoring. For these reasons, attempts have been made to automate aversive control procedures or adapt them to self-administration. Heller and Strang (1973) treated nocturnal bruxism (teeth grinding) by the contingent application of a loud, aversive noise. A device was employed that recorded the sounds of teeth grinding during the night (Bernal, Gibson, Williams, & Pesses, 1971) and activated a sound blast through a tiny speaker worn in the client's ear if the grinding reached a rate of three per five-second interval. Although bruxism was not totally eliminated, over the course of two months it was significantly reduced in both frequency and intensity. The reduction in intensity was largely responsible for the lack of total suppression, because the sound eventually went below the threshold of the recorder. A more sensitive sensing device (e.g., one that measured the contraction of jaw muscles) would probably have produced total suppression.

Another technique for generalizing the contexts in which aversive control procedures can be employed is to put them under self-control and devise a form that may be used reasonably unobtrusively in the natural environment. A more extensive discussion of self-control techniques occurs elsewhere in this book (Chapter 10), so we will not belabor the point here. Mastellone (1974) has proposed a technique that may lack grace but is a good example of a self-administered contingent aversive control in natural context that uses commonly available stimuli. In this case, the aversive stimulus involves wearing a rubber band around the wrist and contingently snapping it following inappropriate behavior. The client is instructed to wear a loose-fitting rubber band of approximately three millimeters in width. The aversive stimulus is self-administered via a strong snap against the underside of the wrist. Mastellone reports that the subjective sensation is a very brief sting, not unlike that of a shock. In introducing this procedure, Mastellone described two case studies in which the technique was used successfully. One involved an adolescent girl who compulsively pulled her hair out (trichotillomania). She was instructed to snap her wrist after each instance of hair pulling or whenever she had the urge to pull her hair. She reported that after using the technique for three consecutive days, she remained totally free of the problem until she suffered a relapse some six months later.

In a second case, a male client who had homosexual fantasies and attractions, but who engaged in no overt homosexual (or heterosexual) behavior, sought treatment to reduce his homosexual leanings. He was instructed to snap his wrist at the first sign of sexual arousal after seeing an attractive man. This treatment regime was combined with procedures to increase the attractiveness of women. Substantial reductions in arousal to male stimuli were achieved within a few weeks, and the remainder dissipated over the period of several months. More recently, Berecz (1979) reported the effective use of "wrist band aversion therapy" in the maintenance of nonsmoking behavior.

A contingent aversion procedure that is common in natural socialization but rarely reported in the clinical literature is that of verbal rebuke and reprimand. While it is often a component of patient control on wards, student control in classrooms, and (often futile) child control in the home, it is seldom mentioned as a formal therapeutic technique. This is most likely because it is often combined with, or ancillary to, some other procedure of behavior control that is seen as the primary one. Adams and associates (1973) report a broad-spectrum reinforcement and punishment treatment regimen for the elimination of self-injurious behavior in an epileptic child. This institutionalized child would repeatedly fall to the floor in a pseudoseizure that could be easily differentiated from the actual seizures that she suffered (this was essential to justify treatment). The staff was instructed to selectively identify rewards and punishers in order to shape compliant and cooperative behavior and eliminate the feigned seizures. The initial major thrust of the treatment was the punishment of the pseudoseizures, since they were common and the desired compliant behavior was relatively rare. The first punishment administered was intense verbal scolding for falling, followed by enforced wearing of a football helmet, which the patient found an enduring aversive experience. The staff made clear to her that the helmet would be removed if consistent absence of falling behavior was demonstrated, but any repeated instances of falling, even with the helmet on, were met with scolding. The girl's parents were also trained in this regimen. Through this treatment, falling was eliminated almost completely within the first 5 days of treatment and gains were maintained over 30 days of hospitalization and during an additional 30-day follow-up period after discharge. The success of this treatment regimen allowed the more accurate diagnosis of actual seizure experiences and the establishment of an effective drug regimen that would control the physiologically induced epileptic phenomena.

A set of aversive stimuli that has proven effective includes aversive aromas and tastes. These are often particularly appropriate for treating problem behaviors that are oral in nature, such as obesity, nail biting, or children's biting of others. Morganstern (1974) reported the use of cigarette smoke as an effective aversive stimulus in the treatment of compulsive eating. In this instance, the client did not smoke and found smoke a particularly aversive stimulus (as is generally the case for nonsmokers) that elicited an immediate gag response followed by sensations of dizziness, nausea, and even vomiting. In another of the frequent cautionary notes required in any discussion of aversion techniques, we should say here that there may be cardiovascular consequences to the use of smoke as an aversive stimulus, such as hypertensive crises. The special vulnerability of the client must be assessed and great care must be taken in structuring the aversive stimulus, such as the density of smoke and length of exposure. Other investigators have also used cigarette smoke as a significant aversive stimulus, even in the treatment of smoking itself (Foreyt & Kennedy, 1971; Franks, Fried, & Ashem, 1966; Wolpe, 1969).

Weitzel and associates (1977) reported details of an apparatus that can be used to deliver aromatic stimuli, controlling for duration and concentration (ppm in air). This apparatus allows the use of such stimuli for either aversive counterconditioning or contingent aversive control, since the perception of odor and its aversive nature is an immediate phenomenon. The range of chemical odorants that can be utilized is rather broad and would allow for tailoring the aversive stimulus to the tastes (distastes, actually) of the particular client. A wide variety of stimuli have been identified, including cigarette smoke, dilute ammonium sulfide, butyric acid and aromatic ammonia, smelling salts, asafetida,

skunk oil, trimethylamine pyrudine, disopropylamine, and methylsulfide.

In an interesting and innovative procedure, Lichstein and Stalgaitis (1980) implemented a "reciprocal aversion" procedure. Working with couples, both of whom smoked, spouses were required to have a cigarette every time their mate smoked one. This procedure thus enforced smoking in both partners at numerous times when they did not wish to, making the act less enjoyable and probably aversive. The treatment was effective in reducing smoking by 74 percent, and after a six-month follow-up there was still a 61 percent reduction.

Matson and Ollendick (1976) have reported the effectiveness of mild mouthwash as a punisher for young children, especially for behaviors that are oral in nature, such as biting other children. In this procedure, the problem behavior is prompted (elicited) subtly and bites or attempted bites are followed by the administration of an acidic mouthwash directly into the child's mouth. This treatment is paired with reinforcement for behavior alternative to the biting behavior in contexts that usually elicited it. The maintenance procedures are continued for a fairly long period of time after the problem behavior is eliminated. These authors report that nine children between the ages of 1½ and 3½ years have been treated with this procedure. Treatment was accomplished in five days and all children but one showed continued freedom from biting over at least six months following treatment. Another substance used in this fashion is lemon juice.

Vargas and Adesso (1976) report a comparative study of the treatment of nail biting, in which electric shock, negative practice, and the use of a bitter substance were contrasted in their effectiveness. Half of the subjects were instructed to monitor carefully their nail-biting behavior, keeping good records on its daily occurrence. None of the three aversion techniques was superior to a self-monitoring control condition for the initial reduction in nail biting, but after a 90-day follow-up, only clients treated with one of the aversion procedures continued to show significant nail growth and a reduction in nail biting. At least for this one class of problem behavior, it appears that the relatively simple and mild procedure involving a taste stimulus has an effectiveness equal to that of a more involved and intense procedure such as shock.

Another mild stimulus that has been used in contingent aversive control is the bright light. Martin and Conway (1976) treated a female toddler (2 years of age) who engaged in nocturnal rocking that eventuated in a sitting posture and that brought her shoulders or head into contact with the crib walls. A 100-watt bulb, unshaded, was placed at the foot of the bed and connected to a noise-activated relay. The light had been demonstrated as aversive to the child, and was probably even more so in her bedroom, since it would be in contrast to the dark room at night. Whenever the relay closed because of noise from the rocking, the light came on and remained on for five seconds. After a treatment period of 10 days, the girl showed an immediate and dramatic drop in nocturnal rocking that was maintained through a year's follow-up.

Overcorrection A technique of relatively mild aversive control, in which the punishment may be said to "fit the crime," is that of *overcorrection*. In this technique, the punishment involves enforced action that corrects, undoes, or is clearly the (desirable) opposite of the problem behavior. Overcorrection also frequently includes mandatory restitution: the environment must be restored to a condition equal to or better than that which existed prior to the performance of the inappropriate behavior.

Originally posed by Azrin and Foxx as a treatment procedure for the control of self-stimulatory or destructive behaviors (Azrin, Kaplan, & Foxx, 1973; Foxx & Azrin, 1972, 1973; Webster & Azrin, 1973), overcorrection has three primary components. First, the problem behavior should be interrupted, if possible, before it has been totally completed. The next

phase typically involves physically guiding (or forcing) the individual through a behavior that corrects any damage or negative outcomes from the problem act, and perhaps constitutes a desired, alternative behavior to the one in question. Finally, the individual is required to engage in repeated corrective acts and to practice proper alternative behaviors that are exaggerated in their appropriateness (hence the term *over*correction).

The technique of overcorrection has been demonstrated as an effective punishment intervention for a variety of different problem behaviors in a broad range of settings. As noted above, Foxx and Azrin and their colleagues have utilized the technique for the control of self-destructive and self-stimulatory behaviors, and similar success has been reported by Kelly and Drabman (1977). Azrin and Wesolowski (1975) and Duker and Seys (1977) have used slightly different forms of an overcorrection treatment to eliminate psychogenic vomiting in retarded patients. Smeets, Elson, and Clement (1975) report the use of an overcorrection procedure with a multihandicapped deaf child for the elimination of problematic nasal discharges that the child commonly smeared over herself, the furniture, and teaching materials used in her instruction and in the instruction of others. Barrett and Shapiro (1980) report long-term effectiveness of overcorrection to treat stereotyped hair pulling by a retarded child, and others have reported its successful use to control self-injurious eye-gouging in blind children (Conley & Wolery, 1980), headbanging (Strauss, Rubinoff & Atkeson, 1983), and miscellaneous stereotyped behaviors in chronic psychiatric patients (Matson & Stephens, 1981).

Recently, issues have been raised regarding the scheduling of overcorrection interventions (cf. the scheduling of reinforcements and punishments). Luiselli, Suskin, and McPhee (1981) compared continuous and intermittent overcorrection for self-injurious behavior in an autistic child. Although intermittent overcorrection (contingent on every third self-injurious response) did reduce the incidence of self-injury, continuous application (every time) was still more effective and produced effects that persisted at two- and six-month follow-ups. Altmann and Krupsaw (1983) used overcorrection to treat aggressive and destructive behavior in a mildly retarded adolescent boy. Since some instances of misbehavior occurred when the child was alone, the overcorrection was often necessarily implemented only after a delay had intervened between the occurrence of the behavior and the intervention. These investigators report that, even under these circumstances, the overcorrection procedure was effective. Although there was no comparison with immediate overcorrection, it seems reasonable that while delayed overcorrection may be effective, immediate intervention may be more so and should be employed unless other circumstances require a delay.

The adaptability of overcorrection to both settings and problems is most easily demonstrated by describing the particular procedures used for the control of self-destructive behavior in a 3-year-old visually handicapped child. The procedure used by Kelly and Drabman (1977) for the control of the boy's self-injurious eye gouging involved brief daily overcorrection sessions. The problem behavior was pressing his index fingers into his eyes, an act that, if continued, would eradicate the little remaining vision he had. During a 10-minute treatment session conducted while seated at a table containing toys (other things for him to do with his hands), whenever the boy would bring his arm and hand up to make contact with his eye, the teacher firmly grasped and lowered the arm back to his side. The arm was then raised again, by the teacher, simulating an eye poke but not actually touching the eye, and this was repeated 12 times. The result of these treatment sessions was a rapid reduction in the rate of manual eye contact that showed clear generalization into other settings.

In one study, Matson, Horne, Ollendick, and Ollendick (1979) attempted to evaluate the relative contributions of the restitution (e.g. repairing or replacing taken or damaged objects) and positive practice components of overcorrection. The subjects were children referred by their teachers for aggressive and disruptive behavior in the classroom. Treatment was implemented during a summer school program that included half-day classes five days a week. For half of the children, aggressive behavior (hitting, kicking, destruction of property, tantrums, taking things from other children, etc.) was treated by enforced restitution, and for the other half, misbehavior led to a period of positive practice of proper behavior. When a child was observed to misbehave, he or she was ordered to stop and then went with a trainer to a separate area where five minutes of restitution or positive practice ensued. After a 6-day baseline period, there was a 10-day treatment period, followed by a 9-day period (children were ordered to stop any misbehavior, but there was no treatment) during which maintenance of any treatment effects were assessed.

Figure 8–1 illustrates the relative effectiveness of these two aspects of the general overcorrection procedure. Both types of treatment were effective, achieving between 84 percent and 89 percent reductions in the frequency of aggressive behavior, and there was no reliable difference in relative effectiveness. These findings suggest that it may not be necessary to include both components in an overcorrection intervention, a result that is consistent with successful interventions reported by others who used only one or the other element of the general overcorrection procedure. It is also of interest to note that the children in this study indicated that they preferred overcorrection procedures to other forms of punishment, important information if one wishes to select aversion procedures that are effective yet no more aversive than necessary.

Finally a cautionary note must be sounded regarding the use of physical force in overcorrection. The procedure may prove dangerous for at least two reasons. First, there is no

---

Figure 8–1   *Mean number of misbehaviors per child for each of the two groups: restitution and positive practice.*

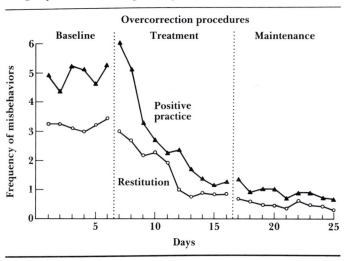

From Matson, Horne, Ollendick, and Ollendick (1979).

way to specify clearly the degree of force with which overcorrection is to be done. There are reported cases, for example, of patients in a state hospital who had limbs broken during overcorrection procedures. Second, poorly trained or vindictive staff members in a hospital or other treatment setting may use overcorrection to abuse recalcitrant clients, justifying their punitive actions under the guise of "treatment."

Aversive Behavior Rehearsal   A technique that is quite similar to negative practice overcorrection and to negative practice (see Chapter 7, "Response Elimination and Extinction Procedures") is *aversive behavior rehearsal.* In this procedure, the problem behavior is not forcibly corrected again and again, but rather is voluntarily practiced repeatedly to the point where its performance becomes quite aversive. This is essentially the same procedure as negative practice, but aversive behavior rehearsal is interpreted to be effective for two reasons: the aversive component of the practice is inherently contingent upon repeated instances and it is also

counterconditioning in nature because the unpleasantness persists throughout the performance of the behavior. Negative practice, on the other hand, is theoretically interpreted in terms of the buildup of inhibition that becomes conditioned to the response, thus canceling out the motivation for performance. Sometimes the behavior itself may be aversive (e.g., vomiting), but negative practice of "neutral" behaviors may be converted into aversive behavior rehearsal by pairing the practice with an aversive stimulus. In this case, it is probably viewed more properly as a procedure of counterconditioning, but we will discuss all the various types of aversive behavior rehearsal in this section.

Spergel (1975) reported the successful treatment of compulsive vomiting by repeatedly inducing it. The case was interpreted in terms of negative practice, but it seems reasonable to include it here because of the unpleasant nature of the behavior involved. Treatment consisted of five trials of forced vomiting in rapid succession by means of manual stimulation of the back of the throat. Although compulsive vomiting had reached the frequency of 9 to 11 times daily, after only the first forced vomiting trial, the patient protested that he did not want to vomit anymore, and by the fifth trial, he was emphatic about it. After the time there was no more compulsive vomiting and a seven-month follow-up revealed no recurrence.

Wickramasekera (1976) developed a procedure that combines direct and vicarious aversive behavior rehearsal. In this treatment of sexual exhibitionism, the patient is given an appointment to come to the office and expose himself at a clearly denoted time and place to people who are familiar with him. The actual (*in vivo*) exhibitionism is videotaped so that patients have the opportunity to view the exhibition of other patients (vicarious aversive behavior rehearsal). Not surprisingly, this has been termed "shame aversion" therapy by some (Serber, 1970). Wickramasekera reports successful treatment in a number of cases, with no remissions in follow-ups that have extended to seven years. Other researchers reported positive results from this procedure (Reitz & Keil, 1971; Serber, 1970; Stevenson & Jones, 1972), though there has not been a continuing effort to document more fully the effectiveness of this procedure. Wickramasekera recommended that this treatment be used for clients who are "introverted, anxious, moralistic and nonassertive" and not extraverted or sociopathic. The reason, presumably, is that the former individuals (particularly those who are anxious or moralistic) are most likely to experience anxiety or other aversive internal states upon viewing the videotapes.

Negative practice can be converted to aversive behavior rehearsal by the addition of an aversive stimulus during the repeated trials. Although we might invoke the theoretical principles cited to account for the effects of negative practice to explain the effects of aversive behavior rehearsal, it seems appropriate to differentiate the two, because one concentrates on the aversive and the other on the fatiguing components of the practice. Knepler and Sewall (1974) report the treatment of a facial eye-blink

tic through the use of massed practice combined with exposure to aromatic ammonia (smelling salts). In this case, a tic of several years' duration declined significantly after only 80 minutes of treatment. Perhaps because of the limited amount of treatment, however, long-term suppression was not good and remission occurred after about six months.

Consistent with the increased cognitive emphasis in behavior therapy, recent reports of punishment procedures describe new and different ways that cognitions may be put to active use in the treatment process. The procedure of covert sensitization (about which we will say more later) has from the start been a totally cognitive technique in which both the change-worthy behavior and the aversive components are imagined. Sensitization, however, is primarily classed as a type of aversive counterconditioning, so it was not until recently that cognitive elaborations were proposed for punishment procedures.

Covert Punishment   Covert punishment involves the imagining of contingent aversive consequences for a problem behavior. There is at least one laboratory research report that assesses the ability of imagined aversive stimuli to act as punishers in a typical instrumental conditioning paradigm, and it concluded that contingent covert stimuli could indeed act as "typical" reinforcers and punishers (Epstein & Peterson, 1973).

In one of the earliest reports of the clinical use of a covert punishment procedure (Davison, 1969), a child's maladaptive behavior was treated by having the child vividly imagine the father's angry mood that would be the consequence of the act. Moser (1974) reported the successful treatment of hallucinatory behavior with covert punishment, a testimony to the potential effectiveness of this technique for the treatment of problem behaviors that are themselves covert. Guidry (1975) utilized the procedure in the treatment of compulsive stealing. In this case, the client was to imagine the incipient components of a stealing incident, and then the aversive consequences that might occur. For example, the client would imagine getting the urge to steal while in a store, and then think of getting caught or looking up and finding the manager of the store watching him closely. This procedure is a good example for the design of any punishment procedure, because elements early in the sequence of problem behaviors were utilized in connection with the punishment. In this particular case, the client's stealing acts were reduced from a frequency of two per month to two instances during a 10-month follow-up period. During that time, he reported several instances of being able to resist the urge to steal while in a store.

Berecz (1972) investigated the feasibility of utilizing self-administered punishment (shock) in the treatment of problem smoking when the behaviors punished were not those of actual smoking but of an imagined scene in which smoking occurred. In this study, one group of clients self-administered an electric shock contingent upon imagined smoking behavior, and another group self-administered shock contingent upon actually smoking. The two groups were compared with each other for changes in smoking, and both groups were compared with nontreated control subjects. For male clients who were moderate smokers, there were no differences in effectiveness between the imagined and the actual smoking treatment; both groups showed a significant decrement in smoking over a nine-week period. Interestingly, among heavy smokers, the imagined smoking treatment was the only effective procedure. This finding suggests that contingent punishment may be most effective in the control of very highly motivated behaviors when cognitive substitutes for the actual behavior are employed, since it is possible that the attractive components of some behaviors, when actually practiced, outweigh the aversive components of the punishment employed. Interestingly, an ancillary finding of this study was that the level of shock clients used tended to increase as treatment proceeded, indicating that highly moti-

vated clients are not likely to minimize the severity of the aversive stimulus employed.

In another study, Berecz (1976) investigated the timing of the contingent punishment in the sequence of imagined behaviors. Problem smoking was also the behavior under treatment, and he found that contingent punishment (shock) administered *early* in the sequence of problem behaviors was most effective and reduced smoking that lasted through a two-year follow-up period. This finding is consistent with the general literature on punishment, primarily with reference to the socialization of children's behavior (Parke, 1974; Walters, Parke, & Crane, 1965). The interpretation of this finding is that punishment early in a sequence of behaviors suppresses the behavior sequence before it is well under way and thus more difficult to stop.

Contingent Aversive Control with Strong Aversive Stimuli

In this section, we will dwell primarily on the use of electric shock as a contingent punishment procedure. Other stimuli can produce an intensely aversive state—drugs that induce nausea or the paralysis of breathing, for example—but these stimuli are typically of slow onset and offset, a characteristic that makes it difficult to define a clear contingency. Electric shock, on the other hand, has a distinct onset and offset and thus can be scheduled to begin immediately after the occurrence of a problem behavior in a contingent fashion, and then to terminate contingent upon cessation of the behavior.

Effective learning may require only a minimally aversive stimulus, but in some instances, such as avoidance training procedures (e.g., Tanner, 1973), stronger aversive stimuli produce better results. Although the possible deleterious effects of aversive treatment should never be regarded lightly, animal research has indicated that response suppression increases as the intensity of the aversive stimulus (shock) increases (Rachlin & Herrnstein, 1969). Tanner treated two groups of homosexuals with electrical aversion techniques, with one group being allowed to set their own level of shock and the other receiving a value determined by the experimenter. With only one exception, self-determined clients invariably selected a level of shock intensity below the one prescribed by the therapist. Tanner found that the higher shock intensity produced significantly greater reduction in homosexual behavior, although there was a slight tendency for the higher shock to induce more clients to drop out of treatment before completion. Also, the clients who expressed a greater fear of shock tended to drop out early, which inclined Tanner to recommend that the assessment of fear could be used to determine shock intensity: clients with greater fear may be best treated with lower shock intensities.

As a powerful punishing, aversive stimulus, electric shock has many advantages over other punishing stimuli used in aversive control. Excepting covert sensitization procedures, shock is the punishment most easily employed, because it requires little special equipment other than the inductorium device used to supply the electric current. Obviously, severe electric shock can cause serious skin burns if applied inappropriately. However, sufficient care in making certain that the client is in good health, the use of an inductorium device specially designed for aversive control of humans,[2] and the appropriate place-

ment of the electrodes (typically in the forearm, fingers, back of legs, or feet) will minimize potential dangers.

As an aversive stimulus, shock has several distinct advantages, some of which we have already noted. It has a highly discrete and controllable onset and offset, so that the timing of the onset of punishment and its termination can be precisely linked to the occurrence and termination of a problem behavior. A clear offset also facilitates the pairing of new stimuli, or alternative behaviors, with termination of punishment in order to increase their attractiveness, as in anxiety-relief and aversion-relief procedures. The intensity of shock is generally adjustable, so the unpleasantness of the stimulus can be varied in accord with clients' individual differences in sensitivity. There are, of course, disadvantages, mostly concerned with the high degree of unpleasantness of electric shock, which may produce aggression or may drive patients from therapy if the level of shock employed is too extreme.

Several types of inductoria and electrodes are available. Some dispense current via electrodes that can be connected to a client's fingers, legs, soles of feet, or forearms. These devices typically operate directly from house current. Other devices are battery operated and provide the client some freedom of movement. This is occasionally necessary when, for example, the client is an active child, or when the behavior to be controlled is sufficiently motoric to require that the client not be hampered by temporarily attached electrodes and wires. Obviously, the administration of the aversive stimulus from a portable device involves care on the part of the therapist to ensure delivery within a short time following the response and to an appropriate part of the body. Battery-operated devices are also used for self-dispensation of shock. These devices can be carried by the client, who can self-dispense shocks when undesired thoughts or motives occur, or when a changeworthy behavior seems imminent. In these cases, the client must be carefully instructed in the procedures

---

[2]Many references in the literature concern proper equipment for the delivery of electric shock as an aversive stimulus. Before employing such a strong aversive stimulus, a therapist should reconsider the ethical issues involved and review the conditions under which the likely effectiveness of such techniques outweighs their liabilities. For electric shock, there should also be careful research on safety and other factors, some relevant references include safety factors of electric shock when used for the aversive conditioning of humans (Butterfield, 1975); telemetric delivery of electric shock (Galbraith, Byrick, & Rutledge, 1970); grid for delivery of shock to soles of feet (Royer, Rynearson, Rice, & Upper, 1971); electrode for delivery of shock to arm (Pfeiffer & Johnson, 1968).

of timing and the identification of instances when self-administered aversive consequences are appropriate.

When shock is to be used as a *contingent punisher,* with no attempt to alter stimulus valences or to establish an avoidance condition, the procedure is quite simple. Whether in the home or in a clinical setting, the client should be provided with stimuli that elicit the changeworthy behavior. Thus, if smoking is to be treated, the client may be given a package of cigarettes and directly asked to smoke. Or he may be asked to form an image of smoking so realistic that he can nearly experience the actual sensations. A client with tendencies toward transvestism might be given women's clothing articles and instructed to put them on. These responses, once performed, can then be followed by shock, either on a continuous schedule (i.e., every time they are performed) or on an intermittent schedule (i.e., every third time or every fourth time, on the average).

Some procedures can involve *escape training.* The paradigm for escape training is one in which a behavior begins, is punished, and then the punishing stimulus continues until the individual ceases the behavior and possibly performs an alternative behavior, at which time the aversive stimulus terminates. In this procedure, punishment cannot be avoided, but rapid execution of a behavior incompatible with the one punished will bring about termination of the punishment. Consequently, ceasing the problem behavior and any alternative behaviors that occur is strongly reinforced by the termination of pain and the anxiety accompanying the punishment. Escape training procedures of this type are one type of *aversion-relief* technique as discussed earlier.

Contingent punishment appears to be most effective when it occurs 0.5 second following a response (Hull, 1952). Most cases described in the literature have attempted to deliver the punishment with this approximate latency, especially in cases that do not involve long chains of behavior. When the treatment is applied in a clinical setting, this delay can often be established precisely by the use of timing equipment. However, when punishment is applied in more naturalistic settings, such as the home, often the person employing the punishment must estimate the time lag or simply apply the punishment as rapidly as possible following the behavior. It is unlikely in such cases that the punisher could be applied any more rapidly than 0.5 second following a response, and great care should be taken to prevent lag of much more than a few seconds, because the effect of punishment decreases rapidly as the lag between response and punishment is increased.

There are no clear guidelines concerning the duration of punishment. Shock is so extremely aversive to most individuals that it seems clear the duration ought to be quite brief. Longer durations become so aversive that they create conditioned emotional responses or drive clients from therapy, neither of which is ethical or desirable. As with all aversive stimuli we discuss, it is possible for clients to form a clear discrimination between the therapy situation and other situations in which the behavior is likely to occur, or between the therapist and other individuals who must exercise control over the client's behavior. As we see in the following examples, the use of portable inductoria allows treatment to proceed in the diverse situations in which problem behaviors are likely to occur. And the use of multiple therapists can prove effective in encouraging the generalization of behavioral extinction when initial results indicated that the behavior is inhibited only in the presence of the therapist, or in the clinical setting. Such procedures have proved particularly effective, for example with autistic children.

Although these are among the most important concerns in the use of shock as an aversion technique, actual procedures vary slightly depending on the behavior under treatment. Problem behaviors may be frequent and discrete, as in the case of a stutter response to certain letters, or the self-destructive behavior of a psychotic child. At other times, the problem may require the alteration of the valence of be-haviors and associated stimuli, as in the treat-ment of homosexuality or alcoholism, when the problem behavior is of lesser frequency and un-likely to occur in the therapy situation. Since the behavior under treatment affects the manner of procedures by which aversive control is utilized, let us turn to some examples of successful cases that have employed electric shock as the aver-sive stimulus. The reader should note that in many of these examples, the aversion technique is employed in combination with other, more positive means of behavior change, although in several cases, aversion techniques were used only after positive techniques had failed.

In the treatment of a case of transvestism, Blakemore, Thorpe, Barker, Conway, and Lavin (1963) employed contingent electric shock, which was administered while the patient was donning women's attire. Treatment sessions were administered at 30-minute intervals, spaced throughout each treatment day (which lasted from 9:00 in the morning to late after-noon). Treatment lasted six days. Each session included five "trials," when the client would be donning female attire. During this time, he stood on a rubber mat into which an electric grid had been embedded. A hand-operated generator could deliver a powerful electrical stimulus (120 VAC, 10,000 ohms resistance; amperage unspecified), and punishment con-sisted of two hand turns of the generator. At some point during each trial, after a varying number of female articles had been put on, the patient either received a shock or heard a buzzer, following either of which he was to be-gin undressing in preparation for the next trial. The shock and buzzer were randomly ordered, so that punishment was on an intermittent schedule, a procedure that appears to maximize the anxiety components of punishment and readily promotes generalization of training to situations and times when it is clear that shock is not likely to ensue. In the present example, the patient did not know how long it would be be-fore he received the signal to undress or

whether the signal would be the shock or buzzer. Neither did he know the frequency with which these would occur over the various trials.

Although treatment lasted only six days, the patient found it quite unpleasant and stressful, and he showed a clear decline in his level of motivation. Consequently, after four days of treatment, a two-day intervening "vacation" was prescribed, following which treatment was resumed and completed. Even during this two-day period, the patient avoided cross-dressing several times in situations that would have stimulated him to cross-dress in earlier times. After the total of six days of treatment, a six-month follow-up revealed that no transvestism had occurred and that the patient had no desire whatsoever to engage in what had been his most satisfying sexual outlet. It should be noted at this point that the procedure failed to build in appropriate sexual-behavior alternatives to the transvestism. Although the treatment appeared to be effective in eliminating cross-dressing, it is not clear whether the client was satisfied with his eventual sexual adjustment. A component of positive training would probably have been a useful addition to this sort of treatment pro-cedure.

Another class of behavior that may often best be controlled by strong contingent punishment is self-injurious behavior. Bucher and Lovaas (1968) worked with a 7-year-old psychotic boy who had shown self-mutilating behaviors since the age of 2. He typically was kept in physical restraints, and when they were removed, he was likely to hit himself nearly 2,000 times in the space of just one hour. When electric shock was applied contingently to such destructive behav-ior, only four treatment sessions and 12 shocks were required to eliminate this behavior almost entirely. In another case reported by the same authors, head banging by a psychotic girl was reliably eliminated after a total of only 15 con-tingent shocks. It is interesting to note that the self-destructive behavior by these children was not the only behavior affected by the treatment. Following treatment, the children whined less and showed much greater tendencies to attend to their therapists. The importance of this latter result cannot be exaggerated, because it paves the way for other forms of treatment, which may involve more benign interventions, such as social reinforcement or modeling.

In another example of the utility of punishment procedures for the control of self-injurious acts, Prochaska, Smith, Marzilli, Colby, and Donovan (1974) reported the use of response-contingent shock to reduce the rate of head banging shown by a profoundly retarded child. In this particular case, strenuous efforts had been made to control the child's behavior through antiseizure and tranquilizing medications, efforts that were of some success for a two-year period but which then failed. When the child was brought for behavior therapy treatment, an interesting problem confronted these authors. Although there were reports of effective contingent aversion treatment for self-injurious behaviors, including head banging (e.g., Lovaas et al., 1965), there had been numerous reports of poor generalization from the treatment context (Corte, Wolf, & Locke, 1971; Lovaas & Simmons, 1969; Miron, 1971; Risley, 1968). The authors decided to utilize a stationary inductory apparatus for the initial treatment and then to employ a portable remote-control unit for the remainder of treatment. The findings were in agreement with their expectations: initial use of the stationary equipment produced suppression of the head banging, but primarily in the treatment context, with little generalization. But subsequent use of the remote-control apparatus overcame the generalization problem and totally eliminated the self-injurious head banging.

It is not necessary that the behavior under treatment be one over which the client has voluntary control, that it be an attractive or enjoyable one, or that the client be of any minimum age. Sachs and Mayhall (1971) reduced the incidence of spasms and involuntary movements in a cerebral palsied individual, and Wright (1973) reported the successful treatment of a 5-year-old boy who had self-induced seizures. Creer, Chai, and Hoffman (1977) reported the effective use of a mild electrical aversion treatment that included but a single contingent punishment to suppress a long-term chronic cough, with suppression still in evidence at a 2½-year follow-up. Kushner (1968) reported similar success with chronic sneezing. In a now-classic study, Lang and Melamed (1969) eliminated ruminative vomiting in a 9-month-old infant, and there have been other reports of similarly successful procedures with infants (Cunningham & Linscheid, 1976; Toister, Condron, Worley, & Arthur, 1975) and with retarded children and adults (Galbraith et al., 1970; Kohlenberg, 1970).

In the case treated by Lang and Melamed (1969), the infant tended to regurgitate small amounts of food all during the day and to vomit most of his food within 10 minutes after feeding. It was possible to recognize the imminent onset of vomiting by observing the vigorous throat movements that would precede vomiting and would occur at no other time. Since vomiting occurred only after feeding, not during it, the use of aversion techniques was deemed appropriate, since there would be little possibility that actual feeding behavior would be affected by the administration of contingent punishment.

In the treatment of this infant, one-second-long electric shocks were administered to the leg. The intensity level was set by two criteria: the shock was judged painful by the therapists and was sufficient to elicit signs of distress in the infant. The shocks were delivered at one-second intervals beginning at the start of vomiting and terminating only when vomiting had ceased. Both the observation of a nurse and electromyographic recording of muscle activity were used to determine the onset of vomiting.

By the end of the first session of aversion procedures, the frequency and duration of vomiting had decreased markedly from earlier levels. After a second session, it was clear the infant had learned to anticipate shocks; he had also begun to avoid the shock by curling his foot. This latter behavior necessitated the therapists' moving the electrodes from the bottom of the foot to the calf. Following this maneuver, the vomiting quickly showed a decrease, and by the end of the sixth session, vomiting had stopped. After two days of nontreatment, there was some indication that the vomiting was beginning to recur. However, after three further days of treatment sessions, the response was reliably eliminated. Six months later, the infant still showed no tendency to vomit following feeding and had regained his normal weight.

One effect of contingent punishment is the potential interruption of the behavior on which it is contingent. This is a helpful characteristic if the termination of the punishment is then to be contingent upon an alternative behavior that takes the place of the problem one since the interruption of one behavior sequence provides the opportunity for other behaviors to occur. In some types of disordered behaviors, the interruption may be of primary importance. Obsessive ideation or continuing hallucinations, for example, are problem behaviors whose interruption may be an important part of treatment. Kenny, Solyom, and Solyom (1973) reported the use of electric shock to disrupt obsessive verbal phrases and mental images in five patients. These authors note that electrical aversion techniques have been used effectively to treat obsessive ruminations (Kushner & Sandler, 1966; McGuire & Vallance, 1964; Wolpe, 1958). Electrical aversion has not been commonly used for the treatment of obsessive fears, doubts, compulsions, rituals, or "horrific temptations," and when it has there have been many reports of poor outcome. Kenny and colleagues (1973) selected patients whose obsessive ideation included fears, doubts, and the like, and examined the effectiveness of a shock technique for the treatment of this type of obsession. They reported one failure, a patient whose obsessions were eliminated but then replaced by psychotic delusions. The remaining four patients all benefited from the treatment, three of them markedly so.

In another example of this type, Alford and Turner (1976) reported the successful interruption and suppression of auditory hallucinations through the use of electrical aversion procedures. In this case study, the individual under treatment had already had the frequency of hallucinations reduced through her relatives' ignoring her whenever she engaged in "crazy talk," but the aversion procedure produced lasting suppression. Earlier reports indicating the effectiveness of aversion procedures in eliminating hallucinations were provided by Bucher and Fabricatore (1970) and McGuigan (1966).

There is at least one other report in the literature of a compulsive behavior responding quite well to contingent aversive treatment. Scholander (1972) reported the case of an epileptic boy, 14 years of age, who developed the compulsion to hold his hands tightly around his neck. As the compulsion developed, the boy became more and more introverted and gradually came to choke himself, keeping his hands tightly around his neck nearly all the time. Naturally, this interfered with his eating, his dressing, and other aspects of daily behavior that required the use of his hands. When treatment involving contingent shock for the self-choking behavior was instituted, the compulsion subsided, without the indications of anxiety or irritation that had occurred earlier whenever he was prevented from choking himself, and his overall adjustment showed improvement. Interestingly, his epileptic seizures also became less frequent.

Contingent Aversive Control by the Withdrawal of Reinforcement

Response Cost Response cost is a punishment procedure involving contingent withdrawal of a reward. Since people generally find the loss of such a reward at least a mildly aversive experience, response cost is generally classified as a punishment, and it has proved very effective in suppressing undesired behaviors.

Response cost in the form of fines is often a component of token economies, although it has also been applied to treat individuals as well (Elliott & Tighe, 1968; Kazdin, 1972; Siegel, Lenske, & Broen, 1969). The concept of response cost should not be confused with that of time-out from reinforcement (see Chapter 5). Although the absence of rewards in time-out procedures and during extinction (see Chapter 7) may be judged aversive, there is no actual withdrawal or removal of an already accrued reward, whereas such removal is the crux of the response cost procedure.

There are two basic procedures for the enactment of a response cost technique. In some instances (and this may be more appropriate for laboratory studies than for clinical application), the individual may be given an amount of reward, such as a number of tokens, and then lose some tokens when she performs inappropriate behaviors. Or, upon the initiation of a treatment program, she may be required to deposit a lump sum of money, and subsequently lose a specified amount for each occurrence or sign of occurrence (e.g., gaining a pound in a weight-loss program) of the changeworthy behavior. Perhaps more realistically, response cost can be embedded within a procedure of contingency management in which the individual gains rewards for appropriate behaviors and loses rewards for inappropriate action. It is easy to see how this latter procedure would maximize an individual's discriminations between behaviors that are appropriate and inappropriate, and at the same time encourage the performance of appropriate behaviors and the suppression of inappropriate behaviors.

In an extensive review of reported uses of response cost procedures, Kazdin (1972) pointed out a number of advantages inherent in this technique and speculated about the mechanisms that may be responsible for its effectiveness. Behaviors suppressed with response cost procedures appear not to recover when the punishment is discontinued, although this conclusion should not be taken as justification for reducing the care with which this or any other behavior change procedure is terminated following positive changes in behavior. It also appears to be the case that the undesirable side effects that may stem from a typical punishment procedure employing a truly aversive stimulus are not present when a response cost procedure is utilized.

Wolf, Hanley, King, Lachowicz, and Giles (1970) utilized a response cost procedure to control the hyperactive behavior of an individual child within a classroom. Points were given out, noncontingently, before class began, and out-of-seat behavior resulted in a loss of points. The out-of-seat behavior ceased rapidly, and the response cost procedure proved even more effective when it was generalized to the entire class, whereby all points remaining at the end of a class were shared by all the members of the class, not just the individual child. Sulzbacher and Houser (1968) utilized points that were worth minutes of recess to suppress obscene gestures. In a procedure similar to covert sensitization (discussed later in this chapter), Weiner (1965) showed that *imagined* loss of reward is nearly as effective as actual reward loss.

The range of behavior disorders that have been effectively treated utilizing response cost procedures is impressive. Smoking (Elliott & Tighe, 1968), overeating (Harmatz & Lapuc, 1968), stuttering (Halvorson, 1968), head banging (le Boeuf, 1974), psychotic talk (Davis, Wallace, Liberman, & Finch, 1976), trichotillomania (McLaughlin & Nay, 1975), nail biting (Ross, 1974), speech disfluencies (Kazdin, 1973a; Siegel et al., 1969), echolalia (Doleys & Slapion, 1975), weight loss (Jeffrey, 1974), academic performance of mildly retarded individuals (Arnold, Forehand, & Sturgis, 1976), and even cash shortages in a small business (Marholin & Gray, 1976) have all been reported to respond favorably to response cost treatments. The populations within which response cost techniques can be utilized are also quite broad, ranging from psychotics, sociopaths, and retarded individuals to delinquents and normal children.

The effectiveness of response cost procedures has been clearly demonstrated in a number of settings. Phillips (1968) included response cost procedures in a token system for predelinquent boys. Whereas threats, corrective feedback, and simple instructions proved ineffective in decreasing verbal aggression, tardiness, and poor grammar, the inclusion of response cost procedures reliably decreased the frequencies of such behaviors. Response cost has also been a small component in token economy systems, although its effectiveness has rarely been evaluated (see Atthowe & Krasner, 1968; Ayllon & Azrin, 1968b; Heap, Boblitt, Moore & Hord, 1970; Packard, 1970; Steffy, Hart, Craw, Torney, & Marlett, 1969). When its effectiveness has been evaluated, it has been found ineffective in suppressing a variety of aggressive and rule-violating behaviors in hospitalized patients (Winkler, 1970; Upper, 1971).

In an innovative application of the response cost principle, Ross (1974) treated nail biting by utilizing a contingency that required the client to contribute money to a strongly disliked organization when, at periodic measurements, there was no increase in nail length. This contingent response cost contract was effective in increasing the client's nail length (and presumably in reducing the tendency toward nail biting), and the increase was maintained at both three- and six-month follow-ups. The response cost procedure utilized by le Boeuf (1974) in the treatment of head banging evidenced by an otherwise normal adult male further indicates the range of stimuli and techniques that can be utilized. For this individual, a response cost procedure was combined with a mild punishment procedure: any instance of head banging resulted in either the interruption of recorded music (response cost) or the sounding of an alarm (punishment), both aversive stimuli that bore some relationship to the problem, since he tended to bang his forehead rhythmically with his arm or wrist in time to music. This seemed be to an adult version of the infantile head banging in which he had engaged and which had just changed form over the years. The treatment procedure was implemented over a 45-day period and produced a total suppression

of the head-banging behavior that was maintained throughout a follow-up period.

We have noted elsewhere the possible importance of the magnitudes of rewards (see the chapters on contingency management) and punishers in determining the effectiveness of contingency management and aversive control procedures. Interestingly, there is no indication thus far in the research literature that the magnitude of response cost has any systematic effects on the effectiveness of the procedure. Elliott and Tighe (1968) included a response cost procedure in their treatment program for cigarette smokers. Clients lost great sums of money for smoking and were able to earn the money back by progressively longer periods of abstinence (self-reported). After 16 weeks of treatment, fully 84 percent of the subjects were abstinent, and of these, 75 percent claimed that it was the fear of losing money that enabled them to abstain from smoking. There are, of course, problems with this particular study, since there was no control group with which abstinence rates might be contrasted, and the use of self-report to determine the giving or withdrawal of rewards may have induced patients to change their reports, not their actual behavior. Although Elliott and Tighe (1968) utilized a large sum of money (up to $65) in their response cost procedure, Siegel and associates (1969) effectively suppressed speech disfluencies in college students by levying fines of only one cent.

Studies of the effectiveness of response cost procedures indicate that it is a powerful manipulation. For example, early research showed clearly how response cost procedures may lead to suppression effects that are as persistent as those following the use of electric shock as a punisher (Azrin & Holz, 1966). And response cost appears to allow less recovery of suppressed responses than do other punishment procedures (McMillan, 1967; Tolman & Mueller, 1964). Several investigators have found that after response cost procedures are discontinued, there is little tendency for the punished response to recover to its original frequency after periods of time up to several months (Harmatz & Lapuc, 1968; Kazdin, 1971, 1972; Phillips, 1968; Siegel et al., 1969). Nevertheless, other reports in the literature cite recovery of the problem behavior when the response cost procedure was discontinued (Birnbrauer, Wolf, Kidder, & Tague, 1965; Burchard, 1967; Phillips, Phillips, Fixsen, & Wolf, 1971; Sulzbacher & Houser, 1968; Winkler, 1970; Wolf et al., 1970).

Several studies have contrasted the effectiveness of response cost with other procedures for the suppression of problem behaviors. Phillips and associates (1971) found that a combination of token reinforcement and response cost (fines) resulted in better attention to current events (televised news) than did either procedure alone (this program is discussed in greater detail in Chapter 5).

Bucher and Hawkins (1971) and Panek (1970) found that positive reinforcement and response cost procedures were of essentially equal effectiveness in the control of disruptive behaviors by children and associative responding by schizophrenics. Harmatz and Lapuc (1968) utilized response cost, group therapy, and diet only in treating obese patients. Response cost involved a loss of money whenever a week went by without some weight loss, whereas group therapy patients were given praise when weight losses were reported and generally discussed the dynamic processes underlying obesity. After six weeks of treatment, group therapy and response cost procedures were equally effective in promoting weight loss. After a one-month follow-up, however, the group therapy patients had regained weight and no longer differed from the diet-only group, whereas response cost patients had actually continued to lose weight.

In a study comparing response cost with other forms of punishment, Schmauk (1970) contrasted the effects of response cost (money loss), physical punishment (shock), and social disapproval in the learning of an avoidance task

by normal individuals and individuals diagnosed as sociopaths. The normal individuals learned equally well under all conditions of punishment. However, although sociopathic individuals typically learn less well than normal people, under response cost conditions they learned equally well; yet under other conditions of punishment, their learning was less efficient than that of normal individuals.

It seems well documented that response cost procedures constitute an effective form of aversive control. Further, it is clearly a procedure that can be easily integrated with more positive forms of control, especially contingency management procedures (indeed, response cost is a form of contingency management). Response cost can produce relatively enduring behavior suppression, with little likelihood of negative side effects, such as disruption of ongoing behavior (Bandura, 1969; Leitenberg, 1965), emotional responding (Schmauk, 1970), or escaping the therapy situation (Baron & Kaufman, 1966; Leitenberg, 1965; Phillips et al., 1971).

Time-out Procedures Whereas typical response cost procedures entail a clear contingency in which specified reinforcers are withdrawn for problem behavior, time-out procedures constitute a highly generalized withdrawal contingency in which the individual is isolated from as much reinforcement as possible, including simple contact with others (social reinforcement) and access to tangible items of reinforcing value. The most common time-out operation, at least in contemporary mythology, is the instance of sending a child to his room, without his supper, as punishment for some misbehavior.

Time-out experiences are probably not entirely aversive. Hyperactivity or aggressive acting out behavior can be effectively controlled through time-outs not simply because of the aversive contingency, but because, in addition, the individual is insulated from ongoing stimulation (e.g., the taunting behavior of others, or the arousal of angry motives to aggress through the sight of an enemy) that may have been maintaining the problem behavior. Given that time-out is a procedure whose effectiveness can rely on more than just its aversive components, the fact that ongoing reinforcement is indeed withdrawn makes this the most appropriate place to classify the technique.

In principle, the implementation of a time-out seems simple, but in operation many complexities arise. The parental practice of banishing a child to his room may not effectively constitute a time-out if toys, books, television, or other sources of interest and enjoyment are still available. Often the best way to effect a time-out is to have access to a place—a small room, for example—that can be kept stark and barren, free from any sources of stimulation that might have reinforcing value. Such rooms can be maintained on treatment wards or in schools, but are less readily accessible in other contexts where behavioral control is desired. Ethical considerations are also a complicating factor, since clearly there are limits to the length of time individuals can be humanely deprived of social contact or reasonable physical comforts.

We introduced the concept of time-outs in Chapter 5 because they are often used in conjunction with a procedure of positive contingency management. In that chapter, cases are described in which tantrum behavior in children was effectively controlled by the use of time-out procedures (Wahler, Winkel, Peterson, & Morrison, 1965; Wolf, Risley, & Mees, 1964). These cases were germane at that point partially because they illustrate one of the other advantages of time-out procedures—that is, insulation of the individual from the behavior of others that may not simply elicit but actually reinforce the problem behavior. For example, the plaintive, compliant, or even negatively attending (yelling, scolding) behavior of a mother may paradoxically maintain tantrum behavior, just as teacher scolding and authoritarian attempts to keep students in their seats may maintain rowdy and apparently uncontrolled classroom behavior (Brown & Elliot, 1965). The range of behaviors

shown to be sensitive to time-out aversive control procedures is broad and extends significantly beyond the tantrum and aggressive actions that originally motivated this sort of treatment (Bostow & Bailey, 1969; Hawkins, Peterson, Schweid, & Bijou, 1966; Pendergrass, 1972; Tyler & Brown, 1967). The literature reports the use of time-out procedures to suppress delusional and hallucinatory speech (Davis et al., 1976), as well as disruptive behaviors of retarded adults (Calhoun & Lima, 1977) and of children (Spitalnik & Drabman, 1976).

Time-out procedures have also been examined as a function of the types of reinforcers that are removed (Bostow & Bailey, 1969; Ramp, Ulrich, & Dulaney, 1971; Tyler & Brown, 1967). In one study of this sort, the use of time-out was also extended to the control of problem drinking in alcoholics. Griffiths, Bigelow, and Liebson (1977) allowed individuals access to a specified amount of alcohol (one ounce of 95-proof ethanol) periodically during the day, but varied the sorts of time-out experiences that were imposed after each drink. The alcohol was available once every 40 minutes, following which were restrictions on the patient's behavior. The conditions compared were (1) no restrictions (baseline); (2) a "social time-out," during which ward staff and patients could not talk, gesture, or play games with the patient; (3) an "activity time-out," during which staff and patients could talk to the patient although he was confined to a particular chair in the day room and could engage in no activities (e.g., movement or games) other than smoking; and (4) a combined social and activity time-out. For the particular problem behavior of drinking, which has its own social ramifications, social time-out occasionally produced a slight reduction in subsequent alcohol consumption, but sometimes actually raised it. On the other hand, activity time-outs and the combined social-activity time-outs suppressed intake to 36 percent and 24 percent of baseline, respectively. Overall, although the social and activity time-out procedures individually showed variable effectiveness, their combined use typically produced a reasonable level of suppression.

There has been some discussion in the literature of a distinction between time-out and social isolation. Drabman and Spitalnik (1973) proposed that isolating an individual from social contact in the absence of any evidence that social contact itself or aspects of the social situation were reinforcing should be termed *social isolation*, whereas the term *time-out* should be reserved for instances in which the isolation procedure clearly deprives the individual of positive reinforcement. These authors propose the distinction on the reasoning that contingent isolation may achieve its effects on behavior because of the aversive quality of the social isolation room and be unrelated to any withdrawal of reinforcement that had been present in the social contact situation.

The decision regarding at least one aspect of time-out, its duration, is rather arbitrary. It is difficult to say exactly how long a time-out *should* be, how long is too long, and how long is too short. In general, longer time-outs seem to be more effective than short ones. White, Nielsen, and Johnson (1972) and Burchard and Barrera (1972) utilized time-out periods that ranged from 1 to 30 minutes in length. Some evidence that the length of a time-out is a relative phenomenon comes from the work of Kendall, Nay, and Jeffers (1975). These investigators contrasted the effects of 5-minute and 30-minute time-outs for the control of both verbal and physical aggression. They found that if a 5-minute time-out was utilized before the clients (male delinquents, in this case) had any experience with a longer time-out period, it was effective in suppressing the problem behaviors. If the clients had already experienced a longer time-out, then the shorter period failed to have any suppressive value, probably because its aversive character was minimized by comparison with the earlier time-out experience.

Another consideration in the design of a treatment procedure employing time-outs is the scheduling of their contingent use. Although there has been no extensive investigation of scheduling for this particular aversive control procedure, the research that is available suggests that, in general, consistency—imposing a time-out for every instance of the problem behavior—is likely to be the most effective procedure (cf. the results reported earlier for overcorrection by Matson, Horne, Ollendick, & Ollendick, 1979). There is some indication (Calhoun & Lima, 1977) that a variable-rate schedule (e.g., once every four occurrences) of time-outs may be effective for the control of high-rate behaviors *if* it is implemented after a consistent time-out procedure has been used to suppress another problem behavior. This indicates that an individual's history of experience with this sort of punishment must be taken into account.

It is important to note that the time-out procedure may be particularly inappropriate for one type of behavior that otherwise can be responsive to punishment techniques: self-stimulatory behavior. The time-out context cannot eliminate opportunities for reinforcing this type of behavior, because it is indigenous to the individual (typically a child) himself. Time-out, therefore, is not a procedure of choice for the control of self-stimulatory behavior.

As with other techniques of aversive control, time-out procedures raise a certain degree of ethical concern. Time-outs of too long a duration and those that have no built-in rules to allow interruption for legitimate reasons (e.g., to go to the bathroom) are certainly inappropriate and examples of misuse. The literature has also noted that there are safety factors that must be taken into account. Neisworth and Madle (1976) have proposed a number of special features that a time-out booth or room should have in order to protect the rights and the physical well-being of the individual being treated, and it would be advisable to review their proposal and discussion before implementing any major program of treatment involving the use of time-out procedures.

It is important to note that there is a subtle but meaningful distinction between time-out-from-positive-reinforcement and seclusion as therapeutic procedures. Time-out can be accomplished by ignoring an individual or expressly eliminating a major source of ongoing reinforcement (e.g., television for a solitary child). Seclusion, although it generally includes a time-out from positive reinforcement, is more than that. Seclusion implies that the individual is insulated from many sources of ongoing stimulation, including even the observation of reinforcing events or contact with other individuals who might be interacting with (reinforcing) him but are not. It is also possible that seclusion will *not* include time-out from positive reinforcement. Consider the child who engages in problematic self-stimulation that may be maintained by both the attention that it draws from others and by its intrinsic reinforcing properties. Mere seclusion from others does not prevent the reinforcing consequences of the self-stimulation, and in this case, a true time-out may be accomplished only by physical restraint. The point to be gleaned from this is that there are seldom specific operations (such as seclusion or ignoring) that automatically implement a desired behavior therapy technique, such as time-out, no matter what the setting, who the client is, or what the maladaptive behavior happens to be.

Aversive Counterconditioning

The term *counterconditioning* is generally used to refer to procedures that alter the valence or attractiveness of a stimulus or behavior. The procedures are generally seen to involve the pairing of a positive or an aversive state (or experience) with the presentation of the stimulus or the occurrence of the behavior. Of course, valences can be changed in two ways. They can be made more attractive, or their attractiveness can be reduced.

Counterconditioning and Sensitization

In the application of techniques of aversive control, one of the most common goals is the reduction of the attractiveness of inappropriate stimuli and behaviors. This goal is usually achieved by having an aversive stimulus occur at the same time as the performance of the problem behavior or the perception of the inappropriate stimuli. Thus, the procedure is one of *counterconditioning*, in which attractive valences of inappropriate behavior and stimuli are replaced by the overpowering aversive qualities of the simultaneously presented aversive stimulus, presumably by the process of classical conditioning. This procedure can also be labeled *sensitization:* the individual becomes "sensitized," in that he or she learns to feel anxious when performing the problem behavior while experiencing (tasting, smelling, etc.) the stimuli associated with the problem behavior (see Chapter 2 for a discussion of one view of desensitization as a counterconditioning procedure; see also Bandura, 1969). The procedure of covert sensitization is the only technique that uses the term "sensitization" in its formal label. However, other counterconditioning procedures utilizing nonimaginal aversive stimuli might well be labeled techniques of *overt* sensitization.

Counterconditioning procedures can also be employed to *de*sensitize an individual to a stimulus or behavior that is anxiety provoking or has other negative characteristics (e.g., the client finds it unpleasant or distasteful). The classical desensitization procedure is sometimes interpreted as one of counterconditioning, in which the relaxation response, which is counter to anxiety, becomes conditioned to the fear-provoking stimulus and replaces the anxiety. Within the sphere of aversive control procedures, the termination of an aversive stimulus is itself a positive experience that can be used in a counterconditioning fashion to replace the distaste associated with a stimulus or behavior, or simply to increase the attractiveness of a stimulus that is neutral or only mildly attractive. Through this sort of counterconditioning, a client can be motivated to undertake behaviors that previously would have elicited little interest.

Contingent punishment procedures can have counterconditioning components added to them easily. This can be done through the presentation of a stimulus or the evocation of a behavior just at the moment of termination of punishment. The stimuli or behaviors would be chosen from the socially approved, adaptive behavior that the client does not perform or value and that typically are mutually exclusive with the behavior or stimulus attraction under treatment. Thus, as we have already noted, male homosexuals can be shown pictures of nude males accompanied by the onset and duration of shock. Subsequently, they may activate a switch that terminates the slides, or the therapist may darken the screen just as the shock terminates. Immediately, a slide depicting a nude female will appear, so that it is paired with the termination of the shock. An alcoholic might be shocked immediately as he quaffs a mouthful of bourbon, but the shock might be terminated immediately upon his spitting out of the bourbon.

Initially, aversive counterconditioning procedures are often *escape* procedures.[3] After this technique has been employed for several treatment sessions or trials, however, a client may be allowed to *avoid* the aversive stimulus by requesting or otherwise self-administering the termination of the display of inappropriate stimuli and the onset of the relief stimuli *before* the punishing event has occurred. Because the anticipation of an aversive experience promotes anxiety, the aversive counterconditioning procedure that allows a client to avoid an impending aversive stimulus has been termed both *anticipatory avoidance* and *anxiety relief*. For example, after the inappropriate stimuli are displayed, the

client may have eight seconds before a shock will occur, during which time he or she can terminate the display, institute the display of more appropriate items, and in doing so avoid the shock (Feldman & MacCulloch, 1971). As noted above, even though punishment may not occur (because the client terminates the display), this period tends to be quite anxiety provoking because of the imminent aversive event. Further, the avoidance response (say, pressing a button that terminates the slide of a nude male and substitutes one of a nude female) does not always produce immediate results. The time period during which the inappropriate stimuli and shock can be avoided varies from trial to trial: 6½ seconds on some trials, 4½ on others, and up to 7½ on others. These procedures promote even more intense anxiety and heighten the subsequent feelings of relief (when the slide is removed and shock is avoided). Since the purpose of all these aspects of this technique is to produce anxiety, and since the internal experience of anxiety constitutes the aversive event, the label *anxiety-relief conditioning* seems appropriate to this procedure. Additionally, such a label differentiates this technique, which is based on *avoidance* training, from aversion-relief procedures, which are based on *escape* training.

Note that in the use of anticipatory avoidance technique (e.g., in which a homosexual client may terminate his viewing of a nude male slide prior to experiencing an aversive stimulus and by so doing avoid that unpleasant experience), it has not been demonstrated that the aversion-relief effect actually operates (MacDonough, 1972). It is clearly a basic theoretical premise, however, that anxiety increases as the client views the slide (and the shock approaches), and that the termination of the viewing of that slide produces a decrement in anxiety. This reduction in anxiety, in turn, is a highly positive event paired with current stimuli (for instance, the presentation of a slide of a nude female) and one that may reinforce the act of terminating the availability of the prohibited stimulus and attention to it.

---

[3]That is, doing something or having something occur (e.g., for a homosexual, withdrawing the picture of a nude male) makes the aversive stimulus cease and the client thus "escapes" from it.

Thus far, we have dwelt almost totally on the use of aversive counterconditioning to *reduce* the attractiveness of a stimulus or even to cause it to induce an unpleasant internal state. In research on the use of aversive procedures to treat alcoholism, for example, the major focus is generally on techniques to induce conditioned taste aversions. Also noteworthy, however, is the applicability of research in this area to a more positive goal, the treatment of problem situations where an unwanted taste aversion is of concern. Generally, such research would be relevant in the general area of behavioral medicine, particularly for situations in which a physical treatment, such as chemotherapy for cancer, induces taste aversions for food (in general) as a side effect (Burish, Levy, & Meyerowitz, 1985). In this instance, research reveals conditions under which aversive counterconditioning procedures *fail* to induce an acquired aversion. In an example of such research, Cannon, Best, Batson, & Feldman (1983) report that a pretreatment familiarization to an unusual taste tended to prevent taste aversion through the use of apomorphine-induced nausea. These results suggest that effective induction of taste aversion will be facilitated by linking the taste with nausea before the trial on which nausea is induced. Contrarily, findings such as these (see also Elkins & Hobbs, 1979) suggest ways that patients undergoing chemotherapy might be protected from acquired taste aversions that induce anorexic complications by careful exposure to foods during times when nausea is not present, thus interfering with the direct conditioning of chemotherapy-induced nausea to the taste of food. See Chapter 11 for an extensive treatment of behavioral medicine procedures, including those based on aversion techniques.

Aversive counterconditioning procedures have most often been employed to treat homosexuality, various sexual deviations, smoking, and alcoholism—all problems for which the typical eliciting stimulus is attractive and compelling to the client. Although the basic procedure utilized in the standard treatment of a particular disorder is the same, there is a fairly wide variation among behavior therapists in the exact procedural details. The next two sections illustrate the use of electrical- and drug-induced aversive states in procedures to negatively sensitize individuals to inappropriate stimuli and behaviors, and occasionally to postively sensitize (i.e., to add reinforcing characteristics) individuals to alternative, appropriate stimuli and behaviors. Major criticisms have been made regarding the degree to which the timing of the aversive state is important, and questions have been raised about the conclusion that classical conditioning is actually occurring in aversion and aversion-relief paradigms since the research evidence has been conflicting (Hallam, Rachman, & Falkowski, 1972; Langevin & Martin, 1975; Levey & Martin, 1975; Russell, Armstrong, & Patel, 1976). In the following sections, we will illustrate procedures for the implementation of aversive counterconditioning, but the reader should remain aware that the psychological principles underlying any effectiveness shown by these techniques are still not fully understood.

The Use of Electric Shock in Aversive Conditioning and Counterconditioning

Two relatively early investigations in the area of aversive counterconditioning provided the clearest examples of the procedural detail that goes into an electrical aversion procedure. Since different therapists and investigators employ individualized treatment programs, the one selected for illustration here and the problems on which they focus (homosexual behavior, or desire not acceptable to the client, and alcoholism) should not be interpreted as prototypes but simply as detailed examples. Bear in mind that a homosexual orientation is not considered a behavioral disorder unless it is "ego dystonic"—that is, unacceptable to the individual involved.

Figure 8–2 *A diagram of the setting and apparatus utilized by Feldman and MacCulloch in the electrical aversion treatment of homosexuality.*

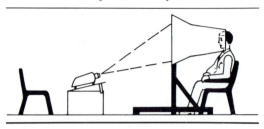

From Feldman and MacCulloch (1971).

Feldman & MacCulloch (1965, 1971) have presented detailed procedures for the treatment of homosexual individuals who wish to change their sexual proclivities. In this procedure, the client viewed slides (and short movie clips) from a chair, with electrodes attached to his leg ("posterior tibial group of muscles, avoiding the tibia and the lateral peroneal nerve"). Provision was made for the use of current at either of two preset levels, to avoid habituation to a stimulus of one particular level of intensity. The client was given a switch that controlled the slide projector, although the therapist had final control. The apparatus is depicted in Figure 8–2. (Feldman and MacCulloch [1971] have presented detailed diagrams of the construction of the treatment apparatus.)

Initially, clients were given a series of pictures of clothed and nude males and were asked to rate their degrees of attractiveness. Eventually, a number of these, including pictures brought in by the client, were arranged into a hierarchy. After this step, a hierarchy of female slides was also formulated, and the two hierarchies were melded into a series of pairs, with the *least* attractive male slide paired with the *most* attractive female slide, and so on. Patients who had appropriate pictures of their own, of a lover, wife, or girl friend, for example, contributed these pictures and they, too, were made

into slides and included in the procedure. In later versions (Feldman & MacCulloch, 1971), short film clips were included as well as slides.

The level of shock was determined by increasing the current gradually to the point identified by the patient as unpleasant. The slides were presented on a small screen in a quiet darkened room. The client was informed that he would see a male slide and after several seconds he might receive a shock. He was further informed that he could turn off the slide by pressing a switch, and that the moment the slide was no longer visible, the shock would no longer be forthcoming (or would terminate if it had already commenced). However, it was stressed that the slide should remain on the screen as long as the client found it sexually attractive.

When the first slide was presented, if the client switched it off within eight seconds, he was not shocked. If he left it on after eight seconds, a shock was given. If the client did not immediately terminate the shock, the intensity of the shock was increased until he did so (this rarely occurred). If the client waited until shock had begun, terminating the slide was termed an escape response. Typically, the first several exposures to the slide resulted in escape responses; next there were some escape trials and some trials when the client pressed the switch prior to shock (anticipatory avoidance); and then there was a series of trials with consistent avoidance. At this point (after three consecutive avoidance trials), the procedure became more complex. Some of the subsequent avoidance attempts were successful, and shock was avoided. Some were not successful: the slide remained on, and after eight seconds the client received a brief shock. Some of the avoidance attempts received delayed success (the slide did not leave the screen for 4½, 6, or 7½ seconds after coming on, the delay times being varied randomly). Immediate success, nonsuccess, and delayed success trials were randomly interspersed.

Feldman and MacCulloch (1971) reported that clients felt relief when the slide to be avoided actually disappeared from view (this is a common report, cited also by Birk, Huddleston, Millers, & Cohler [1971]). Consequently, a corollary to the procedure described above included having a female slide appear upon the termination of a male slide (and, of course, vice versa when treating female homosexuals). This did not happen on each trial (a procedure the authors felt led to better generalization), and the therapist was in control of the termination of the female slides. The client could, however, request the return of the female slide (and a correlated delay in the beginning of the next trial), and randomly this request was or was not granted.

Treatment began with the least attractive male slide and the most attractive female slide. After a client was continuously and quickly rejecting a male slide, the next slide pair was introduced. The frequency with which the female slide appeared on successful avoidance trials (when requested) went from 100 percent to 33 percent. This was intended to establish firmly the behavior of requesting the female slide and to allow maintenance of this behavior despite decreasing success. The maximum number of requested reappearances of the female slide rose from one to three across the first three programs, and then decreased to two for the fourth program. This also was intended to develop the habit of performing active approach behaviors to female stimuli. To accustom the client to viewing female figures, the length of the presentation of the female slide was increased from 4 seconds to 12 seconds across the four programs, and its reappearance increased from 4 to 12 seconds as well.

It is noteworthy that of eight clients who received this treatment regimen and no other, seven were successfully avoiding homosexual behavior three months following treatment, and one engaged only in homosexual fantasy. This treatment procedure was only one of several in an evaluative study that is reported in the final

section of this chapter. When clients who were unsuccessfully treated by one or more treatment procedures were given the anticipatory avoidance regimen, the success rate was far lower, and only one out of six patients could be counted as a success. This latter ratio may be an extreme underestimate to the extent that only the more difficult and trenchant cases were included, ones that has been treated unsuccessfully by other procedures. Indeed, Feldman and MacCulloch felt that their anticipatory avoidance procedure was more applicable to patients who had had some form of heterosexual experience prior to treatment, however minimal, and in whom some heterosexual interest was present, again, however, minimal. These authors classify homosexuals into two categories on this basis: primary homosexuals (having no heterosexual interest or skills) and secondary homosexuals (having such heterosexual interest and skills). They reported that most failures, especially clients who had already had another form of treatment, could be classified as primary homosexuals.

This classification brings us again to a point that must be stressed over and over in the context of aversive control, namely, the importance of the availability (or training in) alternative modes of behavior. In the present instance, although Feldman and MacCulloch's technique contained procedures designed to increase the attractiveness of female stimuli, there was no provision for the acquisition of the requisite skills needed for proper social and sexual interactions with the opposite sex. Provision of training in these behavior patterns would surely increase the success of such therapy and might eradicate the proposed importance of a distinction between primary and secondary homosexuals.

Although the aversive treatment of alcoholism does not usually employ shock as the aversive stimulus, it can be used in the treatment of this disorder. Blake (1965) reported the successful use of a combination of relaxation and shock procedures in the treatment of alcoholism. In this procedure, the client is placed in a room and separated from the therapist by a one-way vision screen. Electrodes for the delivery of shock are attached to the client's forearm. The client is given the liquor of his choice, a glass, and some water, and told to mix his drink as he prefers it. He is then told to sip this drink, but not to swallow any of it. Prior to this time, the therapist and client have established a level of shock that is above the threshold level at which the client begins to report that the shock is unpleasant and painful. Following each sip, a shock may be applied and the client may terminate this shock by spitting out his mouthful of alcohol into a bowl. Half the time, on a random schedule, the client receives a shock, and half the time a green light comes on, signaling that there will be no shock and that he is to spit the liquor into the bowl. Blake's procedure usually lasts over only four to eight days and involves an investment of about five hours per client.

The relaxation Blake uses in addition to aversion procedures is not intended to involve systematic desensitization. Clients are simply instructed in the use of muscular relaxation techniques (Jacobson, 1938) and told to use relaxation as a means to control general tension and to induce natural sleep at night. With this combination of relaxation training and aversive conditioning, Blake reported that up to 54 percent of his clients remain abstinent over a period of 6 months, and 52 percent over a 12-month period.

Sensitization techniques involving electric shock have also been used in cases of drug abuse. As with alcohol, the treatment procedures occasionally employ relaxation training as well, perhaps as a potential substitute for the drug-induced relaxation. Lesser (1967) worked with a 21-year-old college senior who wished to eliminate his drug habit, which involved the self-administration of morphine two or three times a week. The client was not completely addicted, but he had been at an earlier time. He had been able to eliminate his addiction by

dropping out of school and locking himself in a hotel room until the withdrawal symptoms were past.

In the present instance, aversion procedures were designed to associate anxiety with various aspects of injecting drugs. After the client had described in detail his procedure of injecting drugs, he was asked to bring in the equipment he typically used: a hypodermic syringe and a rubber nipple, which he used to squeeze dissolved morphine through the needle. The injection procedure was analyzed into five steps. In each treatment routine, the client was asked to imagine a particular step and to signal when he had a clear image in his mind. Two of the five steps involved the client actually picking up the syringe or nipple while imagining. Once the client signaled that he had a clear image, the shock commenced and ceased only when the client said "stop," indicating that he had ceased to visualize the step, and after he had dropped any object he may have picked up as part of the sequence.

For this particular case, the aversion procedure was administered twice a week, with the client going through the five steps three times each session (for a total of 15 shocks). Each step was shocked for the first 16 sessions, and from then on a partial schedule of punishment was instituted. It is interesting to note that after 8 sessions of aversion procedures, the client accepted an opportunity to take drugs. He reported that he did not get the expected "good feeling" and was disappointed that he had yielded. Apparently, any lack of success of the aversion procedures in inhibiting the behavior is more than overcome by their successful elimination of the positive value of the drug effects. Follow-ups after 7 and 10 months indicated that the client had successfully avoided hard drugs. He did continue to smoke marijuana upon occasion, but had never considered stopping its use when undertaking therapy. Continued use of marijuana did not appear to hamper the successful avoidance of more dangerous drugs.

The Use of Drug-induced Aversive States in Aversive Conditioning and Counterconditioning

A variety of drugs has been used to produce aversive states that can be paired with problem behaviors or stimuli. The most common class of drugs used are *emetics*, notably apomorphine hydrochloride or emetine hydrochloride. Occasionally, given proper respirating equipment, curare-type, short-term paralytic drugs can be used, which cause a temporary inability to breathe—a condition that is extremely aversive.

It should be clear that the use of drugs in aversive treatment requires even more equipment and preparation than the use of shock, and occasionally requires the hospitalization of the patient. Provision must be made for the collection and disposal of emesis if emetics are used, and medical supervision is ethically mandatory since drugs are typically injected and may have undesirable side effects. For example, frequent use of emetine can produce cardiovascular problems (Barker, Thorpe, Blakemore, Lavin, & Conway, 1961). Side effects of this magnitude clearly reduce the desirability of the use of such drugs when any alternative procedures involving less risk may be available.

There are several other problems with the use of drugs in aversive control. Drug-induced aversive states have a relatively gradual onset and offset, thus making it difficult to have the onset contingent upon a response, or the offset simultaneous with the presentation of a relief stimulus. Furthermore, it has been clearly shown (Fromer & Berkowitz, 1964) that aversive stimuli that have a gradual onset produce weaker avoidance responses than do stimuli whose onset is clear and abrupt.

Despite its other disadvantages, emetine has generally been favored over apomorphine, because the latter is a central depressant. Central depressant drugs retard conditioning and are not as effective in aversion procedures (Franks, 1966). When apomorphine is used, however, its depressant effects may be counteracted by the simultaneous administration of a stimulant such as caffeine (Freund, 1960) or dexamphetamine sulphate (Lavin, Thorpe, Barker, Blakemore, & Conway, 1961).

Aversive control utilizing drugs has been employed most often in the treatment of alcoholism. There is no clear reason for this limitation. Perhaps the delayed aversive effects of drugs are less of an impediment when treating abusive use of other drugs whose effects are also somewhat delayed and not of clearly specifiable onset. Along this line, one might expect that the use of emetics and other drugs producing uncomfortable physical states would be extremely effective in the treatment of narcotic drug abuse involving either the oral or injected ingestion of drugs. Such a use of this technique has not yet become common, however.

The use of drug-induced aversive states in the treatment of alcoholism is not new. Procedures involving electric shock were reported as early as 1934 (Kantorovich, 1934), and the systematic application of drugs began a few years later (Lemere, Voegtlin, Broz, O'Hallaren, & Tupper, 1942a, 1942b; Voegtlin, 1940). Recent methods of treatment still resemble those original procedures, typically involving from four to seven sessions devoted to associating the sight, smell, and taste of alcohol with drug-induced nausea.

In a typical treatment regimen, the client will first be given a verbal description of the treatment procedures, and any questions he may have are answered. Often a client is required to drink only liquids on the treatment day. Also, he may be given a stimulant drug, such as benzedrine sulphate, which is intended to augment the conditioning procedure and offset any narcotic effects produced by the emetic drug (say, if apomorphine were used). Since there are many aspects to the presentation of alcohol (smell, sight, taste), treatment typically proceeds in a darkened, sound-proof room, and the client is confronted by an array of liquors clearly lighted in order to focus his attention on them.

At the beginning of a treatment session, the client will be given two large (10 ounce) glasses of warm salt solution containing $1\frac{1}{2}$ grains of emetine and 1 gram of salt, all dissolved in the 20 ounces of water. Following this procedure, the client will be given an injection containing both emetine hydrochloride and $1\frac{1}{2}$ grains of ephedrine sulphate.

After a few minutes, when the client begins to feel nauseated, he or she should be given several ounces of whiskey in a glass. (Because of its properties as a gastric irritant, whiskey is to be preferred at first, although there are compelling reasons to utilize a variety of beverages, certainly the client's favorite ones, if vomiting is likely to occur without the irritation produced by the whiskey.) It is important that treatment eventually encompass a variety of alcoholic beverages. Several authors (Lemere & Voegtlin, 1940; Quinn & Henbest, 1967) have reported cases in which an aversion was established to the alcoholic beverages used in the aversive procedures, but the client subsequently switched his alcoholic preferences to those that had not been included in the treatment. For each beverage presented, the client is to smell, taste, swill around in his mouth, and then (for some therapists) swallow the liquor, following which vomiting usually occurs.

Early investigators suggested that treatment be continued beyond this point, prolonging the nausea. For example, following vomiting, Voegtlin and his associates (Lemere & Voegtlin, 1940; Lemere et al., 1942a, 1942b; Voegtlin, 1940; Voegtlin, Lemere, Broz, & O'Hallaren, 1941, 1942) recommended giving the client a glass of "near beer" containing tartar emetic in order to prolong the nausea. As treatment progressed, subsequent sessions would include an increase in the dosage of injected emetine, increases in the length of treatment sessions, and a variety of alcoholic beverages to enhance generalization. Other therapists have adopted Voegtlin's general procedure, although often their procedures are not as severe. Furthermore, several minor modifications have been proposed, including pretreatment interviews, hospitalization during treatment (Shadel, 1944), and the elimination of the client's swallowing of the alcohol during the treatment session (Kant, 1944a, 1944b) since, unless it is immediately regurgitated, its own effects are likely to impede successful treatment. These aspects of treatment have not received much specific attention in terms of attempts to evaluate their importance for overall effectiveness. The best generalization seems to be that the treatment elements likely to maximize the aversiveness of stimuli are preferred.

Occasionally, reports appear describing the use of aversive drugs to alter sexual orientation in those who wish to change. McConaghy (1971) compared emetic aversion and aversion relief involving shock in the treatment of 40 men who complained of homosexual feelings and behavior. In the drug treatment regimen, patients were given injections of apomorphine, which induced nausea of about 10 minutes' duration, but no vomiting. Approximately 1 minute before the onset of nausea, the patient switched on a slide showing a nude male. Before the nausea reached its maximum level the slide was switched off. The drug treatment included 28 sessions, which were given at two-hour intervals over a period of five days (the patients were hospitalized for the duration of treatment). In the aversion-relief treatment, shock was made contingent upon the patient's reading of homosexually oriented words and phrases that he found attractive. These words and phrases were read at 10-second intervals. After reading 14 of these words and phrases, the patient viewed 1 that was illustrative of heterosexual activity for 40 seconds, and was not shocked. The total procedure occurred five times within each treatment session. There were three treatment sessions daily for five days.

There were no significant differences in the effectiveness of these two types of treatment.

Following treatment, sexual arousal to pictures of nude men was significantly lower than to slides of nude women, which was not the case in a no-treatment control condition. This tendency had not changed after an entire year. One year following treatment, 50 percent of the patients reported a decrease in homosexual leanings, and 50 percent (not necessarily the same individuals) reported an increase in heterosexual feelings; 25 percent reported that they engaged in no homosexual behavior; and 25 percent (again, not necessarily the same individuals) reported that they had commenced heterosexual intercourse or now engaged in it more frequently.

Although emetics are by far the most common class of drugs employed in aversive control, drug-invoked paralysis has also been used. The drug typically used is succinylcholine chloride dyhydrate, which produces a total paralysis of the respiratory system, including, of course, the cessation of breathing, which lasts approximately 60–90 seconds (Campbell, Sanderson, & Laverty, 1964; Sanderson, Campbell, & Laverty, 1963). The onset and offset of the drug's effects are more clear-cut and controllable than those of the emetic drugs, providing an increased possibility of anxiety-relief conditioning procedures. The anxiety produced by this procedure is quite intense, involving a sense of extreme terror and often including the belief that one is going to die.

In the application of this procedure, the client is connected to a polygraph monitoring his GSR (galvanic skin response), respiration, heart rate, and muscle tension. A respirator is always kept at hand. The client is then placed on a stretcher and the needle of a saline drip bottle is inserted into a vein of his forearm. The drip is left running slowly, and the drugs can be injected directly into the tube running from the saline bottle to the needle. Often clients are given injections of atropine to prevent excessive salivation during the period of paralysis, which might interfere with subsequent breathing. However, the paralytic agent also produces cardiac irregularities in some subjects, and since atropine also acts upon the heart, it is not always advisable to use this drug. Obviously, this procedure requires extensive care in its administration, and should never be considered unless all undesirable consequences can be anticipated and controlled.

In the aversive treatment of a behavior problem such as alcoholism, the therapist should prepare an alcoholic beverage prior to the administration of the drug. The client may be given a bottle containing some of his favorite alcoholic beverage to hold and be asked to smell it, look at it, and taste it, then hand it back to the therapist. This is done several times without the administration of the paralytic agent. These trials involve approximately 10–15 seconds and are repeated approximately once a minute. After these trials, however, the succinylcholine is injected into the drip. As soon as the drug enters the bloodstream, there is a characteristic change in GSR, indicating that the effect is imminent. The therapist then hands the bottle to the client and just as the bottle is put to the lips, the drug usually takes effect. The therapist then holds the bottle to the client's lips and puts a few drops of it into the client's mouth. The bottle is taken away as soon as signs of regular breathing begin to reappear.

Alternatives to Electrical- and Drug-induced Aversive States in Overt Sensitization Procedures

Although many aversive counterconditioning procedures utilize electric shock as the aversive stimulus or employ drug-induced aversive states, there has been a growing trend toward the creative use of alternative, less dangerous, or milder techniques to achieve aversive stimulation that should not go unrecognized. We have already discussed cases or experiments in which enforced repeated performances of a behavior itself (aversive behavior rehearsal) or the overcorrection of a particular action may be utilized to produce an aversive state. Those procedures were discussed in the section on punishment, but we noted that the mechanism for their effectiveness was not totally clear: these procedures might be instituted in a contingent fashion, or they might induce an aversive state that is contiguous with the behavior during repeated performances and thereby alter the intrinsic attractiveness of the behavior.

Some problem behaviors even contain their own aversive components that may be put to advantage in a behavior-change program. Smoking, for example, might be treated by aversive rehearsal through induced rapid smoking (Horan et al., 1977), which heightens the irritating components of the smoke itself, or by providing smoke in a density that is automatically aversive to the client. In many cases, however, the problem behavior has intrinsic maladaptive and possibly physically harmful components that lessen the desirability of this procedure.

An innovative procedure to induce nausea that allows the use of the aversive state in treatment while avoiding drugs or the necessity for an attending physician or other personnel is the Pseudo-Coriolis Effect (Dichgans & Brandt, 1973), which induces nausea merely by providing an individual with a specified visual experience while he tilts his head first to one side, then to the other. In this procedure, an individual is exposed to a visual field of laterally moving vertical stripes by seating him within a large cylinder painted with vertical stripes that is then rotated around him. The individual is then instructed to tilt his head repeatedly, first to one side and then the other. The optokinetic input, combined with the stimulation of the vestibular system by the head tilting, produces the illusion that the person himself is spinning, and severe disequilibrium, dizziness, and nausea result (Lamon, Wilson, & Leaf, 1977).

In two experiments, Lamon and associates first demonstrated that the aversive state produced by this procedure would be utilized to reduce the attractiveness of a preferred beverage when it was used as the aversive component of a counterconditioning (sensitization) procedure. Then they contrasted the effectiveness of the nausea induced by the Pseudo-Coriolis Effect with electrical aversive stimulation for the conditioning of aversion to preferred beverages and found it to be superior in reducing subsequent consumption of what was initially a preferred drink. While not a common procedure and one that does involve cumbersome equipment, this technique does present an alternative to the use of drugs and avoids the physiological risks associated with such procedures.

Counteranxiety-Relief Procedures

Before concluding our discussion of overt aversive counterconditioning procedures, there is one final technique that should be discussed. It is not often used but is nevertheless deserving of some consideration. The *counteranxiety-relief* procedure is intended to transform a neutral stimulus into one that evokes such strong positive feelings that it can overcome and displace feelings of anxiety. We have emphasized the problem of generalizing treatment effects beyond the treatment room. Anxiety-relief procedures are typically utilized in cases where anxiety is the primary problem. By taking a verbal stimulus, such as the word *calm*, and associating it with the termination of punishment, one can create a stimulus that a client may provide for himself when faced with an anxiety-provoking situation outside the therapy room, a stimulus that can reduce or even nullify the feelings of anxiety so that adaptive behavior and relearning can occur. The use of verbal stimuli has distinct advantages, since they can be thought rather than said aloud, thereby enabling the patient to control his own behavior without the notice of others (see Chapter 10 for other procedures of self-control).

The procedure for establishing anxiety-relief conditioning is quite simple. Typically, a continuous shock is delivered to a client for as long as she can bear it. The client is instructed to allow the shock to continue until she can simply bear it no longer, at which time she is to say a particular word (for example, "calm") aloud. As she utters the word, the therapist terminates the current. This procedure can be repeated a number of times over a series of sessions, and its effectiveness can be enhanced by slightly increasing the level of shock on each trial. An alternative procedure is to begin with a mild level of shock and to increase the intensity gradually as the current stays on, with the client saying the designated word when the intensity has reached the maximum the client can bear. In any event, care should be taken to utilize a level of shock that is truly aversive to the client and to increase the level whenever the client reports that she is adapting to the point that the unpleasantness of the stimulus seems to be decreased.

One procedure was proposed for counter-anxiety-relief conditioning utilizing a voluntarily induced aversive state (Orwin, 1971; Orwin, le Boeuf, Dovey, & James, 1975). This technique can be an alternative to other counteranxiety procedures, such as desensitization, if it is used alone with exposure to the feared stimulus. In other words, in addition to providing a neutral stimulus, such as a word, with anxiety-abating properties by pairing it with an intense experience of relief from an aversive state, anxiety associated with specific items can be allayed by exposing the individual to those items when he or she is feeling relief from an aversive state. The voluntarily induced aversive state proposed by Orwin and his colleagues involves the self-induced prevention of breathing for the maximum period of time that an individual can tolerate it, with the resumption of breathing constituting the relief experience. Clients are in-

structed to take a deep breath, *then exhale completely,* following which they close their mouths and pinch their nostrils shut with their hand. With the other hand, they then signal the therapist at the point when they can no longer tolerate this respiratory interruption.

Orwin and colleagues (1975) utilized this procedure in the treatment of specific fears, an unusual target for an aversive control technique. In their procedure, at the point when respiration was about to be resumed, a curtain separating the client from the feared object was opened and he (the client) pressed a button that slowly brought the object nearer and nearer to him, holding the button down as long as he could. A control group of clients was included who were simply instructed to expose themselves to the feared object by pressing the button; they engaged in no other procedures that might induce a relief experience. The individuals involved all had phobias for some type of organism ranging from spiders to snakes. The counteranxiety relief procedure produced a significant reduction in both avoidance behavior and subjective reports of anxiety regarding the previously feared item, whereas simple exposure had no effect. A seven-month follow-up revealed only one instance of relapse. Unfortunately, Orwin and his colleagues (Orwin, 1971, 1973; Orwin et al., 1975) are the only individuals who have reported on this treatment procedure, though it clearly has potential and deserves the attention of other investigators.

The Use of Cognitive Stimuli in Aversive Counterconditioning

In treating a variety of disorders, some therapists employ only words that suggest the changeworthy behavior or describe situations or stimuli associated with it. Thus, a male homosexual might be confronted with the words "man in bed with me," or "gay bar," during shock; and then with "woman's breast," "woman in bed with me," or "girl friend," immediately upon the termination of shock (an aversion-relief procedure with anxiety-relief components, as well, since thinking "woman in bed with me" may reduce his anxiety when he advances to that stage of heterosexual behavior).

It seems likely that the use of symbolic representations in any therapy, while effective to a good degree, may not be as effective as employing the true stimulus or behavior. In some instances, however, the symbolic stimuli employed may, in fact, be the operative ones in real life. The fantasy of a nude male or a picture of one may be a common stimulus for sexual arousal in an active homosexual, and even more so in a homosexual who wishes to alter his behavior and consequently is less active with real partners, depending more upon masturbation to homosexual fantasies for sexual outlet. The point remains, however, that even though the use of real stimuli and behaviors may enhance the effectiveness of a modification technique, symbolic representation of stimuli and behaviors is often the only alternative available to a therapist.

The extent to which such symbolic representations may be effective is demonstrated in the effectiveness of systematic desensitization, which uses imaginal stimuli (see Chapter 2). Further, the following section on covert sensitization (see also the discussions of implosive therapy in Chapter 7) shows how imagined circumstances that are highly aversive can be effectively employed as the aversive stimulus in place of "real" stimuli of an aversive nature—such as electric shock or emetic drugs.

Covert Sensitization

Covert sensitization (Cautela, 1966b) involves the use of imagery that includes aversive elements, as well as the imagined depiction of problem behaviors. The simultaneous inclusion of these two factors, aversion and the problem behaviors, is designed to alter the valence of the behavior and any relevant imagined stimuli in a manner similar to the aversion procedures, discussed earlier, that involve physical aversive stimulation.

This technique has been successfully applied to a wide variety of behavior disorders, including alcoholism (Anant, 1968; Ashem & Donner, 1966; Cautela, 1967, 1970b, 1971c; Cautela & Wisocki, 1969; Smith & Gregory, 1976), obesity (Cautela, 1966b; Janda & Rimm, 1972; Stuart, 1967), homosexuality and pedophilia (Barlow, Leitenberg, & Agras, 1969; Maletzky, 1980), fetishism (Kolvin, 1967), transvestite fantasies (Gershman, 1970), sadistic fantasies (Davison, 1968a), gasoline sniffing (Kolvin, 1967), delinquent behavior (Cautela, 1967), shoplifting (Gautlier & Pellerin, 1982), self-destructive behavior (Cautela & Baron, 1969), and smoking (Irey, 1972; Lawson & May, 1970; Sipich, Russell, & Tobias, 1974; Tooley & Pratt, 1967; Wagner & Bragg, 1970; Mullen, 1968). It has also been utilized in the treatment of drug addiction (Götestam & Melin, 1974; Melin & Götestam, 1973; Polakow, 1975), trichotillomania (Levine, 1976), and nailbiting (Daniels, 1974; Paquin, 1977). Although most consistently used with adults, at least one report gives successful case examples of the implementation of covert sensitization with children (Cautela, 1982).

In the application of covert sensitization, the therapist must generate a scene for the client to imagine that combines the problem behavior, relevant stimuli, and aversive aspects into a coherent image or train of images. Since problems treated by aversion procedures often involve behaviors that are highly motivated and quite intrinsically reinforcing, and that are generally elicited powerfully by stimuli themselves quite attractive, treatment by covert sensitization is often performed systematically, much in the manner of systematic desensitization or modeling with guided participation. Thus, at the beginning of treatment, the client might be asked to imagine a highly aversive scene and to combine it with a scene in which the problem behavior is only weakly elicited by the imagined stimuli, or in which the behavior is not totally satisfying. Some work may also be required in advance, such as testing out various aversive images in order to find one that the client can imagine easily and clearly and that he or she finds most aversive.

Davison (1968a) provided a good example of the systematic application of covert sensitization procedures in his account of the treatment of sadistic sexual fantasies in a young man. The client was referred because his sexual gratification was comprised primarily of masturbation to fantasies of sadistic torture inflicted upon young women. The total treatment of this client involved both positive conditioning (instructing the client to masturbate to pictures and images of females in nonsadistic contexts) and covert sensitization to the sadistic fantasies. Therefore, as with the application of aversive procedures in general, care was taken to provide alternative modes of responding, and the aversion procedures were combined with others of a more positive nature.

The aversive images utilized must indeed be aversive. Typically, the client is given a description of a thoroughly nauseating scene that involves urine, feces, or bodily harm. Some adjustment may be necessary to find the scene that is maximally aversive to a particular client. For example, Davison (1968a) originally instructed his client to imagine a typical sadistic scene (an attractive young girl tied to stakes in the ground and tearfully struggling to escape). While imagining this scene, the client was first instructed to imagine that as he looked upon this situation someone was bringing a smoldering branding iron toward his eyes, so close that his eyebrows became singed. When this proved unsuccessful, a second image was described, in which he was kicked viciously in the groin by an angry-looking karate expert. This image also proved

to be only mildly aversive. Finally, the client was instructed to imagine himself viewing the poor struggling girl while peering over a bowl of "soup" comprised of urine with feces floating on top, which was steaming forth an utterly nauseating stench. When this proved effectively aversive (the client displayed facial expressions and groans indicating that it was so), he was instructed to imagine leaning over the bowl, drinking from it, and the accompanying nausea, observing the struggling girl all the while.

There is some evidence to suggest that it is also important to relate the character of the aversive stimulus in the images to the behavior under treatment. Clarke and Hayes (1984) contrasted the effectiveness of nausea-evoking and anxiety-evoking imagery to induce a taste-aversion and then assessed consumption of the target substance. Although the two types of imagery produced equal ratings of unpleasantness, only the nausea-evoking imagery produced a significant reduction in consumption. This suggests, once again, that within general categories of behavior therapy techniques, qualitative aspects of the treatment procedures should be tailored as much as possible to relevant aspects of the behavior under treatment.

Occasionally, the aversive imagery may draw from a client's actual aversive experiences while performing the changeworthy behavior. Miller (1963) reported the treatment of a homosexual whose past experiences had left him nauseated following the performance of fellatio with an uncircumcised partner because of the prevalent odors and taste of urine and perspiration. After several sessions in which the description of these experiences was used as the aversive component of scenes involving homosexual contacts, the client reported that he felt nauseated during the performance of homosexual behavior and eventually ceased his homosexual contacts. As in the case reported by Davison (1968a), Miller combined the aversion procedures with procedures designed to increase the attractiveness of women, and the client reported increasing attraction to and dating of women as treatment progressed.

The problem of finding an aversive scene of sufficient intensity may be helped by the systematic application of relaxation training along with the aversive imagery and by the use of a series of images in which the aversive aspects are decreased and the client imagines himself ceasing the undesirable behavior or leaving a situation just as he begins to feel nauseated or frightened. Finally, the client imagines relief and relaxation when he pictures himself away from the original scene, performing an entirely different behavior. A good application of this procedure is reported by Barlow and associates (1969). These authors treated two clients, a pedophilic and a homosexual, utilizing only covert sensitization. The homosexual client, in one instance, was asked to imagine himself approaching and entering the apartment of a male friend. One scene he has to imagine went as follows:

> As you get close to the door, you notice a queasy feeling in the pit of the stomach. You open the door and see Bill lying on the bed naked and you can sense that puke is filling up your stomach and forcing its way up to your throat. You walk over to Bill and you can see him clearly, as you reach out for him you can taste the puke, bitter and sticky and acidy on your tongue, you start gagging and retching and chunks of vomit are coming out of your mouth and nose, dropping onto your shirt and all over Bill's skin. (Barlow, et al., 1969, p. 598)

These authors included eight imagined scenes in each treatment session. The one just described would have been one of the first, and would have been expanded to last from 30 to 60 seconds. During the final four scenes, however, the procedure would differ considerably. For example, the client might be asked to imagine himself approaching a male, who was a potential sex partner, and just beginning to feel nauseated. At that point, he would visualize himself turning around and walking away from the encounter, feeling more and more relieved and relaxed as he did so. At the beginning of each session, the client was given relaxation instruction, so that the removal of the aversive image and its attendant discomfort would leave him in a pleasant, comfortable state.

It is possible to cast covert sensitization procedures into a simple aversion or an aversion-relief approach (Cautela, 1967; Irey, 1972). The two scenes described next are from a covert sensitization treatment of smoking. Irey utilized these scenes in treatment sessions that included 10 presentations of the sensitization scene, which alternated with 10 presentations of the aversion-relief scene:

SENSITIZATION SCENE

Now I want you to imagine that you've just had your supper and have just decided to have an after-dinner cigarette, a (name of favorite brand). As you are about to reach for the pack, you get a funny feeling in the pit of your stomach. You start to feel queasy, nauseous and sick all over. As you pick up the pack, you can feel food particles inching up your throat. You're just about to vomit. As you pull a cigarette out of the pack, the food comes up into your mouth. You try to keep your mouth closed because you are afraid that you'll spit food out all over the place. You bring the cigarette up to your mouth. As you're about to open your mouth, you puke; you vomit all over your hands, the cigarette, the pack. It goes all over the table, all over the people sitting at the table. Your eyes are watering. Snot and mucous are all over your mouth and nose. Your hands feel sticky and slimy. There's an awful smell and a horrible sour taste in your mouth. As you look at this mess, you just can't help but vomit again and again until only watery stuff is coming out. Finally, nothing more will come up but you've got the dry heaves and just can't stop retching. It feels like the inside of your stomach is tearing loose. As you look up, everybody is staring at you with shocked expressions. You turn away from the cigarette pack and immediately you start to feel better. You run out of the room, and as you run out, you feel better and better. You wash and clean yourself up, and it feels wonderful.

AVOIDANCE (RELIEF) SCENE:

You've just finished eating supper and decide to have an after-dinner cigarette. As soon as you make the decision, you start to get that funny feeling in the pit of your stomach, again. You say to yourself, "Oh, no; I won't have that cigarette." Then you immediately feel calm, comfortable, and relaxed. (1972, p. 89)

The evidence that has appeared in the literature indicates that procedures involving aversive imagery are quite effective. For example, in the cases reported by Barlow and associates (1969), the therapists asked their clients to keep a diary of the urges they felt to perform pedophilic or homosexual acts, and the homosexual client discussed earlier was actually instructed to visit bars several times a week, recording instances when he felt attracted to other men. When the clients came in for treatment, they were also asked to complete a card sort in which they were to rank verbal descriptions of scenes used in the sensitization procedure in terms of their attractiveness. No sensitization trials were conducted during the first five days in order to establish a baseline. Then the period of treatment lasted 6–9 days, during which time sensitization was carried out. Following this stage, there were several treatment sessions where the scenes were presented without the aversive portions of the images, and finally a series of sessions when the aversive portions of the images were reintroduced. Figure 8–3 depicts the results of these procedures for the pedophilic client, and the results were similar for the homosexual one.

These findings suggest that the aversive portion of the treatment was necessary and effective. The fact that the client's urges and attractiveness ratings rose during the extinction period is an important indication that the pairing of the noxious portions of the images with the attractive portions is important. During the extinction, all the other psychotherapeutic variables remained, such as therapeutic instructions, patient expectancies of improvement, and the rapport between patient and therapist. In this

particular study, we must note that the card sort procedure is not specifically behavioral and subject to demand characteristics (the client may sort cards according to how he feels he is expected to feel). Nevertheless it appears that covert sensitization can be an effective procedure for aversive control, though continued research concerning its short- and long-term effectiveness in changing behavior, as well as cognition, will increase.

Although covert sensitization is, by definition, a procedure free from overt aversive stimulation, the effectiveness of this technique may be increased if it is "assisted" by ancillary aversive input. Maletzky (1973, 1977) and Maletzky and George (1973) have reported the enhancement of self-induced aversive states by exposing clients to the odor of valeric acid during the presentation of covert scenes. This procedure arose after reports in the literature of the use of covert sensitization procedures with only marginal effectiveness. In one investigation, Maletzky and George (1973) used the assisted covert sensitization procedure with four homosexual clients who were unhappy with their sexual orientation. Treatment produced significant declines in both overt and covert (fantasy) homosexual behavior, accompanied by an increase in direct and fantasy heterosexual inclinations. Other reports, however, suggest that when used alone, covert sensitization is as effective as electrical aversion therapy (McConaghy, Armstrong, & Blaszcynski, 1981).

Another procedure for the enhancement of therapeutic success is the inclusion of "booster" sessions sometime after initial treatment in order to bolster the permanence of changed behavior. Maletzky (1977) reported on the effectiveness of assisted covert sensitization combined with booster sessions for the long-term reduction in homosexual behavior and exhibitionism in 30 clients. There were three phases to the treatment. First was active treatment, which utilized assisted covert sensitization in bimonthly office sessions over a period of 6 months combined with 15–25 additional sessions at the

Figure 8–3 *Total attractiveness score on card sort and total frequency of pedophilic urges in blocks of four days surrounding each treatment session (○——○: total urges; ●– – –●: card sort).*

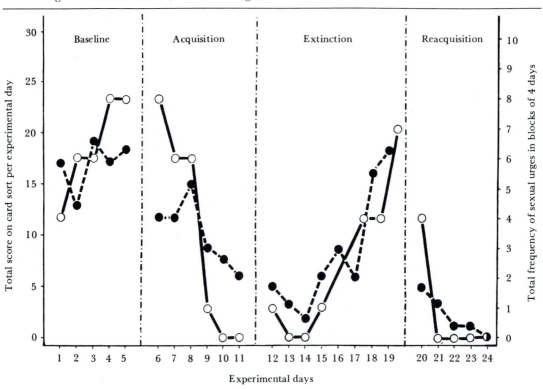

From Barlow, Leitenberg, and Agras (1969).

clients' homes, plus *in vivo* sensitizations whenever the opportunity arose. After the treatment phase, there was a 12-month follow-up with monthly assessments, which was followed by a booster phase with monthly office treatments for the first 3 months and then on each 90 days thereafter, plus monthly assisted sensitization sessions at the client's home for the entire 12-month period.

The effectiveness of this treatment regime can be seen in Figure 8–4. Although there was a gradual remission in homosexual or exhibitionistic behavior during the follow-up period,

the booster sessions very quickly reduced the frequency of overt behavior and maintained it at an extremely low level for the duration of the 12-month period. This treatment regime is a good example of an intense and aggressive program for the reduction of problem behaviors and is noteworthy because of the way treatment was implemented in a variety of settings and over a long period of time. Of the 30 individuals under treatment, only 11 showed behavioral remissions during the follow-up period. The remaining 19 clients showed no relapse to homosexual or exhibitionistic behavior

Figure 8–4 *Effectiveness of assisted covert sensitization combined with booster sessions on homosexual and exhibitionistic behavior (●——●: homosexual behavior; ○– – –○: exhibitionistic behavior).*

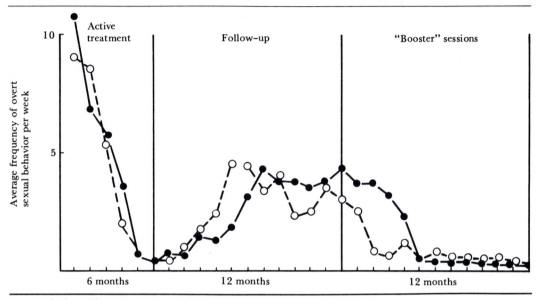

From Maletzky (1977).

and did not, behaviorally, appear to require the booster sessions. It is difficult to fault a study that reports such a thorough attempt to treat such difficult problem behavior patterns as homosexuality and exhibitionism, but we must note that the effectiveness of the booster sessions for the long-term effectiveness of treatment, as opposed to recapturing incipient treatment failures, has yet to be demonstrated. Additional follow-up data beyond the 30 months of treatment for which data are reported would speak to this question.

Some early research suggested that covert sensitization alone may not be a particularly effective treatment for obesity. Foreyt and Hagen (1973) found that obese subjects' liking for favorite foods decreased as much in a suggestion (placebo) control group as it did in a group treated with covert sensitization. Diament and Wilson (1975) also contrasted covert sensiti-

zation procedures with an attention-placebo condition and found no effects on eating, although both conditions evidenced decreased subjective reactions to the taste and odor of a target food while a control group did not.

Other studies reported the effective use of covert sensitization, though nearly all of them included multiple-treatment procedures in addition to covert sensitization (Harris, 1969; Janda & Rimm, 1972; Manno & Marston, 1972; Stuart, 1967). For example, Manno and Marston (1972) found that both a covert sensitization procedure and a covert reinforcement procedure (imagining great pleasure at being able to exercise restraint in eating) produced greater weight losses than an attention-control condition. The covert sensitization procedure in this experiment included a very clear relief component in which nausea was imagined to pass after the subject imagined declining to eat a particular morsel. In addition, in the final sessions of treatment (Nos. 6 and 7), subjects were to imagine saying "I don't want it," to imagine actually not wanting the food, and then to "feel wonderful." These components may have contributed to the observed effectiveness of the covert sensitization procedure in this case. This interpretation that covert sensitization requires, or at least profits from, embellishment in the treatment of obesity is supported by another finding in the literature in which covert sensitization was included in a multimodal treatment that proved effective (Romanczyk, Tracey, Wilson, & Thorpe, 1973). Although this issue is not fully resolved and has not been the focus of recent research, it does not seem inappropriate to suggest that covert sensitization procedures will typically be employed most effectively with other techniques of behavior change, particularly those that promote behaviors and cognitions that are adaptive and alternative to the behavior under treatment.

Some investigators have expressed concern about the possibility that some or all of the effectiveness of covert sensitization procedures was due to the therapeutic instructions with which they were introduced, rather than to the actual procedures themselves. Three studies that addressed this issue have produced conflicting outcomes (Barlow, Agras, Leitenberg, Callahan, & Moore, 1972; Beiman, 1976; Foreyt & Hagen, 1973). Barlow and colleagues (1972) varied the information that was given to a homosexual client under treatment as to the supposed effects of the aversive scenes. Measurements were taken of penis circumference during exposure to slides of nude males to indicate actual sexual arousal. After baseline measurements, a covert sensitization treatment was instituted but the client was told that the scenes would probably *increase* his sexual arousal. Following this was a short baseline period when slides were shown but the aversive imagery was deleted, and finally there was a second treatment phase during which the client was told that his desires would now most likely

decrease. The results are indicated in Figure 8–5. Despite the incorrect information during the second phase of treatment, in both phases employing covert sensitization procedures, the degree of sexual arousal to homosexual stimuli decreased. Aversive imagery, therefore, was obtaining a therapeutic effect despite instructions that would incline the client to expect the opposite.

On the other hand, Foreyt and Hagen (1973) found that obese subjects' *liking* for favorite foods decreased as much by suggestion as by a covert sensitization procedure. Beiman (1976), in a study that examined stress reactions such as heart or respiration rate or muscle tension, found that subjects who expected to have a mild response to aversive imagery did indeed have milder responses than those who expected stronger responses. A reasonable conclusion seems to be that the direction of therapeutic results is indeed a function of actual aversive components of covert sensitization procedures, although the therapeutic instructions accompanying them may exert a degree of influence over the amount of emotional arousal that is induced by the aversive images.

Empirical Findings

In this section we will discuss only two of the many categories of problem behavior that are most often treated by aversive control procedures: sexual and affectional preferences and alcoholism. It should be clear from the many examples throughout the chapter that aversive control procedures can be successfully utilized to reduce or eliminate many divergent patterns of behavior, ranging from those that may be life threatening (or life shortening)—such as self-injurious behavior, obesity, or smoking—to those that are less "important" but problematic nonetheless—such as nail biting, aggressive behavior, psychogenic seizures, hallucinations, or kleptomania. Nevertheless, a great deal of research and much social concern has centered

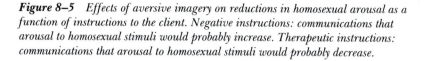

Figure 8–5 *Effects of aversive imagery on reductions in homosexual arousal as a function of instructions to the client. Negative instructions: communications that arousal to homosexual stimuli would probably increase. Therapeutic instructions: communications that arousal to homosexual stimuli would probably decrease.*

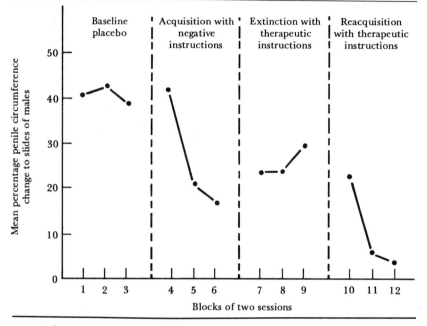

From Barlow, Agras, Leitenberg, Callahan, and Moore (1972).

on sexual- and alcohol-related behavior patterns, and we will attempt a brief summary of the success with which these have been treated using methods of aversive control.

Sexual and Affectional Preferences

Individuals wishing to change their sexual or affectional preference are often persons whose affectional preferences are uncomfortable to them or who engage in sexual behavior that is socially or maritally disruptive or illegal, such as exhibitionism or fetishism. Almost invariably, these persons are male. There is hardly a case report or experiment in the literature involving women, and questions might be raised about the degree to which the demonstrated effectiveness of any technique for the alteration of sexual or affectional preferences indicates that it would be successful in the treatment of women.

We should also note that in the present section we will focus on the change of sexual or affectional preferences other than homosexuality. This reflects in large part the fact that a homosexual orientation is not, in and of itself, maladaptive or disordered. Additionally, we have employed many treatment examples illustrating aversive treatment procedures that happened to focus on ego dystonic homosexual orientations, and these examples generally summarize the empirical findings on that issue.

In this section, we will touch only superficially on multimodal approaches to treatment, although it must be recognized that these are important for successful outcomes. Although abstinence or perhaps moderation is a potential treatment goal for problem drinking, sexual behavior change often involves the development of *alternative* behavior patterns. We have already stressed the importance of alternative behaviors in the utilization of aversive control procedures, and this is a good occasion for a reminder. In some cases, sexual or affectional preference changes may be difficult or impossible to achieve, but alternative treatment goals might be easily constructed. For example, Masters treated a middle-aged man with a lengthy history of pedophilic behavior. This man had never had any sort of heterosexual experience and found the idea of such behavior extraordinarily distasteful. Although he had not had extensive homosexual contact with individuals his own age, he found this much less aversive. The treatment subsequently involved directing the gentleman into a comfortable homosexual existence, free from pedophilic desires.

In general, reports concerning aversion procedures in the treatment of homosexuality indicate that success in modifying this behavior problem is slightly less extensive than the success reported for transvestism or fetishism. Treatment of transvestism typically involves the client's viewing of pictures of himself in female attire or actually cross-dressing during treatment. Drug-induced aversion has been applied during treatment of this disorder, with success reported over follow-up periods of three to seven months (Barker et al., 1961; Glynn & Harper, 1961). One study reported the treatment of transvestism utilizing apomorphine in a treatment regimen of 39 sessions. Of 13 transvestites treated, 7 were reported as "apparently cured" during follow-up periods ranging from eight months to seven years (Morganstern, Pearce, & Rees, 1965). Drug-induced aversion procedures have generally been abandoned in favor of shock procedures, primarily

for the advantages of better timing and the consequent availability of anxiety-relief treatment procedures. In general, these studies report a high degree of success, although most of the literature consists of case studies for which there is no possibility of calculating success "rates" (Blakemore et al., 1963; Clark, 1965; Marks & Gelder, 1967; Thorpe, Schmidt, Brown, & Castell, 1964).

Fetishism is a reasonably rare disorder, or perhaps it is rarely reported, since to some degree normal male sexual arousal is stimulated by a variety of items. Overall, successful treatment appears a common outcome and has included the use of both drug-induced aversive states (Cooper, 1964; Raymond, 1956; Raymond & O'Keefe, 1965) and electric shock aversion (Barker, 1965; Kushner, 1965; Marks & Gelder, 1967; McGuire & Vallance, 1964).

In the treatment of a fetishist, Marks and Gelder (1967) were successful in removing the patient's sexual responsiveness to the various fetish objects, while leaving unaffected his responsiveness toward appropriate sexual stimuli (e.g., a photograph of a nude woman). The measures of sexual arousal typically employed in empirical studies of sexual deviations include increases in penile blood volume (these may be seen as incipient erections), the presence or absence of total erections, or the latency between presentation of a stimulus and the occurrence of an erection. In the case treated by Marks and Gelder, the inappropriate sexual stimuli were treated with aversive control procedures one at a time. After 20 treatment trials to the first inappropriate stimulus (panties), the patient B showed no responsiveness to that stimulus, but undiminished responsiveness to the other inappropriate stimuli (pajamas, skirts and blouses, and slips). As the counterconditioning procedures were applied to the other items, they each, in turn, lost their capacity to induce sexual arousal. Throughout, the responsiveness to appropriate stimuli (nude women) remained undiminished and within the series of treatments of each sexually arousing stimulus the latencies between the presentation of the stimulus and the onset of erection became progressively longer until the erection no longer occurred. The stimuli were thus judged to be no longer sexually arousing.

In a subsequent study, Marks, Gelder, and Bancroft (1970) performed a two-year follow-up to assess treatment effectiveness. The entire sample of 24 transvestite and fetishist males in this study had either significantly reduced the frequency of their problem behavior or had ceased it totally.

Another deviant sexual behavior that has been treated successfully by aversive control techniques is that of exhibitionism. Although little evaluation research has appeared in the literature, it seems apparent that aversion techniques can be employed effectively in the treatment of this problem (Evans, 1967, 1968; Hughes, 1977; Kushner & Sandler, 1966), although there have been several reports of other techniques, notably assertive training and desensitization (Bond & Hutchison, 1960; Wolpe, 1958).

Alcoholism

Although the treatment of sexual and affectional preferences has included primarily electrical aversive control procedures and, to some extent, covert sensitization techniques, the treatment of alcoholism has utilized a much larger range of treatment procedures, including a number of aversive control techniques (chemically induced aversion, electric shock, covert sensitization), as well as other behavior therapy procedures (e.g., contingency management and operant methods of self-control). In the present instance, we will concern ourselves only with the aversive control procedures and attempt to make generalizations about the success with which such techniques have been shown to alter problem drinking behavior.

The treatment goal for more aversive control treatments of alcoholism is generally abstinence from drinking, motivated by a change in the at-tractiveness of alcohol (but not necessarily the inebriated condition that it promotes). This is distinct from other possible treatment goals, such as the inducement of moderate social drinking rather than alcohol abuse. It also reflects the widely accepted assumption that alcoholics can never maintain a controlled pattern of drinking, although there is some debate about the possibility that some alcoholics can either resume moderate drinking after treatment (Davies, 1962; Kendell, 1965) or be effectively treated with the goal of moderate, social drinking (Lazarus, 1965; Miller, 1972; Sobell & Sobell, 1973a, 1973b). This debate has been at a fever pitch of charge and countercharge (Pendery, Maltzman, & West, 1981; Sobell & Sobell, 1984) regarding the veracity of findings supporting the possibility of controlled drinking by alcoholics. It is perhaps fairest to say that this issue is not yet fully resolved, and the possibility of effective treatment leading to controlled consumption should not be ignored.

Among studies of aversion treatments designed to promote total abstinence, the picture is mixed regarding long-term effectiveness in 20 studies published between 1928 and 1977, there is variability in the abstinence rates reported, and only 4 of the studies reported showed rates lower than 50 percent.[4] The variance in these reports probably reflects the differing lengths of follow-up periods during which abstinence was assessed. The general picture is one in which abstinence is quite high during the time immediately following treatment, then there is a

[4]Specifically, the studies reviewed were Anant (1967); Ashem and Donner (1968); Blake (1967); Burt (1974); Claeson and Malm (1973); DeMorsier and Feldmann (1950); Edlin, Johnson, Hletko, and Heilbrunn (1945); Gordova and Kovalev (1961); Kant (1945); Kantorovich (1928); Lemere and Voegtlin (1950); Mestrallet and Lang (1959); Michaelson (1976); Miller (1959); Miller, Dvorak, and Turner (1960); Ruck (1956); Shanahan and Hornick (1946); Thimann (1949); Vogler, Weissbach, and Compton (1977).

very sharp increase in incidence of reversion to drinking 6–12 months following treatment, with only gradually increasing reversion thereafter.

There is some indication that supplementary treatment sessions are important for the long-term success of aversion procedures in the control of behavior. Voegtlin and colleagues (1941) studied the effectiveness of supplementary treatment during the year following the original treatment. Patients were given from one to four supplementary treatment sessions at 30, 60, and then every 90 days following the original treatment. Clients given these supplementary sessions showed consistently lower rates of remission that did clients not offered the opportunity for supplementary treatment. Another study (Voegtlin et al., 1942) found that 91 percent of clients who agreed to participate in periodic retreatment remained abstinent by the end of one year, whereas 71 percent of those who declined such supplementary treatment were similarly successful.

We have already commented on the apparent trend toward the identification of mild stimuli for use in aversion procedures. Relevant to the treatment of alcoholism, an animal study by Phol, Revusky, and Mellow (1980) suggests that taste-aversion and subsequent reductions in alcohol consumption can be accomplished as well by mild drug-induced noxious states as by more powerful ones. In a study contrasting lithium-induced noxious states with those produced by more powerful drugs, such as emetine, ipecac, disulfiram, and succinylcholine, these investigators found that there was no difference in effectiveness between the weaker or stronger drugs. They conclude that aversion treatments of alcoholism may be employing more noxious drugs than are necessary for effective outcomes and illustrate, once again, the ethical wisdom of seeking the least aversive procedure necessary to achieve success.

Within the realm of aversive counterconditioning, both theory and results favor drawing a distinction between chemically induced and electrically induced aversion. Some theorists (Eysenck & Beech, 1971; Franks, 1966) feel that there are reasons to expect a superiority for electrical aversion techniques, but there are no controlled studies to support this contention. On the other hand, the most effective aversion treatment is one that employs a type of aversion related to the behavior in question. In this case, a chemically induced aversive state of nausea seems more relevant to alcoholism than does the pain of electric shock (Wilson & Davison, 1969), and covert sensitization procedures that symbolically induce a state of nausea would also seem appropriate. At least one report in the literature (Miller, Hersen, Eisler, & Hillsman, 1974) notes the total failure of an electrical aversion technique when contrasted with a control or a treatment condition involving very mild shock. In addition, a number of studies indicate that another, non–nausea-related aversion procedure—respiratory paralysis—has a reduced level of effectiveness in the treatment of alcoholism (Farrar, Powell, & Martin, 1968; Holzinger, Mortimer, & Van Dusen, 1967).

Indeed, earlier we noted that the effectiveness of covert sensitization procedures can be enhanced when the character of the aversive imagery is tailored to the response under treatment (e.g., a response involving taste or oral behavior may be most affected by nausea-inducing imagery). Such tailoring, in fact, may assist the effectiveness of aversion procedures in the treatment of alcoholism when the aversive stimulus is not covert or cognitive in nature.

Baker and Cannon (1979) have argued that electrical aversion therapy has not been shown to be particularly effective for the treatment of alcoholism (Elkins, 1975; Hallam, Rachman, & Falkowski, 1972; MacCulloch & Feldman, 1967; Miller et al., 1973; Wilson, Leaf, & Nathan, 1975; Wilson & Tracey, 1976) and reasoned that this might be due to the lack of relatedness between shock-induced aversion (pain) and the nature of drinking behavior. While they did not make a direct comparison between electrical-

and nausea-induced aversion, they did demonstrate that taste aversion procedures do induce a conditioned aversion to the taste and smell of alcohol that promotes malaise and, in their study, vomiting shortly after consumption of alcohol is begun. In subsequent studies (Cannon & Baker, 1981; Cannon, Baker, & Wehl, 1981), these investigators found that when either electrical-aversion or nausea-aversion procedures were employed, only the nausea-evoking procedures were effective in producing an aversion to alcohol.

If the goal of treatment is controlled drinking and not total abstinence, a treatment procedure that addresses not the attractiveness of alcohol but rather drinking behavior itself may be preferable (Wilson & Tracey, 1976). In this case, operant procedures that may be aversive (contingent punishment) or positive in nature may provide an effective treatment regimen. There is relatively clear evidence that alcoholics can learn to moderate their drinking through contingent punishment (Schaefer, 1972; Wilson & Tracey, 1976; Wilson, Leaf, & Nathan, 1975) or through contingent positive reinforcement and discrimination training (Cohen, Liebson, Faillace, & Allen, 1971; Hunt & Azrin, 1973; Lovibond & Caddy, 1970; Sobell & Sobell, 1973a, 1973b). It is currently a familiar platitude, but probably nonetheless a true conclusion, that alcoholism is most likely to be treated effectively by a multiple-component program that focuses on the attractiveness, frequency, and amount of drinking behavior and on the attractiveness of alcohol itself.

The elimination of problem behaviors, especially those that are intrinsically attractive or difficult to control, is one of the treatment goals most likely to confront the behavior therapist. There are many avenues to achieve this goal, as most of the other chapters in this text attest. In this chapter we have reviewed the numerous cognitive, physiological, and behavioral techniques that make use of punishment and aversion procedures, and we have been careful to discuss ethical and procedural considerations as well.

These techniques should be used with caution and perhaps sparingly at best. We have noted the development of techniques for mild aversive stimulation, and this, along with the concern for sparing and judicious use of punishment and aversion, should be taken to reflect the ethical sensitivity that must precede any consideration about the employment of these techniques in behavioral treatment programs aimed at the elimination of problem behaviors or cognitions. It is with these two points that we may best conclude this chapter: punishment and aversion procedures are important techniques of behavior change, but we need continued research regarding the conditions and limits of their effectiveness. The general rule of application should be to employ them only when alternative, effective techniques of behavior change are not available.

9

Cognitive and Cognitive-Behavioral Methods

Probably no area of intervention research has generated more enthusiasm since the mid-1970s than the cognitive and cognitive-behavioral interventions.[1] A variety of therapeutic strategies have been articulated, complete with treatment manuals (e.g. Beck, Rush, Shaw, & Emery, 1979; Ellis, 1962; Kendall & Braswell, 1985; Meichenbaum, 1977; Turk, Meichenbaum, & Genest, 1983), numerous clinical training workshops and seminars have been conducted, scores of controlled empirical outcome trials have been executed, and several journals focused on those approaches have been launched. The first edition of this text, published in 1974, provided only scant coverage of these diverse interventions. The second edition, published in 1979, devoted a chapter to these strategies, but consisted largely of a description of the underlying rationales and recommended procedures. Empirical trials seeking to evaluate the efficacy of these approaches were rather sparse. Since that time, although it is fair to say that little has changed in terms of the nature of the major treatment approaches, there has been a virtual

explosion in the number of controlled empirical trials designed to evaluate their clinical efficacy.[2]

Like behavior therapy before it, and the dynamic approaches before behaviorism, and, indeed, all novel intervention strategies, the cognitive interventions have clearly passed through a honeymoon period during which they were the objects of intense enthusiasm and optimism. Much has been expected of them: that they would produce change more powerfully than other approaches, particularly the dynamic-eclectic and humanistic-existential perspectives; that they would lend themselves more readily than behavioral approaches to the types of issues presented by the typical outpatient psychotherapy candidate; and that the changes produced by these approaches would somehow be more general across situations or more stable over time than those produced by other approaches. This greater stability was presumed to be obtained either by altering relatively intracti-

---

[1]As we shall see, the various approaches described in this chapter differ in the degree to which they utilize behavioral techniques and strategies in their overall treatment package. Each targets cognitive mechanisms for change, but some do so via largely cognitive procedures, whereas others utilize various combinations of cognitive and behavioral procedures.

[2]The chapter on the cognitive learning perspectives in the second edition of this text reviewed a total of 20 controlled empirical trials involving cognitive or cognitive-behavioral interventions, over half involving Ellis's RET. In our present review, through the end of 1986, we have uncovered 84 such controlled trials, nearly half involving Meichenbaum's SIT, and only 3 new trials investigating RET. An exhaustive review of this literature is beyond the scope of this chapter, but the interested reader can consult Hollon and Beck (1986) for such a discussion.

ble "personality" factors (i.e., belief systems) predisposing the individual to psychopathology or by providing relatively permanent coping skills that the client could utilize long after therapy had terminated.

As an ever-increasing number of controlled empirical trials have begun to emerge, we find ourselves in a position to evaluate the actual merits of these approaches. Not unlike any maturing relationship, and not unlike the life histories of the other major intervention strategies, it would be unusual if all of the initial promises were realized. We would not expect the cognitive and cognitive-behavioral interventions to meet all of the field's earlier expectations for them, but they should at least match, if not exceed, the utilities of other major alternative approaches, in particular, the more purely behavioral strategies. As we shall see, this has typically been the case. Whether or not these approaches have added anything new to the existing clinical armanentarium is less clear, although there is growing evidence that, at least for some disorders—such as depression in adults and impulsivity in children—this has probably been the case. The extent to which this same conclusion can be extended to the other nonpsychotic disorders remains to be determined.

Defining the Cognitive Learning Perspective

In this chapter, we deal with the cognitive and cognitive-behavioral methods for effecting changes in maladaptive behavior and emotion. Cognitive psychology is specifically concerned with thinking processes and their products. Hence, the cognitive and cognitive-behavioral methods aim at modifying feelings and actions by influencing the client's patterns of thinking.

Our particular focus in this chapter will be on the approaches that target presumably mediating cognitive mechanisms for change, utilizing at least partially "cognitive" procedures. Some theorists have argued that most clinical change

is mediated by changes in beliefs and information processing (cf. Bandura, 1977a; Frank, 1974), regardless of the actual procedures used to effect that change. Although cognitive mechanisms may or may not prove to be universal mediators of clinical change, other approaches deal only indirectly with these mechanisms.

According to Mahoney, the various cognitive approaches all share the following assumptions:

1. The human organism responds primarily to cognitive representations of its environments rather than to those environments per se.

2. These cognitive representations are functionally related to the processes and parameters of learning.

3. Most human learning is cognitively mediated.

4. Thoughts, feelings, and behaviors are causally interactive. (1977a, pp. 7–8)

Thus, these approaches can be interpreted as the ideological first cousins of the more purely behavioral approaches, adhering to many of the same tenets, but with the addition of a focus on the cognitive mediation of important learning processes. As we shall see, the various approaches differ in terms of how extensively they utilize the more purely behavioral procedures described earlier in this text.

The contemporary cognitive approaches have much in common with behavior therapy. Certainly, when the therapies are divided into three major domains—dynamic, behavior, and humanistic (Davison & Neale, 1978)—most cognitive theorists would regard themselves as behaviorists.[3] The difference between the two

---

[3] This statement does not hold historically. Theorists such as Ellis (RET) and Beck (CB) were originally psychoanalytically trained, whereas theorists such as Meichenbaum (SIT) and Mahoney ("personal science") were originally trained within a behavioral perspective. Goldfried (SRR) was originally trained within a dynamic orientation, then passed through a period in which he was largely identified with behavioral approaches before he increasingly incorporated

approaches is to some extent one of emphasis. Cognitive learning theorists, such as Beck (1976), Mahoney (1974), Meichenbaum (1977), and Ellis (1971, 1974b, 1977a), believe that conscious thoughts play a major role in mediating emotional and instrumental behavior in human beings. Bandura (1977a), in his classic treatise on self-efficacy theory, has gone so far as to suggest that cognitive processes are the *major* mediators of change in all therapies, including behavior therapy, although he maintains that the purely behavioral procedures remain the most effective means of mobilizing those processes.

cognitive elements into his behavioral orientation. Although all of these respective theorists have gradually been converging on a cognitive perspective, some interesting and subtle differences exist in their conceptualizations which may reflect their earlier orientations. Ellis, Beck, and Goldfried, all originally trained within a dynamic perspective, have tended to focus on the clients' idiosyncratic meaning systems, the subtle nuances of connotation and symbolism brought by different individuals to the same event. They have tended to emphasize the reevaluation of existing meaning systems with the expressed purpose of altering what people *believe*. Theorists such as Meichenbaum, on the other hand, have tended to focus on the products of thinking as discrete events (even initially equating "thought" with covert vocalizations, hence the origin of the term "self-statements"). Efforts at change have tended to focus more on altering the probability that a given thought will occur in a given situation (e.g., via use of repetition, rehearsal, and contingency manipulation), than directly influencing the degree to which the individual believes any particular proposition. That is, they focus more on what the individual *thinks* in a given situation, the actual concrete event, than on the degree to which that individual believes that thought. Although it would be a gross oversimplification to suggest that the formerly dynamic theorists deal only with the degree to which clients believe certain propositions, and although the formerly behavioral theorists focus on the occurrence of a thought rather than on the degree of belief ascribed to it, there is an element of truth to this distinction.

Nonetheless, though most advocates of more convential behavior therapy do not deny that mediation may be important in some instances, they stress the direct role of learning history. Thus, Wolpe (1978) argued that noncognitively mediated conditioned anxiety habits, reflecting changes at the synapse, underlie the majority of the neuroses. To be sure, many of the behavior therapy techniques presented in the preceding chapters of this book have important cognitive ingredients. For example, visual imagery is assumed to play a key role in systematic desensitization, flooding, implosive therapy, and covert sensitization. But when these techniques are employed in the conventional manner, the goal of therapy is not to modify the content of cognitions, but rather to modify their emotional valence so that, for example, imagining a dog will no longer be frightening. In contrast, cognitive therapists *do* attempt to modify their clients' thinking, on the assumption that this will have a positive effect on their instrumental and emotional behavior.

In actuality, many of the more traditional forms of psychotherapy operate, at least in part, through mediating cognitive processes (Rice, 1974; Wachtel, 1981; Wexler, 1974). For example, the methods of psychoanalysis, including intense introspection, free association, and dream interpretation, are based on an examination of the client's cognitions. However, as Beck (1970, 1976) notes, cognitive therapy, as it has evolved in recent years, is markedly different from the more traditional, dynamically based methods of treatment in several significant respects. The therapeutic interview is more structured. Treatment focuses on relatively specific problems. Little attention is devoted to childhood experiences, at least early in treatment. Little heed is given to constructs such as infantile sexuality or the unconscious. Further, in contrast to psychodynamic approaches, modern cognitive learning therapy is briefer, its constructs are more readily researched, and its techniques are more easily taught.

Background

The cognitive learning approaches reflect an integration (critics would say an *attempted* integration) of two important perspectives in clinical psychology, *internalism* and *behaviorism* (Mahoney, 1977a). Internalism assumes that the major determinants of human behavior reside within the individual. Traditional approaches to psychopathology and treatment (Freudian and neo-Freudian, Rogerian, humanistic-existential; see Mahoney, 1977a) have been characterized by internalism. The trait psychological approach to personality, discussed in Chapter 1, illustrates internalism. Extreme or radical behaviorism from J. B. Watson (1913) to Skinner (1953, 1974) was partly a reaction to internalism, and as the reader knows, radical behaviorism places great stress on external causality (recall our discussion of situationalism in Chapter 1).

The integration of these two opposing perspectives provided by the cognitive learning approach is an example of interactionalism. Recall from Chapter 1 that the interactionalistic position maintains that behavior is a joint or interactive function of external and internal events: in the cognitive learning approach, the internal events are primarily cognitions (see Bandura's 1978 treatise on *reciprocal determinism*).

The major antecedents of present-day cognitive learning approaches are many and diverse. Among clinical psychologists, Rotter (1954) and Kelly (1955) stressed the importance of conscious thought processes in mediating human behavior. A similar emphasis on cognitive mediational processes is found in Bandura's classic text on behavior modification (1969). In the early 1960s, Schacter, a social psychologist, and his colleagues (Schacter, 1966; Schacter & Singer, 1962; Schacter & Wheeler, 1962) provided data pointing to the importance of attributional cognitions in affecting human emotion and behavior. Although it is somewhat more difficult to assess the impact of cognitively oriented learning theorists—such as Tolman

(1932), Mowrer (1960), Paivio (1971), and Bower (1975)—on the development of cognitive learning therapy, proponents of the latter (e.g., Bandura, 1969; Mahoney, 1974) do rely heavily on data from the learning laboratory to make a strong case for the importance of cognitive mediation. As cognitive learning therapy continues to evolve, the direct impact of researchers in the area of cognitive learning and memory will likely become increasingly apparent (cf. Bower, 1978; Darley & Fazio, 1980; Goldfried & Robins, 1982, 1983; Hollon & Kriss, 1984; Kahneman, Slovic, & Tversky, 1982; Markus, 1977; Nisbett & Ross, 1980; Turk & Salovey, 1985a, 1985b; Turk & Speer, 1983).

The mid-1960s witnessed a developing interest in the psychology of self-control by certain behaviorally oriented psychologists. Although the terminology of published reports (Ferster, Nurnberger, & Levitt, 1962; Goldiamond, 1965; Stuart, 1967) was largely Skinnerian (and Skinner himself had discussed self-control at some length in his 1953 book, never regarding cognitions as unimportant, simply unobservable, and hence an inappropriate object for scientific study), many viewed this as an important departure from the position of extreme situationalism associated with radical behaviorism. This had the effect of encouraging some otherwise dedicated behaviorists to rethink the role of internal processes, and in particular, to reexamine the possibility that conscious thinking plays an important mediational role in human behavior.

Although it would be incorrect to designate any single individual as the founder of the cognitive learning therapy movement, Albert Ellis has been one of the most influential (and prolific) writers in the area (see, e.g., 1962, 1971, 1974b, 1975, 1977a). The specifics of his approach, along with relevant research, will be presented in the section to follow. The work of Aaron Beck (1963, 1964, 1967, 1976) and that of Donald Meichenbaum (1969, 1974, 1977) have also had a major impact on clinical practice as well as theory, and their respective approaches will also be reviewed.

There are, of course, other writers and researchers who have made very important contributions to the cognitive learning therapy movement, including Bandura (1969, 1976, 1977a, 1977b, 1978, 1981), Kanfer (1970, 1971), Mahoney (1974, 1977a), Mischel (1973), and M. R. Goldfried and Goldfried (1975), to mention only a few. The contributions of these writers and many others are just as readily classified under the label *psychology of self-control*—the subject of the next chapter of this text. Although interest in self-control procedures slightly predated interest in cognitive learning therapy in academic departments of psychology (for the practicing clinician and the lay public, the reverse was probably true), content has tended to overlap more and more. Thus, virtually every approach to cognitive learning therapy involves teaching clients some manner of self-control; conversely, many techniques labeled as *self-control* either explicitly or implicitly rely on the modification of the clients' cognitions.

Process Variations

Just how modification in thinking is brought about probably differs as a function of the specific type of intervention. As shown in Table 9–1, at least two of the major approaches, Ellis's Rational Emotive Therapy (RET—Ellis, 1957, 1962, 1971, 1974b, 1977a) and Goldfried and colleagues' systematic rational restructuring (SRR—Goldfried, DeCanteceo, & Weinberg, 1974), a more structured version of RET, appear to rely largely on appeals to reason or logic (*rationality*) to effect change in beliefs.

Beck's cognitive therapy (typically abbreviated as CB, since it is, in essence, an amalgamation of cognitive and behavioral procedures—Beck, 1964, 1967, 1970, 1976; Beck et al., 1979), Mahoney's personal science system (1977b), and Kelly's pioneering work (1955) certainly draw heavily on appeals to rationality, but they place

an additional emphasis on empirical hypothesis testing (*empiricism*) as a means of determining the validity of beliefs. Both approaches based on rationality and those based on empiricism are perhaps best suited to dealing with situations in which clients already possess maladaptive cognitions—that is, when the therapeutic goal is to counter existing erroneous thinking (distortions).

Meichenbaum's self-instructional training (SIT) and, typically but not invariably, stress inoculation training (STI) (Meichenbaum, 1975a, 1977)[4] rely heavily on the process of guided rehearsal (*repetition*) as a means of introducing mediating cognitions when they are absent.[5] Such approaches may be best conceptualized as correcting deficits in information processing.[6]

---

[4]We have elected to save our discussion of stress inoculation training, and the literature supporting its efficacy, for Chapter 10, "Self-control." That is because of our belief that the truly unique feature of this approach is its emphasis on practice and preparation for dealing with specific stressful situations. Although it is an approach that frequently involves cognitive components (as do many of the self-control approaches), it need not. Since the essence of this approach appears to lie in its *preparatory* nature, not its cognitive aspects, we have elected to discuss it in conjunction with the self-control therapies.

[5]To a somewhat lesser extent, Meichenbaumian self-statement modification approaches have also tended to emphasize *functionality*—or the argument that one will feel or perform better if a new thought is substituted for an existing one—as an active change process. As we shall see, self-statement introduction approaches based on repetition have tended to be utilized most clearly when working with impulsive children, whereas self-statement replacement approaches, combining functionality and repetition, have tended to be utilized in working with anxious adults.

[6]There can be little doubt that repetition alone can alter existing beliefs. One need look no further than Joseph Goebbels's successful reliance on the "Big Lie," the incessant reiteration of known falsehoods that formed the basis of the Nazi propaganda machine

Finally, thought-stopping techniques (Wolpe, 1958, 1969, 1973), which work largely via interruption (and, typically, *distraction*), may prove particularly appropriate when existing beliefs are neither necessarily irrational nor inaccurate (distortions), but still dysfunctional. We will organize this chapter around these four major processes: rationality, empiricism, repetition (plus functionality), and distraction, recognizing that although differences exist in emphasis, any particular therapeutic approach may draw on any and all of these processes.

Interventions Primarily Emphasizing Rationality

Rational Emotive Therapy

Rational emotive therapy (RET) derives directly from a theory that psychological disorders arise from faulty or irrational patterns of thinking. The thought patterns that typically manifest themselves in chains of preconscious, implicit verbalizations arise from assumptions that constitute the individual's basic belief system. Actually, there is a relatively long history of treatment approaches stressing the importance of belief systems and self-verbalizations (e.g., Korzybski, 1933; Shaffer, 1947).[7] For example, Shaffer (1947) defined therapy as a "learning process through which a person acquires an ability to speak to himself in appropriate ways so as to control his own conduct." Although Adlerians do not focus quite to the same extent on self-verbalization, their emphasis on problem-solving in the here and now is in the tradition of rationalism that is the hallmark of rational emotive therapy (Ellis, 1974a, 1974b; Harper, 1977).

Ellis's view of the primacy of preconscious (as well as conscious) thinking is at sharp odds with that of classic psychoanalysis with its paramount emphasis on the unconscious, although both approaches stress the fundamental role of primitive, magical, or irrational thinking in the development of psychopathology. Early in his professional career, Ellis (a clinical psychologist) subscribed to the prevailing dynamic point of view but, over the years, evolved an approach that increasingly deemphasized the acquisition of "historical" insight and stressed the here-and-now cognitive factors that directly mediate maladative behaviors and emotions. According to Ellis (1962), an ever-increasing success rate in the clinic resulted from his efforts to modify his approach (keeping in mind that unsystematic clinical observation is no substitute for controlled experimentation).

By the late 1960s, RET had emerged as a major treatment approach, and its popularity

---

during the Second World War (Shirer, 1959), to see the potential power of the approach. Nonetheless, we suspect that for most clinical purposes, repetition is more useful as a means of introducing cognitive mediators, especially as memory prompts for preferred action sequences, than as a means of altering a belief already held.

[7]As suggested earlier, there is probably a subtle distinction between beliefs and self-verbalizations, if only in the historical roots of each term. The term "belief" connotes a proposition held by an individual to which at least some subjective validity is accorded. The term "self-verbalization" (or synonyms such as "self-statement") represents the efforts by radical behaviorists in transition to a cognitivist position to deal with essentially unobservable cognitive phenomena by equating them with covert speech. Hence, "thinking," a forbidden mentalistic concept, was brought into the behavioral domain of inquiry by relabeling it "covert self-verbalizations" and equating it with an observable behavior, overt speech. Early behaviorists actually attempted to "observe" thinking by monitoring minute movements of the vocal chords (Watson, 1913). The consequence of this rather curious history is that cognitive-behavior theorists initially trained within a behavioral perspective often attend largely to the concrete occurrence or nonoccurrence of thoughts (i.e., self-verbalizations or self-statements), without evidencing much concern for the subjective validity (ascribed accuracy) of that belief.

Table 9–1 **Overview of Major Cognitive Change Processes Emphasized by Various Cognitive and Cognitive-Behavioral Approaches**

Processes	Theory of Disorder	Theory of Change	Cognitive Techniques	Behavioral Techniques	Major Metaphor
Rationality-based (RET, SRR, and related cognitive restructuring procedures)	Irrational beliefs produce affective distress and lead to maladaptive behaviors (distortions)	Demonstrating irrationality of beliefs will lead client to discard illogical system of information processing in favor of more rational beliefs (rationality)	Persuasion and reason, provision of alternative conceptualization and "insight" into irrationality	Homework and other behavioral assignments often recommended, but as practice living in accordance with new beliefs, not necessarily for informational value (cognitive or combined cognitive-behavioral)	Adoption of new philosophy of life (RET) or at least tutoring in logic (SRR)
Empirically based (CB, "personal science," etc.)	Inaccurate beliefs mediate affective distress and lead to maladaptive behaviors (distortions)	Empirical hypothesis testing emphasized to reality test beliefs in addition to logical analysis (empiricism/rationality)	Empirical hypothesis testing in which client behaviors used to test validity of beliefs, along with persuasion and reason, provision of alternative conceptualization and "insight" into distortions in information processing	Homework and other behavioral assignments always recommended, integral part of empirical hypothesis testing approach, largely for their informational value (integrated cognitive-behavioral)	Application of scientific methodology (rationally guided empiricism)
Repetition-based approaches (SIT)	Presence of negative self-statements produces affective distress and leads to maladaptive behaviors (distortions) or absence of appropriate cognitive mediators for guiding behavior (deficits)	Repetition and rehearsal of appropriate mediational self-statements produces internalization of those self-statements	Repetition and rehearsal of desired self-statements, typically presented through modeling	Various behavioral procedures; e.g., modeling, manipulation of response cost contingencies, or behavioral rehearsal typically recommended (combined/integrated cognitive-behavioral)	Acquisition of performance skill (e.g., driving a car)
Interruption-based approaches (thought stopping)	Presence of unpleasant cognitions produces affective distress and maladaptive behavior	Interruption of ongoing series of cognitive ruminations temporarily distracts the client	Compelling external stimulus (noise, slap, etc.) used to distract attention, often followed by explicit redirection of attention	Treats cognitions as if behaviors; no effort to change belief in a given thought, simply to interrupt thought as an event in stream of consciousness	(Not applicable)

has continued to grow throughout the 1970s and 1980s. The popularity of RET can be partially attributed to the enthusiasm and productivity of its founder, but in our view, there are more fundamental reasons for its widespread acceptance. First, for many practitioners (and many lay people), the basic assumption that what an individual thinks to himself has a major bearing on the way he feels and acts is incontrovertible. Second, the chief method of RET, a direct (and nonsubtle) attempt on the part of the therapist to modify these beliefs, is a plausible therapeutic corollary to the first assumption. Third, in terms of both theory and practice, Ellis's style of exposition is clear and explicit. Many therapists (justifiably or not) have felt sufficiently knowledgeable in RET to begin to apply it to clients after merely reading the definitive *Reason and Emotion in Psychotherapy* (Ellis, 1962). Kelly's (1955) fixed-role therapy bears a remarkable similarity to RET in terms of its philosophical basis as well as its here-and-now action orientation. Nevertheless, Kelly's manner of presentation, though logically appealing, is quite esoteric, and this may in part account for why his impact on practitioners has not been nearly as great as that of Ellis.

The essence of RET is seen in the A–B–C–D–E paradigm (Ellis, 1971, 1974b, 1977a). *A*, the activating experience, refers to a real external event to which the individual is exposed. *B*, belief, refers to the chain of thoughts or self-verbalizations the person goes through in response to *A*. *C*, the consequences, symbolizes the emotions and behaviors that result from *B*. The A–B–C portion of the paradigm symbolizes Ellis's theory of emotional reactivity. *D* stands for the therapist and client disputing the beliefs when they are irrational. For Ellis, this involves debating, discriminating, and defining—a process involving the "logico-empirical method of scientific questioning, challenging and debating" (1977a, p. 20). *E* symbolizes the effect of appropriately confronting one's irrational beliefs—that is, the client feels better and functions more efficiently.

To illustrate, consider the depressed client who complains to the therapist that no one "loves" him, providing objective evidence that this is, indeed, the case. In particular, the client describes the event that precipitated his present depression: his girlfriend telephoned to inform him she wishes to end the relationship. This is event *A*. The therapist now sets about determining the nature of *B*, the client's chain of thoughts that followed *A*. Initially, the client may not be totally aware of these crucial beliefs, in which case some degree of probing and encouragement on the part of the therapist is required. On the other hand, the client may be able to verbalize them quite readily. In either case, assume that the sequence of thoughts is as follows: "She no longer loves me. . . . Nobody does. . . . I'm a worthless nothing. . . . That's simply terrible." After engaging in this pattern of thinking, the client, now at *C*, is expected to experience considerable negative emotion (anxiety, anger, depression) and to behave accordingly.

The therapist's interventions *(D)* consist of direct efforts at having the client examine, in a scientifically critical manner, the rationality of the beliefs at point *B*. In particular, he or she helps the client make the very critical discrimination between the statements at *B* that are objectively true (e.g., "She no longer loves me. . . . Nobody does") and those that may be irrational (e.g., "I'm worthless").

Once the client makes this discrimination, the therapist may ask the client to provide evidence that the second *B* statement does, in fact, follow logically from the first, as follows:

> You are telling yourself that you are presently unloved, which may be true, and which means that you are lonely and sexually frustrated and so on, which is too bad, but then you are telling yourself that *because* you are unloved, you are worthless. Can you tell me how the second idea follows from the first?

Sooner or later, the client will come to the realization that the second statement does not follow from the first, at which point he is expected to engage in alternative and more flexible ways of thinking. For example, with some coaching from the therapist, he may now think to himself:

> It is true she no longer loves me. No one does. I certainly want this person (or somebody) to love me, but I don't really *need* love. There is nothing terrible about her rejecting me, or nobody loving me, and it certainly doesn't imply that I'm worthless.

The client is now in a position to experience the more positive emotions and consequent behaviors symbolized by *E*.

In summary, event *A* (an objective occurrence) impinges on the individual, giving rise to beliefs at *B*, some of which are irrational and self-defeating and lead to negative emotions and related behaviors at *C*. The RET therapist, at point *D*, helps the client to examine the logical relationship of the beliefs at *B*, resulting in the elimination of irrational thinking and a consequent amelioration of suffering at point *E*.

While in the consulting room, clients may indicate quite strongly that they are convinced of the irrational and self-defeating nature of certain of their beliefs, also indicating alternative, healthier ways of thinking. However, it is unlikely that clients will tend to revert to their habitual ruminative patterns between therapy sessions (especially early in therapy), and the RET therapist must take steps to minimize this. One tactic involves having the client verbalize how he would handle negative feelings when the therapist is not present. For example, the therapist might say, "Now, suppose tomorrow you notice yourself beginning to feel anxious or depressed because your girlfriend rejected you. What would you do to make yourself feel better?" This allows for an additional check on the client's self-verbalizations and serves as added encouragement to practice rational thinking on his own.

Homework is an important element of rational emotive therapy. The client might be asked to read relevant chapters in one or more books authored by Ellis and his associates that are intended for lay audiences (Ellis, 1972a, 1972b, 1975, 1976; Ellis & Harper, 1973, 1975; Ellis, Wolfe, & Moseley, 1972). Homework may be in the form of a kind of *in vivo* desensitization (Ellis, 1974a, 1974b), wherein a shy client may be asked to make overtures to attractive members of the opposite sex (to facilitate social skills, but more importantly, to help clients believe they can function more effectively, or if their performance happens to be deficient, to help them convince themselves it is no catastrophe). Homework assignments also include cognitive exercises. Ellis (1974b) illustrates such exercises with the case of a man who hates his mother-in-law. The client is instructed to keep in contact with her and when he feels anger to uncover and examine what he is saying to himself. When he comes across an irrational belief, he is to dispute it vigorously. Another exercise involves the use of rational emotive imagery. Speech-anxious individuals might be asked to imagine themselves making a speech during the course of which they experience a block and can no longer talk. They are then to imagine people in the audience laughing or sneering at them, at which point they are encouraged to feel panic. The critical elements of the exercise involve determining the thoughts that mediated the panic reaction and confronting and modifying them so that feelings of panic are replaced by milder emotions associated with a sense of disappointment. Exercises of this nature are complex, and initially at least, they should be carried out with the assistance of the therapist (see Ellis, 1974b, p. 323, for a more detailed description of rational emotive imagery). Once mastered, the client is instructed to practice the exercise 5 or 10 minutes a day, perhaps until the next therapy session.

According to Ellis (1977a), irrational thoughts are thoughts that have self-defeating or self-destructive consequences. Irrational thoughts (e.g., beliefs) either are empirically false (Ellis, 1974b) or are of such a nature that they cannot be empirically verified (Ellis, 1971). Thus, the belief that "masturbation causes mental illness" is empirically false, whereas the belief that one is worthless because one is not loved or is not a professional success is without any empirical referent, since personal worth is not quantifiable (Ellis, 1971, 1974b, 1977a). Similarly, the belief that another individual—for instance, a convicted mass murderer—is, in an absolute sense, worthless cannot be taken as correct. Criminals are not *bad* or *evil* in the sense that they are deserving of punishment or damnation (although Ellis is not suggesting that society should not protect itself from their misdeeds), nor is the person who discovers a method for immunizing people against a dreadful disease (e.g., Jonas Salk) considered to be a *good* person, although society is wise to reward such behavior. In short, the philosophy of Ellis allows for neither saint nor sinner.

Ellis (1976, 1977a) believes that humankind has a biological predisposition toward irrationality. He bases this view in part on the apparent pervasiveness of irrational thinking (across cultures, across centuries) and the unwillingness of people to give up irrational ideas, even in the face of insight. On a more positive note, Ellis shares with the existentialists and humanists the view that we are also predisposed toward growth and self-actualization and that we can successfully combat our irrational predisposition. Ellis's emphasis on biological predisposition illustrates an interactionalism somewhat akin to that of Hans Eysenck.

Finally, Ellis (1962, 1971, 1977a) maintains that there are certain irrational beliefs quite common to our culture (and probably to other cultures as well). Thus, although he believes that the propensity for irrationality is an essential part of human nature, he recognizes cultural variation in content, which could only occur if life experience (including what we are taught) played a role in shaping that content.

Examples of Irrational Ideas

The following constitute a set of examples regarding the kinds of irrational ideas targeted by Ellis and colleagues. This list is not exhaustive, but it does provide concrete instances of the main material focused on in RET:

The idea that you must—yes, *must*—have sincere love and approval almost all the time from all the people you find significant

The idea that you must prove yourself thoroughly competent, adequate, and achieving; or that you must at least have real competence or talent at something important

The idea that people who harm you or commit misdeeds rate as generally bad, wicked, or villainous individuals and that you should severely blame, damn, and punish them for their sins

The idea that life proves awful, terrible, horrible, or catastrophic when things do not go the way you would like them to go

The idea that emotional misery comes from external pressures and that you have little ability to control your feelings or rid yourself of depression and hostility

The idea that if something seems dangerous or fearsome, you must become terribly occupied with and upset about it

The idea that you will find it easier to avoid facing many of life's difficulties and self-responsibilities than to undertake some rewarding forms of self-discipline

The idea that your past remains all-important and that because something once strongly influenced your life it has to keep determining your feelings and behavior today

The idea that people and things should turn out better than they do; and that you have to view it as awful and horrible if you do not quickly find good solutions to life's hassles

The idea that you can achieve happiness by inertia and inaction or by passively and un-committedly "enjoying yourself"

The idea that you must have a high degree of order or certainty to feel comfortable; or that you need some supernatural power on which to rely

The idea that you can give yourself a global rating as a human and that your general worth and self-acceptance depend upon the goodness of your performance and the degree that people approve of you (Ellis, 1977a, p. 10)

Ellis (1962) has provided the reader with a detailed account of why each of these beliefs is irrational and self-defeating. For example, believing that one must receive love and approval from significant others is irrational because it is arbitrary (cannot be empirically proved) and self-defeating because it will usually lead to frustration and disappointment.

Note that most of the above irrational ideas are "shoulds" or "musts." The notion that people create psychological havoc for themselves by insisting that they or another *should* or *must* behave in certain ways (see Horney, 1950, for the classic discussion of the "Tyranny of the 'Shoulds' "), or that events *should* happen in some prescribed fashion, is central to RET. Ellis calls this "musturbation," and he takes delight in bandying around phrases such as

Masturbation proves good and delicious,
while musturbation seems bad and pernicious.
Lusturbate, don't musturbate.
Musturbation means self-abuse. (1977a, pp. 28–29)

Since, as the reader may know, a theme common to much of what Ellis has written is that guilt-free sexual expression (including masturbation) is, in general, a positive, healthy thing, his choice of words in these quotations is by no means arbitrary. The quotations also illustrate the lively, provocative style that characterizes much of the writings and public presentations by Ellis and other RET advocates.

The Method of RET

In most general terms, the therapist's task (Ellis, 1971) is threefold. The therapist first determines precipitating external events, then the specific thought patterns (and underlying beliefs) that constitute the internal response to these events and give rise to negative emotions. Third, the therapist assists the client in altering these beliefs and thought patterns. The first task is usually accomplished by relatively standard interviewing techniques. As we have suggested, clients often bring quite specific complaints to the clinic, but when they are of a nonspecific nature (for instance, depression), it is usually not difficult to determine what external events correlated with the onset of the disorder. The therapist's next task involves determining his or her client's internalized response to these events.

To this end, Ellis (1977a) provides some highly specific guidelines. He suggests that therapist and client look for any of the following:

1. "Awfulizing" self-verbalizations that certain things are awful or terrible; for example, "It is *awful* when my date stands me up."

2. Things one "can't stand" or "can't bear"; for example, "I can't *stand* it when my boss ignores my suggestions."

3. *Musturbating*; for example, "I *must* keep my house spotless," "I *should* respect my parents."

4. Damning (blaming) oneself or others; for example, "I'm a worthless nothing for mistreating my wife." "My boss is a rotten bastard who deserves to rot in hell."

What makes detecting such ideas relatively easy is that most clients have little difficulty verbalizing them aloud (this, of course, assumes that overt verbalizations mirror thinking, a basic assumption of cognitive learning approaches). Consider the following client-therapist dialogue. The client, a 39-year-old housewife, for the past two years had been experiencing intermittent bouts of anxiety. The referring psychiatrist characterized her anxiety as "freefloating" (Buss, 1966). However, it was not difficult to tie her anxiety to a specific class of situations: being in public places, but especially eating in restaurants. The following therapy excerpt illustrates how we could use Ellis's guidelines in determining self-defeating patterns of thought, and how we might employ RET principles with them.

Client: I had another anxiety attack yesterday. I was having lunch with some good friends in this really nice restaurant in North Dallas. I felt like I couldn't finish my meal. It was just terrible.

Therapist: Okay. Now think back to when you were in the restaurant yesterday, and tell me what you experienced. You know, how you felt and what you were thinking.

Client: Okay . . . Well, the waiter had just served the main course. I noticed I was really tense. I remember thinking . . . "What if I have another panic attack, right here? I might not be able to continue eating. I might even faint. That would be terrible."

Therapist: Well, you said that you've never actually fainted in situations like this before. And so my guess is you won't . . . but what if you did? How would it be terrible? Do you mean that you would injure yourself physically or something like that?

Client: No . . . not really. I think I imagine myself, you know, slumped over in my chair. And my friends and everybody else are looking at me, just staring.

Therapist: And what are those people thinking?

Client: (Her eyes begin to tear) That . . . I can't even have lunch without making an ass of myself . . . that I'm incompetent . . . worthless.

Therapist: I can see that thinking in that way makes you very tense. Let's try the relaxation technique I taught you. (At this point, the therapist had the client go through three to four minutes of cue-controlled relaxation; see Chapter 2.)

Therapist: How do you feel now?

Client: Better, pretty good.

Therapist: Okay. Now it looks to me like you think the worst thing that could happen would be that you'd faint. First, that is pretty unlikely, right?

Client: Sure, but what if I *did?*

Therapist: Suppose you were in a restaurant and you saw somebody else faint. What would you think about them? Would you judge them to be incompetent and worthless?

Client: I guess I'd think they were, you know, sick . . . I'd probably try to help them. No . . . I wouldn't think they were . . . bad . . . or worthless. I see what you mean. Maybe they wouldn't ridicule me.

Therapist: I think they wouldn't. But *suppose* they did. There you are, slumped in your chair and you are just regaining consciousness. And everyone in the restaurant . . . your friends . . . everyone . . . they are jeering you . . . they are making fun of you. We just agreed that isn't likely to happen, but suppose everybody in the restaurant just happened to behave like purple meanies.

Client: That would be awful . . . I couldn't stand it. I'd just wither up and die.

Therapist: You'd literally physically wither up and die?

Client: Well, when you put it that way . . . I guess not. I'd feel terrible, though.

Therapist: Remember the *A–B–C* thing we discussed last week? *A* is people jeering after you've fainted, *C* is your reaction. True, most people in that situation wouldn't feel terrifically good. But how bad, how crummy you feel depends on what you *choose* to say to yourself at *B*.

Client: That I'm a worthless nothing who can't even handle herself in a restaurant!

Therapist: Not so fast. Let's talk about this idea of worthwhileness.

At this point, the therapist may point out (consistent with Ellis's position) that human worth simply is not ratable, empirically or conceptually; ergo, it is logically impossible for anything one does to diminish human worth. Earlier, Ellis (1962) took the position that human beings are worthwhile simply because they are alive. Both positions lead to the same conclusion: human worth is not contingent on behavior. Let us assume that the client has (at least tentatively) accepted this conclusion:

Therapist: Okay, if you and I agree that just because you passed out and people around you don't approve doesn't have any bearing on your worth, tell me how it is terrible?

Client: Well . . . people *should* be able to handle themselves!

Therapist: Guess what, Helen, . . . you just *musturbated*.

Client: (Looks shocked, then laughs) What do you mean?

Therapist: You said people *should* do such and such, . . . like, people *must* do such and such. . . . That's where the term *musturbation* comes from. The thing is this: as children we are taught we *should* do this, or we *must* do that, or we *shouldn't* do this. And we grow up accepting this without ever thinking about it logically. The reality is that the "shoulds" and "musts" are the rules that other people hand down to us, and we grow up accepting them as if they are absolute truth, which they most assuredly aren't.

Client: You mean it is perfectly okay to, you know, pass out in a restaurant?

Therapist: Sure!

Client: But . . . now I'm confused. . . . I know I wouldn't *like* it to happen.

Therapist: I can certainly understand that. It would be unpleasant, awkward, inconvenient.

But it is illogical and irrational to think that it would be terrible, or that you shouldn't, or that it somehow bears on your worth as a person. Thinking this way is also very self-defeating.

Client: What do you mean?

Therapist: Well, suppose one of your friends calls you up and invites you back to that restaurant. If you start telling yourself, "I might panic and pass out and people might make fun of me and that would be terrible," you are going to *make* yourself uptight. And you might find you are dreading going to the restaurant, and you probably won't enjoy the meal very much.

Client: Well, that *is* what usually happens.

Therapist: But it doesn't have to be that way. That is the really important thing. Remember the A–B–C's. The way you feel, your reaction, C, depends on what you *choose* to believe or think, or say to yourself, at B. A could be anything. Like your friend inviting you to meet her at the restaurant. Or noticing you are tense when the meal is being served.

Client: Well, what *should* I think, Doctor?

Therapist: That was a musturbation! Can you state that in a more rational way?

Client: (Laughs) Hmmm . . . let's see. What would be a healthy . . . thing to think?

Therapist: Let's role-play it. I'll be your friend calling you up to invite you to the restaurant. Then you say aloud the thoughts that you might think that would be, well, healthy, to use your word.

Client and therapist role-play until both are satisfied her reaction at *B* is rational and self-enhancing rather than self-defeating. The therapist may model appropriate verbalizations, but it is advisable to fade out prompts of this nature as quickly as possible. At the close of the session, the therapist would probably give the client a homework assignment; for example, imagining she does actually faint in the restaurant and that people are showing displeasure, but that ultimately she overcomes her intense negative feelings by engaging in rational thinking.

The material presented in this section is intended merely to provide the reader with a general introduction to the theory and method of RET. The therapist seriously interested in implementing RET is advised to refer to any one of the many primary sources currently available. As a point of departure, the reader is referred to Ellis (1974b), a relatively brief but comprehensive statement of the RET position, followed by two recent edited texts (Ellis & Grieger, 1977; Wolfe & Brand, 1977.) Tapes are readily available and workshops conducted by Ellis or associates are now fairly widespread.

As the reader may know, Ellis and many of his followers have a no-nonsense therapeutic style that some might describe as blunt. In fact, we have known graduate students who have been inclined to reject RET as a potential therapeutic tool entirely on this basis. In such instances, the typical response is "I could never come on to a client like that . . . it just isn't me." At such times, we hasten to point out that there is absolutely nothing in the *theory* of RET that necessitates an especially blunt therapeutic *style*. In fact, other well-known therapists working within a cognitive learning therapy framework (e.g., A. T. Beck) have a therapeutic style that is anything but aggressive or blunt.

Case Studies

The use of RET has been described in a variety of case studies. In an early report, Ellis (1957) summarized the results of 172 case histories, all treated by the author. Of this number, some were treated with orthodox psychoanalysis, some with psychoanalytically oriented psychotherapy, and some with RET. According to Ellis, clinical outcomes clearly favored RET over the other two approaches. This report was, of course, largely anecdotal, and should not be interpreted as providing formal support for the differential efficacy of RET. Since that time, a

variety of case reports have been reported, including Gets's (1971) work with a 17-year-old culturally deprived high school student, as well as cases of clients' concerns about homosexuality in a basically heterosexual male (Ellis, 1971d), guilt over religious perfectionism (Ellis, 1971c), sexual impotence (Gullo, 1971), depression (Maultsby, 1975), orgasmic dysfunction (Ellis, 1974b), acting out behavior in children (DiGuiseppe, 1975, 1977), antisocial impulsivity (Watkins, 1977), heterosexual anxiety (Vasta, 1975), and vaginismus (Shahar & Jaffee, 1978). Although there are few problem areas to which RET has not been applied, it is probably fair to say that it is most frequently seen as being useful with nonpsychotic populations—that is, clients who can think rationally, but may not be doing so for one reason or another.

Experimental Studies of RET Theory

Experimental laboratory research investigating the major tenets of RET can be divided into three main categories. These involve research on semantic generalization (see Maltzman, 1968), symbolic self-stimulation (e.g., Platonov, 1959), vicarious learning (Bandura, 1969), and visual image mediation in learning and memory (Bower, 1972a, 1976). In general, although controversy still exists, a strong case can be made for the role of cognitive processes in learning and emotion (see Mahoney, 1974, for a review).

The second category involves studies that provide relatively specific tests of the *A–B–C* cognitive learning paradigm. The general paradigm typically involves asking subjects to engage in thinking various negative or irrational thoughts. Overall, most studies have been supportive (e.g., Hale & Strickland, 1976; Natale, 1977; Velten, 1968; Rimm & Litvak, 1969; May & Johnson, 1973; Russell & Brandsma, 1974; Strickland, Hale, & Anderson, 1975; May, 1977b; Teasdale & Bancroft, 1977), although some exceptions do exist (Rogers & Craighead, 1977). The major problem with this line of research has been that it typically involves rather trivial manipulations long on demand characteristics and short on clinical realism.

Finally, any of a number of studies have demonstrated differences between pathological and nonpathological populations in terms of their endorsement of various beliefs (e.g., Nelson, 1977; Hollon & Kendall, 1980; Rimm, Janda, Lancaster, Nahl, & Dittmar, 1977; Weissman & Beck, 1978). Again, these studies have tended to support the basic cognitive model.

Positive support for the *A–B–C* paradigm of emotional reactivity is *necessary* if a therapeutic derivative of this paradigm (such as RET) is to be considered valid. Such evidence, however, is by no means sufficient. In the section to follow, we shall consider the clinical experimental evidence most specifically relevant to RET: therapeutic outcome research.

Controlled Therapeutic Outcome Research

In this section, we review some of the experimental findings that directly test the efficacy of RET. What is and is not directly pertinent to RET is somewhat problematic, as it turns out (Trexler, 1977). Often, authors of research simply use the term *cognitive therapy* to refer to either RET or a close relative, or the approach of Beck or that of Meichenbaum, or one of these in combination with a behavior technique such as relaxation. Another term used in a somewhat inconsistent fashion is <u>*cognitive restructuring*</u>. This term was popularized by Lazarus (1971), who described an approach very similar to, and in considerable measure derived from, RET. The studies to follow either are presented by their authors as explicit tests of RET or, by virtue of the procedures involved, constitute reasonably fair tests of Ellis's therapeutic approach.

Test Anxiety Three studies have evaluated the efficacy of RET in the treatment of test anxiety. In one study, Maes and Heimann (1970) compared the effectiveness of RET, client-centered therapy, and systematic desensitization with test-anxious male high school students. Treatments were administered during 10 training sessions covering a five-week period. Response measures included anxiety self-report, heart rate, and galvanic skin response. Following treatment, the subject was required to imagine he was about to take an examination, at which time the anxiety inventory was administered. Then he was given a concept mastery test (described as an intelligence test), and as he responded, physiological measures were taken. Although the anxiety inventory failed to distinguish among the treatment groups, for both physiological measures, the desensitization and RET subjects showed significantly less emotional reactivity than either the client-centered subjects or subjects in a fourth, nontreated control group. No follow-up was reported.

Montgomery (1971) also worked with test-anxious students, comparing RET with systematic desensitization and implosive therapy (and a nontreated control condition). The results tended to be supportive of desensitization, but as Trexler correctly points out, the presentation of prerecorded therapy is hardly a fair test of RET, wherein a live therapist is typically expected to dispute the client's irrational beliefs. Finally, Holroyd (1976) evaluated the differential efficacy of a cognitive approach containing aspects of both RET and SIT (self-instructional training) in the treatment of test anxiety. Test-anxious undergraduate volunteers were randomly assigned to one of five conditions: (1) the cognitive approach, (2) systematic desensitization, (3) combined cognitive desensitization, (4) a pseudotreatment meditational control, and (5) no treatment. Treatment was conducted in seven weekly hour-long sessions by graduate students. As shown in Figure 9–1, the cognitive approach (combining RET and SIT) was superior to the other conditions, including combined cognitive-desensitization treatment, on most outcome measures, including subsequent grade point average (a clearly practical criterion), and all active treatment conditions and the pseudotreatment control evidenced greater reductions

Figure 9–1   *Mean digit symbol, State Anxiety, and Anxiety Differential scores by group at preassessment, postassessment, and follow-up assessment (○——○: cognitive therapy; △——△: systematic desensitization; □- - -□: combined; - - -: pseudotherapy; . . . .: waiting list control).*

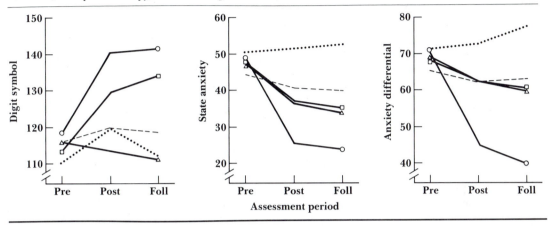

From Holroyd (1976).

in debilitating anxiety than did the no-treatment group. Gains were typically maintained through a one-month follow-up.

In general, these three studies afford only modest support for the utility of RET in the treatment of test anxiety. Although RET and RET–SIT combinations typically outperformed minimal treatment controls, they exceeded the efficacy of systematic desensitization only in one study (Holroyd, 1976). There was little evidence of greater stability of treatment gains over time than for other approaches, although, in general, treatment gains did tend to be maintained over brief follow-up periods. It would appear that RET is better than nothing in the treatment of test anxiety, but it is not necessarily preferable to alternative treatments. A major concern across all three studies involved the wholly nonclinical (i.e., analogue) nature of the populations treated.

Speech Anxiety   In an extremely thorough investigation, Meichenbaum, Gilmore, and Fedoravicius (1971) compared the effectiveness of group RET with group desensitization in treating speech anxiety in an analogue college student population. A third group of subjects received group desensitization followed by a combination of RET and group desensitization. A fourth group served as attention controls, and a fifth comprised waiting-list controls. Treatment was carried out over eight one-hour sessions.

Principal response measures, objective and self-ratings, were made in connection with test speeches occurring prior to and following treatment. As shown in Figure 9–2, the main findings were that subjects receiving desensitization only, or RET only (labeled "insight" in the figure), showed the greatest improvement. In fact, their level of speech performance following treatment generally matched that of an additional group of low speech-anxious subjects that was included in order to provide a standard for adaptive responding in such a situation. Subjects receiving the combination of RET and desensitization did not differ from attention-control subjects in their degree of improvement, and

Figure 9–2A *Mean reduction and increase in manifestations of anxiety from pretreatment to posttreatment on test speech measures (groups not connected by solid line are significantly different at .05 level). (■: desensitization; ▨: insight; ▢:desensitization plus insight; □: speech disc.; ▨: waiting list)*

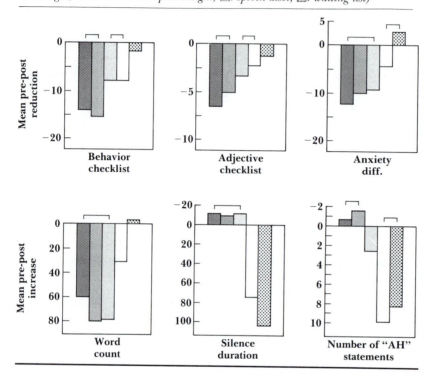

waiting-list controls showed the least improvement. The authors attributed the lack of improvement in the RET plus desensitization group to the insufficient amount of time devoted to each of the component procedures. Self-report follow-up measures taken three months after treatment indicated that the subjects had maintained improvement.

In Chapter 2, we indicated that desensitization appeared to be most effective for clients manifesting relatively few phobias. Results of the just-mentioned study tend to support this. Subjects who experienced anxiety in a wide variety of interpersonal situations benefited lit-

tle from desensitization, whereas subjects whose anxiety was restricted to public-speaking situations improve noticeably. On the other hand, subjects who were anxious in many interpersonal situations benefited considerably from RET. It may well be that cognitively oriented procedures, such as RET (and thought stopping, presented in the section to follow), are more appropriate to clients suffering from multiple fears than are such techniques as desensitization or extinction.

Karst and Trexler (1970) provided yet another early trial of RET. Speech-anxious college students recruited for the project were as-

Figure 9–2B Mean self-report of anxiety on personal report of confidence of a speaker (PRCS), fear of negative evaluation (FNE), and social avoidance and distress (SAD) scales at pretreatment, and posttreatment, and a three-month follow-up. (Note that "improvement" is reflected here by lowered scores.) (○──○: desensitization; ⊠──⊠: low speech anxious; ■──■: speech disc.; ●- - -●: insight; ●──●: desensitization plus insight; △──△: waiting list)

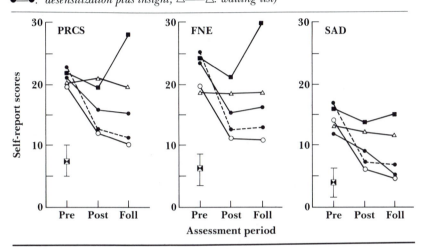

From Meichenbaum, Gilmore, and Fedoravicius (1971).

signed to RET, fixed-role therapy (Kelly, 1955), or a waiting list control. Treatment consisted of three group sessions spaced across several days. Both active interventions proved superior to the waiting list, and fixed-role therapy was superior to RET on one of five self-report anxiety measures. No differences were evident on ratings of performance on a public-speaking task or on a six-month follow-up, although the subjects tended to maintain the treatment gains.

Trexler and Karst (1972), working with speech-anxious college students, compared the effectiveness of RET with that of a relaxation treatment (viewed by the experimenters as a placebo control). A third group of subjects served as nontreated controls. Treatment was carried out during four group sessions spaced several days apart. The somewhat complex experimental design allowed for three-minute test speeches made prior to treatment, immediately

after treatment, and after some delay. Of the several response measures employed, subjects receiving RET showed significantly greater improvement than the placebo and control groups on the Irrational Belief Test (Jones, 1968), a self-report measure designed to operationalize beliefs targeted by Ellis, and on a scale measuring self-confidence while speaking. Since all subjects ultimately received RET, it was possible to increase the statistical power of the tests employed by combining pairs of groups having received RET and comparing them to a third group that had not yet undergone this treatment. The results of this more sensitive analysis revealed the superiority of RET on most of the other measures used, including objective ratings of anxiety while speaking and anxiety concerning speaking in general. Additionally, evidence showed that the effect of RET had generalized to certain problem areas unrelated to public speaking. A questionnaire follow-up made six to seven months after the completion of the study suggested that improvement had been maintained.

In a modified replication of Trexler and Karst, Straatmeyer and Watkins (1974) compared five treatment sessions of RET with and without the disputing element. The treatments, which included videotaped presentations appropriate to each, were compared with a placebo control involving a general discussion of the problems of anxiety and with a nontreated control. No significant treatment effects were found on either of the two behavior measures or two self-report measures relevant to speech anxiety, although trends favoring the RET treatment with the disputing element were apparent. On a generalization measure (a scale reflecting interpersonal anxiety), a significant effect was obtained, but only when the RET groups were compared with the nontreated controls. No follow-up was reported. Thus, the results of the Straatmeyer and Watkins investigation were essentially negative.

Thorpe, Amatu, Blakey, and Burns (1976) examined treatment components of the RET analogue of Meichenbaum and colleagues (1971). Speech-anxious high school students received five 30-minute group sessions involving one of the following treatments:

1. General insight, involving a discussion of Ellis's 11 irrational ideas—that is, why they were irrational—with subjects encouraged to look for such thinking and to "reason themselves" out of it

2. Specific insight, involving a discussion of four irrational ideas relevant to speech anxiety, with an emphasis on how each could lead to discomfort in a public-speaking situation

3. Instructional rehearsal, involving a discussion of four productive ideas designed to counteract the above four irrational ideas—subjects were instructed to rehearse these ideas in the context of an imagined speech

4. Insight plus rehearsal, involving a combination of specific insight and rehearsal of productive ideas

One positive feature of the study was the inclusion of postrationale (but pretreatment) ratings of expected value of treatments; no significant effect was found. Although self-report measures of anxiety revealed a significant treatment effect at posttest and at the three-month follow-up, favoring conditions *not* involving rehearsal, the two behavioral measures (Paul's Timed Behavior Checklist [Paul, 1966] and a measure of speech duration), failed to show significant treatment effects. Thus, the conclusion by Thorpe and associates that insight is the more important ingredient must be viewed as highly tentative.

Weissberg (1977), also working with speech-anxious college student volunteers, compared six hours of direct versus vicarious treatment involving standard desensitization, desensitization with coping instructions, and a cognitive modification procedure. The last, derived from Meichenbaum and colleagues (1971) and Meichenbaum (1972), included RET followed by desensitization with coping instructions (when subjects experienced anxiety, they were to cope with it using appropriate self-instruction and breathing exercises). On two self-report measures of speech anxiety, no significant treatment effect was obtained; for the behavioral checklist obtained while the subjects gave a speech, both cognitive modification and desensitization with coping instructions were significantly better than standard desensitization at posttest, but not at the 11-week follow-up. In a post hoc analysis, individual treatments were compared with a nontreated control condition. Significant differences were obtained on most measures, generally favoring the direct desensitization with coping instruction group and the direct cognitive modification group.

The incorporation of modified desensitization into the cognitive modification package renders the Weissberg study a less than perfect test of classical RET (it was not offered as such). On the other hand, it is difficult to see how the addition of the desensitization would have detracted from the efficacy of the RET treatment component—that is, had cognitive modification emerged as clearly superior, one might have taken this as support for RET. No such clear-cut superiority was obtained, however.

In still another study involving public-speaking anxiety on an analogue student population, Fremouw and Zitter (1978) compared a treatment combining Meichenbaum and colleagues' (1971) RET analogue and relaxation (Goldfried & Trier, 1974) with assertive training. Subjects were seen in groups for a total of five hours. In terms of behavioral measures (a behavioral checklist and an overall anxiety rating), a significant treatment effect was found for both treatments compared to placebo and non-treated controls. In terms of self-rated confidence, the assertive training group was superior to the cognitive therapy group, and both were superior to the control conditions. Only self-report measures were taken at the eight-week follow-up, at which time both treatment conditions showed additional improvement. Reductions in speech anxiety did not generalize to social anxiety.

Fremouw and Zitter were also interested in whether social anxiety (as measured by the Social Anxiety and Distress Scale [Watson & Friend, 1969]) would be predictive of a differential response to the treatment. Though not significant, an interesting trend did emerge: assertive training was equally effective for high and low socially anxious subjects. Cognitive therapy, however, was more effective for subjects showing high social anxiety than for those with low social anxiety.

Again, as for the studies evaluating RET in the treatment of test anxiety, these several studies involving the treatment of public-speaking anxiety offered only modest support for the efficacy of RET, alone or in combination with other approaches. In general, although RET typically exceeded attention placebo or waiting list control conditions, there was little evidence that it was in any way superior to alternative approaches (e.g., desensitization or fixed-role therapy). Further, while treatment gains were typically maintained over follow-up periods ranging from two to six months, there was little

evidence of greater stability for the cognitive approaches relative to the more behavioral ones. There were, however, some tantalizing suggestions of a greater generality of treatment gains for the cognitive approaches, typically involving reductions in general anxiety levels beyond specific speech anxiety (Meichenbaum et al., 1971; Trexler & Karst, 1974). This greater generality was, however, neither large in magnitude nor particularly robust, failing to emerge in at least one other trial (Fremouw & Zitter, 1978). Finally, there were some low-level indications of differential prediction, with subjects higher on general social anxiety tending to do better in the RET conditions than in systematic desensitization (Meichenbaum et al., 1971) or assertion training (Fremouw & Zitter, 1978). The general picture that emerges is one in which RET is not clearly superior on the average to other behavioral interventions in the treatment of speech anxiety, but in which it may be differentially advantageous for subjects with higher general levels of anxiety beyond public-speaking fears.

Social Anxiety   In one of the better-known studies in the literature, DiLoreto (1971) compared RET with systematic desensitization, client-centered therapy, a placebo treatment, and a no-treatment control group. The analogue population, college students all suffering from interpersonal anxiety, were classified as introverts or extroverts on the basis of their responses to a questionnaire. Approximately 11 hours of treatment were presented. In general, subjects in all three treatments experienced significantly greater anxiety reduction than the control group, with the greatest magnitude of anxiety reduction associated with desensitization. For reported interpersonal activity, RET was found to be significantly better than client-centered therapy or desensitization. These findings tended to be maintained at a three-month follow-up. One interesting and potentially useful finding was that RET was more effective for subjects classified as introverts than for those categorized as extroverts, although not necessarily more effective than systematic desensitization for either. DiLoreto solicited critiques from Ellis and others (DiLoreto, 1971) and not surprisingly, the study has been subject to much discussion and criticism (e.g., Ellis viewed the RET procedures as somewhat lacking; also see Bergin & Suinn, 1975; Mahoney, 1974). One flaw in the DiLoreto investigation, and this characterizes most of the remaining research in this section, was the failure to include credibility checks on the placebo treatment.

Overall, probably more has been written about this rather modest study because of its early appearance than for any striking insights into the nature of treatment response that it provided. The best that can be said for RET from this design is that it was arguably comparable to systematic desensitization and client-centered therapy in the treatment of this analogue population. The indication of differential response by introverts and extroverts to RET is somewhat treacherous to interpret. Although introverts clearly did better in RET than did extroverts, we would not want to recommend RET for introverts with social anxiety on that basis. There was no indication that introverts did better in RET than they did in either of the other active interventions; in fact, the data more nearly suggested that it was the extroverts who fared worse in RET than the other approaches, accounting for the treatment by subject interaction. If these data reflect a truly robust clinical phenomenon—and one should, of course, be cautious about overinterpreting any single set of findings—it is that extroverted subjects with social anxiety are better off being treated with something other than RET.

Assertion Problems Three studies have evaluated RET in the treatment of assertion problems. Wolfe and Fodor (1972) recruited unassertive female clinic outpatients via advertisements and assigned them to one of four conditions: (1) behavioral rehearsal, (2) behavioral rehearsal plus RET, (3) consciousness raising, and (4) waiting list. Treatment was limited to two weekly two-hour groups. No differences were evident on various self-report measures, but behavioral performance ratings favored both the behavioral rehearsal and the combined behavioral rehearsal-RET over the other conditions. In short, the addition of RET to behavioral rehearsal provided little gain over behavioral rehearsal alone. Perhaps the most noteworthy feature of this design was the utilization of a population drawn from a psychiatric outpatient clinic, albeit one in which the problems that led them to the clinic were not necessarily the same as the problems treated in the study. This was, curiously, one of the few trials involving the use of RET in a clinical, as opposed to an analogue, population.

Alden, Safran, and Weideman (1978) recruited both community and student volunteers for a trial contrasting behavioral skills training, an amalgamation of RET and SIT, and a no-contact control. Treatment consisted of six two-hour group sessions conducted by graduate students. Both self-report and behavior ratings indicated comparability for the two active interventions, with both superior to the controls. Finally, Carmody (1978) compared RET plus behavioral rehearsal with SIT plus behavioral rehearsal, behavioral rehearsal alone, and a delayed treatment control. Treatment involved four weekly 90-minute group sessions led by graduate students. Few significant between-group differences emerged on either self-report or behavioral performance measures, although those that did rather nonspecifically favored all three active approaches over the control condition. Only the RET plus behavioral rehearsal condition exceeded the control group on one of the measures, an *in vivo* refusal task, but this was not a general pattern across the various dependent variables. Although treatment gains were basically maintained at a three-month follow-up, there was no indication of any greater stability for the cognitive-behavioral over the purely behavioral cells. Thus, the addition of either RET or SIT to behavioral rehearsal appeared to provide little incremental gain over behavioral rehearsal alone.

Thus, while RET may be better than nothing in the treatment of assertion problems (at least when combined with SIT [Alden et al., 1978]), there is little evidence to suggest its superiority to behavioral rehearsal alone on any response dimension, and little evidence that its addition to behavioral rehearsal provides any particular clinical gain. This superiority to no-treatment controls and rough comparability to purely behavioral interventions is, by now, a familiar refrain. The one somewhat more positive feature of this brief literature was the inclusion of at least somewhat more clinically representative populations, although still none of the studies dealt with a population seeking clinical treatment for the actual problem targeted for change.

Stuttering Finally, in an investigation by Moleski and Tosi (1976), stutterers received eight sessions of RET or systematic desensitization. Each treatment was presented with and without homework (e.g., phone calls to friends, discussions with strangers). In terms of objectively rated speech dysfluencies, RET was significantly more effective than desensitization or a nontreated control condition. The superiority of RET to desensitization was also apparent at a one-month follow-up. Paper-and-pencil measures of interpersonal anxiety and attitudes toward stuttering also favored RET over desensitization. Although not entirely consistent, the general effect of homework was to augment each of the treatments. In spite of the investigation's several strong points—for example, the utilization of a bona fide clinical population, more than one therapist, on-going monitoring of the therapists' behaviors, a follow-up (albeit a brief one), and several relevant response measures—strong conclusions supporting RET are mitigated somewhat by the failure to include credibility checks on treatment (whether or not the conditions were seen by subjects as having been equally credible) and an equally credible placebo control.

It is somewhat curious that the only controlled study in the RET literature to utilize a clinically representative population was the study providing the clearest support for the differential efficacy of RET, both in terms of initial response and the stability of treatment gains. Nonetheless, we could hardly say that RET has moved into the forefront of treatment for stuttering, having largely been bypassed in favor of various specific fluency training procedures. Overall, this single study stands as a rather curious anomaly, strongly supportive of RET (relative to systematic desensitization) in its own right, but never replicated and hardly within the mainstream of work with people who stutter.

Summary In general, the conclusions that can be drawn about the *proven* clinical efficacy of RET are really rather modest. In most studies, spanning such problem targets as test, speech, and social anxiety, assertion problems, and speech dysfluencies, the fairest conclusions that can be drawn is that RET was better than nothing and, perhaps, roughly comparable to more purely behavioral approaches. There was little evidence to suggest that RET was superior to those behavioral interventions, or that adding RET to those behavioral interventions enhanced their efficacy in any noticeable fashion. There were virtually no comparisons of RET with any viable nonbehavioral intervention, other than DiLoreto's comparison to client-centered therapy in the treatment of social anxiety (essentially a "tie score" outcome) and Wolfe and Fodor's comparison of combined behavioral rehearsal and RET to consciousness raising in the treatment of assertion problems (essentially favoring the RET combination). Further, little evidence indicated any differential stability of treatment gains. There was some low-level indication of greater response generality in the treatment of speech anxiety (Meichenbaum et al., 1971; Trexler & Karst, 1974), such that general social anxiety was also reduced (at least relative to systematic desensitization). Finally, there was a hint of differential prediction of response, with subjects evidencing more general or more severe social fears perhaps doing better in RET than in purely behavioral approaches (Meichenbaum,

Gilmore, & Fedoravicius, 1971; Fremouw & Zitter, 1978), but these indications were neither large nor robust. Overall, one is struck by the absence of fully clinically representative trials and the generally modest indications of empirical support for the efficacy of RET.

Systematic Rational Restructuring

Systematic rational restructuring, or SRR (Goldfried et al., 1974), was initially presented as a structured set of procedures for operationalizing the theoretical processes seen as underlying change in RET. The approach involves four major components:

1. Providing a rationale, typically a version of Ellis's A–B–C model, with reference to the role of self-fulfilling prophecy in creating aversive consequences (Darley & Fazio, 1980)

2. Presenting various irrational assumptions believed by Ellis to underlie neuroticism

3. Analyzing the client's specific problems from a cognitive perspective to determine which irrational assumptions are operating

4. Teaching the client to modify his or her internal sentences

At this final stage, the client is encouraged to put into practice what he or she has learned during therapy.

The basic approach largely overlaps with RET, differing primarily in terms of the structure provided. Great emphasis is placed on rationality, with the underlying assumption that once the client recognizes the irrationality in his or her thinking, change at the cognitive level will begin to occur. Goldfried and colleagues describe the process as follows:

> In essence, the individual's emotional reaction now takes on the function of a signal or cue for him to stop and think: "What am I telling myself that may be irrational?" In the process of breaking up what heretofore might have been an automatic reaction, the client now becomes more aware of his inappropriate self-statement, and then proceeds to reevaluate this belief more rationally. The irrational self-statement is then replaced with more of a realistic appraisal of the situation, and note is taken of the resulting decrement in anxiety. (1974, p. 251)

Behavioral procedures may or may not be combined with this more purely cognitive approach. When they are, they are presented more frequently as an opportunity to practice living in a way consistent with more rational beliefs than as a means of empirically testing the validity of those beliefs. In this respect, systematic rational restructuring is also more similar to RET than it is to some of its more empirically oriented approaches, such as Beck's cognitive therapy.

Empirical Support

Since the basic theory underlying systematic rational restructuring is virtually identical to that underlying RET, a review of the approach's empirical support can concentrate on the controlled outcome trials in which it has been evaluated. Unlike RET, which although frequently practiced with clinically representative populations has rarely been tested with other than analogue populations, systematic rational restructuring has received at least several trials with recruited community volunteer samples (e.g., Kanter & Goldfried, 1979; Linehan, Goldfried, & Goldfried, 1979; Shahar & Merbaum, 1981). Although such samples are not fully representative of clinical populations, they at least come closer than trials relying solely on undergraduate college students. Nonetheless, fully representative clinical populations are not to be found in any of the trials to be reviewed, limiting the generalizability of the claims that can be made.

Test Anxiety Two trials have evaluated systematic rational restructuring in the treatment of test anxiety. As noted earlier, this is a disorder typically chosen for study more because of its convenience to university-based academicians than for any intrinsic interest in its treatment. Goldfried, Linehan, and Smith (1978) compared systematic rational restructuring with prolonged imaginal exposure and a waiting list control in a study conducted simultaneously at two different sites. It was not clear whether or not the subject population consisted solely of undergraduate college students, or precisely how subjects were recruited, but it would appear that the sample was recruited by advertisement largely from a college community (subject ages ranged from 18 to 49, but no mean was provided). Treatment was conducted in six weekly one-hour sessions by the two senior authors, both experienced clinicians.

Treatment outcome, as assessed by self-reported test anxiety measures, typically favored the systematic rational restructuring over the imaginal exposure, and both over the waiting list control. Measures of the generality of anxiety reduction and a preexamination anxiety self-report were typically inconclusive, although both active treatments looked somewhat better than the control. A six-week follow-up indicated that treatment gains were typically maintained, but offered only slight evidence of greater stability for the SRR group than the imaginal exposure group, with 4 of 17 outcome measures evidencing at least a trend favoring the SRR condition. Overall, this study provided modest support for the utility of SRR in the treatment of test anxiety, with SRR generally superior to a waiting list control, and apparently outperforming the imaginal exposure condition on at least some of the many outcome measures.

Wise and Haynes (1983) attempted to replicate these findings in a study contrasting SRR with both an attentional and a waiting list control in a college student sample recruited via advertisement. Treatment was again provided in a group format, in this study involving five weekly one-hour sessions. In general, although the SRR condition outperformed the waiting list control on measures of test anxiety, it did not exceed the attentional control. However, it did appear to outperform the attentional control condition on measures of generalized anxiety. Although an eight-month follow-up was noted, it was difficult to determine exactly how the respective treatment conditions had fared by that time.

Exactly how much actual improvement was accomplished in clinical terms in either study is not clear (or even how important such change would have been, in clinical terms). Certainly, the Goldfried and colleagues design, one of the nicer studies in the treatment of test anxiety, provided at least reasonable support for SRR in the treatment of this disorder. However, the failure of the SRR condition in the Wise and Haynes design to exceed the attentional control on specific test anxiety measures suggests a lack of robustness for the approach. Similarly, although Goldfried, DeCanteceo, & Weinberg did not find any particular advantage for SRR in terms of generalized anxiety, Wise and Haynes did. Finally, there was some hint of greater stability of gains for SRR in Goldfried's study but little comparable support from Wise and Haynes. Overall, the efficacy of SRR for this problem target appears promising, but hardly overwhelming.

Speech Anxiety Two trials have evaluated SRR in the treatment of speech anxiety. As with test anxiety, this disorder is typically chosen for study more as a matter of convenience than for its intrinsic interest. Lent, Russell, and Zamostony (1981) contrasted SRR, cue-controlled desensitization, attention placebo, and a waiting list control in a sample of undergraduates selected for extreme scores on a self-report measure of speech anxiety. Treatment was again provided in five weekly one-hour group sessions. Treatment outcome on self-reported speech anxiety measures favored the cue-controlled desensitization over SRR, which did not exceed the control groups. There was no evidence of differential generalization to generic anxiety states. Gross and Fremouw (1982) evaluated the interaction between type of speech anxiety and type of treatment. Cognitive restructuring and progressive relaxation were equivalent to one another, and both were superior to a waiting list control in an undergraduate student sample, again recruited on the basis of extreme scores on a self-report measure of speech anxiety. However, those subjects reporting little in the way of physiological responsivity in their speech anxiety responded better to cognitive restructuring than they did to progressive relaxation.

Overall, this pair of studies provided only modest support for the utility of SRR in the treatment of speech anxiety. The rationality-based approach was outperformed by cue-assisted desensitization in one trial (Lent et al., 1981) and was only comparable to progressive relaxation in a second (Gross & Fremouw, 1982). The latter trial did suggest a potentially interesting subject by treatment interaction, with speech-anxious volunteers low in physiological reactivity doing better in SRR than in relaxation training. Whether or not this indication develops into a robust guide to treatment selection will depend on subsequent research.

Social Anxiety Two studies evaluated SRR in the treatment of social anxiety, a more clinically representative disorder. Kanter and Goldfried (1979) recruited community volunteers via advertisement who were randomly assigned to SRR, self-control desensitization (Goldfried & Trier, 1974), combined SRR and self-control desensitization, and a waiting list control. Treatment was provided in seven weekly 1 1/2-hour group sessions. Treatment outcome favored all three active treatment conditions over the waiting list control group, but only on self-report measures, not observational ratings or physiological measures. As shown in Figure 9–3, such differences as were evident between the three active treatment conditions appeared to favor SRR, either alone or in combination with systematic desensitization. A nine-week follow-up indicated that treatment gains, including between-group differences, were either maintained or enhanced following treatment condi-

tion. One additional finding of note was a greater change in the endorsement of irrational beliefs (as measured by Jones's 1968 IBT) for the SRR condition than for either the desensitization or the control group (the combined SRR-desensitization cell was nonsignificantly intermediate on this measure). Thus, greater change was clearly evident on a cognitive *mechanisms* measure, as well as on reported social anxiety. Shahar and Merbaum (1981) contrasted SRR, self-control desensitization, and a waiting list in a similar population of community volunteers. Both active interventions were superior to the control, but again, only on self-report measures. Treatment gains essentially held up through a four-month follow-up, with no differential stability evident between the two active treatments. Neither study found clear evidence of a treatment by subtype interaction (physiologically responsive versus nonphysiologically responsive subjects), although each was designed to explore such a possibility.

Overall, these two studies suggested the comparability of SRR to an alternative behavioral intervention—cue-controlled desensitization—and its superiority to minimal treatment control conditions, but these patterns were largely limited to self-report indices. Further, the only alternative behavioral approach to which SRR was compared was a form of desensitization. It would be interesting to see how SRR fares in comparison with a more skills training and exposure approach. No clear pattern of differential response as a function of subject characteristics emerged, nor was there any evidence of differential generality or stability. In general, this pair of studies, both at least involving recruited community volunteers rather than relying solely on college students, provided modest but hardly overwhelming support for the efficacy of SRR in the treatment of social anxiety.

Assertion Problems Finally, two trials have been conducted utilizing SRR in the modification of assertion problems. Linehan et al., (1979) contrasted SRR versus behavioral re-

Figure 9–3 Mean self-report scores for each treatment condition at pretest, posttest, and follow-up assessments (□——□: systematic rational restructuring; ■----■: rational restructuring plus desensitization; ●——●: self-control desensitization; △- - -△: waiting list).

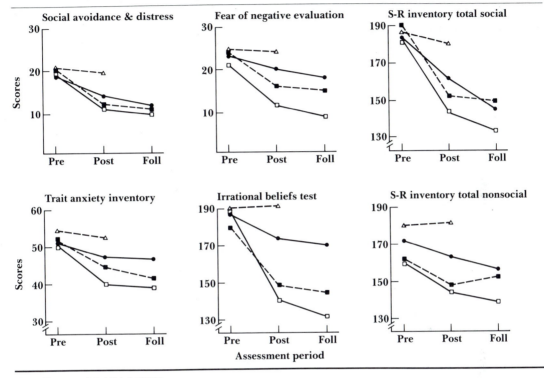

From Kanter and Goldfried (1979).

hearsal (involving modeling, role playing, and feedback), combined SRR and behavioral rehearsal, a relationship control, and a waiting list control. Clients were adult female community volunteers recruited at two geographically distinct centers. Treatment was provided by carefully trained and supervised graduate students in eight weekly individual one-hour sessions. As shown in Figure 9–4, SRR and combined SRR-behavioral rehearsal were superior to the waiting list control on most self-report measures, whereas behavioral rehearsal was not. There were, however, no differences between those three active treatment groups on the self-report

measures. Combined SRR-behavioral rehearsal and behavioral rehearsal alone were superior to SRR on behavioral performance tasks. Treatment gains were generally maintained at a two-month follow-up, with little indication of any differential stability between the active treatment modalities. On the whole, the combined modality appeared to represent the optimal treatment of choice, by virtue of influencing both self-report and behavioral performance measures. Each single modality, on the other hand, appeared to be more limited in its impact, with SRR alone influencing the self-report assertion measures and behavioral rehearsal

Figure 9–4 *Unadjusted mean scores for behavioral role-play test performance and subjective emotional response measures at pretest and posttest assessment. With the exception of base anxiety, all scores reflect averages across six role-played situations (■- - -■: BR/RR, behavior rehearsal/ rational restructuring; ●——● RR, rational restructuring; □——□ BR, behavior rehearsal; △——△ RC, relationship control; ▽——▽ WAIT, waiting list).*

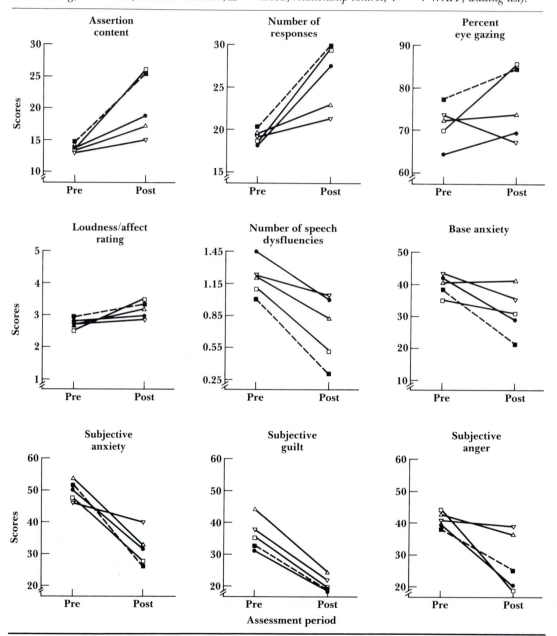

From Linehan, Goldfried, and Goldfried (1979).

influencing the behavioral performance measures. In this study, one of the better designed and executed studies in the literature, the combination of cognitive (SRR) and behavioral (rehearsal) procedures, appeared to provide an advantage over either alone, largely by broadening the range of components of assertion problems changed by treatment.

Hammen, Jacobs, Mayol, and Cochran (1980) compared combined SRR plus social skills training versus social skills training alone in a sample of recruited community volunteers and found both superior to a waiting list control, but not different from one another. Treatment gains were essentially maintained at a one-month follow-up, but there was no evidence of differential stability. The absence of any additive advantage for the combination of SRR and social skills training over social skills training alone stands in contrast to the findings of Linehan and colleagues (1979) just described.

Overall, SRR has fared relatively well in trials investigating assertion training, performing comparably to more purely behavioral approaches and outperforming control conditions in both reported trials, and evidencing an additive advantage over strictly cognitive or strictly behavioral approaches in one of those two trials. If robust, such additivity may reflect underlying differences in the generality of the respective single modalities and, perhaps, point toward the prediction of differential response profiles across potential patients. But little direct evidence existed of either in the two studies reviewed. Although treatment gains appeared to be maintained over time, there was little evidence of any differential stability across treatments.

Summary

In general, the quality of the studies evaluating the efficacy of SRR is superior to those evaluating RET. At the very least, several of the studies were executed by Goldfried and colleagues (Goldfried et al., 1978; Kanter & Goldfried, 1979; Linehan et al., 1979), ensuring that SRR was adequately imple-

mented in at least some of the trials.[8] Given Ellis's concern about the adequacy of the execution of RET in the DiLoreto (1971) trial, and the absence of any clear indication that acknowledged experts in RET had participated in any of those trials (Wolfe & Fodor [1977] was clearly an exception to this statement), it was reassuring that at least some of the SRR trials have been conducted by acknowledged experts in that intervention.

On the whole, the available evidence was at least moderately supportive. SRR typically outperformed various minimal and no-treatment conditions and, with only two exceptions, one negative (Lent et al., 1981) and one positive (Goldfried et al., 1978), typically equaled the performance of more purely behavioral approaches. SRR plus a behavioral intervention outperformed either single modality in one study (Linehan et al., 1979) and, perhaps, in a second (Kanter & Goldfried, 1979), but failed to evidence any additive advantage in a third (Hammen, et al., 1980). There was little evidence of greater generality of treatment gains—other than the Linehan and colleagues (1979) and the Wise and Haynes (1983) trials—and none of greater treatment stability. On the whole, the available literature can be regarded as sounder than that evaluating RET, but yielding a very

[8]It is probably desirable to have some trials in a literature conducted by proponents of a procedure, simply to ensure that it has been adequately executed in at least some studies. Subsequently, it is desirable to have additional trials executed by other investigators, as a means of ensuring that observed findings are not wholly attributable to the subtle influences of experimenter biases. Ideally, any given trial would include proponents of each of the major modalities represented. The Sloan, Staples, Cristol, Yorkston, and Whipple (1975) comparison between behavior therapy and dynamic psychotherapy represents one such example, the Hollon et al. (1986) and the NIMH-sponsored Treatment of Depression Collaborative Research Project, Elkin, Parloff, Hadley, & Autrey (1985) represent others. Few other such examples exist in the literature.

similar set of conclusions. Namely, SRR can be said to be better than nothing, but not necessarily superior to other more purely behavioral alternatives. Although some evidence for the incremental advantage of combining SRR and behavioral approaches was present, it was hardly robust. Finally, within the RET literature, the lack of fully clinically representative samples in the studies reviewed was both striking and regretable. The SRR literature did involve a greater number of recruited community volunteers samples, rather than relying solely on college student samples, but one really must wonder why such a major approach has yet to be scrutinized in a fully clinical trial.

Other Restructuring Approaches

Several of the most interesting controlled treatment trials have involved cognitive restructuring approaches that are not wholly classifiable as either RET or SRR, but that clearly rely heavily on rationality as the main working change process. With two exceptions, these trials have involved fully clinical populations. With few exceptions, these trials have not been particularly supportive of the cognitive restructuring approaches.

Specific Fears In an early trial with students who feared dead animals, D'Zurilla, Wilson, and Nelson (1973) utilized a version of cognitive restructuring that focused on providing subjects with a reattribution of snake fear in terms of learning principles. Though not differing from imaginal exposure on any outcome measure, both active treatments proved superior to a waiting list control on some but not all outcome measures. In a subsequent study, Wein, Nelson, and Odom (1975) utilized the same approach in the treatment of snake-phobic college students. Although treatment outcomes were mixed, the cognitive restructuring approach was at least the equal of systematic desensitization on behavioral measures and arguably more effective in reducing subjective anxiety.

Biran and Wilson (1981) provided one of the more interesting comparisons in the literature. Community residents, recruited via advertisement but carefully screened to ensure that their presenting problems (a range of phobias including heights, darkness, or elevators) were of truly clinical magnitude, were randomly assigned to either guided exposure or cognitive restructuring. The cognitive restructuring involved an amalgamation of relabeling, rational restructuring, and self-instructional training. Treatment was provided by graduate students in five individual sessions over a several-week period. As shown in Figure 9-5, guided exposure proved superior to cognitive restructuring in terms of enhancing approach behavior, reducing subjective fear and decreasing physiological reactivity. A crossover design indicated that subjects not improving in the cognitive condition responded more powerfully when provided with the behavioral intervention. On the whole, this well-conducted study clearly supported the efficacy of the more purely behavioral approach over the purely cognitive one.

Agoraphobia In the first of a pair of studies with agoraphobic patients, Emmelkamp and colleagues (Emmelkamp, Kuipers, & Eggeraat, 1978) utilized the same amalgamation of relabeling, rational restructuring, and self-instructional training used by Biran and Wilson, again in comparison with *in vivo* exposure. Treatment was provided in five two-hour group sessions over a one-week period. As shown in Figure 9-6, *in vivo* exposure proved superior to the cognitive approach on both behavioral and self-report measures. In the second trial, Emmelkamp and Mersch (1982) compared the same cognitive amalgamation versus *in vivo* exposure versus the combination of the two, again in a fully clinical agoraphobic sample. Treatment was provided in eight two-hour group sessions. At posttest, both the *in vivo* exposure and the combined cognitive-exposure groups were superior to the cognitive approach alone. The cognitive-only group did evidence continued

Figure 9-5 *Level of self-efficacy and approach behavior toward different threats at the various stages of the study. (Plotted here is level of self-efficacy assessed prior to the behavioral approach test.) (Guided exposure:* ●——●: *approach behavior;* ●-----●: *level of self-efficacy; cognitive restructuring:* ○——○: *approach behavior;* ○-----○: *level of self-efficacy.)*

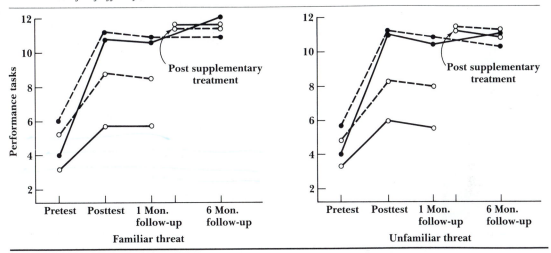

From Biran and Wilson (1981).

improvement after treatment and no longer differed from the other two groups at a one-month follow-up. In a third clinically representative trial, Williams and Rappaport (1983) found that the addition of a cognitive component involving self-distraction, relabeling anxiety, self-statement replacement, and self-instructional training added little to *in vivo* exposure in the modification of driving fears in an agoraphobic population.

These three studies, all involving clinically representative populations of agoraphobic patients, represent some of the strongest challenges to proponents of cognitive approaches. In no trial did a purely cognitive approach even equal behavioral exposure, and in no study did the addition of a cognitive component to exposure enhance the efficacy of that combination over behavioral exposure alone.

We should note that none of these trials were conducted by recognized experts in the cognitive interventions (Emmelkamp, for example, is generally recognized as one of the leading contemporary figures in modern behavior therapy). Whether or not this factor contributed to any lesser competency in the execution of the cognitive approaches is impossible to discern, although the possibility does exist. Further, even if these studies do reflect poorly on cognitive therapy relative to exposure therapy, that relative disadvantage may be limited to agoraphobic populations. Nonetheless, it is striking that the cognitive approaches fared so poorly, relative to behavioral exposure, in the treatment of this clinical disorder.

Obsessive-Compulsive Disorder Finally, in yet another study with a fully clinical population, Emmelkamp, van der Helm, van Zanten, and Plochg (1980) found no particular gain from adding a cognitive component (again, the amalgamation of relabeling, rational

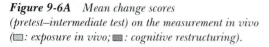

Figure 9-6A *Mean change scores (pretest–intermediate test) on the measurement in vivo (▨: exposure in vivo; ▩: cognitive restructuring).*

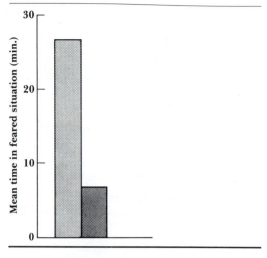

restructuring, and self-instructional training) to *in vivo* exposure in the treatment of obsessive-compulsive disorder, as shown in Figure 9-7. We should note, however, that the time allotted to the cognitive component was relatively brief, averaging 30 minutes in each of the two-hour treatment sessions. As before, it remains unclear how adequately the cognitive component was operationalized by this research group. Nonetheless, there was again little support for proponents of cognitive approaches in this trial with a fully clinical population.

Summary In general, these various trials involving at least partially rationality-based approaches provided little, if any, support for the cognitive approaches. In only two trials, both involving the treatment of specific fears in analogue student populations (D'Zurilla et al., 1973; Wein et al., 1975) did cognitive approaches equal more purely behavioral alter-

Figure 9-6B *Mean change scores (pretest–intermediate test) on phobic anxiety and avoidance scales (▨: exposure in vivo; ▩: cognitive restructuring).*

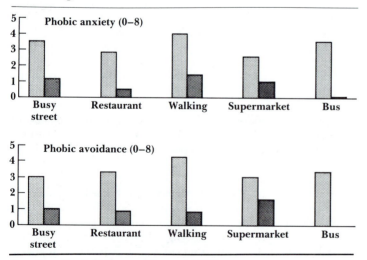

From Emmelkamp, Kuipers, and Eggeraat (1978).

Figure 9-7A *Treatment of obsessive-compulsive patients.*

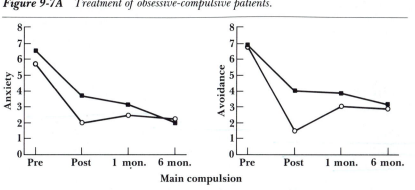

Main compulsion

natives. In each of the remaining trials, all involving fully clinical populations—(or at least carefully screened community volunteers (as in Biran & Wilson, 1981)—cognitive approaches both failed to equal behavioral exposure, and the addition of a cognitive component to behavioral exposure failed to produce any clinical gain over behavioral exposure alone.

The only potentially mitigating factor was the unknown adequacy with which the cognitive components were executed. In each of the fully clinical trials, the cognitive modality was an amalgamation of RET-like rationality and SIT-like self-statement replacement approaches of unknown fidelity designed by investigators more closely associated with behavioral than cognitive interventions. One cannot escape the nagging sense that these particular cognitive representations were designed as much to be plausible nonspecific controls for exposure therapy than bona fide active interventions in their own right. Nonetheless, until (and unless) solid empirical

Figure 9-7B *Contributions of self-instructional training (■-----■: cognitive plus exposure; ○——○: exposure).*

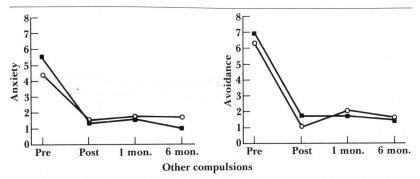

Other compulsions

From Emmelkamp, van der Helm, van Zanten, and Plochg (1980).

evidence is produced suggesting that cognitive interventions can prove more clinically useful with fully clinical populations, the current, rather unfavorable picture of the cognitive approaches eminating from these trials will have to stand.

Overall Evaluation of the Rationality-based Approaches

Overall, there was less well-founded empirical support for the efficacy of the various rationality-based approaches (RET, SRR, and the related other amalgamations) than one might have expected, given the impact of RET on clinical practice and the general enthusiasm that such approaches have generated in the field. RET itself has rarely been evaluated in a truly adequate clinical trial. One comes away with the impression that the perception of the efficacy of this approach has virtually been "grandfathered" into the field, in part due to the rather uncritical claims of its proponents (Ellis, 1977b) and in part due to the reasonableness of the model on which it is based. Although RET was not without empirical support, that data base was hardly overwhelming, which was a conclusion reached by numerous reviewers (e.g., Mahoney, 1974; Mahoney & Arnkoff, 1978; Meichenbaum, 1974; Trexler, 1977).

What was somewhat more disconcerting was the rather modest showing of related rationality-based approaches, such as systematic rationale restructuring and the amalgamations of rational restructuring and self-instructional training. Evidence for the efficacy of the former was derived largely from trials with college student analogue or quasi-analogue community volunteer populations (e.g., test anxiety, speech anxiety, social anxiety, and assertion problems) typically conducted in populations recruited by advertisement. More fully clinical representative trials have typically not been supportive of cognitive components. However, those trials have typically involved rather idiosyncratic amalga-

mations of multiple cognitive approaches (e.g., rational restructuring and self-instructional training). Further, many of those trials have been conducted by researchers more closely associated with behavioral than with cognitive approaches (e.g., Emmelkamp and colleagues), raising questions about the adequacy with which cognitive approaches were executed.

In summary, this literature engenders feelings of dissatisfaction. On the one hand, there is the sense that something important may be going on clinically. On the other hand, there is the sense that researchers with the capacity to execute these approaches adequately have elected to produce rather trivial quasi-analogue trials, while the more clinically representative studies have been left to the more behaviorally oriented researchers. We hope this state of affairs will change in the ensuing years.

Approaches Emphasizing Empiricism

Beck's Cognitive Therapy

Aaron Beck, a psychiatrist, offers a conceptualization of psychopathology not unlike that of Ellis's and an approach to therapy that overlaps in many respects with RET. Despite the overlap, however, there are important points of differentiation that will be discussed below. Like Ellis, Beck's training emphasized psychoanalysis, which he employed for many years before reaching the conclusion, based on both clinical experience and empirical psychopathology studies, that conscious thinking plays a primary role in human emotion and behavior (see Beck, 1963, 1964, 1967, 1976). In contrast to many other contemporary advocates of a cognitive learning orientation (e.g., Goldfried & Goldfried, 1975; Lazarus, 1976; Mahoney, 1974, 1977; Meichenbaum, 1977), Beck developed his theory independently of Ellis, although, not surprisingly, the influence of RET is apparent in his later writing (e.g., Beck, 1976).

Both Beck and Ellis forcefully reject the primacy of Freudian precepts, especially unconscious thought processes. Both conceptualize human behavior and emotion largely in accord with the A–B–C paradigm. Both stress the role of faulty or irrational thinking in generating negative affect. Finally, both stress a here-and-now action orientation (including homework) and relatively short-term treatment.

In what ways, then, do the approaches of Beck and Ellis differ? Perhaps because of his psychiatric training, Beck places greater credence in conventional psychodiagnostic categorization. Thus, Beck (1976) explicitly relates stylistic patterns of maladaptive thinking to many of the categories of psychopathology, most notably depression (Beck, 1967, 1970; Beck is recognized as a leading authority on depressive disorders), but also to manic states, anxiety neuroses, hysteria, obsessional disorders, psychosomatic disorders, phobias, and to some extent schizophrenia. His analysis of the ideational content of certain common phobias (e.g., fear of flying, agoraphobia; see Chapter 7 of Beck, 1976) reflects the relative specificity of his approach, which is also seen in his analysis of the thought patterns associated with different emotional states, including anxiety, sadness, anger, and euphoria. The therapeutic approach of Beck and colleagues is also somewhat more structured than RET (Beck et al., 1979), but recall that there *are* highly structured versions of RET (e.g., Goldfried et al., 1974; Maultsby, 1977). In addition, cognitive therapy frequently follows an inductive pattern, in which abstract beliefs are inferred from repeated concrete instances, rather than RET's more deductive process.

The major difference, however, appears to reside in the role given to empiricism. In cognitive therapy, efforts are continually being made to test the validity of the client's beliefs against external reality by virtue of behavioral experiments; that is, instances in which the clients utilize their own behaviors to test the accuracy of their beliefs. In RET, cognitive change is seen largely as a consequence of reason and persuasion. Ellis (1980) has recognized this distinction as reflecting a basic dichotomy between a purportedly empirical approach (cognitive therapy) and a basically philosophical one (RET).

For example, one of the subjects in a recent controlled outcome trial involving cognitive therapy for depression (Hollon, DeRubeis, Evans, Tuason, Wiemer, & Garvey, 1986) was concerned that she would never be able to have a really serious relationship with a man because she was unable to bear children. In her personal belief system, she could not imagine any eligible male choosing her for a wife because she was barren. A RET therapist might well have concentrated on her belief that not being able to have children or, by extension, not being able to marry, were awful fates that reflected poorly on her self-worth. That is, the RET therapist might well have focused on her philosophical stance toward her predicament. The cognitive therapist in the case, however, elected first to focus on the accuracy of her belief that no one would ever consider having a truly meaningful relationship with her because she was infertile. The client and therapist devised an experiment for her to run in which she polled numerous male colleagues in her office building about her situation, disguising her involvement by relating the details as the plot of a recent daytime television show. To her surprise, 10 of the 12 males she questioned indicated that the childbearing capacity of the potential spouse would have little or no impact on their willingness to initiate or deepen a relationship. Rather, the qualities of the individual were their primary concern. Armed with information disconfirming her beliefs, the client was able to begin dating without being so fearful of the impact of personal disclosure. In cognitive therapy, the emphasis is on a process of *collaborative empiricism* (Hollon &

Beck, 1979), in which client and therapist attempt to devise actual tests of the accuracy of the client's beliefs, not infrequently using the client's own behaviors as "experiments" to provide evidence bearing on these issues.

Beck believes that certain maladaptive beliefs are widely held, especially in psychiatric populations. The nature of these beliefs varies somewhat, depending on the diagnostic category, but in general they can be charted on one of two dimensions. One dimension is *safety–danger:* for example, "It would be awful for someone to form a low opinion of me," or "It would be terrible if someone thought I was ridiculous." The second dimension is *pleasure–pain:* for example, "I can never be happy if I'm not famous." These fundamental ideas are referred to by Beck as *rules*. In contrast to Ellis, he does not view them as *necessarily* irrational. Instead they are characterized as too absolute, too broad or extreme, or too arbitrary. The basic rules give rise to maladaptive self-verbalizations, or possibly visual images, which Beck calls *automatic thoughts* (because that is how they are experienced by clients). Much of therapy involves assisting the client to ferret out automatic thinking and, ultimately, the basic rules, and then to test them both logically and empirically.

Beck's conceptualization of psychological problems is well illustrated in his approach to depression. Behaviorally, depression may be manifested by a variety of symptoms, such as crying, a sad face, suicidal threats, loss of appetite. These symptoms are related to thoughts or desires associated with avoiding activity and possibly committing suicide. More basic than these, however, are the underlying clusters of rules—for example, "I am a loser," "I'll fail at everything." For Beck, basic ideation in depression has three themes (he uses the term *cognitive triad*):

1. *Negative view of the self.* The individual dislikes himself or herself.

2. *Negative view of the world.* Events are interpreted negatively.

3. *Negative view of the future.* The future is appraised negatively.

Clearly, these themes illustrate distortions in thinking. Beck points to several ways in which individuals suffering from psychological disorders manifest such distortions.

Personalization. Incorrectly referring an external event to one's self (e.g., blaming oneself for a plague in a distant land)

Polarized thinking. Dichotomous either/or thinking (e.g., interpreting a mild rebuff as total rejection)

Selective abstraction. Attending to a detail while ignoring the context

Arbitrary inference. Jumping to conclusions in the absence of corroborative evidence

Overgeneralization. Arriving at a sweeping conclusion from a single experience (e.g., concluding one will never do anything right after making one mistake)

The following excerpts, taken from the Beck and colleagues treatment manual, illustrates the method of cognitive therapy:

One woman who complained of severe headache and other somatic disturbances was found to have a very high depression score. When asked about the cognitions that seemed to make her unhappy, she said, "My family doesn't appreciate me"; "Nobody appreciates me, they take me for granted"; "I am worthless."

As an example, she stated that her adolescent children no longer wanted to do things with her. Although this particular statement could very well have been accurate, the therapist decided to determine its authenticity. He pursued the "evidence" for the statement in the following interchange:

Patient: My son doesn't like to go to the theatre or to the movies with me anymore.

Therapist: How do you know that he doesn't want to go with you?

Patient: Teenagers don't actually like to do things with their parents.

Therapist: Have you actually asked him to go with you?

Patient: No, as a matter of fact, he did ask me a few times if I wanted him to take me . . . but I didn't think he really wanted to go.

Therapist: How about testing it out by asking him to give you a straight answer?

Patient: I guess so.

Therapist: The important thing is not whether or not he goes with you but whether you are deciding for him what he thinks instead of letting him tell you.

Patient: I guess you are right, but he does seem to be inconsiderate. For example, he is always late for dinner.

Therapist: How often has that happened?

Patient: Oh, once or twice. . . . I guess that's really not all that often.

Therapist: Is his coming late for dinner due to his being inconsiderate?

Patient: Well, come to think of it, he did say that he had been working late those two nights. Also he has been considerate in a lot of other ways.

Actually, as the patient later found out, her son was willing to go to the movies with her.

Thus, the therapist does not accept the patient's statements at their face value but pursues them to determine their validity. If the patient's conclusions had been valid, then the therapist could explore the way she assigns meanings to her son's "rejection." The therapist could also encourage her to pursue other activities and relationships with other people." (Beck et al., 1979, pp. 105–106).

In dealing with severe depression, the initial focus, perhaps over the first several sessions, is largely behavioral. As Beck notes, depressed people typically see themselves as losers, unable to accomplish anything, and the provision of *any* success experience can have a mood-elevating effect. Thus, graduated tasks or activities are assigned early in treatment. For example, a depressed woman who sees herself as a total failure as a housewife might be asked initially to do nothing more than boil an egg. When she has successfully carried this out, she is given a slightly more difficult assignment. Before long, she may be preparing an entire meal, much to her satisfaction. Obviously, it is important that the therapist not assign a task that is likely to overwhelm the client; after all, additional failure experiences are the last things depressed individuals need.

Beck presents graded task assignments as only one part of his treatment package (and certainly not the heart of it), but the following case history illustrates its therapeutic potential when used as the sole treatment method. Beck describes a middle-aged man who had not moved from his bed in over a year. Antidepressant medications had been to no avail. Beck spent but one session with the patient and devoted it exclusively to encouraging him to walk away from his bed, first 10 yards, then 20 yards, and so on. Within 45 minutes, the man was able to walk about the ward, and soon he was able to avail himself of reinforcements in the hospital (use of vending machines, recreational facilities, and within a week, the hospital grounds). One month later he was discharged. This case is instructive in that it illustrates how resistant (and lacking in confidence) a depressed individual can be. Initially, the patient was convinced he had not the strength to walk at all. Beck was able to persuade him to test his hypothesis, offering to catch him if he fell. Obviously, the patient's hypothesis proved incorrect.

Recall our prior discussions of Bandura's (1977a) concept of self-efficacy (Chapters 1, 3, and 4). For Bandura, successful treatment of problems associated with excessive avoidance of situations perceived as threatening involves enhancing the individual's sense of self-efficacy. Bandura is particularly partial to interventions that involve active participation in threatening situations or tasks in a graduated and structured manner. (Recall participant modeling, discussed in Chapter 4.) Interventions of this nature provide clients with highly credible information that they can indeed cope. Beck's graduated task assignments constitute such an intervention.

Other interventions introduced early in therapy include the following:

1. *Self-monitoring*. Frequently, one of the first assignments in therapy involves training in systematic self-monitoring. As shown in Table 9-2, the client is trained to record events and activities, moods (with "0" representing the worst the client has ever felt and "100" the best), and, perhaps, other notable events, such as "mastery" (M) or "pleasure" (P) experiences. Such self-monitoring provides exquisite detail regarding the specifics of the client's life, serves as a baseline for evaluating change during treatment, and frequently provides information that can be used in specific hypothesis testing. For example, the record presented in Table 9-2 was provided by a former art professor reduced to working as a handyman in an apartment complex. He viewed his depression as a necessary consequence of being "stuck" in his current "dead-end" job. Yet, a careful examination of his own self-monitoring records suggested that his moods were actually rather pleasant when he was at work. His lowest periods came during weekends and evenings when he would lay around the house ruminating about how awful his employment situation was at the moment.

2. *Activity Schedule Making*. Clients and therapists schedule specific daily activities, selected and evaluated strictly on the basis of how effectively they elevate mood.

3. *Mastery and Pleasure Therapy*. The aforementioned activities are rated by the client on dimensions of mastery and pleasure. Depressed clients, who characteristically report they can master nothing and enjoy nothing, are thus confronted with information to the contrary.

As therapy progresses and clients begin to experience more elevated moods, the focus of treatment becomes more cognitive. Clients are instructed to observe and record automatic thoughts, perhaps at a specific time each evening, and when they become aware of increased dysphoria. Typically, the thoughts are negative self-referents—"I'm worthless"; "I'll never amount to anything"–and initially the therapist points out their unreasonable and self-defeating nature. With practice, clients learn "distancing"—that is, dealing with such thoughts objectively, evaluating them rather than blindly accepting them. Homework assignments can facilitate distancing: the client records an automatic thought; next to it he or she writes down a thought that counters the automatic thought, as the therapist might have done. According to Beck, certain basic themes soon emerge, such as being abandoned, as well as stylistic patterns of thinking, such as overgeneralization. The themes reflect the aforementioned rules, and the ultimate goal of therapy is to assist the client to modify them.

Primary emphasis is placed upon evaluating the accuracy of the specific beliefs identified. The client is typically trained to utilize at least three standard questions to facilitate the hypothesis testing process. These prompts are

1. *Evidence:* "What's my evidence for (and against) this belief?"

2. *Alternative Explanation:* "Is there any other way of looking at that?"

3. *Implications:* "Even if it is true, is it as bad as it first seems?"

These questions are, certainly, not exhaustive. For example, there are times when it might be advantageous to try not to dwell on a distressing but relatively accurate belief. For example, focusing on the real dangers of a misdiagnosis probably does little to aid the performance of the young medical resident. In such circumstances, a fourth prompt may be appropriate:

Table 9–2 Weekly Self-Monitoring Record from a Depressed Male

Time	Monday 1/16	Tuesday 1/17	Wednesday 1/18	Thursday 1/12	Friday 1/13	Saturday 1/14	Sunday 1/15
9–10	Did dishes (40), breakfast	Drove to class, eat (50)	Meeting with sales agent (50)	Therapy session (25 P)[a]	Up—out to dentist, nauseous (25)	Up early (60), to work, working with J. (M)[a]	Sleep
10–11	Went to bookstore (45 P)	Sculpture class (55 M)	Meetings (55)	Mail out brochures, eat (50 M,M)	Dentist, toast at diner	Apply hardwall, finish wall (65 P)	Sleep
11–12	Filled gas, read paper (45)	Sculpture class (55 M)	Meeting (55)	Make business calls (M,P)	Home, read magazine (25)	Off to store (60 P)	Read paper (25)
12–1	Looked at mail, real estate ads (45)	Looked at boots at stores (40), guilty	Fill car, buy paper (55)	Read mail (60), phone calls (45), coffee (30)	Call models, truck relay out (25)	Work on alarm system (55 P)	Read magazine (30)
1–2	Went to work (40)	Went to work (50)	Make calls (45)	Work at lumber yard (35)	Replace relay (40 P,M)	Come home read mail, talk to J. (45)	Read magazine, eat (30)
2–3	Cut end rows (45 P)	Talked with boss (50)	Go to work (45)	Lumber yard and hardware store (25)	Work on sculpture, (50 P) still nauseous	Eat lunch (30) wash dishes	Watch tube (30)
3–4	Painted end rows (50 P,M)	Head for home (45)	Install fixtures (30)	Repair tires (25)	Off to work (50)	Clean home (30)	Watch tube (30)
4–5	Installed grill plates (60 P,M)	Leave for night class (45)	Home to eat (35)	Replace tiles, & clean up (25)	Patching wall, and clean up (50)	Clean home (25), wash clothes, relax	Watch tube (30), eat
5–6	Installed grill plates and mike (60 P)	Sculpture class (50 P)	Go to movie (45)	Clean up, head for home (25)	Work on wall, to store (50 P)	Relax, make drinks, dinner (25)	Watch tube (30)
6–7	Come home (50)	Sculpture (50)	Movie (45 P)	Eat, watch tube (25)	Home to eat (25), read magazine	Eat, talk, drink wine (35)	Watch tube (30), read
7–8	Eat dinner, (45) talk to J.	Head home, talk to J. (50)	Movie (35), fight with J.	Watch tube, called therapist (25)	Talk to J. (25), out for ice cream	Relax, talk (35)	Took bath (30–45)
8–12	Watch tube (45), made molds (60 P,M)	Work on sculpture (50)	Coffee out (45), then home	Watch tube, talk to J. (20)	Back home (35), tooth still hurts	Relax, talk (35)	Read magazine bed, 10:30 (35)

[a]M = Mastery Behavior
P = Pleasure
(0–100) = Current mood. 0 is the worst you've ever felt, 100 is the best you've ever felt.
From Hollon and Beck (1979).

4. *Functionality:* "Is it useful for me to think about this right now?"

Table 9-3 presents a sample dysfunctional thoughts record, completed by the same former university art instructor who provided the self-monitoring material in Table 9-2. The form itself is rather common to the various restructuring methods and was probably introduced to the field by Ellis and colleagues. In the first entry, the client dealt with negative self-recriminations regarding work not completed by reminding himself of other recent accomplishments, applying the "evidence" prompt to his belief that "I never get my work done." In addition, he applied the "alternative explanations" prompt to explain why he had accomplished so little in that particular instance, noting that he had tried to tackle too much at one time. Both negative affect and degree of belief in the original automatic thoughts were subsequently reduced. In the second example, the client decided that he did not need to work all of the time, particularly since he was being quite productive some of the time, again with subsequent reductions in negative affects. In the third example, the client demonstrated a common error in cognitive therapy, relying on a shibboleth with little meaning to him to counter the automatic thoughts. In contrast to the two previous examples, the client's response did not involve a review of recent experiences. Rather, he relied on a self-statement with little direct relevance to his situation (note the minimal subjective validity he ascribed to his "rational response"), with little subsequent reduction in negative affect. Beck would assert that it is not what a person "says to himself or herself" that matters, it is what he or she *believes* that counts, and the most powerful way to alter existing beliefs is by uncovering and reviewing evidence that disconfirms those notions.

Frequently, these interchanges lead directly to the specification of behavioral experiments which can further the hypothesis testing pro-

cess. The client providing the thought records in Table 9-3 was, for example, encouraged to try to tackle some tasks in an "all-or-none" fashion and others by breaking them up into smaller steps in order to test the notion more fully that he could be productive when he selected more helpful strategies (Example 1). Other examples of hypothesis testing with this client involved having him restructure his weekends so that he engaged in more activities with his family rather than lying on the couch ruminating, demonstrating that he could impact his mood even before he obtained the kind of job he wanted, and doing volunteer art teaching to community groups to demonstrate to himself that he could pursue his interests even if only as an avocation. The general strategy followed is first to identify beliefs in a given situation, then to explore the broader meaning system surrounding those beliefs, then to evaluate that meaning system by using the various prompts noted to review existing information, and finally to devise empirical tests to gather further information in order to choose between competing hypotheses. Thus, the approach blends cognitive introspection, rational reevaluation, and empirical hypothesis testing in order to evaluate the accuracy of existing beliefs.

In teaching clients to modify self-defeating thinking, Beck stresses distinguishing ideas from the events they symbolize. Other cognitive techniques used in this stage of therapy include the following:

Alternative therapy. Reconceptualizing seemingly insolvable problems so that they have workable solutions (particularly valuable with suicidal clients)

Disattribution. Helping clients disabuse themselves of the belief that they are entirely responsible for problems or difficulties

Decatastrophizing. Helping clients appreciate that certain events or experiences are not catastrophes (in the fashion of RET)

Table 9–3 Evaluating Automatic Negative Thoughts: Client's Record

Date	Situation	Emotion(s)	Automatic Thought(s)	Rational Response	Outcome
			Daily Record of Dysfunctional Thoughts		
	Describe: 1. Actual event leading to unpleasant emotion, or 2. Stream of thoughts, daydream, or recollection, leading to unpleasant emotion.	1. Specify sad–anxious, etc. 2. Rate degree of emotion, 1–100%.	1. Write automatic thought(s) that preceded emotion(s). 2. Rate belief in automatic thought(s), 0–100%.	1. Write rational response to automatic thought(s). 2. Rate belief in rational response, 0–100%.	1. Rerate belief in automatic thought(s), 0–100%. 2. Specify and rate subsequent emotions, 0–100%.
2/5	Not getting filing and lots of other stuff done.	Anxious–Sad–Angry 85%	A failure again, I can never get my work done. I'm no good. 85%	I have gotten filing and other work done in the past, but usually in smaller bites, not all at once. 80%	1. 45% 2. Anxious–Sad 50%
2/7	Sitting and idly looking thru some old books./6:30 a.m.	Depressed 75%	Feeling guilty because I'm not doing work. I'm going to slip back into funk if I'm not careful. 70%	After 12 hours of high-energy work yesterday (phone work, building, filing, letter, therapy, driving) I think its OK to relax from 5:30 a.m. to 6:30 a.m. the following day 95%	1. 10% 2. Joyful, Exuberant 95%
	(Example of misapplication: Applies "Rational Response" in rote fashion without examining belief—note the lack of rated belief in the "Rational Response" and the lack of subsequent effect in belief and emotion in "Outcome.")				
2/9	I can't handle it any more, too much in the past to undo, lack of setting priorities, misuse of time, plus the present seems untenable	Depressed 80%	No options—either direct job in my specialty or nothing at all	The present does not predict the future 20%	1. 95% 2. Depressed 95%

Explanation: When you experience an unpleasant emotion, note the situation that seemed to stimulate the emotion. (If the emotion occurred while you were thinking, daydreaming, etc., please note this.) Then note the automatic thought associated with the emotion. Record the degree to which you believe this thought: 0% = not at all; 100% = completely. In rating degree of emotion: 1 = a trace; 100 = the most intense possible.

From Hollon and Beck (1979).

Expectation therapy. Realistically examining the variables affecting the client's failure, as a way of reducing pessimism

As therapy progresses, the emphasis shifts to identifying the basic assumptions or rules. Among the rules or assumptions likely to presuppose people to depression are

1. "In order to be happy, I have to be successful in whatever I undertake."
2. "To be happy, I must be accepted by all people at all times."
3. "If I make a mistake, it means that I'm inept."
4. "I can't live without love."
5. "If somebody disagrees with me, it means he doesn't like me."
6. "My value as a person depends on what others think of me." (Beck, 1976, p. 295)

These ideas are similar to Ellis's irrational beliefs (1977a), and at this stage, Beck's therapy is also rather similar to Ellis's.

Homework is an important and ongoing component of Beck's approach. The assignments are varied and tailored to the individual. They include the aforementioned graded tasks and activity schedules and checking of automatic thoughts. Homework may also include bibliotherapy (e.g., reading Ellis & Harper's *New Guide to Rational Living* [1975]). Note that when clients are given tasks, they are often presented within the context of hypothesis testing. For instance, a female client who thinks men will reject her if she expresses her positive feelings about women's liberation might be encouraged to test this out on her date. The therapist does not try to provide the expectation that her date will not reject her, but rather that it is an *empirical* matter.

The aforementioned treatment package (see Beck et al., 1979) is specifically designed for 20 hours of treatment. Why does Beck prefer therapy (with depressives) to be so highly structured? In part, the answer is that a time-limited no-nonsense approach discourages both therapist and client from wasting time and provides the client with a much-needed sense of order and discipline. Another consideration, however, is that a highly structured, standardized treatment package is easily researched. We shall now consider some experimental findings directly pertinent to Beck's treatment approach.

Experimental Findings

Empirical findings have tended to be supportive both of cognitive theories of psychopathology and of cognitive therapy, although more clearly so for the latter than the former. In a recent review, Coyne and Gotlib (1983) argued that the evidence supporting a cognitive model of depression was far from conclusive. Reviewing studies across five areas—expectations and evaluations of performance, perception of environmental information, recall of information, cognitive biases, and attributional processes—they suggested that although some support does exist for a cognitive model of depression, the support was not as robust as many might presume. Depressed persons do tend to present themselves negatively on a variety of measures, but those differences could be accounted for either by having encountered more negative life experiences or by adopting a self-derogative interpersonal strategy in the service of manipulating others.

Although Coyne and Gotlib's review was exhaustive, it was not particularly evenhanded. In their critique, they lumped less carefully executed postexperimental questionnaire data with primary dependent variables, failed to discriminate between carefully executed designs and more marginal experiments, and generally considered the failure to reject a null hypothesis to be a refutation of a cognitive model, rather than simply an instance of nonsupport for it. On the whole, although there are many studies suggesting that thinking and subsequent affect and behavior are related, perhaps causally, and numerous studies that fail to show any such relationship, there are few, if any, studies that indicate an inverse pattern of relationship. If Coyne and Gotlib's suggested nonrelatedness were accurate, with observed positive findings contributed only by chance, we would expect to find an equal number of studies evidencing significantly negative relationships.

The larger issue involves the impact of cognitive therapy on manifest symptomatology. In this regard, it is fair to say that considerable empirical evidence has been generated concerning cognitive therapy (at least in the treatment of depression), and that most of the evidence has been quite supportive. Compared with the relative paucity of controlled empirical trials evaluating RET in clinically representative populations, cognitive therapy has clearly lent itself to repeated empirical scrutiny.

Shaw (1977) compared the effectiveness of cognitive and behavior therapy with depressed college students recruited from a university outpatient clinic. Cognitive therapy was derived from Beck (but apparently without Beck's behavioral components), and the behavioral approach involved activity schedules, contracts, and assertive training, each aimed at permitting the subject to obtain more reinforcement (Lewinsohn, 1974b). A total of 16 hours of group treatment was presented over four weeks. The results generally favored the cognitive treatment. At the posttest for the Beck Inventory and for independent behavioral ratings, only the cognitive treatment group showed significantly greater improvement than a nondirective control group and a no-treatment control group. At the follow-up assessment one month later, the two treatment groups no longer differed significantly, although trends clearly favored the cognitive treatment. Unfortunately, only one therapist was used for all treatments, thereby limiting external validity.

Taylor and Marshall (1977) compared a group treated with a cognitive therapy, reportedly derived from Beck, Ellis, and Bandura, with a group treated with behavioral approach-stressing responses that would likely compete

with depression (e.g., assertive behavior, engaging in a wider range of reinforcing activities). A third group received a combination of the cognitive and behavioral approach. Response measures included depression inventories and self-ratings of depression, self-acceptance, and self-esteem. Principal findings were that subjects in all three treatments showed significantly greater improvement on all measures following the six 40-minute treatment sessions than did the nontreated controls. For all measures, the behavioral and cognitive treatments did not differ significantly. However, for the depression inventories and for self-esteem and self-acceptance, the combination of treatments was typically superior to either treatment alone. Of the aforementioned treatments, in our view, the one closest to the treatment package described by Beck and associates (1979)—that is, what we have described in the preceding section—was the combined treatment. Strong support for Beck, however, is mitigated by a lack of a placebo control and a lack of behavior measures (a deficiency characteristic of much of the work in the area of depression).

In a study comparing cognitive therapy and pharmacotherapy, Rush, Beck, Kovacs, and Hollon (1977) pitted the Beck treatment package against imipramine therapy, both presented over a 12-week treatment period. Based on questionnaire data and psychiatric history, the degree of depression could be described as moderate to severe for each subject (e.g., 75 percent reported suicidal ideation; the median number of previous therapists was 2.0). In terms of subjective ratings—that is, the Beck Inventory and behavior observations—both groups showed significant and clinically meaningful reductions in depression, with positive results generally holding up at three- and six-month follow-ups. However, as shown in Figure 9–8, significantly greater pre–post improvement was associated with cognitive therapy. At the follow-ups, the same trend was apparent, but the differences were not statistically significant (see also Kovacs, Rush, Beck, & Hollon, 1981).

Figure 9–8 *Self-reported level of depression: completers only*

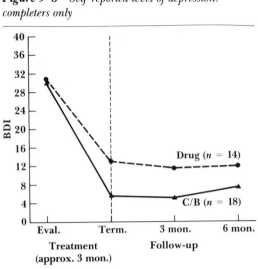

From Rush, Beck, Kovacs, and Hollon (1977).

The dropout rate for the drug condition (8 out of 22) was far higher than that for cognitive therapy (1 out of 19), and whereas 68 percent of the drug group sought additional treatment, only 16 percent of the cognitive therapy group sought additional help. In view of the evidence that imipramine therapy is effective in depression, the results are impressive. On the other hand, it should be noted that the clinical ratings were not blind: raters could determine, from the side effects, which subjects were on the medication. Further, the drug-treated patients responded at a level more comparable to the cognitive therapy patients through the first 10 weeks in therapy, starting to differ only when the medications began to be tapered during the final 2 weeks of active treatment. Also, a sizable number of therapists (18) participated. Although this enhances generalizability, the question of therapist variability was not examined. Finally, postrational credibility checks were not reported (although chemotherapy was *probably* perceived as a credible treatment), nor was the

total amount of therapist-patient contact equated for the two conditions. These objections notwithstanding, the data may be taken as supportive of the Beck approach to the treatment of depression.

Several studies have been designed essentially to replicate the Rush and associates (1977) findings. Beck, Hollon, Young, Bedrosian, and Budenz (1985) contrasted cognitive therapy with combined cognitive therapy and pharmacotherapy (amitriptyline) for depressed outpatients. Using a 12-week, 20-session treatment package similar to that used by Rush and colleagues, no differences were found between modalities, although the cognitive-therapy-only condition was no less effective than cognitive-therapy-only in the earlier Rush et al. trial.

Blackburn, Bishop, Glen, Whalley, and Christie (1981) executed a similar trial in two distinct populations. In that design, implemented in Edinburgh, Scotland, depressed outpatients from both a general medical setting and a psychiatric clinic were randomly assigned to cognitive therapy only, tricyclic pharmacotherapy, or combined cognitive-pharmacotherapy. The combination treatment was superior to pharmacotherapy alone in both populations, whereas cognitive therapy was superior to pharmacotherapy only in the general medical setting. In view of the abysmal performance of the pharmacotherapy condition in that population (only 14 percent of the patients improved, compared to an average of 65–70 percent in the rest of the literature), it is questionable how adequately the drug therapy was executed by the general practitioners providing treatment. Unfortunately, no drug blood plasma levels were obtained, making it impossible to ascertain whether or not patients received an adequate trial of the medications. Nonetheless, this trial, conducted by researchers other than the developers of cognitive therapy and utilizing evaluators blind to treatment condition, suggested at least the comparability, if not the superiority, of cognitive therapy to pharmacotherapy and, perhaps, some evidence of the superiority of the combination of the two treatments over either alone.

Murphy, Simons, Wetzel, and Lustman, (1984) contrasted cognitive therapy, tricyclic pharmacotherapy (desipramine), combined cognitive-pharmacotherapy, and the combination of cognitive therapy with an active placebo in a depressed clinical outpatient population. This trial is particularly noteworthy because it was conducted at the Department of Psychiatry at Washington University in St. Louis, one of the leading centers of biological-pharmacological research in the United States. Thus, if any biases operated in the trial, they should have worked against the cognitive approach. Treatment in all conditions was provided by psychiatric residents according to a protocol similar in most respects to that fol-

lowed in the Rush and associates design. The three major differences involved the continuation of patients on full medication through the end of active treatment (12 weeks), the use of blood plasma levels to ensure compliance with the medication regime, and the utilization of independent evaluators blind to treatment condition.

In essence, as shown in Figure 9–9, although all groups evidenced significant improvement over time, no differences were noted between the conditions. Comparability between cognitive therapy and pharmacotherapy was not inconsistent with the studies already reviewed, but finding no differences between the combined treatment versus drug-only failed to replicate Blackburn et al. Posttreatment follow-up over a one-year period also indicated no differential

Figure 9–9 *Beck Depression Inventory scores and Hamilton Rating Scale for depression scores for four treatment groups by week (means) (■——■: cognitive therapy, CT; □-----□: tricyclic antidepressant, TCA; ○——○: CT and placebo; ●– – –●: CT and TCA).*

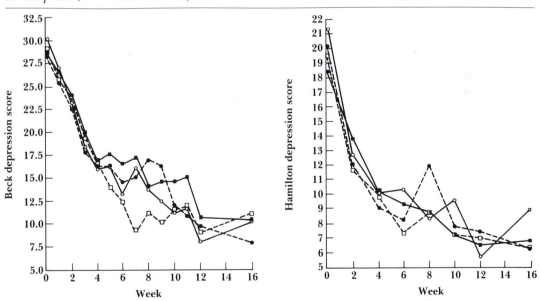

From Murphy, Simons, Wetzel, and Lustman (1984).

advantage for the psychosocial approach, a finding perhaps at variance with indications of a prophylactic effect suggested in other trials (Rush et al., 1977; Hollon et al., 1986). Given the somewhat discrepant pattern of results from earlier studies, it is unfortunate that no measures of the adequacy of the execution of cognitive therapy, analogous to the blood plasma checks, were provided. Such measures have recently been developed (DeRubeis, Hollon, Evans, & Bemis, 1982; Evans, et al., 1983; Hollon, Evans, Elkin, & Lowery, 1984; Young, 1980) and will likely receive increasingly widespread use as trials involving cognitive therapy increase (Kendall & Hollon, 1983).

Two particularly interesting findings from the Murphy et al. design involved differential prediction and differential mechanisms of change. Patients' status on *learned resourcefulness,* a personality variable thought to index an individual's a priori capacity to cope with adversity, predicted differential response to treatment, with patients who score high on learned resourcefulness doing better in cognitive therapy than in pharmacotherapy and patients who score low on that variable evidencing a nonsignificant trend in the opposite direction (Simons, Lustman, Wetzel, & Murphy, 1985). With regard to the mechanisms of action, the change in cognitive processes for patients treated with drug only was equivalent to that of patients treated with cognitive therapy (Simons, Garfield, & Murphy, 1984). Although controversy exists as to whether or not a cognitive model of depression would predict greater change in such cognitive processes as a consequence of cognitive therapy (see the exchange of letters between Beck [1984] and Simons [1984]), such nonspecificity does fail to establish that cognitive processes are causal mediators of the clinical change process.

Hollon et al. (1986) provided yet another trial contrasting cognitive therapy, tricyclic pharmacotherapy, and combined cognitive-pharmacotherapy in the treatment of depressed outpatients. One hundred six primary depres-

sives were randomly assigned to one of four treatment cells (the three listed above and a fourth, drug-only, maintenance cell in which drug treatment was provided through the first year of a two-year follow-up period). The protocol closely followed Rush et al., again with the exceptions of continuing medications through the end of the 12-week active treatment period, executing blood plasma drug level checks, and utilizing independent evaluators blind to treatment.

Sixty-five patients completed active treatment. Response rates were strong, with 75 percent of patients in each of the single modalities (cognitive therapy and tricyclic pharmacotherapy) evidencing full or partial response, along with 88 percent of the patients in combined treatment. A significant difference was evident between the cells on only one of four measures (the MMPI-D—Hathaway & McKinley [1950], favoring the combined treatment over pharmacotherapy alone, but nonsignificant trends were evident on the other three primary dependent measures, with an additive composite based on all four measures evidencing a fully significant effect, again favoring the combined treatment over drugs alone. Most strikingly, there was clear evidence of a prophylactic effect for cognitive therapy, whether combined with medication or provided alone. Across the two-year posttreatment follow-up, patients initially treated with drugs alone, which were then withdrawn, had a higher relapse rate (50 percent) than did patients treated with cognitive therapy (20 percent) or combined treatment (31 percent). Patients who were treated initially with drugs then kept on maintenance medication evidenced an intermediate relapse rate (30 percent), but each instance of relapse was associated with noncompliance with the maintenance regime (Evans et al., 1986).

Unlike the Murphy et al. design, there was some evidence of specificity of mechanism. Although some measures of cognition evidenced nonspecific change in all conditions—for example, the Automatic Thoughts Questionnaire, or ATQ (Hollon & Kendall, 1980)—two others evidenced greater changes in cells involving cognitive therapy, namely the Attributional Styles Inventory, or ASI (Seligman, Abramson, Semmel, & von Baeyer, 1979), and the Dysfunctional Attitudes Scale, or DAS (Weissman & Beck, 1978). The former measure is more nearly a measure of spontaneous, stream-of-consciousness ruminations, whereas the latter two measures more nearly capture patterns of thinking and generic beliefs, respectively. These findings may indicate that although thought content is largely state dependent, changing nonspecifically whenever depression remits, certain underlying information processing tendencies may actually be differentially influenced by the cognitive approaches. It remains unclear why the Murphy et al. design did not reveal this pattern (many of the measures overlapped between the two studies), although subtle differences may have existed in the execution of cognitive therapy between the two studies.

Summary

Overall, there has been an impressive series of studies executed to evaluate cognitive therapy for depression, most involving fully representative outpatient depressed populations. In general, cognitive therapy appears to be at least the equal of any single tricyclic medication in terms of reducing the acute episode, with combined cognitive-pharmacotherapy possibly superior to drugs only. There are indications that cognitive therapy, either alone or in combination with medications, may produce a prophylactic effect, reducing the probability of symptomatic relapse. Both sets of findings are impressive, since the tricyclics have been clearly established as effective change agents in clinical depression (for reviews, see Klein & Davis, 1969; Morris & Beck, 1974). Conversely, other psychosocial approaches to the treatment of depression have typically not fared well in comparisons with medications (cf. Hollon & Beck, 1978).

Nonetheless, important questions still remain. First, the bulk of the trials reviewed have utilized tricyclic pharmacotherapy as the primary comparison condition, rather than nonspecific therapy or placebo controls. Although this may be a more ethical research strategy when an effective change agent has already been well established (O'Leary & Borkovec, 1978), it does risk overinterpreting essentially "tie score" findings. Carroll (1983), for example, has pointed out that since not all placebo-controlled drug trials find significant differences, the reliance on drug-only comparisons and the acceptance of "tie scores" as indicating comparability may involve the acceptance of too lenient a criterion for establishing treatment efficacy. Second, and closely related, in the absence of direct comparisons with other psychosocial approaches, it may be too tempting to conclude that cognitive therapy is specifically effective, when, if it works, it may work through nonspecific mechanisms common to other psychosocial approaches.

Further, the equivocal findings regarding the specificity of cognitive change underline the need for more cognitive therapy–alternate psychotherapy comparisons, since it is still unclear whether or not cognitive therapy works by virtue of changing beliefs and information processing. Finally, there are important limitations to the established generality of the intervention. To date, the bulk of the trials conducted have involved only carefully selected primary unipolar depressed outpatients. Patients that have depressions coexistent with other disorders (e.g., schizophrenia, alcoholism or chemical dependency, or other neurotic disorders) have routinely been screened out of these trials. Similarly, there are, as yet, no published outcome studies evaluating the efficacy of cognitive therapy with either depressed inpatients or affectively ill bipolar populations. Cognitive therapy appears to be a feasible intervention with at least some such patients, especially in conjunction with other established interventions (Hollon, 1984), but clear evidence of its clinical efficacy has yet to be provided. What is clear is that within the unipolar outpatient population, cognitive therapy is not inferior to pharmacotherapy for the treatment of patients evidencing an endogenous symptom pattern (Blackburn et al., 1981; Hollon et al., 1986) and may be superior for those patients with associated personality disorders or "double depressions" (Hollon et al., 1986).

Interventions Emphasizing Repetition and Functionality

Self-instructional Training

In 1963, Donald Meichenbaum, a psychology graduate student, attended a meeting wherein he observed demonstrations of Gestalt therapy, psychoanalytic techniques, and semantic therapy. At the conclusion of the demonstrations, he directed a question to the presenters regarding a possible common component in the three approaches. As one would expect from a bright but fledging graduate student, the question was immersed in a fair bit of jargon. The analyst and Gestalt therapist responded dutifully and predictably, Meichenbaum recalled, "But it was the semantic therapist who was most forceful and direct in his answer: 'Please rise young man. . . . That is complete bullshit!' He went on to explain the nature of irrational beliefs, etc., that gave rise to psychopathology" (1977, pp. 13– 14). The therapist, of course, was Albert Ellis. This incident apparently set the stage for Meichenbaum's research and clinical interest in cognitive learning approaches.

The specific emphasis that Meichenbaum brings to cognitive learning theory grew out of his doctoral dissertation, carried out several years later (Meichenbaum, 1969). Hospitalized schizophrenics were trained to emit "healthy talk" via operant conditioning, and the positive effects generalized to a follow-up interview. What struck Meichenbaum was that during the interview the patients spontaneously verbalized experimental instructions such as "Give healthy talk; be coherent and relevant" (Meichenbaum, 1977, p. 15). It was as if the instructions were actually mediating the observed generalization. This led to Meichenbaum's long-standing interest in the role of self-statements in guiding human behavior, especially in the skill-acquisition and problem-solving area. Note that Meichenbaum does not view his approach as competing with RET (in fact, as we noted earlier Meichenbaum et al. [1971] was one of the first experimental investigations supporting RET). He sees it, instead, as a matter of emphasis. Ellis is primarily concerned with the mitigation of negative emotions by teaching clients to construe external events in a rational, adaptive way. Meichenbaum is more concerned with teaching patterns of implicit verbalization that will facilitate the self-control of overt verbal and motor behavior.

Meichenbaum's view of how individuals acquire control of their own behavior reflects the theorizing of the Russian investigators (Luria, 1969; Vygotsky, 1962). Luria provides a three-stage conceptualization of the acquisition of the control of voluntary behavior in children. In Stage 1, control is exercised by the verbal behavior of others (e.g., parents). In Stage 2, overt speech on the part of the child exercises an important guiding function. Finally, in Stage 3, much of the child's behavior comes under the control of covert self-speech. Covert speech facilitates problem solving in several ways. It directs attention to and discriminates among relevant stimulus attributes and dimensions, it helps the individual formulate hypotheses, and it maintains relevant information in short-term memory. As Meichenbaum points out, self-speech thus exerts control over the individual's behavior in much the same way as speech coming from another person.

A good deal of the research of Meichenbaum and his associates (e.g., Meichenbaum & Goodman, 1969, 1971; see Meichenbaum, 1977, for a review of this and related work) has been with impulsive and aggressive children, who typically engage in less self-regulatory speech than other less impulsive children (Camp, 1977; Meichenbaum & Goodman, 1969, 1971). In one such investigation, Meichenbaum and Goodman (1969) found that among cognitively impulsive children (defined by poor performance on a simple picture-matching task), only 40 percent met a performance criterion of 90 percent correct in another task involving verbal control; the comparable figure for nonimpulsive children was 85 percent. Interestingly, in the verbal control task, impulsive children would often repeat the appropriate instruction aloud, but then proceed to make the wrong response. Thus, impulsivity appears to reflect a dearth of self-instruction *and/or* a weak relationship between verbal cues and motor behavior.

Meichenbaum's approach to treating impulsive children is seen in the following sequence of activities (adapted from Meichenbaum, 1977, p. 32):

1. An adult model performs a task while talking to himself out loud.

2. The child then performs the task, with guidance from the model.

3. The child performs the task while giving himself instructions aloud.

4. The child whispers the instructions to himself while going through the task.

5. The child carries out the task, employing covert self-instructions.

Meichenbaum and Goodman illustrate what an adult might say aloud at Step 1. The task involves copying line patterns.

> Okay, what is it I have to do? You want me to copy the picture with the different lines. I have to go slowly and carefully. Okay, Draw the line down, down, good; then to the right, that's it; now down some more and to the left. Good, I'm doing fine so far. Remember, go slowly. Now back up again. No, I was supposed to go down. That's okay. Just erase the line carefully. . . . Good. Even if I make an error I can go on slowly and carefully. I have to go down now. Finished. I did it! (1971, p. 117)

In the course of training children in self-instruction, a variety of tasks is presented in order of increasing difficulty. Early on, they are of a simple, perceptual motor nature (e.g., copying simple line patterns). The more complex tasks include completing pictorial series or solving concept formation problems (e.g., Raven's Matrices).

Initially applied to schizophrenic adults and then to impulsive children, self-instructional training has been utilized with a variety of disorders. These include various anxiety states (Glass, Gottman, & Shmurak, 1976; Kanfer, Karoly, & Newman, 1975; Meichenbaum, 1972; Woodward & Jones, 1980), agoraphobia (Emmelkamp et al., 1978; Emmelkamp & Mersch, 1982, Williams & Rappoport, 1983), assertion problems (Jacobs & Cochran, 1982; Safran, Alden & Davidson, 1980; Thorpe, 1975), anger management (Camp, Blom, Hebert, & van Doornick, 1977; Foreman, 1980), and obesity (Dunkel & Glaros, 1978). In fact, since the previous revision of this text, it has become the most frequently evaluated cognitive-behavioral intervention. In that earlier edition, a total of 5 controlled studies were listed. In preparing the current edition, a total of 36 controlled outcome trials could be located. We turn now to a review of the empirical literature evaluating self-instructional approaches.

Empirical Studies

Impulsivity As noted, the main body of work has grown up around the treatment of impulsive children, many of whom would be considered to fall within the diagnostic category of attention deficit disorder by current standards (American Psychiatric Association, 1980). The first major trial with this population (drawn from kindergarten and first grade classes) was executed by Meichenbaum and Goodman (1971). In that trial, self-instructional training, relative to placebo and nontreated control conditions, led to significantly greater improvement of a variety of tasks (e.g., Porteus Maze, WISC performance IQ, and a matching figures test), and the improvement was still evident at a one-month follow-up.

Meichenbaum and Goodman (1971) report a second study that compared cognitive modeling (Step 1 of the above procedure) with and without the requirement that the child rehearse the instructions. Although cognitive modeling alone was effective in slowing down the child's behavior on the matching figures test, errors were not reduced. Slowing down and error reduction were associated with cognitive modeling and rehearsal. Other investigations (e.g., Bender, 1976; Finch, Wilkinson, Nelson, & Montgomery, 1975; Karnes, Teska, & Hodgins, 1970; Palkes, Stewart, & Kahana, 1968) support the importance of self-verbalized instructions in controlling behavior.

Not surprisingly, the temporal relationship between the self-instruction and the task is important. Karoly and Dirks (1977) had inner-city preschool children perform the task of extending their arms (a test of tolerance rather than skill). One group practiced self-instruction preceding the task; the second group practiced self-instruction following the task. In terms of correspondence between verbal behavior (i.e., intentions of performing the task) and task performance, the group practicing self-instruction prior to engaging in the task was superior. In the study, reinforcement for verbal behavior was compared with reinforcement for correspondence. For both groups of children, reinforcement for correspondence resulted in a much higher percentage of children showing correspondence between verbalized intentions and actual behavior.

Although the combination of operant and self-instructional procedures has obtained impressive results (e.g., Bornstein & Quevillon, 1976), Meichenbaum offers a note of caution. Attention deficit disorder children may quickly return to baseline when the reinforcement is withdrawn. Whether the child attributes success to "luck" or to "personal effort" appears to predict the relative effectiveness of reinforcement versus self-instruction training, with luck attributors more influenced by external rein-

forcement (Bugental, Whalen, & Henker, 1977). *Self*-reinforcement (discussed in Chapter 10), in the form of self-praise, is incorporated into Meichenbaum's cognitive modeling. One investigation (Nelson & Birkimer, 1978) suggests this may be a critical component: self-instruction with impulsive children was effective *only* when combined with self-reinforcement.

Kendall and Finch (1978) provided the major replication and extension of the Meichenbaum and Goodman (1971) work. A self-instructional training package, which included modeling and response cost contingencies, was contrasted with an attentional control. As shown in Figure 9–10, results indicated improvement on both performance tasks and classroom behavior, the latter an important index of treatment generalization. Treatment gains were maintained through a two-month follow-up.

The package assembled by Kendall and colleagues includes self-instructional training, modeling, and response cost contingencies, a true blending of cognitive and behavioral components. As described by Kendall and Wilcox (1980), each component is targeted at specific deficits observed in impulsive children. Basic descriptive psychopathology research has indicated that non–self-controlled children exhibit cognitive deficits in problem-solving abilities (Ault, 1973), verbal mediation (Camp, 1977), and information seeking (Finch & Montgomery, 1977), which the self-instructional component is designed to ameliorate. Further, non–self-controlled children have been observed to lack appropriate search-and-scan problem-solving behavior (Drake, 1970; Siegelman, 1969), a deficit which is addressed through the use of modeling procedures. Finally, response cost procedures (as well as social praise and self-reward) are typically used to suppress off-task behaviors and to maintain attention (Erickson, Wyne, & Routh, 1973; Nelson, Finch, & Hooke, 1975).

Arnold and Forehand (1978) attempted to dissemble this package. Impulsive children were randomly assigned to SIT, response cost, SIT with response cost, and placebo training. Train-

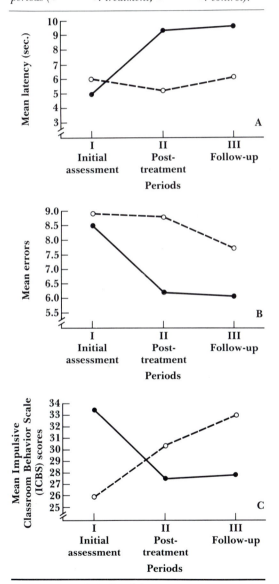

Figure 9–10 *A. Mean latency in seconds for the treatment and control groups at the initial assessment, posttreatment, and follow-up periods. B. Mean errors for the treatment and control groups at the initial assessment, posttreatment, and follow-up periods. C. Mean Impulsive Classroom Behavior Scale (ICBS) scores for the treatment and control group at the initial assessment, posttreatment, and follow-up periods (●———●: treatment; ○— — —○: control).*

From Kendall and Finch (1978).

ing consisted of five sessions over two weeks. Results indicated that error rates were significantly reduced for all groups—an apparent nonspecific effect of exposure—but also that cognitive training, with or without response cost contingencies, facilitated generalization to novel tasks.

Parrish and Erickson (1981) evaluated the contribution of the "scanning strategy" training provided by the modeling component. In a decomposition design, "scanning strategy" instructions alone were contrasted with self-instructional training alone and with self-instructional training plus "scanning strategy" modeling, the full package. All three conditions were superior to an attention control and were equivalent to one another, suggesting that the separate components simply duplicated, rather than complemented, one another, at least on academic performance tasks. Nelson and Birkimer (1978) provided a component analysis focused on the self-reinforcement component. In this study, the addition of self-reinforcement to self-instructional training clearly enhanced performance on various academic tasks.

Finally, Kendall and Braswell (1982) attempted a component analysis which isolated the self-instructional component from the modeling and response cost components. In general, both the full package and the strictly behavior components (modeling plus response cost), proved superior to an attentional control on ratings of self-control and hyperactivity, with the full package superior to the behavorial components alone on the self-control ratings. Parents' ratings failed to evidence any differential effects. Overall, it remains unclear whether or not all of the components of the treatment package really contribute to the treatment's efficacy, but it does appear that at least some do.

Kendall and colleagues have provided two additional studies designed to explore procedures to enhance training generalization. In the first, Kendall and Wilcox (1980) hypothesized that more abstract *conceptual training* would more readily facilitate generalization to nontraining tasks than the more standard task-specific, or *concrete,* training. As shown in Figure 9–11, blind teacher ratings of self-control and hyperactivity indicated that both forms of training produced superior generalization over an attention placebo, with some modest indications of greater generalization for the conceptual training condition. A one-year follow-up indicated that treatment gains were maintained but were not differential (Kendall, 1981). Kendall and Zupan (1981) attempted to facilitate generalization by providing training in a group format, not unlike a classroom situation. Treatment outcomes indicated nonspecific improvement for all groups (including attention controls) on academic performance measures, with superior generalization for the self-instructional training cells, whether provided in an individual or a group format. This latter finding was

clearly not consistent with the investigators' original hypothesis. Again, a one-year follow-up indicated stability of treatment gains (Kendall, 1972).

Overall, studies evaluating self-instructional training have produced somewhat mixed results. Although improved performance on the academic performance tasks used for training has generally been noted, such improvement is often apparent simply as a function of exposure to the materials. Efforts at component analysis have been ambiguous. The preferred treatment package has clearly grown to incorporate a variety of cognitive and behavioral components, but it remains unclear whether or not the rather elegant theories regarding component specificity have been borne out in fact. Most disconcerting is the issue of generalization. Self-

Figure 9–11 *Mean SCRS scores for the concrete labeling, conceptual labeling, and control groups across the three assessment periods. Mean SCRS score (99.3) or 110 randomly selected children (same grades and both sexes) extrapolated over time. The SD is 46.1. Thus, scores between 53.2 and 145.4 would be within 1 SD of the mean of the normative group (○——○: concrete; ■——■: conceptual; △——△: control).*

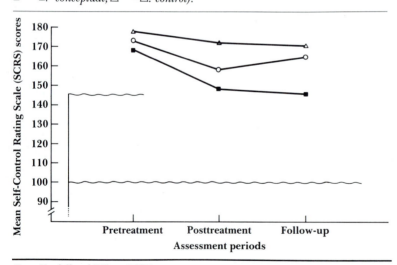

instructional training, as initially implemented, was very narrow in focus. Subsequent studies have tried to expand both the range of the phenomena dealt with in training and the breadth of measures designed to evaluate that effort, but with only mixed results. We complete our review of this literature with almost the opposite sense that we had from our review of RET. In this instance, although it is clear that a careful, cumulative program of research has grown up around self-instructional training for children and that the approach produces change, it is not clear whether the changes obtained are truly clinically meaningful.

Schizophrenia Meichenbaum and Cameron (1973) employed the self-instructional treatment strategy with hospitalized schizophrenics. The treatment, conducted over eight 45-minute sessions, included instructions in self-monitoring (as well as monitoring the reactions of others) and self-instruction training in perceptual motor tasks and then in solving more complex cognitive problems. The following is an example of a modeled instruction for a similarities task ("How are a bird and a flower alike?"):

> I have to figure out how a bird and a flower are alike. A bird and a flower. (Pause) A bird is small and a flower is small. I got it, the bird can eat the flower. (Pause) No, that doesn't help. That doesn't tell me how they are alike. I have to see how they are alike. Go slowly and think this one out. Don't just say the first thing that comes to mind. (Pause, while the model thinks) I want to give the best answer I can. Let me imagine in my mind the objects . . . bird, flower . . . out in fresh air. They both need air to live. That's it; they are both living things. Good, I figured it out. If I take my time and just think about how the two objects are alike, I can do it. (Meichenbaum, 1977, p. 71)

The progression of tasks in the treatment led, during the final session, to a further discussion of the reactions of others to inappropriate behavior and self-statements the patient might employ in the face of such a reaction. In terms of a variety of measures (including digit recall, a proverbs test, level of responding to inkblots, and percent of "sick talk" during an interview), treatment subjects showed significantly greater improvement than control subjects, who had merely been exposed to the practice materials. The results generally held up at a three-week follow-up. Note, however, that the controls also showed improvement on all measures. In the absence of credibility checks for treatment rationales, the possibility that this variable accounted for obtained differences cannot be ruled out. Further, in spite of the short follow-up interval, some decline in performance was apparent for all measures for the treatment subjects (and for the controls as well). One would have hoped that reinforcement from the natural environment would have had the effect of increasing healthy problem-solving behavior. Perhaps in a nonhospital environment this would have been the case.

Further concerns are raised by Margolis and Shemberg (1976). Working with a considerably larger sample, the authors were unable to replicate the earlier Meichenbaum and Cameron findings. They noted particularly that subjects had reported finding the "self-reward" component "silly" and "babyish," and that most had forgotten the SIT techniques by the time of the posttest. Overall, although it is noteworthy that SIT is the only cognitive approach that has been tested in the schizophrenias—primarily a disorder of thinking—the overall effort hardly appears to provide more than an adjunct to other more powerful interventions, such as antipsychotic medications.

Creativity Meichenbaum (1975) described the application of self-instruction training aimed at enhancing creativity in college students. The first step of the training sequence involved gaining awareness of creativity-inhibiting automatic thoughts. Subjects then were trained to generate creativity-enhancing thoughts incompatible with the negative thoughts (an example of thought substitution). In the third step, the experimenter modeled self-statements reflecting several different theoretical conceptualizations of creativity, which the subjects then rehearsed. Treatment was conducted over six one-hour sessions. Relative to a placebo control (trained to focus on present feelings) and a nontreated control, the self-instruction treatment showed significantly greater increases in measures of orginality and flexibility, in preference for complexity, in perception of human movement in inkblot tests, and in self-concept. Unfortunately, no follow-up was reported.

Test Anxiety Programs incorporating SIT, either alone or in combination with other approaches, have also been extensively tested

with various anxiety disorders. The original study in this genre was again contributed by Meichenbaum (1972). Twenty-one test-anxious undergraduate volunteers were assigned to either cognitive modification—consisting of a combination of "insight," self-statement rehearsal, and coping desensitization—standard desensitization, or a waiting list control. Treatment was conducted in eight one-hour group sessions. The "insight" component involved providing a cognitive rationale for test anxiety, identifying specific anxiety-related self-verbalizations, and discussing their impact. The inclusion of this component has led some reviewers to consider this condition an operationalization of RET, but there is little indication that rationality (as op-

Figure 9–12A *Mean reduction and increase in manifestations of test anxiety from pretreatment to posttreatment (groups not connected by solid line are significantly different at .05 level) (■: cognitive modification; ▨: desensitization; ▢: waiting list).*

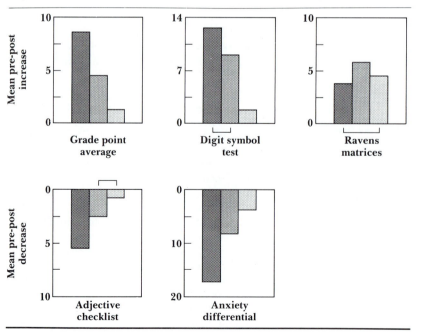

posed to functionality) was appealed to during training. As shown in Figure 9–12, treatment outcome indicated superior improvement for the cognitive-behavior package over both the desensitization and the waiting list control on most of the self-report anxiety measures. The differences were maintained at a one-month follow-up, with somewhat more mixed findings on behavioral performance measures. Subsequent grade point average did, however, favor the cognitive-behavioral package over systematic desensitization. McCordick, Kaplan, Finn, and Smith (1979) attempted a replication and extension, with only partial success. Holroyd (1976)

provided a trial described earlier in which an amalgamation of RET and SIT proved superior to desensitization on both self-report and subsequent academic performance measures. Overall, packages containing SIT are probably effective in the treatment of test anxiety.

Speech Anxiety Several studies have evaluated SIT in the treatment of speech anxiety. The first such design, provided by Meichenbaum et al. (1971), involved an amalgamation of SIT and RET principles and has already been described in the section evaluating RET. In that design, both cognitive modification (combining SIT and RET) and group desensitization were superior to combined cognitive-desensitization (and a control group) on a variety of self-report, cognitive, and behaviorial measures. Weissberg (1977), in a similar amalgamation of RET and SIT, found only equivocal support. That study has also been described in greater detail in the section on RET. Finally, Fremouw and Zitter (1978) also found equivocal support for a RET-SIT amalgamation, with stronger support for a purely behaviorial skills training approach.

Glogower, Fremouw, and McCroskey (1978) provided a component analysis dissembling the "insight" from the self-statement rehearsal components. Speech-anxious college students were assigned to extinction, "insight" into negative self-statements, rehearsal of positive coping statements, combined insight and rehearsal, or a waiting list control. Treatment was conducted during one-hour sessions over a five-week period. Both the combination and the coping self-statement conditions outperformed the other cells, leading the authors to conclude that "while extinction and identification of negative self-statements produce some improvement, the coping self-statement component is the primary factor in the cognitive restructuring procedure" (Glogower et al., 1978, p. 220).

Finally, Cradock, Cotler, and Jason (1978) contrasted a cognitive restructuring approach built largely around coping self-statement rehearsal with systematic desensitization in a

Figure 9–12B *Mean self-report of facilitating and debilitating anxiety on the Alpert-Haber Anxiety Test at pretreatment and posttreatment and a one-month follow-up (●——●: cognitive modification; □——□: waiting list; △- - -△: desensitization; ◪——◪: low test anxious ± ISD).*

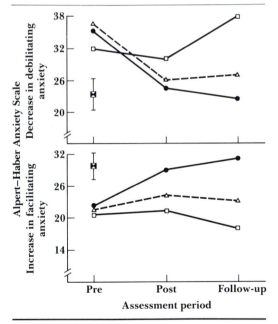

primary prevention study designed to forestall speech anxiety in high school students. The self-statement rehearsal outperformed a waiting list control, something the desensitization condition did not do, but did not differ significantly from that desentization condition.

Overall, self-instructional training can be said to have garnered modest support from this series of largely analogue studies, at least relative to waiting list or attention-placebo controls. It is not clear that it consistently outperformed alternate behavioral procedures. In general, the evidence appears to favor treatment efficacy, although the overall thrust of this literature would hardly inspire great enthusiasm.

Social Anxiety Two studies have evaluated treatment packages involving SIT in the treatment of social anxiety. Glass et al. (1976) provided a trial of self-statement modification in the treatment of males anxious about heterosexuality. Undergraduate college student volunteers were assigned to behavioral skills training, cognitive self-statement modification, combined skills training–cognitive modification, or a waiting list control. In general, the behavioral skills training groups (alone or combined) outperformed the cognitive modification group on role-play vignettes used in training, whereas the cognitive modification groups (alone or combined) outperformed the behavioral skills training group on nontraining, generalization vignettes. Results were essentially maintained through a six-month follow-up. Glass and colleagues concluded that "this study, therefore, failed to find strong evidence that a response-acquisition treatment can lead to transfer-of-training to non-training laboratory situations and to *in vivo* behavior, and supports the efficacy of the cognitive self-statement modification approach to therapy" (1976, p. 525). Elder, Edelstein, and Fremouw (1981) similarly compared a self-statement modification program with response acquisition in an analogue population but failed to find clear evidence of superiority for the self-statement approach. Again, some mixed support for the self-

statement approach is evident, although not overwhelming.

Specific Phobias Several studies have evaluated self-statement approaches in the treatment of anxiety states. Goren (1975) found SIT comparable to systematic desensitization in an analogue population in the treatment of both a general phobia (test anxiety) and a specific phobia (snakes), despite hypothesizing that SIT would be more effective with the former than the latter. Denny, Sullivan, and Thirty (1977) found evidence that self-statement rehearsal added to modeling and behavior rehearsal in the treatment of spider phobias. Kanfer et al. (1975) found that coping self-statements enhanced tolerance for the dark in school-age children. Girodo and Roehl (1978) found little support for the efficacy of SIT in the alleviation of flying fears in an analogue population, and Ladouceur (1983) found participant modeling plus SIT no more effective than participant modeling alone in the treatment of animal phobias in a volunteer population. Finally, in what was by far the most compelling study utilizing SIT in the treatment of phobias, Biran and Wilson (1981) found an amalgamation of cognitive procedures including SIT (and SRR) to be less effective than guided exposure in the treatment of specific phobias in a community volunteer sample. This study was described in greater detail in the earlier section, "Other Restructuring Approaches."

Overall, these various studies again provide at best modest support for SIT in the treatment of phobias. Such support as was evident derived largely from analogue studies and did not appear to generalize to more nearly clinical populations. Even in those analogue trials, SIT rarely outperformed more purely behavioral alternatives.

Agoraphobia This general pattern also appears to hold for studies focused on agoraphobia. The two major studies in this literature (Emmelkamp et al., 1978; Emmelkamp & Mersch, 1982), both involved an amalgamation involving SIT (and RET) in the treatment of a fully clinical population and neither were particularly supportive of the cognitive approach, either in comparison with exposure or as an adjunct to exposure. Both studies were described in detail in an earlier section in this chapter. Finally, Williams and Rappoport (1983) found no incremental benefit from adding a SIT component to *in vivo* exposure for driving fears in an agoraphobic population, despite clear evidence that patients in the combined cognitive-behavior group were indeed making greater usage of coping self-statements in driving situations.

Generalized Anxiety Disorder One of the few exceptions to this rather bleak performance in fully clinical populations was provided by Woodward and Jones (1980), and even in this design that support was rather modest. Working with clinic outpatients diagnosed as having generalized anxiety disorders, the authors contrasted cognitive restructuring via self-statement replacement, systematic desensitization, combined cognitive restructuring–desensitization, and a no-treatment control. Treatment was provided in weekly two-hour group sessions over an eight-week period. In this design, the combined treatment proved superior to either single modality alone (and the no-treatment control) on one self-reported intensity of anxiety measure, whereas desensitization, with or without cognitive modification, proved superior to cognitive modification alone on an anxiety diary measure. Given that numerous other measures failed to evidence group differences, it is hard to accept Woodward and Jones's contention that "combining both cognitive restructuring and modified SD procedures . . . is significantly better than the components of treatment taken separately" (1980, p. 407).

Assertion Problems Finally, a variety of controlled comparisons in the treatment of assertion problems (Alden et al., 1978; Carmody, 1978; Craighead, 1979; Derry & Stone, 1979; Jacobs & Cochran, 1982; Kaplan, 1982; Kazdin & Mascitelli, 1982; Safran et al., 1980; Thorpe,

1975) have generally found cognitive and cognitive behavioral packages incorporating SIT to perform well relative to controls, without outperforming more purely behavior approaches. There is some indication that SIT may more adequately complement the more purely behavioral components than do other cognitive approaches. These studies are reviewed in greater detail in Chapter 3, "Assertion Training."

Summary In general, it is difficult to generate much enthusiasm for SIT approaches for treating anxiety-related disorders based on the existing empirical literature. A relatively large empirical literature has developed, but much of it has involved rather trivial applications in analogue populations. Trials in more fully clinical populations have hardly been encouraging. The strongest statement that can be made is that the approach typically outperforms minimal treatment controls and rarely exceeds the efficacy of more purely behavioral approaches. Although it is important to recognize that the major trials involving clinical populations have typically been conducted by researchers more clearly identified with behavioral interventions (e.g., Emmelkamp or Wilson), one cannot help but wonder why proponents of SIT approaches have focused so exclusively on analogue populations.

Self-instructional training has clearly emerged as a major variant of cognitive interventions, but its empirical support remains somewhat suspect. It continues to appear most appropriate for childhood disorders—such as impulsivity—in which cognitive deficits can be addressed via repetition but remains somewhat suspect for disorders such as the anxiety states, in which existing beliefs may be only partially modified by the repetition of positive self-statements. Clearly, more research needs to be done, focused on the clinical relevance of the changes produced in impulsive children and whether or not meaningful change is produced in anxious clinical populations before clear conclusions can be drawn regarding the clinical utility of SIT.

Approaches Emphasizing Interruption and Distraction

Thought Stopping

Wolpe (1958, 1969, 1973) popularized the method of thought stopping, although he credits Bain with introducing it in 1928, and Taylor (in a personal communication to Wolpe, 1958) for its adoption by contemporary behavior therapists. The basic technique is extremely straightforward. Clients are asked to concentrate on troublesome thoughts and, after a short period of time, the therapist emphatically says "Stop" (any loud noise or even a painful electric shock might be used instead). After this procedure has been repeated several times (and the clients report their thoughts were interrupted or blocked), the usual practice is to shift the locus of control to clients—that is, typically it is presented as a self-control technique. Specifically, clients are encouraged to emit a subvocal "Stop" whenever they begin to engage in self-defeating ruminations.

In the early behavior therapy literature (Wolpe, 1958, 1969), thought stopping was used primarily in dealing with obsessional thinking, much the way aversion therapy might be used in a case of compulsive hand washing. More recently, in keeping with the increasing emphasis on cognitive mediation, usage has broadened. For instance, consistent with the A–B–C paradigm, thought stopping may be employed with phobic reactions.

Thought stopping typically involves four discrete steps:

1. First the therapist interrupts the client's overt thoughts.
2. Next, the therapist interrupts the client's covert thoughts.
3. Then, the client overtly interrupts his or her covert thoughts.
4. Finally, the client covertly interrupts his or her covert thoughts.

After the client has been taught to block out these unwanted thoughts, he is encouraged to practice the exercise on his own, especially in the target situations in which the ruminations were most frequent.

Frequently, thought stopping is combined with distraction and covert assertion. In the former instance, the client is further instructed to direct his or her attention to some other subject after executing the thought stopping procedures. That topic could be left to chance or prearranged. Covert assertion involves attending to positive assertive or coping self-statements after engaging in thought stopping. In these latter instances, it is clear that a version of self-statement replacement has been added to thought stopping.

Empirical Findings

Thought stopping procedures have received rather widespread usage, typically as an adjunct to other procedures. Controlled outcome trials have been few and not terribly supportive. Stern, Lipsedge, and Marks (1973) worked with patients reporting a variety of obsessions but found little efficacy using a tape-recorded thought stopping procedure. Rimm, Saunders, and Westel (1975) found thought stopping plus covert assertion superior to a brief discussion group in the treatment of snake-avoidance in an analogue population. In a related study, Armstrong and Rimm (1974) found thought stopping plus covert assertion comparable to systematic desensitization (and both superior to a placebo control), again in a snake-avoidant analogue population. Hackman and McLean (1975) found thought stopping comparable to flooding in a sample of obsessive-compulsive neurotics, and Matthews and Shaw (1977) found thought stopping superior to a placebo condition in the treatment of anxiety neurotics. Finally, Kenny, Mowbray, and Lalani (1978) found thought stopping, using aversive shock as the distracting stimulus, superior to a placebo control in a small sample of obsessional patients.

The bulk of these studies utilized small samples, mixed treatment packages including but not limited to thought stopping, and marginally representative treatment intervals and outcome criteria. We must conclude that the research support for thought stopping is not impressive to date. Studies are few, results are mixed, and designs tend to be flawed. Although thought stopping is probably a marginally useful adjunct to other types of approaches, it is unlikely that the approach represents a major clinical intervention in its own right.

Other Related Approaches

Personal Science

Michael Mahoney's *personal science* (1977b) is a broad spectrum cognitive-behavioral approach that stresses the acquisition of coping skills. The therapist assumes the role of a coach, encouraging the client to attempt various tactics and strategies, staying with those that are effective and discarding those that are not. Given the personalized nature of the treatment (Mahoney would prefer the term *clinical apprenticeship*) and its breadth, personal science is somewhat less structured than the other cognitive learning approaches presented in this chapter; it does bear a decided similarity to Lazarus's multimodal approach (1976). Like Lazarus, Mahoney provides therapists with an acronym to guide their behavior—**SCIENCE:**

S   Specify general problem area
C   Collect data
I   Identify patterns or sources
E   Examine options
N   Narrow and experiment
C   Compare data
E   Extend, revise, or replace

For more specifics, see Mahoney (1977b). Although it has been available to the field for a number of years, we know of no clinical trials evaluating its efficacy.

False Feedback and Reattribution

The treatments of Ellis, Goldfried, Beck, Meichenbaum, and Mahoney are relatively straightforward in nature: by persuasion, disputation, cognitive modeling, and the like, efforts are directed at modifying self-statements or beliefs. In this section, we will review some research aimed at the therapeutic modification of subjects' cognitions that are of a relatively more indirect nature. The general strategy in these studies is to induce subjects, by some manipulation, into inferring that they are able to cope with certain situations.

One such strategy involves the use of false physiological feedback. A prototypical study was conducted by Valins and Ray (1967). They found that subjects who were fed bogus feedback, identified as heart rate, indicating that they were less fearful of harmless snakes than of electric shock subsequently showed less reluctance to approach a snake than those who heard the same feedback but were told it was irrelevant. However, the experimental effect was rather weak, and attempted replications have yielded mixed results (Borkovec & Glasgow, 1973; Conger, Conger, & Brehm, 1976; Gaupp, Stern, & Galbraith, 1972; Kent, Wilson, & Nelson, 1972; Rosen, Rosen, & Reid, 1972; Sushinsky & Bootzin, 1970).

Another major strategy for inducing positive cognitions involves leading subjects to alter their beliefs regarding certain causes and effects—that is, modifying attributions. In one such experiment, Schacter and Singer (1962) found that the emotional effects of epinephrine injections were mitigated by informing subjects about the nature of the drug. Nisbett and Schacter (1966) and Davison and Valins (1969) both employed reattribution strategies to facilitate the tolerance of physical pain. Davison, Tsujimoto, and Glaros (1973) provided insomniacs with a treatment package including chloral hydrate (a sedative often prescribed for insomnia) and relaxation. Subjects later misinformed that their dosage has been inadequate to produce the sedative effect evidenced more satisfactory sleep patterns after the medication was terminated. Additional studies by Storms and Nisbett (1970); Kellogg and Baron (1975); Ribordy and Denny (1977); and Singerman, Borkovec, and Baron (1976) have utilized similar reattribution strategies, with varying success.

At this time, research findings bearing on the efficacy of false feedback and reattribution are mixed. It would seem that indirect cognitive manipulation of this nature may lead to some degree of behavior change, provided that the information so induced does not sharply conflict with preexisting cognitions. Admittedly, this is of some theoretical interest, but even this tentative conclusion is mitigated by the general lack of follow-up data. From a practical perspective, there is presently little reason to believe that *deceptive* manipulations of this nature are of very much clinical utility (not to mention their questionable ethicality). On the other hand, experience would seem to suggest that manipulations or procedures that are aimed at correcting *faulty* inferences or attributions may be very valuable indeed.

Some Concluding Comments

We have presented a variety of cognitive learning perspectives and some relevant research findings. The reader familiar with the first two editions of this text might well be struck by the length of this chapter and the number of outcome studies reviewed. We believe this increased coverage is an accurate reflection of existing trends in the field. As we noted in Chapter 1 and at the beginning of the present chapter, the role of cognitions—or theorizing about cognitions—remains a subject of heated controversy within the field of behavior therapy (see Ellis, 1977a; Ledwidge, 1978; Mahoney, 1977a; Rachlin, 1977; Wolpe, 1977). As we have seen, the controversy revolves

around the following question: in terms of predicting and controlling human behavior, how useful is it to postulate (and then attempt to manipulate) unseen cognitive processes or entities? Radical behaviorists such as Rachlin believe that it is not very useful because, in the past, certain major psychological systems that have relied heavily on hypothetical constructs have had little success. Clearly, there is some validity to this argument. However, this hardly constitutes a rational basis for summarily dismissing all cognitive theory theorizing. As we noted earlier, contemporary cognitive theorizing has ofttimes led to clear-cut, nontrivial predictions that have been verified (Bower, 1975; Mahoney, 1974; many of the findings reported throughout this text). At the same time, unqualified acceptance of a particular cognitive formulation on the grounds that it is intuitively appealing or because its major proponents are especially enthusiastic is every bit as antiscientific and counterproductive as prejudicial dismissal. Each of the aforementioned cognitive learning therapies (excluding those too new to have been tested) has *some* empirical support, but none can presently be said to have conclusive empirical foundation. "More research is needed" may sound like a shibboleth, but in the present context, it could not be more appropriate.

Largely because of the increasing emphasis on cognitive processes, social learning conceptualizations of psychological disorders have become increasingly complex. The complexity of such formulations reflects an emerging, highly sophisticated interactionalistic view of personality (Bandura, 1978; Mahoney, 1977a; Mischel, 1977) that attempts to take into account a host of variables essentially ignored by earlier, more simplistic formations. To the extent that more complex models allow for better prediction and control, this trend is very positive.

At the beginning of this chapter, we noted that the cognitive and cognitive-behavioral therapies have been expected to add something to the clinical armamentarium that other approaches have not provided. That advantage could be the production of greater change, greater generality for that change over situations or components of the larger problem, or greater stability for that change over time. By and large, although considerable evidence existed that these approaches equaled reasonable alternative interventions (particularly behavioral approaches) in the treatment of many nonpsychotic disorders, little clear evidence indicated superiority on any outcome dimension. The possible additive advantage of combined cognitive-pharmacotherapy over either single modality and the apparent greater stability of treatment gains for cognitive therapy over pharmacotherapy in the treatment of depression, along with the apparent efficacy of cognitive-behavioral integrative SIT packages in the training of impulsive children, may represent exceptions. Excluding those possible exceptions, there was little differential advantage for the cognitive approaches over other reasonable alternatives, in particular the more purely behavioral approaches. Conversely, one could look at this same literature and say that the cognitive and cognitive-behavioral approaches have proven at least the equal of other major alternatives.

One relevant note involves a comment on the quality of research literature evaluating these approaches. First, there is a curious confounding of specific cognitive therapy type and subtype of disorder. RET and SRR have been involved primarily in studies with various anxiety states and assertion problems, Beck's cognitive therapy has been solely restricted to tests with depressed populations, whereas Meichenbaum's

SIT has been utilized somewhat more broadly (impulsivity, anxiety, and schizophrenia). This confounding makes it difficult to discern if differential efficacy is an attribute of the treatment subtype (and the associated change process mobilized), the specific population involved, or some interaction between the two.

Finally, one must remain concerned about the consistency of design limitations within these respective literatures. By and large, the studies involving anxious populations by researchers expert in cognitive approaches have simply relied far too exclusively on analogue populations. RET, SRR, and SIT, as treatments for anxiety, have really not received adequate trials in appropriate *clinical* populations. After more than 15 years, that is really quite distressing. Studies involving CB for depression have typically eschewed minimal treatment or placebo controls, leaving us in a position of interpreting a series of "tie-score" outcomes. Studies involving SIT for impulsivity have not adequately addressed the clinical meaningfulness of the changes produced. Overall, although research activity has been vigorous, it has too often been somewhat stereotypic. Rather than providing conceptual replications and extensions that build on earlier trials while addressing new and interesting questions regarding treatment efficacy, the existing literature has tended to be repetitive, leaving major issues regarding relative efficacy unaddressed. We can only hope that the great vigor shown since the mid-1970s will be translated into efforts to address these concerns in the years to come.

10
Self-Control

Self-control approaches provide clients with active coping strategies for dealing with problem situations. The strategies are typically, but not exclusively, behavioral. The basic rationale of the self-control approach is threefold: (1) some goals may be more powerfully realized when the client is given an active role in the change process (efficacy), (2) clients skilled in self-management techniques can apply these skills to problems not directly approached in treatment (generality), and (3) changes obtained should prove more stable over time if the client can reapply change procedures as needed (stability) (Goldstein & Kanfer, 1979; Karoly & Steffan, 1980).

The self-control approach is in direct contrast with those that rely, theoretically at least, on what might be described as a passive conditioning process (Kanfer & Gaelick, 1986). The self-control versus passive conditioning distinction is well illustrated in two approaches to systematic desensitization discussed in Chapter 2. The Wolpian approach illustrates passive conditioning. After clients have been desensitized, they are not required to *do* anything in particular in the target situation to experience the positive effects of treatment. That is, the theory expects the counterconditioning to effect a more or less automatic reduction in anxiety vis-à-vis the phobic stimulus. In contrast, the Goldfried approach illustrates self-control (Goldfried & Trier, 1974). The client is taught to "relax away" tension elicited by the phobic stimulus— that is, to cope actively with the anxiety. Given this distinction, it should be clear that many of

the approaches presented in the previous chapters of this text implicitly, if not explicitly, reflect a self-control perspective. Assertion training, described in Chapter 3, is an obvious example. The cognitive approaches, discussed in Chapter 9, are very much within the conceptual rubric of self-control. The present chapter deals with additional techniques and empirical findings relevant to the topic of self-control, including operant approaches that emphasize stimulus control and reinforcement; stress-inoculation procedures aimed at helping individuals cope with stress, anger, and pain; and biofeedback.

Operant Methods in Self-control

Problems of self-control usually fall into one of two categories (Kanfer & Phillips, 1970). In the first, clients engage in a behavior pattern that is self-defeating or injurious. A few examples of problems of this nature often encountered in the clinic include eating patterns leading to obesity, excessive smoking or drinking or other forms of drug abuse, and indiscriminate or impulsive sexual behavior. For problems in this category, the therapist must help clients reduce the probabilities of the occurrence of such behaviors. In the second category, clients suffer because they engage in certain adaptive behaviors too infrequently, if at all. Common examples include the inability to study, the failure to initiate social contacts, a low frequency of helping others, and sexual inactivity. Here it is the therapist's goal to aid clients in increasing the probabilities of such responses.

In actual practice, a given self-control program involves simultaneous efforts to increase the likelihood of certain types of responses and to decrease other types of responses. To illustrate, most obese individuals eat excessive amounts of high-calorie food, and the primary goal of the therapist and client is to reduce this behavior. One way is to have clients reward themselves for failing to engage in excessive eating. Another way is to attempt to strengthen responses that would compete with eating. For example, the client might be encouraged to take a walk at a time when he or she would normally engage in eating (Stuart, 1967). In a similar vein, Watson and Tharp (1977) reported a case of a male student who spent most of his study time in the library looking at girls. By eliminating the competing response of girl watching (by having the student study in his room), as well as by allowing for reinforcement of study behavior, the amount of studying was effectively increased. Both examples illustrate a strategy common to most self-control programs: the simultaneous strengthening of desirable behaviors and weakening of competing undesirable behaviors.

Background

In the early 1950s, Skinner (1953) provided a rudimentary conceptual analysis of self-control, including a variety of techniques. In the early and mid-1960s, a small number of writers (e.g., Ferster, Nurnberger, & Levitt, 1962; Goldiamond, 1965; Homme, 1965) made significant inroads into the application of operant principles to problems of the above nature. By the early 1970s, interest in operantly based self-control procedures had increased dramatically (Goldfried & Merbaum, 1973; Kanfer & Phillips, 1970; Mahoney & Thoreson, 1974; Thoreson & Mahoney, 1974; Watson & Tharp, 1972). The field continued to mature into the late 1970s and 1980s (Blankstein & Polivy, 1982; Goldstein & Kanfer, 1979; Kanfer & Goldstein, 1986; Karoly & Kanfer, 1982; Karoly & Steffan, 1980; Stuart, 1977; Watson & Tharp, 1977).

Several factors probably have contributed to the initial wariness on the part of many behaviorists dealing with issues related to self-control. First, when we think of self-control, we almost automatically think of such terms as *willpower* or *strength of character.* Concepts of this nature may be meaningful to the theologian, but certainly not to the deterministically minded psychologist. Second, self-control connotes control from within the individual—that is, control emanating from nonobservable mental processes. In Chapter 1, we dealt with the unfavorable reaction toward "mentalistic" analyses displayed by many behaviorists. Third, self-control, when we do attempt to deal with it in operant terms, implies self-reinforcement. That is, the individual has free access to reward, but does not partake of it until he or she has performed some desired response. Skinner (1953) suggested the necessity for accounting for why a person would behave in this manner (when the most obvious response would be immediate self-reinforcement). He then raised a far more basic question: Will self-reinforcement increase the probability of the behaviors that precede it? Skinner's intimation was that indeed it might not.

By the early 1970s, a great many psychologists had overcome their earlier skepticism, and research into therapeutic application of self-control procedures had become a respectable enterprise. By then, it was clear that self-control could be seen in terms of the systematic manipulation of antecedent stimulus events and response consequences rather than as a mystical exercise in willpower. In particular, researchers (e.g., Bandura & Perloff, 1967) demonstrated that self-reinforcement, one of the mechanisms most fundamental to self-control, could indeed alter the likelihood that an individual would behave in a certain manner. Indeed, the act of self-reinforcement itself could be seen as the second behavior in a two-behavior chain (the first being the original response to be modified), as fully subject to whatever laws of learning operate on any other behaviors (Bandura, 1976).

Although controversy still exists regarding whether self-administered techniques operate through the same mechanisms as externally administered contingencies (Castro, Perez, Albanchez, & deLeon, 1983; Hayes & Nelson, 1983; Nelson, Hayes, Spong, Jarret, & McKnight, 1983), there is little remaining doubt that self-applied contingencies have an impact. Finally, as we noted in Chapter 9, developments in operant approaches to self-control at least indirectly contributed to the development of the cognitive learning therapies. By the early 1970s, the relationship between these two perspectives could be described as *mutually facilitative,* with each stressing an internal locus of control. By the mid-1980s, it has become clear that self-control procedures, sometimes used alone but most often in combination with other behavioral and cognitive-behavioral strategies, have become a major component in the behavior therapy armamentarium. Table 10–1 provides a selective listing of just some of the problem areas to which self-control procedures have been applied. As can be seen, the list is diverse. Arguably, the addictive disorders, and particularly obesity, alcoholism, and smoking, have received the greatest attention (Brownell, 1982b). We will focus our review on these areas.

Applying Operant Procedures to Problems of Self-control

When to Implement a Self-control Program

In principle, the therapist can apply self-control procedures to almost any behavioral problem, provided that the client has the intelligence sufficient to comprehend and carry out such a program (which is probably almost always the case). Consider the male who becomes tongue-tied whenever he approaches an attractive female. A therapist might provide him with instructions in self-control procedures, stressing the maintenance of careful records, attending to those stimuli in the environment that typically give rise to such responding, and possible rewards that the client might provide for himself following more adequate approach responses to attractive females. Before long, it is likely that the client will report some progress, and eventually he may be making frequent and effective overtures to females.

While such a therapeutic approach might well be effective, it is naive, because it ignores the fact that there is a potential immediate and potent external reinforcer in every target situation—namely, a positive response (e.g., a smile on the part of the woman). In other words, there are important *short-term* (as well as long-term) rewards for behaving in a certain manner in such a situation. A more reasonable therapeutic strategy would involve simply providing direct instruction (behavior rehearsal, Chapter 4) in how to behave in such situations. Once the client has acquired such skills, these behaviors will be maintained (perhaps intermittently) by powerful external rewards.

Consider the case of the student who seeks professional help because he seems unable to study. He reports that studying is a "drag," although he thinks he would like to do well in school (receive good grades). The therapist might assume that all that is required is to provide instruction in how to study (i.e., taking effective notes, rehearsing, reciting, etc.). However, this is also naive because it assumes that there is a significant short-term gain in studying in a more efficient manner. Such may be the case for the student who does not have a study problem, but it is probably not true for the person in question. It is quite unlikely that, after 10 minutes of effective study behavior, the professor will burst into the room saying, "Terrific! Here is your A," or even that a friend will happen on the scene and commend the student for more efficient studying. For this individual, in

Table 10–1 **Some Applications of Self-control Approaches (Either Alone or as Part of Larger Treatment Packages)**

Abusing Parents	Barth, Blyth, Schinke, & Schilling, 1983; Nomellini & Katz, 1983
Alcoholism	Foy, Nunn, & Rychartik, 1984; Miller, 1978; Miller & Taylor, 1980; Miller, Taylor, & West, 1980
Depression	Brown & Lewinsohn, 1984; Hamilton & Waldman, 1983; Rehm, 1977, 1983; Kornblith, Rehm, O'Hara, & Lamparski, 1983
Encopresis	Propp, 1985
Enuresis	Meier & Land, 1983
Geriatric	Rodin, 1983
Hiatus Hernia	Calloway, Fonagy, Pounder, & Morgan, 1983
Hyperactivity	Hinshaw, Hencker, & Whalen, 1984; Horn, Chatoos, & Conners, 1983
Insomnia	Bootzin & Nicassio, 1978; Lacks, Bertelson, Gans, & Kunkel, 1983; Nicassio & Buchanan, 1981
Learning Disabilities	Ammer, 1982
Marital	Jacobson, 1977
Menopausal Hot Flashes	Stevenson & Delprato, 1983
Obesity	Abrams & Follick, 1983; Brownell & Stunkard, 1981; Chapman & Jeffrey, 1978; Craighead, 1984; Craighead, Stunkard, & O'Brien, 1981; Foreyt, Mitchell, Gee, Scott, & Gotto, 1982; Jeffery, Gerber, Rosenthal, & Lindquist, 1983; Jeffery, Thompson, & Wing, 1978; Johnson, Wildman, & O'Brien, 1980; Wing & Jeffery, 1979
Obsessive-Compulsive	Hoogduin & Hoogduin, 1984
Psychotic Inpatients	Breier & Strauss, 1983; Levendusky, Berglas, Dooley, & Landau, 1983
Retardates	Guralnick, 1976; Litrownik, 1982
Smoking	Abrams & Wilson, 1979; Colletti & Kopel, 1979; Colletti & Supnik, 1980; Colletti, Supnick, & Rizzo, 1982; Hall, Rugg, Tunstall, & Jones, 1984; Sommer, Schmid-Methfessel, & Seyfferth, 1984; Spring, Sipich, Trimble, & Goeckner, 1978
Study Behavior	Heffernan & Richards, 1981; Kirschenbaum & Perri, 1982; Mercier & Ladoucer, 1983; Richards, 1981; Ronnback, 1983
Trichotillomania	Ottens, 1982
Vomitting (Air Sickness)	Rebman, 1983
Worrying	Borkovec, Wilkinson, Folensbee, & Lerman, 1983
Writer's Block	Rosenberg & Lah, 1982

the short run, there is little in the natural environment to maintain more effective study behaviors. Here is a case where training in self-control is a preferred method of treatment, because one of the main things it would provide for this individual is an immediate incentive for engaging in more desirable behavior. Such an incentive would be expected to bridge the temporal gap between responding and long-term, naturally occurring reinforcements, such as good grades, praise from parents, or a rewarding job. One of the major theoretical controversies to emerge in recent years involves whether self-reinforcement works by virtue of its short-term incentive properties—the traditional view—or by virtue of cueing those long-term rewards (Castro et al., 1983; Hayes & Nelson, 1983; Nelson et al., 1983).

Although there are no hard-and-fast rules, the foregoing examples suggest some general guidelines. When a client is behaving in a self-defeating manner, and there are no immediate and potent reinforcers in the natural environment for behaving otherwise, a self-control regimen might well be the most feasible treatment. Problems that would seem to lie in this category include low frequencies of so-called self-improvement behaviors, associated with relatively long-term rewards—for instance, academic studying, practicing a musical instrument, or participation in strenuous exercise programs. Other problems include overeating, excessive drinking or smoking, and the inability to save money. This list is certainly not exhaustive and it is presented merely to provide the reader with a general feel for the types of problems amenable to self-control programs. (As we implied earlier, when the nature of the problem is such that appropriate behavior change is likely to be reinforced by the natural environment with a relatively minimal delay, therapeutic strategies other than self-control would probably prove to be more efficient.) Naturally, there is nothing to preclude combining the implementation of a self-control program with other therapeutic interventions. For example, the alcoholic might undergo the avoidance conditioning procedures of Chapter 8 while receiving training in self-control.

Introducing the Self-control Program

Having decided that self-control is an appropriate method of treatment for clients, the therapists next orient them to such a treatment strategy. Clients receive what is tantamount to a brief course in the experimental analysis of behavior (see Chapters 5 and 6 of this text). Such an orientation is a very important part of the overall treatment program because the clients themselves are the primary therapists, who must become skilled in the application of relevant learning principles. This task is not especially formidable, since the principles involved are relatively few in number and are not especially complicated. Ordinarily, the orientation can be accomplished in one or two treatment sessions, although the client's understanding and skills will increase as the program unfolds.

One of the major points to be made during this first session is that it is of no use whatsoever for clients to think of themselves as lacking in willpower or backbone. Viewing themselves in such terms can only sabotage their efforts at self-control, for what is the point of trying to change if one's difficulties emanate from an immutable state of inner weakness? No doubt clients can point to certain people they know who appear to have no difficulties in most areas of self-control, intimating that these people are "strong," whereas they are "weak." It must be stressed that what such individuals possess is not strength or moral fiber, but rather a fortunate learning history that enables them, probably without much effort, to behave in self-enhancing rather than self-defeating ways. In fact, studies of successful "self-changers" across a variety of problem behaviors have consistently shown these individuals to differ from unsuccessful "self-changers" not in terms of "willpower" but in their spontaneous utilization of the kinds of cognitive and behavioral coping skills typically incorporated in self-control programs (e.g., DiClemente & Prochaska, 1982; Prochaska & DiClemente, 1982; Shiffman, 1982, 1984). The problem with the clients is not that they are not trying hard enough, but that they simply have not yet learned to employ the most effective tactics. The therapist's role is, of course, to facilitate the learning of those tactics.

Self-control Principles

The therapist may structure the self-control program around Kanfer's multistage model (Kanfer, 1971; Karoly & Kanfer, 1974; Spates & Kanfer, 1977), proceeding from self-monitoring to self-evaluation to self-reinforcement. Self-monitoring involves careful observation and recording of the target behavior (as noted in Chapter 9, self-monitoring plays an important role in many of the cognitive-behavioral interventions). Frequency of the behavior should be noted, as well as other relevant information (e.g., in the case of eating, the quantity, the caloric content, and, depending on the nature of the diet, the relative amounts of protein, carbohydrate, fat). Circumstances under which the behavior occurred should also be noted, including antecedent events, the stimulus environment in which the behavior was carried out, and consequent events. For example, an individual with a drinking problem reported that one drinking episode immediately followed a fight with his wife. Following that negative interaction, he drank a six-pack while watching a football game on television, forgetting about the conflict with his wife after several beers. Such an instance is quite common in various types of substance abuse disorders in which negative emotional states frequently precede instances of maladaptive behaviors, largely because those behaviors reduce subjective distress (cf., Brownell, Marlatt, Lichtenstein, & Wilson, 1986; Cummings, Gordon, & Marlatt, 1980; Shiffman, 1982, 1984).

The client may require some coaching in the most effective way to quantify the target behavior (Watson & Tharp, 1977). Some behaviors, such as cigarette smoking, lend themselves most naturally to a simple counting procedure. Others, such as eating, require a measure representing amount. For still others, time engaged in the target behavior may be the most reasonable measure (e.g., studying or sleeping during the day).

For target behaviors having a very high frequency (smoking, nail biting), some type of portable counter might be helpful. If none is available, the client might take a coin from one pocket and place it in another each time he engages in the response (Watson & Tharp, 1977). Behaviors of this nature (such as smoking) are sometimes performed relatively automatically without any conscious decision being made; in such instances, it might be helpful to have the client deliberately practice the response with a great deal of concentration, in order to increase his awareness of its occurrence (Watson & Tharp, 1977).

As we noted, knowledge of the circumstances in which the behavior occurs is important. For behaviors having a relatively low frequency (sexual encounters, engaging in serious arguments), it is possible to record these events for every occurrence of the target behavior. For high-frequency behaviors, this may not be feasible. For example, consider the heavy smoker who consumes three packs (60 cigarettes) a day. Counting might not be especially difficult, but recording events surrounding each cigarette would be impossible. On the other hand, by periodic examination of the rate of smoking, the client should not have difficulty ascertaining ongoing events or experiences that tend to correlate with gross changes in the rate of smoking. A person who says, "I smoke a lot when I'm studying for exams," is doing precisely this.

Whether clients choose to employ small notebooks or mechanical procedures for reliable on-the-spot observations, they should transcribe the data collected each day into more permanent records that they and their therapists can use during the planning and implementation stages of the program. Data sheets, such as the one presented in Table 10–2, are useful for this purpose.

During the initial phase of the program, perhaps over a period of a week or two, self-monitoring is employed to collect baseline data. It is important that the therapist be aware of the

Table 10–2 **Sample of Portion of One Day's Record for Housewife With Smoking Problem**

Day	Time	Frequency or Amount	Antecedents, Stimulus Environment, Consequences
Monday	8–10 a.m.	4	Awoke, had 1 sitting in bed, felt nauseated; had remainder after drinking coffee while reading newspaper; coughed afterward.
	10–12 a.m.	5	Had 1 after every 20–30 minutes of heavy housecleaning, sat in living room watching TV. Felt relaxed afterward, no coughing.
	12–2 p.m.	2	Right after lunch, felt relaxed, but coughed a lot.
Total for Day		37	

reactive nature of self-monitoring (e.g., Green, 1978; Hayes & Cavior, 1977; Hollon & Kendall, 1981; Komaki & Dore-Boyce, 1978; Nelson, Hay, Hay, & Carstens, 1977; Nelson, Lipinski, & Boykin, 1978). That is, the act of observing one's behavior tends to change the behavior observed. The direction of the change is difficult to predict, although often it is in the desired direction. Empirical examples include weight loss in obese patients (Romanczyk, 1974), reduced smoking in people motivated to stop (Abrams & Wilson, 1979), and improved study habits in students having study problems (Johnson & White, 1971; Richards, 1975). Thus, when an obese person monitors his or her calorie intake, that intake is likely to decrease (Green, 1978), especially if the monitoring occurs *prior to* the eating behavior (Bellack, Rozensky, & Schwartz, 1974). It is likely that one factor contributing to the efficacy of self-monitoring as a tool for positive behavior change is *motivation to change* (see Fremouw & Brown, 1980; Hayes & Nelson, 1983; Kirschenbaum & Tomarken, 1982; Komaki & Dore-Boyce, 1978; and McFall, 1977, for discussions of the determinants of reactivity to self-monitoring). Since high levels of motivation would be likely in a clinical population, positive change during the baseline period would generally be the rule. It is probably wise to point out in advance that self-monitoring may cause behavior change; otherwise, the client may provide an inaccurate and potentially confusing attribution for such change.

Self-monitoring will facilitate the client's appreciation of the importance of stimulus control. Thus, obese persons may learn that they do not gorge themselves all the time, and individuals with study problems will learn that certain external events and circumstances favor study behavior, whereas others do not. The client with the weight problem may observe that she eats excessively only when alone in her apartment before retiring. The student learns that he has no difficulty studying in his dormitory room, but is distracted when he attempts to study in the library where attractive girls are often in view, or in the fraternity house where his friends congregate.

If behavior is under stimulus control, it should be possible for a person to weaken or eliminate undersirable responses and strengthen desirable responses by changing the stimulus environment. The student distracted from studying in the library would be expected to fare better in an isolated room. The alcoholic who is a solitary drinker should attempt to place himself in social situations at those times he is most likely to drink. The housewife who spends excessive amounts of money on clothes should attempt to avoid stimuli, such as fashion magazines, that tend to cue such behavior. In these examples, the individuals are taking advantage of already existing stimulus-response relationships. *They are placing themselves in a different situation, or in some manner changing their environment, and behaving more adaptively.*

Other methods of stimulus control may involve building in appropriate stimulus-response connections. One such method is *narrowing,* or tightening, stimulus control (Ferster et al., 1962). An overall pattern of behavior may be especially maladaptive because it is practiced in a wide variety of situations. Certain obese individuals perhaps have acquired the habit of eating while watching television, listening to the radio, or reading the newspaper. Narrowing restricts the behavior to a limited set of stimuli. For example, eating might be limited to the dinner table at certain times of day, with the television off (Stuart, 1967, 1971).

Another method of building in stimulus control may be used when an adaptive behavior is not strongly conditioned to any set of environmental cues. The technique of *cue strengthening* requires that conditions be made favorable for the person to practice the response in a specific situation. A good example would be the student whose study behavior is virtually absent. He might be encouraged to study in a certain specified location (Fox, 1962) so that stimuli associated with that location come to trigger study behavior.

Once clients have determined environmental cues that give rise to critical patterns of behavior, the therapist may discuss *alternative* or *competing* responses. Such responses keep a person from doing something else in specified situations. If the stated problem involves failure to engage in adaptive behavior (say, a study problem), clients may be asked to specify responses they typically make that interfere with such desired behavior (e.g., talking with friends in the library); the goal, of course, is to eliminate such responses. If the problem involves engaging in some undesirable behavior, such as overeating, clients are encouraged to think of effective and readily available competing responses; for instance, going for walks when one normally snacks. Even the process of self-monitoring instances in which urges are conquered appears to produce desirable reactivity (O'Banion, Armstrong, & Ellis, 1980).

Careful self-monitoring will usually reveal that a particular self-defeating behavior is actually the *termination of a sequence of responses* chained together. To illustrate, consider the alcoholic who does his drinking in a particular neighborhood tavern between the hours of 10 in the evening and 2 in the morning. On a given evening, he looks at the clock and it is 9:45; this cues searching for the car keys, getting in the car, and driving toward the tavern. The closer he gets to his destination, the more likely he is to encounter additional stimuli reminding him of the tavern, such as his first drink, and the feeling he will have after a couple of drinks. By the time he enters the tavern and sits at the bar, he is likely to be overwhelmed by a multitude of cues (any one of which is strongly conditioned to drinking: the bartender, the sight of whiskey bottles, the smell of alcohol, the sight of one or more drinking partners). Naturally, the first drink will act as an additional powerful stimulus for further drinking. Had this person been able to interrupt this behavioral chain at any point prior to, say, having consumed three or four drinks, for that evening, at least, he would not be a problem drinker. Both in terms of the number of cues tending to elicit drinking and the immediacy of reinforcement (the effects of alcohol), it is clear that the likelihood of interrupting this chain is far greater if efforts at self-control occur early rather than late in the sequence (see Fremouw & Brown, 1980, for an example of capitalization on this principle). It may be that as the person progresses in the self-control program, he will be able to interrupt the chain at a point much closer to the terminal behavior. However, for the relative novice, writers in the area tend to agree on the following important principle. *Self-control procedures are most easily implemented early in a response chain.*

The point just made may seem rather obvious, yet many persons with serious self-control problems appear oblivious to it. This can be seen in a dieting obese person who regularly lunches with gluttonous friends, or the philandering husband who, bent on reform, tests his resolve by having a drink with his attractive coworker in her apartment. Certain people seem to believe that the mark of self-control is the ability to withstand any and all temptation. In fact, it is far more correct to say that the mark of self-control is the ability to minimize temptation by early interruption of such behavioral chains.

When people monitor their behavior, they usually engage in a process of self-evaluation. They compare their response with some subjective standard derived from previous experience of a direct or vicarious nature (Bandura, 1969, Karoly & Kanfer, 1974). Evidence suggests that such self-evaluation is critical to effective self-control (Spates & Kanfer, 1977), in all likelihood because it provides the basis for self-reinforcement, itself a key element in self-management programs (Bellack, 1976; Mahoney, 1974; Perri, Richards, & Schultheis, 1977). For example Grimm (1983) found that the tendency to self-reinforce was largely a function of the lack of discrepancy between evaluative standards and actual performance, rather than a direct function of either alone.

Individuals differ considerably with respect to internal or subjective standards. Some persons seem to evaluate their performance against very stringent standards. Depressed individuals, for example, have been found to hold themselves to higher standards than others (cf. Ciminero & Steingarten, 1978; Garber, Hollon, & Silverman, 1979), as have individuals with Type A personalities (Grimm & Yarnold, 1984). If they have the capability of meeting or surpassing those standards, then there is no particular problem. It is unlikely, however, that clients showing problems in self-control will show such a capability, at least initially. If the internal standards are nevertheless high, self-reinforcement will not be forthcoming, and significant behavior change will be unlikely. Clinical experience suggests that individuals with self-control problems do frequently have unrealistically high, perfectionistic standards, and often one of the important treatment goals involves persuading clients to lower those standards.[1] Closely related is the tendency for individuals to adopt temporally distal outcomes as standards, rather than more immediate subgoals leading to those larger goals (Bandura & Simon, 1977), a process which would allow them to reinforce themselves at frequent intervals along the way. To illustrate, consider the following example, all too familiar to those of us who have supervised graduate students.

A 24-year-old male graduate student went to a therapist, complaining that he had not written one page on his thesis proposal in three months and was in danger of being removed from the program.

Therapist: Well, what usually happens when you begin to work? Do you get distracted by your friends, or TV, or something like that?

Student: Not really. I don't know. . . . It's like, I write a paragraph . . . and I start thinking of all the things I have to go through before I get through with this. It's like, you know . . . what's the use.

Therapist: Have you ever been involved in any project as large in scope as a thesis?

[1]When given choices, children typically set very *lenient* standards for self-reward (Bandura & Perloff, 1967; Felixbrod & O'Leary, 1973, 1974). Further, among children, lenient standards may be associated with relatively poor performance (Brownell, Colletti, Ersner-Hershfield, Hershfield, & Wilson, 1977). From these data, one may infer that *certain* individuals who suffer from a lack of self-control select standards for self-reinforcement that are too *lenient* rather than too strict. In our opinion, however, such cases are exceptions and not the rule.

Student: No, not really. The closest thing would be, well, a 10- or 20-page term paper.

Therapist: Let me guess. I'll bet you'd put it off until the last possible moment, and then stay up all night until it was complete. And then you'd feel really good it was done.

Student: You forgot the gallon of coffee! But that is exactly right.

Therapist: Okay, your strategy was to reward yourself—you know, pat yourself on the back, or whatever—only when you completed the *entire task.* And that worked, because you could complete it in *one night.* You are now faced with the problem of having a project that will take months to finish, but I'll bet you still insist on having it all done before you allow yourself to feel good about yourself.

Student: I see what you're getting at. And it's true. But what do I do about it?

Therapist: Set more realistic goals . . . really subgoals. You tell me one.

Student: Okay, writing the introduction, which includes a literature review. (Student shows an obvious look of discouragement)

Therapist: No, I mean what could you complete *tonight,* say in a couple of hours. Think of a goal that you are absolutely *certain* you could reach tonight.

Student: Hmmm. Well (laughs), I could write a page. Maybe two to three pages. . . . Hmmm. I'm less sure of that. Okay, one page, if that is what you mean.

Therapist: That is exactly what I mean! Write your page and then do something to reward yourself.

Student: That seems almost like cheating.

Therapist: I don't agree. And, working at that rate, you'd have the project done inside of two months. Probably sooner, if you gradually increase the number of pages per day,

but let's not worry about that for the present.

Student: Yeah, I guess it does make sense.

In our experience, once students adopt the strategy of setting up permissive, easily attainable subgoals followed by self-reinforcement, they experience little difficulty in completing their projects. Note that in the above example, the therapist set the stage for the student's adopting a permissive standard for self-reinforcement, but that it was the student who provided the specifics of the standard—that is, one page per night, initially at least. Although research findings are not entirely consistent, there is some evidence that self-imposed standards lead to greater behavior change than externally imposed standards (e.g., Brownell Colletti, Ersner-Hershfield, Hershfield, & Wilson, 1977; Lovitt & Curtiss, 1969).

Although the initial response requirements for self-reinforcement are quite lenient, it is common in self-control programs to raise them gradually, similar to the process of shaping we described in Chapter 5. Care should be taken, however, that the steps are easily manageable. After all, in order to reinforce and thereby strengthen a response (whether it be a desirable response or one that competes with an undesirable behavior), the response must first occur. Thus, throughout the program, *response requirements must be modest enough to make it very likely that clients will meet their ongoing behavioral goals.* Recall that immediate reinforcers are far more effective than delayed reinforcers. In the preceding example, the student's standards were such that he would not provide self-reinforcement until the entire project was complete, meaning a delay in reinforcement of many months, which is tantamount to no reinforcement at all. This all-or-nothing attitude is common to individuals with self-control problems and is illustrated in the case of a hospitalized alcoholic. His religious background led him to believe that drinking in any amount was sinful. Another person might have strengthened the behavior of having only one drink by self-reinforcement for a competing response (e.g., leaving the tavern). This person could not, however, because having only one drink was no more deserving of reward than having a dozen. The very brief treatment consisted merely of helping him view drinking on a continuum, so that he was in a position to reward himself for drinking less on any given occassion. He was soon discharged from the hospital, and at a follow-up several months later, he was handling a responsible job and reported no problem with alcohol. He indicated that his new attitude about drinking had been a major factor in his improvement.

The two preceding examples illustrate the two major classes of behaviors to be reinforced: in the case of a behavioral deficit, instances of the target behavior (i.e., writing on a thesis) are to be self-rewarded; in the case of a behavioral surfeit (i.e., alcohol consumption), responses that effectively compete with the behavioral excess (e.g., leaving or avoiding a bar) are to be rewarded. There is evidence (Mahoney, 1974; Saccone & Israel, 1978) that self-reinforcement is far more effective when it is contingent on appropriate behavior than when it is made contingent on the *effects* of that behavior. For instance, the student who had difficulty working on his thesis was advised to reward himself for a specified amount of writing behavior in contrast, for example, to waiting until he received his master's degree before providing self-reinforcement. Similarly, overweight individuals should stress target behaviors that compete with eating for self-reward, as opposed to weight loss. This is not to suggest that there is anything wrong with also rewarding the positive effects of such behavior. But if it is the program strategy to reward *only* these effects or outcomes, such outcomes will probably be very infrequent.

Among the elements of a self-control treatment program, the one that is perhaps the least intrinsically reinforcing is self-monitoring. Obvi-

ously, self-monitoring is essential in gathering baseline data, but it is equally important during later stages of the program when it serves as the main source of information regarding how the program is proceeding. To ensure that careful records are made by the client throughout the program, the client should be encouraged to provide self-reinforcement for such behavior.

The Use of Contracts

A self-control program involves at least an implicit contract between the therapist and client, wherein the client receives approval for achieving the various subgoals. However, formal contractual agreements usually involve more tangible rewards, for example, money refunded from cash deposits according to the degree of progress (see Harris & Bruner, 1971). Contracts may be arranged between the client and a person or persons other than the therapist. The essence of such contracts is the assumption of a reciprocal exchange of rewards, contingent upon certain actions on the part of each party (Tooley & Pratt, 1967). For example, a husband may agree to cut down on his smoking in exchange for periodic telephone calls at work from his wife. The terms of the contract should be very explicit. Thus, in the above example, the husband might contract to reduce his cigarette consumption by 10 cigarettes per day on the understanding that his wife will call him and give him gentle reminders and support. Although contracts may be used by themselves, they may also be incorporated into a broader self-control program employing other principles mentioned in this chapter.

Whether or not the therapist chooses to incorporate formal contractual procedures is a matter of preference, although there are cases for which they might be especially appropriate. Examples include Jacobson's (1977) use of contracting in working with troubled marriages; Jeffery, Gerber, Rosenthal, and Lindquist's (1983) use of contracting to maintain motivation for weight loss; or Spring, Sipich, Trimble, and

Goeckner's (1978) use of contracting in self-control smoking modification program. For persons less adept at delaying gratification (i.e., individuals who tend to self-reward in a noncontingent manner), contractual management that involves external reinforcement may be very helpful. Many individuals in our culture have been conditioned to view contract obligations as virtually sacred. For such persons, the inclusion of some type of formal contractual understanding in the overall program might be a very valuable addition.

In summary, the following are the basic operant principles with which the client should have some familiarity before dealing with a specific problem.

1. Self-control is not a matter of blind willpower. Instead, it comes about as a result of judicious manipulation of antecedent and consequent events, in accord with established principles of learning.
2. The client should be aware of the importance of self-monitoring, how one engages in such behavior, and that self-observation is frequently reactive.
3. The client should take advantage of the fact that behavior is under stimulus control by employing any of the following tactics:
   a. Physically changing the stimulus environment;
   b. Narrowing the range of stimuli eliciting undesirable behaviors;
   c. Strengthening the connection between certain stimuli and desirable behaviors.
4. The client should determine which responses are competing with and thereby inhibiting desirable behavior, with the goal of weakening them. The client should determine which responses might serve as healthy alternatives to undesirable ways of behaving, with the goal of strengthening them.
5. The client should attempt to interrupt behavior chains leading to undesirable responses as early as possible in the chain.
6. The client should self-administer rewards immediately after appropriate responses have occurred.

7. Graduated behavioral goals in a self-control program should always be easily attainable. That is, clients should deliberately plan to achieve their overall goals in a gradual manner.
8. Behavioral contracts may be a useful element of self-control programs.

Relapse Prevention

Probably the major innovation in the area of self-control interventions has been the articulation of Marlatt's relapse prevention program (Marlatt, 1979, 1982; Marlatt & Gordon, 1985). Self-control strategies have long been touted for their potential to create change that should be more stable than that produced by other interventions, if only because clients are presumed to have acquired skills that they can reapply to themselves as needed in the future. Rather than being the passive recipients of curative procedures applied by a therapist, an ideology carried over from the medical model for understanding psychopathology and treatment (Brickman, Rabinowitz, Karuza, Coates, Cohn, & Kidder, 1982), self-control approaches strive to impart behavioral management skills to clients that they can continue to use long after therapy is over. Given such logic, it seems reasonable to expect that such self-control programs should produce greater stability of change than other alternative approaches.

Whether or not they do produce greater stability remains a matter of controversy. Certainly in the area of obesity, behavioral programs incorporating self-control principles evidence better weight loss maintenance than other interventions (e.g., "crash diets," drugs), but greater variability is evident than would be desired. It remains unclear that such programs outperform behavioral programs without the emphasis on self-control (cf. Brownell, 1982b; Craighead, 1985). In the area of alcohol addiction, the whole issue of maintenance of treatment gains has become inexorably tied-up in the controversy between controlled drinking versus abstinence models (see Pendery, Maltzman, &

West, 1982; Marlatt, 1983; for a discussion of the controversy surrounding the work of Sobell & Sobell, 1978, in particular, and controlled drinking in general). Similarly, smoking cessation appears to be easier to obtain than to maintain (Brownell, 1982b). Self-control approaches appear to perform at least as well as any viable alternative interventions with regard to long-term maintenance, but it is not clear that such standard self-control packages are necessarily superior to more traditional behavioral alternatives. What is clear is that nothing works as well as we would like it to work in this regard.

Marlatt's *relapse prevention* program, referred to as RP, is predicated on the notion that addictive behaviors represent overlearned habits, rather than underlying disease processes (Marlatt & Gordon, 1985). In effect, he argues that various acts, such as excessive eating by someone who is overweight, drinking to excess,

or heavy smoking, represent the sacrifice of long-term goals (e.g., physical appearance, stable interpersonal relationships, vocational achievements, and physical health) in the service of short-term gratifications. Frequently, such decisions are made during periods of life stress or emotional distress (Cummings et al., 1980).

Building on a powerful theoretical analysis by Brickman and colleagues (1982), Marlatt notes that both conventional moral (i.e., "People could do better, but won't because of flaws in their character") and medical (i.e., "People can't help themselves because they have a disease that is beyond behavior control") models of addictive disorders undercut long-term maintenance by instilling all-or-none thinking. In essence, any small slip is seen as a prelude to a major relapse which the individual is either unwilling (moral) or unable (medical) to prevent. As shown in Figure 10–1, individuals failing to make initial cop-

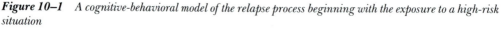

Figure 10–1   *A cognitive-behavioral model of the relapse process beginning with the exposure to a high-risk situation*

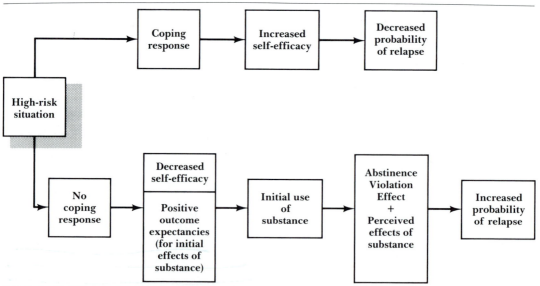

From Marlatt and Gordon (1985).

ing responses in a "high-risk situation" experience decreased self-efficacy (Bandura, 1977) and succomb to the temptation to engage in the maladaptive behavior. The propensity to engage in all-or-none thinking engendered by the moral or medical models leaves the individual unable to distinguish between a minor lapse and a major relapse (Brownell et al., 1986). The person then procedes to making internal, characterological attributions for the slip (Goldstein, Gordon, & Marlatt, 1984). The consequence is that the individual abandons all efforts at self-control in the face of minor lapses, a phenomenon labelled the *abstinence violation effect* (AVE). The paradoxical consequence of those traditional moral or medical models is, according to Marlatt, to increase the likelihood of the very relapses they are trying to forestall.

Relapse prevention programs attempt to utilize self-control and cognitive-behavioral procedures to reduce the risk of relapse. Clients are offered specific help in identifying potential high-risk situations, skills training to help develop compensatory strategies, and practice in applying these strategies (see our discussion of stress-inoculation training later in this chapter). Cognitive decision-making techniques are introduced that look at both short- and long-term consequences of engaging in consumatory behaviors in an effort to overcome the tendency to focus only on the short-term gratification involved. "Programmed relapses" are held with the therapist present, for clients who feel compelled to resume an old habit, in an effort to undercut the pernicious influences of spontaneous relapses (e.g., the client who resumes smoking under unpleasant circumstances is likely to attribute stress-reductive properties to the cigarette). Careful attention is given to coping with initial lapses, rather than allowing them to procede to full-blown relapses (see Brownell et al., 1986, for a discussion of this useful distinction).

The whole notion of programmed lapses remains controversial and, as yet, not demonstrably effective (Brownell et al., 1986). In the

only studies to date to test this component formally, Cooney and colleagues (Cooney & Kopel, 1980; Cooney, Kopel, & McKeon, 1982) found that initial displeasure with smoking and confidence in continued abstinence did not translate into greater long-term abstinence. (A fine line needs to be drawn between preparing a client to deal with possible lapses (and even relapses) in a way that forestalls a full-blown AVE versus giving "permission" for mistakes to occur by implying that they are inevitable.)

Marlatt and Gordon (1985) suggest using a "fire drill" metaphor, in which it is useful to practice escaping from a fire, even though one hopes (and in most instances this hope is realized) that one will never have to use the skills. Brownell (1985) uses a "forest ranger" metaphor in which the client is seen as having a dual task. The first, and preferable task, is to prevent fires (lapses), whereas the second is to put them out if they get started (keeping a lapse from degenerating into a relapse). Finally, attention is paid to promoting a more balanced life-style in an effort to ameliorate the emotional "peaks" and "valleys" that often provoke behavioral loss of control. To the extent that one less dominated by "shoulds" (activities perceived as external demands) and more attuned to "wants" (activities for pleasure or self-fulfillment), this heads off impulsive binges developing in the face of frustration and resentment (Marlatt, 1982).

It is still too early to determine whether RP programs, such as that proposed by Marlatt and colleagues (cf., Marlatt, 1979; Marlatt & Gordon, 1980, 1985), will have a major impact on maintenance rates across the various addictive behaviors. As we shall see when we review the empirical evidence supporting the efficacy of the self-control approaches for obesity, alcoholism, and smoking, the early evidence, although still sparse and not wholly consistent, is generally encouraging. Whatever the ultimate outcome, there can be no doubt that the work has generated more excitement in the field than anything else over the last decade. It builds on a solid theoretical foundation, draws heavily from what is currently known about the psychopathology of the addictive disorders, and expands on procedures that are already at least the equal of anything currently available in the field. The next decade should tell whether the approach's initial promise will be realized, but few innovations have looked so promising over the last several years.

Self-control and Obesity

There are many similarities, and not a few differences, between the problems involved in obesity, alcohol abuse, and smoking, to name only three of the prominent addictive disorders approached from a self-control perspective (cf., Brownell et al., 1986). Detailed descriptions of treatment procedures in each of these three areas would prove to be redundant. Therefore, we have elected to discuss self-control procedures as they apply to obesity in some detail, highlighting at times applications common to the other addictive disorders. In subsequent sections, we will describe the application of self-control principles to alcohol abuse and smoking, albeit in a much more abbreviated fashion.

Recent years have seen an appropriate accentuation of interest in basic metabolic processes and the role of exercise in weight loss. Attention to these factors should be part of any behavioral weight control program. We strongly recommend appropriate medical consultation.

Many people in our culture (certainly persons over 30) have been confronted with the problem of obesity, in some degree at least. In the main, approaches that have relied exclusively on dietary restriction (including the more recent fad diets) have not been very successful (Brightwell & Sloan, 1977; Harris, 1969). Typically, only a relatively small percentage of subjects show marked weight loss, and among those who do, rapid regain of weight is the rule rather than the exception (Brownell, 1982b;

Wilson & Brownell, 1980). The state of affairs has been summarized by Stunkard, who observed that "most obese persons will not stay in treatment for obesity. Of those who stay in treatment, most will not lose weight, and of those who do lose weight, most will regain it" (1958, p. 27). On the other hand, since the 1970s, investigations employing behavioral treatment packages including operant self-control methods have provided some very encouraging results (e.g., Harris, 1969; Mahoney, 1974; Musante, 1976; Stuart, 1967, 1971. See Abramson, 1977; Brownell, 1982b, 1986; Jeffery, Wing, & Stunkard, 1978; and Wilson & Brownell, 1980, for reviews of much of this literature). Some of these results are considered in a later section. The following procedures are derived principally from the writings of Ferster et al. (1962), Stuart (1967, 1971), and Ferguson (1975), as well as our own professional experiences.

Clients may be seen individually, although group treatment is not uncommon (Ferguson, 1975). When practical considerations necessitate only minimal therapist contact, treatment may be presented via a manual. Research findings suggest that frequent therapist-client contacts are *not* necessary for improvement in such a program (Bellack et al., 1974; Hagen, 1974; Hanson, 1974), and in the long run may actually be detrimental. For example, Carter, Rice, & deJulio (1977) found that greater maintenance of weight loss occurred when the therapist was *faded out* during treatment.

Duration of treatment varies considerably from study to study. Jeffery, Wing, and Stunkard (1978) report a range of from 4 weeks to more than 20 weeks. They note that greater weight loss tends to be associated with longer treatment, although the weight loss per week is typically greater over the first several weeks, leveling off as treatment progresses, due in part to physiological processes. As a rule of thumb, 6–8 treatment sessions, once the standard in the field, has tended to be replaced by programs running from 10 to 16 weeks or more, typically with even greater weight loss (Brownell, 1982b).

Initial weight loss has shown remarkable consistency across programs with an average of about 11 pounds in the briefer programs and greater amounts in the longer term programs (Wilson & Brownell, 1980). While this is striking and desirable, there is reason to question the clinical meaningfulness of such a change. It has been estimated that only 5 percent of all obese persons treated will reach their ideal weight (often 30–50 pounds below the level reached at the end of the typical treatment program) and maintain that new weight for a year (Brownell, 1982b; Stunkard, 1980). Weight reductions tend to become more variable over time, suggesting that while some people are regaining, others continue to lose weight.

Exercise   Most therapists (Brownell & Stunkard, 1980; Ferguson, 1975; Stuart, 1971; Thompson, Jarvie, Lahey, & Cureton, 1982) stress the role of exercise in a reducing program. Regular exercise is one of the few factors correlated with long-term success (Cohen, Gelfand, Dodd, Jensen, & Turner, 1980; Graham, Taylor, Hovell, & Siegel, 1983; Katahn, Pleas, Thackery, & Wallston, 1982; Miller & Sims, 1981; Stuart & McGuire, 1978) and numerous studies have shown its impact in terms of improved maintenance of posttreatment weight loss (Dahlkoetter, Callahan, & Linton, 1979; Harris & Hallbauer, 1973; Stalonas, Johnson, & Christ, 1978). As the nutritionist Mayer (1968) has pointed out, inactivity is a major factor accounting for obesity in modern society. Consider the following example. A 150-pound male from his early teens through college has the responsibility for mowing his family's lawn. The task, which requires about one hour per week, is carried out throughout the six-month growing season. After graduation, he obtains a good job and moves into an apartment. At age 28, he marries and purchases his own home, which has a sizable lawn. However, he is now affluent and

hires someone to cut it. He is now age 40. Assuming that in terms of energy expenditure, everything else has been held constant from age 22 to age 40, how much weight has he gained merely as a result of *not mowing his lawn?* Conservatively, 1.5 pounds per year, for a total of 27 pounds (these figures are derived from Ferguson, 1975). This can more than account for the so-called middle-age spread. Roughly comparable gains in weight would result from discontinuation of any of the following activities (carried out 52 weeks per year for a half hour per week): general housework, walking at a moderate rate, engaging in light farm work, or playing golf.

On the other hand, in the short term, losing even a single pound requires an enormous amount of exercise. Thus (again extrapolating from Ferguson, 1975), a 150-pound person jogging at the rate of 5 1/2 miles per hour would be required to jog for close to *six hours* in order to lose a pound. The same individual would have to climb stairs continuously for four hours, and even at a relatively slow rate, starting at sea level, he or she would end up at the cruising altitude of a commercial jet! If the decision is made to incorporate relatively strenuous exercise into the program, it is important that clients be aware of these sorts of data. Obviously, some clients may feel so overburdened by a program that requires self-control activities plus strenuous daily exercises that they may abandon the entire treatment. An alternative might be to have clients begin exercise programs *after* they have lost the desired weight and have gained control over their eating habits.

Internal homeostatic mechanisms play a role in determining the relationship between food intake and subsequent weight status. Different individuals appear to operate at different set points. Reduction of caloric intake may lead to initial weight loss, but is typically followed by rapid alterations in set points, producing increased metabolic efficiency. The result can be a frustrating inability to lose weight after the first several weeks on a weight loss program despite maintaining a reduced caloric intake (Rodin, 1982a, 1982b). In such an event, either further caloric restriction or an active exercise program may be required to overcome this alteration in physiological set point.

A Monetary Deposit

Although the attrition rate in self-control programs may not be as high as that associated with more traditional approaches, it still may present a serious problem. For this reason, during the first session (or before the first session, when logistics allow), the therapist may request that the clients deposit a specified amount of money, to be refunded when the client completes the program (usually the refund is independent of weight loss). Hagen, Foreyt, and Durham (1976) found that deposits as small as $5 reduced attrition, with $20 deposits virtually eliminating dropout. Larger monetary deposits appear to have a larger initial impact, but one that dissipates over time, and contracting in a group context appears to be more effective than setting individual contracts (Jeffery et al., 1983).

Baseline Period

In employing a self-control approach to the treatment of obesity, baseline periods are sometimes omitted. After all, weight would not be expected to vary widely over a one- or a two-week period; ergo, weight immediately before treatment may be considered relatively stable. Further, extended baseline periods may be a source of frustration to clients and may contribute to attrition. On the other hand, *behaviors* leading to obesity would be expected to show considerable variability, depending on which of a multitude of stimulus events influence the client. While information regarding these events could be obtained during treatment, activities associated with treatment might render such information less than valid. Ideally, then, if one wishes to tailor the program to the needs of the individual client (as opposed to presenting a fixed treatment package), a baseline period of from one to two weeks is recommended.

Treatment Goals

Although there is considerable variability among subjects (Jeffery et al., 1978), the average weight loss per week shows some degree of consistency from study to study, approximating one pound per week. Thus, in a typical program, a weekly goal of one pound of weight loss, and certainly no more than two pounds, would seem reasonable. It may also be useful to establish long-term weight-loss goals, and if clients are vague in their specification of such goals, a readily available weight chart may be helpful. However, lest clients become too preoccupied with weight loss, it is important to point out that treatment will focus on *behaviors* that lead to weight loss, and ultimately to maintenance of a desired weight, rather than on weight loss itself.

Self-control procedures for weight loss differ markedly from so-called crash diets that involve levels of deprivation that are usually very aversive to clients. The aversiveness of such diets probably accounts, in part at least, for the oft-noted rapid regain in weight. What clients may learn from such experiences is to equate weight control with pain, which would be expected to detract from their motivation to maintain a desired weight. In contrast, the self-control approach, with its emphasis on small increments in weight loss and psychological interventions that make engaging in appropriate eating behaviors relatively easy (and sometimes pleasant), is a rather painless approach to dieting.

Diet Selection

Although most individuals have some notion of which foods are especially fattening, misconceptions (primarily relating to caloric content) can sabotage any diet. It is not necessary for therapist and client to become expert nutritionists, but knowledge of certain fundamentals is quite helpful. Familiarity with any elementary text on nutrition or, for that matter, a dietary cookbook (e.g., Nidetch's *Weight Watchers' Cookbook*, Hearthside Press, 1966) will suffice. In planning the diet, a food-exchange procedure (Stuart, 1971) may be employed. This involves listing a sizable number of foods of comparable nutritional value from each of several general categories. Meals are then based on selections from differing categories, allowing for greater flexibility.

As the reader undoubtedly knows, there is a plethora of unusual diets on the market; for example, the grapefruit and egg diet and the Atkins diet. All of these diets are controversial, and some may be downright dangerous or even lethal (e.g., the liquid protein diet so popular in the late 1970s). We are not in a position to evaluate the various diets, but if clients wish to go on one of them (obviously, they should not do so without first consulting a knowledgeable physician), there is no reason why self-control principles cannot be incorporated into the program. Thus, Musante (1976) successfully employed self-control procedures in implementing the "Workingman's Diet," which calls for a low intake of fat and carbohydrates and a moderate intake of protein. Under such a program, the client and therapist may wish to set weight-loss goals in excess of one to two pounds per week, depending upon what can *realistically* be expected to be lost under the given diet. Such specific diets require unusually careful monitoring, and a reasonable degree of nutritional sophistication on the part of the client. To illustrate, a young female was very disappointed that she had lost no weight in spite of the fact that she had steadfastly adhered to her low-carbohydrate diet for nearly a month. She made this comment while wolfing down a fruit salad (washed down with a large glass of orange juice!). This, she said was her daily reward for abstaining from eating "high-carbohydrate" items, such as bread and cake. Fortunately, books detailing the nutritional

components of all common foods are readily available, and are recommended if one embarks on such a diet.

Self-control Techniques

1. *Removing undesirable foods from the house.* This includes foods (except those very low in calories) that require no preparation—for instance, breadstuffs, cheese, and many canned goods (Stuart, 1967). Since the purpose of this is to increase the time and effort involved in unplanned eating, this goal may also be accomplished by freezing prepared foods (such as leftovers), which makes it impossible to eat them impulsively.

2. *Modifying consummatory behavior.* In order to decrease the rate of food consumption, while (possibly) increasing the sensuous satisfaction associated with eating, it is recommended (Ferguson, 1975; Harris, 1969; Stuart, 1971) that after the client takes a mouthful of food, he or she return the utensils to the table until that mouthful is swallowed.[2] Additionally, short breaks (five minutes) during the meal may help provide clients with the comforting realization that they do not *have to eat* in the presence of food. Such periods of abstinence may make them aware of feelings of satiety, especially if these periods occur during the latter part of the meal (Harris, 1969).

3. *Stimulus narrowing.* In order to decrease the number of stimuli-eliciting eating behavior, the client is to eat in only one place, such as the kitchen. Food is allowed in no other room in the house. The client is to engage in no other activity (such as watching television, listening to the radio, carrying on a conversation, reading) while eating. The client should be informed that some obese people may be especially susceptible to environmentally, as opposed to viscerally, cued eating (Schacter,

---

[2]The reasonableness of this recommendation should be obvious. However, you should be aware that obese and normally weighted persons probably *do not* differ markedly in eating style in a naturalistic setting (Mahoney, 1975).

1971).[3] Similar procedures have proven quite useful in the treatment of insomnia, with clients trained to restrict bedroom activities to sleeping (and sexual behavior), restricting such activities as worrying, watching television, reading, or eating (Bootzin & Nicassio, 1978; Nicassio & Buchanan, 1981). In the same vein, chronic worriers can benefit from postponing all worrying behavior until a preset time (Borkovec, Wilkinson, Folensbee, & Lerman, 1983).

4. *Changing the stimulus environment.* Clients should take advantage of their particular learning histories by exposing themselves to stimuli that tend to inhibit eating. For instance, if they are too embarrassed to gorge themselves while others are around, they should attempt to eat only in the presence of others. If stimuli associated with the program (such as the diet plan or food or weight charts) have a similar suppressing effect, it would be well to keep them in plain view.

5. *Reinforcement.* Clients should provide self-reward for improvements in eating behavior (eating smaller portions, eating the right foods, etc.). They may also wish to enlist the help of friends or relatives, requesting that they provide social reinforcement for such improvement.

[3]Very briefly, what Schacter and his colleagues (see Schacter, 1971) found was that obese people would eat more food than people of normal weight when the food (or food-related cues) were in plain view. When food was not visible, obese individuals ate less than people of normal weight. Schacter believes that these differences reflect impairment in the functioning of certain parts of the hypothalamus (a lower-brain mechanism that plays a critical role in motivation) that govern cessation of feelings of hunger. Schacter draws a parallel between obese humans and laboratory rats that eat enormous amounts of food following experimental lesions to their hypothalamus, a parallel obese individuals would not find very flattering. Be advised that Schacter's findings and his theorizing are very controversial (see Mahoney, 1975; or Rodin, 1981). The general direction in the field now appears to be one based less on the external-internal distinction and more on the role of differential physiological set points.

6. *Competing responses.* At times when impulsive or otherwise inappropriate eating is likely to occur, the client should engage in competing behavior. Competing responses (e.g., going for a walk or drinking a large glass of water or a diet soft drink) decrease either the availability of food or the desire for food (smoking a cigarette, for obvious reasons, is not strongly recommended). If the competing response is not inherently pleasurable, it should be self-rewarded, although the ideal alternative response is one that is reinforcing in and of itself. The competing response should be initiated as early as possible in the chain that otherwise would lead to eating.

7. *Incorporating shaping principles.* As in the case of all operantly based self-control programs, care must be taken not to overload the client with treatment requirements at any given point in time. The most reasonable way to proceed is to have the client incorporate the above procedures gradually, perhaps one or two per week (Stuart, 1967). Since it is important for the client to experience success at each stage of the program, the procedures should be presented in order of increasing difficulty. This may be accomplished most easily by having the client rank the various tasks according to the likelihood that he or she can successfully carry them out.

You may wonder why the shaping principle is not applied to the amount of weight lost from week to week. There are several reasons for this. First, recall that reinforcement is mainly keyed to behaviors, not weight loss. Second, as we noted, weight loss per week often decreases over the course of the program. Third, even if weight loss did tend to increase from week to week, the increments could easily be obscured by a variety of uncontrollable factors (e.g., a relatively minor change in water retention).

Weekly Sessions

Initially (perhaps over the first three to four weeks of treatment), sessions will be devoted to setting up the program. Thereafter, meetings will be devoted to monitoring clients' progress and making modifications in programs when necessary. After the program is well under way, the decision may be made to wean clients from dependence on the therapist, perhaps by spacing out meetings to every two weeks, then three weeks, and so on. However, until the weight goal has been reached, there is a danger that excessively long periods between meetings may increase the likelihood that clients will lapse into some of their former eating habits. Once clients have begun to approximate their desired weights, naturally occurring reinforcements should do much to maintain appropriate eating behaviors (we note later that booster sessions may be of value). Additionally, it is easier for most individuals to remain on a maintenance diet than on a reduction diet.

Other Techniques

Covert Sensitization Covert sensitization, described in Chapter 8, may be incorporated into the program, especially in connection with foods that the client finds difficult to resist. Recall, however, that research findings bearing on the efficacy of covert sensitization are, at best, equivocal (Little & Curran, 1978). Although we have no good evidence to indicate that the use of the technique would be *detrimental* to treatment, the approach has clearly lost favor with most practicing behavior therapists. If the decision is made to include covert sensitization, an empirical attitude is recommended; that is, if after a few sessions it does not seem to be assisting clients in "turning themselves off" particular foods, it should be abandoned. We also recommend that it be presented to clients as another method of self-control rather than as an externally imposed conditioning procedure.

Use of Contracts Earlier we noted the value of a monetary deposit in reducing attrition. Ordinarily, refunding the money is *not* contingent on weight loss. However, evidence shows (e.g., Harris & Bruner, 1971) that a contractual arrangement wherein so many dollars are re-

turned to the client per pound of weight lost may facilitate weight loss. The amount of money would vary with the magnitude of the deposit, which should be tied to the affluence of the client. One dollar per pound would seem to be a reasonable minimum figure. Naturally, contracts need not involve the therapist directly, or for that matter, the exchange of money. For instance, obese clients may contract with their spouses for rewards such as clothing or special vacations contingent on so much weight loss.

Cognitive Methods Certain of the cognitive methods described in Chapter 9 may readily be incorporated into the self-control program for obesity. Recall the case history data presented in that chapter suggesting that the method of RET may be appropriate to impulsive behavior. Clearly, overeating, or eating inappropriate foods, is often impulsive in nature. Consider the following dialogue:

Therapist: Think back to right before you ordered the chocolate sundae. What did you say to yourself?

Client: Hummm . . . well, that I just *had* to have it! It looked so *delicious.*

Therapist: I'll agree that sundaes do taste good and that eating one would be pleasurable. But do you honestly believe that you *had* to have one. After all, you wouldn't have been in physical pain if you hadn't had it, would you? You wouldn't even have been scared or anxious. Isn't that right?

Client: You are right, of course, but they sure are good.

Therapist: Agreed. But thinking *that* isn't the same thing as thinking that you absolutely have to order one.

Client: I see your point. But, man, when I see somebody else ordering one, I really have trouble controlling myself. I *have* been avoiding those places, you know, like the Dairy Queen, just like you suggested. And it helps a lot. But sometimes you just end up there, like with friends.

Therapist: I understand perfectly. So, in those situations, let's see if we can teach you not to have those self-defeating thoughts that lead to inappropriate eating.

The therapist may now introduce the client to thought-stopping covert assertion, described in Chapter 9.[4] The assertion might be something like "I don't *really* need _____!" or "It will be *great* to be slim."

Another cognitive technique potentially useful in the treatment of obesity involves training clients in the *toleration of noxious stimulation* (Steffen & Myszak, 1978). Many obese individuals (and for that matter, persons with other self-control problems) may be lacking in the cognitive skills associated with tolerance of aversive states such as hunger or they may *view themselves* as lacking such skills. Steffen and Myszak provided pretreatment training in tolerating muscular exertion by having subjects imagine pleasant scenes that were to distract them from their discomfort. In terms of a standard weight-reduction index (weight loss divided by pounds overweight—Mahoney, 1974b), the pretreatment procedure was associated with virtually *twice* the magnitude of improvement obtained for subjects not receiving pretreatment (at posttest and at a three-month follow-up). A somewhat related procedure might be to have subjects abstain from eating for several hours, so they are experiencing a distressing degree of hunger, and then to expose them to desirable but inappropriate foods and have them engage in similar distracting activity. These procedures are akin to the stress inoculation/pain tolerance methods to be discussed later in the chapter.

---

[4]We can make a good case that RET and thought stopping ought to be facilitative in a self-control program for the treatment of obesity. Keep in mind, however, that this is in need of empirical validation.

Assertion Training Individuals with drinking problems often report intense social pressure to "have just one little drink." In terms of *pervasiveness*, the social pressure to imbibe is nothing compared to what dieters regularly experience, especially if their proportions are not elephantine—"You couldn't *possibly* have a weight problem." Indeed, most of us find it difficult to turn down the second portion of a main course our host or hostess spent the better part of the day preparing, or the *first* portion of some exotic dessert in which the preparer takes great pride. Needless to say, in developing responses for such occasions, the emphasis is on diplomacy: "The roast was outstanding, but I promised myself I'd lose ten pounds, so I'll have to turn down that second helping" or "That cream pie looks delicious. You really *are* a superb cook. But, sadly, I must demur. Darn this diet!"

Social Support Much recent work has focused on the impact of spousal involvement in the overall treatment program, with somewhat mixed results. Several studies have found little or no impact of spousal involvement on weight loss (O'Neill, Currey, Hirsch, Riddle, Taylor, Malcolm, & Sexauer, 1979; Weisz & Bucher, 1980; Wilson & Brownell, 1978), whereas in others, typically those giving a greater role to the spouse, such involvement appears to facilitate weight loss and subsequent maintenance (Brownell, Heckerman, Westlake, Hayer, & Monti, 1978; Fremouw & Zitter, 1980; Rosenthal, Allen, & Winter, 1980; Saccone & Israel, 1978). At first, it appeared that the studies that gave spouses greater behavioral responsibilities produced greater impacts (Brownell, 1982b). However, a large-scale effort at replication with a particularly enriched spousal involvement program failed to produce any additive gains (Brownell & Stunkard, 1981). Clearly, more work will be needed to clarify this issue.

Medication Pharmacological agents exist that can produce rapid weight loss but that are almost invariably followed by subsequent relapses and weight gain (Brownell, 1982a). Stunkard (1982) has suggested that such pharmacological agents merely lower body weight set point, which returns to premedication levels once the drug is discontinued. Several studies have attempted to combine behavioral self-control programs with these medications (chiefly fenfluramine, a sympathomimetic amine) in an effort to sustain the rather dramatic weight losses produced by the medications. As shown in Figure 10–2, Craighead, Stunkard, and O'Brien (1981) found somewhat greater weight loss with either drugs alone or the combination of drugs and behavior therapy than for behavior therapy alone over the six-month active treatment phase. A one-year follow-up, however, evidenced a very different pattern, with the behavior-therapy-alone condition evidencing far greater stability of gains than the other two conditions. Brownell and Stunkard (1981) observed a similar pattern in a subsequent study. Craighead (1984) found that introducing fenfluramine part way through a behavioral weight loss program led to greater weight loss than an early introduction, but weight regain was evident once medications were withdrawn, unless behavior therapy was continued, in which case weight regain became evident after behavior therapy was terminated. Finally, neither

Figure 10–2   *Weight changes during 6-month treatment and 12-month follow-up. The three major treatment groups lost large amounts of weight during treatment: behavior therapy (closed circles), 10.9 kg; pharmacotherapy (open circles), 14.5 kg; and combined treatment (squares), 15.3 kg. Behavior-therapy group continued to lose weight for 2 months and then slowly regained it; pharmacotherapy and combined-treatment groups rapidly regained weight. Among control groups, no-treatment (waiting list) group (closed triangles) gained weight; physician's office medication group (open triangles) lost 6.0 kg. Patients in control groups received additional treatment at 6 months and so were not available to follow-up. Vertical lines represent 1 SEM.*

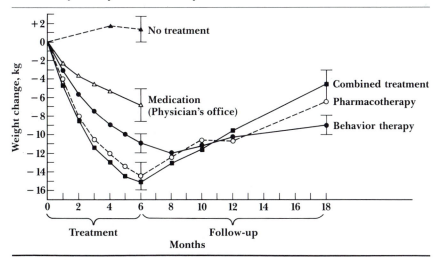

From Craighead, Stunkard, and O'Brien (1981).

Abramson, Garg, Cioffari, and Rutman (1980) nor Brightwell and Naylor (1979) found evidence that combining behavior therapy with drugs blocked postmedication weight gain. These studies indicate that certain drugs can enhance initial weight loss, but not even the inclusion of behavior therapy appears to prevent subsequent relapse.

Relapse Prevention Behavioral weight loss programs, including those with major self-control components, have demonstrated by far the best record with regard to maintenance of weight loss (Craighead, 1985). Nonetheless, maintenance shows considerable variation across individuals, with a tendency for variability to increase following the end of treatment (Brownell, 1982b). Efforts to stabilize weight loss over time with periodic booster sessions have been relatively ineffective (Foreyt, Goodrick, & Gotto, 1981; Wilson & Brownell, 1980).

As noted earlier, Marlatt's relapse prevention model (cf., Marlatt, 1979, 1982; Marlatt & Gordon, 1980, 1985) generated considerable interest in the late 1970s and the 1980s. In brief, Marlatt and colleagues view the propensity to overeat as an overlearned habit that is most likely to benefit from careful training in the application of self-control strategies. Analysis of successful weight loss maintenance has highlighted the importance of the following factors (Craighead, 1985), all consistent with the basic rationale of RP:

1. Exercise
2. Continued self-monitoring of progress
3. Adopting a specific range of weight gain (e.g., three to five pounds) as an indicant to reinitiate self-control strategies
4. Continued use of the specific strategies leading to initial weight loss
5. Spouse support in weight loss efforts
6. Making more general life-style changes
7. Absence of major life events or the capacity to cope effectively with those events and their emotional concomitants

The data linking behavioral relapse and emotional status is particularly compelling, with clear associations between unexpected stressors and strong affective states evident across a variety of studies (Dubbert & Wilson, 1983; Gormally, Rardin, & Black, 1980; Leon & Chamberlain, 1973; Rosenthal et al., 1980).

Relapse prevention programs are of fairly recent origin, so that few studies are available to evaluate its efficacy with regard to weight loss maintenance. Those that have been conducted have been somewhat mixed in their results. Wadden, Stunkard, Brownell, and Day (1984) used RP procedures to block the rapid weight gain that typically follows low caloric diets. Abrams and Follick (1983) found that adding a relapse prevention package to a work setting behavioral program improved long-term results. Sternberg (1985) found a small but significant (five pound) advantage for RP clients over clients treated with a "standard" approach three months following termination of treatment, despite the fact that there had been no differences at posttreatment. Further, twice as many of the "standard" approach clients evidenced weight gain during the follow-up. However, a subsequent effort to replicate using a longer follow-up (Collins, Rothblum, & Wilson, 1986), failed to find any advantage for the RP clients. Perri, McAdoo, Spevak, and Newlin (1984) found better long-term results for a multicomponent maintenance program including relapse prevention features than for a control approach using booster sessions. Finally, Perri, Shapiro, Ludwig, Twentyman, and McAdoo (1984) found superior long-term maintenance with RP, but only when it was combined with extensive telephone and mail contact. Overall, it is probably premature to draw any firm conclusions about the clinical efficacy of RP programs with regard to weight control, but the initial studies have generally been encouraging.

Empirical Studies   Reviews of the literature (Abramson, 1977; Brownell, 1982a, 1982b; Craighead, 1985; Foreyt, Mitchell, Garner, Gee, Scott, & Gotto, 1982; Jeffery et al., 1978; Wilson & Brownell, 1980) point to the value of self-control approaches, typically embedded within larger behaviorally oriented programs, in effecting weight loss. Better than a hundred controlled trials support the efficacy of such general behavior therapy programs (Craighead, 1985), with many incorporating at least some self-control procedures. In studies ranging from Musante's (1976) work with 229 previously unsuccessful dieters, Jeffery, Wing, and Stunkard's (1978) extensive efforts to determine individual difference and treatment program predictors of change, through more recent efforts involving expanded programs, behavior therapy/pharmacotherapy comparisons (Brownell & Stunkard, 1981; Craighead et al., 1981), contracting (Jeffery et al., 1978), and spousal involvement, the following general conclusions can be drawn (adapted largely from Brownell, 1982b; and Craighead, 1985):

1. Behavioral treatment programs are designed for relatively slow weight loss, averaging from 1/2 to 2 pounds per week. Most programs appear to be able to meet this goal with most clients, although attrition is often a problem. The earlier programs were briefer (10–12) weeks) and typically produced an average weight loss of about 11 pounds. More recent programs have typically been longer (from 16 to 25 weeks) and typically report larger losses (from 17 to 24 pounds). While such outcomes are encouraging, they are typically far below the total loss desired.

2. Weight loss is very consistent across programs that vary greatly in terms of types of clients, locations, treatment fees, level of therapist training, and client demographics.

3. Only a few clients continue to lose weight after program termination (approx. 25 percent), but weight loss during the programs is typically well maintained, on the average. The average group mean loss at one-year follow-ups is about 10 pounds, although greater losses have been noted for the longer, more effective programs (e.g., Craighead et al., 1981). Despite the relatively good average maintenance noted, variability in maintenance increases as time passes. There is great interest in the application of Marlatt-type relapse prevention programs to enhance overall maintenance.

Self-control and Alcoholism

The use of alcohol and other drugs is one of the major public health problems in our society. As with obesity, excessive drinking has frequently been approached as a deficiency in self-control behaviors (see Marlatt, 1979; Marlatt & Gordon, 1985). Since the types of programs established for treating chronic drinking within the self-control model are so similar to those adopted to facilitate the control of overeating, we will review only one exemplary program.

Behavioral self-control training (BSCT), developed by Miller and Muñoz (1976), is a comprehensive alcoholism program that includes training in each of the following skills: (1) self-monitoring of alcohol consumption, (2) discussions of appropriate limits for alcohol consumption, (3) drinking rate reduction strategies, (4) self-reinforcement for appropriate self-regulatory behaviors, (5) stimulus control procedures, and (6) training in alternative coping strategies. Many of the same procedures useful in the treatment of obesity are also useful in the treatment of alcoholism, but some areas present special problems. Motivational issues are particularly salient, since many candidates for treatment programs are remanded by the courts or simply responding to pressure from significant others (Brownell et al., 1986). Surprisingly, little systematic work has been done in the area of enhancing motivation for change, although some promising efforts have started to appear

(Prochaska, 1979; Prochaska & DiClemente, 1983, 1984). In recent years, considerable attention has been directed at incorporating explicit relapse control strategies (Marlatt, 1979, 1982; Marlatt & Gordon, 1980, 1985). As with obesity, many instances of problematic relapse appear to occur in response to negative emotional states, including anger and frustration related to interpersonal conflict, as well as direct social pressure (Chaney, Roszell, & Cummings, 1982; Marlatt & Gordon, 1980).

Controlled Drinking Few issues have sparked more controversy in recent years than the debate between proponents of abstinence models versus controlled drinking models (see Marlatt, 1983, for a particularly thoughtful review). Briefly stated, abstinence models, as propounded by organizations such as Alcoholics Anonymous, basically argue that the problem drinker has so lost control of his or her ability to moderate alcohol intake that the only way to maintain sobriety is to abstain from drinking at all. This model is typically tied to a disease concept of alcoholism propounded by Jellinek (1960), which asserts that the pharmacological properties of the substance override any capacity for behavioral self-control. Such popular sayings as "One drink away from a drunk," or "First the man takes a drink, then the drink takes a drink, then the drink takes the man," capture the flavor of this model.

Proponents of controlled drinking argue that drinking behaviors are, like any other behaviors, learned phenomena that respond to all the same internal and external contingencies as any other behaviors. Without getting into a lengthy review of the literature underlying this position (this is ably reviewed elsewhere, chiefly in Marlatt, 1979; Marlatt & Gordon, 1985; and Sobell & Sobell, 1978), it is sufficient to say that considerable evidence has accrued from laboratory studies pointing to the operation of self-fulfilling prophecies (Darley & Fazio, 1980) in the "loss-of-control" drinking phenomenon. That is, if someone believes that one drink will

lead to an uncontrollable binge, the expectation alone may be enough to produce the results (cf., Marlatt, Demming, & Reid, 1973, for an empirical example; or Critchlow, 1986; and Marlatt & Gordon, 1985, for recent reviews).

Efforts to deal with drinking habits, and particularly loss-of-control behaviors, via behavioral (including self-control) procedures have been closely related to this social learning approach to understanding alcohol abuse. Adoption of a social learning theory model of addiction does not compel one to adopt a controlled drinking strategy (Lawson & Boudin, 1985; Marlatt & Gordon, 1985).

One of the first trials focusing on controlled drinking strategies (Sobell & Sobell, 1973a, 1973b) has also become one of the best known, in part because of the controversy surrounding a subsequent reanalysis of their data and methods (Pendery et al., 1982). In brief, Pendery and colleagues reexamined the posttreatment data for the controlled drinking group in the Sobell and Sobell study, obtaining additional archival records and reinterviewing those still accessible, and concluded that the maintenance rates reported by Sobell and Sobell were grossly optimistic. Amid charges of misrepresentation, Pendery and colleagues argued that controlled drinking was greatly overvalued and potentially dangerous. Subsequent independent investigations prompted by the claims of fraud have indicated that the Sobells did not misrepresent their data (Dickens, Doob, Warwick, & Winegard, 1982; Jensen, 1983). Although the success rate for controlled drinking was probably not as benign as originally reported, neither was the rate associated with the traditional abstinence model (a fact omitted from the Pendery et al. critique). Thus, the overall advantage enjoyed by controlled drinking over abstinence did indeed survive the problems in reporting, which were common to both cells (Marlatt, 1983).

There is increasing evidence that the severity of the drinking problem may go a long way to predicting who can handle a controlled drinking program and who cannot (Maisto, Sobell, & Sobell, 1980; Miller, 1980; Polich, Armor, & Braiker, 1980). Although early studies supportive of a controlled drinking approach did deal with the most severe, or "gamma," alcoholic, they typically included only highly motivated volunteers (cf., Sobell & Sobell, 1973a; Vogler, Compton, & Weissbach, 1975). In addition, they often contained design features which reduce confidence in their findings (e.g., absence of fully random assignment to conditions). A more recent controlled comparison between a broad-spectrum behavioral program (including self-management skills training) and that same program with specific training in controlled drinking skills (e.g., blood-alcohol-level discrimination training, responsible-drinking-skills training, and social drinking practice sessions) involving "gamma" alcoholics found significantly poorer performance at six months for the controlled drinking condition in terms of fewer days abstinence and more abusive drinking (only nonsignificant trends were evident at the one-year follow-up) (Fry, Nunn, & Rychtarik, 1984).

On the other hand, studies by several groups (Heather & Robertson, 1981; Miller & Hester, 1980; Pomerleau, Pertschuck, Adkins, & Brady, 1978; Sanchez-Craig, Annis, Bornet, & MacDonald, 1984) have indicated that selected socially stable problem drinkers trained in controlled-drinking techniques typically achieve success rates (defined as abstinence or moderate drinking) of around 70 percent. This is considerably higher than the 46 percent success rate (28 percent abstinence and 18 percent controlled drinking) evident for unselected alcoholics, including "gamma" alcoholics (Polich et al., 1980). The larger issue appears to be one of discriminating subtypes within the larger population of alcoholics (cf., Marlatt, 1983). If a distinction is made between *problem drinkers* (cf., Lang & Marlatt, 1982)—those who have experienced problems with their use of alcohol but who have not evidenced signs of physical dependence—versus the socially and, occasion-

ally, physiologically deteriorated "gamma" alcoholics, then the former group, but not the latter group, may be potential candidates for a controlled-drinking intervention.

Empirical Literature As for obesity, the controlled literature evaluating the efficacy of self-control approaches to the treatment of alcoholism is voluminous and will not be comprehensively evaluated here. Rather, the interested reader is directed to reviews by Brownell (1982a), Lawson and Boudin (1985), and Marlatt (1979). In general, focused programs such as Miller and colleagues' BSCT program (Miller, 1978; Miller & Muñoz, 1976) may be every bit as effective as more time-consuming multifaceted treatment programs (Miller & Taylor, 1980; Miller, Taylor, & West, 1980). Miller and Hester (1980) have calculated average improvement rates at three-month and six-month follow-ups of 79 percent for BSCT, versus 68 percent for the more encompassing multimodal programs.

One particularly noteworthy study involving specific relapse prevention training was provided by Chaney, O'Leary, and Marlatt (1978), who evaluated the efficacy of providing specific skills training designed to forestall relapse in high-risk situations for inpatients going through an abstinence-focused alcohol treatment program. Skills training in this design involved a complex package of instruction, modeling, behavioral rehearsal, and coaching (both for actual behaviors and cognitive reappraisals), with specific problem-solving strategies based on D'Zurilla and Goldfried's (1971) stepwise analysis of problem-solving. Results, based largely on self-report, indicated that patients receiving the additional coping skills training evidenced decreased duration and severity of relapse episodes over a one-year follow-up, relative to patients in either an attention-control or no-additional-treatment group. The authors caution that the skills training program was not designed to carry the full weight of clinical change, but did seem to be an important adjunct to the existing in-patient treatment program (note that that program held abstinence, rather than controlled drinking, as a goal).

Clearly, problem drinking can be approached from a self-control perspective. It appears to be at least as effective as other viable alternatives (Brownell, 1982b; Marlatt, 1983). As for obesity, the results are far from wholly satisfying, although, unlike obesity, the problem seems to be as much one of maintaining promising changes as it is producing them in the first place. Whether the explicit incorporation of relapse prevention strategies, such as those developed by Marlatt and colleagues (Marlatt, 1979, 1982; Marlatt & Gordon, 1980, 1985), with enhance efficacy in this regard remains to be determined, but again, the initial findings appear promising.

Self-control and Smoking

Cigarette smoking, like overeating, is widespread, clearly a health hazard, and not readily eliminated through psychological interventions. Self-control procedures for the reduction or elimination of smoking behaviors correspond closely to those used for the treatment of obesity. That is, typical self-control behavioral treatment strategies make extensive use of procedures such as self-monitoring, monetary deposits, stimulus control procedures, stimulus narrowing, and self-reward procedures. Recent studies have suggested that the instillation of exercise programs as a competing behavior and life-style change may facilitate long-term maintenance (Koplan, Powell, Sikes, Shirley, & Campbell, 1982; Oldridge, Donner, Buck, Jones, Andrew, Parker, Cunningham, Kananaugh, Rechnitzer, & Sutton, 1983). In recent years, considerable attention has been paid to efforts to prevent relapse.

There is little doubt that behavioral programs, typically including self-control com-ponents, can be effective in producing significant reductions in initial smoking rates (Brownell, 1982b; Lichtenstein & Brown, 1980). Nonetheless, it remains unclear whether those rates exceed the rates associated with other interventions. The greater problem involves the long-term maintenance of induced change (Bernstein, 1969; Bernstein & McAlister, 1976; Hunt & Bespalec, 1974; Hunt & Matarazzo, 1973; Keutzer, 1968; Lichtenstein & Danaher, 1976; Ockene, Hymowitz, Sexton, & Broste, 1982). For instance, in the mid-1970s, Hunt and Bespalec (1974) summarized data from over 80 studies and noted that fewer than one-third of those abstinent at the conclusion of treatment were able to maintain abstinence in the long term. By the end of the decade, Lichtenstein and Brown (1980) were able to cite a significantly higher success rate for behavior therapy augmented by self-control procedures, but even longer-term studies (e.g., three- to four-year follow-ups) suggest only moderate stability of change (Colletti, Supnick, & Rizzo, 1982).

Early studies typically found reductions in smoking frequency to a variety of self-control variants (e.g., Lawson & May, 1970; Powell & Azrin, 1968; Azrin & Powell, 1968; Sachs, Bean, & Morrow, 1970; Chapman, Smith, & Layden, 1971). However, these reductions were frequently nonspecific (Lawson & May, 1970), not well maintained after treatment (Bernstein, 1968; Azrin & Powell, 1968; Powell & Azrin, 1968) or weakened by problems in the study design (Sachs et al., 1970; Chapman et al., 1971).

More recent programs have tended to be longer in duration, provide more extensive training in self-control principles, and focus more intensely on maintenance enhancing strategies, with somewhat more, but still not wholly, satisfying results (Brownell, 1982b; Lichtenstein & Brown, 1980). For example, Sommer, Schmid-Methfessel, and Seyfferth (1984) found a full self-control program superior to a self-monitoring control alone. Colletti and Kopel

(1979) and Colletti and Supnick (1980) similarly found evidence of differential initial smoking reduction and greater short-term maintenance using self-control programs. Utilization of contingency contracting appears to enhance treatment effects (Spring et al., 1978), as does the provision of an explicit client treatment manual (Glasgow, 1978). Nonetheless, the problem of long-term maintenance remains, as Colletti et al. (1982) found three- and four-year abstinence rates of only about 24 percent. Whether such a long-term finding is seen as impressive remains a matter of interpretation. The authors did, however, note that overall smoking behaviors were only about 56 percent of the pretreatment baseline, which sounds like a respectable decrement.

Several studies have attempted to determine whether the inclusion of specific relapse prevention strategies, typically, but not invariably, modeled after Marlatt and Gordon (1985), would reduce posttreatment relapse. The findings have been somewhat mixed, but on the whole, still encouraging. Thus, Hall, Rugg, Tunstall, and Jones (1984) found reduced relapse over a one-year follow-up when they examined their own idiosyncratic skills training relapse prevention program against a discussion control. Killen, Maccoby, and Taylor (1984) also found positive effects for a relapse prevention program. Brown, Lichtenstein, McIntyre, and Harrington-Kostur (1984) found similarly positive maintenance enhancement using a Marlatt-type program in an initial pilot study but were unable to replicate that finding in a more carefully controlled trial contrasting RP plus nicotine fading (see following) with nicotine fading alone. Finally, Supnick and Colletti (1984) found no evidence of relapse prevention (and some suggestion of even poorer maintenance) for a Marlatt-type program following standard behavioral training. Whether or not any of these trials have been executed adequately enough to give a fair test to the relapse prevention strategies remains an open question.

Clearly, more work is needed to determine the ultimate utility of relapse prevention programs in the control of smoking.

Three related approaches merit mention. These include *controlled smoking*, *nicotine fading*, and *rapid smoking*. Each will be discussed in turn.

Controlled Smoking Controlled smoking (Frederiksen, 1979) involves a deliberate reduction in three aspects of smoking behavior: (1) nicotine content of the cigarettes smoked, (2) number of cigarettes smoked over a given day, and (3) the amount of each cigarette smoked. Typically, the program calls for a 50 percent reduction in each of these three aspects. Various self-control procedures, particularly stimulus control and self-reinforcement strategies, are used to achieve these reductions. Glasgow, Klesges, Godding, and Gegelman (1983) compared controlled smoking, controlled smoking plus carbon monoxide feedback, and a delayed treatment control, adding a Marlatt-type relapse prevention component to the controlled smoking programs. Smokers in both active treatment conditions successfully reduced nicotine levels, numbers of cigarettes smoked, and amount of each cigarette smoked, with changes largely maintained through a six-month follow-up. Carbon monoxide feedback did not enhance controlled smoking efficacy. In a subsequent study, Glasgow, Klesges, Godding, Vasey, and O'Neill (1984) essentially replicated the earlier efficacy of the controlled smoking program, again finding little additive advantage for the carbon monoxide feedback. In addition, some evidence showed that a gradual program was superior to an abrupt one. Overall, these studies suggest that controlled smoking may have a useful role to play, but the brevity of the existing follow-ups (none was longer than six months) gives reason for continued caution in interpreting these findings.

Nicotine Fading Nicotine fading (Foxx & Brown, 1979) involves decreasing nicotine content over time in an effort to reduce dependence on the substance. Typically, nicotine fading is presented within the context of a larger self-control program. Several studies (Beaver, Brown, & Lichtenstein, 1981; Foxx & Brown, 1979) have presented evidence that such a combination can facilitate both subsequent smoking reductions and abstinence.

Rapid Smoking Among the behavior interventions aimed at reducing smoking, rapid smoking has emerged as a particularly promising approach (Danaher, 1977; Lando, 1976; Lichtenstein, Harris, Birchler, Wahl, & Schmal, 1973; Pechacek & Danaher, 1979). The procedure requires that the subject take a draft of smoke (i.e., a "drag") every 6 seconds or so (Danaher, Lichtenstein, & Sullivan, 1976) while focusing on negative subjective experiences. Subjects are asked to continue until they feel they are unable to take another puff (or until a specific period has elapsed, perhaps 8–10 minutes). Results obtained by Lando (1976) are typical: one to two weeks after treatment, nearly 80 percent of his subjects were abstinent. At the one-month follow-up, the figure was 57 percent, and at six months, 43 percent. Among subjects assigned to nonaversive smoking (one puff every 30 seconds), the number abstinent stayed around 27 percent through the six-month period, with comparable results for subjects who smoked at their own pace during the treatment period.

Recall that Chapman and associates (1971) combined self-control with shock-based aversive conditioning with apparent success. In a parallel investigation, Danaher (1977) examined the effects of combining rapid smoking and self-control. Habitual smokers were assigned to one of four 3-week treatments: rapid smoking plus self-control, rapid smoking plus filler discussion, normally paced smoking plus self-control, normally paced smoking plus filler discussion. Following treatment, subjects in all four conditions were averaging smoking rates no more than 8 percent of their preexperimental level. By 13

weeks, the normally paced discussion subjects had returned to nearly 90 percent of baseline. Rapid smoking plus discussion led to the most improvement at the 13-week follow-up: less than 25 percent of the pretreatment baseline. Interestingly, rapid smoking *plus* self-control showed an average rate at 13 weeks of between 40 and 50 percent. That is, self-control appeared to *detract* from the positive effects of rapid smoking, perhaps, as Danaher suggests, because self-control involved the acquisition of too many skills. The group roughly equivalent to a self-control-alone group (self-control plus normal smoking) showed a smoking rate of about 60 percent of baseline at the 13-week follow-up, a relatively unimpressive figure. Earlier writers had expressed concern regarding the safety of rapid smoking (Hauser, 1974; Horan, Hackett, Nicholas, Linberg, Stone, & Lukaski, 1977; Horan, Linberg, & Hackett, 1977), but more recent studies (e.g., Hall, Sachs, Hall, & Benowitz, 1984) have largely laid this concern to rest.

In conclusion, available evidence would seem to indicate that operantly based self-control procedures are of at least some value in helping people reduce smoking behavior. The Danaher results notwithstanding, such procedures, perhaps in concert with multifaceted behavioral programs or combined with aversive conditioning procedures (specifically, rapid smoking) appear to hold promise, provided care is taken not to overwhelm clients with an excessive number of self-control instructions. Clearly, however, additional research is still needed, particularly in the area of producing stable change not as subject to subsequent relapse.

Self-control and Study Behavior

The practitioner, especially the school psychologist or the member of a university counseling service, frequently encounters students with study problems. Often the difficulty is a function of insufficient time devoted to studying and inefficient study habits (Heffernan & Richards, 1981). For such students, participation in the kind of program presented below may be very helpful.

At the outset, we should mention that the literature supporting the efficacy of self-control as applied to academic problems is not nearly as impressive as the literature supporting the self-control of obesity (see Kirschenbaum & Perri, 1982; or Richards, 1981; for recent reviews). In fact, we are aware of a sizable number of unpublished reports containing negative results. For the most part, these studies were methodologically sound, and we are inclined to think that subject selection was a major problem. That is, the fact that a student volunteers to participate in such an investigation in no way ensures that his or her academic difficulties stem primarily from poor study habits. Any of the following factors may be far more important:

1. The student has unrealistic goals, for example, straight As in a highly competitive university. (Recall the case of the would-be medical student presented in Chapter 9, illustrating RET.)

2. The student has inadequate prior academic preparation, associated perhaps with substandard schooling. Remedial instruction would be in order.

3. The student is lacking in verbal intelligence. Such a conclusion should be reached only after careful consideration of all available evidence. All too often individuals are condemned to a career of academic and professional underachievement as a result of advice rendered on the basis of a single administration of an intellectual aptitude test. If verbal intelligence really is lacking, appropriate academic and career counseling is in order.

4. The student does not personally value his or her present academic goals. Some students select majors thay personally dislike because of parental pressure. In such cases, assertion training (Chapter 3) might be in order. Many stu-

dents select a major or course of study on the basis of a whim and subsequently find that what they are learning is of little interest to them. Here, career counseling might be useful.

Clearly, to the extent that the aforementioned factors operate among the subjects volunteering for a self-control study, one can anticipate unimpressive group data. Another very important consideration, more apropos to the counselor than to the researcher, pertains to students' primary motivation for seeking help. As any experienced therapist in an academic setting well knows, often students with problems not related to academic matters will use a study problem as a "safe" entry into therapy, hoping that the therapist will ask questions that are more pertinent to what is really troubling them.

Nonetheless, there is general consensus that training in self-control study skills can enhance performance for many students (see Kirschenbaum & Perri, 1982; Richards, 1981; Ronnback, 1983). If after careful consultation with the client the aforementioned factors can be ruled out as major causes of poor academic performance, the therapist may turn to self-control methods. The procedures present in this section are adapted mainly from the writings of Fox (1962), Goldiamond (1965), Beneke and Harris (1972), Richards, (1985), Watson and Tharp (1977), as well as from our own experiences.

Baseline

A period of one week is probably adequate. The client should record the total time allocated to studying during a given period, the total time spent in actual studying, where the behavior occurred, and surrounding events (distractions, reinforcements for studying, competing responses). With this information, the therapist can determine to what extent the problem is one of poor stimulus control, inadequate reinforcement, or ineptitude in dealing with the subject matter.

Treatment Goals

As with obesity, goals exist at several levels. Long-term goals include a better appreciation of the subject matter, adequate grades in present and future course work, and graduation. Short-term goals involve the successful completion of periods of effective study. Initially, periods of study should be relatively short (perhaps 10–20 minutes), depending on the individual and the material, with the duration increasing a few minutes each day. As we have noted, many persons with study problems set short-term goals that are unrealistically high. We should mention that unrealistic goals frequently arise from the need to cover an entire term's material the night before the final examination. While students in this predicament might be given a few tips on efficient study techniques (presented below), this is hardly the time to begin a self-control program, which emphasizes modest, incremental goals. A far more propitious time would be the beginning of the new semester.

Self-control Techniques

1. *Changing the stimulus environment.* Most often this involves selecting a study area where undesirable competing behaviors are unlikely to occur. If the client tends to be distracted by other people while at the library or fraternity house, he must find another location where he may study in solitude. On the other hand, he may regularly avoid studying by sleeping, in which case a more suitable locale might *be* the library, where such behavior is less likely to occur. For most people, however, a quiet, well-lighted room is more desirable.

2. *Cue strengthening.* The student should select one study area (a desk) in the room, which is to be used exclusively for studying. Only those materials directly relevant to the study task at hand should be on the desk. In time, stimuli associated with the study area will become powerful, discriminative stimuli for studying.

3. *Reinforcement.* The initial subgoal of 10–20 minutes is based on the assumption that most people can study for such durations without experiencing aversive consequences, such as boredom. Naturally, the precise duration will have to be tailored to the individual on the basis of his self-report. The major point is that he should attempt to avoid exceeding his limit at any stage in the program. Overstudying leads to aversive consequences that only negatively reinforce studying. Fox (1962) has suggested that once the student begins to experience discomfort, he should leave the area, but before doing so, he should complete some easy part of the lesson (rereading a page). It is probably best, however, that he leave *before* experiencing discomfort.

The client should reward himself immediately after completing the desired segment of study behavior. Rewards might include a piece of candy, calling a friend, and the like. As Watson and Tharp (1977) have suggested, a good reinforcer might be engaging in the behavior that in the past has competed with studying ("girl watching" is their example). At what point the client should return to the study area must be worked out on an individual basis. Certain individuals may be sufficiently "revitalized" after a break of only a few minutes, whereas for others, initially at least, no more than one or two study periods per day can be tolerated. As a rule of thumb, if successive study periods tend to be shorter and shorter during a given day, the rest intervals are probably too brief.

Improving Study Efficiency Thus far, we have discussed methods for increasing the amount of time the client spends in study behavior. Now we shall focus on tactics of studying designed to increase what the client is able to learn over a fixed period of time.

The SQ3R method (Fox, 1962; Beneke & Harris, 1972, based on Robinson, 1946) is one means for increasing study efficiency. The client is instructed to begin by *surveying* (S) the material to be covered, attending to chapter and section headings and summaries and to concluding paragraphs. Following this cursory survey, the client is to take the first subheading or introductory sentence and turn it into a *question* (Q), proceeding to *read* (R) the material to follow, in order to answer the question. For example, the preceding subheading might be transformed into "What are the specific ways for improving study efficiency?" (Q). After the client has *read* (R) the section, he or she is to engage in *recitation* (R) of the material, which would involve answering the above question (e.g., "The SQ3R method is one way to increase efficiency. It involves . . ."). The last phase involves *reviewing* (R) the material. Thus, SQ3R stands for Survey, Question, Read, Recite, and Review.

Beneke and Harris (1972) discuss two additional aspects of overall academic skill—the taking of notes and examination performance. As they point out, students tend to err in one of two directions in note taking. Either they attempt to take notes verbatim (which means they are so busy writing that they miss essential points), or they fail to take any notes. Beneke and Harris suggest using outlines and then revising the notes the same day. Some people have difficulty in outlining, so it might be very helpful for the therapist to present a tape or a portion of a typical lecture, having the client make notes in outline form and then, afterward, presenting the therapist with a good outline of the same material.

Debilitating test anxiety is a commonly observed phenomenon. Methods for dealing with this problem (for instance, systematic desensitization) are to be found elsewhere in this text. Unrelated to anxiety, the client may be in need of instruction in testmanship. For example, for essay questions, the client might be asked to write answers (beginning with a brief outline of what is to be said) under simulated examination conditions. She might also be provided with sample answers as models. For objective exams, she might be instructed to go through the exam fairly rapidly, answering only questions she is reasonably certain of (thus providing her with

an initial success experience and ensuring that she not get bogged down by a few difficult items). Following this, she might go through the exam again, this time answering questions she is moderately sure of, and so on. It should be pointed out that the desirability of guessing depends on whether the test involves a penalty for guessing.

Other Techniques

The cognitive modeling approach provided by Meichenbaum and his colleagues (see Chapter 9) may be incorporated into the program. Thus, the SQ3R method may be presented in this way, with the therapist going through a brief chapter or section of a text, verbally modeling thoughts associated with efficient study. The therapist may also provide a cognitive model for taking an examination, incorporating several of the techniques presented in this text. In the following example, the client sits next to the therapist, who is in a simulated examination situation. A third person, acting as the instructor, soberly hands the therapist-as-student an examination:

Instructor: This is an important examination, so do your best . . . good luck.

Therapist as Student (thinking aloud): This *is* important. . . . I've *got* to do well . . . wait a minute . . . not so! . . . I *want* to do well, and that is different. The first question is easy . . . Elizabeth 1 . . . the answer is C . . . I'll just circle it. Question number 2 . . . hmmm . . . hell, it could be any of the first three alternatives . . . this is hard . . . I might fa-STOP!!! I'll probably do *all right,* and it *isn't* a matter of life and death, so I'm gonna take a minute to relax. (Therapist models cue-controlled relaxation) *Now* I feel better. I'm gonna go through the exam and just answer the easy ones, and then go back. Let me see, the next question has got to be the Spanish Armada, so I'll circle A. Okay, what's next . . . hmmm, could be Charles I or Charles II . . . I'll skip it for now and get back to old Charlie later. Let's see, who was the one who shook up Parliament . . . got it, Cromwell! Circle D. What's next? Was that Mary a Tudor or a York? Had to be Tudor, so circle B. I'm doing okay . . . gonna spend a few seconds relaxing. (Therapist models 30 seconds of cue-controlled relaxation) This is almost fun.

In the previous section, we pointed to the value of assertion training in assisting obese individuals to refuse offers of excessive or forbidden food. Assertion training may also be helpful for clients with study problems, particularly in dealing with friends, roommates, and others who are likely to provide tempting competing activities; for example, "Hey, Bill, you can hit the books tomorrow. There's this really great X-rated flick at the Fine Arts! You know you really get off on those movies!" An effective response to role-play might be "I'd like to go, Susan, but how about tomorrow instead. Then I'll be caught up."

Self-control for Depression

Rehm (1977) has provided an interesting conceptualization of depression in terms of deficiency in self-control. Following Kanfer (1971), Rehm believes depressed people show deficits in monitoring (selectively attending to negative events), in self-evaluation (setting unrealistically high goals), and in self-reinforcement (emitting high rates of self-punishment and low rates of self-reward). Rehm's model incorporates elements of Beck (1967, 1976), as well as Lewinsohn (Lewinsohn, 1974, relates depression to a deficit in social skills that leads to insufficient reinforcement). Fuchs and Rehm (1977) have provided a test of the Rehm model with female volunteers. The six-week self-control program involved sequential presentation of instruction in self-monitoring, self-evaluation, and self-reinforcement. On a variety of measures, self-control subjects showed significantly greater improvement than non-specific or nontreatment control subjects on several relevant measures, including the MMPI–D scale, the Beck Depression Inventory, and a measure of group interaction. Group differences were generally maintained at a six-week follow-up. The magnitude of the group differences are somewhat striking, as can be seen in Table 10–3.

In a second project, Rehm, Fuchs, Roth, Kornblith, and Romano (1979) found the self-control approach superior to social skills training on a variety of measures, again in a community volunteer sample. In a pair of dismantling studies, Rehm, Kornblith, O'Hara, Lamparski, Romano, and Volin (1981) found maximum change associated with the self-monitoring component alone, while Kornblith, Rehm, O'Hara and Lamparski (1983), found that the complete self-control package was again outperformed by its components, as well as by a dynamic group psychotherapy. Finally, Rehm, Lamparski, Romano, and O'Hara (in preparation) found the full self-control package comparable to both a cognitively targeted self-control approach and a behaviorally targeted self-control approach, with all three conditions superior to a waiting list. In a companion study, Rehm, Kaslow, Rabin, and Willard (1981) found no differences between the full self-control package and both cognitively and behaviorally targeted self-control packages. Further, no specific differences were evident on cognitive and behavioral variables included as potential mechanism measures.

In one final trial not directly conducted by Rehm's group (although it was conducted by one of his former students), Roth, Bielski, Jones, Parker, and Osborn (1982) contrasted comprehensive self-control therapy versus combined self-control therapy plus antidepressant medication (desipramine). Twenty-six community volunteers were treated over a 12-week interval in individual therapy. No differences were apparent at posttest or at three-month follow-up, although the combined self-control plus pharmacotherapy group appeared to evidence more rapid symptom reduction.

Table 10–3 **Major Response Measures Employed by Fuchs and Rehm**

Measures and Condition	Pretest	Posttest	Follow-up
Beck Depression Inventory[a]			
Self-control	21.38	4.75	6.12
Nonspecific	23.60	14.30	11.67
Waiting list	23.20	21.40	—
MMPI–D scale[a]			
Self-control	85.25	59.88	59.88
Nonspecific	83.90	77.40	71.11
Waiting list	80.90	81.60	—
Group interaction activity			
Self-control	7.25	27.50	—
Nonspecific	6.60	14.00	—

[a]Note that on both the Beck Depression Inventory and the MMPI–D scale, prior to treatment, subjects would be characterized as moderately depressed. Following treatment, every subject in the self-control group scored in the normal range on both measures.
From Fuchs and Rehm (1977).

On the whole, this series of studies appeared to provide some support for the efficacy of self-control therapy, although the general reliance on waiting list controls as the primary control procedure did not provide a particularly stringent test to pass. Only in Rehm et al. (1979) and Kornblith et al. (in press) was the approach directly contrasted with an alternative treatment approach, evidencing superior results relative to social skills training in the first trial and failing to excede dynamic group psychotherapy in the second. Further, the approach has yet to be directly compared with a tricyclic pharmacotherapy, the current standard of treatment (the Roth et al. trial evaluated the additive efficacy of tricyclics combined with self-control). Combined with the exclusive reliance on community volunteer samples and inexperienced graduate student therapists (other than Roth et al., 1982), the tests of self-control therapy have, perhaps, lacked in clinical realism. Although the findings to date have been generally supportive, it would seem that more powerful comparisons in fully clinical populations would be useful in determining the clinical utility of the approach.

Stress Inoculation

Recall that in Chapter 2 we discussed anxiety management training (Suinn, 1975; Suinn & Richardson, 1971), a treatment package designed to help clients cope with anxiety. Recall also the approach and interpretation of systematic desensitization provided by Goldfried and Trier (1974). Both of these are *self-control* approaches to the management of maladaptive emotion, and they stand in sharp contrast to traditional approaches (e.g., Wolpe's version of systematic desensization), which emphasize some manner of deconditioning that is assumed to generalize in more or less automatic fashion in *in vivo* target situations. *Stress inoculation* (Jaremko, 1984; Meichenbaum, 1977; Meichembaum & Cameron, 1972; Meichenbaum & Jaremko, 1982; Meichenbaum & Turk, 1976; Novaco, 1975) is also aimed at helping clients cope with aversive states by enhancing their self-control skills.

The method of stress inoculation involves three relatively discrete phases. Phase 1, which is *educational* in nature, provides clients with a cognitive-behavioral conceptualization of their response to stress, more or less along the lines of the A–B–C paradigm presented in the preceding chapter. Thus, clients are told that maladaptive emotionality (anxiety, anger, reaction to physical pain) has an important and *modifiable* cognitive component, and more specifically that self-statements play a critical role in such states. In this stage, clients are asked to monitor their self-statements.

During Phase 2 of the stress inoculation program, the *acquisition* phase, clients are taught specific coping skills, including relaxation (perhaps pregressive muscle relaxation phased into cue-controlled relaxation—see Chapter 2) and coping self-verbalizations similar in some respects to the self-instruction Meichenbaum and his colleagues used in dealing with psychotic and impulsive behavior (see Chapter 9). Meichenbaum (1977) conceptualizes the stress experience in four sequential stages. The first is preparatory: clients are encouraged to offer self-statements that would assist them in getting ready for a stressful experience or encounter. The preparatory phase might correspond, *in vivo*, to the moments preceding making a speech or asking the boss for a raise, or, if a person is fearful of driving across high bridges, approaching such a bridge in an auto. Examples of these self-statements, and those associated with the remaining stages, are presented in Table 10–4.

In Stage 2, clients engage in self-statements designed to manage negative emotion when they begin the actual confrontation with the stressor (e.g., beginning to address the audience, finding yourself in the boss's office, actually asking for the raise, feeling the car angle upward as you approach the summit of the bridge). In Stage 3, the self-statements are aimed at coping with elements of the stressful situation that might elicit a sense of being overwhelmed or panicked (e.g., the audience responds to your initial joke with cold indifference; the boss glares at you; you realize the car is now 10 stories above cold, deep water, and

there is no turning back).[5] In the final stage, clients are instructed in reinforcing themselves for coping effectively.

Once clients have shown some mastery in the use of the aforementioned self-statements, the final phase of stress inoculation is introduced. Clients are exposed to the stressful experience and are encouraged to use what they have learned in the first two phases. The stressful experience, often presented in graduated fashion, may be imaginal (Suinn, 1975) or it may be real, as in unpredictable electric shock (Meichenbaum & Cameron, 1972). This is referred to as the *application* phase.

There is evidence that Meichenbaum's stress inoculation package is useful in dealing with phobic reactions (Meichenbaum & Cameron, 1972) and general states of chronic overarousal and stress (cf. Long, 1985; Lustman & Sowa, 1983). Similarly, efforts have been made at utilizing stress inoculation training to enable people to deal with particularly stressul occupations, such as police work or adjustment to Marine boot camp, albeit with mixed results (Novaco, 1977b, 1979; Novaco, Cook, & Sarason, 1978; O'Neill, Hanewicz, Fransway, & Cassidy-Riske, 1982; Sarason, Johnson, Berberich, & Siegel, 1979). In general, however, stress inoculation has been applied to two areas that have received considerably less attention in the behavior therapy literature: self-defeating anger and physical pain.

---

[5]When working with a specific phobia, it would be useful to adapt the self-statements in Table 10–4 to that phobia. For instance, as the bridge phobic approaches the bridge, he or she might say, "Just relax, you've driven across bridges before." During the confrontation phase, he or she might say, "Take a deep breath. . . . Some anxiety is useful . . . helps you concentrate." During the critical phase, when the client might otherwise panic, he or she might say, "Just look straight ahead" or "You'll soon be over the bridge." When we use stress inoculation, we routinely teach our clients thought stopping. In this instance, thought stopping would prevent such panic-inducing ruminations as, "What if the car goes out of control and I crash through the guardrail!" (See Chapter 9 for a discussion of thought stopping.)

Table 10–4 **Examples of Coping Self-statements Rehearsed in Stress Inoculation Training**

Preparing for a stressor
   What is it you have to do?
   You can develop a plan to deal with it.
   Just think about what you can do about it.
   That's better than getting anxious.
   No negative self-statements: Just think rationally.
   Don't worry: Worry won't help anything.
   Maybe what you think is anxiety is eagerness to confront the stressor.
Confronting and handling a stressor
   Just psych youself up—you can meet this challenge.
   You can convince yourself to do it. You can reason your fear away.
   One step at a time: You can handle the situation.
   Don't think about fear: Just think about what you have to do. Stay relevant.
   This anxiety is what the doctor said you would feel. It's a reminder to use your coping exercises.
   This tenseness can be an ally: A cue to cope.
   Relax: You're in control. Take a slow deep breath.
   Ah, good.
Coping with the feeling of being overwhelmed
   When fear comes, just pause.
   Keep the focus on the present: What is it you have to do?
   Label your fear from 0 to 10 and watch it change.
   You should expect your fear to rise.
   Don't try to eliminate fear totally: Just keep it manageable.
Reinforcing self-statements
   It worked: You did it.
   Wait until you tell your therapist (or group) about this.
   It wasn't as bad as you expected.
   You made more out of your fear than it was worth.
Reinforcing self-statements
   Your damn ideas—that's the problem. When you control them, you control your fear.
   It's getting better each time you use the procedures.
   You can be pleased with the progress you're making.
   You did it!

From Meichenbaum (1974).

Stress Inoculation in the Treatment of Anger

Recall from Chapter 3 our discussion of assertion training as a means of assisting clients in dealing with anger and antisocial aggression. Another promising approach is seen in Novaco's application of stress inoculation to the control of anger (Novaco, 1975, 1976, 1979). In the fashion of an interactionalist, Novaco conceptualizes anger as being jointly determined by an initial provocation, mediating cognitions, the somatic-affective state of the individual (e.g., the individual's anxiety level), and behaviors that may have the effect of escalating any such encounter.

As Novaco notes (1976), anger may have an adaptive as well as a maladaptive function, and initially care should be taken to determine whether anger is indeed a problem. Thus, anger reactions can be viewed with respect to several dimensions (Novaco, 1977a), including frequency, intensity, duration, mode of expression, effect on performance, and effect on interpersonal relationships. Novaco (1975) also developed the Novaco Anger Scale, a multiitem questionnaire similar in structure to the Fear Survey Schedule (the scale, which is presently being revised, now consists of 80 items; respondents rate each on a five-point anger scale). Whether the therapist uses such a scale or not, attending to the aforementioned dimensions will facilitate determining whether the individual's anger is indeed self-defeating and in what circumstances and to what degree.

Having made the decision to treat the client's anger, the therapist can then commence with the first phase of treatment, cognitive preparation. During this phase, the cognitive-affective-behavioral model of anger is discussed with the client. Clients are asked to identify situations that provoke anger, are assisted in distinguishing anger from aggression and justified anger from less justified anger,[6] and are introduced to coping techniques for dealing with conflict and stress. Clients are also asked to keep a diary of anger experiences, noting the frequency and intensity of such experiences and their own proficiency in managing anger in those situations. Clients then assess self-statements that mediate anger (e.g., "I won't let that son of a bitch get away with that"; "He had no right to treat me that way"). Finally, clients are asked to set up a hierarchy of anger-inducing situations that is used during the application phase.

As would be expected, rehearsal of coping self-statements is an important part of the skills acquisition phase. Novaco divides rehearsal statements into four sequential categories as follows:

1. Preparing for a provocation (e.g., "This could be rough, but I can handle it")
2. Impact and confrontation (e.g., "Be cool," and "I'm in control")
3. Coping with arousal (e.g., "I'm getting tight . . . take a deep breath . . . just relax")
4. Subsequent reflection
   a. *Conflict unresolved* (e.g., "Thinking about what happened only makes me upset . . . shut it off")
   b. *Conflict resolved* (e.g., "Good for me, I handled it well") [7]

The anger hierarchy is employed during the application phase. The client is relaxed and is asked to imagine scenes and to signal if anger is experienced. In the presence of such a signal, the client is to use what he or she has learned to cope with or manage the anxiety.

In one investigation, Novaco (1976) compared the treatment package just listed (i.e., self-instruction combined with relaxation training) with relaxation alone and self-instruction alone, with a fourth group serving as attention controls. Treatment effectiveness was evaluated via the anger inventory and by laboratory provocations (imaginal and role-played), as well as self-report and blood pressure indices in actual situations. The most consistent differences were obtained between the combined treatment condition and the attention-control condition (significant for almost every measure). Less consistent improvement was noted for the instruction-alone group, although this group, in general, showed greater gains than the relaxation-only group (the latter showed significant superiority to the controls on self-report of anger in imaginal situations only). No follow-up has been reported.

Novaco (1977) also reported applying his treatment to a 38-year-old hospitalized patient carrying a diagnosis of depressive neurosis. The patient's intense feelings of depression and worthlessness were apparently related in part to his inability to control his anger: he was verbally

---

[6]The term *justified* has moralistic overtones with which we are not comfortable. We would prefer the term *adaptive*.

[7]See Novaco (1977a) for additional examples.

abusive to his children, threatening them (e.g., "I'll knock your goddamn head off") to the point that one of his sons ran away from home. This pattern of undercontrolled verbal aggression was in sharp contrast to the overcontrol he typically showed at work (see Chapter 3 for a discussion of undercontrolled and overcontrolled aggression). Treatment sessions were conducted three times per week for 3 1/2 weeks in the hospital, and following discharge, biweekly over a 2-month period. On the Novaco Anger Inventory, pretreatment to posttreatment reduction of 43 points (more than one standard deviation) was reported. During the course of treatment, the patient also showed marked reductions in clinical ratings of antagonism and anger. In terms of self-rated frequency of anger and degree of anger management, improvement was also apparent. Further, before treatment, the patient had routinely administered physical punishment in response to fighting on the part of his sons. During the 3-month treatment period, only three such incidents were reported.

The approach presented by Novaco seems promising, although as noted by Wilson (1984), it has still yet to be clearly documented in adequately controlled trials. Although Novaco (1977) alludes to the incorporation of assertion procedures in his treatment package, a particularly useful approach might combine stress inoculation and assertion training in a more systematic way.

Stress Inoculation and Pain Control

Traditional approaches to the control of chronic pain, which have been limited primarily to surgical and pharmacological techniques, are often ineffective and frequently have untoward side effects (Fordyce, 1976; Melzack, 1973; Melzack & Casey, 1968). In recent years, psychologists have become increasingly interested in the problems of physical pain.[8] A variety of approaches has been employed, in-

cluding operant conditioning (the Fordyce, 1976, presentation is highly readable and comprehensive), biofeedback (recall, e.g., the work on migraine and tension headaches, or Raynaud's disease), relaxation (e.g., Bovey & Davidson, 1970; Neufeld & Davidson, 1971), and cognitive modification. As Meichenbaum (1977) observes, the cognitive approaches may be divided into two categories: those that stress imagery manipulation, and those that do not. Among the imagery techniques are goal-directed fantasy (e.g., imagining a scene or situation whose content is antithetical to pain, such as a particularly pleasurable or relaxing experience; Horan & Dellinger, 1974; Worthington, 1978) and techniques aimed at acknowledging the aversive sensations, but relabeling those sensations or the context to decrease discomfort (Bovey & Davidson, 1970; Kanfer & Goldfoot, 1966; Kanfer & Seider, 1973). Thus, an individual might relabel pain as numbness or fatigue or imagine the pain has resulted from an injury incurred while carrying out some noteworthy or heroic act (e.g., a football buff imagining being lofted to the shoulders of his teammates amid tumultous applause after scoring the winning touchdown in the Super Bowl). The nonimagery cognitive strategies include somatization—or concentrating on bodily sensations other than pain (e.g., Evans & Paul, 1970)—or focusing on external stimuli to the exclusion of pain (e.g., Kanfer & Seider, 1973).

The stress inoculation approach to pain management, rather than relying on any single strategy, is multifaceted—that is, clients are presented with a variety of such coping devices and select according to their individual needs

[8]As the reader may know, hypnosis has been used as an analgesic for more than a century. Without demeaning the potential value of hypnosis as an approach to chronic pain, it may be said that theoretical and research issues are complex and controversial. A fair treatment of this fascinating subject would require more space than can be reasonably allocated in the present volume.

(Horan, Hackett, Buchanan, Stone, & Stone, 1977; Meichenbaum, 1977; Meichenbaum & Turk, 1976; Turk, Meichenbaum, & Genest, 1983). As usual, stress inoculation treatment begins with an educational phase, including a conceptualization of pain that stresses sensory, affective, and cognitive components of the pain experience (Turk, 1975, cited in Meichenbaum, 1977). Clients may also be instructed to monitor and examine self-statements that exacerbate rather than alleviate the pain experience.

During the coping training phase, clients may be taught relaxation as one means of dealing with tension characteristics of painful experiences, along with the other aforementioned exercises (transformation of pain and context, goal-directed imagery, distraction—Horan et al., 1977; Meichenbaum & Turk, 1976; Turk, 1975). Naturally, this phase also includes instruction in and rehearsal of coping statements appropriate for pain. Turk (1975) also divided such statements into a sequence of four categories:

Preparping for the painful stressor—"What is it you have to do?"; "You have lots of different strategies you can call upon."

Confronting and handling pain—"You can meet the challenge." "Just relax, breathe deeply."

Coping with feelings at critical moments—"When pain comes, just pause; keep focusing on what you have to do." "When the pain mounts, you can switch to a different strategy; you're in control."[9]

During the application phase, subjects are sometimes exposed to the actual pain. Pain induction may involve immersing one's hand in near-freezing water (Horan et al., 1977; Turk, 1976).

Results employing this general approach to pain management are encouraging. For exam-

[9]For additional statements, see Turk (1975) or Meichenbaum (1977).

ple, Turk (1975, 1976) reported successfully employing the technique with ischemic pain (cited in Meichenbaum, 1977), which comes about when circulation in a limb is cut off for any extended period of time (as might occur with a blood pressure cuff). Stress inoculation procedures (or closely related cognitive-behavioral interventions) have been successfully utilized in the treatment of headache (Holroyd & Andrasik, 1978; Holroyd, Andrasik, & Westbrook, 1977; Kremsdorf, Kochanowicz, & Costello, 1981), pain associated with burn injury (Wernick, Jaremko, & Taylor, 1981), dental fears (Klepac, Hauge, Dowling, & McDonald, 1981; Moses & Hollandsworth, 1985), cardiac catheterization (Kendall, Williams, Pechacek, Graham, Shisslak, & Herzoff (1979), and chronic pain (e.g., Hartman & Ainsworth, 1980; Morgan, Kremer, & Gaylor, 1979; Rybstein-Blinchik & Grzesiak, 1979; Turner, 1982).

If stress inoculation does involve actual exposure to physical pain, is such exposure all that is really necessary to teach people to cope more successfully with pain? The results of the investigation by Horan and colleagues (1977) suggest that it is not. Subjects given the cold pressor exposure (a hand in 33 degree Fahrenheit water) showed little increased ability to tolerate pain in a subsequent cold pressor test. In contrast, large improvements were obtained for subjects provided with a combination of coping instructions, although the most improvement was associated with a treatment that combined coping training *and* application training with the cold pressor. Thus, the findings of Horan and colleagues not only point to the limited value of pain experience per se, but also suggest that application training with an actual painful stimulus is of value in facilitating coping with subsequent pain.

In another investigation, Worthington (1978) found that significantly greater pain tolerance was produced in subjects provided with a *choice* of imagined scenes to use in a subsequent cold pressor test than in subjects provided with the content of the scene to be imagined by the experimenter. Surprisingly, whether the content of the imagined scene was pleasant or neutral appeared to make little difference. Less surprisingly, subjects who were instructed to plan specific coping self-statements to use during the pressor test tolerated significantly more pain than subjects who merely repeated descriptions of a model of pain back to the experimenter.

Finally, Vallis (1984) executed a complex decomposition of the full stress inoculation package in an analogue population. In that study, while the full package was clearly better than various controls, the skills acquisition phase, during which clients were given training in various cognitive and behavioral coping strategies, carried the greatest weight of change.

In summary, the stress inoculation procedure appears to hold considerable promise in the self-control of anxiety, anger, and pain.

Whether or not stress inoculation will prove to be of long-term value in clinical situations is, of course, a major empirical question, but the initial findings are generally positive.

Biofeedback

Biofeedback is the name given to a wide variety of procedures wherein some aspect of an individual's physiological functioning is systematically monitored and fed back to that individual, typically in the form of an auditory or visual signal. The individual's task is to modify that signal in order to change that physiological function or process in some way. For example, consider a client who suffers from tension headaches. The therapist attaches electrodes to the client's frontalis (forehead) muscles; the

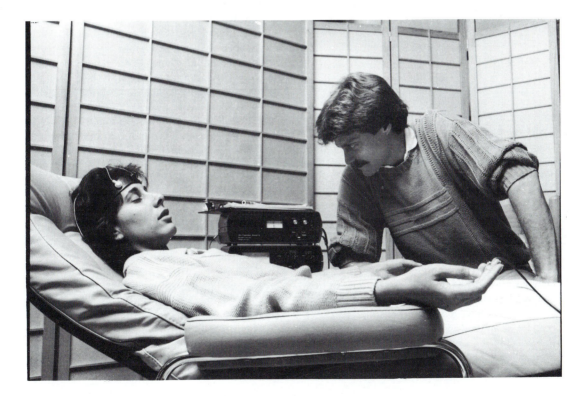

Table 10–5 **Some Physiological Responses and Symptoms Subjected to Attempted Biofeedback Manipulation**

Alpha brain wave activity	Kamiya, 1968; Plotkin, Mazer, & Loewy, 1976
Theta brain wave activity	Sittenfeld, Budzynski, & Stoyva, 1976–1977
Beta brain wave activity	Beatty, 1971
Epileptic brain wave activity	Lubar & Bahler, 1976–1977; Wyler, Lockard, Ward, & Finch, 1976–1977
Heart rate increases and/or decreases	Lang, 1974
Heart rate variability	Lang & Hnatiow, 1965
Cardiac arrhythmias	Weiss & Engel, 1970, 1971
Heart rate control to reduce pain	Sirota, Schwartz, & Shapiro, 1974
Heart rate control to reduce anxiety	Rupert & Holmes, 1978
Heart rate control to reduce phobias	Nunes & Marks, 1975; Prignatano & Johnson, 1972
Galvanic skin response	Kimmel, 1967, 1974a, 1974b
Modification of systolic and/of diastolic blood pressure	Datey, 1978; Benson, Shapiro, Tursky, Gershon, & Stern, 1969; Shapiro, Tursky, & Schwartz, 1970; Shapiro, Tursky, & Schwartz, 1971
Skin temperature reduction to treat migraine headaches	Blanchard, Theobald, Williamson, Silver, & Brown, 1977; Daly, Zimmerman, Donn, & Galliher, 1985; Kewman & Roberts, 1980; Sargent, Green, & Walters, 1972
Raynaud's disease	Blanchard & Epstein, 1978; Freedman, Ianni, & Wenig, 1983; Guglielmi, Roberts, & Patterson, 1982; Jacobson, Manschauk, & Silverberg, 1979; Keefe, Surwit, & Pilson, 1980; Surwit, Pilon, & Fenton, 1978
EMG feedback for "muscle reeducation" (e.g., in the case of partial paralysis following a stroke)	Brudny, Korein, Grynbaum, Friedmann, Weinstein, Sachs-Frankel, & Belandres, 1976a, 1976b
EMG feedback for torticollis	Brudny, Grynbaum, & Korein, 1973
EMG feedback for subvocal speech	Hardyck & Petrinovich, 1976
EMG feedback for stuttering	Guitar, 1975; Lanyon, Barrington, & Newman, 1976

electrodes pick up minute electrical activity associated with contraction of these muscles. These electrical discharges are amplified and sent to a device that emits a tone. The tonal feedback may be of an *analogue* nature—that is, the pitch (or possibly the amplitude) varies with the degree of muscular tension—or it may be *binary,* for example, tension increases cause a tone of constant pitch and loudness, while tension decreases are associated with no tone, in either/or fashion. In the case of analogue feedback, the client's task would be to attempt to maintain a low pitch (or low magnitude). For binary feedback, the client would simply attempt to eliminate the tone altogether. Biofeedback keyed to muscle tension is referred to in the literature as

EMG for muscle-tension headaches	Abramowicz & Bell, 1985; Andrasik & Holroyd, 1980, 1983; Blanchard et al., 1982; Blanchard et al., 1983; Budzynski, Soyva, & Adler, 1970; Carrobles, Cardona, & Santacreu, 1981; Daley, Zimmerman, Donn, & Galliher, 1985; L. H. Epstein & Abel, 1977; L. H. Epstein, Hersen, & Hemphill, 1974; Holroyd, Andrasik & Noble, 1980
EMG feedback to reduce anxiety	Burish, Hendrick, & Frost, 1981; Canter, Kondo, & Knotts, 1975; Lavelle, Lamontagne, Annable, & Fontaine, 1982; LeBoeuf, 1980; Raskin, Bali, & Peeke, 1980; Raskin, Johnson, & Rondestevedt, 1973; Ruppert, Dobbins, & Mathews, 1981; Schandler & Grings, 1976; Townsend, House, & Addario, 1975
EMG feedback for phobias	Budzynski & Stoyva, 1973; Chiari & Mosticoni, 1979; Reeves & Mealiea, 1975; Wickramasekera, 1972
Stomach acidity (pH) (potential treatment for ulcers)	Welgan, 1974; Whitehead, Renault, & Goldiamond, 1975
Functional diarrhea (caused by, say, spastic colon)	Furman, 1973
Encopresis	N. P. Engel, Nikoomanesh, & Schuster, 1974; Whitehead, Burgio, & Engel, 1985
Changes in penile erection	Price, 1973
Homosexuality	Barlow, Agras, Abel, Blanchard, & Young, 1975
Airsickness	Jones, et al., 1985
Asthma	Feldman, 1976; Richter & Bernhard, 1982
Control of visual accommodation	Provine & Enoch, 1975
Vaginal blood flow	Hoon, Wincze, & Hoon, 1977

electromyographic (EMG) feedback (Budzynski, Stoyva, & Adler, 1970; Chesney & Shelton, 1976).

The physiological responses and psychological symptoms that have been subjected to attempts to biofeedback manipulation are virtually without limit (see Table 10–5, which is by no means exhaustive).

Biofeedback did not come into widespread use until the late 1960s. Its acceptance or credibility derives principally from two separate lines of research (Blanchard & Epstein, 1978): (1) studies showing that a variety of presumably nonvoluntary responses could be brought under operant control (e.g., GSR, Kimmel, 1967; the work of Miller and his associates on heart rate, blood pressure, urine formation, and even vaso-constriction in the ear); (2) electroencephalographic (EEG) studies suggesting that alpha brain wave activity could be brought under voluntary control. It should be pointed out that the excitement generated by these early findings was dampened considerably by later studies and applications. First, the tantalizing findings of Miller and his associates were not replicated (see Miller & Dworkin, 1974). Second, the clinical value of GSR control is highly questionable (Blanchard & Epstein, 1978).

Third, the intimation of "mind control" suggested by the early EEG alpha studies remains today little more than a promise. In view of the impact of these alpha studies on the popular as well as on the scientific community, some additional comment is in order. Research by Kamiya (1968, Nowliss & Kamiya, 1970) and B. B. Brown (1970) indicated that alpha brain wave activity normally associated with relaxed wakefulness could be readily brought under voluntary control in human subjects. That is, subjects could be taught to increase their alpha level. In so doing, subjects commonly reported an experience of relaxation or "letting go" similar to subjective reports provided by Zen or yoga meditators. These findings, coupled with the report (see Stoyva, 1976) that Zen masters showed higher alpha amplitude than beginning meditators, suggested to many that EEG alpha training would be an easy and rapid means of entering transcendental states of consciousness heretofore requiring years of disciplined study and practice. The subjective state of relaxation purportedly associated with enhanced alpha activity is commonly referred to as the "alpha experience."

As we noted, later work diminished much of the enthusiasm generated by the early findings. For example, Paskewitz and Orne (1973) found that alpha training did not yield alpha production in excess of baseline. Further, Walsh (1974) reported that alpha training by itself did not result in the alpha experience. To obtain the alpha experience, subjects had to be provided

with instructions regarding what to expect, a finding also reported by Plotkin (1976), who concluded that "alpha feedback per se is neither necessary for nor especially facilitative of the achievement of the alpha experience. Is alpha control of value clinically? Some reports are at least suggestive (Gannon & Sternback, 1971; and McKenzie, Ehrisman, Montgomery, & Barnes, 1974, for the treatment of headaches; Melzak & Perry, 1975, for chronic pain). As Blanchard and Epstein (1978) note, however, the evidence is far from clear-cut. At this stage, the clinical value of alpha control must be viewed as questionable, or at the very least controversial.

A somewhat more optimistic note may be sounded when we examine clinical and experimental evidence dealing with EEG feedback in the control of epileptic seizures (see Blanchard & Epstein, 1978; Mostofsky & Balaschak, 1977). The patient is instructed to generate a particular EEG pattern, or wave form, which is then fed back to the patient visually or auditorily. Sometimes the response is actively rewarded, perhaps with money (or electric shock for epileptiform EEG activity, Stevens, 1962). The use of incentives, especially positive reward, is not uncommon in other types of biofeedback treatment; often the reward accompanies the auditory or visual signal.

The particular brain wave pattern the patient is instructed to produce or strengthen depends in part on the researcher's hypotheses regarding brain wave activity in relation to seizures. For example, the early work of Sterman and his colleagues (e.g., Sterman, LoPresti, & Fairchild, 1969, cited in Mostofsky & Balaschak, 1977) with cats suggested that a rhythm of 12–14 Hz over the sensorimotor region of the cerebral cortex was associated with resistance to drug-induced seizures. Feedback designed to enhance this particular rhythm (known as sensorimotor, or SMR, feedback) has led to some rather dramatic results (Finley, Smith, & Etherton, 1975; Lubar, 1975; Sterman & Friar, 1972; Sterman, MacDonald, & Stone, 1974). Finley and colleagues report a decrease in seizure frequency to 10 percent of baseline (along with a commensurate sixfold increase in SMR 12 Hz rhythm). Finley (1976), in a follow-up with the same patient, reported that after one year of SMR feedback, seizures decreased from eight per hour to less than one every three hours.

As Mostofsky and Balaschak (1977) note, seizure activity appears to be very susceptible to placebo effects. Kuhlman and Allison (in press) provided patients with feedback randomly related to EEG patterns, a reasonable placebo condition, followed by feedback for a specific antiseizure EEG pattern. No consistent EEG changes occurred during the placebo month. However, within two weeks of *contingent* biofeedback (i.e., the legitimate treatment), reductions in seizures occurred. Further evidence that the treatment was not merely functioning as a placebo is seen in the increases in seizures occurring during extended breaks in training. Although results are not uniformly positive (e.g., Kaplan, 1975, obtained negative results), they are clearly promising. As reviewers have noted (Blanchard & Epstein, 1978; Mostofsky & Balaschak, 1977), additional care needs to be taken to rule out placebo effects.

EMG biofeedback has been used for a variety of clinical purposes. We provided a brief illustration of how EMG frontalis feedback might be used in the treatment of tension headaches and, in fact, several early reports point to the value of such a treatment (Budzynski et al., 1970; Epstein, Hersen, & Hemphill, 1974; Epstein & Abel, 1977; Wickramasekera, 1973a). However, other early studies suggested that EMG biofeedback was no more effective than simpler procedures, such as relaxation training, for reducing tension headaches (Chesney & Shelton, 1976; Haynes, Griffin, Mooney, & Parise, 1974; Hutchings & Reinking, 1976, did report more benefit from biofeedback than from relaxation instruction). Thus, in a review of this "first-generation" research, Nuechterlein and Holroyd (1980) concluded that although EMG frontalis biofeedback typically produced statisti-

cally significant and clinically meaningful reductions in tension headache activity, it was no more effective than relaxation training, which was considerably less expensive.

More recent studies have hardly changed this picture. Holroyd, Andrasik, and Noble (1980) found EMG biofeedback superior to both meditation and a self-monitoring control group, a difference maintained at a three-year follow-up (Andrasik & Holroyd, 1983), but they argued that the findings did not support the specific efficacy of biofeedback because that intervention was confounded with other procedures. Carrobles, Cardona, and Santacreu (1981) found EMG frontalis biofeedback superior to a placebo control, but utilized such a minimal control that differential credibility may well have accounted for the results. In a series of single case designs, Kremsdorf et al. (1981), meanwhile, found little evidence that EMG biofeedback was useful in reducing tension headaches, although it did appear to facilitate the maintenance of reductions induced via relaxation. Cott, Goldman, Pavloski, Kirschberg, and Fabich (1981) and Russ, Hammer, and Adderton (1979) found no evidence of greater efficacy for biofeedback over relaxation alone, or any additive increment when biofeedback was added to relaxation.

Reductions in headache levels observed have typically not been directly tied to changes in EMG frontalis tension levels (e.g., Abramowitz & Bell, 1985; Cram, 1980; Daly, Zimmerman, Donn, & Galliher, 1985; Epstein & Abel, 1977; Hart & Cichanski, 1981; Holroyd & Andrasik, 1978; Holroyd, Andrasik, & Westbrook, 1977; Kremsdorf, 1978; Martin & Mathews, 1978; Philips 1978), with only Janssen (1983a) demonstrating such a correlation. In one of the more ambitious projects to date, Blanchard and associates (1982a, 1982b, 1983) first utilized relaxation training to treat tension headaches, then provided EMG frontalis biofeedback for anyone not evidencing greater than 60 percent reduction in headache frequency. A substantial number of those less than fully responsive subjects evidenced additional headache reductions, suggesting that biofeedback may be a useful addition to relaxation training. However, as Reed and colleagues (Reed, Katkin, & Goldband, 1986) point out, without having continued a portion of that sample in additional relaxation training, it is not possible to determine if that effect was specific to biofeedback. Overall, there can be little doubt that EMG frontalis biofeedback is effective in the treatment of tension headaches, but little evidence shows that it is any more effective than basic relaxation training or that when it works it does so by virtue of producing changes in frontalis activity (see Holmes & Burish, 1983; and Reed et al., 1986, for recent extended reviews).

Frontalis EMG feedback has also been used in attempts to reduce general anxiety (Burish, Hendrix, & Frost, 1981; Canter, Kondo, & Knotts, 1975; Lavellee, Lamontagne, Annable, & Fontaine, 1982; leBoeuf, 1980; Raskin, Bali, & Peeke, 1980; Raskin, Johnson, & Rondestvedt, 1973; Rupert, Dobbins, & Mathew, 1981; Schandler & Grings, 1976; Townsend, House, & Addario, 1975). As noted by Reed et al. (1986), these efforts were predicated on two related assumptions: (1) that EMG biofeedback of the frontalis muscles is an effective procedure for inducing general body relaxation, and (2) that deep relaxation leads to the subjective experience of relaxation. As we shall see, neither of these assumptions has been well supported by more recent empirical trials. Although early studies were often positive (cf., Canter et al., 1975; Raskin et al., 1973; Townsend et al., 1975), those that included comparison interventions, such as progressive relaxation, typically found no specific advantage (Schandler & Grings, 1976). Given the inadequacies in these early trials, and the failure of biofeedback to outperform less expensive and more mundane alternatives, the initial wave of review articles typically concluded that there was no conclusive evidence that muscle tension biofeedback was *specifically* effective in reducing anxiety

(Alexander & Smith, 1979; Burish, 1981; Katkin & Goldband, 1979).

More recent studies have, if anything, only reinforced this conclusion (see Reed et al., 1986; Rice & Blanchard, 1982; and Rickels, Onada, & Doyle, 1982, for reviews). Thus, several carefully controlled studies have found EMG biofeedback no more powerful than relaxation training or simple instructions in reducing EMG levels (Burish et al., 1981; leBoeuf, 1980; Raskin et al., 1980), whereas EMG levels have not been found to be related to self-reported anxiety (Burish et al., 1981; leBoeuf, 1980; Raskin et al., 1980; Rupert et al., 1981). The only study to find any correlation between EMG activity and subjective anxiety was one conducted by Lavellee et al. (1982), and then only for subjects who reported a decrease in anxiety. As noted by Reed et al. (1986), although EMG biofeedback of frontalis muscles typically does produce reductions in frontalis muscle activity, it is no more likely to do so than other more general methods (e.g., relaxation training or simple instructions). Further, reduction in frontalis activity does not appear to be directly tied to decreased activity in other muscle groups, nor does it appear to lead to reductions in general autonomic nervous system arousal. Although EMG frontalis biofeedback is not without clinical efficacy, its efficacy appears to derive from nonspecific factors (e.g., "placebo" or expectancy effects) unrelated to the guiding rationale behind its derivation. Further, efficacy appears to be no greater than that associated with less complex (and less expensive) procedures. Similar conclusions can be drawn with respect to efforts to use frontalis EMG biofeedback in the treatment of phobic disorders (Reed et al., 1986).

In general, attempts to produce general relaxation via biofeedback procedures have not been as popular and, apparently, no more successful than those using EMG frontalis biofeedback. Efforts to utilize discrete brainwave (EEG) feedback were quite popular during the early days of biofeedback, but have receded in importance due, in part, to their inherent methodological complexity and controversies surrounding their clinical efficacy (see Reed et al., 1986, for a review). Similarly, heartrate biofeedback did not look promising in a controlled trial (Rupert & Holmes, 1978). In general, there is little evidence to suggest that biofeedback has any specific role to play in the treatment of anxiety disorders.

In our view, one of the most exciting and potentially useful applications of biofeedback is in EMG neuromuscular rehabilitation (Brudny et al., 1976a, 1976b; Inglis, Campbell, & Donald, 1976–1977). Brudny and associates give a large-scale case history presentation covering some 114 patients, including those suffering from hemiparesis, torticollis, dystonia, and spinal cord or peripheral nerve injury. Most had suffered from their debilitating disorder for some time (in one case, 35 years, and in all cases at least 3 months), and all had prior conventional therapy with few positive results. The details of the treatment are complex and well beyond the scope of the present text. In general, however, treatment involved monitoring EMG activity in parts of the body, for example, extremities that were atrophied or showed severe functional paralysis. Naturally, the paralysis could not be total, as would occur when nervous tissue is severed beyond repair, inasmuch as the EMG biofeedback procedure assumes the potential for voluntary control. By receiving signals that a particular muscle is in fact functioning, albeit minimally, the client is in a position to augment or in some way modify movement in an adaptive way, thereby regaining incremental voluntary control. These procedures may be used to increase muscular strength and, in the case of spasmodic torticollis, to decrease involuntary spasmodic activity. Therapeutic sessions were provided 3 to 5 times a week (typically, sessions lasted 30 to 45 minutes) over 8 to 12 weeks. Among the hemiparetics, more than 60 percent showed marked gains; at follow-ups

ranging from three months to three years, the success rate was 50 percent. While formal controls are lacking, it seems unlikely that improvements of this magnitude would have occurred in the absence of treatment or as a result of a credible placebo treatment.

At present, there is a sizable literature dating back to the late 1960s suggesting that biofeedback may assist people in altering their heart rates (e.g., Engel & Hansen, 1966; Headrick, Feather, & Wells, 1971; Hnatiow & Lang, 1965; Sirota, Schwartz, & Shapiro, 1974—see reviews of Blanchard & Epstein, 1978; Blanchard & Young, 1973, 1974; McCanne & Sandman, 1976). In general, the magnitude of the change is not great, and the evidence that subjects are able to raise heart rate is more consistent than the evidence that people can lower heart rate (Blanchard & Epstein, 1978). Further, it should be noted that comparable reductions have been observed with transcendental meditation (Wallace, 1970; Wallace & Benson, 1972) and progressive relaxation (Paul, 1969). In one of the more significant clinical demonstrations involving biofeedback in cardiac control, Weiss and Engle (1970, 1971) worked with patients suffering from cardiac arrhythmias (specifically, premature ventricular contractions—PVC). Patients were trained to increase and decrease heart rate, with biofeedback gradually faded out. In four patients, PVCs went from 10 to 20 per minute to approximately 1 per minute, with evidence of improvement maintained at follow-ups of up to 21 months (see Blanchard & Epstein, 1978, for additional clinical data.)

In addition to PVC, the other major target of cardiac rate biofeedback has been tachycardia. Although several investigators have reported successful case studies (Bleecker & Engel, 1973; Engel & Bleecker, 1974; Janssen, 1983b; Scott, Blanchard, Edmunson, & Young, 1973), little controlled empirical research has been conducted. As Reed et al. (1986) observed, although the results obtained with both PVC and tachycardia have been dramatic, such results are limited to only portions of the patients evaluated, and few of the studies, if any, have provided adequate controls for ruling out nonspecific factors. As we have seen repeatedly, early uncontrolled case reports typically give a far more optimistic picture than do subsequent, more carefully controlled, trials.

Within the cardiovascular sphere, blood pressure modification has also been the target of a variety of biofeedback investigations. Early reports appeared to provide convincing experimental evidence that both systolic and diastolic blood pressure can be modified using biofeedback (e.g., Brener & Kleinman, 1970; Fey & Lindholm, 1975; Shapiro, Schwartz, & Tursky, 1972; Shapiro, Tursky, & Schwartz, 1970), although, as in the case of heart rate modification, the magnitude of the changes typically were modest, roughly 3–4 mm Hg in either direction. Results with clinical populations, however, were mixed, at best. Thus, Benson, Shapiro, Tursky, and Schwartz (1971) obtained marked decreases in systolic pressure for five of seven patients (i.e., 16 mm Hg or greater), with two of the five patients moving into the normal range. (As you probably know, normal systolic pressure for individuals of college age is roughly 120 mm Hg; normal diastolic pressure is around 80 mm Hg.) The report by Benson and associates did suffer from the lack of a control group, and further, Benson (1975) in a follow-up noted that all the patients had returned to the hypertensive range. Schwartz and Shapiro (1973) obtained essentially negative results in their attempts at modifying diastolic pressure. Positive results have been reported by Miller (1972), by Elder, Ruiz, Deabler, and Dillenkoffer (1973), and by Blanchard, Young, and Haynes (1975), with Blanchard and colleagues reporting decreases as high as 51 mm Hg.

In a particularly well controlled investigation (Blanchard & Epstein, 1978), blood pressure biofeedback was compared with frontalis EMG feedback (for relaxation) and instructions simply to relax. Although all three groups showed small decreases in blood pressure, significant differential effects were not obtained. More recent studies have been even less supportive. Surwit, Shapiro, and Good (1978), for example, found evidence that a combination of systolic blood pressure (SBP) and heart rate (HR) biofeedback reduced both systolic and diastolic blood pressure levels, but only within, not across, sessions and to no greater extent than was observed for relaxation training. Blanchard, Miller, Abel, Haynes, and Wicker (1979) observed similar findings, albeit without any changes in diastolic blood pressure. Luborsky and colleagues (1982) similarly found SBP biofeedback no more effective than relaxation (or mild exercise) and less effective than antihypertensive medications. Glasgow, Gaardoner, and Engel (1982) also found SBP biofeedback to be no more effective than relaxation. In general, although SDP biofeedback does appear to reduce systolic blood pressure, and to a lesser extent diastolic blood pressure, it appears to be no more effective than simple relaxation training (see Reed et al., 1986; or Stainbrook, Hoffman, & Benson, 1983, for reviews). Efforts to utilize diastolic biofeedback have been even less successful; whereas efforts to utilize other biofeedback procedures, e.g., EMG feedback (Moeller, 1976), electrodermal activity feedback (Patel, Marmot, & Terry, 1981; Datey, 1978), or temperature biofeedback (Green, Green, & Norris, 1980) have often proven useful, but only as part of larger packages and, again, not more so than simpler, less expensive procedures (see Reed et al., 1986, for a review).

Previously we discussed the use of EMG feedback as therapy for tension headaches. One popular approach to the treatment of *migraine* headaches involves skin temperature biofeedback. As the technique is usually employed, it involves teaching clients to raise the temperature of their *fingers* or *hands*. Although the psychophysiology of migraine headaches is not well understood, it is usually assumed they are caused by, or at least associated with, dilated blood vessels in the head (Dalessio, 1972). Raising the temperature of fingers or hands was presumed to alleviate migraine pain by virtue of blocking the central vasoconstriction which preceded subsequent vasodilation. Early studies suggested that raising finger temperature was clinically effective (Sargent, Green, & Walter, 1972, 1973; Turin & Johnson, 1976; Wickramasekera, 1973b). However, although subsequent research has typically supported the clinical utility of the finger warming procedures, it has not demonstrated its specificity, nor has it provided support for its presumed mechanism. Thus, a series of well-controlled studies have found finger temperature biofeedback no more effective than alternative procedures such as relaxation training, hypnosis, or EMG biofeedback (Barrios & Karoly, 1983; Beasley, 1976; Blanchard, Theobald, Williamson, Silver, & Brown, 1977; Hart, 1984; LaCroix, Clarke, Bock, Doxey, Wood, & Lavir, 1983; Sargent, 1984). Further, hand warming is typically no more effective than hand cooling (Claghorn, Mathew, Largen & Meyer, 1981; Gauthier, Bois, Allaire, & Drolet, 1981; Jessup, 1978; Kewman & Roberts, 1980; Mullinix, Norton, Hock, & Fishman, 1978). Both sets of findings cast real doubt on the notion that this type of biofeedback training has any specific efficacy for the treatment of migraines, although it clearly has a clinical impact.

A more recent direct application of biofeedback to the modification of cephalic blood flow may prove to be a more promising approach to the treatment of migraine, since current theory relates migraine etiology to the dilation of the superficial temporal arteries (Dalessio, 1972). A series of studies have demonstrated that migraine sufferers can learn to control cephalic vasomotor response (CVMR) (Allen & Mills, 1982; Feuerstein & Adams, 1977; Fudge & Adams, 1985; Lichstein, Hoelscher, Nickel, & Hoon, 1983; Price & Clarks, 1979). Biofeedback is usually provided via photoelectric cell measurement of cephalic pulse volume. However, although this approach does appear to provide clinical relief in excess of spontaneous change

noted for untreated controls, it does not appear to be more effective than EMG feedback, at least in the controlled studies to date evaluating its efficacy (Bild & Adams, 1980; Friar & Beatty, 1976; Gauthier, Doyon, Lacroix, & Drolet, 1980; Knapp, 1982). Since CVMR versus EMG biofeedback comparisons appear to have dominated this literature, it is not possible to determine the extent to which CVMR biofeedback operates through specific, rather than nonspecific, mechanisms, unless one is willing to assume that EMG biofeedback operates solely as a nonspecific agent. Theoretically, the CVMR approach would appear to be particularly promising. Empirically, the approach is clearly effective. Whether or not it will prove to be more effective than simple nontechnological relaxation procedures remains to be determined, but the initial data are not that encouraging.

Raynaud's disease is a disorder characterized by painful constriction of blood vessels in the hands and feet. If the rationale for temperature biofeedback is less than clear in cases of migraine headaches, it would seem a very logical treatment for Raynaud's disease. Indeed, Blanchard and Epstein (1978) report at least some success in 20 of 22 such cases (it should be mentioned that they also employed digital volume feedback: the volume of one's fingers or toes is roughly proportional to the amount of blood flow or vessel expansion, and this can be readily recorded and fed back to individuals). Freedman and colleagues (Freedman, Ianni, Hale, & Lynn, 1979; Freedman, Lynn, & Ianni, 1978; Freedman, Lynn, Ianni, & Hale, 1981) have generally reported good success in decreasing Raynaud's symptoms in a series of studies that did not control for nonspecific factors. In a subsequent study, Freedman, Ianni, and Wenig (1983) found finger temperature biofeedback superior to either autogenic training or EMG biofeedback. Nonetheless, other controlled investigations have not been as benign. In the bulk of these trials, finger temperature biofeedback has typically not outperformed simple relaxation or various other control procedures (Guglielmi, Roberts, & Patterson, 1982; Jacobson, Manschreck, & Silverberg, 1979; Keefe, Surwit, & Pilon, 1980; Surwit, Pilon, & Fenton, 1978). In general, although Raynaud's symptoms typically improve after finger temperature biofeedback, there is very little evidence that they do so for any reasons specific to that intervention. Once again, comparable results appear to be obtainable with simpler, less expensive interventions such as relaxation (see Reed et al., 1986, for a comprehensive review).

For a discipline scarcely two decades old, the research and clinical interest in biofeedback can only be described as phenomenal. Considering the cost of biofeedback equipment, not to mention the cost and effort involved in learning to employ it correctly, the time and money devoted to clinical and research investigations, and so on, we may reasonably ask whether the enterprise has been worth the effort. Clearly, the discipline has produced some notable successes (e.g., certain types of seizure disorders and neuromuscular disorders), but, just as clearly, the discipline has been vastly oversold in many other areas (cf. cardiovascular disorders, migraine and tension headaches, anxiety reduction, and Raynaud's disorder, to name just a few). In virtually all of these latter cases, the apparent efficacy indicated by the earlier studies, typically uncontrolled case reports, has given way to a picture in which the various types of biofeedback, although generally evidencing a pattern of clinical efficacy, rarely exceed various alternative procedures such as relaxation training. Further, in most instances, efforts to link the clinical changes to the presumed physiological processes modified have rarely been successful. Given that those alternative procedures are typically less expensive and less time consuming than biofeedback with its complex instrumentation, the continued high level of enthusiasm for biofeedback in clinical circles is hard to justify.

Biofeedback training seminars, instrumentation, and clinical utilization continue to mushroom, despite its rather tepid performance in the controlled literature, leading some observers to lament the nature of clinical training and practice (Poppen, 1983; Roberts, 1985). Although there are clearly problem areas for which biofeedback appears to have a unique contribution to make (e.g., epilepsy and neuromuscular rehabilitation), many of its other applications seem to be supported more by a desire to give the appearance of having a technologically sophisticated, quasi-medical intervention than by any inherent superiority of the procedures over less complex (and less expensive) alternatives.

Some Concluding Comments

On the whole, it is clear that the self-control approaches have emerged as a major component of modern behavior therapy. Their use in the addictive disorders, especially, has become the standard in the field. Typically, whether or not these approaches are presented as part of a larger treatment package remains an open question (the same question could be raised about the other components), but there is little question that such packages have good clinical efficacy.

Despite their demonstrable value, it is also clear that relapse prevention remains a major clinical issue. Recall that one of the primary rationales behind the development of the self-control procedures involved the expectation that such approaches would facilitate both cross-situational generality and the stability of changes over time. Some evidence shows that this may be so, for at least some problems, but the findings of the last two decades have clearly not matched the initial expectations. Whether or not newly developed programs such as Marlatt and colleagues' relapse prevention training programs (Marlatt, 1979, 1982; Marlatt & Gordon, 1980, 1985) will fulfill this hope remains to be determined, but the initial data are at least promising.

Certainly, self-control approaches lend themselves nicely to outpatient settings with relatively intact, sentinent adult populations (they have, of course, other uses as well, but may be particularly palatable to clients who want to maintain an active role in their treatment). Applications to the control of stress, pain, anger, and depression have also proven promising, although clearly in need of further exploration. Finally, biofeedback, discussed in greater length in the behavioral medicine chapter (Chapter 11), has shown mixed results. Clearly, application of biofeedback principles to the control of epileptic seizures and neuromuscular training and rehabilitation represent major breakthroughs. On the other hand, applications of biofeedback to essentially autonomically mediated processes

(e.g., anxiety disorders, tension and migraine headaches, hypertension, etc.) have typically failed to outperform far simpler and less expansive controls.

Overall, it is clear that the self-control perspective has made a major contribution to our understanding and practice of behavior therapy. It has clearly not matched the expectations of its early advocates, but, just as clearly, it has exceeded the expectations of its early critiques. More attention to its underlying theoretical principles and the shaping of its derivative procedures to meet clinical needs, particularly in the area of relapse prevention, should follow in the years to come.

11
Behavioral Medicine

The prior chapters of this text have focused on specific behavioral techniques, such as systematic desensitization, extinction, thought stopping, and so forth. This chapter, however, adopts a different perspective, focusing instead on a particular area of content: behavioral medicine. Specifically, we will briefly define this burgeoning area of behavioral intervention, recount its dynamic history, explore its theoretical underpinnings, and then give examples of how the behavioral techniques presented in previous chapters have been applied to issues relating to physical health and disease. The general point is that behavioral approaches are important not only for traditional problems in psychology, such as depression, fear, nonassertiveness, and aggressive behaviors, but also for influencing our physical health. And we are not referring here only to those illnesses traditionally regarded as being influenced by psychological factors, such as ulcers and headaches. Rather, we are concerned also with physical disorders that have not been traditionally linked to psychological factors, such as heart disease and cancer, the two leading causes of death in most Western cultures. Additionally, behavioral medicine is concerned with procedures that promote health and prevent the initial occurrence or recurrence of physical diseases. In short, medicine today is becoming increasingly *behavioral* in nature, and therefore, professionals trained in behavioral approaches are now playing an increasingly important role in the field of health and illness.

Definition

Behavioral medicine is an area of research and practice that integrates behavioral techniques with the science and application of medicine in order to promote health and prevent, diagnose, and treat disease. The term was used initially in a very narrow sense to refer to the use of specific behavioral techniques, usually based on operant conditioning principles, within a medical context. The first time the term was used in a professional publication was in an article by Birk in 1973, in which he described the use of biofeedback to treat medical disorders (Bradley & Prokop, 1981). Later, in 1979, Pomerleau and Brady published a textbook entitled *Behavioral Medicine: Theory and Practice*. In the introduction of that book, they defined behavioral medicine as

> (a) the clinical use of the techniques derived from the experimental analysis of behavior—behavior therapy and behavior modification—for the evaluation, prevention, management, or treatment of physical disease or physiological dysfunction; and (b) the conduct of research contributing to the functional analysis and understanding of behavior associated with medical disorders and problems in health care. (P. xii)

Clearly, then, in its early history, behavioral medicine was viewed by some as referring only to narrowly defined *behavioral* techniques. This interpretation was developed further in a follow-up article in which Pomerleau (1979) stated that there are really only two basic intervention techniques in the field of behavioral medicine: *biofeedback,* which was defined as "special application of operant conditioning methods to the control of visceral, somatomotor, and CNS activities"; and *self-management strategies,* which Pomerleau believed "provide new reinforcing consequences for adaptive behavior and . . . interfere with or defer immediate reinforcement for maladaptive behavior while making the delayed aversive consequences more potent" (p. 657). Cognitive self-management techniques were not included in this early definition of behavioral medicine.

At about the same time that Pomerleau and others were offering a very narrow definition of behavioral medicine, an interdisciplinary group of investigators suggested a broader conceptualization. Their definition grew out of a seminal conference held at Yale in 1977. In effect, the Yale Conference on Behavioral Medicine launched the current field of behavioral medicine. Its influence was due to a number of factors, including the fact that the conference (a) attracted a large number of highly respected and highly visible scholars whose research had important medical implications; (b) helped to establish a new journal called the *Journal of Behavioral Medicine;* (c) began a new interdisciplinary professional organization, called the Society of Behavioral Medicine; and perhaps most importantly, (d) offered a definition of the field that was relatively broad and widely acceptable to the professional community. The modified version of this definition, which was offered shortly after the conference by Schwartz and Weiss (1977, 1978), is perhaps the most quoted and agreed upon definition of behavioral medicine in the field and is the one we will subscribe to in this chapter:

> Behavioral medicine is the interdisciplinary field concerned with the development and integration of behavioral and biomedical science knowledge and techniques relevant to health and illness and the application of this knowledge and these techniques to prevention, diagnosis, treatment and rehabilitation. (1978, p. 250)

We should emphasize four points about this definition. First, it goes much beyond the narrow operant focus of the Pomerleau and Brady definition. The area is still characterized as "behavioral" in nature, but much like the behavior therapy field as a whole, this behavioral focus now includes a broad range of approaches and techniques, ranging from the modification of classically conditioned responses to the use of cognitive approaches to establish health-related behaviors, such as dental flossing or breast self-examinations. Second, the field is interdisciplinary, integrating not only the approaches of the behavioral sciences but also those of biomedical sciences. It is out of this type of integration that exciting new fields such as psychoneuroimmunology (which we will discuss later) developed. Third, the definition clearly emphasizes both basic science and practical application, thus including both researchers and practitioners within the field of behavioral medicine. Finally, unlike the traditional approaches in medicine that focus primarily on the diagnosis and treatment of disease, the behavioral approach to medicine also emphasizes prevention, rehabilitation, and health promotion. This difference is especially important today because, as we will see shortly, the majority of health problems in Western cultures could be prevented by changes in our behavior.

History

Although the field of behavioral medicine is relatively new, the view that one's behaviors may influence health and disease has existed for thousands of years. For example, ancient cultures often attributed illnesses or diseases to the actions of evil spirits or gods. Since these primitive people held that the wrath of the gods could be evoked by thoughts or behaviors that were displeasing to the gods, they subscribed to one of the first mind–body interaction theories. Unfortunately, although their theory was advanced in terms of its interactionist perspective, their treatment techniques were not. One of the most widely written about procedures was called trephining, a technique whereby the "healer" pounded a small hole in the skull of the patient with a stone or sharp object in order to let the evil spirit escape the body. Apparently, one way or another, the procedure was deemed quite effective in stopping the progression of the illness.

The mind–body interactionist position continued to be advocated for many years, although in scientifically more advanced ways. For example, around 400 B.C. the Greek physician Hippocrates advanced a humoral theory of personality and psychopathology. Hippocrates suggested that the amount of four different fluids, or "humors," in the body helped determine various personality characteristics. The amount of black bile was associated with sadness or melancholia, and the amount of blood affected whether one was sanguine (from the Latin word for blood) or optimistic in outlook. The other two fluids, yellow bile and phlegm, were associated with irritability and listlessness, respectively. Although this theory was eventually abandoned, it was historically significant in that it advanced the notion that there is an interaction between physical and emotional factors.

The interactionist viewpoint lost ground many years later and was replaced by the well-known mind–body dualism position. The philosopher Descartes, who argued that the mind or soul was a separate entity from the body, is perhaps the best known advocate of this position. The position was strengthened within medicine by the confluence of several factors which eventually led to the so-called *disease model,* which is preeminent yet today. In the seventeenth century, technological advances in microscopy allowed researchers to discover and study microorganisms. Then, in the nineteenth century, the work of Pasteur and others led to the revolutionary notion that some diseases were actually caused by the microorganisms that van Leeuwenhoek and others had discovered. Further advances led to aseptic techniques that reduced significantly the complications of surgery and to the development of new anesthetics, vaccines, and sanitation procedures (Miller, 1983). All of these exciting new discoveries and developments reinforced the view that the mind and body are separate, that diseases are due directly to germs and are not influenced by spirits or beliefs or any other mental causes.

The strict mind–body dualism gave way somewhat in the nineteenth and early twentieth centuries when some prominent physicians began to emphasize the role that emotional or behavioral factors can play in health and illness. For example, in 1852, physician Henry Holland published a book entitled *Mental Physiology,* in which he stated:

> Human physiology comprises the reciprocal actions and relations of mental and bodily phenomena, as they make up the totality of life. Scarcely can we have a morbid affection of the body in which some feeling or function of mind is not concurrently engaged—directly or indirectly—as cause or as effect. (Cited in Grinker, 1953, p. 12)

Sigmund Freud's emphasis on the role of unconscious processes in physical as well as emotional functioning had a major influence in promoting the notion that mental functioning can have an impact on one's health. The importance of behavioral and psychological factors in health and illness was also underscored at a workshop entitled "The Relations of Psychology and Medical Education," which was sponsored by the American Psychological Association in 1911. The psychologists and physicians participating in this symposium, including John Watson—who is regarded by some as the father of modern behaviorism—agreed not only that behavioral and psychological factors could have an important influence on disease processes, but also that physicians should be made more aware of these influences. They concluded:

> (a) that medical students enter training with too little knowledge of psychology; (b) that such knowledge is essential to proper medical training; (c) that in fact courses in psychology should precede courses in psychiatry and neurology; and (d) that more hours should be devoted to psychology in the medical curriculum. (Gentry & Matarazzo, 1981, p. 6)

In spite of the considerable support that the interactionist position received from Freud, Watson, and others, it has had little practical impact on the practice of medicine until fairly recently. There are at least three reasons that the disease model remained relatively unaltered during this period. First, the disease model was stunningly effective in the 1800s and early 1900s. During this time infectious diseases accounted for a large proportion of all deaths. The disease model was highly successful in eradicating one infectious disease after another. Second, although several people tried to champion the role of behavioral factors in disease, little research evidence was available to support the position. Comments like Holland's, quoted previously, were based primarily on anecdotal data, and Freud neither conducted himself nor stimulated in his followers much empirical research. Watson and those of a more behavioral persuasion did carry out several experiments, but few were focused on medically related problems. Finally, there was generally a high level of satisfaction within the medical community. Physicians were esteemed members of society, and biomedical scientists were making discoveries and technological advances at startling rates. All in all, there seemed to be little reason to move away from a model and an approach that was serving well the people of America and other Western countries.

Over the years, however, each of these three factors began to change. First, the major health problems changed from infectious diseases such as pneumonia and diphtheria to chronic illnesses such as heart diseases and cancer. In 1900, infectious diseases accounted for 36 of every 100 deaths; today they account for about 6 deaths per 100. In contrast, the death rate from chronic diseases has grown from 20 per 100 deaths in the first part of this century to about 70 per 100 today (Burish & Bradley, 1983). Unfortunately, the disease model is not terribly effective in dealing with chronic diseases, as Glazier has pointed out:

> The medical system of the U.S. is able to meet with high efficiency the kind of medical problem that was dominant until about 40 years ago, namely infectious disease. It also deals effectively with episodes of acute illness and with accidents that call for advanced, hospital-based biomedical knowledge and technology. The system is much less effective in delivering the kind of care that is more often needed today . . . primary (first-contact) care and the kind of care needed at a time when chronic illnesses predominate. . . . For these diseases medicine has few measures and not even much comfort. (1973, p. 13)

Glazier and others have suggested that the disease model is outmoded, at least for many of today's major health problems.

Second, as we will discuss at length later, there is now abundant research evidence that behavioral and psychological factors can play major roles in the development and course of a disease and the promotion of health, and that behavior-change techniques can have a major impact on health status. For example, the U.S. Public Health Service Center for Disease Control has estimated that over half the mortality that results from the 10 leading causes of death in the United States is related to people's behavior, to life-styles (Miller, 1983). An illustration of the types of behaviors involved might help to adumbrate our later discussions. Several years ago, Breslow and Enstrom (1980) published a report on the importance of various health behaviors in prolonging life or, as epidemiologists generally put it, reducing mortality. In 1965, these investigators and their colleagues surveyed almost 7,000 people living in Alameda County, California, in order to determine their health practices and medical histories, and then followed them for over nine years to determine whether there was a relationship between health practices and longevity. Residents were originally asked to indicate whether or not they followed seven specific health practices: not smoking, regular physical exercise, moderate or no alcohol consumption, sleeping seven to eight hours each night, maintaining a proper weight, not eating between meals, and eating breakfast. The investigators also asked the residents to answer several questions about their past and current health. The 1974 follow-up found that 717 of the originally surveyed residents had died. The remaining survivors were asked to respond to a new questionnaire about their health practices and current health. Almost 5,000 of the survivors responded. The results were dramatic. Men who practiced three or fewer of the behaviors were approximately four times as likely to have died as men who followed all seven of the health behaviors. Women practicing three or fewer of the behaviors were approximately twice as likely to have died as women practicing all seven of the behaviors. Thus, at least in a correlational sense, behavior was strongly associated with health. Interest-

ingly, the data suggested that people were very stable in their health behaviors during the nine-year period between surveys. For example, approximately 72 percent of those people who fell into the "poor health practices group" (i.e., followed three or fewer of the behaviors) in 1965 fell into that group or one step above that group (practicing up to four of the behaviors) in 1974. These data suggest that some type of intervention may be necessary in order to motivate people to change, and perhaps also to help them effectuate any desired changes. As we will see later, other data suggest that, at least for some behaviors, such change can indeed result in improved prospects of a longer life free of certain illnesses.

Finally, there is growing dissatisfaction with many aspects of the current medical system, a development which, in an indirect way, helps to promote the rise of alternate models of care. For example, there is tremendous concern outside of as well as within the medical community about rising health costs. As Table 11–1 indicates, health care requires a multibillion dollar budget that equals almost 11 percent of the entire gross national product! The failure of the medical community to come up with effective treatments for many types of major health problems, such as several types of cancers, acquired immune deficiency syndrome (AIDS), and Alzheimer's disease, has also contributed to

Table 11–1 **Health Care Costs in the United States**

Year	Total Health Expenditure (billions)	Health Expenditures, Percentage of GNP	Health Expenditures per person
1960	$ 27	5.3	$ 146
1965	42	6.1	207
1970	75	7.6	350
1975	133	8.6	591
1980	248	9.4	1049
1984	387	10.6	1580
1985	425	10.7	1721

Adapted from Waldo, Levit, and Lazenby (1986).

a disenchantment with the disease model as the only model of health care. Another source of dissatisfaction with the disease model is its lack of focus on *quality of life*. Infectious diseases are usually acute in onset and last for relatively short, predictable periods of time. Even highly aversive medical interventions can usually be tolerated for this brief period. In contrast, chronic diseases often have a slow, insidious onset and may endure for a long, indefinite period. Given this course, prolonged, aversive medical treatments that disregard the quality of life that they permit are becoming increasingly unacceptable. For example, the authors have worked with some cancer patients who have elected an increased chance of an early death rather than undergo prolonged chemotherapy treatments. Behavioral and other interventions that can improve the quality of life thus have become highly sought after as the incidence of chronic disease has increased.

As a result of the changes in the three factors noted above, the disease model has begun to give way to alternate models, although it should be clearly noted that even today the disease model is the dominant model in medical communities. The alternate model that has gained the most acceptance is the *biopsychosocial model* of health and illness (Engel, 1977; Schwartz, 1982). In contrast to the disease model, which looks only at biological or medical factors, this model holds that a person's health status depends on a complex interaction of biological, psychological, and social factors. Taylor highlights the important tenants of the biopsychosocial model:

> The biopsychosocial model maintains that *health and illness are caused by multiple factors and produce multiple effects*. The model further maintains that the *mind and body cannot be distinguished* in matters of health and illness because both so clearly influence an individual's state of health. The biopsychosocial model *emphasizes both health and illness* rather than regarding illness as a deviation from some steady state. (1986, p. 12, emphasis in original)

The biopsychosocial model has several important implications for the study and practice of behavioral medicine (Engel, 1977; Taylor, 1986). First, the biopsychosocial model emphasizes that the interaction of biological, psychological, and social factors must always be considered when assessing a person's health status or treating a health problem. Just as the medical community has erred in overemphasizing the role of biological factors to the exclusion of other factors, some behaviorally oriented professionals have overemphasized the role of behavioral or psychological factors. Although we will be discussing behavioral techniques throughout this chapter, we are not advocating their use to the exclusion of, or without properly assessing the need for, traditional medical interventions. The biopsychosocial model has implications for all health professionals, not only those in the traditional medical community.

Second, the biopsychosocial model is concerned with a much broader array of factors than the disease model. For example, the promotion of health and the prevention of illness are emphasized much more within the biopsychosocial model than the biomedical model. Because these are areas in which behavioral interventions can have a significant effect, behavioral theories and techniques have emerged as an important component of the holistic approach that the biopsychosocial model emphasizes.

Third, the biopsychosocial model does not insist that all deviations from good health are diseases or illnesses. Headaches are seen in the biomedical model as an illness; but in the biopsychosocial model, they may be more appropriately viewed in some situations as emotional reactions to stressful life circumstances. This broader conceptualization fosters an approach to health that might emphasize a behavioral treatment program to eliminate fears or increase social support among family members rather than the prescription of a pill.

Finally, given that biological, psychological, and social factors all interact to affect health and illness, the biopsychosocial model suggests that the best approach to dealing with these issues involves an interdisciplinary team of professionals, each contributing the knowledge and techniques of his or her specialty.

Overall, therefore, the biopsychosocial model clearly advocates a new, broad-based, interdisciplinary approach to health and illness that emphasizes an interaction between the mind and body and advocates a holistic approach to assessing and helping individuals attain and maintain health. Within this approach, learning theory and behavior therapy have emerged as important components, so much so that the biopsychosocial model should be regarded as consistent with, and providing the contextual underpinnings of, the field of behavioral medicine.

Differentiating Behavioral Medicine From Related Fields

Behavioral medicine should be regarded as a broad, multidisciplinary area that deals with the interaction of biomedical and behavioral science knowledge and applications. However, there are also several other fields or subfields that deal in some fashion with mind–body or health–behavior interactions. In order to avoid confusion and to gain a better understanding of what behavioral medicine is, it is helpful to distinguish it from these related areas.

Perhaps the oldest field that emphasizes mind–body interactions as they relate to illness is *psychosomatic medicine*. Psychosomatic medicine is generally considered a specialty area within medicine, composed primarily of psychiatrists, that focuses on the role of *psycho*logical factors in *somatic* or physical disease. A classic example of work in psychosomatic medicine is Graham's *specific-attitude* theory (Grace & Graham, 1952). Graham postulated that certain attitudes are associated with particular patterns of physiological responding, and hence with specific types of disorders. Table 11–2 lists several diseases and

the attitudes which presumably are associated with them. In recent years, psychosomatic medicine has broadened to include nonmedical professionals and to explore areas other than etiology and diagnosis. However, the field is primarily the domain of psychiatrists and, in general, still gives relatively little attention to disease prevention and health promotion (Gentry & Matarazzo, 1981).

In contrast, the field of *behavioral health* gives almost total attention to disease prevention and health promotion. Behavioral health is a relatively new field, championed most strongly by Matarazzo (1980, 1982), a psychologist who is very active in the behavioral medicine movement. Matarazzo believes that behavioral medicine does not emphasize sufficiently the prevention and health promotion components, even though, according to Matarazzo, it is in these areas that behavioral scientists will have their greatest influence. Matarazzo defines behavioral health as an "interdisciplinary subspecialty within behavioral medicine specifically concerned with the maintenance of health and the prevention of illness and dysfunction in currently healthy persons" (1980, p. 807).

There are several other areas of subspecialty that fall under the general rubric of behavioral medicine. Unlike behavioral health, however, most of the other subspecialties are discipline-specific rather than interdisciplinary in nature. For example, *health psychology* is a subdiscipline of psychology devoted to understanding how psychological factors influence health and illness. A subgroup within the American Psychological Association called the Division of Health Psychology defines the area as follows:

Health psychology is the aggregate of the specific educational, scientific, and professional contributions of the discipline of psychology to the promotion and maintenance of health, the prevention and treatment of illness, the identification of etiologic and diagnostic correlates of health, illness, and related dysfunction and the improvement of the health care system and health policy formation. (Matarazzo, 1980, p. 815)

Table 11–2 Examples of Relationships Between Attitudes and Illness, as Proposed by Graham

Uticaria (hives)	Patients see themselves as mistreated and are preoccupied with what is happening to them. Patient is not thinking about retaliation or solving the problem. Typical self-statement: "They did a lot of things to me and I couldn't do anything about it."
Eczema	Patients feel they are being prevented from doing something and cannot think of a way to deal with their frustration. They are preoccupied with the situation. Typical self-statement: "I couldn't do what I wanted but there wasn't anything I could do about it."
Raynaud's Disease	Patients believe they should undertake some type of hostile action, but do not know exactly what to do. Typical self-statement: "I wanted to put a knife through him."
Asthma	Patients feel unloved, rejected, and disapproved of. They wish to shut out or not have anything to do with the person or situation that is making them feel this way. Typical self-statement: "I wanted them to go away."
Duodenal ulcer	Patients feel deprived of what is due them and want to get even. Typical self-statement: "I want revenge."
Migraine headache	Occurs when patients who had been making an intense effort to carry out a planned activity or to achieve a definite objective have stopped their efforts, regardless of whether they succeeded or failed. Typical self-statement: "I had a million things to do before lunch."
Hypertension	Patients believe they must be constantly prepared to meet all possible threats. Typical self-statement: "Nobody is ever going to beat me; I'm ready for everything."
Low back pain	Patients want to carry out some action that involves movement of the entire body, for example running away from home. Typical self-statement: "I want to get out of there."

From Grace and Graham (1952) and Graham et al. (1962).

For example, a health psychologist may be interested in determining why diabetic patients do not comply with their physicians' recommendations concerning diet and daily insulin injections, even though the patients know that following these recommendations is important to their health and longevity. Other health psychologists might be interested in whether increasing the control that a patient feels in a medical setting, for example by allowing the patient to help make important decisions about drug regimens or surgery options, increases patient compliance with the chosen procedures. Much of the work we will describe in this chapter has been conducted by health psychologists.

Medical psychology is also a specialty area within psychology. It is broadly defined as the "practice of psychology within the medical school establishment" (Gentry & Matarazzo, 1981). This activity includes medical education, clinical services, and research. Unlike health psychology, medical psychology does not focus solely on factors that influence physical health and illness, but also on traditional activities in the mental health area, such as projective testing and behavior therapy, with patients who have psychiatric diagnoses. In general, medical psychology is defined primarily by the person performing the activity, not by the nature of the activity itself.

Medical sociology is a subdiscipline within sociology that is concerned with the effect of social influences on health and the health care system. In contrast to psychologists, who focus primarily on individuals—their behaviors, cognitions, attitudes, and so forth—sociologists focus on the interactions among larger groups within society. For example, medical sociologists might study the influence of various societal or cultural influences on health care practices or the utilization of hospital facilities. They might also look at how hospitals generate their own subculture, complete with customs and implicit rules, and how these factors influence the behavior of patients.

Several other disciplines also have specialty areas, including *health economics* and *medical anthropology*. In general, each of these subspecialties focuses on the part of the health care system that is relevant to its own cognate area. Thus, much of the work in each of these areas also falls under the more general rubric of behavioral medicine.

Role of Behavioral Factors in the Development of Health-related Problems

Before reviewing the specific contributions that behavior therapy has made to the promotion of health and the reduction of illness, it is important to discuss how behavioral factors can influence health and disease. Such a discussion will help us to understand, in general, why behavior therapy has and is making such impor-

tant contributions to behavioral medicine, and it will provide the details necessary to determine when and how behavior therapy interventions might be most effectively applied to promote physical health and well-being.

As we have already suggested, the health problems that plague the majority of people in Western cultures today have changed from infectious diseases prevalent up until about the 1930s to chronic diseases, such as cardiovascular problems, cancer, and diabetes, and also to accidents that can often be attributed to a lack of reasonable precautionary behavior. These disorders or problems are characterized by the fact that they can often be prevented, or their course strongly affected, by what we eat, how much alcohol we drink, how much we sleep, whether or not we exercise or smoke, how effectively we cope with stress, whether or not we take precautions such as wearing seat belts, whether or not we engage in prevention or early detection behaviors such as dental flossing and performing testicular or breast self-exams, and so forth. In essence, therefore, many of our medical problems today are essentially behavior problems, and as such they are influenced by the same behavioral principles and techniques that we have discussed in this text.

In general, the processes by which behavior can influence health and illness can be grouped into three major categories (Krantz, Grunberg, & Baum, 1985; Singer & Krantz, 1982). First, behaviors can lead directly to alterations of tissue and bodily function by their effects on neuroendocrine and other physiological processes. Central to this category of effects is the concept of stress. Psychological stress results when a person appraises a certain situation or event as causing, or having the potential to cause, some type of harm (Lazarus & Folkman, 1984). Stress can exert a number of effects, including direct physiological changes. For example, severe, frequent, or prolonged stress can result in potentially harmful changes in cardiovascular functioning (e.g., blood pressure), gastrointestinal secretions, endocrine functioning, and other changes that are directly related to one's physical well-being. Behaviors that lead to an increase in severe, frequent, or prolonged stress will thus increase the probability of disease; behaviors that prevent such levels of stress from occurring or quickly reduce them if they do occur will lead to a decrease in the likelihood of disease.

Perhaps the most well-documented major disorder in which stress plays an important role is cardiovascular disease. Research on variables that can increase the likelihood of myocardial infarctions (heart attacks), for example, has identified a host of physical factors, such as hypertension, elevated levels of blood cholesterol, diabetes, and so on. However, these physical factors alone are not maximally predictive of heart attacks. The best set of predictors includes a number of behavioral factors, including a behavior pattern known as the *Type A,* or coronary-prone behavior pattern. Type A behavior is characterized by three major behaviors (Matthews, 1982): (1) a high level of aggressiveness and easily aroused hostility in pursuing one's goals; (2) a sense of time urgency about almost everything; and (3) being competitive and highly achievement oriented. Early research suggested that the composite Type A behavior pattern was significantly related to developing coronary heart disease. Moreover, knowing that a person was Type A added to our ability to predict the occurrence of coronary heart disease over knowing only the physical risk factors, such as high blood cholesterol level. More recent research has refined our understanding of the relation between Type A behavior and coronary heart disease. Researchers now believe that only people who are high on the hostility and anger component are at increased risk of coronary heart disease (e.g., Dembroski et al., 1985; MacDougall, Dembroski, Dimsdale, & Hackett, 1985). Such a pinpointing of maladaptive health behaviors, made possible by several careful behavior analysis studies, helps us not only to develop specific behavioral interventions for preventing or ameliorating the behaviors (e.g.,

Levekron, Cohen, Mueller, & Fisher, 1983; Thurman, 1985), but also to understand better the processes through which behaviors can influence health by directly affecting bodily functioning.

A second means by which behavior is linked to physical health and illness is through habits and life-styles that can have maladaptive physical effects. This behavioral category has received the most attention in the media and probably comprises the types of problems that are most amenable to behavioral therapies. As we have already noted, behaviors such as cigarette smoking, lack of exercise, poor nutrition habits, and refusal to wear seat belts have been clearly linked to diseases or other forms of physical insult.

Perhaps the most serious maladaptive health behavior is cigarette smoking. Smoking has been linked to several types of cancer, including cancers of the lung, mouth, esophagus, pancreas, bladder, and kidney (Reif, 1981), and to coronary heart disease, chronic obstructive pulmonary diseases, and various diseases of the kidney. Altogether, smoking is regarded as the single most important preventable behavioral factor contributing to illness, disability, and death in the United States (Perry, Killen, Telch, Slinkard, & Danaher, 1980).

Most people probably begin smoking for any of a variety of reasons ranging from curiosity to peer pressure. Modeling and social reinforcement of one type or another typically maintain the behavior, which can quickly become habit-forming. Because of the important role of learning in smoking behavior, the primary approaches to preventing or treating the problem, other than simple education, are behavioral in nature. In fact, almost every behavior therapy technique described in the preceding chapters has been used to help people to stop smoking. As we will illustrate later in the chapter, therapists' success in this area has been mixed, with fairly good initial results but a disappointingly large relapse rate.

The final mechanism by which behavior can

influence health and disease involves people's reactions to perceived illness, actual illness, treatments for illness, and precautions intended to prevent illness or promote health. One of the most prominent examples of behavior that falls in this category is adherence behavior—that is, the extent to which patients adhere to or comply with the health professional's advice. For example, failure to take prescribed medication, to follow a recommended diet, or to comply with a behavior therapist's instructions in a smoking cessation program can have serious effects, ranging from increasing the risk of developing an illness to exacerbating the course of a current illness. Nonadherence can also lead to additional problems. Gatchel and Baum (1983) give the example of a man who failed to follow his physician's prescription, but rather than admit this to the physician, insisted that he took the medicine as prescribed. Because the patient did not improve as expected, and the doctor believed the patient, the physician decided that the initial diagnosis must have been incorrect and thus proceeded to prescribe a new and irrelevant treatment. Obviously, the failure to comply coupled with the failure to admit noncompliance led to a waste of time and money. More importantly, it also might have led to an exacerbation of the disease and the need for more aggressive intervention. Multiply these examples by the millions of times they probably occur each day throughout this country—it is estimated that over 30 percent of all patients fail to follow their health professional's recommendations (Taylor, 1986)—and we can begin to understand one reason why health care costs are so high.

Research has shown that poor learning can contribute to poor compliance. If a patient does not understand the professional's instructions, or is not motivated to follow them, adherence will be low. In a similar vein, behavioral techniques that promote adequate motivation and learning can drastically improve compliance. For example, several studies have suggested that self-monitoring strategies, self-supervision, and

the arrangement of frequent reporting to and reinforcement by medical professionals can increase compliance levels by as much as 60 percent (Gatchel & Baum, 1983).

Sometimes adherence behaviors are aimed at preventing health problems from developing or providing for their early detection and treatment. For example, some people simply ignore such things as an unusual lump on the breast, or a mole that seems to be spreading, or frequent exposure to sunlight, even though they "know" the risks involved in such behavior. Adherence to smoking cessation programs, as we noted previously, is a serious problem. Patients do not limit their noncompliance to instructions given by medical professionals; noncompliance is also a problem for behavior therapists. Figure 11–1, for example, illustrates the characteristic pattern of relapse after treatment for heroin, smoking, and alcohol addiction (Hunt, Barnett, & Ranch, 1971). As the data suggest, many treatment programs are successful in producing immediate effects, but their success in produc-

Figure 11–1 *Relapse rates over time for addictive behaviors following treatment.*

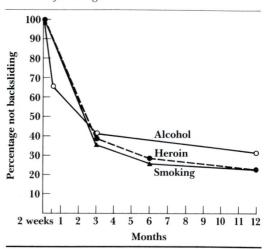

From Hunt et al. (1971).

ing lasting change is disappointing. An important theme that emerges in the use of behavioral (and other) therapies in behavioral medicine is the problem of long-term effectiveness, often due to decreasing compliance with prescribed intervention strategies over time.

A very different example of how people's behaviors can influence their health involves maladaptive approaches to preventing disease or responding to perceived symptoms. Some people overemphasize the importance of certain behaviors in causing or preventing disease and go to unnecessary and unwise lengths to prevent disease. In fact, in some cases the so-called preventive behaviors are so extreme that they may actually increase the likelihood of developing health-related problems. A graphic example of such maladaptive behavior comes from the recent biography of multimillionaire Howard Hughes (Fowler, 1986), a portion of which is reprinted in Figure 11–2. Hughes's extreme behavior apparently resulted at least in part from a phobic concern with illness which he developed in his early childhood. Because of his power and money, Hughes's outrageous demands were not questioned by his staff. What might have been an easily treated fear or avoidance response became a moribund behavioral repetoire.

Behavior, therefore, can decrease health and promote illness and other physical problems through three major mechanisms: direct effects on bodily tissue, health-impairing habits, and maladaptive reactions to illness or health promotion activities. Table 11–3 lists some of the leading causes of death and some of the behaviors known to contribute to them. As the table indicates, many of the health problems that exist today are, at least in part, actually behavioral problems. Table 11–3 also lists some of the behavioral interventions that have shown to be effective in preventing or modifying these maladaptive behaviors. In the remainder of the chapter, we focus on the use of behavioral interventions as applied to behavioral medicine problems.

Use of Behavioral Techniques in the Prevention and Treatment of Behavioral Medicine Problems

Because behavior plays such a critical role in many of today's health problems, behavior change procedures have come to play an increasingly important role in the health and illness field. Over the last 20 years, each of the behavioral techniques discussed in the previous chapters have been applied to health-related problems. In the sections that follow, we will provide examples of the application of major behavior therapy interventions for the promotion of health and the prevention or treatment of disease. The intent of these sections is to be illustrative rather than comprehensive in coverage. They focus on demonstrating the types of problems for which behavioral interventions have had the most success and appear to have the most promise and on describing the types of challenges that face the behavior therapist working in the behavioral medicine area.

Prevention Versus Treatment

Behavior therapy procedures have been used in two primary ways in the behavioral medicine area, for the *prevention of disease and promotion of health* and for the *treatment* of already extant health-related problems. The first way in which behavior therapy techniques have been used focuses on maintaining health by promoting positive life-style habits. This emphasis is sometimes referred to as *primary prevention*. Matarazzo (1980, 1982) and others have convincingly pointed out that this is the area in which interventions based on the behavioral sciences can have their greatest impact. This is true because in terms of expense, effort, and suffering, it is usually easier to prevent a problem from

Figure 11–2   *Howard Hughes: A Disturbed Obsession With Health*

Howard Hughes, Jr., was the child of a hearty, extroverted but often absent father and a quiet, softspoken mother who focused her full attention on her only child. Young Howard, usually called Sonny, was thin and slightly built, and Allene Hughes constantly worried about his health, particularly his teeth, feet, digestion, and bowels, for which she gave him nightly doses of mineral oil as a laxative.

He was separated from his mother for the first time when he went to summer camp at the age of 10. While he was there, his mother worried incessantly and wrote the camp with instructions about caring for his health. Both parents requested reassurance that Howard would be protected from "the violent germs" of polio, which they felt could be so easily carried "even by a well person." Eventually, Allene Hughes took Howard out of camp because of her fear that he might be exposed to polio. . . .

Using illness to escape social pressures, which continued throughout Howard's life, seems to have been well established by the time he reached adolescence. When Howard was 12, he and a group of boys interested in shortwave radio formed a club that met in his room. This atypical involvement with other boys was interrupted when Howard became ill and had to stay out of school for much of the winter and spring.

When he was 13, he developed more frightening symptoms. He was suddenly unable to walk and appeared to be paralyzed. His parents, desperately afraid that he might have polio, brought a physician from New York to care for him full time. Howard was immobilized for several months, but the condition was never diagnosed and disappeared without any specific treatment. Whether the illness was real or imagined, it may well have served as a way for Howard to avoid the increasing social demands characteristic of the early teenage years. . . .

But by the time Hughes was 24, things began to change for the worse. He kept odd hours, hated to be photographed, avoided large parties, and was even shier and more uncomfortable around strangers. His excessive fear of disease and the extraordinary precautions he took to avoid germs added to his growing reputation as an eccentric. He gargled often and avoided people with colds. One time, when he found out that an actress with whom he had been having an affair had been exposed to a venereal disease, he stuffed all of his clothes in canvas bags and ordered them burned.

As a child, Hughes dealt with his anxiety first by avoidant behavior and later by using illness as an escape. His increasing fear of germs as a young man suggests the beginning of an obsessive-compulsive disorder. Obsessions are persistent, recurrent and distressing thoughts. Compulsions are repetitive types of behavior designed to protect against a future situation. Hughes's fear of and precautions against germs had already gone beyond what most people regard as normal and eventually escalated into seriously disruptive behavior. . . .

[In his 40s] his fear of germs became worse. He made people who worked with him carry out elaborate hand-washing rituals and wear white cotton gloves, sometimes several pairs, when handling documents he would later touch. Newspapers had to be brought to him in stacks of three so he could slide the middle, and presumably least contaminated, copy out by grasping it with Kleenex. To escape contamination by dust, he ordered that masking tape be put around the doors and windows of his cars and houses. His employees were told not to touch him, speak directly to him, or even look at him. When asked about his behavior, he defended it by saying, "Everybody carries germs around with them. I want to live longer than my parents, so I avoid germs."

From Fowler (1986).

Table 11–3 **Behaviors Associated With Leading Causes of Death**

Health Problem	Contributing Behaviors	Examples of Behavioral Treatments
Heart disease	Eating excessive animal fats (Lovenberg & Tamori, 1984)	Stimulus control, contingency management (Foreyt, Mitchell, Garner, Gee, Scott, & Gotto, 1982)
	Smoking (Holbrook, Grundy, Hennekens, Kannel, & Strong, 1984)	Satiation (Lando, 1977)
	Inadequate physical activity (Paffenbarger & Hale, 1975)	Stimulus control, self-reinforcement (Keefe & Blumenthal, 1980)
	Type A behavior (Haynes, Feinleib, & Kannel, 1980)	Self-control training, RT (Levenkron, Cohen, Mueller, & Fisher, 1983)
	Excessive calorie consumption (Davidoff, 1983)	Self-monitoring, assertiveness training, stimulus control (Wadden, Stunkard, Brownwell, & Day, 1984)
Malignant neoplasms	Smoking (Mori & Sakai, 1984)	Monitored nicotine fading (Fox & Brown, 1979)
	Insufficient fiber in diet (American Cancer Society Special Report, 1984)	Goal-setting (Wing, Epstein, Nowalk, Koeske, & Hagg, 1985)
Cerebrovascular diseases	Smoking (Mustacchi, 1985)	Contingency management/behavioral contracting (Paxton, 1980)
	Excessive dietary sodium (Werber, Baumbach, Wagner, Mark, & Heistad, 1985)	Self-monitoring, goal-setting (Jacob, Fortman, Farguhar, & Agras, 1985)
	Excessive calorie consumption (Kagan, Popper, Rhoads, & Yano, 1985)	Covert sensitization, chaining, cognitive restructuring (Kirschenbaum, Stalonas, Zostowny, & Tomarken, 1985)

Table 11–3 (continued)

Health Problem	Contributing Behaviors	Examples of Behavioral Treatments
Accidents	Excessive alcohol consumption (Soderstrom, Arias, Carson, & Cowley, 1984)	Flooding/response prevention (Rankin, Hodgson, & Stockwell, 1983)
	Nonuse of seat belts (States, 1985)	Delayed reinforcement (Geller, 1984)
Influenza and pneumonia	Smoking (Kark, Lebiush, & Rannon, 1982)	Rapid smoking (Hall, Sachs, & Hall, 1979)
Diabetes	Excessive caloric consumption (Bonham & Brock, 1985)	Punishment, stimulus control (Rainwater, Ayllon, Fredericksen, Moore, & Bonar, 1982)
	Excessive dietary sugar (Moss & Mayer, 1977)	Contingency management (Green, 1978)
Arteriosclerosis	Smoking (Rabkin, 1984)	Controlled smoking (Frederikson & Simon, 1978a, 1978b)
Cirrhosis of the liver	Excessive alcohol intake (Norick et al., 1985)	Behavioral marital therapy, behavior rehearsal, homework assignments (O'Farrell, Cutter, & Floyd, 1984)
Bronchitis, emphysema, and asthma	Stress reaction (Dudley, Glaser, Jorgenson, & Logan, 1980)	Relaxation training (Atkins, Kaplan, Timms, Reinsch, & Lofbak, 1984)

occurring than to treat it after it has occurred. For example, preventing people from smoking and from developing alcohol and drug addictions, poor nutritional habits, and sick-role behaviors that produce procrastination in seeking help for major symptoms is a much more effective way of promoting health than is trying to diagnose and treat the health problems that the behaviors cause after they have become ingrained habits. Unfortunately, however, up until very recently, relatively little emphasis has been placed on primary prevention by health professionals, including behavior therapists. There are several reasons for this.

Healthy people, even though they may have unhealthy behavior habits, rarely seek help in changing those behaviors. When people are relatively young and feel good, they often are not concerned about health, and in some cases they even believe that they are relatively impervious to health problems. Because of this lack of concern about illness and an absence of immediate health problems, there is often a lack of incentive for practicing positive health habits, especially because many people view health behaviors (e.g., regular exercise, avoiding fatty foods, moderate drinking of or abstinence from alcoholic beverages) as lacking in positive reinforcement value, if not downright painful!

One of the most important times to intervene to teach healthy life-style habits is during the formative school-age years. Habits regarding nutrition, dental hygiene, alcohol, sick-role behavior, exercise, and a host of other health-relevant behaviors develop during this time. But because children are usually healthy and are perceived to be many years away from any likely health problems, adults have little motivation to put forth the effort to teach them good health habits. Fortunately, this thinking is beginning to change, primarily for two reasons. First, adults are becoming more health conscious and are more aware of the importance of health behaviors, and as a result are more likely to model and reinforce similar behaviors in their chil-

dren. Second, recent epidemiological studies are producing alarming data about the development of health problems in school-age individuals. Figure 11–3 illustrates, for example, the number of youths who regularly drink alcoholic beverages and the number who have serious drinking problems. Such figures make clear the need to begin to teach health promotion habits at an early age.

Although behavior change procedures are perhaps most likely to have a major impact in the prevention area, they also play an important role in treating already extant health-related problems. For example, behavior therapy techniques have been widely used to alleviate pain, reduce the distress of surgery, lower blood pressure, and increase adherence to medical interventions, such as medication prescriptions, diet changes, and exercise regimens. In some contexts behavioral techniques are combined with medical interventions to form a comprehensive

Figure 11–3 Percentages of youngsters in grades 7 through 12 who admitted being drinkers or problem drinkers—defined as drunkenness six times during the past year or trouble related to alcohol (male: ▢ drinker, ▨ problem drinker; female: ☐ drinker, ▨ problem drinker).

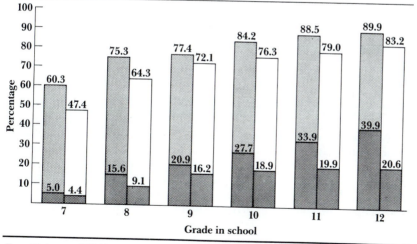

From Matarrazo (1982).

health package, while in other contexts they are applied independent of or instead of medical interventions. Of course, whenever a behavioral scientist treats a person with a medical condition, he or she should first be sure that the patient has had an adequate medical workup and that the prescribed behavioral treatment does not interfere with or lead to a delay in seeking appropriate medical care. Also, behavior therapists working with patients who are under the care of a physician should communicate, with the patient's permission, with the patient's physician in order to coordinate a maximally effective multidisciplinary treatment approach.

In the sections that follow, we illustrate some applications of behavior change procedures that have been the most widely used in the behavioral medicine area. The discussion of each technique is divided into sections that focus on health promotion and primary prevention and on treatment applications.

Behavioral Relaxation Strategies

Behavioral relaxation strategies are perhaps the most commonly used behavior change techniques in the behavioral medicine area. There are at least three reasons for their popularity. First, as we saw in Chapter 2, behavioral relaxation techniques have long been recognized as effective in helping to control stress. Because stress has been known for many years to be a component of many psychiatric problems, most behavior therapists have learned relaxation strategies and frequently use them in their practices. Once it became widely recognized that stress can also play a role in the etiology and course of physical problems, it was a natural development for behavior therapists to use their relaxation techniques within the behavioral medicine area.

A second reason for the popularity of relaxation strategies in the behavioral medicine area is the considerable data suggesting that these techniques can directly affect physiological functioning, making them intuitively appealing even for medical professionals. One of the major historical figures in the development of relaxation strategies, Edmund Jacobson, himself a physician, demonstrated that relaxation training can produce direct changes in physiological functioning, including changes in autonomic arousal and EMG levels. Subsequent research has shown that it can also directly affect noradrenaline levels (Hoffman et al., 1982), and the functioning of the immune system (Kiecolt-Glaser et al., 1985).

A third reason for the popularity of relaxation strategies in the behavioral medicine area is that they are easy to teach and learn, rarely have negative side effects, are inexpensive, and can eventually be applied by the patient him- or herself without continued professional intervention. All of these attributes make relaxation a practical intervention, even within a medical context.

Within the research literature on behavioral medicine, relaxation strategies have been used alone and in conjunction with other behavioral and medical interventions in a wide variety of prevention and treatment contexts. We will focus on published research in which relaxation strategies were the only or the primary intervention employed. However, we should emphasize that, in most clinical contexts, relaxation is usually combined with other treatment approaches.

Health Promotion and Illness Prevention One of the most common health promotion and disease preventive uses of relaxation strategies is to help individuals cope better with stress. Much of the classic research in this area was carried out long before behavioral medicine was recognized as an area of study and application. For example, in the late 1960s, Gordon Paul (1969) demonstrated that progressive muscle relaxation training could produce significant decreases in heart rate, respiratory rate, and muscle tension levels and that these changes were often greater than those that could be produced by other psychological interventions, such as hypnosis. A host of additional research has confirmed these findings.

More recent research has focused on whether relaxation training can alter indices of stress that are believed to be directly involved with the etiology of disease. One of the most intriguing lines of research in this area involves exploring the effect of relaxation training on the functioning of the immune system. Data from a variety of studies suggests that high levels of stress can decrease the competence of the immune system, thereby increasing a person's susceptibility to a variety of diseases (Ader, 1981; Cohen, 1980). The question that several recent studies have explored is whether relaxation training can reduce stress and thereby reverse this potentially deleterious effect on immune functioning. In one of the best studies in this area, Kiecolt-Glaser and her colleagues (1985) randomly assigned 45 geriatric subjects to one of three conditions: progressive muscle relaxation training with guided relaxation imagery; social contact, in which a student simply visited with the subject; and no-contact control. Subjects in the first two groups were visited three times a week for four consecutive weeks. Several measures of immunocompetence were collected from blood samples, both immediately after treatment and at a one-month follow-up testing, including the level of natural killer (NK) cell activity and an index of the amount of certain lymphocytes, both of which help to fight infections. At the end of the intervention period, subjects in the relaxation condition showed a significant enhancement of immune functioning, whereas subjects in the other two groups did not. This positive difference was much reduced at the follow-up time, probably because only four relaxation subjects continued to practice the technique. Nonetheless, these exciting data suggest that the regular practice of relaxation training may produce demonstrable changes in immune functioning. Important questions for future research are whether or not these effects lead to a decrease in subsequent medical problems and whether or not people

who are ill can strengthen an already taxed immune system through relaxation training.

Little and her colleagues (1984) used relaxation training to help prevent problems during pregnancy in a high-risk group. This group consisted of women with somewhat elevated blood pressures (135/85mm Hg). Women who develop high blood pressure during pregnancy have a much higher than normal risk of complications to themselves and to their babies, and therefore it is important to prevent such elevations from occurring. Little et al. assigned 60 pregnant women to groups that received relaxation training, relaxation training plus skin conductance biofeedback, or no behavioral intervention. Subjects in the first two groups received weekly training sessions for six weeks and were given relaxation tapes to practice at home. Results indicated that women in the two intervention groups generally showed significantly lower blood pressures throughout pregnancy than did women in the control group. More importantly, the results also indicated that a significantly greater proportion of patients in the no-intervention group (67 percent) had to be admitted to the hospital for problems developing during the course of pregnancy than in either the relaxation (28 percent) or the relaxation plus biofeedback (28 percent) groups. Moreover, when patients were admitted, their hospital stay was significantly longer if they were in the no-treatment group (6.5 days) than if they were in the relaxation (2.3 days) or relaxation plus biofeedback (1.8 days) groups, which did not differ significantly from each other. These data strongly suggest that relaxation training can be highly effective in helping to prevent complications during pregnancy in women who are at increased risk because of their blood pressures. They also suggest that, in this situation, the biofeedback added little to the relaxation procedure. Other research has suggested that relaxation also can help patients to cope more effectively with a variety of other medical procedures including electromyographic examinations (Kaplan, Metzger, &

Jablecki, 1983) and sigmoidoscopies (Kaplan, Atkins, & Lenhard, 1982).

Treatment Relaxation training has been used to help reduce the distress of almost every type of medical disorder. For example, Wilson (1981) randomly assigned 33 cholescystectomy patients and 37 abdominal hysterectomy patients to one of four preoperative intervention groups: information only, in which patients listened to a taped message describing the sensations and procedures likely to be experienced during their hospitalization for the surgery; taped relaxation training; information plus relaxation training; or usual hospital procedures only. All patients received their intervention the evening before the surgery; relaxation patients were allowed to play the relaxation tape as often as they wished after surgery (45 percent used the tape at least once a day postsurgery). A variety of dependent measures was collected daily during the hospital stay. The results indicated that patients in the relaxation condition reported less pain, asked for fewer pain medications, reported increased strength and energy, and left the hospital sooner than did patients in the control condition. Information-only patients left the hospital sooner than did control patients but did not show any of the other effects. Receiving relaxation plus information generally did not appear to be more effective than receiving only relaxation training.

In addition to examining the general treatment effects of relaxation and information, Wilson (1981) also assessed whether certain individual difference variables affected treatment outcome, including patients' preoperative levels of fear, their aggressiveness, and the extent to which they used denial as a coping strategy. With respect to relaxation training, the results suggested that less frightened patients benefited more than highly frightened patients. With the information manipulation, patients who were less aggressive did not stay as long in the hospital but reported more pain and asked for more pain medication than patients high in aggres-

siveness. Interestingly, patients who were high users of denial showed no negative effects from being given either the information or the relaxation preparation procedures.

One of the most frequent behavioral medicine uses of relaxation training is to treat hypertension. Hypertension, or high blood pressure, affects 10–15 percent of the adult population (Shapiro, Schwartz, Ferguson, Redmond, & Weiss, 1977) and is thought to be a major health problem because it increases substantially the risk of strokes, myocardial infarctions, kidney problems, and a variety of other disorders. The diagnosis of high blood pressure is not made on the basis of a specific blood pressure level, but rather in reference to a gradient: the higher one's blood pressure, the greater one's risk of many other diseases and the greater the reduction in one's life expectancy (Shapiro & Goldstein, 1982). The preferred treatment for hypertension varies as a function of a number of factors, including the severity of the problem. For mild levels of hypertension, a change in diet, weight loss, or the regular use of relaxation procedures may be adequate. For higher levels of hypertension, some type of medication is usually prescribed. However, even in these cases, relaxation may be a useful adjunctive treatment which may sometimes result in a reduction in the level of medication taken.

Table 11-4 lists the outcome of several studies in which relaxation training is used with hypertensives. Although this table is not a complete listing of all the research conducted in the area, it does indicate the overall trend: relaxation training can be a highly effective adjunctive treatment for hypertension. We have already described in Chapter 2 several studies in which relaxation training was successfully used to treat hypertension. Additional research has begun to identify factors that might help to predict which types of hypertensives are most and least likely to benefit from relaxation strategies. For example, Crowther, Taylor, and Hoge (1982) administered eight sessions of relaxation training plus relaxation imagery to 29 hypertensive

Table 11–4 **Results of Representative Studies of Relaxation Techniques on Blood Pressure**

Study	Treatment	N	Initial	SBP (mm Hg) Posttreatment Change	Follow-up Change	Initial	DBP (mm Hg) Posttreatment Change	Follow-up Change
Agras et al. (1983)	PMRT,[a] clinic	12	144	8 wks. + boosters −16	15 months −16	97	−14	−14
	PMRT, work place	12	143	− 9	−12	93	− 6	− 8
	NT, clinic	18	141	− 2	− 6	94	− 2	− 7
	NT, work place	18	140	− 2	− 5	92	+ 2	+ 1
Brauer et al. (1979)	PMRT, therapist	10	153	−10	6 months −17	93	− 5	−10
	PMRT, tape	9	150	− 5	+ 1	95	− 1	− 5
		10	145	− 9	− 1	93	− 4	− 1
Hafner (1982)	Meditation	7	146	−15	3 months −13	103	−14	−15
	Meditation and biofeedback (EMG or SR)	7	160	−22	−21	107	−15	−15
	NTC	7	160	− 8	− 9	98	− 3	− 3
Hatch et al. (1985)	PMRT	13	148	−18	12 months −19	89	− 5	−10
	DBP biofeedback	13	135	− 9	0	87	− 7	− 2
	Instructions only	13	136	− 5	− 2	87	− 3	− 9
	Medication only	13	136	− 7	−11	88	− 5	− 6
Hoelscher et al. (1986)	PMRT, individual	11	153	4 weeks −13	10 weeks −15	97	− 5	− 5
	PMRT, group	12	150	−11	−14	95	− 3	− 5
	PMRT and contingency contract	12	150	−10	−10	95	− 4	− 7
	Waitlist control	12	145	− 1	+ 2	96	0	0
Surwit et al. (1978)	Benson Relaxation Training	8	141	− 5	6 weeks − 5	——	——	——
	EMG biofeedback	8	136	+ 9	− 3	——	——	——
	BP biofeedback	8	136	+ 6	+ 1	——	——	——
Wadden (1983)	PMRT, spouse not involved	16	136	− 6	5 months − 9	91	− 5	− 8
	PMRT, spouse involved	15	143	− 7	− 7	91	− 5	− 7

[a]PMRT: Progressive muscle relaxation training

individuals (all with blood pressures greater than 140/90). During a pretreatment session, subjects completed an assessment battery that included a variety of psychosocial tests. The data indicated first that subjects showed a mean reduction in blood pressure of 16.2mm Hg systolic, and 7.6mm Hg diastolic, following relaxation training. More interestingly, analyses suggested that subjects who had higher trait anxiety scores and who had less competitive and high-pressure occupations were more likely to show postrelaxation reductions in systolic or diastolic blood pressure.

Somewhat similar results were reported by Wadden (1983). He found that hypertensive subjects who had high trait anxiety scores showed greater reductions in systolic blood pressure one month after relaxation training, and that subjects who scored high on measures of job involvement and being hard driving and competitive showed less improvement in systolic and/or diastolic blood pressure. Unfortunately, neither the Crowther et al. nor the Wadden study included any control groups, and as a result their findings must be regarded with caution. For example, possible reductions in blood pressure by simple "regression to the mean" may have contributed to the results in both studies. Nonetheless, altogether, these and other data in the hypertension area suggest that relaxation procedures can help most but not all hypertensive individuals to produce clinically significant reductions in their blood pressure levels.

Another problem for which relaxation training has been used frequently is headaches. For example, following four weeks of collecting baseline levels of headache activity, Blanchard and his colleagues (1982) administered 10 sessions of progressive muscle relaxation training to 91 subjects diagnosed as having tension, migraine, or combined tension and migraine headaches. Posttreatment analyses indicated that subjects in all three groups showed significant reductions in headache intensity and duration and a significant increase in the

number of headache-free days.[1] Comparable results have been found by others who have included placebo treatment groups or no-treatment control groups (see reviews by Adams, Feuerstein, & Fowler, 1980; Blanchard, Ahles, & Shaw, 1979; and Blanchard & Andrasik, 1982). In an overall meta-analysis of published studies on the use of relaxation training with headache patients, Blanchard and his colleagues (1980) calculated that, on the average, relaxation training produces approximately a 59 percent improvement across various indices of outcome by the end of the treatment.

A more recent use of relaxation training within the behavioral medicine context involves cancer patients who receive chemotherapy treatments. Because chemotherapy can be highly aversive in some cases, causing severe side effects, which include intense and prolonged nausea and vomiting, many patients develop conditioned side effects to their treatments. The sight of the chemotherapy nurse, the smell of the drugs, or even the thought of receiving chemotherapy can cause some patients to feel nauseated and even to vomit (Burish & Carey, 1986). Relaxation training has been used to treat these classically conditioned side effects and the high levels of dysphoria that often accompany them. For example, Lyles, Burish, Krozely, and Oldham (1982) assigned 55 cancer chemotherapy patients to one of three conditions: relaxation training with guided relaxation imagery; therapist control, in which a therapist spent an amount of time with each patient equal to that spent with a matched relaxation patient but without administering relaxation; and no-treatment control. Patients in the relaxation condition received training before and during three consecutive chemotherapy infusions and were asked to practice daily at home. They were

[1]Following the administration of relaxation training, patients who did not show substantial improvement were given training in some type of biofeedback treatment. The outcome of the biofeedback intervention is discussed later in the chapter.

then encouraged to use relaxation on their own during a fourth chemotherapy treatment. During the three training treatments, patients in the relaxation condition reported significantly less nausea during and after chemotherapy and had significantly lower levels of postchemotherapy blood pressure, pulse rate, anxiety, and depression. For the most part, these results continued, although at somewhat weaker levels, during the session in which patients self-administered relaxation training.

An interesting question generated by the results of the Lyles et al. (1982) study and several similar reports is why relaxation decreased nausea. In a discussion of that question, we have suggested that it may be due to the effects that relaxation has on biochemical processes in the brain (Burish & Carey, 1984; Burish, 1986). It appears that the effects of relaxation may be similar to those of some antiemetic medications in that they dampen the activity of the "vomiting center," which is located in the lower brain stem, probably through effects on the mediating pathways in the cortex or other brain areas. Although work addressing this question is just beginning, the data that do exist suggest that this could be an important and exciting area of investigation.

In addition to the areas mentioned above, relaxation training procedures have been used in association with the treatment of a variety of other problems, including chronic low back pain (e.g., Turner, 1982), bruxism (e.g., Glaros & Rao, 1977), temporomandibular joint pain (e.g., Funch & Gale, 1984), Raynaud's disease (e.g., Surwit, Allen, Gilgor, & Duvie, 1982), and cystic fibrosis (e.g., Spirito, Russo, & Masek, 1984).

Although relaxation procedures are popular and usually effective, there do appear to be problems for which they are of little use or may even be detrimental. For example, Sigman and Zalman (1982) found that progressive muscle relaxation training had no positive effect on reducing gastric acid output. The researchers had 14 college students swallow an apparatus that allowed an experimenter to measure acid output in the stomach. Acid levels were measured before and after subjects had practiced relaxation eight times. Results indicated that there were no differences between pretraining and posttraining levels. In fact, 8 of the 14 subjects actually increased acid secretion following the relaxation training. Relaxation has also been reported as ineffective in reducing spontaneous bleeding in hemophiliacs (Lichstein & Eakin, 1985); reducing the severity of tinnitus, a disorder that produces an uncomfortable ringing in the ears (Ireland, Wilson, Tonkin, & Platt-Hepworth, 1985); and decreasing the symptoms of primary dysmenorrhea (Bennink, Hulst, & Benthem, 1982).

In summary, behavioral relaxation procedures are among the most popular and effective behavioral interventions used to promote health, prevent illness, and treat health-related problems. In most cases, relaxation procedures are used as part of a multimodal treatment package that usually includes other behavioral, educational, and/or medical intervention components. In spite of the widespread use of relaxation procedures, however, remember that they are not useful for all behavioral medicine problems, and even with problems for which they have proven to be effective, they will not work with all individuals. The careful monitoring of treatment outcome on an individual-by-individual basis is, as with the more traditional areas of behavior therapy, a necessary component of responsible therapy.

Systematic Desensitization

The uses of systematic desensitization within behavioral medicine have been rather straightforward extensions of their most common use within the traditional behavior therapy literature: to reduce maladaptive levels of fear. In some cases, this fear prevents people from engaging in appropriate health promotion–disease prevention behaviors, such as regular dental examinations. In other cases, the fears are associated with extant disease states or aversive treatments, such as asthma and cancer chemo-therapy. Sometimes the health-related problem is, at least in part, a consequence of a more central psychological problem, such as when persistent fear or anxiety leads to gastric ulcers. In other cases, the aversiveness of the disease or its treatment lead to the develop-ment of intensive and maladaptive fears, such as in the development of needle phobias. How-ever, since the basic application of systematic desensitization within the behavioral medicine area is similar regardless of the particular problem, we will not divide our discussion of desensitization into separate sections on health promotion–disease prevention and treatment. Rather, we will present a few general illustra-tions of the application of systematic desensiti-zation that can serve as examples for the area as a whole.

Morrow and Morrell (1982) have described the highly successful use of desensitization to reduce the conditioned side effects of cancer chemotherapy. These investigators worked with cancer patients who had been receiving emeto-genic chemotherapy treatments (i.e., drugs that produce intense nausea and vomiting) and who, as a result, developed conditioned nausea and/or vomiting responses during the days and especially hours immediately before each chemotherapy treatment. Hypothesizing that these responses were similar to phobic reactions to other aversive events, the investigators taught the patients progressive muscle relaxation train-ing and then exposed them to a graduated fear hierarchy. The hierarchy, which was the same for each patient, was as follows:

1. Driving to the chemotherapy clinic
2. After dinner, the evening before the treat-ment
3. Waking up and getting ready to go to the hospital on the morning of treatment
4. Eating breakfast the day of the treatment
5. Waiting in the treatment room for the chemotherapy to start

6. Seeing the chemotherapy nurse enter the room to administer the treatment[2]

All participants completed this hierarchy in two sessions, which were held between the pa-tients' fourth and fifth chemotherapy treat-ments. Patients' nausea and vomiting responses during their fifth and sixth treatments were then recorded on a specially designed scale. Two other groups of patients were included in the study: a placebo group that received two sessions of Rogerian-like counseling, and a no-treatment control group. The results indicated that patients who received systematic desensiti-zation subsequently reported significantly less frequent, less severe, and shorter-lasting nausea and vomiting than did patients in either of the other conditions, who did not differ significantly from each other.

In an interesting follow-up investigation to this study, Morrow taught physicians and nurses who were working with cancer patients to ad-minister the desensitization procedure, instead of using experienced psychologists.[3] The train-ing of medical personnel to administer behavior therapy procedures is becoming increasingly common in medical settings. In general, this trend is to be encouraged because it allows the more widespread application of behavioral in-terventions to a large and growing number of people who can benefit from them. However, behavior therapists must keep in mind that when training professionals in other fields to use behavioral techniques, they are responsible for assuring that the quantity and quality of that training are adequate and that they are available for consultation as appropriate.

Gatchel (1980) used group-administered de-sensitization to reduce fear of dental procedures in a group of people whose fear was so extreme

---

[2]Personal communication from Gary Morrow (De-cember 1985).
[3]Personal communication from Gary Morrow (De-cember 1985).

that they were avoiding making needed appointments with their dentists. Gatchel trained four dentists from the community to administer the treatment. As is usually the case with group-administered desensitization, the same hierarchy was used for all patients (see Gatchel & Baum, 1983):

1. Thinking about going to the dentist
2. Calling for an appointment with the dentist
3. Getting in the car to go to the dentist's office
4. Sitting in the waiting room of the dentist's office.
5. Having the nurse tell you it's your turn
6. Getting into the dentist's chair
7. Seeing the dentist lay out the instruments, one of which is a probe
8. Seeing the dentist lay out the instruments, one of which is pliers used to pull teeth
9. Having a probe held in front of you while you look at it
10. Having a probe placed on the side of a tooth
11. Having a probe placed in a cavity
12. Getting an injection in your gums on one side
13. Having your teeth drilled and worrying if the anesthetic will wear off
14. Getting two injections, one on each side
15. Hearing the crunching sounds as your tooth is being pulled

In addition to the desensitization group, two other groups were included in the study: a discussion group, which met to discuss their dental anxiety and how to deal with it more effectively; and a no-treatment control group. The results indicated that both the desensitization and discussion groups evinced a significantly greater frequency than did the control group in making appointments with their dentists and following through on those appointments. The desensitization subjects also showed a significantly greater reduction in dental anxiety than subjects in either of the other conditions.

A final example demonstrates the use of *in vivo* desensitization within a single-subject design (Redd, 1980). The patient was a 53-year-old female who originally went to her physician because she was feeling weak and was not able to retain solid foods. She reported that each time she swallowed any solid food, she would immediately regurgitate. The patient underwent a thorough medical examination which revealed that she had a cancerous mass on her esophagus. She was successfully treated with radiation therapy and her original symptoms disappeared. However, about five months later she again started to regurgitate solid foods. Subsequent tests revealed that the cancer had recurred. This time the patient underwent an esophagogastrectomy (removal of the esophagus and upper part of the stomach). Although the procedure appeared to be successful, the patient continued to complain of difficulty swallowing and refused to eat. Medical tests suggested that there was nothing physically wrong to cause the problem. Eventually the patient became dehydrated and lost considerable weight. She was rehospitalized and placed on hyperalimentation (intravenous feeding). The medical staff were considering inserting a feeding tube through her nose into her stomach so that she could go home and feed herself by injecting food through the tube. At that point a behavior therapist was consulted.

After four baseline feeding test trials using various foods, the patient was given four sessions of progressive muscle relaxation training alone. During the fifth and subsequent sessions, she was directed through the relaxation and was then given a small amount of increasingly bulky foods (e.g., Session 5, bouillon; Session 7, soft boiled egg; Session 9, tuna salad; Session 13, chicken). These relaxation sessions were held in the morning, and in the afternoon she was given the same food as in the morning but without the relaxation. By the fourteenth session, she was able to retain all solid foods without regurgitating. At a nine-month follow-up assessment, she was still symptom free.

Because many people develop considerable fears about certain medical procedures or develop conditioned symptoms that can continue long after the original medical reasons for those symptoms have been eradicated (as in the preceding case described by Redd), systematic desensitization is frequently used within the behavioral medicine context. In addition to the problems described above, for example, systematic desensitization has been used for ambulance and hospital phobia (Lazarus & Rachman, 1960), blood phobia (Elmore, Wildman, & Westefeld, 1980), injection phobia (Gatchel & Baum, 1983), hemodialysis phobia (Gatchel & Baum, 1983), asthma (Moore, 1965), and fear of childbirth (Kondas & Scetnicka, 1972). While the majority of applications of desensitization have been effective, we emphasize that it is not appropriate for all fears. Frequently, the fears or concerns a medical patient has are largely based in reality rather than being grossly out of proportion. Moreover, medical patients often must repeatedly go through aversive or painful procedures or treatments of one type or another. In such instances, desensitization may not be the treatment of choice.

Biofeedback

Feedback of information is one of the most important behavior change techniques available. Many of the behavioral techniques we have discussed in this text are based in part on feedback—from a therapist to a client, from group members to each other, from self-observation. For example, behavioral rehearsal is essentially designed to allow a person to develop and perfect new behavior repertoires by receiving corrective and reinforcing feedback about successively closer approximations to the target behavior. The shaping of target behav-

iors by contingent reinforcement based on feedback is also a central component of many non-behavioral therapies, including insight therapies and systems therapies.

Biofeedback, as described in Chapter 10, is simply a type of feedback in which information about a *biological* response is *fed back* to a person in order to allow the person to gain increased control over the response. Since biofeedback by its very nature involves biological responses, its applications have largely been biomedical in nature. It is therefore not surprising that our earlier discussion of biofeedback focused on behavioral medicine problems both in health promotion–disease prevention and in the treatment areas. In this chapter, therefore, we will discuss several interesting clinical examples of how biofeedback can be used with various health-related problems. Keep in mind that in most clinical settings, biofeedback is used as one component of a multimodal treatment approach. For example, when used for stress reduction, it is almost always combined with some type of relaxation instructions or cognitive restructuring exercise. However, for the sake of presentation, we will focus here on the biofeedback procedure per se.

Health Promotion and Illness Prevention Since biofeedback's early rise to prominence within behavior therapy in the 1960s, one of its major applications has been to reduce psychophysiological arousal and, therefore, presumably stress. Barbara Brown (1974), for example, one of the early promoters of biofeedback, suggested that it would replace drug addiction because people would prefer to "turn on to biofeedback" rather than to mind-altering drugs. The media referred to it as "electronic yoga" and advertised inexpensive biofeedback units that could be ordered through the mail. Today, professionals often use frontalis electromyographic (EMG) biofeedback to reduce stress, a procedure whereby a person is taught to reduce EMG levels recorded from the forehead area. Unfortunately, this type of biofeedback either does not reduce general levels of arousal or anxiety any better than simply sitting quietly and resting, or if it does, it usually does not do so any better than more economical and less cumbersome relaxation strategies (e.g., see Burish, 1981; Price & Gatchel, 1979). Hence, although we are not opposed to the use of biofeedback to reduce stress, we do not strongly encourage its use—unless it is combined with some other procedure, such as relaxation training—because we believe there are better alternative behavior therapy techniques available.

An important principle of biofeedback, which accounts both for its success in some areas and its failure in others—such as when frontalis biofeedback is used to reduce general distress—is *progressive discrimination* (e.g. Brener, 1974, 1977). As people learn to control a given physiological response, they often learn to become more and more efficient, making the desired changes with minimum effects on any other physiological system. For example, when first learning to decrease the EMG levels measured from electrodes on the forehead, a subject might try to produce a general relaxation effect throughout the entire body. However, as training continues, the subject will probably become more and more skilled at simply reducing the EMG level of the specific muscles affecting the forehead, without altering the EMG levels of other muscles in the body. Although such efficiency is adaptive from a physiological point of view, it may be at odds with the goal of the therapist, which is to produce a general reduction in muscle tension throughout the body. This same principle also applies to a number of other behavior therapy techniques. In fact, it is *because* people tend to learn to become progressively more efficient at changing only the specific behavior that therapists have to be so concerned with programming in generalization effects. Because biofeedback as it is usually provided is response-specific, generalization, if desired, is often problematic.

Other than for general stress reduction, there are few reported attempts to use biofeed-

back for health promotion or disease prevention. In one of the few exceptions, Peavey and her colleagues (1984) used a biofeedback-assisted relaxation procedure to increase the immune functioning in subjects who rated themselves as being under high stress, and who presumably thereby were candidates for increased illness. Sixteen high stress subjects, as determined by two self-report scales, who also had low immune levels (as measured by a test of phagocytic immune functioning) were randomly assigned either to a group that received frontalis EMG biofeedback training and skin temperature biofeedback training in addition to diaphragmatic breathing and progressive muscle relaxation training, or to a no-treatment control group. Biofeedback subjects received twice-weekly training sessions until they reached the criterion of an EMG level of 1.2 microvolts or less, and a hand temperature of 95 degrees Fahrenheit or higher ($M = 10.75$ sessions). The results of posttraining tests indicated that subjects who received biofeedback-assisted relaxation had significantly lower tension levels and a significantly higher level of immune functioning. Although promising, this study must be considered preliminary and inconclusive because it lacked appropriate experimental procedures (e.g., posttests were not carried out to determine whether the EMG and skin temperature levels of the biofeedback group were lower than those of the control group, and no follow-up testing was conducted to determine the longevity of the immune functioning change or whether it was related to illness prevention). Nonetheless, this study is a good example of the type of illness prevention studies that some have claimed illustrate the potential contribution of biofeedback and other stress-reduction procedures to illness prevention.

Treatment Most applications of biofeedback are for the treatment of disorders or symptoms. Perhaps the most consistently promising treatment application of biofeedback is for neuromuscular reeducation. The general goal of biofeedback in this area, which is usually EMG biofeedback, is to teach a person to exert greater control over the firings or tension levels of muscles that have been injured due to disease or accident, that are associated with pain, or that are in some other way causing difficulties. For example, EMG biofeedback has been used to help treat patients with poliomyelitis, loss of motor control resulting from cerebrovascular accidents (strokes), torticollis, nerve injury, temporomandibular joint disorder, bruxism, blepharospasms, and other disorders (Keefe & Surwit, 1978). Unfortunately, much of the research in this area is of the case study or single subject design, and therefore the results must be regarded with caution.

An example involves the treatment of a 23-year-old woman with periorbital facial muscle tension (Ince, 1983). The woman had a number of problems with her vision. She was given twice-weekly visual therapy, and a prescription for special corrective lenses, but she still complained about tension around the eye muscles (i.e., periorbital facial muscle tension). Her doctor decided that EMG biofeedback might help her learn to reduce these elevated tension levels. Miniature electrodes were placed in the inner and outer canthus of each eye. The patient was given a visual oscilloscopic display of the muscle activity. In addition, each time the EMG level

deviated from a criterion level set by the therapist, a tone sounded. The patient's task, therefore, was to keep the signal tone off. Each eye was trained separately. After approximately 25 30–45 minute sessions, the patient displayed fairly good control of the periorbital muscles. Follow-up contact with the patient 11 months after treatment revealed that she was not experiencing any tension around her eyes.

It is interesting to note that although the treatment for this patient was successful, the biofeedback did not reduce her levels of periorbital muscle tension to "normal" levels. Table 11–5 shows the tension levels of four normal subjects in the relevant muscle regions and the levels of the patient both before and following treatment. As the data indicate, although the patient markedly reduced her levels of muscle tension, and the symptoms remitted, her tension levels were still above those of normal individuals. Such findings are not uncommon in the biofeedback area. One implication of these findings is important to keep in mind: although, following treatment, the patient may not be experiencing the symptom that initiated treatment, he or she may still be at increased risk for reexperiencing the symptom at a later point because of elevated base levels. Teaching patients how to become aware of early signs of the redevelopment of a problem, and how to reini-

Table 11–5 **Muscle Tension Levels (in μ V-sec) of Successfully Treated Patient and Normal Subjects**

	Muscle Tension Levels Around Eyes			
	Right Upper Area	*Right Lower Area*	*Left Upper Area*	*Left Lower Area*
Patient before Tx	12.3	12.3	12.0	26.1
Patient after Tx	8.2	5.6	9.6	7.7
Subject 1	5.3	3.2	4.3	6.6
Subject 2	7.3	2.5	4.2	7.0
Subject 3	4.3	2.7	6.3	1.7
Subject 4	6.5	2.5	4.4	4.0

Note: Although the patient was symptom free, her EMG levels were still above normal.
From Ince (1983).

tiate the self-control procedure, can be an important component of biofeedback therapy.

Brantley and his colleagues (1985) used EMG biofeedback to treat a 58-year-old female patient with blepharospasms, a chronic condition characterized by involuntary, spasmodic closure of the eyelid and frequently accompanied by involuntary movements in other facial muscles. The condition usually begins when a person is in his or her 50s or 60s, and it is more frequent in females than males.

A single-case, A-B-A-C-A experimental design was used to examine the relative effects of a typical pharmacological treatment with EMG biofeedback. After 5 days of baseline assessment (A), the patient was put on a trihexyphenidyl (Artane) for approximately 5 weeks (B). She was then taken off the drug, and baseline assessments continued. After 4 weeks, biofeedback therapy (C) was initiated. She was given three sessions of EMG biofeedback each week for approximately 8 weeks. Feedback was given from electrodes placed approximately one inch above each eye, with the patient's task being to reduce EMG levels, especially eyeblinks. Biofeedback was then terminated and follow-up assessments were conducted at 1, 2, 4, 8, 24, and 42 weeks posttreatment. The results are displayed in Figure 11–4. As the figure shows, EMG levels and eyeblink levels were high at baseline, remained high during drug treatment, and fell only after biofeedback training had been initiated. Importantly, they stayed low after the biofeedback was withdrawn, suggesting that the patient learned self-control of her muscle-tension levels and had not become dependent on the biofeedback machines.

Biofeedback has been extensively applied to a number of gastrointestinal disorders, with perhaps the most successful outcomes being with fecal incontinence. This disorder is especially common with institutionalized geriatric patients, having a prevalence rate that is estimated to be between 16 and 60 percent (American College of Physicians, 1985). It is associated with certain diseases (e.g., multiple

sclerosis, diabetes, irritable bowel syndrome, severe constipation), and can be a postsurgical complication of a number of procedures (e.g., hemorrhoidectomy and fistulectomy). In general, the research literature suggests that biofeedback can reduce substantially the frequency of incontinence in approximately 75 percent of patients, and that these effects are still evident at one- to two-year follow-up assessments (Marzuk, 1985).

For example, Whitehead, Burgio, and Engel (1985) treated 15 patients aged 65–92 who had been referred to them by physicians. In the first phase of the study, the patients were divided into two groups, one of which was instructed to perform 50 sphincter exercises per day, whereas the other was not. The purpose of this phase was to determine whether exercises alone might produce increased control of the sphincter muscles and thereby reduce incontinence. Two patients became continent during this phase. The patients who did not become continent and the no-exercise control patients participated in Phase 2, which involved sphincter exercise as described above plus twice-weekly biofeedback sessions. Biofeedback in this disorder is based on the assumption that through adequate feedback, patients can learn to contract more strongly their external sphincter muscles when distention (resulting from the accumulation of intestinal contents) occurs. It consists of inserting a specially designed balloon into the rectum and inflating it with air, so as to create rectal distention. The patient is instructed to increase sphincter muscle contraction and is able to observe contraction levels on a polygraph tracing. Over time, the amount of air in the balloon is decreased, so that the patient is producing contractions to smaller and smaller amounts of rectal distention. Biofeedback training was continued until either the patient became continent (less than one episode of incontinence a month) or failed to show any improvement on two successive visits. Results indicated that the biofeedback produced significant increases in contraction strength of the sphincter muscles. More

Figure 11–4   *Means for EMG and eyeblink activity as a function of treatment session.*

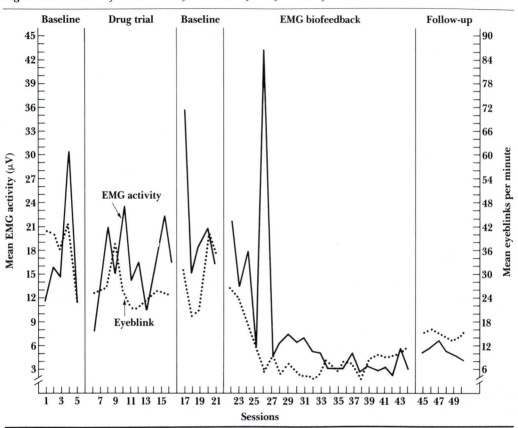

From Brantley, Carnrike, Faulstich, and Barkemeyer (1985).

importantly, 10 of the 13 patients given biofeedback achieved either total continence (6 patients) or at least a 75 percent reduction from their pretreatment levels (4 patients). These gains were maintained in most patients at a 12-month follow-up; in those that showed relapse, the incontinence was associated with a debilitating illness (e.g., stroke).

Biofeedback is not the treatment of choice for all physical problems for which behavioral treatments are appropriate. However, as we have noted several times in prior discussions,

there are tremendous individual differences in response to any intervention, such that biofeedback might work in some cases where the "generally" more effective procedure has proved to be inadequate. Blanchard and his colleagues (1982) have provided an excellent example of this situation. These investigators treated 91 patients with tension, migraine, or combined tension and migraine headaches by providing progressive muscle relaxation training, the intervention that most behavioral clinicians would probably agree is the first-order treatment of choice for headaches. We briefly described this study earlier in the chapter and noted that relaxation training alone produced significant improvement in a large number of patients. However, not all patients benefited, and many of those who did still experienced some headaches. Therefore, following the relaxation training, the investigators gave 49 patients who had not achieved a 60 percent or greater reduction in headache activity 12 sessions of either frontalis EMG biofeedback training (tension headache patients) or skin temperature biofeedback training (migraine and combined headache patients). The results showed that approximately 47 percent of the tension headache patients, 43 percent of the migraine headache patients, and 64 percent of the combined headache patients achieved at least a 50 percent decrease in whatever headache activity remained after relaxation training. Although the lack of a comparison group that continued to receive relaxation training (instead of biofeedback) weakens the study, the data do suggest that biofeedback can be a useful follow-up to relaxation training.

Additional Comment Some believe that the effects of biofeedback therapy, especially when it is applied to bona fide medical or physical problems, are due to the biofeedback per se. As a result, a great deal of attention is devoted to the technology of biofeedback, with relatively little attention devoted to the importance of therapist variables. In our view, this can be a serious clinical error. As with any other behavioral technique, the motivating, instructional, and reinforcing properties of the therapist–client interaction are critical to successful outcome. Biofeedback therapy requires clinical skill, not just mechanical and electronic gadgetry, if it is to be effective. Lazarus (1975) relates the instance of a woman who received 10 weeks of blood pressure biofeedback, during which she successfully reduced her diastolic blood pressure from 97 to about 80mm Hg. The patient was clear about how important the therapist was in the process:

I always depend very heavily on Barry Dworkin's [the therapist] encouragement and on his personality. I think he could be an Olympic Coach. He not only seems aware of my general condition but he is never satisfied with less than my best, and I can't fool him. I feel we are friends and allies—it's really as though *we* were lowering my blood pressure. (1975, p. 555)

Although the specific physiological information that biofeedback provides is critical to its many clinical contributions to behavior medicine, the motivation to use the feedback adaptively, and the reinforcement to continue applying the self-control strategies acquired, often depend heavily on the therapist.

Self-monitoring

Although few behavioral medicine programs use self-monitoring as the sole behavioral treatment, self-monitoring is often an important component of many health-oriented behavioral programs. In general, self-monitoring procedures require that the client record and chart a target behavior each time it occurs (see Chapter 5). By monitoring their behavior, clients are better able to assess the frequency with which the behavior occurs. Keeping careful records of the frequency of health behaviors (e.g., medication intake) may be particularly crucial to the success of a medical intervention. In addition, self-monitoring is thought to have beneficial effects in and of itself (Kazdin, 1974e; Thoresen & Mahoney, 1974). That is, self-monitoring a behavior may actually produce a change in the frequency of the behavior in a desired direction. Therefore, the procedure may help in both increasing positive and decreasing negative health habits. For example, if you are a coffee drinker and would like to cut down on the amount of caffeine you consume, simply recording the number of cups of coffee that you drink in a day may help you reduce your coffee consumption. Self-monitoring procedures have been used in both the prevention and treatment of illness.

Health Promotion and Illness Prevention Self-monitoring techniques have been frequently used to help modify negative health habits. In smoking cessation programs, for example, self-monitoring procedures have been successfully combined with nicotine fading programs to help smokers reduce their tar and nicotine intake (see Lichtenstein, 1982, for a review). In nicotine fading programs, smokers progressively reduce their nicotine intake, often by changing to cigarette brands that contain less tar and nicotine. In addition, smokers self-monitor nicotine and tar reductions, getting feedback on their progress by calculating and graphing their estimated intake of nicotine and tar each day. In general, research has indicated that even if smokers do not completely stop smoking as a result of monitored nicotine fading, most will continue to smoke cigarettes with less tar and nicotine than their baseline brand without increasing their rate of smoking.

For example, Foxx and Axelroth (1983) randomly assigned 12 smokers to one of two groups within a multiple baseline design. Subjects in Group 1 received a one-week baseline whereas subjects in Group 2 received two weeks of baseline conditions. During baseline, subjects were instructed to continue to smoke as they normally would, but were asked to record the frequency and brand of cigarettes smoked each day. During the next three weeks, subjects were instructed to reduce their nicotine intake by changing brands of cigarettes on a weekly basis. Each week the subjects were to change to a brand that contained 30 percent less nicotine than the one they had smoked the week before. In addition, subjects were asked to self-monitor their daily tar and nicotine intake by plotting graphs of each. Subjects were then encouraged to quit smoking completely. A follow-up was taken one week later. Subjects who had not yet completely stopped smoking (83 percent) then participated in a three-week cigarette fading procedure in which they were required to reduce gradually and graph the daily number of cigarettes they smoked. Results indicated that 33 percent of all subjects were abstinent at a one-year follow-up and that all nonabstinent smokers were smoking cigarettes lower in tar and nicotine than their baseline brands. Furthermore, subjects averaged a 28.1 percent reduction in the number of cigarettes smoked from baseline to follow-up.

Treatment The two primary uses of self-monitoring in the treatment of disease have been to increase compliance to medical regimens and to monitor symptoms of the disease as part of the treatment itself.

Several studies have assessed the value of self-monitoring in controlling medication intake. For example, Wandless and Davie (1977) gave geriatric patients a pill calendar to help them keep track of their medication use. The patients simply tore off calendar pages after taking their pills. Results indicated that patients in the calendar group missed fewer pills than did patients who were given verbal instructions or detailed instruction cards. Overall, however, self-monitoring procedures alone do not seem to be as effective in increasing medication compliance as other behavioral techniques, such as reinforcement or feedback approaches (see Epstein & Cluss, 1982, for a review).

For many diseases, it is crucial to the patient's health that he or she monitor disease symptoms. Diabetes, a disease characterized by high blood glucose and insulin deficiency, is an excellent example. Many diabetics must follow a very complex regimen including daily insulin injections, regular exercise, and a prescribed diet in which they must eat specific types of foods at set times of the day. If the regimen is not correctly followed, serious short-term (e.g., hyper- or hypoglycemia) as well as long-term (e.g., heart disease) consequences may occur (Turk & Speers, 1983). Furthermore, because the treatment regimen must be balanced to maintain metabolic control, insulin dosages, diet, and exercise may frequently need to be readjusted. One way that diabetics can help predict whether their treatment regimen is correct is by self-monitoring their glucose levels. Most commonly, diabetics test their urine on a daily basis to check for excess blood sugar that may have been excreted into the urine (Fisher, Delamater, Bertelson, & Kirkley, 1982). Thus, by monitoring their glucose levels, diabetics are better able to plan meals, adjust insulin dosages, or change exercise regimens accordingly. In fact, self-monitoring is so important in diabetes self-regulation that much of the behavioral literature pertaining to diabetes has focused on methods to increase compliance to the self-monitoring procedure itself (see Wing, Epstein, Nowalk, & Lamparski, 1986).

Contingency Management

Because many health habits and illness behaviors can be considered operant responses, in that they are strongly controlled by their environmental consequences, contingency management procedures have been widely used in medical settings to help control the frequency of certain health-related behaviors. As in traditional mental health settings, the goal of contingency management in behavioral medicine is to increase the frequency of desired behaviors and decrease the frequency of undesired behaviors by managing the consequences of these behaviors. Common goals of contingency management programs in medical settings include increasing positive health behavior (e.g., daily exercise), increasing adherence to treatment regimens, decreasing negative health habits (e.g., smoking), and decreasing the frequency of illness behaviors (e.g., excessive crying associated with chronic pain).

There are at least two reasons why contingency management programs may be particularly well-suited for changing health behaviors. First, although changing health behaviors is often associated with reinforcing consequences in the long run, in the short run changing these behaviors may not be at all rewarding, and may even be punishing. For example, veteran exercisers may enjoy increased efficiency of their cardiorespiratory systems, improved muscle tone, and enhanced feelings of well-being, to name but a few of the benefits that have been associated with exercise (Serfass & Gerberich, 1984). However, anyone who has tried to begin exercising after being sedentary for any length of time is probably well aware that the immediate effects of starting an exercise program are anything but rewarding. Because behavior is often more strongly controlled by immediate rather than delayed consequences, it is difficult to change the frequency of behaviors, such as exercise, in which the consequences are primarily delayed. One benefit of contingency management programs is that they can provide immediate reinforcement for the performance (or lack of performance) of health-related behaviors.

Second, illness behaviors (e.g., pain behavior) frequently associated with disease or illness begin as natural responses to a patient's condition but may persist because they are consistently reinforced. For instance, an adaptive response to spraining an ankle is to stay off of it for a while. However, if this inactivity leads to positive consequences (e.g., receiving more attention from others or avoiding responsibilities), that person may be tempted to stay off the ankle much longer than is necessary. Contingency management programs are often used to control illness behaviors by controlling the consequences of these behaviors. To use the example of the sprained ankle, a contingency management program in this case may consist of having the injured person's family ignore the patient whenever he or she complains of pain associated with the ankle and praise the patient whenever he or she performs household duties. It is important to note, however, that we are not suggesting that all illness behaviors are inappropriate. It may be necessary, for example, for some patients to remain inactive for a long period of time. Contingency management programs are most appropriate when there is an *excess* of disability and suffering or when the behavior of the patient becomes a problem to him or her or to those around the person.

A variety of contingency management procedures have been used for both health promotion–illness prevention and the treatment of illness. The following sections will provide examples of various contingency management programs from both of these behavioral medicine areas.

Health Promotion and Illness Prevention The role of contingency management in health promotion and illness prevention has been primarily in modifying behavioral risk factors that are associated with the development of chronic diseases and in promoting positive health behaviors. Several types of contingency management procedures have been used in modifying health-related behaviors. Among the most frequently used of these procedures are social reinforcement, self-reinforcement, and behavioral contracting.

SOCIAL REINFORCEMENT. Social reinforcement procedures most often involve having someone from the individual's environment provide a reward contingent upon the individual's performance of a desired behavior. For example, in trying to promote adolescent compliance to dental hygiene procedures, Blount and Stokes (1984) studied the effectiveness of posting photographs of the children as a reinforcer for having low levels of dental plaque. The investigators used a two-phase design across classrooms in which phase one for Classroom A was continued for four plaque checks, whereas phase one for Classroom B was continued for nine checks. During the first phase, plaque checks were conducted on a variable interval schedule. The children were given feedback regarding the location of the plaque and were praised if the plaque level was low. During phase two, in addition to giving feedback, the investigators posted a photograph of each child who had an acceptable plaque level on a poster board entitled "The Better Brushers." In each photograph, the child was smiling and was holding a toothbrush next to his or her face. As Figure 11–5 indicates, in both classrooms, plaque levels were substantially reduced only during the intervention phase. Other studies that

have used external reinforcement to promote dental hygiene in adolescents have provided similar results (Clauhout & Lutzker, 1981; Dahlquist et al. 1985; Lund & Kegeles, 1984a). Unfortunately, treatment gains do not appear

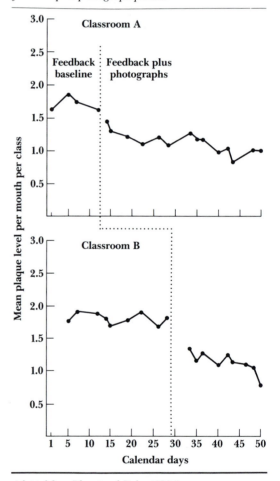

Figure 11–5 *Mean plaque levels as measured by the Simplified Oral Hygiene Index (OHI-S) in Classrooms A and B during the feedback baseline and feedback plus photograph phases.*

Adapted from Blount and Stokes (1984).

to be maintained over time (Lund & Kegels, 1984b).

SELF-REINFORCEMENT. One criticism of external reinforcement programs is that when others control treatment contingencies, the target behavior is not always under their observation. Consequently, the observers may miss a large amount of the target behavior (Gross, 1983), thereby preventing the desired response from being consistently reinforced (Kazdin, 1975). Self-reinforcement may allow responses to be reinforced more consistently. In addition, self-reinforcement may result in stronger maintenance effects than those obtained under external control (O'Leary & Dubey, 1979).

An example of self-reinforcement used in the modification of health habits was provided by Stalonas, Johnson, and Christ (1978). Forty-eight obese subjects were randomly assigned to one of four groups: weight loss program alone, weight loss program plus exercise, weight loss program plus a contingency management component, and weight loss program plus exercise and contingency components. The basic weight loss program included patient education and behavioral tasks (e.g., stimulus control, self-monitoring). The exercise component consisted of weekly attempts to increase physical activity. Finally, subjects who received the contingency component were instructed to self-administer rewards for complying with program strategies. After compiling lists of activities that could serve as self-administered rewards, these subjects made daily checklists in which program activities were converted into points that could be exchanged for rewards from their lists. Although all subjects had lost significant amounts of weight by the end of the 10-week program, only those subjects participating in the self-administered contingency management and/or exercise programs maintained their weight loss at one-year follow up.

BEHAVIORAL CONTRACTING. As described in Chapter 5, behavioral contracting involves the individual whose behavior is to be changed and others acting as contingency managers. The two parties make a formal agreement, or contract, which clearly specifies contingencies of targeted behaviors well in advance of the program. An area of behavioral medicine in which psychologists have found this form of contingency management to be particularly useful is in increasing adherence to exercise programs (Epstein, Wing, Thompson, & Griffin, 1980; Oldridge & Jones, 1981; Wysocki, Hall, Iwata, & Riordan, 1979). Kau and Fischer (1974) described a behavioral contract that Kau established between herself and her husband in order to initiate and maintain a regular exercise program for herself. The plan was put into a written contract which both parties signed. Kau's part of the contract was to jog a certain distance every day. Part of her husband's contract was to pay her 25¢ each time she jogged. In addition, her husband was to engage in one of several prespecified social activities with her each time she accumulated $1.75 (7 days of exercise). Until she accumulated $1.75, none of the social activities was permitted. Fortunately (probably both for Kau and her husband), the contract was successful in promoting exercise behavior. Moreover, Kau continued her program even after the contract was terminated.

A specialized form of behavioral contracting that has been frequently used in attempts at decreasing negative health habits is monetary depositing, in which the client pays a sum of money to the therapist and has it returned only if he or she succeeds in decreasing the frequency of the targeted behavior. Paxton (1980), for example, assessed the value of monetary depositing used in conjunction with a behavioral smoking cessation program. In this study, 60 smokers were randomly assigned to a behavioral-treatment-only condition or to a behavioral-treatment-plus-monetary-deposit condition. The behavioral treatment consisted of a variety of interventions, including aversive procedures and various self-control techniques. In addition to participating in the behavioral program, subjects in the monetary deposit condition were required to deposit approximately $20 at the beginning of a smoking cessation program which was to be repaid at $5 per week for four weeks unless the person smoked during that period. If a subject smoked at all during the four-week period, his or her money was forfeited and was shared by members of the group who had not smoked. After four weeks, the subjects were asked to provide a second deposit of $20 and a similar contract was specified. The results are shown in Figure 11–6. At the end of the program, significantly more subjects in the monetary deposit condition had stopped smoking than had subjects in the no-deposit condition. However, at a two-month follow-up, there were no longer significant differences between the two groups, indicating that treatment gains from the monetary contracting were not maintained over time. Unfortunately, this pattern of results often occurs in contingency management studies when the intervention phase is fairly short and the rewards (or the punishments) are abruptly discontinued.

Treatment Contingency management procedures in the treatment of illness have primarily been applied toward increasing compliance to medical or rehabilitative treatments and decreasing excessive illness behavior. Several types of contingency management procedures have been used for these purposes.

INCREASING COMPLIANCE. Contingency management procedures used to increase compliance behaviors are often based on the assumption that patients are often noncompliant because following medical advice may be more punishing or disruptive than rewarding, at least in the short term. For example, for a child with scoliosis, wearing a back brace may be inconvenient or even embarrassing, and treatment gains may not become obvious for months or even years. As mentioned earlier, a benefit of contingency management programs is that they can provide the patient with more immediate reinforcement.

Probably the contingency management programs most frequently used in increasing compliance among medical patients are behavioral contracting and token economy systems. Cummings, Becker, Kirsch, and Levin (1984), for example, used behavioral contracting to increase dietary compliance among kidney transplant patients who were on hemodialysis. Because abuse of dietary restriction in these patients can result in a buildup of toxic fluids, which in turn may lead to cardiovascular problems, uremic symptoms (e.g., nausea and vomiting), or even death, it is crucial that patients on hemodialysis follow their diets. The investigators randomly assigned 120 patients to one of four conditions: behavioral contract, behavioral contract with a family member or friend, weekly telephone contract, or no-treatment control. The behavioral contract intervention consisted of four phases: (1) the identification of the compliance behavior to be changed; (2) negotiation be-

Figure 11–6 *Percentage of subjects not smoking each week in the behavior-treatment-only (dotted line) and behavior-treatment-plus-deposit (solid line) conditions. Note that the deterrent effects of the monetary deposit ended abruptly when deposits were no longer required.*

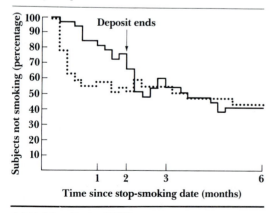

Adapted from Paxton (1980).

tween the nurse and the patient of a timetable that indicated the times by which specified behaviors were to be accomplished, how the behaviors were to be evaluated, and when and how the patient was to be rewarded; (3) the formation of a written contract; and (4) the maintenance of a record of each patient's progress.

Patients contracting with a family or friend followed the same procedure as those patients in the contract-only condition, except that a family member or friend participated in the contracting procedure with the nurse and the patient (see Figure 11–7 for a sample contract). The duties of the family member or friend included helping the patient to comply with his or her treatment. Patients in the telephone contract condition were called once a week for six weeks by their clinic nurses. During these phone calls, the nurses gathered information from the patients about problems they might be having in following their treatment instruction; provided information to the patients about the consequences of following or not following treatment regimens, and about things the patient could do to achieve better compliance; and verbally reinforced the patients for complying with their treatments. Finally, patients in the no-treatment control group were assigned to routine medical care.

In general, results indicated that patients in all three intervention programs exhibited more dietary and fluid limit compliance than did those in the no-treatment control condition. In addition, patients in both of the behavioral contract conditions had mean weight gains (a measure of fluid limit compliance) that were 13 percent lower than patients in the control groups and 9 percent lower than those in the weekly telephone contact group, indicating that the behavioral contract conditions were more effective than the other two conditions in promoting fluid limit compliance. However, results of a three-month follow-up indicated that program effects had tapered off to preintervention levels, suggesting the need for a long-term intervention program.

Epstein et al. (1981) used a multiple-baseline design to assess the effectiveness of a token economy system in increasing compliance to treatment regimens with diabetic children. The intervention phase involved having the childrens' parents praise their child's self-regulatory behaviors (e.g., urine monitoring and insulin adjustment). A token economy system in which the children received points for monitoring their urine was developed to help maintain behavior change. Significant increases in the percentage of negative urine corresponded to the implementation of the intervention across groups, indicating that the intervention was successful in increasing compliant behavior. Moreover, treatment gains were maintained over a two-week follow-up period. Similar results have been found in other studies that have used point systems to increase treatment compliance in adolescents with diabetes (Carney, Schecter, & Davis, 1983; Lowe & Lutzker, 1979).

DECREASING ILLNESS BEHAVIOR. Perhaps the most widely used contingency management technique for decreasing illness behavior is social reinforcement. Social reinforcement procedures have been particularly successful when used as part of comprehensive chronic pain management programs (see Turner & Chapman, 1982). The goal of most of these programs is to decrease operant pain behaviors and replace them with behaviors that are inconsistent with the sick role. To achieve this goal, pain behaviors are not rewarded, whereas "well" behaviors are. For example, in a prototypical operant inpatient pain program developed by Fordyce and his colleagues (Fordyce, Fowler, DeLateur, Sand, & Trieschmann, 1973), 36 chronic pain patients were assessed before and after program participation. In addition to rehabilitation counseling, occupational therapy, physical therapy, and systematic decrease of medications, the program included instructing family members and the medical staff to ignore patients' pain behaviors and to praise behaviors that were inconsistent with the sick role. The

---

Figure 11–7 *A sample behavioral contract between a hemodialysis patient and her nurse aimed at improving dietary compliance.*

We, <u>Jane Doe</u> and <u>Doris Evans</u>, agree to the following

actions to help assure improvement of <u>Jane Doe's</u> health.

1. I agree to gain not more than 3 Kg. of fluid weight gain between dialysis treatments, for which I'll receive 3 points.
2. I agree to follow recommended dietary restrictions so that my pre K+ level is 5.5 or below, for which I will receive 3 points.
3. I agree to keep a diary of the amount of fluid I drink, time taken, and type on a weekly basis for which I will receive 10 points on Saturday, if completed.

Point Schedule
    Accumulated total points of 25 = 1 free lottery ticket
        "   "   "   "   50 = 2 free lottery tickets
        "   "   "   "   75 = 3 free lottery tickets
        "   "   "   " 100 = 4 free lottery tickets

It is understood that this agreement can be revised at a later date. The terms of the

agreement will be reviewed and revision made, if necessary on <u>May 3, 1979</u>.

We agree to follow and abide by the actions outlined above.

<u>Jane Doe</u>	<u>4–12–79</u>
Signed	Date

<u>Doris Evans</u>	<u>4–12–79</u>
Signed	Date

_____	_____
Signed	Date

From Cummings, Becker, Kirsch, and Levin (1984).

patients showed significant increases in physical therapy activities and decreases in medication intake from admission to discharge. Furthermore, patients retrospectively rated themselves as having had significant decreases in pain and increases in activity levels during the treatment program which were maintained after discharge. Although the lack of adequate control groups in this study should be clearly recognized, the consistently positive results that Fordyce and his colleagues have reported in using contingency management procedures to treat chronic pain provides strong clinical support for the use of this technique.

In summary, a variety of contingency management procedures have been used both in promoting health and in preventing and treating illness. Common uses of these procedures have included increasing positive health behaviors, decreasing negative health behaviors, promoting compliance, and reducing maladaptive illness behavior. Contingency management procedures appear to be successful when used alone, as well as when used in conjunction with other behavioral and medical interventions as part of comprehensive multimodal treatment packages.

Stimulus Control

Just as some health behaviors seem to be controlled primarily by their environmental consequences, many other health-related behaviors appear to be controlled, at least in part, by their antecedents. Such control usually occurs through one of two processes. First, through an associative learning process, environmental stimuli that are present immediately before each performance of a behavior can come to serve as discriminative stimuli (i.e., stimuli that are capable of eliciting the behaviors with which they are associated). The conditioned responses developed by cancer chemotherapy patients, which were discussed earlier, are good examples. Cancer chemotherapy often produces severe nausea and vomiting within hours after the treatment. As a result, many chemotherapy patients eventually become conditioned to stimuli associated with the treatment, such as the sight of the chemotherapy nurse or the smell of the drugs. The authors experienced one incident in which a chemotherapy patient who was shopping in a store saw his chemotherapy nurse in the aisle ahead of him and immediately began to vomit! Second, environmental stimuli may serve simply as prompts or reminders to behave in a certain way. For example, taping a reminder note on your bathroom mirror might be an effective cue for making an appointment with your physician when you get up in the morning, or taping to the refrigerator a picture of yourself when you were 30 pounds lighter might be a clear reminder that you are supposed to be cutting down on desserts!

Stimulus control techniques are designed to modify the antecedents of target behaviors. In behavioral medicine, stimulus control interventions usually serve one of two purposes: either to remove from the client's environment stimuli that elicit negative health behaviors (e.g., smoking) or to provide new stimuli that will elicit positive health behaviors (e.g., breast self-examination).

Health Promotion and Illness Prevention One use of stimulus control in promoting health and preventing illness has been in eliminating negative health habits, such as overeating. Stimulus control has frequently been a part of multicomponent weight loss programs (see Hall & Hall, 1982). Specific stimulus control techniques may include eating only in a certain place, taking smaller portions, removing leftovers from the table, and restricting other activity (e.g., watching television) while eating. In addition to learning stimulus control techniques, clients are often taught a variety of other behavioral techniques (e.g., self-monitoring, self-reinforcement), are encouraged to exercise, and are taught the principles of good nutrition.

Stimulus control techniques are frequently included as a component of behavioral treatment packages because they can improve the durability of effects of other interventions. For example, Carroll and Yates (1981) randomly assigned 24 women either to a standard weight loss group or to a group that received stimulus control in addition to the standard treatment. The standard treatment included instruction in self-monitoring, self-reinforcement, self-punishment, response chaining, substitution, nutrition, and exercise. In addition to receiving this treatment, subjects in the stimulus control group were instructed in the importance of stimulus control as a basic technique, and were specifically told to reserve one room and one chair for eating, eat at the same time each day, do nothing else while eating, and store no food

within sight. Covered nontransparent bowls or brown bags were used for storing food in the refrigerator. Each group met for 10 weekly sessions. Subjects in both groups lost approximately the same amount of weight (about five pounds) by the end of the program. However, an eight-month follow-up indicated that subjects in the stimulus control group had lost significantly more weight in the long run than had those in the standard treatment group (see Table 11–6).

Stimulus control techniques have also been applied to encourage women to perform breast self-examination (BSE), a procedure used for the early detection of breast cancer. Despite the markedly improved prognosis of breast cancer

Table 11–6 **The Incremental Utility of Stimulus Control Training in Behavioral Obesity Therapy**

	Behavioral therapy without stimulus control training			Behavioral therapy with stimulus control training		
	WRI[a,b]	kg[a]	lbs.[a]	WRI[a,b]	kg[a]	lbs.[a]
Beginning vs. end of therapy						
Median	20.8	20.0	4.4	18.9	2.0	4.4
Mean	17.2	2.4	5.3	19.6	2.0	4.4
SD	21.0	3.6	8.0	20.1	3.2	7.1
Range (min., max.)	(−15.1, 62.1)	(−0.9, 6.4)	(−2.0, 14.1)	(−18.9, 53.4)	(−1.8, 5.9)	(−4.0, 13.0)
Kurtosis[d]	2.7	1.6	3.5	2.2	2.1	4.6
End of therapy vs. 8 months later						
Median	5.0	0.5	1.1	22.9[c]	1.4[c]	3.1
Mean	6.0	0.8	1.8	20.5	2.5	5.5
SD	27.9	4.1	9.1	65.9	7.9	17.5
Range	(−37.4, 66.2)	(−3.6, 6.4)	(−8.0, 14.1)	(−166.1, 111.8)	(−10.0, 11.3)	(−22.1, 25.0)
Kurtosis[d]	2.8	2.6	5.7	5.8	3.7	8.2

[a]Positive values represent *loss* of bodyweight. Negative values shown in range rows represent weight *gain* during the periods specified on the extreme left.

[b]Weight Reduction Index: [(pre kg − post kg) − (pre kg − ideal kg)] × (pre kg + ideal kg) × 100 (see Wilson, 1978).

[c]The difference between behavior therapy without stimulus control training vs. behavior therapy with stimulus control training is significant, $p < .05$, one-tailed U.

[d]The kurtosis of a distribution should be approximately 3 if it is to be considered normal. Values greater than 3 indicate a more peaked distribution; values less than 3 indicate a flatter distribution.

From Carroll and Yates (1981).

when detected and treated in its early stages (American Cancer Society, 1976) and the affordability and ease with which women can perform BSE, only 24 percent of U.S. women practice BSE regularly (National Cancer Institute, 1980). Furthermore, surveys have indicated that over 91 percent of women are aware of the procedure (National Cancer Institute, 1980) and 80 percent have at one time tried it (Grady, 1981), suggesting that nonpractice of BSE is not a function of ignorance or nonfamiliarity. Instead, some have suggested that, given at least minimum competence, repeated practice is most likely dependent on the stimulus conditions and reinforcement associated with the behavior (Grady, 1984). Unfortunately, there are few intrinsically positively reinforcing outcomes associated with the performance of BSE. Usually, the only outcomes from performing BSE are negative (a suspicious finding) or neutral (no finding). BSE cannot even prevent the negative outcome of cancer, but can only increase the *possibility* of survival. Similarly, because BSE is performed in private and is rarely discussed with family or friends, there is little opportunity for extrinsic reinforcement. Therefore, intervention studies have primarily focused on manipulating the stimulus conditions that may control the performance of BSE.

Mayer and Frederiksen (1986) evaluated the effectiveness of mail and phone prompts in promoting compliance to BSE. In their study, 84 women were assigned to one of three groups: mail prompting, phone prompting, or a no-treatment control. A stratified random assignment procedure matched subjects with respect to previous experience with BSE. All subjects first participated in a one-hour BSE teaching workshop in which they learned the procedure. Subjects were instructed to place baby oil on their fingers before palpating their breasts. After palpating their breasts, subjects were to put a sheet of tissue upon their chests to absorb the oil. They were then asked to send in the tissue, signed and dated, each time they performed this procedure at home so that it could

be used as an indirect behavioral measure of the frequency of BSE. Subjects in the mail prompt group were mailed postcards that contained the brief message, "Now may be a good time for you to perform BSE" (Mayer & Frederiksen, 1986, p. 182). To ensure that at least one prompt per month occurred at a time that was appropriate to perform BSE (i.e., when subjects were not premenstrual or menstruating), postcards were mailed on a biweekly basis. Subjects in the phone prompt group received telephone calls at their homes on the same schedule as mail prompted subjects. The message was the same as that received by the mail prompt group. Prompts were delivered for seven months. Results indicated that women who received prompts, particularly those given by phone, performed BSE significantly more often than did women in the no-treatment control condition. However, the percentage of high compliers did not differ among groups, and compliance decreased over time in all groups.

Other studies (e.g., Grady, 1984) have also suggested that stimulus control techniques may initially increase compliance, but that the effect decreases once the prompts are discontinued. As a result, we suggest that either a prompt or a cuing procedure be developed that does not depend on external agents (e.g., a therapist making a telephone call) and that stimulus control procedures be supplemented with other behavioral techniques that maintain the behavior over time. For example, it may be helpful for a woman to circle an appropriate date on her calendar each month to remind herself to perform BSE. Similarly, some women use the end of menstruation as a prompting cue and perform BSE immediately following menstruation each month.

Treatment Stimulus control techniques have also been effectively used in increasing patients' compliance to their medical treatments. Meyers, Thackwray, Johnson, and Schleser (1983), for example, used prompting strategies to improve the appointment compliance of hypertensive patients. In their study, 148 hypertensives who had missed at least one appointment for treatment at a community health center were randomly assigned to a postcard, phone call, home visit, or rotating contact group. Subjects in the postcard, phone call, and home visit groups received up to three messages in the appropriate modality, one following each of three consecutively missed appointments. Subjects in the rotation contact group also received up to three messages; however, each of the messages was in a different modality. The order of modalities in this group was counterbalanced across subjects. All subjects received the following message in the appropriate modality:

> Dear (Subject's name),
>
> Did you know that high blood pressure can hurt you? Well, it can. High blood pressure can make you feel tired and dragged out all the time. It can even lead to more serious problems like heart disease or crippling strokes. The good news is that high blood pressure can be treated easily and inexpensively if it is identified early.
>
> Your blood pressure was checked on (date and place) and it was too high. Since you missed your (date) appointment, you need to come in (date) to have it (checked again/treated). Why don't you do it? Do it for yourself and for your family. You'll feel better and so will they. (Meyers et al., 1983, p. 270)

Results indicated that the rotating contact, home visit, and phone conditions were all significantly more effective prompts than were postcards in increasing appointment compliance. However, compliance rates produced by all the prompts were significantly greater than compliance rates at the clinic three months prior to the beginning of the study.

Punishment and Aversive Procedures

As in mental health contexts, aversive procedures used in behavioral medicine fall most commonly into one of three basic categories: punishment, aversive counterconditioning, and flooding or response prevention. Punishment is used when the behavior in question is thought, at least in part, to be learned or maintained via operant conditioning processes. More specifically, punishment is often used when the short-term consequences of a health behavior are rewarding but the long-term consequences are punishing. For example, illicit drug-taking behavior may be initially rewarding, but may often lead to severe delayed consequences (e.g., financial difficulties, loss of cognitive function, organ damage, etc.) if the behavior is maintained. The goal of punishment is to make the short-term consequences of the behavior punishing instead of rewarding.

Aversive counterconditioning procedures take advantage of classical conditioning processes in achieving their effects. Specifically, negative health behaviors or their antecedent stimuli are repeatedly paired with unpleasant stimuli in hopes that the negative health behaviors will acquire negative characteristics or associations. For example, if taking a cigarette is repeatedly paired with thoughts of vomiting, the sight of a cigarette may begin to induce feelings of nausea, with a resultant decrease in the frequency of smoking.

Finally, flooding or response-prevention procedures have been used in behavioral medicine contexts when the goal of treatment is to modify a negative health habit. The rationale for using these procedures in modifying negative health habits stems from two basic assumptions, the first of which is that certain negative health habits are thought to be reinforcing because they help people to avoid unpleasant states. For example, drinking alcohol can presumably help one to avoid (or eliminate) feelings of anxiety or despondency. The second assumption is that these negative health behaviors or avoidance responses can be triggered by certain cues. For example, a person might always smoke when at a party or when drinking an alcoholic beverage. The goal of flooding or response prevention procedures is to extinguish the cues so that they no longer elicit the behavior. In general, this is done by repeatedly exposing the person to the cues or discriminative stimuli while at the same time blocking the response (i.e., the unhealthy behavior) to them, until the cues no longer elicit the response.

As discussed in Chapter 8, because of the controversy surrounding the use of aversion techniques, they are usually used only for behaviors that are highly rewarding but physically damaging, and only when there is no better option. Because nonaversive techniques, such as relaxation exercises and positive reinforcement, have enjoyed widespread success in the treatment of disease-related problems, aversion therapies are seldom used as part of treatment protocols. However, as we shall see, aversion techniques have been used with some frequency in the realm of positive health promotion and illness prevention.

Health Promotion and Illness Prevention Perhaps the two negative health behaviors for which aversion techniques have been most frequently used are excessive alcohol consumption and smoking. Although aversion procedures have been used to modify other behaviors (e.g., overeating), they either have been ineffective (Foreyt & Kennedy, 1971) or have not been as effective as other techniques (Mahoney, Moura, & Wade, 1973) in modifying these behaviors, and therefore have been infrequently used.

ALCOHOL. Aversion techniques involving chemically induced aversion, electrical shock, and covert sensitization have been used with problem drinkers and alcoholics to modify drinking behavior. In general, the frequency with which these techniques have been used has declined since the mid-1970s. Due to lack of evidence supporting its effectiveness (Cannon, Baker, & Wehl, 1981), electrical shock techniques are now seldom used (Marlatt, 1983), and chemical conditioning and covert sensitization are used usually only when abstinence, rather than controlled drinking, is the goal of treatment (Carey & Maisto, 1985; Marlatt, 1983).

Another aversion technique used to modify drinking behavior is flooding, or response prevention. In general, the research in this area at best may be regarded as preliminary, consisting primarily of case studies and uncontrolled, small-*n* designs. Nevertheless, findings have been consistently encouraging, suggesting that flooding and other response prevention techniques may be quite effective in modifying drinking behavior. For example, Blakely and Baker (1980) assessed the drinking behavior of six male alcoholics in terms of the behaviors' antecedents and consequences. A list of drinking "triggers" for each patient was then established from this assessment. The treatment procedure included three major components. First, each patient was exposed to the specific stimuli or situations that were thought to elicit his own drinking behavior. During the exposure period, the patient was not allowed to drink. The investigators used a graded exposure procedure in which stimuli presented in the later stages of treatment were considered to be more powerful "triggers" than those presented near the beginning of treatment. Second, successful completion of exercises was socially reinforced. Finally, to help prevent relapse posttreatment, patients were coached in how to deal with difficult home situations in which the temptation to drink could occur. Five of the six subjects attained abstinence by the end of the therapy, and they maintained abstinence over follow-ups of up to nine months. Figure 11–8 shows one of the patient's self-ratings of desire to drink at various stages of the treatment.

In one of the only controlled studies that assessed the effectiveness of flooding/response prevention with alcoholics, Rankin, Hodgson, and Stockwell (1983) assigned 10 alcohol-dependent subjects either to an *in vivo* exposure/response prevention group or to a minimal exposure condition in which the subjects received imaginal cue exposure. Subjects in the *in vivo* exposure condition participated in six 45-minute sessions in which they were instructed to drink two glasses of their favorite alcoholic beverage. The taste, sight, and smell of these drinks

Figure 11–8 *Subject's reported desire for drink during exposure sessions (○—○: first trial; ●—●: second trial; □—□: third trial; ■—■: fourth trial).*

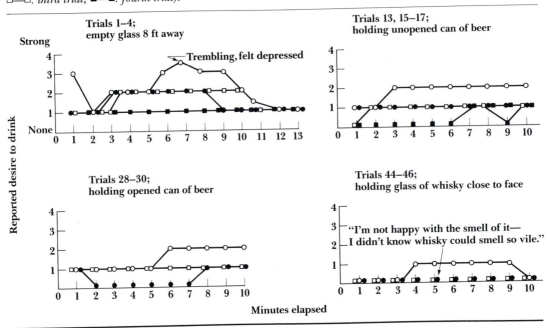

Adapted from Blakely and Baker (1980).

were thought to serve as discriminative stimuli in eliciting drinking behavior. During the exposure period, subjects were instructed first to maintain eye contact with the drink, then to hold the glass at arm's length, and finally to hold the glass near their mouths and sniff the drink. The glass was then removed. Subjects in the imaginal cue exposure condition participated in six sessions in which they were asked to imagine refusing a drink in a situation in which they would normally drink. Results indicated that, compared to subjects in the imaginal cue exposure group, subjects in the *in vivo* group were able to drink alcoholic beverages more slowly, had less of a desire for drinks, and found it less difficult to refuse drinks.

Overall, therefore, flooding/response prevention shows promise as an effective means of modifying negative health habits which serve, at least in part, as avoidance responses. However, additional research examining the effectiveness of this technique within a behavioral medicine context is needed.

An important point in using any aversion technique with problem drinkers is that unless an alternative response to drinking is established early in the treatment procedure, the person will gradually reestablish the old drinking patterns as the effect of the aversion wears off (Marlatt, 1983). In fact, in one study, patients in the aversion group actually drank more 15 months after treatment than did patients in a control group, even though they were drinking less than control group subjects immediately following treatment (Chaney, O'Leary, & Marlatt, 1978). Thus, because aversion techniques when used alone are often ineffective in producing lasting reductions in drinking behavior, most aversion techniques are now used as part of multicomponent packages, which often include relapse prevention techniques (Marlatt, 1983).

SMOKING. The aversion technique that has been researched most thoroughly as a method of smoking cessation is a procedure called *rapid smoking*. As discussed in Chapter 10, this method requires that the client inhale cigarettes as rapidly as possible until he or she is unable to continue or becomes sick. The process is repeated until the client indicates that he or she no longer desires to smoke. The goal of the process is to produce an aversive state which the client will associate with smoking in the hope that the aversiveness will generalize to environmental cues that stimulate smoking. Hall and Hall (1985) list six elements that are crucial to the success of rapid smoking programs:

1. The client should not smoke between rapid smoking sessions. If clients want to smoke, they should wait until the next scheduled rapid smoking session.

2. Sessions should be directed by a therapist.

3. Sessions should continue until the client reports no more urges to smoke. (This usually happens after seven or eight sessions.)

4. The therapist should make the client fully aware of the rationale behind rapid smoking. The client must understand that he or she is to smoke to the point of dysphoria or nausea and that smoking between sessions may hinder the effectiveness of the procedure.

5. The therapist should heighten the client's awareness of aversion. It is essential that clients are not allowed to distract themselves from the procedure; instead, the therapist should aid in helping clients to concentrate on the aversiveness of the experience.

6. The therapist should instruct the client to recall vividly the unpleasantness of the experience, particularly when at home where he or she may need to fight off urges to smoke until the next session.

The results of studies assessing the efficacy of rapid smoking have been mixed. Earlier studies (see Danaher, 1977) provided generally positive results in producing short-term abstinence, although some of the studies indicated a moderate degree of relapse within two to six years posttreatment (Lichtenstein & Rodrigues, 1977). Later studies have provided positive (Hall, Sachs, & Hall, 1979) as well as negative (Raw & Russell, 1980) results (for a review, see Lichtenstein, 1982). Other studies (Tongas, 1979) have included rapid smoking as part of multicomponent programs, in which the specific contribution of rapid smoking alone was not assessed. Overall, it seems that rapid smoking is often effective as a smoking cessation device. As with all aversion techniques, however, its popularity among therapists and clients depends largely on the availability of equally effective, but less unpleasant, alternate treatments.

There has been considerable controversy concerning the risks associated with rapid smoking procedures. Because rapid smoking produces significant increases in heart rate, carboxyhemoglobin, and blood-nicotine levels (Lichtenstein, 1982), there has been some concern about the possibility of nicotine poisoning (Horan, Linberg, & Hackett, 1977) and cardiovascular complications (Hall, Sachs, & Hall, 1979) occurring as a result of the procedure. Direct comparisons of blood-nicotine levels under regular and rapid smoking conditions, however, have indicated that nicotine poisoning is highly unlikely (Russell, Raw, Taylor, Feyerabend, & Saloojee, 1978).

The major concern with rapid smoking, therefore, has been with cardiovascular complications. Whereas some studies have indicated that rapid smoking may be dangerous even for healthy individuals (Hausen, 1974), others have indicated that rapid smoking is safe for healthy individuals (Sachs, Hall, Pechacek, & Fitzgerald, 1979), individuals with mild to moderate cardiopulmonary disease, and for those who have had uncomplicated heart attacks (Hall, Sachs, Hall, & Benowitz, 1984). In fact, Lichtenstein and Glasgow (1977) estimated that rapid smoking procedures had been used with approximately 35,000 people without serious complications. There is a general consensus that appropriate screening procedures (e.g., excluding high-risk subjects and individuals over 55) should be conducted to minimize risks (Gatchel & Baum, 1983).

Because of the high cost of screening and the potential risks associated with rapid smoking, a modification of the procedure, *focused smoking,* is often used as an alternative. This method requires clients to smoke at a normal rate while concentrating on the unpleasant aspects of the smoking experience (e.g., the smoke, the smell, stinging or burning sensations in the throat). Results of studies assessing focused smoking are mixed. For example, Lichtenstein, Harris, Birchler, Wahl, and Schmahl (1973) found that focused smoking was effective in short-term cessation, but not at follow-up. On the other hand, results of other studies have indicated that there are no differences in effectiveness between rapid and focused smoking (Danaher, 1977; Glasgow, 1978).

Treatment As discussed earlier, aversion procedures are seldom used in the treatment of illness. In one of the few studies that used an aversion technique, Creer (1970) successfully instituted a time-out procedure to reduce the length of hospital stays for asthmatic children. Whenever a child was admitted to the hospital, comic books, television, and the opportunity to interact socially with other patients were prohibited. Although they can be effective, procedures such as these are used as infrequently as possible in treating illness, and only when other methods have failed.

In summary, although aversion techniques are seldom used in the treatment of illness, they have been used with some frequency in modifying negative health habits such as smoking and excessive alcohol consumption. Results from studies assessing their effectiveness in modifying these negative health habits have been mixed.

In particular, the efficacy of aversion procedures in maintaining long-term effects and preventing relapse appears to be somewhat equivocal. For that reason, the frequency with which aversion techniques are used as part of multicomponent packages is decreasing.

Modeling

As discussed in Chapter 4, modeling refers to behavior change that occurs from observing others. Within behavioral medicine, modeling procedures may aid in both preventing and treating illness in at least three ways.

First, because observational learning (i.e., imitative learning that occurs without obvious direct reinforcement) may influence the performance of certain health behaviors, modeling procedures may be an effective means by which health habits can be acquired, changed, or extinguished. For example, a child who sees his or her parents exercise daily may be more likely to exercise than a child whose parents are sedentary.

Second, modeling may provide patients with effective methods of managing their illnesses. Through the observation of others who have had to face similar situations, patients may be able to acquire skills that will help them better manage their own health problems. Many chronic pain programs, for example, hold group meetings in which patients model effective coping and rehabilitative techniques for each other.

Finally, modeling procedures may help reduce patients' fears or anxiety through a vicarious extinction process (see Chapter 7 for a discussion of vicarious extinction). For example, a child who is afraid to go to the dentist may be less fearful if he or she first observes other children visiting the dentist without experiencing severely negative consequences.

Health Promotion and Illness Prevention Given that many negative health habits (e.g., smoking) seem to be resistant to change, the most effective strategy for decreasing the incidence of negative health behaviors may be to prevent individuals from acquiring them in the first place. Because observation of others often influences whether or not health behaviors are learned, modeling may serve as an important tool in preventing the acquisition of negative health habits.

Botvin, Eng, and Williams (1980) have illustrated how modeling can be used as part of a smoking prevention program. In their study, two schools were assigned to either an experimental or control condition. Students in the experimental condition participated in a 10-session smoking prevention program, which consisted of group discussion and special skills training. Basic life skills, as well as special skills in how to deal with the issue of smoking, were taught through modeling and behavioral rehearsal. Skills training topics included self-image, decision making, coping with anxiety, communication skills, social skills, and assertion training. A brief description of the training materials is given in Table 11–7. Overall, significantly fewer students in the experimental group began smoking during the course of the study than did students in the control condition. Other smoking prevention studies that have included modeling components have produced similar results (Hurd et al., 1980).

Treatment Modeling procedures have frequently been effective in preparing children for invasive medical procedures (see Anderson & Masur, 1983). The goal of most of these studies has been to reduce surgery-related anxiety. Melamed and Siegel (1975), for example, had 60 children who were scheduled to undergo elective surgery for hernias, tonsillectomies, or urinary-genital tract difficulties watch one of two films before undergoing their surgeries. Children in the relevant film condition watched a film about a 7-year-old boy who was about to undergo a hernia operation. The film depicted various events that most children undergoing elective surgery encounter during their hospital stay, for example, having a blood test and being separated from their parents. Some of the scenes are narrated by the child, who describes his concerns and feelings regarding each event. A coping model is used, in which the child is initially anxious but eventually overcomes his anxiety through the use of various coping techniques. Children in the irrelevant film condition watched a film that was about a preadolescent male taking a nature trip to the country. Results indicated that children who watched the coping film fared much better on behavioral, subjective, and physiological indices of postoperative anxiety than did the control group of children who watched the film unrelated to surgery.

Although modeling procedures have been consistently successful in adolescent populations, surprisingly few studies have assessed modeling procedures as preparatory treatments in adult populations. Of those studies that have used modeling procedures to prepare adults for a medical procedure, it seems that modeling was most effective in reducing anxiety in patients who had not had much previous experience with a given medical procedure (Shipley, Butt, Horwitz, & Furbe, 1978). Presumably, these patients are able to learn much more from a model than are people who have already developed negative perceptions or maladaptive behaviors as a result of prior experiences with the given procedure.

Cognitive-Behavioral Interventions

The goal of cognitive techniques, as discussed in Chapter 9, is to modify the feelings and behaviors of a client by influencing his or her patterns of thought. The use of cognitive therapies is based on the assumption that thoughts or cognitions are important mediators of both the emotional and behavioral responses associated with any given event. For example, depending on what their thoughts are, two people who are approached by an unfamiliar

Table 11–7 **Description of Skills Training Program**

Session	Material Covered
Orientation	General introduction to the program, administration of pretest questionnaire, overview of forthcoming sessions
Smoking: myths and realities	Common attitudes and beliefs about smoking; prevalence of smoking, reasons for and against smoking, the process of becoming an addicted smoker, and the decreasing social acceptability of smoking
Self-image and self-improvement	Self-image and how it is formed, the relationship between self-image and behavior, the importance of a positive self-image, and ways of improving self-image
Decision making and independent thinking	A general decision-making strategy, decision making and sources of influence affecting decisions, resisting persuasive tactics, and the importance of independent thinking.
Advertising techniques	Use and function of advertising, ad techniques, identifying ad techniques used in cigarette advertising and how they are designed to affect consumer behavior, alternative ways of responding to these ads
Coping with anxiety	Situations causing anxiety, demonstration, and practice of techniques for coping with anxiety
Communication skills	Verbal and nonverbal communication, techniques for avoiding misunderstandings, basic conversational skills, giving and receiving compliments, making introductions, etc.
Social skills	Boy-girl relationships, conversing with the opposite sex, the nature of attraction, asking or being asked out for a date
Assertiveness	Difference between assertion and aggression, standing up for one's rights, common situations calling for an assertive response, reasons for not being assertive, responding to peer pressures to smoke
Conclusion	Brief review, conclusions, posttest

From Botvin, Eng, and Williams (1980).

dog may react quite differently to the situation. Whereas one person may react with warmth and approach the dog, the other person may become very anxious and run the other way. In mental health settings, cognitive therapies are used specifically to modify cognitions (e.g., irrational fears) that are thought to hinder the client's day-to-day functioning in some way.

Cognitive techniques are used in medical settings with a similar goal: to modify thoughts that may negatively influence the client's health. A person's health may be influenced negatively by his or her cognitions in at least three ways. First, may people hold irrational beliefs about themselves which influence whether or not they will perform certain health-related behaviors. For example, one theory holds that eating disorders often stem from irrational beliefs regarding body image. Many anorexics do not eat because they falsely believe that they are overweight. On the other hand, people who overeat are often correct in their perceptions about their body weight, but do not stay on diet or exercise programs because they hold irrational beliefs regarding their ability to complete these programs. That is, because they do not think that they are capable of losing weight under any circumstance, they give up before giving the program a chance.

Second, due to maladaptive cognitive appraisals of potential stressors, individuals may experience excessive amounts of stress, putting them at greater risk for the development of chronic illness.

Finally, a patient's cognitions about his or her illness may cause the person to experience anxiety and depression which, in turn, may exacerbate existing symptoms or increase illness-related distress. For instance, if a patient is excessively afraid of undergoing surgery, he or she may actually feel worse and experience more minor complications postoperatively than might another patient who does not hold these fears. Thus, cognitive strategies can be used both to modify health-related behavior and to reduce illness- or treatment-related distress.

Health Promotion and Illness Prevention The primary role of cognitive techniques in promoting health and preventing illness has been in modifying negative health behaviors. For example, bulimia, a behavioral disorder characterized by cycles of excessive binge eating and self-induced vomiting, fasting, or laxative use, has been the focus of several cognitive-behavioral programs. Bulimic behavior is relatively widespread among young women, occurring in as many as 5 to 20 percent of college women (Halmi, Falk, & Schwartz, 1981; Pyle et al., 1983). Unfortunately, not only is the disorder widespread, but it appears to result in a variety of serious health consequences, including the depletion of electrolytes (Wallace, Richards, Chesser, & Wrong, 1968; Wolff et al., 1968), dental problems (Hurst, Lacey, & Crisp, 1977; Reinhardt & Reinhardt, 1977), and glandular swelling (Harris, 1983).

The basis for using cognitive techniques with bulimics is often centered around client reports of irrational preoccupation with food and body weight, as well as obsessive and unrealistic fears of fat and its consequences (Ordman & Kirschenbaum, 1985). Most cognitive-behavioral programs aimed at reducing bulimic behavior are comprised of cognitive restructuring procedures used in conjunction with a variety of behavioral techniques, such as contracting, flooding/response prevention, stimulus control, and self-monitoring. For example, Ordman and Kirschenbaum (1985) randomly assigned 20 bulimics to either a cognitive-behavioral intervention condition or a minimal treatment comparison condition. Subjects in the cognitive-behavioral condition attended from 10 to 24 sessions in which they underwent cognitive, behavioral, and process-oriented therapy. The cognitive component of the program involved a restructuring procedure in which clients were to identify any self-defeating and unrealistic cognitions that were influencing their eating behavior. The following is an example of the type of cognition the clients were to modify:

> If I gain two pounds, I'll continue to gain weight until I become obese. Vomiting is the only way I can control my weight. Sweets are bad foods and if I eat them I'm a bad person. If I can lose just five pounds, my life will drastically improve. My appearance, especially my weight, is the basis of my self-worth. (P. 307)

The behavioral component included self-monitoring, flooding/response prevention, and behavioral contracting, and the process-oriented component consisted primarily of supportive counseling. Subjects in the minimal treatment condition attended one session in which a therapist explained that binge eating is often maintained by the availability of vomiting as an escape response, and that vomiting is often maintained by the relief from discomfort that follows it. These subjects were asked to practice eating without purging. In addition, other behavioral strategies (e.g., self-monitoring) were reviewed.

Results indicated that, compared to the brief intervention clients, clients in the cognitive-behavioral condition reduced the frequency of their binging-vomiting, improved their general psychological adjustment, and changed their attitudes about food, dieting, and body image. Several other studies have also supported the use of cognitive-behavioral interventions in reducing bulimic behavior (Grinc, 1982; Wilson, Rossiter, Kleifield, & Lindholm, 1986).

Cognitive-behavioral interventions have also been used to decrease the Type A or coronary-prone behavior pattern. As mentioned earlier, Type A behavior, especially hostility and anger, has been linked to coronary heart disease (Dembroski et al., 1985; MacDougall et al., 1985). The basis for using cognitive-behavioral techniques in modifying Type A behavior stems from the assumption that Type A individuals respond to daily stress in an "all or none

fashion," in which they usually accomplish their goals, but only with an unnecessarily "high cost in energy expenditure and disturbed interpersonal relations" (Roskies et al., 1986, p. 49). The goal of cognitive-behavioral techniques has been to teach the Type A individual to respond to potential stressors in a less stereotyped, more differentiated manner, drawing from a broad range of cognitive and behavioral strategies (Roskies et al., 1986). For example, Roskies and colleagues (1986) assessed the relative effectiveness of cognitive-behavioral techniques, aerobic exercise, and weight training in reducing behavioral reactivity among Type A individuals. In this study, 107 Type A individuals were randomly assigned to one of the three treatment conditions. Each of the treatments spanned a 10-week period. Subjects in the cognitive-behavioral condition received training that emphasized "discriminating between 'good' and 'bad' stress perceptions and responses, and of devising and implementing coping strategies for turning the latter into the former" (p. 49). Specific coping strategies included relaxation training, communication skills, cognitive relabeling, stress inoculation, and problem solving. The aerobic training condition consisted of 27–30, 20-minute jogging sessions. Finally, the weight-training condition served as a control. Subjects in this condition participated in 20 20-minute sessions of weight-training exercises that were too short to produce aerobic conditioning. Behavioral reactivity was measured by the Structured Interview (Dembroski, MacDougall, Shields, Petito, & Lushene, 1978; Rosenman, 1978), a 20-minute interview that poses questions, in a manner likely to evoke Type A behavior, about habits and daily activity. Results indicated that subjects in the cognitive-behavioral condition showed greater reductions from pre- to posttreatment on all components of the Structured Interview, including hostility, than did subjects in either the aerobic or weight training conditions. Other studies have provided similar results, indicating that cognitive-behavioral techniques are effective in modifying

Type A behavior patterns (Levenkron, Cohen, Mueller, & Fisher, 1983; Thurman, 1985a) and in maintaining their effects over a long-term follow-up period (Thurman, 1985b).

Treatment Several types of cognitive techniques (e.g., attentional diversion, positive self-statements) have been used in association with the treatment of illness. Two of the more common uses of these techniques have been helping patients cope with invasive medical procedures and treating chronic pain.

Perhaps the most frequently used cognitive technique with patients undergoing stressful medical procedures is attentional diversion or distraction. The goal of attentional diversion strategies is to redirect patients' attention away from unpleasant or disturbing aspects of the medical procedure onto either neutral or pleasant thoughts. For example, Corah and his colleagues (1979a, 1979b) found that patients who underwent relaxation training or played video Ping-Pong during dental restorations exhibited less anxiety as measured by self-reports and dentist ratings than did patients who did not receive these interventions. Diversionary techniques have also been used successfully in reducing treatment-related distress associated with a number of other medical procedures, including major and minor surgery (Langer, Janis, & Wolfer, 1975), cancer chemotherapy (Kolko & Rickard-Figueroa, 1985; Redd et al., in press), and childbirth (e.g., Stevens, 1977).

To assess the efficacy of cognitive techniques in managing chronic pain, Rybstein-Blinchik (1979) compared three cognitive strategies (stimulus reinterpretation, attentional diversion, and sensation focusing) and an attention-placebo control. Patients in the stimulus reinterpretation group were instructed to reinterpret painful sensations as being nonpainful and to replace them with new sensory descriptions, such as "I feel ticklish," "I feel numbness," "I feel aroused" (p. 98). Those in the diversion condition were instructed to replace thoughts regarding their pain experience with "new ones

concerning important events in their lives" (p. 97). Patients in the sensation focusing condition were instructed to identify and analyze pain-related sensation, such as "I feel sharpness," "I feel stabbing," "I feel burning" (p. 97). Finally, patients in the attention-placebo condition participated in a group discussion of their pain experiences. Results indicated that whereas the attentional diversion condition was more effective than the reinterpretation and control conditions in reducing subjective indices of pain, the stimulus reinterpretation condition was more effective than all three of the other groups in reducing both behavioral and subjective indices of pain.

Although it is apparent that cognitive techniques may be successfully used alone in treating chronic pain conditions, these techniques are more often used as components of more comprehensive treatment programs. One such comprehensive treatment program, recently developed by Meichenbaum and Turk (1976), is stress inoculation. Stress inoculation programs most commonly include a number of cognitive and behavioral coping skills, which are taught during a skills training phase and are later practiced during a rehearsal phase in which the patient is encouraged to test his or her newly acquired skills imaginally or *in vivo*. The goal of these programs is to provide patients with a variety of coping skills that can be used across different stressful situations.

Bradley et al. (1985) implemented a stress inoculation program to help manage pain in patients with rheumatoid arthritis. Thirty-three patients were randomly assigned to a cognitive-behavioral stress inoculation group, a structured social support group, or a no-treatment control group. Patients in the stress inoculation group participated in 5 individual sessions of biofeedback training and 10 group meetings consisting of four phases. The first phase was *educational*, in which the rationale for the cognitive-behavioral interventions was given. The second phase consisted of *skills acquisition*, during which patients were taught palliative coping strategies (i.e., deep muscle relaxation and imagery techniques) and were taught how to set and achieve pain-related behavioral goals (e.g., reducing excess weight). The third stage included *self-instructional training* in the use of self-rewards and cognitive coping strategies. The fourth stage was the *rehearsal phase* in which patients practiced the skills they had just learned and reported on their progress in group sessions. Patients in the social support condition attended 15 group sessions, which included an educational component similar to that used in the stress inoculation condition and a support component in which patients received support from the therapist and the other members of the group and interacted with family members and friends. Patients in this condition were encouraged to develop their own coping strategies. Patients in the no-treatment control condition did not receive therapy of any type.

The results indicated that patients in both the stress inoculation and social support conditions experienced significant decreases in anxiety and depression from pretreatment to posttreatment. However, only patients in the stress inoculation condition exhibited decreases in pain behavior, self-reported pain intensity, and rheumatoid factor titer (a physiological index of rheumatoid arthritis). Furthermore, decreases in Health Locus of Control scores across assessment periods among patients in the stress inoculation condition suggested that the stress inoculation procedures may have provided these patients with more confidence in their ability to control their health outcomes. Other studies assessing cognitive-behavioral programs among chronic pain patients have provided similar results (see Turner & Chapman, 1982).

Multimodal Behavior Therapy

Up to this point in the chapter, the primary focus within each individual section has been on a single behavioral procedure. Even so, many of the behavioral interventions discussed thus far have involved more than one behavioral technique. For example, the successful smoking prevention program for adolescent school children instigated by Botvin et al. (1980) and discussed previously in relation to its modeling procedures also included behavior rehearsal, didactic instruction, and general assertion training. Likewise, as presented in the section on cognitive interventions, the treatment package developed by Ordman and Kirschenbaum (1985) specifically for bulimics included cognitive strategies as well as a behavioral component consisting of self-monitoring, flooding/response prevention, and behavioral contracting. Rather than relying on a single behavioral technique, in actual practice of behavior therapy, one behavioral method is often combined with others to form a more comprehensive treatment package. The use of selected, complementary behavioral techniques in the treatment of a specified problem is called *broad spectrum behavior therapy* (Lazarus, 1971) or *multimodal therapy*. Because much of the research presented thus far has in fact been multimodal, an additional section providing examples of the application of multimodal behavior therapy to health issues would be redundant. As such, this section will diverge from the others in format in an attempt to discuss the basic points associated with multimodal therapy and provide some explicit examples of those topics. Because the multimodal approach has only been referred to in this chapter in an off-hand manner and has not been addressed directly, it deserves elaboration.

There are two major advantages to the multimodal approach. First, many health-related problems are multifaceted, involving a complex interaction of many factors in both the development and maintenance of the problem. For example, a man at high risk for stroke who consistently avoids controlling his dietary salt intake may do so for several reasons. First, he may notice his family and friends eating salty foods and may follow their example. Second, he may find that reaching for the salt shaker at the dinner table is a difficult habit to break. Finally, he may not fully comprehend the implications of sodium intake on the onset and course of cerebrovascular disease. Clearly, then, to manage his salt-eating behavior successfully, all these contributing factors should be addressed. To change health behaviors most effectively, it is often necessary to use a variety of carefully integrated techniques that form a comprehensive behavioral management program. Multimodal behavior therapy is designed specifically to provide such a comprehensive program.

Second, multimodal therapy emphasizes the individual needs of each patient. As we have seen repeatedly throughout the textbook, a given behavioral technique or a behavioral management program usually is not equally effective for everyone, even if all the recipients have the same problem. Multimodal therapy not only permits the inclusion of more than one behavioral procedure but also posits that these techniques should be carefully selected to influence the target behavior in the most effective way.

Unfortunately, the individualization of a behavior therapy regimen is an advantage that has not been fully developed in psychological research. That is, to ensure standardization, the rigors of experimental design require that no differences exist between separate applications of a single intervention. Nevertheless, the preponderance of published case studies that have incorporated a multimodal approach illustrates the importance of and the need for individualized treatment. For example, Ducko, Pollard, Bray, and Schieter (1984) applied a comprehensive behavioral program in the treatment of complex tinnitus, a condition characterized by ringing or buzzing in the ear that is not caused by an external audio stimulus. An intense psychological and behavioral assessment of the patient through questionnaires, direct observation, and self-monitoring revealed social skills deficits, depression and recurrent negative self-statements, marital problems, and eromophobia (i.e., fear of solitude). Most importantly, self-monitoring indicated that the tinnitus worsened in stressful situations.

The patient was first taught progressive muscle relaxation and a biofeedback procedure to allow him to control his reaction to stressful events. To combat the depression that accompanied and apparently exacerbated the physical disability, reinforcement of positive self-statements was included in the program. Social skills were developed through assertion training and by negatively reinforcing attentive listening and succinct speech. The patient's eromophobia was treated with *in vivo* exposure to time spent alone. Finally, the patient and his wife received marital therapy with a focus on communication skills. By dealing with issues such as depression, social skills, eromophobia, and marital problems, it was predicted that the patient would be able to reduce the discomfort associated with those situations which he had once found stressful, thereby reducing the incidence of tinnitus. After nine days of treatment, the patient reported a marked reduction in the severity ratings of his tinnitus and improved functioning in all targeted psychological and behavioral areas. Furthermore, treatment effects were maintained during the three-month follow-up period. This case study clearly illustrates the unique and varied agents that may directly and indirectly contribute to a maladaptive behavior or health problem and also how a comprehensive program of behavioral techniques might successfully manage that problem.

For multimodal therapy to work most effectively, however, the individualization of treatment extends beyond being simply an advantage of a multicomponent program and becomes a necessity. In other words, it is vital that the particular program implemented, whether standardized or not, meets the needs of the patient. A demonstration of this principle is provided by Wing, Epstein, Norwalk, Koeske, and Hagg (1985) in an obesity study with Type II (non–insulin dependent) diabetic patients.

Fifty-three obese diabetic patients were randomly assigned to a multimodal therapy condition, a nutrition education condition, or a standard-care condition. The multimodal therapy condition included self-monitoring of high-sugar foods, reinforcement for eating foods high in fiber, modeling and social reinforcement of exercise, contingency contracting for weight loss, stimulus control, and a cognitive intervention to modify self-statements concerning food. The nutrition education condition provided information concerning diabetes, diet, and exercise, but contained no specific behavioral procedures, while the standard-care condition acted as a control condition. The patients in the multimodal therapy condition lost significantly more weight during the first four months of the treatment program than did patients in the nutrition education condition or the standard-care condition. These differences, however, were not maintained at the end of the 16-month study. Wing and colleagues suggest that this lack of maintenance behavior may be due to the fact that this particular weight control program was inappropriate for Type II diabetic patients. That is, perhaps a program dealing with diabetic patients should have had a greater emphasis on monitoring glucose levels and on helping patients perceive the relationship between diet, exercise, and glucose control. Therefore, not only does this study present another means by which a multimodal technique might be applied to the area of health promotion, it also points out the importance of matching the treatment to the needs of the patient.

On the other hand, even large, standardized behavioral programs can be successful when they specifically address the issues at hand in a manner appropriate for the participants. For instance, Rakos, Grodek, and Mack (1985) assessed the effectiveness of "Superstuff," a self-help, self-administered behavioral program for asthmatic children. Superstuff incorporated behavioral procedures such as relaxation training, self-control techniques, and social reinforcement within the context of games and puzzles designed for children aged 7–12. The authors reported that the children who had received the intervention evidenced increased asthma self-control skills, fewer asthma-related interruptions of parents, greater improvements in the progression of asthma, and a trend toward decreased school absenteeism than children assigned to the no-treatment control condition. In this treatment package, both the techniques chosen and the means by which they were administered met the needs of the patients involved, a fact which certainly contributed to its success.

The term *multimodal therapy* is sometimes used to refer to comprehensive treatment packages consisting of both behavioral interventions and nonbehavioral procedures. The basis for combining treatments of different modalities is the hope of an additive or synergistic effect that would be greater than the effect of either intervention alone. One popular combination is behavior therapy and pharmacotherapy. For instance, Taylor, Farguar, Nelson, and Agras (1977) assigned 31 pharmacologically treated hypertensive patients to one of three conditions: relaxation training plus medication, nonspecific psychotherapy plus medication, and medication only. Prior to their participation in the study, all patients received at least two months' medical care for hypertension, during which time their medications were stabilized. The results of the study are shown in Figure 11–9. At the end of treatment, the patients who received relaxation training plus medication had significantly lower blood pressures than did patients in either of the other two conditions. By the end of the six-month follow-up, the relaxation training plus medication patients continued to have lower blood pressures, though the difference was no longer statistically significant.

These results suggest that behavior therapy enhanced the effectiveness of medication alone in reducing blood pressure. It might be noted that there was not a relaxation-only comparison group, and therefore, some might argue that relaxation alone might have been as effective as the mutimodal package of relaxation plus medication. However, it is important to keep in mind that in some medical contexts, it is not ethically

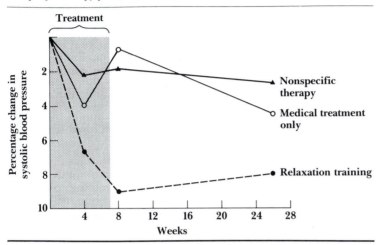

Figure 11–9 *Percentage of systolic blood pressure change before, during, and after treatment, which included relaxation training plus medication, nonspecific therapy plus medication, and medication alone.*

Adapted from Taylor et al. (1977).

appropriate to remove a person from medical interventions, even if this would provide a perfectly balanced experimental design. When such is the case, the important question is whether a behavioral treatment adds to the effectiveness of appropriate medical intervention. In many cases, as suggested by the Taylor et al. study, the answer is yes.

In addition to pharmacotherapy, other treatment modalities have been successfully combined with behavior therapy. Research in the treatment of obesity has suggested that exercise combined with a behavioral and dietary intervention produces significantly greater weight loss than does a single intervention strategy (see review by Thompson, Jarvie, Lahey, & Cureton, 1982). Furthermore, follow-up data indicate that the combination package appears to maintain treatment effects better than a single treatment modality. Finally, another possible combination of behavior therapy and non–behavior therapy involves not a simultaneous administra-

tion of both procedures but instead a sequential application.

The potential use of behavior therapy to maintain follow-up effects of a preceding non–behavioral intervention has been advocated by Heinrich et al. (1985). The researchers compared physical therapy to multimodal behavior therapy in the treatment of chronic low back pain. The patients received either a traditional physical therapy intervention designed to increase low back function or a multimodal behavioral treatment addressing the environmental, social, and psychological issues associated with chronic low back pain. Outcome data suggested that both groups reported significantly less perceived pain at follow-up than at pretreatment. Behavior therapy demonstrated a slight advantage over physical therapy in decreasing emotional distress, but did relatively poorly in controlling lower back function. Though physical therapy significantly increased lower back control and back protection skills, these effects were not maintained at follow-up. The authors suggested that behavioral techniques such as modeling and reinforcement be implemented following the physical therapy intervention specifically to increase maintenance behavior.

The examples that have been presented here illustrate the broad range of health-related issues to which a comprehensive behavioral program might be applied. In general, the results of multimodal approaches in behavioral medicine have been positive. For instance, combining behavioral techniques has been associated with significant reductions in cigarette smoking, weight loss, and decreased pain (e.g., Botvin et al., 1983; Bradley et al., 1985; Wing et al., 1985). Clearly, though, a multicomponent treatment approach is not always as effective as one might hope it would be. Particularly in investigations targeting obesity and smoking, behavioral interventions are frequently unable to maintain their effects at follow-up (see Brownwell, 1982; Hunt & Bespalec, 1974), and even a comprehensive behavioral program may not bring the desired long-term maintenance effects. Despite the primary advantage of a multimodal program (i.e., combining behavioral interventions to build an individualized treatment package), one should not automatically assume that a comprehensive behavioral intervention is always better. That is, a multimodal package is often more expensive and more time consuming than a single behavioral intervention, and consequently, the pros and cons of the multimodal intervention should be weighed and compared with the advantages and disadvantages of a single behavioral technique. Therefore, when considering implementation of a multicomponent behavioral treatment, the researcher and the clinician should consider the cost-effectiveness of that package and alternative strategies.

Conclusion

Behavior therapy techniques have become widely used procedures within the multidisciplinary area of behavioral medicine. In this chapter we have attempted to illustrate how the behavioral procedures described in prior chapters have been applied within the behavioral medicine context. As the studies described in this chapter illustrate, behavioral techniques are often used to promote health, prevent disease, and treat patients with physical illness or problems. Since many of the health problems that plague us today are really behavioral, not medical, in nature, altering behavior patterns can be one of the most successful and cost-effective approaches available to promoting health and treating illness.

Clinical and experimental work in the area of behavioral medicine is relatively new. Most behavioral therapists still work primarily in mental health settings, focusing on the treatment of psychopathology. As a result, some of the studies we have described were conducted by medical specialists (e.g., nurses) rather than behavioral scientists, and many showed the methodological limitations that often characterize the early stages of field research. Nonetheless, we believe that one of the most exciting areas for behavior therapy in coming years, both in terms of application and in terms of theoretical and procedural innovation, will be behavioral medicine.

Appendix A
Reinforcers and Contingencies of Reinforcement

Reinforcers and Reinforcement

When tailoring a contingency management program to a particular individual, the therapist often attempts to utilize reinforcers (and punishers perhaps) that have proved effective for that particular individual in the past. When attempting to define these effective reinforcers, there are some basic types of reinforcers and reinforcing events for which to look, and often there are stimuli or events within these categories that are effective reinforcers for nearly everyone. The types of reinforcers and reinforcing events can be *material, social, activity, token,* and *covert.*

In the natural environment, reinforcers are rarely directly dispensed to adults immediately following a desired behavior. In view of this, the therapist should take great care to direct the client into environments where his or her new behaviors will be reinforced and thus maintained. The difficulty in guiding the client to a more favorable environment is compounded when the reinforcers are social, or perhaps activity, and not material.

For children, the therapist or an agent such as a parent, teacher, or nurse may dispense reinforcement of just about any category—material, social, or activity—and the child may be directly *placed* in environments that reinforce the desired behaviors (with adults, self-exposure to the desired environment is generally *encouraged* or *directed,* but children have less freedom than adults in our society). Institutionalized adults, or adults who are retarded but not institutionalized, can receive direct reinforcement from therapists, ward personnel, or caretakers.

Types of Reinforcers

Material Reinforcers Material reinforcers are perhaps most effective for children—or at least most common—although they have their place in adult life. Candy, toys, and food treats are often dispensed to children who have been "good," done their chores on time, and so on. Adults often receive bonuses or raises, and some business organizations also give trips as prizes for jobs well done. On a person-to-person basis, material rewards are not as common among adults, although husbands and wives probably consent more readily to let their mates buy some desired items when prior behavior has met a particular standard or preference.

The use of material and other types of reinforcers (e.g., activity or negative reinforcers based on the termination of aversive events) has one rather important and desirable side effect. When the reinforcer is consistently delivered by a single individual (or group) delivering the reinforcement, the person (or persons) delivering the reinforcement begins to acquire a positive, reinforcing valence himself. This quality then predisposes the client to respond to the other person's presence, approval, and other behaviors as though they were

549

reinforcers. Thus, we have the class of *social reinforcers.*

Social Reinforcers A vast majority of all reinforcing events that come to affect human behavior are social events involving the nearness, smiles, praise, or even physical contact with other individuals. Humans learn to value other humans because they are consistently paired with material, unlearned reinforcers, especially in early infancy (e.g., the early feeding experience, which involves being held while feeding or even being breast-fed directly). Some authors believe that the human organism innately shows social responsivity (Bowlby, 1969). For our purposes, the argument is largely academic. It remains the case that people are, or become, responsive to people. There is some evidence, however, that individuals who are not responded to as reinforcing will become so if they are paired with established reinforcers; and autistic children, who appear to find no social contact reinforcing, may be (socially) responsive to an individual who is consistently paired with a very powerful existing reinforcer (Lovaas, 1968).

Table A-1 presents some common social reinforcers. Certainly different individuals respond more or less positively (and sometimes negatively) to each of these. They are common, however, and people dispense and receive these reinforcers all the time. In most instances, these reinforcers are acquired *contingently*. Mothers are loving to their children, and husbands are affectionate to their wives after behaviors or interactions pleasing to them and not at all during arguments or spats. A person can dispense reinforcers contingently without even knowing it. But our point here is that social reinforcers are quite prevalent in the natural environment, are quite powerful, and can be manipulated in order to modify behavior. The therapist's attentiveness and facial expression in more traditional, non–behavior-modification forms of therapy can even be largely responsible for the changes that occur in various client behaviors (Bandura, 1962).

Table A–1 **Common Social Reinforcers: Examples**

	Praise (Verbal Reinforcer)	
Good	Good Job	That's interesting
That's right	Good thinking	I'm pleased with that
Excellent	Thank you	Show this to your father
That's clever	Great	Show Grandma your picture
Exactly		I love you
	Facial Expressions	
Smiling	Looking interested	
Laughing		Winking
	Nearness	
Walking together	Eating together	Playing games together
Talking and/or listening to each other for a while		
	Physical Contact	
Touching	Shaking hands	Sitting in lap
Hugging	Holding hands	Patting head, shoulder, or back

Adapted from Becker (1971).

Activity Reinforcers Although many of the social reinforcers discussed above involve activity as well, we wish to stress that the occasion, or privilege, to perform preferred activities of any sort (social or not) may be used to reinforce activities or behaviors that are less preferred. Some authors, (Becker, 1971; Homme, 1971) refer to "Grandma's Rule," which states, "First you work, then you play." Or, "You do what I want you to do before you get to do what you want to do." Clearly this principle has been around a long time as simple common sense, and it was defined as a formal principle delineating one type of reinforcer by Premack in 1965. Typically it is referred to as the *Premack principle* (Danaher, 1974).

The Premack principle, quite simply, states that an activity, or behavior, may be reinforced by the privilege to engage in another behavior of greater baseline frequency. Thus, sitting quietly in a classroom for a few minutes can be reinforced by the privilege of running around, or studying at home can be reinforced by periods of watching television. Another clever application of the Premack principle in the classroom is the procedure of "topic sequencing" in which topics of study that are most preferred are used to reinforce work on less preferred topics (e.g., boys who enjoy math might be given the privilege of working on it only after the English assignment has been completed) (Hartje, 1973).

Often the frequency with which a behavior is performed is an index of the degree to which it is valued. Not all valued behaviors can be performed that frequently, so there are other activities that may be reinforcing even though they are not performed as frequently as the behavior to be reinforced. Watching television may reinforce a less frequent behavior, such as studying, for an individual who is an avid video fan. In another instance, a poor child who has little access to television may also find watching it reinforcing even though in the past he has seen television less frequently than he has per-

formed the behavior to be reinforced (e.g., studying). A particular activity reinforcer will not reinforce all other activities. For one child, getting to study with a friend, rather than alone, might reinforce reading a new book. For another child, who reads a great deal, the opportunity to read after studying (with a friend or alone) might increase the frequency of studying.

For children, the privileges to engage in various activities may often be dictated by parents, teachers, and the like, and hence these individuals can control the sequence of these activities, making more preferred ones contingent upon the performance of less preferred activities. For adults, contingency management of this sort can be placed within the control of the client. After discussion with the therapist of the problematic low frequencies of some behaviors and the designation of others, more preferred activities, the client may be instructed in the sequencing of various behaviors. For example, a student with poor study habits may be told to read five pages and then go down to the student lounge for a while, or to read his five pages before seven p.m. and then watch a half-hour TV show before returning to study. A writer may organize his day so that he works for three hours in the morning, and then relaxes with his family, working in the afternoon again only if he feels like it.

Token Reinforcers Although many material objects in the natural environment, such as food, cars, toys, and jewelry, have clear reinforcing value, a majority of reinforcing experiences probably involve token reinforcers. A token reinforcer is an object with redeemable value, one that can be traded for an "actual" reinforcer of another kind (material, social, or activity), and is termed a "backup reinforcer." The most prevalent token reinforcer for adults (and possibly older children) is money, with which we all can purchase food, company, or activity privileges. Credit cards are another example of objects that may have periodic token

reinforcement value since they are used to secure desired objects or privileges.

In a contingency management program,
then, token reinforcers can be introduced by
identifying a particular token and then establishing a procedure to give it reinforcing value.
A hospital ward may implement a broad token
economy utilizing poker chips and create an extensive list of the objects and privileges for
which they can be redeemed. Although group
settings, such as a hospital ward or cottage (for
delinquent children), may be the most commonplace settings for token economies, they may
also be used in the treatment of individual
clients, either with a therapist dispensing tokens
and maintaining control over their redemption
or by the establishment of a small token economy in a natural unit such as a household
(Popler, 1976).

Covert Reinforcers The final category of
reinforcers includes the thoughts and self-evaluations that an individual may engage in contingent upon his own behavior. The thoughts,
images, and evaluations that individuals engage
in following particular acts may exert a maintaining influence over those acts, and a contingency management procedure may enlist
covert reinforcement in support of a behavior
change program. Generally, the manipulation
of covert reinforcers involves alterations in the
degree to which individuals evaluate desired behavior positively.

Types of Reinforcement

Extrinsic and Intrinsic Reinforcement Often the question arises as to whether training an
individual by means of externally administered
reinforcement will enslave such a person to the
use of reinforcement forever and doom him (or
the behavior in question) to extinction whenever
the planned reinforcement of that behavior
ceases. This is clearly not the case since newly
acquired desirable behaviors tend to be reinforced by others (not just the contingency

managers) and will be reinforced in new situations as well (O'Leary, O'Leary, & Becker, 1967;
Wahler & Erickson, 1969). Often, individuals participating in a program of contingency
management object to the overt use of extrinsic
reinforcers as "bribery." They may feel it is a
child's moral duty to empty the trash or help
with the dishes, or a husband's responsibility to
take out the trash. They may feel that they were
never reinforced (untrue though this may be)
for the behaviors in question, so why should
someone else be treated differently. Often an
effective counter to this position is to draw a
sharp distinction between socially desirable and
undesirable behaviors. It can be pointed out
that bribery refers to a payoff for irresponsible,
undesirable, or morally offensive behaviors,
whereas desired behaviors are often reinforced
under such conceptualizations as salary, bonuses, commission, praise, approval, or even reward.

Several procedures help ensure the enduring
effectiveness of a reinforcement-based therapy
program. The procedure of *leaning* is often
evoked in a reinforcement paradigm. The procedure involves gradually omitting reinforcement that has been externally administered and
is extrinsic in nature. The result of such a procedure is often not the extinction of the behavior in question, but rather the adoption by the
individual of intrinsic reinforcement such as
feelings of pride, approval of his own behavior,
or perhaps self-professed enjoyment of the behavior in question. Many individuals dislike coffee or cigarettes at first but indulge in their consumption for other reasons (wanting to be
"grown-up," needing to stay awake, etc.). In
most cases, the consumption of these products
eventually comes to be intrinsically reinforcing.
Individuals who engage in a particular behavior
and are insufficiently rewarded for it come to
prefer that behavior (Festinger, 1957; Festinger
& Carlsmith, 1959; Masters & Mokros, 1973).
This effect is termed "the psychology of
insufficient reward" (Festinger, 1961). Interestingly, the use of reinforcers that are highly

valued may deter learning and behavior change (Masters & Mokros, 1973; Miller & Estes, 1961), perhaps via a process of distraction: an individual's attention may become riveted on the prospect of coming rewards to such an extent that he or she attends only poorly to the behaviors he is learning.

We wish to make two points here. First, there is a tendency for behaviors that have been acquired through reinforcement techniques to become intrinsically reinforcing, especially if the reinforcement manipulated during learning is effective, but not of grandiose proportions, and if it is carefully and gradually withdrawn as the behavior becomes an established part of the person's repertoire. Second, it is simply not true that all "normal" behaviors are primarily internally motivated. The social environment continually reinforces (and punishes) everyday behaviors, and a client may be guided into environments that respond appropriately to newly acquired behaviors (and away from environments that respond inappropriately).

Positive and Negative Reinforcement

Many people equate negative reinforcement and punishment, and this is incorrect. The term *reinforcement,* as we noted earlier, refers to increasing either the likelihood that a behavior will be performed or the intensity with which it will be performed. The term *positive reinforcement* is used to describe the occurrence of a reinforcing event following the performance of a desired behavior. Conversely, *negative reinforcement* describes the termination of an aversive event following the performance of a desired behavior. The addition of a positive event and the termination of an aversive event both have the same effect on behavior: they increase the frequency of the behavior upon whose occurrence they are contingent.

Self-reinforcement A final type of reinforcement deserving of mention is self-reinforcement, the dispensation of reinforcing consequences to oneself. Although people, especially children, often dispense material reinforcers (e.g., buying a soda or a candy bar) or even activity reinforcers (e.g., going to a movie after doing well on an exam) in a clearly contingent fashion, the primary form of self-reinforcement that has relevance for contingency management procedures is the almost automatic act of evaluating one's own behavior when it reaches a standard of excellence or a goal (producing positive reinforcement), or when it fails to do so (producing punitive self-criticism).

We have already discussed covert reinforcers, and this section might well have been labeled *covert reinforcement* since such reinforcement is always self-delivered. In any event, one common step in a contingency management program—one that is often implicit in the training or encouragement of self-monitoring—is the invocation of behavior standards that describe the eventual desired behavior. The mere establishment of such a goal may ensure that self-reinforcement in the form of positive evaluations or appropriate behavior will augment any program of extrinsic contingency management. Recent research suggests, however, that self-reinforcement effects may be a function of *public* (as opposed to private) goal setting (Hayes et al., 1985). A particular contingency management program may also address itself directly to self-reinforcement behavior. Clients who complain of depression or low self-concept may benefit from retraining in self-reinforcement so that their behavior standards are not set so high as to ensure self-rated failure, or from retraining designed to refocus their attention on their own behavior so that successes and positive self-attributes are attended to more than failures or shortcomings (Mischel, Ebbesen, & Zeiss, 1973, 1976).

Parameters of Reinforcement

In both the assessment of the problem and its treatment by contingency management, it is important to determine the schedule of reinforcement that pertained for the client prior to treatment and to train the change agent in the proper, most effective utilization of reinforcement. There are several important principles to be grasped here.

Immediacy Versus Delay of Reinforcement
The longer the time between the completion of a behavior and the delivery of a reinforcing consequence, the less effect the reinforcer will have. This is often termed the *temporal gradient of reinforcement*. Thus, if a desired behavior is of low frequency even though it generally elicits reinforcement, it is important to determine whether the reinforcement is delivered soon after the completion of the behavior. Thanking a child at night for finally making his own bed that morning is likely to be ineffective, or slightly effective at best.

A procedure to maximize the effectiveness of reinforcement or punishment that has already been delayed long after the act on which it is contingent has been performed is to verbally restate the contingency (e.g., "I am awarding you three bonus tokens because the nursing staff reports that you helped clean up after lunch and engaged in pleasant conversation with other patients during the morning"). In general, however, a reinforcer (or punisher) is most effective when it is delivered immediately after the completion of the desired response.

Delay of Reinforcement in Behavior Sequences When an individual is expected to acquire an extended sequence of behaviors (most "behaviors" are actually sequences of more elementary component behaviors), it may be necessary to insert reinforcement into the sequence while it is being learned. Often this is termed *shaping* (we discuss this procedure in a later section). Since some sequences are quite long, they are not always completed quickly, and a reinforcer delivered at the end may be relatively ineffective overall. Diagnostically, the therapist is faced with two questions. First, he or she must decide whether or not the behavior is actually such a long sequence that reinforcement should be given following components, as well as at the end. Second, he or she must ascertain whether or not reinforcement is being administered with little delay upon the completion of a low-frequency desired behavior. A verbal clarification of the contingency could also be used in this case.

Verbal Clarification of Behavior and the Contingent Relationship Between Behavior and Reinforcer Behavior is clearly a complex, ongoing stream; thus, a reinforcer that suddenly appears may not have any clear contingency. When a reinforcer follows a long sequence of behaviors, or when it is somewhat delayed after the completion of a behavior, its effectiveness may be enhanced by a clear spelling out of the contingency. "You have been a good boy today," followed by a kiss or special treat is less informative than "You mowed the lawn without being asked!" Often, too, spelling out a contingency includes specification of the behaviors involved in the sequence. "You put your underwear, socks, pants, and shirt on *all* by yourself," said with a smile while mother buttons a little boy's shirt is likely to be more powerful than commenting before dinner that night, with a smile, "You nearly got dressed all by yourself this morning" (Stevenson, 1971).

Discriminative cues can also be enhanced by verbal explication ("When you go play after school and don't tell me before you go, I am unhappy"). Similarly, it seems plausible that family or marital therapy often provides a forum for individuals to discover that the contingency they surmised for reinforcers or punishers is not, in truth, the intended contingency. "I thought you were crabby on those days because it was just that time of the month. I didn't know that those were the days I forgot to clean the sink after shaving." Or, "When you complained about my not cleaning the sink, I didn't know you were generally ticked off because I didn't let you have the bathroom first and you were in a hurry. I thought you were just mad in general 'cause there are lots of times I don't clean the sink and you don't say anything." From these examples it is clear that communication skills and reinforcement skills may often be similar, and perhaps even identical.

Incentive Value and the Power of a Reinforcer   Often individuals inadvertently assume that what is a powerful reinforcer for them is also one for others. For this and a variety of other reasons, a behavior may remain at low frequency because it is reinforced by a reward of slight value to the individual. Some individuals do not respond as powerfully to praise as others. Some people feel less pride in completing a task and, therefore, may not behave as though they have a sense of responsibility (whether or not they *should* have this feeling is not under consideration). Thus, the fact is simply this: desired behaviors that are infrequent when followed by certain reinforcements can be increased in frequency by utilization of a more powerful or more effective (for that person) reinforcer. The only caution here is that one should be careful not to employ reinforcers of such high value that they excite or distract to the point of *reducing* the learning of new behaviors (Masters & Mokros, 1973). On the other hand, common reinforcing events that have been paired with unpleasant experiences or that have become so frequent as to provoke satiation are likely to be ineffective because they are of such low power. Food, candy, praise, and even sex are prone to temporary satiation. Exchangeable reinforcers, such as tokens or money, appear less prone to satiation, probably because they can always be redeemed for new and different backup reinforcers.

Shaping New Behaviors: Schedules of Reinforcement

The technique of shaping behavior is often termed *successive approximation* or *response differentiation* (Bandura, 1969; Skinner, 1937). If a

behavior is not exhibited by an individual, it cannot be reinforced. Shaping is simply a general procedure designed to induce the performance of new behaviors by the initial reinforcement of behaviors in the individual's repertoire that have some similarity to the desired behavior. Then, gradually, reinforcement is withdrawn from the less similar behaviors and concentrated on the more similar ones, which progressively become more and more similar to the desired behavior until they are one and the same. In a striking example of the technique, Wolf, Risley, and Mees (1964) used shaping to get a 3 1/2-year-old autistic boy to wear glasses. Initially, a conditioned reinforcer was established by pairing the clicks of a toy noisemaker with a small bit of candy or fruit. Very quickly the child learned to approach the bowl where food was immediately delivered after the click. Initially, since the prescription lenses required were quite powerful and changed the visual field radically—a condition that might itself have been aversive—the child was rewarded for wearing the *frames* only. Even this proved difficult, since they could not be placed appropriately upon his head because he became active and upset whenever anyone touched his head. Furthermore, the staff of the hospital ward was reluctant to deprive the child of food, so the candy and fruit were minimally powerful reinforcers.

To counter these problems, Wolf et al. reported,

> We attempted to increase deprivational control by using breakfast as a shaping session, bits of breakfast now being dependent upon approximations to the wearing of glasses. . . . Later we added to the glasses . . . a "roll bar" which would go over the top of his head and guide the pieces up and over the ears.
>
> After wearing the glasses was established in these sessions, it could be maintained with often less manipulable reinforcers. For example, the attendants would tell Dicky, "Put your glasses on and let's go for a walk." Dicky was usually required to wear the glasses during meals, snacks, automobile

rides, walks, outdoor play, etc. If he removed the glasses, the activity was terminated. At the time of Dicky's release from the hospital he had worn the glasses for more than 600 hours and was wearing them about 12 hours a day. (1964, pp. 309–310)

In this case, there is also a good example of counterconditioning components that may be embedded within a contingency management program. Later, we will discuss counterconditioning as a relatively common component of aversive control procedures. In the present instance, it is simply important to state that having the child wear the glasses at the same time that he was engaged in a pleasant activity, such as walking, provided the necessary conditions for the positive valence of walking to become conditioned to the act of wearing glasses, replacing *(counterconditioning)* the negative valence the glasses had initially.

The use of shaping is not limited to simple behaviors, young children, or highly disturbed individuals. Schwitzgebel (1967) and Schwitzgebel and Kolb (1964) effectively used a shaping procedure to treat noninstitutionalized adolescent juvenile delinquents. In this procedure, the therapist went directly into areas of high crime on the pretext of hiring subjects for a research project. It was explained that the purpose of the research was to find out what teenagers think and feel about things, and one of the "qualifications" for the job was that the person have a court record.

Schwitzgebel and Kolb (1964) paid adolescents an hourly wage to give tape-recorded "interviews." When the juveniles seemed to enjoy these interviews, the meetings were gradually modified toward therapeutic ends and the payment was withdrawn. The adolescents were seen an average of three times per week for approximately nine months in a therapy setting where the therapist was highly directive. A three-year follow-up revealed a significant reduction in the frequency and severity of crimes the subjects committed when compared to a matched-pair control group.

Schwitzgebel (1967) similarly elicited the therapeutic cooperation of juvenile delinquents for a series of 10 interviews over a period of two to three months. One group of adolescents received positive consequences for statements of concern about other people and prompt arrival at the session. For example, they might be given cigarettes, candy bars, or even cash bonuses of 25¢ to $1 for statements such as "Joe is a good guy." Another group received negative consequences for hostile statements about people. For example, the therapist might become inattentive or mildly disagree following expressions of antagonism toward, or depreciation of, another person's status. The juveniles were observed in a social situation (a restaurant). When positive consequences had followed statements of concern for other people, there was a significant increase in such statements in a natural social interaction. Juveniles punished for hostile comments showed a significant decrease in such comments in the social situation. The use of contingent positive consequences also induced the adolescents to arrive promptly for their appointments.

Arrangement of Contingencies

Usually the term *schedule of reinforcement* is limited to the actual relationship between the occurrence of a response (or the passage of time) and the provision of a reinforcing event. There has been extensive research concerning the effects of various schedules of reinforcement on the behavior of lower organisms and of man (Ayllon & Azrin, 1965; Ferster & Skinner, 1957). The schedules of reinforcement most prevalent in the practice of behavior therapy are continuous and intermittent reinforcement and ratio and interval schedules.

Continuous Reinforcement Under *continuous reinforcement* (CRF), *every* appropriate response is followed by reinforcement. Under these conditions, the acquisition of a particular behavior is likely to be quite rapid, but upon the cessation of reinforcement, extinction also occurs quite rapidly. Thus, a CRF schedule may be used in shaping a particular behavior, but other schedules are likely to be employed later in order to increase the "endurance" of the response. The natural environment very rarely provides a CRF schedule or reinforcement for a particular behavior. More often, some or most instances of a response are reinforced, but some are not.

Intermittent Reinforcement Under *intermittent reinforcement* schedules, not every response is followed by a reinforcer, and the schedule is denoted by the letters FR or FI followed by a number indicating how often reinforcement occurs. An FR1 schedule, for example, is the same as a continuous schedule (every response is reinforced) and so one seldom sees this particular denotation. All *ratio* (except FR1) and *interval* schedules (see the next two sections) are intermittent schedules. When not every response is reinforced, the behaving individual is always in extinction to some degree since extinction is supposedly the result of the repeated occurrence of a response without ensuing reinforcement. The result of an intermittent schedule is less rapid acquisition (if this schedule is used from the start) and a rather unsteady rate of responding, with rapid responding sometimes, slow responding at other times: the individual tends to pause after the delivery of a reinforcer then begin responding at an increasingly rapid rate until another reinforcer is dispensed.

When extinction is instituted and the designated responses are no longer reinforced at all, the individual only gradually ceases to respond. The onset of an extinction procedure (withdrawal of contingent reinforcement) is difficult to recognize in this case since one is "used to" responding without reinforcement (there is some controversy over the proper explanation of this phenomenon; e.g., see Deese & Hulse, 1967). In practice, it is quite common to begin a training procedure utilizing a continuous schedule, to transform the schedule gradually into an intermittent one (variable ratio), and then, as environmental and self-managed contingencies become increasingly effective, gradually, to phase out the therapeutic reinforcement schedule completely.

Ratio Schedules Most schedules of reinforcement are *ratio schedules* that are either fixed or variable in nature. *Fixed-ratio (FR) schedule* describes cases in which every *n*th response (second, third, fourth, etc.) is reinforced. If every second response is reinforced, the schedule is an FR2; if every third, an FR3, and so on. Obviously this type of schedule requires close monitoring of the precise number of times a response occurs and is not very common in everyday life. In practice, however, it may be a useful way in which to "lean out" a continuous schedule (or a "rich" intermittent one, "rich" indicating that the ratio is quite small, say, 2 or 3) in a gradual, regulated way; for example, by going from FR4 to FR5 to FR7, and so on.

By far the more common ratio reinforcement is the *variable-ratio (VR) schedule*. Variable ratio means simply that the ratio between the number of responses and reinforcements changes from time to time. For example, a reinforcer may occur after three responses, then after the very next one, then not until five responses have occurred. A VR schedule is described by referring to the *average* number of responses that occur before a reinforcement is administered (e.g., a VR3 means that even though the ratio is variable, *on the average* every third response is reinforced). Variable-ratio schedules tend to produce steady and high rates of responding without the pause associated with a fixed-ratio schedule. An example of a variable-ratio schedule in everyday life would be the praise and approval parents might give their child when he or she works on homework during the evening. One night the parents may look in at 9:00, another night at 8:00 and again at 9:30, and another night not at all. Note how this schedule of reinforcement would be best for preventing extinction, since it is usually impossible to know for sure when the next reinforcement is going to occur. This is quite necessary for human behavior, since often a desired behavior must be performed many times before it gains any reinforcement. Also, variable ratios give training in responding to highly delayed reinforcement—an occurrence that is also characteristic of natural environments.

Interval Schedules   Finally there are *interval schedules,* which may be either fixed (FI) or variable (VI). Interval schedules, unlike ratio schedules are not solely tied to an individual's rate of behavior, but are primarily concerned with the amount of time between reinforcement. Nonetheless, they do have an effect on his or her behavior. Fixed-interval schedules, in which reinforcement is given after fixed periods of time, tend to produce or maintain behavior in a manner similar to that of a fixed-ratio schedule, with pauses after the receipt of each reinforcement. Recess in school is a good exam-

ple of a fixed-interval schedule (unless the teacher makes it contingent upon good behavior!). Variable-interval schedules produce steadier responding. An example of a variable interval would be the coffee or smoking breaks called by a director during rehearsals. Interval schedules are not particularly common in behavior therapy, except in instances such as a token economy when, for example, a fixed-interval privilege (for instance, sleeping in a single bedroom) is contingent upon some minimal behavior standards. Even in this example, the reinforcement—though itself interval in nature—is a ratio as well, since some occurrence (response rate) is necessary to maintain the privilege. Salaries, with fixed-interval paydays; recesses in schools; meals—all these are fixed-interval reinforcers in the natural environment. To be utilized in therapy procedures, however, they are typically changed to a ratio basis: behave yourself, or go to bed without dinner (a poorly specified contingency, with threatened time-out).

Appendix B
Detailed Examples of Token Systems and Economies in Institutional Settings

Institutional Use of Contingency Management Procedures

Schaefer and Martin (1969) employed token systems that were very much oriented to each individual patient. Table B-1 contains treatment programs for two patients treated by these authors. Note how the behaviors are simple, specific, and clearly have reference to the behavior problems characterizing each patient.

Schaefer and Martin (1969) also used jobs as sources of token reinforcement. Their purpose, of course, was to benefit the patient and not simply to obtain cheap labor. Toward this end, one goal was to enable the patient to complete the entire task or job by himself—an extended chain of behaviors—without reinforcement or reminders in the midst of the job sequence. Table B-2 presents two job descriptions for a patient at different phases of his treatment. Note how, via fading techniques, greater and greater reliance was placed on the patient himself for remembering the equipment he needed and the various individual tasks included in the total job.

Ayllon & Azrin (1968b) used a larger number of on- and off-ward jobs for which patients could earn tokens. These were the sorts of jobs available in any large institution, such as being a meal-server, cleaning up halls and dormitories (sweeping, mopping), picking up laundry from units and delivering it to the central laundry, and so forth. Ayllon & Azrin (1968b) also allowed patients to select the jobs they wished to perform. Each job was described to the patient, with attention given to details about the time, place, and number of tokens to be earned by successful completion. They allowed patients to sign up for a job at any time and, initially, to keep signing up for a job as long as they liked. They recommended, however, that patients be encouraged or forced to rotate from job to job to prevent the bored, rote, stereotyped performance that comes to characterize performance of a particular job after a time.

Although token economies with many considerations for individual patients may be elaborate and lengthy, an economy for a total ward may sometimes be described quite succinctly. The following is an account of the token economy—in terms of information presented (in written form) to the patient—at a Veterans Administration hospital (Petrick, 1971).

In order to . . . teach responsible behavior, this ward has a Token Economy. You can *earn* over 200 tokens weekly for being responsible in three

Table B–1 **Sample Treatment Program Form**

Name _____
Date _____

Behavior	Reinforcer	Schedule	Control Stimuli
Smiling	Tokens	Each time detected	As part of greeting
Talking to other patients	Tokens	Each time detected	
Sitting	Tokens	Each time detected	Patients must be with others; not alone
Reading (patient looking at printed material)	Tokens	Each time detected	Appropriate time and place: especially not in group meetings or at medications
Grooming—hair	Tokens or praise	Each time detected	Only when hair is not pulled tightly against head; prefer "feminine"
Completion of specific assignment	Tokens or free trip out-of-doors	Each time detected	Prior to reinforcement patient must say something positive about the job she completed

Example of treatment program displayed as wall chart for quick reference.

Current Treatment Plan for: Helen			
Behavior	**Reinforcer**	**Schedule**	**Control Stimulus**
talking softly	tokens	each time	especially in groups
working	1 token per task	once each day	at 9:00 a.m.
combed hair	1 cigarette	each hour	9:00 a.m. to 9:00 p.m.

From Schaefer and Martin (1969).

areas: Appearance, Work Assignment, Use of Free Time and Social Skills. Bonus Tokens for other behaviors are also available. How tokens may be *spent* is explained later in the handout.

How to Earn Tokens

I. *Appearance:* Possible 12 tokens daily or 84 weekly.

  A. *Personal Appearance:* Five areas will be inspected at about 8:00 a.m. and 4:15 p.m. daily. You will receive one token for

each of the following areas which are satisfactory:

1. Hair—neatly combed and clean.
2. Face and hands—clean shave, clean face and hands.
3. Shirt—clean, buttoned, tucked in, good repair, clean undershirt.
4. Trousers—clean, pressed, zippered, good repair, belt, proper fit.
5. Shoes and socks—clean, tied, good repair, shined, pulled up socks.

Table B–2 **Patient Job Descriptions:**
              Specification and Fading Behavior

Job: Dorm Cleaner[a]   Time: 9:00–9:30 a.m.

Equipment: 1 Dust mop
           1 Dust rag
           1 Dust pan
           1 Cleaning rag
           1 Pail of water

Requirements:
  1. Pick up equipment at 9:00
  2. Dust all ledges, partitions, and sills
(everyday)
  3. Dust-mop entire dorm floor except area
under beds
  4. Shake out dust rag and dust mop outside
behind the ward
  5. Empty and clean water pail
  6. Rinse out cleaning rag
  7. Turn in all equipment at 9:30 or before
  8. Wash insides of all dorm windows (each
Saturday)

Job: Dorm Cleaner[b]   Time: 9:00–9:30 a.m.

Equipment: 1 Dust mop
           1 __ __
           1 Dust __
           1 Cleaning rag
           1 __ of water

Requirements:
  1. Pick up at __ o'clock
  2. Dust all partitions, ledges and __
  3. __ __ __ __ __ __ __ __ __ __ __
  4. Shake out dust rag and dust mop outside
behind the ward
  5. Empty and __ __ __
  6. Rinse out __ rag
  7. Turn in all equipment at about __
  8. Wash insides of all dorm windows
(each __)

From Schaefer and Martin (1969).
[a]Job description of dorm cleaner during early phase.
[b]Job description of dorm cleaner during later phase.

B. *Bed and Locker Appearance:* Checked daily
   at 8:00 a.m. One token for each if satisfactory.
C. *Comments:* Not all patients will be required to stand close personal inspection
   but everyone is subject to a five-token
   penalty for inappropriate appearance at
   any time. Wearing pajamas in public
   areas before 9:00 p.m. daily is considered inappropriate and the five-token
   penalty applies. Persons not required to
   stand daily inspection will receive 84 tokens credited to their account at weekly
   token counting time. Persons on close
   personal inspection will receive tokens at
   the time of inspection unless they have
   deficiencies to correct. Each person has
   15 minutes to correct the deficiencies
   and report back to the inspector, and if
   the corrections are made, he will receive
   tokens as earned on the initial inspection. Failure to correct the deficiency in
   15 minutes results in loss of all tokens
   for that inspection. There is a ten-token
   penalty for still being in bed at 8:00
   a.m., seven days a week.

II. *Work Assignment:* Four tokens per satisfac-
    tory hour as recorded on time card, or
    about 100 per week. Ten-token penalty for
    missing work assignment each half-day.
    Penalty for missing three consecutive half-
    days on assignment is to lose all earned to-
    kens at that time and go on daily food plan.
    No token credit for work assignment at a
    time other appointments are scheduled,
    e.g., groups and ward meetings. You are re-
    quired to know the name of your work su-
    pervisor and to inform him if you will be
    absent from work.

III. *Use of Free Time and Social Skills:* Possible
     ten tokens per evening or 70 tokens per
     week. Constructive use of free time and so-
     cial skills will be judged daily for the entire
     evening period from about 4:00 p.m. to
     9:00 p.m. Tokens are given according to a
     general impression of the whole evening
     activity as follows:
     Tokens:
       0 Little or no activity alone, e.g., sitting

alone in chair, in bed, or in chair sleeping.

2 Minimal activity alone, e.g., watching TV, listening to radio, reading.

5 Part of the evening spent on minimal activity, and part of the evening spent participating more with others.

10 Participation most of the evening in activities with others, e.g., playing pool, cards, conversation, going to off-ward activities, such as dances or bowling.

Comments: Use of inappropriate talk, including statements implying lack of responsibility for change, will limit ratings to two or zero. No tokens given to anyone in pajamas.

Bonus Tokens as Follows

I. *Attendance at Group Meetings:* Two tokens for attendance and up to three more for appropriate participation; also three for being at doctor's rounds. Five token penalty for missing groups without adequate excuse.

II. *Dayroom and Porch Clean-up:* Two men will be assigned daily and should finish the clean-up by 8:00 a.m. and 6:30 p.m. Five tokens per man for satisfactory work. Penalty for unsatisfactory ward appearance is no TV until the next inspection period.

III. *Other Behavior:* Tokens will be available from staff for satisfactory performance of other tasks such as laundry sorting, better personal hygiene, and cleaning except for routine ward cleaning which is everyone's responsibility.

IV. *Watching 10:00 p.m. News:* Two tokens at 10:30 for persons watching entire newscast and who can satifactorily report some news they viewed.

V. *Explaining Token Economy to Guests:* You may earn ten tokens for touring guests and explaining the program.

How You May Spend Tokens

Tokens must be spent for board and room, just like outside the hospital. In addition, tokens can be converted into weekly cash allowances, passes, and privileges of various kinds.

I. *Room and Board:* Your first obligation is to spend 140 tokens per week for room and board. These tokens will be collected Thursday afternoon for the next week beginning on Friday. If you do not have the necessary 140 tokens you will be placed on a daily food payment plan. In order to make the beginning stages of the Token Economy somewhat easier, you will pay 15 tokens daily for food; however, after your second Thursday on the ward (after about 10 days) you will be required to pay 20 tokens daily or 140 for the entire week. You must pay the full amount for an entire day and you will receive all meals on a given day after payment is made in full.

Comments: Earning 20 tokens daily for room and board is not difficult, but it does make you responsible for some constructive behavior in order to receive your food. You can earn 12 tokens daily for appearance, up to 10 daily for social interaction and about 20 for an average day on assignment, or about 40 tokens per day.

In order to reward persons who have been doing well but haven't many tokens left at the end of the week because of the required daily food payment, there are two plans.

A. If you earned 225 or more tokens in the previous week, the staff will return to you the full amount of tokens paid for daily food during the previous week.

B. If you earned 150 or more tokens in the previous week, the staff will return to you 2/3 of the tokens you paid for daily food during the previous week.

II. *Weekly Cash Allowance:* You may exchange tokens for funds from your account at the rate of ten tokens per dollar. Except for persons on canteen books, drawing funds more than once a week will be at the rate of 15 tokens per dollar. Persons on canteen books may exchange tokens for books at the same rate, ten tokens for one dollar.

III. *Passes*

A. *Continuous passes into town:* You may request a continuous Saturday, Sunday, and holiday pass, or an evening pass, and if it is approved, you may use it without a token charge, unless:

1. You are on daily food.
2. You must stand personal inspection.
3. You do not take medication satisfactorily.

(You must correct these problems before you are eligible for a continuous pass.)

B. *Weekend or overnight passes:* You may request a weekend or overnight pass prior to the weekly team meeting, and if the pass is approved, you may use it according to the following guidelines:

1. The usual weekend pass from after work Friday afternoon until Sunday evening is 60 tokens including $10.00 of your fund.
2. Funds over $10.00, within limits, are available at three tokens per dollar.
3. In order to receive money at this rate, you must be gone from the hospital at least 24 hours, otherwise you will be required to pay additional tokens at the usual rate for weekly cash allowance.
4. If you sign up for a pass, but don't have enough tokens, you will be fined 20 tokens, so plan carefully.
5. Recreational passes during duty hours are 20 additional tokens for each 1/2 day. You must clear with your work supervisor before you may use a pass during duty hours.

IV. *Other Cost Items*

A. Sleeping on bed during work hours (weekdays 8:00 a.m.) and (1:00 p.m. to 3:30 p.m.): five-token penalty if you get up, or 10 tokens per hour if you choose to rest. This does not apply if a physician agrees you are sick and prescribes bed rest.
B. Missing roll call or being late for medication: five-token penalty, more for repeat offenders.
C. Smoking in small bedrooms: 20 tokens and transfer to dorm; smoking in dorm: 20 tokens, more for repeat offenders.
D. Hitting another person or damaging property: 20-token penalty for the first offense and more for repeat offenders.
E. Persons off grounds without a valid pass lose all tokens in their possession or banked at that time and are placed on daily food.
F. Inability to pay any token fine results in loss of advanced room and board payment, and being placed on daily food.

GOOD LUCK! WE HOPE TO PROMOTE YOU OFF THE TOKEN PLAN AS SOON AS POSSIBLE!

References

Abramowitz, S. I., & Bell, N. W. (1985). Biofeedback, self-control, and tension headache. *Journal of Psychosomatic Research, 29,* 95–99.

Abrams, J. L., & Allen, G. J. (1974). Comparative effectiveness of situational programming, financial payoffs, and group pressure in weight reduction. *Behavior Therapy, 5,* 391–400.

Abrams, D. B., & Follick, M. J. (1983). Behavioral weight loss intervention at the worksite: Feasibility and maintenance. *Journal of Consulting and Clinical Psychology, 51,* 226–233.

Abrams, D. B., & Wilson, G. T. (1979). Self-monitoring and reactivity in the modification of cigarette smoking. *Journal of Consulting and Clinical Psychology, 47,* 243–251.

Abramson, E. E. (1977). Behavior approaches to weight control. *Behavior Research and Therapy, 15,* 355–363.

Abramson, L. Y., Seligman, M. E. P., & Teasdale, J. D. (1978). Learned helplessness in humans: Critique and formulation. *Journal of Abnormal Psychology, 87*(1), 49–74.

Abramson, R., Garg, M., Cioffari, A., & Rutman, P. A. (1980). An evaluation of behavioral techniques reinforced with an anorectic drug in a double-blind weight loss study. *Journal of Clinical Psychiatry, 41,* 234–237.

Adams, H. E., Doster, J. A., & Calhoun, K. S. (1977). A psychologically based system of response classification. In A. R. Ciminero, K. S. Calhoun, & H. E. Adams (Eds.), *Handbook of behavioral assessment.* New York: Wiley.

Adams, H. E., Feuerstein, M., & Fowler, J. L. (1980). Migraine headache: Review of parameters, etiology, and intervention. *Psychological Bulletin, 87,* 217–237.

Adams, K. M., Klinge, V. K., & Keiser, T. W. (1973). The extinction of a self-injurious behavior on a epileptic child. *Behaviour Research and Therapy, 11,* 351–356.

Ader, R. (Ed.). (1981). *Psychoneuroimmunology.* New York: Academic Press.

Agras, W. S. (1967). Behavior therapy in the management of chronic schizophrenia. *American Journal of Psychiatry, 124,* 240–243.

Agras, W. S., Horne, M., & Taylor, C. B. (1982). Expectations and the blood-pressure-lowering effects of relaxation. *Psychosomatic Medicine, 44*(4), 389–395.

Agras, W. S., Jacob, R. G., & Lebedeck, M. (1980). The California drought: A quasi-experimental analysis of social policy. *Journal of Applied Behavior Analysis, 13,* 561–570.

Agras, W. S., Southam, M. A., & Taylor, C. B. (1983). Long-term persistence of relaxation-induced blood pressure lowering during the working day. *Journal of Consulting and Clinical Psychology, 51,* 792–794.

Alabiso, F. (1975). Operant control of attention behavior: A treatment of hyperactivity. *Behavior Therapy, 6,* 39–42.

Alberti, R. E. (1977). Comments on "Differentiating assertion and aggression: Some behavioral guidelines." *Behavior Therapy, 8,* 353–354.

Alberti, R. E., & Emmons, M. L. (1978). *Your perfect right: A guide to assertive behavior* (3rd ed.). San Luis Obispo, CA: Impact Press.

Alden, L. (1984). An attributional analysis of assertiveness. *Cognitive Therapy and Research, 8,* 607–618.

Alden, L., Safran, J., & Weideman, R. (1978). A comparison of cognitive and skills training strategies in the treatment of unassertive clients. *Behavior Therapy, 9,* 843–846.

Alexander, A. B., & Smith, D. D. (1979). Clinical applications EMG biofeedback. In R. J. Gatchel & K. P. Price (Eds.), *Clinical applications of biofeedback: Appraisal and status.* Elmsford, NY: Pergamon.

Alexander, F., & French, T. M. (1946). *Psychoanalytic therapy.* New York: Ronald.

Alexander, R. N., Corbett, T. F., & Smigel, J. (1976). The effects of individual and group consequences on school attendance and curfew violations with predelinquent adolescents. *Journal of Applied Behavior Analysis, 9,* 221–226.

Alford, G. S., & Turner, S. M. (1976). Stimulus interference and conditioned inhibition of auditory hallucinations. *Journal of Behavior Therapy and Experimental Psychiatry, 7,* 155–160.

Allen, K. E., & Harris, F. R. (1966). Elimination of a child's excessive scratching by training the mother in reinforcement procedures. *Behaviour Research and Therapy, 4,* 79–84.

Allen, K. E., Hart, B. M., Buell, J. S., Harris, F. R., & Wolf, M. M. (1964). Effects of social reinforcement on isolate behavior of a nursery school child. *Child Development, 35,* 511–518.

Allen, K. E., Henke, L. B., Harris, F. R., Baer, D. M., & Reynolds, N. J. (1967). Control of hyperactivity by social reinforcement of attending behavior. *Journal of Educational Psychology, 58,* 231–237.

Allen, R. A., & Mills, G. K. (1982). The effects of unilateral plethysmographic feedback of temporal artery activity during migraine head pain. *Journal of Psychosomatic Research, 26,* 133–140.

Altman, K. (1977). Use of contingent lemon juice to eliminate public masturbation by a severely retarded boy. *Behaviour Research and Therapy, 16,* 131–134.

Altman, K., Haavik, S., & Cook, J. W. (1978). Punishment of self-injurious behavior in natural settings using contingent aromatic ammonia. *Behaviour Research and Therapy, 16,* 85–96.

Altman, K., & Krupsaw, R. (1983). Suppressing aggressive-destructive behavior by delayed overcorrection. *Journal of Behavior Therapy and Experimental Psychiatry, 14*(4), 359–362.

Alvord, J. R. (1973). *Home token economy: An incentive program for children and their parents.* Champaign, IL: Research Press.

American Cancer Society. (1976). *76 cancer facts and figures.* New York: American Cancer Society.

American Psychiatric Association. (1980). *Diagnostic and statistical manual of mental disorders* (3rd ed.). Washington, DC: American Psychiatric Association.

Ammer, J. J. (1982). Managing learning disabled students' academic frustration through self-control. *Pointer, 27,* 17–20.

Anant, S. S. (1967). A note on the treatment of alcoholics by a verbal aversion technique. *Canadian Psychologist, 8,* 19–22.

Anant, S. S. (1968). The use of verbal aversion (negative conditioning) with an alcoholic: A case report. *Behaviour Research and Therapy, 6,* 695–696.

Anderson, K. O., & Masur, F. T., III. (1983). Psychological preparation for invasive medical and dental procedures. *Journal of Behavioral Medicine, 6,* 1–40.

Andrasik, F., & Holroyd, K. A. (1980). A test of specific and non-specific effects in the biofeedback treatment of tension headache. *Journal of Consulting and Clinical Psychology, 48,* 575–586.

Andrasik, F., & Holroyd, K. A. (1983). Specific and nonspecific effects in the biofeedback treatment of tension headache: 3-year follow-up. *Journal of Consulting and Clinical Psychology, 51,* 634–636.

Andresen, B. L. (1981). A comparison of systematic desensitization and directed masturbation in the treatment of primary orgasmic dysfunction in females. *Journal of Consulting and Clinical Psychology, 49,* 568–570.

Anthony, J., & Edelstein, B. A. (1975). Thought stopping treatment of anxiety attacks due to seizure related obsessive ruminations. *Journal of Behavior Therapy and Experimental Psychiatry, 6,* 343–344.

Anton, W. D. (1976). An evaluation of outcome variables in the systematic desensitization of test anxiety. *Behaviour Research and Therapy, 14,* 217–224.

Appel, K. G., Amper, J. M., & Schefler, G. G. (1961). Prognosis in psychiatry, *AMA Archives of Neurology and Psychiatry, 70,* 459–468.

Aragona, J., Cassady, J. & Drabman, R. S. (1975). Treating overweight children through parental training and contingency management. *Journal of Applied Behavior Analysis, 8,* 269–278.

Arkowitz, H., Lichenstein, E., McGovern, K., & Hines, P. (1975). The behavioral assessment of social competence in males. *Behavior Therapy, 6,* 3–13.

Armor, D. J., Polich, J. M., & Stambul, H. B. (1976). *Alcoholism and treatment.* Santa Monica, CA: Rand Corporation.

Armstrong, D., & Rimm, D. C. (1974). *Thought stopping-covert assertion vs. systematic desensitization in the treatment of snake phobias.* Unpublished master's thesis, Southern Illinois University.

Arnkoff, D. B., & Stewart, J. (1973). The effectiveness of modeling and videotape feedback on personal problem solving. *Behaviour Research and Therapy,* 1973, *13,* 127–133.

Arnold, J. E., Levine, A. G., & Patterson, G. R. (1975). Changes in sibling behavior following family intervention. *Journal of Consulting and Clinical Psychology, 43*, (5), 683–688.

Arnold, S. C., & Forehand, R. (1978). A comparison of cognitive training and response cost procedures in modifying cognitive styles of impulsive children. *Cognitive Therapy and Research, 2*, 183–188.

Arnold, S. C., Forehand, R., & Sturgis, E. T. (1976). Effects of a response cost procedure on the academic performance of retarded students. *Journal of Behavior Therapy and Experimental Psychiatry, 7*, 191–192.

Arora, M., & Murthy, R. S. (1976). Treatment of writer's cramp by progression from paintbrush in supinated hand. *Journal of Behavior Therapy and Experimental Psychiatry, 7*, 345–347.

Arrick, C., Voss, J., & Rimm, D. C. (1975). *Thought stopping vs. covert assertion vs. thought stopping plus covert assertion in the treatment of snake phobics.* Unpublished master's thesis, Southern Illinois University.

Ascher, L. M., & Phillips, D. (1975). Guided behavior rehearsal. *Journal of Behavior Therapy and Experimental Psychiatry, 6*, 215–218.

Ashem, B., & Donner, L. (1966). Covert sensitization with alcoholics: A controlled replication. *Behaviour Research and Therapy, 6*, 7–12.

Ashem, B., & Donner, L. (1968). Covert sensitization with alcoholics: A controlled replication. *Behaviour Research and Therapy, 6*, 7–12.

Association for Advancement of Behavior Therapy, Ethical issues for human services. (1977). *Behavior Therapy, 8*, v-vi.

Atkins, C. J., Kaplan, R. M., Timms, R. M., Reinsch, S., & Lofbak, K. (1984). Behavioral exercise programs in the management of chronic obstructive pulmonary disease. *Journal of Consulting and Clinical Psychology, 52*, 591–603.

Atthowe, J. A. (1973). Behavior innovations and persistence. *American Psychologist, 27*, 34–41.

Atthowe, J. M. Jr., & Krasner, L. (1968). Preliminary report on the application of contingent reinforcement procedures (token economy) on a "chronic" psychiatric ward. *Journal of Abnormal Psychology, 73*, 37–43.

Ault, R. L. (1973). Problem-solving strategies of reflective, impulsive, fast-accurate, and slow-inaccurate children. *Child Development, 44*, 259–266.

Ayllon, T. (1963). Intensive treatment of psychotic behavior by stimulus satiation and food reinforcement. *Behaviour Research and Therapy, 1*, 53–62.

Ayllon, T. & Azrin, N. H. (1965). The measurement and reinforcement of behavior of psychotics. *Journal of the Experimental Analysis of Behavior, 8*, 357–383.

Ayllon, T. & Azrin, N. H. (1968a). Reinforcement sampling: A technique for increasing the behavior of mental patients. *Journal of Applied Behavior Analysis, 1*, 13–20.

Ayllon, T., & Azrin, N. H. (1968b). *The token economy: A motivational system for therapy and rehabilitation.* New York: Appleton.

Ayllon, T., Garber, S., & Pisor, K. (1975). The elimination of discipline problems through a combined school-home motivational system. *Behavior Therapy, 6*, 616–626.

Ayllon, T., & Haughton, E. (1964). Modification of symptomatic verbal behavior of mental patients. *Behaviour Research and Therapy, 2*, 87–97.

Ayllon, T., Layman, D., & Kandel, H. J. (1975). A behavioral-educational alternative to drug control of hyperactive children. *Journal of Applied Behavior Analysis, 8*, 137–146.

Ayllon, T., & Michael, J. (1959). The psychiatric nurse as a behavioral engineer. *Journal of the Experimental Analysis of Behavior, 2*, 323–334.

Azrin, N. H. (1956). Some effects of two intermittent schedules of immediate and non-immediate punishment. *Journal of Psychology, 42*, 3–21.

Azrin, N. H. (1958). Some effects of noise on human operant behavior. *Journal of the Experimental Analysis of Behavior, 1*, 183–200.

Azrin, N. H. (1959). A technique for delivering shock to pigeons. *Journal of the Experimental Analysis of Behavior, 2*, 161–163.

Azrin, N. H. (1960). Use of rests as reinforcers. *Psychological Reports, 7*, 240.

Azrin, N. H., & Holz, W. C. (1966). Punishment. In W. K. Honig (Ed.), *Operant behavior: Areas of research and application.* New York: Appleton.

Azrin, N. H., Holz, W. C., & Hake, D. (1963). Fixed-ratio punishment. *Journal of the Experimental Analysis of Behavior, 6*, 141–148.

Azrin, N. H., Kaplan, N. H., & Foxx, R. M. (1973). Autism reversal: Eliminating stereotyped self-stimulation of retarded individuals. *American Journal of Mental Deficiency, 78*, 241–248.

Azrin, N. H., & Powell, J. (1968). Behavioral engineering: The reduction of smoking behavior by a conditioning apparatus and procedure. *Journal of Applied Behavior Analysis, 1,* 193–200.

Azrin, N. H., Sneed, T. J., & Foxx, R. M. (1973). Drybed: A rapid method of eliminating bedwetting (enuresis) of the retarded. *Behaviour Research and Therapy, 11,* 427–434.

Azrin, N. H., & Wesolowski, M. D. (1975). Eliminating habitual vomiting in a retarded adult by positive practice and self-correction. *Journal of Behavior Therapy and Experimental Psychiatry, 6,* 145–148.

Bach, R., & Moylan, J. H. (1975). Parents administer behavior therapy for inappropriate urination and encopresis: A case study. *Journal of Behavior Therapy and Experimental Psychiatry, 6,* 239–241.

Baer, A. M., Rowbury, T., & Baer, D. M. (1973). The development of instructional control over classroom activities of deviant preschool children. *Journal of Applied Behavior Analysis, 6,* 289–298.

Baer, D. M., Peterson, R. F., & Sherman, J. A. (1967). The development of imitation by reinforcing behavioral similarity to a model. *Journal of the Experimental Analysis of Behavior, 10,* 405–416.

Baer, D. M., & Sherman, J. A. (1969). Appraisal of operant therapy techniques with children and adults. In C. M. Franks (Ed.), *Behavior therapy: Appraisal and status.* New York: McGraw-Hill.

Baer, D. M., Wolf, M. M. (1967). *The entry into natural communities of reinforcement.* Paper presented at the American Psychological Association, Washington, D. C., September 1967.

Bailey, J. S., Wolf, M. M., & Phillips, E. L. (1970). Home-based reinforcement and the modification of pre-delinquents' classroom behavior. *Journal of Applied Behavior Analysis, 3,* 223–233.

Bailey, K. G. & Sowder, W. T. (1970). Audiotape and videotape confrontation in psychotherapy. *Psychological Bulletin, 74,* 127–137.

Bain, J. A. (1928). *Thought control in everyday life.* New York: Funk & Wagnalls.

Bajtelsmit, J. W., & Gershman, L. (1976). Covert positive reinforcement: Efficacy and conceptualization. *Journal of Behavior Therapy and Experimental Psychiatry, 7,* 207–212.

Baker, T. B., & Cannon, D. S. (1979). Taste aversion therapy with alcoholics: Techniques and evidence of a conditioned response. *Behaviour Research and Therapy, 18,* 71–78.

Bancroft, J. H. J. (1969). Aversion therapy for homosexuality. *British Journal of Psychiatry, 115,* 1417–1431.

Bander K. W., Steinke, G. V., Allen, G. J., & Mosher, D. L. (1975). Evaluation of three dating-specific treatment approaches for heterosexual dating anxiety. *Journal of Consulting and Clinical Psychology, 43,* 259–265.

Bandura, A. (1962). Social learning through imitation. In M. R. Jones (Ed.), *Nebraska Symposium on Motivation.* Lincoln: University of Nebraska Press.

Bandura, A. (1965). Influence of models' reinforcement contingencies on the acquisition of imitative responses. *Journal of Personality and Social Psychology, 1,* 589–595.

Bandura, A. (1969). *Principles of behavior modification.* New York: Holt, Rinehart and Winston.

Bandura, A. (1971). Psychotherapy based on modeling principles. In A. E. Bergin & S. L. Garfield (Eds.), *Handbook of psychotherapy and behavior change.* New York: Wiley.

Bandura, A. (1976). Self-reinforcement: Theoretical and methodological considerations. *Behaviorism, 4,* 135–155.

Bandura, A. (1977a). Self-efficacy: Toward a unifying theory of behavioral change. *Psychological Review, 84,* 191–215.

Bandura, A. (1977b). *Social learning theory.* Englewood Cliffs, N. J.: Prentice-Hall.

Bandura, A. (1978). The self-system in reciprocal determinism. *American Psychologist, 33*(4), 344–358.

Bandura, A., (1981). In search of pure undirectional determinants. *Behavior Therapy, 12,* 30–40.

Bandura, A. (1982). The assessment and predictive generality of self-percepts of efficacy. *Journal of Behavior Therapy and Experimental Psychiatry, 13,* 195–199.

Bandura, A., Adams, N. E., Beyer, J. (1977). Cognitive processes mediating behavioral change. *Journal of Personality and Social Psychology, 35,* 125–139.

Bandura, A., Blanchard, E. B., & Ritter, R. (1969). The relative efficacy of desensitization and modeling approaches for inducing behavioral, affective, and attitudinal changes. *Journal of Personality and Social Psychology, 13,* 173–199.

Bandura, A., Grusec, J. E., & Menlove, F. L. (1967a). Some social determinants of self monitoring reinforcement systems. *Journal of Personality and Social Psychology, 5,* 449–455.

Bandura, A., Grusec, J. E., & Menlove, F. L. (1967b). Vicarious extinction of avoidance behavior. *Journal of Personality and Social Psychology, 5,* 16–23.

Bandura, A., Jeffery, R. W., & Gajdos, E. (1975). Generalizing change through participant modeling with self-directed mastery. *Behaviour Research and Therapy, 13,* 141–152.

Bandura, A. Jeffery, R. W., & Wright, C. L. (1974). Efficacy of participant modeling as a function of response induction aids. *Journal of Abnormal Psychology, 83*(1), 56–64.

Bandura, A., & Kupers, C. J. (1964). Transmission of patterns of self-reinforcement through modeling. *Journal of Abnormal and Social Psychology, 69,* 1–9.

Bandura, A., & Menlove, F. L. (1968). Factors determining vicarious extinction of avoidance behavior through symbolic modeling. *Journal of Personality and Social Psychology, 8,* 99–108.

Bandura, A., & Perloff, B. (1967). Relative efficacy of self-monitored and externally imposed reinforcement systems. *Journal of Personality and Social Psychology, 7,* 111–116.

Bandura, A., Reese, L., & Adams, N. E. (1982). Microanalysis of action and fear arousal as a function of differential levels of perceived self-efficacy. *Journal of Personality and Social Psychology, 43,* 5–21.

Bandura, A., Ross, D., & Ross, S. A. (1963). Vicarious imitative learning. *Journal of Personality and Social Psychology, 67,* 601–607.

Bandura, A., & Schunk, D. H. (1981). Cultivating competence, self-efficacy, and intrinsic interest through proximal self-motivation. *Journal of Personality and Social Psychology, 41,* 586–598.

Bandura, A., & Simon, K. M. (1977). The role of proximal intentions in self-regulation of refractory behavior. *Cognitive Therapy and Research, 1,* 177–193.

Bandura, A., & Walters, R. H. (1959). *Adolescent aggression.* New York: Ronald.

Bandura, A., & Whalen, C. K. (1966). The influence of antecedent reinforcement and divergent modeling cues on patterns of a self-reward. *Journal of Personality and Social Psychology, 3,* 373–382.

Barden, R. C., Garber, J., Leiman, B., Ford, M. E., & Masters, J. C. (1985). Factors governing the effective remediation, of negative affect and its cognitive and behavioral consequences. *Journal of Personality and Social Psychology, 49,* 1040–1053.

Barker, J. C. (1965). Behavior therapy for transvestism: A comparison of pharmicological and electrical aversion techniques. *British Medical Journal, 111,* 268–276.

Barker, J. C., Thorpe, J. G., Blakemore, C. B., Lavin, N. I., & Conway, C. G. (1961). Behaviour therapy in a case of transvestism. *Lancet, 1,* 510.

Barker, R. G., & Wright, H. F. (1955). *Midwest and its children: The psychological ecology of an American town.* New York: Harper.

Barkley, R. A., & Zupnick, S. (1976). Reduction of stereotypic body contortions using physical restraint and DRO. *Journal of Behavior Therapy and Experimental Psychiatry, 7,* 167–170.

Barlow, D. H. (1973). Increasing heterosexual responsiveness in the treatment of sexual deviation: A review of the clinical and experimental evidence. *Behavior Therapy, 4,* 655–671.

Barlow, D. H., Agras, W. S., Abel, G. G., Blanchard, E. B., & Young L. D. (1975). Biofeedback and reinforcement to increase heterosexual arousal in homosexuals. *Behaviour Research and Therapy, 13,* 45–50.

Barlow, D. H., Agras, W. S. Leitenberg, H., Callahan, E. J., & Moore, R. C. (1972). Case histories and shorter communications. *Behaviour Research and Therapy, 10,* 411–415.

Barlow, D. H., Agras, W. S., Leitenberg, H., & Wincze, J. P. (1970). An experimental analysis of the effectiveness of 'shaping' in reducing maladaptive avoidance behavior: An analogue study. *Behaviour Research and Therapy, 8,* 165–173.

Barlow, D. H., & Hersen, M. (1984). *Single case experimental designs: Strategies for studying behavior change* (2nd ed.). New York: Pergamon Press.

Barlow, D. H., Leitenberg, H., & Agras, W. S. (1969). Experimental control of sexual deviation through manipulation of the noxious scene in covert sensitization. *Journal of Abnormal Psychology, 74,* 596–601.

Barnard, J. D., Christophersen, E. R., & Wolf, M. M. (1977). Teaching children appropriate shopping behavior through parent training in the supermarket setting. *Journal of Applied Behavior Analysis, 10,* 49–59.

Baron, A., & Kaufman, A. (1966). Human, free-operant avoidance of "time-out" from monetary reinforcement. *Journal of the Experimental Analysis of Behavior, 9,* 557–565.

Barrett, C. L. (1967). *Systematic desensitization therapy (SDT) versus implosive therapy (IT): A comparative study of two methods of reducing the snake phobic behavior of otherwise normal adults.* Unpublished doctoral dissertation, University of Louisville.

Barrett, C. L. (1969). Systematic desensitization versus

implosive therapy. *Journal of Abnormal Psychology, 74*, 587–592.

Barrett, R. P., & Shapiro, E. S. (1980). Treatment of stereotyped hair-pulling with overcorrection: A case study with long term follow-up. *Journal of Behavior Therapy and Experimental Psychiatry, 11*, 317–320.

Barrios, F. X., & Karoly, P. (1983). Treatment expectancy and therapeutic change in treatment of migraine headache: Are they related? *Psychological Reports, 52*, 59–68.

Barrish, H. H., Saunders, M., & Wolf, M. M. (1969). Good behavior game: Effects of individual contingencies on disruptive behavior in a classroom. *Journal of Applied Behavior Analysis, 2*,119–124.

Barron, F., & Learly, T. (1955). Changes in psychoneurotic patients with and without psychotherapy. *Journal of Consulting Psychology, 19*, 239–245.

Barth, R. P., Blythe, B. J., Schinke, S. P., & Schilling, R. F. (1983). Self-control training with maltreating parents. *Child Welfare, 62*, 313–324.

Barton, E. (1981). Developing sharing: An analysis of modeling and other behavioral techniques. *Behavior Modification, 5*, 386–398.

Barton, E. S. (1970). Inappropriate speech in a severely retarded child: A case study in language conditioning and generalization. *Journal of Applied Behavior Analysis, 3*, 299–307.

Bassett, J. E. (1974). *Behavior management program: Applied behavior analysis in an adult male correctional facility.* Unpublished manuscript.

Bassett, J. E., & Blanchard, E. B. (1977). The effect of the absence of close supervision on the use of response cost in a prison token economy. *Journal of Applied Behavior Analysis, 10*, 375–379.

Bassett, J. E., Blanchard, E. B., & Koshland, E. (1977). On determining reinforcing stimuli: Armchair versus empirical procedures. *Behavior Therapy, 8*, 205–212.

Bates, H. D., & Zimmerman, S. F. (1971). Toward the development of a screening scale for assertive training. *Psychological Reports, 28*, 99–107.

Baum, M. (1966). Rapid extinction of an avoidance response following a period of response prevention in the avoidance apparatus. *Psychological Reports, 18*, 59–64.

Baum, M. (1968). Efficacy of response prevention (flooding) in facilitating the extinction of an avoidance response in rats: The effect of overtraining the response. *Behaviour Research and Therapy, 6*, 197–203.

Baum, M. (1969a). Extinction of an avoidance response following response prevention: Some parametric investigations. *Canadian Journal of Psychology, 23*, 1–10.

Baum, M. (1969b). Extinction of an avoidance response motivated by intense fear: Social facilitation of the action of response prevention (flooding) in rats. *Behaviour Research and Therapy, 7*, 57–62.

Baum, M. (1970). Extinction of avoidance responding through response prevention (flooding). *Psychological Bulletin, 74*, 276–284.

Baum, M. (1973). Extinction of avoidance in rats: The effects of chlorpromazine and methylphenidate administered in conjunction with flooding response (prevention). *Behaviour Research and Therapy, 11*, 165–169.

Baum, M., & Poser, E. G. (1971). Comparison of flooding procedures in animals and man. *Behaviour Research and Therapy, 9*, 249–254.

Bawkart, B., & Elliott, R. (1974). Extinction of avoidance in rats: Response availability and stimulus presentation effects. *Behaviour Research Therapy, 12*, 53–56.

Beasley, J. (1976). Biofeedback in the treatment of migraine headaches. *Dissertation Abstracts International, 36*, (11-B) 5850B-5851B (abstract).

Beatty, J. (1971). Effects of alpha wave abundance and operant training procedures on occipital alpha and beta wave activity. *Psychonomic Science, 23*, 197–199.

Beaver, C., Brown, R. A., & Lichenstein, E. (1981).Effects of monitored nicotine fading and anxiety management training on smoking reduction. *Addictive Behaviors, 6*, 301–305.

Beck, A. T. (1963). Thinking and depression. I. Idiosyncratic content and cognitive distortions. *Archives of General Psychiatry, 9*, 324–333.

Beck, A. T. (1964). Thinking and depression. II. Theory and therapy. *Archives of General Psychiatry, 10*, 561–571.

Beck, A. T. (1967a). *Depression: Causes and treatment.* Philadelphia: University of Pennsylvania Press.

Beck, A. T. (1967b). *Depression: Clinical, experimental, and theoretic aspects.* New York: Harper.

Beck, A. T. (1970). Cognitive therapy: Nature and relation to behavior therapy. *Behavior Therapy, 1*, 184–200.

Beck, A. T. (1972a). *Depression: Causes and treatment.* (2nd ed.). Philadelphia: University of Pennsylvania Press.

Beck, A. T. (1972b). The phenomena of depression: A synthesis. In D. Offer & D. X. Freemon (Eds.), *Modern psychiatry and clinical research.* New York: Basic Books.

Beck. A. T. (1976). *Cognitive therapy and the emotional disorders.* New York: International Universities Press.

Beck, A. T. (1984). Cognition and therapy. *Archives of General Psychiatry 41,* 1112–1114.

Beck, A. T., Hollon, S. D., Young, J. E., Bedrosian, R. C., & Budenz, D. (1985). Combined cognitive-pharmacotherapy versus cognitive therapy in the treatment of depressed outpatients. *Archives of General Psychiatry, 42,* 142–148.

Beck, A. T., Rush, A. J., Shaw, B. F., & Emery, G. (1979). *Cognitive therapy of depression: A treatment manual.* New York: Guilford Press.

Beck, A. T., Ward, C. H., Mendelson, M., Mock, J., & Erbaugh, J. (1961). An inventory for measuring depression. *Archives of General Psychiatry, 4,* 561–571.

Beck, A. T., Weissman, A., Lester, D., & Trexler, L. (1974). The measurement of pessimism. *Journal of Consulting and Clinical Psychology, 42*(6), 861–865.

Beck, J. G., & Heimberg, R. G. (1983). Self-report assessment of assertive behavior: A critical analysis. *Behavior Modification, 7,* 451–487.

Becker, H. G., & Costello, C. G. (1975). Effects of graduated exposure with feedback of exposure times on snake phobia. *Journal of Consulting and Clinical Psychology, 43,* 478–484.

Becker, W. C. (1971). *Parents are teachers.* Champaign, IL: Research Press.

Beiman, I. (1976). Case histories and shorter communications. *Behaviour Research and Therapy, 14,* 175–179.

Beiman, I., Israel, E., & Johnson, S. A. (1978). During training and postraining effects of live and taped extended progressive relaxation, self-relaxation, and electromyogram biofeedback. *Journal of Consulting and Clinical Psychology, 46,* 314–321.

Bellack, A. S. (1976). A comparison of self-reinforcement and self-monitoring in a weight reduction program. *Behavior Therapy, 1,* 68–75.

Bellack, A. S. (1979). A critical appraisal of strategies for assessing social skills. *Behavioral Assessment, 1,* 157–176.

Bellack, A. S. (1985). Covert rehearsal. In A. S. Bellack & M. Hersen (Eds.), *Dictionary of behavior therapy techniques.* New York: Pergamon.

Bellack, A. S., & Hersen, M. (1977). *Behaivor modification: An introduction.* Baltimore: Williams & Wilkins.

Bellack, A. S., Hersen, M., & Turner, S. M. (1979). Relationship of role playing and knowledge of appropriate behavior to assertion in the natural environment. *Journal of Consulting and Clinical Psychology, 47,* 670–678.

Bellack, A. S., Rozensky, R., & Schwartz, J. (1974). A comparison of two forms of self monitoring in a behavioral weight reduction program. *Behavior Therapy, 5*(4), 523–530.

Bem, D. J., & Allen, A. (1974). On predicting some of the people some of the time: The search for cross-situational consistencies in behavior. *Psychological Review, 81,* 506–520.

Bender, N. N. (1976). Self-verbalization versus tutor-verbalization in modifying impulsivity. *Journal of Educational Psychology, 44,* 490–491.

Beneke, W. N., & Harris, M. B. (1972). Teaching self control of study behavior. *Behaviour Research and Therapy, 10,* 35–41.

Bennink, C. D., Hulst, L. L., & Benthem, J. A. (1982). The effects of EMG biofeedback and relaxation training on primary dysmenorrhea. *Journal of Behavioral Medicine, 5,* 329–341.

Bensberg, G. J., Colwell, C. N., & Cassell, R. H. (1965). Teaching the profoundly retarded self-help activities by behavior shaping techniques. *American Journal of Mental Deficiency, 69,* 674–679.

Benson, H. (1975). Voluntary control of and reactivity of heart rate. *Psychophysiology, 12,* 339–348.

Benson, H. (1978). *The relaxation response.* New York: Avon.

Benson, H., Shapiro, D., Tursky, B., & Schwartz, G. E. (1971). Decreased systolic blood pressure through operant conditioning techniques. *Science, 173,* 740–742.

Berah, E. F. (1981). Influence of scheduling variations on the effectiveness of a group assertion-training program for women. *Journal of Counseling Psychology, 28,* 265–268.

Berecz, J. M. (1972). Modification of smoking behavior through self-administered punishment of imagined behavior: A new approach to aversion therapy. *Journal of Consulting and Clinical Psychology, 38,* 244–250.

Berecz, J. M. (1976). Treatment of smoking with cognitive conditioning therapy: A self-administered aversion technique. *Behavior Therapy, 7,* 641–648.

Berecz, J. M. (1979). Maintenance of nonsmoking behavior through self-administered wrist-band aversion therapy. *Behavior Therapy, 10,* 660–675.

Bergin, A. E. (1962). The effect of dissonant persuasive communications upon changes in a self-referring attitude. *Journal of Personality, 30,* 423–438.

Bergin, A. E. (1966). Some implications of psychotherapy research for therapeutic practice. *Journal of Abnormal Psychology, 71,* 235–246.

Bergin, A. E. (1969). A self-regulation technique for impulse control disorders. *Psychotherapy: Theory, Research, and Practice, 6,* 113–118.

Bergin, A. E., & Suinn, R. M. (1975). Individual psychotherapy and behavior therapy. *Annual Review of Psychology, 26,* 509–556.

Berkowitz, B. P., & Graziano, A. M. (1972). Training parents as behavior therapists: A review. *Behaviour Research and Therapy, 10,* 297–317.

Bernal, M. E. (1969). Behavioral feedback in the modification of brat behaviors. *Journal of Nervous and Mental Disease, 148,* 375–385.

Bernal, M. E., Duryee, J. S., Pruett, H. L., & Burns, B. J. (1968). Behavior modification and the brat syndrome. *Journal of Consulting and Clinical Psychology, 32,* 447–455.

Bernal, M. E., Gibson, D. M., Williams, D. E., & Pesses, D. I. (1971). A device for automatic audio tape recording. *Journal of Applied Behavior Analysis, 4,* 151–156.

Bernsberg, G. J., Colwell, C. N., & Cassel, R. H. (1965). Teaching the profoundly retarded self-help activities by behavior shaping techniques. *American Journal of Mental Deficiency, 69,* 674–679.

Bernstein, D. A. (1968). *The modification of smoking behavior.* Unpublished doctoral dissertation, Northwestern University.

Bernstein, D. A. (1969). The modification of smoking behavior: An evaluative review. *Psychological Bulletin, 71,* 418–440.

Bernstein, D. A., & Borkovec, T. D. (1973). *Progressive relaxation training: A manual for the helping professions.* Champaign, IL: Research Press.

Bernstein, D. A., & Given, B. A. (1984). Progressive relaxation: Abbreviated methods. In R. L. Woolfolk & P. M. Lehrer (Eds.), *Prinicples and practice of stress management.* New York: Guilford.

Bernstein, D. A., & Kleinknecht, R. A. (1982). Multiple approaches to the reduction of dental fear. *Behavior Therapy and Experimental Psychiatry, 13,* 287–292.

Bernstein, D. A., & McAlister, A. (1976). The modification of smoking behavior: Progress and problems. *Addictive Behaviors, 1,* 89–102.

Bild, R., & Adams, H. E. (1980). Modification of migraine headaches by cephalic blood volume pulse and EMG biofeedback. *Journal of Consulting and Clinical Psychology, 48,* 51–57.

Biran, M., & Wilson, G. T. (1981). Treatment of phobic disorders using cognitive and exposure methods: A self-efficacy analysis. *Journal of Consulting and Clinical Psychology, 49,* 886–899.

Birk, L., Huddleston, W., Millers, E., & Cohler, B. (1971). Avoidance conditioning for homosexuality. *Archives of General Psychiatry, 25,* 314–323.

Birnbrauer, J. S., Bijou, S. W., Wolf, M. M., & Kidder, J.D. (1965). Programmed instruction in the classroom. In L. P. Ullman & L. Krasner (Eds.), *Case studies in behavior modification.* New York: Holt.

Birnbrauer, J. S., Wolf, M. M., Kidder, J., & Tague, C. E. (1965). Classroom behavior of retarded pupils with token reinforcement. *Journal of Experimental Child Psychology, 2,* 219–235.

Bitgood, S. C., Crowe, M. J., Suarez, Y., & Peters, R. D. (1980). Immobilization: Effects and side effects on stereotyped behavior in children. *Behavior Modification, 4*(2), 187–208.

Blackburn, I. M., Bishop, S., Glen, A. I. M., Whalley, L. J., & Christie, J. E. (1981). The efficacy of cognitive therapy in depression: A treatment trial using cognitive therapy and pharmacotherapy, each alone and in combination. *British Journal of Psychiatry, 139,* 181–189.

Blake, B. G. (1965). The application of behaviour therapy to the treatment of alcoholism. *Behaviour Research and Therapy, 3,* 75–85.

Blake, B. G. (1967). A follow-up of alcoholics treated by behaviour therapy. *Behaviour Research and Therapy, 5,* 89–94.

Blakemore, C. B., Thorpe, J. G., Barker, J. C., Conway, C. G., & Lavin, N. I. (1963). The application of faradic aversion conditioning in a case of transvestism. *Behaviour Research and Therapy, 1,* 29–34.

Blakey, R., & Baker, R. (1980). An exposure approach to alcohol abuse. *Behaviour Research and Therapy, 18,* 319–325.

Blanchard, E. B. (1969). *The relative contributions of modeling, informational influences, and physical contact in the extinction of phobic behavior.* Unpublished doctoral dissertation, Stanford University.

Blanchard, E. B. (1970). The relative contributions of modeling, information influences, and physical contact in the extinction of phobic behavior. *Journal of Abnormal Psychology, 76,* 55–61.

Blanchard, E. B. (1975). Case histories and shorter communications: Brief flooding treatment for a debilitating revulsion. *Behaviour Research and Therapy, 13,* 193–195.

Blanchard, E. B., Ahles, T. A., & Shaw, E. R. (1979). Behavioral treatment of headaches. In M. Hersen, R. M. Eisler, & P. M. Miller (Eds.), *Progress in behavior modification* (Vol. 18). New York: Academic Press.

Blanchard, E. B., & Andrasik, F. (1982). Psychological assessment and treatment of headache: Recent developments and emerging issues. *Journal of Consulting and Clinical Psychology, 50,* 859–879.

Blanchard, E. B., Andrasik, F., Ahles, T. A., Teders, S. J., & O'Keefe, D. (1980). Migraine and tension headache: A meta-analysis review. *Behavior Therapy, 11*(5), 613–631.

Blanchard, E. B., Andrasik, F., Neff, D. F., Arena, J. G., Ahles, T. A., Jurish, S. E., Pallmeyer, T. P., Saunders, N. L., Teders, S. J., Barron, K. D., & Rodichok, L. D. (1982). Biofeedback and relaxation training with three kinds of headache: Treatment effects and their prediction. *Journal of Consulting and Clinical Psychology, 50,* 562–575.

Blanchard, E. B., Andrasik, F., Neff, D. F., Saunders, N. L., Arena, J. G., Pallmeyer, T. P., Teders, S. J., & Jurish, S. E. (1983). Four process studies in the behaviorial treatment of chronic headache. *Behaviour Research and Therapy, 21,* 209–220.

Blanchard, E. B., Andrasik, F., Neff, D. F., Teders, S. J., Pallmeyer, T. P., Arena, J. G., Jurish, S., Saunders, N. L. Ahles, T. A., & Rodichok, L. (1982). Sequential comparisons of relaxation training and biofeedback in the treatment of three kinds of chronic headaches or, the machines may be necessary some of the time. *Behaviour Research and Therapy, 20,* 469–481.

Blanchard, E. B., & Epstein, L. H. (1977). Clinical applications of biofeedback. In M. Hersen, R. M. Eisler, & P. M. Miller (Eds.), *Progress in behavior modification* (Vol. 4). New York: Academic Press.

Blanchard, E. B., & Epstein, L. H. (1978). *A biofeedback primer.* Reading, MA: Addison-Wesley.

Blanchard, E. B., Miller, S. T., Abel, G. G., Haynes, M. R., & Wicker, R. (1979). Evaluation of biofeedback in the treatment of borderline essential hypertension. *Journal of Applied Behavior Analysis, 12,* 99–109.

Blanchard, E. B., Theobald, D. E., Williamson, R. A., Silver, B. V., & Brown, P. A. (1978a). Temperature biofeedback in the treatment of migraine headaches: A controlled evaluation. *Archives of General Psychiatry, 35,* 581–588.

Blanchard, E. B., & Young, L. D. (1973). Self-control of cardiac functioning: A promise as yet unfulfilled. *Psychological Bulletin, 79,* 145–163.

Blanchard, E. B., & Young, L. D. (1974). Clinical applications of biofeedback training: A review of evidence. *Archives of General Psychiatry, 30,* 530–589.

Blanchard, E. B, Young, L. D., & Haynes, M. R (1975). A simple feedback system for the treatment of elevated blood pressure. *Behavior Therapy, 6,* 241–245.

Blankstein, K. R., & Polivy, J. (Eds.). (1982). *Self control and self-modification of emotional behavior.* New York: Plenum.

Blechman, E. A. (1985). *Solving child behavior problems at home and at school.* Champaign, IL: Research Press.

Blechman, E. A., Olson, D. H. L., Schornagel, C. Y. Halsdorf, M., & Turner, A. J. (1976). The family contract game: Technique and case study. *Journal of Consulting and Clinical Psychology, 44,* 449–455.

Blechman, E. A., Taylor, C. J., & Schrader, S. M. (1981). Family problem solving versus home notes as early intervention with high-risk children. *Journal of Consulting and Clinical Psychology, 49*(6), 919–926.

Bleecker, E. R., & Engel, B. T. (1973). Learned control of cardiac rate and cardiac conduction in the Wolff-Parkinson-White syndrome. *New England Journal of Medicine, 288,* 560–562.

Blount, R.L., & Stokes, T. F. (1984). Contingent public posting of photographs to reinforce dental hygiene: Promoting effective toothbrushing by elementary school children. *Behavior Modification, 8,* 79–92.

Bolstad, O. D., & Johnson, S. M. (1972). Self-regulation in the modification of disruptive classroom behavior. *Journal of Applied Behavior Analysis, 5,* 430–453.

Bond, I. K., & Hutchison, H. C. (1960). Application of reciprocal inhibition therapy to exhibitionism. *Canadian Medical Association Journal, 83,* 23–25.

Bondy, A. S., & Erickson, M. T. (1976). Comparison of modeling and reinforcement procedures in increasing question-asking of mildly retarded children. *Journal of Applied Behavior Analysis, 9,* 108.

Bonham, G. S., & Brock, D. B. (1985). The relationship of diabetes with race, sex, and obesity. *American Journal of Clinical Nutrition, 41,* 776–783.

Bootzin, R. R., & Nicassio, P. (1978). Behavioral treatment for insomnia. In M. Hersen, R. Eisler, & P. Miller (Eds.), *Progress in behavior modification* (Vol 6). New York: Academic Press.

Borgeat, F., Stravynski, A., & Chalou, H. L. (1983). The influence of two different sets of information and suggestions on the subjective effects of relaxation. *Journal of Human Stress, 9,*(3) 40–45.

Borkovec, T. D. (1970). *The comparative effectiveness of systematic desensitization and implosive therapy and the effect of expectancy manipulation on the elimination of fear.* Unpublished doctoral dissertation, University of Illinois.

Borkovec, T. D. (1972). Effects of expectancy on the outcome of systematic desensitization and implosive treatments for analogue anxiety. *Behavior Therapy, 3,* 29–40.

Borkovec, T. D. (1982).Insomnia. *Journal of Consulting and Clinical Psychology, 50,* 880–895.

Borkovec, T. D., & Bernstein, D. A. (1985). Forward. In J. C. Smith (Ed.), *Relaxation dynamics: Nine world approaches to self-relaxation.* Champaign, IL: Research Press.

Borkovec, T. D., & Glasgow, R. E. (1973). Boundary conditions of false heart rate feedback effects on avoidance behavior: A resolution of discrepant results. *Behaviour Research and Therapy, 11,* 171–177.

Borkovec, T. D., & Grayson, J. B. (1980). Consequences of increasing the functional impact of internal emotional stimuli. In K. Blankstein, P. Pliner, & J. Polivy (Eds.), *Assessment and modification of emotional behavior.* New York: Plenum Press.

Borkovec, T. D., Grayson, J. B., & Cooper, K. M. (1978). Treatment of general tension: Subjective and physiological effects of progressive relaxation. *Journal of Consulting and Clinical Psychology, 46,* 518–528.

Borkovec, T. D., Kaloupek, D. G., & Slama, K. M. (1975). The facilitative effect of muscle tension-release in the relaxation treatment of sleep disturbance. *Behavior Therapy, 6,* 301–309.

Borkovec, T. D., & Nau, S. D. (1972). Credibility of analogue therapy rationales. *Journal of Behavior Therapy and Experimental Psychiatry, 3,* 257–260.

Borkovec, T. D., & Sides, J. K. (1979). Critical procedural variables related to the physiological effects of progressive relaxation: A review. *Behaviour Research and Therapy, 17,* 119–125.

Borkovec, T. D., Wall, R. L., & Stone, N. M. (1974). False physiological feedback and the maintenance of speech anxiety. *Journal of Abnormal Psychology, 83,* 164–168.

Borkovec, T. D., Weerts, T. C., & Bernstein, D. A. (1977). Assessment of anxiety. In A. R. Ciminero, K. S. Calhoun, & H. E. Adams (Eds.), *Handbook of behavioural assessment.* New York: Wiley.

Borkovec, T. D., Wilkinson, L., Folensbee, R., & Lerman, C. (1983). Stimulus control applications to the treatment of worry. *Behaviour Research and Therapy, 21,* 247–251.

Bornstein, P., & Quevillon, R. (1976). The effects of a self-instructional package on overactive preschool boys. *Journal of Applied Behavior Analysis, 9,* 179–188.

Bostow, D. E., & Bailey, J. B. (1969). Modification of severe disruptive and aggressive behavior using brief time-out and reinforcement procedures. *Journal of Applied Behavior Analysis, 2,* 31–37.

Botvin, G. J., Eng, A., & Williams, C. L. (1980). Preventing the onset of cigarette smoking through life skills training. *Preventive Medicine, 9,* 135–143.

Boudin, H. M. (1972). Contingency contracting as a therapeutic tool in the deceleration of amphetamine use. *Behavior Therapy, 3,* 604–608.

Boulougouris, J. C., & Bassiakos, L. (1973). Case histories and shorter communications: Prolonged flooding in cases with obsessive-compulsive neurosis. *Behaviour Research and Therapy, 11,* 227–231.

Boulougouris, J. C., & Marks, I. M. (1969). Implosion (flooding): A new treatment for phobias. *British Medical Journal, 2,* 721–723.

Boulougouris, J. C., Marks, I M., & Marset, P. (1971). Superiority of flooding (implosion) to desensitization for reducing pathological fear. *Behaviour Research and Therapy, 9,* 7–16.

Bovey, M., & Davidson, P. (1970). Psychological factors affecting pain tolerance. *Journal of Psychosomatic Research, 14,* 371–376.

Bower, G. H. (1967). *Mental imagery and memory.* Colloquium, Arizona State University, May.

Bower, G. H. (1972a). *Mental imagery and associational learning in memory.* New York: Wiley.

Bower, G. H. (1972b). Mental imagery and associative learning. In L. W. Gregg (Ed.), *Cognition in learning and memory.* New York: Wiley.

Bower, G. H. (1975). Cognitive psychology: An introduction. In W. K. Estes (Ed.), *Handbook of learning and cognitive processes* (Vol. 1). Hillsdale, NJ: Lawrence Erlbaum Associates.

Bower, G. H. (1976). *Asserting yourself: A guide for positive change.* Reading, MA: Addison-Wesley.

Bower, G. H. (1978). Contacts of cognitive psychology with social learning theory.*Cognitive Therapy and Research, 2*(2), 123–146.

Bower, G. H., & Bower, S. (1976). *Asserting yourself: A practical guide for positive change.* Reading, MA: Addison-Wesley.

Bower, G. H., & Hilgard, E. R. (1981). *Theories of learning* (5th ed). Englewood Cliffs, NJ: Prentice-Hall.

Bowlby, J. (1969). *Attachment and loss* (Vol. 1). New York: Basic Books.

Bradley, L. A., Turner, R. A., Young, L. D., Agudelo, C. A., Anderson, K. O., & McDaniel, L. K. (1985). Effects of cognitive-behavioral therapy on pain behavior of rheumatoid arthirtis (RA) patients: Preliminary outcomes. *Scandinavian Journal of Behaviour Therapy, 14,* 51–64.

Brady, J., & Lind, D. L. (1961). Experimental analysis of hysterical blindness. *Archives of General Psychiatry, 4,* 321–339.

Brady, J. P. (1967). Comments of methohexitone-aided systematic desensitization. *Behaviour Research and Therapy, 5,* 259–260.

Brady, J. P., Luborsky, L., & Kron, R. E. (1974). Blood pressure reduction in patients with essential hypertension through metronome-conditioned relaxation: A preliminary report. *Behavior Therapy, 5,* 203–209.

Brantley, P. J., Carnike, C. L. M., Faulstich, M. E., & Barkemeyer, C. A. (1985). Blepharospasm: A case study comparison of tritrexphenidyl (artane) versus EMG biofeedback. *Biofeedback and Self-Regulation, 10,* 173–180.

Brauer, A. P., Horlick, L., Nelson, E., Farquhar, J. W.,

& Agras, W. S. (1979). Relaxation therapy for essential hypertension. *Journal of Behavioral Medicine, 2,* 21–29.

Brawley, E. R., Harris, F. R., Allen K. E., Fleming, R. S., & Peterson, R. F. (1969). Behavior modification on an autistic child. *Behavioral Science, 14,* 87–97.

Breger, L., & McGaugh, J. L. (1965). Critique and reformulation of "learning theory" approaches to psychotherapy and neurosis. *Psychological Bulletin, 63,* 338–358.

Breier, A., & Strauss, J. S. (1983). Self-control in psychotic disorders. *Archives of General Psychiatry, 48,* 1141–1145.

Brener, J. (1974). A general model of voluntary control applied to the phenomena of learned cardiovascular change. In P. A. Obrist, A. H. Black, J. Brener, & L. V. DiCara (Eds.), *Cardiovascular psychophysiology: Current issues in response mechanisms, biofeedback, and methodology.* Chicago: Aldine.

Brener, J., & Kleinmen, R. A. (1970). Learned control of decreases in systolic blood pressure. *Nature* (London), *226,* 1063–1064.

Brethower, D. M., Reynolds, G. S. (1962). A facilitative effect of punishment on unpublished behavior. *Journal of the Experimental Analysis of Behavior, 5,* 191–199.

Breyer, N. L., & Allen, G. J. (1975). Effects of implementing a token economy on teacher attending behavior. *Journal of Applied Behavior Analysis, 8,* 373–380.

Brickman, P., Rabinowitz, V. C., Karuza, J., Coates, D., Cohn, E., & Kidder, L. (1982). Models of helping and coping. *American Psychologist, 37,* 368–384.

Brierley, H. (1964). Electrical aversion therapy. *British Medical Journal, 1,* 631.

Brigham, T. A., Graubard, P. S., & Stans, A. (1972). Analysis of the effects of sequential reinforcement contingencies on aspects of composition. *Journal of Applied Behavior Analysis, 5,* 421–429.

Brightwell, D. R., & Naylor, C. S. (1979). Effects of a combined behavioral and pharmacological program on weight loss. *International Journal of Obesity, 3,* 141–148.

Brightwell, D. R., & Sloan, C. L. (1977). Long-term results of behavior therapy for obesity. *Behavior Therapy, 8,* 898–905.

Bristol, M. M., & Sloane, H. N., Jr. (1974). Effects of contingency contracting on study rate and test performance. *Journal of Applied Behavior Analysis, 7,* 271–285.

Brock, L. D. (1967). *The efficacy of various extinction procedures on a conditioned avoidance response in humans: An experimental analogue.* Unpublished doctoral dissertation, Southern Illinois University.

Broden, M., Hall, R. V., Dunlap, A., & Clark, R. (1970). Effects of teacher attention and a token reinforcement system in a junior high school special education class. *Exceptional Children, 36,* 341–349.

Brody, G. H., Lahey, B. B., & Combs, M. L (1978). Effects of intermittent modeling on observational learning. *Journal of Applied Behavior Analysis, 11,* 87–90.

Brown, B. (1974). *New mind, new body: Biofeedback; new directions for the mind.* New York: Harper & Row.

Brown, B. B. (1970). Recognition aspects of consciousness through association with EEG alpha activity represented by a light signal. *Psychophysiology, 6,* 442–452.

Brown, G. E. (1978). Self-administered desensitization of a cemetary phobia using sexual arousal to inhibit anxiety. *Journal of Behavior Therapy and Experimental Psychiatry, 9,* 73–74.

Brown, P., & Elliot, R. (1965). Control of aggression in a nursery school class. *Journal of Experimental Child Psychology, 2,* 103–109.

Brown, R. A., & Lewinsohn, P. M. (1984). A psychoeducational approach to the treatment of depression: Comparison of group, individual, and minimal contact procedures. *Journal of Consulting and Clinical Psychology, 52,* 774–783.

Brown, R. A., Lichtenstein, E., McIntyre, K. D., & Harrington-Kostur, J. (1984). Effects of nicotine fading and relapse prevention on smoking cessation. *Journal of Consulting and Clinical Psychology, 52,* 307–308.

Brownell, K. D. (1982a). Obesity: Understanding and training a serious prevalent, and refractory disorder. *Journal of Consulting and Clinical Psychology, 50,* 820–840.

Brownell, K. D. (1982b). The addictive disorders. In C. M. Franks, G. T. Wilson, P. C. Kendall, & K. D. Brownell (Eds.), *Annual review of behavior therapy* (Vol. 8). New York: Guilford Press.

Brownell, K. D. (1985). *The LEARN Program for weight control.* Unpublished treatment manual, University of Pennsylvania.

Brownell, K. D. (1986). Public health approaches to obesity and its management. *Annual Review of Public Health, 7,* 521–533.

Brownell, K. D., Colletti, G., Ersner-Hershfield, R., Hershfield, S. M., & Wilson, G. T. (1977). Self control in school children: Stringency and leniency in self determined and externally imposed performance standards. *Behavior Therapy, 8,* 442–455.

Brownell, K. D., Heckerman, C. L., Westlake, R. J., Hayes, S. C., & Monti, P. M. (1978). The effects of couples training and partner cooperativeness in the behavioral treatment of obesity. *Behaviour Research and Therapy, 16,* 323–333.

Brownell, K. D., Marlatt, G. A., Lichenstein, E., & Wilson, G. T. (1986). Understanding and preventing relapse. *American Psychologist, 41,* 765–782.

Brownell, K. D., & Stunkard, A. J. (1980). Physical activity in the development and treatment of obesity. In A. J. Stunkard (Ed.), *Obesity* (pp. 300–324). Philadelphia: Saunders.

Brownell, K. D., & Stunkard, A. J. (1981). Couples training, pharmacotherapy, and behavior therapy in the treatment of obesity. *Archives of General Psychiatry, 38,* 1224–1229.

Bruch, M. A. (1975). Influence of model characteristics on psychiatric inpatients interview anxiety. *Journal of Abnormal Psychology, 84,* 290–294.

Brudny, J., Grynbaum, B. B., & Korein, J. (1973). New therapeutic modality in the treatment of spasmodic torticollis. *Archives of Physical Medicine and Rehabilitation, 54,* 575.

Brudny, J., Korein, J., Grynbaum, B. B., Friedman, L. W., Weinstein, S., Sachs-Frankel, G., & Belandres, P. V. (1976a). EMG feedback: Review of treatment of 114 patients. *Biofeedback and Self-Control,* 47–66.

Brudny, J., Korein, J., Grynbaum, B. B., Friedman, L. W., Weinstein, S., Sachs-Frankel, G., & Belandres, P. V. (1976b). EMG feedback therapy. *Archives of Physical and Medical Rehabilitation, 57,* 55–61.

Bucher, B., & Fabricatore, J. (1970). Use of patient-administered shock to suppress hallucinations. *Behavior Therapy, 1,* 383–385.

Bucher, B., & Hawkins, J. (September, 1971). *Comparison of response cost and token reinforcement systems in a class for academic underachievers.* Paper presented at the Association for the Advancement of Behavior Therapy, Washington, D.C.

Bucher, B., & Lovaas, O. I. (1968). Use of aversive stimulation in behavior modification. In M. R. Jones (Eds.), *Miami Symposium on the Prediction of Behavior 1967: Aversive Stimulation.* Coral Gables, FL: University of Miami Press.

Bucher, B., & Reaume, J. (1979). Generalization of Reinforcement Effects in a token program in the home. *Behavior Modification, 3*(1), 63–72.

Bucher, B., Reykdal, B., & Albin, J. (1976). Brief physical restraint to control PICA in retarded children. *Journal of Behavior Therapy and Experimental Psychiatry, 7,* 137–140.

Buckley, N. R., & Walker, H. M. (1970). *Modifying classroom behavior: A manual of procedure for classroom teachers.* Champaign, IL: Research Press.

Budd, K. S., Green, D. R., & Baer, D. M. (1976). An analysis of multiple misplaced parental social contingencies. *Journal of Applied Behavior Analysis, 9,* 459–470.

Budzynski, T. H., & Stoyva, J. (1973). Biofeedback techniques in behavior therapy. In D. Shapiro, T. X., Barber, L. V. DiCasa, J. Kamiya, N. E. Miller, & J. Stoyva (Eds.), *Biofeedback and self-control 1972: An Aldine annual on the regulation of bodily processes and consciousness.* Chicago: Aldine.

Budzynski, T. H., Stoyva, J., & Adler, C. S. (1970). Feedback-influenced muscle relaxation: Applications to tension headache. *Journal of Behavior Therapy and Experimental Psychiatry, 1,* 205–211.

Budzynski, T. H., Stoyva, J. M., & Peffer, K. E. (1980). Biofeedback techniques in psychomatic disorders. In A. Goldstein & E. B. Foa (Eds.), *Handbook of behavioral interventions.* New York: Wiley.

Buell, J., Stoddard, P., Harris, P. R., & Baer, D. M. (1968) Collateral social development accompanying reinforcement of outdoor play in a preschool child. *Journal of Applied Behavior Analysis, 1,* 167–173.

Bugental, D. B., Whalen, C. K., & Henker, B. (1977). Causal attributions of hyperactive children and motivational assumptions of two behavioral-change approaches: Evidence for an interactionist position. *Child Development, 48,* 874–884.

Burchard, J. D. (1967). Systematic socialization: A programmed environment for the habilitation of antisocial retardates. *Psychological Record, 17,* 461–476.

Burchard, J. D., & Barrera, F. (1972). An analysis of timeout and response cost in a programmed environment. *Journal of Applied Behavior Analysis, 5,* 271–282.

Burchard, J. D., & Tyler, V., Jr. (1965). The modification of delinquent behaviour through operant conditioning. *Behaviour Research and Therapy, 2,* 245–250.

Burish, T. G. (1981). EMG biofeedback in the treatment of stress-related disorders. In C. K. Prokop & L. A. Bradley (Eds.), *Medical psychology: Contributions to behavioral medicine.* New York: Academic Press.

Burish, T. G. (1986). Behavioral treatments for the conditioned side effects of cancer chemotherapy: Why are they effective? In W. H. Redd, *Physiological arousal and cognitive distraction in the control of conditioned nausea and vomiting: Assessment issues.* Symposium presented at meeting of Society of Behavioral Medicine, March, San Francisco.

Burish, T. G., & Bradley, L. A. (1983). Coping with chronic disease: Definitions and issues. In T. G. Burish & L. A. Bradley (Eds.), *Coping with chronic disease: Research and applications.* New York: Academic Press.

Burish, T. B., & Carey, M. P. (1984). Conditioned responses to cancer chemotherapy: Etiology and treatment. In B. H. Fox & B. H. Newberry (Eds.), *Impact of psychoendocrine systems in cancer and immunity.* Toronto: Hogrefe.

Burish, T. B., & Carey, M. P. (1986). Conditioned aversive responses in cancer chemotherapy patient: Theoretical and developmental analysis. *Journal of Consulting and Clinical Psychology, 54*(5), 593–600.

Burish, T. G., Hendrix, E. M., & Frost, R. O. (1981). Comparison of frontal EMG biofeedback and several types of relaxation instructions in reducing multiple indices of arousal. *Psychophysiology, 18,* 594–602.

Burish, T. G., Levy, S. M., & Meyerowitz, B. E. (Eds.). (1985). *Cancer, nutrition, and eating behavior: A bio behavioral perspective.* Hillsdale, N. J.: Erlbaum.

Burt, D. W. (1974). Case histories and shorter communications. *Behaviour Research and Therapy, 12,* 121–123.

Bushell, D., Jr., Wrobel, P. A., & Michaelis, M. L. (1968). Applying "group" contingencies to the classroom study behavior of preschool children. *Journal of Applied Behavior Analysis, 1,* 55–61.

Buss, A. H. (1966). *Psychopathology.* New York: Wiley.

Butterfield, H. (1975). Electric shock: safety factors

when used for the aversive conditioning of humans. *Behavior Therapy, 6,* 98–110.

Cahoon, D. D. (1968). Symptom substitution and the behavior therapies: Reappraisal. *Psychological Bulletin, 69,* 149–156.

Calef, R. A., & MacLean, G. D. (1970). A comparison of reciprocal inhibition and reactive inhibition therapies in the treatment of speech anxiety. *Behavior Therapy, 1,* 51–58.

Calhoun, A., & Koenig, K. P. (1973). Classroom modification of elective mutism. *Behavior Therapy, 4,* 700–702.

Calhoun, K. S., & Lima, P. (1977). Effects of varying schedules of timeout on high- and low-rate behaviors. *Journal of Behavior Therapy and Experimental Psychiatry, 8,* 189–194.

Callner, D. A., & Ross, S. M. (1976). The reliability and validity of three measures of assertion in a drug addict population. *Behavior Therapy, 7,* 659–667.

Calloway, S. P., Fonagy, P., Pounder, R. E., & Morgan, M. J. (1983). Behavioral techniques in the management of aerophagia in patients with hiatus hernia. *Journal of Psychosomatic Research, 27,* 499–502.

Camp, B. W. (1977). Verbal mediation in young aggressive boys. *Journal of Abnormal Psychology, 86*(2), 145–153.

Camp, B. W., Blom, G. E., Hebert, F., & van Doornick, W. J. (1977). "Think aloud": A program for developing self-control in young aggressive boys. *Journal of Abnormal Child Psychology, 5,* 157–169.

Campbell, D., Sanderson, R. E., & Laverty, S. G. (1964). Characteristics of a conditioned response in human subjects during extinction trials following a single traumatic conditioning trail. *Journal of Abnormal and Social Psychology, 68,* 627–639.

Campbell, L. M. (1973). A variation of thought stopping in a twelve year old boy: A case report. *Journal of Behavior Therapy and Experimental Psychiatry, 4,* 69–70.

Cannon, D. S., & Baker, T. B. (1981). Emetic and electric shock alcohol aversion therapy: Assessment of conditioning. *Journal of Consulting and Clinical Psychology, 49*(1), 20–33.

Cannon, D. S., Baker, T. B., & Wehl, C. K. (1981). Emetic and electric shock alcohol aversion therapy: Six- and twelve-month follow-up. *Journal of Consulting and Clinical Psychology, 49,* 360–368.

Cannon, D. S., Best, M. R., Batson, J. D., & Feldman, M. (1983). Taste familiarity and apomorphine-induced taste aversions in humans. *Behaviour Research and Therapy, 21*(6), 669–673.

Canter, A., Kondo, C. Y., & Knotts, J. P. (1975). A comparison of EMG feedback and progressive relaxation training in anxiety neurosis. *British Journal of Psychiatry, 127,* 470–477.

Cantrell, R. P., Cantrell, M. L., Huddleston, C. M., & Woolridge, R. L. (1969). Contingency contracting with school problems. *Journal of Applied Behavior Analysis, 2,* 215–220.

Carek, R. G. (1969). *A comparison of two behavioral therapy techniques in the treatment of rat "phobias."* Unpublished doctoral dissertation, University of Iowa.

Carey, K. B., & Maisto, S. A. (1985). A review of the use of self-control techniques in the treatment of alcohol abuse. *Cognitive Therapy and Research, 9,* 235–251.

Carey, M. P., & Burish, T. B. (1985). Anxiety as a predictor of behavioral therapy outcome for cancer chemotherapy patients. *Journal of Consulting and Clinical Psychology, 53,* 860–865.

Carey, M. P., & Burish, T. B. (1986). Providing relaxation training to cancer chemotherapy patients: A comparison of three delivery techniques. *Journal of Consulting and Clinical Psychology, 53,* 860–865.

Carey, R. M. (1983). Clinical applications of relaxation training. *Hospital Practice,* July, 83–87, 91–94.

Carkhuff, R. R. (1969). *Helping and human relations.* New York: Holt.

Carlson, C. S., Arnold, C. R., Becker W. C., & Madsen C. H. (1968). The elimination of tantrum behavior of a child in an elementary classroom. *Behaviour Research and Therapy, 6,* 117–119.

Carney, R. M., Schechter, K., & Davis, T. (1983). Improving adherence to blood glucose testing in insulin-dependent diabetic children. *Behavior Therapy, 14,* 247–254.

Carmody, T. P. (1978). Rational-emotive, self-instructional, and behavioral assertion training: Facilitating maintenance. *Cognitive Therapy and Research, 2,* 241–254.

Carpenter, R., & Casto, G. (1982). A simple procedure to improve a token economy. *Journal of Behavior Therapy and Experimental Psychiatry, 13,* 331–332.

Carrobles, J. A. I., Cardona, A., & Santacreu, J. (1981). Shaping and generalization procedures in the EMG biofeedback treatment of tension headache. *British Journal of Consulting and Clinical Psychology, 45,* 503.

Carroll, B. J. (1983). Neurobiologic dimensions of depression and mania. In J. Angst (Eds.), *The origins of depression: Current concepts and approaches.* New York: Springer-Verlag.

Carroll, L. J., & Yates, B. T. (1981). Further evidence for the role of stimulus control training in facilitation weight reduction after behavioral therapy. *Behavior Therapy, 12,* 287–291.

Carter, E. N., Rice, A. P., & deJulio, S. (1977). Role of the therapist in the self control of obesity. *Journal of Consulting and Clinical Psychology, 45*(3), 503.

Carter, R. D. (1972). *Help! These kids are driving me crazy.* Champaign, IL: Research Press.

Case, H. M. (1940). *Stuttering and speech blocking: A comparative study of maladjustment.* Unpublished doctoral dissertation, University of California, Los Angeles.

Castro, L., Perez, G. C., Albanchez, D. B., & de Leon, E. P. (1983). Feedback properties of "self-reinforcement": Further evidence. *Behavior Therapy, 14,* 672–681.

Catania, C. A. (1975). The myth of self reinforcement. *Behaviorism, 3,* 192–199.

Caudill, B. D., & Lipscomb, T. R. (1980). Modeling influences on alcoholics' rates of alcohol consumption. *Journal of Applied Behavior Analysis, 13,* 355–365.

Cautela, J. R. (1966a). A behavior therapy approach to pervasive anxiety. *Behaviour Research and Therapy, 4,* 99–109.

Cautela, J. R. (1966b). Treatment of compulsive behavior by covert sensitization. *Psychological Record, 16,* 33–41.

Cautela, J. R. (1967). Covert sensitization. *Psychological Reports, 74,* 459–468.

Cautela, J. R. (1970a). Covert reinforcement. *Behavior Therapy, 1,* 33–50.

Cautela, J. R. (1970b). The use of covert sensitization in the treatment of alcoholism. *Psychotherapy: Theory, Research and Practice, 7,* 86–90.

Cautela, J. R. (1971a). Covert conditioning. In A. Jacobs & L. B. Sachs (Eds.), *The psychology of private events.* New York: Academic Press.

Cautela, J. R. (1971b). Covert extinction. *Behavior Therapy, 2,* 192–200.

Cautela, J. R. (1971c). Covert sensitization for the treatment of sexual deviations. *Psychological Record, 21,* 37–48.

Cautela, J. R. (1977). The use of covert conditioning in modifying pain behavior. *Journal of Behavior Therapy and Experimental Psychiatry, 8,* 45–52.

Cautela, J. R. (1982). Covert conditioning with children. *Journal of Behavior Therapy and Experimental Psychiatry, 13*(3), 209–214.

Cautela, J. R., & Baron, M. G. (1969). *The behavior therapy treatment of self-destructive behavior.* Unpublished study, Boston College.

Cautela, J. R., & Baron, M. G. (1973). Multi-faceted behavior therapy of self injurious behavior. *Journal of Behavior Therapy and Experimental Psychiatry, 4,* 125–131.

Cautela, J. R, Flannery, R., Jr., & Hanley, S. (1974). Covert modeling: An experimental test. *Behavior Therapy, 5,* 494–502.

Cautela, J. R., & Kastenbaum, R. (1967). A reinforcement survey schedule for use in therapy, training and research. *Psychological Reports, 20,* 1115–1130.

Cautela, J. R., Walsh, K., & Wish, P. (1971). The use of covert reinforcement to modify attitudes toward retardates. *Journal of Psychology, 77,* 257–260.

Cautela, J. R., & Wisocki, P. A. (1969). The use of male and female therapists in the treatment of homosexual behavior. In I. R. Rubin & C. Franks, (Eds.), *Advances in behavior therapy.* New York: Academic Press.

Chadwick, B. A., & Day, R. C. (1971). Systematic reinforcement: Academic performance of underachieving students. *Journal of Applied Behavior Analysis, 4,* 311–319.

Chaney, E. F., O'Leary, M. R., & Marlatt, G. A. (1978). Skill training with alcoholics. *Journal of Consulting and Clinical Psychology, 46,* 1097–1104.

Chaney, E. F., Roszell, D. K., & Cummings, C. (1982). Relapse in opiate addicts: A behavioral analysis. *Addictive Behaviors, 7,* 291–297.

Chapel, J. L. (1970). Behaviour modification techniques with children and adolescents. *Canadian Psychiatric Association Journal, 15,* 315–318.

Chapman, R. F., Smith, J. W., & Layden, T. A. (1971). Elimination of cigarette smoking by punishment and self management training. *Behaviour Research and Therapy, 9,* 255–264.

Chapman, S. L., & Jeffrey, D. B. (1978). Situational management, standard setting, and self-reward in a behavior modification weight loss program. *Journal of Consulting and Clinical Psychology, 46,* 1588–1589.

Chartier, G. M., Ainley, C., & Voss, J. (1976). Effects

of vicarious reward and punishment on social imitation in chronic psychotics. *Behaviour Research and Therapy, 14,* 303–304.

Chesney, M. A., & Shelton, J. L. (1976). A comparison of muscle relaxation and electromyogram biofeedback treatments for muscle contraction headache. *Journal of Behavior Therapy and Experimental Psychiatry, 7,* 221–225.

Chiari, G., & Mosticoni, R. (1979). The treatment of agoraphobia with biofeedback and systematic desensitization. *Journal of Behavior Therapy and Experimental Psychiatry, 10,* 109–113.

Chittenden, G. E. (1942). An experimental study in measuring and modifying assertive behavior in young children. *Monographs of the Society for Research in Child Development, 7*(Whole No. 31).

Christensen, A., Arkowitz, H., & Anderson, J. (1975). Practice dating as a treatment for college dating inhibitions. *Behaviour Research and Therapy, 13,* 321–331.

Christensen, D. E., & Sprague, R. L. (1973). Reduction of hyperactive behavior by conditioning procedures alone and combined with methylphenitate. *Behaviour Research and Therapy, 11,* 331–334.

Christoff, K. A., & Kelly, J. A. (1985). A behavioral approach to social skills training. In L. L'Abate & M. A. Milan (Eds.), *Handbook of social skills training and research.* New York: Wiley.

Christy, P. R. (1975). Does use of tangible rewards with individual children affect peer observers? *Journal of Applied Behavior Analysis, 8,* 187–196.

Ciminero, A. R. (1977). Behavioral assessment: An overview. In A. R. Ciminero, K. S. Calhoun, & H. E. Adams (Eds.), *Handbook of behavioral assessment.* New York: Wiley.

Ciminero, A. R., Calhoun, K. W., & Adams, H. E. (Eds.). (1986). *Handbook of behavioral assessment* (2nd ed.) New York: Wiley.

Ciminero, A. R., Steingarten, K. A. (1978). The effects of performance standards on self-evaluation and self-reinforcement in depressed and nondepressed individuals. *Cognitive Therapy and Research, 2,* 179–182.

Claerhout, S., & Lutzker, J. R. (1981). Increasing children's self-initiated compliance to dental regimens. *Behavior Therapy, 12,* 165–170.

Claeson, L. E., & Malm, U. (1973). Electro-aversion therapy of chronic alcoholism. *Behaviour Research and Therapy, 11,* 663–665.

Claeson, L. E., & Malm, U. (1976). Social training in chronic schizophrenia: A comparative study of treatment with and without a token economy system. *European Journal of Behavioral Analysis and Modification, 3,* 169–175.

Claghorn, J. L, Mathew, R. J., Largen, J. W., & Meyer, J. S. (1981). Directional effects of skin temperature self-regulation on regional cerebral blood flow in normal subjects and migraine patients.

Clark, D. F., (1965). A note on avoidance conditioning techniques in sexual disorder. *Behaviour Research and Therapy, 3,* 203–206.

Clark, D. F. (1967). Behavior therapy of Gilles de la Tourette's syndrome. *British Journal of Psychiatry, 113,* 375–381.

Clement, P. W. (1970). Elimination of sleepwalking in a seven-year-old boy. *Journal of Consulting and clinical Psychology, 34,* 22–26.

Clements, C. B., & McKee, J. M. (1968). Programmed instruction for institutionalized offenders: Contingency management and performance contracts. *Psychological Reports, 22,* 957–964.

Clingman, J., & Fowler, R. L. (1976). The effects of primary reward on the I.Q. performance of grade-school children as a function of initial I.Q. level. *Journal of Applied Behavior Analysis, 9,* 19–23.

Coates, T. J. (1978). Successive self-management strategies towards coping with night eating. *Journal of Behavior Therapy and Experimental Psychiatry, 9,* 181–183.

Cohen, A. S., Barlow, D. H., & Blanchard, E. B. (1985). Psychophysiology of relaxation-associated panic attacks. *Journal of Abnormal Psychology, 94,* 96–101.

Cohen, D. C. (1977). Comparison of self-report and overt behavioral procedures for assessing acrophobia. *Behavior Therapy, 8,* 17–23.

Cohen, E. A., Gelfand, D. M., Dodd, D. K., Jensen, J., & Turner, C. (1980). Self-control practices associated with weight loss maintenance in children and adolescents. *Behavior Therapy, 11,* 26–37.

Cohen, F. (1980). Personality, stress, and the development of physical illness. In G. C. Stone, F. Cohen, & N. E. Adler (Eds.), *Health psychology.* San Francisco: Jossey-Bass.

Cohen, M., Liebson, I. A., Faillace, L. A., & Allen R. P. (1971). Moderate drinking by chronic alcoholics. *Journal of Nervous and Mental Disease, 53,* 434–444.

Coleman, S. L, & Stedman, J. M. (1974). Use of peer model in language training in an echolalic child.

Journal of Behavior Therapy and Experimental Psychiatry, 5, 275–279.

Colletti, G., & Kopel, S. A. (1979). Maintaining behavior change: An investigation of three maintenance strategies and the relationship of self-attribution to the long-term reduction of cigarette smoking. *Journal of Consulting and Clinical Psychology, 47,* 614–617.

Colletti, G., & Supnick, J. A. (1980). Continued therapist contact as a maintenance strategy for smoking reduction. *Journal of Consulting and Clinical Psychology, 48,* 665–667.

Colletti, G., Supnick, J. A., & Rizzo, A. A. (1982). Long-term follow-up (3–4 years) of treatment for smoking reduction. *Addictive Behaviors, 7,* 429–433.

Collins, R. L., Rothblum, E., & Wilson, G. T. (1986). The comparative efficacy of cognitive and behavioral approaches to the treatment of obesity. *Cognitive Therapy and Research, 10,* 299–317.

Colsen, C. (1972). Olfactory aversion therapy for homosexual behavior. *Journal of Behavior Therapy and Experimental Psychiatry, 3,* 185–187.

Condiotte, M. M., & Lichtenstein, E. (1981). Self-efficacy and relapse in smoking cessation programs. *Journal of Consulting and Clinical Psychology, 49,* 648–658.

Condon, T. J., & Allen, G. J. (1980). Role of psychoanalytic merging fantasies in systematic desensitization: A rigorous methodological examination. *Journal of Abnormal Psychology, 89,* 437–443.

Cone, J. D. (1977). The relevance of reliability and validity for behavioral assessment. *Behavior Therapy, 8,* 411–426.

Conger, J. C., Conger, A. J., & Brehm, S. S. (1976). Fear level as a moderator of false feedback effects in snake phobics. *Journal of Consulting and Clinical Psychology, 44*(1), 135–141.

Conrin, J., Pennypacker, H. S., Johnston, J., & Rast, J. (1982). Differential reinforcement of other behaviors to treat chronic rumination of mental retardates. *Journal of Behavior Therapy and Experimental Psychiatry, 13,* 325–329.

Conway, J. B., & Bucher, B. D. (1974). "Soap in the mouth" as an aversive consequence. *Behavior Therapy, 5,* 157–163.

Cook, J. W., Altman, K., Shaw, J., & Blaylock, M. (1978). Use of contingent lemon juice to eliminate public masturbation by a severely retarded boy. *Behaviour Research and Therapy, 16,* 131–134.

Cooke, T. P., & Apolloni, T. (1976). Developing positive social-emotional behaviors: A study of training and generalization effects. *Journal of Applied Behavior Analysis, 9,* 65–78.

Cooney, N. L., Kopel, S. A. (1980). *Controlled relapse: A social learning approach to preventing smoking recidivism.* Paper presented at the meeting of the American Psychological Association, Montreal.

Cooney, N. L., Kopel, S. A., & McKeon, P. (1982). *Controlled relapse training and self-efficacy in ex-smokers.* Paper presented at the meeting of the American Psychological Association, Washington, DC.

Cooper, A., Furst, J. B., & Bridger, W. H. (1969). A brief commentary on the usefulness of studying fears of snakes. *Journal of Abnormal Psychology, 74,* 413–414.

Cooper, A. J. (1964). A case of of fetishism and impotence treated by behavior therapy. *British Journal of Psychiatry, 109,* 649–652.

Cooper, M. L., Thompson, C. L., & Baer, D. M. (1970). The experimental modification of teacher attending behavior. *Journal of Consulting and Clinical Psychology, 3,* 153–157.

Corah, N. L., Gale, E. N., & Illig, S. J. (1979a). Stress reduction during dental procedures. *Journal of Dental Research, 58,* 1347–1351.

Corah, N. L., Gale, E. N., & Illig, S. J. (1979b). The use of relaxation and distraction to reduce psychological stress during dental procedures. *Journal of the American Dental Association, 98,* 390–394.

Cornelio, R., Levine, B. A., & Wolpe, J. (1980). The treatment of handwriting anxiety by an in-vivo desensitization procedure. *Journal of Behavior Therapy and Experimental Psychiatry, 11,* 49–51.

Corte, H. E., Wolfe, M. M., & Locke, B. J. (1971). A comparison of procedures of eliminating self-injurious behavior of retarded adolescents. *Journal of Applied Behavior Analysis, 4,* 201–203.

Costello, C. G. (1978). A critical review of Seligman's laboratory experiments on learned helplessness and depression in humans. *Journal of Abnormal Psychology, 87*(1), 21–31.

Cotharin, R. L., & Mikulas, W. L. (1975). Systematic desensitization of racial emotional responses. *Journal of Behavior Therapy and Experimental Psychiatry, 6,* 347–348.

Cotler, S. B. (1970). Sex differences and generalization of anxiety reduction with automated desensitization and minimal therapist interaction. *Behaviour Research and Therapy, 8,* 273–285.

Cotler, S. B., & Guerra, J. J. (1976). *Assertion training: A humanistic behavioral guide to self dignity.* Champaign, IL: Research Press.

Cott, A., Goldman, J. A., Pavloski, R. P., Kirschberg, G. J., & Fabich, M. (1981). The long-term therapeutic significance of the addition of electromyographic biofeedback to relaxation training in the treatment of tension headaches. *Behavior Therapy, 12,* 556–559.

Cox, D. J., Freundlich, A., & Meyer, R. G. (1975). Differential effectiveness of electromyograph feedback, verbal relaxation instructions, and medication placebo with tension headaches. *Journal of Consulting and Clinical Psychology, 43,* 892–899.

Coyne, J. C., & Gotlib, I. H. (1983). The role of cognition in depression: A critical appraisal. *Psychological Bulletin, 94,* 472–505.

Cradock, C., Cotler, S., & Jason, L. A. (1978). Primary prevention: Immunization of children for speech anxiety. *Cognitive Therapy and Research, 2,* 389–396.

Craig, K. D., & Neidemayer, H. (1974). Autonomic correlates pain thresholds influenced by social modeling. *Journal of Personality and Social Psychology, 29,* 246–252.

Craighead, L. W. (1979). Self-instructional training for assertive-refusal behavior. *Behavior Therapy, 10,* 529–543.

Craighead, L. W. (1984). Sequencing of behavior therapy and pharmacotherapy of obesity. *Journal of Consulting and Clinical Psychology, 52,* 190–199.

Craighead, L. W. (1985). A problem-solving approach to the treatment of obesity. In M. Hersen & A. S. Bellack (Eds.), *Handbook of clinical behavior therapy with adults.* New York: Plenum Press.

Craighead, L. W., Stunkard, A. J., & O'Brien, R. (1981). Behavior therapy and pharmacotherapy for obesity. *Archives of General Psychiatry, 38,* 763–768.

Craighead, W. E., Kazdin, A. E., & Mahoney, M. M. (1976). *Behavior modification: Principles, issues and applications.* Hopewell, NJ: Houghton Mifflin.

Craighead, W. E., Mercatoris, M. & Bellack, B. (1974). A brief report on mentally retarded residents as behavioral observers. *Journal of Applied Behavior Analysis, 7,* 333–340.

Cram, J. R. (1980). EMG biofeedback and the treatment of tension headache: A systematic analysis of treatment components. *Behavior Therapy, 11,* 699–710.

Creer, T. L. (1970). The use of a time-out from positive reinforcement procedure with asthmatic children. *Journal of Psychosomatic Research, 14,* 117–127.

Creer, T. L. (1982). Asthma. *Journal of Consulting and Clinical Psychology, 50,* 912–921.

Creer, T. L., Chai, H., & Hoffman, A. (1977). A single application of an aversive stimulus to eliminate chronic cough. *Journal of Behavior Research and Experimental Psychiatry, 8,* 107–109.

Critchlow, B. (1986). The powers of John Barleycorn: Beliefs about the effects of alcohol in social behavior. *American Psychologist, 41,* 751–764.

Crowe, M. J., Marks, I. M., Agras, W. S., & Leitenberg, H. (1972). Time-limited densensitization, implosion and shaping for phobic patients: A crossover study. *Behaviour Research and Therapy, 10,* 319–328.

Crowther, J. H., Taylor, M. L., & Hoge, D. (1982). *Factors predicting blood pressure response to relaxation training for hypertension.* Paper presented at the meeting of the American Psychological Association, Washington, D.C.

Csapo, M., & Agg, B. (1976). Educational rehabilitation of delinquents in a community setting. *Canadian Journal of Criminology and Corrections, 18,* 42–48.

Cummings, C., Gordon, J. R., & Marlatt, G. A. (1980). Relapse: Prevention and prediction. In W. R. Miller (Ed.), *The addictive disorders: Treatment of alcoholism, drug abuse, smoking, and obesity.* New York: Pergamon Press.

Cummings, K. M., Becker, M. H., Kirscht, J. P., & Levin, N. W. (1984). Intervention strategies to improve compliance with medical regimens by ambulatory hemodialysis patients. *Journal of Behavioral Medicine, 4,* 111–127.

Cunningham, C. E., & Linscheid, T. R. (1976). Elimination of chronic infant ruminating by electric shock. *Behavior Therapy, 1,* 231–234.

Curran, J. P. (1975). Social skills training and systematic desensitization in reducing dating anxiety. *Behaviour Research and Therapy, 13,* 65–68.

Curran, J. P. (1977). Skills training as an approach to the treatment of heterosexual-social anxiety: A review. *Psychological Bulletin, 84,* 140–157.

Curran, J. P., & Gilbert, F. S. (1975). A test of the relative effectiveness of a systematic desensitization program and an interpersonal skills training program with date anxious subjects. *Behavior Therapy, 6,* 510–521.

Dahlkoetter, J., Callahan, E. J., & Linton, J. (1979). Obesity and the unbalanced energy equation: Exercise vs. eating habit change. *Journal of Consulting and Clinical Psychology, 47,* 898–905.

Dahlquist, L. M., Gil, K. M., Hodges, J., Kalfus, G. R., Gunsberg, A., & Halborn, S. W. (1985). The effects of behavioral intervention on dental flossing skills in children. *Journal of Pediatric Psychology, 10,* 403–412.

Dalessio, D. J. (1972). *Wolff's headaches and other head pain.* New York: Oxford University Press.

Daly, E. J., Zimmerman, J. S., Donn, P. A., Galliher, M. J. (1985). Psychophysiological treatment of migraine and tension headaches: A 12-month follow-up. *Rehabilitation Psychology, 30,* 3–10.

Danaher, B. G. (1974). Theoretical foundations and clinical applications of the Premack principle: Review and critique. *Behavior Therapy, 5,* 307–324.

Danaher, B. G. (1977). Rapid smoking and self control in smoking treatment. *Journal of Consulting and Clinical Psychology, 45*(6), 1068–1075.

Danaher, B. G., Lichtenstein, E., & Sullivan, J. M. (1976). Comparative effects of rapid and normal smoking on heart rate and carboxyhemoglobin. *Journal of Consulting and Clinical Psychology, 44,* 556–563.

Danet, B. N. (1968). Self-confrontation in psychotherapy reviewed. *American Journal of Psychotherapy, 22,* 245–258.

Daniels, L.K. (1974). Rapid extinction of nail biting by covert sensitization: A case study. *Journal of Behavior and Experimental Psychiatry, 5,* 91–92.

Darley, J. M., & Fazio, R. (1980). Expectancy confirmation processes arising in the social interaction sequence. *American Psychologist, 35,* 867–881.

Datey, K. K. (1978). Biofeedback training and hypnosis in the management of hypertension. *Biofeedback and Self-regulation, 3,* 206–207 (abstract).

Davanloo, H. (Ed.) (1980). *Short-term Dynamic Psychotherapy.* New York: Jason. Aronson.

Davidoff, F. (1980). Diet and cardiovascular disease: An introductory statement. *Connecticut Medicine, 47,* 257–258.

Davidson, P., & Bucher, B. (1978). Intrinsic interest and extrinsic reward: The effects of a continuing

token program on continuing nonconstrained preference. *Behavior Therapy, 9,* 222–234.

Davidson, R. J., & Schwartz, G. E. (1976). Psychobiology of relaxation and related states. In D. Mostofsky (Eds.), *Behavior modification and controls of physiological activity.* Englewood Cliffs, NJ: Prentice-Hall.

Davies, D. L. (1962). Normal drinking in recovered alcohol addicts. *Quarterly Journal of Studies on Alcohol, 23,* 94–104.

Davis, J. O. (1976). Refractorial extinction of homosexual fantasy. *Behavior Therapy, 7,* 698.

Davis, J. R., Wallace, C. J., Liberman, R. P., & Finch, B. E. (1976). The use of brief isolation to suppress delusional and hallucinatory speech. *Journal of Behavior Therapy and Experimental Psychiatry, 7,* 269–275.

Davison, G. C. (1968a). Elimination of a sadistic fantasy by a client-controlled counter-conditioning technique: A case study. *Journal of Abnormal and Social Psychology, 73,* 84–90.

Davison, G. C. (1968b) Systematic desensitization as a counter-conditioning process. *Journal of Abnormal Psychology, 73,* 91–99.

Davison, G. C. (1969). Self-control through "imaginal aversive contingency" and "one downmanship." *Behavioral counseling: Cases and techniques.* New York: Holt.

Davison, G. C. (1976). Homosexuality: The ethical challenge. *Journal of Clinical and Consulting Psychology, 44,* 157–162.

Davison, G. C., & Neale, J. M. (1978). *Abnormal Psychology* (2nd Ed.). New York: Wiley.

Davison, G. C., & Stuart, R. B. (1975). Behavior therapy and civil liberties. *American Psychologist, 30,* 755–763.

Davison, G. C., Tsujimoto, R. N., & Glaros, A. G. (1973). Attribution and the maintenance of behavior change in falling asleep. *Journal of Abnormal Psychology, 82,* 124–133.

Davison, G. C., & Valins, S. (1969). Maintenance of self-attributed and drug-attributed behavior change. *Journal of Personality and Social Psychology, 11,* 25–33.

Davison, G. C., & Wilson, G. T. (1972). Critique of desensitization social and cognitive factors underlying the effectiveness of Wolpe's procedure. *Psychological Bulletin, 78,* 28–31.

Dawley, H. H., Jr., Ellithorpe, D. B., & Tretola, R. (1976). Aversive smoking: Carboxyhemoglobin levels before and after rapid smoking. *Journal of Behavior Therapy and Experimental Psychiatry, 7,* 13–15.

Dawley, H. H., Jr., & Wenrich, W. W. (1976). Group implosive therapy in the treatment of test anxiety: A brief report. *Behavior Therapy, 4*, 261–263.

Dawley, H. H., Jr., & Wenrich, W. W. (1976). *Achieving assertive behavior: A guide to assertive training.* Monterey, CA: Brooks/Cole.

Day, L., & Reznikoff, M. (1980). Preparation of children and parents for treatment at a children's psychiatric clinic through videotaped modeling. *Journal of Consulting and Clinical Psychology, 48*, 303–304.

Dayton, M. P., & Mikulas, W. L. (1981). Assertion and nonassertion supported by arousal reduction. *Journal of Behavior Therapy and Experimental Psychiatry, 12*, 307–309.

Dee, C. K. (1970). *Instructions and the extinction of a learned fear in the context of taped implosive therapy.* Unpublished doctoral dissertation, University of Iowa.

Deese, J., & Hulse, S. H. (1967). *The psychology of learning.* New York: McGraw-Hill.

Deitz, S. M., Slack, D. J., Schwarzmueller, E. B., Wilander, A. P., Weatherly, T. J., & Hilliard, G. (1978). Reducing inappropriate behavior in special classrooms by reinforcing average interresponse times: Interval DRL. *Association for Advancement of Behavior Therapy.* Paper presentation, Georgia State University, 1976.

Delahunt, J., & Curran, J. P. (1976). Effectiveness of negative practice and self-control techniques in the reduction of smoking behavior. *Journal of Consulting and Clinical Psychology, 44*, 1002–1107.

Dembroski, T. M., MacDougall, J. M., Shields, J. L., Petito, J., & Lushene, R. (1978). Components of the Type A coronary-prone behavior pattern and cardiovascular response to psychomotor challenge. *Journal of Behavioral Medicine, 1*, 159–176.

Dembroski, T. M., MacDougall, J. M., Williams, R. B., Harvey, T. L., & Blumenthal, J. A. (1985). Components of Type A, hostility, and anger in: Relationship to angiographic findings. *Psychomatic Medicine, 47*, 219–233.

De Moor, W. (1970). Systematic desensitization versus prolonged high intensity stimulation (flooding). *Journal of Behavior Therapy and Experimental Psychiatry, 1*, 45–52.

DeMorsier, G., & Feldmann, H. (1950). Le traitement biologique de l'alconolisme chronique par l'apomorphine. Etude de 200 cas. (The biological treatment of chronic alcoholism with apomorphine. Study of 200 cases.) *Schweizer Archiv fuer Neurologie und Psychiatrie, 65*, 472–473.

Denney, D. R. (1982). Relaxation and stress management training. In C. E. Waller (Ed.), *Handbook of Clinical Psychology.* Homewood, IL: Dorsey Press.

Denney, D. R., & Sullivan, B. J. (1976). Desensitization and modeling treatments of spider fear using two types of scenes. *Journal of Consulting and Clinical Psychology, 44*(4), 573–579.

Denney, D. R, Sullivan, B. J., & Thiry, M. R. (1977). Participant modeling and self-verbalization training in the reduction of spider fears. *Journal of Behavior Therapy and Experimental Psychiatry, 8*, 247–253.

Depue, R. A., & Fowles, D. C. (1973). Electrodermal activity as an index of arousal in schizophrenics. *Psychological Bulletin, 79*, 233–238.

DeRicco, D. A., & Niemann, J. E. (1980). In vivo effects of peer modeling on drinking rate. *Journal of Applied Behavior Analysis, 13*, 149–152.

DeRicco, D. A., & Niemann, J. E. (1982). Effects of concurrent fast and slow models on drinking rate. *Behavior Modification, 6*, 85–93.

DeRisi, W. J., & Butz, G. (1974). *Writing behavioural contracts: A case simulation practice manual.* Champaign, IL: Research Press.

Derry, P. A., & Stone, G. L. (1979). Effects of cognitive-adjunct treatments on assertiveness. *Cognitive Therapy and Research, 3*, 213–222.

DeRubeis, R. J., Hollon, S. D., Evans, M. D., & Bemis, K. M. (1982). Can psychotherapies for depression be discriminated? A systematic investigation of cognitive therapy and interpersonal therapy. *Journal of Consulting and Clinical Psychology, 50*, 744–756.

de Silva, P., Rachman, S., & Seligman, M. E. P. (1977). Prepared phobias and obsessions: Therapeutic outcome. *Behaviour Research and Therapy, 15*, 65–77.

Dewhurst, D. L. T., & Cautela, J. R. (1980). A proposed reinforcement survey schedule for special needs children. *Journal of Behavior Therapy and Experimental Psychiatry, 11*, 109–112.

Diament, C., & Wilson, G. T. (1975). An experimental investigation of the effects of covert sensitization in an analogue eating situation. *Behavior Therapy, 6*, 499–509.

Dichgans, J., & Brandt, T. (1973). Optokinetic motion sickness and psuedo-Coriolis effects induced by moving visual stimuli. *Acta Oto-Laryngologica, 76*, 339–348.

Dickens, B. M., Doob, A. N., Warwick, O. H., & Winegard, W. C. (1982). *Report of the Committee of Enquiry into Allegations Concerning Drs. Linda and Mark Sobell.* Toronto: Addiction Research Center, Addiction Research Foundation.

DiClemente, C., & Prochaska, J. (1982). Self-change and therapy change of smoking behavior: A comparison of processes of change in cessation and maintenance. *Addictive Behaviors, 7,* 133–142.

Diebert, A. N., & Harmon, A. J. (1973). *New tools for changing behavior.* Champaign, IL: Research Press.

DiGiuseppe, R. A. (1975). The use of behavioral modification to establish rational-self statements in children. *Rational Living, 10*(2), 18–20.

DiGiuseppe, R. A. (1977). The use of behavior modification to establish rational self statements in children. In A. Ellis & R. Grieger (Eds.), *Handbook of rational emotive therapy.* New York: Springer-Verlag.

DiLoreto, A. O. (1971). *Comparative psychotherapy.* Chicago: Aldine-Atherton.

Dobes, R. W. (1977). Amelioration of psychosomatic dermatosis by reinforced inhibition of scratching. *Journal of Behavior Therapy and Experimental Psychiatry, 8,* 185–188.

Doleys, D. M., & Doster, J., & Cartelli, L. M. (1976). Parent training techniques: Effects of lecture-roleplaying followed by feedback and self-recording. *Journal of Behavior Therapy and Experimental Psychiatry, 7,* 359–362.

Doleys, D. M., & Slapion, J. J. (1975). The reduction of verbal repetitions by response cost controlled by a sibling. *Journal of Behavior Therapy and Experimental Psychiatry, 6,* 61–63.

Dollard, J., & Miller, N. E. (1950). *Personality and psychotherapy.* New York: McGraw-Hill.

Donner, L., & Guerney, B. G. (1969). Automated group desensitization for test anxiety. *Behaviour Research and Therapy, 7,* 1–13.

Doster, J. A., & Brooks, S. J. (1974). Interviewer disclosure modeling information revealed, and interviewee verbal behavior. *Journal of Consulting and Clinical Psychology, 42*(3), 420–426.

Doster, J. A., & McAllister, A. (1973). Effect of modeling and model status on verbal behavior in an interview. *Journal of Consulting and Clinical Psychology, 40*(2), 240–243.

Doty, D. W., McInnis, T., & Paul, G. L. (1974). Remediation of negative side effects on an ongoing response-cost system with chronic mental patients. *Journal of Applied Behavior Analysis, 7,* 191–199.

Dougherty, E. H., & Lane, J. R. (1976). Naturalistic alternatives to extinction: An application to self-injurious bedtime behavior. *Journal of Behavior Therapy and Experimental Psychiatry, 7,* 373–376.

Dowrick, P. W., & Dove, C. (1980). The use of self-modeling to improve the swimming performance of spina bifida children. *Journal of Applied Behavior Analysis, 13,* 51–56.

Drabman, R. S., Ross, J. M., Lynd, R. S., & Cordura, G. D. (1978). Retarded children as observers, mediators, and generalization programmers using an icing procedure. *Behavior Modification, 2,* No. 2, Sage Publication, Inc.

Drabman, R. S., & Spitalnik, R. (1973). Social isolation as a punishment procedure: A controlled study. *Journal of Experimental Child Psychology, 16,* 236–249.

Drabman, R. S., Spitalnik, R., & O'Leary, K. D. (1973). Teaching self-control to disruptive children. *Journal of Abnormal Psychology, 82,* 110–116.

Drabman, R. S., Spitalnik, R., & Spiltalnik, K. (1974). Sociometric and disruptive behavior as a function of four types of token reinforcement programs. *Journal of Applied Behavior Analysis, 7,* 93–101.

Drake, D. M. (1970). Perceptual correlates of impulsive and reflective behavior. *Developmental Psychology, 2,* 202–214.

Dubbert, P. M., & Wilson, G. T. (1983). Treatment failures in behavior therapy for obesity: Causes, correlates, and consequences. In E. Foa & P. M. G. Emmelkamp (Eds.), *Treatment failures in behavior therapy,* 263–288. New York: Wiley.

Dudley, D., Glaser, E. M., Jorgenson, B. N., & Logan D. L. (1980). Psychosocial concommitants to rehabilitation in chronic obstructive pulmonary disease: 1. Psychosocial and psychological considerations. *Chest, 77,* 413–420.

Duker, P. C., & Seys, D. M. (1977). Elimination of vomiting in a retarded female using restitutional overcorrection. *Behavior Therapy, 8,* 255–257.

Du Nann, D. G., & Weber, S. J. (1976). Short, and long-term effects of contingency managed instruction on low, medium, and high GPA students. *Journal of Applied Behavior Analysis, 9,* 375–376.

Dunkel, L. D., & Glaros, A. G. (1978). Comparison of self-instructional and stimulus control treatments for obesity. *Cognitive Therapy and Research, 2,* 75–78.

Dunlap, K. (1932). *Habits, their making and unmaking.* New York: Liveright.

Dyckman, J. M., & Cowan, P. A. (1978). Imaging vividness and the outcome of in vivo and imagined scene desensitization. *Journal of Consulting and Clinical Psychology, 46,* 1155–1156.

D'Zurilla, T. J., & Goldfried, M. R. (1971). Problem solving and behavior modification. *Journal of Abnormal Psychology, 78,* 107–126.

D'Zurilla, T. J., Wilson, G. T., & Nelson, R. N. (1973). A preliminary study of the effectiveness of graduated prolonged exposure in the treatment of irrational fear. *Behavior Therapy, 4,* 672–685.

Edelman, R. I. (1972). Vicarious fear induction and avowed autonomic stereotypy. *Behaviour Research and Therapy, 10,* 105–110.

Edelstein, B. A., & Eisler, R. M. (1976). Effects of modeling and modeling with instructions and feedback on the behavioral components of social skills. *Behavior Therapy, 7,* 382–389.

Edinger, J. D. (1982). Incidence and significance of relaxation treatment side effects. *Behavior Therapist, 5,* 137–138.

Edlin, J. V., Johnson, R. H., Hletko, P., & Heilbrunn, G. (1945). The conditioned aversion treatment of chronic alcoholism. Preliminary report. *Archives of Neurology and Psychiatry, 53,* 85–87.

Edlund, C. V. (1972). The effect on the behavior of children as reflected in the IQ scores, when reinforced after each correct response. *Journal of Applied Behavior Analysis, 5,* 317–319.

Edwards, N. B. (1972). Case conference: Assertive training in a case of homosexual pedophilia. *Journal of Behavior Therapy and Experimental Psychiatry, 3,* 55–63.

Egel, A. L., Richman, F. S., & Koegel, R. L. (1981). Normal peer models and autistic children's learning. *Journal of Applied Behavior Analysis, 14,* 3–12.

Einstein, A. (1953). *The meaning of relativity.* Princeton, NJ: Princeton University Press.

Eisler, R. M., Blanchard, E. B., Fitts, H., & Williams, J. G. (1978). Social skill training with and without modeling for schizophrenic and non-psychotic hospitalized psychiatric patients. *Behavior Modification, 2,* 147–172.

Eisler, R. M., Hersen, M., & Agras, W. S. (1973a). Effects of videotape and instructional feedback on nonverbal marital interaction: An analog study. *Behavior Therapy, 4,* 551–558.

Eisler, R. M., Hersen, M., & Agras, W. S. (1973b). Videotape: A method for the controlled observation of nonverbal interpersonal behavior. *Behavior Therapy, 4,* 420–425.

Eisler, R. M., Miller, P. M., & Hersen, M. (1973). Components of assertive behavior. *Journal of Clinical Psychology, 29,* 295–299.

Eisler, R. M., Miller, P. M., Hersen, M., & Alford, H. (1974). Effects of assertive training on marital interaction. *Archives of General Psychiatry, 30,* 643–649.

Elder, J. P., Edelstein, B. A., & Fremouw, W. J. (1981). Client by treatment interactions in response acquisition and cognitive restructuring approaches. *Cognitive Therapy and Research, 5,* 203–210.

Elder, S. T., Ruiz, Z. B., Deabler, R. L., & Dillenkoffer, R. L. (1973). Instrumental conditioning of diastolic blood pressure in essential hypertensive patients. *Journal of Applied Behavior Analysis, 6,* 377–382.

Elefthedrious, C. P., Shoudt, J. T., & Strang, H. R. (1972). The game machine: A technological approach to classroom control. *Journal of School Psychology, 10,* 55–60.

Elkin, I. E., Parloff, M. B., Hadley, S., & Autrey, J. (1985). NIMH Treatment of Depression Collaborative Research Program: Background and research program. *Archives of General Psychiatry, 42,* 305–316.

Elkins, R. L., Feldman, M. P., Orford, J. F., & MacCulloch, M. L. (1966). Anticipatory avoidance learning in the treatment of alcoholism: A record of therapeutic failure. *Behaviour Research and Therapy, 4,* 187–196.

Elkins, R. L., & Hobbs, S. H. (1979). Forgetting, preconditioning CS familiarization and taste aversion learning treatment. *Behaviour Research and Therapy, 17,* 567–573.

Elliott, P. A., Barlow, F., Hooper, A., & Kingerlee, P. E. (1979). Maintaining patients' improvements in a token economy. *Behaviour Research and Therapy, 17,* 335–367.

Elliott, R., & Tighe, T. (1968). Breaking the cigarette habit: Effects of a technique involving threatened loss of money. *Psychological Record, 18,* 503–513.

Ellis, A. (1957). Outcome of employing three techniques of psychotherapy. *Journal of Clinical Psychology, 13,* 344–350.

Ellis, A. (1962). *Reason and emotion in psychotherapy.* New York: Lyle Stuart.

Ellis, A. (1971a). A critique. In A. O. DiLoretto (Ed.) *Comparative psychotherapy.* Chicago: Aldine-Atherton.

Ellis, A. (Ed.). (1971a). *Growth through reason.* Palo Alto, CA: Science & Behavior Books.

Ellis, A. (1971b). A twenty-three-year-old girl guilty

about not following her parents' rules. In A. Ellis (Ed.), *Growth through reason*. Palo Alto, CA: Science & Behavior Books.

Ellis, A. (1971c). A young male who is afraid of becoming a fixed homosexual. In A. Ellis (Ed.), *Growth through reason*. Palo Alto, CA: Science & Behavior Books.

Ellis, A. (1972a). *How to master your fear of flying.* New York: Curtis Books.

Ellis, A. (1972b). Psychotherapy and the value of a human being. In J. W. Davis (Ed.), *Value and valuation. Axiological studies in honor of Robert S. Hartman.* Knoxville: University of Tennessee Press. (Reprinted, New York: Institute for Rational Living, 1972.)

Ellis, A. (1973). *Humanistic psychotherapy: The rational-emotive approach.* New York: Julian Press.

Ellis, A. (1974a). Experience and rationality: The making of a rational emotive therapist. *Psychotherapy: Theory, Research, and Practice, 11,* 194–198.

Ellis, A. (1974b). *Humanistic psychotherapy: The rational emotive approach.* McGraw-Hill.

Ellis, A. (1974c). Rational emotive therapy. In A. Burton (Ed.), *Operational theories of personality.* New York: Brunner/Mazel.

Ellis, A. (1975). *How to live with a "neurotic"* (rev. ed.). New York: Crown.

Ellis, A. (1976). *Sex and the liberated man.* New York: Lyle Stuart.

Ellis, A. (1977). Can we change thoughts by reinforcement? A reply to Howard Rachlin. *Behavior Therapy, 8,* 666–672.

Ellis, A. (1977a). The basic clinical theory of rational-emotive therapy. In A. Ellis & R. Grieger (Eds.), *Handbook of rational-emotive therapy.* New York: Springer.

Ellis, A. (1977b). Research data supporting the clinical and personality hypotheses of RET and other cognitive-behavior therapies. In A. Ellis & R. Grieger (Eds.), *Handbook of rational-emotive therapy.* New York: Springer.

Ellis, A. (1980). Rational-emotive therapy and cognitive behavior therapy: Similarities and differences. *Cognitive Therapy and Research, 4,* 325–340.

Ellis, A., & Grieger, R. (Eds.). (1977). *Handbook of rational emotive therapy.* New York: Springer-Verlag.

Ellis, A. & Harper, R. A. (1973). *A guide to successful marriage.* North Hollywood: Wilshire.

Ellis, A., & Harper, R. A. (1975). *A new guide to rational living.* Englewood Cliffs, NJ: Prentice-Hall.

Ellis, A., Wolfe, J. L., & Moseley, S. (1972). *How to raise an emotionally healthy, happy, child.* North Hollywood: Wilshire.

Elman, D., Schroeder, H. E., & Schwartz, M. F. (1977). Reciprocal social influence of obese and normal-weight persons. *Journal of Abnormal Psychology, 86,* 408–413.

Elmore, R. T., Jr., Wildman, R. W., II, & Westefeld, J. S. (1980). The use of systematic desensitization in the treatment of blood phobia. *Journal of Behavior Therapy and Experimental Psychiatry, 11,* 277–279.

Emmelkamp, P. M. G., Hout, A., & deVries, K. (1983). Assertive training for agoraphobics. *Behaviour Research and Therapy, 21,* 63–68.

Emmelkamp, P. M. G., Kuipers, A. C. M., & Eggeraat, J. B. (1978). Cognitive modification versus prolonged exposure in vivo: A comparison with agoraphobics as subjects. *Behaviour Research and Therapy, 16,* 33–42.

Emmelkamp, P. M. G., & Mersch, P. P. (1982). Cognition and exposure in vivo in the treatment of agoraphobia: Short-term and delayed effects. *Cognitive Therapy and Research, 6,* 77–90.

Emmelkamp, P. M. G., & Straatman, H. A. (1976). A psychoanalytic reinterpretation of the effectiveness of systematic desensitization: Fact or fiction. *Behaviour Research and Therapy, 14,* 245–249.

Emmelkamp, P. M. G., van der Helm, M., van Zanten, B. L., & Plochg, I. (1980). Treatment of obsessive-compulsive patients: The contribution of self-instructional training to the effectiveness of exposure. *Behaviour Research and Therapy, 18,* 61–66.

Emmelkamp, P. M. G., & Wessels, H. (1975). Flooding in imagination vs. Flooding in vivo: A comparison with agoraphobics. *Behaviour Research and Therapy, 13,* 7–15.

Emshoff, J. G., Redd, W. H., & Davidson, W. S. (1976). Generalization training and the transfer of prosocial behavior in delinquent adolescents. *Journal of Behavior Therapy and Experimental Psychiatry, 5,* 141–144.

Endler, N. S., & Magnusson, D. (1976). Toward an interactional psychology of personality. *Psychological Bulletin, 83*(5), 956–974.

Engel, B. T., & Bleecker, E. R. (1974). Application of operant conditioning techniques to the control of the cardiac arrhythmias. In P. A. Obrist, A. H. Black, J. Brener, L. V. DiCara (Eds.), *Cardiovascular psychophysiology.* Chicago, IL: Aldine.

Engel, B. T., & Hansen, S. P. (1966). Operant conditioning of heart rate slowing. *Psychophysiology, 3,* 176–187.

Engel, N. P., Nikoomanesh, P., & Schuster, M. M. (1974). Operant conditioning of rectosphincteric responses in treatment of fecal incontinence. *New England Journal of Medicine, 290,* 646–649.

Epstein, L. H., & Abel, G. G. (1977). Analysis of biofeedback training effects for tension headache patients. *Behavior Therapy, 8,* 37–47.

Epstein, L. H., & Beck, S., Figueroa, J., Farkas, G., Kazdin, A. E., Daneman, D., & Becker, D. (1981). The effects of targetting improvements in urine glucose on metabolic control in children with insulin dependent diabetes. *Journal of Applied Behavior Analysis, 14,* 367–375.

Epstein, L. H., & Cluss, P. A. (1982). A behavioral medicine perspective on adherence to long-term medical regimens. *Journal of Consulting and Clinical Psychology, 50,* 950–971.

Epstein, L. H., Hersen, M., & Hemphill, D. P. (1974). Music feedback in the treatment of tension headache: An experimental case study. *Journal of Behavior Therapy and Experimental Psychiatry, 5,* 59–63.

Epstein, L. H. & McCoy, J. F. (1977). Bladder and bowel control in Hirschsprung's disease. *Journal of Behavior Therapy and Experimental Psychiatry, 8,* 97–99.

Epstein, L. H., Miller, P. M., & Webster, J. S. (1976). Effects of reinforcing concurrent behavior on self-monitoring. *Behavior Therapy, 1,* 89–95.

Epstein, L. H., Parker, L., McCoy, J. F., & McGee, G. (1976). Descriptive analysis of eating regulation in obese and nonobese children. *Journal of Applied Behavior Analysis, 9,* 407–415.

Epstein, L. H., & Peterson, G. L. (1973). Differential conditioning using covert stimuli. *Behavior Therapy, 4,* 96–99.

Errickson, E. A., Wyne, M. D., & Routh, D. K. (1973). A response-cost procedure for reduction of impulsive behavior of academically handicapped children. *Journal of Abnormal Child Psychology, 1,* 350–357.

Estes, W. K. (1944). An experimental study of punishment. *Psychological Monographs, 57* (Whole No. 263).

Evans, D. R. (1967). An exploratory study into the treatment of exhibitionism by means of emotive imagery and aversive conditioning. *Canadian Psychologist, 8,* 162.

Evans, D. R. (1968). Masturbatory fantasy and sexual deviation. *Behaviour Research and Therapy, 6,* 17–19.

Evans, D. R. (1976). A systematized introduction to behavior therapy training. *Journal of Behavior Therapy and Experimental Psychiatry, 7,* 23–26.

Evans, M., & Paul, G. (1970). Effects of hypnotically suggested analgesia on physiological and subjective responses to cold stress. *Journal of Consulting and Clinical Psychology, 35,* 362–371.

Evans, M. D., Hollon, S. D., DeRubeis, R. J., Auerbach, A., Tauson, V. B., & Wiemer, M. (1983, July). *Development of a system for rating psychotherapies for depression.* Paper presented at the Annual Meeting of the Society for Psychotherapy Research, Sheffield, England.

Evans, M. D., Hollon, S. R., DeRubeis, R. J., Piasecki, J. M., Tuason, V. B., & Garvey, M. J. (1986). *Relapse/recurrence following cognitive therapy and pharmacotherapy for depression: 4. Two-year follow-up in the CPT project.* Unpublished manuscript, University of Minnesota and the St. Paul-Ramsey Medical Center, Minneapolis-St. Paul, Minnesota.

Evans, P. D., & Kellam, A. M. P. (1973). Semi-automated desensitization: A controlled clinical trait. *Behaviour Research and Therapy, 11,* 641–646.

Evans, G. W., & Oswalt, G. L. (1968). Acceleration of academic progress through the manipulation of peer influence. *Behaviour Research and Therapy, 6,* 189–195.

Evans, M., & Paul, G. (1970). Effects of hypnotically suggested analgesia on physiological and subjective responses to cold stress. *Journal of Consulting and Clinical Psychology, 35,* 362–371.

Evans, P. D., & Kellam, A. M. P. (1973). Semi-automated desensitization: A controlled clinical trial. *Behaviour Research and Therapy, 11,* 641–646.

Everaerd, W. T. A. M., Rijken, H. M., & Emmelkamp, P. M. G. (1973). A comparison of "flooding" and "successive approximation" in the treatment of agoraphobia. *Behaviour Research and Therapy, 11,* 105–117.

Evaraerd, W., & Dekker, J. (1982). Treatment of secondary orgasmic dysfunction: A comparison of systematic desensitization and sex therapy. *Behaviour Research and Therapy, 20,* 269–274.

Everett, P. B., Hayward, S. C., & Meyers, A. W. (1974). The effects of a token reinforcement procedure on bus ridership. *Journal of Applied Behavior Analysis, 7,* 1–9.

Eysenck, H. J. (1952). The effects of psychotherapy:

An evaluation. *Journal of Consulting Psychology, 16,* 319–324.

Eysenck, H. J. (1959). Learning theory and behaviour therapy. *Journal of Mental Science, 105,* 61–75.

Eysenck, H. J. (Ed.). (1960). *Behavior therapy and the neuroses.* Oxford: Pergamon.

Eysenck, H. J. (1968). A theory of the incubation of anxiety/fear responses. *Behaviour Research and Therapy, 6,* 309–322.

Eysenck, H. J., & Beech, H. R. (1971). Counterconditioning and related methods. In A. E. Bergin & S. L. Garfield (Eds.), *Handbook of psychotherapy and behavior change.* New York: Wiley.

Eysenck, J. J., & Eysenck, S. B. G. (1968). *Personality, structure and measurement.* London: Routledge & Kegan Paul.

Fairweather, G. W. (1964). *Social psychology in treating mental illness: An experimental approach.* New York: Wiley.

Fairweather, G. W., Sanders, D. H., Maynard, H., & Cressler, D. L. (1969). *Community life for the mentally ill: An alternative to institutional care.* Chicago: Aldine.

Fairweather, G. W., & Simon, R. (1963). A further follow-up comparison of psychotherapeutic programs. *Journal of Consulting Psychology, 27,* 186.

Fairweather, G. W., Simon, R., Gebhard, M. E., Weingarten, E., Holland, J. I., Sanders, R., Stone, G. B., & Reahl, J. E. (1960). Relative effectiveness of psychotherapeutic programs: A multicriteria comparison of four programs for three different patient groups. *Psychological Monographs, 74* (Whole No. 492).

Fantuzzo, J. W., & Clement, P. W. (1981). Generalization of the effects of teacher and self-administered token reinforcers to nontreated students. *Journal of Applied Behavior Analysis, 14,* 435–447.

Farber, I. E. (1963). The things people say to themselves. *American Psychologist, 18,* 185–197.

Farina, A., Arenberg, D., & Guskin, S. (1957). A scale for measuring minimal social behavior. *Journal of Consulting Psychology, 21,* 265–268.

Farina, A., Gliha, D., Boudreau, L. A., Allen, J. G., & Sherman, M. (1971). Mental illness and the impact of believing others know about it. *Journal of Abnormal Psychology, 77,* 1–5.

Farina, A., & Ring, K. (1965). The influence of perceived mental illness on interpersonal relations. *Journal of Abnormal Psychology, 70,* 47–51.

Farrar, C. H., Powell, B. J., & Martin, L. K. (1968). Punishment of alcohol consumption by apneic paralysis. *Behaviour Research and Therapy, 6,* 13–16.

Fazio, A. F. (1970). Treatment components in implosive therapy. *Journal of Abnormal Psychology, 76,* 211–219.

Fehrenbach, P. A., & Thelen M. H. (1981). Assertive-skills training for inappropriately aggressive college males: Effects on assertive and aggressive behaviors. *Journal of Behavior Therapy and Experimental Psychiatry, 12,* 213–217.

Feldman, G. M. (1976). The effects of biofeedback training on respiratory resistance of asthmatic children. *Psychosomatic Medicine, 38,* 27–34.

Feldman, M. P., & MacCulloch, M. J. (1965). The application of anticipatory avoidance learning to the treatment of homosexuality. 1. Theory, technique, and preliminary results. *Behaviour Research and Therapy, 2,* 165–183.

Feldman, M. P., & MacCulloch, M. J. (1971). *Homosexual behaviour: Therapy and assessment.* Oxford: Pergamon.

Feldman, R. B., & Werry, J. S. (1966). An unsuccessful attempt to treat a tiqueur by massed practice. *Behaviour Research and Therapy, 4,* 111–117.

Felixbrod, J. J., & O'Leary, K. D. (1973). Effects of reinforcement on children's academic behavior as a function of self determined and externally imposed contingencies. *Journal of Applied Behavior Analysis, 6,* 241–250.

Felixbrod, J. J., & O'Leary, K. D. (1974). Self determination of academic standards by children. *Journal of Educational Psychology, 66,* 845–850.

Fenichel, O. (1945). *The psychoanalytic theory of neurosis.* New York: Norton.

Ferguson, J. M. (1975). A clinical program for the behavioral control of obesity. In B. J. Williams, S. Martin, & J. P. Foreyt (Eds.), *Obesity: Behavioral approaches to dietary management.* New York: Brunner/Mazel.

Ferritor, D. C., Buckholt, D. Hamblin, R. L., & Smith, L. (1972). The non-effects of contingent reinforcement for attending behavior on work accomplished. *Journal of Applied Behavior Analysis, 5,* 7–18.

Ferster, C. B., Nurnberger, J. I., & Levitt, E. B. (1962). The control of eating. *Journal of Mathematics, 1,* 87–109.

Ferster, C. B., & Skinner, B. F. (1957). *Schedules of reinforcement.* New York: Appleton.

Feshbach, S. (1970). *Aggression.* In P. H. Mussen (Ed.), *Carmichael's manual of child psychology* (Vol. 2). New York: Wiley.

Festinger, L. (1957). *A theory of cognitive dissonance.* Stanford, CA: Stanford University Press.

Festinger, L. (1964). Behavioral support for opinion change. *Public Opinion Quarterly, 28,* 404–417.

Festinger, L., & Carlsmith, J. M. (1959). Cognitive consequences of forced compliance. *Journal of Abnormal and Social Psychology, 58,* 203–210.

Feuerstein, M., & Adams, H. E. (1977). Cephalic vasomotor feedback in the modification of migraine headache. *Biofeedback and Self-regulation, 2,* 241–254.

Fey, S. G., & Lindholm, E. (1975). Systolic blood pressure and heart rate changes during three sessions involving biofeedback or no feedback. *Psychophysiology, 12,* 513–519.

Fichter, M. M., Wallace, C. J., Liberman, R. P., & Davis, J. R. (1976). Improving social interaction in a chronic psychotic using discriminated avoidance ("nagging"): Experimental analysis and generalization, *Journal of Applied Behavior Analysis, 9,* 377–386.

Finch, A. J., Jr., & Montgomery, L. E. (1973). Reflection-impulsivity and information seeking in emotionally disturbed children. *Journal of Abnormal Child Psychology, 1,* 358–362.

Finch, A. J., Jr., Wilkinson, M. D., Nelson, W. M., III, & Montgomery, L. E. (1975). Modification of an impulsive cognitive tempo in emotionally disturbed boys. *Journal of Abnormal Child Psychology, 3,* 49–52.

Finley, W. W. (1976). Effects of sham feedback following successful SMR training in an epileptic: Follow up study. *Biofeedback and Self Regulation, 1,* 227–235.

Finley, W. W., Smith, H. A., & Etherton, M. D. (1975). Reduction of seizures and normalization of EEG in a severe epileptic following biofeedback training. *Biological Psychology, 2,* 195–209.

Finley, W. W., Wansley, R. A., & Blenkarn, M. M. (1977). Conditioning treatment of enuresis using a 70% intermittent reinforcement schedule. *Behaviour Research and Therapy, 15,* 419–427.

Fischer, J., & Nehs, R. (1978). Use of commonly available chore to reduce a boy's rate of swearing. *Journal of Behavior Therapy and Experimental Psychiatry, 9,* 81–83.

Fisher, E. B., Jr. (1979). Overjustification effects in to-

ken economies. *Journal of Applied Behavior Analysis, 12,* 407–415.

Fisher, E. B., Delmater, A. M., Bertelson, A. D., & Kirkley, B. G. (1982). Psychological factors in diabetes and its treatment. *Journal of Consulting and Clinical Psychology, 50,* 993–1003.

Fisher, E. B., & Winkler, R. C. (1975). Self control over intrusive experiences. *Journal of Consulting and Clinical Psychology, 43*(6), 911–916.

Fisher-Beckfield, D., & McFall, R. M. (1982). Development of a competence inventory for college men and evaluation of relationships between competence and depression. *Journal of Consulting and Clinical Psychology, 50,* 697–705.

Fishman, H. C. (1937). A study of the efficiency of negative practice as a corrective for stammering. *Journal of Speech Disorders, 2,* 67–72.

Fixsen, D. L., Phillips, E. L., & Wolf, M. M. (1972). Achievement place: The reliability of self-reporting and peer-reporting and their effects on behavior. *Journal of Applied Behavior Analysis, 5,* 19–30.

Flannery, R. (1970). *An investigation of differential effectiveness of office vs. in vivo therapy of a simple phobia: An outcome study.* Unpublished doctoral dissertation, University of Windsor.

Fordyce, W. E. (1976). *Behavioral methods for chronic pain and illness.* St. Louis: Mosby.

Fordyce, W. E., Fowler, R. S., Jr., Lehmann, J. F., DeLateur, B. J., Sand, P. L., & Trieschmann, R. B. (1973). Operant conditioning in the treatment of chronic pain. *Archives of physical medicine and rehabilitation, 54,* 399–408.

Forehand, R., & Atkeson, B. M. (1977). Generality of treatment effects with parents as therapists: A review of assessment and implementation procedures. *Behavior Therapy, 8,* 575–593.

Foreyt, J. P., Goodrick, G. K., & Gotto, A. M. (1981). Limitations of behavioral treatment of obesity: Review and analysis. *Journal of Behavioral Medicine, 4,* 159–174.

Foreyt, J. P., & Hagen, R. L. (1973). Covert sensitization: Conditioning or suggestions? *Journal of Abnormal Psychology, 82*(1), 17–23.

Foreyt, J. P., & Kennedy, W. A. (1971). Treatment of overweight by aversion therapy. *Behaviour Research and Therapy, 9,* 29–34.

Foreyt, J. P., Mitchell, R. E., Garner, D. T., Gee, M., Scott, L. W., & Gotto, A. M. (1982). Behavioral treatment of obesity: Results and limitations. *Behavior Therapy, 13,* 153–161.

Foreman, S. A. (1980). A comparison of cognitive training and response cost procedures in modifying aggressive behavior of elementary school children. *Behavior Therapy, 11,* 594–600.

Fowler, R. D., (1986, May). Howard Hughes: A psychological autopsy. *Anthropology 2nd Education Quarterly, 20*(5), 22–23.

Fowler, S. A., & Baer, D. M. (1981). "Do I have to be good all day?" The timing of delayed reinforcement as a factor in generalization, *Journal of Applied Behavior Analysis, 14,* 13–24.

Fox, L. (1962). Effecting the use of efficient study habits. *Journal of Mathematics, 1,* 75–86.

Fox, R. M., & Hake, D. F. (1977). Gasoline conservation: A procedure for measuring and reducing the driving of college students. *Journal of Applied Behavior Analysis, 10,* 61–74.

Foxx, C. L., Foxx, R. M., Jones, J. R., & Keily, D. (1980). Twenty-four hour social isolation. *Behavior Modification, 4,* 130–144.

Foxx, R. M., & Axelroth, E. (1983). Nicotine fading, self-monitoring and cigarette fading to produce cigarette abstinence of controlled smoking. *Behaviour Research and Therapy, 21,* 111–125.

Foxx, R. M., & Azrin, N. H. (1972). Restitution: A method of eliminating aggressive-disruptive behavior of retarded and brain-damaged individuals. *Behaviour Research and Therapy, 10,* 15–27.

Foxx, R. M., & Azrin, N. H. (1973). The elimination of autistic self-stimulatory behavior by overcorrection. *Journal of Applied Behavior Analysis, 6,* 1–4.

Foxx, R. M., & Brown, R. A. (1979). Nicotine fading and self-monitoring for cigarette abstinence or controlled smoking. *Journal of Applied Behavior Analysis, 12,* 111–125.

Foxx, R. M., & Shapiro, S. T. (1978). The timeout ribbon: A nonexclusionary timeout procedure. *Journal of Applied Behavior Analysis, 11,* 125–136.

Foy, D. W., Eisler, R. M., & Pinkston, S. (1975). Modeled assertion in a case of explosive rages. *Journal of Behavior Therapy and Experimental Psychiatry, 6,* 135–138.

Foy, D. W., Nunn, L. B., & Rychtarik, R. G. (1984). Broad-spectrum behavioral treatment for chronic alcoholics: Effects of training controlled drinking sills. *Journal of Abnormal Psychology, 52,* 218–230.

Frame, C., Matson, J. L., Sonis, W. A., Fialkoo, M. J., & Kazdin, A. E. (1982). Behavioral treatment of depression in a prepubertal child. *Journal of Behavior Therapy and Experimental Psychiatry, 13,* 239–243.

Framer, E. M., & Sanders, S. H. (1980). The effects of family contingency contracting on disturbed sleeping behaviors in a male adolescent. *Journal of Behavior Therapy and Experimental Psychiatry, 11,* 235–237.

Franchina, J. J., Hauser, P. J., & Agee, C. M. (1975). Persistence of response prevention effects following retraining of escape behavior. *Behaviour Research and Therapy, 13,* 1–6.

Franchina, J. J., Hauser, P. J., & Agee, C. M. (1975). *Per therapy assessment.* New York: Springer-Verlag.

Frankel, P. B. (1977). A factor analytic study of measures of assertiveness. *Dissertation Abstracts International, 37,* 4676–4677B.

Frankosky, R. J., & Sulzer-Azaroff, B. (1978). Individual and group contingencies and collateral social behaviors. *Behavior Therapy, 9,* 313–327.

Franks, C. M. (1963). Behavior therapy, the principles of conditioning and the treatment of the alcoholic. *Quarterly Journal of Studies on Alcohol, 24,* 511–529.

Franks, C. M. (1966). Conditioning and conditioned aversion therapies in the treatment of the alcoholic. *International Journal of Addictions, 1,* 61–98.

Franks, C. M. (Ed.). (1969a). *Behavior therapy: Appraisal and status.* New York: McGraw-Hill.

Franks, C. M. (Ed.) (1969b). Introduction: Behavior therapy and its Pavlovian origins: Review and perspectives. In *Behavior therapy: Appraisal and status.* New York: McGraw-Hill.

Franks, C. M. (1973). *Persuasion and healing* (2nd ed.). Baltimore: Johns Hopkins University Press.

Franks, C. M. (1976). Foreword. In E. J. Mash & L. G. Terdal (Eds.), *Behavior therapy assessment.* New York: Springer-Verlag.

Franks, C. M., Fried, R., & Ashem, B. (1966). An improved apparatus for the aversive conditioning of cigarette smokers. *Behaviour Research and Therapy, 4,* 301–308.

Franzini, L. R., & Tilker, H. A. (1972). On the terminological confusion between behavior therapy and behavior modification. *Behavior Therapy, 3,* 279–282.

Frederiksen, L. W. (1979). Controlled smoking. In N. A. Krasnegor (Ed.), *Behavioral analysis and treatment of substance abuse.* (Research Monograph 25, pp. 128–139; DHEW Publication No. ADM

79–839). Washington, DC: U.S. Government Printing Office.

Frederiksen, L. W., Jenkins, J. O., & Carr, C. R. (1976). Indirect modification of adolescent drug abuse using contingency contracting. *Journal of Behavior Therapy and Experimental Psychiatry, 7,* 377–378.

Frederikson, L. W., & Simon, S. J. (1978a). Modification of smoking topography: A preliminary analysis. *Behavior Therapy, 9,* 146–149.

Frederikson, L. W., & Simon, S. J. (1978b). Modifying how people smoke: Instructional control and generalization. *Journal of Applied Behavior Analysis, 11,* 431–432.

Freedman, B. J., Rosenthal, L., Donahoe, C. P., Jr., Schlundt, D. G., & McFall, R. M. (1978). A social-behavioral analysis of skill deficits in delinquent and nondelinquent adolescent boys. *Journal of Consulting and Clinical Psychology, 46,* 1448–1462.

Freedman, R. R., Ianni, P., Hale, P., & Lynn, S. (1979). Treatment of Raynaud's phenomenon with biofeedback and cold desensitization. *Psychophysiology, 16,* 182 (abstract).

Freedman, R. R., Ianni, P., & Wenig, P. (1983). Behavioral treatment of Raynaud's disease. *Journal of Consulting and Clinical Psychology, 51,* 539–549.

Freedman, R. R., Lynn, S. J., & Ianni, P. (1978). Biofeedback treatment of Raynaud's phenomenon. *Biofeedback and Self-regulation, 3,* 320 (abstract).

Freedman, R. R., Lynn, S. J., Ianni, P., & Hale, P. A. (1981). Biofeedback treatment of Raynaud's disease and phenomenon. *Biofeedback and Self-regulation, 6,* 355–365.

Freeman, W., & Meyer, R. G. (1975). A behavioral alteration of sexual preferences in the human male. *Behavior Therapy, 6,* 206–212.

Fremouw, W. J., & Brown, J. P. (1980). The reactivity of addictive behaviors to self-monitoring: A functional analysis. *Addictive Behaviors, 5,* 209–217.

Fremouw, W. J., & Zitter, R. E. (1978). A comparison of skills training and cognitive restructuring-relaxation for the treatment of speech anxiety. *Behavior Therapy, 1978, 9,* 248–259.

Fremouw, W. J., & Zitter, R. E. (1980). Individual and couple behavioral contracting for weight reduction and maintenance. *Behavior Therapist, 3,* 15–16.

Freud, S. (1922–1923). Two encylopedic articles: Psychoanalysis. *Standard Edition, 18,* 235–254.

Freund, K. (1960). Some problems in the treatment of homosexuality. In H. J. Eysenck (Ed.), *Behaviour therapy and the neuroses.* Oxford: Pergamon.

Freund, K. (1977). Psychophysiological assessment of change in erotic preferences. *Behaviour Research and Therapy, 15,* 297–301.

Friar, L. R., & Beatty, J. (1976). Migraine: Management by trained control of vasoconstriction. *Journal of Consulting and Clinical Psychology, 44,* 46–53.

Friedman, P. H. (1968). *The effects of modeling and role playing on assertive behavior.* Unpublished doctoral dissertation, University of Wisconsin, Madison.

Fromer, R., & Berkowitz, L. (1964). Effect of sudden and gradual shock onset on the conditioned fear response. *Journal of Comparative and Physiological Psychology, 57,* 154–155.

Fuchs, C. Z., & Rehm, L. P. (1977). Self-control depression program. *Journal of Consulting and Clinical Psychology, 45(2),* 206–215.

Fudge, R., & Adams, H. E. (1985). The effects of discrimination training on voluntary control of cephalic vasomotor activity. *Psychophysiology, 22,* 300–306.

Funch, D. P., & Gale, E. N. (1984). Biofeedback and relaxation therapy for chronic temporomandibular joint pain: Predicting successful outcomes. *Journal of Consulting and Clinical Psychology, 52,* 928–935.

Furman, S. (1973). Intestinal biofeedback in functional diarrhea: A preliminary report. *Journal of Behavior Therapy and Experimental Psychiatry, 4,* 317–321.

Futch, E. J., Scheirer, C. J., & Lisman, S. A. (1982). Factor analyzing a scale of assertiveness: A critque and demonstration. *Behavior Modification, 6,* 23–43.

Galassi, J. P. (Review of Dawley, H. H., & Wenrick, W. W. (1978). *Achieving assertive behavior: A guide to assertive training.* Monterey, CA: Brooks/Cole, 1976). *Behavior Research, 9,* 132–133.

Galassi, J. P., DeLo, J. S., Galassi, M. D., Bastien, S. (1974). The College Self-Expression Scale: A measure of assertiveness. *Behavior Therapy, 5,* 165–171.

Galassi, M. D., & Galassi, J. P. (1977). *Assert yourself: How to be your own person.* New York: Human Sciences Press.

Galbraith, D. A., Byrick, R. J., & Rutledge, J. T. (1970). An aversive conditioning approach to the inhibition of chronic vomiting. *Canadian Psychiatric Association Journal, 1970, 15,* 311–313.

Gallagher, J. J. (1953). MMPI changes concomitant

with client-centered therapy. *Journal of Consulting Psychology, 17,* 443–446.

Gambrill, E. D. (1985). Assertiveness training. In A. S. Bellack & M. Hersen (Eds.), *Dictionary of behavior therapy techniques.* New York: Pergamon.

Gambrill, E. D., & Richey, C. A. (1975). An assertion inventory for use in assessment and research. *Behavior Therapy, 6,* 550–561.

Gannon, L. & Sternbach, R. A. (1971). Alpha enhancement as a treatment for pain. A case study. *Journal of Behavior Therapy and Experimental Psychiatry, 2,* 209–211.

Garber, J., Hollon, S. D., & Silverman, V. (1979, December). *Evaluation and reward of self vs. others in depression.* Paper presented at the meeting of the Association for the Advancement of Behavior, San Francisco.

Garcia, E., Baer, D. M., & Firestone, I. (1971). The development of generalized imitation within topographically determined boundaries. *Journal of Applied Behavior Analysis, 4,* 101–112.

Gardner, J. E. (1967). Behavior therapy treatment approach to a psychogenic seizure case. *Journal of Consulting Psychology, 31,* 209–212.

Garfield, Z. H., Darwin, P. L., Singer, B. A., & McBreaty, J. F. (1967). Effect of "in vivo" training on experimental desensitization of a phobia. *Psychological Reports, 20,* 515–519.

Garfield, Z. H., McBreaty, J. F., & Dichter, M. (1969). A case of impotence treated with desensitization combined with *in vivo* operant training and thought substitution. In R. D. Rubin & C. M. Franks (Eds.), *Advances in behavior therapy.* New York: Academic Press.

Garlington, W. K., & Dericco, D. A. (1977). The effects of modeling on drinking rate. *Journal of Applied Behavior Analysis, 10,* 207–211.

Gatchel, R. J. (1980). Effectiveness of two procedures for reducing dental fear: Group-administered desensitization and group education and discussion. *Journal of the American Dental Association, 101,* 634–637.

Gatchel, R. J., & Baum, A. (1983). *An introduction to health psychology.* Reading, MA: Addison-Wesley.

Gatchel, R. J., Hatch, J. P., Watson, P. J., Smith, D., & Gaas, E. (1977). Comparative effectiveness of voluntary heart rate control and muscular relaxation as active coping skills for reduction speech anxiety. *Journal of Clinical and Consulting Psychology 45,* 1093–1100.

Gaupp, L. A., Stern, R. M., & Galbraith, G. G. (1972).

False heartrate feedback and reciprocal inhibition by aversion relief in the treatment of snake avoidance behavior. *Behavior Therapy, 3,* 7–20.

Gauthier, J., Bois, R., Allaire, D., & Drolet, M. (1981). Evaluation of skin temperature biofeedback training at two different sites for migraine. *Journal of Behavioral Medicine, 4,* 407–419.

Gauthier, J., Doyon, J., Lacroix, R., & Drolet, M. (1983). Blood volume pulse biofeedback in the treatment of migraine headache: A controlled evaluation. *Biofeedback and Self-regulation, 8,* 427–442.

Gauthier, J., & Pellerin, D. (1982). Management of compulsive shoplifting through covert sensitization. *Journal of Behavior Therapy and Experimental Psychiatry, 13*(1), 73–75.

Gay, M. L., Hollandsworth, J. G., & Galassi, J. P. (1975). An assertiveness inventory for adults. *Journal of Counseling Psychology, 22,* 340–344.

Gaylon, W. (1973, October). Skinner redux. *Harper's Magazine,* pp. 48–56.

Geer, J. H. (1965). The development of a scale to measure fear. *Behaviour Research and Therapy, 3,* 45–53.

Geis, H. J. (1971). Rational emotive therapy with a culturally deprived teenager. In A. Ellis (Ed.), *Growth through reason.* Palo Alto, CA: Science & Behavior Books.

Gelder, M. G., Bancroft, J. H. J., Gath, D. H., Johnston, D. W., Mathews, A. M., & Shaw, P. M. (1973). Specific and non-specific factors in behavior therapy. *British Journal of Psychiatry, 123,* 445–462.

Gelfand, D. M., Gelfand, S., & Dobson, W. R. (1967). Unprogrammed reinforcement of patients' behavior in a mental hospital. *Behaviour Research and Therapy, 5,* 201–207.

Geller, S. E. (1984). A delayed reward strategy for large scale motivation of safety belt use: A test of long-term impact. *Accident Analysis and Prevention, 16,* 457–463.

Gershman, L. (1970). Case conference: A transvestite fantasy treated by thought-stopping, covert sensitization, and aversive shock. *Journal of Behavior Therapy and Experimental Psychiatry, 1,* 153–161.

Gesell, A. (1938). The conditioned reflex and the psychiatry of infancy. *American Journal of Orthopsychiatry, 8,* 19–30.

Gewirtz, J. L., & Baer, D. M. (1958a). The effect of brief social deprivation on behaviors for a social reinforcer. *Journal of Abnormal and Social Psychology, 56,* 549–556.

Gewirtz, J. L., & Baer, D. M. (1958b). Deprivation and

satiation of social reinforcers as drive conditions. *Journal of Abnormal and Social Psychology, 57,* 165–172.

Giles, D. K., & Wolf, M. M. (1966). Toilet training in institutionalized, severe retardate: An application of operant behavior modification techniques. *American Journal of Mental Deficiency, 70,* 766–780.

Gill, M. M. (Ed.). (1967). *The collected papers of David Rapaport.* New York: Basic Books.

Girardeau, F. L., & Spradlin, J. E. (1964). Token rewards in a cottage program. *Mental Retardation, 2,* 345–351.

Girodo, M. (1974). Yoga meditation and flooding in the treatment of anxiety neurosis. *Journal of Behavior Therapy and Experimental Psychiatry, 5,* 157–160.

Girodo, M., & Roehl, J. (1978). Cognitive preparation and coping self-talk: Anxiety management during the stress of flying. *Journal of Consulting and Clinical Psychology, 46,* 978–989.

Gittelman, M. (1965). Behavior rehearsal as a technique in child treatment. *Journal of Child Psychology and Psychiatry, 6,* 251–255.

Gladstone, B. W., & Sherman, J. (1975). Developing generalized behavior-modification skills in high-school students working with retarded children. *Journal of Applied Behavior Analysis, 8,* 169–180.

Gladstone, B. W., & Spencer, C. J. (1977). The effects of modeling on the contingent praise of mental retardation counselors. *Journal of Applied Behavior Analysis, 10,* 75–84.

Glaros, A. G., & Rao, S. M. (1977). Bruxism: A critical review. *Psychological Bulletin, 84,* 767–781.

Glasgow, M. S., Gaardoner, K. R., & Engle, B. T. (1982). Behavioral treatment of high blood pressure. II: Acute and sustained effects of relaxation and systolic blood pressure biofeedback. *Psychosomatic Medicine, 44,* 155–170.

Glasgow, R. E. (1975). In vivo prolonged exposure in the treatment of urinary retention. *Behavior Therapy, 6,* 701–702.

Glasgow, R. E. (1978). Effects of a self-control manual, rapid smoking, and amount of therapist contact on smoking reduction. *Journal of Consulting and Clinical Psychology, 46,* 1439–1447.

Glasgow, R. E., Klesges, R. C., Godding, P. R., & Gegelman, R. (1983). Controlled smoking, with or without carbon monoxide feedback, as an alternative for chronic smokers. *Behavior Therapy, 14,* 386–397.

Glasgow, R. E., Klesges, R. C., Godding, P. R., Vasey, M. W., & O'Neill, H. K. (1984). Evaluation of a worksite-controlled smoking program. *Journal of Consulting and Clinical Psychology, 52,* 137–138.

Glass, C. R., Gottman, J. M, & Shmurak, S. H. (1976). Response acquisition and cognitive self-statement modification approaches to dating skills training. *Journal of Counseling Psychology, 23,* 520–526.

Glogower, F. D., Fremouw, W. J., & McCroskey, J. C. (1978). A component analysis of cognitive restructuring. *Cognitive Therapy and Research, 2,* 209–224.

Glogower, F. D., & Sloop, E. W. (1976). Two strategies of group training of parents as effective behavior modifiers. *Behavior Therapy, 7,* 177–184.

Glover, J., & Gary, A. L. (1976). Procedures to increase some aspects of creativity. *Journal of Applied Behavior Analysis, 9,* 79–84.

Glynn, E. L., Thomas, J. D., & Shee, S. M. (1973). Behavioral self-control of on-task behavior in an elementary classroom. *Journal of Applied Behavior Analysis, 6,* 105–113.

Glynn, J. D., & Harper, P. (1961). Behaviour therapy in transvestism. *Lancet, 1,* 619.

Gnagey, T. D. (1975). *How to put up with parents: A guide for teenagers.* Ottawa, IL: Facilitation House.

Goetz, E. M., & Baer, D. M. (1973). Social control of form diversity and the emergence of new forms in children's blockbuilding. *Journal of Applied Behavior Analysis, 6,* 209–217.

Goetz, E. M., Holmberg, M. C., & LeBlanc, J. M. (1975). Differential reinforcement of other behavior and noncontingent reinforcement as control procedures during the modification of a preschooler's compliance. *Journal of Applied Behavior Analysis, 8,* 77–82.

Gold, S., & Neufeld, I. L. (1965). A learning approach to the treatment of homosexuality. *Behaviour Research and Therapy, 3,* 201–204.

Goldblatt, M., & Munitz, H. (1976). Behavioral treatment of hysterical leg paralysis. *Journal of Behavior Therapy and Experimental Psychology, 7,* 259–263.

Goldenberg, H. (1983). *Contemporary clinical psychology* (2nd ed.). Monterey, CA: Brooks/Cole.

Goldfried, M. R. (1971). Systematic desensitization as training in self-control. *Journal of Consulting and Clinical Psychology, 37,* 228–234.

Goldfried, M. R., DeCanteceo, E. T., & Weinberg, L. (1974). Systematic rational restructuring as a self control technique. *Behavior Therapy, 5,* 247–254.

Goldfried, M. R., & Davison, G. C. (1976). *Clinical behavior therapy.* New York: Holt.

Goldfried, M. R., & Goldfried, A. P. (1975). Cognitive change methods. In F. Kanfer & A. Goldstein

(Eds.), *Helping people change*. Oxford: Pergamon Press.

Goldfried, M. R., & Goldfried, A. P. (1977). Importance of hierarchy content in the self-control of anxiety. *Journal of Consulting and Clinical Psychology, 45,* 124–134.

Goldfried, M. R., & Kent, R. N. (1972). Traditional versus behavioral assessment: A comparison of methodological and theoretical assumptions. *Psychological Bulletin, 77,* 409–420.

Goldfried, M. R., Linehan, M. M., & Smith, J. L. (1978). Reduction of test anxiety through cognitive restructuring. *Journal of Consulting and Clinical Psychology, 46,* 32–39.

Goldfried, M. R., & Merbaum, M. (Eds.). (1973). *Behavior change through self-control.* New York: Holt.

Goldfried, M. R., & Robins, C. (1982). On the facilitation of self-efficacy. *Cognitive Therapy and Research, 6,* 361–380.

Goldfried, M. R., & Robins, C. (1983). Self-schema, cognitive bias, and the processing of therapeutic experiences. In P. C. Kendall (Ed.), *Advances in cognitive-behavioral research and therapy* (Vol. 2). New York: Academic Press.

Goldfried, M. R., & Trier, C. (1974). Effectiveness of relaxation as an active coping skill. *Journal of Abnormal Psychology, 83,* 348–355.

Goldiamond, I. (1965). Self-control procedures in personal behavior problems. *Psychological Reports, 17,* 851–868.

Goldiamond, I. (1976). Self-reinforcement. *Journal of Applied Behavior Analysis, 9,* 509–514.

Goldsmith, J. B., & McFall, R. M. (1975). Development and evaluation of an interpersonal-skill training program for psychiatric inpatients. *Journal of Abnormal Psychology, 84,* 51–58.

Goldstein, A. P., & Kanfer, F. H. (Eds.). (1979). *Maximizing treatment gains: Transfer enhancement in psychotherapy,* New York: Academic Press.

Goldstein, A. P., Martens, J., Hubben, J., van Belle, H. A., Schaaf, W., Wiersma, H., & Goedhart, A. (1973). The use of modeling to increase independent behavior. *Behaviour Research and Therapy, 11,* 31–42.

Goldstein, S., Gordon, J. R., & Marlatt, G. A. (1984). *Attributional processes and relapse following smoking cessation.* Paper presented at the meeting of the American Psychological Association, Toronto.

Golin, S., Terrel, F., & Johnson, B. (1977). Depression and the illusion of control. *Journal of Abnormal Psychology, 86,* (4), 440–442.

Goodwin, S. E., & Mahoney, M. J. (1975). Modification of aggression through modeling: An experimental probe. *Journal of Behavior Therapy and Experimental Psychiatry, 6,* 200–202.

Gordova, T. N., & Kovalev, N.K. (1961). Unique factors in the hypnotic treatment of alcoholism. In R. B. Winn (Ed.), *Psychotherapy in the Soviet Union.* New York: Philosophical Library.

Goren, E. (1975). *A comparison of systematic desensitization and self-instruction in the treatment of phobias.* Unpublished Masters Thesis, Rutgers University.

Gormally, J. (1982). Evaluation of assertiveness: Effects of gender, rater involvement, and level of assertiveness. *Behavior Therapy, 13,* 219–225.

Gormally, J. Rardin, D., & Black, S. (1980). Correlates of successful response to a behavioral weight control clinic. *Journal of Counseling Psychology, 27,* 179–191.

Götestam, K. G., & Melin, L. (1974). Covert extinction of amphetamine-dependent addiction. *Behavior Therapy, 5,* 90–92.

Grace, W. J., & Graham, D. T. (1952). Relationship of specific attitudes and emotions to certain bodily diseases. *Psychosomatic Medicine, 14,* 243–251.

Grady, K. E. (1984). Cue enhancement and the long-term practice of breast self-examination. *Journal of Behavioral Medicine, 7,* 191–204.

Graham, L. E., II, Taylor, C. B., Hovell, M. F., & Siegel, W. (1983). Five-year follow-up to a behavioral weight loss program. *Journal of Consulting and Clinical Psychology, 51,* 322–323.

Grandy, G. W., Madsen, C. H., Jr., & deMersseman, L. M. (1973). The effects of individual and interdependent contingencies on inappropriate classroom behavior. *Psychology in the Schools, 10,* 488–492.

Gray, J. (1971). *The psychology of fear and stress.* London: World University Library.

Green, E. E., Green, A. M., & Norris, P. A. (1980, March). Self-regulation training for control of hypertension. *Primary Cardiology,* 126–127.

Green, L. (1978). Temporal and stimulus factors in self monitoring by obese persons. *Behavior Therapy, 9,* 328–341.

Green, R. W. (1978). Self-regulated eating behaviors in a diabetic mental patient. *Behavior Therapy, 9,* 521–525.

Greenspoon, J. (1955). The reinforcing effect of two spoken sounds on the frequency of two responses. *American Journal of Psychology, 68,* 409–416.

Greenspoon, J. (1962). Verbal conditioning in clinical

psychology. In A. J. Bachrach (Ed.), *Experimental foundations of clinical psychology.* New York: Basic Books.

Greenwood, C. R., Sloane, H. N., Jr., & Baskin, A. (1974). Training elementary aged peer-behavior managers to control small group programmed mathematics. *Journal of Applied Behavior Analysis, 7,* 103–114.

Greiner, J. M., & Karoly, P. (1976). Effects of self-control training on study activity and academic performance: An analysis of self monitoring, self reward, and systematic planning components. *Journal of Counseling Psychology, 23*(6), 495–502.

Griffin, J. C., Locke, B. J., & Landers, W. F. (1975). Manipulation of potential punishment parameters in the treatment of self-injury. *Journal of Applied Behavior Analysis, 8,* 458.

Griffiths, R. D. P. (1974). Videotape feedback as a therapeutic technique: Retrospect and prospect. *Behaviour Research and Therapy, 12,* 1–8.

Griffiths, R. R., Bigelow, G., & Liebson, I. (1977). Comparison of social time-out and activity time-out procedures in suppressing ethanol self-administration in alcoholics. *Behaviour Research and Therapy, 15,* 329–336.

Grimm, L. G. (1980). The evidence for cue-controlled relaxation. *Behavior Therapy, 11,* 283–293.

Grimm, L. G. (1983). The relation between self-evaluation and self-reward: A test of Kanfer's self-regulation model. *Cognitive Therapy and Research, 7,* 245–250.

Grimm, L. G., & Yarnold, P. P. (1984). Performance standards and the type A behavior pattern. *Cognitive Therapy and Research, 8,* 59–66.

Grinc, G. A. (1982). A cognitive-behavioral model for the treatment of chronic vomiting. *Journal of Behavioral Medicine, 5,* 135–141.

Grinker, R. R., & Spiegel, J. P. (1945). *War neurosis.* New York: McGraw-Hill (Blakiston).

Gross, R. T., & Fremouw, W. J. (1982). Cognitive restructuring and progressive relaxation of treatment of empirical subtypes of speech-anxious subjects. *Cognitive Therapy and Research, 6,* 429–436.

Grossberg, J. M. (1965). Successful behavior therapy in a case of speech phobia ("Stage fright"). *Journal of Speech and Hearing Disorders, 30,* 285–288.

Grossberg, J. M., & Wilson, H. K. (1968). Physiological changes accompanying the visualization of fearful and neutral situations. *Journal of Personality and Social Psychology, 10,* 124–133.

Grusec, J. E., Kuczynski, L., Rushton, J. P., & Simutis, Z. M. (1978). Modeling, direct instruction, and attributions: Effects on altruism. *Developmental Psychology, 14,* 51–57.

Guglielmi, R. S., Roberts, A. H., & Patterson, R. (1982). Skin temperature biofeedback for Raynaud's disease: A double-blind study. *Biofeedback and Self-regulation, 7,* 99–120.

Guidry, L. S. (1975). Use of a covert punishing contingency in compulsive stealing. *Journal of Behavior Therapy and Experimental Psychiatry, 6,* 169.

Guitar, B. (1975). Reduction of stuttering frequency using analogue electromyographic feedback. *Journal of Speech & Hearing Research, 18,* 672–685.

Gulanick, N., Woodburn, L. T., & Rimm, D. C. (1975). Weight gain through self-control procedures. *Journal of Consulting and Clinical Psychology, 43*(4), 536–539.

Gullo, J. M. (1971). A husband and wife who have not had intercourse during thirteen years of marriage. In A. Ellis (Ed.), *Growth through reason.* Palo Alto, CA: Science & Behavior Books.

Guralnick, M. J. (1976). Solving complex discrimination problems: Techniques for the development of problem solving strategies. *American Journal of Mental Deficiency, 81,* 18–25.

Guthrie, E. R. (1952). *The psychology of learning.* New York: Harper.

Gutride, M. E., Goldstein, A. P., & Hunter, G. F. (1973). The use of modeling and roleplaying to increase social interaction among asocial psychiatric patients. *Journal of Consulting and Clinical Psychology, 40,* 408–415.

Gutride, M. E., Goldstein, A. P., Hunter, G. F., Carrol, S., Clark, L., Furia, R., & Lower, W. (1974). Structured learning therapy with transfer training for chronic inpatients. *Journal of Clinical Psychology, 30,* 277–279.

Hackmann, A., & McLean, C. (1975). A comparison of flooding and thought stopping in the treatment of obsessional neurosis. *Behaviour Research and Therapy, 13,* 263–269.

Hafner, R. J. (1982). Psychological treatment of essential hypertension: A controlled comparison of meditation and meditation plus biofeedback. *Biofeedback and Self-Regulation, 7,* 305–316.

Hagen, R. L. (1974). Group therapy versus bibliotherapy in weight reduction. *Behavior Therapy, 5,* 222–234.

Hagen, R. L., Foreyt, J. P., & Durham, T. W. (1976). The dropout problem: Reducing attrition in obesity research. *Behavior Therapy, 7,* 463–471.

Hain, J. D., Butcher, H. G., & Stevenson, I. (1966). Systematic desensitization therapy: An analysis of results in twenty-seven patients. *British Journal of Psychiatry, 112,* 295–307.

Hale, W. D., & Strickland, B. R. (1976). Induction of mood states and their effects on cognitive and social behaviors. *Journal of Consulting and Clinical Psychology, 44,* 155.

Hall, R. G., Sachs, D. P., & Hall, S. M. (1979). Medical risk and therapeutic effectiveness of rapid smoking. *Behavior Therapy, 10,* 249–259.

Hall, R. G., Sachs, D. P., Hall, S. M., & Benowitz, N. L. (1984). Two-year efficacy and safety of rapid smoking therapy in patients with cardiac and pulmonary disease. *Journal of Consulting and Clinical Psychology, 52,* 574–581.

Hall, R. V., Axelrod, S., Tyler, L., Grief, E., Jones F. C., & Robertson, R. (1972). Modification of behavior problems in the home with a parent as observer and experimenter. *Journal of Applied Behavior Analysis, 5,* 53–64.

Hall, R. V., Lund, D., & Jackson, D. (1968). Effects of teacher attention on study behavior. *Journal of Applied Behavior Analysis, 1,* 1–12.

Hall, R. V., Panyan, M., Rabon, D., & Brodin, M. (1968). Instructing beginning teachers in reinforcement procedures which improve classroom control. *Journal of Applied Behavior Analysis, 1,* 315–322.

Hall, S. M. (1972). Self-control and therapist-control in the behavioral treatment of overweight women. *Behaviour Research and Therapy, 10,* 59–68.

Hall, S. M., Hall, G. H., DeBoer, G., & O'Kulitch, P. (1977). Self and external management compared with psycho-therapy in the control of obesity. *Behaviour Research and Therapy, 15,* 89–95.

Hall, S. M., Hall, R. G. (1982). Clinical series in the behavioral treatment of obesity. *Health Psychology, 1,* 359–372.

Hall, S. M., Hall, R. G. (1985). Treatment of cigarette smoking. In J. R. Blumenthal & D. McKee (Eds.), *Applications in behavioral medicine and health psychology: A clinician's source book.* Sarasota: Professional Research Exchange.

Hall, S. M., Hall, R. G., Borden, B. I., & Hanson, R. W. (1975). *Behaviour Research and Therapy, 13,* 167–172.

Hall, S. M., Hall, R. G., Hanson, R. W., & Borden, B. I. (1974). Permanence of two self-managed treatments of overweight in university and community populations. *Journal of Consulting and Clinical Psychology, 42,* 781–786.

Hall, S. M., Rugg, D., Tunstall, C., & Jones, R. T. (1984). Preventing relapse to cigarette smoking by behavioral skill training. *Journal of Consulting and Clinical Psychology, 52,* 372–382.

Hallam, R., Rachman, S., & Falkowski, W. (1972). Subjective, attitudinal and physiological effects of electrical aversion therapy. *Behaviour Research and Therapy, 10,* 1–13.

Halmi, K. A., Falk, J. R., & Schwartz, E. (1981). Binge eating and vomiting: A survey of a college population. *Psychological Medicine, 11,* 697–706.

Halonen, J. S., & Passman, R. H. (1985). Relaxation training and expectations in the treatment of postpartum distress. *Journal of Clinical and Consulting Psychology, 53,* 839–845.

Halvorson, J. (1968). *The effects of stuttering frequency of paired punishment (response cost) with reinforcement.* Unpublished doctoral dissertation, University of Minnesota.

Hamilton, J., Stephens, L., & Allen, P. (1967). Controlling aggressive and destructive behavior in severely retarded institutionalized residents. *American Journal of Mental Deficiency, 71,* 852–856.

Hamilton, S. B., & Waldman, D. A. (1983). Self-modification of depression via cognitive-behavioral intervention strategies: A time series analysis. *Cognitive Therapy and Research, 7,* 99–105.

Hammen, C. L., Jacobs, M., Mayol, A., & Cochran, S. D. (1980). Dysfunctional cognitions and effectiveness of skills and cognitive-behavioral assertion training. *Journal of Consulting and Clinical Psychology, 48,* 685–695.

Hannie, T. J., Jr., & Adams, H. E. (1974). Modification of agitated depression by flooding: A preliminary study. *Journal of Behavior Therapy and Experimental Psychiatry, 5,* 161–166.

Hanson, R. W. (1974). *Effects of programmed learning and therapist-group contact in treating obesity.* Paper presented at the annual meeting of the Western Psychological Association, San Francisco.

Hanson, R. W., Borden, R. I., Hall, S. M., & Hall, R. G. (1976). Use of programmed instruction in teaching self-management skills to overweight adults. *Behavior Therapy, 7,* 366–373.

Hardyck, C., & Petrinovich, L. F. (1966). Feedback of speech muscle activity during silent reading. *Science, 54,* 1467–1468.

Harmatz, M. G., & Lapuc, P. (1968). Behavior

modification of overeating in a psychiatric population. *Journal of Consulting and Clinical Psychology, 32,* 383–387.

Harper, R. A. (1977). RET's place and influence in contemporary psychotherapy. In J. Wolfe & E. Brand (Eds.), *Twenty years of rational therapy.* New York: Institute for Rational Living.

Harris, G., & Johnson, S. B. (1980). Comparison of individualized covert modeling, self-control desensitization, and study skills training for alleviation of test anxiety. *Journal of Consulting and Clinical Psychology, 48,* 186–194.

Harris, M. B. (1969). Self-directed program for weight control: A pilot study. *Journal of Abnormal Psychology, 74,* 264–270.

Harris, M. B., & Bruner, C. G. (1971). A comparison of self-control and a contract procedure for weight control. *Behaviour Research and Therapy, 9,* 347–354.

Harris, M. G., & Hallbauer, E. S. (1973). Self-directed weight control through eating and exercise. *Behaviour Research and Therapy, 11,* 523–529.

Harris, R. T. (1983). Bulimarexia and related serious eating disorders with medical complications. *Annals of Internal Medicine, 99,* 800–807.

Harris, V. W., & Sherman, J. A. (1973a). Effects of peer tutoring and consequences on the math performance of elementary classroom students. *Journal of Applied Behavior Analysis, 6,* 587–597.

Harris, V. W., & Sherman, J. A. (1973b). Use and analysis of the "Good Behavior Game" to reduce disruptive classroom behavior. *Journal of Applied Behavior Analysis, 6,* 405–417.

Harris, V. W., & Sherman, J. A. (1974). Homework assignments, consequences, and classroom performance in social studies and mathematics. *Journal of Applied Behavior Analysis, 7,* 505–519.

Harrison, J. A., Carlsson, S. G., & Berggren, U. (1985). Research in clinical process and outcome methodology: Psychophysiology, systematic desensitization, and dental fear. *Journal of Behavior Therapy and Experimental Psychiatrty, 16,* 201–209.

Hart, B. M., Reynolds, N. J., Baer, D. M., Brawley, E. R., & Harris, F. R. (1968). Effect of contingent and non-contingent social reinforcement on the cooperative play of a preschool child. *Journal of Applied Behavior Analysis, 1,* 73–76.

Hart, J. D. (1984). Temperature biofeedback, frontal EMG biofeedback, and relaxation training in the treatment of migraine. *Biofeedback and Self-regulation, 9,* 84–85 (abstract).

Hart, J. D., & Cichanski, K. A. (1981). A comparison of frontal EMG biofeedback & neck EMG biofeedback in the treatment of muscle-contraction headache. *Biofeedback and Self-regulation, 6,* 63–74.

Hart, R. R. (1979). Utilization of token economy within a chronic dialysis unit. *Journal of Consulting and Clinical Psychology, 47,* 646–648.

Hartje, J. C. (1973). Premackian reinforcement of classroom behavior through topic sequencing. *Journal of Psychology, 84,* 61–74.

Hartman, L. M., & Ainsworth, K. D. (1980). Self-regulation of chronic pain. *Canadian Journal of Psychiatry, 25,* 38–43.

Harvey, J. R., Karan, O. C., Bhargara, D., & Morehouse, N. (1978). Relaxation training and cognitive behavioral procedures to reduce violent temper outbursts in a moderately retarded woman. *Journal of Behavior Therapy and Experimental Psychiatry, 9,* 347–351.

Hathaway, S. R., McKinley, J. C. (1951). *The Minnesota Multiphasic Personality Inventory Manual.* New York: Psychological Corporation.

Hatzenbeuhler, L. C., & Schroeder, H. E. (1978). Desensitization procedures in the treatment of childhood disorders. *Psychological Bulletin, 85,* 831–844.

Hausen, R. (1974). Rapid smoking as a technique of behavior modification: Caution in selection of subjects. *Journal of Consulting and Clinical Psychology, 42,* 625–626.

Hawkins, R. P., Peterson, R. F., Schweid, E., & Bijou, S. W. (1966). Behavior therapy in the home: Amelioration of problem parent-child relations with the parent in a therapeutic role. *Journal of Experimental Child Psychology, 4,* 99–107.

Hay, W. M., Hay, L. R., & Nelson, R. O. (1977a). The adaptation of covert modeling procedures to the treatment of chronic alcoholism and obsessive-compulsive behavior: Two case reports. *Behavior Therapy, 8,* 70–76.

Hay, W. M., Hay, L. R., & Nelson, R. O. (1977b). Direct and collateral changes in on-task and academic behavior resulting from on-task versus academic contingencies. *Behavior Therapy, 8,* 431–441.

Hayes, S. C., & Cavior, N. (1977). Multiple tracking and the reactivity of self-monitoring. *Behavior Therapy, 8,* 819–831.

Hayes, S. C., & Cone, J. D. (1977). Reducing residential electrical energy use: Payments, information, and feedback. *Journal of Applied Behavior Analysis, 10,* 425–435.

Hayes, S. C., & Nelson, R. C. (1983). Similar reactivity produced by external cues and self-monitoring. *Behavior Modification, 7,* 183–196.

Haynes, S. M., Griffin, D., Mooney, D., & Parise, M. (1974). Electromyographic feedback and relaxation instructions in the treatment of muscle tension. *Psychophysiology, 12,* 547–553.

Hays, V., & Waddell, K. J. (1976). A self-reinforcing procedure for thought stopping. *Behavior Therapy, 7,* 559.

Headrick, M. W., Feather, B. W., & Wells, D. T. (1971). Unidirectional and large magnitude heart rate changes with augmented sensory feedback. *Psychophysiology, 8,* 132–142.

Heap, R. F., Bobblitt, W. E., Moore, C. H., & Hord, J. E. (1970). Behavior-milieu therapy with chronic neurospychiatric patients. *Journal of Abnormal Psychology, 76,* 349–354.

Heather, N., & Robertson, I. (1981). *Controlled drinking.* London: Methuen.

Hedberg, A. G., & Campbell, L. (1974). A comparison of four behavioural treatments of alcoholism. *Journal of Behavior Therapy and Experimental Psychiatry, 5,* 251–256.

Hedquist, F. J., & Weingold, B. K. (1970). Behavioral group counseling with socially anxious and unassertive college students. *Journal of Counseling Psychology, 17,* 237–242.

Heffernan, T., & Richards, C. S. (1981). Self-control of study behavior: Identification of natural methods. *Journal of Counseling Psychology, 28,* 361–364.

Heide, F. J., & Borkovec, T. D. (1983). Relaxation-induced anxiety: Paradoxical anxiety enhancement due to relaxation training. *Journal of Consulting and Clinical Psychology, 51,* 171–182.

Heide, F. J., & Borkovec, T. D. (1984). Relaxation-induced anxiety: Mechanisms and theoretical implications. *Behaviour Research and Therapy, 22,* 1–12.

Heimberg, R. G., & Harrison, D. F. (1980). Use of the Rathus Assertiveness Schedule with offenders: A question of questions. *Behavior Therapy, 11,* 278–281.

Heimberg, R. G., Montgomery, D., Madsen, C. H., Jr., & Heimberg, J. S. (1977). Assertion training: A review of the literature. *Behavior Therapy, 8,* 953–971.

Heine, R. W. (1953). A comparison of patients' reports on psychotherapeutic experience with psychoanalytic, non-directive and Adlerian Therapists. *American Journal of Psychotherapy, 7,* 16–23.

Hekmat, H. (1973). Systematic versus semantic sensitization and implosive therapy: A comparative study. *Journal of Consulting and Clinical Psychology, 40,* 202–203.

Heller, R. F., & Strang, H. R. (1973). Controlling bruxism through automated aversive conditioning. *Behaviour Research and Therapy 11,* 327–329.

Henson, F. O., II. (1975). An investigation of the effects of token reinforcement on divergent verbal responding. *Journal of Applied Behavior Analysis, 8,* 459.

Herbert, E. W., & Baer, D. M. (1972). Training parents as behavior modifiers: Self-recording contingent attention. *Journal of Applied Behavior Analysis, 5,* 139–149.

Herrnstein, R. J. (1977). The evolution of behaviorism. *American Psychologist, 32*(8), 593–603.

Hersen, M., & Bellack, A. S. (1977). Assessment of social skills. In A. R. Ciminero, K. S. Calhoun, & H. E. Adams (Eds.), *Handbook of behavioral assessment.* New York: Wiley.

Hersen, M., Bellack, A. S., & Turner, S. M. (1978). Assessment of assertiveness in female patients: Motor and autonomic measures. *Journal of Behavior Therapy and Experimental Psychiatry, 9,* 11–16.

Hersen, M., Bellack, A. S., Turner, S. M., Williams, M. T., Harper, K., & Watts, J. G. (1979). Psychometric properties on the Wolpe-Lazarus Assertiveness Scale. *Behaviour Research and Therapy, 17,* 63–69.

Hersen, M., Eisler, R. M., & Miller, P. M. (1973). Development of assertive responses: Clinical measurement and research considerations. *Behaviour Research and Therapy, 11,* 505–521.

Hersen, M., Eisler, R. M., & Miller, P. M. (1974). An experimental analysis of generalization in assertive training. *Behaviour Research and Therapy, 12,* 295–310.

Hersen, M., Eisler, R. M., Miller, P. M., Johnson, M. B., & Pinkston, S. G. (1973). Effects of practice, instructions, and modeling on components of assertive behavior. *Behaviour Research and Therapy, 11,* 443–451.

Herzberg, A. (1941). Short treatment of neuroses by graduated tasks. *British Journal of Medical Psychology, 19,* 36–51.

Hillenberg, J. B., & Collins, F. L. (1982). A procedural

analysis and review of relaxation training research. *Behaviour Research and Therapy, 20,* 251–260.

Hillenberg, J. B., & Collins, F. L. (1983). The importance of home practice for progressive relaxation training. *Behaviour Research and Therapy, 21,* 633–642.

Hinshaw, S. P., Henker, B., & Whalen, C. K. (1984). Self-control in hyperactive boys in anger-inducing situations: Effects of cognitive-behavioral training and of methylphenidate. *Journal of Abnormal Child Psychology, 12,* 55–77.

Hirsch, S. (1975). *An experimental investigation of the effectiveness of assertion training with alcoholics* (Res. Rep.). Texas Department of Mental Health and Mental Retardation, Austin, Texas. [Contract No. (74–75)–1973, Texas Commission on Alcoholism.].

Hnatiow, M., & Lang, P. J. (1965). Learned stabilization of cardiac rate. *Psychophysiology, 1,* 330–336.

Hobbs, T. R., & Holt, M. M. (1976). The effects of token reinforcement on the behavior of delinquents in cottage settings. *Journal of Applied Behavior Analysis, 9,* 189–198.

Hodgson, R. J., & Rachman, S. (1970). An experimental investigation of the implosion technique. *Behaviour Research and Therapy, 8,* 21–27.

Hodgson, S., Rachman, S., & Marks, I. (1972). The treatment of chronic obsessive-compulsive neurosis: Follow-up and further findings. *Behaviour Research and Therapy, 10,* 181–189.

Hoelscher, T. J., Lichstein, K. L., & Rosenthal, T. L. (1986). Home relaxation practice in hypertensive treatment: Objective assessment and compliance induction. *Journal of Consulting and Clinical Psychology, 54,* 217–221.

Hoffman, J. W., Benson, H., Arns, P. A., Stainbrook, G. L., Landsberg, L., Young, J. B., & Gill, A. (1982). Reduced sympathetic nervous system responsivity associated with the relaxation response. *Science, 215,* 190–192.

Hogan, R. A. (1963). *The implosive technique: A process of reeducation through the application of principles of learning for emotionally disturbed individuals.* Unpublished doctoral dissertation, Case Western Reserve University.

Hogan, R. A. (1966). Implosive therapy in the short term treatment of psychotics. *Psychotherapy: Theory, Research and Practice, 3,* 25–32.

Hogan, R. A. (1968). The implosive technique. *Behaviour Research and Therapy, 6,* 423–432.

Hogan, R. A. (1969). Implosively oriented behavior modification: Therapy considerations. *Behaviour Research and Therapy, 7,* 177–184.

Hogan, R. A., DeSoto, C. B., & Solano, C. (1977). Traits, tests, and personality research. *American Psychologist, 32*(4), 255–264.

Hogan, R. A., & Kirchner, J. H. (1967). A preliminary report of the extinction of learned fears via short term implosive therapy. *Journal of Abnormal Psychology, 72,* 106–111.

Holbrook, J. H., Grundy, S. M., Hennekens, C. H., Kannel, W. B., & Strong, J. P. (1984). Cigarette smoking and cardiovascular diseases: A statement for health professionals by a task force appointed by the steering committee of the American Heart Association, *Circulation, 70,* 1114A–1117A.

Hollandsworth, J. G. (1977). Differentiating assertion and aggression: Some behavioral guidelines. *Behavior Therapy, 8,* 347–352.

Hollon, S. D. (1984). Cognitive therapy for depression: Translating research into clinical practice. *The Behavior Therapist, 7,* 126–127.

Hollon, S. D., & Beck, A. T. (1978). Psychotherapy and drug therapy: Comparisons and combinations. In S. L. Garfield & A. E. Bergin (Eds.), *The Handbook of psychotherapy and behavior change* (2nd ed.). New York: Wiley.

Hollon, S. D., & Beck, A. T. (1979). Cognitive therapy of depression. In P. C. Kendall, S. D. Hollon (Eds.), *Cognitive-behavioral interventions: Theory, research, and procedures.* New York: Academic Press.

Hollon, S. D., & Beck, A. T. (1986). Cognitive and cognitive-behavioral interventions. In A. E. Bergin & S. L. Garfield (Eds.), *Handbook of psychotherapy and behavior change* (3rd ed.). New York: Wiley.

Hollon, S. D., DeRubeis, R. J., Tuason, V. B., Weimer, M. J., Evans, M. D., & Garvey, M. J. (1986). *Cognitive therapy, pharmacotherapy, and combined cognitive-pharmacotherapy in the treatment of depression: 1. Differential outcome.* Unpublished manuscript, University of Minnesota and the St. Paul-Ramsey Medical Center, Minneapolis-St. Paul.

Hollon, S. D., Evans, M. D., Elkin, I., & Lowery, A. (1984, May). *System for rating therapies for depression.* Paper presented at the Annual Meeting of the American Psychiatric Association, Los Angeles.

Hollon, S. D., & Kendall, P. C. (1980). Cognitive self-statements in depression: Development of an automatic thoughts questionnaire. *Cognitive Therapy and Research, 4,* 383–395.

Hollon, S. D., & Kendall, P. C. (1981). *In vivo* assessment techniques for cognitive-behavioral processes. In P. C. Kendall & S. D. Hollon (Eds.), *Assessment strategies for cognitive-behavioral interventions.* New York: Academic Press.

Hollon, S. D., & Kriss, M. R. (1984). Cognitive factors in clinical research and practice. *Clinical Psychology Review, 3,* 35–76.

Holmes, D. S., & Burish, T. G. (1983). Effectiveness of biofeedback for treating migraine and tension headaches: A review of the evidence. *Journal of Psychosomatic Research, 27,* 515–532.

Holroyd, K. A. (1976). Cognition and desensitization in the group treatment of test anxiety. *Journal of Consulting and Clinical Psychology, 44,* 991–1001.

Holroyd, K. A., & Andrasik, F. (1978). Coping and the self-control of chronic tension headache. *Journal of Consulting and Clinical Psychology, 46,* 1036–1045.

Holroyd, K. A., Andrasik, F., & Noble, J. (1980). A comparison of EMG biofeedback and a credible pseudotherapy in treating tension headache. *Journal of Behavioral Medicine, 3,* 29–39.

Holroyd, K. A., Andrasik, F., & Westbrook, T. (1977). Cognitive control of tension headache. *Cognitive Therapy and Research, 1,* 121–133.

Holsopple, J. Q., & Vanouse, I. (1929). A note on the beta hypothesis of learning. *School Sociology, 29,* 15–16.

Holt, M. M., & Hobbs, T. R. (1979). The effects of token reinforcement, feedback and response cost on standardized test performance. *Behaviour Research and Therapy, 17,* 81–83.

Holz, W. C., & Azrin, N. H. (1962). Interactions between the discriminative and aversive properties of punishment. *Journal of the Experimental Analysis of Behavior, 5,* 229–234.

Holz, W. C., & Azrin, N. H. (1963). A comparison of several procedures for eliminating behavior. *Journal of the Experimental Analysis of Behavior, 6,* 399–406.

Holzinger, R., Mortimer, R., & Van Dusen, W. (1967). Aversion conditioning treatment of alcoholism. *American Journal of Psychiatry, 124,* 246–247.

Homme, L. E. (1965). Perspectives in psychology. XXIV. Control of coverants, the operants of the mind. *Psychological Record, 15,* 501–511.

Homme, L. E. (1971). *How to use contingency contracting in the classroom.* Champaign, IL: Research Press.

Homme, L. E., deBaca, P. C., Devine J. V., Steinhorst, R., & Rickert, E. J. (1963). Use of the Premack principle in controlling the behavior of nursery school children. *Journal of the Experimental Analysis of Behavior, 6,* 544.

Hoogduin, C. A., & Hoogduin, W. A. (1984). The out-patient treatment of patients with an obsessional-compulsive disorder. *Behaviour Research and Therapy, 22,* 455–459.

Hoon, E. F., Wincze, J. P., & Hoon, P. (1977). Sexual arousal in women: A comparison of cognitive and physiological responses by continuous measurement. *Archives of Sexual Behavior, 6*(2), 121–133.

Horan, J. J., & Dellinger, J. (1974). "In vivo" emotive imagery; a preliminary test. *Perceptual and Motor Skills, 39,* 359–362.

Horan, J. J., Hackett, G., Buchanan, J. D., Stone, C. I., & Stone, D. D. (1977). Coping with pain: A component analysis of stress inoculation. *Cognitive Therapy and Research, 1*(3), 211–221.

Horan, J. J., Hackett, G., Nicholas, W. C., Linberg, S. E., Stone, C. I., & Lukaski, H. C. (1977). Rapid smoking: A cautionary note. *Journal of Consulting and Clinical Psychology, 45,* 341–343.

Horan, J. J., Lindberg, S. E., & Hackett, G. (1977). Nicotine poisoning and rapid smoking. *Journal of Consulting and Clinical Psychology, 45,* 344–347.

Horn, W. F., Chatoor, I., & Conners, C. K. (1983). Additive effects of dexedrine and self-control training: A multiple assessment. *Behavior Modification, 7,* 383–402.

Horne, A. M., & Matson, J. L. (1977). A comparison of modeling, desensitization, flooding, study skills, and control groups for reducing test anxiety. *Behavior Therapy, 8,* 1–8.

Horner, R. D., & Keilitz, I. (1975). Training mentally retarded adolescents to brush their teeth. *Journal of Applied Behavior Analysis, 8,* 301–310.

Horney, K. (1950). *Neurosis and human growth: The struggle toward self-realization.* New York: Norton.

Horowitz, M. J, & Becker, S. S. (1971). Cognitive response to stress and experimental demand. *Journal of Abnormal Psychology, 78*(1), 86–92.

Horowitz, M. J., Becker, S. S., & Moskowitz, M. L. (1971). Intrusive and repetitive thought after stress: A replication study. *Psychological Reports, 29,* 763–767.

Horton, A. M., & Johnson, C. H. (1977). The treatment of homicidal obsessive ruminations by thought stopping and covert assertion. *Journal of Behavior Therapy and Experimental Psychiatry, 8,* 339–340.

Hosford, R. E. (1969). Overcoming fear of speaking in a group. In J. D. Krumboltz & C. E. Thoresen (Eds.), *Behavioral Counseling.* New York: Holt.

Houston, J. P. (1976). *Fundamentals of learning.* New York: Academic Press.

Howard, W. A., Murphy, S. H., & Clarke, J. C. (1983). The nature and treatment of fear of flying: A controlled investigation. *Behavior Therapy, 14,* 557–567.

Huey, W. C., & Rank, R. C. (1984). Effects of counselor and peer-led group assertive training on black adolescent aggression. *Journal of Counseling Psychology, 31,* 95–98.

Hugdahl, K., Fredrickson, M., & Ohman, A. (1977). "Preparedness" and "arousability" as determinants of electrodermal conditioning. *Behaviour Research and Therapy, 15,* 345–353.

Hughes, R. C. (1977). Covert sensitization treatment of exhibitionism. *Journal of Behavior Therapy and Experimental Psychiatry, 8,* 177–179.

Hull, C. L. (1943). *Principles of behavior.* New York: Appleton.

Hull, C. L. (1952). *A behavior system.* New Haven, CT: Yale University Press.

Humphrey, J. (1966). Personal communication.

Hundert, J. (1976). The effectiveness of reinforcement, response cost, and mixed programs on classroom behaviors. *Journal of Applied Behavior Analysis, 9,* 107.

Hundziak, M., Mowrer, R. A., & Watson, L. S., Jr. (1965). Operant conditioning in toilet training of severely mentally retarded boys. *American Journal of Mental Deficiency, 70,* 120–124.

Hunt, G. M., & Azrin, N. H. (1973). A community-reinforcement approach to alcoholism. *Behaviour Research and Therapy, 11,* 91–104.

Hunt, W. A., Barnett, L. W., & Ranch, L. G. (1971). Relapse rates in addiction programs. *Journal of Clinical Psychology, 27,* 455–456.

Hunt, W. A., & Bespalec, D. A. (1974). An evaluation of current methods of modifying smoking behavior. *Journal of Clinical Psychology, 30,* 431–438.

Hunt, W. A., & Matarozzo, J. E. (1973). Three years later: Recent developments in the experimental modification of smoking behavior. *Journal of Abnormal Psychology, 81,* 107–114.

Hunziker, J. C. (1972). *The use of participant modeling in the treatment of water phobias.* Unpublished master's thesis, Arizona State University.

Hurd, P. D., Johnson, C. A., Pechacek, T., Bast, L. P., Jacobs, D. R., & Luepker, R. V. (1980). Prevention of cigarette smoking in seventh-grade students. *Journal of Behavioral Medicine, 3,* 15–28.

Hurley, A. D. (1976). Covert reinforcement: The contribution of the reinforcing stimulus to treatment outcome. *Behavior Therapy, 7,* 374–378.

Hurst, B. S., Lacey, J. H., & Crisp, A. H. (1977). Teeth, vomiting and diet: A study of the dental characteristics of seventeen anorexia nervosa patients. *Postgraduate Medical Journal, 53,* 298–305.

Hussain, M. Z. (1970). Thiopentone-facilitated implosion of treatment of phobic disorders. *Canadian Medical Association Journal, 103,* 768–769.

Hussain, M. Z. (1971). Desensitization and flooding (implosion) in treatment of phobias. *American Journal of Psychiatry, 127,* 85–89.

Hutchings, D. F., & Reinking, R. H. (1976). Tension headaches: What form of therapy is most effective? *Biofeedback and Self-control, 1,* 183–190.

Ince, L. P. (1983). The utilization of EMG biofeedback for the treatment of periorbital facial muscle tension. *Biofeedback and Self-Regulation, 8,* 377–382.

Ingham, R. J., & Andrews, G. (1973). An analysis of a token economy in stuttering therapy. *Journal of Applied Behavior Analysis, 6,* 219–229.

Inglis, J., Campbell, D., & Donald M. W. (1976–1977). EMG feedback therapy: Review of treatment of 114 patients. *Biofeedback and Self-control, 3–22.*

Ingram, E. M. (1967). *Discriminative and reinforcing functions in the experimental development of social behavior in a preschool child.* Unpublished master's thesis, University of Kansas.

Irey, P. A. (1972). *Covert sensitization of cigarette smokers with high and low extraversion scores.* Unpublished master's thesis, Southern Illinois University.

Israel, E., & Beiman, I. (1977). Live versus recorded relaxation training: What form of therapy is most effective? *Biofeedback and Self-Regulation, 8,* 251–254.

Iwata, B. A., & Bailey, J. S. (1974). Reward versus cost token systems: An analysis of the effects on students and teacher. *Journal of Applied Behavior Analysis, 7,* 567–576.

Jacob, R. G., Fortman, S. P., Kraemer, H. C., Farquhar, J. W., Agras, W. S. (1985). Combining behavioral treatments to reduce blood pressure. *Behavior Modification, 9,* 32–54.

Jacobs, M. K., & Cochran, S. D. (1982). The effects of cognitive restructuring on assertive behavior. *Cognitive Therapy and Research, 6,* 63–76.

Jacobsen, R., & Edinger, J. D. (1982). Side effects of relaxation treatment. *American Journal of Psychiatry, 139,* 952–953.

Jacobson, A. M., Manschreck, T. C., & Silverberg, E. (1979). Behavioral treatment for Raynaud's disease: A comparative study with long-term follow-up. *American Journal of Psychiatry, 136,* 844–846.

Jacobson, E. (1938). *Progressive relaxation.* Chicago: University of Chicago Press.

Jacobson, E. (1970). *Modern treatment of tense patients.* Springfield, IL: Charles C. Thomas.

Jacobson, E. (1977). The origins and development of progressive relaxation. *Journal of Behavior Therapy and Experimental Psychiatry, 8,* 119–123.

Jacobson, J. A. (1970). *Reciprocal inhibition and implosive therapy: A comparative study of a fear of snakes.* Unpublished doctoral dissertation, Memphis State University.

Jacobson, N. S. (1977). Problem-solving and contingency contracting in the treatment of marital discord. *Journal of Consulting and Clinical Psychology, 45,* 92–100.

Jacobson, N. S. (1978). Specific and nonspecific factors in the effectiveness of a behavioral approach to the treatment of marital discord. *Journal of Consulting and Clinical Psychology, 46,* 442–452.

Jacobson, N. S., & Baucom, D. H. (1977). Design and assessment of nonspecific control groups in behavior modification research. *Behavior Therapy, 8,* 709–719.

Jaffe, P. G., & Carlson, P. M. (1976). Relative efficacy of modeling and instructions in eliciting social behavior from chronic psychiatric patients. *Journal of Consulting and Clinical Psychology, 44,* 200–207.

James, J. E., Hampton, A. M., & Larson, S. A. (1983). The relative efficacy of imaginal and *in vivo* desensitization in the treatment of agoraphobia. *Journal of Behavior Therapy and Experimental Psychiatry, 14,* 203–207.

Janda, H. L., & Rimm, D. C. (1972). Covert sensitization in the treatment of obesity. *Journal of Abnormal Psychology, 80,* 37–42.

Janssen, K. (1983a). Differential effectiveness of EMG-feedback versus combined EMG-feedback and relaxation instructions in the treatment of tension headache. *Journal of Psychosomatic Research, 27,* 243–253.

Janssen, K. (1983b). Treatment of sinus tachycardia with heart-rate feedback. *Journal of Behavioral Medicine, 6,* 109–114.

Jaremko, M. (1984). Stress inoculation training: A generic approach for the prevention of stress-related disorders. *Personnel and Guidance Journal, 62,* 544–550.

Jeffery, R. W., Gerber, W. M., Rosenthal, B. S., & Lindquist, R. A. (1983). Monetary contracts in weight control: Effectiveness of group and individual contracts of varying size. *Journal of Consulting and Clinical Psychology, 51,* 242–248.

Jeffery, R. W., Thompson, P. D., & Wing, R. R. (1978). Effects on weight reduction of strong monetary contracts for caloric restriction on weight loss. *Behaviour Research and Therapy, 16,* 363–369.

Jeffery, R. W., Wing, R. R., & Stunkard, A. J. (1978). Behavioral treatment of obesity. The state of the art. (1976). *Behavior Therapy, 9,* 189–199.

Jeffrey, D. B. (1974). A comparison of the effects of external control and self-control on the modification and maintenance of weight. *Journal of Abnormal Psychology, 83,* 404–410.

Jellinek, E. M. (1960). *The disease concept in alcoholism.* New Brunswick, NJ: Hill House Press.

Jensen, J. E. (1983, March 23). Letter to Drs. Mark and Linda Sobell. Investigator, Subcommittee on Investigations and Oversight, U.S. Congress.

Jessup, B. (1978). *Autogenic feedback for migraine: A bidirectional control group study.* Unpublished paper, University of Western Ontario, London, Ontario.

Jessup, B. A., & Neufeld, R. W. (1977). Effects of biofeedback and "autogenic relaxation" techniques on physiological and subjective responses in psychiatric patients: A preliminary analysis. *Behavior Therapy, 8,* 160–167.

Johnson, D. F., & Geller, E. S. (1974). Operations manual for a contingency management program in a maximum security institution. *JSAS Catalog of Selected Documents in Psychology, 4,* 23.

Johnson, J. H., & Thompson, D. J. (1974). Modeling in the treatment of enuresis: A case study. *Journal of Behavior Therapy and Experimental Psychiatry, 5,* 93–94.

Johnson, S. M., Christensen, A., & Bellamy, G. T. (1976). Evaluation of family intervention through unobtrusive audio recordings: Experiences in "bugging" children. *Journal of Applied Behavior Analysis, 9,* 213–219.

Johnson, S. M., & White, G. (1971). Self-observation as an agent of behavioral change. *Behavior Therapy, 2,* 488–497.

Johnson, W. G., Ross, J. M., & Mastria, M. A. (1977). Delusional behavior: An attributional analysis of development and modification. *Journal of Abnormal Psychology, 86*(4), 421–426.

Johnson, W. G., Wildman, H. E., & O'Brien, T. (1980). The assessment of program adherence: The Achilles' heel of behavioral weight reduction? *Behavioral Assessment, 2,* 297–301.

Johnston, M. S., Kelley, C. S., Harris, F. R., & Wolf, M. (1966). An application of reinforcement principles to development of motor skills of a young child. *Child Development, 37,* 379–387.

Jones, F. D., Stayer, S. J., Wichlacz, C. R., Thomes, L., & Livingstone, B. L. (1977). Contingency management of hospital diagnosed character and behavior disorder soldiers. *Journal of Behavior Therapy and Experimental Psychiatry, 8,* 333.

Jones, H. G. (1956). The application of conditioning and learning techniques to the treatment of a psychiatric patient. *Journal of Abnormal and Social Psychology, 52,* 414–419.

Jones, H. G. (1960). Continuation of Yates' treatment of a tiquer. In H. J. Eysenck (Ed.), *Behaviour therapy and the neuroses.* Oxford: Pergamon.

Jones, M. C. (1924). The elimination of children's fears. *Journal of Experimental Psychology, 7,* 382–390.

Jones, R. G. (1968). A factored measure of Ellis' irrational belief system, with personality and maladjustment correlates. Doctoral dissertation, Texas Technological College (University Microfilms, No. 69–6443).

Jones, et al., (1985). Self-control of psychophysiologic response to motion stress: Using biofeedback to treat airsickness. *Aviation, Space, & Environmental Medicine, 56,* 1152–1157.

Josiassen, R. C., Fantuzzo, J., & Rosen, A. C. (1980). Treatment of pedophilia using multistage aversion therapy and social skills training. *Journal of Behavior Therapy and Experimental Psychiatry, 11,* 104–108.

Kahneman, D., Slovic, P., & Tversky, A. (1982). *Judgment under uncertainty: Heuristics and biases.* Cambridge: Cambridge University Press.

Kallman, W. M., & Feuerstein, M. (1977). Psychophysiological procedures. In A. R. Ciminero, K. S.

Calhoun, & H. E. Adams (Eds.), *Handbook of behavioral assessment.* New York: Wiley.

Kallman, W. M., Hersen, M., & O'Toole, D. H. (1975). The use of social reinforcement in a case of conversion reaction. *Behavior Therapy, 6,* 411–413.

Kamano, D. K. (1972). Using drugs to modify the effect of response prevention on avoidance extinction. *Behaviour Research and Therapy, 10,* 367–370.

Kamiya, J. (1968). Conscious control of brain waves. *Psychology Today, 1,* 57–60.

Kandel, H. J., Ayllon, T., & Rosenbaum, M. S. (1977). Flooding or systematic exposure in the treatment of extreme social withdrawal in children. *Journal of Behavior Therapy and Experimental Psychiatry, 8,* 75–81.

Kanfer, F. H., (1970). Self-regulation: Research, issues and speculations. In C. Neuringer & J. L. Michael (Eds.), *Behavior modification in clinical psychology.* New York: Appleton-Century-Crofts.

Kanfer, F. H. (1971). The maintenance of behavior by self-generated stimuli and reinforcement. In A. Jacobs & L. Sachs (Eds.), *The psychology of private events.* New York: Academic Press.

Kanfer, F. H., & Gaelick, L. (1986). Self-management methods. In F. H. Kanfer & A. P. Goldstein (Eds.). *Helping people change* (3rd ed.). New York: Pergamon Press.

Kanfer, F. H., & Goldfoot, D. (1966). Self-control and tolerance of noxious stimulation. *Psychological Reports, 18,* 79–85.

Kanfer, F. H., & Goldstein, A. P. (Eds.). (1986). *Helping people change* (3rd ed.). New York: Pergamon Press.

Kanfer, F. H., Karoly, P., & Newman, A. (1975). Reduction of children's fear of the dark by competence-related and situational threat-related verbal cues. *Journal of Consulting and Clinical Psychology, 43,* 251–258.

Kanfer, F. H., & Phillips, J. S. (1969). A survey of current behavior therapies and a proposal for classification. In C. M. Franks (Ed.), *Behavior Therapy: Appraisal and status.* New York: McGraw-Hill.

Kanfer, F. H., & Phillips, J. S. (1970). *Learning foundations of behavior therapy.* New York: Wiley.

Kanfer, F. H., & Saslow, G. (1969). Behavioral diagnosis. In C. M. Franks (Ed.), *Behavior therapy: Appraisal and status.* New York: McGraw-Hill.

Kanfer, F. H., & Seider, M. (1973). Self control factors enhancing tolerance of noxious stimulation. *Journal of Personality and Social Psychology, 25,* 381–389.

Kant, F. (1944a). Further modifications in the technique of conditioned-reflex treatment of alcohol addiction. *Quarterly Journal of Studies on Alcoholism, 5,* 228–232.

Kant, F. (1944b). The conditioned-reflex treatment in the right of our knowledge of alcohol addiction. *Quarterly Journal of Studies on Alcoholism, 5,* 371–377.

Kant, F. (1945). The use of conditioned reflex in the treatment of alcohol addicts. *Wisconsin Medical Journal, 44,* 217–221.

Kanter, N. J., & Goldfried, M. R. (1979). Relative effectiveness of rational restructuring and self-control desensitization in the reduction of interpersonal anxiety. *Behavior Therapy, 10,* 472–490.

Kantorovich, N. V. (1928). An attempt of curing alcoholism by associated reflexes. *Novoye Refleksologii nervnoy i fiziologii Sistemy, 3,* 436–445. [Cited by Razran, G. H. S. (1934). Conditioned withdrawal responses with shock as the conditioning stimulus in adult human subjects. *Psychological Bulletin, 31,* 111–143.]

Kaplan, B. J. (1975). Biofeedback in epileptics: Equivocal relationship of reinforced EEG Frequency to seizure reduction. *Epilepsia, 16,* 477–485.

Kaplan, D. A. (1982). Behavioral, cognitive, and behavioral-cognitive approaches to group assertion training therapy. *Cognitive Therapy and Research, 6,* 301–314.

Kaplan, R. M., Metzger, G., & Jablecki, C. (1983). Brief cognitive and relaxation training increases tolerance for a painful clinical electromyographic examination. *Psychosomatic Medicine, 45,* 155–162.

Karnes, M. B., Teska, J. A., & Hodgins, A. S. (1970). Educational intervention at home by mothers of disadvantaged infants. *Child Development, 41*(4), 925–935.

Karoly, P., & Dirks, M. (1977). Developing self control in pre-school children through correspondence training. *Behavior Therapy, 8,* 398–405.

Karoly, P., & Kanfer, F. H. (1974). Situational and historical determinants of self reinforcement. *Behavior Therapy, 5,* 381–390.

Karoly, P., & Kanfer, F. H. (Eds.). (1982). *Self-management and behavior change: From theory to practice.* Elmsford, NY: Pergamon Press.

Karoly, P., & Steffen, J. J. (Eds.). (1980). *Improving the long-term effects of psychotherapy.* New York: Gardner Press.

Karst, T. O., & Trexler, L. D. (1970). An initial study using fixed role and rational-emotive therapies in treating public speaking anxiety. *Journal of Consulting and Clinical Psychology, 34,* 360–366.

Kass, R. E., & O'Leary, K. D. (1970, April). *The effects of observer bias in field-experimental settings.* Paper presented at a symposium *Behavior Analysis in Education,* University of Kansas.

Kass, W., & Gilner, F. H. (1974). Drive level, incentive conditions and systematic desensitization. *Behaviour Research and Therapy, 12,* 99–106.

Katahan, M., Pleas, J., Thackery, M., & Wallston, K. A. (1982). Relationship of eating and activity self-reports to follow-up weight maintenance in the massively obese. *Behavior Therapy, 13,* 521–528.

Katkin, E. S., & Goldband, S. (1979). The placebo effect and biofeedback. In R. Gatchel & K. Price (Eds.), *Clinical applications of biofeedback: Appraisal and status.* Elmsford, NY: Pergamon Press.

Kauffman, J. M., & Hallahan, D. P. (1973). Control of rough physical behavior using novel contingencies and directive teaching. *Perceptual and Motor Skills, 36,* 1225–1226.

Kaufman, K. F., & O'Leary, K. D. (1972). Reward cost, and self-evaluation procedures for disruptive adolescents in a psychiatric hospital school. *Journal of Applied Behavior Analysis, 5,* 293–309.

Kaufmann, P. (1950). Changes in the MMPI as a function of psychiatric therapy. *Journal of Consulting Psychology, 70,* 337–342.

Kazdin, A. E. (1971). The effect of response cost in suppressing behavior in a pre-psychotic retardate. *Journal of Behavior Therapy and Experimental Psychiatry, 2,* 137–140.

Kazdin, A. E. (1972). Response cost: The removal of conditioned reinforcers for therapeutic change. *Behavior Therapy, 3,* 533–546.

Kazdin, A. E. (1973a). The effect of response cost and aversive stimulation in suppressing punished and nonpunished speech disfluencies. *Behavior Therapy, 4,* 73–82.

Kazdin, A. E. (1973b). The effect of vicarious reinforcement on attentive behavior in the classroom. *Journal of Applied Behavior Analysis, 6,* 71–78.

Kazdin, A. E. (1974a). Comparative effects of some variations of covert modeling. *Journal of Behavior Therapy and Experimental Psychiatry, 5,* 225–231.

Kazdin, A. E. (1974b). Covert modeling, model similarity and reduction of avoidance behavior. *Behavior Therapy, 5,* 325–340.

Kazdin, A. E. (1974c). The effect of model identity

and fear-relevant similarity on covert modeling. *Behavior Therapy, 5*, 624–625.

Kazdin, A. E. (1974d). Effects of covert modeling and model reinforcement on assertive behavior. *Journal of Abnormal Psychology, 83*, 240–252.

Kazdin, A. E. (1974e). Self-monitoring and behavior change. In M. J. Mahoney & C. E. Thoresen (Eds.), *Self-control: Power to the person*. Monterey, CA: Brooks/Cole, 1974.

Kazdin, A. E. (1975). Covert modeling, imagery assessment, and assertive behavior. *Journal of Consulting and Clinical Psychology, 43*, 716–724.

Kazdin, A. E. (1976a). Assessment of imagery during covert modeling of assertive behavior. *Journal of Behavior Therapy and Experimental Psychiatry, 7*, 213–219.

Kazdin, A. E. (1976b). Effects of covert modeling, multiple models and model reinforcement on assertive behavior. *Behavior Therapy, 7*, 211–222.

Kazdin, A. E. (1977). Assessing the clinical or applied importance of behavior change through social validation. *Behavior Modification, 1*, 427–452.

Kazdin, A. E. (1978). Effects of covert modeling and coding of modeled stimuli on assertive behavior. *Behaviour Research and Therapy, 17*, 53–61.

Kazdin, A. E. (1979). Imagery elaboration and self-efficacy in covert modeling treatment of unassertive behavior. *Journal of Consulting and Clinical Psychology, 47*, 725–733.

Kazdin, A. E. (1980). Covert and overt rehearsal and elaboration during treatment in the development of assertive behavior. *Behaviour Research and Therapy, 18*, 191–201.

Kazdin, A. E. (1982). The separate and combined effects of covert and overt rehearsal in developing assertive behavior. *Behaviour Research and Therapy, 1*, 17–25.

Kazdin, A. E., & Bootzin, R. (1972). The token economy: An evaluative review. *Journal of Applied Behavior Analysis, 5*, 343–372.

Kazdin, A. E., & Mascitelli, S. (1980). The opportunity to earn oneself off a token system as a reinforcer for attentive behavior. *Behavior Therapy, 11*(1), 68–78.

Kazdin, A. E., & Mascitelli, S. (1982a). Behavioral rehearsal, self-instructions, and homework practiced in developed assertiveness. *Behavior Therapy, 13*, 346–360.

Kazdin, A. E., & Mascitelli, S. (1982b). Covert and overt rehearsal and homework practice in develop-ing assertiveness. *Journal of Consulting and Clinical Psychology, 50*, 250–258.

Kazdin, A. E., & Wilcoxon, L. A. (1976). Systematic desensitization and nonspecific treatment effects: A methodological evaluation. *Psychological Bulletin, 83*, 729–758.

Keane, T. M., & Kaloupek, D. G. (1982). Imaginal flooding in the treatment of a posttraumatic stress disorder. *Journal of Consulting and Clinical Psychology, 50*(1), 138–140.

Keane, T. M., Prue, D. M., & Collins, F. L., Jr. (1981). Behavioral contracting to improve dietary compliance in chronic renal dialysis patients. *Journal of Behavior Therapy and Experimental Psychiatry, 12*, 63–67.

Keane, T. M., St. Lawrence, J. S., Himadi, W. G., Graves, K. A., & Kelly, J. A. (1983). Black's perceptions of assertive behavior: An empirical evaluation. *Behavior Modification, 1*, 97–111.

Keane, T. M., Wedding, D., & Kelly, J. A. (1983). Assessing subjective responses to assertive behavior: Data from patient samples. *Behavior Modification, 1*, 317–330.

Keefe, F. J., & Surwit, R. S. (1978). Electromyographic biofeedback: Behavioral treatment of neuromuscular disorders. *Journal of Behavioral Medicine, 1*, 13–24.

Keefe, F. J., Surwit, R. S., & Pilon, R. N. (1980). Biofeedback, autogenic training, and progressive relaxation in the treatment of Raynaud's disease: A comparative study. *Journal of Applied Behavior Analysis, 13*, 3–11.

Keeley, S. M., Shemberg, K. M., & Carbonell, J. (1976). Operant clinical intervention: Behavior management or beyond? Where are the data? *Behavior Therapy, 7*, 292–305.

Kelleher, R. T. (1966). Chaining and conditioned reinforcement. In W. K. Honig (Ed.), *Operant behavior: Areas of research and application*. New York: Appleton.

Kelley, M. L., & Stokes, T. F. (1982). Contingency contracting with disadvantaged youths: Improving classroom performance. *Journal of Applied Behavior Analysis, 15*, 447–454.

Kellogg, R., & Baron, R. S. (1975). Attribution theory, insomnia, and the reverse placebo effect: A reversal of Storm's and Nisbett's findings. *Journal of Personality and Social Psychology, 32*, 231–236.

Kellogg, W. N., & White, R. E. (1935). A maze test of Dunlap's theory of learning. *Journal of Comparative Psychology, 19*, 119–148.

Kelly, G. A. (1955). *The psychology of personal constructs*, (vol. II). New York: Norton.

Kelly, J. A., & Drabman, S. (1977). Generalizing response suppression of self-injurious behavior through an overcorrection punishment procedure: A case study. *Behavior Therapy, 8,* 468–472.

Kelly, J. A., Kern, J. M., Kirkley, B. G., Patterson, J. N., & Keane, T. M. (1980). Reactions to assertive versus unassertive behavior: Differential effects for males and females and implications for assertiveness training. *Behavior Therapy, 11,* 670–682.

Kelly, J. A., St. Lawrence, J. S., Bradlyn, A. S., Himadai, W. G., Graves, K. A., & Keane, T. M. (1982). Interpersonal reactions to assertive and unassertive styles when handling social conflict situations. *Journal of Behavior Therapy and Experimental Psychiatry, 13,* 33–40.

Keltner, A., & Marshall, W. L. (1976). Attribution and subject control factors in experimental desensitization. *Behavior Therapy, 7,* 626–633.

Kempler, W. (1973). Gestalt therapy. In R. Corsini (Ed.), *Current psychotherapy.* Itasco, IL: Peacock.

Kendall, P. C. (1981). One-year follow-up of concrete versus conceptual cognitive-behavioral self-control training. *Journal of Consulting and Clinical Psychology, 49,* 748–749.

Kendall, P. C. (1982a). Individual versus group cognitive-behavioral self-control training: 1-year follow-up. *Behavior Therapy, 13,* 241–247.

Kendall, P. C., & Braswell, L. (1982). Cognitive-behavioral self-control therapy for children: A components analysis. *Journal of Consulting and Clinical Psychology, 50,* 672–689.

Kendall, P. C., & Braswell, L. (1985). *Cognitive-behavior therapy with impulsive children.* New York: Guilford.

Kendall, P. C., & Finch, A. J. (1978). A cognitive-behavioral treatment for impulsivity: A group comparison study. *Journal of Consulting and Clinical Psychology, 46,* 110–118.

Kendall, P. C., & Hollon, S. D. (1983). Callibrating the quality of therapy: Collaborative archiving of tape samples from therapy outcome trials. *Cognitive Therapy and Research, 7,* 199–204.

Kendall, P. C., Moses, J. A., & Finch, A. J. (1980). Impulsivity and persistence in adult inpatient "impulse" offenders. *Journal of Clinical Psychology, 36*(1), 363–365.

Kendall, P. C., Nay, W. R., & Jeffers, J. (1975). Timeout duration and contrast effect: A systematic evaluation of a successive treatments design. *Behavior Therapy, 6,* 609–615.

Kendall, P. C., & Wilcox, L. E. (1980). Cognitive-behavioral treatment for impulsivity: Concrete versus conceptual training in non-self-controlled problem children. *Journal of Consulting and Clinical Psychology, 48,* 80–91.

Kendall, P. C., Williams, L., Pechacek, T. F., Graham, L. E., Shisslak, C., & Herzoff, N. (1979). Cognitive-behavioral and patient education interventions in cardiac catheterization procedures: The Pala Alto medical psychology project. *Journal of Consulting and Clinical Psychology, 47,* 49–58.

Kendall, P. C., & Zupan, B. A. (1981). Individual versus group application of cognitive-behavioral self-control procedure with children. *Behavior Therapy, 9,* 209–221.

Kendell, R. E. (1965). Normal Drinking by former alcohol addicts. *Quarterly Journal of Studies on Alcoholism, 26,* 247–257.

Kennedy, R. E. (1976). Behavior modification in prisons. In W. E. Craighead, A. E. Kazdin, & M. J. Mahoney, (Eds.), *Behavior modification: Principles, issues, and applications.* Boston: Houghton Mifflin.

Kenny, F. T., Mowbray, R. M., & LaLani, S. (1978). Faradic disruption of obsessive ideation in the treatment of obsessive neurosis. *Behavior Therapy, 9,* 209–221.

Kenny, F. T., Solyom, L., & Solyom, C. (1973). Faradic disruption of obsessive ideation in the treatment of obsessive neurosis. *Behavior Therapy, 4,* 448–457.

Kent, R. N., O'Leary, K. D., Diament, C., & Dietz, A. (1973). "Expectations biases in observational evaluation of therapeutic change." *Journal of Consulting and Clinical Psychologist, 42,* 474–480.

Kent, R. N., Wilson, T., & Nelson, R. (1972). Effects of false heart rate feedback on avoidance behavior: An investigation of "cognitive desensitization." *Behavior Therapy, 3,* 1–6.

Kern, J. M. (1982). Predicting the impact of assertive, empathic-assertive and nonassertive behavior: The assertiveness of the assertee. *Behavior Therapy, 13,* 486–498.

Kern, J. M., Cavell, T. A., & Beck, B. (1985). Predicting differential reactions to males' versus females' assertions, empathic-assertions, and nonassertions. *Behavior Therapy, 16,* 63–75.

Kern, J. M., & MacDonald, M. L. (1980). Assessing

assertion: An investigation of construct validity and reliability. *Journal of Consulting and Clinical Psychology, 48,* 431–439.

Keutzer, C. S. (1968). Behavior modification of smoking: The experimental investigation of diverse techniques. *Behaviour Research and Therapy, 6,* 137–157.

Kewman, D. G., Roberts, A. H. (1980). Skin temperature biofeedback and migraine headaches: A double-blind study. *Biofeedback and Self-regulation, 5,* 327–345.

Kiecolt-Glaser, J. K., Glaser, R., Willinger, D., Stout, J., Messick, G., Sheppard, S., Richer, D., Romisher, S. C., Briner, W., Bonnell, G. & Donnerberg, R. (1985). Psychosocial enhancement of immune competence in a geriatric population. *Health Psychology, 4,* 25–41.

Kiesler, D. J. (1966). Some myths of psychotherapy research and the search for a paradigm. *Psychological Bulletin, 65,* 110–136.

Kifer, R. E., Lewis, M. A., Green, D. R., & Phillips, E. I. (1974). Training predelinquent youths and their parents to negotiate conflict situations. *Journal of Applied Behavior Analysis, 7,* 357–364.

Killen, J. D., Maccoby, N., & Taylor, C. B. (1984). Nicotine gum and self-regulation training in smoking relapse prevention. *Behavior Therapy, 15,* 234–248.

Kimble, F. A. (1961). *Hilgard and Marquis' Conditioning and learning.* New York: Appleton.

Kimble, F. A., & Kendall, J. W., Jr. (1953). A comparison of two methods of producing experimental extinction. *Journal of Experimental Psychology, 45,* 87–90.

Kimmell, H. D. (1967). Instrumental conditioning of autonomically mediated behavior. *Psychological Bulletin, 67,* 337–345.

Kimmell, H. D. (1974a). Instrumental conditioning of autonomically mediated responses. *American Psychologist, 29,* 325–335.

Kimmell, H. D. (1974b). Instrumental conditioning of autonomically mediated responses in human beings. *Biofeedback and Self-Control, 29*(5), 41–52.

King, G. F., Armitage, S. G., & Tilton, J. R. (1960). A therapeutic approach to schizophrenics of extreme pathology. *Journal of Abnormal and Social Psychology, 61,* 276–286.

Kintsch, W. (1970). *Learning, memory, and conceptual processes.* New York: Wiley.

Kirby, F. D., & Shields, F. (1972). Modification of arithmetic response rate and attending behavior in a seventh-grade student. *Journal of Applied Behavior Analysis, 5,* 79–84.

Kirby, F. D., & Toler, C. H., Jr. (1970). Modification of preschool isolate behavior: A case study. *Journal of Applied Behavior Analysis, 3,* 309–314.

Kirchner, J. H., & Hogan, R. A. (1966). The therapist variable in the implosion of phobias. *Psychotherapy: Theory, Research and Practice, 3,* 102–104.

Kirigin, K. A., Braukmann, C. J., Atwater, J. D., & Wolf, M. M. (1982). An evaluation of teaching-family (achievement place) group homes for juvenile offenders. *Journal of Applied Behavior Analysis, 15,* 1–16.

Kirkland, K., & Hollandsworth, J. G. (1980). Effective test taking: Skills-acquisition versus anxiety-reduction technique. *Journal of Consulting and Clinical Psychology, 48,* 431–439.

Kirschenbaum, D. S., & Perri, M. G. (1982). Improving academic competence in adults: A review of recent research. *Journal of Counseling Psychology, 32,* 279–305.

Kirschenbaum, D. S., Stalonas, P. M., Zastowny, T. R., & Tomarken, A. J. (1985). Behavioral treatment of adult obesity: Attentional controls and a 2-year follow-up. *Behaviour Research and Therapy, 23,* 675–682.

Kirschenbaum, D. S., & Tomarken, A. J. (1982). On facing the generalization problem: The study of self-regulatory failure. In P. C. Kendall (Ed.), *Advances in cognitive-behavioral research and therapy* (Vol. 1). New York: Academic Press.

Kirschner, N. M. (1976). Generalization of behaviorally oriented assertive training. *Psychological Record, 26,* 117–125.

Klein, D. F., & Davis, J. M. (1969). *Diagnosis and drug treatment of psychiatric disorders.* Baltimore: Williams & Wilkins.

Klepac, R. K., Hauge, G., Dowling, J., & McDonald, M. (1981). Direct and generalized effects of three components of stress inoculation for increased pain tolerance. *Behavior Therapy, 12,* 417–424.

Knapp, T. W. (1982). Treating migraine by training in temporal artery vasoconstriction and/or cognitive behavioral coping: A one-year follow-up. *Journal of Psychosomatic Research, 26,* 551–557.

Knepler, K. N., & Sewall, S. (1974). Negative practice paired with smelling salts in the treatment of a tic.

Journal of Behavior Therapy and Experimental Psychiatry, 5, 189–192.

Knight, M. F., & McKenzie, H. S. (1974). Elimination of bedtime thumbsucking in home settings through contingent reading. *Journal of Applied Behavior Analysis, 7*, 33–38.

Koch, L., & Breyer, N. L. (1974). A token economy for the teacher. *Psychology in the Schools, 11*, 193–200.

Koegel, R. L., & Covert, A. (1972). The relationship of self-stimulation to learning in autistic children. *Journal of Applied Behavior Analysis, 5*, 381–387.

Koegel, R. L., Firestone, P. B., Kramme, K. W., & Dunlap, G. (1974). Increasing spontaneous play by suppressing self-stimulation in autistic children. *Journal of Applied Behavior Analysis, 7*, 521–528.

Koegel, R. L., & Rincover, A. (1977). Research on the difference between generalization and maintenance in extra-therapy responding. *Journal of Applied Behavior Analysis, 10*, 1–2.

Koenig, K. P., & Masters, J. C. (1965). Experimental treatment of habitual smoking. *Behaviour Research and Therapy, 3*, 235–243.

Kohlenberg, R. J. (1970). The punishment of persistent vomiting: A case study. *Journal of Applied Behavior Analysis, 3*, 241–245.

Kohlenberg, R. J., Phillips, T., & Proctor, W. (1976). A behavioral analysis of peaking in residential electrical-energy consumers. *Journal of Applied Behavior Analysis, 9*, 13–18.

Kolko, D. J., & Rickard-Figueroa, J. L. (1985). Effects of video games on the adverse corollaries of chemotherapy in pediatric oncology patients: A single-case analysis. *Journal of Consulting and Clinical Psychology, 53*, 223–228.

Kolvin, I. (1967). "Aversive imagery" treatment in adolescents. *Behaviour Research and Therapy, 5*, 245–248.

Komaki, J., & Dore-Boyce, K. (1978). Self-recording: Its effects on individuals high and low in motivation. *Behavior Therapy, 9*, 65–72.

Konarski, E. A., Jr., Johnson, M. R., Crowell, C. R., & Whitman, T. L. (1981). An alternative approach to reinforcement for applied researchers: Response deprivation. *Behavior Therapy, 12*, 653–666.

Kondas, O., & Scetnicka, B. (1972). Systematic desensitization as a method of preparation for childbirth. *Journal of Behavior Therapy and Experimental Psychiatry, 3*, 51–54.

Koplan, J. P., Powell, K. E., Sikes, R. K., Shirley, R. W., & Campbell, C. C. (1982). An epidemiologic study of the benefits and risks of running. *Journal of the American Medical Association, 248*, 3118–3121.

Kornblith, S. J., Rehm, L. P., O'Hara, M. W., & Lamparski, D. M. (1983). The contribution of self-reinforcement training and behavioral assignments to the efficacy of self-control therapy for depression. *Cognitive Therapy and Research, 7*, 499–528.

Korzybski, A. (1933). *Science and sanity.* Lancaster, PA: Lancaster Press.

Kovacs, M., Rush, A. J., Beck, A. T., & Hollon, S. D. (1981). Depressed outpatients treated with cognitive therapy or pharmacotherapy: A one-year follow-up. *Archives of General Psychiatry, 38*, 33–39.

Kozloff, M. A. (1973). *Reaching the autistic child: A parent training program.* Champaign, IL: Research Press.

Krapfl, J. E. (1967). *Differential ordering of stimulus presentation and semi-automated versus live treatment in the systematic desensitization of snake phobia.* Unpublished doctoral dissertation, University of Missouri.

Krasner, L. (1976a). Behavior modification: Ethical issues and future trends. In H. Leitenberg (Ed.), *Handbook of behavior modification and behavior therapy.* Englewood, Cliffs, NJ: Prentice-Hall.

Krasner, L. (1976b). On the death of behavior modification: Some comments from a mourner. *American Psychologist, 31*, 387–388.

Krasner, L., & Ullman, L. P. (Eds.). (1965). *Research in behavior modification.* New York: Holt.

Krawitz, G., Rimm, D. C., & Zimmerman. (1978). *Flooding versus an equally credible placebo in treatment of acrophobia.* Unpublished master's thesis, Old Dominion University, Norfolk, VA.

Kremsdorf, R. R. (1978). *Biofeedback and cognitive skills training: An evaluation of their relative efficacy.* Paper presented at the ninth meeting of the Biofeedback Society of America, Albuquerque, NM.

Kremsdorf, R. R., Kochanowicz, N. A., & Costello, S. (1981). Cognitive skills training versus EMG biofeedback in the treatment of tension headaches. *Biofeedback and Self-regulation, 6*, 93–102.

Kristt, D. A., & Engel, B. T. (1975). Learned control of blood pressure in patients with high blood pressure. *Circulation, 51*, 370–378.

Kropp, H., Calhoon, B., & Verrier, R. (1971). Modification of the "self-concept" of emotionally disturbed children by covert reinforcement. *Behavior Therapy, 2*, 201–204.

Krueger, J. R. (1961). An early instance of conditioning from the Chinese dynastic histories. *Psychological Reports, 9*, 117.

Kuhlman, W. N., & Allison, T. (In press). EEG feedback training in the treatment of epilepsy. *Pavlovian Journal of Biological Science.*

Kumar, K., & Wilkinson, J. C. M. (1971). Thought stopping: A useful treatment for phobias of "internal stimuli." *British Journal of Psychiatry, 119*, 305–307.

Kuriansky, J. B., Sharpe, L., & O'Connor, D. (1982). The treatment of anorgasmia: Lay-term effectiveness of a short-term behavioral group therapy. *Journal of Sex and Marital Therapy, 8*, 29–43.

Kushner, M. (1965). The reduction of a long-standing fetish by means of aversive conditioning. In L. P. Ulmann & L. Krasner (Eds.), *Case studies in behavior modification.* New York: Holt.

Kushner, M. (1968). The operant control of intractible sneezing. In C. D. Spielberger, R. Fox, & D. Masterton (Eds.), *Contributions to general psychology.* New York: Ronald.

Kushner, M., & Sandler, J. (1966). Aversion therapy and the concept of punishment. *Behaviour Research and Therapy, 4*, 179–186.

Lacks, P., Bertelson, A. D., Gans, L., & Kunkel, J. (1983). The effectiveness of three behavioral treatments for different degrees of sleep onset insomnia. *Behavior Therapy, 14*, 593–605.

LaCroix, M., Clarke, M. A., Bock, J. C., Doxey, N., Wood, A., & Lavis, S. (1983). Biofeedback and relaxation in the treatment of migraine headaches: Comparative effectiveness and physiological correlates. *Journal of Neurology, Neurosurgery, and Psychiatry, 46*, 525–532.

Lader, M. H. (1967). Palmar skin conductance measures in anxiety and phobic states. *Journal of Psychosomatic Research, 11*, 271–281.

Lader, M. H., Gelder, M. G., & Marks, I. M. (1967). Palmar skin conductance measures as predictors of response to desensitization. *Journal of Psychosomatic Research 11*, 283–291.

Ladouceur, R. (1974). An experimental test of the learning paradigm of covert positive reinforcement. *Journal of Behavior Therapy and Experimental Psychiatry, 5*, 3–6.

Ladouceur, R. (1983). Participant modeling with or without cognitive treatment for phobias. *Journal of Consulting and Clinical Psychology, 51*, 942–944.

Lahey, B. B., McNees, M. P., & Brown, C. C. (1973). Modification of deficits in reading for comprehen-

sion. *Journal of Applied Behavior Analysis, 6*, 475–480.

Lamon, S., Wilson, G. T., & Leaf, R. C. (1977). Human classical aversion conditioning: Nausea versus electric shock in reduction of target beverage consumption. *Behaviour Research and Therapy, 15*, 313–320.

Lamontagne, Y., Marks, I. M. (1973). Psychogenic urinary retention: Treatment of prolonged exposure. *Behavior Therapy, 4*, 581–585.

Landau, P., & Paulson, T. (1977). Cope: A wilderness workshop in AT. In R. E. Alberti (Ed.), *Assertiveness: Innovations, applications, issues.* San Luis Obispo, CA: Impact.

Lando, H. A. (1976). Self-pacing in eliminating chronic smoking: Serendipity revisited. *Behavior Therapy, 7*, 634–640.

Lando, H. A. (1977). Successful treatment of smokers with a broad-spectrum behavioral approach. *Journal of Consulting and Clinical Psychology, 45*, 361–366.

Lang, A. R., & Marlatt, A. G. (1982). Problem drinking: A social learning perspective. In R. J. Gatchel, A. Baum, & J. E. Singer (Eds.), *Handbook of psychology and health.* Hillsdale, NJ: Erlbaum.

Lang, P. J. (1969). The mechanics of desensitization and laboratory studies of human fear. In C. M. Franks (Ed.), *Behavior therapy: Appraisal and status.* New York: McGraw-Hill.

Lang, P. J. (1974). Learned control of human heart rate in a computer directed environment. In P. A. Obrist, A. H. Black, J. Brener, & L. V. DiCara (Eds.), *Cardiovascular psychophysiology.* New York: Aldine.

Lang, P. J., & Hnatiow, P. J. (1965). Learned stabilization of cardiac rate. *Psychophysiology, 1*, 330–336.

Lang, P. J., & Lazovik, A. D. (1963). Experimental desensitization of a phobia. *Journal of Abnormal and Social Psychology, 66*, 519–525.

Lang, P. J., Lazovik, A. D., & Reynolds, D. J. (1965). Desensitization, suggestibility, and pseudotherapy. *Journal of Abnormal Psychology, 70*, 395–402.

Lang, P. J., & Melamed, B. G. (1969). Avoidance conditioning therapy of an infant with chronic ruminative vomiting. *Journal of Abnormal Psychology, 74*, 1–8.

Lang, P. J., Melamed, B. G., & Hart, J. (1970). A psychophysiological analysis of fear modification using an automated desensitization procedure. *Journal of Abnormal Psychology, 76*, 220–234.

Lange, A. J., & Jakubowski, P. (1976). *Responsible assertive behavior*. Champaign, IL: Research Press.

Langer, E. J., Janis, I. E., & Wolfer, J. A. (1975). Reduction of psychological stress in surgical patients. *Journal of Experimental and Social Psychology, 11*, 155–165.

Langevin, R., & Martin, M. (1975). Can erotic responses be classically conditioned? *Behavior Therapy, 6*, 350–355.

Lanyon, R. I., Barrington, C. C., & Newman, A. C. (1976). Modification of stuttering through EMG biofeedback: A preliminary study. *Behavior Therapy, 7*, 96–103.

Lanyon, R. I., Primo, R. Terrell, F., & Weiner, A. (1972). An aversion-desensitization treatment for alcoholism. *Journal of Consulting and Clinical Psychology, 38*, 394–398.

LaPointe, K. A., & Rimm, D. C. (1980). Cognitive, assertive and insight oriented group therapies in the treatment of reactive depression in women. *Psychotherapy: Theory, Research, and Practice 17*, 312–321.

Lavelle, Y., Lamontagne, Y., Annable, L., & Fontaine, F. (1982). Chraracteristics of chronically anxious patients who respond to EMG feedback training. *Journal of Clinical Psychiatry, 43*, 229–230.

Lavigueur, H. (1976). The use of siblings as an adjunct to the behavioral treatment of children in the home with parents as therapists. *Behavior Therapy, 7*, 602–613.

Lavin, N. I., Thorpe, J. G., Barker, J. C., Blakemore, C. B., & Conway, C. G. (1961). Behavior therapy in a case of transvestism. *Journal of Nervous and Mental Disease, 133*, 346–353.

Lawrence, P. S. (1970). *The assessment and modification of assertive behavior*. Unpublished doctoral dissertation, Arizona State University.

Lawson, D. M., & Boudin, H. M. (1985). Alcohol and drug abuse. In M. Hersen & A. S. Bellack (Eds.), *Handbook of clinical behavior therapy with adults*. New York: Plenum Press.

Lawson, D. M., & May, R. B. (1970). Three procedures for the extinction of smoking behavior. *Psychological Record, 20*, 151–157.

Lawson, R. (1960). *Learning and behavior*. New York: Macmillan.

Layne, C. C. (1970). *The effects of suggestion in implosive therapy for fear of rats*. Unpublished doctoral dissertation, Southern Illinois University.

Lazarus, A. A. (1960). Objective psychotherapy in the treatment of dysphemia. *Journal of South African Logopedic Society, 6*, 8–10.

Lazarus, A. A. (1961). Group therapy of phobic disorders by systematic desensitization. *Journal of Abnormal and Social Psychology, 63*, 505–510.

Lazarus, A. A. (1963). The results of behavior therapy in 126 cases of severe neurosis. *Behaviour Research and Therapy, 1*, 69–79.

Lazarus, A. A. (1964a). Crucial procedural factors in desensitization therapy. *Behaviour Research and Therapy, 2*, 65–70.

Lazarus, A. A. (1964b). Behavior rehearsal vs. nondirective therapy vs. advice in effecting behavior change. *Behaviour Research and Therapy, 4*, 209–212.

Lazarus, A. A. (1965). Behavior therapy, incomplete treatment and symptom substitution. *Journal of Nervous and Mental Disease, 140*, 80–86.

Lazarus, A. A. (1966). Behavior rehearsal vs. nondirective therapy vs. advice in effecting behavior change. *Behaviour Research and Therapy, 4*, 209–212.

Lazarus, A. A. (1971). *Behavior therapy and beyond*. New York: McGraw-Hill.

Lazarus, A. A. (Ed.). (1972). *Clinical behavior therapy*. New York: Brunner/Mazel.

Lazarus, A. A. (1973). On assertive behavior: A brief note. *Behavior Therapy, 4*, 697–699.

Lazarus, A. A. (1974a). Multimodal behavioral treatment of depression. *Behavior Therapy, 5*, 549–554.

Lazarus, A. A. (1974b March). Multimodal therapy: Basic ID. *Psychology Today 7*(10), 59–63.

Lazarus, A. A. (1976). *Multimodal behavior therapy*. New York: Springer.

Lazarus, A. A. (1977). Has behavior therapy outlived its usefulness? *American Psychologist, 32*, 550–554.

Lazarus, A. A., & Fay, A. (1975). *I can if I want to*. New York: William Morrow.

Lazarus, A. A., & Rachman, S. (1957). The use of systematic desensitization in psychotherapy. *South African Medical Journal, 31*, 934–937.

Lazarus, A. A., & Rachman, S. (1960). The use of systematic desensitization in psychotherapy. In H. J. Eysenck (Ed.), *Behavior therapy and the neuroses*. Oxford: Pergamon.

Lazarus, A. A., & Serber, M. (1968). Is systematic desensitization being misapplied? *Psychological Reports, 23*, 215–218.

Lazarus, R. S. (1975). A cognitively oriented psychologist looks at biofeedback. *American Psychologist, 30*, 553–561.

Leal, L. L., Baxter, E. G., Martin, J., & Marx, R. W. (1981). Cognitive modification and systematic desensitization with test anxious high school students. *Journal of Counseling Psychology, 26,* 371–377.

le Boeuf, A. (1974). Aversion treatment of headbanging in a normal adult. *Journal of Behavior Therapy and Experimental Psychiatry, 5,* 197–199.

le Boeuf, A. (1980). Effects of frontalis biofeedback on subjective ratings of relaxation. *Perceptual and Motor Skills, 50,* 99–103.

Lederhendler, I., & Baum, M. (1970). Mechanical facilitation of the action of response prevention (flooding) in rats. *Behaviour Research and Therapy, 8,* 43–48.

Ledwidge, B. (1978). Cognitive behavior modification: A step in the wrong direction. *Psychological Bulletin, 85,* 353–375.

Lee, C. (1983). Self-efficacy and behaviour as predictors of subsequent behaviour in an assertiveness training programme. *Behaviour Research and Therapy, 21,* 225–232.

Lee, C. (1984). Accuracy of efficacy and outcome expectations in predicting performance in a simulated assertiveness task. *Cognitive Therapy and Research, 8,* 37–48.

Lehrer, P. M. (1978). Psychophysiological effects of progressive relaxation in anxiety neurotic patients and of progressive relaxation and alpha feedback in nonpatients. *Journal of Consulting and Clinical Psychology, 46,* 389–404.

Lehrer, P. M. (1982). How to relax and how not to relax: A re-evaluation of the work of Edmund Jacobson: 1. *Behaviour Research and Therapy, 20,* 417–428.

Lehrer, P. M., & Woolfolk, R. L. (1984). Are stress reduction techniques interchangeable, or do they have specific effects: A review of the comparative empirical literature. In R. L. Woolfolk & P. M. Lehrer (Eds.), *Principles and practice of stress management.* New York: Guilford Press.

Leitenberg, H. (1965). Is time-out from positive reinforcement an aversive event? A review of the experimental evidence. *Psychological Bulletin, 64,* 428–441.

Leitenberg, H., Agras, S., Butz, R., & Wincze, J. (1971). Relationship between heartrate and behavioral change during the treatment of phobias. *Journal of Applied Behavior Analysis, 78,* 59–68.

Leitenberg, H., Agras, S., Thompson, L. E., & Wright, D. E. (1968). Feedback in behavior modification: An experimental analysis in two phobic cases. *Journal of Applied Behavior Analysis, 1,* 131–137.

Leitenberg, H., Burchard, D., Burchard, N., Fuller, E. J., & Lysaght, T. V. (1977). Using positive reinforcement to suppress behavior: Some experimental comparisons with sibling conflict. *Behavior Therapy, 8,* 168–182.

Lemere, F., & Voegtlin, W. L. (1940). Conditioned reflex therapy of alcoholic addiction: Specificity of conditioning against chronic alcoholism. *California and Western Medicine, 53,* 268–269.

Lemere, F., & Voegtlin, W. L. (1950). An evaluation of the aversion treatment of alcoholism. *Quarterly Journal of Studies on Alcohol, 11,* 199–204.

Lemere, F., Voegtlin, W. L., Broz, W. R., O'Hallaren, P., & Tupper, W. E. (1942a). Conditioned reflex treatment of chronic alcoholism: 7, Technic. *Diseases of the Nervous System, 3,* 243–247.

Lemere, F., Voegtlin, W. L., Broz, W. R., O'Hallaren, P., & Tupper, W. E. (1942b). The conditioned reflex treatment of chronic alcoholism: 8, A review of six years' experience with this treatment of 1526 patients. *Journal of the American Medical Association, 120,* 269–270.

Lent, R. W., Russell, R. K., & Zamostny, K. P. (1981). Comparison of cue-controlled desensitization, rational restructuring, and a credible placebo in the treatment of speech anxiety. *Journal of Consulting and Clinical Psychology, 49,* 608–610.

Leon, G. R., & Chamberlain, K. (1973). Comparison of daily eating habits and emotional states of overweight persons successful or unsuccessful in maintaining a weight loss. *Journal of Consulting and Clinical Psychology, 41,* 108–115.

Lepper, M. R., Greene, D., & Nisbett, R. E. (1973). Undermining children's intrinsic interest with extrinsic rewards: A test of the overjustification hypothesis. *Journal of Personality and Social Psychology, 28,* 129–137.

Lesser, E. (1967). Behavior therapy with a narcotics user: A case report. *Behaviour Research and Therapy, 5,* 251–252.

Levendusky, P. G., Berglas, S., Dooley, C. P., & Landau, R. J. (1983). Therapeutic Contract Program: Preliminary report on a behavioral alternative to the token economy. *Behaviour Research and Therapy, 21,* 137–142.

Levenkron, J. C., Cohen, J. D., Mueller, H. S., & Fisher, E. B. (1983). Modifying the Type A coronary-prone behavior pattern. *Journal of Consulting and Clinical Psychology, 51,* 192–204.

Levey, A. B., & Martin, I. (1975). Classical conditioning of human "evaluative" responses. *Behaviour Research and Therapy, 13,* 221–226.

Levin, R. B., & Gross, A. M. (1985). The role of relaxation in systematic desensitization. *Behaviour Research and Therapy, 23,* 187–196.

Levine, B. A. (1976). Treatment of Trichotillomania by covert sensitization. *Journal of Behavior Therapy and Experimental Psychiatry, 7,* 75–76.

Levine, B. A., & Wolpe, J. (1980). In vivo desensitization of a severe driving phobia through radio contact. *Journal of Behavior Therapy and Experimental Psychiatry, 11,* 281–282.

Levis, D. J. (1967). Implosive therapy: Part 2, The subhuman analogue, the strategy, and the technique. In S. G. Armitage (Ed.), *Behavior modification techniques in the treatment of emotional disorders.* Battle Creek, MI: Veterans Administration Publication, 1967.

Levis, D. J., & Carrera, R. N. (1967). Effects of 10 hours of implosive therapy in the treatment of outpatients: A preliminary report. *Journal of Abnormal Psychology, 72,* 504–508.

Levitt, E. E. (1963). Psychotherapy with children: A further evaluation. *Behaviour Research and Therapy, 1,* 45–51.

Levy, R., & Meyer, V. (1971). Ritual prevention in obsessive patients. *Proceedings of the Royal Society of Medicine, 64,* 1115–1118.

Lewinsohn, P. M. (1974a). A behavioral approach to depression. In R. M. Friedman & M. M. Katz (Eds.), *The psychology of depression: Contemporary theory and research.* New York: Wiley.

Lewinsohn, P. M. (1974b). The behavioral study and treatment of depression. In M. Hersen, R. M. Eisler, & P. M. Miller (Eds.), *Progress in behavior modification* (Vol. 1). New York: Academic Press.

Lewinsohn, P. M., & Shaffer, M. (1971). Use of home observations as an integral part of the treatment of depression. Preliminary report and case studies. *Journal of Consulting and Clinical Psychology, 37,* 87–95.

Lewis, S. (1974). A comparison of behavior therapy techniques in the reduction of fearful avoidance behavior. *Behavior Therapy, 5,* 648–655.

Ley, R., & Walker, H. (1973). Effects of carbon dioxide-oxygen inhalation on heart rate, blood pressure, and subjective anxiety. *Journal of Behavior Therapy and Experimental Psychiatry, 4,* 223–228.

Liberman, R. P. (1968). A view of behavior modification projects in California. *Behaviour Research and Therapy, 6,* 331–341.

Liberman, R. P., King, L. W., DeRisi, W. J., & McCann, M. (1975). *Personal effectiveness.* Champaign, IL: Research Press.

Libet, J. M., & Lewinsohn, P. M. (1973). Concept of social skill with special reference to the behavior of depressed persons. *Journal of Consulting and Clinical Psychology, 40,* 304–312.

Lichstein, K. L., & Eakin, T. L. (1985). Progressive versus self-control relaxation to reduce spontaneous bleeding in hemophiliacs. *Journal of Behavioral Medicine, 8,* 149–162.

Lichstein, K. L., Hoelscher, T. J., Nickel, R., & Hoon, P. W. (1983). An integrated blood volume pulse biofeedback system for migraine treatment. *Biofeedback and Self-regulation, 8,* 127–134.

Lichtenstein, E. (1982). The smoking problem: A behavioral perspective. *Journal of Consulting and Clinical Psychology, 50,* 804–819.

Lichtenstein, E., & Brown, R. A. (1980). Smoking cessation methods: Review and recommendations. In W. R. Miller (Ed.), *The addictive behaviors: Treatment of alcoholism, drug abuse, smoking, and obesity.* New York: Pergamon Press.

Lichtenstein, E., & Danaher, B. G. (1976). Modification of smoking behavior: A critical analysis of theory, research, and practice. In M. Hersen, R., M. Eisler, & P. M. Miller (Eds.), *Progress in behavior modification* (Vol. 3). New York: Academic Press.

Lichtenstein, E., & Glasgow, R. E. (1977). Rapid smoking: Side effects and safeguards. *Journal of Consulting and Clinical Psychology, 45,* 815–821.

Lichtenstein, E., Harris, D. E., Birchler, G. R., Wahl, J. M., Schmahl, D. P. (1973). Comparison of rapid smoking, warm, smoky air, and attention placebo in the modification of smoking behavior. *Journal of Consulting and Clinical Psychology, 40,* 92–98.

Lichtenstein, E., & Rodrigues, M. R. P. (1977). Long-term effects of rapid smoking treatment for dependent cigarette smokers. *Addictive Behaviors, 2,* 109–112.

Lick, J. R. (1975). Expectancy, false galvanic skin response feedback and systematic desensitization in the modification of a phobic behavior. *Journal of Consulting and Clinical Psychology, 43,* 557–567.

Liebert, R. M., Spiegler, M. D., Hall, W. M. (1970). Effects of the value of contingent self administered and non-contingent externally imposed reward on children's behavioral productivity. *Psychonomic Science, 18,* 245–246.

Linehan, M. M., Goldfried, M. R., & Goldfried, A. P. (1979). Assertion therapy: Skill training or cognitive restructuring. *Behavior Therapy, 10,* 372–388.

Linscheid, T. R., & Cunningham, C. E. (1977). A controlled demonstration of the effectiveness of electric shock in the elimination of chronic infant rumination. *Journal of Applied Behavior Analysis, 10,* 500.

Lippit, R., & Hubbell, A. (1956). Role playing for personnel and guidance workers: Review of the literature with suggestions for application. *Group Psychotherapy, 9,* 89–114.

Lira, E. T., Nay, R., McCullough, J. P., & Etkin, M. W. (1975). Relative effects of modeling and role playing in the treatment of avoidance behaviors. *Journal of Consulting and Clinical Psychology, 43,* 608–618.

Litrownik, A. J. (1982). Special considerations in the self-management of training of the developmentally disabled. In P. Karoly & F. H. Kanfer (Eds.), *Self-management and behavior change: From theory to practice.* Elmsford, NY: Pergamon Press.

Litrownik, A. J., Franzini, L. R., & Turner, G. L. (1976). Acquisition of concepts by TMR children as a function of type of modeling, rule verbalization and observer gender. *American Journal of Mental Deficiency, 80,* 620–628.

Little, B. C., Hayworth, J., Benson, P., Hall, F., Beard, R. W., Dewhurst, V., & Priest, R. G. (1984, April). Treatment of hypertension in pregnancy by relaxation and biofeedback. *Lancet,* 865–867.

Little, L. M., & Curran, J. P. (1978). Covert sensitization: A clinical procedure in need of some explanations. *Psychological Bulletin, 85,* 513–531.

Little, L. M., Curran, J. P., & Gilbert, F. S. (1977). The importance of subject recruitment procedures in therapy analogue studies on heterosexual-social anxiety. *Behavior Therapy, 8,* 24–29.

Locke, E. A. (1971). Is "behavior therapy" behavioristic? An analysis of Wolpe's psychotherapeutic methods. *Psychological Bulletin, 76,* 318–327.

Lomont, J. F., Gilner, F. H., Spector, N. J., & Skinner, K. K. (1969). Group assertion training and group insight therapies. *Psychological Reports, 25,* 463–470.

London, P. (1964). *The modes and morals of psychotherapy.* New York: Holt.

Long, B. C. (1985). Stress-management interventions: A 15-month follow-up of aerobic conditioning and stress inoculation training. *Cognitive Therapy and Research, 9,* 471–478.

Long, J. D., & Williams, R. L. (1973). The comparative effectiveness of group and individually contingent free time with inner-city junior high school students. *Journal of Applied Behavior Analysis, 6,* 465–474.

Lovaas, O. I. (1966). *Reinforcement therapy* (16 mm sound film). Philadelphia: Smith, Kline, & French Laboratories.

Lovaas, O. I., (1967). A behavior therapy approach to the treatment of childhood schizophrenia. In J. P. Hill (Ed.), *Minnesota Symposium on Child Psychology* (Vol 1). Minneapolis: University of Minnesota Press.

Lovaas, O. I. (1968). Some studies in the treatment of childhood schizophrenia. In J. M. Schlien (Ed.), *Research in psychotherapy.* Washington, DC: American Psychological Association.

Lovaas, O. I., Berberich, J. P., Kassorla, I. C., Klynn G. A., & Meisel, J. (1966). *Establishment of a texting and labeling vocabulary in schizophrenic children.* Unpublished manuscript, University of California, Los Angeles.

Lovaas, O. I., Berberich, J. P., Perloff, B. F., & Schaeffer, B. (1966). Acquisition of imitative speech by schizophrenic children. *Science, 151,* 705–707.

Lovaas, O. I., Dumont, D. A., Klynn, G. A., & Meisel, J. (1966). *Establishment of appropriate response to, and use of, certain prepositions and pronouns in schizophrenic children.* Unpublished manuscript, University of California, Los Angeles.

Lovaas, O. I., Freitag, G., Gold, V. J., & Kassorla, I. C. (1965). Experimental studies in childhood schizophrenia: Analysis of self-destructive behavior. *Journal of Experimental Child Psychology, 2,* 67–84.

Lovaas, O. I., Freitag, G., Kinder, M. I., Rubenstein, B. D., Schaeffer, B., & Simmons, J. Q. (1966). Establishment of social reinforcers in two schizophrenic children on the basis of food. *Journal of Experimental Child Psychology, 4,* 109–125.

Lovaas, O. I., Freitag, L., Nelson, K., & Whalen, C.

(1967). The establishment of imitation and its use for the development of complex behavior in schizophrenic children. *Behaviour Research and Therapy, 5,* 171–181.

Lovaas, O. I., & Simmons, J. Q. (1969). Manipulation of self-destruction in three retarded children. *Journal of Applied Behavior Analysis, 2,* 143–157.

Lovenberg, W., & Tamori, T. (1984). Nutritional factors and cardiovascular disease. *Clinical and Experimental Hypertension, 6A,* 417–426.

Lovibond, S. H., & Caddy, G. (1970). Discriminated aversive control in the moderation of alcoholics' drinking behavior. *Behavior Therapy, 1,* 437–444.

Lovitt, T. C., & Curtiss, K. A. (1969). Academic response rate as a function of teacher and self imposed contingencies. *Journal of Applied Behavioral Analysis, 2,* 49–53.

Lovitt, T. C., Guppy, T. E., & Blattner, J. E. (1969). The use of free-time contingency with fourth graders to increase spelling accuracy. *Behaviour Research and Therapy, 7,* 151–156.

Lowe, K., & Lutzker, J. P. (1979). Increasing compliance to a medical regimen with a juvenile diabetic. *Behavior Therapy, 10,* 57–64.

Lowe, M. L., & Cuvo, A. J. (1976). Teaching coin summation to the mentally retarded. *Journal of Applied Behavior Analysis, 9,* 483–489.

Lubar, J. F. (1975, June). Behavioral management of epilepsy through sensori-motor rhythm EEG biofeedback conditioning. *National Spokesman,* pp. 6–7.

Lubar, J. F., & Bahler, W. W. (1976–1977). Behavioral management of epileptic seizures following EEG biofeedback training of sensorimotor rhythm. *Biofeedback and Self-Control,* pp. 475–502.

Luborsky, L., Crits-Christoph, P., Brady, J. P., Kron, R. E., Weiss, T., Cohen, M., & Levy, L. (1982). Behavioral versus pharmacological treatments of essential hypertension: A needed comparison. *Psychosomatic Medicine, 44,* 203–213.

Luce, S. C., Deliquadrix, J., & Hall, R. V. (1980). Contingent exercise: A mild but powerful procedure for suppressing inappropriate verbal and aggressive behavior. *Journal of Applied Behavioral Analysis, 13,* 583–594.

Lucero, R. J., Vail, D. J., & Scherber, J. (1968). Regulating operant-conditioning programs. *Hospital and Community Psychiatry, 19,* 53–54.

Luiselli, J. K., & Greenridge, A. (1982). Behavioral treatment of high-rate aggression in a rubella child. *Journal of Behavior Therapy and Experimental Psychiatry, 13,* 152–157.

Luiselli, J. K., Suskin, L., & McPhee, D. F. (1981). Continuous and intermittent application of overcorrection in a self-injurious autistic child: Alternating treatments design analysis. *Journal of Behavior Therapy and Experimental Psychiatry, 12*(4), 355–358.

Lund, A. K., Kegeles, S. S. (1984). Rewards and adolescent health behavior. *Health Psychology, 3,* 351–369.

Luria, A. (1961), *The role of speech in the regulation of normal and abnormal behavior.* New York: Liveright.

Lustman, P. J., & Sowa, C. J. (1983). Comparative efficacy of biofeedback and stress inoculation for stress reduction. *Journal of Clinical Psychology, 39,* 191–197.

Lyles, J. N., Burish, T. G., Krozely, M. G., & Oldham, R. K. (1982). Efficacy of relaxation training and guided imagery in reducing the aversiveness of cancer chemotherapy. *Journal of Consulting and Clinical Psychology, 50,* 509–524.

MacCulloch, M. J., Birtles, C. J., & Feldman, M. P. (1971). Anticipatory avoidance learning for the treatment of homosexuality: Recent developments and an automatic aversion therapy system. *Behavior Therapy, 2,* 151–169.

MacCulloch, M. J., & Feldman, M. P. (1967). Aversion therapy in the management of 43 homosexuals. *British Medical Journal, 2,* 594–597.

MacCulloch, M. J., Feldman, M. P., & Pinschof, J. S. (1965). The application of anticipatory avoidance learning to the treatment of homosexuality. II. Avoidance response latencies and pulse rate changes. *Behaviour Research and Therapy, 3,* 21–43.

MacDonough, T. S. (1972). A critique of the first Feldman and MacCulloch avoidance conditioning treatment for homosexuals. *Behavior Therapy, 3,* 104–111.

MacDougal, J. M., Dembroski, T. M., Dimsdale, J. C., & Hackett, T. P. (1985). Components of Type A, hostility, and anger-in: Further relationships to angiographic findings. *Health Psychology, 4,* 137–152.

MacPherson, E. M., Candee, B. L., & Hohman, R. J. (1974). A comparison of three methods for eliminating disruptive lunchroom behavior. *Journal of Applied Behavior Analysis, 7,* 287–297.

Madsen, C. H., Jr., Becker, W. C., Thomas, D. R., Koser, L., & Plager, E. (1968). An analysis of the reinforcing function of "sit down" commands. In R. K. Parker (Ed.), *Readings in educational psychology*. Boston: Allyn & Bacon.

Madsen, C. H., Jr., Madsen, C. K., & Thompson, F. (1974). Increasing rural head start children's consumption of middle-class meals. *Journal of Applied Behavior Analysis, 7*, 257–262.

Maes, W. R., & Heimann, R. A. (1970). *The comparison of three approaches to the reduction of test anxiety in high school students* (Final report, Project 9–1049). Washington, DC: Office of Education, Bureau of Research, U.S. Department of Health, Education and Welfare.

Magrab, P. R., & Papadopoulou, Z. I. (1977). The effect of a token economy on dietary compliance for children on hemodialysis. *Journal of Applied Behavior Analysis, 10*, 573–578.

Mahoney, K., & Mahoney, M. J. (1976a). *Permanent weight control*. New York: Norton.

Mahoney, K., Mahoney, M. J. (1976b). Treatment of obesity: A clinical exploration. In B. J. Williams, S. Martin, & J. P. Foreyt (Eds.), *Obesity: Behavioral approaches to dietary management*. New York: Brunner/Mazel.

Mahoney, M. J. (1971). The self management of covert behavior: A case study. *Behavior Therapy, 2*, 575–578.

Mahoney, M. J. (1974a). *Cognition and behavior modification*. Cambridge, MA: Ballinger.

Mahoney, M. J. (1974b). Self-reward and self monitoring techniques for weight control. *Behavior Therapy, 5*, 48–57.

Mahoney, M. J. (1975). Fat fiction. *Behavior Therapy, 6*, 416–418.

Mahoney, M. J. (1976a). *Scientist as subject: The psychological imperative*. Cambridge, MA: Ballinger.

Mahoney, M. J. (1976b). Terminal terminology: A self-regulated response to Goldiamond. *Journal of Applied Behavior Analysis, 9*, 515–517.

Mahoney, M. J. (1977a). Cognitive therapy and research: A question of questions. *Cognitive Therapy and Research, 1*, 1–3.

Mahoney, M. J. (1977b). On the continuing resistance to thoughtful therapy. *Behavior Therapy, 8*, 673–677.

Mahoney, M. J. (1977c). Personal science: A cognitive learning therapy. In A. Ellis & R. Grieger (Eds.), *Handbook of rational-emotive therapy*. New York: Springer-Verlag.

Mahoney, M. J. (1977d). Reflections on the cognitive learning trend in psychotherapy. *American Psychologist, 32*(1), 5–13.

Mahoney, M. J., & Arnkoff, D. (1978). Cognitive and self-control therapies. In S. Garfield & A. Bergin (Eds.), *Handbook of psychotherapy and behavior change* (2nd ed.). New York: Wiley.

Mahoney, M. J., & Bandura, A. (1972). Self reinforcement in pigeons. *Learning and Motivation, 3*, 292–303.

Mahoney, M. J., Moura, N. G. M., & Wade, T. C. (1973). The relative efficacy of self-reward, self-punishment, and self-monitoring techniques for weight loss. *Journal of Consulting and Clinical Psychology, 40*, 404–407.

Mahoney, M. J., & Thoresen, C. E. (Eds.). (1974). *Self-control: Power to the person*. Monterey, CA: Brooks/Cole.

Maier, S. F., & Seligman, M. E. (1976). Learned helplessness: Theory and evidence. *Journal of Experimental Psychology, 105*, 3–46.

Main, G. C., & Monro, B. C. (1977). A token reinforcement program in a public junior-high school. *Journal of Applied Behavior Analysis, 10*, 93–94.

Maisto, S. A., Sobell, M. B., & Sobell, L. C. (1980). Predictors of treatment outcome for alcoholics treated by individualized behavior therapy. *Addictive Behaviors, 5*, 259–264.

Malan, D. H. (1976). *The frontier of brief psychotherapy: An example of the convergence of research and clinical practice*. New York: Plenum Press.

Maletzky, B. M. (1973). "Assisted" covert sensitization: A preliminary report. *Behavior Therapy, 4*, 117–119.

Maletzky, B. M. (1977). "Booster" sessions in aversion therapy: The permanency of treatment. *Behavior Therapy, 8*, 460–463.

Maletzky, B. M. (1980). Self-referred versus court-referred sexually deviant patients: Success with assisted covert sensitization. *Behavior Therapy, 11*, 306–314.

Maletzky, B. M., & George, F. S. (1973). The treatment of homosexuality by "assisted" covert sensitization. *Behaviour Research and Therapy, 11*, 655–657.

Malleson, N. (1959). Panic and phobia. *Lancet, 1*, 225–227.

Malmo, R. B. (1962). Activation. In A. J. Bachrach (Ed.), *Experimental foundations of clinical psychology*. New York: Basic Books.

Maloney, D. M., Harper, T. M., Braukmann, C. M.,

Fixsen, D. L., Phillips, E. L., & Wolf, M. M. (1976). Teaching conversation-related skills to predelinquent girls. *Journal of Applied Behavior Analysis, 9,* 371.

Maloney, K. B., & Hopkins, B. L. (1973). The modification of sentence structure and its relationship to subjective judgments of creativity in writing. *Journal of Applied Behavior Analysis, 6,* 425–433.

Maltzman, I. (1968). Theoretical conceptions of semantic conditioning and generalization. In T. R. Dixon & D. L. Horton (Eds.), *Verbal behavior and general behavior theory.* Englewood Cliffs, NJ: Prentice-Hall.

Mann, R. A. (1972). The behavior-therapeutic use of contingency contracting to control an adult behavior problem: Weight control. *Journal of Applied Behavior Analysis, 5,* 99–109.

Mann, R. J., & Flowers, J. V. (1978). An investigation of the reliability and validity of the Rathus Assertiveness Schedule. *Psychological Reports, 42,* 632–634.

Manno, B., & Marston, A. R. (1972). Weight reduction as a function of negative covert reinforcement (sensitization) versus positive covert reinforcement. *Behaviour Research and Therapy, 10,* 201–207.

Mansdorf, I. J. (1977). Reinforcer isolation: An alternative to subject isolation in time-out from positive reinforcement. *Journal of Behavior Therapy and Experimental Psychiatry, 8,* 391–393.

Marburg, C. C., Houston, B. K., & Holmes, D. S. (1976). Influence of multiple models on the behavior of institutionalized retarded children: Increased generalization to other models and other behaviors. *Journal of Consulting and Clinical Psychology, 44,* 514–519.

Margolis, R. B., & Shemberg, K. M. (1976). Cognitive self-instruction in process and reactive schizophrenics: A failure to replicate. *Behavior Therapy, 7,* 668–671.

Marholin, D., II, & Gray, D. (1976). Effects of group response-cost procedures on cash shortages in a small business. *Journal of Applied Behavior Analysis, 9,* 25–30.

Marholin, D., II, & Steinman, W. M. (1977). Stimulus control in the classroom as a function of the behavior reinforced. *Journal of Applied Behavior Analysis, 10,* 465–478.

Marks, I. M., & Gelder, M. G. (1967). Transvestism and fetishism: Clinical and psychological changes during faradic aversion. *British Journal of Psychiatry, 113,* 711–729.

Marks, I. M., Gelder, M. G., & Bancroft, J. (1970). Sexual deviants two years after electric aversion. *British Journal of Psychiatry, 117,* 173–185.

Marks, I. M., Viswanathan, R., & Lipsedge, M. S. (1972). Enhanced relief of phobias by flooding during waning diazepam effect. *British Journal of Psychiatry, 121,* 493–505.

Markus, H. (1977). Self-schemata and processing information about the self. *Journal of Personality and Social Psychology, 35,* 63–78.

Marlatt, G. A. (1979). Alcohol use and problem drinking: A cognitive-behavioral analysis. In P. C. Kendall & S. D. Hollon (Eds.), *Cognitive-behavioral interventions: Theory, research, and procedures.*

Marlatt, G. A. (1982). Relapse prevention: A self-control program for the treatment of addictive behaviors. In R. B. Stuart (Ed.), *Adherence, compliance and generalization in behavioral medicine.*

Marlatt, G. A. (1983). The controlled-drinking controversy: A commentary. *American Psychologist, 38,* 1097–1110.

Marlatt, G. A., Demming, B., & Reid, J. B. (1973). Loss of control drinking in alcoholics: An experimental analogue. *Journal of Abnormal Psychology, 81,* 223–241.

Marlatt, G. A., & Gordon, J. R. (1980). Determinants of relapse: Implications for the maintenance of behavior change. In P. O. Davidson & S. M. Davidson (Eds.), *Behavioral Medicine: Changing health lifestyles.* New York: Brunner/Mazel.

Marlatt, G. A., & Gordon, J. R. (Eds.) (1985). *Relapse prevention.* New York: Guilford Press.

Marquis, J. N., & Morgan, W. G. (1969). *A guidebook for systematic desensitization.* Palo Alto, CA: Veterans Administration Hospital.

Marrone, R. L., Merksamer, M. A., & Salzberg, P. M. (1970). A short duration group treatment of smoking behavior by stimulus saturation. *Behaviour Research and Therapy, 8,* 347–352.

Marshall, W. L., Boutilier, J., & Minnes, P. (1974). The modification of phobic behavior by covert reinforcement. *Behavior Therapy, 5,* 469–480.

Marshall, W. L., Parker, L., & Hayes, B. M. (1982). Treating public speaking problems. *Behavior Modification, 6*(2), 147–170.

Marshall, W. L., Presse, L., & Andrews, W. R. (1976). A self-administered program for public speaking anxiety. *Behaviour Research and Therapy, 14,* 33–39.

Marshall, W. L., Stoian, M., & Andrews, W. R. (1977). Skills training and self-administered desensitization in the reduction of public speaking anxiety. *Behaviour Research and Therapy, 15*, 115–117.

Marston, A. R. (1965). Imitation, self-reinforcement, and reinforcement of another person. *Journal of Personality and Social Psychology, 2*, 225–261.

Martin, P. R., & Matthews, A. M. (1978). Tension headache: A psychophysiological investigation. *Journal of Psychosomatic Research, 22*, 389–399.

Martin, R., & Lauridsen, D. (1974). *Developing student discipline and motivation: A series for teacher in service training*. Champaign, IL: Research Press.

Martin, R. D., & Conway, J. B. (1976). Aversive stimulation of eliminate infant nocturnal rocking. *Journal of Behavior Therapy and Experimental Psychiatry, 7*, 200–201.

Marzillier, J. S., Lambert, C., & Kellett, J. (1976). A controlled evaluation of systematic desensitization and social skills training for socially inadequate psychiatric patients. *Behaviour Research and Therapy, 14*, 225–238.

Marzuk, D. M. (1985). Biofeedback for gastrointestinal disorder: A review of the literature. *Annals of Internal Medicine, 103*, 240–244.

Mash, E. J., Hamerlynck, L. A., & Handy, L. C. (Eds.). (1976). *Behavior modification and families*. New York: Brunner/Mazel.

Mash, E. J., Handy, L. C., & Hamerlynck, L. A. (Eds.). (1976). *Behavior modification approaches to parenting*. New York: Brunner/Mazel.

Mash, E. J., & Terdal, L. G. (Eds.). (1976). *Behavior therapy assessment*. New York: Springer-Verlag.

Masserman, J. H. (1943). *Behavior and neurosis*. Chicago: University of Chicago Press.

Mastellone, M. (1974). Aversion therapy: A new use for the old rubber band. *Journal of Behavior Therapy and Experimental Psychiatry, 5*, 311–312.

Masters, J. C., Furman, W., & Barden, R. C. (1977). Effects of achievement standards, tangible rewards, and self-dispensed achievement evaluations on children's task mastery. *Child Development, 48*, 217–224.

Masters, J. C., Gordon, F. R., & Clark, L. V. (1976). Effects of self-dispensed and externally dispensed model consequences on acquisition, spontaneous and oppositional imitation, and long-term retention. *Journal of Personality and Social Psychology, 33*, 421–430.

Masters, J. C., & Mokros, J. R. (1973). Effects of incentive magnitude upon discriminative learning and choice preference in young children. *Child Development, 44*, 225–231.

Masters, J. C., & Pisarowicz, P. A. (1975). Self-reinforcement and generosity following two types of altruistic behavior. *Child Development, 46*, 313–318.

Masters, J. C., & Santrock, J. (1976). Studies in the self-regulation of behavior: Effects of contingent cognitive and affective events. *Development Psychology, 12*, 334–348.

Masters, W. H., & Johnson, V. E. (1966). *Human sexual response*. Boston: Little, Brown.

Masters, W. H., & Johnson, V. E. (1970). *Human sexual inadequacy*. Boston: Little, Brown.

Masur, F. T., III. (1976). Behavior therapy in a case of Pollakiuria. *Journal of Behavior Therapy and Experimental Psychiatry, 7*, 175–178.

Matarazzo, J. D. (1980). Behavioral health and behavioral medicine: Frontiers for a new health psychology. *American Psychologist, 35*, 807–817.

Matarazzo, J. D. (1982). Behavioral health's challenge to academic scientific, and professional psychology. *American Psychologist, 37*, 1–14.

Matson, J. L. (1982). Independence training vs. modeling procedures for teaching phone conversation skills to the mentally retarded. *Behaviour Research and Therapy, 20*, 505–511.

Matson, J. L., Horne, A. M., Ollendick, D. G., & Ollendick, T. H. (1979). Overcorrection: A further evaluation of restitution and positive practice. *Journal of Behavior Therapy and Experimental Psychiatry, 10*, 295–298.

Matson, J. L., & Ollendick, T. H. (1976). Elimination of low-frequency biting. *Behavior Therapy, 7*, 410–412.

Matson, J. L., & Stephens, R. M. (1978). Increasing appropriate behavior of explosive chronic psychiatric patients with a social-skills training package. *Behavior Modification, 2*, 61–76.

Matson, J. L., & Stephens, R. M. (1981). Overcorrection treatment of stereotyped behaviors. *Behavior Modification, 5*(4), 491–502.

Matthews, A., & Shaw, P. (1977). Cognitions related to anxiety: A pilot study of treatment. *Behaviour Research and Therapy, 15*, 503–505.

Matthews, K. (1985). Psychological perspectives on the Type A behavior pattern. *Psychological Bulletin, 91*, 293–323.

Maultsby, M. C., Jr. (1975). *Help yourself to happiness*. New York: Institute for Rational Living.

Maultsby, M. C., Jr. (1977). Rational-emotive imagery. In A. Ellis & R. Grieger (Eds.), *Handbook of rational emotive therapy*. New York: Springer-Verlag.

May, J. R. (1977a). A psychophysiological study of self and externally regulated phobic thoughts. *Behavior Therapy, 8,* 849–861.

May, J. R. (1977b). Psychophysiology of self regulated phobic thoughts. *Behavior Therapy, 8,* 150–159.

May, J. R., & Johnson, H. J. (1973). Physiological activity to internally elicited arousal and inhibitory thoughts, *Journal of Abnormal Psychology, 82,* 239–245.

Mayer, J. (1968). *Overweight: Causes, cost, and control.* Englewood Cliffs, NJ: Prentice-Hall.

Mayer, J. A., & Frederiksen, L. W. (1986). Encouraging long-term compliance with breast self-examination: The evaluation of prompting strategies. *Journal of Behavioral Medicine, 9,* 179–189.

Mayhew, G., & Harris, F. (1979). Decreasing self-injurious behavior: Punishment with citric acid and reinforcement of alternative behavior. *Behavior Modification, 3,* 322–336.

McAllister, L. W., Stachowiak, J. G., Baer, D. M., & Conderman, L. (1969). The application of operant conditioning techniques in a secondary school classroom. *Journal of Applied Behavior Analysis, 2,* 277–285.

McCanne, T. R., & Sandman, C. A. (1976). Human operant heart rate conditioning: The importance of individual differences. *Psychological Bulletin, 83*(4), 587–601.

McConaghy, N. (1971). Aversive therapy of homosexuality: Measures of efficacy. *American Journal of Psychiatry, 127,* 141–144.

McConaghy, N., Armstrong, M. S., & Blaszczynski, A. (1981). Controlled comparison of aversive therapy and covert sensitization in compulsive homosexuality. *Journal of Behavior Therapy and Experimental Psychiatry, 19,* 425–434.

McCordick, S. M., Kaplan, R. M., Finn, M. E., & Smith, S. H. (1979). Cognitive behavior modification and modeling for test anxiety. *Journal of Consulting and Clinical Psychology, 47,* 419–420.

McCullough, J. P., Huntsinger, G. M., & Nay, R. W. (1977). Self control treatment in a 16 year old male. *Journal of Consulting and Clinical Psychology, 45*(2), 322–331.

McCutcheon, B. A., & Adams, H. E. (1975). The physiological basis of implosive therapy. *Behaviour Research and Therapy, 13,* 93–100.

McFall, R. M. (1976). *Behavioral training: A skill acquisi-tion approach to clinical problems.* Morristown, NJ: General Learning Press.

McFall, R. M. (1977). Parameters of self-monitoring. In R. B. Stuart (Ed.), *Behavioral self-management: Strategies, techniques and outcomes.* New York: Brunner/Mazel.

McFall, R. M. (1982). A review and reformulation of the concept of social skills. *Behavioral Assessment, 4,* 1–33.

McFall, R. M., & Lillesand, D. B. (1971). Behavioral rehearsal with modeling and coaching in assertion training. *Journal of Abnormal Psychology, 77,* 313–323.

McFall, R. M., & Marston, A. R. (1970). An experimental investigation of behavior rehearsal in assertive training. *Journal of Abnormal Psychology, 76,* 295–303.

McFall, R. M., & Twentyman, C. (1973). Four experiments on the relative contribution of rehearsal, modeling and coaching to assertion training. *Journal of Abnormal Psychology, 81,* 199–218.

McGlynn, F. D. (1968). *Systematic desensitization, implosive therapy and the aversiveness of imaginal hierarchy items.* Unpublished doctoral dissertation, University of Missouri.

McGlynn, F. D., Reynolds, E. J., & Linder, L. H. (1971). Experimental desensitization following therapeutically oriented and physiologically oriented instructions. *Journal of Behavior Therapy and Experimental Psychiatry, 2,* 13–18.

McGuigan, F. J. (1966). Covert oral behavior and auditory hallucinations. *Psychophysiology, 3,* 73–80.

McGuigan, F. J. (1984). Progressive relaxation: Origins, priniciples, and clinical applications. In R. L. Woolfolk & P. M. Lehrer (Eds.), *Principles and practice of stress management.* New York: Guilford Press.

McGuire, D. M., Thelen, M. H., & Amolsch, T. (1975). Interview self-disclosure as a function of length of modeling and descriptive instructions. *Journal of Consulting and Clinical Psychology, 43,* 356–362.

McGuire, R. J., & Vallance, M. (1964). Aversion therapy by electric shock, a simple technique. *British Medical Journal, 1,* 151–152.

McIntyre, T. J., Jeffreys, D. B., & McIntyre, S. L. (1984). Assertion training: The effectiveness of comprehensive cognitive-behavioral treatment package with professional nurses. *Behaviour Research and Therapy, 22,* 311–318.

McKenzie, R. E., Ehrishman, W. J., Montgomery,

P. S., & Barnes, R. H. (1974). The treatment of headache by means of electroencephalographic biofeedback. *Headache, 14,* 164–172.

McLaughlin, J. G., & Nay, W. R. (1975). Treatment of trichofillomania using positive coverants and response cost: A case report. *Behavior Therapy, 6,* 89–91.

McLaughlin, T. F., & Malaby, J. (1971). Development of procedures for classroom token economies. In E. A. Ramp & B. L. Hopkins (Eds.). *A new direction for education: Behavior analysis.* Lawrence: University of Kansas Press.

McLaughlin, T. F., Malaby, J. (1972a). Intrinsic reinforcers in a classroom token economy. *Journal of Applied Behavior Analysis, 5,* 263–270.

McLaughlin, T. F., & Malaby, J. (1972b). Reducing and measuring inappropriate verbalizations in a token classroom. *Journal of Applied Behavior Analysis, 5,* 329–333.

McMillan, D. E. (1967). A comparison of the punishing effects of response-produced shock and response-produced time out. *Journal of the Experimental Analysis of Behavior, 10,* 439–449.

McMillan, W. (1974). The effectiveness of tangible reward systems with sixth grade ghetto children in a regular classroom situation: An experimental investigation. *Psychology in the Schools, 11,* 373–378.

McNamara, J. R. (1972). The use of self-monitoring techniques to treat nail biting. *Behaviour Research and Therapy, 10,* 193.

McReynolds, L. J. (1969). Application of timeout from positive reinforcement for increasing efficiency of speech training. *Journal of Applied Behavior Analysis, 2,* 199–205.

McReynolds, W. T., Barnes, A. R., Brooks, S., & Rehagen, N. J. (1973). The role of attention-placebo influences in the efficacy of systematic desensitization. *Journal of Consulting and Clinical Psychology, 41,* 86–92.

McReynolds, W. T., & Lutz, E. N. (1976). Weight loss resulting from two behavior modification procedures with nutritionists as therapists. *Behavior Therapy, 7,* 282–291.

McReynolds, W. T., & Tori, C. A. (1972). Further assessment of attention-placebo effects and demand characteristics in studies of systematic desensitization. *Journal of Consulting and Clinical Psychology, 38,* 261–265.

Mealiea, W. L., & Nawas, M. M. (1971). The comparative effectiveness of systematic desensitization and implosive therapy in the treatment of snake phobia. *Journal of Behavior Therapy and Experimental Psychiatry, 2,* 85–94.

Medland, M. B., & Stachnik, T. J. (1972). Goodbehavior game: A replication and systematic analysis. *Journal of Applied Behavior Analysis, 5,* 45–51.

Megargee, E. I. (1966). Undercontrolled and overcontrolled personality types in extreme antisocial aggression. *Psychological Monographs, 3,* (Whole No. 611).

Meichenbaum, D. H. (1969). The effects of instructions and reinforcement on thinking and language behaviors of schizophrenics. *Behaviour Research and Therapy, 7,* 101–114.

Meichenbaum, D. H. (1972a). Cognitive modification of test-anxious college students. *Journal of Consulting and Clinical Psychology, 39,* 370–380.

Meichenbaum, D. H. (1972b). Examination of model characteristics in reducing avoidance behavior. *Journal of Behavior Therapy and Experimental Psychiatry, 3,* 225–227.

Meichenbaum, D. H. (1974). *Cognitive behavior modification.* Morristown, N.J.: General Learning Press.

Meichenbaum, D. H. (1975a). Toward a cognitive theory of self control. In G. Schwartz & D. Shapiro (Eds.), *Consciousness and self regulation: Advances in research.* New York: Plenum.

Meichenbaum, D. H. (1975b). A self-instructional approach to stress management: A proposal for stress inoculation training. In I. Sarason & C. D. Spielberger (Eds.), *Stress and anxiety* (Vol. 2). New York: Wiley.

Meichenbaum, D. H. (1977). *Cognitive-behavior modification.* New York: Plenum Press.

Meichenbaum, D. H., Bowers, K. S., & Ross, R. R. (1968). Modification of classroom behavior of institutionalized female adolescent offenders. *Behaviour Research and Therapy, 6,* 343–353.

Meichenbaum, D. H., & Cameron, R. (1972). *Stress inoculation: A skills training approach to anxiety management.* Unpublished manuscript, University of Waterloo, Canada.

Meichenbaum, D. H., Cameron, R. (1973). Training schizophrenics to talk to themselves: A means of developing attentional controls. *Behavior Therapy, 4,* 515–534.

Meichenbaum, D. H., Gilmore, J. B., & Fedoravicius, A. (1971). Group insight vs. group desensitization in treating speech anxiety. *Journal of Consulting and Clinical Psychology, 36,* 410–421.

Meichenbaum, D. H., & Goodman, J. (1969). Reflection, impulsivity, and verbal control of motor behavior. *Child Development, 40,* 785–797.

Meichenbaum, D. H., & Goodman, J. (1971). Training impulsive children to talk to themselves: A means of developing self control. *Journal of Abnormal Psychology, 77,* 115–126.

Meichenbaum, D. H., & Jaremko, M. E. (Eds.). (1982). *Stress prevention and management: A cognitive-behavioral approach.* New York: Plenum Press.

Meichenbaum, D. H., & Turk, D. (1976). The cognitive behavioral management of anxiety, anger, and pain. In P. Davidson (Ed.), *The behavioral management of anxiety, depression, and pain.* New York: Brunner/Mazel.

Meier, F., & Land, H. (1983). Use and process evaluation of a self-control program in case of diurnal enuresis. *Praxis der Kinder-psychologie und Kinderpsychiatrie, 32,* 181–186.

Melamed, B. G., & Siegel, L. J. (1975). Reduction of anxiety in children facing hospitalization and surgery by use of filmed modeling. *Journal of Consulting and Clinical Psychology, 43,* 511–521.

Melamed, B. G., Yurcheson, R., Fleece, E. L., Hutcherson, S., & Hawes, R. (1978). Effects of film modeling on reduction of anxiety-related behaviors in individuals varying in level of previous experience in the stress situation. *Journal of Consulting and Clinical Psychology, 46,* 1357–1367.

Melin, L., & Götestam, K. G. (1973). A contingency-management program on a drug-free unit for intravenous amphetamine addicts. *Journal of Behavior Therapy and Experimental Psychiatry, 4,* 331–337.

Mellstrom, M., & Gelsomino, J. (1976). Contingency management of an adult's inappropriate urination and masturbation in a family context. *Journal of Behavior Therapy and Experimental Psychiatry, 7,* 89–90.

Melnick, J. A. (1973). A comparison of replication techniques in the modification of minimal dating behavior. *Journal of Abnormal Psychology, 81,* 51–59.

Melnick, J. A., & Stocker, R. B. (1977). An experimental analysis of the behavioral rehearsal with feedback technique in assertiveness training. *Behavior Therapy, 8,* 222–228.

Melzack, R. (1973). *The puzzle of pain.* Harmondsworth, England: Penguin.

Melzack, R., & Casey, K. (1968). Sensory motivational and central control determinants of pain: A new conceptual model. In D. Kenshalo (Ed.), *The skin senses.* Springfield, IL: Thomas.

Melzack, R., & Perry, C. (1975). Self-regulation of pain: The use of alpha-feedback and hypnotic training for the control of chronic pain. *Experimental Neurology, 46,* 452–469.

Mercier, P., & Ladouceur, R. (1983). Modification of study time and grades through self-control procedures. *Canadian Journal of Behavioural Science, 15,* 70–81.

Mertens, G. C., & Fuller, G. B. (1964). *The therapist's manual.* Willmar State Hospital, Willmar Minnesota. (Mimeograph)

Mestrallet, A., & Lang, A. (1959). Indications, techniques et resultats du traitement par l'apomorphine de l'alcoolisme psychiatrique. (Indications, technique, and results in apomorphine therapy of psychiatric alcoholism). *Journal de Medecine de Lyon, 40,* 279–285.

Meyer, R. G. (1975). A behavioral treatment of sleepwalking associated with test anxiety. *Journal of Behavior Therapy and Experimental Psychiatry, 6,* 167–168.

Meyer, V. (1957). The treatment of two phobic patients on the basis of learning principles. *Journal of Abnormal and Social Psychology, 55,* 261–266.

Meyer, V., Liddell, A., & Lyons, M. (1977). Behavioral interviews. In A. R. Ciminero, K. S. Calhoun, & H. E. Adams (Eds.), *Handbook of behavioral assessment.* New York: Wiley.

Meyer, V., Robertson, J., & Tatlow, A. (1975). Home treatment of an obsessive-compulsive disorder by response prevention. *Journal of Behavior Therapy and Experimental Psychiatry, 6,* 37–38.

Meyers, A. W., Thackwray, D. E., Johnson, D. B., & Schleser, R. (1983). A comparison of prompting strategies for improving appointment compliance of hypertensive individuals. *Behavior Therapy, 14,* 267–274.

Meyers-Abel, J. E., & Jansen, M. A. (1980). Assertive therapy for battered women: A case illustration. *Journal of Behavior Therapy and Experimental Psychiatry, 11,* 301–305.

Michaelson, G. (1976). Short-term effects of behavior therapy and hospital treatment of chronic alcoholics. *Behaviour Research and Therapy, 14,* 69–72.

Michelson, L., Mavissakalian, M., & Marchione, K. (1985). Cognitive and behavioral treatments of agoraphobia: Clinical, behavioral, and psychophysiological outcomes. *Journal of Consulting and Clinical Psychology, 53,* 913–925.

Milan, M. A., & McKee, J. M. (1976). The cellblock token economy: Token reinforcement procedures in a maximum security correctional institution for adult male felons. *Journal of Applied Behavior Analysis, 9,* 253–275.

Milby, J. B., Meredith, R. L., & Rice, J. (1981). Videotaped exposure: A new treatment for obsessive-compulsive disorders. *Journal of Behavior Therapy and Experimental Psychiatry, 12,* 249–255.

Miller, B. V., & Levis, D. J. (1971). The effects of varying short visual exposure times to a phobic test stimulus on subsequent avoidance behavior. *Behaviour Research and Therapy, 9,* 17–21.

Miller, E. C., Dvorak, A., & Turner, D. W. (1960). A method of creating aversion to alcohol by reflex conditioning in a group setting. *Quarterly Journal of Studies on Alcohol, 21,* 424–431.

Miller, H. R., & Nawas, M. M. (1970). Control of aversive stimulus termination in systematic desensitization. *Behaviour Research and Therapy, 8,* 57–61.

Miller, L. B., & Estes, B. W. (1961). Monetary reward and motivation in discrimination learning. *Journal of Experimental Psychology, 6,* 501–504.

Miller, M. M. (1959). Treatment of chronic alcoholism by hypnotic aversion. *Journal of the American Medical Association, 171,* 1492–1495.

Miller, M. M. (1963). Hypnotic-aversion treatment of homosexuality. *Journal of the National Medical Association, 55,* 411–415.

Miller, M. P., Murphy, P. J., & Miller, T. P. (1978). Comparison of electromyographic feedback and progressive relaxation training in treating circumscribed anxiety stress reactions. *Journal of Consulting and Clinical Psychology, 46,* 1291–1298.

Miller, N. E. (1972). Postscript. In D. Singh, & C. T. Morgan (Eds.), *Current status of physiological psychology. Readings.* Monterey, CA: Brooks/Cole.

Miller, N. E., & Dollard, J. (1941). *Social learning and imitation.* New Haven: Yale University Press.

Miller, N. E., & Dworkin, B. R. (1974). Visceral learning: Recent difficulties with curarized rats and significant problems for human research. In D. A. Obrist et al. (Eds.), *Cardiovascular psychophysiology.* Chicago: Aldine.

Miller, P. M. (1972). The use of behavioral contracting in the treatment of alcoholism: A case report. *Behavior Therapy, 3,* 593–596.

Miller, P. M. (1975). Social skills training to teach alcoholics to refuse drinks effectively. *Journal of Studies on Alcohol, 37,* 1340–1345.

Miller, P. M. (1982). *Behavioral treatment of alcoholism.* Elmsford, NY: Pergamon.

Miller, P. M., Hersen, M., Eisler, R. M., & Hemphill, D. P. (1973). Electrical aversion therapy with alcoholics: An analogue study. *Behaviour Research and Therapy, 11,* 491–497.

Miller, P. M., Hersen, M., Eisler, R. M., & Hilsman, G. (1974). Effects of social stress on operant drinking of alcoholics and social drinkers. *Behaviour Research and Therapy, 12,* 67–72.

Miller, P. M., & Sims, K. L. (1981). Evaluation and component analysis of a comprehensive weight control program. *International Journal of Obesity, 5,* 57–66.

Miller, R. L., Brickman, P., & Bolen, D. (1975). Attribution versus persuasion as a means for modifying behavior. *Journal of Personality and Social Psychology, 31,* 430–441.

Miller, S. J., & Sloane, H. N., Jr. (1976). The generalization effects of parent training across stimulus settings. *Journal of Applied Behavior Analysis, 9,* 355–370.

Miller, T. W. (1983). Assertiveness of coaches: The issues of healthy communication between coaches and players. *Journal of Sport Psychology, 4,* 107–114.

Miller, W. H. (1975). *Systematic parent training: Procedures, cases and issues.* Champaign, IL: Research Press.

Miller, W. R. (1978). Behavioral treatment of problem drinkers: A comparative outcome study of three controlled-drinking therapies. *Journal of Consulting and Clinical Psychology, 46,* 74–86.

Miller, W. R. (1980). *The addictive behaviors.* London: Pergamon Press.

Miller, W. R., & DiPilato, M. (1983). Treatment of nightmares via relaxation and desensitization: A controlled evaluation. *Journal of Consulting and Clinical Psychology, 51,* 870–877.

Miller, W. R., & Hester, R. K. (1980). *Treating the problem drinker: Treatment of alcoholism, drug abuse, smoking, and obesity* (111–142). New York: Pergamon Press.

Miller, W. R., & Muñoz, R. F. (1976). *How to control your drinking.* Engelwood Cliffs, NJ: Prentice-Hall.

Miller, W. R., & Seligman, M. E. (1975). Depression and the perceptions of reinforcement. *Journal of Abnormal Psychology, 82,* 62–73.

Miller, W. R., & Taylor, C. A. (1980). Relative effectiveness of bibliotherapy, individual and group-control training in the treatment of problem drinkers. *Addictive Behaviors, 5,* 13–24.

Miller, W. R., Taylor, C. A., & West, J. C. (1980).

Focused versus broad-spectrum behavior therapy for problem drinkers. *Journal of Consulting and Clinical Psychology, 48,* 590–601.

Mills, K. C., Sobell, M. B., & Schaefer, H. H. (1971). Training social drinking as an alternative to abstinence for alcoholics. *Behavior Therapy, 2,* 18–27.

Minge, M. R., & Ball, T. S. (1967). Teaching of self-help skills to profoundly retarded patients. *American Journal of Mental Deficiency, 71,* 864–868.

Mira, M. (1970). Results of a behavior modification training program for parents and teachers. *Behaviour Research and Therapy, 8,* 309–311.

Miron, N. B. (1971). Behavior modifications techniques in the treatment of self-injurious behavior in institutionalized retardates. *Suicidology, 8,* 64–70.

Mischel, W. (1968). *Personality and assessment.* New York: Wiley.

Mischel, W. (1973). Toward a cognitive social learning reconceptualization of personality. *Psychological Review, 80,* 252–283.

Mischel, W. (1977). On the future of personality measurement. *American Psychologist, 32,* 246–254.

Mischel, W., Ebbesen, E. B., & Zeiss, A. (1973). Selective attention to the self: Situational and dispositional personality determinants. *Journal of Personality and Social Psychology, 27,* 129–142.

Mischel, W., Ebbesen, E. B., & Zeiss, A. (1976). Determinants of selective memory about the self. *Journal of Consulting and Clinical Psychology, 44,* 92–103.

Mischel, W., & Liebert, R. M. (1966). Effects of discrepancies between observed and imposed reward criteria on their acquisition and transmission. *Journal of Personality and Social Psychology, 3,* 45–53.

Mitchell, K. R., & White, R. G. (1976). Self management of tension headaches: A case study. *Journal of Behavior Therapy and Experimental Psychiatry, 7,* 387–389.

Mithaug, D. E., & Wolfe, M. S. (1976). Employing task arrangements and verbal contingencies to promote verbalizations between retarded children. *Journal of Applied Behavior Analysis, 9,* 301–314.

Moeller, L. E. (1976). EMG biofeedback facilitation of progressive relaxation and autogenic training: A comparative study. *Dissertation Abstracts International, 36,* 4168B (abstract).

Mogar, R. E., & Savage, C. (1964). Personality change associated with psychodelic (LSD) therapy: A preliminary report. *Psychotherapy: Theory, Research and Practice, 1,* 154–162.

Mogel, S., & Schiff, W. (1967). "Extinction" of a head-bumping symptom of eight years' duration in two minutes: A case report. *Behaviour Research and Therapy, 5,* 131–132.

Moleski, R., & Tosi, D. J. (1976). Comparative psychotherapy: Rational-emotive therapy versus systematic desensitization in the treatment of stuttering. *Journal of Consulting and Clinical Psychology, 44,* 309–311.

Montegar, C. A., Reid, D. H., Madsen, C. H., Jr., & Ewell, M. D. (1977). Increasing institutional staff to resident interactions through inservice training and supervisor approval. *Behavior Therapy, 8,* 533–540.

Montgomery, A. (1971). *Comparison of the effectiveness of systematic desensitization rational-emotive therapy, implosive therapy, and no therapy, in reducing test anxiety in college students.* Unpublished doctoral dissertation, Washington University.

Moore, B. L., & Bailey, J. S. (1973). Social punishment in the modification of a preschool child's "autistic-like" behavior with mother as therapist. *Journal of Applied Behavior Analysis, 6,* 497–507.

Moore, N. (1965). Behavior therapy in bronchial asthma: A controlled study. *Journal of Psychosomatic Research, 9,* 257–276.

Moreno, J. L. (1946). *Psychodrama* (Vol. 1). New York: Beacon House.

Moreno, J. L. (1955). The discovery of the spontaneous man with special emphasis upon the technique of role reversal. *Group Psychotherapy, 8,* 103–129.

Moreno, J. L. (1963). Behavior therapy. *American Journal of Psychiatry, 120,* 194–196.

Moreno, Z. T. (1965). Psychodramatic rules, techniques and adjunctive methods. *Group Psychotherapy, 18,* 73–86.

Morgan, B., & Leung, P. (1980). Effects of assertion training on acceptance of disability by physically disabled university students. *Journal of Counseling Psychology, 27,* 209–212.

Morgan, D. C., Kremer, E., & Gaylor, M. (1979). The behavioral medicine unit: A new facility. *Comprehensive Psychiatry, 20,* 79–89.

Morgan, W. G. (1974). The shaping game: A teaching technique. *Behavior Therapy, 5,* 271–272.

Morganstern, F. S., Pearce, J. F., & Rees, W. L. (1965). Predicting the outcome of behaviour therapy by psychological tests. *Behaviour Research and Therapy, 2,* 191–200.

Morganstern, K. P. (1973). Implosive therapy and

flooding procedures: A critical review. *Psychological Bulletin, 79,* 318–334.

Morganstern, K. P. (1974). Cigarette smoke as a noxious stimulus in self-managed aversion therapy for compulsive eating: Technique and case illustration. *Behavior Therapy, 5,* 255–260.

Morris, J. B., & Beck, A. T. (1974). The efficacy of anti-depressant drugs: A review of research (1958–1972). *Archives of General Psychiatry, 30,* 667–674.

Morris, R. J., & Suckerman, K. R. (1974). Therapist warmth as a factor in automated systematic desensitization. *Journal of Consulting and Clinical Psychology, 42,* 244–250.

Morrow, G. R., & Morrell, C. (1982). Behavioral treatment for the anticipatory nausea and vomiting induced by cancer chemotherapy. *New England Journal of Medicine, 307,* 1476–1480.

Moser, A. J. (1974). Covert punishment of hallucinatory behavior in a psychotic male. *Journal of Behavior Therapy and Experimental Psychiatry, 5,* 297–299.

Moses, A. N., III, & Hollandsworth, J. G., Jr. (1985). Relative effectiveness of education alone versus stress inoculation training in the treatment of dental phobia. *Behavior Therapy, 16,* 531–537.

Mostofsky, D. I., & Balaschak, B. A. (1977). Control of seizures. *Psychological Bulletin, 84,* (4), 723–750.

Mowrer, O. H. (1950). Identification: A link between learning theory and psychotherapy. In O. H. Mowrer (Ed.), *Learning theory and personality dynamics.* New York: Ronald Press.

Mowrer, O. H. (1960). *Learning theory and the symbolic processes.* New York: Wiley.

Muehlenhard, C. L., & McFall, R. M. (1983). Automated assertion training: A feasibility study. *Journal of Social and Clinical Psychology, 1,* 246–258.

Mullen, F. G. (1968). *The effect of covert sensitization on smoking behavior.* Unpublished study, Queens College, Charlottesville, NC.

Mullinix, J. M., Norton, B. J., Hock, S., & Fishman, M. A. (1978). Skin temperature biofeedback and migraine. *Headache, 17,* 242–244.

Munjack, D. J. (1975). Overcoming obstacles to desensitization using *in vivo* stimuli and brevital. *Behavior Therapy, 6,* 543–546.

Munjack, D. J., & Razani, J. (1974). Side effects of brevital-aided desensitization: Some clinical impressions. *Behavior Therapy, 5,* 423–427.

Murphy, G. E., Simons, A. D., Wetzel, R. D., & Lustman, P. J. (1984). Cognitive therapy and phar-macotherapy, singly and together, in the treatment of depression. *Archives of General Psychiatry, 41,* 33–41.

Murphy, G. M., & Bootzin, R. R. (1973). Active and passive participation in the contact desensitization of snake fear in children. *Behavior Therapy, 4,* 203–211.

Murray, J. A., & Epstein, L. H. (1981). Improving oral hygiene with videotape modeling. *Behavior Modification, 5,* 360–371.

Murry, R. G., & Hobbs, S. A. (1977). The use of a self imposed timeout procedure in the modification of excessive alcohol consumption. *Journal of Behavior Therapy and Experimental Psychiatry, 8,* 377–380.

Musante, G. J. (1976). The dietary rehabilitation clinic: Evaluative report of a behavioral and dietary treatment of obesity. *Behavior Therapy, 7,* 198–204.

Mustacchi, P. (1985). Risk factors in stroke. *Western Journal of Medicine, 143,* 186–192.

Mylar, J. L., & Clement, P. W. (1972). Prediction and comparison of outcome in systematic desensitization and implosion. *Behaviour Research and Therapy, 10,* 235–246.

Natale, M. (1977). Induction of mood states and their effects on gaze behaviors. *Journal of Consulting and Clinical Psychology, 45*(5), 960.

National Cancer Institute. (1980). *Breast cancer: A measure of progress of public understanding,* (OHHS Publication No. 81–2306). Washington, DC: U.S. Government Printing Office.

Nawas, M. M., Welsch, W. V., & Fishman, S. T. (1970). The comparative effectiveness of pairing aversive imagery with relaxation, neutral tasks and muscular tension in reducing snake phobia. *Behaviour Research and Therapy, 6,* 63–68.

Neisworth, J. T., & Madle, R. A. (1976). Time-out with staff accountability: A technical note. *Behavior Therapy, 6,* 261–263.

Neisworth, J. T., Madle, R. A., & Goeke, K. K. (1975). "Errorless" elimination of separation anxiety: A case study. *Journal of Behavior Therapy and Experimental Psychiatry, 6,* 79–82.

Neisworth, J. T., & Moore, F. (1972). Operant treatment of asthmatic responding with the parent as therapist. *Behavior Therapy, 3,* 95–99.

Nelson, C. M., Worell, J., & Polsgrove, L. (1973). Behaviorally disordered peers as contingency managers. *Behavior Therapy, 4,* 270–276.

Nelson, G. L., & Cone, J. D. (1979). Multiplebaseline analysis of a token economy for psychiatric inpatients. *Journal of Applied Behavior Analysis, 12,* 255–271.

Nelson, R. E. (1977). Irrational beliefs in depression. *Journal of Consulting and Clinical Psychology, 45* (6), 1190–1191.

Nelson, R. O., Hay, L. R., Hay, W. M., & Carstens, C. B. (1977). The reactivity of teachers' self monitoring and negative classroom verbalizations. *Behavior Therapy, 8,* 972–985.

Nelson, R. O., Hayes, S. C., Spong, R. T., Jarret, R. B., & McKnight, D. L. (1983). Self-reinforcement: Appealing misnomer or effective mechanism? *Behaviour Research and Therapy, 21,* 557–566.

Nelson, R. O., Lipinski, D. P., & Boykin, R. A. (1978). The effects of self recorders training and the obtrusiveness of the self recording device on the accuracy and reactivity of self monitoring. *Behavior Therapy, 9,* 200–208.

Nelson, W. J., & Birkimer, J. C. (1978). Role of self-instruction and self-reinforcement in the modification of impulsivity. *Journal of Consulting and Clinical Psychology, 46,* (1), 183.

Nelson, W. M., III, Finch, A. J., Jr., & Hooke, J. F. (1975). Effects of reinforcement and response-cost on cognitive style in emotionally disturbed boys. *Journal of Abnormal Psychology, 84,* 426–428.

Nemetz, G. H., Craig, K. D., & Reith, G. (1978). *Journal of Consulting and Clinical Psychology, 46,* 62–73.

Neufield, R., & Davidson, P. (1971). The effects of vicarious and cognitive rehearsal on pain tolerance. *Journal of Psychosomatic Research, 15,* 319–325.

Newton, J. R. (1968). Considerations for the psychotherapeutic technique of symptom scheduling. *Psychotherapy: Theory, Research and Practice, 5*(2), 92–103.

Nicassio, P. M., & Bootzin, R. (1974). A comparison of progressive relaxation and autogenic training as treatments for insomnia. *Journal of Abnormal Psychology, 83,* 253–260.

Nicassio, P. M., & Buchanan, D. C. (1981). Clinical application of behavior therapy for insomnia. *Comprehensive Psychiatry, 22,* 512–521.

Nidetch, J. (1966). *Weight watchers' cookbook.* New York: Hearthside Press.

Nietzel, M. T., Martorano, R. D., & Melnick, J. (1977). The effects of covert modeling with and without reply training on the development and generaliza-

tion of assertive responses. *Behavior Therapy, 8,* 183–192.

Nisbett, R. E., & Ross, L. (1980). *Human inference.* Englewood Cliffs, NJ: Prentice-Hall.

Nisbett, R. E., & Schacter, S. (1966). Cognitive manipulation of pain. *Journal of Experimental and Social Psychology, 2,* 227–236.

Nolan, J. D. (1968). Self control procedures in the modification of smoking behavior. *Journal of Consulting and Clinical Psychology, 32,* 92–93.

Nomellini, S., & Katz, R. C. (1983). Effects of anger control training on abusive parents. *Cognitive Therapy and Research, 7,* 57–67.

Nordyke, N. S., Baer, D. M., Etzel, B. C., & LeBlanc, J. M. (1977). The implications of the stereotyping and modification of sexrole. *Journal of Applied Behavior Analysis, 10,* 553–557.

Norton, G. R., Rhodes, L., Hauch, J., & Kaprowy, E. A. (1985). Characteristics of subjects experiencing relaxation and relaxation-induced anxiety. *Journal of Behavior Therapy and Experimental Psychiatry, 16,* 211–216.

Novaco, R. W. (1975). *Anger control: The development and evaluation of an experimental treatment.* Lexington, MA: Heath.

Novaco, R. W. (1976). The functions and regulation of the arousal of anger. *American Journal of Psychiatry, 133,* 1124–1128.

Novaco, R. W. (1977a). Stress inoculation: A cognitive therapy for anger and its application to a case of depression. *Journal of Consulting and Clinical Psychology, 45,* (4), 600–608.

Novaco, R. W. (1977b). A stress inoculation approach to anger management in the training of law enforcement officers. *American Journal of Community Psychology, 5,* 327–346.

Novaco, R. W. (1979). The cognitive regulation of anger and stress. In P. C. Kendall & S. D. Hollon (Eds.), *Cognitive-behavioral intervention: Theory, research, and procedures.* New York: Academic Press.

Novaco, R. W., Cook, T., & Sarason, I. B. (1982). Military recruit training: An area of stress coping skills. In D. H. Meichenbaum & M. E. Jaremko (Eds.). *Stress prevention and management: A cognitive-behavioral approach.* New York: Plenum Press.

Novick, D. M., Enlow, R. W., Gelb, A. M., Stenger, R. J., Fotino, M., Winter, J. W., Yancovitz, S. R., Shoenberg, M. D., & Kreck, M. J. (1985). Hepatic cirrhosis in young adults: Association with adolescent onset of alcohol and parental heroin abuse. *Gut, 26*, 8–13.

Nowliss, D. P., & Kamiya, J. (1970). The control of electroencephalographic alpha rhythms through auditory feedback and the associated mental activity. *Psychophysiology, 6*, 476–484.

Neuchterlein, K. H., & Holroyd, J. C. (1980). Biofeedback in the treatment of tension headache: Current status. *Archives of General Psychiatry, 37*, 866–873.

Nunes, J. S., & Marks, I. M. (1975). Feedback of true heart rate during exposure *in vivo. Archives of General Psychiatry, 32*, 933–936.

Nurnberger, J. I., & Zimmerman, J. (1970). Applied analysis of human behavior. An alternative to conventional motivational inferences and unconscious determination in therapeutic programming. *Behavior Therapy, 1*, 1–3.

O'Banion, D., Armstrong, B. K., & Ellis, J. (1980). Conquered urge as a means of self-control. *Addictive Behaviors, 5*, 101–106.

Obler, M. (1973). Systematic desensitization in sexual disorders. *Journal of Behavior Therapy and Experimental Psychiatry, 4*, 93–101.

O'Brien, F., Azrin, N. H., & Bugle, C. (1972). Training profoundly retarded children to stop crawling. *Journal of Applied Behavior Analysis, 5*, 131–137.

Ockene, J. K., Hymowitz, N., Sexton, M., & Broste, S. K. (1982). Comparisons of patterns of smoking behavior change among smokers in the Multiple Risk Factor Intervention Trial (MRFIT). *Preventive Medicine, 11*, 621–638.

O'Connor, R. D. (1969). Modification of social withdrawal through symbolic modeling. *Journal of Applied Behavior Analysis, 2*, 15–22.

O'Donnell, C. R., & Worell, L. (1973). Motor and cognitive relaxation in the desensitization of anger. *Behaviour Research and Therapy, 11*, 473–482.

O'Farrell, T. J., Cutter, H. S., & Floyd, F. J. (1984). Evaluating behavioral marital therapy for male alcoholics: Clinical procedures from a treatment outcome study in progress. *American Journal of Family Therapy, 12*, 33–46.

Ohman, A., Erixon, G., & Lofberg, I. (1975). Phobias and preparedness: Phobic versus neutral pictures as conditioned stimuli for human autonomic responses. *Journal of Abnormal Psychology, 84*, 41–45.

Oldridge, N. B., Donner, A. P., Buck, C. W., Jones, N. L., Andrew, G. M., Parder, J. O., Cunningham,

D. A., Kavanaugh, T., Rechnitzer, P. A., & Sutton, J. R. (1983). Predictors of dropout from cardiac exercise rehabilitation: Ontario exercise-heart collaborative study. *American Journal of Cardiology, 51*, 70–74.

O'Leary, K. D., & Becker, W. C. (1967). Behavior modification of an adjustment class: A token reinforcement program. *Exceptional Children, 33*, 637–642.

O'Leary, K. D., Becker, W. C., Evans, M. B., & Saudargas, R. A. (1969). A token reinforcement program in a public school: A replication of systematic analysis. *Journal of Applied Behavior Analysis, 2*, 3–13.

O'Leary, K. D., & Borkovec, T. D. (1978). Conceptual, methodological, and ethical problems of placebo groups in psychotherapy research. *American Psychologist, 33*, 821–830.

O'Leary, K. D., & Kent, R. N. (1973). Behavior modification for social action: Research tactics and problems. In C. L. Hamerlynck et al. (Eds.). *Critical issues in research and practice.* Champaign, IL: Research Press.

O'Leary, K. D., O'Leary, S. G., & Becker, W. C. (1967). Modification of a deviant sibling interaction pattern in the home. *Behaviour Research and Therapy, 5*, 113–120.

O'Leary, K. D., & Wilson, G. T. (1975). *Behavior therapy: Application and outcome.* Englewood Cliffs, NJ: Prentice-Hall.

O'Leary, S. G., & Dubey, D. R. (1979). Application of self-control procedures by children: A review. *Journal of Applied Behavior Analysis, 12*, 449–466.

O'Leary, S. G., & O'Leary, K. D. (1977). Ethical issues of behavior modification research in schools. *Psychology in the Schools, 14*(3), 299–307.

Oldridge, N. B., & Jones, N. L. (1981). Contracting as a strategy to reduce dropout in exercise rehabilitation. *Medicine and Science in Sports and Exercise, 13*, 125–126.

Ollendick, T. H., Shapiro, E. S., & Barrett, R. P. (1982). Effects of vicarious reinforcement in normal and severely disturbed children. *Journal of Consulting and Clinical Psychology, 50*, 63–70.

O'Neill, M. W., Hanewicz, W. B., Fransway, L. M., & Cassidy-Riske, C. (1982). Stress inoculation training and job performance. *Journal of Police Science & Administration, 10*, 388–397.

O'Neill, P. M., Currey, H. S., Hirsch, A. A., Riddle,

F. E., Taylor, C. I., Malcolm, R. J., & Sexauer, J. D. (1979). Effects of sex of subject and spouse involvement on weight loss in a behavioral treatment program: A retrospective investigation. *Addictive Behavior, 4,* 167–178.

Ordman, A. M., & Kirschenbaum, D. S. (1985). Cognitive-behavioral therapy for bulimia: An initial outcome study. *Journal of Consulting and Clinical Psychology, 53,* 305–313.

Orenstein, H., & Carr, J. (1975). Implosion therapy by tape-recording. *Behaviour Research and Therapy, 13,* 177–182.

Orenstein, H., Orenstein, E., & Carr, J. E. (1975). Assertiveness and anxiety: A correlational study. *Journal of Behavior Therapy and Experimental Psychiatry, 6,* 203–207.

Orne, M. (1962). On the social psychology of the psychological experiment: With particular reference to demand characteristics and their implications. *American Psychologist, 17,* 776–783.

Orwin, A. (1971). Respiratory relief: A new and rapid method for the treatment of phobic states. *British Journal of Psychiatry, 119,* 636–637.

Orwin, A. (1973). Augmented respiratory relief: A new use in Co2 therapy in the treatment of phobic conditions: A preliminary report on two cases. *British Journal of Psychiatry, 122,* 171–173.

Orwin, A., le Boeuf, A., Dovey, O., & James, S. (1975). A comparative trial of exposure and respiratory relief therapies. *Behaviour Research and Therapy, 13,* 205–214.

Osborn, S., & Harris, G. (1974). *Assertive training in women.* Springfield, IL: Thomas.

Osborne, J. G. (1969). Free-time as a reinforcer in the management of classroom behavior. *Journal of Applied Behavior Analysis, 2,* 113–118.

Ottens, A. J. (1982). A cognitive-behavioral modification treatment of trichotillomania. *Journal of American College of Health, 31,* 78–81.

Overmeir, J. B., & Seligman, M. E. P. (1967). Effects of inescapable shock upon subsequent escape and avoidance learning. *Journal of Comparative and Physiological Psychology, 63,* 23–33.

Pachman, J. S., Foy, D. W., Massey, F., & Eisler, R. M. (1978). A factor analysis of assertive behaviors. *Journal of Consulting and Clinical Psychology, 46,* 347–348.

Packard, R. G. (1970). The control of "classroom attention": A group contingency for complex behavior. *Journal of Applied Behavior Analysis, 3,* 13–28.

Paffenberger, R. J., & Hale, W. E. (1975). Work activity and coronary heart mortality. *New England Journal of Medicine, 292,* 545.

Page, T. J., Iwata, B. A., & Neef, N. A. (1976). Teaching pedestrian skills to retarded persons: Generalization from the classroom to the natural environment. *Journal of Applied Behavior Analysis, 9,* 433–444.

Paivio, A. (1971). *Imagery and verbal processes.* New York: Holt.

Paivio, A., & Yuille, J. (1967). Mediation instructions and word attributes in paired-associate learning. *Psychonomic Science, 8,* 65–66.

Palkes, H., Stewart, W., & Kahana, B. (1968). Porteus maze performance of hyperactive boys after training in self directed verbal commands. *Child Development, 39,* 817–826.

Panek, D. M. (1970). Word association learning by chronic schizophrenics on a token economy ward under conditions of reward and punishment. *Journal of Clinical Psychology, 26,* 163–167.

Paquin, M. J. (1977). The treatment of a nail-biting compulsion by covert sensitization in a poorly motivated client. *Journal of Behavior Therapy and Experimental Psychiatry, 8,* 181–183.

Parke, R. D. (1974). Rules, roles, and resistance to deviation: Recent advances in punishment, discipline and self-control. In A. D. Pick (Ed.), *Minnesota symposia on child psychology* (Vol. 8). Minneapolis: University of Minnesota Press.

Parrish, J. M., & Erickson, M. T. (1981). A comparison of cognitive strategies in modifying the cognitive style of impulsive third grade children. *Cognitive Therapy and Research, 5,* 71–84.

Parsonson, B. S., Baer, A. M., & Baer, D. M. (1974). The application of generalized correct social contingencies: An evaluation of a training program. *Journal of Applied Behavior Analysis, 7,* 427–437.

Paskewitz, D. A., & Orne, M. T. (1973). Visual effects on alpha feedback training. *Science, 181,* 360–363.

Passman, R. H. (1976). A procedure for eliminating writer's block in a college student. *Journal of Behavior Therapy and Experimental Psychiatry, 7,* 297–298.

Patel, C., Marmot, M. G., & Terry, D. J. (1981). Controlled trial of biofeedback-aided behavioral methods in reducing mild hypertension. *British Medical Journal, 6281,* 2005–2008.

Patterson, C. H. (1974). *Relationship counseling and psychotherapy.* New York: Harper.

Patterson, G. R. (1965). A learning theory approach to

the treatment of the school phobic child. In L. P. Ullmann, & L. Krasner (Eds.), *Case Studies in behavior modification.* New York: Holt.

Patterson, G. R. (1974a). Interventions for boys with conduct problems: Multiple settings, treatments, and criteria. *Journal of Consulting and Clinical Psychology, 42,* 471–481.

Patterson, G. R. (1974b). Retraining of aggressive boys by their parents: Review of recent literature and follow-up evaluation. *Canadian Psychiatric Association Journal, 19,* 142–158.

Patterson, G. R. (1975). *Families: Applications of social learning to family life.* Champaign, IL: Research Press.

Patterson, G. R., & Cobb, J. A. (1971). A dyadic analysis of "aggressive" behaviors. In J. P. Hill (Ed.), *Minnesota Symposium on Child Psychology* (Vol. 5). Minneapolis: University of Minnesota Press.

Patterson, G. R., Cobb, J. A., & Ray, R. S. (1973). A social engineering technology for retraining the families of aggressive boys. In H. Adams, & Unikel (Eds.), *Issues and trends in behavior therapy.* Springfield, IL: Thomas.

Patterson, G. R., & Gullion, M. E. (1976). *Living with children: New methods for parents and teachers.* Champaign, IL: Research Press.

Patterson, G. R., Jones, R., Whittier, J., & Wright, M. A. (1965). A behavior modification technique for the hyperactive child. *Behaviour Research and Therapy, 2,* 217–226.

Paul, G. L. (1966). *Insight versus desensitization in psychotherapy: An experiment in anxiety reduction.* Stanford, CA: Stanford University Press.

Paul, G. L. (1967). Insight vs. desensitization in psychotherapy two years after termination. *Journal of Consulting Psychology, 31,* 333–348.

Paul, G. L. (1969a). Behavior modification research: Design and tactics. In C. M. Franks (Ed.), *Behavior therapy: Appraisal and status.* New York: McGraw-Hill.

Paul, G. L. (1969b). Outcome of systematic desensitization: 1. Background and procedures, and uncontrolled reports of individual treatments. In C. M. Franks (Ed.), *Behavior therapy: Appraisal and status.* New York: McGraw-Hill.

Paul, G. L. (1969c). Outcome of systematic desensitization: 2. Controlled investigations of individual treatment, technique variations, and current status. In C. M. Franks (Ed.), *Behavior Therapy: Appraisal and status.* New York: McGraw- Hill.

Paul, G. L. (1969). Physiological effects of relaxation training and hypnotic suggestion. *Journal of Abnormal Psychology, 74,* 425–437.

Paul, G. L., & Shannon, D. T. (1966). Treatment of anxiety through systematic desensitization in therapy groups. *Journal of Abnormal Psychology, 71,* 124–135.

Paul, G. L., & Trimble, R. W. (1970). Recorded vs. "live" relaxation training and hypnotic suggestions: Comparative effectiveness for reducing physiological arousal and inhibiting stress response. *Behavior Therapy 1,* 285–302.

Paulsen, K., Rimm, D. C., Woodburn, L. T., & Rimm, S. A. (1977). A self-control approach to inefficient spending. *Journal of Consulting and Clinical Psychology, 45*(3), 433–435.

Pavlov, I. P. (1927). *Conditioned reflexes: A investigation of the physiological activity of the cerebral cortex* (G. V. Anrep, trans.). London & New York: Oxford Univ. Press.

Pavlov, I. P. (1928). *Lectures on conditioned reflexes* (W. H. Gantt, trans.) (Vol. 1). London: Lawrence & Wishart.

Paxton, R. (1980). The effects of a deposit contract as a component in a behavioral programme for stopping smoking. *Behaviour Research and Therapy, 18,* 45–50.

Paxton, R. (1981). Deposit contracts with smokers: Varying frequency and amount of repayments. *Behaviour Research and Therapy, 19,* 117–123.

Peak, H. M. *Credit union family financial counseling: A survey course.* Sacramento, Calif. Credit Union League, Department of Education.

Peavey, B. S., Lawlis, G. F., & Goven, A. (1984). *Biofeedback assisted relaxation: Effects on phagocytic immune functioning.* Paper presented at annual meeting of the American Psychological Association, Toronto, Ontario.

Pechacek, T. F., & Danaher, B. G. (1979). How and why people quit smoking: A cognitive-behavioral analysis. In P. C. Kendall & S. D. Hollon (Eds.), *Cognitive-behavioral interventions: Theory, research, and procedures.* New York: Academic Press.

Pendelton, M. G., & Higgins, R. L. (1983). A comparison of negative practice and systematic desensitization in the treatment of agoraphobia. *Journal of Behavior Therapy and Experimental Psychiatry, 14,* 317–323.

Pendergrass, V. E. (1972). Time-out from positive reinforcement following persistent high-rate behavior in retardates. *Journal of Applied Behavior Analysis, 5,* 85–91.

Pendery, M. L., Maltzman, I. M., & West, L. J. (1982). Controlled drinking by alcoholics? New findings and a reevaluation of a major affirmative study. *Science, 217,* 169–174.

Penick, S. B., Filion, R., Fox, S., & Stunkard, A. J. (1971). Behavior modification in the treatment of obesity. *Psychosomatic Medicine, 33,* 49–55.

Pentz, M. (1980). Assertion training and trainer effects on unassertive and aggressive adolescents. *Journal of Counseling Psychology, 27,* 76–83.

Pentz, M. A., & Kazdin, A. E. (1982). Assertion modeling and stimuli effects on assertive behavior and self-efficacy in adolescents. *Behaviour Research and Therapy, 20,* 365–371.

Percell, L. P., Berwick, P. T., & Biegels, A. (1974). The effects of assertive training on self-concept. *Archives of General Psychiatry, 31,* 502–504.

Perri, M. G., McAdoo, W. G., Spevak, P. A., & Newlin, D. B. (1984). Effect of a multicomponent maintenance program on long-term weight loss. *Journal of Consulting and Clinical Psychology, 52,* 480–481.

Perri, M. G., Richards, C. S., & Schultheis, K. R. (1977). Behavioral self-control and smoking reduction: A study of self-initiated attempts to reduce smoking. *Behavioral Therapy, 8,* 360–365.

Perri, M. G., Shapiro, R. M., Ludwig, W. W., Twentyman, C. T., & McAdoo, W. G. (1984). Maintenance strategies for the treatment of obesity: An evaluation of relapse prevention training and posttreatment contacts by mail and telephone. *Journal of Consulting and Clinical Psychology, 52,* 404–413.

Peters, H. N., & Jenkins, R. L. (1954). Improvement of chronic schizophrenic patients with guided problem-solving motivated by hunger. *Psychiatric Quarterly Supplement, 28,* 84–101.

Pfeiffer, E. A., & Johnson, J. B. (1968). A new electrode for the application of electrical shock in aversive conditioning therapy. *Behaviour Research and Therapy, 6,* 393–394.

Phelps, S., & Austin, N. (1974). *The assertive woman.* San Luis Obispo, CA: Impact.

Philips, C. (1978). Tension headache: Theoretical problems. *Behaviour Research and Therapy, 16,* 249–261.

Phillips, D., Fisher, S. C., & Singh, R. (1977). A children's reinforcement survey schedule. *Journal*

of Behavior Therapy and Experimental Psychiatry, 8, 131–134.

Phillips, E. L. (1968). Achievement place: Token reinforcement procedures in a home-style rehabilitation setting for "predelinquent" boys. *Journal of Applied Behavior Analysis, 1,* 213–223.

Phillips, E. L., Phillips, E. A., Fixsen, D. L., & Wolf, M. M. (1971). Achievement place: Modification of the behaviors of pre-delinquent boys within a token economy. *Journal of Applied Behavior Analysis, 4,* 45–59.

Phillips, E. L., Phillips, E. A., Wolf, M. M., & Fixsen, D. L. (1973). Achievement place: Development of the elected manager system. *Journal of Applied Behavior Analysis, 6,* 541–561.

Pierce, C. H., & Risley, T. R. (1974a). Improving job performance of neighborhood youth corps aides in an urban recreation program. *Journal of Applied Behavior Analysis, 7,* 207–215.

Pierce, C. H., & Risley, T. R. (1974b). Recreation as a reinforcer: Increasing membership and decreasing disruptions in an urban recreation center. *Journal of Applied Behavior Analysis, 7,* 403–411.

Pikoff, H. (1984). A critical review of autogenic training in America. *Clinical Psychology Review, 4,* 619–639.

Pitts, C. E. (1976). Behavior modification—1787. *Journal of Applied Behavior Analysis, 9,* 146.

Platonov, K. I. (1959). *The word as a physiological and therapeutic factor.* Moscow: Foreign Langauges Publishing House.

Plotkin, W. B. (1976). On the self regulation of the occipital alpha rhythm: Control strategies, states of consciousness, and the role of physiological feedback. *Journal of Experimental Psychology, 105,* 66–99.

Plotkin, W. B., Mazer, C., & Loewy, D. (1976). Alpha enhancement and the likelihood of an alpha experience. *Psychophysiology, 13,* 466–471.

Plummer, S., Baer, D. M., & LeBlanc, J. M. (1977). Functional considerations in the use of procedural time out and an effective alternative. *Journal of Applied Behavior Analysis, 10,* 689–706.

Pohl, R. W., Revusky, S., & Mellor, C. S. (1980). Drugs employed in the treatment of alcoholism: Rat data suggest they are unnecessarily severe. *Behaviour Research and Therapy, 18,* 71–78.

Poindexter, A. (1936). The factor of repetition in learning to type. *Kentucky Personality Bulletin, 17,* 3–4.

Polakow, R. L. (1975). Covert sensitization treatment of a probationed barbiturate addict. *Journal of Behavior Therapy and Experimental Psychiatry, 7,* 53–54.

Polich, J. M., Armor, D. J., & Braiker, H. B. (1980). *The course alcoholism: Four years after treatment.* Santa Monica, CA: Rand Corporation.

Polin, A. T. (1959). The effects of flooding and physical suppression as extinction techniques on an anxiety motivated avoidance locomotor response. *Journal of Psychology, 47,* 235–245.

Pomerleau, O. F., Pertschuck, M., Adkins, D., & Brady, J. P. (1978). A comparison of behavioral and traditional treatment methods for middle-income problem drinkers. *Journal of Behavioral Medicine, 1,* 187–200.

Poole, A. D., & Bodeker, G. C. (1975). Using time restriction to modify compulsive rocking. *Journal of Behavior Therapy and Experimental Psychiatry, 6,* 153–154.

Popler, K. (1976). Token reinforcement in the treatment of nocturnal enuresis: A case study and six month follow-up. *Journal of Behavior Therapy and Experimental Psychiatry, 7,* 83–84.

Poppen, R. L. (1968). *Counterconditioning of conditioned suppression.* Unpublished doctoral dissertation, Stanford University.

Poppen, R. L. (1970). Counterconditioning of conditioned suppression in rats. *Psychological Reports, 27,* 659–671.

Poppen, R. L. (1983). Clinical practice and biofeedback research: Are the data really necessary? *Behavior Therapist, 6,* 145–148.

Potter, S. (1952). *One-upsmanship, being some account of the activities and teachings of the Lifemanship Correspondence College of One-upness and Games lifemastery.* New York: Holt.

Powell, J., & Azrin, N. (1968). The effects of shock as a punisher for cigarette smoking. *Journal of Applied Behavior Analysis, 1,* 63–71.

Powers, R., & Powers, E. (1971). Responding of retarded children on a backscratch schedule of reinforcement. *Psychological Aspects of Disability, 18,* 27–34.

Premack, D. (1959). Toward empirical behavioral laws. I. Positive reinforcement. *Psychological Review, 66,* 219–233.

Premack, D. (1965). Reinforcement theory. In D. Levine (Ed.), *Nebraska Symposium on Motivation.* Lincoln: University of Nebraska Press.

Price, K. P., & Clarke, L. K. (1979). Classical conditioning of digital pulse volume in migraineurs and normal controls. *Headache, 19,* 328–332.

Price, K. R. (1973, May). *Feedback effects on penile tumescence.* Paper presented to Eastern Psychological Association, Washington, DC.

Prignatano, G., & Johnson, H. (1972). Biofeedback control of heart rate variability to phobic stimuli: A new approach to treating spider phobia. *Proceedings of the 80th Association Convention* (pp. 403–404). Washington, D. C.

Prochaska, J. D. (1979). *Systems of psychotherapy: A transtheoretical analysis.* Homewood, IL: Dorsey.

Prochaska, J. D., & DiClemente, C. O. (1982). Transtheoretical therapy: Toward a more integrative model -of change. *Psychotherapy: Theory, Research, and Practice, 19,* 276–288.

Prochaska, J. D., & DiClemente, C. O. (1983). Stages and processes of self-change of smoking: Toward an integrative model of change. *Journal of Consulting and Clinical Psychology, 51,* 390–395.

Prochaska, J. D., & DiClemente, C. O. (1984). *The transtheoretical approach: Crossing traditional boundaries of therapy.* Homewood, IL: Dow Jones/Irwin.

Prochaska, J. O., Smith, N., Marzilli, R., Colby, J., & Donovan, W. (1974). Remote-control aversive stimulation in the treatment of head-banging in a retarded child. *Journal of Behavior Therapy and Experimental Psychiatry, 5,* 285–289.

Propp, L. (1985). A self-control treatment for encopresis combining self-charting with paradoxical instructions: Two case examples. *Journal of Child & Adolescent Psychotherapy, 2,* 26–31.

Provine, R. R., & Enoch, J. M. (1975). On voluntary ocular accommodation. *Perception & Psychophysics, 17,* 209–212.

Pyle, R., Mitchell, J. E., Eckert, E., Halverson, P., Neuman, P., & Goff, G. (1983). The incidence of bulimia in freshman college students. *International Journal of Eating Disorders. 2,* 75–85.

Quay, H. C., Glavin, J. P., Annesley, P. R., & Werry, J. S. (1972). The modification of problem behavior and academic achievement in a resource room. *Journal of School Psychology, 10,* 187–193.

Quilian, J., Besing, S., & Dinning, D. (1977). Standardization of the Rathus Assertiveness Schedule, *Journal of Clinical Psychology, 33,* 418–422.

Quinn, J. T., & Henbest, R. (1967). Partial failure of generalization in alcoholics following aversion therapy. *Quarterly Journal of Studies on Alcoholism, 28,* 70–75.

Quinsley, V. L., Maguire, A., & Varney, G. W. (1983). Assertion and overcontrolled hostility among mentally disturbed murderers. *Journal of Consulting and Clinical Psychology, 51,* 550–556.

Quinsley, V. L., & Varney, G. W. (1977). Social skills game: A general method for the modeling and practice of adaptive behaviors. *Behavior Therapy, 8,* 279–281.

Rabavilas, A. D., & Boulougoris, J. C. (1974). Physiological accompaniments of ruminations, flooding and thought-stopping in obsessive patients. *Behaviour Research and Therapy, 12,* 239–243.

Rabavilas, A. D., Boulougoris, J. C., & Stefanis, C. (1977). Compulsive checking diminished when over-checking instructions were disobeyed. *Journal of Behavior Therapy and Experimental Psychiatry, 8,* 111–112.

Rabkin, S. W. (1984). Effect of cigarette smoking cessation on risk factors for coronary atherosclerosis. *Atherosclerosis, 53,* 173–184.

Rachlin, H. (1977a). Reinforcing and punishing thoughts. *Behavior Therapy, 8,* 659–665.

Rachlin, H. (1977b). Reinforcing and punishing thoughts: A rejoinder to Ellis and Mahoney. *Behavior Therapy, 8,* 678–681.

Rachlin, H., & Herrnstein, R. J. (1969). Hedonism revisited: On the negative law of effect. In B. A. Campbell, & R. M. Church (Eds.), *Punishment and aversive behavior.* New York: Appleton.

Rachman, S. (1965). Aversion therapy: Chemical or electrical? *Behaviour Research and Therapy, 2,* 289–299.

Rachman, S. (1966a). Studies in desensitization II: Flooding. *Behaviour Research and Therapy, 4,* 1–6.

Rachman, S. (1966b). Studies in desensitization. III. Speed of generalization. *Behaviour Research and Therapy, 4,* 7–15.

Rachman, S. (1968). The role of muscular relaxation in desensitization therapy. *Behaviour Research and Therapy, 16,* 159–166.

Rachman, S. (1969). Treatment by prolonged exposure to high intensity stimulation. *Behaviour Research and Therapy, 7,* 295–302.

Rachman, S. (1977). The conditioning theory of fear-acquisition: A critical examination. *Behaviour Research and Therapy, 15,* 375–387.

Rachman, S., Hodgson, R., & Marks, I. (1971). The treatment of chronic obsessive-compulsive neurosis. *Behaviour Research and Therapy, 9,* 237–247.

Rachman, S., Marks, I. M., & Hodgson, R. (1973). The treatment of obsessive-compulsive neurotics by modeling and flooding in vivo. *Behaviour Research and Therapy, 11,* 463–471.

Rachman, S., & Teasdale, J. (1969). *Aversion therapy and behaviour disorders: An analysis.* Coral Gables, FL: University of Miami Press.

Rainey, C. A. (1972). An obsessive-compulsive neurosis treated by flooding *in vivo. Journal of Behavior Therapy and Experimental Psychiatry, 3,* 117–121.

Rainwater, N., Ayllon, T., Frederiksen, L. W., Moore, E. J., & Bonar, J. R., (1982). Teaching self-management skills to increase diet compliance in diabetics. In R. Stuart (Ed.), *Adherence, compliance and generalization in behavioral medicine.* New York: Brunner/Mazel.

Ramp, E., Ulrich, R., & Dulaney, S. (1971). Delayed timeout as a procedure for reducing disruptive classroom behavior: A case study. *Journal of Applied Behavior Analysis, 4,* 235–239.

Rankin, H., Hodgson, R., & Stockwell, T. (1983). Cue exposure and response prevention with alcoholics: A controlled trial. *Behaviour Research and Therapy, 21,* 435–446.

Rapport, M. D., & Bostow, D. E. (1976). The effects of access to special activities on the performance in four categories of academic tasks with third-grade students. *Journal of Applied Behavior Analysis, 9,* 372.

Raskin, M., Bali, L. R., & Peeke, H. V. (1980). Muscle biofeedback and transcendental meditation: A controlled evaluation of efficacy in the treatment of chronic anxiety. *Archives of General Psychiatry, 37,* 93–97.

Raskin, M., Johnson, G., & Rondestevedt, J. W. (1973). Chronic anxiety treatment by feedback induced muscle relaxation: A pilot study. *Archives of General Psychiatry, 28,* 263–267.

Rathus, S. A. (1972). An experimental investigation of assertive training in a group setting. *Journal of Behavior Therapy and Experimental Psychiatry, 3,* 81–86.

Rathus, S. A. (1973a). A 30-item schedule for assessing assertive behavior. *Behavior Therapy, 4,* 398–406.

Rathus, S. A. (1973b). Instigation of assertive models and directed practice. *Behaviour Research and Therapy, 11,* 57–65.

Rathus, S. A., & Nevid, J. S. (1977). Concurrent validity of the 30-item assertiveness schedule with a psychiatric population. *Behavior Therapy, 8,* 393–397.

Raw, M., & Russell, M. A. H. (1980). Rapid smoking, cue exposure and support in the modification of smoking. *Behaviour Research and Therapy, 18,* 363–372.

Raymond, M. J. (1956). Case of fetishism treated by aversion therapy. *British Medical Journal, 2,* 854–857.

Raymond, M. J., & O'Keefe, K. (1965). A case of pin-up fetishism treated by aversion conditioning. *British Journal of Psychiatry, 111,* 579–581.

Rebman, V. L. (1983). Self-control desensitization with case-controlled relaxation for treatment of a conditioned vomiting response to air travel. *Journal of Behavior Therapy and Experimental Psychiatry, 14,* 161–164.

Redd, W. H. (1969). Effects of mixed reinforcement contingencies on adults' control of children's behavior. *Journal of Applied Behavior Analysis, 2,* 249–254.

Redd, W. H. (1980). In vivo desensitization in the treatment of chronic emesis following gastrointestinal surgery. *Behavior Therapy, 11,* 421–427.

Redd, W. H., Jacobsen, P. B., Die-Trill, M., Dermatis, H., McEvoy, M., & Holland, J. L. (1987). Cognitive/attentional distraction in the control of conditioned nausea in pediatric cancer patients receiving chemotherapy. *Health Psychology.*

Reed, S. D., Katkin, E. S., & Goldband, S. (1986). Biofeedback and behavioral medicine. In F. H. Kanfer & A. P. Goldstein (Eds.), *Helping people change: A textbook of methods* (3rd ed.). New York: Pergamon Press.

Reeves, J. L., & Mealiea, W. L. (1975). Biofeedback assisted cue-controlled relaxation for the treatment of flight phobias. *Journal of Behavior Therapy and Experimental Psychiatry, 6,* 105–109.

Rehm, L. P. (1977). A self-control model of depression. *Behavior Therapy, 8,* 787–804.

Rehm, L. P. (1983). Outcome for self-control therapy for depression with subpopulations. *Psychotherapy in Private Practice, 1,* 15–19.

Rehm, L. P., Fuchs, C. Z., Roth, D. M., Kornblith, S. J., & Romano, J. M. (1979). A comparison of self-control and assertion skills treatments of depression. *Behavior Therapy, 10,* 429–442.

Rehm, L. P., Kaslow, N. J., Rabin, A. S., & Willard, R. (1981, Aug.). *Prediction of outcome in a behavior therapy program for depression.* Paper presented at the Annual Meeting of the American Psychological Association, Los Angeles.

Rehm, L. P., Kornblith, S. J., O'Hara, M. W., Lamparski, D. M., Romano, J. M., & Volin, J. (1981). An evaluation of major components in a self-control behavior therapy program for depression. *Behavior Modification, 5,* 459–490.

Rehm, L. P., Lamparski, D. M., Romano, J. M., & O'Hara, M. W. (In preparation). *Cognitive, behavioral and combined versions of a self-control therapy program for depression.* Unpublished manuscript, University of Houston, Houston, TX.

Reichle, J., Brubakken, D., & Tetreault, G. (1976). Eliminating perservative speech by positive reinforcement and time-out in a psychotic child. *Journal of Behavior Therapy and Experimental Psychiatry, 1,* 179–183.

Reinhardt, R. A., & Reinhardt, R. C. (1977). Dental implications of anorexia nervosa: Report of a case. *Journal of the Nebraska Dental Association, 54,* 709.

Reisinger, J. J. (1972). The treatment of "anxiety-depression" via positive reinforcement and response cost. *Journal of Applied Behavior Analysis, 5,* 125–130.

Reisinger, J. J., Frangia, G. W., & Hoffman, E. H. (1976). Toddler management training: Generalization and marital status. *Journal of Behavior Therapy and Experimental Psychiatry, 7,* 335–340.

Reitz, W. E., & Keil, W. E. (1971). Behavioral treatment of an exhibitionist. *Journal of Behavior Therapy and Experimental Psychiatry, 2,* 67–69.

Rekers, G. A. (1977). Atypical gender development and psychosocial adjustment. *Journal of Applied Behavior Analysis, 10,* 559–571.

Rekers, G. A., Yates, C. E., Willis, T. J., Rosen, A. C., & Taubman, M. (1976). Childhood gender identity change: Operant control over sex-typed play and mannerisms. *Journal of Behavior Therapy and Experimental Psychiatry, 7,* 51–57.

Repp, A. C., & Deitz, S. M. (1974). Reducing aggressive and self-injurious behavior of institutionalized retarded children through reinforcement of other behaviors. *Journal of Applied Behavior Analysis, 7,* 313–325.

Resick, P. A., Forehand, R., & McWhorter, A. (1976). The effect of parent treatment with one child on an untreated sibling. *Behavior Therapy, 7,* 544–548.

Retter, J. B. (1954). *Social learning and clinical psychology.* Englewood Cliffs, NJ: Prentice-Hall.

Rettig, E. B. (1973). *ABC's for parents: An educational workshop in behavior modification.* North Hollywood, CA: Associates for Behavior Change.

Rettig, E. B., & Paulson, T. L. (1975). *ABC's for teachers: An in-service training program in behavior modification.* North Hollywood, CA: Associates for Behavior Change.

Ribordy, S. C., & Denney, D. R. (1977). The behavioral treatment of insomnia: An alternative to drug therapy. *Behaviour Research and Therapy, 15,* 39–50.

Rice, K. M., & Blanchard, E. B. (1982). Biofeedback in the treatment of anxiety disorders. *Clinical Psychology Review, 2,* 557–577.

Rice, L. N. (1974). The evocative function of the therapist. In D. A. Wexler & L. N. Rice (Eds.), *Innovation in client-centered therapy.* New York: Wiley-Interscience.

Richards, C. S. (1975). Behavior modification of studying through study skills advice and self-control procedures. *Journal of Counseling Psychology, 22,* 431–436.

Richards, C. S., (1981). Improving college students' study behaviors through self-control techniques: A brief review. *Behavioral Counseling Quarterly, 1,* 159–175.

Richards, C. S. (1985). Work and study problems. In M. Hersen & A. S. Bellack (Eds.), *Handbook of clinical behavior therapy with adults.* New York: Plenum Press.

Richardson, F. C. (1976). Anxiety management training: A multimodal approach. In A. A. Lazarus (Ed.), *Multimodal behavior therapy.* Berlin & New York: Springer-Verlag.

Richardson, F. C., & Suinn, R. M. (1973). A comparison of traditional systematic desensitization, accelerated massed desensitization, and anxiety management training in the treatment of mathematics anxiety. *Behavior Therapy, 4,* 212–218.

Richter, R., & Bernhard, D. (1982). Bronchial asthma in adults: There is little evidence for the effectiveness of behavioral therapy and relaxation. *Journal of Psychomatic Research, 26,* 533–540.

Rickels, W. H., Onoda, L., & Doyle, C. C. (1982). Task force study section: Biofeedback as an adjunct to psychotherapy. *Biofeedback and Self-regulation, 7,* 1–33.

Rimm, A., & Somerville, J. W. (1977). *Abnormal psychology.* New York; Academic Press.

Rimm, D. C. (1967). Assertive training used in treatment of chronic crying spells. *Behaviour Research and Therapy, 5,* 373–374.

Rimm, D. C. (1973). Thought stopping and covert assertion in the treatment of phobias. *Journal of Consulting and Clinical Psychology, 41,* 466–467.

Rimm, D. C. (1976). Behavior therapy: Some general comments and a review of selected papers. In R. L. Spitzer, & D. F. Klein (Eds.), *Evaluation of psychological therapies.* Baltimore: John Hopkins University Press.

Rimm, D. C. (1977a). Assertive training and the expression of anger. In R. E. Alberti (Ed.), *Assertiveness: Innovations, applications, issues.* San Luis Obispo, CA: Impact Publishers.

Rimm, D. C. (1977b). Treatment of antisocial aggression. In G. G. Harris (Ed.), *The group treatment of human problems.* New York: Grune & Stratton.

Rimm, D. C., & Bottrell, J. (1969). Four measures of visual imagination. *Behaviour Research and Therapy, 7,* 63–69.

Rimm, D. C., deGroot, J. C., Boord, P., Heiman, J. Dillow, P. V. (1971). Systematic desensitization of an anger response. *Behaviour Research and Therapy, 9,* 273–280.

Rimm, D. C., Hill, G. A., Brown, N. N., & Stuart, J. E. (1974). Group-assertive training in treatment of expression of inappropriate anger. *Psychological Reports, 34,* 791–798.

Rimm, D. C., Janda, L. H., Lancaster, D. W., Nahl, M., & Dittmar, K. (1977). An exploratory investigation of the origin and maintenance of phobias. *Behaviour Research and Therapy, 15,* 231–238.

Rimm, D. C., & Litvak, S. B. (1969). Self verbalization and emotional arousal. *Journal of Abnormal Psychology 74,* 181–187.

Rimm, D. C. & Madieros, D. C. (1970). The role of muscle relaxation in participant modeling. *Behavior Research and Therapy, 8,* 127–132.

Rimm, D. C., & Mahoney, M. J. (1969). The application of reinforcement and participant modeling procedures in the treatment of snake-phobic behavior. *Behaviour Research and Therapy, 7,* 369–376.

Rimm, D. C., & Masters, J. C. (1979). *Behavior therapy: Techniques and empirical findings* (2nd ed.). New York: Academic Press.

Rimm, D. C., Saunders, W. D., & Westel, W. (1975). Thought stopping and covert assertion in the treatment of snake phobias. *Journal of Consulting and Clinical Psychology, 43,* 92–93.

Rimm, D. C., Snyder, J. J., Depue, R. A., Haanstad, M. J., & Armstrong, D. P. (1976). Assertive training versus rehearsal, and the importance of making assertive response. *Behaviour Research and Therapy, 14,* 315–321.

Rincover, A., & Koegel, R. L. (1975). Setting generality and stimulus control in autistic children. *Journal of Applied Behavior Analysis, 8,* 235–246.

Ringer, V. M. J. (1973). The use of a "token helper" in the management of classroom behavior. *Journal of Applied Behavior Analysis, 6,* 671–678.

Rinn, R. C., Vernon, J. C., & Wise, M. J. (1975). Training parents of behaviorally-disordered children in groups: A three years' program evaluation. *Behavior Therapy, 6,* 378–387.

Risley, T. R. (1968). The effects and side effects of punishing the autistic behaviors of a deviant child. *Journal of Applied Behavior Analysis, 1,* 21–34.

Risley, T. R., & Wolf, M. M. (1967). Establishing functional speech in echolalic children. *Behaviour Research and Therapy, 5,* 73–88.

Ritter, B. (1968a). The effect of contact desensitization on avoidance behavior, fear ratings, and self-evaluative statements. *Proceedings of the 76th Annual Convention of the American Psychological Association, 3,* 527–528.

Ritter, B. (1968b). The group treatment of children's snake phobias, using vicarious and contact desensitization procedures. *Behaviour Research and Therapy, 6,* 1–6.

Ritter, B. (1969a). Eliminating excessive fears of the environment through contact desensitization . In J. D. Krumboltz, & C. E. Thoreson (Eds.), *Behavioral counseling: Cases and techniques.* New York: Holt.

Ritter, B. (1969b). Treatment of acrophobia with contact desensitization. *Behaviour Research and Therapy, 7,* 41–45.

Ritter, B. (1969c). The use of contact desensitization, demonstration-plus-participation, and demonstration alone in the treatment of acrophobia. *Behaviour Research and Therapy, 7,* 157–167.

Rizley, R. (1978). Depression and distortion in the attribution of causality. *Journal of Abnormal Psychology, 87,*(1), 32–48.

Robbins, L. C. (1963). The accuracy of parental recall of aspects of child development and of child rearing practices. *Journal of Abnormal and Social Psychology, 66,* 261–270.

Roberts, A. H. (1985). Biofeedback: Research, training, and clinical roles. *American Psychologist, 40,* 938–941.

Roberts, M. C., Wurtele, S. K., Boone, R. R., Ginther, L. J., & Elkins, P. D. (1981). Reduction of medical fears by use of modeling: A preventive application in an general population of children. *Journal of Pediatric Psychology, 6,* 293–300.

Robertson, S. J., DeReus, D. M., & Drabman, R. S. (1976). Peer and college-student tutoring as reinforcement in a token economy. *Journal of Applied Behavior Analysis, 9,* 169–177.

Robinson, F. P. (1946). *Effective study.* New York: Harper.

Rodin, J. (1981). Current status of the internal-external hypothesis for obesity: What went wrong? *American Psychologist, 36,* 361–372.

Rodin, J. (1982a). Biopsychosocial aspects of self-management. In P. Karoly & F. H. Kanfer (Eds.), *Self-management and behavior change: From theory to practice.* Elmsford, NY: Pergamon Press.

Rodin, J. (1982b). Obesity: Why the losing battle? In B. B. Wolman (Ed.), *Psychological aspects of obesity: A handbook.* New York: Van Nostrand.

Rodin, J. (1983). Behavioral medicine: Beneficial effects of self-control training in aging. *International Review of Applied Psychology, 32,* 153–181.

Roeper, G., Rachman, S., & Marks, I. (1975). Passive and participants modeling in exposure treatment of obsessive-compulsive neurotics. *Behaviour Research and Therapy, 13,* 271–279.

Rogers, C. R. (1961). *On becoming a person.* Boston: Houghton Mifflin.

Rogers, T., & Craighead, W. E. (1977). Physiological responses to self-statements: The effects of statement valence and discrepancy. *Cognitive Therapy and Research, 1*(2), 99–119.

Rogers-Warren, A., & Baer, D. M. (1976). Correspondence between saying and doing: Teaching children to share and praise. *Journal of Applied Behavior Analysis, 9,* 335–354.

Romanczyk, R. G. (1974). Self-monitoring in the treatment of obesity: Parameters of reactivity. *Behavior Therapy, 5,* 531–540.

Romanczyk, R. G., Kent, R. N., Diament, C., & O'Leary, K. D. (1973). Measuring the reliability of observational data: A reactive process. *Journal of Applied Behavior Analysis, 6,* 175–184.

Romanczyk, R. G., Tracey, D. A., Wilson, G. T., & Thorpe, G. L. (1973). Behavioral techniques in the treatment of obesity: A comparative analysis. *Behaviour Research and Therapy, 11,* 629–640.

Romano, J. L., & Cabianca, W. A. (1978). EMG biofeedback training versus systematic desensitization for test anxiety reduction. *Journal of Consulting Psychology, 34,* 791–798.

Ronnback, B. E. (1983). Self-management of study habits: A review. *Scandinavian Journal of Behavior Therapy, 12,* 73–110.

Roos, P. (1965). Development of an intensive habit-training unit at Austin State School. *Mental Retardation, 3,* 12–15.

Rosekrans, M. A. (1966). *Vicarious reinforcement and the acquisition and performance of imitative response as a function of perceived similarity to a social model.* Unpublished Ph.D. thesis, University of Minnesota.

Rosekrans, M. A., & Hartup, W. W. (1967). The effects on inconsistent consequences to the model on imitation. *Journal of Personality and Social Psychology, 7,* 429–434.

Rosen, G. M. (1976). Subjects' initial therapeutic expectancies and subject's awareness of therapeutic goals in systematic desensitization: A review. *Behavior Therapy, 7,* 14–27.

Rosen, G. M., Rosen, E., & Reid, J. R. (1972). Cognitive desensitization and avoidance behavior. *Journal of Abnormal Psychology, 80,* 176–182.

Rosen, R. C., & Schnapp, B. J. (1974). The use of a specific behavioral technique (thought stopping) in the context of conjoint couples therapy. *Behavior Therapy, 5,* 261–264.

Rosenbaum, M. S., & Breiling, J. (1976). The development and functional control of reading-comprehension behavior. *Journal of Applied Analysis, 9,* 323–333.

Rosenberg, H., & Lah, M. I. (1982). A comprehensive behavioral-cognitive treatment of writer's block. *Behavioural Psychotherapy, 10,* 356–363.

Rosenberg, H., Upper, D., Connors, G. J., & Dicroce, E. (1982). Applying behavioral contracting to alcohol abuse in a spinal cord injured patient. *Journal of Behavior Therapy and Experimental Psychiatry, 13,* 341–346.

Rosenfeld, G. W. (1972). Some effects of reinforcement on achievement and behavior in a regular classroom. *Educational Psychology, 63,* 189–193.

Rosenman, R. H. (1978). The interview method of assessment of the coronary-prone behavior pattern. In T.M. Dembroski, S. M. Weiss, J. Shields, S. G. Haynes, & M. Feinleib (Eds.), *Coronary-prone behavior.* New York: Springer-Verlag.

Rosenthal, B., Allen, G. J., & Winter, C. (1980). Husband involvement in the behavioral treatment of overweight women: Initial effects and long-term follow-up. *International Journal of Obesity, 4,* 165–173.

Rosenthal, R. (1963). On the social psychology of the psychological experiment: The experimenter's hypothesis as unintended determinant of experimental results. *American Scientist, 51,* 268–282.

Rosenthal, T. L., Linehan, K. S., Kelley, J. E., Rosenthal, R. H., Theobald, D. E., & Davis, A. F. (1978). Group aversion by imaginal, vicarious and shared recipient-observer shocks. *Behaviour Research and Therapy, 16,* 421–427.

Rosenthal, T. L., & Reese, S. L. (1976). The effects of covert and overt modeling on assertive behavior. *Behaviour Research and Therapy, 14,* 463–469.

Ross, D. M., Ross, S. A., & Evans, T. A. (1971). The modification of extreme social withdrawal by modeling with guided participation. *Journal of Behavior Therapy and Experimental Psychiatry, 2,* 273–279.

Ross, J. A. (1974). The use of contingency contracting in controlling adult nailbiting. *Journal of Behavior Therapy and Experimental Psychiatry, 5,* 105–106.

Ross, S. M., & Proctor, S. (1973). Frequency and duration of hierarchy item exposure in an systematic desensitization analogue. *Behaviour Research and Therapy, 11,* 303–312.

Roth, D., Bielski, R., Jones, M., Parker, W., & Osborn, G. (1982). A comparison of self-control therapy and combined self-control therapy and antidepressant medication in the treatment of depression. *Behavior Therapy, 13,* 133–144.

Rotter, J. B. (1954). *Social learning and clinical psychology.* Englewood Cliffs, NJ: Prentice-Hall.

Rotter, J. B. (1966). Generalized expectancies for internal vs. external control of reinforcement. *Psychological Monographs, 80* (Whole No. 609).

Rovetto, F. M. (1983). In vivo desensitization of a severe driving phobia through radio contact with telemonitoring of neurophysiological reactions. *Journal of Behavior Therapy and Experimental Psychiatry, 14,* 49–54.

Rowbury, T. G., Baer, A. M., & Baer, D. M. (1976).

Interactions between teacher guidance and contingent access to play in developing preacademic skills of deviant pre-school children. *Journal of Applied Behavior Analysis, 9,* 85–104.

Royce, W. S., & Arkowitz, H. (1977). Clarification of some issues concerning subject recruitment procedures in therapy analog studies. *Behavior Therapy, 8,* 64–69.

Royer, F. L., Rynearson, R., Rice, W., & Upper, D. (1971). An inexpensive quickly built stock grid for use with humans. *Behavior Therapy, 2*(2), 251–252.

Rozensky, R. H., & Bellack, A. S. (1974). Behavior change and individual differences in self-control. *Behaviour Research and Therapy, 12,* 267–268.

Ruck, F. (1956). Alkoholentziehungskur mit Hilfe eines bedingten Reflexes (Apomorphinentziehungskur). (Conditioned reflex treatment of alcoholism). *Psychiatrie, Neurologie und Mdezinsche Psychologie, 8,* 88–92.

Ruhl, R. A. (1935). Negative practice versus positive practice in the eliminating of typing errors. *Journal of General Psychology, 13,* 203–211.

Rupert, P. A., Dobbins, K., & Mathew, R. J. (1981). EMB biofeedback and relaxation instructions in the treatment of chronic anxiety. *American Journal of Clinical Biofeedback, 4,* 52–61.

Rupert, P. A., & Holmes, D. S. (1978). Effects of multiple series of true and placebo heart rate biofeedback training on the heart rates and anxiety levels of anxious patients during and following treatment. *Psychophysiology, 15,* 582–590.

Rush, A. J., Beck, A. T., Kovacs, M., & Hollon, S. D. (1977). Comparative efficacy of cognitive therapy and pharmacotherapy in the treatment of depressed outpatients. *Cognitive Therapy and Research, 1*(1), 17–37.

Russ, K. L., Hammer, R. L. & Adderton, M. (1979). Clinical follow-up: Treatment and outcome of functional headache patients treated with biofeedback. *Journal of Clinical Psychology, 35,* 148–153.

Russell, M. A. H., Armstrong, E., & Patel, U. A. (1976). Temporal contiguity in electric aversion therapy for cigarette smoking. *Behaviour Research and Therapy, 14,* 103–123.

Russell, M. A. H., Raw, M., Taylor, L., Feyeraband, C., & Saloojee, V. (1978). Blood nicotine and carboxyhemoglobin levels after rapid-smoking aversion therapy. *Journal of Consulting and Clinical Psychology, 46,* 1423–1431.

Russell, P. L., & Brandsma, J. M. (1974). A theoretical and empirical investigation of the rational-emotive and classical conditioning theories. *Journal of Consulting and Clinical Psychology, 42,* 389–397.

Russell, R. K., & Sipich, J. F. (1973). Cue-controlled relaxation in the treatment of test anxiety. *Journal of Behavior Therapy and Experimental Psychiatry, 4,* 47–49.

Russell, R. K., Sipich, J. F., & Knipe, J. (1976). Progressive relaxation training: A procedural note. *Behavior Therapy, 7,* 566–568.

Russo, D. C., Bird, B. L., & Masek, B. J. (1980). Assessment issues in behavioral medicine. *Behavior Assessment, 2,* 1–18.

Rutherford, B. R. (1940). The use of negative practice in speech therapy with children handicapped by cerebral palsy, athetoid type. *Journal of Speech Disorders, 5,* 259–264.

Rybstein-Blinchik, E., & Grzesiak, R. C. (1979). Effects of different cognitive strategies on chronic pain experience. *Journal of Behavioral Medicine, 2,* 93–101.

Rybstein-Blinchik, E., & Grzesiak, R. C. (1979). Reinterpretative cognitive strategies in chronic pain management. *Archives of Physical Medicine and Rehabilitation, 60,* 609–612.

Saccone, A. J., & Israel, A. C. (1978). Effects of experimenter versus significant other controlled reinforcement and choice of target behavior on weight loss. *Behavior Therapy, 9,* 271–278.

Sachs, D. A., & Mayhall, B. (1971). Behavioral control of spasms using aversive conditioning with a cerebral palsied adult. *Journal of Nervous and Mental Disorders, 152,* 362–363.

Sachs, D. P. L., Hall, R. G., Pechacek, T. F., & Fitzgerald, J. (1979). Clarification on risk-benefit issues in rapid smoking. *Journal of Consulting and Clinical Psychology, 47,* 1053–1060.

Sachs, L. B., Bean, H., & Morrow, J. E. (1970). Comparison of smoking treatments. *Behavior Therapy, 1,* 465–472.

Safran, J. D., Alden, L. E., & Davidson, P. O. (1980). Client anxiety level as a moderator variable in assertion training. *Cognitive Therapy and Research, 4,* 189–200.

Sailor, W., & Taman, T. (1972). Stimulus factors in the training of prepositional usage in three autistic children. *Journal of Applied Behavior Analysis, 5,* 183–192.

Sajwaj, T., Libet, J., & Agras, S. (1974). Lemon-juice therapy: The control of life-threatening rumination in a six-month old infant. *Journal of Applied Behavior Analysis, 7,* 557–563.

Salter, A. (1949). *Conditioned reflex therapy.* New York: Farrar, Straus & Giroux.

Salter, A. (1964). The theory and practice of conditioned reflex therapy. In A. Salter, J. Wolpe, & L. J. Reyna (Eds.), *The conditioning therapies: The challenge in pscyhotherapy.* New York: Holt.

Samaan, M. (1975). Thought stopping and flooding in a case of hallucinations, obsessions, and homicidal suicidal behavior: 1. *Journal of Behavior Therapy and Experimental Psychiatry, 6,* 65–67.

Sanchez, V. C., Lewinsohn, P. M., & Larson, D. W. (1980). Assertion training: Effectiveness in the treatment of depression. *Journal of Clinical Psychology, 36,* 526–529.

Sanchez-Craig, M., Annis, H. M., Bornet, A. R., & MacDonald, K. R. (1984). Random assignment to abstinence and controlled drinking: Evaluation of a cognitive-behavioral program for problem drinkers. *Journal of Consulting and Clinical Psychology, 52,* 390–403.

Sanders, B. D. (1967). *Behavior rehearsal and imaginal desensitization in reducing public speaking anxiety.* Unpublished doctoral dissertation, Stanford University.

Sanders, M. R., & Glynn, T. (1977). Functional analysis of a program for training high and low preference peers to modify disruptive classroom behavior. *Journal of Applied Behavior Analysis, 10,* 503.

Sanderson, R. E., Campbell, D., & Laverty, S. G. (1963). An investigation of a new aversive conditioning treatment for alcoholism. *Quarterly Journal of Studies on Alcoholism, 24,* 261–275.

Sank, L. I., & Biglan, A. (1974). Operant treatment of a case of recurrent abdominal pain in a 10-year-old boy. *Behavior Therapy, 5,* 677–681.

Sanson-Fisher, B., Seymour, F., Montgomery, W., & Stokes, T. (1978). Modifying delinquents conversation using token reinforcement of self-recorded behavior. *Journal of Behavior Therapy and Experimental Psychiatry, 9,* 163–168.

Sarason, I. G. (1968). Verbal learning, modeling, and juvenile delinquency. *American Psychologist, 23,* 254–266.

Sarason, I. G., & Ganzer, V. J. (1969). Social influence techniques in clinical and community psychology. In C. D. Spielberger (Ed.), *Current Topics in Clinical and Community Psychology.* New York: Academic Press.

Sarason, I. B., Johnson, J. H., Berberich, J. P., & Siegel, J. M. (1979). Helping police officers to cope with stress: A cognitive-behavioral approach. *American Journal of Community Psychology, 7,* 593–603.

Sarason, S. (1958). Interrelationships among individual difference variables, behavior in psychotherapy, and verbal conditioning. *Journal of Abnormal and Social Psychology, 56,* 339–351.

Sargent, J. D. (1984). Results of a controlled, experimental, outcome study of non-drug treatments for the control of migraine headache. *Biofeedback and Self-regulation, 9,* 106 (abstract).

Sargent, J. D., Green, E. E., Walters, E. D. (1972). The use of autogenic feedback training in a pilot study of migraine and tension headaches. *Headache, 12,* 120–125.

Sargent, J. D., Green, E. E., & Walter, E. D. (1973). Preliminary report on the use of autogenic feedback training in the treatment of migraine and tension headaches. *Psychosomatic Medicine, 35,* 129–135.

Saunders, A. (1974). *Behavior management program: Applied behavior analysis in an adult male correctional facility.* Unpublished manuscript.

Schacter, S. (1966). The interaction of cognitive and physiological determinants of emotional states. In C. D. Spielberger (Ed.), *Anxiety and behavior.* New York: Academic Press.

Schacter, S. (1971). Some extraordinary facts about obese humans and rats. *American Psychologist, 26,* 129–144.

Schacter, S., & Singer, J. E. (1962). Cognitive, social, and physiological determinants of emotional state. *Psychological Review, 69,* 379–399.

Schacter, S., & Wheeler, L. (1962). Epinephrine chlorpromazine, and amusement. *Journal of Abnormal and Social Psychology, 65,* 121–128.

Schaefer, H. H. (1972). Twelve month follow-up of behaviorally trained ex-alcoholic social drinkers. *Behavior Therapy, 3,* 286–289.

Schaefer, H. H., & Martin, P. L. (1966). Behavior therapy for "apathy" of hospitalized schizophrenics. *Psychological Reports, 19,* 1147–1158.

Schaefer, H. H., & Martin, P. L. (1969). *Behavioral therapy.* New York: McGraw-Hill.

Schandler, S. L., & Grings, W. W. (1976). An examination of methods for producing relaxation during short term laboratory sessions. *Behaviour Research and Therapy, 14,* 419–426.

Scheiderer, E. G. (1977). Effects of instructions and modeling in producing self-disclosure in the initial clinical interview. *Journal of Consulting and Clinical Psychology, 45,* 378–384.

Schlundt, D. G., & McFall, R. M. (1985). New directions in the assessment of social competence and social skills. In L. L'Abate & M. A. Milan (Eds.), *Handbook of social skills training and research.* New York: Wiley.

Schmauk, F. J. (1970). Punishment, arousal, and avoidance learning in sociopaths. *Journals of Abnormal Psychology, 76,* 325–335.

Schmidt, E., Castell, D., & Brown, P. (1965). A retrospective study of 42 cases of behaviour therapy. *Behaviour Research and Therapy, 3,* 9–20.

Schneider, J. W. (1982). Lens-assisted *in vivo* desensitization to heights. *Journal of Behavior Therapy and Experimental Psychiatry, 13,* 333–336.

Schnelle, J. F. (1974). A brief report on invalidity of parent evaluations of behavior change. *Journal of Applied Behavior Analysis, 7,* 341–343.

Schofield, W. (1950). Changes in responses to the Minnesota Multiphasic Inventory following certain therapies. *Psychological Monographs, 64,* (Whole No. 311).

Schofield, W. (1953). A further study of the effects of therapies on MMPI responses. *Journal of Abnormal Psychology, 48,* 67–77.

Scholander, T. (1972). Case reports and technique innovations treatment of an unusual case of compulsive behavior by aversive stimulation. *Behavior Therapy, 3,* 290–293.

Schroeder, H. E., Rakos, R. F., & Moe, J. (1983). The social perception of assertive behavior as a function of response class and gender. *Behavior Therapy, 14,* 534–544.

Schroeder, H. E., & Rich, A. R. (1976). The process of fear reduction through systematic desensitization. *Journal of Consulting and Clinical Psychology, 44,* 191–199.

Schubot, E. D. (1966). *The influence of hypnotic and muscular relaxation in systematic desensitization of phobic behavior.* Unpublished doctoral dissertation, Stanford University.

Schultz, J. H., & Luthe, W. (1959). *Autogenic training.* New York: Grune & Stratton.

Schultz, J. H., & Luthe, W. (1969). *Autogenic therapy: 1. Autogenic methods.* New York: Grune & Stratton.

Schumaker, J. B., Hovell, M. F., & Sherman, J. A. (1977). An analysis of daily report cards and parent-managed privileges in the improvement of adolescents' classroom performance. *Journal of Applied Behavior Analysis, 10,* 449–464.

Schwartz, G. E., & Shapiro, D. (1973). Biofeedback and essential hypertension: Current findings and theoretical concerns. In L. Birk (Ed.), *Biofeedback: Behavioral medicine.* New York: Grune & Stratton.

Schwartz, R., & Gottman, J. M. (1976). Toward and task analysis of assertive behavior. *Journal of Consulting and Clinical Psychology, 44,* 910–920.

Schwitzgebel, R. (1960). A new approach to understanding delinquency. *Federal Probation,* 5–9.

Schwitzgebel, R. (1963, January). Delinquents with tape recorders. *New Society.*

Schwitzgebel, R. (1967). Short-term operant conditioning of adolescent offenders on socially relevant variables. *Journal of Abnormal Psychology, 72,* 134–142.

Schwitzgebel, R., & Kolb, D. A. (1964). Inducing behavior change in adolescent delinquents. *Behaviour Research and Therapy, 1,* 297–304.

Scott, R. W., Blanchard, E. B., Edmunson, E. D., & Young, L. D. (1973). A shaping procedure for heart rate control in chronic tachycardia. *Perceptual and Motor Skills, 37,* 327–338.

Seaver, W. B., & Patterson, A. H. (1976). Decreasing fuel-oil consumption through feedback and social commendation. *Journal of Applied Behavior Analysis, 9,* 147–152.

Seidner, M. L., & Kirshenbaum, D. S. (1980). Behavioral Contracts: Effects of pretreatment information and intention statements. *Behavior Therapy, 11,* 689–698.

Seitz, P. F. (1953). Dynamically-oriented brief psychotherapy: Psychocutaneous excoriation syndromes. *Psychosomatic Medicine, 15,* 200–213.

Seligman, M. E. P. (1971). Phobias and preparedness. *Behavior Therapy, 2,* 307–320.

Seligman, M. E. P., Abramson, L. Y., Semmel, A., & von Baeyer, C. (1979). Depression attributional style. *Journal of Abnormal Psychology, 88,* 242–247.

Seligman, M. E. P., & Maier, S. F. (1967). Failure to escape traumatic shock. *Journal of Experimental Psychology, 74,* 1–9.

Semat, H. (1954). *Introduction to atomic and nuclear physics.* New York: Holt.

Serber, M. (1970). Shame aversion therapy. *Journal of Behavior Therapy and Experimental Psychiatry, 1,* 213–215.

Serber, M., & Nelson, P. (1971). The ineffectiveness of systematic desensitization and assertive training in hospitalized schizophrenics. *Journal of Behavior Therapy and Experimental Psychiatry, 2,* 107–109.

Serfass, R. L., & Gerberich, S. G. (1984). Exercise for

optimal health: Strategies and motivational considerations. *Preventive Medicine, 13,* 79–99.

Seymour, F. W., & Stokes, T. F. (1976). Self-recording in training girls to increase work and evoke staff praise in an institution for offenders. *Journal of Applied Behavior Analysis, 9,* 41–54.

Shadel, C. A. (1944). Aversion treatment of alcohol addiction. *Quarterly Journal of Studies on Alcoholism, 5,* 216–228.

Shaffer, L. F. (1947). The problem of psychotherapy. *American Psychologist, 2,* 459–467.

Shafto, F., & Sulzbacker, S. (1977). Comparing treatment tactics with a hyperactive preschool child: Stimulant medication and programmed teacher intervention. *Journal of Applied Behavior Analysis, 10,* 13–20.

Shahar, A., & Jaffee, Y. (1978). Behavior and cognitive therapy in the treatment of vaginismus: A case study. *Cognitive Therapy and Research, 2*(1), 57–60.

Shaher, A., & Merbaum, M. (1981). The interaction between subject characteristic and self-control procedures in the treatment of interpersonal anxiety. *Cognitive Therapy and Research, 5,* 221–224.

Shanahan, W. M., & Hornick, E. J. (1946). Aversion treatment of alcoholism. *Hawaii Medical Journal, 6,* 19–21.

Shapiro, A. P., Schwartz, G. E., Ferguson, D. C. E., Redmond, D. P., & Weiss, S. M. (1977). Behavioral methods in the treatment of hypertension: A review of their status. *Annals of Internal Medicine, 86,* 626–636.

Shapiro, D., & Goldstein, I. B. (1982). Biobehavioral perspectives on hypertension. *Journal of Consulting and Clinical Psychology, 50,* 841–858.

Shapiro, D., Schwartz, G. E., & Tursky, B. (1972). Control of diastolic blood pressure in man by feedback and reinforcement. *Psychophysiology, 9,* 296–304.

Shapiro, D., Tursky, E., Gershon, E., & Stern, M. (1969). Effects of feedback and reinforcement on control of human systolic blood pressure. *Science, 163,* 558–590.

Shapiro, D., Tursky, E., Schwartz, G. E. (1970). Differentiation of heart rate and stystolic blood pressure in man by operant conditioning. *Psychosomatic Medicine, 32,* 417–423.

Shaw, B. F. (1977). Comparison of cognitive therapy and behavior therapy in the treatment of depression. *Journal of Consulting and Clinical Psychology, 45*(4), 543–551.

Shaw, B. F., & Beck, A. T. (1977). The treatment of depression with cognitive therapy. In A. Ellis, & R. Grieger (Eds.), *Handbook of rational emotive therapy.* New York: Springer-Verlag.

Shelton, J. L. (1973). Murder strikes and panic follows: Can behavior modification help? *Behavior Therapy, 4*(5), 706–708.

Shepphard, W. C., Shank, S. B., & Wilson, D. (1973). *Teaching social behavior to young children.* Champaign, IL: Research Press.

Sherman, J. A. (1965). Use of reinforcement and imitation to reinstate verbal behavior in mute psychotic. *Journal of Abnormal Psychology, 70,* 155–174.

Sherrington, C. S. (1906). *Integrative action of the nervous system.* New Haven, CT: Yale University Press.

Sherry G. S., & Levine, B. A. (1980). An examination of procedural variables in flooding therapy. *Behavior Therapy, 11,* 503–508.

Shiffman, S. (1982). Relapse following smoking cessation: A situational analysis. *Journal of Consulting and Clinical Psychology, 50,* 71–86.

Shiffman, S. (1984). Coping with temptations to smoke. *Journal of Consulting and Clinical Psychology, 52,* 261–267.

Shipley, R. H., & Boudewyns, P. A. (1980). Flooding and implosive therapy: Are they harmful? *Behavior Therapy, 11,* 503–508.

Shipley, R. H., Butt, J. H., Horwitz, B., & Farbry, J. E. (1978). Preparation for a stressful medical procedure: Effect of stimulus preexposure and coping style. *Journal of Consulting and Clinical Psychology, 46,* 499–507.

Shirer, W. L. (1959). *The rise and fall of the Third Reich: A history of Nazi Germany.* New York: Simon and Schuster.

Shorkey, C., & Himple, D. P. (1974). Systematic desensitization treatment of a recurring nightmare and related insomnia. *Journal of Behavior Therapy and Experimental Psychiatry, 5,* 97–98.

Sidman, M. (1960). *Tactics of scientific research.* New York: Basic Books.

Siegel, G. M., Lenske, J., & Broen, P. (1969). Suppression of normal speech disfluences through response cost. *Journal of Applied Behavior Analysis, 2,* 265–276.

Siegel, R. K. (1977). Stimulus selection and tracking during urination: Autoshaping directed behavior with toilet targets. *Journal of Applied Behavior Analysis, 10,* 255–266.

Siegelman, E. (1969). Reflective and impulsive observing behavior. *Child Development, 40,* 1213–1222.

Siegeltuch, M. B., & Baum, M. (1971). Extinction of well-established avoidance responses through response prevention (flooding). *Behaviour Research and Therapy, 9,* 103–108.

Sifneos, P. (1979). *Short-term dynamic psychotherapy: Evaluation and technique.* New York: Plenum Press.

Sigman, M., & Zalman, A. (1982). Progressive relaxation exercises and human gastric acid output: A study using telemetric measurements. *Behaviour Research and Therapy, 20,* 605–612.

Silverman, L. H., Frank, S. G., & Dachinger, P. A. (1974). A psychoanalytic reinterpretation of the effectiveness of systematic desensitization: Experimental data bearing on the role of merging fantasies. *Journal of Abnormal Psychology, 83,* 313–318.

Silverman, P. J. (1977). The role of social reinforcement in maintaining an obsessive compulsive neurosis. *Journal of Behavior Therapy and Experimental Psychiatry, 8,* 325–326.

Simmons, F. T., & Wasik, B. H. (1973). Small group contingencies and special activity times to manage behavior in a first-grade classroom. *Journal of School Psychology, 11,* 228–238.

Simons, A. D. (1984). In reply. *Archives of General Psychiatry, 41,* 1114–1115.

Simons, A. D., Garfield, S. L., & Murphy, G. E. (1984). The process of change in cognitive therapy and pharmacotherapy for depression. *Archives of General Psychiatry, 41,* 45–51.

Simons, A. D., Lustman, P. J., Wetzel, R. D., & Murphy, G. C. (1985). Predicting response to cognitive therapy of depression: The role of learned resourcefulness. *Cognitive Therapy and Research, 9,* 79–89.

Singerman, K. J., Borkovec, T. D., & Baron, R. S. (1976). Failure of "misattribution therapy" manipulation with a clinically relevant target behavior. *Behavior Therapy, 7,* 306–313.

Sipich, J. F., Russell, R. K., & Tobias, L. L. (1974). A comparison of covert sensitization and "nonspecific" treatment in the modification of smoking behavior. *Journal of Behavior Therapy and Experimental Psychiatry, 5,* 201–203.

Sirota, A. D., Schwartz, G. E., & Shapiro, D. (1974). Voluntary control of human heart rate: Effect on reaction to aversive stimulation. *Journal of Abnormal Psychology, 83,* 261–267.

Sittenfield, P., Budzynski, T., & Stoyva, J. (1976-1977). Differential shaping of EEG. Theta rhythms. *Biofeedback and Self Control,* 339–406.

Skinner, B. F. (1938). *The behavior of organisms: An experimental analysis.* New York: Appleton.

Skinner, B. F. (1950). Are theories of learning necessary? *Psychological Review, 57,* 193–216.

Skinner, B. F. (1953). *Science and human behavior.* New York: Macmillan.

Skinner, B. F. (1966). Operant behavior. In W. K. Honig (Ed.), *Operant behavior: Areas of research and application.* New York: Appleton.

Skinner, B. F. (1969). *Contingencies of reinforcement: A theoretical analysis.* New York: Appleton.

Skinner, B. F. (1971). *Beyond freedom and dignity.* New York: Knopf.

Skinner, B. F. (1974). *About behaviorism.* New York: Knopf.

Skinner, B. F. (1978). *Reflections on behaviorism and society.* Englewood Cliffs, NJ: Prentice-Hall.

Slack, C. W. (1960). Experimenter-subject psychotherapy: A new method of introducing intensive office treatment for unreachable cases. *Mental Hygiene, 44,* 238–256.

Slater, S. L., & Leavy, A. (1966). The effects of inhaling a 35% carbon dioxide, 65% oxygen mixture upon anxiety level in neurotic patients. *Behaviour Research and Therapy, 4,* 309–316.

Sloane, H. N., Jr., Johnston, M. K., & Bijou, S. W. (1967). Successive modification of aggressive behavior and aggressive fantasy play by management of contingencies. *Journal of Child Psychology and Psychiatry, 8,* 217–226.

Sloane, H. N., Jr., Johnston, M. K., & Harris, F. R. (1968). Remedial procedures for teaching verbal behavior to speech deficient or defective young children. In H. N. Sloane, Jr., & B. A. MacAulay (Eds.), *Operant procedures in remedial speech and language training.* Boston: Houghton Mifflin.

Sloane, R. B., Staples, F. R., Cristol, A. H., Yorkston, J. J., & Whipple, K. (1975). *Psychotherapy versus behavior therapy.* Cambridge, MA: Harvard University Press.

Smeets, P. M., Elson, L. E., & Clement, A. (1975). Eliminating nasal discharge in a multihandicapped deaf child. *Journal of Behavior Therapy and Experimental Psychiatry, 6,* 264–266.

Smeets, P. M., & Striefel, S. (1975). The effects of different reinforcement conditions on the test performance of multihandicapped deaf children. *Journal of Applied Behavior Analysis, 8,* 83–89.

Smith, J. M., & Smith, D. E. P. (1976). *Child management: A program for parents and teachers.* Champaign, IL: Research Press.

Smith, M. L., & Glass, G. V. (1977). Meta-analysis of psychotherapy outcome studies. *American Psychologist, 32*(9), 752–760.

Smith, R. E. (1973). The use of humor in counter-conditioning of anger responses: A case study. *Behavior Therapy, 4,* 576–580.

Smith, R. E., & Gregory, P. B. (1976). Covert sensitization by induced anxiety in the treatment of an alcoholic. *Journal of Behavior Therapy and Experimental Psychiatry, 7,* 31–33.

Sobell, M. B., & Sobell, L. C. (1973a). Alcoholics treated by individualized behavior therapy: One year treatment outcome. *Behaviour Research and Therapy, 11,* 599–618.

Sobell, M. B., & Sobell, L. C. (1973b). Individualized behavior therapy for alcoholics. *Behavior Therapy, 4,* 49–72.

Sobell, M. B., & Sobell, L. C. (1978). *Behavioral treatment of alcohol problems.* New York: Plenum Press.

Sobell, M. B., & Sobell, L. C. (1984). The aftermath of heresy: A response to Pendery et al.'s (1982) critique of "Individualized Behavior Therapy for Alcoholics." *Behaviour Research and Therapy, 22*(4), 413–440.

Soderstrom, C. A., Arias, J. D., Carson, S. L., & Cowley, R. A. (1984). Alcohol consumption among vehicular occupants injured in crashes. *Alcoholism: Clinical and Experimental Research, 8,* 269–271.

Solnick, J. V., Rincover, A., & Peterson, C. R. (1977). Some determinants of the reinforcing and punishing effects of time-out. *Journal of Applied Behavior Analysis, 10,* 415–424.

Solomon, R. L. (1964). Punishment. *American Psychologist, 19,* 239–253.

Solomon, R. L., Kamin, L. J., & Wynn, L. C. (1953). Traumatic avoidance learning: The outcomes of several extinction procedures with dogs. *Journal of Abnormal and Social Psychology, 48,* 291–302.

Solomon, R. W. (1973). Peers as behavior modifiers for problem classmates. *Dissertation Abstracts International, 33*(8–A), 4189.

Solomon, R. W., & Wahler, R. G. (1973). Peer reinforcement control of classroom problem behavior. *Journal of Applied Behavior Analysis, 6,* 49–56.

Solyom, L., & Miller, S. B. (1965). A differential conditioning procedure as the initial phase of the behavior therapy of homosexuality. *Behavior Research and Therapy, 3,* 147–160.

Solyom, L., & Miller, S. B. (1967). Reciprocal inhibition by aversion relief in the treatment of phobias. *Behaviour Research and Therapy, 5,* 313–324.

Sommer, G., Schmid-Methfessel, I., & Seyfferth, H. (1984). Development and evaluation of a complex self control program for smokers. *Zeitschrift fur Kinische Psychologie: Forschung und Praxis, 13,* 39–60.

Southam, M. A., Agras, W. S., Taylor, C. B., & Kraemer, H. C. (1982). Relaxation training: Blood pressure lowering during the working day. *Archives of General Psychiatry, 39,* 715–717.

Spates, C. R., & Kanfer, F. H. (1977). Self-monitoring, self-evaluation, and self-reinforcement in children's learning: A test of multistage self-regulation model. *Behavior Therapy, 8,* 9–16.

Speltz, M. L., Shimamura, J. W., & McReynolds, W. T. (1982). Procedural variations in group contingencies: *Journal of Applied Behavior Analysis, 15,* 533–544.

Spergel, M. (1975). Induced vomiting treatment of acute compulsive vomiting. *Journal of Behavior Therapy and Experimental Psychiatry, 6,* 85–86.

Spiegel, D. (1973). The prevention of the dropout syndrome via token reinforcement contingencies. *Dissertation Abstracts International, 33*(8–A), 4190.

Spielberger, C. D., & De Nike, L. D. (1966). Descriptive behaviorism versus cognitive theory in verbal operant conditioning. *Psychological Review, 73,* 306–326.

Spirito, A., Russo, D. C., & Masek, B. J. (1984). Behavioral interventions and stress management training for hospitalized adolescents and young adults with cystic fibrosis. *General Hospital Psychiatry, 6,* 1–8.

Spitalnik, R., & Drabman, R. (1976). A classroom timeout procedure for retarded children. *Journal of Behavior Therapy and Experimental Psychiatry, 7,* 17–21.

Spring, D., Prochaska, J., & Smith, N. (1974). Fear reduction in rats through avoidance blocking. *Behaviour Research and Therapy, 12,* 29–34.

Spring, F. L., Sipich, J. F., Trimble, R. W., & Goeckner, D. J. (1978). Effects of contingency and noncontingency contracts in the context of a self-control-oriented smoking modification program. *Behavior Therapy, 9,* 967–968.

Srnec, J., & Freund, K. (1953). Treatment of male homosexuality through conditioning. *International Journal of Sexology, 7,* 92–93.

St. Lawrence, J. S. (1981). Efficacy of a money deposit contingency on clinical outpatients' attendance and participation in assertive training. *Journal of Behavior Therapy and Experimental Psychiatry, 12,* 237–240.

Staats, A. W., & Butterfield, W. H. (1965). Treatment of non-reading in a culturally deprived juvenile delinquent: An application of reinforcement principles. *Child Development, 36,* 925–942.

Stainbrook, G. L., Hoffman, J. W., & Benson, H. (1983). Behavioral therapies of hypertension: Psychotherapy, biofeedback, and relaxation/meditation. *International Review of Applied Psychology, 32,* 119–135.

Stake, J. E., & Pearlman, J.(1980). Assertiveness training as an intervention technique for low performance self-esteem women. *Journal of Counseling Psychology, 27,* 276–281.

Stalonas, P. M., Johnson, W. G., & Christ, M. (1978). Behavior modification for obesity: The evaluation of exercise, contingency management, and program adherence. *Journal of Consulting and Clinical Psychology, 46,* 463–469.

Stambaugh, E. E., II. (1977). Audio-taped flooding in outpatient treatment of somatic complaints. *Journal of Behavior Therapy and Experimental Psychiatry, 8,* 173–176.

Stampfl, T. G. (1961). Implosive therapy: A learning theory derived psychodynamic therapeutic technique. In Lebarba & Dent (Eds.), *Critical issues in clinical psychology.* New York: Academic Press.

Stampfl, T. G. (1967). Implosive therapy. Part I. The theory. In S. G. Armitage (Ed.), *Behavioral modification techniques in the treatment of emotional disorder.* Battle Creek, MI: V. A.

Stampfl, T. G., Levis, D. J. (1967a). Essentials of implosive therapy: A learning-theory-based psychodynamic behavioral therapy. *Journal of Abnormal Psychology, 72,* 496–503.

Stampfl, T. G., & Levis, D. J. (1967b). Phobic patients: Treatment with the learning theory approach of implosive therapy. *Voices: The Art and Science of Psychotherapy, 3,* 23–27.

Stampfl, T. G., & Levis, D. J. (1968). Implosive-therapy—A behavioral therapy? *Behaviour Research and Therapy, 6,* 31–36.

States, J. D. (1985). Violence on the highway: A national public health problem. *New York State Journal of Medicine, 85,* 69–71.

Staub, E. (1968). Duration of stimulus-exposure as determinant of the efficacy of flooding procedures in the elimination of fear. *Behaviour Research and Therapy, 6,* 131–132.

Stawar, T. L. (1976). Fable mod: Operantly structured fantasies as an adjunct in the modification of fire-setting behavior. *Journal of Behavior Therapy and Experimental Psychiatry, 7,* 285–288.

Steffen, J. J., & Myszak, K. A. (1978). Influence of pretherapy induction upon the outcome of a self-control weight reduction program. *Behavior Therapy, 9,* 404–409.

Steffy, R. A., Hart, J., Craw, M., Torney, D., & Marlett, N. (1969). Operant behavior modification techniques applied patients. *Canadian Psychiatric Association Journal, 14,* 59–67.

Steinmark, S. W., & Borkovec, T. D. (1974). Active and placebo treatment effects on moderate insomnia under counterdemand and positive demand instructions. *Journal of Abnormal Psychology, 83,* 157–163.

Stephens, C. E., Pear, J. J., Wray, L. D., & Jackson, G. C. (1975). Some effects of reinforcement schedules in teaching picture names to retarded children. *Journal of Applied Behavior Analysis, 8,* 435–447.

Sterman, M. B., & Friar, L. (1972). Suppression of seizures in an epileptic following sensorimotor EEG feedback training. *Electroencephalography and Clinical Neurophysiology, 89,* 95.

Sterman, M. B., LoPresti, R. W., & Fairchild, M. D. (1969). *Electroencephalographic and behavioral studies of monomethylhydrozinetoxicity in the cat* (Tech.Rep. AMRL-TR-69-3). Wright-Patterson Air Force Base, Ohio: Air force Systems Command, Aerospace Medical Division.

Sterman, M. B., MacDonald, L. R., & Stone, R. K. (1974). Biofeedback training of the sensorimotor electroencephalograph in man: Effects on epilepsy. *Epilepsia, 15,* 395–416.

Stern, R. S., Lipsedge, M. S., & Marks, I. M. (1973). Obsessive ruminations: A controlled trial of thought-stopping technique. *Behaviour Research and Therapy, 11,* 659–662.

Sternberg, B. (1985). Relapse in weight control: Definitions, processes, and prevention strategies. In G. A. Marlatt & J. R. Gordon (Eds.), *Relapse prevention: Maintenance strategies in the treatment of addictive behaviors.* New York: Guilford Press.

Stevens, J. R. (1962). Endogenous conditioning to abnormal cerebral electrical transients in man. *Science, 137,* 974–976.

Stevens, R. J. (1977). Psychological strategies for management of pain in prepared childbirth: 2. A study of psychoanalgesia in prepared childbirth. *Birth and Family Journal, 4,* 4–9.

Stevens-Long, J., & Rasmussen, M. (1974). The acquisition of simple and compound sentence structure in an autistic child. *Journal of Applied Behavior Analysis, 7,* 473–479.

Stevenson, D. W., & Delprato, D. J. (1983). Multiple component self-control program for menopausal hot flashes. *Journal of Behavior Therapy & Experimental Psychiatry, 14,* 137–140.

Stevenson, H. W. (1965). Social reinforcement of children's behavior. In L. P. Lipsitt, & C. C. Spiker (Eds.), *Advances in child development and behavior* (Vol. 2). New York: Academic Press.

Stevenson, H. W. (1971). *Children's learning.* New York: Appleton.

Stevenson, I. (1959). Direct instigation of behavioral changes in psychotherapy. *AMA Archives of General Psychiatry, 1,* 115–123.

Stevenson, I., & Wolpe, J. (1960). Recovery from sexual deviations through overcoming non-sexual neurotic response. *American Journal of Psychiatry, 116,* 737–742.

Stevenson, J., & Jones, I. H. (1972). Behavior Therapy techniques for exhibitionism. *Archives of General Psychiatry, 27,* 239–241.

Stewart, M. A. (1961). Psychotherapy by reciprocal inhibition. *American Journal of Psychiatry, 118,* 175–177.

Stokes, T. F., & Baer, D. M. (1977). An implicit technology of generalization. *Journal of Applied Behavior Analysis, 10,* 349–367.

Stokes, T. F., Baer, D. M., & Jackson, R. L. (1974). Programming the generalization of a greeting response in four retarded children. *Journal of Applied Behavior Analysis, 7,* 599–610.

Stokes, T. F., & Kennedy, S. H. (1980). Reducing child uncooperative behavior during dental treatment through modeling and reinforcement. *Journal of Applied Behavior Analysis, 13,* 41–49.

Stollak, G. E. (1967). Weight loss obtained under different experimental procedures. *Psychotherapy: Theory Research and Practice, 4,* 61–64.

Storms, M. D., & Nisbett, R. E. (1970). Insomnia and the attribution process. *Journal of Personality and Social Psychology, 16*(2), 319–328.

Stoyva, J. (1976). Self-regulation and the stress-related disorders: A perspective on biofeedback. In D. I. Mostofsky, (Ed.), *Behavior control and modification of physiological activity.* Englewood Cliffs, NJ: Prentice-Hall.

Stoyva, J., & Budzynski, T. (1974). Cultivated low arousal: An antistress response? In L. DiCara (Ed.), *Limbic and autonomic nervous system research.* New York: Plenum.

Straatmeyer, A. J., & Watkins, J. T. (1974). Rational emotive therapy and the reduction of speech anxiety. *Rational Living, 9*(1), 33–37.

Strahley, R. F. (1965). *Systematic desensitization and counterphobic treatment of an irrational fear of snakes.* Unpublished doctoral dissertation, University of Tennessee.

Strain, P. S., Shores, R. E., & Kerr, M. M. (1976). An experimental analysis of "spillover" effects on the social interaction of behaviorally handicapped preschool children. *Journal of Applied Behavior Analysis, 9,* 31–40.

Straughan, J. H. (1968). The application of operant conditioning to the treatment of elective mutism. In H. N. Sloane, Jr., & B. A. MacAulay (Eds.), *Operant procedures in remedial speech and language training.* Boston: Houghton Mifflin.

Strauss, C. C., Rubinoff, A., & Atkeson, B. M. (1983). Elimination of nocturnal headbanging in a normal seven-year-old girl using overcorrection plus rewards. *Journal of Behavior Therapy and Experimental Psychiatry, 14*(3), 269–273.

Strickland, B. R., Hale, W. D., & Anderson, L. K. (1975). Effect of induced mood states on activity and self reported affect. *Journal of Consulting and Clinical Psychology, 43,* 587.

Strum, I. E. (1965). The behavioristic aspect of psychodrama. *Group Psychotherapy, 18,* 50–64.

Strupp, H. H. & Binder, J. L. (1984). *Psychotherapy in a new key: A guide to time-limited dynamic psychotherapy.* New York: Basic Books.

Stuart, R. B. (1967). Behavioral control over eating. *Behaviour Research and Therapy, 5,* 357–365.

Stuart, R. B. (1969). Token reinforcement in marital treatment. In R. D. Rubin, & C. M. Franks (Eds.), *Advances in behavior therapy 1968.* New York: Academic Press.

Stuart, R. B. (1971). A three-dimensional program for the treatment of obesity. *Behaviour Research and Therapy, 9,* 177–186.

Stuart, R. B. (Ed.) (1977). *Behavioral self-management: Strategies, techniques and outcomes.* New York: Brunner/Mazel.

Stuart, R. B., & Lott, L. A. (1972). Behavioral contracting with delinquents: A cautionary note. *Journal of Behavior Therapy and Experimental Psychiatry, 3,* 161–169.

Stuart, R. B., & McGuire, K. (1978). Some correlates

of the maintenance of weight loss through behavior modification. *International Journal of Obesity, 2,* 225–235.

Stunkard, A. J. (1958). The management of obesity. *New York State Journal of Medicine, 58,* 79–87.

Stunkard, A. J. (Ed.). (1980). *Obesity.* Philadelphia: Saunders.

Stunkard, A. J. (1982). Anorectic agents lower a body weight set point. *Life Sciences, 30,* 2043–2055.

Suarez, Y., McCutcheon, B. A., & Adams, H.E. (1976). Flooding and systematic sensitization: Efficacy in subclinical phobics as a function of arousal. *Journal of Consulting and Clinical Psychology, 44,* 872.

Sue, D. (1975). The effect of duration of exposure on systematic desensitization and extinction. *Behaviour Research and Therapy, 13,* 55–60.

Suinn, R. (1975). Anxiety management training for general anxiety. In R. Suinn, & R. Weigel (Eds.), *Innovative therapies: Critical and creative contributions.* New York: Harper.

Suinn, R., & Richardson, F. (1971). Anxiety management training. A nonspecific behavior therapy program for anxiety control. *Behavior Therapy, 2,* 498–510.

Sulzbacher, S. I., & Houser, J. E. (1968). A tactic to eliminate disruptive behaviors in the classroom: Group contingent consequences. *American Journal of Mental Deficiency, 73,* 88–90.

Sulzer-Azaroff, B., & Mayer, J. R. (1977). *Applying behavior analysis procedures with children and youth.* New York: Holt.

Supnick, J. A., & Colletti, G. (1984). Relapses coping and problem solving training for treatment for smoking. *Addictive Behaviors, 9,* 401–404.

Surwit, R. S., Allen, L. M., Gilgor, R. S., & Duvic, M. (1982). The combined effect of praeosin and autogenic training on cold reactivity in Raynaud's phenomenon. *Biofeedback and Self-Regulation, 7,* 537–544.

Surwit, R. S., Pilon, R. N., & Fenton, C. H. (1978). Behavioral treatment of Raynaud's disease. *Journal of Behavioral Medicine, 1,* 323–335.

Surwit, R. S., Shapiro, D., & Good, J. I. (1978). Comparison of cardiovascular biofeedback, neuromuscular biofeedback, and meditation in the treatment of borderline essential hypertension. *Journal of Consulting and Clinical Psychology, 46,* 252–263.

Sushinsky, L., Bootzin, R. (1970). Cognitive desensitization as a model of systematic desensitization. *Behaviour Research and Therapy, 8,* 29–34.

Swift, M. S., & Spivack, G. (1975). *Alternative teaching strategies: Helping behaviorally troubled children achieve.* Champaign, IL: Research Press.

Switzer, E. B., Deal, T. E., & Bailey, J. S. (1977). The reduction of stealing in second graders using a group contingency. *Journal of Applied Behavior Analysis, 10,* 267–272.

Switzky, H. N., & Haywood, H. C. (1974). Motivational orientation and the relative efficiency of self-monitored and externally imposed reinforcement systems in children. *Journal of Personality and Social Psychology, 30,* 360–366.

Szasz, T. S. (1961). *The myth of mental illness: Foundations of a theory of personal conduct.* New York: Harper.

Tanner, B. A. (1973). Shock intensity and fear of shock in the modification of homosexual behavior in males by avoidance learning. *Behaviour Research and Therapy, 11,* 213–218.

Tanner, B. A., & Zeiler, M. (1975). Punishment of self-injurious behavior using aromatic ammonia as the aversive stimulus. *Journal of Applied Behavior Analysis, 8,* 53–57.

Tasto, D. L. (1977). Self-report schedules and inventories. In A. R. Ciminero, K. S. Calhoun, & H. E. Adams (Eds.), *Handbook of behavioral assessment.* New York: Wiley.

Tavormina, J. B. (1975). Relative effectiveness of behavioral and reflective group counseling with parents of mentally retarded children. *Journal of Consulting and Clinical Psychology, 43*(1), 22–31.

Taylor, C. B., Agras, W. S., Schneider, J. A., & Allen, R. A. (1983). Adherence to instructions to practice relaxation exercises. *Journal of Consulting and Clinical Psychology, 51,* 952–953.

Taylor, D. W. A. (1971). A comparison of group desensitization with two control procedures in the treatment of test anxiety. *Behaviour Research and Therapy, 9,* 281–284.

Taylor, F. G., & Marshall, W. L. (1977). Experimental analysis of a cognitive behavioral therapy for depression. *Cognitive Therapy and Research, 1*(1), 59–72.

Taylor, J. G. (1963). A behavioral interpretation of obsessive compulsive neurosis. *Behaviour Research and Therapy, 1,* 237–244.

Taylor, S. E. (1986). *Health psychology,* New York: Random House.

Teasdale, J. D., & Bancroft, J. (1977). Manipulation of thought content as a determinant of mood and corrugator electromyographic activity in depressed patients. *Journal of Abnormal Psychology, 86*(3), 235–241.

Terrace, H. S. (1966). Stimulus control. In W. K. Honig (Ed.), *Operant behavior.* New York: Appleton.

Terrell, G., & Ware, R. (1961). Role of delay of reward in speed and form discrimination learning in children. *Child Development, 32,* 409–415.

Tharp, R. G., & Wetzel, R. J. (1969). *Behavior modification in the natural environment.* New York: Academic Press.

Thelen, M. H., & Fry, R. A. (1981). The effect of modeling and selective attention on pain tolerance. *Journal of Behavior Therapy and Experimental Psychiatry, 12,* 225–229.

Thelen, M. H., Fry, R. A., Dollinger, S. J., & Paul, S. C. (1976). Use of videotaped models to improve the interpersonal adjustment of delinquents. *Journal of Consulting and Clinical Psychology, 44,* 492.

Thelen, M. H., & Lasoski, M. C. (1980). The separate and combined effects of focusing information and videotape self-confrontation feedback. *Journal of Behavior Therapy and Experimental Psychiatry, 11,* 173–178.

Thimann, J. (1949). Conditioned reflex treatment of alcoholism. II. The risks of its application, its indications, contraindications, and psychotherapeutic aspects. *New England Journal of Medicine, 241,* 406–410.

Thomas, J. D. (1976). Accuracy of self-assessment of on-task behavior by elementary school children. *Journal of Applied Behavior Analysis, 9,* 209–210.

Thompson, J. K., Jarvie, G. J., Lahey, B. B. & Cureton, K. J. (1982). Exercise and obesity: Etiology, physiology, and intervention. *Psychological Bulletin, 91,* 55–79.

Thompson, T., & Grabowski, J. (1972). *Reinforcement schedules and multi-operant analysis.* Englewood Cliffs, NJ: Prentice-Hall.

Thompson, T., & Grabowski, J. (Eds.). (1977). *Behavior modification of the mentally retarded.* London & New York: Oxford University Press.

Thoresen, C. E., & Mahoney, M. J. (1974). *Behavioral self-control.* New York: Holt.

Thorndike, E. L. (1898). Animal intelligence: An experimental study of the associative processes in animals. *Psychological Review, 2* (No. 8). (Monograph Supplement).

Thorndike, E. L. (1911). *Animal intelligence.* New York: Macmillan.

Thorndike, E. L. (1913). *The psychology of learning* (Educational Psychology, II). New York: Teachers College.

Thorpe, G. L. (1975). Desensitization, behavior rehearsal, self-instructional training and placebo effects on assertive-refusal behavior. *European Journal of Behavior Analysis and Modification, 1,* 30–44.

Thorpe, G. L., Amatu, H. I., Blakey, R. S., & Burns, L. E. (1976). Contribution of overt instructional rehearsal and specific insight to the effectiveness of self instructional training. *Behavior Therapy, 7,* 504.

Thorpe, J. G., Schmidt, E., Brown, P. T., & Castell, D. (1964). Aversion-relief therapy: A new method for general application. *Behaviour Research and Therapy, 2,* 71–82.

Thorpe, J. G., Schmidt, E., & Castell, D. (1963). A comparison of positive and negative (aversive) conditioning in the treatment of homosexuality. *Behaviour Research and Therapy, 1,* 357–362.

Thurman, C. W. (1985). Effectiveness of cognitive-behavioral treatments in reducing Type A behavior among university faculty, one year later. *Journal of Counseling Psychology, 32,* 445–448.

Todd, D. T., Scott, R. B., Bostow, D. E., & Alexander, S. B. (1976). Modification of the excessive inappropriate classroom behavior of two elementary school students using home-based consequences and daily report-card procedures. *Journal of Applied Behavior Analysis, 9,* 106.

Toister, R. P., Condron, C. J., Worley, L., & Arthur, D. (1975). Faradic therapy of chronic vomiting in infancy: A case study. *Journal of Behavior Therapy and Experimental Psychiatry, 6,* 55–59.

Tolman, C. W., & Meuller, M. R. (1964). Laboratory control of toe-sucking in a young rhesus monkey by two kinds of punishment. *Journal of the Experimental Analysis of Behavior, 7,* 323–325.

Tolman, E. C. (1932). *Purposive behavior in animals and men.* New York: Appleton.

Tongas, P. N. (1979). The Kaiser-Permanente smoking control program: Its purpose and implications for an HMO. *Professional Psychology, 10,* 409–418.

Tooley, J. T. & Pratt, S. (1967). An experimental procedure for the extinction of smoking behavior. *Psychological Record, 17,* 209–218.

Townsend, R. E., House, J. F., & Addario, D. (1975). A comparison of biofeedback-mediated relaxation and group therapy in the treatment of chronic anxiety. *American Journal of Psychiatry, 132,* 598–601.

Trexler, L. D. (1977). A review of rational-emotive psychotherapy outcome studies. In J. Wolfe, & E. Brand (Eds.), *Twenty years of rational therapy.* New York: Institute of Rational Living.

Trexler, L. D., & Karst, T. O. (1972). Rational emotive therapy, placebo, and no treatment effects on public speaking anxiety. *Journal of Abnormal Psychology. 79,* 60–67.

Trotter, S. (1974). ACLU scores token economy. *APA Monitor, 5,* 7.

Turin, A., & Johnson, W. G. (1976). Biofeedback therapy for migraine headaches. *Archives of General Psychiatry, 33,* 517–519.

Turk, D. C. (1975). *Cognitive control of pain: A skills training approach for the treatment of pain.* Unpublished master's thesis, University of Waterloo.

Turk, D. C. (1976). *An expanded skills training approach for the treatment of experimentally induced pain.* Unpublished doctoral dissertation, University of Waterloo.

Turk, D. C., Meichenbaum, D., & Genest, M. (1983). *Pain and behavioral medicine: A cognitive-behavioral perspective.* New York: Plenum.

Turk, D. C., Salovey, P. (1985a). Cognitive structures, cognitive processes, and cognitive-behavior modification: 1. Client issues. *Cognitive Therapy and Research, 9,* 1–17.

Turk, D. C., Salovey, P. (1985b). Cognitive structures, cognitive processes, and cognitive-behavior modification: 2. Judgments and inferences of the clinician. *Cognitive Therapy and Research, 9,* 19–33.

Turk, D. C., & Speers, M. A. (1983). Cognitive schemata and cognitive processes in cognitive-behavioral interventions: Going beyond the information given. In P. C. Kendall (Ed.), *Advances in cognitive-behavioral research and therapy* (Vol. 2). New York: Academic Press.

Turk, D. C., & Speers, M. A. (1983). Diabetes mellitus: A cognitive-functional analysis of stress. In T. G. Burish & L. A. Bradley (Eds.), *Coping with chronic disease.* New York: Academic Press.

Turkat, I. D. (1982). An investigation of parental modeling in the etiology of diabetic illness behavior. *Behaviour Research and Therapy, 20,* 547–552.

Turner, J. A. (1982). Comparison of group progressive-relaxation training and cognitive-behavioral group therapy for chronic low back pain. *Journal of Consulting and Clinical Psychology, 50,* 757–765.

Turner, J. A. & Chapman, C. R. (1982). Psychological interventions for chronic pain: A critical review: 2. Operant conditioning, hypnosis, and cognitive-behavioral therapy. *Pain, 12,* 23–46.

Turner, S. M., & Luber, R. F. (1980). The token economy in day hospital settings: Contingency management or information feedback. *Journal of Behavior Therapy and Experimental Psychiatry, 11,* 89–94.

Tuso, M. A., & Geller, E. S. (1976). Behavior analysis applied to environmental/ecological problems: A review. *Journal of Applied Behavior Analysis, 9,* 526.

Twentyman C. T., & McFall, R. M. (1975). Behavioral training of social skills in shy males. *Journal of Consulting and Clinical Psychology, 43,* 384–395.

Twentyman, C. T., Pharr, D. R., & Connor, J. M. (1980). A comparison of three covert assertion training procedures. *Journal of Clinical Psychology, 36,* 520–525.

Tyler, V. O., & Brown, G. D. (1967). The use of swift, brief isolation as a group control device for institutionalized delinquents. *Behaviour Research and Therapy, 5,* 109.

Ullmann, L. P., & Krasner, L. (Eds.). (1965). *Case studies in behavior modifications,* New York: Holt.

Ullmann, L. P., & Krasner, L. (1969). *A psychological approach to abnormal behavior.* Englewood Cliffs, NJ: Prentice-Hall.

Ultee, C. A., Griffoen, D., & Schellekens, J. (1982). The reduction of anxiety in children: A comparison of the effects of "systematic desensitization *in vitro*" and "systematic desensitization *in vivo.*" *Behaviour Research and Therapy, 20,* 61–67.

Underwood, B. J. (1957). *Psychological research.* New York: Appleton.

Uno, T. Greer, S. E., & Goates, L. (1973). Observational facilitation of response prevention. *Behaviour Research and Therapy, 11,* 207–212.

Upper, D. (1971, September). *A ticket: system for reducing ward rules violations on a token economy program.* Paper presented at the Association for Advancement of Behavior Therapy, Washington, D.C.

Vaal, J. V. (1975). The Rathus assertiveness schedule: Reliability at the junior high school level. *Behavior Therapy, 6,* 566–567.

Valerio, H. P., & Stone, G. L. (1982). Effects of behavioral, cognitive and combined treatments for assertion as a function of differential deficits. *Journal of Counseling Psychology, 29,* 158–168.

Valins, S. (1966). Cognitive effects of false heart-rate feedback. *Journal of Personality and Social Psychology, 4,* 400–408.

Valins, S., & Ray A. (1967). Effects of cognitive desensitization on avoidance behavior. *Journal of Personality and Social Psychology, 7,* 345–350.

Vallis, T. M. (1984). A complete component analysis of stress inoculation for pain tolerance. *Cognitive Therapy and Research, 8,* 313–329.

Van Houten, R., Hill, S., & Parsons, M. (1975). An analysis of a performance feedback system: The effects of timing and feedback, public posting, and praise upon academic performance and peer interaction. *Journal of Applied Behavior Analysis, 8,* 449–457.

Varenhorst, B. B. (1969). Helping a client speak up in class. In Krumboltz, J. E., & Thoresen, C. E. (Eds.), *Behavioral counseling.* New York: Holt.

Vargas, J. M., & Adesso, V. J. (1976). A comparison of aversion therapies for nailbiting behavior. *Behavior Therapy, 7,* 322–329.

Vasta, R. (1975). Coverant control of self-evaluations through temporal cueing. *Journal of Behaviour Therapy and Experimental Psychiatry, 7,* 35–37.

Vasta, R. (1981). On token rewards and real dangers. *Behavior Modification, 5,* 129–140.

Velten, E. A. (1968). A laboratory task for induction of mood states. *Behaviour Research and Therapy, 6,* 473–482.

Ventis, W. L. (1973). Case history: The use laughter as an alternative response in systematic desensitization. *Behavior Therapy, 4,* 576–580.

Voegtlin, W. L. (1940). The treatment of alcoholism by establishing a conditioned reflex. *American Journal of Medical Science, 199,* 802–810.

Voegtlin, W. L., & Broz, W. R. (1949). The conditioned reflex treatment of chronic alcoholism: An analysis of 3125 admissions over a period of ten and a half years. *Annals of Internal Medicine, 30,* 580–597.

Voegtlin, W. L., Lemere, F., Broz, W. R., & O'Hallaren, P. (1941). Conditioned reflex therapy of chronic alcoholism. IV. A preliminary report on the value of reinforcement. *Quarterly Journal of Studies of Alcoholism, 2,* 505–511.

Voegtlin, W. L., Lemere, F., Broz, W. R., & O'Hallaren, P. (1942). Conditioned reflex therapy of alcoholic addiction. VI. Follow-up report of 1042 cases. *American Journal of Medical Science, 203,* 525–528.

Vogler, R. E., Compton, J. V., & Weissbach, T. A. (1975). Integrated behavior change techniques for alcoholics. *Journal of Consulting and Clinical Psychology, 43,* 233–243.

Vogler, R. E., Lunde, S. E., Johnson, G. R., & Martin, P. L. (1970). Electrical aversion conditioning with chronic alcoholics. *Journal of Consulting and Clinical Psychology, 34,* 302–307.

Vogler, R. E., Lunde, S. E., & Martin, P. L. (1971). Electrical aversion conditioning with chronic alcoholics: Follow-up and suggestions for research. *Journal of Consulting and Clinical Psychology, 36,* 450.

Vogler, R. E., Weissbach, T. A., & Compton, J. V. (1977). Learning techniques for alcohol abuse. *Behaviour Research and Therapy, 15,* 31–38.

Voss, J., Arrick, C., & Rimm, D. C. (1976). *The role of task difficulty and modeling in assertive training.* Unpublished master's thesis, Southern Illinois University.

Vygotsky, L. (1962). *Thought and language.* New York: Wiley.

Wachtel, P. L. (1981). Transference, schema, and assimilation: The relevance of Piaget to the psychoanalytic theory of transference. In Chicago Institute for Psychoanalysis (Eds.), *Annual of Psychoanalysis* (Vol. 8). New York: International Universities Press.

Wadden, T. A. (1983). Predicting treatment response to relaxation therapy for essential hypertension. *Journal of Nervous and Mental Disease, 171,* 683–689.

Wadden, T. A., Stunkard, A. J., Brownell, K. D., & Day, S. C. (1984). Treatment of obesity by behavior therapy and very-low-caloric diet: A pilot investigation. *Journal of Consulting and Clinical Psychology, 52,* 692–694.

Wagner, M. K., & Bragg, R. A. (1970). Comparing behavior modification approaches to habit decrement—smoking. *Journal of Consulting and Clinical Psychology, 34,* 258–263.

Wahler, R. G. (1969). Setting generality: Some specific and general effects of child behavior therapy. *Journal of Applied Behavior Analysis, 2,* 239–246.

Wahler, R. G. (1975). Some structural aspects of deviant child behavior. *Journal of Applied Behavior Analysis, 8,* 27–42.

Wahler, R. G., & Erickson, M. (1969). Child behavior therapy: A community program in Appalachia. *Behaviour Research and Therapy, 7,* 71–78.

Wahler, R. G., & Pollio, H. R. (1968). Behavior and insight: A case study in behavior therapy. *Journal of Experimental Research in Personality, 3,* 45–56.

Wahler, R. G., Winkel, G. H., Peterson, R. F., & Morrison, D. C. (1965). Mothers as behavior therapists for their own children. *Behaviour Research and Therapy, 3,* 113–124.

Wakeham, G. (1928). Query on "A revision of the fundamental law of habit formation." *Science, 68,* 135–136.

Wakeham, G. (1930). A quantitative experiment on Dr. K. Dunlap's "Revision of the fundmental law of habit formation." *Journal of Comparative Psychology, 10,* 235–236.

Waldo, D., Levit, K. R., & Lazenby, H. (1986). National health expenditures, (1985). *Health Care Financing Review, 8*(1), 1–21.

Walker, H. M., & Buckley, N. K. (1968). The use of positive reinforcement in conditioning attending behavior. *Journal of Applied Behavior Analysis, 1,* 245–250.

Wallace, C. J., Davis, J. R., Liberman, R. P., & Baker, V. (1973). Modeling and staff behavior. *Journal of Consulting and Clinical Psychology, 41,* No. 3, 425–432.

Wallace, C. J., Tiegen, J. R., Liberman, R. P., & Baker, V. (1973). Destructive behavior treated by contingency contracts and assertive training: A case study. *Journal of Behavior Therapy and Experimental Psychiatry, 4,* 273–274.

Wallace, J. A. (1949). The treatment of alcoholism by the conditioned-reflex method. *Journal of the Tennessee Medical Association, 42,* 125–128.

Wallace, M., Richards, P., Chesser, E., & Wrong, O. (1968). Persistent alkalosis and hypokalaemia caused by surreptitious vomiting. *Quarterly Journal of Medicine, 37,* 577–588.

Wallace, R. K. (1970). Physiological effects of transcendental meditation. *Science, 167,* 1751–1754.

Wallace, R. K., & Benson, H. (1972). The physiology of meditation. *Scientific American, 226,* 85–90.

Walsh, D. H. (1974). Interactive effects of alpha feedback and instructional set on subjective state. *Psychophysiology, 11,* 428–435.

Walters, R. H., Parke, R. D., & Crane, V. A. (1965). Timing of punishment and the observation of consequences to others as determinants of response inhibition. *Journal of Experimental Child Psychology, 2,* 10–30.

Walton, D. (1960). The application of learning theory to the treatment of a case of neurodermatitis. In H. J. Eysenck (Ed.), *Behaviour therapy and the neuroses.* Oxford: Pergamon.

Walton, D. (1961). Experimental psychology and the treatment of a tiquer. *Journal of Child Psychology and Psychiatry, 2,* 148–155.

Walton, D. (1964). Massed practice and simultaneous reduction in drive level: Further evidence of the efficacy of this approach to the treatment of tics. In H. J. Eysenck (Ed.), *Experiments in behaviour therapy.* Oxford: Pergamon.

Walton, D., Mather, M. D. (1963a). The relevance of generalization techniques to the treatment of stammering and phobic symptoms. *Behaviour Research and Therapy, 1,* 121–125.

Walton, D., & Mather, M. D. (1963b). The application of learning principles to the treatment of obsessive-compulsive states in the acute and chronic phases of illness. *Behaviour Research and Therapy, 1,* 163–174.

Wandless, I., & Davie, J. W. (1977). Can drug compliance in the elderly be improved? *British Medical Journal, 1,* 359–361.

Waranch, H. R., Iwata, B. A., & Wohl, M. K. (1981). Treatment of a retarded adult's mannequin phobia through in vivo desensitization and shaping approach responses. *Journal of Behavior Therapy and Experimental Psychiatry, 12,* 359–362.

Ward, M. H., & Baker, B. L. (1968). Reinforcement therapy in the classroom. *Journal of Applied Behavior Analysis, 1,* 323–328.

Ware, R., & Terrell, G. (1961). Effects of delayed reinforcement on associative and incentive factors. *Child Development, 32,* 789–793.

Warren, S. F., Rogers-Warren, A., & Baer, D. M. (1976). The role of offer rates in controlling sharing by young children. *Journal of Applied Behavior Analysis, 9,* 491–497.

Waters, W. F., McDonald, D. G., & Koresko, R. L. (1972). Psychophysiological responses during analogue systematic desensitization and non-relaxation control procedures. *Behaviour Research and Therapy, 10,* 381–393.

Watkins, J. T. (1977). The rational emotive dynamics of impulsive disorders. In A. Ellis & R. Grieger (Eds.), *Handbook of rational emotive therapy.* New York: Springer-Verlag.

Watson, D., & Friend, R. (1969). Measurement of social evaluative anxiety. *Journal of Consulting and Clinical Psychology, 33,* 448–457.

Watson, D. L., & Tharp, R. G. (1972). *Self-directed be-*

havior: Self-modification for personal adjustment. Monterey, CA: Brooks/Cole.

Watson, D. L., & Tharp, R. G. (1977). *Self-directed behavior: Self-modification for personal adjustment* (2nd ed.). Monterey, CA: Brooks/Cole.

Watson, J. B. (1913). Psychology as the behaviorist views it. *Psychological Review, 20,* 158–177.

Watson, J. B. (1916). The place of the conditioned reflex in psychology. *Psychological Review, 23,* 89–116.

Watson, J. B., & Rayner, R. (1920). Conditioned emotional reactions. *Journal of Experimental Psychology, 3,* 1–14.

Watson, J. P., Mullett, G. E., & Pillay, H. (1973). The effects of prolonged exposure to phobic situations upon agoraphobic patients treated in groups. *Behaviour Research and Therapy, 11,* 531–545.

Watts, F. N. (1973). Desensitization as an habituation phenomenon: 2. Studies of interstimulus interval lengths. *Psychological Reports, 33,* 715–718.

Watts, F. N. (1974). The control of spontaneous recovery of anxiety in imaginal desensitization. *Behaviour Research and Therapy, 12,* 57–59.

Weathers, L., & Liberman, R. P. (1975). Contingency contracting with families of delinquent adolescents. *Behaviour Research and Therapy, 6,* 356–366.

Webster, D. R., & Azrin, N. H. (1973). Required relaxation: A method of inhibiting agitative-disruptive behavior of retardates. *Behaviour Research and Therapy, 11,* 67–78.

Webster-Stratton, C. (1982). The long-term effects of a videotape modeling parent-training program: Comparison of immediate and 1-year-follow-up results. *Behavior Therapy, 13,* 702–714.

Wein, K. S., Nelson, R. O., & Odom, J. V. (1975). The relative contributions of reattribution and verbal extinction to the effectiveness of cognitive restructuring. *Behavior Therapy, 6,* 459–474.

Weiner, H. (1965). Real and imagined cost effects upon human fixed-interval responding. *Psychological Reports, 17,* 659–662.

Weinman, B. K., Gelbart, P., Wallace, M., & Post, M. (1972). Inducing assertive behavior in chronic schizophrenics. A comparison of socioenvironmental desensitization, and relaxation therapies. *Journal of Consulting and Clinical Psychology, 39,* 246–252.

Weintraub, M., Segal, R. M., & Beck, A. T. (1974). An investigation of cognition and affect in the depressive experiences of normal men. *Journal of Consulting and Clinical Psychology, 42*(6), 911.

Weiss, R. L., Birchler, G. R., & Vincent, J. P. (1974). Contractual models for negotiation training in marital dyads. *Journal of Marriage and the Family, 36,* 321–330.

Weiss, R. L., Hops, H., & Patterson, G. R. (1972, April). *A framework for conceptualizing marital conflict, a technology for altering it, and some data for evaluating it.* Paper presented at the meeting of the International Conference of Behavior Modification. Banff, Alberta, Canada.

Weiss, T., & Engel, B. T. (1970). Voluntary control of premature ventricular contractions in patients. *American Journal of Cardiology, 26,* 666 (abstract).

Weiss, T., & Engel, B. T. (1971). Operant conditioning of heart rate in patients with premature ventricular contractions. *Psychosomatic Medicine, 3,* 1–25.

Weissberg, M. (1975). Anxiety inhibiting statements and relaxation combined in two cases of speech anxiety. *Journal of Behavior Therapy and Experimental Psychiatry, 6,* 163–164.

Weissberg, M. (1977). A comparison of direct and vicarious treatments of speech anxiety: Desensitization, with coping imagery, and cognitive modification. *Behavior Therapy, 8,* 606–620.

Weissman, A., & Beck, A. T. (1978, November). *Development and validation of the Dysfunctional Attitude Scale (DAS).* Paper presented at the 12th Annual Meeting of the Association for the Advancement of Behavior Therapy, Chicago.

Weisz, G., & Bucher, B. (1980). Involving husbands in the treatment of obesity: Effects on weight loss, depression, and marital satisfaction. *Behavior Therapy, 11,* 643–650.

Weitzel, W. B., Horan, J. J., & Addis, J. W. (1977). A new olfactor aversion appartus. *Behavior Therapy, 8,* 83–88.

Welgen, P. R. (1974). Learned control of gastric acid secretions in ulcer patients. *Psycosomatic Medicine, 36,* 411–419.

Wells, U. C., Forehand, R., Hickey, K., & Green, K. D. (1977). Effects of a procedure derived from the overcorrection on manipulated and nonmanipulated behavior. *Journal of Applied Behavior Analysis, 10,* 679–688.

Werber, A. H., Baumback, G. L., Wagner, D. V., Mark, A. L., & Heistad, D. D. (1985). Factors that influence stroke in Dahlsalt-sensitive rats. *Hypertension, 7,* 59–64.

Wernick, R. L., Jaremko, M. E., & Taylor, P. W. (1981). Pain management in severely burned adults: A test of stress inoculation. *Journal of Behavioral Medicine, 4,* 103–109.

Wetzel, R. J., Baker, J., Roney, M., & Martin, M. (1966). Outpatient treatment of autistic behavior. *Behaviour Research and Therapy, 4,* 169–177.

Wexler, D. A. (1974). A cognitive theory of experiencing, self-actualization, and therapeutic process. In D. A. Wexler & L. N. Rice (Eds.), *Innovations in client-centered therapy.* New York: Wiley-Interscience.

White, G. D., Nielsen, G., & Johnson, S. M. (1972). Timeout duration and the suppression of deviant behavior in children. *Journal of Applied Behavior Analysis, 5,* 111– 120.

White, J. G. (1962, April). *Neurotic habit formations and the experimental analysis of learning (conditioning).* Paper read to the Ulster Neuropsychiatric Society.

Whitehead, W. E., Burgio, K. L., & Engel, B. T. (1985). Biofeedback treatment of fecal incompetence in geriatric patients. *Journal of the American Geriatrics Society, 33,* 320–324.

Whitehead, W. E., Renault, P. F., & Goldiamond, I. (1975). Modification of human gastric acid secretion with operant conditioning procedures. *Journal of Applied Behavior Analysis, 8,* 147–156.

Whiteman, T. L., Zakaras, M., & Chardos, S. (1971). Effects of reinforcement and guidance procedures on instruction-following behavior of severely retarded children. *Journal of Applied Behavior Analysis, 4,* 283–290.

Whitman, T. L. (1972). Aversive control of smoking behavior in a group context. *Behaviour Research and Therapy, 10,* 97–104.

Whitman, T. L., & Dussault, P. (1976). Self control through the use of a token economy. *Journal of Behavior Therapy and Experimental Psychiatry, 7,* 161–166.

Wickramesekera, I. (1972). Instructions and EMG feedback in systematic desensitization: A case report. *Behavior Therapy, 3,* 461–465.

Wickramesekera, I. (1973a). The application of verbal instruction and EMG feedback training to the managment of tension headache: Preliminary observations. *Headache, 13,* 74–76.

Wickramasekera, I. (1973b). Temperature feedback for the control of migraine. *Journal of Behavior Therapy and Experimental Psychiatry, 4,* 343–345.

Wickramesekera, I. (1976). Aversive behavior rehearsal for sexual exhibitionism. *Behavior Therapy, 7,* 167–176.

Wijesinghe, B. (1974). A vomiting phobia overcome by one session of flooding with hypnosis. *Journal of Behavior Therapy and Experimental Psychiatry, 5,* 169–170.

Wilde, G. J. S. (1964). Behaviour therapy for addicted cigarette smokers: A preliminary investigation. *Behaviour Research and Therapy, 2,* 107–109.

Wilkins, W. (1971). Desensitization: Social and cognitive factors underlying the effectiveness of Wolpe's procedure. *Psychological Bulletin, 76,* 310–317.

Williams, C. D. (1959). The elimination of tantrum behavior by extinction procedures. *Journal of Abnormal and Social Psychology, 59,* 269.

Williams, L., Martin, G. L., McDonald, S., Hardy, L., & Lambert, L., Sr. (1975). Effects of a backscratch contingency of reinforcement for table serving on social interaction with severely retarded girls. *Behavior Therapy, 6,* 220–229.

Williams, R. L., & Anandam, K. (1973). The effect of behavior contracting on grades. *Journal of Educational Research, 66,* 230–236.

Williams, S. L., & Rappaport, A. (1983). Cognitive treatment in the natural environment for agoraphobics. *Behavior Therapy, 14,* 299–313.

Williamson, D. A., Sewell, W. R., Sanders, S. H., Haney, J. N., & White, D. (1977). The treatment of reluctant speech using contingency management procedures. *Journal of Behavior Therapy and Experimental Psychiatry, 8,* 151–156.

Willis, J., & Giles, D. (1978). Behaviorism in the twentieth century: What we have here is a failure to communicate. *Behavior Therapy, 9,* 15–27.

Willis, R. W. (1968). *A study of the comparative effectiveness of systematic desensitization and implosive therapy.* Unpublished doctoral dissertation, University of Tennessee.

Willis, R. W., & Edwards, J. A. (1969). A study of the comparative effectiveness of systematic desensitization and implosive therapy. *Behaviour Research and Therapy, 7,* 387–395.

Wilson, C. C., Robertson, S. J., Herlong, L. H., & Haynes, S. N. (1979). Vicarious effects of time-out in the modification of agression in the classroom. *Behavior Modification, 3,* 97–111.

Wilson, G. T. (1973). Effects of false feedback on avoidance behavior: "Cognitive" desensitization revisited. *Journal of Personality and Social Psychology, 28,* 115–122.

Wilson, G. T. (1978). On the much discussed nature of the term "Behavior Therapy." *Behavior Therapy, 9,* 89–98.

Wilson, G. T. (1985). Psychological prognostic factors

in the treatment of obesity. In J. Hirsch & T. B. Van Itallie (Eds.), *Recent advances in obesity research* (Vol. 4). London: Libbey.

Wilson, G. T., & Brownell, K. D. (1978). Behavior therapy for obesity: Including family members in the treatment process. *Behavior Therapy, 9,* 943–945.

Wilson, G. T., & Brownell, K. D. (1980). Behavior therapy for obesity: An evaluation of treatment outcome. *Advances in Behavior Therapy, 3,* 49–86.

Wilson, G. T., & Davison, G. C. (1969). Aversion techniques in behavior therapy: Some theoretical and metatheoretical considerations. *Journal of Consulting and Clinical Psychology, 33,* 327–329.

Wilson, G. T., Leaf, R. C., & Nathan, P. E. (1975). The aversive control of excessive alcohol consumption by chronic alcoholics in the laboratory setting. *Journal of Applied Behavior Analysis, 8,* 13–26.

Wilson, G. T., Rossiter, E., Kleifield, E. I., & Lindholm, L. (1986). Cognitive-behavioral treatment of bulimia nervosa: A controlled evaluation. *Behaviour Research and Therapy, 24,* 277–288.

Wilson, G. T., & Tracey, D. A. (1976). An experimental analysis of aversive imagery vs. electrical aversive conditioning in the treatment of chronic alcoholics. *Behaviour Research and Therapy, 14,* 41–51.

Wilson, J. F. (1981). Behavioral preparation for surgery: Benefit or harm? *Journal of Behavioral Medicine, 4,* 79–102.

Wilson, S. H., & Williams, R. L. (1973). The effects of group contingencies on first graders' academic and social behaviors. *Journal of School Psychology, 11,* 110–117.

Wilson, R. (1984). A review of self-control treatments for aggressive behavior. *Behavioral Disorders, 9,* 131–140.

Wincze, J. P., & Caird, W. K. (1976). The effects of systematic desensitization and video desensitization in the treatment of essential sexual dysfunction in women. *Behavior Therapy, 7,* 335–342.

Winett, R. A., & Vachon, E. M. (1974). Group feedback and group contingencies in modifying behavior of fifth graders. *Psychological Reports, 34,* 1283–1292.

Wing, R. R., Epstein, L. H., Norwalk, M. P., Koeske, R., & Hagg, S. (1985). Behavior change, weight loss, and psychological improvements in Type Ii diabetic patients. *Journal of Consulting and Clinical Psychology, 53,* 111–122.

Wing, R. R., Epstein, L. H., Norwalk, M. P., & Lamparski, D. M. (1986). Behavioral self-regulation in the treatment of patients with diabetes mellitus. *Psychological Bulletin, 99,* 78–89.

Wing, R. R., & Jeffrey, R. W. (1979). Outpatient treatments of obesity: A comparison of methodology and clinical results. *International Journal of Obesity, 3,* 261–79.

Winkler, R. C. (1970). Management of chronic psychiatric patients by a token reinforcement system. *Journal of Applied Behavior Analysis, 3,* 47–55.

Winkler, R. C. (1977). What types of sex-role behavior should behavior modifiers promote? *Journal of Applied Behavioral Analysis, 10,* 549–552.

Wise, E. H., & Haynes, S. N. (1983). Cognitive treatment of test anxiety: Rational restructuring versus attentional training. *Cognitive Therapy and Research, 7,* 69–78.

Wisocki, P. A. (1973). A covert reinforcement program for the treatment of test anxiety. *Behavior Therapy, 4,* 264–266.

Wodarski, J. S. (1976). Procedural steps in the implementation of behavior modification programs in open settings. *Journal of Behavior Therapy and Experimental Psychiatry, 7,* 133–136.

Wolf, M. M., Hanley, E. L., King, L. A., Lachowicz, J., & Giles, D. K. (1970). The timer-game: A variable interval contingency for the management of out-of-seat behavior. *Exceptional Children, 37,* 113–117.

Wolf, M. M., Risley, T., & Mees, H. L. (1964). Application of operant conditioning procedures to the behavior problems of an autistic child. *Behaviour Research and Therapy, 1,* 305–312.

Wolfe, B. E. (1979). Behavioral treatment of childhood gender disorders: A conceptual and Empirical Critique. *Behavior Modification, 3,* 550–575.

Wolfe, J. L. & Brand, E. (Eds.). (1977). *Twenty years of rational therapy.* New York: Institute for Rational Living.

Wolfe, J. L., & Fodor, I. G. (1977). Modifying assertive behavior in women: A comparison of three approaches. *Behavior Therapy, 8,* 567–574.

Wolff, H. P., Vecsei, P., Kruck, F., Roscher, S., Brown, J. J., Dusterdieck, G. O., Lever, A. F., & Robertson, J. I. S. (1968). Psychiatric disturbance leading to potassium depletion, sodium depletion, raised plasma-renin concentration and secondary hyperaldosteronism. *Lancet, 1,* 257–261.

Wolff, J., & Desiderato, O. (1980). Transfer of assertion-training effects to roommates of program participants. *Journal of Counseling Psychology, 27,* 484–491.

Wollersheim, J. P. (1970). The effectiveness of group therapy based upon learning principles in the treatment of overweight women. *Journal of Abnormal Psychology, 76,* 462–474.

Wolpe, J. (1952). Objective psychotherapy of the neuroses. *Southern African Medical Journal, 26,* 825–829.

Wolpe, J. (1954). Reciprocal inhibition as the main basis of psychotherapeutic effects. *AMA Archives of Neurology and Psychiatry, 72,* 205–226.

Wolpe, J. (1958). *Psychotherapy by reciprocal inhibition.* Stanford, CA: Stanford University Press.

Wolpe, J. (1961). The systematic desensitization treatment of neuroses. *Journal of Nervous and Mental Disease, 132,* 189–203.

Wolpe, J. (1964). Behavior therapy in complex neurotic states. *British Journal of Psychiatry, 110,* 18–34.

Wolpe, J. (1969). *The practice of behavior therapy.* Oxford: Pergamon.

Wolpe, J. (1971). Dealing with resistance to thought stoppage: A transcript. *Journal of Behavior Therapy and Experimental Psychiatry, 2,* 121–125.

Wolpe, J. (1973). *The practice of behavior therapy* (2nd ed.). Oxford: Pergamon.

Wolpe, J. (1976a). Behavior therapy and its malcontents: 1. Denial of its bases and psychodynamic fusionism. *Journal of Behavior Therapy and Experimental Psychiatry, 7,* 1–5.

Wolpe, J. (1976b). Behavior therapy and its malcontents: 2. Multimodal eclecticism, cognitive exclusivism and "exposure" empiricism. *Journal of Behavior Therapy and Experimental Psychiatry, 7,* 109–116.

Wolpe, J. (1976c). *Theme and variations: A behavior therapy casebook.* Elmsford, NY: Pergamon.

Wolpe, J. (1977). Inadequate behavior analysis: The Achilles heel of outcome research in behavior therapy. *Journal of Behavior Therapy and Experimental Psychiatry, 8*(1), 1–3.

Wolpe, J. (1978). Cognition and causation in human behavior and its therapy. *American Psychologist, 33,* 437–446.

Wolpe, J. (1982). *The practice of behavior therapy* (3rd ed.). Oxford: Pergamon.

Wolpe, J., & Lang, P. J. (1964). A fear survey schedule for use in behavior therapy. *Behaviour Research and Therapy, 2,* 27–30.

Wolpe, J., & Lazarus, A. A. (1966). *Behavior therapy techniques: A guide to the treatment of neuroses.* Oxford: Pergamon.

Wolpin, M., & Pearsall, L. (1965). Rapid deconditioning of a fear of snakes. *Behaviour Research and Therapy, 3,* 107.

Woodward, R., & Jones, R. B. (1980). Cognitive restructuring treatment: A controlled trial with anxious patients. *Behaviour Research and Therapy, 18,* 401–407.

Woodworth, R. S., & Schlosberg, H. (1954). *Experimental psychology.* New York: Holt.

Worthington, E. L. (1978). The effects of imagery content, choice of imagery content, and self verbalization on the self control of pain. *Cognitive Therapy and Research, 2*(3), 225–240.

Wright, D. F., & Busch, G. (1977). Parental intervention in the treatment of chronic constipation. *Journal of Behavior Therapy and Experimental Psychiatry, 8,* 93–95.

Wright, H. F. (1960). Observational child study. In P. H. Mussen (Ed.), *Handbook of research methods in child development.* New York: Wiley.

Wright, J. C. (1976). A comparison of systematic desensitization and social skill acquisition in the modification of a social fear. *Behavior Therapy, 7,* 205–210.

Wright, L. (1973). Aversive conditioning of self-induced seizures. *Behavior Therapy, 4,* 712–713.

Wulbert, M., & Dries, R. (1977). The relative efficacy of methylphenidate (ritalin) and behavior-modification techniques in the treatment of a hyperactive child. *Journal of Applied Behavior Analysis, 1977, 10,* 21–31.

Wyler, A. R., Lockard, J. S., Ward, A., & Finch, C. A. (1976, 1977). Conditioned EEG desynchronization and seizure occurrence in patients. *Biofeedback and Self-Control 41*(5), 503–512.

Wysocki, T., Hall, G., Iwata, B., & Riordan, M. (1979). Behavioral management of exercise: Contracting for aerobic points. *Journal of Applied Behavior Analysis, 12,* 55–64.

Yamagami, T. (1971). The treatment of an obsession by thought stopping. *Journal of Behavior Therapy and Experimental Psychiatry, 2,* 133–135.

Yates, A. J. (1958). Symptoms and symptom substitution. *Psychological Review, 65,* 371–374.

Yates, A. J. (1970). *Behavior Therapy.* New York: Wiley.

Yates, A. J. (1975). *Theory and practice in behavior therapy.* New York: Wiley.

Young, E. R., Rimm, D.C., & Kennedy, T. D. (1973).

An experimental investigation of modeling and verbal reinforcement in the modification of assertive behavior. *Behaviour Research and Therapy, 11,* 317–319.

Young, J. (1980). *The development of the Cognitive Therapy Scale.* Unpublished manuscript, Center for Cognitive Therapy, Philadelphia, PA.

Yule, W., Sacks, B., & Hersov, L. (1974). Successful flooding treatment of a noise phobia in an eleven-year-old. *Journal of Behavior Therapy and Experimental Psychiatry, 5,* 209–211.

Zemore, R. (1975). Systematic desensitization as a method of teaching a general anxiety-reducing skill. *Journal of Consulting and Clinical Psychology, 43,* 157–161.

Ziesat, H. A. (1976). Self control methods of increasing efficiency of study. *Dissertation Abstracts, 37*(6-B), 3102.

Zifferblatt, S. M. (1970). *Improving study and homework behaviors.* Champaign, IL: Research Press.

Zimmerman, E. H., Zimmerman, J., & Russell, C. D. (1969). Differential effects of token reinforcement in instruction-following behavior in retarded students instructed as a group. *Journal of Applied Behavior Analysis, 2,* 101–112.

Zimmerman, J., & Ferster, C. B. (1963). Intermittent punishment of S responding in matching to sample. *Journal of the Experimental Analysis of Behavior, 6,* 349–356.

Zytowski, D. G. (1966). The study of therapy outcomes via experimental analogues: A review. *Journal of Consulting Psychology, 13,* 235–240.

The following citations are late additions to the References:

Black, J. L., & Keane, T. M. (1982). Implosive therapy in the treatment of combat related fears in World War II veteran. *Journal of Behavior Therapy and Experimental Psychiatry, 13*(2), 163–165.

Bradley, L. A., & Prokop, C. K. (1981). The relationship between medical psychology and behavioral medicine. In Charles K. Prokop & Laurence A. Bradley (Eds.), *Medical psychology: Contributions to behavioral medicine,* (pp. 1–4). New York: Academic Press.

Breslow, L., & Enstrom, J. E. (1980). Persistence of health habits and their relationship to mortality. *Preventive Medicine, 9,* 469–483.

Chambless, D. L., Foa, E. B., Groves, G. A. & Godstein, A. J. (1979). Flooding with Brevital in the treatment of agoraphobia: Countereffective? *Behaviour Research and Therapy, 17*(3), 243–251.

Clarke, J. E., & Hayes, K. (1984). Covert sensitization, stimulus relevance and the equipotentiality premise. *Behaviour Research and Therapy, 22*(4), 451–454.

Conley, O. S., & Worley, M. R. (1980). Treatment by overcorrection of self-injurious eye gouging in preschool blind children. *Journal of Behavior Therapy and Experimental Psychiatry, 11,* 121–125.

Duckro, P. N., Pollard, C. A., Bray, H. D., & Scheiter, L. (1984). Comprehensive behavioral management of complex tinnitus: A case illustration. *Biofeedback and Self-regulation, 9,* 459–469.

Elkins, R. L. (1976). A note on aversion therapy for alcoholism. *Behaviour Research and Therapy, 14*(2), 159–160.

Engel, G. L. (1977). The need for a new medical model: A challenge for biomedicine. *Science, 196,* 129–136.

Epstein, L. H., Wing, R. R., Thompson, J. K., & Griffin, W. (1980). Attendance and fitness in aerobics exercise: The effects of contract and lottery procedures. *Behavior Modification, 4*(4), 465–479.

Fleischman, M. J., Horne, A. M., & Arthur, J. L. (1983). *Troubled families: A treatment program.* Champaign, IL: Research Press.

Foy, D. W., Nunn, L. B., & Rychtarik, R. B. (1984). Broad-spectrum behavioral treatment for chronic alcoholics: Effects of training controlled drinking skills. *Journal of Consulting and Clinical Psychology, 52*(2), 218–230.

Franzini, L., & Grimes, W. B. (1980). Contracting and Stuart's three-dimensional program in behavior modification of the obese. *Psychotherapy: Theory, Research and Practice, 17*(1), 44–51.

Gentry, W. D., & Matarazzo, J. D. (1981). Medical psychology: Three decades of growth and development. In Charles K. Prokop & Laurence A. Bradley (Eds.), *Medical psychology: Contributions to behavioral medicine,* (pp. 5–15). New York: Academic Press.

Glazier, W. H. (1973). The task of medicine. *Scientific American, 228,* 13–17.

Gresham, F. M., & Nagle, R. J. (1980). Social skills training with children: Responsiveness to modeling and coaching as a function of peer orientation. *Journal of Consulting and Clinical Psychology, 48*(6), 718–729.

Grinker, R. R. (1953). *Psychosomatic research.* New York: W. W. Norton.

Gross, A. M. (1983). Self-management training and medication compliance in children with diabetes. *Child & Family Behavior Therapy, 4*, 47–55.

Hatch, J. P., Klatt, K. D., Supik, J. D., Rios, N., Fisher, J. G., Bauer, R. L., & Shimotsu, G. W. (1985). Combined behavioral and pharmacological treatment of essential hypertension. *Biofeedback and Self-regulation, 10*, 119–138.

Hay, W. M., Barlow, D. H., & Hay. L. R. (1981). Treatment of stereotypic cross-gender motor behavior using covert modeling in a boy with gender identity confusion. *Journal of Consulting and Clinical Psychology, 49*(3), 388–394.

Hayes, S. C., et al. (1985). Self-reinforcement effects: An artifact of social standard setting? *Journal of Applied Behavior Analysis, 18*(3), 201–214.

Haynes, S. G., Feinleib, M., & Kannel, W. B. (1980). The relationship of psychosocial factors to coronary heart disease in the Framingham study: III. Eight-year incidence of coronary heart disease. *American Journal of Epidemiology, 111*(1), 37–58.

Heinrich, R. L., Cohen, M. J., Nailiboff, B. D., Collins, G. A., & Bonebakker, A. D. (1985). Comparing physical and behavior therapy for chronic low back pain on physical abilities, psychological distress, and patients' perceptions. *Journal of Behavioral Medicine, 8*, 61–78.

Ireland, C. E., Wilson, P. H., Tonkin, J. P., & Platt-Hepworth, S. (1985). An evaluation of relaxation training in the treatment of tinnitus. *Behaviour Research and Therapy, 23*, 423–430.

Kagan, A., Popper, J. S., Rhoads, G. G., & Yano, K. (1985). Dietary and other risk factors for stroke in Hawaiian Japanese men. *Stroke, 16*, 390–396.

Kark, J. D., Lebiush, M., & Rannon, L. (1982). Cigarette smoking as a risk factor for epidemic (ACH_1N_1) influenza in young men. *New England Journal of Medicine, 307*, 1042–1046.

Kau, M. L., & Fischer, J. (1974). Self-modification of exercise behavior. *Journal of Behavior Therapy and Experimental Psychiatry, 5*(2), 213–214.

Keefe, F. J., & Blumenthal, J. A. (1980). The life fitness program: A behavioral approach to making exercise a habit. *Journal of Behavior Therapy and Experimental Psychiatry, 11*, 31–34.

Krantz, D. S., Grunberg, N. E., & Baum, A. (1985). Health Psychology. *Annual Review of Psychology, 36*, 349–383.

Lazarus, R. S., & Folkman, S. (1984). *Stress, appraisal, and coping.* New York: Springer.

Lewinsohn, P. M., & Amenson, C. S. (1978). Some relations between pleasant and unpleasant mood-related events and depression. *Journal of Abnormal Psychology, 87*(6), 644–654.

Lichstein, K. L., & Stalgaitis, S. J. (1980). Treatment of cigarette smoking in couples by reciprocal aversion. *Behavior Therapy, 11*(1), 104–108.

Matthews, K. A. (1982). Efforts to control by children and adults with the Type A coronary-prone behavior pattern. *Child Development, 50*(3), 842–847.

Mori, W., & Sakai, R. (1984). A study on chronologic change of the relationship between cigarette smoking and lung cancer based on autopsy diagnosis. *Cancer, 54*, 1038–1042.

Moss, N. H., & Mayer, J. (1971). *Food and nutrition in health and disease.* New York: New York Academy of Sciences.

Novick, D. M., Enlow, R. W., Gelb, A. M., Stenger, R. J., Fotino, M., Winter, J. W., Yancovitz, S. R., Shoenberg, M. D., & Kreck, M. J. (1985). Hepatic cirrhosis in young adults: Association with adolescent onset of alcohol and parental heroin abuse. *Gut, 26*, 8–13.

Oldridge, N. B., & Jones, N. L. (1981). Contracting as a strategy to reduce dropout in exercise rehabilitation. *Medicine and Science in Sports and Exercise, 13*, 125–126.

Perry, C., Killen, J., Telch, M., Slinkard, L. A., & Danaher, B. G. (1980). Modifying smoking behavior of teenagers: A school based intervention. *American Journal of Public Health, 70*(7), 722–725.

Pomerleau, O. F., & Brady, J. P. (Eds.). (1979). *Behavioral medicine: Theory and practice.* Baltimore: Williams & Wilkins.

Price, K. P., & Gatchel, R. J. (1979). A perspective on clinical biofeedback. In R. J. Gatchel and K. P. Price (Eds.), *Clinical biofeedback: Appraisal and status.* Elmsford, New York: Pergamon.

Rakos, R. F., Grodek, M. V., & Mack, K. K. (1985). The impact of a self-administered behavioral intervention program on pediatric asthma. *Journal of Psychosomatic Research, 29*, 101–108.

Reif, A. E. (1981). The causes of cancer. *American Scientist, 69*, 437–446.

Roskies, E., Seraganian, P., Oseasohn, R., Hanley, J. A., Collie, R., Martin, N., & Smilga, C. (1986). The Montreal Type A intervention project: Major findings. *Health Psychology, 5*, 45–69.

Sarason, I. G., & Sarason, B. R. (1981). Teaching cognitive and social skills to high school students. *Journal of Consulting and Clinical Psychology, 49*(6), 908–918.

Saunders, D. G. (1976). A case of motion sickness treated by systematic desensitization and *in vivo* relaxation. *Journal of Behavior Therapy and Experimental Psychiatry, 7,* 381–382.

Schultz, J. H. (1932). *Das autogene training.* Thieme, Stuttgart, F.R.G.

Schwartz, G. E. (1982). Testing and biophysical model: The ultimate challenge facing behavioral medicine? *Journal of Consulting and Clinical Psychology, 50,* 1040–1053.

Schwartz, G. E., & Weiss, S. (1977). What is behavioral medicine? *Psychosomatic Medicine, 36,* 377–381.

Schwartz, G. E., & Weiss, S. (Eds.) (1978). Proceedings of the Yale Conference on Behavioral Medicine. *Journal of Behavioral Medicine, 1,* 3–12.

Singer, J. E., & Krantz, D. S. (1982). Perspectives on the interface between psychology and public health. *American Psychologist, 37,* 955–960.

Smith, G. P., & Coleman, R. E. (1977). Processes underlying generalization through participant modeling with self-directed practice. *Behaviour Research and Therapy, 15*(2), 204–206.

Speltz, M. L., & Bernstein, D. A. (1979). The use of treatment of participant modeling for claustrophobia. *Journal of Behavior Therapy and Experimental Psychiatry, 19*(3), 251–255.

Taylor, C. B., Farquhar, J. W., Nelson, E., & Agras, W. S. (1977). Relaxation therapy and high blood pressure. *Archives of General Psychiatry, 34,* 339–342.

Copyrights and Acknowledgments

Tables

3-1 From Beck, J. G., and Heimberg, R. G., Self-assessment of assertive behavior: A critical analysis, *Behavior Modification* (1983). **3-2** From McFall, R. M., and Lillesand, D. B., Conflict Resolution Inventory, 1971. Reprinted by permission of the authors. **3-4** From Beck, J. G., and Heimberg, R. G., Self-report assessment of assertive behavior: A critical analysis, *Behavior Modification* (1983).

6-2 Copyright © 1968 by the Society for the Experimental Analysis of Behavior, Inc. Reprinted by permission.

9-2, 9-3 Copyright © 1979 by Academic Press. Reprinted by permission.

10-3 From Fuchs, C. Z., and Rehm, L. P., Self-control depression program, *Journal of Consulting and Clinical Psychology*, 45, No. 2(1977): 206-215. Copyright © 1977 by the American Psychological Association. Reprinted by permission of the publisher and authors. **10-4** From Meichenbaum, D. H., *Cognitive Behavior Modification*, Morristown, NJ: General Learning Press.

11-2 From Grace, W. J., and Graham, D. T., Relationship of specific attitudes and emotions to certain bodily diseases, *Psychosomatic Medicine* 14 (1952): 243-251. **11-5** From Ince, L. P., The utilization of EMG Biofeedback for the treatment of preorbital facial muscle tension, *Biofeedback and Self-Regulation*, 8 (1983): 377-382. Reprinted by permission of the publisher Plenum Publishing Corporation. **11-6** From Carroll, L. J., and Yates, B. T., Further evidence for the role of stimulus control training in facilitating weight reduction after behavioral therapy, *Behavior Therapy*, 12 (1981): 288. Copyright © 1981 by Academic Press. **11-7** From Botvin, G. J., Eng, A., and Williams, C. L., Preventing the onset of cigarette smoking through life skills training, *Preventive Medicine*, 9 (1980): 136. Copyright © 1980 by Academic Press. Reprinted by permission.

A-1 Adapted from Becker, W. C., *Parents are teachers: A child management program*. Champaign, IL: Research Press Co., 1971, p. 100. Reprinted by permission. **B-1, B-2** From Schaefer, H. H., and Martin, P. L., *Behavior therapy*. Copyright © 1969 by McGraw-Hill. Reprinted by permission.

Text

Passim Reprinted with permission from Wolpe, J., and Lazarus, A. A., *Behavior Therapy Techniques: A guide to the Treatment of Neuroses*. Copyright © 1966, Pergamon Books, Ltd. **Pp. 39-40** Reprinted with permission from Research Press Co. Bernstein, D. A., and Borkovec, T. D. (1973). *Progressive Relaxation Training: A Manual for the Helping Professions* (pp. 19-20). Champaign, IL: Research Press. **46-47** Excerpted from Pikoff, H., A critical review of autogenic training in America, *Clinical Psychology Review* (1984):620-621. **115-119** Excerpted from Rimm, D. C., Assertive training and the expression of anger. In R. A. Alberti (ed.), *Assertiveness: Innovations, Applications, Issues*. Copyright © 1977. Reprinted by permission of Impact Publishers, Inc., P. O. Box 1094, San Luis Obispo, CA 93406. Further reproduction prohibited. **172-173** Excerpted from Kelly, G., *The Psychology of Personal Contsructs*, Vol, 2. New York: Norton, 1955. **212** Excerpted from Tharp, R. G., and Wetzel, R. J., *Behavior Modification in the Natural Environment*. Copyright © 1969 by Academic Press. Reprinted by permission. **305** Excerpted from Cautela, J. R., Covert extinction, *Behavior Therapy*, 2 (1971): 192-200. Copyright © 1971 by Academic Press. Reprinted by permission. **316** Reprinted with permission from *Behaviour Research and Therapy*, 6. Hogan, R., The implosive technique. Copy-

Illustration Credits

4-1 From Bandura, A. *Social Learning Theory,* Englewood Cliffs, NJ: Prentice-Hall, 1977. Fig. 1., p. 23. Copyright © 1977 by Prentice-Hall, Inc. **4-2** From Chittenden, G. E., An experimental study in measuring and modifying assertive behavior in children, *Monographs of the Society for Research in Child Development,* 1942, 7 (Whole No. 31). Copyright © 1942 by the Society for Research in Child Development. Reprinted by permission. **4-3** From Lovaas, O. I., Berberich, J. P., Perloff, B. F., and Schaeffer, B. Acquisition of imitative speech by schizophrenic children. *Science,* 11 February 1966, 151, 706. Fig. 1. Copyright © 1966 by the American Association for the Advancement of Science. **4-4** From Lovaas, O. I. A behavior therapy approach to the treatment of childhood schizophrenia. In John P. Hill (Ed.), *Minnesota Symposia on Child Psychology,* Vol. 1. Minneapolis: University of Minnesota Press, 1967. Copyright © 1967, University of Minnesota. **4-5** From O'Connor, R.D. Modification of social withdrawal through symbolic modeling. Journal of Applied Behavior Analysis, 1969, 2, 19. Fig. 1. Copyright © 1969 by the Society for the Experimental Analysis of Behavior, Inc. **4-6** From Kazdin, A. E. The effect of vicarious reinforcement on attentive behavior in the classroom. *Journal of Applied Behavior Analysis,* 1973, 6, 71-78. Fig. 2. Copyright © 1973 by the Society for the Experimental Analysis of Behavior, Inc. **4-7** From Bandura, A., Grusec, J. E., and Menlove, F. L. Vicarious extinction of avoidance behavior. *Journal of Personality and Social Psychology,* 1967, 5, 21. Fig. 1. Copyright © 1967 by the American Psychological Association. Reprinted by permission. **4-8 and 4-9** From Bandura, A., and Menlove, F. L. Factors determining vicarious extinction of avoidance behavior through symbolic modeling. *Journal of Personality and Social Psychology,* 1968, 8, 102, 103. Figs. 1 and 4. Copyright © 1968 by the American Psychological Association. Reprinted by permission.

4-10 From Kazdin, A. E. Effects of covert modeling and model reinforcement on assertive behavior. *Journal of Abnormal Psychology,* 1974, 83, 240-252. Fig. 1. Copyright © 1974 by the American Psychological Association. Reprinted by permission. **4-11** From Kazdin, A. E. Covert modeling, imagery assessment, and assertive behavior. *Journal of Consulting and Clinical Psychology,* 1975, 43, 716-724. Fig. 1. Copyright © 1975 by the American Psychological Association. Reprinted by permission. **4-12 and 4-13** From Bandura, A., Jeffery, R. W., and Wright, C. L. Efficacy of participant modeling as a function of response induction aids. *Journal of Abnormal Psychology,* 1974, 83(1), 56-64, Figs. 2 and 3. Copyright © 1974 by the American Psychological Association. Reprinted by permission. **4-14** From Bandura, A. Jeffery, R. W., and Gajdos, E. Generalizing change through participant modeling with self-directed mastery. *Behavior Research and Therapy,* 1975, 13, 144-152. Figs. 2 and 3. **4-15** From Ritter, B. The use of contact desensitization, demonstration-plus-participation, and demonstration alone in the treatment of acrophobia. *Behavior Research and Therapy,* 1969, 7(1),160, Table 1. **4-16 and 4-17** From Blanchard, E. B. The relative contributions of modeling, informational influences, and physical contact in the extinction of phobic behavior. Unpublished doctoral dissertation, Stanford University, 1969. **4-18 and 4-19** From Bandura, A., Adams, N. E., and Beyer, J. Cognitive processes mediating behavioral change. *Journal of Personality and Social Psychology,* 1977, 35, 125-139. Figs. 2 and 1. Copyright © 1977 by the American Psychological Association. Reprinted by permission. **4-20** From Bandura, A., Reese, L., and Adams, N. E. (1982) Microanalysis of action and fear arousal as a function of differential levels of perceived self-efficacy. *Journal of Personality and Social Psychology,* 43, 601-607. Copyright © 1982 by the American Psychological Association. Reprinted with permission. **4-21** From Bandua, A., Adams, N. E., and Beyer, J. Cognitive processes mediating behavioral change. *Journal of Personality and Social Psychology,* 1977, 35, 125-139. Fig. 3. Copyright © 1977 by the American Psychological Association. Reprinted by permission.

5-3 From Wahler, R.G., Winkel, G.H., Peterson, R.F., and Morrison, D.C. Mothers as behavior therapists for their own children. *Behaviour Research and Therapy,* 1965, 3, 121. Fig. 5. **5-4** From Glynn, E.L., Thomas, J.D., and Ghee, S.M. Behavioral self-control of on-task behavior in an elementary classroom. *Journal of Applied Behavior Analysis,* 1973, 6, 105-113. Fig. 1. Copyright © 1973 by the Society for the Experimental Analysis of Behavior, Inc. **5-5** From Solnik, J.V., Rincover, A., and Peterson, C.R. Some determinants of the reinforcing and punishing effects of time-out. *Journal of Applied Behavior Analysis,* 1977, 10, 415-424. Fig. 1. Copyright © 1977 by the Society for the Experimental Analysis of Behavior, Inc. **5-6** From Weathers, L. and Liberman, R.P. Contingency contracting with families of delinquent adolescents. *Behavior Therapy,* 1975, 6, 356-366. Fig. 2. **5-7** From Ayllon, T., and Azrin, N.H. Reinforcer sampling: A technique for increasing the behavior of mental patients. *Journal of Applied Behavior Analysis,* 1968, 1, 15-18. Figs. 2, 4, and 6. Copyright © 1968 by the Society for the Experimental Analysis of Behavior, Inc.

6-1 From Allen, K.E., Hart, B.M., Buell, J.S., Harris, F.R., and Wolf, M.M. Effects of social reinforcement on isolate behavior of a nursery school Child. *Child Development,* 1964, 35, 511-518. Copyright © 1964 by the Society for Research in Child Development. Reprinted by permission. **6-2** From Hay, W.M. Hay, L.R., and Nelson, R.O. Direct and collateral changes in on-task and academic behavior resulting from on-task versus academic contingencies. *Behavior Therapy,* 1977, 8, 431-441. Fig. 1. **6-3** From Rekers, G.A., Yates, C.E., Willis, T.J., Rosen, A.C., and Taubman, M. Childhood gender identity change: Operant control over sex-typed

play and mannerisms. *Journal of Behavior Therapy and Experimental Psychiatry,* 1976, 7, 51-57, Fig. 2. **6-4** From Christensen, D.E., and Sprague, R.I. Reduction of hyperactive behavior by conditioning procedures alone and combined with methylphenitate. *Behaviour Research and Therapy,* 1973, 11, 331-334. Fig. 1. **6-5** From Harris, V.W., and Sherman, J.A. Use and analysis of the "good behavior game" to reduce disruptive classroom behavior. *Journal of Applied Behavior Analysis,* 1973, 405-417. Fig. 2. Copyright © 1973 by the Society for the Experimental Analysis of Behavior, Inc. **6-6** From Solomon, R.W., and Wahler, R.G. Peer reinforcement control of classroom problem behavior. *Journal of Applied Behavior Analysis,* 1973, 6, 49-56. Fig. 1. Copyright © 1973 by the Society for the Experimental Analysis of Behavior, Inc. **6-7** From Lovitt, T.C., Guppy, T.E., and Blattner, J.R. The use of a free-time contingency with fourth-graders to increase spelling accuracy. *Behaviour Research and Therapy,* 1969, 7, 153, Fig.1. **6-8** From Chadwick, B.A., and Day, R.C. Systematic reinforcement: Academic performance of underachieving students. *Journal of Applied Behavior Analysis,* 1971, 4, 311-319. Fig. 1. Copyright © 1971 by the Society for the Experimental Analysis of Behavior, Inc. **6-9** From McLaughlin, T.F., and Malaby, J. Intrinsic reinforcers in a classroom token economy. *Journal of Applied Behavior Analysis,* 1972, 5, 263-270, Fig. 2. Copyright © 1972 by the Society for the Experimental Analysis of Behavior, Inc. **6-10 and 6-11** From Kirby, F.D., and Shields, F. Modification of arithmetic response rate and attending behavior in a seventh-grade student. *Journal of Applied Behavior Analysis,* 1972, 5, 79-84. Figs. 1 and 2. Copyright © 1972 by the Society for the Experimental Analysis of Behavior, Inc. **6-12** From Goetz, E.M., and Baer, D.M. Social control of form diversity and the emergence of new forms in children's block-building. *Journal of Applied Behavior Analysis,* 1973, 6, 209-217. Fig. 1. Copyright © 1973 by the Society for the Experimental Analysis of Behavior, Inc. **6-13** From Williams, L., Martin, G.L., McDonald, S., Hardy, L., Lambert, Sr., L.

Effects of a backscratch contingency of reinforcement for table serving on social interaction with severely retarded girls. *Behavior Therapy,* 1975, 6, 220-229. Fig. 2. **6-14** From Bostow, D.E., and Bailey, J.S. Modification of severe disruptive and aggressive behavior using brief timeout and reinforcement procedures. Journal of Applied Behavior Analysis, 1969, 2, 34, 36. Figs. 1 and 2. Copyright © 1969, by the Society for the Experimental Analysis of Behavior, Inc. **6-15** From Philips, E. L. Achievement place: Token reinforcement procedures in a home-style rehabilitation setting for "predelinquent" boys. *Journal of Applied Behavior Analysis,* 1968, 1, 217. Fig. 1. Copyright © 1968 by the Society for the Experimental Analysis of Behavior, Inc. **6-16** From Phillips, E.L., Phillips, E.A. Fixsen, D.L., and Wolf, M.M. Achievement place: Modification of the behaviors of predelinquent boys within a token economy. *Journal of Applied Behavior Analysis,* 1971, 4, 45-59. Fig. 5. Copyright © 1971 by the Society for the Experimental Analysis of Behavior, Inc. **6-17 and 6-18** From Phillips, E.L., Phillips, E.A., Wolf, M.W., and Fixsen, D.L. Achievement place: Development of the elected manager system. *Journal of Applied Behavior Analysis,* 1973, 6, 541-561. Copyright © 1973 by the Society for the Experimental Analysis of Behavior, Inc. **6-19** From Bailey, J.S., Wolf, M.M., and Phillips, E.L. Home-based reinforcement and the modification of pre-delinquents' classroom behavior. *Journal of Applied Behavior Analysis,* 1970 by the Society for the Experimental Analysis of Behavior, Inc. **6-20** From Bassett, J.E., and Blanchard, E.B. The effect of the absence of close supervision on the use of response cost in a prison token economy. *Journal of Applied Behavior Analysis,* 1977, 10, 375-379. Fig. 1. Copyright © 1977 by the Society for the Experimental Analysis of Behavior, Inc. **6-21** Reprinted from George Fairweather et al., Community life for the mentally ill. Chicago: Aldine Publishing Company, 1969. Figs 12.1 and 12.2. Copyright © 1969 by Aldine Publishing Company. Reprinted by permission of the authors and Aldine Publishing Company.

6-22 From Wahler, R.G. Setting gererality: Some specific and general effects of child behavior therapy. *Journal of Applied Behavior Analysis,* 1969, 2, 243, Copyright © 1969 by the Society for Experimental Analysis of Behavior, Inc.

7-1 From Williams, C. The elimination of tantrum behavior by extinction procedures. *Journal of Abnormal and Social Psychology,* 1959, 59, 269. Fig. 1. Copyright © 1959 by the American Psychological Association. Reprinted with permission. **7-2** From Ayllon, T., and Haughton, E. Modification of symptomatic verbal behavior of mental patients. *Behaviour Research and Therapy,* 1964, 2, 94. Fig. 3. Reproduced with the permission of Microform International Marketing Corporation, exclusive copyright licensee of Pergamon Press Journal back files. **7-3** From Mansdorf, I.J. Reinforcer isolation: An alternative to subject isolation in time-out from positive reinforcement. *Journal of Behavior Therapy and Experimental Psychiatry,* 1977, 8, 391-393. Fig. 1. **7-4** From Madsen, C.H., Jr., Becker, W.C., Thomas, D.R., Koser, L., and Plager, E. An analysis of the reinforcing function of "sit down" commands. In R.K. Parker (Ed.), *Readings in educational psychology.* Boston: Allyn and Bacon, 1968. **7-5** From Ayllon, T., and Haughton, E. Modification of symptomatic verbal behavior of mental patients. *Behaviour Research and Therapy,* 1964, 2, 87-97. Fig. 1. **7-6** From Neisworth, J.T., and Moore, F. Operant treatment of asthmatic responding with the parent as therapist. *Behavior Therapy,* 1972, 3, 95-99. Fig. 1. Copyright © 1972 by Academic Press. **7-7** From Neisworth, J.T., Madle, R.A., Goeke, K.E. "Errorless" elimination of separation anxiety: A case study. *Journal of Behavior Therapy and Experimental Psychiatry,* 1975, 6, 79-82. Fig. 1. Reprinted by permission of Pergamon Press, Ltd. **7-8** From Sue, D. Case histories and shorter communications: The effect of duration of exposure on systematic desensitization and extinction. *Behaviour Research and Therapy,* 1975, 13, 55-60. Fig. 1. Reprinted by permission of Pergamon Press, Ltd. **7-9** From Poppen, R.L. Counterconditioning of conditioned suppression in rats. *Psychological Reports,* 1970, 27, 659-671. Reproduced by permission. **7-10** From Yates, A.J. The application of learning theory to the treatment of tics. *Journal of Abnormal and Social Psychology,* 1958, 56, 179. Fig. 1. Copyright © 1958 by the American Psychological Association. Reprinted by permission. **7-11** From Delahunt, J., and Curran, J.P. Effectiveness of negative practice and self-control techniques in the reduction of smoking behavior. *Journal of Consulting and Clinical Psychology,* 1976, 44, 1002-1007. Fig. 1. Copyright © 1976 by the American Psychological Association. Reprinted by permission. **7-12** From Ayllon, T. Intensive treatment of psychotic behavior by stimulus satiation and food reinforcement. *Behaviour Research and Therapy,* 1963, 1, 57. Fig. 2. **7-13** From Orenstein, H., and Carr, J. Implosion therapy by tape-recording. *Behaviour Research and Therapy,* 1975, 13, 177-182. Fig. 4. Reprinted by permission of Pergamon Press, Ltd. **7-14** From Blanchard, E.B. Case histories and shorter communications: Brief flooding treatment for a debilitating revulsion. *Behaviour Research and Therapy,* 1975, 13, 193-195. Fig. 1. Reprinted by permission of Pergamon Press, Ltd.

8-1 Matson, J.L., Horne, A.M., Ollendick, D.G., & Ollendick, T.H. (1979). Overcorrection: A further evaluation of restitution and positive practice. *Journal of Behaviour Therapy and Experimental Psychiatry,* 10, 295-298. **8- 2** From Feldman, M.P., and MacCullock, M.J. Homosexual behavior: Therapy and assessments. Oxford: Pergamon Press, 1971. Reproduced with the permission of Microform International Marketing Corporation, Exclusive copyright licensee of Pergamon Press Journal back files. **8-3** From Barlow, D. H., Leitneberg, H., and Agras, W.S. Experimental control of sexual deviation through the manipulation of the noxious scene in covert sensitization. *Journal of Abnormal Psychology,* 1969, 75(5), 599. Fig. 1. Copyright © 1969 by the American Psychological Association. Reprinted by permission. **8-4** From Maletzky, B.M. "Booster" sessions in aversion therapy: The permanency of treatment. *Behavior Therapy,* 1977, 8, 460-463. Copyright © by Academic Press. **8-5** From Barlow, D.H., Agras, W.S., Leitenberg, H., Callahan, E.J., and Moore, R.C. Case histories and shorter communications. *Behaviour Research and Therapy,* 1972, 10, 411-415. Fig. 1. Reprinted by permission of Pergamon Press, Ltd.

9-1 From Holroyd, K.A. (1976). Cognition and desensitization in the group treatment of test anxiety. *Journal of Consulting and Clinical Psychology* 44: 991-1001. Copyright © 1976 by the American Psychological Association. Reprinted by permission of the publisher and author. **9-2** Meichenbaum, D., Gilmore, J.B., and Fedoravicius, A. (1971). Group insight vs. group desensitization in treating speech anxiety. *Journal of Consulting and Clinical Psychology* 36: 410-21. Copyright © 1971 by the American Psychological Association. Reprinted by permission of the publisher and author. **9-3** From Kanter, J.J., and Goldfried, M.R. (1979). Relative effectiveness of rational restructuring and self-control desensitization in the reduction of interpersonal anxiety. *Behavior Therapy* 10: 472-91. Copyright © 1979 by the Association for the Advancement of Behavior Therapy. **9-4** From Linehan, M.M., Goldfried, M.R., and Goldfried, A.P. (1979). Assertion therapist: Skill training or cognitive restructuring. *Behavior Therapy* 10: 372-88. Copyright © 1979 by the Association for the Advancement of Behavior Therapy. **9-5** From Biran, M., and Wilson, G.T. (1981). Treatment of phobic disorders using cognitive and exposure methods: A self-efficacy analysis. *Journal of Clinical Psychology* 49:886-99. Copyright © 1981 by the American Psychological Association. Reprinted by permission of the publisher and author. **9-6** Reprinted with permission from *Behavior Research and Therapy,* 16. Emmelkamp, P.M.G., Kuipers, A.L.M., and Eggeraat, J.B., "Cognitive modification versus prolonged exposure in vivo: a comparison with agoraphobics as subjects." Copyright © 1978, Pergamon Press, Ltd. **9-7** Reprinted with per-

Index of Disorders

Page numbers in italics indicate that an entry is presented as a full case study or in a description of an experimental investigation; remaining numbers indicate that an entry is only mentioned.

Author Index

Abel, G. G., 485, 487, 490
Abramowitz, S. I., 485, 487
Abrams, D. B., 447, 450, 466
Abramson, E. E., 458, 467
Abramson, L. Y., 429
Abramson, R., 466
Adams, H. E., 27, 317, 319, 321, 323, 327, 491, 514
Adams, K. M., 344
Adams, N. E., 131, 183–185
Addario, D., 485, 488
Adderton, M., 487
Ader, R., 511
Adesso, V. J., 345
Adkins, D., 469
Adler, C. S., 485
Agg, B., 263
Agras, S., 302
Agras, W. S., 51, 122, 376, 372, 378, 379, 485, 506, 513, 546
Ahles, T. A., 514
Ainley, C., 142
Ainsworth, K. D., 482
Alabiso, F., 236, 241
Albanchez, D. B., 446
Alberti, R. E., 79, 97, 119
Alden, L. E., 83, 108, 127, 404, 405, 431, 439
Alexander, A. B., 488

Alexander, F., 11
Alexander, R. N., 237
Alexander, S. B., 237
Alford, G. S., 355
Allaire, D., 491
Allen, A., 9
Allen, G. J., 58, 236, 249, 464
Allen, J. G., 15
Allen, K. E., 217, 231, 233, 236, 237
Allen, L. M., 52, 515
Allen, R. A., 491
Allen, R. P., 383
Allison, T., 487
Allsey, 258
Almit, Z., 515
Altman, K., 206, 347
Altwater, J. D., 268
Alvord, J. R., 197
Amatu, H. I., 402
Amenson, C. S., 192
Ammer, J. J., 447
Amolsch, T., 150
Amper, J. M., 3
Anandam, K., 249, 251
Anant, S. S., 372, 381
Anderson, J., 128
Anderson, K. O., 539
Anderson, L. K., 397
Andrasik, F., 482, 485, 487, 514
Andresen, B. L., 75
Andrew, 470
Andrews, G., 238
Annable, L., 485, 488
Annis, H. M., 469
Anton, W. D., 60, 77

Apolloni, T., 236, 281
Appel, K. G., 3
Aragona, J., 219, 297
Arenberg, D., 177
Arias, J. D., 507
Arkowitz, H., 21, 94, 128
Armitage, S. G., 238
Armor, D. J., 469
Armstrong, B. K., 451
Armstrong, D., 440
Armstrong, E., 363
Armstrong, M. S., 375
Arnkoff, D. B., 167, 416
Arnold, J. E., 284, 285
Arnold, S. C., 215, 356, 432
Arora, M., 300
Arthur, D., 354
Ascher, L. M., 147, 150
Ashem, B., 312, 345, 372, 382
Atkeson, B. M., 280, 346
Atkins, C. J., 507, 512
Atthowe, J. A., 279
Atthowe, J. M., Jr., 357
Ault, R. L., 432
Austin, N., 119
Author, J. L., 197
Autrey, J., 411
Axelrod, S., 197
Axelroth, E., 524
Ayllon, T., 206, 227–229, 241, 236–238, 263, 272, 274, 275, 278, 290, 294, 296, 311, 312, 323, 357, 507, 556

Azrin, N. H., 227–229, 238, 258, 263, 272, 274, 275, 342, 346, 357, 383, 470, 556

Bach, R., 297
Baer, A. M., 238, 249
Baer, D. M., 141, 236, 239, 238, 249, 256, 258, 260, 278–281, 283, 284, 292, 312
Bahler, W. W., 484
Bailey, J. B., 260, 262, 359
Bailey, J. S., 219, 226, 238, 260, 262, 263, 270, 271, 286
Bajtelsmit, J. W., 218
Baker, B. L., 245
Baker, J., 238
Baker, R., 535, 536
Baker, T. B., 383, 535
Baker, V., 137
Balaschak, B. A., 486, 487
Bali, L. R., 485, 488
Ball, T. S., 237, 258
Bancroft, J., 381, 397
Bandura, A., 3, 7, 9–12, 22, 28, 70, 71, 83, 109, 110, 131, 132, 134, 135, 137, 138, 140, 143, 147, 154–157, 167–170, 176, 183–186, 210, 300, 358, 361, 385, 387, 388, 397, 418,

667

Subject Index